THE URBAN
ETHNOGRAPHY READER

THE URBAN ETHNOGRAPHY READER

Edited by

MITCHELL DUNEIER,

PHILIP KASINITZ, AND

ALEXANDRA K. MURPHY

UNIVERSITY PRESS

OXFORD

UNIVERSITY PRESS

Oxford University Press is a department of the University of Oxford.
It furthers the University's objective of excellence in research, scholarship,
and education by publishing worldwide.

Oxford   New York
Auckland   Cape Town   Dar es Salaam   Hong Kong   Karachi
Kuala Lumpur   Madrid   Melbourne   Mexico City   Nairobi
New Delhi   Shanghai   Taipei   Toronto

With offices in
Argentina   Austria   Brazil   Chile   Czech Republic   France   Greece
Guatemala   Hungary   Italy   Japan   Poland   Portugal   Singapore
South Korea   Switzerland   Thailand   Turkey   Ukraine   Vietnam

Oxford is a registered trademark of Oxford University Press
in the UK and certain other countries.

Published in the United States of America by
Oxford University Press
198 Madison Avenue, New York, NY 10016

Library of Congress Cataloging-in-Publication Data
The urban ethnography reader / edited by Mitchell Duneier, Philip Kasinitz,
and Alexandra K. Murphy.
   pages cm
Includes bibliographical references.
ISBN 978–0–19–974358–2 (hardcover : alk. paper)—ISBN 978–0–19–974357–5 (pbk. : alk. paper)
1. Sociology, Urban.   2. City and town life.   3. Social psychology.   I. Duneier, Mitchell.
HT151.U663 2013
307.76—dc23
     2013002495

CONTENTS

ACKNOWLEDGMENTS

This volume has been many years in the making, and it would not have come about without the wise council, boundless enthusiasm and apparently inexhaustible patience of our brilliant editor, James Cook. We also thank Mary Jo Rhodes for shepherding the book through a complicated production process, Chris Dahlin and Irina Oryshkevich for their work copyediting this lengthy manuscript, and Alexandra Mele for her efforts to market the volume. Thank you to our four anonymous reviewers for their useful suggestions. Chase Robinson, Provost of the Graduate Center of the City University of New York, generously provided support for the effort, and Rati Kashyap, also of the Graduate Center, was invaluable in locating funds seemingly lost forever in a maze of bureaucracy. Marjorie Crowell and Christine Vidmar assisted early on with acquiring permissions for the readings in this volume; Peter Worger at Oxford assisted in finalizing this acquisitions process.

THE URBAN
ETHNOGRAPHY READER

AN INVITATION TO

URBAN ETHNOGRAPHY

You have been told to go grubbing in the library, thereby accumulating a mass of notes and liberal coating of grime. You have been told to choose problems wherever you can find musty stacks of routine records based on trivial schedules prepared by tired bureaucrats. This is called "getting your hands dirty in real research." Those who counsel you are wise and honorable; the reasons they offer are of great value. But one more thing is needful: first hand observation. Go and sit in the lounges of the luxury hotels and on the doorsteps of flophouses; sit on the Gold Coast settees and the slum shakedowns; sit in the Orchestra Hall and in the Star and Garter burlesque. In short, gentlemen, go get the seat of your pants dirty in *real* research.

—An unpublished 1920s quote by Robert E. Park,
recorded by Howard Becker.[1]

In the 1920s, Professor Robert Park, one of the founding fathers of American social science, enticed his students on a most unconventional quest. Through his lectures at the University of Chicago, he drew them into his effort to make sense of the forces that were transforming social life. All around them in the great metropolis they could see the effects of massive growth: the convergence of diverse peoples, the creation of new forms of community, the uprooting of traditions, and the swirling balance of order and chaos that constituted the modern city. They were not alone in this effort. Like the social workers and bureaucrats who had compiled these "musty stacks of routine records," scholars and intellectuals, artists and writers, were all in their different ways trying to understand these new forms

of social life. Park, however, urged his students to take up a somewhat paradoxical method of investigation—one associated with the study of "exotic" members of traditional communities—and to apply it to their own society. He urged them to look at the commonplace with new eyes, to try to understand the world of the stranger next door, and to examine everyday life with both the discipline of scientists and the adventurous spirit of explorers.

At the risk of extreme immodesty, we would like to renew this invitation. With this volume we invite you on a journey into one of the richest traditions in social science: the firsthand study of urban community life.

"Ethnography" is a method of social science research that investigates people's lives, actions, and beliefs within their everyday context. Surveys, experiments, and formal interviews are all situations created and largely controlled by the social scientist. The ethnographer, by contrast, seeks to understand life as it is lived. His or her conclusions are based primarily on "fieldwork," which involves entering the world of the people under study as a close observer or even as a participant over an extended period of time. By sharing in the daily life experiences of his or her subjects, the ethnographer becomes more attuned to the less visible conditions and situations that shape these lives.

This method has its origins in late nineteenth- and early twentieth-century anthropology. In a classic ethnographic anthropological study, the researcher typically goes to live among members of a different society, usually geographically and culturally distant from his or her own. He or she learns the people's language and, to the extent possible, shares their daily life activities in an effort to understand their beliefs, worldviews, and systems of meaning-making. Of course, the anthropologist never fully closes the gap between him- or herself and "the other." Indeed, generations of anthropologists have been warned about the dangers of losing a critical distance or of coming to see themselves as members of (or, worse, spokespersons for) a different and usually less powerful society. Still, the assumption is that the more anthropologists immerse themselves in a social context, the better they will come to understand it.

But what does it mean to apply such a method to one's own society? The modern metropolis is full of strangers and "others," persons whose worldview may be fundamentally different from one's own. Yet the various "villages" that make up the modern city are less clearly bounded and sharply differentiated than the typical subject of classic ethnography, that is, the traditional small community dominated by face-to-face communication and dense social ties. Modern people may simultaneously belong to many overlapping social groups, or they may experience a sense of isolation from all of them. Still, at the core of the urban ethnographic enterprise lies the idea that observing people in their everyday contexts, in various unstructured situations over an extended period of time, may offer clues as to how they construct and make sense of their world.

Ethnography emphasizes the utility of personal experiences—the experiences of both the people being studied and the people doing the study. On the one hand, ethnographers are interested in what it is like to be alive at a particular moment, in the daily experiences of ordinary people on ordinary days, and in the interpretations that they themselves bring to these experiences. Over time, in fact, good ethnography can turn into great social history. On the other hand, ethnographers believe that they cannot know such things without relying on their own experiences of standing in (or at least near) other people's shoes. By subjecting themselves as much as possible to the daily circumstances of the people they write about, they hope to come to understand, although not necessarily to share, their worldview.

Engaging in a study of this kind requires an investigator to have the "nerve" to go up to strangers and enlist their help and cooperation. This is most difficult when researchers take on roles as participant observers that are not their own. This is also a method that frequently requires courage or naiveté (or both) from research subjects, who must trust that a researcher will not exploit or take advantage of them. Much ethnography involves a complex negotiation between the observer and the observed, as well as considerable self-reflection as each party interrogates his or her own position in relation to that of "the other."

It is in this interaction between the personal experience of the subject and that of the investigator that ethnography lies. The method requires a commitment to "being there" for an extended period, to spending a great deal of time with research subjects, and to ensuring that the subjects are able to accept the researcher's presence at least on a minimal level. It also entails a kind of subjectivity that is often absent in more statistical types of research, meaning that the ethnographer needs to work very hard to maintain a scientific disposition. Striking the right balance of subjective insight, empathy, and scientific rigor is never easy.

Ethnography is not based exclusively on interviews, even though interviews frequently form part of the research. It is difficult to know about people's practices without talking to them about the meanings these practices have to them (Wuthnow 2012, vii.). But while interviews have great value, even the best ones are limited to what subjects actually know and are able or willing to articulate to a relative stranger. This is true regardless of whether the results are quantified, as in a survey, or presented in narrative form. Although ethnography is sometimes said to "give voice" to its subjects, one of its greatest strengths lies in its ability to examine the relationship between what people *say* and what they actually *do*. For this reason, the ethnographer must come to grips with the subject's understanding of his or her situation but also go beyond simple reportage in his or her own analysis. Great studies often emerge from efforts to understand the unspoken rules and *"definition of the situation"* (Thomas 1923) that make a life reasonable, meaningful, and normal to the people who live it (Hughes 1971) as well as the social categories that people use to make sense of their world.

The ethnographer needs to understand things that are taken for granted but never defined (Hughes 1971). This usually requires him or her to observe how social life operates in the long run. In this respect

the old canard that ethnography is merely "slow journalism" is half true; good ethnographic work *is* slow! It has to be, because, unlike all but the best journalism, it seeks to go beyond what people might say in interviews and to reveal understandings that emerge only after countless interactions over the course of time.

Furthermore, while the survey researcher, interviewer, or experimenter needs to have a pretty good idea of the kinds of topics he or she will learn about through questionnaires or experiments, the ethnographer who puts him- or herself in a "natural" setting is more likely to be surprised by what he or she discovers. Indeed, one of the method's great strengths is that it is not limited to questions composed in advance. Ethnographic researchers do not—or at least should not—"insulate" themselves from insights that are only tangentially related to the questions with which they begin. They must deal with "surprise data, things [they] didn't ask about but were told anyway" (Becker 1996, p. 56). One of the founding stories of urban ethnography allegedly occurred on a morning in 1910 when W. I. Thomas, Professor of Sociology at the University of Chicago, "had to duck to avoid some garbage being tossed into an alley on Chicago's West Side. The bundle contained several packages of letters in Polish" (Bennett 1981, p. 123), which became the basis of Thomas and Florian Znaniecki's classic, *The Polish Peasant in Europe and America* (1918-1920). Such surprises are the essence of ethnography, in which research is sometimes indebted to serendipity and the discovery of valuable things that had not been originally sought. Of course, good luck is not a methodological tool, and interviews too may take unintended directions. But a pivotal aspect of ethnography is that it does not depend heavily on a research design or an initial research question.

For many years after Park taught that first generation of students in the 1920s, urban ethnography ranked among the mainstays of social scientific research. Practiced by anthropologists, social workers, political scientists, urban studies specialists, and most often by sociologists, it made many important contributions to the conceptual vocabulary of scholars and social theorists, journalists, and social critics. From the mid-1960s to the late 1980s, however, urban ethnographic research was reduced to a somewhat marginal position within the social scientific profession due to advances in, survey techniques, statistical methods, and computer technology. It began to appear outmoded, if not quaint. Fine work continued to be done and leading practitioners of the craft were much honored as elder statesmen, but few aspiring social scientists were encouraged to follow in their footsteps.

More recently, things have changed. Since the early 1990s the field has been experiencing an extraordinary revival as demonstrated by many new books, journal articles, and conferences in the discipline as well as the many ethnographers currently holding tenure or tenure-track positions in universities across the United States. Two decades ago, there were only a handful of sociology departments with ethnographers on their faculty. Today, there are only a handful of major departments that do not have any. After a long period of marginalization, methods that privilege the meanings people bring to their situations and the organization of everyday life are once again deemed vital and necessary.

***

What is the "urban" in urban ethnography? The term as commonly used today is something of a misnomer. While most "urban" ethnographic research does take place in cities, it is also conducted outside politically defined city limits, in suburbs, or (to quote the title of a classic study) in a "small town in Mass Society" (Vidich and Bensman 1958). The term is a legacy of the

nineteenth-century notion that "urban" society, with its complex division of labor and reliance on impersonal, often utilitarian social bonds, is the quintessential "modern" society. According to this line of reasoning, "urban" is the converse of "traditional," that is, premodern or precapitalist communities frequently epitomized by the rural village with its deep social ties and priority on face-to-face relationships. For most early twentieth-century anthropologists, ethnographic work meant living for a long stretch of time in a traditional community in a social world largely bound by relations among a few hundred or at most a few thousand people. "Urban" or "modern" ethnography, by contrast, took place in communities where social bonds were looser and social connections extended across a much broader network but were assumed to be more tenuous, contingent and less all-consuming. Of course, social scientists know that the urban/modern vs. rural/traditional dichotomy is a huge oversimplification. Cities do not always destroy dense primary relationships. Indeed, in the modern world, the social life of a dense urban neighborhood may be more village-like than it is in smaller communities (see, for example, Herbert Gans's selection in Part VII).

In another important respect urban ethnography is clearly "urban." It was only with the massive growth and unprecedented diversity of the mid-nineteenth-century city that there arose a nonfiction literary genre in which the conventions of travel writing and the emerging field of anthropology were applied to the developed world. In the early twentieth century such literature began assuming the form and discipline of a social science. Of course, authors have been writing about the ways of life of other groups of people since antiquity, yet their efforts to understand the lives of "the other" have usually focused on populations physically distant from their and presumably their readers' homes. The appeal of the classic traveler's tale lay in its ability to provide readers with a view of the lives of strange and different people and the vicarious thrill of identifying with the adventurous traveler, who had journeyed to distant lands and come back to tell the tale!

In early urban ethnography we see that the city—the familiar "home turf" of the literate minority in most societies—is a place of mystery, a strange collection of social worlds that begs to be explained and understood or, as is too often the case, to be exoticized, gawked at, or "reformed." The earliest proto-urban ethnography published in Britain and France in the mid-nineteenth century shares the intellectual climate of the period's popular fiction in bringing presumably middle-class urban readers into the mysterious worlds of the poor, the working class, bohemians, immigrants, and other exotic subcultures inhabiting strange worlds across town. High-minded social reformers often made direct analogies between their work among "denizens" of working-class districts and popular accounts of the "savage" colonial world. Margaret Harkness's 1889 social documentary of the East End, for example, was entitled *In Darkest London*! At their best, proto-ethnographic accounts such as Henry Mayhew's classic *London Labor and the London Poor* (1861) combined rich descriptions of the daily life of various communities with early quantitative analyses and trenchant social criticism.

In these publications and in much of the ethnographic work that followed, it was the modern city that was the world of "strangers," albeit the strangers next door. Once familiar territory, rapidly growing cities like Park's Chicago had become places of mystery. As with the social realism of novelists and the sensationalism of muckraking journalists, so too with early urban ethnography—its allure lay in its voyeurism into diverse social worlds that were all too close and yet so far from those of middle-class readers.

Park and his contemporaries in the Chicago School tried hard to play down this aspect of ethnography. Indeed, the more potentially sensational or lurid the social situations they sought to investigate, the more they assumed an "objective" scientific pose (see Cressey's account of "taxi dancers"). For them, the goal was to portray situations that appeared bizarre, impenetrable, and threatening from the outside as understandable, reasonable, and even ordinary through the presentation of an "inside" point of view. All the same, there is a perennial danger that the ethnographer will create a narrative in which the reader identifies with the researcher and his or her journey, thus making the researcher the focal point of the story.

Yet we hope readers of this volume will agree that, at its best, urban ethnography can do exactly the opposite. At a time when so much urban life is so often seen in the most sensationalist terms, urban ethnography can help readers make sense of worlds that seem impenetrable during the first encounter. We hope readers will also agree that this literature clarifies how patient, skilled, and hard-working observers can render individuals of other than their own race, class, gender, and circumstances recognizable and understandable.

Finally, urban ethnography is also "urban" in the sense that over the years it has sought to reflect the ways in which people tend to think about cities and the social "problems" popularly associated with them. As the following pages illustrate, urban ethnographic accounts reflect issues confronting societies at the time in which they were written. When the discipline came into being in Chicago early in the last century, immigration was one of the most pressing issues facing American cities and American social science. Many US cities had a minority of native English speakers. Thus some of the earliest social scientific studies sought to comprehend how immigrants adapted to their new environment. Within a decade of this first wave of scholarship, black migration from southern states to northern cities turned race into the second great problem tackled by US sociology. At this point, the questions faced by urban ethnographers had to do with the adaptation of former black sharecroppers and small farmers to their new surroundings as they flocked to look for better jobs and decent housing stock.

Recent arrivals in growing cities, regardless of their race or ethnic backgrounds, began negotiating new ways of life. The "rules" controlling social behavior often differed from those of the communities in which these people had grown up. Some observers saw such cities as inherently "disorganized" and beset with "deviance" and "anomie." For others, however, the communities of the modern metropolis enabled the creation of new types of social connections and the rise of complex subcultures that might not have been possible in less populous settings. Thus, in one form or another, the great problems of early urban ethnography had to do with migration, race, and the changing nature of social bonds.

As time passed and as the first generation of European migrants achieved upward mobility, African Americans were often left behind in urban slums. Whereas in the 1920s, it was Jews who lived in so-called ghettos on the Lower East Side of New York or the West Side of Chicago, by the end of World War II it was blacks who were exclusively identified with this type of living condition. Social scientists began to think of the ghetto as the central arena of African-American life.

New questions revolved around this community context of poor black people. In studies of the South Side of Chicago, Harlem, and Philadelphia, for example, ethnographers wrote about life in places where various kinds of people, who would normally have never lived together, were being forced to live among each other because they could not move elsewhere. In doing so, they focused on understanding values within the ghetto and explaining the differences between the value systems of ghetto dwellers and those outside.

In the wake of the social upheavals of the 1960s and 1970s, urban African-American communities were once again defined as a social problem. Many citizens and politicians came to the conclusion that the values of the poor, particularly poor African Americans, were fundamentally at odds with those of the wider society. While some ethnographic studies appeared to show just this, others produced evidence that when it came to work and family, the aspirations of the poor were not so different from those of the rest of society; their life styles and values were adaptations to the racism and high unemployment they faced (for examples, see the chapters by Elliot Liebow and Carol Stack).

Around the same time, students of middle-class life in both the United States and Europe were trying to make sense of new modes of community emerging in the suburbs. Gender relations were changing, and domestic life was to an unprecedented degree becoming spatially separated from work life. What was more, the very organization of work life was changing in response to new technologies and changing class relations. Finally, the postwar reorganization of cities gave rise to new questions concerning the use of public space. All these issues offered fertile ground for ethnographic research.

Subsequent urban ethnography turned to examine the implications of major policy shifts such as deindustrialization, "broken windows" policing, hypersegregation, gentrification, and mass incarceration, as well as the resumption of mass immigration to both the United States and Western Europe. This tradition has not been distinguished merely by its attention to the details of local contexts. The investigating ethnographer also strives to understand how parts relate to the whole, including that largest context, which transcends the local community. His or her interpretations can make visible the social forces of the time, which include local labor markets, policy regimes, and forces such as institutional racism, capitalism, and globalization. These connections extend from the macro to the micro and back again.

In all of these studies, old and new alike, we can see how the ethnographer's findings are shaped by a larger structural context and how his or her interpretations reveal the social forces of a particular period. The earlier studies in this volume were based on the social structure of their time. Urban ethnography lights up "structure" and is always interacting with it. As structure changes, ethnographers need to be aware of those shifts in order to "see" more clearly what is before them and to speak in a relevant voice. But this is also why they need to keep at it: ethnography must be continuous because the undergirding reality keeps changing. As in Park's day, armchair theorizing and trips to the library, or for that matter, excursions on the Internet, are not enough. Ethnographers need *to be* in a place to show how things work.

***

Making the fifty-two selections for this volume from nearly a century's worth of scholarship involved many hard choices. We have tried to create a balance between older and newer pieces and to include well-written presentations of social life on the level at which it occurred. We have not included pieces that we felt show only as much of the people or scene as is absolutely necessary for making a theoretical point. In general, we have probably erred on the side of choosing compelling descriptions and insightful accounts of people's worldviews over more theoretical contributions and works that, however valuable, seemed overly focused on the inner life of the researchers or on how they knew what they knew. While such works are important to the connoisseurs of the discipline, we feel that they have a lesser place in a work for a broader audience.

Indeed, we do hope that after studying these selections, both undergraduates and graduate students will take up our invitation to urban ethnography and appreciate these works as readers. For as much as urban ethnography is a rigorous form of social science, it is also an influential form of literature—one that informs, challenges, and, at its best, captivates readers by helping them engage with a changing world. After spending time with the works in this volume we hope you will agree that ethnographic work can be both good science and a darn good read.

NOTE

1. Quoted in John C. McKinney, *Constructive Typology and Social Theory*, p. 71.

REFERENCES

Becker, Howard S. 1996. "The Epistemology of Qualitative Research." In *Ethnography and Human Development: Context and Meaning in Social Inquiry*. Richard Jessor, Anne Colby, and Richard A. Schweder (eds.). Chicago: University of Chicago Press, pp. 53–72.

Bennett, James. 1981. *Oral History and Delinquency: The Rhetoric of Criminology*. Chicago: University of Chicago Press.

Hughes, Everett C. 1971. *The Sociological Eye, Selected Papers*. Chicago: Aldine-Atherton.

McKinney, John C. 1966. *Constructive Typology and Social Theory*. New York: Appleton-Century-Crofts.

Thomas, William I. and Florian Znaniecki. 1918-1920. *The Polish Peasant in Europe and America: Monograph of an Immigrant Group*, Vol. 1, *Primary-Group Organization* (1918). Chicago: University of Chicago Press; Vol. 2, *Primary Group Organization* (1918). Chicago: University of Chicago Press; Vol. 3, *Life Record of an Immigrant* (1919). Boston: Badger; Vol. 4, *Disorganization and Reorganization in Poland* (1920). Boston: Badger; Vol. 5, *Organization and Disorganization in America* (1920). Boston: Badger.

Thomas, William I. 1923. *The Unadjusted Girl: With Cases and Standpoint for Behavior Analysis*. Boston, MA: Little, Brown and Company.

Vidich, Arthur J. and Joseph Bensman. 1958. *Small Town in Mass Society: Class, Power, and Religion in a Rural Community*. Princeton, NJ: Princeton University Press.

Wuthnow, Robert. 2012. *The God Problem: Expressing Faith and Being Reasonable*. Berkeley: University of California Press.

PART I

FINDING COMMUNITY IN THE MODERN CITY

///

Since ancient times people have been fascinated by the lives of people different from themselves. Over the centuries, many talented writers have sought to make the "other" understandable to themselves and their readers.

In the mid-nineteenth century, the growth of the modern city saw a particular flowering of proto-ethnographic work in Europe and a bit later in the United States. Much of this American work, undertaken by journalists, social reformers, and the first generation of empirical social scientists, was focused on two groups of "strangers": immigrants and African Americans, both of whom were establishing enclaves in the nation's rapidly growing cities at the time.

"Chinatown," the selection by Jacob Riis from his book *How the Other Half Lives*, is an example of this type of proto-ethnographic work. In many ways it presages later ethnographic accounts by combining meticulous observation, analysis of official data, interviews, and the then new technology of mobile photography. A social reformer, Riis felt that by documenting conditions in growing urban slums he could help arouse the indignation of his middle-class audience. In retrospect, however, as Riis opens the lives of the "exotic" poor to middle-class inspection,

his admirable reform impulse seems mixed with an appeal to his readers' voyeurism. In many ways Riis's use of photography to make his points and his career as a lecturer foreshadows the popularity of ethnographic film in later decades. The reader may notice, however, that in Chinatown not a single member of the Chinese community is consulted for an opinion or view. Everything the author says about the Chinese comes from inferences he makes on the basis of reports from police officers and other officials. Despite its many innovations in description and documentation of the lives of the urban poor, Riis's work is therefore not really ethnographic, though it clearly foreshadows much future ethnography.

W. E. B. Du Bois's *The Philadelphia Negro*, published in 1898, should probably be regarded as the first work of American urban ethnography, as well as one of the earliest empirical pieces of modern sociology. Du Bois spent fifteen months living with and talking to people in the Seventh Ward of Philadelphia. He later added census data to create a comprehensive portrait of African-American life in this neighborhood. His pioneering work was an effort to firmly establish the study of the black community as a central topic in American social science.

Fieldwork came into formal existence as a recognized method of social science under the direction of Robert Park at the University of Chicago in the 1920s. Although Du Bois's work predates Robert Park's by decades, it was soon confronted by the racism that pervaded early twentieth-century academic life. Despite his efforts, Du Bois was never able to obtain sufficient funding to establish a program of sociological research at the nation's black colleges, nor did his work gain much attention in white institutions. In the decades after the publication of *The Philadelphia Negro*, Du Bois left academia to concentrate on political and historical writings.[1]

One thing Du Bois (and Riis) share with later urban ethnographers is their focus on the community context as a setting in which urban issues are played out. The profound impact of the physical and social atmosphere on people's lives has been a key insight of sociology since the discipline's founding. Du Bois's *The Philadelphia Negro*, for example, focuses on an urban black neighborhood in late nineteenth-century Philadelphia by looking at it as a site of interaction (and lack of interaction) among a wide variety of social classes. These classes are best understood not on their own but in relation to each another and to the physical community.

Du Bois is careful in explaining the grounds for differentiating classes, and the reader will notice that his criteria are not simply quantitative indices but aspects of everyday life that can be discerned only through a careful reading. In describing the stable working class of the black community, for example, Du Bois focuses on how its members see and define their condition. He documents their sense of discouragement when their jobs are not equal to their talents and their pay far less than what they feel they deserve. Their situation reflects a clear difference between the black and white working classes of the era, one that would have been impossible to understand without talking to the people described. Du Bois has shown the subtle ways in which aspects of society that are held to be separate actually merge together in the everyday life of the community. When he notes that "often in the same family one can find respectable and striving parents weighed down by idle, impudent sons and wayward daughters" (p. 315), he gives due recognition to the complexity of the situation.

Du Bois's attention to social classes in relation to each other makes the excerpt here exemplary of another key dimension of urban ethnography. While people (particularly whites) outside the neighborhood that he discusses usually saw the black population as homogeneous, the people inside were aware of massive social differentiation. Du Bois emphasizes the subjective states of middle-class blacks and notes their reactions to being lumped together with the poor people with whom—due to segregation—they share the community. However, Du Bois's insight comes at a price. The reader struggles in *The Philadelphia Negro* to find instances in which the perspective of a member of the poorer classes is taken into account. This is a common problem in urban ethnography. Most investigators—including those, like Du Bois, who may share a racial identity with the people they study—are themselves members of the "better classes." Thus, particularly in studies of African-American communities, the emphasis is often on how the middle class feels about being lumped with the lower classes, while much less is said on how the poor feel about their position within the community.

In the 1920s, urban ethnography was institutionalized in the academy as a form of empirical social science. Qualitative inquiries into the nature of modern life came about in dialogue with quantitative methods as social science slowly shifted away from being a largely theoretical field.

In American sociology this empirical turn was particularly well represented among the group of scholars who worked with or were trained by Park. A newspaperman turned sociologist, Park remained a leading figure from the late 1910s until his death in 1943 in what came to be called the "Chicago School" of urban sociology. He arrived at social science via a circuitous route. Having studied philosophy with the American pragmatists John Dewey and William James, Park had done postgraduate work in Germany, where he was greatly influenced by the social theorist Georg Simmel and the philosopher Wilhelm Windelband. He also worked as a reporter for the *Minneapolis Star* and spent several years as a scholar-activist working closely with Du Bois's adversary, Booker T. Washington, at the Tuskegee Institute, where he wrote about the issue of race in the United States and published exposés of brutal conditions in colonial Africa. In 1914, at the age of fifty, he accepted an academic appointment at the University of Chicago where he remained for the rest of his career. He soon became a dominant force in a department increasingly dedicated to empirical research on the great city around it.

At this time, Chicago, Sandberg's "city of the big shoulders," was among the fastest growing cities in the world. An industrial behemoth, Chicago symbolized the forces of modernity, capitalism, and the emergence of mass media and consumption for many Americans. It was a rapidly changing city in which most residents were migrants. Trying to make sense of this churning metropolis, Park and his students, most notably Louis Wirth, drew on European theorists such as Simmel, Ferdinand Toennies, and Emile Durkheim. These authors had seen the modern city, and perhaps modernity in general, as a destroyer of traditional community ties and one in which human relations had become tinged with rootless individualism, alienation, and anomie. In the modern city, they argued, bonds of social control were loosened, giving rise to feelings of marginality and behavioral deviance. Despite suffusing early Chicago School studies, however, these views were often in tension with the researchers' discovery of emerging new bases of social solidarity and forms of community developing out of the city's dense neighborhoods and of their ethnic, social, and occupational subcultures.

Furthermore, though Park was interested in developing theory, he felt that theoretical ideas had to relate directly to the actual lives of people and thus needed to be based on the careful accumulation of evidence. To this end, Park felt it was vital that social scientists experience the city, in all its nooks, crannies, and out-of-the-way corners. New forms of community emerging in the city needed to be understood in the same terms as the urbanites themselves understood them. For this to happen, he told his students, they had to meet the subjects of sociological theories and understand how they made sense of their worlds.

Many did just that. Following Park's lead, the University of Chicago's sociology department used the city as a laboratory. These early sociologists took on roles in communities as "participant observers," combining interviews with "fieldwork" that entailed detailed observations of social life, often over long periods of time. Much of their work was oriented toward improving conditions in the city and the country as a whole. Yet unlike Riis and most of the other reform-minded journalists and social workers who had preceded them (and even more so than Du Bois), they usually privileged the definition of the situation that ordinary people brought to the scene.

A number of works that came out of this tradition have been included in this volume, including our third selection from *Black Metropolis* by St. Clair Drake and Horace

Cayton. Studying the African-American community on the South Side of Chicago in the 1940s, these two young black scholars demonstrated the ability of ethnographic studies to treat lower-class populations with dignity and to take the inner life of such communities seriously. Like Du Bois, Drake and Cayton situate the black ghetto of Chicago in terms of the larger social forces that created it. In doing so, however, they also take the reader into the lives of the poorest residents of black neighborhoods. We see how the poor define their own situation, which gives us insight into the conditions that lead them to behave in ways that the middle class defines as problematic. We see what can be gained from hearing the voices of the poor, as well as the power of urban ethnography in presenting the everyday life of subjects in fine-grained detail. In this selection, Drake and Cayton take their readers inside a typical, impoverished South Side home, and they use the experimental device of fictionalized composite characters to great effect.

In the 1960s, this kind of complex portrait of the inner city was updated by the Swedish anthropologist Ulf Hannerz, who asked what was distinctive about ghetto living. Depicting the various life styles of poor residents in Winston Street, a slum community in Washington, D.C., in a period when the United States was focused on race riots and the alleviation of poverty, his study addressed the many Americans who wondered whether poor black ghetto residents were committed to the same values as those harbored by society at large. Hannerz's study takes readers into the world of a ghetto not far from the White House, and he draws a complex picture of different kinds of community members—"mainstreamers," "swingers," and "street families"—in regular interaction with each other. Hannerz demonstrated that many local residents were committed to the same values as those embraced by the broader American society, though some

were quite different in their orientation. All in all, he argued, black culture was a subculture of American culture.

The selection by Harvey Molotch, written just a few years after Hannerz's, highlights yet another key dimension of the study of urban life at the community level: the nature of social integration between racial and ethnic groups. One of the most difficult questions for social scientists to address is how people interact across racial lines. We know that historically blacks and whites have lived quite separately, yet sometimes quite near one another. What is the nature of their social interactions under these conditions? Molotch's research required that he count the number of black and white patrons in various shops and commercial spaces. His discovery that blacks and whites shopped in the same places but did not otherwise socialize or do business in intimate settings was a benchmark finding. Also noteworthy is that most quantitative studies of urban neighborhoods based on official data, such as the census, focus on where people "live," that is, where they sleep. By focusing instead on sites of commercial activity, Molotch offers a sense of how urban space was actually defined, used, lived in, and racialized within everyday interactions.

Likewise, writing about interaction across racial lines on the South Side of Chicago almost two decades later, Mitchell Duneier observed something very different. In his study of the interactions between black and white men in a cafeteria in the Hyde Park neighborhood, Duneier observed how interactions between the races could occur in such commercial spaces. Indeed, such interactions could be quite profound, even intimate. They could also involve people who were seen as (and who might consider themselves to be) quite different from each other—in this case, an older black working-class man who had long lived in the black ghetto and an older white man raised in the South. In showing how these men came to develop strong ties with one another inside and outside the cafeteria, Duneier reveals the power that routine interactions in such spaces had to challenge stereotypes and facilitate understanding among urban dwellers.

While Duneier uncovered the formation of unlikely friendships across racial lines, John L. Jackson Jr. discovered something quite different in his study of the historically African-American neighborhood of Harlem in New York City. There, many residents claimed to have no "friends" at all. This was especially curious because Jackson observed that people who claimed to have no friends interacted and spent time hanging out with people in ways that frequently looked, to the ethnographer, like friendship. Jackson shows us that Harlemites are embedded in class-stratified social networks and that the way in which class is "performed" in everyday life is complex and constantly negotiated. This can result in people claiming to have no friends beyond their family members. Jackson's close attention to the nuanced ways in which people define and enact their relationships reminds us that the relationships composing a community are intricate, evolving, and often situational in ways not always captured in concepts such as "neighbor" or "friend."

Urban ethnographers often think of "communities" geographically. In most cases they are studying neighborhoods, and sometimes use "community" and "neighborhood" almost synonymously, as we do in common talk. Of course, we know that human communities rarely correspond to precise geographic locations, though the two are often related. In the contemporary world, high-speed travel and communication make it increasingly possible for small, bounded communities to occupy different physical spaces, sometimes in different parts of the world, simultaneously. Robert Courtney

Smith's *Mexican New York* is a study of one such transnational community. "Ticuani" (a pseudonym) is a small village in central Mexico. By the 1990s most of its population had migrated to New York City in search of work. Yet even today Ticuani's people remain closely tied to each other and to their home village. They continue to frequently visit and send financial support; the village remains important to their social identity. Moving between the United States and Mexico does change the community's social life and culture, however, both in New York and in Ticuani. Rather than view the villagers as migrants who leave the "old country" and "assimilate" (or not) into the new one, Smith portrays them as being embedded in an ongoing transnational social field that links Ticuani and New York. Like his subjects, Smith travels back and forth between Ticuani and the Mexican neighborhoods of New York while conducting his research. His work has become a model of the sort of "mobile ethnography" that is increasingly undertaken by those wishing to study transnational communities in an era of globalization.

Of course, not all studies of urban community focus on the poor. We thus end this section with two selections that discuss transformations in certain American cities that occur when run-down neighborhoods see an influx of artists, students, and new middle-class residents, a phenomenon known as gentrification. In the excerpt from *Neo-Bohemia*, Richard Lloyd takes readers inside the Chicago neighborhood of Wicker Park during the 1990s. We meet young white newcomers, who are very different from the whites that Harvey Molotch encountered in Chicago in the 1960s. Moving into a neighborhood that was once poor and Latino, the new residents celebrate the grit and danger surrounding them as constituents of an "authentic" urban bohemian experience. Lloyd demonstrates the power of urban ethnography to display with rich detail how people experience the community setting in which they live. We come to know the young men and women who move to Wicker Park and what inspires them to take up residence with other like-minded young people.

The last piece in this section is a study of neighborhood change in the Venice Beach community of Los Angeles. Andrew Deener studied the transformation of Abbot Kinney Boulevard from a poor area into a mixed-income "bohemian" neighborhood with many affordable "hip" stores and then into a community where grit has been completely stamped out in favor of multimillion-dollar "artist" lofts and elite boutiques. Although these newer stores are affordable to only the wealthy, they were created in the image of the artistic and bohemian identities that they ironically displaced. Noteworthy too is that by putting commercial life at the center of his analysis, Deener provides us with some unusual insights into how the area is now being used and perceived, not only by local residents but also by shoppers and store owners who live in other parts of the city.

In each of these pieces, the ability of urban ethnography to document the latest urban transformation stands out. Just as Du Bois examined a Northern city as it adjusted to the emancipation of African Americans in the decades after the Civil War, so today's ethnographers document the social transformations that are remaking the city of the twenty-first century.

NOTE

1. Ironically, Park, who led the department that would one day make urban ethnography one of the founding traditions of American sociology, had previously worked for Booker T. Washington, Du Bois's nemesis. The Park/Washington/Du Bois connection and its possible role in marginalizing Du Bois in early twentieth-century social science is discussed in Aldon Morris's book manuscript on the role of Du Bois in the founding of American sociology. We are indebted to Professor Morris for allowing us to read his work in advance of publication.

1

JACOB RIIS

CHINATOWN

from *How the Other Half Lives* (1890)

In *How the Other Half Lives,* the Danish-born social reformer, journalist, and photographer Jacob Riis affords middle-class readers a glimpse into the "exotic" social world of an urban immigrant neighborhood. Riis's goal was to inform readers about what he considered scandalous slum conditions. For contemporary readers, the piece also provides one of the earliest descriptions of New York's Chinatown.

Between the tabernacles of Jewry and the shrines of the Bend, Joss[1] has cheekily planted his pagan worship of idols, chief among which are the celestial worshippers' own gain and lusts. Whatever may be said about the Chinaman being a thousand years behind the age on his own shores, here he is distinctly abreast of it in his successful scheming to "make it pay." It is doubtful if there is anything he does not turn to a paving account, from his religion down, or up, as one prefers. At the risk of distressing some well-meaning, but, I fear, too trustful people, I state it in advance as my opinion, based on the steady observation of years, that all attempts to make an effective Christian of John Chinaman will remain abortive in this generation; of the next I have, if anything, less hope. Ages of senseless idolatry, a mere grub-worship, have left him without the essential qualities for appreciating the gentle teachings of a faith whose motive and unselfish spirit are alike beyond his grasp. He lacks the handle of a strong faith in something, anything, however wrong, to catch him by. There is nothing strong about him, except his passions when aroused. I am convinced that he adopts Christianity, when he adopts it at all, as he puts on American clothes, with what the politicians would call an ulterior motive, some sort of gain in the near prospect— washing, a Christian wife perhaps, anything he happens to rate for the moment above his cherished pig-tail. It may be that I judge him too harshly. Exceptions may be found.

Indeed, for the credit of the race, I hope there are such. But I am bound to say my hope is not backed by lively faith.

Chinatown as a spectacle is disappointing. Next-door neighbor to the Bend, it has little of its outdoor stir and life, none of its gaily-colored rags or picturesque filth and poverty. Mott Street is clean to distraction: the laundry stamp is on it, though the houses are chiefly of the conventional tenement-house type, with nothing to rescue them from the everyday dismal dreariness of their kind save here and there a splash of dull red or yellow, a sign, hung endways and with streamers of red flannel tacked on, that announces in Chinese characters that Dr. Chay Yen Chong sells Chinese herb medicines, or that Won Lung & Co.—queer contradiction—take in washing, or deal out tea and groceries. There are some gimcracks in the second story fire-escape of one of the houses, signifying that Joss or a club has a habitation there. An American patent medicine concern has seized the opportunity to decorate the back-ground with its cabalistic trade-mark, that in this company looks as foreign as the rest. Doubtless the privilege was bought for cash. It will buy anything in Chinatown, Joss himself included, as indeed, why should it not? He was bought for cash across the sea and came here under the law that shuts out the live Chinaman, but lets in his dead god on payment of the statutory duty on bric-à-brac. Red and yellow are the holiday colors of Chinatown as of the Bend, but they do not lend brightness in Mott Street as around the corner in Mulberry. Rather, they seem to descend to the level of the general dulness, and glower at you from doors and windows, from the telegraph pole that is the official organ of Chinatown and from the store signs, with blank, unmeaning stare, suggesting nothing, asking no questions, and answering none. Fifth Avenue is not duller on a rainy day than Mott Street to one in search of excitement. Whatever is on foot goes on behind closed doors. Stealth

and secretiveness are as much part of the Chinaman in New York as the cat-like tread of his felt shoes. His business, as his domestic life, shuns the light, less because there is anything to conceal than because that is the way of the man. Perhaps the attitude of American civilization toward the stranger, whom it invited in, has taught him that way. At any rate, the very doorways of his offices and shops are fenced off by queer, forbidding partitions suggestive of a continual state of siege. The stranger who enters through the crooked approach is received with sudden silence, a sullen stare, and an angry "Vat you vant?" that breathes annoyance and distrust.

Trust not him who trusts no one, is as safe a rule in Chinatown as out of it. Were not Mott Street overawed in its isolation, it would not be safe to descend this open cellar-way, through which come the pungent odor of burning opium and the clink of copper coins on the table. As it is, though safe, it is not profitable to intrude. At the first foot-fall of leather soles on the steps the hum of talk ceases, and the group of celestials, crouching over their game of fan tan,[2] stop playing and watch the comer with ugly looks. Fan tan is their ruling passion. The average Chinaman, the police will tell you, would rather gamble than eat any day, and they have ample experience to back them. Only the fellow in the bunk smokes away, indifferent to all else but his pipe and his own enjoyment. It is a mistake to assume that Chinatown is honeycombed with opium "joints." There are a good many more outside of it than in it. The celestials do not monopolize the pipe. In Mott Street there is no need of them. Not a Chinese home or burrow there but has its bunk and its layout, where they can be enjoyed safe from police interference. The Chinaman smokes opium as Caucasians smoke tobacco, and apparently with little worse effect upon himself. But woe unto the white victim upon which his pitiless drug gets its grip!

The bloused pedlars who, with arms buried half to the elbow in their trousers' pockets, lounge behind their stock of water-melon seed and sugar-cane, cut in lengths to suit the purse of the buyer, disdain to offer the barbarian their wares. Chinatown, that does most things by contraries, rules it holiday style to carry its hands in its pockets, and its denizens follow the fashion, whether in blue blouse, in gray, or in brown, with shining and braided pig-tail dangling below the knees, or with hair cropped short above a coat collar of "Melican" cut. All kinds of men are met, but no women—none at least with almond eyes. The reason is simple: there are none. A few, a very few, Chinese merchants have wives of their own color, but they are seldom or never seen in the street. The "wives" of Chinatown are of a different stock that comes closer home.

From the teeming tenements to the right and left of it come the white slaves of its dens of vice and their infernal drug, that have infused into the "Bloody Sixth" Ward a subtler poison than ever the stale-beer dives knew, or the "sudden death" of the Old Brewery.[3] There are houses, dozens of them, in Mott and Pell Streets, that are literally jammed, from the "joint" in the cellar to the attic, with these hapless victims of a passion which, once acquired, demands the sacrifice of every instinct of decency to its insatiate desire. There is a church in Mott Street,[4] at the entrance to Chinatown, that stands as a barrier between it and the tenements beyond. Its young men have waged unceasing war upon the monstrous wickedness for years, but with very little real result. I have in mind a house in Pell Street that has been raided no end of times by the police, and its population emptied upon Blackwell's Island, or into the reformatories, yet is to-day honeycombed with scores of the conventional households of the Chinese quarter: the men worshippers of Joss; the women, all white, girls hardly yet grown to womanhood, worshipping nothing save the pipe that has enslaved them body and soul.

Easily tempted from homes that have no claim upon the name, they rarely or never return. Mott Street gives up its victims only to the Charity Hospital or the Potter's Field. Of the depth of their fall no one is more thoroughly aware than these girls themselves; no one less concerned about it. The calmness with which they discuss it, while insisting illogically upon the fiction of a marriage that deceives no one, is disheartening. Their misery is peculiarly fond of company, and an amount of visiting goes on in these households that makes it extremely difficult for the stranger to untangle them. I came across a company of them "hitting the pipe" together, on a tour through their dens one night with the police captain of the precinct. The girls knew him, called him by name, offered him a pipe, and chatted with him about the incidents of their acquaintance, how many times he had "sent them up," and their chances of "lasting" much longer. There was no shade of regret in their voices, nothing but utter indifference and surrender.

One thing about them was conspicuous: their scrupulous neatness. It is the distinguishing mark of Chinatown, outwardly and physically. It is not altogether by chance the Chinaman has chosen the laundry as his distinctive field. He is by nature as clean as the cat, which he resembles in his traits of cruel cunning and savage fury when aroused. On this point of cleanliness he insists in his domestic circle, yielding in others with crafty submissiveness to the caprice of the girls, who "boss" him in a very independent manner, fretting vengefully under the yoke they loathe, but which they know right well they can never shake off, once they have put the pipe to their lips and given Mott Street a mortgage upon their souls for all time. To the priest, whom they call in when the poison racks the body, they pretend that they are yet their own masters; but he knows that it is an idle boast, least of all believed by themselves. As he walks with them the few short steps to the Potter's

Field, he hears the sad story he has heard told over and over again, of father, mother, home and friends given up for the accursed pipe, and stands hopeless and helpless before the colossal evil for which he knows no remedy.

The frequent assertions of the authorities that at least no girls under age are wrecked on this Chinese shoal, are disproved by the observation of those who go frequently among these dens, though the smallest girl will invariably, and usually without being asked, insist that she is sixteen, and so of age to choose the company she keeps. Such assertions are not to be taken seriously. Even while I am writing, the morning returns from one of the precincts that pass through my hands report the arrest of a Chinaman for "inveigling little girls into his laundry," one of the hundred outposts of Chinatown that are scattered all over the city, as the outer threads of the spider's web that holds its prey fast. Reference to case No. 39,499 in this year's report of the Society for the Prevention of Cruelty to Children, will discover one of the much travelled roads to Chinatown. The girl whose story it tells was thirteen, and one of six children abandoned by a dissipated father. She had been discharged from an Eighth Avenue store, where she was employed as cash girl, and, being afraid to tell her mother, floated about until she landed in a Chinese laundry. The judge heeded her tearful prayer, and sent her home with her mother, but she was back again in a little while despite all promises of reform.

Her tyrant knows well that she will come, and patiently bides his time. When her struggles in the web have ceased at last, he rules no longer with gloved hand. A specimen of celestial logic from the home circle at this period came home to me with a personal application one evening when I attempted, with a policeman, to stop a Chinaman whom we found beating his white "wife" with a broom-handle in a Mott Street cellar. He was angry at our interference, and declared vehemently that she was "bad."

"S'ppose your wifee bad, you no lickee her?" he asked, as if there could be no appeal from such a common-sense proposition as that. My assurance that I did not, that such a thing could not occur to me, struck him dumb with amazement. He eyed me a while in stupid silence, poked the linen in his tub, stole another look, and made up his mind. A gleam of intelligence shone in his eye, and pity and contempt struggled in his voice. "Then, I guess, she lickee you," he said.

No small commotion was caused in Chinatown once upon the occasion of an expedition I undertook, accompanied by a couple of police detectives, to photograph Joss. Some conscienceless wag spread the report, after we were gone, that his picture was wanted for the Rogues' Gallery at Headquarters. The insult was too gross to be passed over without atonement of some sort. Two roast pigs made matters all right with his offended majesty of Mott Street, and with his attendant priests, who bear a very practical hand in the worship by serving as the divine stomach, as it were. They eat the good things set before their rice-paper master, unless, as once happened, some sacrilegious tramp sneaks in and gets ahead of them. The practical way in which these people combine worship with business is certainly admirable. I was told that the scrawl covering the wall on both sides of the shrine stood for the names of the pillars of the church or club—the Joss House is both— that they might have their reward in this world, no matter what happened to them in the next. There was another inscription overhead that needed no interpreter. In familiar English letters, copied bodily from the trade dollar, was the sentiment: "In God we trust." The priest pointed to it with undisguised pride and attempted an explanation, from which I gathered that the inscription was intended as a diplomatic courtesy, a delicate international compliment to the "Melican Joss," the almighty dollar.

Chinatown has enlisted the telegraph for the dissemination of public intelligence, but it has got hold of the contrivance by the wrong end. As the wires serve us in newspaper-making, so the Chinaman makes use of the pole for the same purpose. The telegraph pole, of which I spoke as the real official organ of Chinatown, stands not far from the Joss House in Mott Street, in full view from Chatham Square. In it centres the real life of the colony, its gambling news. Every day yellow and red notices are posted upon it by unseen hands, announcing that in such and such a cellar a fan tan game will be running that night, or warning the faithful that a raid is intended on this or that game through the machination of a rival interest. A constant stream of plotting and counterplotting makes up the round of Chinese social and political existence. I do not pretend to understand the exact political structure of the colony, or its internal government. Even discarding as idle the stories of a secret cabal with power over life and death, and authority to enforce its decrees, there is evidence enough that the Chinese consider themselves subject to the laws of the land only when submission is unavoidable, and that they are governed by a code of their own, the very essence of which is rejection of all other authority except under compulsion. If now and then, some horrible crime in the Chinese colony, a murder of such hideous ferocity as one I have a very vivid recollection of, where the murderer stabbed his victim (both Chinamen, of course) in the back with a meat-knife, plunging it in to the hilt no less than seventeen times, arouses the popular prejudice to a suspicion that it was "ordered," only the suspected themselves are to blame, for they appear to rise up as one man to shield the criminal. The difficulty of tracing the motive of the crime and the murderer is extreme, and it is the rarest of all results that the police get on the track of either. The obstacles in the way of hunting down an Italian murderer are as nothing to the opposition encountered in

Chinatown. Nor is the failure of the pursuit wholly to be ascribed to the familiar fact that to Caucasian eyes "all Chinamen look alike," but rather to their acting "alike," in a body, to defeat discovery at any cost.

Withal the police give the Chinese the name of being the "quietest people down there," meaning in the notoriously turbulent Sixth Ward; and they are. The one thing they desire above all is to be let alone, a very natural wish perhaps, considering all the circumstances. If it were a laudable or even an allowable ambition that prompts it, they might be humored with advantage, probably, to both sides. But the facts show too plainly that it is not, and that in their very exclusiveness and reserve they are a constant and terrible menace to society, wholly regardless of their influence upon the industrial problems which their presence confuses. The severest official scrutiny, the harshest repressive measures are justifiable in Chinatown, orderly as it appears on the surface, even more than in the Bend, and the case is infinitely more urgent. To the peril that threatens there all the senses are alert, whereas the poison that proceeds from Mott Street puts mind and body to sleep, to work out its deadly purpose in the corruption of the soul.

This again may be set down as a harsh judgment. I may be accused of inciting persecution of an unoffending people. Far from it. Granted, that the Chinese are in no sense a desirable element of the population, that they serve no useful purpose here, whatever they may have done elsewhere in other days, yet to this it is a sufficient answer that they are here, and that, having let them in, we must make the best of it. This is a time for very plain speaking on this subject. Rather than banish the Chinaman, I would have the door opened wider—for his wife; make it a condition of his coming or staying that he bring his wife with him. Then, at least, he might not be what he now is and remains, a homeless stranger among us. Upon this hinges the real Chinese question, in our city at all events, as I see it. To assert that the victims of his drug and his base passions would go to the bad anyhow, is begging the question. They might and they might not. The chance is the span between life and death. From any other form of dissipation than that for which Chinatown stands there is recovery; for the victims of any other vice, hope. For these there is neither hope nor recovery; nothing but death—moral, mental, and physical death.

NOTES

1. *Joss*: a Pidgin English word derived from the Portuguese *deos*, meaning god.

2. *fan tan*: from the Chinese *fan* (number of times) and *t'an* (apportion), a gambling game involving guessing the remainder, after progressive elimination by fours, of a quantity of cards, counters, or beans.

3. *the Old Brewery*: a five-story building erected in 1792 on the bank of the Collect Pond and run as a brewery until 1837, when it became a vast tenement of mythic lore, alleged to have housed a thousand people at a time, as well as to have been the site of numerous murders. It was bought and razed in 1852 by the Ladies' Home Missionary Society of the Methodist Episcopal Church.

4. *a church in Mott Street*: the Church of the Transfiguration at 29 Mott, which still stands.

2

W. E. B. DU BOIS

SOCIAL CLASSES AND AMUSEMENTS

from *The Philadelphia Negro* (1899)

In one of the first empirical works of American social science, W. E. B. Du Bois studied the African-American ghetto of Philadelphia at the end of the nineteenth century. In this selection, Du Bois focuses on social differentiation within this community. While not denying that blacks have a common history, he focuses his attention on the distinctions that community residents draw among themselves. This selection emphasizes the anger experienced by the "better class of Negroes" when their distinctiveness is ignored by whites who lump them together with their poorer or less "respectable" neighbors.

Notwithstanding the large influence of the physical environment of home and ward, nevertheless there is a far mightier influence to mold and make the citizen, and that is the social atmosphere which surrounds him; first his daily companionship, the thoughts and whims of his class; then his recreations and amusements; finally the surrounding world of American civilization, which the Negro meets especially in his economic life. Let us take up here the subject of social classes and amusements among Negroes....

There is always a strong tendency on the part of the community to consider the Negroes as composing one practically homogeneous mass. This view has of course a certain justification: the people of Negro descent in this land have had a common history, suffer to-day common disabilities, and contribute to one general set of social problems. And yet if the foregoing statistics have emphasized any one fact it is that wide variations in antecedents, wealth, intelligence and general efficiency have already been differentiated within this group. These differences are not, to be sure, so great or so patent as those among the whites of to-day, and yet they undoubtedly equal the difference among the masses of the people in certain sections of the land fifty or one hundred years ago; and there is no surer way of misunderstanding the Negro or being misunderstood by him than by ignoring manifest differences of condition and power in the 40,000 black people of Philadelphia.

And yet well-meaning people continually do this. They regale the thugs and whoremongers and gamblers of Seventh and Lombard streets with congratulations on what the Negroes have done in a quarter century, and pity for their disabilities; and they scold the caterers of Addison street for the pickpockets and paupers of the race. A judge of the city courts, who for years has daily met a throng of lazy and debased Negro criminals, comes from the bench to talk to the Negroes about their criminals: he warns them first of all to leave the slums and either forgets or does not know that the fathers of the audience he is speaking to, left the slums when he was a boy and that the people before him are as distinctly differentiated from the criminals he has met, as honest laborers anywhere differ from thieves.

Nothing more exasperates the better class of Negroes than this tendency to ignore utterly their existence. The law-abiding, hard-working inhabitants of the Thirtieth Ward are aroused to righteous indignation when they see that the word Negro carries most Philadelphians' minds to the alleys of the Fifth Ward or the police courts. Since so much misunderstanding or rather forgetfulness and carelessness on this point is common, let us endeavor to try and fix with some definiteness the different social classes which are clearly enough defined among Negroes to deserve attention. When the statistics of the families of the Seventh Ward were gathered, each family was put in one of four grades as follows:

Grade 1. Families of undoubted respectability earning sufficient income to live well; not engaged in menial service of any kind; the wife engaged in no occupation save that of house-wife, except in a few cases where she had special employment at home. The children not compelled to be bread-winners, but found in school; the family living in a well-kept home.

Grade 2. The respectable working-class; in comfortable circumstances, with a good home, and having steady remunerative work. The younger children in school.

Grade 3. The poor; persons not earning enough to keep them at all times above want; honest, although not always energetic or thrifty, and with no touch of gross immorality or crime. Including the very poor, and the poor.

Grade 4. The lowest class of criminals, prostitutes and loafers; the "submerged tenth."

Thus we have in these four grades the criminals, the poor, the laborers, and the well-to-do.[1] The last class represents the ordinary middle-class folk of most modern countries, and contains the germs of other social classes which the Negro has not yet clearly differentiated. Let us begin first with the fourth class.

The criminals and gamblers are to be found at such centres as Seventh and Lombard streets, Seventeenth and Lombard, Twelfth and Kater, Eighteenth and Naudain, etc. Many people have failed to notice the significant change which has come over these slums in recent years; the squalor and misery and dumb suffering of 1840 has passed, and in its place have come more baffling and sinister phenomena: shrewd laziness, shameless lewdness, cunning crime. The loafers who line the curbs in these places are no fools, but sharp, wily men who often outwit both the Police Department and the Department of Charities. Their nucleus consists of a class of professional criminals, who do not work, figure in the rogues' galleries of a half-dozen cities, and migrate here and there. About these are a set of gamblers and sharpers who seldom are caught in serious crime, but who nevertheless live from its proceeds and aid and abet it. The headquarters of all these are usually the political clubs and pool-rooms; they stand ready to entrap the unwary and tempt the weak. Their organization, tacit or recognized, is very effective, and no one can long watch their actions without seeing that they keep in close touch with the authorities in some way. Affairs will be gliding on lazily some summer afternoon at the corner of Seventh and Lombard streets; a few loafers on the corners, a prostitute here and there, and the Jew and Italian plying their trades. Suddenly there is an oath, a sharp altercation, a blow; then a hurried rush of feet, the silent door of a neighboring club closes, and when the policeman arrives only the victim lies bleeding on the sidewalk; or at midnight the drowsy quiet will be suddenly broken by the cries and quarreling of a half-drunken gambling table; · then comes the sharp, quick crack of pistol shots—a scurrying in the darkness, and only the wounded man lies awaiting the patrol-wagon. If the matter turns out seriously, the police know where in Minster street and Middle alley to look for the aggressor; often they find him, but sometimes not.[2]

The size of the more desperate class of criminals and their shrewd abettors is of course comparatively small, but it is large enough to characterize the slum districts. Around this central body lies a large crowd of satellites and feeders; young idlers attracted by excitement, shiftless and lazy ne'er-do-wells, who have sunk from better things, and a rough crowd of pleasure seekers and libertines. These are the fellows who figure in the police courts for larceny and fighting; and drift thus into graver crime or shrewder dissoluteness. They are usually far more ignorant than their leaders, and rapidly die out from disease and excess. Proper measures for rescue and reform

might save many of this class. Usually they are not natives of the city, but immigrants who have wandered from the small towns of the South to Richmond and Washington and thence to Philadelphia. Their environment in this city makes it easier for them to live by crime or the results of crime than by work, and being without ambition—or perhaps having lost ambition and grown bitter with the world—they drift with the stream.

One large element of these slums, a class we have barely mentioned, are the prostitutes. It is difficult to get at any satisfactory data concerning such a class, but an attempt has been made. There were in 1896 fifty-three Negro women in the Seventh Ward known on pretty satisfactory evidence to be supported wholly or largely by the proceeds of prostitution; and it is probable that this is not half the real number;[3] these fifty-three were of the following ages:

14 to 19	2
20 to 24	11
25 to 29	9
30 to 39	17
40 to 49	3
50 and over	2
Unknown	9
Total	53

Seven of these women had small children with them and had probably been betrayed, and had then turned to this sort of life. There were fourteen recognized bawdy houses in the ward; ten of them were private dwellings where prostitutes lived and were not especially fitted up, although male visitors frequented them. Four of the houses were regularly fitted up, with elaborate furniture, and in one or two cases had young and beautiful girls on exhibition. All of these latter were seven- or eight-room houses for which $26 to $30 a month was paid. They are pretty well-known resorts, but are not disturbed. In the slums the lowest class of street walkers abound and ply their trade among Negroes, Italians and Americans. One can see men following them into alleys in broad daylight. They usually have male associates whom they support and who join them in "badger" thieving. Most of them are grown women though a few cases of girls under sixteen have been seen on the street.

This fairly characterizes the lowest class of Negroes. According to the inquiry in the Seventh Ward at least 138 families were estimated as belonging to this class out of 2395 reported, or 5.8 per cent. This would include between five and six hundred individuals. Perhaps this number reaches 1000 if the facts were known, but the evidence at hand furnishes only the number stated. In the whole city the number may reach 3000, although there is little data for an estimate.[4]

The next class are the poor and unfortunate and the casual laborers; most of these are of the class of Negroes who in the contact with the life of a great city have failed to find an assured place. They include immigrants who cannot get steady work; good-natured, but unreliable and shiftless persons who cannot keep work or spend their earnings thoughtfully; those who have suffered accident and misfortune; the maimed and defective classes, and the sick; many widows and orphans and deserted wives; all these form a large class and are here considered. It is of course very difficult to separate the lowest of this class from the one below, and probably many are included here who, if the truth were known, ought to be classed lower. In most cases, however, they have been given the benefit of the doubt. The lowest ones of this class usually live in the slums and back streets, and next door, or in the same house often, with criminals and lewd women. Ignorant and easily influenced, they readily go with the tide and now rise to industry and decency, now fall to crime. Others of this class get on fairly well in good times, but never get far ahead. They are the ones who earliest feel the weight of hard times and their latest blight. Some correspond to the "worthy poor" of most charitable organizations, and some fall a little below that class. The children of this class are the feeders of the criminal classes. Often in the same family one can find respectable and striving parents weighed down by idle, impudent sons and wayward daughters. This is partly because of poverty, more because of the poor home life. In the Seventh Ward 30½ per cent of the families or 728 may be put into this class, including the very poor, the poor and those who manage just to make ends meet in good times. In the whole city perhaps ten to twelve thousand Negroes fail in this third social grade.

Above these come the representative Negroes; the mass of the servant class, the porters and waiters, and the best of the laborers. They are hard-working people, proverbially good-natured; lacking a little in foresight and forehandedness, and in "push." They are honest and faithful, of fair and improving morals, and beginning to accumulate property. The great drawback to this class is lack of congenial occupation especially among the young men and women, and the consequent wide-spread dissatisfaction and complaint. As a class these persons are ambitious; the majority can read and write, many have a common school training, and all are anxious to rise in the world. Their wages are low compared with corresponding classes of white workmen, their rents are high, and the field of advancement opened to them is very limited. The best expression of the life of this group is the Negro church, where their social life centers, and where they discuss their situation and prospects.

A note of disappointment and discouragement is often heard at these discussions and their work suffers from a growing lack of interest in it. Most of them are probably best fitted for the work they are doing, but a large percentage deserve better ways to display their talent, and better remuneration. The whole class deserves credit for its bold advance in the midst of discouragements, and for the distinct moral improvement in their family life during the last quarter century. These persons form 56 per cent or 1,252 of the families of the Seventh Ward, and include perhaps 25,000 of the Negroes of the city. They live in 5–10-room house, and usually have lodgers. The houses are always well furnished with neat parlors and some musical instrument. Sunday dinners and small parties, together with church activities, make up their social intercourse. Their chief trouble is in finding suitable careers for their growing children.

Finally we come to the 277 families, 11.5 per cent of those of the Seventh Ward, and including perhaps 3,000 Negroes in the city, who form the aristocracy of the Negro population in education, wealth and general social efficiency. In many respects it is right and proper to judge a people by its best classes rather than by its worst classes or middle ranks. The highest class of any group represents its possibilities rather than its exceptions, as is so often assumed in regard to the Negro. The colored people are seldom judged by their best classes, and often the very existence of classes among them is ignored. This is partly due in the North to the anomalous position of those who compose this class; they are not the leaders or the ideal-makers of their own group in thought, work, or morals. They teach the masses to a very small extent, mingle with them but little, do not largely hire their labor. Instead then of social classes held together by strong ties of mutual interest we have in the case of the Negroes, classes who have much to keep them apart, and only community of blood and color prejudice to bind their together. If the Negroes were by themselves either a strong aristocratic system or a dictatorship would for the present prevail. With, however, democracy thus prematurely thrust upon them, the first impulse of the best, the wisest and richest is to segregate themselves from the mass. This action, however, causes more of dislike and jealousy on the part of the masses than usual, because those masses look to the whites for ideals and

largely for leadership. It is natural therefore that even to-day the mass of Negroes should look upon the worshipers at St. Thomas' and Central as feeling themselves above them, and should dislike them for it. On the other hand it is just as natural for the well-educated and well-to-do Negroes to feel themselves far above the criminals and prostitutes of Seventh and Lombard streets, and even above the servant girls and porters of the middle class of workers. So far they are justified; but they make their mistake in failing to recognize that however laudable an ambition to rise may be, the first duty of an upper class is to serve the lowest classes. The aristocracies of all peoples have been slow in learning this and perhaps the Negro is no slower than the rest, but his peculiar situation demands that in his case this lesson be learned sooner. Naturally the uncertain economic status even of this picked class makes it difficult for them to spare much time and energy in social reform; compared with their fellow they are rich, but compared with white Americans they are poor, and they can hardly fulfill their duty as the leaders of the Negroes until they are captains of industry over their people as well as richer and wiser. To-day the professional class among them is, compared with other callings, rather over-represented, and all have a struggle to maintain the position they have won.

This class is itself an answer to the question of the ability of the Negro to assimilate American culture. It is a class small in numbers and not sharply differentiated from other classes, although sufficiently so to be easily recognized. Its members are not to be met with in the ordinary assemblages of the Negroes, not in their usual promenading places. They are largely Philadelphia born, and being descended from the house-servant class, contain many mulattoes. In their assemblies there are evidences of good breeding and taste, so that a foreigner would hardly think of ex-slaves. They are not to be sure people of wide

culture and their mental horizon is as limited as that of the first families in a country
town. Here and there may be noted, too,
some faint trace of careless moral training.
On the whole they strike one as sensible,
good folks. Their conversation turns on the
gossip of similar circles among the Negroes
of Washington, Boston and New York; on
questions of the day, and, less willingly, on
the situation of the Negro. Strangers secure
entrance to this circle with difficulty and
only by introduction. For an ordinary white
person it would be almost impossible to
secure introduction even by a friend. Once
in a while some well-known citizen meets
a company of this class, but it is hard for
the average white American to lay aside his
patronizing way toward a Negro, and to talk
of aught to him but the Negro question; the
lack, therefore, of common ground even for
conversation makes such meetings rather
stiff and not often repeated. Fifty-two of
these families keep servants regularly; they
live in well-appointed homes, which give
evidence of taste and even luxury.[5]

Something must be said, before leaving this subject, of the amusements of
the Negroes. Among the fourth grade and
the third, gambling, excursions, balls and
cake-walks are the chief amusements. The
gambling instinct is wide-spread, as in all
low classes, and, together with sexual loose-
ness, is their greatest vice; it is carried on
in clubs, in private houses, in pool-rooms
and on the street. Public gambling can be
found at a dozen different places every night
at full tilt in the Seventh Ward, and almost
any stranger can gain easy access. Games of
pure chance are preferred to those of skill,
and in the larger clubs a sort of three-card
monte is the favorite game, played with a
dealer who gambles against all comers. In
private houses in the slums, cards, beer and
prostitutes can always be found. In the public pool-rooms there is some quiet gambling
and playing for prizes. For the newcomer
to the city the only open places of amusement are these pool-rooms and gambling

clubs; here are crowds of young fellows, and
once started in this company no one can say
where they may not end.

The most innocent amusements of this
class are the balls and cake-walks, although
they are accompanied by much drinking,
and are attended by white and black prostitutes. The cake-walk is a rhythmic prom-
enade or slow dance, and when well done
is pretty and quite innocent. Excursions are
frequent in summer, and are accompanied
often by much fighting and drinking.

The mass of the laboring Negroes get
their amusement in connection with the
churches. There are suppers, fairs, con-
certs, socials and the like. Dancing is forbidden by most of the churches, and many of
the stricter sort would not think of going to
balls or theatres. The younger set, however,
dance, although the parents seldom accompany them, and the hours kept are late,
making it often a dissipation. Secret societies and social clubs add to these amusements by balls and suppers, and there are
numbers of parties at private houses. This
class also patronizes frequent excursions
given by churches and Sunday schools and
secret societies; they are usually well conducted, but cost a great deal more than is
necessary. The money wasted in excursions
above what would be necessary for a day's
outing and plenty of recreation, would foot
up many thousand dollars in a season.

In the upper class alone has the home
begun to be the center of recreation and
amusement. There are always to be found
parties and small receptions, and gatherings at the invitations of musical or social
clubs. One large ball each year is usually
given, which is strictly private. Guests from
out of town are given much social attention.

Among nearly all classes of Negroes there
is a large unsatisfied demand for amusement. Large numbers of servant girls and
young men have flocked to the city, have no
homes, and want places to frequent. The
churches supply this need partially, but
the institution which will supply this want

better and add instruction and diversion, will save many girls from ruin and boys from crime. There is to-day little done in places of public amusement to protect colored girls from designing men. Many of the idlers and rascals of the slums play on the affections of silly servant girls, and either ruin them or lead them into crime, or more often live on a part of their wages. There are many cases of this latter system to be met in the Seventh Ward.

It is difficult to measure amusements in any enlightening way. A count of the amusements reported by the *Tribune*, the chief colored paper, which reports for a select part of the laboring class, and the upper class, resulted as follows for nine weeks.[6]

Parties at homes in honor of visitors	16
” ” homes	11
” ” ” with dancing	10
Balls in halls	10
Concerts in churches	7
Church suppers, etc.	7
Weddings	7
Birthday parties	7
Lectures and literary entertainments at churches	6
Card parties	4
Fairs at churches	3
Lawn parties and picnics	3
	91

These, of course, are the larger parties in the whole city, and do not include the numerous small church socials and gatherings. The proportions here are largely accidental, but the list is instructive.

NOTES

1. It will be noted that this classification differs materially from the economic division in Chapter XI. In that case grade four and a part of three appear as the "poor": grade two and the rest of grade three, as the "fair to comfortable"; and a few of grade two and grade one as the well-to-do. The basis of division there was almost entirely according to income; this division brings in moral considerations and questions of expenditure, and consequently reflects more largely the personal judgment of the investigator.

2. The investigator resided at the College Settlement, Seventh and Lombard streets, some months, and thus had an opportunity to observe this slum carefully.

3. These figures were taken during the inquiry by the visitor to the houses.

4. This includes not simply the actual criminal class, but its aiders and abettors, and the class intimately associated with it. It would, for instance, include much more than Charles Booth's class A in London.

5. A comparison of the size of families in the highest and lowest class may be of interest:

Number in Family	First Grade	Fourth Grade
One	22–8%	17–12%
Two	66–24%	58–42%
Three	54–19%	27–20%
Four	48 ⎫	21 ⎫
Five	25 ⎬ –33%	6 ⎬ –24%
Six	18 ⎭	6 ⎭
Seven	20 ⎫	2 ⎫
Eight	7 ⎬ –12%	0 ⎬ –2%
Nine	5 ⎭	1 ⎭
Ten	7 ⎫	0 ⎫
Eleven	0 ⎬ –4%%	0 ⎬ –0%
Twelve or more	5 ⎭	0 ⎭
Total	277	138

Average size of family, first grade, 4.07%: fourth grade, 2.08%.

This certainly looks like the survival of the fittest, and is hardly an argument for the extinction of the civilized Negro.

6. These weeks were not consecutive but taken at random.

REFERENCE

Charles Booth. 1892. *Life and Labour of the People.* London-New York: Macmillan and Co.

3

ST. CLAIR DRAKE AND HORACE CAYTON

LOWER CLASS: SEX AND FAMILY

From *Black Metropolis* (1945)

In this excerpt from their study of the South Side of Chicago in the 1940s, Drake and Cayton experiment with a "fictionalized" composite account to communicate the inner lives of middle- and lower-class African Americans.

It was Christmas Eve, 1938. Dr. Maguire had just finished a hard day.[1] Now for a highball, and then to bed. The doctor stepped back and admired the electric star at the top of the Christmas tree and the gifts neatly stacked beneath it. Judy would certainly be a happy girl in the morning when she bounced downstairs to find the dolls and dishes and baby carriage and candy that Santa Claus had brought her. The doctor smiled, drained his glass, and headed for the bathroom. He caught himself musing in the shower. Not so bad, not so bad. Three years out of med school, in the middle of a depression. A pretty wife with smooth olive skin and straight black hair. A sweet little girl, image of her mother. And buying a home. Well, it was just the "breaks"—lucky breaks ever since he quit picking cotton in Georgia and went off to Howard University in Washington. Plenty of other fellows were better students, but a lot of them were still sleeping in their offices. One or two who were supposed to turn out as distinguished surgeons were Red Capping. He reflected a moment. Yes—the breaks. Suppose he hadn't married a woman like Sylvia. He'd be "on the turf," too, perhaps. Dr. Maguire sharply pulled himself to heel. No, he didn't really believe it had been luck. He prided himself on "having some get-up about him," enough ambition to have made his way anyhow. If he could do it, the other fellows could have, too. He looked at his wife, peacefully sleeping, kissed her lightly on the forehead, and crawled into bed.

Man, what a tough day this Christmas Eve had been! Three appendectomies in the morning and a hernioplasty in the early afternoon. Making the rounds in the midafternoon. Then a few minutes out to help distribute baskets for the Christmas Fund; time out to sign some checks for the legal defense committee of the NAACP; and an emergency meeting of the YMCA executive board. That Y meeting had looked as if it were going to last all night. Negroes talk too damn much. He had hoped to be home by ten o'clock, but it was midnight before he parked his Plymouth. Three late emergency calls—TB patients who ought to be in the sanatorium. Not enough bods—Negro quota filled. Damn this country anyhow. Negroes always get the dirty end of the stick. Christmas! Peace on Earth, Goodwill... Bull...Sometimes I think the Communists are right. And those old fogies over at the hospital yell "socialized medicine" every time somebody wants to extend medical care. Aw, hell, what am I bellyaching about? I haven't had it too rough. He shrugged his shoulders and relaxed. He was just drifting off to sleep when the 'phone rang.

Sylvia bounded from the bed like a tennis ball coming up after a smash from the net. She was that way, always ready to protect him and conserve his strength. What would he do without her?

"Are you one of the doctor's regular patients?...Well, why don't you call your regular doctor?...I know, but Dr. Maguire is..." He snatched the 'phone from her hand in time to catch the stream of denunciation. "That's the way you dicty niggers are. You so high 'n' mighty nobody kin reach ya. We kin lay here 'n' die. White doctor'd come right away. Yore own people treat ya like dogs."

Dr. Maguire winced. He always shuddered when this happened. And it happened often. He waited until the hysterical tirade stopped, then said calmly but firmly: "Now listen, you want me to do you a favor. I'll come over there, sure. I'm a doctor. That's my business. But I'm not coming unless you have the money. Have you got five dollars?" He hung up and began to dress wearily.

"Do they have it?" queried his wife.

"I don't know," he snapped, irritated at himself for having to ask such a question, and at his wife for pressing the point. "You know I'm going whether they have it or not. I'm a doctor. I always go. But you might just as well scare them—it'll be hard enough to collect anyhow." He slammed the door and went down the snowdrifted path that led to the garage.

When he arrived at the building, the squad car was at the door. He and the police went in together. Dr. Maguire pushed his way through the ragged group of children and their excited elders who jammed the hall of the dilapidated building.

"Right this way, Doc," someone called.

"What is it?" he asked jauntily. "Shooting or cutting?"

"She stabbed him," volunteered a little girl.

"Boy, she shore put that blade in him too!" A teen-age boy spoke with obvious admiration, while a murmur of corroboration rippled through the crowd fascinated by tragedy.

For a moment, Dr. Maguire felt sick at his stomach. "Are these my people?" he thought. "What in the hell do I have in common with them? This is 'The Race' we're always spouting about being proud of." He had a little trick for getting back on an even keel when such doubts assailed him; he just let his mind run back over the "Uncle Tomming" he had to do when he was a Pullman porter; the turndown he got when he wanted to intern at the University of Chicago hospital; the letter from the American Medical Association rejecting his application for membership; the paper he wrote for a white doctor to read at a Mississippi medical conference which no Negroes could attend. Such thoughts always restored his sense of solidarity with "The Race." "Yeah, I'm just a nigger, too," he mumbled bitterly.

Then he forgot everything—squalor, race prejudice, his own little tricks of psychological adjustment. He was a doctor treating a patient, swiftly, competently, and with composure. Anger and doubt were swallowed up in pride. His glow of satisfaction didn't last long, however, for the woman who had cut the man was now blubbering hysterically. He barked at her, "Shut up. Get a pan of water, quick! He isn't dead, but he will be if you don't help me." He prepared a hypodermic, gave the shot, and dressed the wound.

"How'dja like to have to give him that needle, honey?" A teen-age girl shivered and squeezed her boy friend's hand, as she asked the question.

"Me? I ain't no doc. But, girl, he flipped that ol' needle in his shoulder sweet. Just like Baby Chile did when she put that blade in Mr. Ben. You gotta have education to be a doc. Lots of it, too."

"I'm gonna be a doctor, I am." A small, self-confident urchin spoke up. The crowd tittered and a young woman said, "That's real cute, ain't it? You be a good one too, just like Doc Maguire." Dr. Maguire smiled pleasantly. An elderly crone mumbled, "Doctor? Humph! Wid a hophead daddy and a booze houn' mammy. How he ever gonna be any doctah? He bettah get his min' on a WPA shovel." Everybody laughed.

"The old man will be all right, now." Dr. Maguire was closing his bag. "Just let him lie quiet all day tomorrow and send him down to the Provident Hospital clinic the day after Christmas. The visit is five dollars."

Baby Chile went for her purse. There was nothing in it. She screamed a frantic accusation at the crowd. "I been robbed. You dirty bastards!" Then a little girl whispered in her ear, while the crowd tittered knowingly. Baby Chile regained her composure and explained: "Sorry, Doc. I had

the money. I was gonna pay you. But them goddam policemen was gonna take me off on a 'sault and batt'ry charge. My little girl had to give 'em the ten dollars I had in this here bag, and the folks out there had to raise another ten to make 'em go away. Them policemen's got it all. I ain't even got a red cent left for Christmas tomorrow. You got anything, Ben?"

The sick man growled: "You know I ain' got nuthin'! You know I can't help you."

The doctor didn't say a word. He just picked up his bag and left. But he ostentatiously took out a pencil and wrote down the number of the apartment before he went out. The crowd seemed pleased at his discomfiture. One woman remarked: "He got the number. Them doctors don't never disremember."

"What was it, dear?" Mrs. Maguire asked as her husband once more prepared for bed.

"Same old thing. Niggers cutting each other up over nothing. Rotgut whisky and women, I guess. They ought to start cutting on the white folks for a change. I wonder how they got my number?"

"*Did you get the five dollars?*" his wife asked.

"Nope. Told me some lie about bribing the police. Maybe they did—I don't know. Let's forget it and go to sleep. Judy will have us both up before daybreak. Tomorrow's Christmas."

Mrs. Maguire turned over and sighed. The doctor went to sleep.

Baby Chile crawled into the bed with Mr. Ben. She cried and cried and stroked the bulky dressing on his shoulder. "Honey, I didn't mean to do that. I love you! I do! I do!"

Mr. Ben didn't say a word. The needle was wearing off and his shoulder hurt. But he wasn't gonna let no woman know she'd hurt him. He bit his lip and tried to sleep. He pushed her hand away from his shoulder. He cursed her.

"Hush up, dammit, shet up!" he growled. "I wanna sleep."

Baby Chile kept moaning, "Why'd I do it? Why'd I do it?"

"Shet up, you bitch," Mr. Ben bawled. "I wisht they'da let them creepers take you to the station! Cain't you let me sleep?"

Baby Chile didn't say another word. She just lay there a-thinking and a-thinking. She was trying to remember how it happened. Step by step she reconstructed the event in her mind as though the rehearsal would assuage her feeling of guilt.

She'd been living with Mr. Ben six months now. Of course he was old and he hadn't ever got the country outa him yet. But he had a good job s'long as he kept the furnace fired and the halls swept out. And he got his room free, bein' janitor. She had a relief check coming in reg'lar for herself and her little girl. They could make it all right as long as the case-worker didn't crack down on 'em. But Mr. Ben was so suspicious. He was always watching her and signifyin' she was turning tricks with Slick who helped him with the furnace and slept in the basement. She wouldn't turn no tricks with Slick. He had bad blood and wouldn't take his shots reg'lar. But you couldn't convince old Mr. Ben. Ben didn't treat her little girl right, either. 'Course, it wasn't his child. But he oughta act right. She cooked for him and slept with him and never held her relief check back on him. He could treat her child right. That was the cause of it all, anyhow.

Baby Chile had come home near dark after a day of imbibing Christmas cheer. She must have been a little slug-happy. All she remembered was chasing her little girl outa Mamie's kitchenette next door, telling her to stay outa that whorehouse. "I ain't raisin' you to be a goddammed whore! Why I send you to Sunday school! Why I try to raise you right? For you to lay up in there with them whores?" You just couldn't keep her outa that place listening to the vendor playing boogie-woogie and seein' things only grown folks oughta see. Then she remembered stretching out on the bed. Just before she

lay down she'd asked her daughter, "What Ben get you for Christmas, chile?"

"Nothin', Mother Dear."

"Nothin'?"

"No, ma'am."

Her eyes fell on the sideboard covered with new, shiny bottles of whisky and beer and wine—plenty of "Christmas cheer." A turkey was cooking in the stove. "An' that no-'count bastard didn't get *you* nothin'?" She remembered throwing herself on the bed in a rage. The radio was playing Christmas carols—the kind that always made her cry because it sounded like church back down in Mississippi. She lay there half drunk, carols ringing in her ears from the radio, boogie-woogie assailing them from the juke-box across the hall, the smell of turkey emanating from the kitchen, and her little girl whimpering in the comer.

She recalled the "accident" vividly. She was dozing on the bed in the one large room which along with the kitchen made up their home. She woke up when Ben came into the room. She didn't know how long she'd been sleeping. Whisky and beer don't mix anyhow, and when you been in and outa taverns all day Christmas Eve you get enough to lay you out cold.

When Mr. Ben opened the door near midnight she was almost sober, but mad as hell. Her head ached, she was so mad. Ben grunted, walked into the kitchen, and started to baste the turkey. She challenged him:

"You buy Fanny May a present?"

"Naw," he grunted. "I spent my money for the turkey and the drinks. Tomorrow's Christmas, ain't it? What you do with yore relief check? Drink it up? Why'n you get her a present? She's yore chile, ain't she?"

Ben wouldn't have been so gruff, but he was tired and peeved. That damn furnace hadn't been acting right and everybody was stayin' up all night to see Christmas in, and pestering him for more heat. And all the time he was trying to get the turkey cooked, too. Baby Chile oughta been doing it—she had been sashayin' roun' all day drinking other men's liquor. How'd anybody expect him to think about a present for Fanny May? That girl didn't like him and respect him, nohow—always walling her eyes at him, but polite as hell to "Mother Dear." Crap! Mr. Ben didn't say any of this out very loud. He just mumbled it to himself as he bent over the stove basting the turkey.

Baby Chile stood up and stared at him. She felt her hell arising. She didn't say a word. She walked deliberately to the kitchen table and took up a paring knife, studied it for a moment, and then—with every ounce of energy that anger and frustration could pump into her muscles—she sank it between his shoulders and fled screaming into the hall. "Oh, I've killed Mr. Ben! I've killed my old man! I've killed him!"

Her little girl raced over to the noisy room next door and asked Miss Mamie to call the doctor. And Mamie interrupted her Christmas Eve business to help a neighbor.

Now Baby Chile was in bed with Mr. Ben. His shoulder was all fixed. She squeezed him right, kissed him, and went to sleep.

Everybody had a good time on Christmas Day at Mr. Ben's. Fanny May went to church. The old folks began a whist game in the morning that ran continuously until midnight, with visitors dropping in to take a hand, eat a turkey sandwich, and drink from Mr. Ben's sideboard. The janitor sat in his rocking chair like a king holding court, as the tenants streamed in and out and Baby Chile bustled about making him comfortable. Baby Chile was "high" enough to be lively, but was careful not to get drunk. No one mentioned the tragedy of the night before. Only Slick was uncomfortable.

Bronzeville's Lower Depths

Slick felt "left out of things." He had teamed up with Mr. Ben a month before Christmas after his mother and father had evicted him

from their two rooms because his drunken escapades were bringing trouble to the household. Nearly thirty, Slick was a floater with two deserted wives behind him, an insatiable appetite for liquor, and spirochetes in his veins. He was not unattractive and he liked women. But he had an ugly scar over his entire left side where wife number one, in a fit of jealous rage, had thrown a bucket of lye on him. "She tried to hit my privates, but I turned over too fast," was Slick's comment. *"Now* what girl wants me? My side's enough to turn her nature." Yet, during the Twenties, when he had a job and money, he had girls. Now, during the Depression, he was, to use his own words, "a bum."

Slick's family had migrated to Chicago from St. Louis where his mother, a lower middle-class woman who "married a no-'count Negro," had worked as a seamstress. She had tried to make something out of her only son, but according to her, "It didn't take." With a chronic alcoholic for a husband and a delinquent for a son, Slick's mother had resigned herself to being lower-class, although she refused to take a job in domestic service. When the Depression began, she went on the relief. She kept her two rooms and her person spotlessly clean, tried to make the old man hold a WPA job, and in 1938 got a job as housekeeper in a lower-class kitchenette building. But Slick jeopardized her steady income, and she threw him out.

Slick drifted about. Now he was thinking that he'd better move again as soon as Ben's shoulder got well. Ben was beginning to give him the evil eye. Slick hadn't turned a trick with Baby Chile yet, but he was sure she did want "to be with him." He was gonna stay outa trouble. Just as soon as Ben's shoulder got well, he was gonna cut out—danger was on his trail.

Slick had already propositioned Betty Lou about living with him. He had met her at Streeter's Tavern, bought her a few beers, and "jived" her. She had agreed to live with him if one of Slick's employed friends would consent to board with them until Slick could get a WPA job. This would provide a steady income for food. So Slick wheedled ten dollars from his mother and rented a basement room in the center of the Black Belt—three-and-a-half a week for room, bed, chair, and table. Life began—with Betty Lou, though without a stove or even a hot-plate.

Betty Lou, a native of Alabama, had come north to Detroit in the early days of the Depression and entered domestic service. A rather attractive light-brown-skinned girl in her early twenties, fond of good clothes and with a great deal of personal pride, she worked for three years, went to night school intermittently, and then married a common laborer. One year of married life and they separated after a furious fight. She then came to Chicago to stay with a married sister whose husband worked in the steel mills. Later she secured a job in private family and lived "on premises" for several months. She didn't like living with white folks, but when she decided to return to her sister's home, a lodger was sleeping on the sofa in the living-room where she had formerly slept. Betty Lou had to occupy a pallet on the floor in the bedroom with her sister and husband. Slick's offer of a home provided an avenue of escape.

Slick and Betty Lou lived together in the basement for about a month. He made the rounds of various employment agencies, but spent most of his time trying to work his acquaintances for enough money to buy drinks and pay the rent. Betty Lou, faced with the problem of cooking, made a deal with the unmarried janitor who let her use his kitchen in return for a share of the food. She took a great deal of pride in her biscuits and occasional hot rolls. She was enjoying domesticity.

Here, beneath Bronzeville's surface were a variety of living patterns. The twenty households, sharing four bathrooms, two common sinks in the hallway, and some dozen stoves and hot-plates between them, were forced into relationships of neighborliness and reciprocity. A girl might "do the hair" of a neighbor in return for permission to use her pots and pans. Another woman might trade some bread for a glass of milk. There was seldom any money to lend or borrow, but the bartering of services and utensils was general. Brawls were frequent, often resulting in intense violence. A supper interrupted by the screams of a man with an ice-pick driven into his back might be unusual—but a fight involving the destruction of the meager furniture in these households was not uncommon.

Slick's immediate neighbors were two teen-aged boys, recently discharged from a CCC camp. They were now making their way by robbing laundry trucks and peddling "hot" shirts, towels, socks, and handkerchiefs among the kitchenette dwellers. Each afternoon their room was a rendezvous for schoolgirls—truants and morning-shift pupils—who pooled their lunch money, prepared pots of steaming spaghetti and hot dogs, and spent the afternoon "rug-cutting," drinking whisky, smoking reefers, and "making love." Slick gave strict orders to Betty Lou to "stay outa that reefer den with all them hustlers and reefer smokers."

Betty Lou's best "girl friend" in the basement was Ella, whose husband, "Poke," had recently been jailed for breaking a liquor store window and stealing a pint of whisky. "I just as well not have no ol' man. Stays in jail all the time," Ella confided one day in a pensive mood. Several days later she was living with another man for the interim. "My baby's got to have some milk," she apologized, "an' that damn worker won't get me a job on the WPA 'cause I have a baby. I can run a power-machine, too!"

Down the hall was Joe, a former cook on the railroad who had been fired for stealing Pullman towels and who was now a dishwasher. Living with a waitress, he was currently much agitated because of a letter he had received from his legal wife in Detroit notifying him that she was en route to Chicago. He kept his bags packed.

Strangest of all was Lily, a tall, husky, masculine woman who was subsequently thrown out of the building and warned never to return. "A damn bull-diker[2] who's been messing with the women in here," was Slick's terse comment.

During this period, Slick's mother visited him several times, and professed to be very fond of her son's new common-law wife. Betty Lou's married sister came to visit them too, as did a woman friend who borrowed the room for a few hours each week on her night off so that she could entertain a boy friend. These visitors sometimes brought a little food when they came.

Slick spoke often of wishing to regularize his alliance if he could get an annulment and if Betty Lou could get a divorce. He fantasized too (usually when drunk) about getting on his feet, taking a civil service examination for a post-office job and showing the world, his boarder, and his mother that he wasn't a derelict.

After two months in the basement, the couple decided to raise their standard of living. Slick had got a $55-a-month WPA job, so they decided to move into a first-floor kitchenette[3] with a stove and an ice-box. Thus began the second phase of their joint life.

From Kitchenette to Penitentiary. The three months in the kitchenette started on a note of confidence and ended in tragedy. During this period Betty Lou's sister and her brother-in-law visited occasionally, made the acquaintance of Slick's family, tried to mediate quarrels, and in general functioned as approving relatives. Betty Lou's conception of her role was that Slick should work and support her. Slick, however, insisted that she too should get a job, and often charged her with running around during the day "turning tricks." Such "signifying" became the focal point for continuous quarrels and occasional fights; it eventually resulted in separation.

Betty Lou was anxious to join a church and a social dub, and, as soon as she could, became a member of an usher board at a lower-middle-class church. Slick resented this attempt at mobility, especially since he had neither the personal organization nor the money and clothes to maintain such social connections. He was often torn with doubts about her motives, and on one occasion said, "I think Betty Lou is just tryin' to work me till she gets another man or gets on her feet."

For a month, Slick worked steadily on the WPA labor project, drank far less than usual, and seemed to achieve a moderate amount of emotional stability. He cashed his first check and allowed Betty Lou to purchase groceries and pay the rent. As for the second check, he spent at least half of it on a "good time." After the first month of fairly steady employment, Slick began to miss work frequently, and it was soon evident that he was spending his time watching Betty Lou in an attempt to catch her with other men. This behavior resulted in some serious fights and a threat on the part of her sister to take Betty Lou back home. In one drunken fit, Slick chased her through the building with a butcher knife, and the housekeeper was forced to call a policeman. On another occasion an argument, which began with the passing of mutual insults, ended in Slick's tearing up Betty Lou's clothing and breaking some cherished china souvenirs which she had patiently gathered at a neighboring tavern over a period of several months.

With the approach of Easter, Slick worked steadily in order to make a down payment on some clothing for himself and Betty Lou. On Easter day both were "togged down."[4] Within two days, however, all of Slick's clothes were in a pawn shop and he was again in rags. This contributed to the ultimate breakup of the alliance, since Betty Lou was now able to go to church and to dances, while Slick, lacking clothes, was never able to participate in any public social activities with her except at taverns.

The fights continued. Then one night Betty Lou stormed out, vowing never to return. Slick was in a disorganized and drunken state for several days, plotting vengeance one moment and crying the next. His mother, who had been friendly toward Betty Lou, now insisted that she had always known she was no good, and that she was probably a prostitute anyway. Betty Lou decided a few days later to return to Slick, but what she saw when she entered their apartment permanently estranged her. There in the room was a white girl ensconced in her bed! Betty Lou snatched her clothing from the closet, cursed the woman roundly, reported the incident to the housekeeper, and left. Slick insisted to the housekeeper that he had met the white woman wandering in the cold and like a gentleman had invited her in. To his cronies he proudly told a different story. The woman, he said, was a "hustling woman" he had known when he worked at a North Side "resort." She had befriended him and given him money. Now she was down and out, and when he met her at a Black Belt tavern he decided to bring her in, sleep with her, and to play the role of pimp for a day or two in order to make some extra change. Slick was given three hours to vacate the room under threat of arrest. He moved into a liquor joint for several days and then rented a single room.

One morning several weeks later, a WPA research project in the basement of a church near Slick's lodging place was thrown into an uproar when he rushed through the premises followed by "Two-Gun Dick" and another officer with drawn revolvers. Having met Betty Lou on the street walking with another man, Slick had followed her until her escort left her, and then stabbed her in the breast. His first impulse was to flee to the WPA project, where he had acquaintances who had befriended him in the past. He did not tarry, however, for the police were close behind. He hurried to his mother's home and hid there for the rest of the day. Returning in the evening to the area in which he had committed the crime, he was arrested. His mother borrowed money

on her insurance policies for bail and a lawyer. Her only comment on the girl was: "She ought to be glad my boy didn't mark her in the face. She kin get another man since she ain't marked in the face." When it became evident that Betty Lou would recover, the judge sentenced Slick to a mere six months in the Bridewell Prison.

On his release Slick was at the peak of physical condition; regular treatment for his various bodily ailments, disciplined labor, and regular food had made him almost a different person. But within two months he was once more thoroughly disorganized. Another two months and he was back in prison, this time on a charge of stealing. On his release he departed for St. Louis, whence he had originally come to Black Metropolis.

Slick and Betty Lou—Baby Chile and Mr. Ben; there were hundreds of them in Bronzeville during the Lean Years.

NOTES

1. This account of a doctor's Christmas experience is based on an actual incident witnessed by one of the authors, when he was a participant-observer in a group of lower-class households for six months, and on interviews with the physician involved and his wife. The principal characters' inner thoughts are obviously fictionalized. But the other quoted material...has been selected from interview-documents gathered by trained interviewers and has not been subjected to imaginative recasting.

2. "Bull-diker"—homosexual woman reputed to have male genitalia.

3. Bronzeville's kitchenettes are single rooms, rented furnished and without a lease. Sometimes a hot-plate is included for cooking, but often there are no cooking facilities despite the name. Hundreds of large apartment buildings have been cut up into kitchenettes to meet the chronic housing shortage in the Black Belt.

4. Exceptionally well-dressed.

4

ULF HANNERZ

LIFE STYLES

from *Soulside* (1969)

Amid the upheavals of the 1960s, the Swedish anthropologist Ulf Hannerz moved into the largely poor, African-American area of Winston Street in Washington, D.C. Hannerz quickly realized that, contrary to much of its popular depictions at the time, the ghetto was home to diverse life styles, attitudes, and beliefs. Despite providing ideal type descriptions of different social groups in the neighborhood, he also shows how fluid and situational "culture" can be. Behavior that may seem to exemplify a "culture of poverty" to outsiders was in fact a set of individual and collective adaptations developed in response to economic, social, and political constraints.

Since ghetto dwellers are not much involved with one another in relationships of power and livelihood, the social structure of the ghetto community is made up primarily of a multitude of connecting personal networks of kinsmen, peers, and neighbors. Overarching institutions under community control are lacking. The networks, of course, cannot provide the ghetto with a particularly "tight" structure. Neighborship, mutual acquaintances, place of work, and other unpredictable contingencies influence which ghetto dwellers gain access to each other. Functional differentiation in stable social relationships is limited to age and sex roles, peer roles and kinship roles. However, there is another important kind of differentiation which we may refer to as a diversity of life styles. "Life style" is admittedly a vague term; this may be one of its advantages, at least for a while, in that it does not commit us to some well-established form of analysis which may be less suitable for this particular case. Preliminarily, we may view a life style as the involvement of an individual with a particular set of modes of action, social relationships, and contexts. It goes beyond any more formal definition of a single role, although as we shall see later, ghetto life styles as understood here are not wholly independent of the basic roles of age and sex.[1]

The diversity of life styles has a great impact on the ordering of ghetto social relations. People of different life styles have different kinds of networks, and the difference influences the quantity and quality of interaction between them. Thus there are noticeable social cleavages between people following different walks of life, although one must also note that there are instances when life styles complement one another. To get an overview of ghetto social structure, then, we may attempt to delineate typical social relations within and between life styles.

Two Styles—a Ghetto View

The people of Winston Street often describe themselves and their neighbors in the community as comprising two categories distinguished according to way of life. However, they do not stand quite united in their choice of terms. Some refer to one category—in which they then usually include themselves—as "respectable," "good people," or, more rarely and somewhat facetiously, as "model citizens." More seldom do they refer to this category as "middle class," in this case apparently more a reference to a life style ideal than to socio-economic status, although some of them would qualify as lower-middle class in terms of income and occupation. They use these labels to distinguish themselves from what they conceive of as their opposites, people they describe as "undesirables", "no good", "the rowdy bunch", "bums" or "trash", as well as in other similar terms. The "undesirables", or whatever label is used, are felt by the self-named "respectables" to be characterized collectively by drinking and drunkenness in public, spontaneous brawls, unwillingness to work, sexual licence, and occasional trouble with the police. The "respectables", then, impute to themselves an absence of such character blemishes, or

stated in more positive terms, an allegiance to American mainstream morality.

There is, of course, a category of people who in some ways conform to the "respectable's" description of the "undesirables". Among them the consumption of liquor is high and sometimes beyond the manners and away from the places prescribed by mainstream norms. They engage in occasional violence (which together with drinking and drunkenness is the main source of conflict with the law). Their concern with sexual activity is certainly noticeable. The unemployment rate is high, although this, of course, need not be interpreted as general reluctance toward work as some "respectables" understand it.

How do these people describe themselves and their opposites? In fact, they do not use any corresponding labels very frequently, probably because they are not as concerned with the maintenance of the boundary between themselves and others as the "respectables" are. The most common self-references among these people at Winston Street are simply such vague expressions as "people like us ..." or "us brothers down here ...". These can sometimes refer to ghetto dwellers in general, while at other times they are used in opposition to the more mainstream-oriented members of the community. These may be described occasionally as "stuck up", as people who "think they're really something" or, in a different set of terms, as "house niggers", "handkerchief heads" and "Toms" (or in the more complete form, "Uncle Toms"). These latter terms, of course, imply servility toward white rulers. A "house nigger" during slavery was the personal servant of the white master whose close relationship to the latter brought a somewhat better life and greater sophistication than those of the ordinary plantation slave or "field nigger" but sometimes also some reputation as a renegade. The tied headcloth imputed to a "handkerchief head" is similarly symbolic of the lowly black servant woman's status in the Old South, and "Uncle Tom", of course, is the stereotype of the docile servant of whites. This kind of label, naturally, implies that those who view themselves as "respectable" can somehow be seen as disloyal to the more dispossessed members of the ghetto community. True, the self-styled "respectables" often have closer contacts with whites, in particular at work, and have more confidence in whites than those people have whose most intensive contacts with whites may involve the welfare people, the police, and the arrogant owner of the liquor store. However, the perceived disloyalty of the "respectables" which makes them susceptible to such labeling need not necessarily involve interaction with whites as much as moral alignment with them. In accepting the mainstream morality of most white Americans, the "respectables" also pass judgment on the "undesirable" behavior of other ghetto dwellers and thus commit an infraction against the solidarity of ghetto dwellers. This, perhaps, is the most significant way in which a "respectable" is a renegade. However, we must remember again that those who show less inclination toward mainstream "respectability" do not continuously refer to the mainstream-oriented as "house niggers"—terms of this kind only crop up in conversations now and then. Also, they are occasionally used to refer to other people as well.

The sharp division of ways of life suggested by the use of such terms implies that the ghetto community is clearly divided into two large groups, opposed to each other but internally rather homogeneous. However, a closer look at the actual lives and group formations of people at Winston Street suggests that the picture is not quite so neat. This folk model of social cleavage is not a particularly accurate description of what real lives are like, or of how they are intertwined. Above all, even if there are some people who live rather consistently "respectable" lives, and some whom these people quite consistently view as "no good," these

two categories are only the opposite poles of a rather complex continuum. It is much too easy, judging by the native terms, to see these two categories as residual in relation to one another—whoever is not a typical "respectable" is not therefore a typical "no good."

It seems wiser to see the dichotomy as one of elements of behavior concerning which ghetto dwellers have a well-developed vocabulary of social and moral designations. This vocabulary need not be applied consistently and unambiguously to specific persons. Rather, it is an image bank from which one draws as the situation calls for it and as it befits one's own position. Some people are thus more given to such labeling, and some people are more liable to be labeled. Naturally, however, others find themselves in more of an in-between position with respect to such terms or change between different positions over time. These latter tend to disappear into the dark corners of the picture as ghetto dwellers and outside observers alike point out the most clear-cut examples which fit the moral vocabulary, for maximal contrast.

This point may need to be emphasized because the simple dichotomy seems often to emerge from social science writing, about poor black people or the lower classes in general, as well—perhaps because the observers have simply accepted the moral taxonomy of the natives as an acceptable way of ordering descriptions of the community, or because a similar dichotomy fits the outsider's moral precepts, or his concern for "social problems."[2] In the latter case, the least "respectable" people become the "multi-problem families" or the "hard-to-reach poor"— terms which may lend themselves well to the professional outlook of social workers or persons in similar positions but are not necessarily relevant or adequate for ghetto ethnography. Yet they are no worse than labels such as "respectable" and "nonrespectable" as adopted by social scientists to denote people's total life styles. This often leads rather absurdly to the extension of apparently moral judgments to such life style items as unemployment, intensive peer group life, and flexible household composition, all of which tend to occur together with the original "nonrespectability": drinking, loose sexual liaisons, and interpersonal violence. Yet if such items tend to occur together, it may be convenient to have a label for them, useful in a sociocultural analysis of the ghetto community, yet distinct from those occurring in the dichotomous conscious model of ghetto dwellers.[3] The category suggested for this purpose is "ghetto-specific" modes of action, as opposed to "mainstream-oriented" modes of action. Mainstream-oriented acts are those held appropriate, acceptable or normal by most Americans of the wider society, while ghetto-specific acts occur more frequently in the ghetto than outside it. This, of course, does not necessarily mean that the latter are all unique to the black ghetto, nor that they occur there with greater frequency than mainstream-oriented acts. Although the distinction is probably not one of great precision, it may still function reasonably satisfactorily.

The argument for this distinction, of course, should not rest simply in the interest of a separate ghetto trait list. The modes of behavior identified as ghetto-specific need also be understood in relation to each other and to the background and the peculiar social niche of the ghetto dwellers. Certainly these factors will be at work particularly strongly on some people, so that these will have an entire life style more ghetto-specific than that of other people in the community. Yet for a number of reasons we will largely avoid making this new dichotomy the only basis of a classification of life styles and people. Even the people whose behavior is most ghetto-specific are mainstream-oriented in some ways; furthermore, as we have noted, it is not possible to distinguish clearly between two categories in the ghetto on the basis of this criterion in such a way as to include everybody in either one or the other.

Finally, other criteria than ghetto-specificity and mainstream orientation are influential in life style differentiation.

A slightly more complex categorization of people into four main life styles seems to suit at least the realities of the Winston Street neighborhood better: we will call them mainstreamers, swingers, street families, and streetcorner men. The scheme is not perfect. The four categories are still only "ideal types", approximations of a reality which is hard to depict with any reasonable economy of conceptual equipment and descriptive detail. While it is possible to see the population at least of the Winston Street neighborhood as composed largely of four nuclei around these life styles, there are many individuals who are less clearly oriented toward any one of them. They are, from our point of view, life style straddlers. A major difficulty rests in the fact that a life style in this case is to a great extent an orientation toward participation in a certain social context in which given modes of action tend to prevail; since individuals usually do not participate exclusively in that context, there are necessarily instances when their behavior differs from that which we will consider typical of their life style as a whole. The streetcorner men, for instance, are seen here as oriented particularly toward the peer group context, but a great many of them are also more or less attached to street families. To an extent which varies from one man to another, they are thus involved in a second life style. The more the men become oriented toward the domestic context, however, the more do they remove themselves from the life style of the streetcorner man; and the street family life style, in its most clearcut form one which involves women more than men and which is complementary to that of streetcorner men, then begins to approach the mainstreamer life style.

Another problem is that the life style concept to some may seem to presume an independence of more basic criteria of social differentiation such as age, sex, and marital status; as we shall…there is no total independence of this kind. The swingers are an age category, the streetcorner men are men, the mainstreamers are usually married. But there is no strict determinism, for the swingers do not include all people of the given age, the streetcorner men not all the men, and the mainstreamers not all the married people. The life styles are thus not simply direct expressions of these orders of differentiation, although influenced by them in certain ways.

As we shall see, one of the things which distinguishes our four-way differentiation of life styles from a simple dichotomy of the type discussed above is the joint attention to such basic role criteria and the ghetto-specific/mainstream-oriented distinction.

When we noted above that the categorization of life styles attempted here seems to coincide reasonably well with the nuclei of people discernible in the Winston Street neighborhood, we did not simply mean that this appears to be a realistic way of classifying individuals. It also has sociological correlates, as there tends to be more interaction between people leading similar lives than between those who do not share life styles. However, since there are certain complementary, largely instrumental relationships between people of different age and sex—factors which also involve life style differences—it may be added that the choice of companions with a similar life style is most visible in sociable interaction. It should also be pointed out that the designations for life styles used here are not native ghetto terms, as the ghetto vocabulary lacks clear-cut, stable, and frequently used terms of this kind. However, they seem to be reasonably informative capsule characterizations of the respective life styles.[4]

The Mainstreamers

The people we will call mainstreamers are, of course, those who conform most closely to mainstream American assumptions about the "normal" life. Consequently, they are also those who are most apt to refer to themselves as "respectable" or by similar terms. Most of those at Winston Street who own the houses they live in belong to this category. However, there are also quite a few mainstreamers who rent apartments in the neighborhood. Some of the latter are younger families who expect to be able to move out of the area later, either by way of some social mobility with accompanying higher economic standards or by way of accumulated savings. One man in his early thirties who had lived in the Winston Street neighborhood most of his life said, as he packed up his belongings to take his family to another apartment in an area of town generally regarded as "better":

> "We want to get to a place where it isn't so noisy, and where people aren't so rowdy. Sometimes when summer comes you just can't sleep around here, you know, 'cause there is so much noise. In this place we're going to now you don't have to have anything to do with neighbors if you don't want to. This new place isn't much bigger, though. Next time I hope it'll be a house, out of town somewhere."

The fact that the mainstreamers are home owners or have strong hope of social and concomitant spatial mobility implies that many of them are among the better-off members of the ghetto community. There is hardly any unemployment in this category. While almost all the males in white-collar jobs in the neighborhood who are functioning fathers and husbands—not a very large number—are mainstreamers, most of the membership of this category is made up of relatively stable working-class people. In many families both husband and wife are employed, thus pushing the economic standard considerably higher. The members of the category—we are only talking about the adults here—are usually in ages between the upper twenties and the fifties, that is, in childrearing ages. In fact, most of them are married and live in nuclear families with a quite stable composition. Consensual unions, divorces, and separations are much more infrequent in this group than among the ghetto population in general. However, in some cases one or two of the children are those of only one of the spouses—almost always of the wife—in an earlier marriage or in premarital affairs. In a later stage of the household developmental cycle, a mainstreamer household may include the young children of daughters; the children may have been born out of wedlock or in a marriage which has broken up, and the young mother may either stay with her parents herself or she may have left her child or children in the care of her parents while she continues for some time to live a freer life. With such exceptions, there is only rarely anybody outside the nuclear family present in the household. When it happens, it is most likely to be the sole surviving parent of one of the spouses—usually this turns out to be the mother of one of them.

It is usually not very hard to detect from the outside which houses on Winston Street are the homes of mainstreamers. The new metal screen doors, the venetian blinds, and the flower pots in the windows are usually absent from other people's houses. Yet basically the small row houses in the neighborhood all look rather much alike, whether the dark bricks have a coat of paint or not, and thus it may be quite a surprise to enter a mainstreamer's home and find that behind the drab exterior there is often a home which looks quite out of place in a predominantly low-income neighborhood. One family on Winston Street has a living room set of imitated Italian antique furniture, bought at a price of about $1500 and encased in fitted clear plastic covers; in a couple of homes the occupant-owners have had their living rooms paneled. Some have modern although usually relatively inexpensive Scandinavian-style furniture, and there are many large table lamps,

sometimes matched in pairs, one on each side of the couch. New TV and stereo sets are not unusual; although the record collections include a lot of black rock-and-roll and jazz, there is often also some white pop and, less frequently, some classical music. On the shelves there may be some vases and rather inexpensive china figurines, as well as framed graduation or wedding pictures of the inhabitants of the house or of close relatives. Similar pictures may be on the wall, perhaps sharing the space with some picture prints. There may be a picture or a color memorial plate of the late President Kennedy, whose memory is as greatly esteemed by many mainstreamers as by most other ghetto dwellers. This may be what the inside of the house looks like. During the warmer months one may see something of the mainstreamers' concern with contemporary comfort outside as well; while other people on the street sit on the stairs in front of the doors or make use of old chairs which are on their way to complete discardment, some of the mainstreamers take out new aluminum garden chairs and set them up on the sidewalk for an early evening look at the newspaper. A couple of people in the group even have small barbecue sets in their tiny back yards.

The mainstreamers are clearly very concerned with the style and comfort of their homes. This is visible in their reading habits as well. Not only are they the people on Winston Street who most regularly read newspapers—some of them take both the morning *Washington Post* and one of the evening papers, the *Evening Star* or the more popular *Daily News*—they also hold by far the greater number of subscriptions to periodicals in the neighborhood, and most of these are to publications oriented toward home and family such as *Better Homes and Gardens, the American Home, Ladies' Home Journal* and *McCall's.* However, some also take such magazines as *Life, Look, Reader's Digest* and the Negro picture magazine *Ebony.* The latter, of course, is strongly oriented toward mainstream concerns and occupational achievement, although it also has articles about the problems of the black proletariat.

Book reading is certainly less frequent although not absent. There are many more mainstreamers than other people on Winston Street who have public library cards, but those who most frequently visit the branch office of the library—which is rather far away—are the children, in their pre-teens or lower teens, and many mainstreamers certainly never go there at all.

If one gets a good idea of the typical concerns of mainstreamers just by seeing their homes, they are certainly even more visible in everyday household life. "A nice home," "a good family" and "taking good care of the family" are things mainstreamers often mention as important things in life, and as moral imperatives when they talk about other ghetto dwellers whom they think are not overly concerned with such matters. In mainstreamer households, there is a set dinner hour for all members of the household, if this is made possible at all by working hours and other factors. If there are school-age children in the house, parents try to see to it that home work gets done and that the children can do it somewhere where it is possible to study uninterruptedly. The men take more part in work "around the house" than most ghetto men, take their children on walks and rides (many mainstreamers have cars of late models), and generally spend much time at home. The spouses are together a great deal during their leisure hours, whether they are alone or in the company of relatives or common friends—as we shall see, in some ghetto families the husband and the wife often both interact very little with people close to the other spouse, but this is more seldom the case with mainstreamers.[5]

The distribution of authority in mainstreamer families is somewhat variable. There is hardly ever any doubt that the husband and father is regarded as the head of the household, with the greatest influence on those household affairs in which he wants to have a say—much day-to-day management of the household is of course delegated to the wife. However, while in some families it is quite clear that the husband can make rather independent decisions and enforce them, there are many among the younger couples in particular which have a more companionate type of marital relationship with a greater amount of joint decision-making.

The mainstreamer families on Winston Street are in most cases close only to a few similarly oriented families in the neighborhood. Most of their friends are scattered over town—particularly in the ghetto, of course, but some friends have also moved to somewhat more affluent areas. Many households maintain contacts with friends, and in particular with kin, in the South or in other Northeastern cities, and on occasional weekends and holidays the family may drive for example to New York or Philadelphia for a visit, or receive visitors from such cities. During summer weekends many also drive to the Maryland and Virginia beaches.

The majority of the mainstreamers are not members of any voluntary associations. The parent-teachers associations at the children's schools may be an exception, as their meetings may be seen as a part of the concern with family life. The times seem to have passed when practically all "respectable" black people were active supporters of a church and regular participants in its services.[6] Most mainstreamers on Winston Street go to church only very occasionally, and in particular in connection with the great ceremonies of life, although a great many of them send their children to Sunday school. Perhaps their lack of active church participation has something to do with the fact that most mainstreamers in the Winston Street neighborhood, and perhaps generally, are not migrants from the South, where the black church seems to be a stronger institution, but are born and bred in the city. One of the few mainstreamers in the neighborhood who has moved with his family from the South to Washington very recently is quite active, with his wife and children, in a neighborhood storefront church. When this man sat on the front step of his house one evening, talking to one of the middle-aged alcoholics who hang out in the vicinity, he commented on the religious habits of the people in his new surroundings.

"I've never been in a place where so many people don't go to church as on this street. It's a funny thing, you know. Now, let me tell it to you this way. I know you drink, and you like a drink now and then, 'cause you're used to it. I mean, it's like that. Now, I take a drink myself sometimes. Not all the time, I mean, but I'm no saint. Anyway, so if you don't drink, you won't like drinking that much. You may want to sample it, but it's no big thing with you, like it is when it's a habit. Now me, I've got the church habit, you see. I feel there's something wrong if I don't get to church, 'cause I'm so used to going every Sunday morning, and I wouldn't want to miss it. See what I mean? So if you ain't used to going to church, you might think up lots of reasons for not going, like your clothes ain't right, or your shoes ain't clean, or something like that. But that's only 'cause you don't want to go in the first place, and that's 'cause you ain't got that habit."

It may well be that this man and his family are just still in the churchgoing "habit". Most of the other mainstreamers in the neighborhood are clearly out of it, and they certainly do not need the kind of excuses he suggests to stay home on a Sunday morning. But clearly there are still many enough people in the ghetto, and many of them are undoubtedly mainstreamers, who flock on Sunday morning to fill a considerable number of churches.

Despite their lack of participation in church life one organizational venture of some mainstreamers in the neighborhood recently had a relationship to the church. A small, predominantly white middle-class church group in Washington wanted to sponsor community activities in the neighborhood and made its entry into it through contacts with a storefront church. Most of the activities were aimed at children for whom various programs were run for a period, largely under the supervision of the preacher at the storefront church. The white volunteers also became friendly with some adult mainstreamers, however, and together with these they opened a Friday night open house to which everybody in the neighborhood was welcome for coffee, donuts and ice cream at cost—"so we can all get to know each other". As it turned out, the idea apparently did not appeal to very many. A few young swingers dropped in together very occasionally and usually briefly, some street-corner men made it a Friday evening habit for a while, and some pre-teens dropped in now and then, but often the black and white organizers were a majority of those present. White wellwishers from the sponsoring congregation drove up "to see how things were going" quite frequently in the beginning, but their presence seems above all to have scared neighborhood people away. Too high dress standards for just a coffee hour was mentioned by some of them as a reason for not going, and some who went were irritated by the condescending attitude they felt in the behavior of some white visitors. Others complained that the taped music was not soul music but some classical music which one of the mainstreamer organizers preferred—he mentioned at one time that "some better music can't hurt." Quite a few, finally, felt that Friday night is the big night when you really "let your hair down," not a night for sitting around politely sipping coffee. Randy, who came to the coffee house once or twice, seemed to find the right words to express the unnaturalness he sensed there, as he explained mockingly to an acquaintance: "It's very nice, you can come there and converse with people on different subjects."

Thus the open house did not accomplish what the sponsors had wanted it to—the goals were never very clearly defined but they had something to do with more neighborliness, perhaps in pursuit of neighborhood improvement of some kind, and possibly with giving neighborhood people a more wholesome setting for their Friday night sociability. Giving up their efforts, the mainstreamer organizers just said that the same people had to do the work all the time and that nobody else seemed to care. By then the white church group was not directly concerned with the neighborhood any more.

The Swingers

The people we may call swingers are somewhat younger on the average than the mainstreamers, and many of them have brothers and sisters or parents who are mainstreamers. In due course, some of them will become mainstreamers, because it is hard to be a swinger when one gets older. However, some remain swingers longer than others, and many swingers later take another road than the mainstreamer one.

Swingers are usually somewhere between the late teens and the middle thirties in age. This means that many of them have not yet married and started families on their own, so that familial obligations would naturally be less demanding in terms of time, money, and emotional investments. But there are many swingers who are married and have children and who even so are not family-oriented. Of course, married men are more able to take part in the swinger life than are married women, as they can leave children and household affairs more readily in the hands of their spouses, However, some women manage to continue as swingers by leaving young children with the grandparents, as we noted in describing the mainstreamers. Also, quite a few marriages are broken as one or both spouses prefer to continue the swinger's life.

Swingers typically spend relatively little of their free time just sitting around at home alone or with the family. Weekday nights and particularly weekends are often spent going visiting, whether one travels alone—by private car, taxi, or bus—or in the company of a few friends. The spontaneous gatherings are not complete without some gin, whiskey, or beer, and the talk involves joking, banter, reminiscences of past shared experiences, and exchanges about the trivia of the day such as football results, forecasts of coming boxing bouts, and local grapevine items.

Of course, girl friends also visit boy friends and vice versa, for a few hours or over night. If the girl has a child or two, she might take them along if no babysitter in the form of a mother or sister is available, and on weekends they may all go window-shopping, to the Zoo, or to the movie theater together. Some of the young men are thus on close terms with their girl friends' children.

Friday and Saturday nights are the great nights for parties, with a lot of music and the latest dances, and many swingers manage to take in quite a few if they would not rather stay all the time at one party. After one New Year's Eve, a particularly big party night, one young bachelor on Winston Street announced that he had been to nine parties, none of which was in his own neighborhood and a few of which were in widely separated parts of the Washington ghetto. And Marvin, 22, reminisces about one evening a couple of years earlier:

> "This was a Friday, and I had just got paid, and so I was going out with Geraldine. So we went to one party after another, and we were in and out of taxis all the time, and were going drinking at different places. And then I woke up the next morning and I had to go to work, and I put my hand in my pocket, and there was only two dollars! Two dollars left of all that money! I felt so bad I went right back to sleep."

Other nights when one does not go visiting, one may spend time at the bowling alley or in a pool room, at a bar, at the movies, or at the Howard Theatre. There may be a lot of driving around for no particular reason, or a group may drive over to nearby Baltimore—approximately a 45 minute ride—for a visit to its ghetto entertainment establishments which enjoy a more lively reputation than those in Washington. But all evenings cannot be spent like this, of course, and quite a few evenings most swingers can be found just passing time in front of a TV set. However, swingers, unlike mainstreamers, often talk of this as one of the dullest possible ways of spending one's time.

A rather small number of swingers, but more of them than of any other category in the ghetto, belong to voluntary associations of a rather purely sociable character. These are for men or for women but hardly ever mixed. On the other hand, the activities they organize are practically all occasions for meeting the other sex. Nobody at Winston Street is a member of such an organization, but a number of young men and women in the neighborhood are close friends of members of the Midcity Brotherhood Club, a kind of group with many counterparts in the city. When this club organizes an event, many of the neighborhood swingers will thus be present. Some of them also attend the events organized by other clubs they might hear of through friends and neighbors. As one young man said, "There's always something on somewhere you can go to. You hear about them through the nigger network, if you pardon the expression."

The Midcity Brotherhood Club, with a membership of about fifteen men, organizes a couple of "cabarets"—that is, dances with a band and some other entertainment—as well as a picnic annually, with the members as well as their friends selling tickets to friends, neighbors, and relatives. The dances are held at the premises of an old middle-class Negro fraternity lodge, and hardly anybody but swingers—perhaps a

couple of hundred of so—is present. The ticket says B.Y.O.L., which means Bring Your Own Liquor. Potato chips, ice, and soft drinks for a mixer are supplied by the club. The summer picnic, on the other hand, is a family affair for those who have families, and there is a mixture largely of swingers and mainstreamers. The outing is in a Washington park with large picnic grounds, and the club members, all in the same kind of sports coat with the club name embroidered on the back, provide the visitors—usually two or three hundred—with hot dogs, hamburgers, corn-on-the-cob, and soft drinks. Park regulations forbid the serving of alcoholic beverages, but many visitors bring their own beer or perhaps something stronger. For the adults it is a good place to meet old friends for a few hours or make new ones, the teenagers do likewise or play a game of football, and the smaller children just follow their parents or try the swings. There is an age graded series of dance contests with records for prizes, where teenagers usually excel, and a raffle on the numbered tickets—first prize, a portable TV set, second, a case of whiskey, third, a transistor radio. The proceeds are donated to charitable organizations active in ghetto work.

Swingers thus lead lives full of company and spend much time away from home. This often means that a swinger who is married has friends relatively unknown to his (or her) family. In many cases, this means extramarital affairs, but often it is not a question of intentionally shielding the two spheres of life from one another. Sociability for swingers is simply an individual thing, not a sphere of activity where the couple is the "natural" unit.

It is possible to be a swinger on a variety of economic bases, although swingers have certain concerns which are hard to satisfy on a minimal income. It helps to have a car if one leads a mobile wide-ranging life, and many go to great efforts to keep abreast with fashion trends, for men as well as for women, as these are presented in certain downtown stores as well as on the ghetto main streets. Among the swingers on Winston Street and among their friends there is relatively little long-term unemployment but somewhat more periodical unemployment. A few of the men who are regularly without jobs earn money living off the incomes of women or through illegal pursuits such as robbery, burglary, or gambling. Most of the others in the category frown upon these activities and wonder how long the people in question can get away with it, but they usually do not break altogether with people they may have grown up with or may be closely related to.

A fact partially related to periodical unemployment is that of a rather high rate of job changes. These contribute to the swingers' widening social circles, as they accumulate new friends from among their work mates. Other friends remain from childhood and school days, and yet others are people you met at parties or in the company of other friends and took a liking to. Some acquaintances do not last very long, of course; "It's just a hi and bye thing, you meet and then you see a lot of each other for a while, and then somehow you don't see each other too much, and that's the end of it," as one young woman said.

Yet one more factor in the wide and shifting friendship networks of many swingers is their residential mobility, but this is one which they share with many other ghetto dwellers. When ghetto buildings are condemned as unsanitary, or torn down in urban renewal, the residents have to move; poor people are often expelled when they cannot pay rent; and it is natural that with little money to spare for extra space as a luxury, ghetto dwellers often adjust the size of their quarters to the minimum necessary for the household at its particular point in the developmental cycle—which means that as a family grows larger, there is a continuous pressure for more space.

The swingers' particular reasons for moving may have to do with these, or they may be of other kinds. Since swingers break up old marital and consensual alliances or form new ones rather often compared to other groups, this may influence the question of residence now and then. Other swingers on the move just say that they didn't like the neighborhood they were in— at times because some neighbors seem to feel that swingers should extend the same hospitality and sociability to them as they do to other swingers.

All factors taken together, with their investment of time and effort in sociability and entertainment, their mobility, and their living in a large metropolis where people's paths need not often cross accidentally, the swingers are in a position to make a great number of friendships and acquaintances, but these also easily come to an end if not pursued actively. Stated in somewhat more exact structural terms, the many more or less fluctuating relationships may be seen as making up networks in which large segments are relatively loose-knit and where there is a relatively low frequency of interaction as well as a low degree of permanence in many of the relationships.[7] "Loose-knit", in this case, means that a person's friends and acquaintances are not in direct relationships with each other, independently of their indirect contact through that person. Thus he knows a great many persons unknown to any particular one of his friends and acquaintances and is on the other hand as ignorant of parts of their social circles. Furthermore, and just as significant, even in segments of the network which are close-knit in the sense that persons who know each other also know of mutual friends and acquaintances, people are not always constantly in touch with one another. The often low frequency of interaction and low degree of permanency in sociable relationships mean that in part, the networks are only latently close-knit.

There are phenomena, however, which work toward the renewal of dormant relationships. Large-scale and widely known gatherings such as social club dances and picnics bring together many swingers who have not seen each other for a long time—indeed, this is frequently mentioned as an important reason for going to them. In a different way, mutual friends can prevent people from dropping completely out of one another's awareness. News of people whom one knows but seldom if ever sees are thus often received through intermediaries. Discussions of what is on the grapevine, we have already seen, are often on the agenda when swingers come together. This informative gossip may deal with who has a new job, who has moved, and where, who has married, or separated, whose little sister has grown up and is looking good, or who has got a new car.[8]

While mainstreamers in a way often encapsulate themselves in a few close relationships, many of which are with relatives, and enjoy the stable day-to-day life with home and family, the swingers' interests thus span out over the ghetto and seek variety and entertainment. The difference between them tends to be somewhat like that between "routine-seekers" and "action-seekers" which Gans describes from an Italian-American working-class and lower-class community in Boston (Gans 1962 b). In that case there was also a relationship between age and life style, as well as between marital status and life style, but both among black ghetto dwellers and Italian-Americans there is less than a perfect fit, in that there is a period in one's life when one can live either way irrespective of marital status. When that period is over, however, a swinger has to become something else.

The Street Families[9]

Some of the swingers then become members of street families, as many of them were when they were children. They are called street families here simply because they are conspicuous in the open-air life of ghetto street corners and sidewalks. Probably it is their way of life, and the complementary life style of streetcorner men, which most closely correspond to an outsider's image of typical ghetto life. It is often the members of street families who are conspicuously engaging in affairs with the other sex outside marriage, whose children are born out of wedlock and engage in juvenile delinquency as they grow up, and who drink and fight in public. Although not all street families, or all members of street families, engage in such behavior, and hardly anybody does so all the time, it is to them and their way of life their mainstreamer neighbors occasionally voice moral objections. (It may be added immediately that the members of the street families are not much given to idealizing the life style either.) Little attention is then given to the fact that some members of such families, in particular middle-aged and older women, may attend church quite regularly, and express quite puritanical views about what goes on around them. Of course, there are also women who only go to church on weekday evenings, to play bingo.

The street families are childrearing households. This means that there is practically always an adult woman in the household who is the mother of all, most, or at least some of the children there, and whose age is somewhere between the upper twenties and the fifties in the great majority of cases. (This, of course, means that this category is parallel to the mainstreamers agewise.) The women may or may not have a husband who is a member of the household—among the street families on Winston Street, between one-third and one-half are headed by women without husbands.[10] In the majority of these cases, however, the woman has been married previously.

A childrearing couple in a street family seldom has anybody from an ascending generation present in the household. A single woman with children, on the other hand, often shares her home with her mother. In a very few cases in the Winston Street neighborhood a woman has both her husband and her mother under the same roof, but these households have intensive mother-in-law troubles, and in other cases where this arrangement had been tried, it did not last very long. Thus, in general, street families are either two or three generation conjugal union[11] households, with husband, wife, and one or two descending generations (as young daughters' children may be included in the household), or two to four generation husbandless households, with an adult woman, sometimes with her mother and/or one or more brothers and sisters, and with the same one or two descending generations as those of conjugal union households. In both cases, of course, the younger daughter whose small child or children are in the household may be of the swinger set, just as the young women who leave their children with mainstreamer grandparents.

Naturally, this is only an outline of what may be seen as the two major types of household composition. Particular households with a large number of members of many generations and with age divergencies between members of the same generation can turn out to be quite complex. In the Winston Street neighborhood, for example, one older woman lives with three children—two daughters, one of whom is considerably older than the other, and a son. The elder daughter has nine children, and her oldest teenage daughter in turn has a son. The older woman's other daughter has one child. As a fifteen person household, this is one of the largest in the neighborhood. Those which compete with it in size and complexity are also husbandless. This is hardly surprising, as they are made up primarily of a combination of mother-and-child units with a common grandmother. Such combinations with husbands present in the procreating generation are not apt to occur.

Another aspect of the apparent complexity of households similar to the one just mentioned has to do with the relatively low ages at which many women first give birth and their relatively long periods of childbearing. Most teenage pregnancies in the Winston Street neighborhood occur among the street families, and many women who bear their first children early proceed to get quite large families. This means that generation spans are short, and the age difference between the oldest and youngest children of the same mother may be considerable. The consequence of this is often that a woman and her oldest daughter (or daughters) are childbearers and childrearers at the same time. In a number of households, then, children grow up in the company of uncles and aunts not much older, and sometimes younger, than they are themselves. Also, of course, if childrearing sisters share a household, cousins are raised under the same roof. However, there is no established pattern of etiquette between cousins or between aunts and uncles on the one hand and nieces and nephews on the other when they are of similar age and raised in the same household, so they function as close playmates and almost siblings—each child is aware, of course, that among the adult women of the household, he has a particular relationship to his own mother. Occasionally, in play such as wrestling, an uncle may playfully demand deference from his nephew, but otherwise their exact kinship status with respect to each other is of little importance.

As far as the mothers in a household like this are concerned, they tend to duplicate a mother and household manager role in that they usually all take some part in child care, cooking, cleaning and so forth. There are some dangers of conflict in an ambiguous arrangement like this, of course, over for example individual responsibilities or the proper way of handling a matter (particularly as the young woman either begins to take on her mother role or neglects to do so). On the other hand, it gives a certain flexibility for the participants in the work pool, as people with similar competences can substitute for each other. For one thing, it may permit at least one of the women to hold a job some of the time; for another, a young woman who wants more leisure time to spend in the company of friends can leave her children in the care of her mother.

Such an arrangement necessarily also means that an aunt or grandmother is somewhat like a mother to her sister's or daughter's children. This leads her to take on more authority as a disciplinarian toward these than an aunt or grandmother usually does. The indulgence which particularly a grandmother normally showers over grand-children is thus circumscribed to the extent that she is behaviorally also like the chil-dren's mother.

Thus far it may have seemed here as if the husbandless households among the street families are completely without adult male members. However, this is not nec-essarily the case, as the case of the fifteen person household mentioned above shows. Relatively often the presence of the older woman also brings the brother of the child-rearing woman into the household. The brother may be unmarried, separated, or divorced—if he does not have a home of his own, moving home to mother is a com-mon solution, and in this case it brings him into the household of his sister. Usually, however, a brother of this kind has a very tenuous position in the household, as he is linked to it primarily through the oldest member who might not live much longer and because an unattached man of this kind often behaves in ways which are discomfort-ing to other members of the household. On Winston Street, Reinhardt Ross, 45, is a good example of this.

Reinhardt lives with his 39-year old sis-ter Grace, her eight children and her first grandchild, and his and Grace's 72-year old mother. Reinhardt is unemployed except for occasional day work (several years ago he worked regularly in a streetcorner gro-cery store), and he spends most of his time together with some other unemployed men at the street corner or in the back alley.

However, he also frequently brings the other men into the house at practically any hour, and just like outside, they drink and get drunk there. Although Grace is on rea-sonably good terms with most of the men she would rather not have them around so much and at such inconvenient times, partially because she thinks they are a bad influence on the children. Besides, she wants more privacy. As it is, an evening in the Ross house is frequently like this:

The front room is crowded. One of Reinhardt's friends is asleep under a blanket on one of the two decrepit couches, while two of Grace's youngest children sit on the edge of it. Reinhardt and two other men are on the other couch, with another of Grace's sons between them. There are three tables. One has two TV sets on it, one of which is broken, while the other set shows a Western to which the smaller children are tuned in. The two other tables, on the other side of an oil burner, have heaps of clothes on them, as closet space in the house is very limited. Occasionally a roach runs up a table leg and disappears among the clothes. The edges of one of the tables are kept free so that some can take their meals there while others eat in the adjoining kitchen and the rest wait for their turn and watch TV meanwhile. After the meal, the women clean up care-fully, the smaller children are asked to go upstairs, while the older ones go out or hang around. Reinhardt and his friends are sharing a drink—one of them just returned from the liquor store. Grace's 17-year old son David is inconspicuously leafing through a pornographic maga-zine. When Grace sees it, she snatches it from him and says, "You know you're not allowed to read that kind of trash. Didn't I raise you better than that?" A little later, David goes out. Now only the adults are left downstairs. Grace and her mother work in the kitchen and talk to each other while Grace's sister who is visiting sits half asleep in the front room. The men are also still there. They try to draw her into the conversation but she says nothing. One of them looks appreciatively at her and says, "You know, you're a fine-looking woman, big fat legs, good color, a mouthful on each side..." Grace's sister still says nothing but smiles with half-closed eyes. Later, when Reinhardt and his friends are still there but the older woman and the children have gone to bed, Grace and her sister leave the house to go and play cards at a friend's house.

It is this kind of presence of Reinhardt's friends, as well as Reinhardt's own unruliness and untrustworthiness, which Grace objects to, and which generates much conflict between her and her brother. Both Grace's children and Reinhardt's friends say that Reinhardt only lasts in the house as long as his mother is there. Grace sometimes threatens, in harsh words, to put him out even earlier—"I'll have to get that nigger's ass out of here."

In cases such as this, it is clear that the man included in the household of his mother has little or no household authority. On the other hand, he also has very little responsibility and is hardly at all under the control of anybody in the household. Thus he does not alter the functioning of the household to any significant extent by his presence, except perhaps by being an irritant.

Another frequently occurring type of extra member in the households of street families—both those including a husband and the husbandless ones—is the boarder, taken in to give some additional income, but sometimes also or even primarily because someone in the household pities him. He, too, is usually an unattached male who cannot afford his own apartment and who has no relatives or is simply not accepted into the home of his kinsmen. In some cases, of course, he does not want to stay with relatives either. In many cases, the boarder in

a street family is like a member of it, in that he eats with the family, uses its living room, and is an intimate of the people in the house. On the other hand, of course, he has no particular responsibilities in the organization of household life, and no authority except perhaps to a minor degree over the children, in the absence of their adult guardians. In some cases, boarders stay with the same household for many years, but many shift homes frequently because of failure to pay rent, because the landlord dislikes the boarder's behavior—drunkenness etc.—or because of other quarrels between them.

Finally, more frequently than other ghetto households, those of street families include additional children, usually related to household members but not directly descended from them, who stay there for longer or shorter periods. These are present only in a small number of the households, yet frequently enough to deserve mention. Sometimes, one gets no other reason for the presence of such a child than such explanations as "my sister and I thought Eric (the sister's son) ought to get to know his cousins a little better, so he'll stay with us for a while", but at other times, and more often, it is a question of an adaptive response to particular circumstances. If there is a severe lack of space, for instance, it may be seen as a good idea to let one or two children stay with relatives with more room, and if an older child does not get along with a stepfather it may be a solution to let it stay with an aunt or an uncle. Other reasons may be more complicated; a divorced man's former wife is becoming an alcoholic, and since he cannot himself take care of the children he asks a brother or sister with a family to do so.

All this goes to show that the household composition of street families is quite variable, both between households and in a single household over time. To a certain extent, this is undoubtedly due to strains arising from external pressures—the many separations and divorces, for instance, which result in husbandless households, and the economic pressure which makes it more or less a necessity to take boarders even when there is hardly any extra space to spare. But one should also see the variability as an adaptive flexibility, as in the pooling of resources of adult husbandless sisters or an old mother and her adult daughter with children. Perhaps it is the habituation to this kind of flexibility in household arrangements, and to the adaptive relaxation of mainstream rules of household composition, that makes it easier to accept boarders even if the economic benefit is doubtful, or additional children even when it is not an absolute necessity. A streetcorner man throws the point into relief with this statement:

> "I bet if you couldn't pay your rent and you were evicted from your place you couldn't just go to any of your white people and expect they'd take you in, they'd just be thinking of all the trouble. But you could come over here and stay with somebody 'cause we're used to helping each other out."

It can perhaps be said, then, that it is in the style of life of street families to maintain relatively open household membership boundaries. The mainstream American notion of the composition of a household is that it ought to be stable and coincide with the nuclear family in some stage of its development. Ghetto households often diverge considerably from this type. If we allow ourselves the luxury of making the point a little too strongly for the sake of contrast, they are more in the nature of temporary coalitions of persons relating to the household core in a variety of kinship, friendship, and landlord-boarder ties, for whom sharing residence is expedient even if it may only be for a short period.

Street families clearly have looser internal relationships than mainstreamer families. Compared to the latter, a person's relationships to the other household members have a lower salience and those to outside persons considerably higher. This means that whoever is the manager of the household (usually a woman or a team of women) had less influence on the lives of household members. The whole household is less often united for meals (something which may often also be made difficult by the large number of household members), and there is less control over children's home work. Attempts to steer the lives of household members often fail. In some households this results in recurrent open conflict. Children are given verbal thrashings, a lash with a leather belt, or a sentence of confinement to their rooms, but the disagreements continue. Some children are threatened with reform school by their mothers and regard it as a real possibility that they will be sent there at the initiative of their own family, although it is actually much more likely to be the result of outside intervention. Managing the male-female relationship in the street family where a husband is present may be no easier as he is frequently drawn to his friends at the hangout and perhaps to some outside sexual affair. There may be continuous and sometimes physically violent quarrels over this, and one can notice how many men ignore household hours when these come into conflict with peer group life....

Husbands are included in some street families, while others are husbandless. However, most adult women without a man in the house have been married. Usually they are divorced or simply separated—a legal divorce takes more trouble and some expenses to get, and therefore many only become interested in getting a divorce when a new marriage is to follow. When people who have been married contract new unions, however, these often remain common-law unions. A great many men and women enter new relationships of one kind or other, and as these result in children, the offspring of more than one union will often live together in one household, generally that of the children's common mother. As the children are usually given the last name of their father—sometimes even when they are the result of a short-term extraresidential union—they often have different last names, a fact which adds to the complexity of many street families. However, it happens that as a consensual relationship is broken and the father loses contact with the household his children are in, the last name of the mother also comes to be used for her children out of wedlock. Apparently, no particular usage is very definitely established for children's last names under these circumstances.

Obviously "having husband" and "not having husband" are neither very stable nor very clearcut as attributes of women in street families. One may have a more or less close male companion within or outside the household without being married to him, and the position of such a male partner in household affairs may be quite variable. Whether or not a woman is equipped with a husband or a male partner at one point in time, this is not necessarily her lasting status. A number of the marriages which exist at any given time are likely to split sooner or later.

Most husbands and wives in street families are not very close to each other. One may well characterize their relationships as segregated.[12] They spend most of their leisure time apart. The women (who have less leisure time, being in charge of most household affairs) tend to spend their time with an intimate circle of close kin—mother, sisters and daughters if these live close enough—and a few neighbor women. The men on the other hand, spend their time with a somewhat larger peer group of more fluctuating composition, in which male relatives may or may not be included. A great number of the men have rather marginal involvements with family life, and apart from these their life style is that of the streetcorner men described below. Others, however, are somewhat more oriented toward home and family, which means that their

family relationships are a little closer to those typical of mainstreamer families.

The segregation of relationships between man and wife means that they may know little of each other's company, and in particular that the wife hardly knows the wives and girl friends of her husband's friends at all, while the husband is as unfamiliar with the male company of his wife's female friends—unless these are her close kin, of course. Patricia Jones, a Winston Street woman, sees a great deal of some of her husband Harry's friends, as they often assemble on the front staircase of the Jones house, and sometimes in the Jones living room—it is an "open house" to a greater extent than most—but their wives and girl friends are usually unknown to her except by name and some-times by sight, as they have been pointed out to her on the street. The following incident, involving Harry Jones' friend Sylvester's relationship to his girl friend Diane, shows some of this. Sylvester is a liquor store messenger and a boarder in "Miss Gladys' house" down the street.

Harry, Sylvester, Sonny, and Wes are sharing a pint of whiskey in the Joneses' parlor. As Patricia comes in from the kitchen to get a drink, Sylvester starts making a little show of leaving the group to go over to Diane, ostensibly to stay over night. The other men tease him, as they often do, about the risk of finding some other man with Diane. Patricia says the risk must be small. If Diane thinks Sylvester is good enough for her, she must be an ugly old hag without a tooth in her mouth. The other men laugh as Sylvester indignantly says that she is not like that at all. Patricia keeps on deriding Diane, claiming that she has heard from somebody who had seen Sylvester and Diane together on the street that she was the ugliest thing she ever saw. Sylvester asks who said so, and Patricia finally laughs and says she was just kidding. Actually the only thing she knows about Diane is what Sylvester says, but then that is probably not very reliable either, Patricia says.

More than mainstreamers or swingers, the street families have their leisure lives rooted in a rather small area around the neighborhood. A greater number of relatively close neighbors become engaged in sociable interaction, while one sees less of friends in other parts of town. No doubt, this is partially due to the fact that compared to mainstreamers, many of whom have cars, the members of street families cannot move around so easily. But it seems, too, that the members of street families are less reluctant to engage in interaction with people they have met by chance, such as through repeated encounters in the neighborhood.

It should also be added here that Winston Street has a nucleus of street families who have lived a long time in this area. Some of them have even been present on this street for two or three decades, although they may have moved from one house to another on it as better houses have become available or as eviction notices have forced a move. These families, of course, are well acquainted, and in some cases temporary alliances have been formed between their members and children have resulted from them, as boys and girls have grown up together or as some woman's unattached brother has cast eyes on the divorcee next door.

The participation in street life may cause strains on domestic organization; however, it also has its rosy sides. The informal communications passing between friends may be useful social capital. If a man knows of a job opening at his place of work, he may tell an unemployed neighbor about it in a street-corner conversation; if there is some day work anywhere in the area—moving, painting, cleaning, or carpentry, for instance—the men who are in the midst of street life are apt to hear about it first.

Furthermore, in a society where life on a small income is a continuously unfolding series of instant crises, the small informal loans and services granted between neighbors may ease the burden by channeling resources each moment to the point where there is a current need. This may be a problem for a person who is repeatedly called upon to help but who is seldom in need of assistance himself; but to the extent that these relationships really work out as balanced reciprocity, they are helpful to all involved. The case which follows provides a picture of how a man with good contacts in the Winston Street neighborhood engages in a series of small transactions of this kind in the course of a couple of hours.

I met George about 4.30 p.m. outside Rubin's grocery. Mrs. Dunham just passed by. She was in a hurry to get to her job and borrowed a quarter from George—his last—for her bus fare. Since George is usually at work at this hour, I asked him how it came that he was off, and he said he had been changed to a new shift, from 5 a.m. to 1 p.m. Since he works in Virginia, I said it was a good thing he had just gotten a car; he had paid 200 dollars for it.

"Yeah, but I tore that thing up yesterday," he said. "I wrapped it around a tree."

It turned out he had been working two shifts in a row to get into his new shift, and afterwards he had been out drinking with a work mate. On his way home he had obviously been a little drunk and more than a little tired, so he had probably fallen asleep.

"So I called Lewis, you know, he works at this garage, so he got a buddy from over there to come and tow my car back here."

After we had taken a look at the car which was in uncertain condition, George asked if he owed me any money, and I replied I was afraid he did not.

"Could you stand for a half pint?" he asked. We got one and finished it on our way to Sonny's place, but Sonny was not at home, so we went to look for him and Sylvester at Diane's place—Diane is Sylvester's girl friend. They were not there either, however, so we went back to Winston Street, first to

Albert McNeill, a truck driver and amateur but expert auto mechanic who promised to take a look at George's car "first thing in the morning". George had the next day off and would not have to show up at his job again until the day after. Of course, if the car was not running by then he might be in trouble, since there was no public transport to his job in Virginia between midnight and 6 a.m. But another neighbor knew someone who also started work somewhere out there at an early hour, so perhaps he could arrange a ride.

We then went on to Mr. Clark, and George told him about the car, and Mr. Clark thought it was a shame. But the visit failed as far as its real purpose was concerned. Since George's wife was away he would not get dinner at home, so he needed some money to go to the carry-out. Mr. Clark could not help; he pulled out the lining of his pockets to show that they were empty. So we continued to Mr. Lewis, the man at the garage who had helped George get his car towed the night before. George borrowed a dollar there and went to the carry-out to get a barbecued rib sandwich which he brought back to his friend Harry Jones' house. Harry was asleep, but his wife Patricia was getting ready to go to a church to play bingo. She asked George to come along, so he went across the street to another neighbor to borrow money so that he could play, too.

Street families have a lower average income than mainstreamer families, and a great number of them fall below the poverty line. Many of the men in street families are in unskilled manual work, and a number of them are at least periodically unemployed. The women with jobs are also in unskilled work—many are domestics and cleaning women. A number of the husbandless households receive welfare payments. There is clearly a relationship between low income and elements of the street family organization; we have touched on some of them here....

The Streetcorner Men[13]

Our sketch of the street families dwelt particularly on the life of women and children—even when there are men in these households, they are often peripheral to domestic life. To give a view of the life of men, we must direct our attention to the peer group life of men, much of which takes place at street corners but also in other settings such as some people's houses—at the Ross house and the Jones house on Winston Street, for instance, as described above—carry-out shops, back alleys, or pool halls. Some streetcorner men, we have found, are members of street families, but others are unattached and live as boarders, have their own apartments, or just drift around staying for a while with anybody willing to put them up. In the latter cases contacts with kin may be minimal or altogether absent. This became tragically clear when Rufus, a long-time resident of the Winston Street neighborhood who had been boarding with Patricia and Harry Jones for a couple of years, suddenly died of a heart attack. His friends among the streetcorner men tried to locate his closest relatives—only at this time did some of his peers find out what his last name was. It was impossible to trace any brothers or sisters at all, however, although Rufus had mentioned their existence now and then. The men also knew that Rufus had been married once and had also had a common-law union of some longevity, but they only found his first wife after several days' work. She said bitterly that she had not seen Rufus for years and that since he had contributed nothing to the care of their children for so many years, she did not think it mattered one way or the other if he was dead. Thus she saw no reason to contribute to meeting funeral costs. Nobody else could or would raise the money either, so Rufus was finally cremated at public expense. His friends were quite upset but could not do anything about it.

We mentioned above that male members of street families usually hold low-paying, unskilled jobs and are sometimes unemployed. The unattached men are even more likely to be unemployed for long periods or even permanently. They have often dropped out of school early, and many of them are relatively recent migrants from the rural South.

The streetcorner men usually return day after day to the same hangout. There they talk and drink, play cards and shoot crap, or just do nothing. Some go home to eat, others get something from the carry-out or the streetcorner grocer—some bread and cold cuts, perhaps, things they can eat while they are standing at the corner. There is continuous drinking—a lot of gin and somewhat less whiskey, while some men drink only cheap wine. If they are not already alcoholics, they are well on their way. Many of them have had attacks of *delirium tremens*; the symptoms of "deetee" are familiar to most ghetto dwellers. Now and then somebody at the corner mentions that yet another friend has got cirrhosis of the liver, and everybody knows of friends and acquaintances who have died from ailments caused by their drinking. Quite a few men have attended rehabilitation classes for alcoholics, but these are usually seen as a farce.

> "Those classes are a lot of bullshit. Lot of niggers bring their bottles right into class, and then there's one of these fellows standing up there telling you about how he stopped drinking, and you can see he's half drunk right up there, and he's gonna get more drunk as soon as he gets out of there."

There is not much beer drinking except during the summer. This is also the season of most beer commercials on the black radio stations.

Collections for liquor are taken among the streetcorner men themselves, but there is also a lot of begging from people who pass by. Most of it is quite friendly—from neighbors whom the streetcorner men know quite well—but some men can also behave in rather threatening ways or engage in robbery. Many of the men have some kind of police record. In the case of a relative few the record is serious and may include housebreaking, robbery, and aggravated assault. These are the people known in the ghetto as "gorillas". In other cases there are charges for minor assaults or petty larceny such as shoplifting and purse snatching. Most of the men's records, however, involve drinking and drunkenness in public places, and in some streetcorner groups the members are much more law-abiding than in others.

Some of the unattached men may have extraresidential relationships to women in street families. However, others rely largely on prostitutes for meeting their sexual needs, which is one reason for the spread of venereal disease among them. A couple of single women in the Winston Street neighborhood eke out a meager living as prostitutes catering to the desires of the streetcorner men who hang out there. One of them, a sickly woman named Ruby, occasionally lives with one man or another for a while, but these unions do not last very long. Her one-room apartment is also used as a kind of lounge by some of the men, particularly during the winter when it is too cold to be outside much. One evening at Ruby's place may be like this.

The one room has a concrete floor and is partially below the street level. There is a couch and a few small tables, a couple of old upholstered chairs into which cigarettes have burned many holes over the years (usually as drunken smokers have fallen asleep) and a couple of kitchen chairs. There is no rug. Of the three holders in the ceiling only one holds a bare lightbulb, while the other two are empty. On one of the tables there is a porcelain lamp in the shape of a half-naked woman. Its shade is broken. On this day neither lamp is lighted, since Ruby has failed to pay the electricity bill so that the current has been switched off. Instead, there are a few candles. The walls are adorned by one picture of president Kennedy, three of Jesus Christ, one of a group of black rock-and-roll artists, and one print of a landscape with a beer advertisement pasted on the frame. There are also a plastic wall clock advertising another beer brand (a type of clock usually found in cheap beer taverns) and a calendar from a nearby liquor store. Roaches are running all over the walls and the furniture.

As the men begin to gather this evening Ruby is not yet there. There is an elderly man, Nathan, who talks about his hunting and fishing trips down South; there is Jimmy Wilson, Percy, and Reinhardt; and there is Joshua who came up from North Carolina some eight months ago and has been talking about getting a job since then but has not succeeded so far. Joshua wants to impress people as one who knows his way around and as a smart dresser. His flat, smallbrimmed hat, his coat and his tie are all in matching colors, but by now they are all very dirty, and his coat is torn here and there. His baggy, dirty pants and muddy shoes also fail to contribute toward the image he wants to promote.

> The men pool their resources for a pint of gin and a bottle of soda for a chaser. Old Nathan provides most of the funds. He has a job right now, and besides he is on his way home to his wife and wants a taste before he leaves. Percy goes to the liquor store to get it. He has a fresh knife wound on his cheek after Bee Jay cut him the night before. When he returns, Dennis, the man who has been living with Ruby for several months, is with him. Percy mentions that Lorraine, the 14-year old girl across the street, is pregnant. "Those fellows had better watch out," Dennis says. "You don't go around knocking off young broads like

> that. That's statutory rape, and the judge won't pay it no mind if she wanted to or not." There are some reminiscences of other early pregnancies, about men who got away with it and about men who did not. Then Ruby comes in. "Lord have mercy," she says. "You all here, and you got a taste, too." Then she tells Dennis she is tired of him, so he will have to go. Dennis is silent, but Jimmy Wilson says Dennis will soon find another woman. Nathan leaves to go home. Joshua takes his harmonica out of his pocket and starts playing old country blues. He is not particularly good. Reinhardt and Percy have become more and more drowsy after the gin; now they both sleep on their chairs. Ruby, Dennis, and Jimmy Wilson ask for tunes, and Joshua tries to play them. Even if he is not very successful they are all enjoying themselves. Jimmy Wilson, a jet black man with processed hair and a very hoarse voice, stands up to sing to Joshua's accompaniment. He stands in front of Ruby and leans over her as he sings. "You ain't good looking, but you're my kind of woman…" Ruby smiles, and after Jimmy stops singing she stands up and dances with him on the small space which is free in the middle of the flour. They clench each other tightly and move slowly. Joshua laughs and plays his harmonica, and Dennis looks on. Reinhardt and Percy still sleep, their heads hanging down toward their chests. After a while the men who are awake leave to go and try to find something to eat, and Ruby is left alone with her two sleeping guests.

When the members of a streetcorner men's peer group describe themselves, they lay much emphasis on solidarity. Sometimes, this is a general solidarity among all the members; "When they drink wine, I drink wine; when they drink gin, I drink gin; when they drink whiskey, I drink whiskey." More often, however the solidarity refers to bonds between one man and another. "Dennis is my main man. If he gets into trouble, I'll be right there with him." Many streetcorner men, like Joshua, and like many younger swingers, are acutely conscious of male clothing fashion, although they can usually ill afford to do anything about it. It is another fitting expression of friendship, then, when Fats says, "Freddy can use anything in my closet, and he'd let me use anything in his." And Percy remembers how Lonnie helped pour wine down his thirsty throat when Percy himself had the shakes so badly that he could not hold the bottle.

But all is not peace and friendship in the circle of streetcorner men, and there is much to show that the rosy view of close relationships lasting through thick and thin is considerably exaggerated.[14] The speech style of streetcorner sociability is often tough and scornful, and hospitality is not always liberally extended. If a collection is taken for a half pint of gin and one man has no money, he cannot be too sure to get anything to drink. Fats specifically denies Reinhardt a drink out of his bottle because "That damn motherfucker never brushes his teeth. I ain't gonna let him get close to my bottle with his dirty mouth." In this case Reinhardt says nothing, but at other times a man might be less happy to accept abusive comments on his appearance, behavior, or intelligence. While streetcorner peer groups vary when it comes to the members' reaction to slights upon their honor, there are some where a challenge often leads not only to a heated argument but on to a violent fight.... It happens that knives, bottles or other objects are used, which is one explanation for the scars on the faces and bodies of many streetcorner men. Sometimes, such quarrels lead to lasting animosity, and people who are good friends one day may be bitter enemies from the next day and on. And the conflicts are easily expressed in violence again, as the two enemies continue to hang out at

the same place and with peers they have in common.

Violence also easily erupts in the streetcorner men's relationships with women as some men are no more ready to take insults from these than from other men. Besides, the fast-changing and by no means clearly defined relationships between streetcorner men and the women they interact with easily breed disagreement and distrust about sexual faithfulness, and violence occasionally erupts over such matters as well. Although some women are quite ready to defend themselves with a knife or a razor, many would rather call the police. This, of course, adds to the police records of some men.

It might seem from what has been said that the life of streetcorner men presents a lurid picture of sex, drinking, and violence. This may be true to the extent that the men show much and continuous concern with getting "a taste" and "a piece of pussy", and in that they are undoubtedly well acquainted with violence. But after all, fights occur only now and then, and many men have so limited access to sexual relationships that they must turn to prostitutes. Most days in the life of a streetcorner man, then, are filled with the same faces, the same hangout, the same struggle for money for food and drink, the same kind of talk—in short, the same routine.

* * *

Naturally, some people do not quite fit into anyone of these categories. Some of the old people, for instance, living alone outside childrearing households and without much interaction with neighbors or anybody else, cannot easily be placed in a category, although they may still lean toward the street family, streetcorner man, or mainstreamer orientations which were theirs during their more active lives. A few unattached women without significant household obligations are a kind of female counterparts of the streetcorner men with whom they interact rather intensively. Some of them, like Ruby who was mentioned above, make some money from prostitution but are hardly professionals; rather, they "turn a trick" when an opportunity presents itself, but mostly with friends and acquaintances as customers, people they may often "do it" with anyway. Other people are not so much left out of the four categories as they are left between them. It is not difficult to see that it is possible to follow a middle course between mainstreamer and street family, between swinger and mainstreamer, between swinger and street family, or between swinger and street-corner man. A curious case of such straddling is that of some households in the Winston Street neighborhood which are well established in illegal businesses—bootlegging and the numbers game. Except for these means of income, the households seem to lead mainstreamer lives. Their houses are well kept, the families keep largely to themselves, although they are friendly with their neighbors and well liked by most people, and they sometimes voice concern with the improvement of the neighborhood. Other people are aware of the incongruity between on the one hand the respectable front and the mainstreamer life, on the other hand the kind of business they engage in. As one mainstreamer neighbor said about one of the men involved: "Of course Jimmy Thompson is a crook, but he is a good man." Other people in illicit businesses may be more aligned with other life styles. Many bootleggers, dope pushers, pimps, and other hustlers are in street families, and some of the more successful ones are well-known "men about town" swingers—very well dressed, with expensive cars, and well known in those ghetto bars which are the main settings of the fast life. Illegal activities can thus be combined with a variety of life styles....

NOTES

1. A "basic role," according to Banton's (1965: 33 ff.) usage is one which affects conduct in a wide range of situations; it influences the allocation of other roles to the individual as well as his enactment of them. The sex role is probably the best example of a basic role in most societies.

2. Such dichotomies are more or less prominent for example in studies by Hylan Lewis (1955: 3 ff.), Drake and Cayton (1962: 519 ff.), and Jessie Bernard (1966: 27 ff.)

3. The concept of conscious model is employed here in conformity with the usage by Lévi-Strauss (1953: 526–527).

4. Those who are interested in comparing this to other categorizations of urban life ways in the United States may turn to the general paper by Gans (1962 a), the same author's study of an Italian-American community (Gans 1962 b: 28 ff.), Seeley's paper on the use of the slum (1959), and Drake's and Cayton's study of Black Chicago (1962: 519 ff.).

5. In the terms suggested by Bott (1957: 52 ff.), the mainstreamers often have a joint conjugal role-relationship, particularly in sociability—with husband and wife carrying out activities together—as opposed to a segregated conjugal role-relationship, where husband and wife tend to have separate interests and activities.

6. This seemed still to be the case during Drake's and Cayton's research in Chicago in the late thirties and early forties (Drake and Cayton 1962: 525, 612 ff.).

7. The network concept, as it is used somewhat loosely here, refers to an "egocentric" social structure, with one individual at the center and consisting of his relationships to other individuals as well as the relationships which these individuals may have to one another. The distinction between degrees of network connectedness, that is, between close-knit and loose-knit networks, was suggested by Bott (1957: 59). Other important discussions of "network" and related concepts are those by

Barnes (1954, 1968), Mayer (1966), Mitchell (1966), and Boissevain (1968). It should be noted that the usage of network terminology has been rather varied. Mayer (1966) and Barnes (1968) have recently suggested that other terms should be used for "egocentric" structures, but the usage adopted here seems to have become rather well established.

8. Further comments on the functioning of gossip in the ghetto are made in Hannerz (1967).

9. It should be pointed out that "family" in "street family" should be understood to mean "residential unit with a core of members held together by kinship." To a great extent, the unit is also served by a common organization of domestic activities. The somewhat ambiguous term "family" is used here simply as the least cumbersome term available. Although the term "household" may have been more correct from some points of view, its use would more easily lead the thought too exclusively toward domestic activities. Cf. Solien de González (1960), Bender (1967).

10. It is difficult to give a more exact figure because the proportion varies somewhat over time and in particular because it depends on how people are classified into life style categories. Without a clearcut criterion for classification, one will necessarily find cases which are on the margin of a street family life style and about which one may be in doubt as far as classification is concerned. There is a clear tendency, however, for most husbandless households to be among those which show the strongest street family characteristics in other ways.

11. "Conjugal union" is here taken to include long-term consensual unions as well as legal marriages.

12. See note 5 of this chapter on segregated conjugal role-relationships. This seems to be a common pattern of working class and lower class marriage not only among black Americans; see for instance Dennis et al. (1956: 180 ff.), Rainwater et al. (1959), Rainwater (1964), Gans (1962 b: 50 ff.), and Komarovsky (1964).

13. The concept streetcorner men is used in the same sense by Liebow (1967). His description of this category appears generally valid also for the groups of men who hang out in the Winston Street neighborhood. Here and in following chapters we will discuss their relationship to other segments of the ghetto community, as well as aspects of this life style not discussed in great detail by Liebow. To some extent, some disagreement with details of Liebow's analysis will also be aired. However, those results of field work in the Winston Street neighborhood which parallel Liebow's work largely agree with his results.

14. Liebow also discusses this point (1967: 176 ff.).

REFERENCES

Banton, Michael. 1955. *The Coloured Quarter.* London: Cape.

Barnes, J. A. 1954. "Class and Committees in a Norwegian Island Parish." *Human Relations,* 7: 39–58.

———. 1968. "Networks and Political Process." In *Local-Level Politics.* Marc J. Swartz (ed.). Chicago: Aldine.

Bender, Donald R. 1967. "A Refinement of the Concept of Household: Families, Co-residence, and Domestic Functions." *American Anthropologist,* 69: 493–504.

Bernard, Jessie. 1966. *Marriage and Family among Negroes.* Englewood Cliffs, N.J.: Prentice-Hall.

Boissevain, Jeremy. 1968. "The Place of Non-groups in the Social Sciences." *Man,* n.s., 3: 542–556.

Bott, Elizabeth. 1957. *Family and Social Network.* London: Tavistock.

Dennis, Norman. Fernando Henriques, and Clifford Slaughter. 1956. *Coal Is Our Life.* London: Eyre & Spottiswoode.

Drake, St. Clair, and Horace R. Cayton. 1962. *Black Metropolis.* New York: Harper Torchbooks. (First edition 1945, Harcourt, Brace.)

Gans, Herbert J. 1962a. "Urbanism and Suburbanism as Ways of Life: A Re-evaluation of Definitions." In

Human Behavior and Social Processes. Arnold
M. Rose (ed.). Boston: Houghton Mifflin.

———. 1962b. *The Urban Villagers.*
New York: Free Press.

Hannerz, Ulf. 1967. "Gossip, Networks and
Culture in a Black American Ghetto."
Ethnos, 32: 35–60.

Komarovsky, Mirra. 1964. *Blue Collar Marriage.*
New York: Random House.

Lévi-Strauss, Claude. 1953. "Social Structure."
In *Anthropology Today.* A. L. Kroeber (ed.).
Chicago: University of Chicago Press.

Lewis, Hylan. 1955. *Blackways of Kent.*
Chapel Hill, N.C.: University of North
Carolina Press.

Liebow, Elliot. 1967. *Tally's Corner.*
Boston: Little, Brown.

Mayer, Adrian C. 1966. "The Significance of
Quasi-Groups in the Study of Complex
Societies." In *The Social Anthropology of
Complex Societies* (ASA 4). Michael Banton
(ed.). London: Tavistock.

Mitchell, J. Clyde. 1966. "Theoretical
Orientations in African Urban Studies."
In *The Social Anthropology of Complex
Societies* (ASA 4). Michael Banton (ed.).
London: Tavistock.

Rainwater, Lee. 1964. "Marital Sexuality in Four
Cultures of Poverty." *Journal of Marriage and
the Family*, 26: 457–466.

Rainwater, Lee, Gerald Handel, and Richard
P. Coleman. 1959. *Workingman's Wife.*
New York: Occana.

Seeley, John R. 1959. "The Slum: Its Nature, Use,
and Users." *Journal of the American Institute
of Planners*, 25: 7–14.

Solien De Gonzalez, Nancie L. 1960. "Household
and Family in the Caribbean: Some
Definitions and Concepts." *Social and
Economic Studies*, 9: 101–106.

5

HARVEY MOLOTCH

PATTERNS OF BLACK-WHITE INTERACTION

from *Managed Integration* (1972)

In the midst of the social turmoil that hit American cities in the 1960s, Harvey Molotch became interested in understanding how racial integration could be achieved through policy and urban development practices. One striking finding of his study of a racially mixed South Side Chicago neighborhood—illustrated in this excerpt—is that even when blacks and whites occupy the same public spaces, their social lives rarely intersect in a meaningful way.

Although South Shore was becoming virtually an all-black community, it is possible that during the transition period, geographical propinquity may have led to some degree of racial integration. Three forms of integration are possible during the transition process: *demographic* integration, whereby a given setting contains both blacks and whites in some specified proportions; *biracial interaction,* whereby non-antagonistic social interaction is occurring between blacks and whites to some specific extent; *trans-racial solidarity,* defined as conditions in which whites and blacks interact freely and without constraint so that race ceases to function as an important source of social cleavage or as a criterion for friendship and primary group selection. This chapter describes the extent, form, and most common contexts of these kinds of integration in South Shore. With the data gathered, I will try to explain the more general processes which, in the context of black-white propinquity, inhibit or promote the cross-racial sharing of social life. Interpersonal racial integration was not a salient goal of the South Shore Commission, but it is possible that, under certain circumstances, it nevertheless came into being.

General Strategy

We have many descriptions of communities striving for integration, yet seldom does information on the subject of actual interracial contact go beyond the anecdotal level. Many community studies cheerfully recount instances when whites and blacks serve on the same committee or come together in a constructive joint enterprise.[1] No precise information indicates the frequency of the contacts, the contexts in which they most often occur, or the dynamics of their development. The absence of such information inhibits the development of a sound theory of cross-racial interaction and, at a more practical level, precludes rigorous comparative analysis or evaluation of various forms of intervention which have integration as their goal.

In this study, counts were made of blacks and whites participating in given community settings. Although it is not a direct measure of all possible kinds of biracial interaction occurring in the area, much can be learned by an examination of racial patterns in various community public and quasi-public locales. Various loci of community activity in South Shore were investigated including schools, churches, recreational facilities, retail shops, and voluntary organizations. The basic technique was simply to take head-counts of blacks and whites participating in given organizations or observed in specific settings. In some instances I used reports of organizational chairmen and presidents; in others, I inspected organizational group photographs appearing in the community newspaper. In most instances, however, I was present to count the numbers of whites and blacks in the setting.

Although data gathered in this manner do not directly measure the degree of *neighboring* across racial lines, it is perhaps safe to assume that if people routinely neighbor across racial lines they also go to places such as stores, parks, and churches with one another and will appear at least occasionally in the same community settings. It is also assumed that if whites and blacks are participating together in the same community institutions, they will, as a minimum criterion, be present in the same settings at the same time.

Ordered Segmentation in South Shore

The inhibitions to integration in an area like South Shore cannot be properly understood by reliance upon such concepts as "prejudiced attitudes," "bigotry," or white "status anxiety," as these terms are ordinarily employed to explain interracial avoidance behavior. We can assume that what Suttles[2] refers to as "ordered segmentation" is natural to any community; the fact that South Shore blacks differed from South Shore whites in religion (few black Catholics, no Jews), ethnicity, economic status (blacks lower),[3] stage of life cycle (blacks younger with more children), and length of residency in the area would all act to deter biracial contact. That is, racial distinctions coincided with other common bases for social differentiation.

Urban settings have as their critical social characteristic the fact that intimate relationships between all parties are precluded by [the] sheer vastness of the numbers of people.[4] Selection is thus necessary. In South Shore, as everywhere else in American society, people are "uptight" in the presence of persons who are unknown, unproven, and thus, to them, undependable. The genuine psychic (and occasionally, physical) risks, which accompany encounters with strangers, lead local residents to develop certain techniques for "gaining associates, avoiding enemies and establishing each other's intentions."[5] These techniques evolve in the search for cues which bespeak similarity, or existence of some other form of personal tie (e.g., mutual friendship, blood relationship), which would imply dependability and trustworthiness. Where such cues are not forthcoming, mutual avoidance behavior (or outright hostility) results.

In South Shore not only do authentic social and demographic differences exist between the black and white populations, but there are also more subtle differences in virtually all black-white confrontations. A few examples may be cited. Whites and blacks in South Shore *sound* different; among whites, speech varies with length of residence in Chicago, family status background, and ethnicity. Blacks have an analogous internal pattern of speech differentiation—in addition to a common touch of Southern Negro dialect, not quite absent even among many middle-class Chicago-born blacks. Young blacks *walk differently* from young whites; many, boys especially, use a swagger which sets them apart from their white schoolmates.[6] Without carrying out a complete inventory of black and white habits and folkways, we know these differences exist, and that, whether they speak of them or not, both blacks and whites in South Shore were sensitive to them.

Public Places and Private Behavior

These distinctions, some obvious and some subtle, are more or less problematic for the persons involved, depending upon the public place in which whites and blacks happen to come together. Public places are defined, for this discussion, as settings in which no *explicit* criteria exist for the exclusion of any person or group. Yet public places vary in the degree to which they tend to actually exclude certain types of persons or social groups. Given the inhibitions to random intimacy which exist in urban settings, public places can be viewed as exclusive insofar as they serve as arenas for the kinds

of informal, intimate, and uninhibited sorts of behaviors ordinarily associated with peer group activity. In contrast, public places are inclusive insofar as they act as settings in which formalized roles are routinely attended to by participants, who expect that others will also attend to the performance of prescribed activity and behavior. Thus, public places may be differentiated according to the degree to which they serve as arenas for public as opposed to more private behavior.

Retail Stores

An example of a relatively *public* place for *public* behavior is the local retail store. In South Shore they are rather formal; patrons arrive to purchase merchandise and then exit. Although various forms of informal activity occur, including chats between owners and customers, the usual undirected patter and diffuse banter evident in some lower-class business settings[7] tend to be absent.

Yet despite the relatively formal nature of shopping in South Shore (relative both to shopping in other kinds of areas and to other South Shore public settings), it is indeed a social activity as well as a utilitarian one. Shopping is the social activity which most frequently takes adult residents out of their homes and into the community. An examination of racial compositions of shopping settings may, in addition to providing benchmark data on the status of demographic integration in this important social setting, also indicate something of the extent to which a significant opportunity context exists for the promotion of other kinds of integration.

South Shore has two major internal shopping strips (71st and 79th Streets) both of which run east-west traversing black, mixed, and white residential areas...I visited each of the shopping strips during business hours on shopping days, and made racial head-counts for all street-level retail establishments (including restaurants and taverns) on both streets.[8]

Racial retail shopping patterns were found generally to coincide with racial residential patterns. That is, individual stores and business blocks surrounded by predominantly black residents were patronized almost exclusively by blacks; those in white areas, by whites; those in mixed areas, by members of both races. Table 5.1 presents the results of head counts taken of shopping blocks; Table 5.2 presents results of the same operation in terms of composition of individual stores.

If a setting is arbitrarily considered to be demographically integrated if at least 10 percent of its population consists of members of each race, then it can be said that the 71st Street area is integrated for its entire length and that 70 percent of its shops are integrated. However, 79th Street is generally segregated in its entire length with only 22 percent of its shops integrated.

The congruence of this pattern with the nature of the surrounding residential areas indicates that the factor of distance outweighs other possible considerations (for example, the desire for psychically safe shopping territory) in determining shopping patterns.

Certain interesting exceptions to the pattern are provided by those establishments which by their nature or traditional neighborhood usage render personal services or which serve as settings for informal, more intimate interaction. All barber and beauty shops, regardless of location, were segregated. Establishments catering to recreational and social needs were often segregated; three of seven restaurants on otherwise integrated 71st Street were serving only whites, whereas all six supermarkets on the street were integrated. Perhaps consistent with its attraction for customers of a particular ethnicity and with its function as a social setting, the kosher butcher shop was the only food store not serving a biracial clientele.

TABLE 5.1. Racial composition of South Shore shopping areas[*]

Street and Hundred Block[a]	Number of Black Patrons in Shops	Number of White Patrons in Shops	Total Both Races	Percent of All Patrons White
71st Street				
1600, 1700	35	6	41	15
1800, 1900	67	36	103	35
2000, 2100	74	142	216	65
2200, 2300	19	148	167	89
79th Street				
1600, 1700	49	3	52	6
1800, 1900	33	40	73	55
2000, 2100	2	29	31	94
2200, 2300	5	36	41	88
2400, 2500	0	41	41	100
2600, 2700	8	211	219	96
2800, 2900	5	92	97	95
3000	1	93	94	99

[*] Based on a single visit, daytime weekday count, April 1967.
[a] Each row represents two sides of two shopping blocks.

TABLE 5.2. Racial composition of individual stores on two shopping strips, daytime South Shore[*]

Shopping Street	Number of White Stores[a]	Number of Persons in White Stores	Number of Black Stores[*]	Number of Persons in Black Stores	Number of Integrated Stores[a]	Number of Persons in Integrated Stores	Percent of All Stores Integrated	Percent of All Persons Integrated
71st Street	4	85	2	16	14	235	70	70
79th Street	12	212	2	21	4	67	22	22

[*] Consideration was given only to shops serving eight or more persons.
[a] Stores classified White or Black were those in which at least 90 percent of persons on the premises were of the same race. "Integrated" stores were those in which fewer than 90 percent of persons on the premises were of the same race.

Saturday Night Racial Patterns

This tendency toward greater segregation of social and recreational settings is confirmed by analogous data collected on a Saturday night during the same time period. Americans typically reserve Saturday night as a social, festive occasion and almost all activities during those hours partake of a heightened air of sociability.[9] With many retail stores closed, but with bars and restaurants open and catering to large numbers of persons, both 71st and 79th Streets were more segregated at night than during the day.[10] Table 5.3 presents the results of a head-count made of business establishments open on a Saturday night.

The integrated types of settings on Saturday night included motion picture theaters (a leisure setting, ordinarily with minimal interaction), several restaurants, and those grocery stores and supermarkets keeping late hours. Yet even in the case of restaurants and groceries, there was a tendency toward increased segregation on Saturday night, as compared to weekdays. South Shore's two bowling alleys, integrated by day, become all-black at night.

The tendency toward Saturday night segregation (including a significant increase in the numbers of blacks over whites on the streets) may be explained in various ways. It may be due to a white fear of being in a black setting at night when "crime in the streets" is a more salient concern. Or whites may simply be experiencing different forms of recreation than blacks—forms which are only available outside of South Shore (as in the Loop area). The increased segregation of non-recreation settings may simply reflect that these are the hours in which black housewives, more likely to be working during the day, are shopping for household goods. Such factors notwithstanding, the fact that South Shore's business district is integrated by day but segregated (and heavily black) at night, is consistent with the observation that intimate contexts tend to inhibit integration. It is reasonable to find that during the hours reserved for intimacy, segregation increases.

Special scrutiny of one sort of segregated leisure setting, the neighborhood tavern, can provide some insight into explaining the metamorphosis of places from white to black status. There was almost total racial segregation in taverns with, in certain places, *alternating* black and white establishments along a given block.[11] Tavern owners can themselves influence racial patterns by, in the words of one bartender-owner, "give them (blacks) the big hello." But the several tavern owners who were interviewed felt that although the owner can influence the racial process, he cannot determine it. A bar "just becomes colored" as blacks patronize it

TABLE 5.3. Racial composition of South Shore shopping areas, Saturday night[*]

Shopping Street	Number of White Stores[a]	Number of Persons in White Stores	Number of Black Stores[*]	Number of Persons in Black Stores	Number of Integrated Stores	Number of Persons in Integrated Stores	Percent of All Stores Integrated	Percent of All Persons Integrated
71st Street	4	120	10	300	10	141	42	34
79th Street	14	359	7	272	2	19	9	3

[*] Consideration was given only to establishments observed to be serving eight or more persons.
[a] Stores classified as White or Black were those in which at least 90 percent of persons on the premises were of the same race. Integrated stores were those in which fewer than 90 percent of persons on the premises were of the same race.

with increasing frequency. For white tavern patrons, it is a matter of "the colored took the place over" or "the colored forced everybody out." These phrases were used again and again to explain "what happened" to a particular establishment which once was frequented by whites but eventually became a black setting.

To make sense of this "explanation" of tavern change, it must be noted that of all public settings in South Shore, probably none was more private than the neighborhood tavern. Although the tavern is officially open to the public, it is in fact (at least in South Shore) an intimate setting frequented by a small and stable group of regulars who use the establishment as a focal point of their social lives.[12] For the few middle-class taverns in South Shore (which also were segregated) this characterization is likely less accurate than for working-class establishments. But even here, the tavern is a place where people let their hair down, where backstage and on-stage behavioral routines[13] tend to merge and thus where increased social vulnerability makes for anxiety in the presence of persons who fail to give satisfactory signals of trustworthiness and forgiving acceptance of what may be transgressions of various normative codes. Thus blacks, who share mannerisms, clothing tastes, musical preferences and other tavern-specific behavior habits at variance with white cultural counterparts are

outsiders in the white environment. Their very presence serves to inhibit the kind of interactions for which the tavern is sought out by neighborhood whites; they can thus "take over" an establishment by simply being in it.[14]

Outdoor Recreation

Parks are a day-time setting in which informal social activity is routine.[15] Sports activities, especially for unathletic adults, carry potential for awkward displays of poor coordination, falls, and other evidence of incompetence and indignity. For some, parks are places where psychic vulnerability runs high.

A head-count was made at South Shore's largest park (Rainbow Beach), which provides facilities available nowhere else in South Shore—for example, tennis, beach bathing, formal gardens, and field houses. On a sunny Sunday in May 1967, only two of the several thousand persons at the park were black, and these were small children in the company of white adults. Rainbow Beach Park in 1962 was the scene of a non-violent civil rights "wade-in," protesting the racial segregation of some of the city's beaches (including Rainbow). Ironically, this much publicized event and the accompanying acrimonious remarks by whites may have served to dramatize Rainbow

Beach's *de facto* status as a white public place thus deterring blacks from risking the cost of a subsequent spontaneous visit. That Rainbow Beach was also a place where individuals routinely appear in abbreviated costume (bathing suits, tennis clothes, etc.), and thus routinely expose body areas ordinarily considered private, would act to increase anxieties stemming from interpersonal vulnerability.

Yet the special circumstances of Rainbow Beach were not significant because almost all of South Shore's parks were racially segregated—including those inside the community area and without any known history of incidents. I inspected seven smaller parks and playlots on the same warm Sunday; almost all were catering exclusively to small children with a few parents supervising. The only park catering to adult passive recreation (located on South Shore Drive at 68th Street) was occupied by thirteen white adults and three white children, all of whom sat on benches, and one black child who sat with his dog on the grass at an opposite end of the small greensward.

South Shore's six remaining parks were all scenes of active recreation. In those parks located in segregated areas (either all black or all white), participation was limited to persons of the same race as the surrounding area. At a soccer field at Phillips and 82nd, all game participants and spectators (approximately 200) were white; only black children were present at two playlots (one at Parkside School, 69th at East End, and one at O'Keeffe School, 69th at Merrill) in predominately (although not exclusively) black areas.

One park in a racially mixed residential area (69th at Oglesby) served only black children. The playlot at Bryn Mawr School (74th at Chappel), also in a biracial residential area, was used by approximately fifty black children and forty white children. One ball game was in progress; all players were white. Of the various playgroups, only one—a dyad—was racially mixed, although

the two playlots were serving equal numbers of white and black children.

Rosenblum Park, at 76th Street and Bennett, stands contiguous to both black and white residential areas. Seven ball games were in simultaneous progress while I observed, all being played by adolescent boys. Four games were all-black; two were all white; one was racially mixed. The two tot lots in the park are situated in diagonally opposite corners of the recreation area, with clear visibility from one to the other. The tot lot in the northwest corner was used by approximately thirty-five black children, one white child, and seven supervising black adult women. The tot lot in the southwest corner of the park showed an opposite racial pattern; it was being utilized by twenty white children, one black child and four white supervisors. It is noteworthy that two such playlots in the same park situated at a distance of no more than 200 feet from one another should be almost completely racially segregated.

The lack of evidence of demographic integration leads to the suspicion that South Shore residents, when taking outdoor recreation as well as public indoor recreation, do not lead integrated social lives. Members of different races do not accompany one another to parks and do not mingle once they arrive in parks. For children, some limited cross-racial contact seems to occur; for adults, there seems to be none whatsoever.

Schools

Schools in a community are a crucial determinant of the social lives of children; they provide settings for intimate interaction and their attendance boundaries tend to circumscribe a child's opportunities for friendship formation.[16] For some parents, schools are also a social setting (for example, PTA, volunteer work), but because of parents' more numerous alternative sources of social interaction, and because of the relative small proportion of their time spent in school contexts, the school is of much less social significance.

The racial composition of South Shore's public schools from 1963 through 1966 is presented in Table 5.4. In 1966, two of the community's six elementary schools were demographically integrated (using the 10 percent convention). The South Shore High School and one of the three Catholic schools also were demographically integrated.[17]

PTA meetings held in 1966 at the three integrated public schools (Mann, Bryn Mawr, and the high school) were attended by members of both races and so were PTA meetings at the predominantly black O'Keeffe school which drew an approximately equal number of whites and blacks to its meetings, although its student body was 74 percent black. In general, whites participated most in South Shore's school affairs, including in its biracial schools. In all schools in which any appreciable number of white children were enrolled, whites dominated the adult organizations. All newly elected officers of the high school PTA were white despite the fact that over 42 percent of the school's student body was black at the time of the 1967 PTA Spring elections. In other biracial schools, as in almost all of South Shore's biracial settings, blacks were always underrepresented in top leadership positions.

Religious Institutions

South Shore's religious organizations provide settings which are a mix of formality and informality. During worship services individuals find themselves in a situation where every move of every participant, including gestures and signs of affect, is determined either by explicit ritual, tradition, or local habit. In other church activities, such as funerals, weddings, bowling games, and club meetings, social interaction is more spontaneous, intense, and intimate.

It is thus not surprising to find that whatever integration existed in church organizations existed primarily in terms of worship activity and not in terms of church para-religious social life. Four of South Shore's sixteen Protestant churches hold integrated (again, by the 10 percent criterion) church services; one had an integrated *membership* list. Table 5.5 presents a detailed summary of the racial composition of South Shore's churches and church-related schools.[18]

TABLE 5.4. Racial composition of South Shore public schools, 1963, 1964, 1965, 1966

| School | Proportion of Student Body Black | | | |
	1963	1964	1965	1966
Parkside	90.3	96.6	97.8	99.1
O'Keeffe	39.8	67.3	85.4	93.9
Bryn Mawr	16.3	37.2	55.2	66.1
Mann	7.0	26.6	43.0	55.1
Bradwell	0.1	0.2	0.7	3.7
Sullivan	0.0	0.0	0.0	2.3
South Shore High[a]	1.5	7.0	24.8	41.8

[a] High school boundary zone was modified between 1964 and 1965 with the inclusion of Parkside and O'Keeffe and the exclusion of a larger all-black elementary school as "feeder" schools in the fall of 1965. The net effect of this change on the high school's racial composition was negligible.

Sources: 1963 data, *Chicago Sun-Times*, October 24, 1963; 1964, 1965 data, *Southeast Economist* (Chicago), October 17, 1965; 1966 data, *Southeast Economist* (Chicago), October 23, 1966.

TABLE 5.5. Racial composition of South Shore's Christian churches and church-related schools

Denomination of Church	Number of Church Members	Number of Blacks in Membership	Percent of Membership Black	Number Sunday Attenders	Number Black Sunday Attendees	Percent Sunday Attenders Black	Number Enrolled in Sunday School	Number of Blacks in Sunday School	Percent of Sunday School Black
Protestant									
Community	1,775	14	0.8	625	27	4.3	350	160	45.0
Episcopal	450	30	6.6	250	25	10.0	87	20	23.0
Lutheran	305	25	8.0	113	10	8.8	45	25	55.0
Methodist	650	25	3.8	200	30	15.0	390	250	64.0
Methodist	210	21	10.0	90	9	10.0	159	157	99.0
Christian Science	250	1	0.4	250	7	2.8	160	12	7.5
Bible Church	75	5	6.6	65	35	53.0	150	100	66.0
Sub-Totals	3,715	121	3.3	1,593	143	8.9	1,360	724	53.0
Nine Other	2,285	0	0	994	0	0	140	0	0
Protestant Churches									
Protestant Totals	6,000	121	2.0	2,587	143	5.5	1,500	724	48.0
Catholic[a]									
(1) Catholic	1,200[b]	70[b]	5.0	4,000	100	2.5	485	110	23.0
(2) Catholic	1,900[b]	1[b]	0.5	3,000	0	0	200	10	5.0
(3) Catholic	2,700[b]	325[b]	12.0	9,000	477	53.0	732	40	5.5
Catholic Totals	5,800[b]	396[b]	6.8	16,000	577	3.6	1,417	160	11.0

[a] Catholic school data refer to day school enrollments, not Sunday school. Except for Church No. 3, attendance data based on actual head counts on a Sunday, Spring 1966.

[b] Refers to number of families rather than individuals.

Other sources: Reports of clergymen to the writer and to E. Maynard Moore, III. See Maynard Moore, III, "The Church and Racial Change in South Shore" (unpublished paper, The Divinity School, University of Chicago, 1966).

Church life, outside of worship services, was virtually completely segregated and completely white. Two church membership screening committees had a black member (to help find the "good element," according to the white chairman); several churches had black Sunday school teachers and one church had two black women helping to establish a youth program. These active blacks (as was true of most black church members in South Shore) were all women.

Another important variation in church racial patterns, one strikingly revealed in Table 5.5, was the difference in the degree to which black children, compared to black adults, were being served by South Shore churches. Eight church Sunday schools were at least 10 percent black; in one case a church with only 10 percent black membership had a Sunday school which was 98 percent black. Fully 48 percent of Protestant Sunday school attenders were black; 11 percent of those enrolled in Catholic day schools were black.

The contrast between adult and child integration in church settings is again suggestive of the significance of interpersonal vulnerability as a determinant of racial patterns. Parents of both races were willing to place their children in racially mixed settings because such settings provided no psychic difficulties for *them* (the parents). Children, perhaps having different criteria for mutual identification and for establishing boundaries of community (such as sex, age, territory, athletic standing), were possibly less likely to find the settings painful, although the segregation patterns at play, as well as evidence presented by Suttles,[19] would suggest otherwise. In any event, children are not as free as their parents to pick and choose their social settings, regardless of the inconvenience or personal discomfort they might experience.

This lack of widespread adult black participation in South Shore church life may simply be due to black inhibitions, to black preferences for the ecclesiastical style of all-black congregations, or perhaps to black hostility toward whites. But in some cases, it is clear that blacks were deliberately excluded from South Shore church activities. In one instance, revealed with dismay by the pastor of the church (and confirmed subsequently in an interview with the victim), a black woman was invited by the pastor's wife to join an all-white church bowling team. The other bowlers' subsequent demand that the black woman be excluded from the team was resisted by the clergyman. The issue was resolved by the bowlers who, rather than accept the black as a team member, severed formal ties between the church and the bowling league. The church was in a biracial residential area and the exclusionist bowlers had been praying in an integrated sanctuary for many months before the incident occurred.

Perhaps because of such events, one South Shore black woman was prompted to remark: "The church people here feel like the churches belong to them and we are coming to take it away from them. That's just how they feel....They tolerate us, because it's their Christian duty to tolerate us, but not to love us or have us join in their fellowship." Another black woman, when asked what churches in the community could be doing to help the situation, remarked: "They could invite all the members to take part in the various church organizations. As it is, the woman's groups meet in people's homes so that they can refuse you, and they have said that they will refuse you. Mrs. X asked, me to come to one, but another lady told me that we weren't welcome."

Both of the women quoted were members of the church where the bowling incident occurred. The church minister was outspokenly liberal in his racial views, active in the community, and committed to an "open church." His was one of the first South Shore churches to take in a black member. He told me: "Generally we try to use the church as a setting for new forms of social interaction. When the whites meet the Negroes within the church, they see what fine people they are and their fears are allayed. I think this adds to the stability of the area; the people say 'Well, if the people moving into South Shore are like these people, I see no reason to move.' I think that is the effect we are having." Yet in light of the exclusionist practices of the church's social institutions and the black responses to them, as quoted above, it would seem that the effects upon whites have been less than dramatic, and that the embittered feelings of exclusion among blacks may be among the significant results of the "new forms of social interaction."

Pastoral Role Conflict

In order to understand the general racial patterns among South Shore's churches, one must consider the strain which neighborhood change places upon the clergyman's role. The pastor is under pressure from his flock to exclude blacks—if not from Sunday morning pews, at least from church social activities. If the clergyman defies his congregation, he risks an institutional setback like the one experienced by the pastor whose church lost its bowling league—a major social activity. Most clergymen reported that at least a few of the members had threatened to withdraw from the church if a black was ever admitted to worship—although significantly, all clergymen were surprised to learn that no resignations were ever forthcoming even in those instances in which a large number of blacks became church members. Even so, such threats were taken seriously by many clergymen.

On the other hand, only increased black participation could prevent the loss of a self-supporting church for the denomination. One South Shore minister analyzed the situation this way:

In the past the church has generally handled racial change in an unintelligent manner: total exclusion of Negroes. This meant that Negroes entered the area but not the church; the opportunity of the church to render service to these newcomers was lost; the opportunity to render stability to these lives and to the community was lost.... Finally, the church was left with ten or twenty white members and could no longer maintain itself financially. So it would have to be turned into a mission and draw upon funds from the hierarchy for maintenance. The policy here, however, is to avoid this mistake. This is not a new policy; I like to think of it rather as the continuation of the old policy: the ready acceptance of newcomers. We do this from the standpoint of financial need and also of Christian morality.

It was characteristic of South Shore Christian clergymen to perceive the moral and financial imperatives of integrating blacks into the church. Some clergy stated that they thought there were not going to be enough denominational blacks to go around and that only those churches which aggressively proselytized among the newcomers were going to survive. Still most clergymen were reluctant to push their people too far.

A common method of handling this conflicting set of expectations—one from the white flock to whom one is responsible, the other from one's professional and institutional duty—was to compromise. Blacks were not sought, but when they appeared at the church door they were welcomed. Lay members could be confronted with explicit policies handed down by denomination authorities and with the clear-cut moral imperative that, at least, for purposes of praying, blacks should not be excluded from white environments. But the clergy left the church's social institutions in the hands of laymen to manage on an exclusionist basis—though in their Sunday sermons included references to "brotherly love" and appropriate quotes from the Bible in the hope that communicants would "make the connection."

Meanwhile, the clergy hoped that as whites left the community, blacks could be assimilated fast enough (although *only* fast enough) to keep operations solvent. Many South Shore ministers, judged from the rather sturdy financial condition of their churches,[20] seemed to be accomplishing their goal. And while following that policy, they could view their black members as evidence that theirs was an integrated church in which blacks had been accepted. The dictates of an urban ministry were being obeyed; new forms of social interaction and fellowship were being created. The actual results were sanctuaries which were biracial on Sunday mornings but located in churches which, as institutions, remained largely segregated. This "compromise" rested on the formality and unstrained behavior characteristic of the church service (which included blacks), in contrast to the more informal and intimate nature or church "social life" (from which blacks were excluded).

An Exception: The Baptist Church

A fundamentalist Baptist church, located in a predominantly black area, stood apart from all other religious institutions in South Shore in that equal numbers of whites and blacks attended services; it was, in other respects as well, the most completely integrated of all South Shore religious institutions.[21] It was also distinct in that worship services were a more basic part of the life of the church than in other denominations. Worship was a time of spontaneity and much animated social interaction. Members were working class and lower-middle class; it was among the poorer churches in South Shore—both in terms of its worshippers' income and its

annual institutional budget. Among South Shore clergy, its minister was least familiar with the liberal conventional wisdom concerning the role of the urban ministry and the "crisis in the city"—utterances which permeated interview responses from most other area clergy. This fundamentalist minister was the only South Shore clergyman to ever indicate a past history of "prejudice" toward blacks.

That such conditions gave rise to the only case of trans-racial solidarity in a church context is perhaps surprising.... For the moment, it should be noted that the conditions of spontaneity and intimacy characteristic of fundamentalist religion could lead *only* to one of two states: either complete racial exclusion *or* complete racial integration with concomitant total acceptance. If blacks were to be present at all, their presence would have to be unreservedly accepted; otherwise, the resultant inhibitions would have destroyed the nature of the religious experience and thus the very reason for the coming together.

Voluntary Associations

The many national charity and service organizations (such as Lions, American Legion, Veterans of Foreign Wars, B'nai B'rith) serving South Shore, were all exclusively white.[22] None of the more than fifty organizational group photographs of South Shore residents published in the *Southeast Economist*[23] included blacks. The South Shore Country Club, the boards and officer corps of two local hospitals and of the Chamber of Commerce were also without black participants.

There was in South Shore a pervading theme in the manner in which residents discussed the possible "integration" of their local institutions: a tendency to demarcate certain institutions in the community as "white" and others (few in number), as "Negro," "nigger," or "colored." White South Shore residents spoke of "our church," and "our neighborhood." The major characteristic of the collectivity being spoken of was that members were similar to the speaker—and in South Shore that meant (among other things) that members were white. In the face of the rather ambiguous legal ownership status of most churches, clubs, and associations, long-term, community residents truly regarded the institutions as their *own:* institutions which their funds and efforts had created and maintained, and which were seen to exist for the perpetual use of themselves and persons like themselves. It is likely that many blacks moving into the community shared this perspective—at least to some degree—and except for a few militants or pioneers, they believed white South Shore institutions "belonged" to other kinds of people. Several blacks interviewed seemed surprised and awed (and somewhat uncomfortable) by the fact that they were actually being welcomed into some white institutions. Only slowly and often with a good deal of organizational in-fighting, soul-searching, and, for blacks, a summoning of confidence, was such a perspective being slightly modified.

The South Shore Commission

The most prominent exception to the general pattern of black exclusion (or omission) from the ranks of important community groups was the South Shore Commission, which at least after 1964 was biracial in its leadership and membership. Although blacks remained greatly underrepresented in commission leadership positions during the study period, several on the board of directors and one of six officers were black. Many commission sub-groups were also biracial, including several committees and various block club organizations. But it is safe to say, because only a small proportion of South Shore's residents involved

themselves in any block club or other commission activity, that its effectiveness in creating biracial contacts was probably limited to a small leadership group in the community.

From its very inception, the commission was not an informal social organization; as an association of Protestants, Catholics, and Jews, it had from the beginning brought together persons who were less than completely at ease in each other's presence. As blacks were brought into membership it continued to function primarily as an instrumental organization, not as a setting for intimate socializing. The commission provided a series of public meetings, outings, and fund-raising entertainments wherein public behavior was the accepted norm.

In the context of commission activity, as in the case of other biracial voluntary organizations in South Shore, cross-racial inter action was more formal and guarded than were interactions (also quite formal) between members of the same race. Became of the uniqueness of biracial interaction in American, society, blacks and whites were in the difficult situation of having to create *de novo* a formal mode for social interaction, given the obvious and subtle differences between blacks and whites and the lack of mutual knowledge of what the other party might consider appropriate talking behavior. Thus there was a need to avoid the unknown transgressions which might occur if spontaneous behavior were to run in course. It was accomplished by both blacks and whites resorting to a zealous interpersonal courtesy (to ward off any conceivable slight or "misunderstanding"), unrelenting pleasantness, and a well-understood, tacit, mutual agreement to limit the subject of all conversation to small talk. Behavior was carefully guarded; words and expressions were selected with extraordinary care.

For blacks, the heightened self-consciousness generally resulted in deferential postures toward their white colleagues, and an ongoing monitoring of behavior to avoid any possible controversy which might set them in opposition to policies favored by any significant number of whites. I recall several substantive examples: The commission was known by black members to be cooperating through its tenant referral service with landlords who refused to rent housing to non-whites. The actions entailed in such cooperation were probably illegal under the Chicago Fair Housing Ordinance and were a source of distress to black commission members. Yet they preferred, in the words of one, not to "make a fuss" against a policy which they indicated (to me) that they found obnoxious. Similarly, black commission members assented to quota systems for maintaining whites in buildings and blocks which otherwise would have become predominantly black. Again, there was public acquiescence in spite of privately held feelings that such policies were improper and also in violation of the housing ordinance.

When blacks volunteered to speak, as at commission board meetings, their comments were sometimes irrelevant to the topics under discussion and not presented in a manner under which action could easily be taken. Rather than make motions, blacks tentatively *expressed* themselves—resulting in statements which, when not acted upon by others, simply died—even when a majority in the room seemed in sympathy with the point being made. In committee work, blacks were not, in local parlance, "take charge people." Black participants in South Shore activities seemed to be self-conscious to the point where forthright expression of opinion and resultant effective action was inhibited.

That this effect of biracial interaction was most pronounced in the case of blacks, and not whites, is perhaps explicable (at least in part) in terms of another important feature of biracial interaction in South Shore: blacks and whites seldom come together as equals. This fact adds an

additional dimension to the vulnerability of the alien persons who were not only in a numerical minority but, because of status differences, were especially vulnerable to the sanctions of those who possessed so disproportionate an amount of wealth, power, and expertise.

These status differences were pervasive. In general, blacks moving into South Shore were of lower socioeconomic status than the whites they replaced.[24] The same status differentiation was reflected within organizational contexts such as the commission. White males of the commission's governing board were almost all proprietors, lawyers, physicians, and stock brokers, and black members were generally salesmen, schoolteachers, and low-level supervisors.

Unlike white leaders, blacks did not find their way to the board because of their personal wealth, power, or expertise, but instead because of their race and an acceptance of commission goals. Blacks were originally "brought in" the commission for fear that without some black "representation" on the board of directors, the organization could be accused of being segregationist and thus lose black constituents to the Woodlawn Organization on the north. After one black became active in the commission, other blacks were recruited into the organization—in a way described in an interview with a white commission leader who shared responsibility for nominating new board members:

There has been a great need to get Negro leaders involved in the commission; that's extremely important. We need to get Negroes and whites who will work together without resorting to special, selfish interests. We need strong Negro leadership in the area and it's best it we can do it through the commission.

We asked Mr Y [the first black to be active in the commission] to recommend some Negroes for us for the board. He came up with four and we said how about six. So six it was; hell, we took them all.

Thus, as is evidenced by the means by which they came into the organization, commission blacks were largely interchangeable with any number of other blacks, with the consequence that their status vis-à-vis their white colleagues could only suffer. Several black members were viewed approvingly by whites as "real work horses" who make a "fine contribution," but none had the contacts with the political, religious, and business leaders of Chicago which were seen to be the really important determinants of South Shore's future. A good work horse may be hard to find, but a member of the Chicago School Board or the editor of a Chicago daily newspaper is impossible to replace. Such differences in the degree to which people are important to an organization's goals do not bode well for parity in interpersonal relationships.

The case of biracial interaction in the Commission would seem to provide an explanation for the findings generated by tests of the contact hypothesis. A large body of literature suggests that more favorable white attitudes toward blacks result from biracial interaction in which whites and blacks share the same status, are in mutually dependent roles, and where contact is intimate rather than superficial.[25] These are the conditions in which social vulnerability to alien and unknown individuals is minimized for members of both races. Where the conditions are not present, the contact hypothesis suggests that biracial interaction is expected to yield either no effects or an increased amount of "negative" white evaluation of blacks.

Indeed, the latter results were the consequences in such groups as the commission. For whites, participation with blacks led to the observation that they (blacks) "aren't real leaders." The middle-class analogue of the lazy colored boy remained the dominant white stereotype. For blacks, interaction in such settings would seem to debilitate energies as whites come to be seen as the real makers of decisions and holders of power.[26] The really crucial organizational skills which blacks observed were those involving the use of contact (such as friends in high places) and resources (such as personal fortunes) which they neither possessed nor stood a good chance of ever possessing.

"Marginal Groups": Instances of Transracial Solidarity

In addition to the Baptist church, there were three other contexts in South Shore in which transracial solidarity seemed to exist. These were marginal organizations—marginal in that meetings were held only on an irregular basis and in that they were organizations founded on premises of dissent and protest which limited their appeal to only a small number of participants. One such group was a local branch of Veterans for Peace in Vietnam, an organization with leftist political orientations (including several persons of Marxist ideology) which held occasional meetings above a South Shore store during the study period. Another group was the O'Keeffe Area Council—technically a part of the South Shore Commission but with an active leadership which, because of its rather "pro-Negro," "anti-establishment" orientation, was often independent of the commission in spirit and in action.

Finally, there was the South Shore Organization for Human Rights, a group active in fostering open occupancy and other civil rights goals in South Shore and metropolitan Chicago. This group was indigenous to South Shore, having been stimulated by a young clergyman during his rather brief association with a South Shore Protestant church. Like Veterans for Peace and the O'Keeffe Area Council, its active membership consisted of only a handful of persons;

it carried out independent programs such as "testing" the racial practices of local real estate firms and the commission's Tenant Referral Service.

These three organizations differed from other South Shore institutions not only in terms of their marginality, but also in terms of the "tone" of biracial interactions shared by members. In all of these contexts, as in the case of the Baptist church, interaction across racial lines seemed to come easily; interaction was unstilted, informal and direct. Except possibly for the Veterans for Peace, these were all informal social organizations, with blacks and whites living out shared social as well as shared institutional lives. Race largely disappeared as a source of cleavage or a determinant of institutional roles.

In other respects, these groups were quite diverse. The Baptist church was largely working class with many recent migrants from the South and Appalachia. The O'Keeffe Council consisted of young well-educated professionals; to a lesser extent, the same was true of the Organization for Human Rights. Veterans for Peace was an extremely diverse group of blue-collar workers, small businessmen, and a few professionals. Parishioners of the Baptist church were apolitical, religious fundamentalists; members of the other groups were identified with secular, left-leaning ideologies.[27]

Within each of these groups, race and status differences were not obviously correlated; businessmen or professionals within each were as likely to be black as white. In addition, these groups were alike in that each was in an alien environment. The church was surrounded by more stolid, richer congregations; Veterans for Peace, the Organization for Human Rights, and the O'Keeffe Council existed in the shadow of the powerful South Shore Commission and other "moderate" or conservative institutions which supported Chicago's and the nation's existing

political arrangements. The various deviant traits of these groups' members thus created a situation in which organizational alternatives within the South Shore area were lacking. The result may have been an organizational commitment of sufficient strength to overcome any inhibitions which racial differences might have created. Finally, members of these groups were similar in that most were either new to the South Shore area or, because of their youth, new to South Shore organizational life. A lack of previous ties to existing structures may thus similarly facilitate commitments to organizations which, in that they are biracial, operate with new kinds of *modus vivendi*.

Conclusions

Although South Shore's total racial composition provided initial evidence of some forms of racial integration in the area, social life is essentially segregated. The nature of the contexts in which varying forms of integration are found suggests that fear of exposure and mutual suspiciousness between members of the two races inhibit biracial sharing of public places which serve as loci of private behavior. Thus some degree of demographic integration and a slight amount of biracial interaction can occur in public places in which public behavior traditionally ensues. That is, extensive integration (primarily by demographic indices) occurs in places like retail shops, church chapels, and formal organizations oriented toward the accomplishment of instrumental goals. In such settings, social interaction across racial lines is not reflective of transracial solidarity. Nor can the results of such interaction be assumed to promote eventual solidarity, given the problematic power disparities which are general concomitants of such black-white interaction. Presumably because of the greater psychic and practical dilemmas it would create, integration of any sort is absent from informal settings like church socials, service clubs, taverns, Saturday night bowling, and parks.

Because their activities and commitments tend to be local, women are more likely than men to find themselves in biracial circumstances. Protestants are more likely than are Catholics or Jews, and children—perhaps because they are less free to vary their milieu according to preference—are likely to have the most experience of biracial contact.

Although both blacks and whites face common problems under conditions of biracial propinquity and contact, the consequences on the two groups are not identical. In South Shore, as in the rest of the society, the integration experiment opens with the most important and useful institutions, organizations and settings as white, and the "challengers" or "invaders" as black. *The circumstances are thus not parallel.* The widely shared community conceptions so generated of intruders versus preservers, applied to blacks and whites respectively, provide still another distinction consistent with the status and power disparities widely observed to exist between blacks and whites. Not only is the development of transracial solidarity made more difficult as a result, but, in addition, the psychic difficulties which blacks must face when entering the alien white context are further intensified.[28] That is, biracial interaction challenges members of both races to overcome certain fears of the dissimilar, the unproven, and the threatening. But for blacks, there is the added problem of knowing that in presenting oneself in a biracial setting, one is challenging and pushing to gain something otherwise unavailable. The modal black response would seem to be either hostility (as in some manifestations of the civil rights movement) or, as was common in South Shore, a show of deference and total capitulation to white preferences.

Integration of a thoroughgoing type, what has been termed transracial solidarity, occurred in South Shore in only a few settings. These were instances in which there were cross-racial communalities of a shared and deviant ideology (mutual recognition of which provided bases for the development of needed social alternatives); an equality in occupational status and organizational usefulness (providing cross-racial parity in interpersonal vulnerability); and, among both blacks and whites, a lack of previously constituted local organizational ties (precluding habit or social pressures from inhibiting affiliation with groups which have integration as one of their innovative features).

All settings observed in South Shore (I attempted to be exhaustive) which shared these characteristics were found to approximate the circumstance of transracial solidarity; no other instances of this form of integration were found. If other possible contingencies to racial integration are to be uncovered, or if those observed in South Shore are to be confirmed as determinant (either singly, or in some value-added combination), additional case studies and eventual comparative analysis will be necessary. But for the present, it is well to note that the conditions cited as concomitants of transracial solidarity in South Shore are precisely those which are likely to provide the overarching cues of similarity, reliability, and trust which would seem requisite for the building and maintenance of racially integrated associations, institutions, and community.

Perhaps if given enough years (years for which the commission was fighting), South Shore would be transformed into a community in which transracial solidarity (or at least biracial interaction) was a routine part of social life. Seven years after large-scale black in-migration had begun, a few signs of such a transformation were in evidence, although not nearly enough to alter the conclusion that South Shore would pass through its transition without a major alteration of the racially segregated lives of the blacks and whites who temporarily shared its neighborhoods, schools, and some of its churches and associations.

NOTES

1. See Philip A. Johnson, *Call Me Neighbor, Call Me Friend* (New York: Doubleday, 1965); William Biddle and Loureide Biddle, *The Community Development Process: The Rediscovery of Local Initiative* (New York: Holt, Rinehart and Winston, 1965).
2. Gerald D. Suttles, *The Social Order of the Slum: Ethnicity and Territory in the City* (Chicago: University of Chicago Press, 1968).
3. Changes in South Shore's welfare case loads and crime rates add some evidence for this point.... Although differences in net income between black and white family units is generally small (or nonexistent) in changing areas, the fact that black households are more likely to have multiple breadwinners and that black males are more likely to hold blue-collar jobs, constitute real status differences. See Karl Taeuber and Alma Taeuber, *Negroes in Cities* (Chicago: Aldine, 1965), p. 159 and Chapters 7 and 8.
4. See Louis Wirth, "Urbanism as a Way of Life," in Albert Reiss, Jr., ed., *Louis Wirth on Cities and Social Life* (Chicago: University of Chicago Press, 1964), pp. 61–83.
5. Suttles, *The Social Order of the Slum.*
6. *Ibid.* See also Harold Finestone, "Cats, Kicks, and Color," *Social Problems*, V (July 1957), pp. 3–13.
7. Suttles, *The Social Order of the Slum.*
8. For some establishments, such as beauty shops, there was no way to make a complete count unobtrusively; in such instances, only those patrons visible through plate glass windows were counted. Employees, detectable by uniforms, positions behind counters, or general demeanor, were excluded from the counts.
9. For persons excluded from social activity on Saturday night, these hours are, as the lyrics of the popular song imply, "the loneliest night of the week."
10. For example, the 71st Street daytime count included only one segregated bar whereas

the night count included six segregated bars. Because many retail shops are closed at night, the prevalence of open bars has the consequence of dramatically increasing the *proportion* of segregated establishments and the absolute number of segregated establishments.

11. Except for one bar I observed that had one black patron and nine white patrons, all twenty-one South Shore taverns were completely segregated on Saturday night.
12. Herbert Gans, *The Urban Villagers: Group and Class in the Life of Italian-Americans* (New York: Free Press of Glencoe) has confirmed that this is also the pattern for Italian-American working-class males.
13. See Erving Goffman, *The Presentation of Self in Everyday Life* (New York: Doubleday, 1959).
14. The same phenomenon can be observed in the case of houseguests' "taking over" a home by simply being in it for a period longer than that desired by the hosts. Guests, who often cannot "understand" if confronted with such an accusation, can avoid the problem by either "becoming just like a member of the family" (that is, host accepts guest as an intimate) or by devising schemes whereby extensive absences from the scene can be gracefully arranged.
15. The situation is not strictly comparable to taverns, for the relative expansiveness of space may permit a greater degree of insularity to an intimate gathering.
16. Marion Roper, "The City and the Primary Group" (unpublished Ph.D. dissertation, University of Chicago, 1934).
17. No intensive observations were made of student life within schools.
18. Interviews with local clergy were carried out during the summer of 1965 and spring of 1966. I personally interviewed twelve clergymen: additional interview material was provided by E. Maynard Moore, III, who based part of his interview schedule on mine, thus generating a total of twenty-three comparable cases. Respondents interviewed by both investigators generally gave identical responses to the two researchers. (See Moore 1966.)
19. Suttles, *The Social Order of the Slum*, Chapters 9, 10.

20. Sec E. Maynard Moore, III, "The Church and Racial Change in South Shore" (unpublished paper, The Divinity School, University of Chicago, 1966).

21. The divergence in this church between the number of black *attenders* and number of black *members* (as indicated by data in Table 5.5) was due to the fact that a personal revelation was a requisite for formal membership; many blacks were in the situation of having formal induction pending such a revelation.

22. I was informed that a tutoring center at the South Shore YMCA was racially integrated. Pressures of time did not permit a first-hand investigation of its program.

23. The *Southeast Economist* serves South Shore as well as a much larger region of the South Side as a community newspaper. An organization was considered to be located in South Shore if at least half of all addresses of those photographed were within the study area.

24. See note 3.

25. Various studies have yielded somewhat conflicting evidence on the validity of the contact hypothesis. Three classic studies which indicate a positive relationship between "improvement" in white attitudes toward blacks with increasing contact are Morton Deutsch and Mary Collins, *Interracial Housing: A Psychological Evaluation of a Social Experiment* (Minneapolis: University of Minnesota Press, 1951); Shirley Star, Robin M. Williams, Jr., and Samuel A. Stouffer, "Negro Soldiers," in Samuel Stouffer *et al., The American Soldier: Adjustment During Army Life*, Vol. I (Princeton University Press, 1949); and Robert K. Merton *et al.*, "Social Facts and Social Fictions: The Dynamics of Race Relations in Milltown" (New York: Columbia University Bureau of Applied Social Research, 1949). Three reports providing evidence for the opposite conclusion are Gordon Allport and Bernard Kramer, "Some Roots of Prejudice," *Journal of Psychology*, XXI (Fall, 1949), pp. 9–39; Bernard M. Kramer, "Residential Contact as a Determinant of Attitudes toward Negroes" (unpublished Ph.D dissertation, Harvard University, 1950); and Alvin Winder, "White Attitudes towards Negro-White Interaction in an Area of Changing Racial Composition" (unpublished Ph.D dissertation, Committee on Human Development, University of Chicago, 1952). A synthesis of these mixed findings, consistent with the criteria for affective positive attitude change as specified in the above text, appears in Daniel Wilner, Rosabelle Walkley and Stuart Cook, *Human Relations in Interracial Housing: A Study of the Contact Hypothesis* (Minneapolis: University of Minnesota Press, 1955).

26. Francis Fox Piven and Richard Cloward, "The Case against Racial Integration," *Social Work*, XII (January, 1957), pp. 12–21.

27. These findings are consistent with other studies which have uncovered the extremely diverse conditions under which racial integration occurs and the seeming irrelevance of "prejudice" or racial "attitude" in determining when and where integration exists. George Grier and Eunice Grier, *Privately Developed Interracial Housing: An Analysis of Experience* (Berkeley: University of California Press, 1960), found integrated housing developments to be heterogeneous in terms of the income, education, ethnicity, stage of life cycle, and geographical origin of residents. Supporting findings are also reported in Chester Rapkin and William Grigsby, *The Demand for Housing in Racially Mixed Areas* (Berkeley: University of California Press, 1960), and Albert Mayer, "Russel Woods: Change without Conflict, a Case Study of Neighborhood Racial Change in Detroit" in Nathan Glazer and Davis McEntire, eds., *Studies in Housing and Minority Groups* (Berkeley: University of California Press, 1960). Membership status of the Baptist church was relatively homogeneous. Veterans for Peace was led by a well-to-do black funeral director and several of his black business colleagues, whereas whites included in their ranks (along with a few professionals) a TV repairmen and a sign painter. The O'Keeffe Council included in its top leadership cadre a black businessman and a black lawyer along with

a white businessman and a white engineer. The Organization for Human Rights was dominated by a white clergyman and a group of black and white women who were either white-collar workers or had lower-middle class husbands.

28. Charles J. Levy, *Voluntary Servitude: Whites in the Negro Movement* (New York: Appleton-Century-Crofts, 1968) provides a description of an instance (whites in the southern civil rights movement) in which the tables are turned, that is, where biracial interaction occurs in a black dominated context (with analogous intensification of difficulties for whites).

REFERENCES

Allport, Gordon and Bernard Kramer. 1949. "Some Roots of Prejudice." *Journal of Psychology* 21 (Fall): 9–39.

Biddle, William, and Loureide Biddle. 1965. *The Community Development Process: The Rediscovery of Local Initiative*. New York: Holt, Rinehart and Winston.

Deutsch, Morton and Mary Collins. 1951. *Interracial Housing: A Psychological Evaluation of a Social Experiment*. Minneapolis: University of Minnesota Press.

Finestone, Harold. 1957. "Cats, Kicks, and Color." *Social Problems* 5 (July): 3–13.

Gans, Herbert. 1962. *The Urban Villagers: Group and Class in the Life of Italian-Americans*. New York: Free Press of Glencoe.

Fox Piven, Francis and Richard Cloward. 1957. "The Case against Racial Integration." *Social Work* 12 (January): 12–21.

Goffman, Ernest. 1959. *The Presentation of Self in Everyday Life*. New York: Doubleday.

Grier, George and Eunice Grier. 1960. *Privately Developed Interracial Housing: An Analysis of Experience*. Berkeley: University of California Press.

Kramer, Bernard M. 1950. "Residential Contact as a Determinant of Attitudes toward Negroes." Unpublished Ph.D dissertation, Harvard University.

Levy, Charles J. 1968. *Voluntary Servitude: Whites in the Negro Movement*. New York: Appleton-Century-Crofts.

Mayer, Albert. 1960. "Russel Woods: Change without Conflict, a Case Study of Neighborhood Racial Change in Detroit." In *Studies in Housing and Minority Groups*. Nathan Glazer and Davis McEntire (eds.). Berkeley: University of California Press.

Merton, Robert K. et al. 1949. "Social Facts and Social Fictions: The Dynamics of Race Relations in Milltown." New York: Columbia University Bureau of Applied Social Research.

Moore, E. Maynard III. 1966. "The Church and Racial Change in South Shore." Unpublished Paper. The Divinity School, University of Chicago.

Johnson, Philip A. 1965. *Call Me Neighbor, Call Me Friend*. New York: Doubleday.

Rapkin, Chester and William Grigsby. 1960. *The Demand for Housing in Racially Mixed Areas*. Berkeley: University of California Press.

Roper, Marion. 1934. "The City and the Primary Group." Unpublished Ph.D. dissertation. University of Chicago.

Star, Shirley, Robin M. Williams, Jr., and Samuel A. Stouffer. 1949. "Negro Soldiers." In *The American Soldier: Adjustment During Army Life*. Vol. I. Samuel A. Stouffer et al. (eds.). Princeton: Princeton University Press.

Suttles, Gerald D. 1968. *The Social Order of the Slum: Ethnicity and Territory in the City*. Chicago: University of Chicago Press.

Taeuber, Karl, and Alma Taeuber. 1965. *Negroes in Cities*. Chicago: Aldine.

Wilner, Daniel, Rosabelle Walkley, and Stuart Cook. 1955. *Human Relations in Interracial Housing: A Study of the Contact Hypothesis*. Minneapolis: University of Minnesota Press.

Winder, Alvin. 1952. "White Attitudes towards Negro-White Interaction in an Area of Changing Racial Composition." Unpublished Ph.D dissertation, Committee on Human Development, University of Chicago.

Wirth, Louis. 1964. "Urbanism as a Way of Life." In *Louis Wirth on Cities and Social Life*, pp. 61–83. Albert Reiss, Jr. (ed.). Chicago: University of Chicago Press.

6

MITCHELL DUNEIER

SLIM AND BART

From *Slim's Table* (1992)

In this excerpt from his study of black and white patrons of a cafeteria on the South Side of Chicago, Mitchell Duneier shows how the relationship between unlikely friends develops through mundane interactions.

They both came of age at the height of segregation. Sixty-five, a lifelong Chicagoan, Slim is a black mechanic in a back-alley garage in the ghetto. Bart, white, and ten years older, is a retired file clerk who grew up in the rural South. Both are regular patrons of the Valois "See Your Food" cafeteria.

I first met Bart during my early days as a university student, long before I ever set foot inside Valois. Like many older residents of the Hyde Park neighborhood, he ate regularly in the cafeteria of International House, or I-House, as it was called, a dormitory for graduate students close to the University of Chicago campus.

Tall and skeletal in his mid-seventies, Bart dressed in fine suits and sported a Dobbs hat. Sometimes when he'd be sitting alone at one of the cafeteria's long wooden tables, I'd join him and ask about his past. He did not have any strong family ties. His only brother lived in Colorado, and he hadn't seen him in about five years. They spoke on the telephone no more than once a year. He had retired from a long career as a clerk at Swift's, one of the major meat-packing companies, during the era when Chicago was still "hog butcher for the world." Then he took a job as a file clerk at one of Chicago's largest law firms.

Bart moved to Hyde Park in 1928 to attend the University of Chicago as a pre-medical student and supported himself for a time by working at the Streets of Paris section of the 1933 Century of Progress Exposition. He had little to say about that experience. He had been a ticket collector at the entrance to the shows but had never gone inside to look.

Bart was a very incurious person, one of many odd human beings who become attached to a university community as students and continue the association for decades. His explanation for not marrying was that "some people just never find a person to jive with." His biggest dream had been to become a physician like his father, but the hardships of the Depression made it impossible for him to continue his studies.

He wasn't bitter about his life. The only resentment he ever displayed was toward blacks in the local community. With the southern drawl of the Kentucky town in which he had been raised, he often complained that Hyde Park had long ago turned into a "high-class slum."

Because I thought about Bart only when I saw him sitting in "his" chair after dinner at I-House, many weeks may have gone by before I realized that the old man had been absent for some time. I wondered if he had taken ill. Months passed with no sign of him. I asked the front desk clerk and other residents if they had seen Bart. No one had, and I finally decided that he might have died.

Two years later, when I entered Valois Cafeteria for the first time, I was startled to see Bart sitting by himself eating a bowl of radishes, amidst black men sipping coffee at the surrounding tables. On a chair next to him was the same Dobbs hat I had seen him wearing before he abandoned I-House. He asked me how I had been and inquired about some of the people he remembered from the dormitory cafeteria. He told me that although he had liked being around the students, prices there were high and the quality of food very poor. He had been eating at Valois for a year. I asked what he could tell me about the restaurant, which is known locally by its motto "See Your Food."

"I don't know anything about the place."

"But you eat here every day?"

"Yes, but I don't pay any attention to the place. I just eat my meal and go home."

As our conversation came to a close, he informed me that I might direct my questions about Valois to the owner. ·

Over the weeks and months that followed, I would see Bart constantly. Despite his claims, he seemed to be well aware of the other habitual patrons of the restaurant, including the group of black regulars that congregated at Slim's table.

I came to learn that Slim's table has, for over a decade, been the meeting place of a group of black men who regularly patronize this cafeteria on the margin of the ghetto. Slim, who comes to the restaurant every day, is usually joined by Harold, a self-employed exterminator; Cornelius, a retired meter inspector; Ted, a film developer for *Playboy Magazine* who received an honorable discharge from the army after twenty years of service; and Earl, an administrator at the Chicago Board of Education. These and others constitute a core group that frequents the restaurant daily. Besides them, hundreds of other black men frequent Valois less often, some only on weekends. Ties binding members of the larger collectivity have developed over decades, and it is not uncommon for someone entering the restaurant to be playfully scolded by Slim or his buddies: "Now, don't you go hiding from us again" or "Come by and see us more often," if he has been absent for any significant amount of time.

The spectrum of social classes among the black men is very broad. At one end of the spectrum are a few men like Earl from the Board of Education, middle class and college educated. In the middle, most of the men are solidly working class. At the other end of the spectrum are a significant number who have been downwardly mobile in their later years and have incomes which would place them among the working poor. These are individuals whose wages would place them at or below the poverty line.[1] But even this description is tidier than the reality because most of the men have social characteristics which would place them in various classes at the same time.[2] Most of the men live in small apartments in Hyde Park or local ghettos, but some like Slim own small homes.

By the standards of mainstream American society, none of these men are members of the "underclass" or "undeserving poor," though they are sometimes treated as such by whites from the nearby university.

These black men were very much aware of Bart. Sometimes they would refer to him as "the gentleman" because he wore a Dobbs hat and a suit and tie. And then, after another year had passed and they had come to regard his eccentricities with affection, as Bartie. Although Bart seemed to want to remain detached from the blacks around him, he had a neighborly, jocular relationship with them. He found himself inextricably drawn into the social life at Valois as the men began to greet him cordially:

"How you feeling today, Bartie?" Harold once asked him.

"I feel with my hands," was his response.

He continued to sit alone, and the black men came to know him only gradually. Through comments back and forth, from their table to his, they developed a sense for the kind of man he was:

"I bet you got the cleanest kitchen in that building you live in."

"You're right. I don't put nothing on that stove. Not even boiling water."

Interaction between blacks and whites is common on the outskirts of American ghettos.[3] Many American universities are in or close to black neighborhoods, and the territorial margins of these locales are typified by interaction between middle-class whites like Bart and blacks like the regulars at Valois who come from nearby neighborhoods. Whites in such areas often see clusters of single black men routinely passing time together in public places like barbershops, street corners, bars, and restaurants, and blacks who live in these districts have a category in their minds for the "university types" and other gentrifying forces who settle on the margins of their neighborhoods.

Bart was an object of curiosity to many of the men. When he was out of earshot, they would often try to size him up. "Bart's unusual," Leroy, an electrician, once said. "He is antisocial. He don't care about nobody. He comes in. He eats. Sometimes he just sits there and don't say nothin'."

Slim balanced his chin on his thumb and forefinger, trying not to look in the direction of the old man. "He don't bother nobody."

After a brief silence Harold glanced at Bart and ended the sober appraisal. "You ever notice sometimes he fidgets around when he's eating? He be looking to see if anything is on his tie."

The group of men broke out laughing. "You notice that too?" Leroy chortled hysterically. "Then he'll take his coat and look it over to make sure there's nothin' on it." Bart's little quirks were amusing to the men, but they were also endearing. Later that night, when he started looking at his coat, the men joked with him about his ways:

"Bartie, what are you looking for on your coat?"

"Oh, just looking to see if it's okay."

"Bart, you can stop looking at your tie now."

"Oh, I can?"

"Yes, you can."

"Thank you, Harold."

Through such conversations, the men learned very little about Bart's beliefs and values, but they began to comprehend something about his temperament. As far as they were concerned, these certain habits and idiosyncrasies of Bart's disclosed much they needed to know about the old man who sat near them every day.

Bart had once let it be known that during the fifty years of his working life he had never been late or missed a day of work. The only technical exception was on account of a famous crash of the Illinois Central Railroad. Having been aboard the train on his way to the office, he once described the devastation for the men—seats flew out of the train, people were hanging out of windows, others were lying in the aisles screaming. Bart somehow remained unscathed. Stepping over bodies, he picked his way out of the car and got to work a few minutes late. He seemed proud to let the men know that under the circumstances, and given his prior work record, the supervisor decided to mark him on time.

"Did you help anybody?" Harold asked.

"No. 'Cause I figured there was nothing I could do, and anyway I didn't want to be late for work."

"Didn't it bother you to just leave like that?"

"Why should it bother me? Wasn't a damn thing I could do. I was on my way to work."

The old man's machinelike routines and indifference became lore among the regulars.

In part, Bart developed a connection to the men through Hughes, a white contractor originally from North Carolina who had a close rapport with several of the black regulars. Like a handful of other white patrons—like the meat-packer Werner Mandlebaum, the landlord Morton Fruchman, and the longtime Hyde Parker Lou Ann Davis—Hughes commanded a great deal of respect. Both blacks and whites in the restaurant thought of him as the finest of men, one who took a deep and abiding interest in others. Like Bart, Hughes was raised in the South, but unlike the older man he was an outgoing, easy-mannered person.

During Bart's first few weeks at Valois, a year before, Hughes had become apprehensive when he saw that the old man walked home alone. He told Bart that anytime he wanted a ride, there was "no problem." For over a year, the regulars at Valois knew that Bart was Hughes's passenger.

At times, Hughes found the old man's inflexible ways to be burdensome and aggravating. Sometimes he would be ready long before Bart, but he would patiently wait for the old man to finish his dinner. Often he would be relieved as Bart took his last bite and seemed to be moving toward the coat rack, only to be disheartened when he realized Bart was actually edging toward

the front counter to pick up another bowl of radishes or a dish of vanilla ice cream.

One evening Hughes was expecting an important phone call at his home at exactly 9:00 P.M. He told the old man, who had long since finished eating, that he had to go. But in a characteristically rigid manner, Bart said that he wouldn't be ready till 9:30. Hughes had no choice but to leave. The regulars at Valois feared more for the old man than he feared for himself.

On other occasions Bart would be ready a few minutes before Hughes. His way of hinting that he was ready to leave was a source of both amusement and annoyance to the regulars. First he would pick up his hat and coat, bringing them over to Hughes's table. There he would stand, slowly putting on the coat, one sleeve at a time, and then the hat. The entire ritual would last several minutes. Hughes might still be in the middle of a meal. Although he was tolerant of Bart's ways, he found the old man's attempts to hurry him annoying.

During one two-week period in the middle of August, Hughes had to work late. When Slim saw Bart walking home alone, he was horrified: he knew that the streets around Valois were dangerous for an old man at night. Bart accepted Slim's offer of a ride. Slim told Bart that he should never walk home again, that he would be glad to take him from then on, and Bart accepted the offer.

Slim is a reserved black man, who has lived near the Hyde Park neighborhood for most of his life. Slim has an unimposing but self-assured and dignified presence. He wears the navy blue uniform of a car mechanic with a zipper jacket that says his name; a wool cap in winter or a black and white Chevy "Heartbeat of America" cap in warm weather; and on Sunday, like many of his contemporaries, Florsheim or Stacy Adams dress shoes. The Stacy Adams lace up shoes popular among this generation of men come in two styles, ankle high or low cut. For the black men, Stacy Adams shoes are to respectability what a Dobbs hat is for an older white man like Bart.

In his pockets, Slim keeps a chain with many keys (a symbol of responsibility in the ghetto), and a plastic wallet compliments of the Internal Auto Parts Co. Inside are family pictures, an Aamco bond card, a driver's license, and an automobile I.D. He also carries a pack of Camel cigarettes, business cards from some of the firms he relies on as a mechanic, and loose papers with information related to the various jobs he is engaged in down at the garage.

Slim usually comes to the cafeteria for breakfast and for after-dinner coffee. His back-alley garage off Forty-seventh Street, a ghetto thoroughfare, rented as part of a larger parking establishment, is not visible to pedestrians. But Slim is one of the most respected mechanics on the South Side, and local folks have no trouble finding him. Most of his days, including many weekends, are spent there in the heart of the ghetto. At Valois, Slim is a central figure among the black male patrons, although he is hardly outgoing and rarely demonstrative. To most people who don't know him, he seems aloof and proud. Some people think it is hard to get a fix on him.

The relationship between Slim and Bart intrigued me. Slim seemed to harbor little resentment about injustices of the past, though it was evident from occasional remarks that he had unpleasant dealings with whites once in a while. At the same time, he was a human being with strong moral sensibilities. He viewed himself as a member of a social world characterized by general standards that applied equally to people of all colors.

In the black belt, ... people often develop substitute kinship ties, in which many of the functions served by traditional families are taken up by other caring individuals.[4] Thus a man such as Slim might take a liking to a senior citizen and do the kinds of things for him that in white society would more normally be done by the man's son,

if at all. At Valois, the black counter ladies sometimes even referred to Bart as Slim's "pappy" ("Where's your Pappy tonight?") indicating that in their minds Slim had developed a substitute kinship tie with Bart.

By contrast to Slim's universal morality, Bart was a reserved Southerner who believed that white people were naturally superior to black people. He had not been pleased by the civil rights movement of the 1960s. The fact that he took his meals in the same restaurants as black folks was to him a natural consequence of living in the integrated Hyde Park–Kenwood district.

The two men seldom sat with one another, but at closing time Bart would usually move to a table near Slim's and wait for him to finish his conversation. Bart didn't dare take the firm and resolute Slim for granted as he did Hughes, a fellow white Southerner. He rarely stood up and hinted to the black man that he wanted to leave. He never resisted when Slim told him that it was "time." Usually he would stay by himself until around 9:45, sometimes nodding or even falling asleep at his table. Slim would tap Bart affectionately on the knee to wake him up. The regulars knew that when Slim gave Bart "the tap," the two men would soon be walking out together. Once in a while, Bart would first go to the adjacent liquor store to get himself a pack of Chuckles candy and, on rare occasions, a pack of Camels for Slim.

One November night, some friends and I took Bart with us to dinner at an old German restaurant, the Golden Ox. Werner Mandlebaum, a regular white patron of Valois, had recommended the restaurant to us. As the owner of Chicago's last slaughterhouse, Werner supplied meat to the Golden Ox (as he did to Valois) and vouched for the quality of the steaks. On our way back to Hyde Park from the Golden Ox, Bart asked us to stop by the cafeteria. He explained that he needed to talk to someone for a minute. "My man is still in there, and he'll be wondering where I am." In Bart's vocabulary, there was perhaps no better way to describe the chauffeur that Slim was to him, a man with whom he could occasionally exchange cigarettes for rides.

Given Bart's upbringing and background, there was nothing surprising about his remark. But many months later, the language changed. A young woman who had known him when she was a student came to town for a visit. She later told me that Bart took her to dinner at Valois and said that he had a "friend" in the restaurant, that the friend was a black man, "but"—he emphasized—"he is very nice and he *is* a friend."

The fact that Bart made a point of calling the man his friend, instead of trying to disassociate himself from him in advance, indicated that he had come to value his relationship with Slim. Perhaps Bart was now willing to ignore boundaries that had been vital to him before he grew old and lonely. It seemed also that the very trust he had placed in Slim's reserved but caring behavior had changed Bart's conception of himself vis-à-vis a black person.

I knew that at Christmas time, and for Slim's birthday, Bart would usually ask Hughes to shop for his gifts. Once Bart said to Hughes, "You know what Slim likes. Get him whatever you think he needs 'cause you been to where he works, and I hate to just give him five or ten dollars. The present will show more thought. If you don't mind wrapping the present, I'll get the card."[5]

Though he knew that Bart was trying to show his appreciation, Hughes believed that the old man was being cheap. "Bart, I'm gonna get whatever I think he needs. I'm not gonna insult him by giving him a five or ten dollar pair of socks. Not after what that man's done for you. If you needed that man in the middle of the night, he would be there."

"Well, Hughes, use your own judgment. That's why I want you to do it."

When Hughes picked out a rechargeable flashlight for one of Slim's birthdays and an electric heater on another occasion, it made Bart very happy.

Yet, I sometimes wondered to what extent Bart's use of a more respectful designation, "friend," to describe his relationship with Slim, implied a degree of intimacy. In addition to his feelings of racial superiority, Bart possessed a conception of the male role that militated against vulnerability and closeness with another man, black or white. What kinds of things did these two human beings, raised in a society that earlier in their life-times discouraged social interaction between the races, talk about on their way home each night? The answer to my question came more easily than I ever expected it would.

On one of the rare days when I did not go to Valois, I ran into Earl, the middle-class man who was one of the most consistent regulars at Slim's table. On the street near the restaurant, he told me that Slim's old man had died. As all of the regulars knew, many years ago Slim had taken a man in the ghetto "for his father," rather the way he had Bart. In recent months be had been deeply concerned about the older man's health, moving him into a nursing home when he became very ill. Earl told me the details of the death. He had come from the funeral earlier that day, as had some others at the restaurant. Apparently they had all stopped by Valois after the service was over.

When I spoke to Bart the next day, I decided to ask him about what had happened. I hoped that by inquiring into some of the details, I might learn something about the nature of his friendship with Slim.

"What's new, Mitch?" Bart asked.

"Oh, nothing much," I replied. "I ran into Earl and he told me Slim's father died."

"Slim? Yeah. Funeral's tomorrow, I guess."

"Tomorrow?"

"Yeah."

I knew that the funeral had occurred twenty-four hours ago and I took this as a first hint that Bart was not really aware of what had been going on.

"I thought the funeral was yesterday."

"Well, I don't know, Mitch. I just heard that his father died. He didn't mention nothing to me about it, and I didn't say anything to him. A friend of mine gave me the information."

"Who was this?"

"Hughes."

I asked if Hughes had been dressed in a suit the day before. "Yeah, why?"

"Maybe he was coming from the funeral."

"The funeral isn't until tomorrow."

"Are you going to the funeral, Bart?"

"No."

"I see."

After a brief silence, Bart continued, "No, I don't know when the funeral is. Maybe the funeral's tomorrow. I'll be damned if I know."

"Okay, I guess I'll just ask Slim about it when I see him. Did he look like he was depressed tonight?"

"No. Why would he be? He's a grown man. His father was at the age when they all go. It isn't like when you're young. It can happen any time. He lived a long time. You know a lot of them blacks don't live that long. He hadn't been depressed as far as I know. He hasn't been depressed all week. I think his father was in a nursing home for a while. I don't talk to him much about his affairs. I figure if there's something he wants me to know he'll tell me. I don't think he wants me to ask him any questions."

"Well, I don't know. I thought you might have mentioned it to him on the way home one night."

"No, no, no. I don't talk to him about that."

"Did you drive home with him last night?"

"Oh, yes."

"And he seemed okay to you?"

"He seems okay to me all the time. He wasn't any different last night than any other time."

Again there was silence. I decided to try one more time to learn about Bart's private time with Slim.

"I figure that the funeral must have been yesterday, Bart, because I thought Earl said something about that."

"Well now, I may be wrong. I don't say I'm right. I don't know anything about it really. Slim tells me nothing, and I ask him nothing. I figure he figured it's none of my business 'cause if it was any of my business he'd tell me. He don't want me asking him any questions. You know, that's the way I look at it. What he wants you to know he'll tell you, and what he don't want you to know he's not gonna tell you and he don't want you asking."

"Okay, Bart. I'll see you later on tonight."

"Okay, then."

When I entered the cafeteria later that evening, the old man waved me over to his table. He informed me that the funeral had indeed been the day before.

It is evident that the relationship between Slim and Bart is not one of great depth. Yet Slim places a value on Bart that goes beyond the occasional exchange of a pack of cigarettes or a Christmas gift for a car ride home. Slim often tells me he doesn't think it right that people neglect their elders. His attitude of caring exists within a framework of barriers to closeness set up by Bart, perhaps to protect himself from developing too much intimacy with a black man, or simply with any man.

The standards by which Slim treats Bart are universal, applying equally to any elderly person, black or white, in or out of the ghetto. Inside this restaurant on the margins of the ghetto the black regulars have entered into an affirmative relationship with the wider society, orienting themselves to situations that make it possible for them to apply their high standards and adopting unique social forms, like the substitute kinship tie, beyond the fringes of the black districts.

One day Bart collapsed inside the restaurant and was rushed by ambulance to the University of Chicago hospital. As it turned out, he was merely dehydrated, and within a day he was back at Valois on his usual schedule. Many of the regulars asked about his health, and on one occasion Leroy, the electrician, began telling him what he should do, how much water he should drink, and which foods he should eat. After a few minutes, Bart responded in his typically direct manner: "I appreciate your concern. But it's none of your business and please change the subject."

Leroy responded, "Bart, it's because I love you and I think a lot of you. That's why I'm saying these things...."

But Bart wasn't pleased. "Well, thank you for your concern, Leroy. But I can manage pretty well." And that was that.

Others asked Bart about his health, too. As Hughes explained to me, "It was a constant thing, because people don't have anything to talk to Bart about. I have to dig to the bottom of everything to find anything to talk to him about."

So Bart was annoyed.

A few weeks after he first collapsed in the restaurant, he began to feel dizzy again. This time he was at home, and he telephoned Hughes. The men agreed to meet at the hospital later on that day. When they arrived, Bart decided to check in for tests, and he told Hughes that nobody in the restaurant was to know he was there: "Don't say nothing to anybody in the shop about it. I hate for everybody to see me and say, 'Oh, how are you feeling? Oh, I hear you're sick.'"

Hughes recalled the conversation he had with the old man. Bart was tired of being asked about his health, all right. With a smile he concluded, "So don't tell anybody, Hughes. If anybody asks me about it, I'll know you told them."

"Don't you think we should tell Slim?" Hughes responded.

"What do you think?" Bart asked.

"Well, Bart, think about it..."

"Well..."

"Bart, Slim's your friend. And you know all the things we do for each other. And if

Slim finds out somehow that you been in the hospital when you wasn't at Valois and didn't let him know.... You owe it to Slim to let him know."

"Well, you're right. I hadn't thought of it that way."

The two men tried to figure out what Hughes would tell the others at Valois.

Bart came up with the solution. "Just tell them that in this cold weather I'm eating in a restaurant closer to home until the weather breaks."

Hughes said, "Bart, that's real good. That way we don't have to get into details or anything. I can tell them and be so casual and change the subject so fast that they won't have any reason to come back with another question."

After he left the hospital, Hughes stopped by Valois to tell Slim the news. The instant Hughes walked in, Slim asked, "What have you done with my daddy?" Hughes sat down and explained what had happened.

Slim said, "He probably never should have been sent home the last time."

Hughes explained, "He was getting rid of more liquid than he was taking in, and through evaporation and everything, that can kill you. Even a severe diarrhea can dehydrate you. Everything's checked out okay other than that. All he needs is the right blood pressure medicine and to drink his fluids."

Slim said, "Well, he's like a machine. He has a glass of orange juice in the morning at home. Then he walks six blocks to the restaurant and has two cups of coffee. And then a little later he has a glass of water. Then at night he has two cups of coffee and a cup of tea."

With a laugh Hughes added, "And that's it. And if they tell him to add three glasses of water, he'll add three glasses."

Both men had ambivalent feelings about Bart, some positive and some not. It was not uncommon for sentimentality and humor to mingle when they talked of him. As they sat together at the table, Hughes told

Slim more about what had happened at the hospital:

"I took him a couple of candy bars. I went over to the liquor store because I know he always goes in there before you drive him home. I described Bart to the guy behind the counter. He said, 'Oh, yes.' I said to him, 'What kind of candy does he buy?' He laughed, 'Chuckles.'

"So I took a couple of Chuckles to him. When I walked into the hospital room, he said, 'What do you got?'

"I said, 'Chuckles.'

"He said, 'Hughes, I don't eat candy. I don't eat candy.'"

Slim and Hughes laughed together.

"I said, 'Well, they're here. And if you get hungry you can have them.'

"He said, 'Well, why don't you take them with you and eat them?'

"As I reached for them, he put his hand in the air and said, 'Leave one.' I don't know if he didn't know how to…all he had to do was say thanks.

"Then later on I said, 'Bart, would you like a cup of coffee or something.' He was a bit chilly.

"So I went down to the restaurant, and it was like a maze in that hospital. I've gotten well acquainted with most people who work there because there's hardly an employee there I haven't asked for directions! When I finally reached the cafeteria, I figured I'd get him some toast to go along with the coffee. Sometimes he tells me he eats a cookie or something before he goes to bed.

"So I finally found my way back to his room. I said, 'Bart, here's the coffee.'

"He said, 'Well, put it down. I'll only have two sips of it anyway.'

"And two sips is what he took."

"He said, 'Hughes, you finish it. And I wish you wouldn't get me anything more than I ask you for. I don't want any toast.' I said, 'No problem, Bart.' I wanted to say, 'Stick it up your ass!' But I said, 'Bart, it's better to have it and not want it than to want it and not have it.'"

Slim and Hughes laughed. Together they had gone through so much with the old man that they understood each other's feelings exactly. As Hughes later described it, "Oh, last night I could have chopped him up into little pieces and today I like him." Hughes told Slim how he had felt earlier that day when he went to Bart's apartment to pick up the things Bart had asked for at the hospital:

"As soon as I walked into his apartment his real pretty overcoat, the real nice one, was over a chair. And right next to it on the table was his Dobbs hat. When I saw him again later on I said, 'Bart, everything in your apartment was okay. But one thing really upset me. When I saw your hat. I know the complete history of the hat. And the hat is you up and down. And when I saw your hat and realized where you were, and not knowing just what the outcome would be, I really had a few seconds of feeling sad at that moment. 'Cause I thought ahead and I said, "Oh my God. That poor hat!"'"

Again, Slim and Hughes laughed hard. Then, before he went away, Hughes went over the official story with Slim, emphasizing that not a soul was to know Bart was in the hospital.

At the restaurant that night, before I'd heard anything about the conversation between Slim and Hughes, I sat with Harold, Earl, and Slim. It was very slow. We were about the only ones present, and it was one of those evenings when it seemed that nobody had anything to say. The biggest event was when a Greek accent would yell, "Cheeseburger's ready!" and the men would look to make sure someone had risen to pick it up from the counter.

Suddenly I turned around to check where Bart was and found that he was nowhere to be seen. Turning to Slim, I asked about the old man. He responded that Bart was having his meals at home until the cold weather let up. Later, as the workers cleaned the steam table in preparation for closing, Spring and Ruby, the counter ladies, yelled across the room to Slim: "Where's your Pappy tonight?"

Slim repeated what he had just told me. Harold asked Slim if Bart was okay and Slim said, "Yes."

I thought nothing of this incident until later on that evening. On my way home from the restaurant I stopped by Bart's apartment to see if there was anything he needed in the freezing weather. I rang his bell for five minutes and got no answer. When I arrived home, I attempted to reach him by phone and again received no answer. It occurred to me that Bart might have gone back to the hospital. I called the switchboard and asked whether Bart was listed. He was. When I finally reached Hughes the next day and told him I had spoken to Bart, he explained why Slim hadn't told the truth. Before we hung up, Hughes said, "Whatever you do, don't let Slim know you know. Because he might think I told you."

As I reflected on the previous evening, I was struck that Hughes conceived of himself as living up to standards which were not his alone but were also embodied in the moral authority of Slim. Although middle-class blacks are usually conceptualized as potential role models for other blacks, here an exceptionally sensitive middle-class white man sought the respect of a working-class black man as he attempted to live in accordance with high ideals.

I took note of the willpower and self-control that Slim exhibited on a night when nobody seemed to have anything to say. After all, the whole circle could have gotten a lot of mileage out of that news. Despite his complicated feelings for the old man, he demonstrated a tremendous respect for Bart's privacy. Slim's perception of his own moral worth could not be separated from a disposition to act in accordance with standards appropriate to his associates, whose worthiness was taken for granted in that setting. A person of the weak moral constitution portrayed in major accounts of

the black male would have preferred to let his friends know that he was on the inside. At Valois, Slim and his sitting buddies demonstrate an inner strength characterized by self-control and willpower that is seldom, if ever, attributed to the black male in social scientific and journalistic reports. Though black men are usually portrayed as so consumed with maintaining a cool pose that they are unable to "let their guard down and show affection,"[6] these black men had created a caring community in which one of the men, Leroy, had even expressed his feelings for Bart by telling him the men were interested in his illness because they loved him.... Here, on the margins of the ghetto, I witnessed the adaptation of one of the ghetto's prevalent social forms, the substitute kinship tie, to show, through little acts of caring, an alternative conception of civility and of what it means to be a black man.

Bart died alone in his studio. When, one Tuesday evening, he didn't show up at the cafeteria, Slim notified Hughes, who called the manager of Bart's building.

"The manager just called me back," Hughes told Slim an hour later. "He had opened the door, but the chain was on it. He is waiting for the police to come. I can't say a thing about it, but it doesn't look good."

Slim suggested that Hughes call Bart's brother in Colorado. "They haven't spoken in a year, and he'll want to know."

Hughes got the number from directory assistance, reached the brother, and reported back to Slim: "I just tried to tell him that Bart might be in trouble. But he cut me off, saying, 'He isn't nothing but a bachelor. Who's gonna miss him?'"

"That's a horrible thing to say," said Slim. "How could a man say that about his own brother?"

"I told him we were waiting for the police to enter the room," said Hughes. "That I would call him back when we knew. But he told me he takes his phone off the hook when he goes to sleep. I said, 'Don't take it off tonight. That way if he's gone we can get hold of you.'"

Bart was found dead at the side of his bed, one leg in his pajamas, one leg out.

Hughes dialed Bart's brother, but the line was busy. The building manager referred the Chicago police to Hughes for the brother's number, and an officer called Colorado himself. A few minutes later he called Hughes back to report the constant busy signal. "That's all you're gonna get," Hughes told him.

Bart stayed in the city morgue three weeks. Hughes says he died the way he lived. "We all die alone, but he died totally alone, being in the morgue for so long." In truth Bart wasn't completely by himself. He had Slim, and he had Hughes, and he had the entire caring community at Valois.

Bart did not have to be intimate with Slim to feel affection for him. The moral authority embodied in Slim's caring behavior had pushed Bart to the limits of his own potential for tolerance, friendship, and respect.

Yet, the power of integration over ingrained beliefs is slow and incremental and should not be exaggerated. Years later I asked Hughes, who had himself so clearly looked up to the black man, whether he believed that Bart had changed as a consequence of his relationship with Slim. "There was only so much he could change. But it certainly made him more accepting. He saw what it means to care for another person. It gave him an understanding about the caring behavior of the black race. He probably figured at least some could be human."

NOTES

1. For an excellent article, see Mary Jo Bane and David Ellwood, "Is American Business Working for the Poor?" *Harvard Business Review*, September–October, 1991, pp. 58–66. See also Ellwood, *Poor Support: Poverty and the American Family* (New York: Basic Books, 1988).

2. In this book, I adopt the assumptions about social class enunciated by Christopher Jencks, who writes,

We use terms such as "middle class" and "underclass" because we know that occupation, income, educational credentials, cognitive skills, a criminal record, out-of-wedlock childbearing, and other personal characteristics are somewhat correlated with one another. Class labels provide a shorthand device for describing people who differ along many of these dimensions simultaneously. The term "middle class," for example, evokes someone who has attended college, holds a steady job, earns an adequate income, got married before having children, and has never murdered, raped, robbed, or assaulted anyone. The term "underclass," in contrast, conjures up a chronically jobless high school dropout who has had two or three children out of wedlock, has very little money to support them, and probably has either a criminal record or a history of welfare dependence.

Relatively few people fit either of these stereotypes perfectly. Many people are "middle class" in some respects, "working class" in others, and "underclass" in still others. Those who use class labels always assume, however, that everyone is a member of some class or another. In order to assign everyone to a class, they allow their classes to be internally heterogeneous. If they assign people to classes on the basis of how they make their living, for example, they allow the members of these classes to differ with regard to income, educational credentials, cognitive skills, family structure, and arrest record. Everyone who stops to think recognizes that the world is untidy in this sense. We use class labels precisely because we want to make the world seem tidier than it is. The purpose of these labels is to draw attention to the differences between classes. But by emphasizing differences between classes, such labels inevitably encourage us to forget about the much larger differences that exist *within* classes.

See Christopher Jencks, *Rethinking Social Policy* (Cambridge, Mass.: Harvard University Press, 1992).

Thus a man like Ted, who works for *Playboy* magazine in the photographic lab and retired from a long career in the army, might be considered a member of the working class by virtue of the jobs he has held. His use of large words might demonstrate a verbal ability associated with a middle-class education. His many trips abroad might also show a middle-class orientation, and his views may fluctuate between a working-class orientation most of the time and a middle-class orientation on occasions.

A man like Jackson, a crane operator and longshoreman, who saw much of the world during the Korean war, will engage in a conversation about Paris that might normally be expected from a middle-class person. He reads newspapers and a high school history book and has a working knowledge of western history. But he lives in a small one-bedroom apartment, has no telephone, and writes all of his checks at the currency exchange. His wages put him below the poverty line. He has a small wardrobe and very few possessions and can only afford to eat one meal a day.

Because of the difficulties involved in any system of classification, I am wary of making claims regarding what these men typify within the class structure of the black community. Though most of their occupations, lifestyles, and values place them in the working and lower-working class, I leave it to readers to draw their own conclusions for individual members of the group. With regard to the composition of the black class structure, William Julius Wilson writes, "To be somewhat schematic, of the 29 million American blacks, about 20 percent are in the professional middle class, with another 15 percent in non-credentialed white-collar positions. About 33 percent are working class, with half of them vulnerable to job loss, and 33 percent poor. I'd say about half of that poor population is truly disadvantaged, a sort of destitute population." "The Poor Image of Black Men,"

New Perspectives Quarterly 8, no. 3 (summer 1991): 26.

Readers can draw their own conclusions from the table (cited in Martin Kilson and Clement Cottingham, "Thinking about Race Relations," *Dissent*, Fall 1991, p. 521), which summarizes some relevant statistics.

3. "The margins of the ghetto can be scenes of tension as they become gentrified and are slowly absorbed by a wider community made up primarily of middle- and upper-income people who for the most part are white." See Elijah Anderson, *Streetwise: Race, Class, and Change in an Urban Community* (Chicago: University of Chicago Press, 1990), p. 1.

4. Variations of such relations have been referred to as pseudo-kinship ties. See Elliott Liebow, *Tally's Corner: A Study of Negro Streetcorner Men* (Boston: Little, Brown, 1967), pp. 166–167. "One of the most striking aspects of these overlapping relationships is the use of kinship as a model for the friend relationship.... The most common form of the pseudo-kin relationship between two men is known as 'going for brothers.' This means, simply, that two men agree to present themselves as brothers to the outside world and to deal with one another on the same basis." For similar observations, see Elijah Anderson, *A Place on the Corner* (Chicago: University of Chicago Press, 1978), pp. 17–23. Because there was no effort on the part of my subjects to present themselves as kin or pass these relationships off as genuine, I have refrained from using the word "pseudo" in describing their relations. The substitute kinship tie is characterized by the assumption of obligations normally associated with kinship. For the best discussions of kin-structured social networks, see Carol Stack, *All Our Kin: Strategies of Survival in a Black Community* (New York: Harper Colophon Books, 1974) and Ward Goodenough, *Description and Comparison in Cultural Anthropology* (Chicago: Aldine Publishing Co., 1970).

5. Hughes told me about this conversation after it occurred. I often asked him questions about conversations and occurrences between him and Bart or between him and Slim. When it was not awkward, I often verified Hughes's version with either Slim or Bart. Once I asked Hughes about a particular conversation years after it occurred, because I thought I had lost my notes on it. Hughes told me what he recalled of the conversation. Weeks later I found the old notes and discovered that Slim had used precisely the same words to describe the conversation a few years before. I only used reports which I felt certain had a high degree of reliability. The occasions on which I asked various subjects what others had said were normal conversations and occurred through normal interaction rather than formal interviews. Unless otherwise indicated, this is the only chapter in which I quote from a conversation at which I was not present. Most of the notes I took for more than four years with the men at Valois were written down afterward, upon my return home.

6. See Richard Majors, "Cool Pose: The Proud Signature of Black Survival," in Michael S. Kimmel and Michael A. Messner, *Men's Lives* (New York: Macmillan Publishing Co., 1989), pp. 83–87.

REFERENCES

Anderson, Elijah. 1978. *A Place on the Corner.* Chicago: University of Chicago Press.

Anderson, Elijah. 1990. *Streetwise: Race, Class, and Change in an Urban Community.* Chicago: University of Chicago Press.

Bane, Mary Jo and David Ellwood. 1991. "Is American Business Working for the Poor?" *Harvard Business Review* (September–October): 58–66.

Ellwood, David T. 1988. *Poor Support: Poverty and the American Family.* New York: Basic Books.

Goodenough, Ward. 1970. *Description and Comparison in Cultural Anthropology.* Chicago: Aldine Publishing Co.

Jencks, Christopher. 1992. *Rethinking Social Policy.* Cambridge, Mass.: Harvard University Press.

Kilson, Martin and Clement Cottingham. 1991. "Thinking about Race Relations." *Dissent* (Fall).

Liebow, Elliott. 1967. *Tally's Corner: A Study of Negro Streetcorner Men.* Boston: Little, Brown.

Majors, Richard. 1989. "Cool Pose: The Proud Signature of Black Survival." In *Men's Lives.* Michael S. Kimmel and Michael A. Messner (eds.). New York: Macmillan Publishing Co.

Stack, Carol. 1974. *All Our Kin: Strategies of Survival in a Black Community.* New York: Harper Colophon Books.

Wilson, William Julius. 1991. "The Poor Image of Black Men." *New Perspectives Quarterly* 8 (3).

7

JOHN L. JACKSON JR.

NO FRIENDS

from *Harlemworld* (2001)

In this piece, John Jackson explores how people who live in Harlem, the quintessential American "black community," understand, theorize, and perform race and class. Drawing on more than four years of participant observation and extended interviews, Jackson documents the complex, intricate relationships that black Harlemites have with people of different classes. He finds that sometimes people are able to negotiate class differences in their relationships quite well, while at other times class differences create barriers to the creation and maintenance of these same types of relationships.

...Sometimes, when I tried to get at the issue of friendship networks head-on, specifically querying Harlemites about their friends, many adamantly maintained that they did not have any friendships with differently classed people at all. It seemed evident, however, that some of these folks did have powerfully class-stratified social relationships—even if they were not willing to call them friendships during formal, tape-recorded interviews.... Paul (a person whose varied social networks I know first-hand)... made a case, during one of our more formal interview sessions early in my fieldwork, for the fact that he only had friendships with people in the same socioeconomic position he occupies:

JOHN: Tell me more about your friends. Who are they, and what do they do?

PAUL: I hang out with people at work. People at the gym where I work out. People who do what I do or go places where I go, and they are mostly pretty well-off, I guess. We can relate to each other.

JOHN: Why do you think that is? That you hang out with people from work?

PAUL: We relate. You share things with people that have experienced some of the same things. You know what I'm talking about? That is important. You won't agree on everything, but you have things in common.

JOHN: Things like what?

PAUL: The job for one. Things you like to do. They'll be people you went to school with. You have those things in common. Or you just happen to do the same work.

The first time I ever met Paul face to face, I conducted the interview from which the above is excerpted. I can almost remember him saying the words. They seemed clear, precise, measured, and sensible. However, half a year later...after going back through some of this material, it stood out as problematic. Paul did have friends that he called "friends" who were not colleagues from the job, who did not share the same occupation, and who weren't even working full-time. I was able to revisit these earlier responses,...asking him again about the class stratification he did not mention earlier:

> JOHN: What about your boys, the ones from the party? Jimmy and those guys.
> PAUL: Dev and Jimmy and those guys. I guess that is true. It's definitely true. Yeah, but I don't see them that often. I'm usually busy working.
> JOHN: How often do you see them?
> Paul: Maybe once a month, but they are definitely my boys. I can't forget them.

There was a kind of pattern with respect to class and friendship networks among many of the Harlem folks with whom I spoke. Like Paul...several other Harlemites at different points in time tended to dismiss or "forget" their contacts with people from different rungs of the socioeconomic ladder. Many people found it easy to minimize all nonfamilial relationships, often going so far as to say that they have no close friendships whatsoever—not with anybody, regardless of class differences or similarities; that it is too "dangerous" and leads to "bullshit" or "drama." Many people claimed that they choose to keep to themselves instead:

DEXTER: I don't have no friends. I know people. But all motherfuckers is triflin'. I've seen it. It's real out here. You know what I'm saying. I mean I know heads. I know heads, no doubt. And they know me. And we may talk or give each other a pound or hang for a minute, but you can't be thinking that means it's all good. That ain't what it means. Not at all.

Brandi, too, doesn't have real friends. "I'm not interested in that," she offers. "People try to use you. They try to use you like that. Then you get thrown into bullshit for some 'friend,' for 'that's my friend.' "

Brandi, Dexter, and others reiterate time and again that they don't necessarily have friends or the time to actively cultivate friendships with anyone—let alone with people of different classes. This is an interesting theme that comes out of many of my interviews and discussions with Harlemites. Folks are sometimes quick to argue that they don't have any friends at all. They don't know people of different classes very intimately and don't really have any relationships outside of their familial circles that they would characterize as particularly close. But is that the end of the story? As in Paul's case, many of my informants do have nonfamilial interactions with individuals that look and sound like friendships even though they may be hesitant in applying the term. Zelda, for example, is quick to say that she, too, is a loner:

ZELDA: I have always been the one who stayed to herself. Always. That's what I did, I still do. I just don't feel like I got to be up under somebody to be happy. I don't need that. I can have fun home. If I go out, to the movies or something, I'll take myself. That is fine. I like that. It's less problems.

Zelda's statement that friendships lead to "problems"...would imply that she too has no friends, that she even avoids friendships. Still, Zelda has an active social life, going out every few weekends with several women from her job. "We usually, when we go out, it's like party, have a few drinks, wink at some cuties and then go home." And a couple of ladies in her "regular posse" are doing really well in terms of most socioeconomic indicators; a few are even "bigwigs" like Kate, that fairly high-level supervisor at the center. Kate hangs with Zelda all the time at work and work-related recreational activities. "We are like just running around. She is mad cool, too. And she has juice, so people always want to be kissing her ass. I don't kiss her ass, though. She's cool, but I'm not trying to kiss her ass for it."

Even if he doesn't consider them his "friends," Dexter knows just about everybody he passes on the street. The kids, the cops, the local shop owners—many even call out to him by name. But they aren't friends, he says, they are just "people you know." According to Cynthia, thirty-two, a college graduate and office manager at a Harlem-based educational institution, a woman named Karen "used to be" a friend back when they were in high school but now is "not really" a friend. When I first met Karen, wiry and tall, she was hanging out on the corner of 133rd Street and Seventh Avenue. It was early in the afternoon, and she had on dark and dirty clothes. I had stopped there to meet Cynthia, who was connecting up with me for a visit to the Studio Museum of Harlem. Cynthia is a bit of a fledgling artist, and I figured it would be nice for her to see the exhibit, particularly since she didn't get a chance to get out to museums very much. Karen spotted Cynthia as soon as we passed by and immediately smiled.

The two women exchanged pleasantries: what was going on with families; who had seen whom; details about Cynthia's Aunt Rita moving to Atlanta with some doctor she recently married. After about three minutes, Cynthia and I took our leave of Karen and headed down the block toward 125th Street. As we walked, Cynthia and I discussed Karen a bit. Cynthia is particularly clean-cut, well-groomed, and professional-looking if one's standards are creased pant suits and beauty salon hair. And Cynthia's well-groomed look made Karen's disheveled appearance that much more noticeable. In spite of their obvious history (a history I, as yet, knew nothing about, but could sense even from their brief conversation in the street that day), Cynthia seemed a bit cold and aloof toward Karen— even a bit rude, which wasn't like her at all. I'm not sure if Karen recognized it, but I most certainly thought that I did. Cynthia was cordial and polite enough, I guess, but she kept Karen at something of a distance— possibly because she was a bit anxious about being fifteen minutes late already. Even with Cynthia's purposeful social distance vis-à-vis Karen, I wanted to think that I could still glimpse, hidden beneath all of that nonchalance and indifference, a closeness and affection that Cynthia held for this woman who looked old enough to be Cynthia's mother:

CYNTHIA: She's my age. Drugs and stuff done that to her. Because she is not that old, I know she looks it though.
JOHN: That's awful.
CYNTHIA: Oh yeah. She and I used to be girls. We still cool, but I mean we used to hang hard, We were always together. She got pregnant and got hooked on smoke.... She is still my girl, I guess, we do go back, but she's on some other tip now. Off the hook, you know. She's done some stupid shit, too, and all that is, she needs to try to get help.
JOHN: Does she work?
CYNTHIA: No. On the street. Selling her body for a smoke. And I am like, girl, are you crazy. Her apartment is in a shambles. She has a pretty baby, Shannon. I feel so bad for that baby sometimes. That's who I feel bad for.

Sometimes I'll watch her [the baby] for a bit....[S]ome people don't have money, but that is not the same thing as living in a pig pen. We never had money when I was growing up, but we still had a nice home. Clean, you know. With nice stuff. Being broke ain't the same thing as being nasty and dirty.

Cynthia voices a popular perception about the difference between being a "deserving" poor person who still has American values and being one of those freeloading, lazy, shiftless, dirty, and pig-pen-dwelling poor people who are poor because they refuse to do anything positive with their lives. At the time, Cynthia had a full-time job and a well-kept apartment. Karen was on welfare and hadn't worked full-time in years. That was especially terrible, in Cynthia's opinion, because the two women started out on the same road. Karen just veered off track. Cynthia can begin to offer the beginnings of an argument about her difference from Karen as a function of the simple things her own mother did, such as keeping their apartment clean and neat when she was a child:

> CYNTHIA: Drugs will do that, I guess, but she was always not clean. And when you not clean and on drugs you just a different kind of nasty. She looked at least decent when me and you saw her. The last time I saw her before that, she was looking crazy. She just looked terrible. I mean, it makes me want to cry to think that I grew up with her. I know her family, her mom. We were all kinds of close. My mom wasn't very sociable, but she hung out with [Karen's mother]. Our parents did the same things. I can't believe it. I just thank God, I really thank God. A lot of people have fallen to the drugs and stuff. But God has been good. I just feel almost like it's my responsibility or something. I know she is like her own problem and

all of that, but I just feel as though if I wasn't so busy, I would just be able to help her....

Zelda...also doesn't have many friends that she'd label as such. She does see a guy named Jordan all the time around her block. He isn't a friend, but he's always making passes at her. Zelda is sure that he doesn't really want "anything to be serious even though he can say that." She has a baby, she isn't making a lot of money, and she is admittedly "not bringing all that much to the table" in terms of forming a long-term relationship. Jordan is a "big professional, a big-time social worker. You know, suit and tie....He has a good job. He is that kind. Fly." Zelda feels that his flirting with her is either just being "nice" or "trying to get a piece," but it can't be anything more substantive because of the social distance (signified by dress and occupation) that she believes separates the two of them.

The first time I met Cynthia's high school friend Karen, Cynthia and I had just bumped into her on the street. The two women shared a very brief conversation—as if Cynthia was uncomfortable with the whole scenario, and as if Karen wanted to respect the fact that her high school "homegirl" was walking about town on a breezy morning with a black man she didn't know who was wearing a suit and tie. When I first asked Cynthia about her friend, she had very little to say, dismissing Karen as simply "off the hook" (someone who is crazy and beyond explanation), as someone she "used to know." We ran into Karen again on another day, this time on 125th Street. Cynthia seemed a bit more comfortable as they talked and laughed at length about that crazy boy who got their other high school friend, Liz, pregnant at fourteen— and about when and if Cynthia's Aunt Rita would ever move back to New York City. The conversation ended with Cynthia sliding Karen a few dollars and a hug. Once we are out of earshot, Cynthia, unsolicited, seemed to feel the need to justify her generosity.

"At first I wouldn't give her shit," she admitted, "'cause I knew what she was doing with it, but then I said you know what. I'm just gonna pray on it and ask God to step in and just do what I can."

When I accompanied Cynthia to Karen's apartment for the first time several weeks later, any reservations Cynthia held about their closeness seemed to dissolve in the warm heat of their laughter and stories. The two joked and reminisced with one another—and were even joined in their merriment later on by Liz, the woman who had grown up with them and gotten pregnant very young. I don't know what the three women talked about that night. I only walked Cynthia over to Karen's apartment, was introduced to Liz, chatted for a minute, and then left. In those few moments, I could see that these women shared a great deal and still, despite what I had interpreted as Cynthia's attempts at downplaying their relationship, gained tremendous amounts of pleasure and enjoyment from one another. A few days later, in another discussion I had with Cynthia about her relationship with Liz and Karen, the weight of the two other women's difficult lives almost brought her to tears:

> CYNTHIA: I don't know what happened. But it's fucked up. [Pause.] They used to be my girls. I mean that was it and a bag of chips. You don't know. I feel like now that is all fucked up. They are still cool, but they are so fucked up now with all of this shit. And not just the welfare. Shit happens like that sometimes, I guess. Fine. But they are like just not trying to get out of that, they are just like accepting it and getting deeper down the hole.

When Cynthia offers that Karen and Liz "used to be my girls," she's still placing the friendship in the distant past as opposed to the very real present of, say, that joy-filled get-together where the three of them were able to catch up with one another. Cynthia isn't sure where Liz is living these days, since Liz's mother threw her out about a year ago because of all "the stupid shit she pulled." Even given this ambivalence about her relationships with these women, Cynthia is just as quick to help them out as she is to downplay the importance of such assistance and to argue against the significance of the relationships in general:

> JOHN: Are they good examples of the people you grew up with? I mean, are most of your friends in the same boat that those two are in?
>
> CYNTHIA: No. I don't have a lot of friends. They aren't really my friends, I mean, Liz used to be, and I'm not nasty to her, I feel sorry for her, but she isn't my friend. I can't do anything with her, unless I wanted to do something stupid.

One Sunday morning, I spied Cynthia and Karen through the window of a local eatery. Karen was finishing off a breakfast that Cynthia had paid for. It was only the fourth time Karen had seen me over a two-month period, but she treated me like an old friend. And I appreciated her warmth.

Weeks later, Cynthia again downplayed her relationship with Karen, describing buying Karen a meal on Sunday morning as "nothing really, I'm just like, I got some time, she is, she needs food in her belly, what? I can do that." However, Cynthia did admit that she wanted to try making their weekend breakfasts a more regular thing. She thinks that's the least she can do, especially since Karen "used to be" such a good friend.

8

ROBERT COURTNEY SMITH

"IN TICUANI, HE GOES CRAZY": THE SECOND GENERATION RENEGOTIATES GENDER

from *Mexican New York* (2006)

For more than fifteen years Robert Smith studied a transnational community of people who migrated from a Mexican village he refers to as "Ticuani" to New York City. In this selection we see how the migrants and their children renegotiate their ideas about gender roles as they move back and forth between the two spaces. Contrary to the idea that immigrants and their children are torn between "two worlds," Smith shows how they manage to navigate between very different social expectations in the two locations.

The gender negotiations of the first generation must seem easy to their children. For the first generation, ranchero masculinity is still a dominant ideology, even if other gender practices coexist with it. But the second generation negotiates gender in three contexts: various hegemonic and non-hegemonic "Mexican" and "American" notions of masculinity and femininity, nagging generational questions of ethnic authenticity and nostalgia, and an immigrant narrative of upward mobility that they experience as an "immigrant bargain" with their parents. Hence, second-generation Mexican American boys must figure out how to become Mexican American men while trying to fit the hegemonic images of the macho ranchero, the white middle-class man, the striving immigrant, and other Mexican and American stereotypes, while also redeeming their parents' sacrifice in coming to the United States by succeeding in school and at work. Similarly, second-generation Mexican American girls must figure out how to become Mexican American women while engaging the images of the deferential ranchers, the autonomous and pioneering female migrant, and the second-generation New York career woman, and doing well in school, taking care of the men in their parents' home, and marrying good men and having careers and children. If this is exhausting to read, imagine living it![1]

Transnational life offers a clear view of second-generation Mexican American gender ideologies, bargains, and practices because it is a site in which they are challenged and renegotiated, and through which members of the second generation seek to authenticate or legitimize their Mexicanness. I was able to observe at length the relationship of Julia and Toño, the son of Tomás Maestro, novios in their mid-twenties who grew up in New York and regularly returned together to Ticuani. (Although the word novios is translated as meaning simply a boyfriend-girlfriend couple, in Spanish it implies that the couple will eventually get married, though it does not connote a formal engagement.) They visited friends and relatives, went to parties, and reconnected with Mexico, but they also used their return in other ways. While Toño attempted to reclaim the lost Mexican gender privilege that he felt his father had in Ticuani, Julia attempted to recover dimensions of Mexican culture and "authenticate" herself while retaining her autonomy. Their respective pursuits of their ethnic and gender projects sometimes put them in conflict, and this conflict reveals how each one thinks and lives gender. I have known Toño for more than ten years, and I met Julia when she and Toño first began dating seriously. My research team, especially Sara Guerrero-Rippberger and I, followed their return to Ticuani for three consecutive years, from 1999 to 2001. We spent time with them and their friends and families in New York and interviewed both of them several times, thus observing them both from their early courtship until their breakup more than four years later.

I examine how their relationships with each other, their families, and others were affected by their return to Ticuani, thus tracing how gender is lived in, and structures, transnational life.

Ranchero masculinity still thrives in the imaginations and lives of young men like Toño, but it coexists and sometimes competes with the hegemonic masculinity of the white middle-class career man and with three other notions of masculinity—the hardworking immigrant, the American rapper, and the Mexican gangster, or pandillero—each of which can be dominant in a particular context. These masculinities are also refracted through ethnicity. Hence, many young men like Toño, who was born in Ticuani but moved to New York at age ten (technically making him of the 1.5 generation in my definition), feel they have been made to forfeit the privileges they would have enjoyed had they been born in or stayed in Mexico, where they imagine ranchero masculinity to reign unchallenged. Yet they also feel drawn to "white" middle-class masculinity, wherein a man acquires postsecondary education and a career—meaning a "clean job" in an office—and makes decisions jointly with his wife on the presumption of gender equality. Moreover, their second-generation girlfriends and wives largely reject ranchero masculinity and the family life based on it. Finally, American rapper and Mexican pandillero masculinity resonate a great deal with many youths. Both are what Robert Connell would call "marginalized" hypermasculinized stances arising from exclusion by society. Both prize aggressiveness, power, money, and the potential use of violence as means to dominate both men and women. But both also defend an ethnic masculinity these young men feel has been violated. They feel they are denied the chance to realize the American dream and middle-class masculinity, to be somebody, and instead are seen as being nobody. The image of the hardworking immigrant—the

New York alternative and close cousin to the ranchero—who legitimizes his masculinity through his enduring capacity to work and sacrifice thus upholds their Mexicanness but is a less attractive option for these young men because it lacks the second-generation narrative of upward mobility. In Ticuani, however, enacting ranchero masculinity places Toño squarely in the center of Ticuani's hegemonic, though not exclusive or unchallenged, masculinity.

Second-generation women face similar complexities. While they are almost uniformly told not to be rancheras—women who defer to their husbands in all things and content themselves with child rearing and housework—they are still expected to do the lion's share of the domestic work, as daughters and as wives, and not to assert themselves in ways that create rancor at home. They are simultaneously expected, and expect themselves, to get a postsecondary education and pursue a career that will enable them to demand equality in their relations with their future husbands or to be independent from them in the event of a bad match.[2] The first image is that of the hegemonic second-generation Ticuanense woman, and the second that of the hegemonic New York woman. These sometimes incompatible images can be partly reconciled in the image of *in pionera* (the pioneer), a working immigrant woman autonomously making her way in a man's world, bucking the system when necessary. This nonhegemonic image offers a strong role model for these young women.

The impossibility of fully realizing all the dimensions of these different images of masculinity and femininity is not unique to Mexican or second-generation culture....What makes second-generation migrants' gender practices different from imagined middle-class white ones is that they are negotiated as part of the "immigrant bargain" with parents.[3] "Bargain" describes the expectation that sacrifice by the parents will be redeemed and validated through the children's achievement. While such a bargain occurs in most families, immigrant and nonimmigrant, the life-defining sacrifices of migration convert it into an urgent tale of moral worth or failure. Especially in cases where the second-generation youth's success is uncertain, parents often tell their children, effectively, "We sacrificed our homeland, struggled with English, and lived in fear of the Migra [the immigration authorities] so you would have a better life in New York. All we ask in return is that you succeed in school and at work." Second-generation success validates parental sacrifice, but failure incurs a burden of shame: "You have it so easy, you are a U.S. citizen and speak English, and you cannot even do well in school and get a career." Parents and children both ask: "What was all this sacrifice for, if the children end up doing the same work as the parents?" The children understand the implication that their parents, who overcame long odds, would have done better, and they judge themselves harshly.

This bargain elicits three main responses from the second generation, which resonate strongly with the work of Marcelo and Carola Suarez-Orozco: some try harder, some withdraw, and some reject this narrative and come to feel that their parents' expectations fail to take account of their children's difficulties and greatly exceed their ability to help the children live up to them.[4]

The immigrant bargain orients my analysis somewhat differently from research using the cultural gap or family tightrope as central metaphors.[5] Rather than positing a balancing of old, traditional with new, modern cultures, my perspective recognizes that the cultures of the countries of origin and destination are themselves both evolving and internally inconsistent. Moreover, gender frames how one engages these cultures. Toño, as we will see, embraces the old, traditional ranchero image of masculinity in an attempt to enjoy the privileges he believes it should offer him and that American middle-class masculinity and femininity deny him. He also uses dimensions of *pandillero* and rapper culture. He must balance his assertions of such gender privilege with the need to uphold his part of the immigrant bargain and prove himself as an upwardly mobile second-generation youth.

"Two Kinds of Mexicans"

"Me and Toño are two kinds of Mexicans," says Julia in contrasting Toño's macho, traditional ideas with her more equal vision of their relationship. Ticuani is charged terrain for the two of them when they visit because they both presume that Ticuani norms will approximate the macho ranchero ideal. For example, Toño attempts to control his sisters' and girlfriend's movements to such an extent, and is so prone to fighting, that Magda sums up his return by simply saying. "In Ticuani, he goes crazy." Returning to Ticuani enables Toño to make demands on Julia and his sisters in a context where he believes others will expect them to obey him, while they feel they must transgress local norms to demonstrate their autonomy. These gender negotiations take on added weight because return has become a key ritual in second-generation adolescence. In this context, examining Toño and Julia's relationship offers a strategic research site for gaining what one might call "relational leverage" into gender: because masculinity and femininity are defined relative to each other (or to other forms of themselves), closely examining an evolving relationship can give us insight into the broader process of negotiating gender.

Toño's macho stance toward his sisters (and Julia) is not the only option available. Indeed, my study team followed other older brother–younger sister pairs with very different gender dynamics. In one case, Teresa wanted to spend all her time in Ticuani with her boyfriend, who lives there and whom

she had been seeing during vacations for two years, despite her parents' disapproval. One night, Teresa stayed out past her curfew. When she wandered away with her boyfriend from her group of friends, which included her brother Leo, others in the zocalo began to comment. A friend of Leo's who lives in Ticuani urged him, "Yell at her about this, if you want to," implying that Leo had the right and responsibility to confront her for aberrant behavior. Leo refused, responding, "She can take care of herself." Leo's refusal to criticize his sister and his assertion of her competence and autonomy stand at odds with Toño's belief that controlling his sisters and girlfriend is his right and responsibility. The ranchero masculinity and moral framework inhering in the friend's invitation for Leo to criticize Teresa's behavior is the same one that Toño attempts to mobilize in his renegotiation of his gender bargain with Julia and also with his sisters.[6]

Julia and Toño met in a traditionally Mexican way, when he attended her *quinceñera*, or "sweet fifteen," party in Brooklyn, and he was stereotypically macho in pursuing her. He got into a fight at her party, apologizing profusely the next day and attempting to court her. She expressed scant interest at first, but eventually relented, and they became *novios*. Toño then broke it off because she seemed unenthusiastic. Several years later, they met on the subway, and their attraction became more mutual. Though Julia commented that "he's not my ideal of a perfect man...Toño's the opposite skinny, no eyebrows or facial hair, and short,"[7] they were dating exclusively. Through 2002 they seemed likely to marry, which was what their families expected from a serious relationship.

Julia sees Toño as more traditionally Mexican and herself as more Americanized, a view consistent with their individual and family histories. When Toño came to the United States at age ten, he spoke no English. He was first placed in a special-education class (because of a lack of classes for Spanish speakers) but moved quickly into bilingual and then into all English-language classes. His family's gender dynamics were more traditional, Mexican, and macho than those of Julia's family. His parents, Tomás and Xochitl, eloped and married as teenagers, and Xochitl left school. Tomás, who was a teacher in Mexico, keenly felt his loss of status and power when he became a busboy in New York. He told me: "[In Mexico] I was accustomed to being in charge. [In New York] I felt inferior. And here they were in charge of me.... I felt bad, bad, totally inferior." Now that he has learned more English and been promoted at his job, he feels better.

Tomás Maestro asserts traditional "Mexican" male privilege in his relations with his wife and daughters: "In the house, the man is the law." He outlines the hierarchy in the household: "It is an authority not due to *machismo,* it is an authority idiosyncratic to Mexican culture: where there is a man and a woman, the man is the law. And after the man comes the wife, and after her the oldest son." For Tomás, as for Toño, this male authority is part of being Mexican; ethnicity, gender, and power are intertwined.

Interestingly, Tomás does not demand that his daughters enact this model in their own relationships with men. He says that he hopes they will follow his and Xochitl's example but that he suspects they will want more egalitarian relationships with their husbands. That will make sense, given that they have their own careers and think differently because of growing up in the United States.[8] This change can be interpreted simply as a result of migration to the United States. But older Mexican men, and especially women, also want more egalitarian relations for their young-adult children. Jennifer Hirsch and Gail Mummert see this change as part and parcel of the modernization of gender relations in Mexico, born of economic and other changes in society. While such changes are also fostered by the "modernizing" journey of migration to New York, there is a more overt conflict—between the requirements of the family's gender ideology and that of second-generation mobility—inherent in that migration. Tomás and his daughters see their upward mobility as trumping the ranchero gender model that would require deference from them. In fact Tomás undercuts this gender ideology when he uses the accomplishments of Magda, Toño's younger sister, to pressure Toño to improve his lackluster performance at school. Moreover Toño's jobs in college have not paid as well as Magda's or Julia's, though he did graduate in 2002 with a business degree and computer training. If Toño's role in the family were defined mainly by his lack of educational or job success in comparison with his sisters, then his privileged position as the eldest son would be eroded. Without his father's support in upholding this gender ideology, Toño risks losing it. Here the definition of the generation gap is contingent both on Toño's performance as an upwardly mobile second-generation male and on Tomás's willingness to privilege gender ideology over second-generation ideology.

Magda intuitively understands Toño's precarious position and attempts to push him to work harder and do better in school. In 2001, Toño was having a hard time finding a job, which for her has never been a problem.

> MAGDA: I can't tell my brother... You are doing good, we are happy for you... because I feel he needs a bit more. I don't... compliment him, 'cause I feel he needs to do more. I feel I am in competition with my brother, at least from his side.
> RS: Do you feel competitive with him too?
> M: Yeah, basically, but I am not even trying to do that, you know? I get job offerings like everyday.... Do I look like I need a job? (*laughs*)

Her stronger position with regard to the immigrant bargain translates into greater privileges, such as being allowed to travel without family to Ticuani and, even against her parents' wishes, to another place in Mexico.

Toño, for his part, joins his father in chiding Magda for being lazy, for not cleaning the house, and especially for not learning to cook, something her family tells her that her husband will expect her to do. Their message to her, she says, "'cause I am a woman, [I] have to follow that role." The family sometimes discusses and laughs at Magda's ineptitude at cooking: by her own reporting, their mother has tried to teach both daughters, but both have failed to learn. But both also fail to see it as a necessary skill, telling their mother they will order food in if they come home from work late and do not feel like cooking. Magda's friends even call her a "feminist" because she does not know how to cook, and she sees herself "as more Americanist, since Mexicans do know how to cook, every girl knows how to cook except me." The family invokes ranchera femininity (which resonates with more traditional American culture as well), which casts cooking as women's work and a skill men require in a potential mate. The issue of Toño's learning to cook was not raised in this discussion.

Xochitl has alternatively worked in factories and stayed home to care for the children. While she usually stays silent when her husband asserts his authority, she asserts herself within limits, in other ways. She was present when I was interviewing Tomás and occasionally participated. While she prepared food for Tomás and me, Tomás expounded on male authority. When he said, "Inside the house, the man is the law," Xochitl laughed out loud, covering her mouth with her hand, but kept preparing the food. And while she rarely challenges him openly when he asserts authority over their daughters, she secretly encourages them to resist him when they disagree.[9] Hence, while Xochitl conforms, in the main, to the model of a ranchera wife, she sometimes departs from it.

Several months later I interviewed Xochitl and her two daughters while Tomás and Toño were out of the house and asked her why she had not contradicted Tomás in front of me, when her laughter so clearly expressed her disagreement. She told me, "When I want to say something to him, I say it, that is,...when he is saying things he should not say, I do not say it to him in front of the people because I don't like to lack respect for him or for the people, because I don't like to...be arguing about foolishness, because I will tell him this is foolishness....And I don't like to be fighting....I don't like to yell." She also told me later that after I had left, she did challenge Tomás on his remarks. This knowledge makes her performance when I was there even more skilled: her laugh was a stage whisper, clearly registering her disapproval of Tomás's assertion of privilege, but she continued to cook, staying on the periphery of the conversation while her husband held forth at the table. Xochitl showed both her modern migrant woman's disagreement with her husband and an appropriate ranchera demeanor.

Tomás played the encounter with equal skill, passing over her laugh, which he surely heard, without remark. By not commenting on it, he also upheld their gender bargain. During our interview, in which I had hoped they would both participate, I asked Xochitl questions to draw her into the interview. She responded sometimes by saying that she thought "the same as him," nodding to Tomás, and sometimes expressing her own opinion. But no matter how hard I tried, the conversation never became truly three-way. The dynamic kept returning to that of a conversation between two males, Tomás and me, with myself mainly in the role of listener and questioner.

Julia's household was very different. Her mother assumed adult responsibilities after her own father died when she was young in Mexico, and she never adopted the role of subservient wife and mother with her husband, whom she ended up divorcing. Julia described her mother's influence to Sara Guerrero-Rippberger in 1999:

> I admire my mother a lot for that....She's very independent, too, for a woman who...was born out there [Ticuani],...because some of them from her age group seem more, I don't know, not so independent....Not that they're dependent on a man, but they will do whatever the husband said; basically, they will follow the husband's rules. And my mother, she never went for that. Like she did her part, her thing, and my father did other things. And you know, she told him, "Don't expect for you to come home and me have everything ready on the table, 'cause I work, too, just like you do." And I see that other Mexican mothers—they're like, "Oh, my God, my husband is coming, I gotta get the food ready." And my mother was never like that. And I think that's why I told myself that I would never be like that either. I mean, I'm not saying that I would never give—I'll take care of my house, and I'll cook dinner, if my husband is good, you know, he provides for me, you know, good, caring. I don't see why not. But I don't expect him to tell me, "When I come back, it has to be ready."...If I work like he does, he has no right to learn [expect] to have it ready.

Julia sees her mother as a model of an autonomous, pioneer migrant woman who has pursued her dreams without letting the gender norms of her youth force her into a life she did not want. Julia does not reject domestic life—she says she will cook "if my husband is good"—but wants womanhood on her own terms, embracing things she values but not being forced by a man to do so. Julia says she did not grow up "Mexican";

she spoke both languages at home, but her English is much better than her Spanish; she cannot tolerate spicy Mexican food; her family does not always eat together; and she prefers American music like R&B to traditional Mexican ranchero or *cumbia* music. She is embarrassed when Toño howls along loudly in a traditional *grito* (shout) to Mexican ranchero music and dislikes the convention in dancing *cumbia* that the girl always follows: "His rhythm, his steps, and how he wants her to turn....But it's always like that, the girl has to follow the guy." And she even "had to learn how to act around Toño's family, how to be polite and greet each one of them."[10] Despite rocky periods in her teens, she did well in school, and in her early twenties she was seen by her family as successful, working at a well-paid job as a medical secretary while attending college. Here the image of a cultural or generational gap could be transformed (just this once) into a military or football analogy: Julia's mother has created a gap in the gender line by living as a *pionera,* and Julia has followed her through the breach.

In other ways, Julia and Toño had similar panethnic adolescences. Both had Puerto Rican and Black friends in elementary and middle school. Their friendship circles became more Mexican through adolescence and in early adulthood, a process coinciding with their evolving relationship and returns to Ticuani. Both also emerged from what they describe as "crazy" periods in their mid-teens without major mishap. Toño had hung out with a panethnic crew (gang) that included Puerto Ricans and Blacks at school during the week and with an all-Mexican gang on the weekends. He left the gangs after being shot at and after an ultimatum by his father to leave the gang or leave the family. His father offered him a trip to Mexico if he made the right choice and did better in school. He improved his grades and went to Mexico for several weeks over winter break. Before he and Julia began dating, he fell in love with a girl in Ticuani and saw a different way to be Mexican as he hung out with the Ticuani youth, who were all studying to be professionals. It changed his life: "I started doing better in school, and realizing about a lot of things, you know, go to college, have a degree, you know," and he began to think that Mexicans in New York needed "more Mexican professionals." He also feels he became somebody in Ticuani: people there are glad when he returns. "Since then I like been going back once [per year]...like everybody in the town, the young people, the young crowd, knows me now. When I go, they're like, 'He's back.'" Even his sister Magda acknowledges that Toño is somebody bigger in Ticuani than in New York. "The fact that he knows a lot of people over there, I guess it makes him feel recognized...like, wow, someone really knows what I am doing."

Much as Toño asserted different identities through membership in Mexican, and Black, and Puerto Rican crews, he adopted both a traditional ranchero masculinity and the hypermasculinized image of rappers such as Puff Daddy (Sean Combs) and Biggie Smalls, who was shot and killed in 1997, shortly before our interview. He idolized Smalls, he told me, because of "the words he used to say in his songs, the way he used to be, he used to talk...he was like a major—womanizer, you know. He used to have all the women, all the money—everybody used to envy him. That's why I believe he got shot.... He was like a Selena, he was like a Selena for us, the guys." His idolization of these two rappers is in fact consistent with some aspects of a macho, Mexican ranchero culture. Both project images of violence, fearlessness, and power and enjoy the company of many women. In simultaneously thinking of himself as a Mexican macho, a Ticuani ranchero, and a thuglike rapper, Toño has adopted some of the most hypermasculinized images in Mexican and American culture. Interestingly, though he expressed admiration for the Mexican

American actor James Edward Olmos, he did not discuss a Mexican male role model. Moreover, he identified Biggie Smalls as his role model as a "Selena for us, for the guys," referring to the female Mexican American pop singer.

For Julia, trips to Ticuani had less immediate and dramatic effects, but they did engage her with a set of Mexican practices, such as preparing food with her female relatives and participating in adolescent rituals such as the Grand Dance. These rituals heightened her sense of being Mexican, which was affirmed when others treated her as Mexican. When Julia expressed the feeling that she was not as Mexican as others, Meche, her friend from Ticuani, told her, "You are more Mexican than a cactus!" This increased involvement with a Mexican world in New York and Ticuani also coincided with renegotiating her place in her house in New York, getting her mother to acknowledge and appreciate how much housework she did for the family. Both Toño's and Julia's social worlds have become increasingly Mexican through their adolescence and courtship. Now in their mid-twenties, they hang out mainly with their cousins and other relatives and go to family parties, though Julia still has a fair number of non-Mexican friends. While Toño's life has always been more Mexican than Julia's, together they became more involved in Mexican activities, including trips to Ticuani.

Machismo and Female Autonomy and Labor in Ticuani

Toño and Julia participate in a transnational life that creates both harmony and conflict in their gender bargain. Julia attempts to renew her connection with Mexico in ways that respect her autonomy. She enjoys working with her grandmother in preparing religious feasts and attending *las Mañanitas*. She also permits Toño more authority over her than she allows in New York. Yet she also resists some gender practices, and this resistance sometimes places her in conflict with Toño, who uses Ticuani to live a certain image of ranchero masculinity. Toño embraces these more traditional gender roles because they enable him to be Mexican in a different way than he is in New York, including having a relationship with his girlfriend that is more like that between his parents. In 1997 he told me it was good that relations between men and women "are more equal than they used to be" and that even "girls back in Ticuani and Puebla want their rights and careers...they go to Puebla to study," but that now men could not control relationships as he thought they should. He referred approvingly to his parents' relationship, saying his father "keeps my mother in check....I would love that...with my future wife." In Ticuani, Toño expects and asks Julia to do what he sees as traditional Mexican women's work, things he would not usually ask of her and she would not usually do. Julia and his sisters report he acts more macho in Ticuani than in New York.

In embracing this macho image, Toño presumes authority over his girlfriend and sisters in public and expects them to take care of him at home. He provokes conflict with other young men, drinks a lot, and spends time with older male migrants, including his father, of whom he speaks with great respect as his *jefe* (boss or leader), a slang term for father. Sara Guerrero-Rippberger notes that Toño said being Ticuanense was about " 'wearing a cowboy hat, getting drunk every night—like a true Ticuanense. What Ticuanense doesn't like to drink?'...listening to Ranchera music and Ayyah-yahhhhhingl at the dance."[11]

The changes in Toño's behavior are clear to anyone who knows him. He becomes involved in many more conflicts in Ticuani and Julia says she "hates the ways guys act when they come here [Ticuani] to drink....They act 'macho,' then act stupid,

then end up fighting." His sister agreed but noted that their father's presence there partly counteracts these tendencies. She told me: "My father has totally [sic] control of him when he's around. When he's not, I don't know....When will he grow up? Over here [in New York], he's calm. Like my father said, he can have all the fun in his life in Ticuani....He's crazy over there." By enacting this ranchero masculinity, Toño is also authenticating his Mexicanness and expressing his essential *ticuanensidad,* thus co-constructing ethnicity and gender.

Toño's performance of masculinity is made more urgent by the immigrant bargain, which is different for him and for his sister Magda. During 2000, Tomás and Xochitl refused to give Toño, who was in his mid-twenties and, like most of his peers, still living at home, permission to go to Ticuani alone. They told him that it would not be safe for him to go because his habit of hanging out on the street drinking put him at risk when there were *pandilleros* in Ticuani. Xochitl described their talk: "[We said] he cannot go alone,...so that we could keep a close eye on him so that nothing happens." In contrast, Magda went to a friend's wedding in Mexico alone, despite her father's forbidding it. She had "begged him" for a month, but he said that she could go only with another family member. "He said that just because I have my money, that doesn't mean that I can do whatever I want." According to her sister, her father had insisted that "as long as she lives under his roof, she has to abide by his rules." But in the end, Magda simply purchased the tickets using money she earned. Although Xochitl had supported Tomás's blocking of Toño's solo journey to Ticuani, she spoke to Tomás privately on Magda's behalf: "I told him that she is already grown, that she behaves well in the house, that she has a right to go on vacation." In the end Tomás had to relent.

Toño's heightened displays of masculinity also result from the nonstop party atmosphere in Ticuani during the Feast. There are parties or dances literally every night, but the same kind of dense social interaction that takes place in large Mexican parties in New York is intensified in Ticuani because everyone is there night after night, so that *broncas* (problems) and *chisme* (gossip) that might evolve over months in New York evolve over a few days. Hence, Ticuani offers Toño a stage on which to create an entire play, so to speak, about his masculinity during the week of the Feast. Conflicts that might lie dormant or die in New York because of lack of contact between the parties are more likely to escalate. In Ticuani, too, since everyone sees the initial conflict, those involved feel greater pressure to save face or seek revenge.

Gendered Roles and Expectations in Ticuani and New York

In New York, Julia's and Toño's lives are connected but largely autonomous. Both of them live with their parents, and they spend little time together because they both work and attend college. Thus, for example, they do not negotiate the division of household tasks. In Ticuani, the scope of potentially gendered labor involving Julia and Toño together expands significantly. Julia, like other returning young women, helps older women relatives by doing housework, such as preparing meals and a special "hangover soup" called *guashmole* for Toño and other male returnees who often eat at her house. The social fields in which they move also differ in Ticuani. In New York, they attend family or Mexican parties, in a more "Mexican" style of courtship, but the two also spend time alone in a more "American," companionate dating style. In Ticuani, they spend a much lower portion of their free time alone together; instead they spend time with the "American" clique of second-generation returnees or the "Mexican" clique of first-generation migrants and Ticuani residents. This separation in their socialization

supports Toño's ranchero gender ideology, giving him lots of time to spend hanging out and drinking with his male friends.

On a typical day in Ticuani, Julia gets up early, helps her grandmother or aunt, and spends time with her girlfriends and sister and sometimes with Toño relaxing, going shopping in Puebla, or visiting a local pool. In the evening, she might spend some time with Toño in the zocalo, hang out with her friends there or at a party until midnight or a little later, and then go home. Toño's day begins and ends later. He gets up at noon or later and might go to the zocalo and to Feast events, such as the rodeo, and then spend time with Julia. When leaving to hang out with the men, he might shake a finger and admonish Julia to be good and not to get into trouble.[12] Toño hangs out more than other 1.5- or second-generation youth with young men living in Ticuani. For example, he goes away overnight to run the Antorcha and hang out with the older Ticuani men organizing the event. He is also more warmly greeted by older men from Ticuani than are most other young returnees, and might drink with some of them all night, coming home early in the morning. In one case, he stayed at the local bar, which only admits men, until well past dawn, when his aunt dragged him home. He regularly gets into confrontations, including fistfights, spurring constant fear among Julia and his family that he could be hurt or killed.

In New York, Julia and Toño live a fairly "American" life. Although she dislikes the traditional role Toño attempts to force her into, she does not reject entirely the compromises required by her relationship with what she calls a "real Mexican." This stance is clear in response to Sara Guerrero-Rippberger's question "How would Toño characterize you?"

> Oh, he always tells me, "Oh, you should just be [her brother] and he should be Julia."...He says that I try to be like the man. I said, "What do

you mean, like the man?" He said, "You used to go to karate school, you thinks you could do it all, you have such an attitude, you're such a hard-head, and you're too independent, and I hate it!" That's exactly what he tell me.... Well,... I'll tell him: "How about this? That's exactly what I'm gonna do, and if you don't like it, too bad—that's what I'm doing. I'm just letting you know." He hates that [chuckles].... I don't act a certain way when I'm around him. I mean, yeah, you do have to act a certain way around family, you know, but at the same time it doesn't mean that I'm gonna change completely, like, "Oh, okay, I'll do whatever you want."

Julia is struggling to maintain her independence in a relationship with a man who expects deference. Her New York woman struggles to accommodate his Ticuani ranchero. She resists his attempts to control her directly but compromises and "acts a certain way" around his family. Indeed, Toño attempts to use this family context to try to make Julia behave as he thinks women should, to make her display an appropriate sense of ranchera shame. But she keeps refusing him, not only by not responding but by openly rejecting his demands. For example, when with his family, he wants her not to drink, and to openly show her devotion to him, behavior she sees as reflecting his notion of a traditional Mexican woman:

When I'm with him, and he's, say, with a bunch of family, he has to tell me, "Uh, come and walk next to me and hold my hand." And I'm like, "If I don't want to, I don't have to hold your hand." And he's like, "Yes, you do, because you're my woman." So I feel like, What am I, property to you? No, if I want to hold your hand, I'll hold your hand.... Sometimes we get in a lot of disagreements because of

that.... Oh, like once I got really upset because he told me, it was a birthday party and... I was having a couple of drinks, and he said, "Oh, don't drink that much, or don't hold that bottle, it doesn't look right on a woman." So I really got upset, and I said, "No, if I want to drink, there's nothing wrong with that, I'll drink. And I don't care who sees me, and what people think about me." And he said, "Oh, there you go again."... So we get into problems because of that sometimes. And I feel that sometimes I can't see myself in a future with him, 'cause he's so old-fashioned in a way. And... he talks marriage, which I don't. And I said that, well, if you want that, you have a long way to go, and if you do, I tell him that everything's gonna be fifty-fifty—meaning the bills, cleaning, changing diapers, whatever it takes. I said just because, you know... your mother was... how you see your family, but I will never,... never live like that. And at first it was hard for him to accept it, but then he finally said okay. 'Cause nothing was changing my mind. And so I guess in that sense he is... like a Mexican—not just Mexican, but I think Hispanic men in general. It's like a macho thing—Oh, my woman has to do this and do that for me.... They say it nicely, but I tell him, "No, you know, if you want it that bad, you get up, and you have hands, so go and serve yourself your own soda."[13]

Yet despite these conflicts and Julia's protestations that she does not see a future with him, three years later, in 2002, she seemed even more committed to working through the imperfections in their relationship.

In Ticuani these differences manifest themselves in conflict as well as in assertions of gender privilege by Toño that Julia does not contest. She not only does his laundry and meals but also arranges her other responsibilities so that she can do so. Sara

Guerrero-Rippberger described one scene this way:

> On the morning of the 25th [the Feast day], [Julia's sister] and I went early, at 6:00 A.M., to [her aunt's] house to help prepare the food. Julia met us later, because she had to wait to make the boys' breakfast [Toño and his cousin]. The night before, Julia told me Toño had told her, "Don't go to help out your Tia before you serve us breakfast." Julia agreed, as if she took relish in the idea.... It turned out that the boys didn't want to eat that early, so Julia met us at her aunt's house soon after we got there. Later, while Julia was scrubbing her brother's and Toño's dirty socks, they woke up, and Toño called to Julia, "Serve us to eat, babe." "Oh," she said, and quickly got up to prepare their lunch.[14]

Hence, in Ticuani Julia often accedes to Toño's demands that she adopt the traditional woman's role that she otherwise rejects. Once she even went to his house to wash his clothes because "he doesn't have anyone else to do it for him." In doing such work, and in thinking about it this way, Julia moves closer to embracing, for that time, a deference to male authority and what Toño would see as an appropriate sense of shame.

Toño sees his role in Ticuani as increasing not his gender privilege but his male responsibilities. For example, when two male friends failed to meet him to help escort Julia, her sister, and Sara Guerrero–Rippberger to Puebla from the Mexico City airport late at night, he felt a special responsibility and burden. He said, "I don't like this. I'm the only guy—with three girls. I don't like to travel like this, with all girls. Now I'm responsible." When Julia rolled her eyes and asked what the problem was, he said, "Oh, yeah, right, you're gonna protect us. I'm responsible." Toño not only feels responsible but also resents the fact that the women for whom he feels responsible do not respect his authority. His worry was not

wholly misplaced. As it turned out, the other young men who were supposed to have met them had been robbed at gunpoint within half an hour of arriving in Mexico City. While Toño's perception of threat was valid, his gender logic does not hold: the other car had three men in it, but they were still robbed. (Of course, he may have worried about the risk of rape or abduction, which would be less likely if the group included only men.) At any rate, Toño clearly felt he alone was responsible for keeping the three "girls" safe, and if anything had happened to them, he would have been seen as having failed to protect them.

Even in her more deferential role in Ticuani, Julia does not acquiesce in all Toño's attempts to assert masculine privilege. She reacted angrily to the many fights he got into while drinking. One morning, when she came to his house to clean, he sought sympathy, saying his lip hurt from getting punched the night before. She chided him for drinking and fighting, telling him "that if he came to have a good time, then have a good time and relax, but if he came here to do stupid things like get drunk, get macho, and start fights, then he should leave or 'take it like a man'"[15] and not complain. In 2000, on one of their last nights in Ticuani, Toño and Julia went to the *gallos* (cockfights). Julia spent the time with returning second-generation youths, including her sister, other friends, and Sara Guerrero-Rippberger. Toño hung out most of the night with Ticuani-born men but periodically went to see how she was. I moved among the various groups. During the last few cockfights, Toño told me he had been betting on every fight and had lost more than US$150. My field notes record the following exchange: "Running out of money to bet on the *gallos*, Toño turned to Julia and said, 'You got my back, right?' to which she responded. 'What?!' impatiently. They spoke more and Julia ended the conversation by saying loudly to him. 'Don't ask me for money for *los gallos*. If you lose your money and don't have any more, that's your problem!' He turned away sullenly from her without saying anything and went back to the hangout with the guys he was drinking with."

Julia thus limited the extent to which she would cooperate in Toño's attempts to live out an entitled, ranchero masculinity. She refused to play the woman who supports her man no matter what. First she tells him that as a macho, he must not complain about his lip; if he cannot take a punch, he should avoid fights or go back to New York. She deftly limits his demand for sympathy from an unconditionally supporting girlfriend or wife by invoking the image of a real macho, who would not complain about his lip. She also refuses to lend him money to bet more on the *gallos*, again invoking the image of a macho ranchero who would not need to ask his woman for money because he would win, or have more money to bet. She was not interested in helping him live the image of the hard-drinking, hard-betting macho; she herself works hard and spends prudently. In both cases, she successfully set limits on his demands.

Masculine Displays

Toño's gender ideology led him to explosive confrontations with both men and women, especially about control over and responsibility for the women in his life. These issues invoked powerful emotions of jealousy, empowerment, and tests of a man's true *mexicanidad* or *ticuanensidad*. One incident in January 2000 is notable for the way a trivial incident yielded dramatic jealousy. Toño spends a lot of time in Ticuani talking to girls whom he introduces as his "cousins," thus dismissing the possibility of romantic entanglement. Julia asked her friends if they thought Toño was having an affair; though many thought she had grounds to

be angry, she did not publicly confront him. Toño, however, reacted with fury to a similar suggestion about Julia. She had gone with her sister and some girlfriends to Puebla to buy some souvenirs. While she was away, the brother of one of the young women, a mutual friend, teased Toño that Julia had gone to Puebla with three guys whom she was supposed to have met the night before while Toño was off "with his boys." On their return, Toño immediately and angrily confronted Julia, screaming, "Where were you? Who were you with? I know what you were doing!" The resolution was described by Sara Guerrero-Rippberger:

> Julia calmed Toño down, and they talked it out in the other room. I was surprised that the end result was not that Julia got mad at Toño for being so stupid, but that she calmed him down and then stayed with him to hang out for the rest of the evening (or at least the beginning, until he went to hang out with the guys), almost to prove to him that she really wanted to be with him. When Julia and Toño came out of the room from talking, [Julia's sister] and I asked her if she wanted to join us in the Centro while we waited for Toño to get ready. Julia said, "Nah," and then Toño, smiling, said proudly, "She's staying right here with me while I get ready."

By placating Toño in such a situation, Julia seems to conform to the traditional, ranchera role of supporting her man at all times and disallowing anger—that most "inappropriate sentiment"—at being unjustly accused. Toño's jealously possessive behavior without real cause fits a ranchero masculinity.

Other performances of masculinity involve controlling women's access to public space and their relations with "inappropriate" men, which also implicate Toño's relations with these men and imbue these encounters with even more masculine charge. One such encounter happened early in the morning of January 26, 2000, as revelers left the Grand Dance. This is a rarified time because the revelers move from an area of heavy police and adult presence outside the dance down the road to the zocalo, where there is less adult supervision. Add alcohol, and the mix becomes volatile. When Toño saw his sister Magda getting a ride with a *pandillero,* he became angry. She told him to back off and later described the scene to me in this way: "He screamed, '¡Pendeja! [Asshole!] Go home!'...But [the *cholo,* or gang member] thought it was at him, so they got into a pushing match.... I told him [the *cholo*], 'You misunderstood,' so he went back [to his car]....The next day the guy apologized to me and my brother....Neither one of them remembered what happened, because they were drunk." The brewing fight was quickly broken up by older men, who told Toño, "Don't be an asshole. Those guys carry guns," as they pulled him away. Both men were still angry as they separated but allowed the older, adult men to calm them down, preventing the dispute from escalating.

In another example, Toño wanted his sisters to go straight home after the last night of the *gallos,* at dawn, because he did not think they should be out that late. They ignored him until he finally yelled repeatedly and loudly at them in the zocalo: "Go home!" to which his younger sister, Marisol, responded, "Shut up, shut up, shut up!" This infuriated him, and he yelled a threat to his other sister, Magda, who yelled back so that everyone in the zocalo could hear, "Oh, really? Then why don't you come over here and hit me?" He responded sullenly and yanked Julia roughly by the arm, saying, "Julia, let's go home." Julia glared at him but went, while his sisters stayed with their friends. When he got to Julia's house, he knocked loudly on the windows of her grandmother's house, alarming her so much that she forbade Julia to leave the house again. Toño's

father Tomás Maestro watched all these events from a distance, following his son and Julia back to her house, then following Toño, again at a distance, back to the zocalo.[16]

This incident was witnessed by four members of my research team and followed up closely by Sara Guerrero-Rippberger and me. Each actor interpreted the events differently in the service of different gender ideologies and projects. Toño saw his demand that Magda leave the car as his attempt to keep her safe, thus fulfilling his masculine ranchero responsibility and also protecting the family's honor. He told her getting a ride with the *pandillero* did not look good. Yet Magda felt no danger, as she had known these young men since childhood and had been hanging out having fun independently all week.

Magda's view was almost the opposite. She told me and Sara separately that she had purposely stayed in the zocalo after Toño's confrontations in order to watch out for him. She described her position to me this way: "I would never leave until my brother went to sleep. The whole house [family] would monitor him....My dad didn't go to the dance on the twenty-fifth because of a swollen leg. I woke him up" to bring him to the zocalo. She said, and Xochitl confirms, that in New York her father calls from his job to check up on Toño, asking both Toño and his sisters how he is behaving. Tomás told me, "I got up at five in the morning to keep an eye on my son" in Ticuani, saying that he wanted to let Toño have his freedom and his fun in Ticuani but not endanger himself. Hence even as Toño saw himself as taking up his male responsibilities by protecting his sisters and his girlfriend, he was the object of a family collusion to safeguard him from the dangers of his own ranchero masculinity. In Magda's words, his entire family is "on alert" to protect him from himself.

This group protection of macho young men was noted among others we observed both within families and within friendship groups of youths. Fascinatingly, there are simultaneous gender dynamics: while Toño asserts male power by claiming the authority to send his sisters home, they not only refuse him but are collaborating with his parents in an exercise by the whole family to keep him safe from his masculinity. Toño's family and girlfriend both indulge his desire to assert masculine power but treat him as a child by secretly protecting him from himself. To my knowledge, family members did not tell him about these efforts, even though his parents had told him that they would not let him go to Ticuani alone.

Julia's interpretation of these events shows the compromises in her gender bargain in Ticuani. She was angry at Toño for treating her badly in front of her friends (including members of our research team, especially Sara). She told Sara she went home with Toño not because she felt she should obey him but because of Toño's father; she "felt ashamed that he would think bad things of her if she didn't stop drinking and leave the party when Toño told her to," a shame that intensified because Tomás "wouldn't even look at her" but followed them the whole way home at a distance. Toño's skillful amplification of the perceived risks to Julia's person and honor combined with Tomás's silence to make her feel such shame that she was unable to defy Toño. My later conversations with Tomás indicate that he was trying not to meddle but still to keep his son out of trouble, as I watched him do again in 2001. He saw himself as exercising vigilance from a distance. He would have intervened if the situation had escalated physically, with Julia or with others, but, short of that, he saw the episode as an issue between the couple. When a member of the research team asked Julia the next day if she had felt safe allowing Toño to walk her home under these circumstances, she laughed off the question.

After dropping Julia at home, Toño returned to the zocalo, walking past his father and pointing his finger at him, saying, "Go home!" quickly and directly, an unusual challenge. Tomás let the slight go, but continued to be vigilant as Toño rejoined his male friends, eating tacos, drinking beer, and joking around in the zocalo past sunrise. Interestingly, Toño was attempting to enforce a code of conduct for his sisters that was stricter and more traditional than the one their father enforced. Tomás Maestro's passiveness in the matter seems to suggest he found nothing wrong with his daughters' being there so early in the morning but did not entirely disagree with his son's attempts to control them, either. Hence, Tomás also seems to vacillate between different gender ideologies and practices. With his wife, he practices a stronger form of ranchero masculinity than he does with his daughters, whose relationship is negotiated within a second-generation narrative of upward mobility. With his son, he supports a shared ranchero masculinity while exhorting Toño to take the narrative of mobility more seriously.

The interpretation of these events by Julia's Ticuani friends offers insight into local gender ideologies and the difficult situation they create for Julia. Magda expressed anger that Toño had treated Julia this way and shock that she had allowed him to do so. She added, "And he doesn't even let her go out with her friends!? This is not the way to treat your girlfriend, because she is not your wife." Her sister echoed. "This is not the way to treat your girlfriend, she's not your wife!" and then added, "You shouldn't treat your wife this way either, but it's different." This clearly implies that Toño overstepped the limit. They also expected that as an independent New Yorker, educated, and working at a professional job, Julia should have been able to negotiate a more egalitarian relationship with her boyfriend. And although people apparently expected her to become Toño's obedient wife, they would be disappointed in her if she did, because they also expected her to become an independent, autonomous, New York woman—what Sara Guerrero-Rippberger insightfully calls a "New Ticuanense."[17] Julia is in a catch-22: she is too independent for a ranchera but not independent enough for a New York woman.

For Toño, these conflicts were ideal opportunities to display ranchero masculinity. First, he defended "his" women's honor by attempting to get them to "go home...for their own good," thereby discharging his responsibility as an older brother. In his view, an authoritarian and possessive tone toward his women is justified by their resistance to the authority he possesses by virtue of his responsibility to take care of them. Second, he not only asserts authority over women but does so by getting into a violent, if aborted, conflict with someone dangerous, a *pandillero*. He later further asserted his masculinity by fighting with a *pandillero* who had asked for Julia's telephone number. He thus showed that, though small in size, he had "heart"— the courage to fight anyone who disrespected him, his girlfriend, or his sisters. His courage—and Julia's anger at his recklessness—appeared even greater afterward, when members of the gang spray-painted their gang symbol on Julia's grandmother's house. Moreover, Toño fought while drinking a lot of alcohol, "like a real Ticuanense," whose behavior can run to excess during the Feast, just as Ticuani "blood" is seen by older men to run hot in politics. Toño was thus not only displaying behavior appropriate to a man and older brother but also affirming his authenticity as a Ticuanense and a Mexican.

Gender Performance and Other Young Men

Toño also negotiated his gender role through a set of conflicts over who "lowers their eyes" to whom—or, as Jack Katz frames it, which men command respect and generate fear and dread in others.[18] During the Feast in 2001, Toño became involved in a conflict between his group of cousins, the Zavalas, and another group, the Buendias. He involved himself in some fights and was also present at a tense set of negotiations between the leaders of the two groups on the last night of the Feast. The negotiations were held inside the tent housing the cockfights and ended in the early hours of the morning. Emerging onto the street after the danger of conflict had passed, Toño told me without irony that "I'm just a thug...living a thug life," with his hands splayed out in rapper fashion, with the inner and outer fingers of his hands pointing out at different angles. I immediately thought of his interview in 1997, when he told me of his admiration of the rappers Puffy Combs and Biggie Smalls. Involvement in these confrontations and negotiations gave Toño a sense of being strong and dangerous, a man to be reckoned with—someone ignored at one's peril. While significant differences exist between ranchero masculinity and rapper masculinity—for example, the latter emphasizes money much more—they are similar in imagining power over women, fearlessness in response to challenges from other men, and willingness to use violence to defend one's honor if someone else "lacks respect."

These encounters also clearly illustrate the accelerated and intensified nature of such confrontations set in Ticuani transnational life. The Buendia and the Zavala youths were almost all born or raised in New York and had developed rules of engagement for their adolescent conflicts based both in New York and in the kinship networks that their migrant parents had brought with them....Being back in Ticuani for two weeks speeds up the evolutionary cycle of conflicts, as events develop by the hour and involve others....

Conclusion

The second generation renegotiates their gender bargains and strategies in different physical and relational contexts in New York and Ticuani. Julia embraces Mexican rituals on her own terms, but must do so through negotiation with a boyfriend who wants her to be more traditionally "Mexican" and who pressures her to act more deferentially in Ticuani. His pressures resonate with a powerful gendered memory in Ticuani of a macho, ranchero past lost to migration. In his negotiations with Julia, Toño also invokes images of the rapper who fears no one and who gets all the girls—a player. Ticuani offers a kind of secular sacred space for renegotiating gender bargains and ideologies.[19] It creates "accelerated social time" by bringing into close, extended, intensive social contact people whose social interactions usually occur over longer periods in dispersed locales. The intensity and stakes of these interactions are fueled by the urgency of asserting adolescent identity and the reauthenticating function that Ticuani has assumed in the lives of many young returnees.

Ticuani is a key site for practicing and developing gender strategy, one in which young men can exhibit a hypervigorous, macho ranchero masculinity. They can enjoy the traditional customs like the rodeo or *gallos* and drink or get into confrontations with other men. Returning *pandilleros* have heightened both the danger and the appeal of such conflicts. Young men like Toño see the *pandilleros* as posing a danger to women's honor and offering a chance to demonstrate their own honor and heart by refusing to shrink from conflict with them.

Ticuani's gender reality approximates the images of masculinity that some, like Toño, believe their fathers enjoy and that offers them relief from the need to compete with more economically or educationally successful siblings or peers. Ironically, Toño,

as a college graduate, is educationally way ahead of most of his male peers. But his sisters have done better at living out the immigrant narrative of upward mobility. Toño uses the setting of Ticuani to prove his masculinity and renegotiate his gender bargain with Julia. He simultaneously invokes the images of the Mexican macho and the fearless rapper: he can imagine himself a cousin to both the revolutionary Emiliano Zapata and to Puffy Combs and Biggie Smalls, who fear no man and get "all the women" and "all the money."

Julia's return to Ticuani causes conflict with her New York gender strategy. Although in New York her gender ideology is not unproblematic, conflicts there are not irreconcilable. In Ticuani, her conduct is always making someone unhappy. In this setting Toño sees her as too independent for a Mexican woman, but her friends from Ticuani see her as too accommodating for a New York woman. When she is with Toño's family, she feels pressure to become a more submissive (that is, "Mexican") woman, to attend to Toño's needs and hide her inappropriate sentiments. Her taking care of Toño, which she does because she loves him, becomes blurred with the pressure of the conflicting expectations of her peers and her family and by Toño's leverage of such expectations. She thus goes along with his demands—for example, going home when Toño aggressively insists—that directly contradict her imagined future as an independent, New York woman and inheritor of her mother's very "un-Mexican" autonomy.

Julia negotiated Toño's demands more easily in one-on-one situations not involving his family. One example is her rejection of his request for more money to bet on the cockfights. But she gave into his demands and tolerated his irrational accusations of jealousy. She also clearly felt pressured to submit to him in the presence of his family, especially his father, whose silence she interpreted as an endorsement of the same ranchero masculinity. Yet Toño's family was not a united front imposing such a gender bargain on her. She had bonded quite closely with his two sisters and his mother, who supported each other's independence and rejected Toño's harsher gender ideology. When Julia and Toño eventually broke up, the three women in his family all felt they had lost one of their number. My speculation is that in addition to feeling pressured by Toño's father, Julia was attempting to find ways to make the relationship work by accommodating Toño when she did not want to. The loving relations she had with his family made her try harder, but she came to resent and react against these compromises.

Transnational life is structured in part by these renegotiations of gender bargains, drawing on various Mexican and American gender idioms. Julia and Toño's renegotiation of their gender bargains is interesting and complex because they both use Ticuani to authenticate their Mexicanness but must also engage the gender notions they have learned in New York. Moreover, in the early-morning confrontations in the zocalo, Toño pursues a more macho masculinity with his sisters in Ticuani than his father does precisely because Ticuani is so important for demonstrating his masculinity. His rage when his sisters and girlfriend defy him reflects his fear that his male authority is not respected. He exploits the Ticuani context to enforce his gender bargain on Julia and send her home in silent, shamed, protesting compliance to a gender norm she resents and rejects.

Transnational life is also structured by the interaction between the second-generation narrative of upward mobility and the various competing gender ideologies. Hence, Tomás Maestro asserts tighter control over his son in New York, giving him more freedom to "have his fun" in Mexico, but also implies that his son's lack of effort toward educational and professional success imperils the male authority to which his status as the oldest son entitles him.

Finally, the modeling and renegotiation of gender roles by Julia and Toño and their parents both resonate and dash with the images of the migrant family walking a tightrope or "straddling the gap."[20] Xochitl and Tomás live as a fairly traditional Mexican couple, and she continues to defer to his authority even in New York. She does not work outside the home and use that economic power to renegotiate power relations with her husband, the situation literature posits as the impetus to renegotiation. But neither is she always subservient; indeed, she openly laughs at him, though without an overt challenge.

These metaphors are of no help in interpreting Julia's mother's gender mentorship, though they shed some light on Julia's experience. Julia's mother is not attempting to straddle traditional and modern ways; she has struck out on her own. But Julia attempts to embrace aspects of her "Mexican" culture in Ticuani while trying to preserve her autonomy. Similarly, Toño is not railing against the strictures of Mexican culture in favor of a freer American culture. Rather, he seeks to use dimensions of Mexican ranchero culture to alter the more Americanized gender bargain that Julia has struck with him.

NOTES

1. This chapter draws on my own research over many years, work by Sara Guerrero-Rippberger over more than two years, and work by other team members, including Griscelda Perez and Sandra Lara. Unless otherwise noted, fieldwork observations come from my own notes.

    I first came to know Toño as the son of a Committee member, and I interviewed him and his sister and their father and mother in 1997 when I began in earnest my research on the second generation. He was then reinterviewed for the NSF-funded part of the project by Sara, who also came to know his girlfriend Julia and her sisters well. Sara and I also did ethnography with them in New York and Ticuani. Sara interviewed Julia and her sisters for her 1999 Barnard College senior thesis (Guerrero-Rippberger 1999). Over several years of fieldwork, we observed the evolution of Toño and Julia's relationship, especially during return trips to Ticuani by Toño in 1999 and 2001 and Julia in 1999 and 2000.

2. See Zhou and Bankston's (1998) and Kibria's (1995) work on Vietnamese youths in the United States.

3. Suarez-Orozco and Suarez-Orozco 1995, C. Suarez-Orozco 1999, M. Suarez-Orozco and Paez 2002, and Ainslie 2002 write persuasively on these points. Guerrero-Rippberger also writes about the immigrant bargain.

4. See M. Suarez-Orozco and Paez 2002.

5. Zhou and Bankston 1998; Kibria 1993.

6. In retrospect, it would have been interesting to compare, for example, Toño's gender bargains with his girlfriend and sisters to those of others. While other gender strategies were observed—Leo's refusal to chastise his sister is one example—no similarly rich case presented itself. Leo, who was younger, more restricted in his movements, and without a girlfriend, did not offer a valid comparison to Toño. Toño's relations with Julia and his family fascinated me, and I was in a position to study them because of my long-standing relationships with those involved. Moreover, their theoretical importance emerged only as the action unfolded. My work here thus reflects an ethnographic reality whereby selecting cases is not always possible: instead one follows the stories as they unfold and then attempts to make theoretical sense of them.

7. Guerrero-Rippberger 1998–2000.

8. According to Zhou and Bankston (1998) and Kibria (1993), Vietnamese parents similarly accommodate their second-generation children. For example, Zhou and Bankston explain that fathers view their daughters' educational and occupational mobility as an indirect sign of obedience. Their mothers see it as a way to make them better able to fight the hard gender-role strictures they face in the Vietnamese community.

9. Guerrero-Rippberger 1998–2000.

10. Guerrero-Rippberger 1998–2000.

11. Guerrero-Rippberger 1998–2000: 7.

12. Guerrero-Rippberger 1998–2000.

13. Quote taken from an interview done by Sara Guerrero-Rippberger for her 1999 thesis.

14. Guerrero-Rippberger 1998–2000: 9.

15. Guerrero-Rippberger 1998–2000.

16. Ticuani field notes from 2000 by Guerrero-Rippberger, G. Perez, and R. Smith.

17. Men also noticed these dynamics. One young man who now lives in New York told me that if he had a girlfriend like Julia, he would not spend so much time away from her.

18. Katz 1988.

19. Flores and Resaldo (1997) cite Gottdiener (1985) in discussing a different but similar notion of places that come to have sacred, nonreligious meanings.

20. See Zhou and Bankston 1998; Kibria 1993.

REFERENCES

Ainslie, Ricardo. 2002. "The Plasticity of Culture and Psychodynamic and Psychosocial Processes in Latino Immigrant Families." In *Latinos: Remaking America*. Marcelo Suarez-Orozco and Mariela Paez (eds.). Berkeley: University of California Press.

Flores, William, and Renato Resaldo. 1997. "Identity, Conflict, and Evolving Latino Communities: Cultural Citizenship in San Jose, California." In *Latino Cultural Citizenship*. William Flores and Rena Benmayor (eds.). Boston: Beacon.

Gottdiener, Mark. 1985. *The Social Production of Urban Space*. Austin: University of Texas Press.

Guerrero-Rippberger, Sara. 1998–2000. Notes for Rob Smith's Second-Generation Project.

———. 1999. But for the Day of Tomorrow: Negotiating Femininity in a New York Mexican Identity. Senior thesis, Barnard College.

Katz, Jack. 1988. *Seductions of Crime*. New York: Basic Books.

Kibria, Nazli. 1993. *Family Tightrope: The Changing Lives of Vietnamese Families*. Princeton, NJ: Princeton University Press.

Suarez-Orozco, Carola. 1999. Adolescence and Gender in the Second Generation. Address to the annual meeting of the American Psychological Association.

Suarez-Orozco, Carola, and Marcelo Suarez-Orozco. 1995. *Transformations: Immigration, Family Life, and Achievement Motivation among Latino Adolescents.* Stanford, CA: Stanford University Press.

Suarez-Orozco, Marcelo, and Mariela Paez. 2002. *Latinos: Remaking America.* Berkeley: University of California Press.

Zhou, Min, and Carl Bankston III. 1998. *Growing Up American.* New York: Russell Sage Foundation.

9

RICHARD LLOYD

GRIT AS GLAMOUR

From *Neo-Bohemia* (2006)

Since the 1970s, many once down-at-the-heels urban neighborhoods have emerged as "hip" centers for art, culture, and upscale consumption thanks to a process commonly known as "gentrification." In his study of the Wicker Park section of Chicago, Richard Lloyd tries to understand the role of "creative" communities of artists, writers, musicians, and various young "hangers-on" in this process. Documenting how "grit" has turned into "glamour," Lloyd shows how "creative" communities have changed the visual aesthetic of the neighborhood and how the media contributes to the production of its "hip" scenes.

On the Edge

It is the spring of 2000, and Michael Watson and I sit in the Borderline, a classic Chicago corner bar across the street from the Flat Iron that has been a constant through the neighborhood's transition from the late 1950s. Michael, a thickly muscled African American in his late thirties, worked for several years as a bouncer for this bar and for the Red Dog, the "underground" nightclub that occupies the upstairs. Both businesses, along with a restaurant next door called Café Absinthe, are owned by the same people, and all three venues have reaped the benefits of neighborhood transition by steadfastly expressing neo-bohemian chic, each in its own way. My tape recorder running, Michael and I engage in a long conversation about his colorful history in the neighborhood. A good-natured ex-enforcer, Michael laughs easily while explaining that his job was "to handle the stupid shit": "I was a bouncer here for a number of years. I was a bartender and bouncer at Dreamerz [a bar up the street on Milwaukee, now called Nick's] for a couple of years. I ended up living upstairs from Dreamerz when the owner got shot. I got involved in Wicker Park through violence. Everything at some point had violence."

Despite his imposing physical presence, Michael is no stereotypical urban thug. During the time that he was policing bars, Michael, a poet and writer, was active in the local literary community nurtured in such places as the Guild Complex, the Urbus Orbis café, and the Afrocentric bookstore Lit X. He no longer lives in Wicker Park, but he still is involved in the neighborhood as the poetry director for the Around the Coyote (ATC) art fair.

Michael moved into Wicker Park in 1988, the year before Urbus Orbis opened for business a half block east of the Borderline on North. "Strange enough, what Urbus Orbis was before—there was a big shooting gallery there," Michael says, using the common slang for a site for selling, buying, and injecting heroin. "That's where all the junkies would go. You knew where they were, and considering where it was, this was like, this little walkway, all of this, this is where they would hide." He indicates the stretch between Urbus' former home and the Borderline.

> From there to the bar, it was a [transient] hotel called the Victory Hotel, and they would congregate there. This six corners was always live, and this is where they would go, they would go and hide in the small places. If they could get in there they would do their shit there, or they would go into the park itself. That was called Needle Park, and you would see hypodermics just out there in the grass.

Given this less-than-bucolic portrait, why did Wicker Park increasingly become attractive to so many young people, often from far more sanitized, middle-class origins? In part, artists' interest in locating in marginal neighborhoods whose majority population is poor and nonwhite involves the desire to occupy inexpensive space adequate to their needs. They are a transient population, breaking ground in marginal urban areas that may be targeted for redevelopment. Christopher Mele notes that, "because of their limited economic resources and/or preferences for residing in alternative neighborhoods, these groups endure above average levels of crime, noise and drug related problems."[1] However, it appears that many Wicker Park residents do not merely tolerate these drawbacks, although there remain limits to the extent that any resident with other options would allow his or her personal safety to be compromised. Participants in Wicker Park's arts community profess an ideological commitment to race and class diversity, although, as we will see, the practical definition of diversity is complicated and often fetishistic. Sharing the streets with working-class and nonwhite residents, even if personal interaction remains superficial, is part of their image of an authentic urban experience.

Uniformly, the young artists whom I interviewed who moved into the neighborhood during the late 1980s recall it in terms similar to those of Michael Watson. Many speak of "gang bangers" congregating around the six corners and, along Division Street on the neighborhood's southern border, members of the West Side Latin Kings.[2] Checking these recollections against empirical indicators supports the depiction of a high-crime neighborhood, and no doubt illicit elements had a disproportionate impact on the street ethos, even if the majority of residents confined themselves to law-abiding activities.[3] Yet, if we ordinarily assume that criminal activity like drug dealing and prostitution would repel most residents or at least be endured grudgingly, the picture for young artists in the neighborhood is more complicated than that. Indeed, the recollections of this period tend toward the nostalgic, as the manifest dangers of the neighborhood coincided with the bohemian disposition to value the drama of living on the edge. As one local entrepreneur puts it, "There's a sense of vitality in the streets. Along with the danger there's a vitality that you lose when you're sure about your personal safety. There's a certain edge that goes away. And there's something exciting about having that edge. There's something [exciting] about having drug dealers right up the street."

Other new residents to the neighborhood in the late 1980s also demonstrated a surprising lack of aversion to those elements of garish street life that standard narratives of urban renewal and community policing identify as social disorder.[4] Nina, a painter who was employed for more than a decide in the local bar scene, also moved into the neighborhood during the late 1980s. "It was mostly Puerto Rican and some Mexicans. A lot of Hispanic families and hookers. And when we moved in, the first people that talked to me were the hookers, and they were pretty nice." She recalls the environment as gritty and dangerous, although her take is somewhat more complicated than simple bravado. Rather than treating danger as a source of allure in itself, she remembers the way that she constructed a sense of safety through the forging of ties with the local community.

> After a while people got to know me by sight, and I felt really safe there. And I remember one time I left my house, and I saw all these people chasing this one guy down the street, and they started beating the shit out of him. I thought, "Oh my God." And one guy came over who lived next door, and he said, "That guy just tried to steal this girl's purse. I just want you to know that you have nothing to worry about in this neighborhood, you will always be safe."

This story suggests a different relationship to the neighborhood than that presented by the entrepreneur who trumpeted the thrill of the edge. Nina does not simply stride willfully through a landscape of stimulating dangers. Instead, she locates a sense of community forged through shared space,

offering security for members via practices of informal—and apparently brutal—social control. Even the prostitutes, committing victimless crimes, are incorporated into the sense of community; they are remembered as "pretty nice." For Nina, activities that might suggest to outsiders the breakdown of social order were in fact governed by deep norms of community. Further, this community offered her a veil of protection: "I felt safe because people knew me, and although they were mostly gang bangers, they were also...It was a neighborhood and that made me part of it."

Unlike many of the artists and hipsters entering the neighborhood, Nina was born in the city and was already confident about negotiating a heterogeneous street environment. She is of mixed race background, which she acknowledges as a potential factor in her acceptance by the local Hispanic community. "I have the kind of skin tone that I can kind of pass. Here in the United States, people tend to think I'm Puerto Rican. In Europe, people think I'm Arabic. I blend in a lot." A graduate of Lincoln Park High School on the near North Shore, she studied dance for five years of her adolescence and attended the Art Institute, studying Fine Arts for several years without taking a degree. In fact, she was enrolled in the Art Institute during the late 1980s, and she worked as a manager at the Blue Note, a popular bar with hip young urbanites in the community area of Backtown, next door to Wicker Park. Nina's education and involvement in the arts largely distinguished her from the Hispanic community that was mostly working class, with a high proportion of foreign-born residents. Nonetheless, the combination of being a woman in the heavily male-dominated neighborhood arts scene and being nonwhite may have contributed to her being more readily accepted by the locals, at least provisionally.

Their greater risk of sexual assault no doubt makes women less likely to glamorize the threat of urban violence. Nina did not experience her navigation of the streets as an affirmation of her own roughness: rather, she emphasized the importance of forging provisional bonds with the varying groups within the neighborhood as a key to personal security. On several occasions I was told similar stories by female participants in the arts scene about the young Hispanic men who patrolled the streets offering a "heads-up" on potential dangers and indicating that they would keep an eye out for the woman's safety.

White male informants likewise indicated that over time they would be "recognized" by Hispanic locals and thus were less likely to be hassled, but this arrangement was generally described as implicit, a sign of respect rather than of community per se. Jimmy Garbe, a musician and longtime bartender at the Rainbo Club, recalls, "We coexisted pretty well, I think. In terms of violence, if you kept to yourself you'd feel like you weren't involved in it. I think it scared a lot of people, but for me I'd be walking down the street, hear gunshots, and I'd make sure it wasn't around me, and I'd be alright."

Whatever the level of reported interaction, young Hispanic men enjoyed a peculiar hegemony on the streets, similar to the situation Elijah Anderson describes of young black men in a gentrifying Philadelphia neighborhood,[5] in contrast to their marginal positions in the larger social order.

For male participants in the arts scene, who were mostly white and hailed from relatively privileged backgrounds, navigating the gritty streets involved adopting an "outlaw aesthetic," expressed through both dress and demeanor, that was similar to the persona that Norman Mailer attributed to the "existential hipster" during the 1950s. Such personal styles were intended to mark them as different from mainstream society and to help them blend into the local scene as they experienced it. This persona was not something that they necessarily arrived with; instead, they typically tell a story of an evolutionary process in which hip mastery

of the street grows out of the situational context of the local field. The sculptor Alan Gugel, who received an art degree from a rural midwestern university, describes himself as having initially been "like a total outsider from all this. I came here [to Chicago, in the mid-1980s] from South Dakota, so I'm a bumblefuck; yeah, I grew up on a farm, went to a little college town in Minnesota. I never saw a city of larger than about forty-five hundred people."

He clearly viewed his inexperience as making him inadequate to the challenges posed by the neighborhood street. But that would change.

Alan adopted an aesthetic typical of the 1990s urban hipster—tattoos, secondhand clothes, and stringy, unwashed hair—in order to successfully navigate the uneven neighborhood social terrain.

> [Wicker Park] was not a place for folks who in any way look like they're a part of regular society to be hanging out in. And that was one of the things I learned real quickly in Wicker Park, is that if you don't fit in, you're going to have trouble. If you don't look like the greasy slimy artist, you know, you're just going to be accosted left and right. And it happened to me many times when I moved here. I got beat up and pushed around and robbed and everything else. [So I said,] "Okay, I'll turn into a vampire." And it wasn't like I actually make a conscious decision. It was sort of like a gradual process, over a period of time, it was like my whole appearance, from "good little white boy from South Dakota" changed into like "now I can walk down an alley street in the city of Chicago and deal with the scariest people you'd meet there."

The mode of social performance Alan describes is not affected simply to repel danger, though; artists in the scene perform for their peers at least as much as for potential assailants. Adoption of the appropriate demeanor and dress quickly became a means through which insiders were distinguished from outsiders in the art and music scene, especially as gentrification increasingly eased the sense of real danger. Further, through the circuits of fashion and media, such styles are spread from the gritty urban milieu, evoking only an enticing *fantasy* of grit and danger in more sanitized locales.[6]

Though women in the neighborhood certainly had their own methods of distancing themselves from mainstream society, I never heard one describe the navigating of alley streets with the same level of bravado. While women were a visible nonentity, and well represented among the success stories of the arts scene, there is nonetheless a distinct articulation of male privilege in the normative neo-bohemian construction of the edge.[7] Liz Phair, who was among the first Wicker Park musicians to achieve wide-spread critical and popular recognition (*Spin* named her recording debut its "album of the year" for 1993), has often tweaked the macho pretensions of the male-dominated neighborhood music scene, for example by titling her first album "Exile in Guyville." . . .

"The Odd and Charming Refuse of Humanity"

As we can see, the evocation of diversity, both the key value of multiculturalists and the linchpin of much contemporary marketing discourse,[8] is an important part of the ideology expressed by the avatars of Wicker Park's new bohemia. In contrast to theories of the city as trending toward increased homogenization and sanitization in response to the demands of new residents, diversity here is taken to be a central principle of urban authenticity, and the definition of diversity typically proffered by local artists gives special value to the illicit

and the bizarre. For an admittedly small but disproportionately influential class of taste makers, elements of the urban experience that are usually considered to be an aesthetic blight become instead symbols of the desire to master an environment characterized by marginality and social instability.

Many of the young artists and aspirants making their way into the scene in its nascent stages came from backgrounds quite different from the world of the streets they would encounter in Wicker Park. Still, they were steeped in the long traditions of the artist in the city, traditions that provided a particular lens with which to interpret their new environment. Delia, a film student at the Art Institute, recalls:

> being a corn-fed midwestern girl walking into Wicker Park, I had never seen a six-way intersection before. But it kind of reminded me of how Greenwich Village looked on TV. Kind of gritty inner city, cars, *homeless people*. So it was pretty much a big culture shock. I had spent most of my time in either [a] rural kind of pseudo suburban area, or a medium-sized town like Columbus. So there was nothing like that kind of energy. I loved it. I loved the colors and the people and the sounds and the streets and the whole bustle. It was great.

With this account, Delia calls to mind what has become a bohemian cliché—the wide-eyed novitiate both shocked and seduced by the gritty glamour of the big city. This narrative animated literary efforts in nineteenth-century Paris that included Balzac's *Lost Illusions* and Flaubert's *Sentimental Education*.[9] But now the stranger in a strange land is not a French lad from the provinces but a striking black woman with a head of flaring dreadlocks, and her fantasies of the city were nurtured not only by books but by mass-mediated images—Greenwich Village on television.

Of further interest is Delia's inclusion of the visibly unhoused in her description of the energy-infused street. The years of gentrification since the period Delia describes have not eradicated this presence, and it complicates a general story in which city elites wage war on the homeless population as part of a comprehensive strategy to render the streets more pleasing to elite consumers. Regenia Gagnier observes the tendency among developers and politicians to cast homelessness as an aesthetic rather than a social problem with the homeless ineligible for civic consideration because of the twin crimes of being propertyless and unsightly.[10] When the Viacom-owned network MTV, the contemporary avatar of hip consumerism, set up shop in the neighborhood to film its reality TV program *The Real World*, cameras were reportedly turned off whenever a homeless person entered the frame.

The assumption is that the class of residents and/or viewers that commercial interests wish to attract will hold a uniformly adverse view of these unwashed street people. Yet Delia tells a different story, one in which homelessness is still an aesthetic principle, but now as part of a street panorama that she equates with gritty authenticity. Moreover, Delia, a film student at the Art Institute whose own dramatic persona helped to make the local scene as she worked in important neo-bohemian venues like Urbus Orbis, belongs to a category of residents whose aesthete dispositions cannot be quickly dismissed as unimportant.

Indeed, though the park is no tent city, there are elements of the neighborhood that contribute to its providing what Mitchell Duneier refers to as a "sustaining habitat" for a limited population of unhoused individuals.[11] Some of these elements are enhanced by the economic development of the neighborhood, since the new economic activity increases the density of pedestrian traffic and thus opportunities to make money for panhandlers and informal vendors. As Duneier notes of Greenwich Village, one of the keys to being a sustaining habitat is that at least some of the local residents have dispositions tolerant of the presence of the truly destitute in their midst. Greenwich Village, pretty much the proto-bohemia of United States cultural history, has become an upscale neighborhood, but the educated professionals who reside there nonetheless often evince socially liberal attitudes toward the homeless, particularly insofar as the homeless maintain a certain informally proscribed decorum. The young artists and lifestyle aesthetes who congregate in Wicker Park likewise are sympathetic to the homeless population, whose visible presence continues to counter the overall trend toward increasingly sanitized streets, and thus helps local artists to maintain their sense of neighborhood diversity.

As Duneier indicates, those who make a life on the streets in the neighborhood need not be simply blight on the landscape, but instead may become integrated into the local fabric and flavor of neighborhood life. They become like the "public characters" Jane Jacobs describes,[12] difficult to displace in a neighborhood that continues to trade on gritty bohemian aesthetics despite ongoing gentrification—at least so long as their behavior remains circumspect and their numbers remain manageable. Resourceful street entrepreneurs assure themselves to the distinct local dynamic. One panhandler in the late 1990s made a habit of studying the *Chicago Reader* so that he could alert nighttime revelers to the various entertainment opportunities surrounding them, as in "There's poetry at the Mad Bar tonight. And Subterranean has two bands—$5 cover."

This brings us to the late Wesley Willis, the most unusual of the successes to emerge from the widely hailed Wicker Park music scene of the 1990s. Willis, an African American man born in Chicago's public housing, passed away at the age of 40 in 2003. Willis was a diagnosed schizophrenic intermittently homeless, who in the 1990s came to play an important role in the constitution of the neighborhood as a site of offbeat, funky urban culture. He was unmistakably one of Wicker Park's "public characters." Jim DeRogatis, music critic for the *Chicago Sun-Times*, wrote in 1995, "If you've been to Wicker Park, chances are you've run into Wesley Willis. Willis is a big, burly 31-year-old who's a fixture in Chicago's hippest neighborhood. He walks the streets having agitated conversations with the voices he says he hears in his head."[13]

One of the few individuals from the neighborhood who might reasonably bear the tag "outsider artist," Willis also engaged tangible people on the sidewalks with his push to sell his drawings and CDs, a contemporary version of Greenwich Village's indigent poet Maxwell Bodenheim in the 1960s.[14]

In a different neighborhood, Willis might have languished as an unfortunate casualty of nationwide deinstitutionalization; in Wicker Park, he became a local and then a national celebrity who would tour the country with a backup band of genuine musicians, a group named the Wesley Willis Fiasco, performing his bizarre music. DeRogatis provides this description: "As the group plays powerful, free flowing grooves, Willis takes to the stage to rave about his favorite bands (everyone from Radiohead to Sabalon Glitz) and rant about the things that tick him off (a man who assaulted his mother, the bar closing early, or Casper the Friendly Ghost)."[15]

Though music critics have for the most part discerned little actual talent on display in these performances, Willis numbers among his fans and promoters the local band Urge Overkill and nationally successful musicians including the Beastie Boys, Henry Rollins, and the Red Hot Chili Peppers. With the help of such high-profile support, Willis performed in well-known venues around the country, cut a two-album deal with American Records, and appeared on MTV. When not on tour or hospitalized,

Willis continued to spend his time raving and vending on Wicker Park's sidewalks.

Like many other features of the neo-bohemian scene in Wicker Park, the cult following that Willis achieved has bohemian precedent. Jean-Michel Basquiat's teenage bouts of homelessness in Washington Square Park are a part of the late East Village artist's enduring legend.[16] Even more to the point is the fame afforded to Joe Gould, the Greenwich Village street person sometimes referred to as the "last bohemian," immortalized in Joseph Mitchell's classic essay "Joe Gould's Secret."[17] Ross Wetzsteon writes of Gould, "He transformed vagrancy into an ideal.... Joe Gould wasn't just a bum, he was a bum of a certain genius. He was the leading beneficiary of the Villager's enduring fantasy of a link between the social misfit and the cultural rebel—after all, who better understood society's hypocrisies than society's outcasts?"[18]

A half century after Gould prowled the streets of the Village, Willis would animate similar fantasies among the hip in Chicago and around the country.

Some critics expressed concern over the exploitative nature of turning a mentally ill street person into a rock 'n' roll novelty act. Buddy Seigal wrote in the *Los Angeles Times*, "In trumpeting Willis, [rock musicians] seem to be laughing not so much with him as at him, in a 'let's hang out with a retard and have a giggle' display of rank insensitivity, mindless pack mentality and rampant egotism."[19] But as Libby Copeland notes in a *Washington Post* feature on Willis, for others "he's the ultimate punk. He says what he wants. He's so...authentic!"[20] Erik Wulkowicz, a longtime participant in the local arts scene, argues that Willis' appeal lay in his authenticity. "Here's a guy that just because he's crazy and absolutely real has entertainment value. Some people for a good reason want to do something with him. The rest of them suspect that they are trying to cash in on the guy." Meanwhile, Willis seemed to genuinely enjoy performing and clearly benefited materially, as his minor celebrity showed surprising longevity. The money he earned rescued him from the streets, and his band mates doubled as caretakers on the road: "They forward messages to him, remind him to bathe," Copeland wrote.[21] Things could have been worse, and, of course, for many who are similarly afflicted, things are worse.

The celebration of Wesley Willis by hip tastemakers runs counter to the elite strategies of concealment and containment that Mike Davis demonstrates are typically directed against the homeless, some of whom are mentally ill, in Los Angeles.[22] On the other hand, the spotlight shone on this "outsider" also obscures the legions of uninvited schizophrenic individuals trapped in destitution and desperation. They occupy quasi-visceral street environments and the overcrowded prisons of their own minds, often doing harm to themselves and sometimes, dramatically, to others. The revanchist policies enacted by civic elites around the country against such individuals show that those individuals lack rights in the city. How can they be citizens in a neoliberal landscape where participating in the consumer cornucopia is the mark of legitimate belonging?

Willis, on the other hand, is granted citizenship in the world of hipster culture, but it is what Lauren Berlant might call an "infantile citizenship," secured by the schizophrenia that renders him apparently transparent and therefore "real" for his audience. Willis embodies nostalgia for jaded culture-industry veterans like Rollins or the Beastie Boys for a time when bohemia could be experienced as simple utopia, the fantasy of the rock 'n' roll lifestyle. Licensed by a mental illness that made him "like a child" and therefore free to articulate any sentiment, Willis could happily declare desires that bohemians typically let go unspoken: "I want to be famous and rich." Meanwhile, a young neighborhood Internet entrepreneur whom I interviewed was effusive about Willis as evidence of the neighborhood's offbeat character, and, yes, diversity.

Heroin Chic

The relationship to the exotic on Wicker Park streets whether represented by Willis' schizophrenia or by the presence of gang members, prostitutes, and users of illegal drugs, was not limited to cool voyeurism. For Alan, the industrial sculptor and erstwhile self-described "bumblefuck" from South Dakota, development of a heroin habit of his own sped the acquisition of the appropriate dispositions for negotiating the terrain and becoming in some sense an insider. Indeed, drug use was one way that newcomers would straddle multiple worlds in the streets. The norms of this complex street environment, in which definitions of hipness became intertwined with the "underworld," are embodied in the dispositions of participants—the drug habit bleeds into habitus, with this new style not necessarily experienced as a "conscious decision."

The Wicker Park drug scene captured many participants who were also active in the arts, and it had an impact on the articulation of style on Wicker Park streets even for non-users. This aesthetic made its way into the mass fashion market during the 1990s in the form of "heroin chic," valorizing forms of the street found in locales like Wicker Park and New York's East Village. Michael Warson confirms that "every now and then the two worlds [of artists and drug dealers] merged. There were a few artists I know that had to leave the neighborhood because they got involved in the drug aspect.... You'd always know that so-and-so was in rehab." Alan himself successfully kicked his habit, and has gone on to commercial and critical success as an artist.

Drug use in the neighborhood does not merely reflect reckless hedonism. Experimentation with narcotics is also part of the bohemian tradition, a well-known feature of the biography of many admired cultural producers. In a *New York Times* article marking the death of Layne Staley, lead singer of the Seattle-based grunge rock band Alice in Chains, John Pareles writes, "A Romantic ideology that predates rock glorifies the self-destructive artist as one who's too honest and delicate for this world. As the myth goes, artists use drugs or alcohol to free up inspiration and insulate their sensitive souls from ordinary life."[23]

Continually informed and updated by songs like the Velvet Underground's "Heroin" and "Waiting for the Man," or books like William S. Burroughs' *Naked Lunch* and *Junky* and Jim Carroll's *The Basketball Diaries*,[24] a mythos surrounding drug abuse forms among the bohemian urban intelligentsia, and in Wicker Park, track marks were available for interpretation as markers of bohemian authenticity. Though drug use is stigmatized in many social venues, occasionally it seemed to have the opposite effect in Wicker Park. Daniel, a young denizen of the scene who did not use hard drugs, recalls, "When I moved into the neighborhood, I was told, 'You've got a good look for this neighborhood. Skinny, the stringy hair, the beard— you look like you *might* do heroin.'" In another interaction I witnessed, a young woman was being advised against romantically pursuing a local artist who had a well-known heroin habit. "But he's so cool," she protested.

For the young artists in Wicker Park, the effect of heroin is not merely sensual; it conditions aesthetic appearance and nurtures a profoundly blasé outlook, the very epitome of a "cool" disposition. One Wicker Park artist and recovering addict suggests that sensual and aesthetic effects dovetail in the scene: "It's part of the idea of being relaxed and enjoying yourself and being willing to participate in what might be victimless crimes for the sake of *aesthetics* or entertainment." Still, the drawbacks

of heroin use are also well known, and most people, including most Wicker Park residents, resist heavy involvement. But the "look" associated with drug use, like other aesthetic principles, can be disembodied from the practice. Heroin chic represented the crossover of this aesthetic to mass consumption. Model Zoë Fleischaeur seemed to blame her own addiction on the aesthetic principles dominating the New York fashion world in the mid-1990s. "They wanted models that looked like junkies. The more skinny and fucked up you look, the more everyone thinks you're fabulous."[25]

NOTES

1. Christopher Mele, "The Process of Gentrification in Alphabet City," in *From Urban Village to East Village*, ed. Janet L. Abu-Lughod (Oxford, UK: Blackwell, 1994), p. 186.

2. Reymundo Sanchez's memoir detailing his life as a Latin King takes place around Wicker Park and the neighboring district of Humboldt Park in the mid-1980s. Sanchez, *My Bloody Life* (Chicago: Chicago Review Press, 2000).

3. See Elijah Anderson, *Code of the Street: Decency, Violence, and the Moral Life of the Inner City* (New York: Norton, 1999), for a discussion of the relationship between respectability and criminality in a low-income urban community.

4. Simple loitering in low-income communities has been increasingly construed as a sign of disorder and, according to the "broken windows" model of community control, is therefore likely to contribute to more serious criminal activities. See Robert Jackal, "What Kind of Order?" *Criminal Justice Ethics* (summer 2003): 54–67; Robert J. Sampson and Steven Raudenbush, "Seeing Disorder: Neighborhood Stigma in the Social Construction of 'Broken Windows,'" *Social Psychology Quarterly* 67 (2003): 319–342.

5. Elijah Anderson, *Streetwise: Race, Class, and Change in an Urban Community* (Chicago: University of Chicago Press, 1990).

6. See Malcolm Gladwell, "The Coolhunt," and Alex Kotlowitz, "False Connections," both in *The Consumer Society Reader*, ed. Juliet B. Schot and Douglas B. Holt (New York: New Press, 2002).

7. See Angela McRobbie's critique of the masculinist assumptions of subcultural studies, "Settling Accounts with Subcultures: A Feminist Critique," *Screen Education* 34 (1980): 37–49.

8. Naomi Klein, *No Logo: Money, Marketing, and the Growing Anti-Corporate Movement* (New York: Picador, 1999).

9. Honore de Balzac, *Lost Illusions* (New York: Viking, [1843] 1976); Gustave Flaubert, *Sentimental Education* (New York: Viking, [1869] 1991).

10. Regenia Gagnier, *The Insatiability of Human Wants* (Chicago: University of Chicago Press, 2000), p. 210.

11. Mitchell Duneier, *Sidewalk* (New York: Farrar, Straus, and Giroux, 1999).

12. Jane Jacobs, *The Death and Life of Great American Cities* (New York: Basic Books, 1961).

13. Jim DeRogatis, "Outsider Influence: Singer's Raves Spur Exploitation Debate," *Chicago Sun-Times*, 1995, p. NC5.

14. Maxwell Bodenheim, *My Life and Loves in Greenwich Village* (New York: Bridgehead Press, 1954).

15. DeRogatis, "Outsider Influence," p. 4.

16. Phoebe Hoban, *Basquiat:A Quick Killing in Art* (New York: Penguin, 1998).

17. Joseph Mitchell, *Up in the Old Hotel* (New York: Vintage, 1993).

18. Ross Wetzsteon, *Republic of Dreams:Greenwich Village, the American Bohemia 1910–1960* (New York: Simon and Schuster, 2002), p. 419.

19. Buddy Seigal, "Willis: Both Disturbed, Disturbing," *Los Angeles Times*, March 16, 1996, p. F2.

20. Libby Copeland, "Songs in His Head: Wesley Willls Is Haunted by Voices. His Music Helps to Drown Them Out," *Washington Post*, November 24, 2000, p. C1.

21. Ibid.

22. Mike Davis, *City of Quartz* (New York: Verso, 1990). See also Madeleine Stoner, "The Globalization of Urban Homelessness," in *From Chicago to L.A.*, ed. Michael Dear (Thousand Oaks, CA: Sage, 2002).

23. John Pareles, "When the Suffering Undoes the Artist," *New York Times*, April 28, 2002, 2:1.

24. William S. Burroughs, *Junky* (New York: Ace, 1953); Burroughs, *Naked Lunch* (Paris: Olympia, 1959); Jim Carroll, *The Basketball Diaries* (Bolinas, CA: Tombouctou, 1978).

25. Quoted in Katie Schoemer, "Rockers, Models, and the New Allure of Heroin," *Newsweek*, August 26, 1996.

REFERENCES

Anderson, Elijah. 1990. *Streetwise: Race, Class, and Change in an Urban Community.* Chicago: University of Chicago Press.
———. 1999. *Code of the Street: Decency, Violence, and the Moral Life of the Inner City.* New York: Norton.
Balzac, Honore de. [1843] 1976. *Lost Illusions.* New York: Viking.
Burroughs, William S. 1953. *Junky.* New York: Ace.
———. 1959. *Naked Lunch.* Paris: Olympia.
Carroll, Jim. 1978. *The Basketball Diaries.* Bolinas, CA: Tombouctou.
Davis, Mike. 1990. *City of Quartz.* New York: Verso.
Duneier, Mitchell. 1992. *Slim's Table.* Chicago: University of Chicago Press.
———. 1999. *Sidewalk.* New York: Farrar, Straus, and Giroux.
Flaubert, Gustave. [1869] 1991. *Sentimental Education.* New York: Viking.
Gagnier, Regina. 2000. *The Insatiability of Human Wants.* Chicago: University of Chicago Press.
Gladwell, Malcolm. 1997. "The Coolhunt." In *The Consumer Society Reader.* Juliet B. Schor and Douglas B. Holt (eds.). New York: New Press, 2002.

Hoban, Phoebe. 1998. *Basquiat: A Quick Killing in Art*. New York: Penguin.

Jackal, Robert. 2003. "What Kind of Order?" *Criminal Justice Ethics* (summer): 54–67.

Jacobs, Jane. 1961. *The Death and Life of Great American Cities*. New York: Basic Books.

Klein, Naomi. 1999. *No Logo: Money, Marketing, and the Growing Anti-Corporate Movement*. New York: Picador.

Kotlowitz, Alex. 2002. "False Connections," in *The Consumer Society Reader*, Juliet Schor and Douglas Holt, eds. New York: New Press.

Mailer, Norman. 1959. "The White Negro." In *Advertisements for Myself*. New York: Putnam.

McRobbie, Angela. 1980. "Settling Accounts With Subcultures: A Feminist Critique." *Screen Education* 34: 37–49.

Mele, Christopher. 1994. "The Process of Gentrification in Alphabet City." In *From Urban Village to East Village*, Janet L. Abu-Lughod, ed. Oxford, UK: Blackwell.

Mitchell, Joseph. 1998. *Up in the Old Hotel*. New York: Vintage.

Sampson, Robert, and Steven Raudenbush. 2003. "Seeing Disorder: Neighborhood Stigma in the Social Construction of 'Broken Windows.'" *Social Psychology Quarterly* 67: 319–342.

Sanchez, Reymundo. 2000. *My Bloody Life*. Chicago: Chicago Review Press.

Schoemer, Katie. 1996. "Rockers, Models, and the New Allure of Heroin." *Newsweek*, August 26.

Siegler, Dylan. 1998. "Phair's Rise Gave Women More Industry Validity." *Billboard*, July 4.

Wetzsteon, Ross. 2002. *Republic of Dreams: Greenwich Village, the American Bohemia 1910–1960*. New York: Simon and Schuster.

10

ANDREW DEENER

NEIGHBORHOOD SYMBIOSIS (2011)

In this account, Andrew Deener documents neighborhood change in Venice, the famous beach-front neighborhood in Los Angeles that underwent rapid gentrification in the 1990s and 2000s. He examines how retailers, residents, activists, and real-estate agents worked together to take "symbolic ownership" of the area and to market it to the affluent as a "hip" place to live, visit, and do business.

Abbot Kinney Boulevard is a commercial artery that runs diagonally through the center of Venice, a famous coastal community in Los Angeles. In recent years, the street has gained national and international popularity as a site of innovative design, dining, and commerce due to its array of home-design shops, restaurants, cafés, and trendy boutiques. The street consists of independently owned businesses that activists and merchants furiously protect, resisting the encroachment of corporate retailers, or what they call "formula retail chains." Many residents and merchants describe the street's stores and their wares as "anticorporate." When Tom, a shop owner in his early forties, began to remodel his commercial space to open in the early 2000s, he said that residents stopped by on a daily basis to voice their concerns about rumors, although untrue, that his business would become the street's first chain store. "I think the greatest fear of everybody on Abbot Kinney and maybe even in Venice," Tom said, "is that Abbot's Habit will become a Starbucks."

Handmade, vintage, and craft themes are central to the street's new identity. Store owners purposely organize their spaces and seek out objects to sell that constitute a vintage look and feel. They are selling both a type of product and a particular set of values. A jewelry boutique displays its one-of-a-kind products on top of a giant recycled pharmacy chest with dozens of small drawers, which the owner says she found on the street. In another store, a craftswoman has constructed display tables and wooden shelves from scratch, handpainted them, and strategically scraped and damaged the wood so that it appears weathered and old. The street incorporates a new incarnation of the all-in-one store. Instead of the once popular five and dimes or the classic thrift shops or even the omnipresent warehouse stores of the modern era, the all-in-one theme matches the street's artisanal trends. One shop integrates vintage clothing, works of art, and a hair salon. An arts and crafts co-op sells handmade cards, jewelry, lampshades, and other original works of art. Paintings for sale hang on the walls of various stores that claim to be both "clothing boutique and art exhibit," "coffee bar and art exhibit," "bookstore and art exhibit," or "hair salon and art exhibit." Even restaurateurs, architects, and developers abide by this logic. Developers label new innovative apartment designs where units sell for several million dollars each as "artist lofts." A *Los Angeles Magazine* writer, reviewing a new restaurant, describes its "broad wooden counters and wrought-iron inside and its yard sale furniture amid stone bulwarks in the courtyard" as lending the space an "appealing frankness."[1]

New retailers, residents, activists, and real-estate capitalists have collectively produced rituals, themes, and symbols on and around Abbot Kinney Boulevard that are attractive to a new, wealthier class of hip urban consumers who prefer ethically and carefully manufactured products, foods, and designs. They claim *symbolic ownership* over the street's identity; that is, they control the aesthetic presentation, public perception, and social and economic utility of this social space in order to secure the street's distinguishing features in Los Angeles. One neighborhood newspaper celebrated the street's newfound success as "Brand Venice," defining it according to the principles of "innovation, independence, and community."[2]

The new identity of Abbot Kinney builds on Venice's bohemian reputation, which dates back to the 1950s. Venice was once the center of Southern California's beat culture, a major site of hippie movements, and the home of L.A.'s most influential artists. Despite the attention to creative designs and craftsmanship, the street's new features and functions are quite different from its previous social and economic organization. Called West Washington Boulevard prior to 1989, Abbot Kinney was once a racial, ethnic, and socioeconomic mixing ground. Long-standing residents recall black-owned businesses, a teen center for African-American youth, artist studios, wholesale businesses, and affordable secondhand thrift stores. Political activists, from different racial, ethnic, and socioeconomic backgrounds, worked and organized in offices on the street. They advocated for more affordable housing; wrote about the protection of low-income residents in the left-wing neighborhood newspaper, *Free Venice Beach Head*; and planned a statewide and then national Peace and Freedom Party to counter the pro-war stances of the two major political parties (Haag 1978). Moreover, the street was home to Project Action, an African-American community organization responsible for building fourteen housing projects during the 1970s in the adjacent section of Venice called Oakwood.

Abbot Kinney's diversity of uses has gradually disappeared, and its overarching collective identity has been transformed into a more exclusive locale. Despite its current reputation as a site of high-status consumption, it maintains its proximity to racially, ethnically, and socioeconomically diverse residential surroundings. Oakwood is historically a low-income and working-class black and Latino neighborhood. It has long withstood the pressures of gentrification when compared to other adjacent Venice districts where middle- and upper-class invasions have been commonplace for more than four decades. Oakwood houses an aging homeowning black community, contains fourteen federally subsidized housing projects largely occupied by Latinos and African Americans, and remains the home of the Shoreline Crips, an African-American gang that has engaged in wars with local Latino gangs, such as the Venice 13 from Venice and the Culver City Boys from the nearby Mar Vista Gardens Projects in Culver City. The worst of the violence occurred during a ten-month span in 1993 and 1994 when seventeen people were murdered in Oakwood and over fifty more people were injured (Umemoto 2006).

Different sets of local actors, embedded in networks and coalitions with distinct agendas, have reshaped the symbiotic relationship between Abbot Kinney Boulevard and Oakwood. At one time, Oakwood's identity and residents influenced the daily interactions of this up-and-coming locale. Yet as retailers, activists, and developers take symbolic ownership of the street they also distance themselves from this recent past. The new classification of the street as a site of creative and high-status consumption idealizes middle- and upper-income buying habits as authentic community practices, imposing a clear-cut boundary between Oakwood's diversity and Abbot Kinney Boulevard's exclusivity. This social and economic distance enables real-estate agents to redirect the symbiotic relationship between these two places, readily using the boulevard as a symbol to propel Oakwood's gentrification.

Commercial Change and Competing Cultures

Over the last four decades, West Washington Boulevard became Abbot Kinney Boulevard. Reinventing the street's identity was a gradual process that required local actors to take into account existing community functions.

Different groups maintained ties to West Washington Boulevard, and the street housed a range of social, political, and economic activities. As newcomers moved in and tried to change the boulevard's identity, they faced competing interests and interpretations of its local function.

African Americans who still live in Oakwood have fond memories of Abbot Kinney as a place where as recently as the 1980s they had felt comfortable spending time. Marcella, in her late fifties, whose family has lived in Oakwood for decades, says, "There was a time when this street had a lot of artists' studios and bargain stores and inexpensive restaurants. It wasn't all expensive stores like it is now, and there were none of those buildings, those office buildings or artist lofts. It wasn't just for rich people." James, a black man in his early forties, grew up in Oakwood and his cousins, uncle, and grandparents still live there. He claims, "Everybody from Oakwood, this used to be all the stomping grounds right here on Abbot Kinney. This used to be everything. Used to have the beauty salon, the night clubs, the youth foundation. It was all good." Natasha, an African-American woman in her early fifties who has lived in Venice her entire life, also recalls the historical connections between Oakwood and Abbot Kinney.

> When I was a kid, Abbot Kinney had restaurants, like Lucy's restaurant. We used to have the barbeque place that's [still] there now. We used to have a haircut—the barbershop, ya know, just like the movie *Barbershop*. You could go in there and learn everything you ever wanted to know about anybody and everybody in the community. There were also artists and they would allow us kids to come in there and if we wanted to work with the paints or tempers or whatever, they'd let you. It was really a fun place to be…. In the

'70s and early '80s…there was the teen center, which was great. We could go in there and play pool and watch movies. Kane Davis [who directed it] was good. He had books, all kinds of books on everything.…Any kid, free of charge [could participate]. All you had to do was sign in, because I guess he had to show to his funding that he was servicing the community, and it was somewhere to go, and it kept you out of trouble. You could go there after school, and the first thing that he wanted you to do was your homework. And that was great. Because everybody did their homework. Then after you did, he and the people that were helping him checked your homework. Then and only then could you go play pool or do the weightlifting, the dancing, the drumming. He had all kinds of activities.

Before the boulevard became a popular commercial zone, merchants had a difficult time surviving solely from retail sales. Many stores on the street were a mixture of wholesale and retail, and others provided a range of services to increase their profits and consumer base. For instance, a restaurant called the Merchants of Venice, now the site of a popular and upscale restaurant and lounge called Hal's Bar and Grill, combined retail, restaurant, and repair functions. It sold the very furniture on which people eating breakfast and lunch were sitting, and to make some extra cash, the owners also took on furniture refinishing projects.

Leslie, a white woman in her midfifties, moved her business and home from her boardwalk apartment to West Washington Boulevard in 1982 because she needed more space for her growing manufacturing and wholesale jewelry business, and she wanted to remain close to her employees. She describes the street at that time as mixed in its economic activity.

LESLIE: I went looking for a commercial space to move our business into, but all my workers lived here [in Oakwood] and many of them didn't have cars. So they walked to deliver the work to me and so I was really looking for a commercial location that my workers could still access, but that I could have a regular location to do my shipping and billing and do my office work and whatever.

ANDREW: Were you among the first to do this [establish a retail store] on this street?

LESLIE: No, there were stores here when I came and they came and went and came and went and came and went. It was always changing. People trying out the street, not figuring out what it takes to make it here, and usually blowing it in some way.… [T]he ones who stayed the longest were like ourselves because we weren't relying on the retail business to stay here. We had this whole manufacturing business in the back and that was really the core of our business. Back in the '80s, there were like ten of us who were kind of the stable merchants here. And everybody else came and left, and we all had a wholesale business. We all had retail too, but people who didn't know about the wholesale, well, they never talked to us. They never came and said, "How do you pay the rent every month?" Because I would have said, let me show you our back room.

Many of the stores opening during this period failed, and the ones that remained often stood next to aging beach cottages; abandoned, boarded-up, and graffiti-laced buildings; and empty and overgrown lots. Moreover, store owners faced complications when it came to manufacturing an orderly retail environment on the border of Oakwood, especially due to the ongoing and traumatizing gang violence. Lila, a lifelong African-American resident in her sixties, says that Oakwood's citizens viewed the attempt to change the reputation and character of Abbot Kinney in the early 1990s to make it attractive to upper-income cultural consumers as bizarre, both a sign of the enormous social distance (if not physical distance) between the two neighborhoods and a sign of ignorance among shoppers who seemed unaware of the fact that violence readily spilled over to the commercial street.

> You'd be surprised, how many people that weren't black were walking through the neighborhood [of Oakwood] when there was a race war going on.... And we sit there and look at them, and say, "They are so unaware of what's going on. They just don't know, and the police are trying to keep it so quiet." People are down here on Abbot Kinney and they're having their tea and coffee, and just kicking it and just having a grand ol' time, looking at the little boutiques, and meanwhile, there's murder going on around them. It's stupid, ya know? But it was happening.

Gang-related events in bordering Oakwood seeped into the commercial scene, producing moments of fear and danger that impeded the street's transformation. At the height of the violence during 1994, a group of Oakwood activists influenced the street's reputation by getting people to pay attention to Oakwood's internal strife. A local African-American group called Pathfinders distributed two thousand flyers to the boulevard's customers. The flyers read: "WARNING: UNSAFE AREA. White Customers Shopping in this Section of Venice May be Shot Dead by Mexican Gangs—Without Notice." Timothy Crayton, a lead member of the group, told a *Los Angeles Times* reporter at that time, "We're not really here to hurt anyone, but we're dying here....We're tired of carrying casket after casket. The smell of death is everywhere, and we're trying to share our misery."[3]

As new retailers moved in, they quickly learned about the potential dangers of the area. Amy, who opened up a store in the late '90s, describes the street during that time as more "hoodish" and a "dicey place" to live and work.

> I would be here [at the store] till ten or eleven at night, painting, making things to sell, and the guy who owned the [store] two doors down would wait for me, because he didn't like me being in the neighborhood by myself.... There was a drive-by shooting when I first came here, ya know? That was some scary shit happening.... There was a dead guy that was right in front of this house [pointing]. And I had rented this house [right near the house she pointed to] when I had the store too. I lived here and then had the store for a while. And the things we saw. You had to be aware, much more aware, because it was definitely scary.

In order to distance the street from its connections with Oakwood's identity, activists, merchants, developers, and journalists publicized a new set of meanings about this commercial artery as "Brand Venice." The branding of the street had a cumulative impact: it attracted new stores, enticed new development, increased rent values, and reconfigured the relationship between Abbot Kinney and Oakwood.

Publicizing a New Symbol as Brand Venice

In response to a cycle of false starts, local business owners and activists proposed to change the name of the street from West Washington Boulevard to Abbot Kinney Boulevard. Naming it after the original developer of Venice, they hoped to publicize it, as one store owner says, as "the newest street in Los Angeles." In the past, people looking to shop there would commonly get lost, because the street runs diagonally to other main roads. Often visitors traveled to the other Washington Boulevard that separates Venice from Marina Del Rey to the south. Sarah, a white woman in her early fifties who has rented an apartment in Venice since 1980, explains: "I had no idea Abbot Kinney was even there. At that time, it was West Washington, but for years, I didn't even know it existed."

Leslie was influential in organizing the street's name change. She describes how a small group with intimate knowledge of the political process was able to bring enough pressure to bear on public officials to facilitate this change. They organized locally and established connections with city representatives.

> LESLIE: When it was still called West Washington that was a dilemma, because I used to do print advertising, in like the *LA Weekly* and the *LA Reader* who were the two big weekly papers at the time. And I always knew when the papers hit the streets because people would start calling and say, "Which Washington are you on?"...Then the Venice Action Committee was the one that did the main push for the name change of Abbot Kinney, and I was very, very much involved in that. There were really like three of us who did most of the work on that. And it took us two years to get the name change. Ruth Galanter was a new councilwoman at the time and she was, well, she didn't want to piss anyone off so she was very conservative. Ya know, we got all the signatures of the property owners, which is the requirement—50 percent plus 1. But then she also wanted us to get a majority of the tenants, which meant doing another additional whole campaign.
>
> ANDREW: Getting renters?

> LESLIE: Yeah. So that was a long haul and we wanted it so bad and we got all organized and went downtown to city council and had a great session with the planning and land use committee who was hearing it. And we all came with our little thirty-second speeches so that we wouldn't bore them. And we'd give them the positive reasons why this should happen and you could see these three committee members going like, oh yeah, I've been lost down there before.

At the time of the name change, the West Washington Boulevard Association amended its name to the Abbot Kinney District Association. As an open-membership neighborhood organization made up of a coalition of business owners, developers, and residents who lived on the street, the association took as its first order of business to arrange a beautification effort, much of which resulted in seventy-four palm trees lining the street. With the addition of garbage cans, bike racks, planters around the trees, crosswalks, and an extensive Internet website to catalogue the stores, the association facilitated the appearance of a more contained and orderly shopping atmosphere that slowly attracted new businesses and made the street more appealing to pedestrians and customers.

Despite the name change, newcomers faced the continuing constraints of proximity to Oakwood. In order to further encourage a new neighborhood identity, they "invented rituals" (Hobsbawm and Ranger 1983) that accentuated certain neighborhood historical features while simultaneously ignoring others (Zukin 1995). They endorsed the artistic and bohemian identity of Venice and overlooked the lower-income surroundings, the community's multiclass history, and the recent gang violence. By establishing neighborhood festivals, organizers broke up the monotony of everyday life and allowed certain events to stand out as representative of the neighborhood. For example, the Abbot Kinney District Association drew attention to the neighborhood's artistic history by establishing a small-scale outdoor arts and crafts festival in the 1980s. By the late 1990s and early 2000s, the association became more organized in publicizing the festival, growing it into a large attraction that brings in upward of thirty thousand people each year, as a source of recognition for local business owners (Komaiko 2003, p. E-34). The festival became so central to the street's commercial organization that it renamed itself as the Abbot Kinney Festival Association.

Also, the Venice Art Walk remains one of the most important Los Angeles art events, in which people pay to visit artist studios. Although the individual studios are distributed throughout Venice, the cashiers, the silent auction, and other festivities, including food vendors and musical performances, take place on Abbot Kinney. This event also reframes people's attention toward the narrative of Venice as an influential artistic haven while it physically brings people into this emerging retail zone.

Residents, activists, and merchants draw on certain themes in Venice's history to invent an authentic commercial identity that is disconnected from its actual history. They framed the fashionable bohemia as "anticorporate" and organized a local political movement to ban chain stores. Two local activists, who moved to Venice in the late '80s and late '90s, started a petition campaign called Venice Unchained to preserve the distinct street scene from the invasion of corporate commerce.[4] These activists and their local supporters worry that large-scale, corporate forces threaten the unique character of the commercial neighborhood. They gathered more than four thousand signatures and received the support of the Venice Chamber of Commerce and the Venice Neighborhood Council—a city-funded, locally elected advisory board that represents Venice's interests to the Los Angeles

City Council—to push for an ordinance that would ban future "formula retail" establishments. On the petition they define formula retail as "businesses that are required by contractual or other arrangements to be virtually identical to businesses in other communities including, but not limited to, businesses with standardized architecture, signs, décor, menus, food preparation policies, uniforms, or products."[5]

While activists were struggling to get this ordinance passed in the Los Angeles City Council, the first chain store, a popular purveyor of frozen yogurt called Pinkberry, opened on the street in 2007. Residents were very concerned, because rumors swirled that a Starbucks would follow. Although the Starbucks rumor was untrue, political activists and residents responded by strongly opposing the arrival of any other chain stores. Residents attended meetings and wrote letters to city officials. According to the editors of the local newspaper, *Venice Paper*, "No story since we began covering Venice in 2001 has catalyzed as much spontaneous e-mail and communication as the arrival of the first corporate chain on Abbot Kinney Boulevard."[6]

The response was so overwhelming because newer residents and merchants embraced an official meaning of Abbot Kinney as an anticorporate commercial center despite the retail theme's short-lived history, which only emerged during the '90s following the street's name change and its new retail focus on independent and creative commerce. Nevertheless, one of the founders of Venice Unchained claims, "We feel that so much of L.A. and metropolitan cities look more and more similar....We want to preserve our great city [of Venice] and its originality and character."[7] These relative newcomers to Venice want to safeguard a distinct life style and commercial identity as the "authentic" version of the Venice community experience. Three years after it opened and after the informal boycott by Venice residents, Pinkberry closed its Abbot Kinney store, claiming that it was "underperforming."[8]

The media works with these local actors, taking a central role in providing free discursive publicity for stores and the new cultural trends they create. According to the merchants I interviewed, collectively they have been written up in such magazines and newspapers as *Cargo*, *Casa Brutus* (a Japanese design magazine), *Dwell*, *Interior Design*, the *Los Angeles Times*, the *New York Times*, *Travel Leisure Magazine*, and *Western Interior and Designs*, among others, thus solidifying and publicizing a collective representation of Abbot Kinney as an innovative, trendy, and upscale retail zone. For example, a *Los Angeles Times* article describes the new character of the street in this passage:

> Welcome to the new Abbot Kinney: upscale Abbot Kinney, a place to see and be seen, spot celebrities, eat $8 pancakes, buy $200 jeans, a $1,000 vintage wood school chair ($985 to be exact), or maybe a $2-million loft. (Komaiko 2003, p. E-34)

In addition, there have been a number of articles dedicated to specific businesses, such as this excerpt from the *New York Times* about a long-standing neighborhood bar, which was transformed from a biker bar into a new hip hangout:

> In recent years it had iconic status and few customers. Now the Brig, a 40-year-old bar on Abbot Kinney Boulevard in Venice, has been transformed from a seedy dive for old-timers into a seething hangout for 20-somethings who like their beer served in an environment with attitude. (Anderton 2001, p. F-3)

The attention that the stores and restaurants receive in the media serves as further justification by merchants claiming symbolic ownership over the space and treating Abbot Kinney Boulevard as the "legitimate center" of the Venice neighborhood. Robert, a white man in his early thirties who owns an interior design studio, sums it up by comparing the new street scene to the famous boardwalk attraction at Venice Beach, which is just a short walk away: "The boardwalk is for tourists," he says. "The *real* people from Venice hang out here."

The new symbolic distinction provides an incentive for new store owners looking for an edgy and creative commercial street in Los Angeles. Michael, a white man in his mid-30s who owns a home-design store, moved to Venice from New York City in 2003. He says,

> I was attracted to Venice...just from things I've seen in magazines, like good architecture magazines or design magazines or retail-related stuff. Just that everything that I was ever drawn to in L.A. was in Venice, so I called a friend of mine that has a business....I told her what I wanted to do and she said, well, you definitely need to look at Abbot Kinney. You know, because I told her I wanted to be at the beach. I didn't want to be in town and I also didn't want to be in the traditional home-design area.

Once potential merchants make the decision to open up a store, they reinforce the community theme by presenting storefronts in such a way that sets the stage for how they want others who pass by, window shop, or come into the stores to interpret their commercial identities. They sell handmade products and seek to fuse art, fashion, design, and style. Kim, a white woman in her late twenties, owns a store with her boyfriend, an artist who creates products from scratch. She says, "He's down there himself doing finishing work. Which, I think, that's another response to the corporate thing. They [customers on Abbot Kinney Boulevard] want something that you can't recreate, so you can't Pottery Barn it."

Kazuko, a Japanese woman in her early thirties, moved to Abbot Kinney in 2003 from Tokyo with her husband to open a store that promotes small-time Japanese craftsman and women. She says,

> When we heard of Abbot Kinney, we wanted to try to have a store here. In Japan, many people like to buy a product with the brand name, but here, well, actually there is no brand name. People like to hear a story, like who makes it, like the stories behind it. So it's kind of interesting to talk with customers. Many of our customers like to create things too—like artists, designers, film people, or architects and they like the thing itself. So they check like this way or that way [pretending to hold up an object at different angles and squinting to get a better view of the object].

Developers and architects also design and build in an innovative fashion that blends into the street's overall aesthetic identity by renovating storefronts and breaking ground on new construction sites. Artist lofts carry asking prices of over $3 million for a street-level work studio and a living space above it, bringing together development, commerce, and wealth through the street's cohesive lifestyle theme. As if recognizing the absurdity of calling them artist lofts, one influential developer, Frank Murphy, claims, "Not just artists, but movie producers can work and live here. The location has everything you need: great restaurants and good commercial opportunities."[9] Relative newcomers to Venice want to safeguard a distinct life style, aesthetic appeal, and commercial identity as an authentic version of the Venice community experience. Yet, in doing so, they rewrite history and

further influence the relationship between Abbot Kinney Boulevard and Oakwood.

Neighborhood Symbiosis: Abbot Kinney and Oakwood Revisited

During early attempts to transform Abbot Kinney into an upscale commercial street, Oakwood's residents continued to influence the boulevard scene. African Americans established community organizations on the street and opened businesses; gang members and violence invaded the space; and activists trying to stop the violence used the street as a platform to inform consumers about the detriments of gang activity in the surrounding neighborhood. However, manufacturing Abbot Kinney Boulevard as a symbol of high-class consumption has turned the commercial street into a social and economic boundary. For store owners, craftsmen, and consumers, the changes on the street are about the incorporation of authentic products and life styles. But the choices they make also create a more complex set of neighborhood consequences.

First, they facilitate a set of social norms, such that people can now pinpoint certain behaviors and social categories as signifying "disorder," making it easier to target activity that does not belong. Amy, the owner of a furniture store, reports that she can identify "the normal crew" on the street:

> I would say, in the last three years, it had a big turnover of things that have made it like safer, but at the same time, it goes in waves. There are phases, where all of a sudden, we'll say, who are these people hangin' out? You know, hangin' out in the alley or on the sidewalks even. They don't look like the normal crew. And then there will be like, something will get stolen

that day. We've actually had very few break-ins, but the ones that we had, like the one we left the window open this much [showing about an inch or two between her fingers] and they pulled the phone through the window.

Second, newcomers have come to see Abbot Kinney and Oakwood as disconnected from each other. Leslie says, "There's like an invisible wall along Electric [which runs parallel to Abbot Kinney, directly north of the street], and it's pretty astounding." I ask her, "Even in terms of walking on this street now, if you didn't know there was this Oakwood section, would you have a sense that it existed?" She responds simply, "No!" Paul, a store owner in his late forties, describes the separation in moralistic terms, defining Oakwood as a site of crime and Abbot Kinney as a very safe place to live and work.

> I could be here till one in the morning if I'm doing projects, or midnight and I've never even been hassled.... The crime is in the area, they call it the hood [referring to Oakwood]. And it's just inner-city gang stuff. It doesn't have anything to do with us.... Here's the thing. We leave things outside all the time. We leave that glass table, we leave all the potted stuff and the round metal table. It all stays out and it's still here every morning. We've accidentally left wind chimes hanging. Nothing ever happens.

Third, the coherent retail theme does not simply serve as a magnet for upper-income consumers; it has also become a deterrent for lower-income residents, informing them of their collective position as outsiders. Instead of perceiving Abbot Kinney Boulevard as an example of authentic consumption, longtime Oakwood residents view the street and its commerce as a symbol of social and economic exclusion.

Natasha, an African-American woman and a third-generation Venetian, explains:

> They say it's beautiful now, but beauty is in the eye of the beholder. I don't see it as being beautiful. I don't think walking down Abbot Kinney and looking at a $300 chair that looks like they pulled it out of the alley is beautiful. Because it's been whitewashed or whatever they call that now [referring to the process that makes the products appear worn out]. I don't think a $1,000 dress on Abbot Kinney or what *we* used to call Washington Boulevard is what's beautiful. I just don't. I don't get that kind of beauty and I don't want to. I liked how it was before when it really was bohemian. That's the street I liked.

Mildred, an African-American woman in her late sixties who has lived in Oakwood since she was a child, understands the popular narrative about this retail space, but she does not regard the types of stores on Abbot Kinney Boulevard as more authentic than the corporate formula retail chains in other places. To her, it all signifies "upscale retail." When I ask her if she ever shops on Abbot Kinney Boulevard, she responds,

> No, no. It's much too expensive. It's like Melrose, those—well, any area of that style, it's sort of like, well, it's for tourists. Any place that's for tourists is always [priced] higher. People that don't live here don't know anything about Abbot Kinney, so it's like the same option as Beverly Hills and Melrose. We're at the point where we lump a lot of stuff together in our mind, and ya know, it just sells, just like those other ones do. It's just to sell the image.

Oakwood residents complain that even the yearly festival, which began in the

'80s, has dramatically changed. According to Cynthia, a third-generation African-American woman in her early seventies, the festival formerly celebrated the neighborhood's economic and cultural diversity. Now, older residents with lesser economic resources do not readily participate in the events.

> You can tell the neighborhood's different now. [At the festival] there was no flavor. There were no blacks or Latinos with booths. Or even just walking around, you could see they didn't go. And the reason is it costs too much now to get a booth. Much more than it used to cost. Who can afford over $200 for one day? I went to buy my kids some burgers—$6! I was like, "Kids, we're not eating here today!"

Lastly, creating a visible separation between the two neighborhoods has redirected the symbiotic relationship between them. Abbot Kinney Boulevard has become a mounting symbol of Venice's gentrification, helping to redefine the process of neighborhood change in Oakwood. The new identity of this commercial neighborhood and its wide range of amenities have become important pieces of the selling narrative, overshadowing stories of gang violence. This transformation is quite a change from a decade earlier, when real-estate agents, without any other selling options, would contact existing white homeowners to see if they wanted to purchase additional properties that were vacated. I regularly attended open houses in Oakwood during the 2000s to get a picture of the buying and selling process, and brokers repeatedly brought up the relationship between Oakwood and Abbot Kinney. For example, I asked one broker about the location of a house in terms of safety, and she told me that although the area has had its problems, especially with the housing projects, "Oakwood is now cleaned up." She continued to talk about

the street's proximity to Abbot Kinney Boulevard, which has "all the cute shops and restaurants."[10]

In fact, real-estate companies now advertise Oakwood properties as offering to newcomers a beachfront life style that includes visits to Abbot Kinney Boulevard. A flyer that I received at an open house in 2005, for example, describes an Oakwood home on the market for $1,089,000 in this way:

> This incredibly charming 1908 Venice Beach Craftsman cottage is drenched in sunlight. From the private front yard and garden to the Zen-like backyard with gracious Ash tree, patio, and fountain pond, this home offers the perfect respite from city life! Walk to the beach or Abbot Kinney from this spacious 2+1 with skylights, hardwood and tile floors, high wood beamed ceilings, and an updated kitchen with marble counters and updated full bath. Plus there is an unpermitted detached 1+1 guest house with a secret garden.[11]

Different sets of local actors, embedded in disparate networks, manufactured a new neighborhood symbol that illuminates a particular layer of community life while overlooking others. Venice's anticorporate, bohemian, and artistic identity is used to promote a specific set of community values that stands opposed to wider social, cultural, and economic monotony at the same time that it excludes those without resources to influence the rising consumption narrative.

Conclusion

Many sociologists and urban planners have noted that commerce generates community vitality by drawing people into public spaces.[12] This type of vitality gives rise to a vision of community in which people idealize street-level interactions as integrative and authentic. Yet, when discussing the relationship between commerce and community in a changing neighborhood, we must also ask whose definition of community and whose preferences about commerce are privileged. The construction of a new neighborhood brand for Abbot Kinney Boulevard has had consequences for lower-income and long-term residents who are increasingly excluded from playing a role in defining the neighborhood's future.

The street was formerly the site of a diversity of uses and multiple economic interests, as a wide range of people sustained connections to its social space. By adapting Venice's historic bohemianism into a popular retail theme, people are now able to have distance from the neighborhood's economic diversity, as well as its history of gang violence, both of which were once widely pervasive local narratives. In turn, long-term African-American Oakwood residents, whose definitions of community life clash with the successful thematic creation, are no longer able to influence the uses of this public space or the popular perceptions of the neighborhood in ways that benefit their social position.

Neighborhoods and urban spaces are not isolated zones. The relationship between Oakwood and Abbot Kinney further highlights the interdependence of proximate spaces with distinct identities. Collective actions influencing one place can have a direct spillover effect on another. But it is also important to think about how such relationships change over time. Oakwood's identity formerly had a strong influence on the everyday culture of Abbot Kinney Boulevard, stabilizing its identity as a bohemian scene with diverse uses and functions. The new commercial theme has marked Abbot Kinney as a dividing line between these neighborhoods. As a mounting symbol of high-class consumption, real-estate brokers now use Abbot Kinney Boulevard as part of a new selling narrative for Oakwood. The pervasive commercial symbol has redirected the symbiotic relationship between these two spaces, further compelling the influx of wealthier newcomers who seek out a range of amenities but maintain strong preferences for artisanal trends.

NOTES

1. Kuh (2009).
2. See Rothman (2004). Branding has recently become a major concept in the social sciences. See Greenberg (2008) for a discussion of branding a city.
3. Kramer (1994), p. B-18.
4. See the website www.veniceunchained.org, accessed June 2006.
5. Echavaria (2006).
6. *Venice Paper* (2007).
7. Echavaria (2006).
8. Walker (2010).
9. Wedner (2008).
10. Throughout the 1980s and 1990s, Oakwood slowly was gentrified. The median household value grew from $150,000 in 1979 to $280,000 in 1989 (Umemoto 2006). However, the gang violence in the mid-1990s impacted the gentrification process and the median price of houses sold in Oakwood dramatically decreased. In 1997, for instance, the median sale price was at $161,000 (Goldman 2006) over $100,000 less than the median household value eight years earlier.
11. This is from a document acquired at an open house in Oakwood.
12. See the works of Jane Jacobs (1961), Ray Oldenburg (1999), and Richard Florida (2002) as examples.

REFERENCES

Anderton, Frances. 2001. "A Modernist Temple Replaces a Dive." *New York Times* (September 13): F-3.

Echavaria, Vince. 2006. "Groups Want Chain Store Ban on Boardwalk, Abbot Kinney." *Argonaut* (June 22).

Florida, Richard. 2002. *The Rise of the Creative Class*. New York: Basic Books.

Goldman, Betsy. "Venice Neighborhood Real Estate Sales," Available at http://www.betsysellsvenice.com/convertedpages/realestatesalesneighborhoodpage.html (Accessed June 27, 2006).

Greenberg, Miriam. 2008. *Branding New York: How a City in Crisis Was Sold to the World*. New York: Routledge.

Haag, John. 1978. "The Venice Peace and Freedom Party." *Free Venice Beachhead*, no. 100 (April).

Hobsbawm, Eric, and Terence Ranger (eds.). 1983. *The Invention of Tradition*. New York: Cambridge University Press.

Jacobs, Jane. 1961. *The Death and Life of Great American Cities*. New York: Vintage.

Komaiko, Leslee. 2003. "Between Yesterday and Today." *Los Angeles Times* (September 25): E-34.

Kramer, Jeff. 1994. "Venice Leaders Call Warning Flyers Racist Activism." *Los Angeles Times* (June 26): B-18.

Kuh, Patric. 2009. "Fired Up." *Los Angeles Magazine* (February).

Oldenburg. Ray. 1999. *Great Good Places: Cafés, Coffee Shops, Bookstores, Bars, Hair Salons, and Other Hangouts at the Heart of a Community*. New York: Marlowe.

Rothman, Tibby. 2004. "Brand Venice." *Venice Paper* (September/October).

Umemoto, Karen. 2006. *The Truce: Lessons from an LA Gang War*. Ithaca, N.Y.: Cornell University Press.

Venice Paper. 2007. "This Ain't No Disco—Venice Ain't Loving That Chain Story Feeling" (June 1). http://www.venicepaper.net/pmt_more.php?id=347_0_1_0_M.

Walker, Gary. 2010. "Venice: Effectiveness of Pinkberry Boycott by Anti-Chain Group Debated after Frozen Yogurt Store Closes Its Abbott Kinney Location." *Argonaut* (May 5).

Wedner, Diane. 2008. "The Art of the Venice Art Loft." *Los Angeles Times* (February 17): Real Estate section.

Zukin, Sharon. 1995. *The Cultures of Cities*. Cambridge, Mass.: Blackwell.

PART II

SOCIAL WORLDS, PUBLIC SPACES

//

To be in public in the presence of strangers is perhaps the quintessential urban experience. Physical spaces in which strangers can come together to meet, communicate, conduct business, or simply enjoy the sight and sound of each other are at the very core of modern urban life. At least in theory, "public spaces" are open to all members of a community. In practice, of course, access to many "public" spaces is restricted by race, class, gender, or age.

Public spaces emerge from social practice and are thus a particularly rich area for ethnographic study. Although urban ethnography was forged from the recognition of the importance of the community context in which social life unfolds, it has been equally concerned with social interaction in public spaces within and between these communities. As much effort as it takes to understand the life of an entire district or neighborhood, ethnographers have found that it is as demanding a task to make sense of people's collective activity in specific locales. A simple space such as a bar or restaurant, a street or even a public restroom can reveal a complex social life that takes months or even years to disentangle. In all of these cases, ethnographers have found that what may appear as an unstructured and even spontaneous set of activities at a site may, in fact, be highly structured and predictable once they grasp how it is understood by the people in the situation.

The work of Erving Goffman has greatly influenced urban ethnographic studies of social life in public spaces. Goffman was interested in developing a microsociology of the self in interaction. His project emphasized identifying neglected and taken-for-granted situations and then focusing on how each actor within them defined the situation. While Goffman did conduct some ethnographic research at various points of his career—for example, his in-depth study of a mental hospital—most of the work that inspired later urban ethnographers was not actually ethnographic *per se*. All the same, his attempt—particularly his work to create a sort of lexicon of public behavior in the early 1960s—laid the micro-level groundwork for much urban sociology to follow. Since then, a number of ethnographers have tried to blend Goffman's micro-level insights with more macro-level elements of social structure to see how social identities, such as class, race, gender and sexuality, are created and performed in everyday interactions in public spaces. Their attempt to do so is reflected in each of the selected readings in this section.

The first of these, an excerpt from Laud Humphreys's *Tearoom Trade*, focuses on the self and microinteractions in public.

When reading this excerpt it is important to remember that in the 1960s homosexual relations were stigmatized and "closeted". People who have come of age in recent decades may find it hard to imagine that it was ever that way. At the time, "tearoom" was a slang term for a public restroom in which men had anonymous sexual encounters with other men. As a graduate student in sociology, Humphreys had initially sought to understand the world of gay men by conducting participant observation in gay clubs and bars, places publicly recognized for their gay clientele. He soon realized, however, that such an approach did not encompass the large population of men who engaged in covert sexual relations with each other but who were not generally regarded as "gay" and often did not think of themselves as such. Humphreys spent three years studying "tearooms" which, in this case, were restrooms in public parks. He documented the roles people played in them, the rituals that sustained their actions, the risks involved, and the ways in which these activities related to the men's identities outside the setting. He observed how men announced their desire to engage in anonymous sexual encounters through bodily signals and eye contact. In this excerpt, we see the highly patterned stages of the encounters. Humphreys's research demonstrates how people with a set of interests can come together to carry on activities with complete strangers and how they can do so through agreed-upon patterns of action, without the awareness of others who may be using the space for different purposes.

Humphreys supplemented his observations with interviews. In one of the most debated ethical aspects of his work, he recorded the license plate numbers of those who visited the tearoom. He used this information to identify and find the men, then interview them about many aspects of their lives in the guise of conducting a health survey that made no mention of homosexual behavior. This was an extremely controversial method both because the data were collected surreptitiously and because it posed risks to his subjects, most of whom were understandably desperate to keep their "tearoom" activities private. It is probably fair to say that today's institutional review boards would not permit a university researcher to conduct a study in this way. Yet despite the ethical debates his research methods generated, *Tearoom Trade* remains a valuable, if troubling, sociological text. Written at a time when men who had sex with men were often characterized as dangerous "perverts" and "deviants," the study reveals that many of these men led otherwise "normal" and unremarkable lives. Many were husbands and fathers in heterosexual families. Noteworthy too is that this was a time when police were vigilant about enforcing laws against such behavior. Many lives were ruined when police "set up" gay men and accused them of "coming on" to "innocent" restroom users. Humphreys, however, demonstrates that sexual encounters may be initiated through a series of small interactional cues; rarely, if ever, did anyone make an overt sexual gesture to a stranger that did not elicit the desired response. His meticulous observations made him an important expert witness in cases of false prosecution, seeing that his data demonstrated how unlikely it was for an unwanted sexual encounter to occur within the social world of the public bathroom.

The next selection from James P. Spradley and Brenda J. Mann's *The Cocktail Waitress* is a study of a college bar in a midsized Midwestern city. Spradley and Mann provide an early example of how social interactions are not simply something to be understood on their own terms, as Goffman demonstrated, but must be analyzed in relation to a larger system of gender inequality, represented by the ways in which male privilege is negotiated in public spaces.

In "The Black Male in Public," Elijah Anderson extends the analysis of microinteractions to racial inequality and demonstrates how race and class shape interactions on public streets. He draws on Goffman's insights, which were largely formulated in reference to middle-class white American society, but applies them to potentially racially charged encounters between blacks and whites while asking what types of behavioral cues make up the vocabulary of public interaction in the contemporary inner city. Examining how the rules of daily interaction are shaped by statuses such as race, class, and gender, Anderson, like Spradley and Mann, shows that we cannot develop a full understanding of the situation by looking at microinteractions in isolation; instead, these interactions must be linked to social structure.

"'Empowering the 'Gaze': Personal Stereos and the Hidden Look," comes from Michael Bull's British study of social interactions on the street after the emergence of the Walkman and the cell phone. While Goffman's studies of social interaction have a certain timeless quality, Spradley and Mann, as well as Anderson, brought his ideas into dialogue with contemporary gender and racial social stratification. Bull, in turn, shows how such studies can be updated in light of technological change. Bull is interested in the mundane situation of a person walking down the street or riding a train among many strangers. What is it like to be that individual? How does the personal stereo influence his or her perception of the experience? In the course of his research, he discovers how the civil

inattention described by Goffman operates in the present world, in which people can use technology to remove themselves from the physical world around them. This selection illustrates the need for ongoing ethnographic research to update classic studies for each generation.

The next selection, Jack Katz's "Pissed Off in L.A.," is a study of social life on the streets of Los Angeles. Unlike other studies of social interaction since Goffman, Katz's research looks at interactions between people who are in public but yet occupy a kind of private space, that is, they sit in their private automobiles yet interact with each other on L.A.'s freeways. He tries to explain the absurdity (from the perspective of his subjects as well as of outsiders) of people yelling at people who are behind closed windows and can barely hear them. By focusing his attention on the distinctive aspects of this social situation, he shows that here too what appears as an unstructured and even spontaneous set of activities is actually highly structured and predictable once we understand the way it is experienced by the people in the situation.

In the final reading of this section, "Feeding the Pigeons," Colin Jerolmack shows us that even when people think they are alone in urban public spaces, such as city parks, they often are not. Animals also occupy those spaces. Jerolmack's study of how people interact with pigeons, the most ubiquitous animals in urban public space, demonstrates that the pigeons' presence creates opportunities for social interaction that can mitigate the loneliness of city life. He does so by drawing on Goffman's insights on how surroundings can serve as "props" that facilitate people's interactions with strangers and how people draw on "usable others" to create sociability in public. Jerolmack reveals that the act of feeding pigeons grants people an opportunity to interact with others in a public space; pigeon feeding offers strangers a shared experience to discuss. He also shows how pigeon feeding leads to interactions between feeders and pigeons that are mutually fulfilling and capable of suspending—for the duration of the feeding—human feelings of social isolation.

11

LAUD HUMPHREYS

PATTERNS OF COLLECTIVE ACTION

from *Tearoom Trade* (1970)

In this controversial study, Humphreys documents activities that take place in a "tearoom"—a 1960s slang word for a public restroom in which men went to have anonymous sexual encounters with other men. He reveals how men looking for such encounters use highly patterned systems of signals, body language, and gaze to make their intentions known, generally without speaking. In this manner, the men manage to find each other, usually going undetected by other users of the facilities or the police.

O.K., here goes–no self-respecting homosexual in his right mind should condone sex in public places, but let's face it, it's fun.... The danger adds to the adventure. The hunt, the cruise, the rendezvous, a great little game. Then more likely than not, "instant sex." That's it.[1]

The nature of sexual activity presents two severe problems for those who desire impersonal one-night-stands. In the first place, except for masturbation, sex necessitates collective action; and all collective action requires communication. Mutually understood signals must be conveyed, intentions expressed, and the action sustained by reciprocal encouragement. Under normal circumstances, such communication is ritualized in those patterns of word and movement we call courtship and love-making. Verbal agreements are reached and intentions conveyed. Even when deception is involved in such exchanges, as it often is, self-revelation and commitment are likely by-products of courtship rituals. In the search for impersonal, anonymous sex, however, these ordinary patterns of collective action must be avoided.

A second problem arises from the cultural conditioning of Western man. For him, sex is invested with personal meanings: interpersonal relationship, romantic love, and an endless catalogue of sentiments. Sex without "love" meets with such general condemnation that the essential ritual of courtship is almost obscured in rococo accretions that assure those involved that a respectable level of romantic intent has been reached. Normal preludes to sexual action thus encourage the very commitment and exposure that the tearoom participant wishes to avoid. Since ordinary ways reveal and involve, special ritual is needed for the impersonal sex of public restrooms.

Both the appeal and the danger of ephemeral sex are increased because the partners are usually strangers to one another. The propositioning of strangers for either heterosexual or homosexual acts is dangerous and exciting—so much so that it is made possible only by concerted action, which progresses in stages of increasing mutuality. The special ritual of tearooms, then, must be both non-coercive and noncommittal.

Approaching

The steps, phases, or general moves I have observed in tearoom games all involve somatic motion. As silence is one of the rules of these encounters, the strategies of the players require some sort of physical movement: a gesture with the hands, motions of the eyes, manipulation and erection of the penis, a movement of the head, a change in stance, or a transfer from one place to another.

The approach to the place of encounter, although not a step within the game, resembles moves of the latter sort. Although occurring outside the interaction membrane, the approach may affect the action inside. An automobile may circle the area a time or two, finally stopping in front of the facility. In what I estimate to be about a third of the cases, the driver will park a moderate distance away from the facility—sometimes as far as 200 feet to the side or in back, to avoid having his car associated with the tearoom.

Unless hurried (or interested in some particular person entering, or already inside, the facility), the man will usually wait in his auto for five minutes or longer. While waiting, he looks the situation over: Are there police cars near? Does he recognize any of the other autos? Does another person waiting look like a desirable partner? He may read a newspaper and listen to the radio, or even get out and wipe his windshield, invariably looking up when another car approaches. The purpose here is to look as natural as possible in this setting, while taking the opportunity to "cruise" other prospective players as they drive slowly by.

Sometimes he will go into the restroom on the heels of a person he has been watching. Should he find the occupant of another auto interesting, he may decide to enter as a signal for the other man to follow. If no one else approaches or leaves, he may enter to see what is going on inside. Some will wait in their autos for as long as an hour, until they see a desirable prospect approaching or sense that the time is right for entry.

From the viewpoint of those already in the restroom, the action of the man outside may communicate a great deal about his availability for the game. Straights do not wait; they stop, enter, urinate, and leave. A man who remains in his car while a number of others come and go—then starts for the facility as soon as a relatively handsome, young fellow approaches—may be revealing both his preferences and his unwillingness to engage in action with anyone "substandard."

Whatever his behavior outside, any man who approaches an occupied tearoom should know that he is being carefully appraised as he strides up the path. While some are evaluating him from the windows, others may be engaged in "zipping the fly."

Positioning

Once inside the interaction membrane, the participant has his opportunity to cruise those already there. He will have only the brief time of his passage across the room for sizing-up the situation. Once he has positioned himself at the urinal or in a stall, he has already begun his first move of the game. Even the decision as to which urinal he will use is a tactical consideration. If either of the end fixtures is occupied, which is often the case, an entering party who takes his position at the center of the three urinals is "coming on too strong." This is apt to be the "forward" sort of player who wants both possible views. Should both ends be occupied, it is never considered fair for a new arrival to take the middle. He might interrupt someone else's play. For reasons other than courtesy, however, the skilled player will occupy one of the end urinals because it leaves him more room to maneuver in the forthcoming plays.

If the new participant stands close to the fixture, so that his front side may not easily be seen, and gazes downward, it is assumed by the players that he is straight. By not allowing his penis to be seen by others, he has precluded his involvement in action at the urinals. This strategy, followed by an early departure from the premises, is all that those who wish to "play it straight" need to know about the tearoom game. If he makes the positioning move in that manner, no man should ever be concerned about being propositioned, molested, or otherwise involved in the action. (For defecation, one should seek a facility with doors on the stalls.)

A man who knows the rules and wishes to play, however, will stand comfortably back from the urinal, allowing his gaze to shift from side to side or to the ceiling. At this point, he may notice a man in the nearest stall peer over the edge at him. The next step is for the man in the stall (or someone else in the room) to move to the urinal at the opposite end, being careful to leave a "safe" distance between himself and the other player.

My data indicate that those who occupy a stall upon entering (or who move into a stall after a brief stop at the urinal) are playing what might be called the Passive-Insertee System. By making such an opening bid, they indicate to other participants their intention to serve as fellator. In the systematic observation of fifty encounters ending in fifty-three acts of fellatio, twenty-seven of the insertees opened in this manner (twenty-five sitting on stools, two standing). Only two insertors opened by sitting on stools and four by standing in stalls.

Positioning is a far more "fateful" move for those who wish to be insertees than for others. In sixteen of the observed encounters, the fellator made no further move until the payoff stage of the game. The strategy of these men was to sit and wait, playing a distinctly passive role. Those who conclude as insertors, however, are twice as apt to begin at the urinals as are the insertees. A few of each just stood around or went to a window during the positioning phase of the game.

Signaling

The major thesis of Scott's work on horse racing is that "the proper study of social organization is the study of the organization of information."[2] To what extent this holds for all organizations is not within my realm of knowledge. For gaming encounters, however, this is undoubtedly true, with "skill" inhering in the player's ability to convey, interpret, assimilate, and act upon the basis of information given and received. Every move in the gaming encounter is not only a means of bettering one's physical position in relation to other participants but also a means of communication.

Whereas, for most insertees, positioning is vital for informing others of their intentions, about half of the eventual insertors convey such information in the signaling phase. The primary strategy employed by the latter is playing with one's penis in what may be called "casual masturbation."

> RESPONDENT: The thing he [the potential insertee] is watching for is "handling," to see whether or not the guy is going to play with himself. He's going to pretend like he is masturbating, and this is the signal right there....
>
> INTERVIEWER: So the sign of willingness to play is playing with oneself or masturbation?
>
> RESPONDENT: Pseudomasturbation.

The willing player (especially if be intends to be an insertor) steps back a few inches from the urinal, so that his penis may be viewed easily. He then begins to stroke it or play with the head of the organ. As soon as another man at the urinals observes this signal, he will also begin autoerotic manipulation. Usually, erection may be observed after less than a minute of such stimulation.

The eyes now come into play. The prospective partner will look intently at the other's organ, occasionally breaking his stare only to fix directly upon the eyes of the other. "This mutual glance between persons, in distinction from the simple sight or observation of the other, signifies a wholly new and unique union between them."[3] A few of the players have been observed to move directly from positioning to eye contact, but this seems to happen in only about 5 per cent of the cases.

Through all of this, it is important to remember that showing an erection is, for the inserter, the one essential and invariable means of indicating a willingness to play. No one will be "groped" or otherwise involved in the directly sexual play of the tearooms unless he displays this sign. This touches

on the rule of not forcing one's intentions on another, and I have observed no exceptions to its use. On the basis of extensive and systematic observation, I doubt the veracity of any person (detective or otherwise) who claims to have been "molested" in such a setting without first having "given his consent" by showing an erection. Conversely, anyone familiar with this strategy may become involved in the action merely by following it. He need not be otherwise skilled to play the game.

Most of those who intend to be insertors will engage in casual masturbation at a urinal. Others will do so openly while standing or sitting in a stall. Rarely, a man will begin masturbation while standing elsewhere in the room and then only because all other facilities are occupied.

In about 10 per cent of the cases, a man will convey his willingness to serve as insertee by beckoning with his hand or motioning with his head for another in the room to enter the stall where he is seated. There are a few other signals used by men on the stools to attract attention to their interests. If there are doors on the stalls, foot-tapping or note-passing may be employed. If there is a "glory hole" (a small hole, approximately three inches in diameter, which has been carefully carved, at about average "penis height," in the partition of the stall), it may be used as a means of signaling from the stall. This has been observed occurring in three manners: by the appearance of an eye on the stool-side of the partition (a very strong indication that the seated man is watching you), by wiggling fingers through the hole, or by the projection of a tongue through the glory hole.

Occasionally, there is no need for the parties to exchange signals at this stage of the game. Others in the room may signal for a waiting person to enter the stall of an insertee. There may have been conversation outside the facility—or acquaintance with a player—which precludes the necessity of any such communication inside the interaction membrane. This was the case in about one-sixth of the acts I witnessed.

Maneuvering

The third move of the game is optional. It conveys little information to other players and, for this reason, may be skipped. As the Systematic Observation Sheets show, twenty-eight of the eventual insertees and thirty-five of the insertors (out of fifty-three sexual acts) made no move during this phase of the interaction. This is a time of maneuvering, of changing one's position in relation to other persons and structures in the room. It is important at this point in the action, first, because it indicates the crucial nature of the next move (the contract) and, second, because it is an early means of discerning which men wish to serve as insertees.

Twenty of the thirty-three players observed in motion during this stage of the encounter later became insertees. Two-thirds of these used the strategy of moving closer to someone at the urinal:

> X entered shortly and went to third urinal. Y entered in about a minute and went to first urinal.... O stood and watched X and Y. Y was masturbating, as was X. X kept looking over shoulder at me. I smiled and moved over against far wall, lit cigarette. *X moved to second urinal* and took hold of Y's penis and began manipulating it. I moved to door to observe park policeman (in plain clothes with badge), who was seated on park bench. Then I went back to position by wall. By this time, X was on knees in front of urinals, fellating Y. I went back to door, saw A approaching, and coughed loudly.

Others may use this stage to move closer to someone elsewhere in the room or to move from the urinal to an unoccupied stall. All of these strategies are implemental but nonessential to the basic action patterns. The restroom's floor plan, I have found, is the strongest determinant of what happens during this phase of the game. If there are only two urinals in the facility, the aggressor's maneuver might be no more than to take a half-step toward the prospective partner.

Contracting

Positions having been taken and the signals called, the players now engage in a crucial exchange. Due to the noncoercive nature of tearoom encounters, the contract phase of the game cannot be evaded. Initially, participants have given little consent to sexual interaction. By means of bodily movements, in particular the exposure of an erect penis, they have signaled such consent. Now *a contract must be agreed upon,* setting both the terms of the forthcoming sexual exchange and the expression of mutual consent.

Eighty-eight per cent of the contracts observed are initiated in one of two ways, depending upon the intended role of the initiator. One who wishes to be an insertee makes this move by taking hold of his partner's exposed and erect penis. One who wants to be an insertor under the terms of the contract steps into the stall where the prospective insertee is seated. If neither of these moves is rejected, the contract is sealed.

Manipulation of the other's organ is reciprocated in about half of the cases. Some respondents have indicated that they appreciate this gesture of mutuality, but it is not at all essential to the agreement reached. The lack of negative response from the recipient of the action is enough to seal the contract. It is interesting, in this connection, to note that such motions are seldom met with rejection (only one of my systematic observations records such a break in the

TABLE 11.1. Major strategy systems in tearoom encounters.

	Insertee	Insertor
Active	position: urinal	position: urinal
	signal: casual masturbation	signal: casual masturbation
	contract: manipulates partner's penis	contract: steps into partner's stall
	(27%)*	(41%)**
Passive	position: sits in stall	position: urinal
	signal: masturbation (sometimes beckoning)	signal: masturbation
	contract: accepts partner's entry	contract: accepts partner's manipulation
	(50%)*	(27%)**
Totals	N = 37 (77%)*	N = 33 (68%)**

* Percentage of total insertees.
** Percentage of total insertors.
Note: Eleven insertees (23%) and fifteen insertors (32%) followed a variety of minor strategy systems, combining elements of the major systems with idiosyncratic moves.
(*Source*: systematic observations of 48 encounters ending in fellatio.)

action). By moving through gradual stages, the actors have achieved enough silent communication to guarantee mutuality.

In the positioning and signaling phases of the game, the players have already indicated their intentions. This stage, then, merely formalizes the agreement and sets the terms of the payoff. One should note, in this connection, that a party's relative aggressiveness or passivity in this phase of the game does not, in itself, indicate the role to be acted out at the climax of the interaction. In connection with the positioning of the first move, however, it does provide an indication of future role identification: the man who is seated in the stall *and* is the passive party to the contract will generally end up as an insertee; the man who stands at the urinal *and* is passive in the contract stage, however, will usually be an insertor at the payoff. The more active insertees play from the urinal and initiate the contract by groping, but active insertors play from the urinal (or elsewhere in the room) and initiate the contract by entering the stall of a passive insertee (see Table 11.1).

The systems of strategy illustrated in Table 11.1 account for 77 per cent of the patterns of play for the insertees observed and for 68 per cent of the insertors' moves. (Again, the insertee role seems to be most stable in the encounters.) The Active-Insertee

and Passive-Insertor Systems have already been illustrated and discussed in detail. An illustration from the systematic observation reports of the other two systems follows:

[This was the fourth encounter observed in this tearoom within an hour. The man here identified as X had been the fellator in the second of these actions and had remained seated on the stool throughout the third. I estimated his age at about fifty. He was thin, had grey hair, and wore glasses. Y was about thirty-five, wearing white jeans and a green sport shirt, and was described as "neat." He was well-tanned, had black hair, was balding, and drove up in a new, luxury-class automobile.]

Saw Y approaching tearoom from bridge, so I got into room just before him. I stood at first urinal for a minute, until he began to masturbate at other one—then I moved to the window and looked out on the road. I could see X peering through glory hole at Y when I was at the urinal. Y moved to opposite window and looked out. He then turned to look at X and me. He was stroking his penis thru his pants, maintaining erection. I nodded to him to go ahead. He moved into first stall where X began to fellate him. This took less than five minutes. He wiped penis on tissue and left. X got up, zipped pants and left.

"X" played the Passive-Insertee System throughout these encounters. "Y" followed the Active-Insertor System, with some reassurance from the observer. The total time of this encounter—from entry of "Y" until his departure—was ten minutes. Note that the glory hole has three functions (the first two of which were employed in this encounter): as a peephole for observation, as a signalling device, and as a place of entry for the penis into the insertee's stall. The latter is very rare in the tearooms observed, and I have only twice seen these openings used in such a manner.

There may be forms of contracting other than the two I have described. I once observed a contract effected by the insertor's unzipping his pants directly in front of a prospective partner in the middle of the restroom. Another time, I noticed an active insertee grope a man whose erection was showing while his pants were still zipped. The move was not rejected, and the object of this strategy then played the insertor role. In a very few instances, my observations indicate that the insertee entered a stall where the eventual insertor was seated or that the insertor took hold of the partner's exposed penis at the urinals. These exceptions, while rare, make it necessary to withhold judgment as to what roles are being played until the payoff phase itself.

Foreplay

Although optional and quite variable, sexual foreplay may be seen as constituting a fifth phase of the tearoom encounters. Like maneuvering, it has very little communicative function and is not essential to production of the payoff. From positioning to payoff, nearly all players—and some of the waiters—engage in automanipulation. There is little need, therefore, to prepare the insertee for fellatio by any other means of stimulation.

Unlike coitus, oral-genital sex does not require rigidity of the organ for adequate penetration of the orifice. Whereas an erection is a necessary signal in the early phases of the game, interruptions and repositioning between the contract and payoff stages occasionally result in the loss of an erection by the prospective insertor. The observer has noted that it is not uncommon for a fellator to take the other man's penis in his mouth even in its flaccid state. The male sex organ is a versatile instrument. With the proper psychosocial circumstances (varying with the individual's prior conditioning), it can reach the orgasmic phase in less than a minute. The authors of *Human Sexual Response* briefly discuss the many factors that intersect in determining the length of the "sexual response cycle":

The first or excitement phase of the human cycle of sexual response develops from any source of somatogenic or psychogenic stimulation. The stimulative factor is of major import in establishing sufficient increment of sexual tensions to extend the cycle. If the stimulation remains adequate to individual demand, the intensity of response usually increases rapidly. In this manner the excitement phase is accelerated or shortened. If the stimulative approach is physically or psychologically objectionable, or is interrupted, the excitement phase may be prolonged greatly or even aborted. This first segment and the final segment (resolution phase) consume most of the time expended in the complete cycle of human sexual response.[4]

Foreplay may help in maintaining the level of stimulation required for advancing the response cycle. Such strategies as mutual masturbation and oral contact in the pubic area may not only add appreciably to the sensual pleasure of the players but may help to precipitate orgasm when the participants are operating under the pressure of time and threatened intrusion:

It was now raining hard. O remained standing at window, saw X leave car and enter. Y drove up as X was walking toward tearoom, waited for about three minutes in car and ran thru rain to tearoom. X went to urinal nearest window. Y went to other urinal, urinated and began to play with his penis, stroking head slowly. Couldn't see what X was doing. X then moved over by Y (they had both been looking at one another) and took hold of his penis. Y did not reciprocate or withdraw. Y then moved over to far stall, still masturbating. X went over and stood by him, taking hold of his penis again. X's pants were zipped and I could not see evidence of an erection. He unbuttoned Y's pants and slipped them down to his knees, as he did with his shorts. Playing with Y's testicles and stroking his legs, he began to fellate him....

It should be noted that, due to the danger of interruption, participants in this gaming encounter seldom lower their pants to the floor or unbutton any other clothing. They generally remain ready to engage in covering action at a moment's notice. Perhaps the rain gave these men what we shall later see to be a false sense of invulnerability.

The Payoff

The action now moves into its culminating stage. As is illustrated by continuing the above narrative, intrusions may temporarily detach the payoff phase from the action that leads up to it, providing moments of incongruous suspense:

Two kids, B and C, came running toward facility with fishing poles. I coughed. Y sat down on stool and X moved over to window. B and C entered, talking loudly and laughing at the rain. They rearranged some fishing gear in a box, then ran back outside, the rain having let up slightly.

D, an older boy around fourteen, came riding up on a bicycle from the bridge. I did not see him coming, but X and Y were still separated. D entered, went to urinal, urinated, looked out window by me and said, "Sure is raining out!" I remarked that it was letting up. "Guess I'll make a dash for it," he said. He left and rode off toward street. [This is an example of the lack of "consent to copresence" in these settings. See Chapter 8.]

X and Y resumed activity with X working his head back and forth and rubbing his hands up under shirt of Y, who was again standing. I saw A coming up walk and coughed. X and Y broke—Y sat down—X moved back to window. A entered and I recognized him. I nodded to X and Y, who resumed fellating position. A peered around edge of stall to watch, then stood up and looked over partition to get a better view, masturbating as he stood. Y moaned at orgasm and pressed on back of X's head. X stood up and continued masturbating Y even after orgasm. Y withdrew in a minute and pulled up pants. X moved back to window. Y looked for paper in other stall but it had been used up. He tucked his penis in pants, zipped up and left. X came over to window by me and looked me over. I smiled and left. A remained on stool.

Among other things illustrated here, one may notice the importance of hand play in the sexual act itself. The observations indicate that body and hand movements carry the action through stages that, lacking conversation, might otherwise be awkward. Primarily by means of the hands, the structure of the encounter is well maintained, in spite of the absence of verbal encouragement. Caresses, friendly pats, relaxed salutes, support with the hands, and thrusting motions are all to be observed throughout the action. Normally, the man who takes the insertor role will sustain the action of the fellator by clasping the back of his head or neck or by placing his hands on the partner's shoulders. As a frequent insertee points out:

When you are having sex, it's not just that the sexual organ is being activated. The whole body comes into it. And you want to use your whole body, and your hands are a very important part in sex. Next to the organs themselves, I think the hands are the most important part, even more important than the mouth for kissing. I really think the hands are more important—because you can do fantastic things, if you know how to do them. You can do fantastic things with your hands to another person's body.

Without the use of scientific instruments other than the human eye, it is impossible to say what proportion of the hand play during the sexual act is voluntary or involuntary. During the orgasmic phase, undoubtedly, there is a great deal of involuntary, spasmodic movement of the extremities, such as that described by Masters and Johnson:

This involuntary spasm of the striated musculature of the hands and feet is an indication of high levels of sexual tension. Carpopedal spasm has been observed more frequently during male

masturbatory episodes than during intercourse, regardless of body positioning.[5]

For physiological reasons, such spasmodic clutching of the hands is engaged in only by the insertor and confined mostly to the period surrounding orgasm.

The insertee, however, may have certain functional reasons for handling his partner. Some respondents have spoken of clutching the base of the penis with a hand, in order to ward off a thrust that may cause them to gag or choke:

If the man has a very large piece of meat—I know from experience—I will not have somebody ram that thing down my throat. I'm sorry, but that hurts! It can cause a person to vomit. [Like if you put your fingers down your throat?] Exactly, and this can be very embarrassing. So, ordinarily, I will try to hold on. I know just about how much I can take.

Then I am going to put my hand in a certain place, and I know it can't go any further than my hand. . . .

The same participant continues by describing another functional use of the hands during fellatio:

Then I use my hands on the balls, too—on the scrotum. This can do wild things! [You said something about the hips. Or did I imagine that?] The hips or the backs of the legs. Now, there is one value in this which some people don't realize: these muscles contract first at the point of orgasm. This is one of the first signs of orgasm. When these muscles back in here begin to contract (the legs stiffen, these muscles contract or flex, or whatever—they get hard), you can tell at this point the orgasm is about to be reached. It is very helpful to know these things, especially if you are doing somebody.

Because you can tell to go faster—or keep doing what you are doing. You can at least get ready and know not to pull away all of a sudden.

I suspect that, if one were to concentrate on observing peripheral matters in a study of heterosexual intercourse, he would find the same pattern of hand involvement: exploration of the partner's body, support of the head or pressure on the back, stimulation of the erotic zones, numerous caresses. At least in the payoff phase, silence in sexual encounters is not confined to the tearooms. When body communicates directly with body, spoken language is no longer essential. Thus far in history, the action of sex is the only universal language—perhaps because the tongue is but one among many members to convey the message, and the larynx is less important than the lips.

As has been indicated, it is a lack of such physical involvement—along with the silence—that tends to make tearoom sex less personal. When hand play does occur, therefore, it tends to raise the involvement level of the sexual action. Perhaps for that reason, some people attempt to avoid it:

I saw X's hand as he motioned Y over into his stall. Y entered, stood facing X and unzipped. X ran his hands all over Y's buttocks, the back of his legs and up under his shirt while sucking. Y stood rather still with hands held out just far enough from his sides to give X freedom of movement *without touching him.*

The primary physical connection between the partners is that of the mouth, lips, and tongue of the fellator with the penis of the insertor. The friction and sucking action in the meeting of these organs is what produces the orgasm upon which the encounter focuses. A number of my respondents claim that the physical sensation of oral-genital copulation, while not

unlike that of coitus, is actually more stimulating—or "exciting," as they generally word it. While some of the married men among the cooperating participants say that they actually prefer the sensations of fellatio to those of coitus, most agree that this is true only when certain other variables are held constant, when both acts take place in bed, for example. Many tend to look on tearoom sex as only a substitute for "the real thing."

It's different—and I like both. I guess you could say I'd rather have sex with my wife. Getting a blow job isn't like having the real thing, but it has its points, too. I just don't know. I hadn't thought about it that way. I guess you really can't compare the two. Let's just say I like them both.

Some insertees retain the seminal fluid and swallow it: others clear their throats and spit it out. In one-fifth of the encounters observed, I noted that the insertee spit following the ejaculation of his partner. One respondent claimed that he only spits it out "when it tastes bad":

The variety of tastes is unbelievable! You can almost tell what a person's diet is by what it tastes like. A person with a good, well-balanced ordinary diet, the fluid has a very mild, tangy, salty flavor. A person who has been drinking heavily—even if they aren't drunk or suffering from a hang-over, if they drink a lot—the stuff tastes like alcohol. And I mean pure, rot-gut alcohol, the vilest taste in the world!

I was unable to find any medical references to the taste of ejaculatory fluid, so I have not been able to verify this connoisseur's judgment. Other respondents will say only that they do think "some men taste different than others."

Acts of fellatio generally take place within the stall. This puts the insertee in a more comfortable position than crouching on his haunches elsewhere in the room. It also has an advantage in case of an intrusion, in that only one party to the action needs to move. There are certain tactical advantages as well. If the man who prefers the insertee position takes a stall and remains there for any length of time, he legitimizes himself, indicates the role he wishes to play, and needs only to wait for a partner to arrive.

Another twenty-nine percent of the observed acts took place in front of the urinals. From that position, both may turn to face the fixtures in case of an intrusion. The fellator is poorly braced for his action, however, and probably quite uncomfortable. Occasionally, the act will occur in front of a window. I am informed that this is especially true when no lookout is present, because it has the advantage of enabling the insertor to double as lookout. When the oral-genital contact takes place away from the stool, the insertee will generally squat or drop to his knees to make the necessary contact.

During oral copulation, other men may come from around the room into viewing position. Many will proceed to masturbate while watching, sometimes without opening their pants for the automanipulation. Seldom does the exchange that is the focal point of this attention last more than a few minutes. In looking over my data, I found indications that I had grossly overestimated the amount of time lapsed between insertion and orgasm. What seemed to me like "a long time" (sometimes recorded as five or ten minutes) was probably a reflection only of my nervousness during the payoff stage. Since I was attempting to pass as a voyeur-lookout (both aspects of the role requiring my closest attention during these moments), it was impossible for me to use my watch in timing. No true voyeur would glance at his watch in the middle of a sex act! Actually, I suspect that the oral penetration ranged from ten seconds to five minutes, not counting interruptions.

I have twice seen couples engaging in anal intercourse. This is a form of sexual activity rare in most tearooms, probably due to the greater amount of time required and the drastic rearrangement of clothing involved, both of which tend to increase the danger of being apprehended in the act. Mutual masturbation is an occasional means of reaching orgasm, particularly by the urinals or elsewhere in a crowded room.

Clearing the Field

Once the sexual exchange is accomplished, most insertors step into a stall to use the toilet paper. After the penis is cleansed, clothes are rearranged and flies zipped. In those rare cases in the observed facilities where a workable wash basin is provided, the participants may wash their hands before leaving.

Nearly always in the observation records, when a man took the inserter role he left for his car immediately after cleansing. The insertee may leave, too, but he frequently waits in the tearoom for someone else to enter. Sometimes he becomes the insertor in a subsequent encounter, as in the following account:

[X is about forty-five, wearing a green banlon shirt, light blue slacks, driving a red, late model sports coupe. Y is about thirty, driving a green Ford convertible. He wears a light blue shirt, dark blue slacks, and a conservative tie. He is described as being tan, masculine, well dressed. B is about forty, balding, thin, tanned, wearing horn-rimmed glasses and a grey sport shirt. It is 2:25 on a beautiful Thursday afternoon, and there are few people in the park.]

B was seated on stool when O entered. O stood at urinal a minute, noticed B watching him through glory hole. Crossed to far window, looked out and lit cigarette. Y entered and went to first urinal. X came in soon after Y and went to third urinal. They stood there for about five minutes. X kept peering over edge of stall at B and also at me. I crossed to opposite window and looked out missing pane. X was masturbating. Y went to second stall, lowered pants and sat down. I went back to window on right. Y spread his legs and began masturbating. (He had removed his coat and hung it over edge of stall.) He had slumped on the stool seat as if sitting in camp chair, legs stretched out almost straight in front of him but spread apart and was masturbating obviously. I went back to window overlooking street. X then moved to window by Y, stood there a minute, then leaned over and took hold of Y's penis and began stroking it. He then knelt on the floor to begin fellatio. B just sat in his stall and masturbated. Y moaned a bit at climax. He then wiped and X stood back by window and masturbated while watching Y. Y flushed toilet, put on his coat, zipped pants and left. X stepped into B's stall and was sucked by him. This didn't take more than a minute. X then went to urinal, cleared throat, spit and left. (I was able to see autos of both X and Y through window.)

This is what I have labeled a series encounter. Generally, in order to facilitate the eventual analysis, I have broken these up into "Encounter A," "Encounter B," etc. In the above instance and in a few others among my systematic observations, I was not able to do so because of the rapid succession of events. During the hunting season, series encounters are the most common variety. Once the action begins to "swing," a series may last throughout the day, each group of participants trading upon the legitimation process of the previous game.

Another type of action that tends to swell the volume of sexual acts in a given facility is the simultaneous encounter, in which more than one sexual act is in process at the same time. The payoff phases are seldom reached at exactly the same time in these encounters, but they are staggered as in a round.

[It is a warm, humid, Friday afternoon. A few youngsters are playing ball in the park and some heterosexual couples are parked nearby. X is about thirty-five, tough looking, tattooed, dirty working clothes, drives an old Chevrolet. Y is about forty-five, lean and tanned, wearing tan work clothes. A is about thirty-two, neatly dressed with sport shirt and tie. I describe him as "masculine looking but wore pinky ring." He drove a new, foreign economy car. B is about fifty, heavy set, grey hair, sports clothes, rather unkempt. C is about forty, with a pot belly, wearing white sports shirt, dark blue pants.]

When O entered, X and Y were seated on stools with A standing by far window facing into room. While O urinated, he noticed that X was watching him through glory hole. O lingered at urinal for about four minutes, during which time A moved into stall with X (X is a noisy sucker, much "slurping," so I could tell what was happening but could not see). O crossed to far window, lit cigarette and peered out. A left first stall and stepped into space between Y and O. He stood there, masturbating both himself and Y, who had stood up. Meanwhile, C, who was sitting on bridge watching tearoom when O entered, came into the room. O saw him approaching thru window and coughed. Y and A broke contact for the moment but, recognizing C, returned to action. C stood at urinal less than a minute, halted for another minute opposite stalls, then went into stall with X, who proceeded to fellate him. Y then stood on the toilet seat, watching X and C, while A sucked Y (A had to crouch but continued to masturbate). It was getting crowded on that side of the room, so O moved to opposite window. From this position, he could only see part of A's backside, Y's face and shoulders, and the backside of C. X kneaded C's buttocks and ran his hands up and down the backs of C's legs. When C finished, he left without wiping. A finished with Y about this time, went to urinal number three and spit. Y wiped and left. A stepped over to window by O, peered out through broken pane. His pants were still unzipped and he proceeded to masturbate and to look at O suggestively. O, feeling uncomfortable, went back to far window. B entered and A zipped up pants. B looked around as he went to middle urinal but stayed there for a brief time. He then moved over to stall with X. No one seemed to be made uncomfortable by B and seemed to recognize him. O then left, followed closely by A, who engaged him in conversation by water fountain....All of this took place in twenty-five minutes.

The reader should be able to sense, at this point, that what I have described as a rather simple, six-step game (only four of which are essential to the action) may be acted out with infinite variety and confusing modifications. Every encounter reduces, ultimately, to the basic steps of positioning, signaling, contracting, and payoff; but no two of them are quite alike.

A pat on the shoulder, a wave of the hand, an occasional whispered "thanks" concludes the action. The departure ritual is simple and brief. Once the field is cleared, some individuals go to their homes or jobs, others return to their cars and await the arrival of fresh players, and a few may venture to a different tearoom to take their positions in another encounter.

The length of these games was observed to range between five and forty minutes, with an average duration of about eighteen minutes. Tearoom encounters, then, require relatively little time—a quarter of an hour if one knows where to go and how to play the game. Many suburban housewives may think their husbands delayed by the traffic when, in reality, the spouses have paused for a tearoom encounter.

Coping with Intrusions

Intrusion of a new person through the interaction membrane nearly always causes a break in the action. The man entering *must* be legitimized or the game will be disrupted, at least for the duration of his presence. Until the legitimation or departure of the intruder, a sort of panic reaction ensues; play becomes disorganized and the focus of strategies shifts from the payoff—first to self-protection and then to appraisal of the membrane-violator:

Okay, they're making out or doing something in the tearoom; and, all of a sudden, the door bangs open and in comes someone. They break off right away. There is this twisting of bodies; one twists around in the stall; the other turns, stands up....They change positions. The third party goes over to one of the urinals. Then they look over the top of the stall. He's looking over the tops of the stalls, too. They're thinking: "Do I know him? Have I seen him in here or not?" That's the first thing....So you watch and see: "How long is he going to stay there? Is he urinating or just standing there?" All these different things come into it. So then you decide: "Alright, I'm safe." You hope he is not a cop playing games.

Other than by "cutting out," giving up on the game altogether, I find three chief means of coping with the tension generated by such intrusions into the gaming encounter. The first is the almost automatic and universal response of zipping the fly. The first reaction of a man, when threatened, is to cover his exposure. Since (in the case of deviant action such as a sexual game) the exposure is not so much physical as moral, this covering mechanism is a matter of hiding the incriminating evidence rather than "taking cover." In the game of warfare, where physical protection is paramount, the first response to the crisis of intrusion is "hitting the dirt." Because the negative consequences of a deviant game are more apt to be realized in a courtroom than in a base hospital, however, the immediate problem is one of disposing of potentially damaging evidence. Thus pot-smokers "stash the shit," thieves "ditch the loot," and tearoom players zip the fly.

Actually, I find that zipping the fly occurs not only when the players are threatened by intrusion crises but whenever there is penetration of the interaction membrane. At all points where the outer world impinges upon the inner world, zipping the fly is apt to occur.[6] (Such "involuntary" movements as checking the fly to make sure it is zipped should be included within this general category of protective action.) Few tearoom participants fail to engage in this action just prior to leaving the restroom scene. Likewise, hip persons generally check the "pad" to make certain the "shit" is "stashed" and all "roaches" disposed of, before venturing out into the world.

The second common coping mechanism is looking innocent, by which means participants dissociate themselves from the deviant action. One of my respondents described this as a "huge elaborate disinterest." On many occasions, when my entry into a tearoom disrupted the action, I encountered this sort of elaborate non chalance; however, it was never maintained for long.

There is a remarkable tendency for the normal, payoff-focused action of a gaming encounter to overcome disruption and reorganize. Legitimation never seems to take long: straights seldom stay for more than two minutes; waiters tend either to begin the opening moves of the game or to commence service as lookouts: teen-agers generally cause permanent disruption of the encounter. It may be that legitimation constitutes less of a problem in the city where most observations took place because the metropolitan police no longer use decoys in the tearooms. Where decoys are a threat, the legitimation process would be longer and more elaborate.

The third observed means whereby participants in the tearoom game cope with disruptive entries involves what I would call "speculative inquiry." As illustrated in the previous quotation, every man becomes his own, self-appointed investigating committee. Speculative inquiry requires careful observation, by which the participants pick up identification clues dropped by the new arrival. Once someone decides the newcomer is safe, nods may pass around the room, the action is resumed (somewhat cautiously at first), and the crisis of intrusion passes.

Some intrusion crises are not so easily resolved, and the tearoom game may end in disaster rather than payoff. In spite of the development of patterns of collective action to maintain the noncoercive and noncommittal nature of the encounters, defenses may fail and the feared consequences materialize. The most careful and elaborate structuring of rules, roles, and strategies sometimes collapses....

NOTES

1. Letter in "Open Forum: Sex in Public Places," edited by Larry Carlson in *Vector*, Vol. 3, No. 6 (May, 1967), p. 15. In my opinion, *Vector* is the best of the homophile journals. It is published monthly by the Society for

Individual Rights, 83 Sixth Street, San Francisco, California.

2. Marvin B. Scott, *The Racing Game* (Chicago: Aldine, 1968), p. 3.

3. From George Simmel, *Soziologie,* as quoted in Goffman, *Behavior in Public Places* (New York: The Free Press, 1963), p. 93. For a thorough discussion of the use of eye contact in face-to-face engagements, see pp. 91–96 of Goffman's book.

4. William H. Masters and Virginia E. Johnson, *Human Sexual Response* (Boston: Little, Brown, 1966), pp. 5–6.

5. *Ibid.,* p. 173. See also pp. 296–297.

6. Erving Goffman, *The Presentation of Self in Everyday Life* (Garden City, New York: Doubleday Anchor, 1959), p. 137. These points may be compared with Goffman's discussion of the dramaturgical problem of segregating audiences.

REFERENCES

Carlson, Larry (ed.). 1967. Letter in "Open Forum: Sex in Public Places," Vector 3 (6) (May).

Goffman, Ernest. 1963. *Behavior in Public Places.* New York: The Free Press.

Goffman, Ernest. 1959. *The Presentation of Self in Everyday Life.* Garden City, New York: Doubleday Anchor.

Scott, Marvin B. 1968. *The Racing Game.* Chicago: Aldine.

Masters, William H. and Virginia E. Johnson. 1966. *Human Sexual Response.* Boston Little, Brown.

JAMES P. SPRADLEY
AND BRENDA J. MANN

THE TERRITORIAL IMPERATIVE

from *The Cocktail Waitress* (1975)

At the height of the women's movement, the anthropologists James Spradley and Brenda Mann became interested in how American culture defined the roles of women and how those roles were performed in public places. Taking the work lives of cocktail waitresses in a college bar as their case study, they show how these women had to learn to function in a highly gendered space in which even routine activities were shaped by gender roles, scripts, and expectations.

Humankind cannot escape the territorial dimension of existence, and cocktail waitresses learn this by firsthand experience. The ebb and flow of social life in every society occurs in the context of *place*: a cave, an open campsite, a village square, a convent, an adobe house with kitchen and sleeping room, a locker room, a home, an office, a bar. And always we live under the territorial imperative *to give meaning to space, to define the places of our lives, large and small, in cultural terms.*

Territoriality in humans refers to the means by which space is defined, allocated, and maintained; it is a cultural phenomenon. The physical world is not presented to all humans in the same way; we do not merely use our eyes, ears, and sense of touch to adapt to our environment. Although our perceptions of distance, weight, height, color, and area have a physical basis, such perceptions are always filtered through the culture we have learned. The way we respond to physical perceptions and how we use our senses are culturally learned responses. What people see, feel, hear, and experience in any setting depends on their cultural background. According to different criteria, people everywhere divide, allocate, stake claims on, and attach meaning to space in ways that reflect their cultural knowledge of the world. It comes as no surprise to learn that the villages of Indians like the Tsimshian of Southeast Alaska were not designed like the farm towns of Iowa. The large cedar plank houses of the Tsimshian were arranged to reflect their larger kinship groups, the basic idiom of their social organization. Many towns in the United States are laid out so that people who literally live "across the tracks" belong to a lower economic level than those who live "on the hill." Inside our houses space is divided up and allocated so that even young children may feel a kind of private ownership over certain territory. "Stay out of my room," cries a child of seven or eight to an older brother. On the other hand, among the Zapotec of Oaxaca State in Mexico, all the family sleeps together in a single room. A son will bring his new bride home on their wedding right to share these crowded sleeping quarters. Space, location, territory, distance, direction—all are bound up with cultural meanings.

At the level of face-to-face encounters, people also organize the territory around them. An executive in a large corporation situates his desk behind the doors of a large corner office, partitioned off from the ten women who are his secretaries and assistants. Strangers meeting in our society on a sidewalk or crowded into an elevator avoid direct eye contact with one another. A father has his favorite chair, a child her seat at the dinner table. In Brady's Bar, Mark has his place behind the bar, and Sharon has hers at the waitress station. Wherever people work, live, or play they stake claims on space and attach meanings to them.

The Hidden Dimension

Because space is an ever-present feature of human experience, we learn its meaning and quickly forget we learned it. No one has done more to elucidate the hidden dimension of space than the anthropologist Edward Hall. Maintaining that the spatial cues of a culture are largely outside of awareness, he writes, "...we treat space somewhat as we treat sex. It is there but we don't talk about it."[1] We seldom isolate spatial cues but treat them as background events and activities. As Hall has said, "Literally thousands of experiences teach us unconsciously that space communicates. Yet this fact would probably never have been brought to the level of consciousness if it had not been realized that space is organized differently in each culture."[2]

In our study of Brady's Bar we found that space was one of the most difficult things to examine. The bar is rather small, hardly more than a small home. The patterns of spatial arrangement such as table location, human movement, crowding, backstage areas, and restricted places were easy to observe but also easy to take for granted. The cultural meaning of space in the bar sometimes only came to light when it was disregarded. Territory, we found, was an invisible dimension of social interaction and people in Brady's Bar tended to make unconscious use of it in structuring their social relationships. Let us look briefly at a sequence of activities in the bar, to see how each one is intimately involved with spatial meanings.

Two uniformed policemen enter Brady's. They smile and nod to the bartender as they walk straight to the back of the lower section, past the men's room, and into the *kitchen*. Rob mixes a Screwdriver and a scotch and water, then turns to Sharon: "These are for the kitchen." Sharon drops what she's doing and takes the drinks back to the kitchen to the waiting policemen. She hands the

Screwdriver to the one leaning against the large refrigerator in the corner. The scotch and water goes to the other policeman who is standing in the center of the small room, next to the stainless steel table. Sharon stops to chat with them for a few minutes and then heads back to the bar.

It's nine o'clock and Stephanie is punched in and ready to work. She emerges from the kitchen where she stored her purse, and walks up to Sharon who is standing at the *lower waitress station.*

"Which section do you want?" Stephanie asks.

"I don't know. Which one do you want?"

"Well, I'm kind of tired, would you mind if I took the upper?"

"No. That's fine with me."

Stephanie picks up her tray, some matches and napkins, and goes to the *upper section* to begin work. There are only five tables in this section, and so Stephanie won't have much to do for now.

The bar is quite dark, but when Stephanie glances down to the lower section, she recognizes the familiar figures of Larry, Bobby, and Skeeter silhouetted in the dim light of the juke box *near the end of the bar.* She can't make out faces from that distance or in the poor light, but she knows who they are. They form a permanent tableau in that corner, and she would think it strange not to find them there, drinking and talking.

It's early in the evening and not crowded. There are four or five empty tables in the lower section, yet Sharon can barely squeeze past the group of men standing *around her waitress station* at the bar. She is forced to shove her way through with her tray, muttering repeatedly: "Scuse me, Scuse me," in a useless attempt to force them to change the location of their conversation. They move enough to let her through but settle back into place as soon as she leaves the area.

Eight girls walk in carrying a box that, to Stephanie, looks suspiciously like a birthday cake. She shakes her head and braces herself. She knows they are headed for her

section and the big table in the *corner.* She is right. They cross the lower section, climb the stairs and go to the corner, where they proceed to push one of the smaller tables up next to the big one. The girls move some extra chairs over, remove their coats, and settle down to celebrate someone's twenty-first birthday.

Meanwhile, Steve, the bouncer, wants a drink. Sharon picks one up for him at the bar, and on her way around the tables in her section, she stops *by the door.* "I would only do this for you, Stevie," she says with mock affection. Steve thanks her and she continues on her *circular path around the tables* in her section, stopping here and there and there to check her customers. She makes this trip dozens of times during an evening, taking care of the nine tables she is responsible for in this section.

Five minutes later Sharon makes it back to the bar with only an order for two beers. Her tables are still relatively empty. But neither Rob nor Mark are behind the bar. She glances around and doesn't see them anywhere, they must be in the backroom. So, she walks around to the end of the bar, crawls under the opening, and gets two beers from the coolers *behind the bar.* As she opens them, Mark comes up behind her, and in a voice loud enough so that everyone seated at the bar can hear, he says: "What are *you* doing? You know my uncle doesn't like women behind *his* bar!" Several of the men seated at the bar watch the scene in amusement. Sharon smiles and points to the beers in her hand. She tells Mark she hasn't rung them up yet. "Could he do it?" She doesn't know how. And she crawls back out to take the beer to her waiting customers.

Approaching the table, Sharon sets the beer down, one in front of each of the guys at the table. As she *reaches across the table* to check for empty beer bottles, one of them *grabs her around the waist.* "Hey! Did you know this is my favorite waitress?" he asks his friend. The friend smiles and nods his head. "Yep. She takes good care of me whenever I come in. Don't you, sweetie?" He smiles up at her, his arm still around her waist. Sharon finishes cleaning up the table, smiles as she removes his hand, and moves on to check her other tables.

Each of the foregoing examples reveals some of the ways that space is used and defined in Brady's Bar. We set about to investigate systematically the way waitresses defined the spatial aspects of the bar. We found, for example, that they divided the bar into several different kinds of places: the kitchen, the backroom, the lower waitress station, the door, the restrooms. They not only conceptualized the bar in these terms, but they also, as we shall see, associated various places in the bar with different kinds of people and activities. For example, Saturday night is a big night for dates and Sharon knows that if she works the *upper section* the turnover will be slow; there will be less work; and the section will be filled with couples. Because this *place* in Brady's has such territorial definitions, she can expect substantial tips from the customers there. Stephanie, on the other hand, working the lower section, knows she will have large groups of men or women, the turnover will be relatively fast, and that she will have to work hard for fewer and smaller tips. At the same time, the evening will go by quickly, something Stephanie wants tonight. Each waitress has come to know these and other meanings of space in the bar.

One of the most pervasive messages communicated by territorial arrangements in Brady's Bar was the importance of sexual differences. As our research progressed we began to discover more and more ways that space reinforced the way our culture defines masculinity and femininity. Territoriality reflected the basic definitions of sexual gender as expressed in the division of labor and social structure of Brady's Bar. In the remainder of this chapter we want to examine some of the ways that space expresses these cultural definitions of sex.[3] We begin with the bar as a place distinct from other places in the city of Oakland, and then go on to look at other uses of space and objects within the bar.

The Place Called Brady's

Insulated from the outside by its double doors, an inner cocoon of soft warm lights, music, and controlled temperature, Brady's Bar is like a world unto itself. When people cross the threshold, push open the heavy doors, and enter the bar, they come into a place apart, a place designed for a special kind of social life. For it is here that the ordinary male values of our culture are given ceremonial treatment. It is in such bars as this that the meaning of American masculinity is announced, restated, and underlined for all to know. Like the coffee houses in Greece, or the ritual clubhouses of New Guinea where men gather in isolation from the females in their society, men come to the bar to bask in their masculinity, to glean what reassurances and support they can from one another. Unlike men's ceremonial centers in other cultures, however, some females are allowed to enter this ritual men's house. And unlike the world outside the bar, where women may make demands on men, threaten their masculinity and, of late, compete with them in their places of work, women have no such freedom here. The men in Brady's Bar retain command; every female who enters knows she stands on sacred male turf. In contrast to other places where etiquette requires men to defer, the "ladies first" rule is suspended here.

Even the atmosphere at Brady's Bar seems masculine. Trophies won by bar-sponsored teams glitter from their shelves above the bar and occasionally bring forth play-by-play reminiscences of the victories they represent. The heavy furniture isn't designed for female comfort. There are special amenities and service granted to male customers but not extended to the female, such as the adjustment of barroom temperature to suit *his* comfort.

> There have been nights when I have been freezing in the bar and women come in and sit with their coats on. But it's not until a male customer complains that anything is done. I've seen it happen over and over again. I'll complain and nothing happens, but if a football player complains, the heat goes on.

The choice of television channel or juke box selections are also determined by male whims. Stephanie recalls a specific incident that could occur on any night.

> It was early, there were about seven guys sitting at the bar, drinking beer. Four girls walked in, took a table and they put a dollar in the juke box. I remember this because they were some friends of mine. But it was time for the big game and so Mark turned the juke box off and the television on. The girls lost their money.

But the obvious manifestations of male design and control are far less important than the unseen messages that fill the atmosphere. From the moment a man crosses the threshold into the bar he assumes territorial rights. This is *his place,* created expressly for men like him. He exudes confidence and ownership. It can be seen in the way he surveys the bar, orders his drinks, or looks over the women. All these belong to men. His presence here announces to everyone that he has come of age; no longer a boy, he can do those things reserved for adult males. And if he has doubts about his masculinity he can come to the bar where the very air seems to reassure him, giving him courage. After all, this place is for men, evidence enough that all is well.

For a woman to enter Brady's Bar requires a certain amount of courage. Other than waitresses, they seldom come here alone, seeking safety in numbers. Their approach is hesitant, as if they had entered a precarious world, they do not take time to visually examine the men but move quickly to a table, if possible some distance from the bar. And if she has doubts about her womanliness, the atmosphere increases that insecurity. As she enters the give and take of social encounter, the female waitress and the customer alike will find their presence important for men, as audience, as sexual object, as marginal participant. This does not mean women are not highly valued at Brady's Bar; in one sense they are required if the ceremonial life is to function properly.

No sign hangs above the door at Brady's announcing "Male Territory," but such a claim is written into the customs and mores that guide male and female behavior alike. College girls, or recent graduates from several local schools, come to the bar to drink, occasionally to celebrate a friend's birthday, to work as waitresses, and if unattached, to wait for and respond to male attention. Female customers must monitor even the smallest action, maintaining a kind of muted expressiveness. Even a momentary eye contact can be read by some unwanted man as an open invitation. Dianne and Barbara arrive shortly after 9 P.M. and hesitate briefly in the doorway. The tables are empty and there is plenty of room for them at the bar, but they pause to discuss where to sit. They maintain a casual but studied inattention to the man at the bar. As they make their way to the upper section and the table in the corner, everyone at the bar watches their progress. Once seated, they remove their coats and wait patiently for Sharon to wait on them. Unlike male customers, they don't whistle for the waitress or wave their hands to indicate they want service, nor do they yell across the bar, "Miss. Miss," or "Hey, waitress, we want you over here." They merely sit and wait for Sharon to notice them and to approach their table. They order Cokes, as women sometimes do, hoping some guy will offer to buy them drinks. If Bill, or one of the other men seated at the bar comes over to their table, they will most likely smile, listen to his jokes, and play the coy flirting games they have learned so well. While some girls enter Brady's merely to enjoy a drink or two, many come in hopes of meeting men and finding dates for the evening. For them, to take direct steps in this nightly courting game is culturally taboo.

The men who visit Brady's also come to work, to drink, and to encounter members of the opposite sex. But the range of activities open to a man stands in stark contrast to those a woman finds. It is Friday night and two guys arrive early in the evening. It is snowing outside: a sure sign that Brady's will be crowded with customers seeking escape from apartments and dorm rooms. They stand in the entryway and survey the whole bar, sizing up the possibilities for the evening. Sharon, the only female present, leans against the bar at her station and smokes a cigarette. John washes glasses and the three men seated at the bar talk quietly, drinking beer from tall dark bottles. In the background the juke box drones its quiet music. The two guys decide that things are dead, talk briefly, turn around and leave the bar. They came looking for girls, for action, and they feel no compulsion, once inside this place, to remain. Later in the evening when things have "picked up" they will probably return to stay and drink a while.

The three men at the bar came this evening to watch the Chicago Bears play the Miami Dolphins. The game won't begin for another hour, so they pass the time talking. Even though each came alone and has never met the others before this evening, they are comfortable and at ease. No girl ever comes to Brady's to sit with strangers and watch television, but this is a frequent occurrence for men. Other men become regular customers in order to play on the bar sponsored softball or hockey teams or to participate in Brady's annual golf tournament. And they will return night after night to discuss the games with other men and to make plans for future ones. Some men come to place bets on the next pro football game, to play

cards, and to visit with other friends who they expect will be there. For a man, the bar is a social center. It may be a place to transact business, to enlist the services of a lawyer friend, to make contacts, to close a special deal and celebrate. And yes, to also look over the women who venture in, to hustle them, to buy them drinks, and sometimes to leave with them at closing time. But even if the male customer does not succeed at the latter game, as is often the case, the bar still offers him a great deal and he will return again and again.

Male and Female Drinks

But the reasons men and women come to Brady's is not the only thing that announces that this is male territory, a kind of men's locker room where women are allowed to sit and passively observe, hoping to gain some sort of entry. It is also seen in the drinks that are symbolically defined in sexual terms. For waitresses, this dual classification not only proves arousing at times but is also useful in remembering orders.

Holly is working the lower section this Wednesday night, and it is jammed with people. At the bar she gives Mark her order, not in the sequence she received it from her customers, but as Mark and the other bartenders like the orders arranged; all the beers together, the fancy drinks together, and the bar booze arranged by liquor. She rattles off the order; a Schlitz, a Bud, a scotch and water, a bourbon sour, a vodka tonic, and two frozen daiquiris. She has taken orders from two separate tables. Mark prepares them in the order she recites to him, and sets them on Holly's tray. As she turns from the bar with her loaded tray, she approaches the first table occupied by Tom, Bill, and their dates. Without checking she quickly gives the daiquiris to the girls, the Bud and the scotch and water to the men. She collects their money and moves on to the next table where she deposits the remaining drinks with the three men seated there. "Part of the hassle of remembering who gets what drink is taken care of if you know which drinks the men drink and which ones the women drink," says Holly. "A man would never order a frozen daiquiri, and women seldom order scotch or bourbon."

The pressure to order drinks that correspond to your sex is ever present. Sandy recalls an unusual experience with one customer. "This one guy kept coming in and he always sat at the bar. He kept ordering scotch and water, and he would just sit there and drink it and make the most horrible faces the whole time he was drinking it. It was too much. Finally, I asked him if he really liked scotch and water, and I told him I had been watching him and it didn't seem like he did. He said he was a businessman and went to a lot of lunches with clients and they always ordered scotch and water, and he was trying to get used to the taste."

Men most often drink beer or alcohol such as bourbon, brandy, scotch, and whiskey, all with a minimum of mix. Or else they drink their alcohol straight. Men also drink Old Fashioneds, martinis, or Manhattans. Once in a while, a man will order a gimlet. They tend to abstain from "female" drinks; no man in Brady's has been known to drink a banana daiquiri or a Pink Lady.

Female drinks include daiquiris (especially frozen or banana ones), Gold Cadillacs, Singapore Slings, Pink Ladies, Margueritas, Grasshoppers, Bacardis, Smith and Currants, Sloe Screws, gin fizzes, and alcohol heavily laced with soda pop, grenadine, or other sweet liqueurs. Bartenders consider these drinks a nuisance to make and often discriminate against the women who order them, as well as take out their anger on the waitress who brings the order. Their reaction is a subtle reminder that the bar is fundamentally a male place. "Everytime I give Dave an order for something like a frozen daiquiri or a Smith and Currants," says Sue, "you should see him. He always says 'Fuck!' and then makes this horrible face." The

girls know that bartenders hate mixing the fancy drinks and as a joke, sometimes give the bartenders fake orders. One night, just to get his reaction, Sandy told Mark that she needed six Grasshoppers. "You should have seen his face when I told him I was just kidding. Pure relief."

Bartenders sometimes simply refuse to make some of the drinks. One night close to Christmas, four girls came in and wanted Tom and Jerrys, and because John didn't want to bother with it, he told Joyce to tell the girls he was all out of the batter for the drinks, which wasn't true. Or, bartenders may simply put off making the order until they feel more like making the drink, an attitude they never have when mixing "male" drinks.

There are a few sexually neutral drinks, however, such as Bloody Marys, Screwdrivers, Black Russians, Stingers, and martinis, which convey messages about the drinker other than sexual ones. For example, martinis, Black Russians, and Stingers are usually consumed by experienced drinkers, while Screwdrivers or Bloody Marys by less-experienced drinkers. What one chooses to drink, conveys a message to others in the bar and is symbolic of one's sophistication and sexual status.

Carding

When a person walks into Brady's he passes over a physical boundary between the outer world and the inner world. He enters a well-defined territory. But once inside, there is still a social boundary yet to cross, one symbolized by "carding." Carding is a gatekeeping activity, allowing some persons to remain within the territorial limits of the bar and excluding others. Officially, carding is designed to insure the bar is off limits to anyone under twenty-one.[4] In practice, carding often expresses the masculine nature of the bar. Denise is standing at the bar, smoking a cigarette and talking to Mark. Three girls walk in and take a table in the lower section so Denise leaves her station to wait on them. As she puts napkins down in front of each customer, she says: "I'm sorry, but I will have to see some I.D.'s here." The girls look at one another and one reaches into her purse, pulls out her driver's license, and hands it to Denise. She checks the birthdate and hands it back to her. "May I see yours too?" Denise asks the other girls. "I forgot mine." "I did too."

"I'm sorry, but you'll have to leave. I can't serve you."

"But we've been in here lots of times. Just ask Mark. We just forgot our I.D.'s."

"If Mark says you can stay, it's okay," replies Denise and she walks back to the bar to stand and wait. The girls put on their coats and leave without making an appeal to Mark. If you fail to pass this test, as these girls did, you are unwelcome in this territory. It would seem a simple age test, but it soon became clear it was much more than this and provided further insight into the territorial nature of Brady's Bar.

Whether or not to card a customer is, for the most part, left up to the girls, and it is not always an easy decision for a waitress to make. New girls are told to be careful about carding and Mark gives each new girl a spiel. "There's a $200 fine for serving minors. In this state, that means people under twenty-one. They'll fine you $100 and the bartender $100, and close the place for the rest of the night. That's for a first offense. So card people. If you have any doubts about their ages, card 'em. Understand?" he says, obviously forgetting momentarily that for quite some time one of his waitresses was a minor. So, new girls find themselves squinting at customers across the darkness of the bar when people enter, or as they place napkins on the table in front of each customer, quickly trying to estimate ages and calculate dates as they check proffered I.D.'s.

Carding is an art and the waitresses soon learn the many complicated rules surrounding this action. They learn when to card, whom to card, and how to deal with sensitive situations. Only a new waitress, for example, cards everyone—male and female—who looks underage. More experienced waitresses learn to be more selective about whom they single out for this test. The cultural rules for carding guide the girls in deciding whom to exclude from the process as well as whom to check. "I remember one of the things Sharon told me one of my first nights on the job," recalls Sue. "I was madly carding everyone at my tables and thinking I was doing such a great job. Boy, I wasn't going to let anyone get by me. But Sharon took me aside and pointed out a couple of people I should leave alone—like Mark's girlfriend and some of her own friends. I guess I was naive, but I was a little shocked. Between that and the first time I served the cops in the backroom, well, it was quite an eye opener for me. When I look back on it now, I'm kind of embarrassed." The girls are responsible for carding until 10 P.M., when the bouncer comes in to work the door. From that point on, he checks I.D.'s at the door and the waitress need no longer perform this duty.

The decision to card or not to card is based on many cues. Sometimes a waitress can give a detailed explanation as to why she decided to card a certain individual or group of individuals. Other times, she can only say, "They looked like they should be carded." For example, Denise decided to card the three girls who just came in for several reasons she can make explicit: they look young, they hesitated at the door, and they were dressed to look older. In addition, she hasn't seen them in Brady's before.

But one of the most important factors in carding is sex. Nearly all the customers at Brady's are college students and this means the waitress must make careful discriminations as to their relative age. Men are more often left alone while women are invariably carded with great frequency. Not only do bouncers single them out for carding at the door but so do the waitresses. It is usually easier for a waitress to guess a girl's age than that of a male: "A guy, even if he's under-age, knows something about booze and bars and can fake it," says Holly: "Besides, he's bigger than you are." Waitresses are intimidated more easily by a male customer. "How do you ask a three-hundred-pound football player for his I.D.? Better yet, how do you ask him to leave if he doesn't have one?"

In addition to physical intimidation, a waitress knows that carding males is often an exercise in futility. One night when Sharon was new on the job, she started to card a table of football players. "I was asking them for their I.D.'s and I heard a whistle and my name called across the room." Sharon turned to find the bartender looking at her and vigorously shaking his head, "No." Embarrassed, she turned to the guys and said, "Never mind. What would you like to drink?" They saw the scene between Sharon and the bartender, smiled and waved at him in thanks. "That happens a lot and you learn to just leave most of the men alone when it comes to carding. It's less of a hassle and you don't risk scenes like that."

An important influence on waitresses is the different reactions of customers when they are carded. Men, for example, often feel insulted when asked to show their I.D.'s. It is an affront to be mistaken for a *boy* instead of the *man* he so obviously is. One evening Denise asked two guys for their I.D's. They looked at her in complete disbelief and each said, "Me?" They made a big show of digging around in their pockets while Denise stood waiting uncomfortably. They disgustedly threw their I.D.'s on the table instead of handing them to her. "By this time I felt so flustered that I really didn't look at the birthdate, I just glanced at the card and returned them." Denise apologized for the inconvenience and took their order. She had placed herself, a female, in the role of questioning the right of these males to enter the bar. Their response of incredulity was less in regards to their suspected age as to the

fact that a woman had acted as gatekeeper into this distinctly male territory.

But women, especially women who are over twenty-one, often passively accept the carding process or are delighted that someone thinks they are really younger and wants to see an I.D. One slow Saturday night Sandy asked two women in the upper section for their I.D.'s. They were more than happy to comply. One of the girls asked Sandy, "Do you really think I look that young?" The other one said, "I haven't been carded in ages!" But neither woman took offense at Sandy's request. Sandy took their order and went back to the bar to give it to Steve. While he was preparing the drinks Steve asked her: "Did you really card those two broads up there?" "Yes. Why?" But Steve just shook his head and finished fixing the drinks.

Young girls come into the bar early, hoping to escape the bouncer who doesn't come on until later and to hopefully slip past the waitress. Some get in because of a friendship with one of the waitresses, but even that is not a foolproof strategy. Holly was extremely embarrassed one night when she carded one of her fellow waitress's roommates and she wasn't twenty-one. She didn't have an I.D. and she had been counting on Sandy to see to it that she wasn't carded. The girl had to leave, but such "mistakes" are made only once.

Females, sans men, are prime targets for carding, according to the waitresses. "They come in, dressed to the teeth, lots of makeup and sexy clothes. The first thing they do is to light up a cigarette and try to look nonchalant," says Sue. Studied sophistication is a dead give away, especially when the girls get a good look at them and get an opportunity to take their order. As Sue says, "They never know what to drink."

Waitresses sometimes make carding a game, leading on female customers they know will have to leave. Instead of carding the customers immediately, they lead them through a mild denigration ritual in which the waitress exerts what little power she has over them. For example, Joyce approaches a table of three girls, places the napkins down in front of each one and waits. "What would you like to drink?" she asks, pretending they know all about such things. The girls look at each other and one finally says. "I'll have a beer." The others agree.

"What kind?" inquires Joyce.

"Uh, what kind do you have?" Joyce knows at this point that they are under-age or they would have ordered by brand. She rattles off the brands as quickly as she can: "Grain Belt. Budweiser, Hamm's, Pabst, Michelob, Heinekin, Schlitz, Special Export, and Lowenbrau." The girls look at one another. "Oh, make it a Budweiser."

"Me, too."

"The same for me." Then comes the clincher. "Can I see your I.D.'s?" Joyce asks. But they don't have any and so she asks them to leave. They do, sheepishly and without argument. Joyce watches to make sure they leave and don't go to the bar and try to order. Then she sits down near her station, thankful to be rid of a table of female customers. Waitresses usually reserve this ritual for girls. Again, males are relatively safe from such harassment. "Unless," laughs Holly, "they walk in wearing a high school jacket!"

The dignity of higher status male customers is carefully protected by the waitresses. For example, when such customers are carded, the waitress assumes an apologetic and nonvindictive stance. "I'm very sorry, sir, but I will have to see some identification." Or, "Excuse me, sir, but I am afraid that I have to ask you for your I.D. It's the rules." Such requests are usually accompanied by submissive gestures communicating to the customer the waitress's extreme regret for having to submit him to such indignities. She tries to communicate that, as a female, she would not think of questioning their territorial rights on her own. She is merely "following orders."

The rules for carding are inconsistent and applied according to a rather rigid double standard. A customer who is drinking one night at Brady's may be thrown out the next for not having an I.D., and then be back in the night after drinking again. After a girl works at Brady's for a while, however, she begins to make mental lists of which familiar customers are cardable and which are not. The Cougar football players, most males, friends of the employees, and Mark's girlfriend are not cardable. But lower-status customers such as people off the street and most females do not have this immunity. This is one advantage to being a regular at Brady's. If the waitress recognizes you, chances are you won't be carded.

Carding operates as a kind of "toll gate" controlling access to Brady territory. While it is a process based on legal rules constituted outside the institution of Brady's, it quite effectively operates on another level, allowing Brady's to exercise control over their clientele. Waitresses, stringently applying the law, use carding to reduce the female population in their sections. Stretching the rules, they allow underage friends to remain. Managers and bouncers use carding in similar ways. Thus, the rules for carding are often modified to meet the social as well as the legal requirements of Brady's.

Favorite Places

It's 10 P.M. on a Wednesday evening and Brady's is full of people busy drinking, laughing, and talking. The jukebox and the air conditioning are on full blast. All the seats at the bar are occupied by the first string of the Cougar football team, and the real regulars Skeeter, Larry, and Bob complete the group seated there. Behind the bar, Steve and Mark work rapidly mixing drinks for the men seated there and for the other customers seated elsewhere. Several men stand in the aisles near the bar forming a tight crowd in that area. A few stand near the door, talking with John, who's bouncing this evening. Most of the men are congregated at the bar or in the area immediately surrounding it. A few sit at tables in the lower section. Three policemen are in the kitchen drinking.

Most of the tables are vacant, but here and there is a group of females, some seated in the upper section, others in the lower. But there are no women seated at the bar or standing with the men in that area. A couple on a date sit in the corner of the upper section.

Holly and Sandy are really getting around however. They aren't just waiting on tables. Both wear out a path between the bar and the tables in their sections. Sandy serves John at the door and makes trips to the cigarette machine and the juke box for her customers. Holly serves the policemen in the kitchen, ends up later in the backroom making phone calls for Mark, or runs to the cooler to get more beer and juice for him. One of them may get behind the bar to work if Mark lets her. In the name of service, both get around Brady's, going places where men are usually present and where few other women may go.

The dispersal of these people in Brady's is not random, and where people choose to sit or stand in Brady's is closely related to their sex and status in the Brady social hierarchy. Customers usually come into Brady's, select their favorite place, and spend the greatest amount of their time at this single location. Thus Larry and Skeeter, as well as other real regulars, always find their way to the horseshoe end of the bar where they stand or sit near the juke box; the "rum and coke couple" always sit at the small table under the thermostat in the lower section; Bill always sits at the bar next to the waitress station where the girls are always within speaking and grabbing distance; "JB-and-water-with-a-twist-of-lime" prefers the bar; groups of males such as the Cougars or Brady's hockey team usually occupy the bar or sit in the lower section; groups of Annies sit in the upper section as do couples on dates. There is little moving

around once social groups have been established for the evening. Denise, as well as all the other waitresses, can thus tell you precisely who is drinking what at each of the tables in her section. She can point out as many as thirty-six people and name the drinks she has served each one. The normal turnover of customers and hustling may, of course, alter utilization of space from time to time during an evening.

As an evening moves into high gear, more and more people arrive. Even so, crowding does not force people from their favorite places and into other areas of Brady's. Customers simply move in as close as they can to the place they normally prefer to occupy if their favorite place is already taken. It is not unusual to see people standing three and four deep around the bar while tables remain empty.

The bar is the center of male activity in Brady's and therefore a favorite place for many men. From behind the bar the two male bartenders control the juke box, the television, the loudspeaker, the cash registers, and everything necessary for mixing and dispensing drinks. Waitresses must rely on the bartenders to give them the things they need to serve customers at the tables. Mark, John, Steve, and the other bartenders share feelings of possessiveness over this territory, much the same way that a woman does over her kitchen. Joyce was behind the bar one night, picking up a couple of beers for her customers because both the bartenders were somewhere in the back room. She removed the beers from the cooler, opened them, and left the bottle caps lying on top of the cooler. Once Mark was back behind the bar he was perturbed to find the bottle caps sitting on top of the cooler. "They belong here, in the trash can near the cooler," he told Joyce. "If you leave those there it will make a mess and make me spill things. That's one reason we don't let you bitches behind the bar." Bartenders work diligently at keeping this territory neat and orderly; arranging rows of clean glasses, keeping the counters clean of melting ice, rinsing out the blender after each use, and so forth.

Regulars and off-duty bartenders crowd around the bar to exchange jokes, to discuss sports and the intimate details of last night's date. From this locale originate the loud verbal displays, taunting, and laughter that follow the exchange of personal experiences or the telling of a story. Take a typical night, for example. Four men are seated at the bar and they have been there drinking since 7:15 P.M. It's now 8:30 P.M. Two girls walk in and head for one of the smaller tables in the upper section. They don't even consider sitting at the bar although there is plenty of room for them to do so. The guys turn around and watch their progress through the bar, and once the girls are seated the men turn and whisper to one another. They burst out laughing and then all is quiet again. Mark walks in and while he too could sit at the bar, he walks over and stands at the waitress station where he can talk to Steve and Joyce. Three Cougars enter and take seats at the bar. Brady's slowly fills up, a male crowd begins to form around the bar, leaving tables empty. The two girls seated in the upper section remain in isolation from the social activity emanating from the bar and not reaching the area where they sit. Joyce is the only female at the bar. The invisible barrier between the bar and the tables is extremely difficult to cross and for most girls, sitting at the bar is trespassing: only the waitresses seem to have the right or the audacity to do so.

If a woman is at the bar physically, she may still be excluded socially. Here we see men interacting in the presence of women *as if they weren't there*. While waitresses become adjusted to such behavior, it is a good reason for other women not to venture to seats at the bar. Sandy was working alone one night and there was quite a crowd of men at the bar, discussing their experiences with women, and they eventually got around to attacking the bartender's sexual prowess. This quickly led into a story that Skeeter began

telling: "There was this man who thought he had crabs," began Skeeter. Skeeter tells one particularly crude part of the story and pauses. The men look over at Sandy and laugh and elbow one another. Sandy stands there shaking her head and smiling. "How am I supposed to react?" she asks. Skeeter continues. "Well, the man went to the doctor and the doctor examined him and told the man he would have to do some tests to find out what is wrong. Pretty soon, the doctor comes back and the man is all upset. "Tell me, doctor. What's wrong with me?'" Skeeter pauses to make sure everyone is listening. "'I hate to tell you this, son, but those aren't crabs. They're fruit flies. Your banana died.'" The men laugh and picking up on the joke, begin insulting one another: "Hey George, what's that buzzing around your pants?" and "Sandy, watch out for those flies around Bill!" Although present, the fact that she is on sacred male territory gives the men courage to treat her as if she were only marginally a part of the situation.

Waitresses are often drawn into the telling of such stories as unwilling audience but not as a participant. If Sandy, for example, were to actively join in this camaraderie to the extent of sharing a joke she knows, the men would be astonished and most likely change the subject. Instead, the men tell their stories as if she were not there, yet observe closely her reactions to their crudeness. Like talking in the presence of a child, they ignore her presence as a fully sentient being. Sandy, as well as the other girls, adapt to ritual displays such as these while most female customers would find it intimidating to find themselves in the midst of such male-oriented talk. And since the bar is the center for this kind of activity, it is easier and more comfortable for women to simply avoid the bar altogether.

If a man brings his girlfriend or wife to sit with him at the bar, however, such talk diminishes or dies down altogether. George is the only married bartender and one night when he and his wife were seated at the bar, someone began telling a dirty joke. He didn't get very far for as soon as he began the story, one of the guys seated at the bar piped up: "Hey, watch it. There's a lady present." The presence of a waitress at the bar, however, does not bring forth such chivalrous statements. Unattached females are automatically excluded from the category "lady"; only such girls can provide the kind of audience needed if a man is to gain the full benefit from recounting his sexual exploits or telling some off-color story.

When the men tire of telling jokes, they often turn to the waitress for amusement and include her as the object of verbal displays meant to demonstrate one's masculinity. Denise recalls one evening:

> There were about five guys sitting at the bar talking to Steve. I was just standing at my station listening to their stories and jokes. They were talking and laughing rather loudly about some girl who comes into the bar and who has a large chest. Then they decided they were going to discuss mine. So they started laughing and elbowing one another and yelling across the bar for me to tell them my bra size. That went on for about five minutes but they became bored and switched subjects. A lot of that happens. It used to embarrass me at first but you get used to it.

In this type of interaction, Denise is forced to respond as an object. She cannot, for example, indicate that she is offended by such behavior. An indignant response on her part would increase their taunts and invading questions. The waitress herself is not the focus of attention in these cases; she is merely an artifact used by men to display their prowess. It is as if they were announcing to all within earshot, "Look at me, I can ask this girl intimate questions right here in public. You must admit there's nothing unmanly about me."

The Waitress Station

There are two waitress stations located at the bar, one in each section. The girls work in these areas and it is the only place where they can give their orders to the bartender and pick up drinks. While a strong taboo prevents female customers from invading the most important male territories, neither taboo nor the limited authority of the waitress can keep men from taking over the waitress station. Territorial displacement is often found in primate societies such as baboon troops. In these cases, as in Brady's Bar it reflects the relative status of individuals. Sandy relates a common experience:

> It wasn't very crowded but there were a lot of guys standing at my station and there were places to sit. It made me really mad because I kept saying, "I have to get through. I work in here." As soon as I left the station, they would get right back in there and settle in to have a conversation. It made me so mad because I would come through with a tray load of empty beer bottles that are really tipsy. I was trying to get through with all of them so I could clean off my tray and fill an order. They wouldn't move. I was afraid they would hit me with their elbows and the whole thing would go. This went on for a couple of hours. Finally, I was so mad that I said, "Look, you guys. I really mean it. You are going to have to move." They still didn't move. They just smiled and said, "Let the little lady through." They let me through and then they would get right back. I had to go through it all over again the next time I came to the station. They were big football players so I wasn't going to cause any trouble.

It is a constant and exhausting battle as they attempt to clear their stations by saying, "Scuse me, Scuse me," all the time tapping shoulders, and nudging with the edge of their trays. The girls hesitate to use such tactics against some men and fall back on feminine displays of weakness and helplessness to get them to move. Sue taps them on the arm and waits for them to turn around, then smiles and says, "Please?" This particular tactic works for the moment, but they are right back in the station soon after that.

Some customers are impossible to move, especially a few of the real regulars, who feel particularly secure in their right to be in the waitress station. On occasion, they will turn and look at the waitress as she requests them to move, then resume conversation, completely ignoring her. Bartenders are little help in this matter since they are often busy talking with the customers and do not want to ask them to move for fear of offending them. The bartender may even be engaged himself in conversations with the offending male, and thereby contribute to excluding the waitress from her station. And it is often the case that the offending male is an off-duty bartender. When Mark is not working as a bartender, he stands in the waitress station because from there he can talk to the bartenders, the waitresses, direct activity behind and at the bar, and he can quickly get service there.

This territorial displacement of the waitress from her station not only announces to everyone the dominance of males, that females cannot control any space in the bar, but it also makes work for the waitress more difficult. Holly, for example, squeezes through the crowd to the bar. She starts to give the bartender her order, despite one customer who is still crowding her out of the area and not paying attention to the fact that she needs to be there. His elbow knocks a Harvey Wallbanger, which the bartender has just fixed for her, and it spills down the front of her dress. "The guy just looked at me like, 'Clumsy!' and didn't even apologize!" says Holly. The girls unanimously agree that this is a constant problem in their work and they feel helpless to combat it. The

waitress station is like the rest of the bar, a place where men in the bar enjoy standing and they feel they have the right to utilize this space.

The girls also have a difficult time getting though the aisles and up and down the steps in order to wait on tables and make it to the bar. When it is crowded, they don't complain, but customers often choose to stand in the aisles and on the steps when there is other space available. Again, they spend an inordinate amount of energy yelling, "Scuse me, Scuse me," as they literally fight their way through the aisles with their tray loads of drinks. An empty tray can be a very effective weapon, but balancing a tray full of drinks is a precarious and delicate situation. The girls become infuriated as they say, "Excuse me" for the hundredth time and the response is just a glance from the male blocking the aisle. Similar to the situation at the bar where women are a part of the scenery in male rituals, waitresses must struggle to retain their rights over any space in the aisles, to make their presence and need to be there known to the customers who would prefer to ignore her.

But waitresses also have numerous encounters with customers in which the situation is reversed: the customer won't leave her alone and she must do her best to ignore *him*....

NOTES

1. See Edward Hall, *The Hidden Dimension,* for an excellent study of space uses in cross-cultural perspective.
2. Ibid. (145–149).
3. Erving Goffman, in his book *Relations in Public* emphasizes the importance of the use of space in social interaction and posits a relationship between social status and space. "In general, the higher the rank, the greater the size of all territories of the self and the greater the control across the boundaries" (1971:40–41). Since men in our

society generally enjoy a higher status than do women, we would expect to find males in Brady's exercising more control over territory.

4. At the time of our research, the legal drinking age for the state was twenty-one. It has since been changed to eighteen.

REFERENCES

Goffman, Erving. 1971. *Relations in Public*. New York: Basic Books.
Hall, Edward T. 1966. *The Hidden Dimension*. New York: Doubleday.

13

ELIJAH ANDERSON

THE BLACK MALE IN PUBLIC

from *Streetwise* (1990)

In his book *Streetwise*, Anderson studies two adjacent, formerly working-class neighborhoods: one overwhelmingly African American and increasingly poor, the other racially mixed and gentrifying. The two communities are close enough to share a commercial strip, mass transit lines, and a serious crime problem. In this excerpt he explores how one sector of the local population—young black men—navigate relations in public places here. For them, simply walking the streets safely requires careful attention to the presentation of self as they seek a balance between the need to be seen as "tough" enough to avoid being challenged or victimized by other neighborhood youth, while not being perceived as a threat to whites or the police.

An overwhelming number of young black males in the Village are committed to civility and law-abiding behavior. They often have a hard time convincing others of this, however, because of the stigma attached to their skin color, age, gender, appearance, and general style of self-presentation. Moreover, most residents ascribe criminality, incivility, toughness, and street smartness to the anonymous black male, who must work hard to make others trust his common decency.

This state of affairs is worth exploring at some length for at least two reasons. First, the situation of young black men as a group encapsulates the stigmatizing effect of "negative" status-determining characteristics, in this case gender and race. Because public encounters between strangers on the streets of urban America are by nature brief, the participants must draw conclusions about each other quickly, and they generally rely on a small number of cues. This process is universal, and it unavoidably involves some prejudging—prejudice—but its working out is especially prominent in the public spaces of the Village-Northton.

Second, in the Village itself,...the presence and behavior of anonymous young black men is the single dominating concern of many who use its public spaces. The central theme in maintaining safety on the streets is avoiding strange black males....The consequences for the black males themselves are my concern here.

Anonymous black males occupy a peculiar position in the social fabric of the Village. The fear and circumspection surrounding people's reactions to their presence constitute one of the hinges that public race relations turn on. Although the black male is a provocative figure to most others he encounters, his role is far from simple. It involves a complex set of relationships to be negotiated and renegotiated with all those sharing the streets. Where the Village meets Northton, black males exercise a peculiar hegemony over the public spaces, particularly at night or when two or more are together. This influence often is checked by the presence of the local police, which in turn has consequences for other public relationships in the Village.

The residents of the area, including black men themselves, are likely to defer to unknown black males, who move convincingly through the area as though they "run it," exuding a sense of ownership. They are easily perceived as symbolically inserting themselves into any available social space, pressing against those who might challenge them. The young black males, the "big winners" of these little competitions, seem to feel very comfortable as they swagger confidently along. Their looks, their easy smiles, and their spontaneous laughter, singing, cursing, and talk about the intimate details of their lives, which can be followed from across the street, all convey the impression of little concern for other pedestrians. The other pedestrians, however, are very concerned about them.

When young black men appear, women (especially white women) sometimes clutch their pocketbooks. They may edge up against their companions or begin to walk stiffly and deliberately. On spotting black males from a distance, other pedestrians often cross the street or give them a wide berth as they pass. When black males deign to pay attention to passersby, they tend to do so directly, giving them a deliberate once-over; their eyes may linger longer than the others consider appropriate to the etiquette of "strangers in the streets." Thus the black males take in all the others and dismiss them as a lion might dismiss a mouse. Fellow pedestrians in turn avert their eyes from the black males, deferring to figures who are seen as unpredictable, menacing, and not to be provoked—predators.

People, black or white, who are more familiar with the black street culture are less troubled by sharing the streets with young black males. Older black men, for instance, frequently adopt a refined set of criteria. In negotiating the streets, they watch out particularly for a certain *kind* of young black male: "jitterbugs" or those who might belong to "wolf packs," small bands of black teenage boys believed to travel about the urban areas accosting and robbing people.

Many members of the Village community, however, both black and white, lack these more sophisticated insights. Incapable of making distinctions between law-abiding black males and others, they rely for protection on broad stereotypes based on color and gender, if not outright racism. They are likely to misread many of the signs displayed by law-abiding black men, thus becoming apprehensive of almost any black male they spot in public....

Two general sociological factors underlie the situation in which the black man in the Village finds himself. The first, the "master status-determining characteristic" of race (Hughes 1945), is at work in the most casual street encounter. Becker's application of Hughes's conception of the contradictions and dilemmas of status has special relevance:

> Some statuses, in our society as in others, override all other statuses and

have a certain priority. Race is one of these. Membership in the Negro race, as socially defined, will override most other status considerations in most situations; the fact that one is a physician or middle class or female will not protect one from being treated as a Negro first and any of these other things second. The status of deviant (depending on the kind of deviance) is this kind of master status. One receives the status as a result of breaking a rule, and the identification proves to be more important than most others. One will be identified as a deviant first, before other identifications are made. The question raised: "What kind of person would break such an important rule?" And the answer given: "One who is different from the rest of us, who cannot or will not act as a moral human being and therefore might break other important rules." The deviant identification becomes the controlling one.

Treating a person as though he were generally rather than specifically deviant produces a self-fulfilling prophecy. It sets in motion several mechanisms which conspire to shape the person in the image people have of him. (Becker 1963, 33, 34)

In the minds of many Village residents, black and white, the master status of the young black male is determined by his youth, his blackness, his maleness, and what these attributes have come to stand for in the shadow of the ghetto. In the context of racism, he is easily labeled "deviant" in Becker's sense. In public, fellow pedestrians are thus uncertain about his purpose and have a strong desire to make sense of him quickly, so that they can get on with their own business. Many simply conclude that he is dangerous and act accordingly. Thus in social encounters in the public spaces of the Village, before he can be taken for anything as an individual (that is, "specifically" in Becker's terms), he is perceived first and foremost as a young black man from the ghetto (that is, "generally").

Here the second element comes into play. An assessment like this is really a *social definition*, normally something to be negotiated between labeler and labeled. Goffman's description of the process is classic:

> When an individual enters the presence of others, they commonly seek to acquire information about him or to bring into play information already possessed. They will be interested in his general conception of self, his attitude toward them, his competence, his trustworthiness, etc. Although some of this information seems to be sought almost as an end in itself, there are usually quite practical reasons for acquiring it. Information about the individual helps to define the situation, enabling others to know in advance what he will expect of them and what they may expect of him. Informed in these ways, the others will know how best to act in order to call forth a desired response from him. (Goffman 1959, 1)

In a city one has many encounters with anonymous figures who are initially viewed as strangers, about whom little is known or understood. As Goffman suggests, there are ways strangers can rapidly become known or seen as less strange. In negotiating public spaces, people receive and display a wide range of behavioral cues and signs that make up the vocabulary of public interaction. Skin color, gender, age, companions, clothing, jewelry, and the objects people carry help identify them, so that assumptions are formed and communication can occur. Movements (quick or slow, false or sincere, comprehensible or incomprehensible) further refine this public communication. Factors like time of day or an activity that "explains" a person's presence can also affect in what way and how quickly the image of "stranger" is neutralized (see Simmel 1971; Wirth 1928; Schutz 1969; Goffman 1971).

If a stranger cannot pass inspection and be assessed as "safe" (either by identity or by purpose), the image of predator may arise, and fellow pedestrians may try to maintain a distance consistent with that image. In the more worrisome situations—for example, encountering a number of strangers on a dark street—the image may persist and trigger some form of defensive action.

In the street environment, it seems, children readily pass inspection, white women and white men do so more slowly, black women, black men, and black male teenagers most slowly of all. The master status assigned to black males undermines their ability to be taken for granted as law-abiding and civil participants in public places: young black males, particularly those who don the urban uniform (sneakers, athletic suits, gold chains, "gangster caps," sunglasses, and large portable radios or "boom boxes"), may be taken as the embodiment of the predator. In this uniform, which suggests to many the "dangerous underclass," these young men are presumed to be troublemakers or criminals. Thus, in the local milieu, the identity of predator is usually "given" to the young black male and made to stick until he demonstrates otherwise, something not easy to do in circumstances that work to cut off communication (see Becker 1963; Goffman 1963).

In the Village a third, concrete factor comes into play. The immediate source of much of the distrust the black male faces is the nearness of Northton. White newcomers in particular continue to view the ghetto as a mysterious and unfathomable place that breeds drugs, crime, prostitution, unwed mothers, ignorance, and mental illness. It symbolizes persistent poverty and imminent danger, personified in the young black men who walk the Village streets (see Katz 1988, 195–273). The following narrative of a young black indicates one response of Villagers to the stereotype they fear so much:

A white lady walkin' down the street with a pocketbook. She start walkin' fast. She get so paranoid she break into a little stride. Me and my friends comin' from a party about 12:00. She stops and goes up on the porch of a house, but you could tell she didn't live there. I stop and say, "Miss, you didn't have to do that. I thought you might think we're some wolf pack. I'm twenty-eight, he's twenty-six, he's twenty-nine. You ain't gotta run from us." She said, "Well, I'm sorry." I said, "You can come down. I know you don't live there. We just comin' from a party." We just walked down the street and she came back down, walked across the street where she really wanted to go. So she tried to act as though she lived there. And she didn't. After we said, "You ain't gotta run from us," she said, "No. I was really in a hurry." My boy said, "No you wasn't. You thought we was gon' snatch yo' pocketbook." We pulled money out. "See this, we work." I said, "We grown men, now. You gotta worry about them fifteen-, sixteen-, seventeen-year-old boys. That's what you worry about. But we're grown men." I told her all this. "They the ones ain't got no jobs; they're too young to really work. They're the ones you worry about, not us." She understood that. You could tell she was relieved and she gave a sigh. She came back down the steps, even went across the street.

We stopped in the middle of the street. "You all right, now?" And she smiled. We just laughed and went on to a neighborhood bar.

Experiences like this may help modify the way individual white residents view black males in public by establishing conditions under which blacks pass inspection by disavowing the image of predator, but they do little to change the prevailing public relationship between blacks and whites in the community. Common racist stereotypes persist, and black men who successfully make such disavowals are often seen not as the norm but as the exception—as "different from the rest"—thereby confirming the status of the "rest."

In the interest of security and defense, residents adopt the facile but practical perspective that informs and supports the prevailing view of public community relations: whites are law-abiding and trustworthy; anonymous young black males are crime-prone and dangerous. Ironically, this perceived dangerousness has become important to the public self-identity of many local black men.

Greetings

Among blacks, the art of greeting is of great cultural importance. Children are often chastised at home if they fail to "speak" to their elders when they enter a room. The caretaking adult may become indignant when a charge fails in his duty to "be polite." A visitor will then comment, "Young man, can't you speak?" This places the blame squarely on the child, who then may sheepishly say, "Hi, Mr. Jones."

To some degree this practice may derive from "southern" or rural norms, but it has been brought to northern urban areas and survived. In the days of strict racial segregation, the black community was a haven to blacks, who tended to see every other black person as an ally in the fight against oppression (see Cox 1948: Doyle 1937). Furthermore, blacks were ready to see one another as special—as a "friend," a "brother," or someone with whom they had much in common. In this social context, even unacquainted blacks were inclined to greet each other easily and comfortably. Blacks in the Village still spontaneously greet other blacks they are sure they do not know. In fact Northton blacks, many of whom have southern roots, seem to be

more forthcoming with such greetings to fellow blacks on the streets of the Village than they are on their home turf, reflecting a need to express color-caste solidarity. In contrast, middle-income blacks of the Village are more likely to greet their white counterparts, while remaining somewhat reserved in their overall behavior.

To many blacks, greetings carry an obligation to respond in kind. Not to return a greeting is uncommon, and the person is considered "strange." Blacks are more likely to speak to those they do not know, including whites, than whites are to speak to unfamiliar whites or to blacks in public places. When with a black person, a white person may be amazed that so many "unknown" blacks will speak. In this way, unacquainted blacks can give the appearance of a unified public community on the streets of the Village. Such greeting behavior is not simply an ingrained ritual; it may be viewed as instrumental, as a way for Northton blacks in the Village to come to terms with an environment they see as not always welcoming or safe.

Codified forms of greeting, or lack of greeting, clearly provide a means for negotiating encounters with strangers, so it is hardly surprising that many black males use such behavior as a device, even a ploy, of getting safely past the next black male of uncertain purpose. These greetings become tools for gauging intent and for assessing the safety of a public situation. Black youths are well aware of how "dangerous" they are seen to be, and they may help place each other in that category, which can be advantageous. When one black youth encounters another on the street, he may be circumspect and somewhat cautious, and he will try to read his counterpart. As one young black man said:

> You know by the way they respond to you that you get a certain ease in the relationship. If they respond a certain way, I know a lot of times when I'm not sure

about someone, and see, they'll be the same age as me. I know we doing this for each other. If I see a young black male that I'm not sure about, well, you know, he doesn't exactly put me at ease right away. I might say. "What's up?" or "How ya feel?" You then can kinda know, by the way he responds to you, like if he don't answer you, or if one of your own people [a black person] don't say something to you, then kinda automatically you kinda put a shield around you. You just makin' sure. You act differently than you woulda acted if he hada responded to you in some compatible way. You have to establish something, especially if you never saw the person before.

I can automatically pick up on when somebody's going at me. I mean like a lot of times, I can tell if a brother I see on the street comes from my old neighborhood: I can feel at ease a bit. But if a brother is coming from some other neighborhood, I don't consciously try to predict their acts. But the way I react to them is just saying to them that I'm not sure. I don't perceive them to be necessarily about the same things that I'm about. I don't know whether he's about snatching a pocketbook or holding somebody up. See, I have to wonder when I see a strange black male. I have to watch my back.

When the stranger responds in kind to a greeting on the street, the situation is over: the other youth leaves, and the young black can relax. Typical passing rituals between strange young black males include: "Hey, now," "Hey, hometown," "Hey, home," "Alright," "Hey," "What's up?" "How ya feel," or even an audible grunt. In the streets there is a profound need to acknowledge the presence of the other, to communicate awareness of the other's awareness, but this communication is intended to be superficial and not to go further. Typically, as the two continue on their

ways, neither looks back; they have thus said much by not saying more. The hidden tension among black males is elaborated by a young black man from Northton:

When I go down the street, I go straight to my friends. I watch out for certain people I don't know from the neighborhood. I go straight to my friends; they be on the corner. I watch my back. I observe everything, look in the bushes. I know which way to go home. I never walk in the middle of the street, unless there's a dog on the side. I don't trust no dogs. And I never cross the street when I see dudes [other black males] coming, because I feel as though they see you doin' that, they feel as though, "What's up with him?" When you cross the street, that means you're scared or you can't fight.

But you walk on the same side, first thing they think—he might got a knife, he might be into martial arts, or he might be a boxer. Shit, that means you intimidatin' them. I can come right to 'em: I don't give a shit how many are there. I'm too dumb to run. When people cross the street rather than meet me, I know they scared to death. When I pass some dude, I just say. "How ya doin'?" They say, "What's up?" If he starts to say somethin' to you, you keep walking. At times, I have an expression on my face that I'm not to be messed with. I stare at the person. Intimidate a person. Eye to eye. See who back off first, things like that. I don't pay 'em no mind. If someone bump into me on purpose, I keep on rollin'.

The greeting used in this manner is intended to evade or defuse interaction rather than to move toward personal involvement. An important, if subtle, rule is that participants remain within the negotiated confines of the simple initiation. An attempt to go beyond the superficial greeting might, in the words of Erving Goffman

(1959), "flood out" the situation. Further advances may undermine the delicate relationship between passersby, particularly those of different colors and genders.

The greeting becomes particularly important at night, when it is a kind of peace offering, a means of communication designed to advise the next person of one's civil intentions, or even of one's ability to deal with trouble. A variety of signs may be given to help the individual feel more at ease on the streets, even if they are not understood or taken seriously by his counterpart. The following field note illustrates this:

On successive summer nights I walked or drove around the Village streets. Weather permitting, people sit on their porches in lawn chairs and swings, sometimes completely hidden from passersby. The streets are often quiet except for the faint chirps of crickets or the sound of cars. Occasionally the silence is broken by the clamor of a passing youth's radio, but then it grows quiet again. One weeknight, at about 9:00, I saw a young black woman walking. As we met, she said "Hi." I returned her greeting and continued. Then I saw an elderly black man on the other side of the street, and though the streets are not wide, he did not acknowledge me. Next I saw a young black woman pushing a stroller, with her three- or four-year-old child walking eight to ten feet behind her. Acknowledging me, she said "Hi," and I said "Hey," politely returning her greeting. Farther down the street I encountered four black youths. As we approached I said, "How y'all feelin'?" a greeting common among blacks of the city. One youth returned, "Alright." They continued, and I went on my way.

Such greetings run the social gamut from relatively simple to highly complex: they may signal superficial acceptance of the next person on the street or exhibit varying degrees of personal closeness between sender and recipient. Because most local blacks, regardless of where they reside, are not culturally far removed from the ghetto and are at least conversant with its rules and symbols, they are often better able to read such public situations than are whites or blacks with very limited urban experience. Blacks tend to think of themselves as streetwise in a way whites are not—to feel that they have a special empathy and connection with those blacks who might be dangerous in public. With such attitudes in mind, they have developed a number of strategies for dealing with the anonymous black male, including sometimes aggressive greeting behavior. The "street" repertoire of such individuals includes the strategy of "getting ignorant," which they invoke in conversations with others and enact in public to deal with supposed adversaries. Getting ignorant is taken to mean getting down to the level of a street-oriented person and capably adopting the supposed behavior of underclass blacks who would engage in loud talk and profanity and if necessary violence to deal with a public dispute. For instance:

In an adjacent community that shares some social and cultural patterns with the Village, Thomas Waters, a well-educated middle-class black man, became involved in a dispute with his underclass neighbor. The exchange on the street went something like this: Robert Johnson, the less well-off man, complained, "I don't like you parking in front of my house with your big car [Lincoln Town Car], because you break up my curb. Look at that, see. Now, don't do it again, and ruin my curb, or you gon' pay for it." "What? What are you talking about, man? You want me to pay for your curb? Well, you can just hold your breath on that one. You'll sip ice water in hell before I'll pay for your curb! Do you hear me? That's what you can do!" This exchange grew louder and verged on violence. It never got to that point, but those looking on were worried, not knowing whether to call the police.

In the words of middle-class blacks, the posture and behavior Thomas Waters assumed is "getting ignorant," and because of caste experience, particularly familiarity with an underclass code of behavior, such individuals can sometimes act out the script rather convincingly. It is just this familiarity, and the ability to switch codes situationally, going back and forth between middle-class propriety and an assumed "street" orientation, that allows many middle-income blacks to feel less nervous and constricted in public than their white counterparts. The following field note illustrates this:

On a Saturday night in November at about 11:00, I was at a self-service gas station on the edge of the Village. Because it was cold, I pumped my gas with one hand on the nozzle and the other in my pocket. Suddenly a young black man appeared. He walked over and asked if I had the time. Instinctively I looked him in the eye and said, "What's up, buddy?" as though I expected an answer. There was silence. Then I said, "I ain't got no watch, man." Experience on the streets had taught me that one ruse muggers use is to ask the intended victim a question that distracts him, getting him to drop his guard and setting him up for the mugging. By saying "What's up, buddy?" I gave him pause and made him rethink his intentions. In a stickup or a mugging, timing is crucial. My body language, my tone of voice, and my words, all taken together in that instant, may have thrown him off, possibly averting an attempted stickup. Context was important here. The rules of the streets say that a strange black male does not approach another black male around midnight on a Saturday and ask for the time. Such a person, goes the rule, deserves what he gets in the way of an answer. I understood that, and I presume the possible mugger did too. I was able to switch codes from that of the middle class to that of the street—to "get ignorant."

Claiming Turf Rights

Yet both blacks and whites are cautious with strangers and take special care in dealing with anonymous young blacks. This caution is encouraged by a certain style of self-presentation that is common on the street. Many black youths, law-abiding or otherwise, exude an offensive/defensive aura because they themselves regard the streets as a jungle. A young black man said:

A friend of mine got rolled. He was visiting this girl up near Mercer Street. He come out of this house, and somebody smacked him in the head with a baseball bat. He had all these gold chains on. Had a brand new $200 thick leather jacket, $100 pair of Michael Jordan sneaks, and they were brand new, first time he had them on his feet. He had leather pants on too. And I'm surprised they didn't take his leather pants. I mean, he had a gold chain this thick [shows quarter-inch with his fingers]. I mean pure gold—$800 worth of gold. He came out this girl's house, after visiting his baby. Cats hit him in the head with a baseball bat, and they took everything. Took his sneaks, his coat, everything. When the paramedics got there he had no coat, no sneaks on. They took his belt, took his Gucci belt, the junkies did. I went to visit him in the hospital, and I'm sorry I went in there. I seen him. The boy had stitches...they shaved his head, stitches from here to all the way back of his head. Beat him in the head with a baseball bat. They say it was two guys. They was young boys, typical stupid young boys. Now my boy's life is messed up. He home now, but poor guy has seizures and everything. It's a jungle out here, man. But he sold drugs; the cops found cocaine in his underwear. They [the muggers] got what they wanted.

The young black males' pose is generally intended for people they perceive as potentially aggressive toward them. But at the same time it may engender circumspection and anxiety in law-abiding residents, both black and white, whose primary concern is safe passage on the streets.

In this public environment, pedestrians readily defer to young black males, who accept their public position. They walk confidently, heads up and gazes straight. Spontaneous and boisterous, they play their radios as loud as they please, telling everyone within earshot that this is their turf, like it or not. It may be that this is one of the few arenas where they can assert themselves and be taken seriously, and perhaps this is why they are so insistent.

Other pedestrians withdraw, perhaps with a defensive scowl, but nothing more. For the Village is not defended in the way many working-class neighborhoods are. As the black youths walk through late at night with their radios turned up, they meet little or no resistance. This lack of challenge shows how "tame," weak, or undefended the neighborhood is, except in certain areas where white college students predominate and fraternity boys succeed in harassing apparently defenseless blacks such as women with children, lone women, and an occasional single black man. Black youths tend to avoid such areas of the Village unless they are in groups.

The same black youths might hesitate before playing a radio loud in the well-defended territories of Northton, however. There they would likely be met by two or three "interceptors" who would promptly question their business, possibly taking the radio and punching one of the boys, or worse, in the process. No such defending force exists within the Village.

At about 5:30 on a Tuesday evening in September, three black youths appeared on quiet Linden Avenue. One carried a large box radio, with the volume turned high. The sound was distinctively "rap" [music], and the boys were "jamming" to the beat. They seemed to be in their own world, oblivious to others on the sidewalk and on the porches they passed. Halfway down the block, they stopped at an inviting stoop. They sat on the steps, legs sprawled, as though they were used to the spot. While the music played, the youths spoke loudly, in competition with the radio. One boy sang along with the tape, bobbing his head to the beat. No one complained. The three boys sat there on the stoop, enjoying themselves and filling the air with their music for fifteen to twenty minutes. Then they left as suddenly as they had appeared, transporting their "rap" music down the street, the sounds becoming fainter as they moved on.

Another aspect of claiming turf rights is public talk—its idiom, duration, intensity, and volume. At times the language of young black males, even those who are completely law-abiding, is harsh and profane. This language is used in many public spaces, but especially at trolley stops and on trolleys and buses. Like the rap music played loudly on boom boxes, it puts others on the defensive. The "others" tend not to say much to the offenders; rather, they complain to one another (though some residents have in fact come to appreciate the young males and enjoy the music).

On public transportation young blacks, including some girls, may display raucous behavior, including cursing and loud talk and play. Because most people encounter the youths as strangers, they understand them through the available stereotypes. Law-abiding black youths often don the special urban uniform and emulate this self-presentation, a practice known as "going for bad" and used to intimidate others. As one young black man said:

You see the guys sometimes on the bus having this air about them. They know that the grown people on the bus hope that these guys are not problems. The boys play on that. I'm talking about with women old enough to be their mothers. Now, they wouldn't be doing this at home. But they'll do it on that bus. They'll carry on to such an extent.... Now, I know, especially the young boys. I know they [older people] be scared. They really wondering, 'cause all they know is the headlines, "Juvenile Crime...." "Problems of Youth Kids," or "Chain Snatchers." This is what they know. And these people are much more uncertain than I am, 'cause I know.

In some cases black males capitalize on the fear they know they can evoke. They may "put on a swagger" and intimidate those who must momentarily share a small space on the sidewalk. When passing such a "loud" dark-skinned person, whites usually anticipate danger, though they hope for a peaceful pass. Whites and middle-income blacks are often more than ready to cross the street to avoid passing a "strange" black person at close range. Young blacks understand this behavior and sometimes exploit the fear, as illustrated in the following narrative by a young white woman:

I went out for something at the store at about 9:00, after it was already dark. When I came back, there was no place to park in front of my house anymore. So I had to park around the corner, which I generally don't do because there's a greater chance of getting your car broken into or stolen over there, since a lot of foot traffic goes by at night. So I parked the car, turned out the lights, and got out. I began walking across the street, but I got into a situation I don't like to get into— of having there be some ominous-looking stranger between me and my house. So I have to go around or something. And he was a black fellow between twenty and thirty, on the youngish side. He certainly wasn't anybody I knew. So I decided not really to run, just sort of double-time, so I wouldn't meet him at close distance at the corner. I kind of ran diagonally, keeping the maximum distance between him and me. And it must have been obvious to him that I was running out of fear, being alone at night out

in the street. He started chuckling, not trying to hide it. He just laughed at what I was doing. He could tell what he meant to me, the two of us being the only people out there.

At times even civil and law-abiding youths enjoy this confusion. They have an interest in going for bad, for it is a way to keep other youths at bay. The right look, moves, and general behavior ensure safe passage. However, this image is also a source of subtle but enduring racial and class distinctions, if not overt hostility, within the community.

Some black youths confront others with behavior they refer to as "gritting," "looking mean," "looking hard," and "bumping." Youths have a saying. "His jaws got tight." Such actions could easily be compared to threatening animal behavior, particularly dogs warning other dogs away from their territory or food. Gritting is a way of warning peers against "messing with me." To grit is to be ready to defend one's interests, in this case one's physical self. It conveys alertness to the prospect of harmful intent, communicating and defining personal boundaries. As one young black man said concerning strategies for negotiating the Northton streets near the Village:

When I walk the streets, I put this expression on my face that tells the next person I'm not to be messed with. That "You messing with the wrong fellow. You just try it, try it." And I know when cats are behind me. I be just lookin' in the air, letting them know I'm checkin' them out. Then I'll put my hand in my pocket, even if I ain't got no gun. Nobody wants to get shot, that shit burns, man. That shit hurt. Some guys go to singing. They try to let people know they crazy. 'Cause if you crazy [capable of anything], they'll leave you alone. And I have looked right in they face [muggers] and said, "Yo. I'm not the one." Give 'em that crazy look, then walk away. 'Cause I know what they into. They catch your drift quick. Another young black man described his use of body language this way:

It's certain ways you can give him body language that you're not to be messed with. Some people ball their fists up or just walk, or they're built a certain way. You move the hand. Walk with his hand like this, means he's a fighter. I handle myself. I can handle three guys. See, if you're fightin' three guys, if you swing at the same time they swing, you get tired first, you fightin' three guys. But you use your head. One swing, you snatch him, knock the shit out of him. Another one comes, bam! Throw him off balance. You don't go swinging as much as they do. Use your head.

The youth is caught up here in a cultural catch-22: to appear harmless to others might make him seem weak or square to those he feels a need to impress. If he does not dress the part of a young black man on the streets, it is difficult for him to "act right." If he is unable to "act right," then he may be victimized by strangers in his general peer group. The uniform—radio, sneakers, gold chain, athletic suit—and the selective use of the "grit," the quasi-military swagger to the beat of "rap" songs in public places, are all part of the young man's pose. Law-abiding and crime-prone youths alike adopt such poses, in effect camouflaging themselves and making it difficult for more conventional people to know how to behave around them, since those for whom they may not be performing directly may see them as threatening. By connecting culturally with the ghetto, a young black may avoid compromising his public presentation of self, but at the cost of further alienating law-abiding whites and blacks.

In general, the black male is assumed to be streetwise. He also comes to think of himself as such, and this helps him negotiate public spaces. In this sense others

collectively assist him in being who he is. With a simple move one way or the other, he can be taken as a "dangerous dude." He is then left alone, whereas whites may have more trouble.

Civility and law-abidingness are stereotypically ascribed to the white male, particularly in the public context of so many "dangerous" and "predatory" young blacks. (In fact, white men must campaign to achieve the status of being seen as dangerous in public places.) The white male is not taken seriously on the streets, particularly by black men, who resist seeing him as a significant threat. They think that most white men view conflict in terms of "limited warfare," amounting to little more than scowls and harsh words. It is generally understood that blacks from Northton do not assume this but are open to unlimited warfare, including the use of sticks, stones, knives, and guns, perhaps even a fight to the death.

Most conventional people learn to fear black youths from reading about crimes in the local papers and seeing reports of violence on television, but also by living so near and having the chance to observe them. Every time there is a violent crime, this image of young blacks gains credibility. Such public relations attribute to blacks control over the means and use of violence in public encounters, thus contributing to dominant stereotypes and fear. As is clear from the following interview, black men pick up on that fear:

They [white men] look at you strange, they be paranoid. Especially if you walkin' behind 'em. They slow down and let you walk in front or they walk on the other side. You know they got their eye on you. I walk past one one time. My mother live on Fortieth and Calvary and I did that. I said, "You ain't gotta slow down, brother. I ain't gonna do nothin' to you, I ain't like that." He looked at me and laughed. He knew what I meant, and I knew what he was thinkin'. He had a little smile. It was late at night, about 1:00 A.M. He let me get in front of him. He was comin' from a bar, and he had a six-pack. I'm a fast walker anyway; you can hear my shoes clickin'. I see him slowing down. I said, "I ain't gonna do nothin' to you, I ain't like that." He just laughed; I kept on walking and I laughed. That's the way it went.

Whereas street interactions between black strangers tend to be highly refined, greetings of whites toward blacks are usually ambiguous or have limited effectiveness. This general communication gap between blacks and whites is exacerbated by the influx of white newcomers. In contrast to the longtime residents, the newcomers are unaccustomed to and frequently intolerant of neighboring blacks and have not learned a viable street etiquette. The run-ins such new people have with blacks contribute to a general black view of "the whites" of the Village as prejudiced, thus undermining the positive race relations promoted over many years by egalitarian-minded residents.

The result is that the white and black communities become collapsed into social monoliths. For instance, although blacks tend to relate cautiously to unknown black youths, they are inclined to look at them longer, inspecting them and noting their business to see whether they deserve to be trusted. Whites, on the other hand, look at blacks, see their skin color, and dismiss them quickly as potential acquaintances; then they furtively avert their gaze, hoping not to send the wrong message, for they desire distance and very limited involvement. Any follow-up by black youths is considered highly suspect unless there are strong mitigating factors, such as an emergency where help is needed.

A common testimonial from young blacks reflects the way whites encounter them. They speak about the defensiveness of whites in general. White women are said to plant broad grins on their faces in hopes of not being accosted. The smile may

appear to be a sign of trust, but it is more likely a show of deference, especially when the woman looks back as soon as she is at a safe distance. When the black stranger and the perceived danger have passed, the putative social ties suggested by the smile are no longer binding and the woman may attempt to keep the "dangerous" person in view, for a sudden move could signal an "attempted robbery" or "rape."

A young black man who often walks through the Village reports this reaction from white women:

They give the eye. You can see 'em lookin' right at you. They look at you and turn back this way, and keep on walkin'. Like you don't exist, but they be paranoid as hell. Won't say hello. But some of 'em do. Some of 'em say hi. Some of 'em smile. But they always scared.

One young white woman confirmed this: "I must admit, I look at a black [male] on the street just for a few seconds, just long enough to let him know I know of his presence, and then I look away." The black man just quoted gave an observant report of the general behavior of white Village women on the streets:

Most of the white women will wear pants. You don't see a white woman with a dress on unless she with her boyfriend. She by herself, she'll go right on a porch when she see some [black] guys comin' this way. Most girls walk with a pack of girls. They feel safe they got at least two girls with 'em. Two don't feel too safe. You get a group of three or four, they feel they have a better chance. They have a dog with 'em, a man, or a pack of four or five. And they dress in jeans. You can tell they paranoid. They don't know what to do. They say: "Are they good blacks or bad blacks?" Most of 'em will take a chance. Chance is good; nobody do that no more, they know they got the cops. In the Village, cops sit on the porch, park between cars; they lookin' at every move you makin' and you don't even see 'em. But they see you and waitin'! The women'll stay home. And they have a car. Don't come out at certain times. Especially after eleven or twelve at night. They don't go in bars. They go to clubs downtown.

The young black men are the ones they [women] got to worry about. The young ones walk around lookin' mean and tough. They don't care about the white guys. No. they goin' to catch the trolley to the movies. You gotta go through the Village to catch the trolley, bus, el [subway].

Out of a sense of frustration, many young blacks mock or otherwise insult the whites they see in public spaces, trying to "get even" with them for being part of the "monolithic" group of whites. When they encounter whites who display fear, they may laugh at them or harass them. They think, "What do I have to lose?" and may purposely create discomfort in those they see as "ignorant" enough to be afraid of them. Of course the whites of the Village are anything but a monolithic group. But it is convenient for certain blacks to see things this way, placing all whites, whom they see as the source of their troubles, into an easily manageable bag. In this way blacks as well as whites become victims of simplistic thinking.

Black men's resentment, coupled with peer-group pressure to act tough, may cause them to shift unpredictably from being courteous to whites to "fulfilling the prophecy" of those who are afraid and uncomfortable around blacks. When confronting a white woman on the streets some youths may make lewd or suggestive comments, reminding her that she is vulnerable and under surveillance. The following account describes such an encounter:

On a Wednesday afternoon in June at about 2:00, Sandra Norris pushed her nine-month-old daughter down Cherry Street. The gray stone facades of the Victorian buildings sparkled in the sun. The streets seemed deserted, as the Village usually is at this time. Suddenly three black youths appeared. They looked in their late teens. As they approached her, one of the young men yelled to the others, "Let's get her! Get her!" Making sexual gestures, two of the youths reached for her menacingly. She cringed and pulled the stroller toward her. At that the boys laughed loudly. They were playing with her, but the feigned attack was no fun for Mrs. Norris. It left her shaking.

As indicated above, an aggressive presentation—though certainly not usually so extreme—is often accepted as necessary for black youths to maintain regard with their peers. They must "act right" by the toughest ghetto standards or risk being ridiculed or even victimized by their own peers. Feeling a certain power in numbers, some groups will readily engage in such games, noisily swooping down on their supposed "prey" or fanning out in a menacing formation. Children, white and black, sometimes are intimidated and form fearful and negative feelings about teenage "black boys."

Such demeanor may be a way of identifying with the ghetto streets, but it is also a way of exhibiting "toughness" toward figures who represent the "overclass," which many view as deeply implicated in the misfortunes of their communities. Such conduct is easily confused with and incorporated into ordinary male adolescent behavior, but the result is complicated by race and gender and the generalized powerlessness of the black community. Understandably, middle-class residents, black and white, become even more likely to place social distance between themselves and such youths, conceptually lumping anonymous black males together for self-defense.

Of course not everyone is victimized by crime, but many people take incivility as an indication of what could happen if they did not keep up their guard. When representatives of Northton walking through the Village intimidate residents either verbally or physically, many middle-class people—whites in particular—become afraid of black males in general. They may have second thoughts about "open" and to some degree friendly displays they may previously have made toward blacks in public. Blacks and whites thus become increasingly estranged. In fact there is a vicious circle of suspicion and distrust between the two groups and an overwhelming tendency for public relations between them to remain superficial and guarded.

Public Disavowal

It is not surprising that the law-abiding black man often feels at a disadvantage in his interactions with whites. Most whites, except possibly those who are streetwise…and empathic about the plight of inner-city blacks, are conditioned to consider all black male strangers potential muggers. The average black, because of his own socialization on the streets and his understanding of the psychology of whites, understands this position very well and knows what whites are thinking.

Many blacks and whites seem alarmed when a black youth approaches them for any reason, even to ask the time. Such overtures may simply be the youth's attempt to disavow criminal intent or to neutralize the social distance generally displayed on the streets. But these attempts are easily interpreted as a setup for a mugging, causing the other person to flee or to cut off the interaction. The public stigma is so powerful that black strangers are seldom allowed to be civil or even helpful without some suspicion of their motives (see Becker 1963; Goffman 1963; Hughes 1944; Simmel 1971).

Even law-abiding black men who befriend whites and belong to biracial primary groups face "outsider" status. For example,

when a black visits a white friend's house, knocks on the door or rings the bell and waits, he risks being taken by the neighbors as someone whose business on the stoop is questionable. Some people will keep an eye on him, watching every move until their neighbor comes to the door. It may not matter how well the visitor is dressed. His skin color indicates his "stranger" status, which persists until he passes inspection when the white person answers the door. A white man with the same self-presentation would pass much sooner.

Although they do not usually articulate the problem in just this manner, many black middle-income Villagers feel somewhat bitter about the prejudice of their white neighbors, who are caught up in a kind of symbolic racism. Dark skin has a special meaning, which Village residents have come to associate with crime. Though white Villagers may not have contempt for blacks in general, they do experience anxiety over the prospect of being victimized. So, since blacks are believed to make up a large proportion of the criminals, pedestrians tend to be defensive and short with strange black males. The same people may have intimate black friends and may pride themselves on their racial tolerance. Yet, concerned with safety, they regard blacks as an anonymous mass through which they must negotiate their way to their destination. They may pass right by black "friends" and simply fail to see them because they are concentrating not on the friend but on the social context. Such reactions frustrate many black-white friendships before they have a chance to begin. Blacks generally complain more than whites about such shortcomings of friendly relations. But as blacks make their way around the streets, they too may miss a "friend" of the other color. Such events may have more to do with the ambiguous nature of public race relations than with racial feeling itself. But whatever the cause, these problems are an impediment to spontaneous and biracial interactions.

Although blacks and whites may harbor similar cognitive views of the dangers of life in the Village, their perceptions of real situations commonly vary. Blacks generally feel less threatened than whites by anonymous blacks, because they are better able to read the signs indicating another person's intentions and to determine whether a situation is safe or dangerous. But there are times for them too when a "mock attack" signals real alarm. The following instance of harassment was witnessed by a forty-year-old black man living near the Village:

> On Sunday night at about 11:30 I was walking home when I saw these eight young brothers [black men] messing with this older white man. He was riding an old three-speed down the street when he met the young black men. They assaulted him. One shouted, "Hey! Gimme that bicycle." Another said, "Hey old man, where you going?" With that, they surrounded him. It must have scared the shit out of him. It seemed like that was just what they wanted to do. They didn't really want his bicycle. It wasn't like the bicycle was a new ten-speed. They just wanted to mess with him. One guy grabbed the handlebars and shook the whole bicycle. I thought about saying something, but I was worried about my own safety. You know how these wolf packs can be. After a while one of the guys slapped him upside his helmet, and then they all left the man, laughing as they walked. The old man was very frightened, I know. And down the street a ways he flagged down a police car. The cop was a sister [black woman]. Some other cars soon came, and they put his bicycle in the trunk of one of the cars, and they went looking for the brothers.

In this situation the black man empathized with the victim, but he was concerned for his own safety during the assault. Also, he felt that any attempt to help might be taken by the victim or the police as further harassment, or even that he might be mistaken for one of the perpetrators.

An impressive number of blacks deplore such antagonism and feel somewhat responsible to change it. They may view themselves as among the few members of their race who can help bridge the gap. To play this role, not only must they be outstanding (to set an example of what a black person is capable of for those powerful whites who are in a position to judge), but they must also set an example for other blacks. Thus a number of black men try very hard to disabuse whites of their misjudgments. Often they go to great lengths to behave contrary to the assumed expectations of whites, and they encourage other blacks to do so. They respond to prejudice by putting on a performance of civility.

A young black man in street uniform may extend obvious courtesies such as moving over to allow a white person extra space to pass, making friendly eye contact, or offering a greeting. He may try to confront and allay the stranger's fear. For example, when walking down a dark street behind a white person, he might say, "Hey, you don't have to be afraid, I'm not that man. I'm not out to rob you. You don't have to worry." Unfortunately, the person is likely to be startled and often does not know how to respond. The actions are in such contrast to the common black male dress and self-presentation that only an unusual person would immediately trust the verbal message over the visual image. Furthermore, the words go beyond the expected superficiality in greetings and threaten some personal involvement. Thus the plea to look beyond the black's self-presentation is rarely successful, and the stereotype of the dangerous black persists.

The black man who is determined to fight his bad image may handle what is often an uncomfortable situation for the white person by being too nice:

> On Saturday afternoon at Lee's grocery store, on the edge of the Village, a young white woman was standing in line. She

had bought many items and had two large bags full. As she picked them up off the counter and started for the front door, one bag slipped out of her hands and spilled on the floor. Three black men aged nineteen to twenty-two quickly came to her aid. Within seconds they were on their knees retrieving the groceries. They worked silently, while other customers watched them. They picked up every item and helped rebag the groceries. After this one young man asked, "Want me to take these out for you. Miss?" Clearly grateful but surprised, she sheepishly declined the offer and quickly left the store.

Such shows can be witnessed repeatedly around the Village and may be considered public demonstrations for whites who know little about the black community. They try to say, "We're not all like that [bad]," and at times they are a direct attack on the presumed prejudiced thinking of whites and an attempt to discredit such views—a public disavowal of incivility and criminality.

In public interactions between anonymous blacks and whites, there seems to be a strong concern with the immediate situation. The black person wants to get out with his self-esteem intact, which requires that the white person do the same. Because the black has the upper hand, he can in principle define the situation in a positive manner, such as by being gracious. In practice this is very difficult, as the last few examples illustrate. He hopes that, by his behavior, whites who are inclined to be suspicious of all black males will change their opinions.

The result of this informal public relations campaign is that whites may receive better treatment than blacks do from such people. Fellow blacks are not the primary object of this campaign; presumably they "understand" the existence of integrity and civility in the average black. A young black man made these comments:

I find myself being extra nice to whites. A lot of times I be walking down the streets, you know. And I see somebody white. Going back to my street smarts, I know they are afraid of me. They don't know me, but they intimidated. I pick that intimidation up, so I might smile, just to reassure them. And I know I'm doing that consciously, I know it. At other times I find myself opening doors, you know. Holding the elevator. Putting myself in a certain light, you know, to change whatever doubts they may have. Look, I do this in my neighborhood, when I go downtown to work, because I know how uptight white people are in their relationship with young blacks in town. In the building I work in, I see them. They look at me all funny, so I'll go in the men's room and use the key. I say to a complete stranger, "Hey, how you doing?" I speak [offer a greeting]. I don't have to speak. But it's because I want them to feel comfortable with me in the bathroom. I find myself doing this all the time.

It might be tempting to attribute such behavior to the "race man" ethic...but such an evaluation would be one-dimensional: there may be some of this ideology motivating the black man who acts as a paragon of civility in the presence of whites, but there is an instrumental element as well. Dealing with others in public requires an enormous amount of effort from the black male and produces unwanted distraction. Such a young man must put strangers at ease so he can go about his own business. He can sense when his presence makes whites nervous and unsettled. Blacks who must repeatedly endure this reaction feel emotional stress and want to relieve themselves of the burden.

In adapting to this reality, blacks assume the general principle of public order that trustworthiness is an ascribed characteristic for whites but that blacks, particularly young males, must work to achieve it. One consequence is the development of public communities based on color. Usually the relationships between anonymous whites and blacks in public are truncated and perfunctory, since most people are concerned with "just getting by" and reaching their destination and do not want relations to go further. The intimate biracial friendships that do occur tend to be sponsored through third parties or fostered by an institutional framework. The release of tension when a black male turns out to be "known" is evident in the following incident recounted by a middle-aged white Village resident, which occurred one Halloween:

> I know this kid named Tommy Hatfield; he was in Sarah Taylor's class, third or fourth grade. I forget now which one it was. But anyway. Tommy was having some problems with his family. He was a very angry boy. He wasn't a bad kid, but he was very angry. Sarah was very patient with him, and he liked her a whole lot. And I knew him for these eight weeks. Once a week I'd meet him in the class of about thirty or forty kids for an hour and a half to two hours. We got along fairly well. Anyway, he graduated, and he began going to another school. I hadn't seen him for a while, but then one time just at Halloween, my kids and I were sitting out on the steps.
>
> A group of young black boys were coming to our stoop, we live on Spencer Street. And we could see that they were sidling up next to one another, and they were thinking, "How are we going to get candy off of this guy, now?" They didn't have any masks on or anything. Was he going to give them a hard time? Now maybe I was reading a lot into this. You could see that they were sort of moping around. They were not going to do anything bad, but you could see they were trying to figure out how to handle this situation. Well, Tommy looked up and saw that it was me and said, "Oh, it's Mr. Regis," and he poked his other friend with his elbow, and said, "It's Mr. Regis. He's taught us architecture."
>
> And I looked up at him, and I said, "Oh, it's Tommy." And you could see there was just a whole difference in feeling. You could see that his facial expression changed, and mine probably did. And I said, "Tommy, you'll have to have some candy, here. What would you like?" He probably got more than he would have before. It was resolved in a good way. It was a good feeling. And it could have been a tension-filled situation [had the boys been strangers]. Not dangerous, but a tension-filled situation.

In what circumstances can the anonymous black male become known as something other than a predator? Older black men earn greater trust through their appearance and demeanor, which suggest maturity and even a caretaking role toward others on the street. They often go so far as to become guardians of the public peace, concerned for the safe passage of others. They inform strangers about certain corners, warning them where not to go. Most often they offer advice only to whites who, they presume, are ignorant of the ways of the streets. There is an element of patronage in such interactions.

In determining the degree to which a man is seen as predator, the main question is What's his business? The extent to which he seems to be preoccupied, engaged in doing something, determines whether he is taken as being "up to no good." Daytime generally makes a black man in the Village seem less suspicious, mainly because others can see what he is doing, with the implication that because he can be watched he is also controlled and is less likely to commit a crime. A black man pushing a baby stroller at 3:00 in the afternoon would probably be taken as safe, whereas the same man alone at 11:30 at night would not. Eating an ice-cream cone can lessen a fearsome image, since watchers might reason that such an image is inconsistent with this "human" action. The time of day, the season of the year, the neighborhood's social history—events of the past thirty years or of the past few days—all affect the meaning this black man has for the residents who watch and informally guard the streets and public spaces.

Another important consideration here is what Goffman (1971) has described as the "with" and how its nature defines the individuals involved. Seeing a black man walk down the street with a conservatively dressed white man or woman mitigates what may otherwise be taken as a "tough" image or an unknown quantity and introduces elements of "weakness" or law-abidingness into the social equation.

In trying to take precautions, people look for signs that will indicate the nature of the black male. Whether he wears the uniform of the streets makes a difference in how he will be regarded. Also, the way he walks, whether he makes "false" or suspicious moves, is important. Blacks who desire the public trust feel a great need to distance themselves publicly from the black males who seem most untrustworthy, those wearing street attire or displaying the emblems of the underclass that increase their estrangement from conventional society. Black men who want to be seen as "safe" often display cultural emblems that suggest a connection with this conventional society and, by implication, public civility. Probably the most evocative emblem is the business suit and tie, which suggests that its wearer is committed to civility and thus is unlikely to engage in street fighting, to rob others, or to curse at passersby. Carrying books is another emblem, and black university students might display their books and briefcases to gain trust. Moreover, these are emblems known to be controlled by members of the "overclass"—people who can take for granted the full rights, duties, and civil obligations of ordinary citizens.

Yet even a black man in a suit and tie or carrying books is not necessarily by himself a "full person" in the minds of prejudiced whites concerned about their safety. Rather, he must be considered relative to his "ghetto" counterparts; in contrast to them, he can be seen as trustworthy and possibly law-abiding. That the person may be seen as symbolically negotiating his way suggests that his public identity is precarious and that he is thus discreditable (see Goffman 1963), particularly compared with those who start with the "master status-determining characteristic" of white skin. The anonymous black male is a person apart until he proves he has a connection, and therefore he is more persistently a stranger on the streets.

On the streets and in public places, young blacks are repeatedly sent the message that they are crime-prone and that their neighbors have little faith in their willingness to be law-abiding. And certainly, as the crime statistics and reports of victims illustrate, there are many of whom this is true. But for others this state of affairs creates a gnawing dilemma, for they are victimized from two sides. They must simultaneously prove that they are worthy of respect for their common decency, and they must protect themselves from predatory youths by looking tough and capable of "handling the streets."

This situation further polarizes racial attitudes in the special circumstances of the Village. By encouraging both whites and blacks to see those of the other color not as individuals but as representatives of their "untrustworthy" race, it is eroding the biracial harmony the previous generation of Village residents worked so hard to achieve.

One might wonder what all the second-guessing and fear on the part of middle-income people—black and white—does to the young black men who must live and operate in the Village. Certainly it gives them the sense that they are, if not losers, then at least not "born winners" in the local community or in life in general.

In their campaign for respectability, some young black men have become crusaders, particularly in those city areas that whites and blacks share. In their quest for positive judgment, they have become some of the most generous, helpful, kind, and courteous people around, contributing, to an often unacknowledged degree, to public safety. Nonetheless, it is impossible for them to overcome the pervasive stereotype. In the Village, no young black male has an easy time on the streets. The residents fear him. The police generally consider him out to rob people or insult passersby. Perceiving him as a threat, they view him as someone they must contain. This is one of the reasons many middle-class blacks are deflected from moving into the area or may leave soon after they arrive: they do not want such easy confusion of themselves and their children with the black underclass, particularly as it becomes caught up with the working conceptions and stereotypes of others in the neighborhood.

REFERENCES

Becker, Howard S. 1963. *Outsiders: Studies in the Sociology of Deviance*. New York: Macmillan.

Cox, Oliver C. 1948. *Caste, Class, and Race: A Study in Social Dynamics*. New York: Modern Reader Paperbacks.

Doyle, Bertrand W. 1937. *The Etiquette of Race Relations*. New York: Schocken Books.

Goffman, Erving. 1959. *The Presentation of Self in Everyday Life*. Garden City, N.Y.: Doubleday.

———. 1963. *Behavior in Public Places*. New York: Free Press.

———. 1971. *Relations in Public*. New York: Harper and Row.

Hughes, Everett C. 1945. "Dilemmas and Contradictions of Status." *American Journal of Sociology* 50:353–359.

Katz, Jack. 1988. *Seductions of Crime: Moral and Sensual Attractions in Doing Evil*. New York: Basic Books.

Schulz, David A. 1969. *Coming up Black: Patterns of Ghetto Socialization*. Englewood Cliffs, N.J.: Prentice-Hall.

Simmel, Georg. 1971. *Georg Simmel on Individuality and Social Forms*. Donald N. Levine (ed.). Chicago: University of Chicago Press.

Wirth, Louis. 1928. *The Ghetto*. Chicago: University of Chicago Press.

14

MICHAEL BULL

EMPOWERING THE "GAZE": PERSONAL STEREOS AND THE HIDDEN LOOK

from Sounding Out the City (2000)

Cities today are filled with people walking, waiting for the bus or train, or shopping while listening to personal stereos. How has this transformed urban life? Bull explores this new sonic dimension of public life in his study of London, *Sounding Out the City*. In this excerpt he shows how people are able to create private spaces within public places as well as construct a unique, personal experience of moving through the city.

The interpersonal relationships of people in big cities are characterised by a markedly greater emphasis on the use of the eyes than of the ears. This can be attributed to the institution of public conveyances. Before buses, railroads and trains became fully established during the nineteenth century, people were never in a position to have to stare at one another for minutes or even hours on end without exchanging words ... [Urban conditions require] an inner barrier between people, a barrier, however, that is indispensable for the modern form of life. For the jostling crowdedness, and the motley disorder of metropolitan communication would simply be unbearable without psychological distance. Since contemporary urban culture, with its commercial, professional and social intercourse, forces us to be physically close to an enormous number of people, sensitive and nervous people would sink into despair if the objectification of social relationships did not bring with it an inner boundary and reserve.

—Simmel, *The Metropolis and Mental Life*

People stood on local platforms staring nowhere. A look they'd been practising for years. Speeding past, he wondered who they really were.

—D. DeLillo, *Libra*

In ordinary railway and bus seating in America, passengers who feel overcrowded may be able to send their eyes out the window, thereby vicariously extending their personal space.

—E. Goffman, *Relations in Public*

Not knowing where to put one's eyes whilst travelling through the spaces of the city is a dominant concern amongst urban theorists. The above quotes reflect strategies that subjects use to avoid the perceived social discomfort and embarrassment of the urban "look." How do personal-stereo users manage the "look"? We know that users often establish a zone of separateness within urban spaces in order to create a measure of control over that environment. Yet how does this fit in with the standard accounts of urban looking expressed above? Simmel, in the first quote, describes Berlin at the beginning of this century where the immense changes in urban geography of the period resulted in the forcible mixing of different sections and classes of people in the city. The fragile strategies whereby subjects attempt to maintain those bourgeois rituals of civility and etiquette are highlighted in his analysis. These strategies are the "mute stare" coupled with a sense of vulnerability and unease as to where the eyes should rest. This results, in Simmel's analysis, in a retreat into a self-enclosed mode, referred to as an "inner barrier," that creates a sense of "reserve" in the urban traveller that becomes "second nature" to them.

Goffman's subject, in contrast to this, stares out into space through the windows of a railway carriage in order to create a space. Possessed space thus becomes the horizon of the subjects' vision. Other people lose their materiality because they are not seen or attended to. If the subjects' thoughts are placed literally in front of them, then the sense of subjective space is increased to the visual horizon of the subject. This constitutes, for Goffman, a successful method of avoiding the stare and any resultant sense of discomfort.

DeLillo's New Yorkers stand on tube platforms looking distractedly out into an amorphous space. They are careful to avoid the direct glance of the "other" using this as a strategy of urban survival. The spaces of the city, at least the underground, are described as places of incipient danger and in order to ensure survival one mustn't engage the "look" of the "other" for fear of intruding, much the same as drinkers in some public houses will sit and stare at their drinks for fear of offending anyone with a "look." These observations, Simmel's, Goffman's and DeLillo's, all have a certain exteriority attached to them. Subjects are perceived to be responding to the immutability of their surroundings. Common to all is the defending of some assumed notion of private space. Their responses are all externalist; the woman looks vacantly out of the window; subjects practice their non-looks on station platforms and so on. Common to these observations is an absent interiority. My account of auditory looking and the nature of a technologized auditory construction of urban space is rather undertaken through an analysis of users' accounts. In doing so I provide a micro-study of urban "looking" devoted to an exposition of the distinctive features of auditory looking, addressing what it means to "look," "see," or to be "seen" in public via the use of technology. I refer to personal-stereo looking as a form of "auditory gazing" constituted through personalized sound. It differs fundamentally from the "look" constituted through the randomized sounds of the street.

Managing the Gaze

The use of a personal stereo permits the user to control the "gaze" through a variety of interpersonal strategies. The specificity of auditory looking comes across clearly in the following account:

> When you start commuting it's very unsettling not to know where to put your eyes. The Walkman makes you one step removed from the situation. Also the music is quite comforting, or is something familiar superimposed on everything else...It's a way of passively acknowledging that they're not going to talk to anyone, and that what's around them is not relevant to them. It blocks out and it certainly alters reality. You're not full there...It emphasises the step of removal from where you are. I was thinking about it today watching someone's conversation. I couldn't hear what they were saying at all. So it wasn't like being within five feet of two people having a conversation. (Chris: interview number 11)

Users consistently claim to be "somewhere else" whilst using personal stereos. Their physical embodiment appears to be of secondary importance whilst their management of their mental state appears to be of primary importance. Significantly the circumstances surrounding these states often differ from those examples given above by Simmel and the others, as these mental states are being driven by the facility of the personal stereo and are not necessarily merely a response to the urban

environment. The personal stereo replaces the sounds of the outside world with the sounds chosen by the user. Thus, whatever the experiential process is, it is inevitably attended to and mediated by the sound coming through the machine. The sound is immediate and often loud and works to rearrange the senses producing an experience of being "one step removed" from the physical world. Yet, when users do respond to urban overload, in a manner similar to Simmel's description, the use of a personal stereo removes this unsettled feeling by replacing it with itself, thereby acting to distance any feelings of unsettledness. Personal-stereo use acts to transform users' horizons of experience by superimposing itself onto that environment, cloaking the alien with the familiar and in doing so transforms the subjective response to it. The respondent quoted above describes this process as a passive response to the social situation tinged with an element of guilt, "as if" what was around him should in some sense be relevant to him. This attitude to the social is not typical of users and in this instance resulted in the person using their personal stereo less and less. More typical is the following quote from a woman in her mid twenties:

> It's easier to have eye contact with people, because you can look but you're listening to something else. You don't feel you're intruding in on people, because you're in your own little world. (Stephanie: interview number 42)

The above user both looks and does not look. Eye contact has a different meaning if the recipient of the gaze can see that the person is "somewhere else," signifying that the gaze is not a penetrative gaze but rather an unintentional or distracted gaze. This type of gaze, according to this user, does not constitute an "incursion" into the private space of another due to the lack of intentionality held in the gaze. In a sense the look isn't a look at all. The subject is somewhere else in "her own little world." The term "one's own little world" is used repeatedly by respondents to describe their personal-stereo states both in public and in private. This particular respondent goes on to make the following observation:

> I'm not always aware of who else has a Walkman on. I wonder where they are because whoever's wearing one is somewhere else. (Stephanie: interview number 42)

Users are often indifferent to the presence of others as this rather common response indicates:

> I often think they are thinking about nothing. They're just going. And I don't see them because I'm so used to it and I've got my Walkman. So I don't see them. (Sirah: interview number 15)

This negation of the external environment can be a totalizing experience and is often encapsulated by an attendant burdensome awareness of the "eversame" of the everyday urban. The "other" is often perceived in terms of a blank object, exteriorized automatons on their way to work devoid of thoughts, invisible and of no concern to this user at least. There also appears to be a staving off of the awareness that she too might be like them if not for the use of her personal stereo that secures her in her own subjectivity. The user is a twenty-year-old woman who is performing her daily journey across London on public transport. The use of her personal stereo relieves the boredom of the journey, but for this user there is also the fear of the anonymity of the urban, of losing oneself within it, coupled with a fear of the unknown. The city for her has a kind of anonymous danger attached to it:

> I think it's good to keep yourself apart from other people. I feel vulnerable with people I don't know. (Sirah: interview number 15)

She uses technology as a kind of security fix. Along with her personal stereo she now has a mobile phone which she also claims not to be able to be without. The arsenal of mobile technology becomes her "lifeline" whilst traversing those empty but potentially fearful public spaces (Bauman 1991). Another user describes the world beyond the personal stereo in the following terms:

> When you've got your Walkman on it's like a wall. Decoration. Surroundings. It's not anyone. (Ed: interview number 59)

The metaphor of a "wall" aptly describes the impenetrability of the user's state, or desired state, in relation to the geographical space of experience. The world becomes the backcloth to one's own thoughts; people become adjuncts to this, or alternatively are not noticed at all. The following user is not motivated by apprehension as our other user appeared to be, but merely by the superfluity of it all:

> I look around, look out the window. I guess because from Finchley to High Darnet you're above ground. But you won't really be seeing it. You're just staring blankly at it. You watch the people in the carriage and wonder what they're about but you don't think too hard about it because you've got something else in your head. (Mags: interview number 31)

The dreamlike state of use and the consequent non-look of the user is brought out clearly by the following quote:

> Some people might think you're staring at them but I don't. You just look straight ahead, sometimes you don't look around. Then you come to consciousness and realize you've been staring at them for half an hour—and you've not really

been looking at them. When you've got your Walkman on your brain tends to— you're listening to the music—nothing else—but when you've got nothing else. You look around. You're just conscious. (Jana: interview number 47)

The look here is a totally unrecognized one; it merely appears. The object of the gaze may not know it, but it isn't a look at all. This user is surprised when she realizes that he has been staring at another person. The awareness comes with the breaking into real time as distinct from personal-stereo time. During personal-stereo time the subject does not look. Looking is reserved for states when the world floods in. The first respondent whilst thinking vacantly about other passengers also does not really look and is equally "somewhere else." The gaze on occasion might also be more aggressive in the sense of being bolstered by the person's own soundtrack and the resulting sense of security derived from this, as is the case in these two young males where use works to empower the gaze:

> I feel a bit more confident. So I can just stare at them. (Dan: interview number 22)
> Yeh. I stare at people. I won't be staring at them. I'll just be looking at them. (Michael: interview number 40)

Users are sometimes aware of the difference between a personal-stereo "look" and other forms of looking:

> [On the bus] I look up, usually I'm looking behind or up at the person if the person opposite is interesting, But I don't look at him or her as a person and I don't even think I'm looking at them. I just, kind of stare straight through them. But I get a lot of people looking straight back. There's different ways of looking at somebody. (Gemma: interview number 24)

Using a personal stereo also permits users to negotiate potentially embarrassing looks from others. The following user expresses feelings of discomfort at being "stared at" in the close proximity of the tube. A feeling more frequently mentioned by female users:

> I'm completely lost on the tube. Completely absorbed. It's just another distraction. I feel quite uncomfortable with that sort of eye contact. It's just so raw on the tube. In the tube I'm just completely out of it. No. I look down really. Sometimes I might have my eyes closed. (Jo: interview number 30)

Whilst the above respondent, a woman in her late twenties, is equally absorbed or "lost" on the tube this appears to be more of a reaction to embarrassment and as a method of fending off unwanted or incursive looks. Listening to her personal stereo does not make her feel braver on the tube although elsewhere, on the street it does make her feel more assertive. On the tube it merely occupies her time. She avoids glances, looks down and closes her eyes. This differs from the quote below where for this female user the auditory look becomes an omnipotent one with reciprocal gazing perceived as being impossible:

> It's like looking through a one-way mirror. I'm looking at them but they can't see me. (Julie: interview number 12)

It is a recurring theme amongst users to refer to looking without being seen. The above description of vision as a one-way mirror is merely the most succinct metaphor for escaping the "reciprocal gaze." In this account the viewing subject disappears into an unobserved gaze. In essence a voyeur's gaze of omnipotent control. The role of the personal stereo in this is to make the person's gaze invisible, At the same time her private space remains inviolable whilst she wears her personal stereo, permitting her to perceive the situation as being under control. This can be referred to conceptually as a form of non-reciprocal gazing that embodies an extreme form of asymmetry. This avoidance of the reciprocal gaze means that the subject cannot be fixed. Only as exteriority can she be grasped. This response is mirrored in the following response of a thirty-year-old woman:

> I feel more invisible if anything. Just detached. An observer. Invisible in the sense of a detached observer. I feel very, very detached. I can't say I'm detached from other people looking at me. I'm just detached from the normal rigmarole of sirens and screeching brakes...I feel more detached from it all, then I feel I can look at them more. Just look at them. See them. I just perceive it differently. I see it. I feel I see it for what it truly is. You see deeper...I can really study them and they can't see me. (Jay: interview number 33)

Two processes are operative here: the blocking out of sounds and the auditory look. By blocking out, Jay claims to be able to see more clearly, as if the sounds in her head were constructing a true image or facilitating a true understanding of the subjects of her gaze. It would appear in this instance that the narcissistic gaze is a complement to an empowered gaze. The personal stereo in these cases facilitates a voyeuristic gaze which might be seen to empower the gazer merely because they have worked out a strategy to look and not be seen. In doing so they protect their space and identity from the reciprocal stare. The above example, along with others, demonstrates that the "voyeuristic" gaze cannot merely be understood in terms of gender categories. Both male and female users feel a sense of empowerment through the use of personal stereos. This does not mean however, that the social dynamic is the same for both sexes. More women users refer to resorting

to personal-stereo use in order to avoid the stare of others.

Avoiding the Gaze: Personal-Stereo Use and Social Invisibility

How then do users absent themselves from the gaze of others? Intrinsic to these processes is the reconceptualization of subjective placement in the urban domain. The use of personal stereos replaces the sounds of the outside world with an alternative soundscape which is more immediate and subject to greater control. This replacement function of the personal stereo can be controlled in the sense that the user can adjust the sound levels to suit their circumstances, desire or mood. A consensus is demonstrated in user accounts concerning the transformative nature of use on the subjects' experiences of journeying and their relationship to the outside world. Users typically describe the sound as overwhelmingly enveloping them:

> You become more aware of you and less aware of what's going on. The music is not like a background. It's all around you. It takes over your senses. It can be quite isolating. Walking around I don't feel part of anything. I tend to drift off into nothingness. I'm not thinking about anything or looking at anything. I'm just there physically. I just disappear. (Mags: interview number 31)
>
> It's just me in my own world. After doing that journey you just ignore people and you're just going. You don't even look. It makes you feel almost, like more powerful, I feel much more comfortable with a Walkman on, standing at the bus stop than with nothing at all. (Paul: interview number 9)

It's very insular you know. It's just very much me. You know. On my own sort of stuff and obviously I snap out of it once I get to my destination. (Betty: interview number 34)

It enables me to sort of bring my own dreamworld. Because I have familiar sounds with my music that I know and sort of cut out people around me. So the music is familiar. There's nothing new happening. I can go into my own perfect dreamworld where everything is as I want it. (Magnus: interview number 21)

Users appear to achieve, at least subjectively, a sense of public invisibility. They essentially "disappear" as interacting subjects withdrawing into various states of the purely subjective. Subjective in the sense of focusing or attending to themselves. This attention can be non-intentional and is described by some users passively as taking over their senses. The immediacy of the personal stereo experience overrides the functioning of the other senses which become subordinate to the vivid mental and physical experience of listening to music. Sometimes this appears to be intentional whilst at other times it is merely the response to the music understood as a form of distracted drifting. Users frequently report that they drift in and drift out of their journeys. The power to drift in and out at will is again seen as a pleasurable form of control.

The relationship between public and private space also appears to be transformed in the above accounts as users negate any meanings that the public might have or might accurately be seen as having. Public spaces are voided of meaning and are represented as "dead" spaces to be traversed as easily and as pleasurably as possible. Alternatively, environments such as trains or buses which merely transport the user through urban space to somewhere they either want to go or have to go are put to one side. Public space in this instance is not merely transformed into a private sphere but rather negated so as to prioritize the private. As such, personal stereos facilitate a host of new options for dealing with both the public in its immediacy together with helping the user deal with their own private experiences, desires and moods. This activity isn't fully grasped by merely transposing categories of active or passive onto the behavior. In the following example the use of a personal stereo becomes a self conscious barrier, a shield against the social, against both the "look" as well as a shield to hide feelings of insecurity:

I'm a shy person at times. My Walkman hides me away from that. (Jade: interview number 13)

The use of a personal stereo can also function to enhance any situation by turning a potential anxiety into a pleasurable and personal experience. Personal, inasmuch as the following user maintains that other people in the street merely have the same experience, whilst she possesses something unique which is "hers." The user, in effect, transcends her empirically viewed self:

I'm aware of the fact that I'm different from other people walking down the street because I'm not listening to the sounds they can hear. I'm listening to my music. But it doesn't make me feet anxious. It puts me in a good mood actually. You don't feel lonely. It's your own environment. It's like you're making something pleasurable you can do by yourself and enjoy it. (Sara: interview number 50)

The above example is also an alternative way of claiming private space. Personal space, as we have seen, is often represented in terms of the users' thoughts, mood or volition and can be understood either as an active focusing on the experience of being elevated beyond the spatial present or in the giving oneself up to it:

I might be concentrating on the music but my mind might be somewhere else as well…It depends what you're listening to. You might start marching to the music or the other extreme. Being in a total dream. Not being aware of anything. I kind of feel it's more unreal in a way. It's a kind of escapism. It's time out. (Gemma: interview number 24)

Users frequently describe experience in terms of two "worlds"; the world in the head of the user with its own rearrangement of the senses and the world in which this takes place and which has a different arrangement and often a different sense of time and movement attached to it:

It just separates you really. Because there's just you and the music and there's just nothing else that you need to talk about with anyone. If you want to think you can. (Donna: interview number 52)

Escape is also a frequent metaphor used by users. The following respondent, a 27-year-old woman, lists what she might successfully be escaping from whilst using her personal stereo:

Your nightmare journey. Listening to people arguing or yapping on the bus. Time out before the reality of where you're going. It depends on the end of the journey. You might be pretending that really you're not going to where you're going and the situation you're going into. So it's time out in a nice way. Or alternatively it could be psyching yourself up for whoever you're seeing. (Louise: interview number 16)

Personal stereos can be used to cope with, to avoid or to transform both public experience and/or the subjective, intentional narrative of the user. Transforming the perceived unpleasantness of the journey and the interruptive nature of time spent in public is an important method of coping with or enhancing one's own personal intentions or projects. These strategies of management are not necessarily derived, as the above accounts demonstrate, as a response to the physical environment moved through, in contrast to those accounts stemming from the work of Simmel.

Clearing a Space for Looking

Paradoxically some users claim that they see more clearly through the use of a personal stereo. In the light of the analysis above of the ways in which personal stereos are used to create non-reciprocal gazing, this claim needs to be investigated. The following examples are typical:

I like to see. I like to see exactly and I feel I'm absorbing more because the music is helping me concentrate and because it's so familiar to me I don't have to listen to it so attentively. I know what's coming and I can almost look for that. (Ron: interview number 58)

I'm locking myself in a bit more. It locks the rest of the world out, but then, maybe it doesn't. I think the music also helps me to relate to the outside world. I'll start to notice things more because of the music sometimes. There's nothing to distract you. There's just the journey and the music. (Robina: interview number 35)

Personal stereos appear to function as a clarifier in the above examples. The perceived auditory chaos of the urban environment is overlain by the managed industrialized sounds of the personal stereo which are "known." It is this sense of the familiar that enables the users to clarify their looking. In the following example the "look" accompanies the user's own movement and sound:

I do feel engaged because I'm seeing it. If I look at a mountain I can see its peak, you know. I can see it. If I'm listening to something beautiful in the background it can only add to it. (Jay: interview number 33)

This look is an aestheticized look in which the narcissistic orientation of the looker predominates. The engagement with the visual becomes real with the added "beautiful background" to heighten the visual component of experience. In doing so the experience becomes phantasmagoric (Benjamin), a spectacle (Debord). The following user describes lingering on a train platform entranced by the scene, too entranced to catch his train:

In a way when you're walking it does make you engage with your surroundings more than I otherwise would. I wouldn't normally stop and watch people walking up and down the stairs. Whereas I would do that, or miss a train just so I could hear this tune in this space. (Chris: interview number 11)

Cyclists increasingly wear personal stereos as they traverse the city. Life expectancy demands that they remain visually attentive. Users describe the chaotic sounds of the road as being recessed and replaced by the clarity and predictability of personal-stereo sounds. For cyclists, who cannot hear the sounds of the street, it is necessary to have to "look" more clearly. This is translated into more effective viewing in the sense of clearing space in the mind for the uninterrupted concentration of the cyclist. The fact that nothing can be heard behind the cyclist is conveniently ignored by the following user:

I'm visually more aware [on the bike]. Because you're aware that you're not listening. I'm more focused. More visually defined. I never lose myself in the

music completely. (Stephanie: interview number 42)

Ironically, some cyclists claim that they would be too frightened to cycle around London without using a personal stereo. This despite the awareness that reaction time to the unexpected is often slower with its use. In effect hearing has to be replaced by sight:

I think I become more aware when I've got my Walkman because you have to. I'm not stupid enough to walk in the middle of the road with it. But you become more aware because normally when you cross the road you can hear the sound of the cars. You have to be more aware. So I feel you're more connected with things around you in a way. I'm a very aware person. So I'm always looking around. (Ben: interview number 41)

The complexity and potentially contradictory nature of auditory looking is brought out in the following quote:

I suppose it makes everything surreal, like a dreamlike state because without the sound to go with your vision...disorientates everything and there's a different sound to the visual side...the world around. Well. It just doesn't fit in with it...it's strange. I suppose more distant because I can't hear. I suppose I am more distant. But I'm more aware visually. I'm quite a visual person. (Karin: interview number 18)

This perceptive comment points to an awareness of a parallel sense of being in the world and the disorientation that stems from an awareness of this coupling. The expectation that certain movements will be attended by specific sounds that are being replaced by one's own sounds creates a feeling or visual image in this user that she associates with surrealism by which she means the juxtaposing of two dissimilar things placed into a naturalistic setting. However, respondents, in discussing visual clarity, appear to refer to an awareness of a generalized "outside" rather than to the process of interactive gazing. When an auditory look is focused it often appears to be an aestheticized one. Alternatively, the auditory gaze functions as an urban strategy whereby users attempt to manage the nature of the urban "look" so as to control it.

REFERENCES

Bauman, Z. 1991. *Modernity and Ambivalence.* Cambridge: Polity Press.

Benjamin, W. 1973a. *Charles Baudelaire: A Lyric Poet in the Era of High Capitalism.* London: New Left Books.

Benjamin, W. 1973b. *Illuminations.* London: Penguin.

Benjamin, W. 1986. *Reflections: Essays, Aphorisms, Autobiographical Writings.* ed. P. Demetz. New York: Schocken Books.

Benjamin, W. 1991. *Gesammelte Schriften*, vols 1–7. Frankfurt: Suhrkamp Verlag.

Benjamin. W. 1999. *Selected Writings.* Volume 2: 1927–1934. Cambridge, Mass.: Harvard University Press.

Debord, G. 1977. *Society of the Spectacle.* Detroit: Black and Red.

DeLillo, D. 1988. *Libra.* London: Penguin.

Goffman, E. 1971. *Relations in Public: Microstudies of Public Order.* London: Penguin.

Simmel, G. 1997. "The Metropolis and Mental Life." In *Simmel on Culture.* Frisby and Featherstone (eds.) London: Sage Publications.

15

JACK KATZ

PISSED OFF IN L.A.

from *How Emotions Work* (1999)

In sprawling cities like Los Angeles, people find themselves occupying public space most frequently when driving in their cars. In this piece Katz examines the phenomenon of getting angry while driving in Los Angeles. This study was part of a larger intellectual project, published in the book *How Emotions Work*, in which Katz sought to understand how the different emotions we see and experience in our everyday lives unfold within interactions, are rooted within specific situations but also transcend them, and become sensual experiences that shape future action.

Behind a Los Angeles preschool, a three-year-old boy is using his feet to propel a bottomless plastic car around a crowded playground. As be maneuvers he shouts, "move, fucking asshole" and "go away, fucking asshole." Occasionally he turns his car sharply to a child who had not been interacting with him and yells, "I don't know, fucking asshole." Soon a scatological epidemic has entered the classrooms and is raging throughout the school. The parents of the original cursing child are called to the director's office and they appear sincerely surprised, insisting that "he could not have picked up the phrase in our house." Just before addressing a remedial talk to the child, the director thinks to ask the child if he knows what the phrase means. "Yes," he says brightly, "bad driver."

Becoming "pissed off" when driving may be an unfortunately inescapable fact of public life in many places, but in Los Angeles it is a naturally occurring cornucopia for social psychology. Because this form of anger is known in memorably dramatic instances by virtually everyone who drives in L. A., because it is a brief and infinitely recurring experience, and because angry responses to other motorists are typically felt to be so deeply justified that they can be recounted readily to strangers without concern for loss of face, the experience of becoming "pissed off" while driving provides extraordinarily useful data for exploring fundamental issues about the nature and contingencies of anger as it emerges and declines in social interaction. The near universality of the experience means that we can examine its workings across a wide range of ethnic, gender, socioeconomic, age, and personality divides, in a diverse set of driving circumstances, and at very different moments in drivers' quotidian routines and life histories.

My materials come primarily from about 150 detailed reports in which people, mostly thirty years of age or older, were asked by an equal number of college student interviewers to recount one or more experiences of becoming pissed off while driving around Los Angeles.

When emotions are studied in their naturally occurring contexts, it is useful to kick off the search for relevant ideas by highlighting what initially seem to be absurdities in the phenomena. The search for explanation can then be guided by patterns that, in the light of existing knowledge and upon self-reflection by the people studied, remain as haunting enigmas.

What, for example, is going on when solo drivers gesticulate emphatically and curse vociferously in cars with windows that are completely closed up? It is not as if they believe that their expressions are so powerful that they will pass through the glass, cut through the traffic noise, and penetrate the awareness of an offender who may have provoked their indignation.

> Mike, a thirty-one-year-old paralegal, recalls that he "usually yells at the other drivers from inside his car. At this point he laughed to himself and remarked that he knows that they can't hear him."

While the appearance of this madness may be striking, it is equally intriguing that, despite its absurdity, the practice seems to work to resolve emotional tension.

Lori, who is originally from Georgia but has lived in L.A. for many years, prefers public transportation but must drive here routinely. When "a big new brown truck...decided to cut her off, Lori turns to the truck, 'What do you think you are doing? You know better than that!' She talks to herself and uses hand motions. She looks toward the driver in a sideways glance and then talks facing straight ahead....' She does not want to lose her life over a driving dispute.'" But after she goes through scolding motions "she [can] drop it."

Also intriguing are incidents in which the participants make extraordinary commitments to secure what can only be articulated as the most minor aspects of personal advantage. One example is a battle between two mothers who compete for priority at a McDonald's restaurant while driving station wagons that are packed with kids. The drivers repeatedly tap bumpers and the battle ends only when the police arrive in response to a call from the "losing" mother, who managed to call 911 on her car phone while struggling for advantage in the queue. In another example, a fellow "came to his senses" after racing to "return the favor" to a driver who had cut him off, when he found his car straddling a cement lane divider.

To characterize such scenes as absurd is to take an outsider's perspective, and that would violate a primary rule for developing empirically grounded explanations. But what do we do about the fact that such a characterization is often made by the participants themselves a few moments beyond the heat of the struggle? Thus:

> Mrs. Minh, a Vietnamese immigrant who came to Los Angeles after living in Nebraska, is astonished at the rudeness of drivers in L.A. She is even more astonished, and deeply embarrassed as well, when, after a fellow cuts her off and she shakes her head at

his rudeness, he gives her "the finger" and she finds herself saying "shit" in front of her children.

Jan, who lives with her husband and two children in Orange County and works as an athletic coach at a major university, is late to a practice as she drives her red Corvette convertible with a stick shift along a curvy road in Palos Verdes. At a stop sign, a fellow in front of her who is slow to depart irritates her. As she drives behind him, she finds that he slows up. She waits for an opportunity to pass and as they approach a long curve she downshifts forcefully to second, accelerates, and pulls out into the lane of oncoming traffic, only to find that he speeds up, preventing her from passing until they have driven in parallel around a long curve. A few moments later, she stops her car, "dead in the road," forcing him to stop behind her. She walks briskly to his car, puts her head through his window and yells, ' "You ASSHOLE! You could have killed me!!!" ' He responds with ' "Shut up, you stupid CUNT!" ' Jan immediately 'smacked him across the face.' After speeding off, she 'could not believe she hit the guy.' ' "That guy could have chased me and pulled a gun on me and shot me." '

Even when the theme of personal danger does not apply, there is something enigmatic in the effort of pissed-off drivers to "teach a lesson" to the offending other, for instance by tailgating a tailgater. Self-interest cannot make such responsive actions sensible; even if the lesson is well learned, the teacher is unlikely personally to reap the benefit of the student's progress. If the motivation is explicated as altruistic it is no less mysterious. Moving into the role of the teacher, the angry driver defines other drivers as students against their will. Perhaps there is a wisdom here that angry drivers share with

university teachers who know that a class can be taught perfectly well even though no student learns anything of lasting value from it. But an aura of mystery trails after this wisdom.

That there is something tricky to explain about becoming pissed off on the road is indicated also by its frequently sudden dissipation. A driver who, in being cut off, had just rushed to the brink of madness, often will be pulled back by nothing more than a retrospective nod of acknowledgment. What requires explanation is a mysterious metamorphosis. Powerful forces develop against the drivers' wills, "taking" them against their better judgment. Just as suddenly, the disturbing forces may vanish.

A final paradox that helps orient the search for explanation is the routine production of a sense of incredulity. Accounts of experiences of anger while driving are full of such phrases as "I can't *believe* that asshole!" and "Would you look at that jerk? How can people *do* that?" What is astonishing is that these phrases pop incessantly into the same driving heads day after day. For many, no amount of experience with road "assholes" is sufficient to overcome this learning disability, it may be commendable that so many drivers avoid a hardheaded cynicism; a posture of incredulity, after all, professes faith in the possibility of collective improvement. But given that nothing has been done to reform the driving public since one confronted the last unpleasant incident, why be amazed when one confronts yet another asshole?

In addition to noting seemingly contradictory and absurd patterns in the phenomena, another strategy for orienting inquiry is to consider the inadequacies of prevailing explanations. One explanation that is very commonly invoked is that something awful happened to the angry driver before and independent of starting the drive in question, perhaps a fight with a spouse or child; maybe a conflict with clients, colleagues, superiors, or everyone at work; perhaps just the recognition at some time before getting on the road of a "bad hair day." This explanation fits some of the originating contexts of motorists' anger, but certainly not all. Thus the current sample of some 150 reports describes anger arising while:

- a psychoanalyst, who is returning to her Laguna Hills home, is enjoying nostalgic recollections of her son's recent bar mitzvah;
- a young man, driving home from his girlfriend's house, is enjoying a sustained reverie after "having finished sex";
- many drivers, listening to music on radio, tape, or CD, sing accompaniments in gay, earnest, or seductive voices.

Another very common explanation is that becoming pissed off while driving arises in reaction to fear. Again the facts sometimes but not always fit this hypothesis. People often become pissed off when there is little if any danger to them. At times their cars are not moving at all, as when another driver slips into a space while one is waiting to park. Often the response of the pissed-off driver creates far more danger than the precipitating event. And in any case it is not clear why anger should be a natural, sensible, or likely upshot of fear. If one looks closely at accounts that cite fear, the irritating elements are not necessarily connected closely to the fearful aspects. Thus Dana, a woman of thirty-four who was returning to Westwood from an overnight party in Fountain Valley, cited fear and the need to slam on her brakes as the provocation for her angry response to a driver who cut her off on the 405, but she also noted that what "great[ly] upset her was that the driver of the Infiniti drove off as if nothing had ever happened." Not simply fear but the other's driving off, in and to "infinity," left her stuck in anger.

Drivers often use a version of frustration-aggression theory to explain their anger. The accounts of pissed-off drivers may be divided into two numerically

unequal but morally balanced moieties, those who emphasize prudence and a pragmatic attitude (a favorite expression of their philosophy: "driving is only a way of getting from point A to point B") and those who celebrate their tactics for cutting through and around obstacles. The frustration-aggression hypothesis roughly fits many of the former accounts but it does not handle well the following shark, a not uncommon type who appears to be delightedly aggressive in searching for driving challenges.

> Marc, who sells plastics and chemicals to petroleum and chemical companies over a sales territory stretching from his home in Orange County up to Santa Barbara, speaks of his driving anger almost as a kind of therapy. . . . He is self-conscious about his construction of his anger: ' "I'm always in a rush even if I don't have to be." ' Marc "repeatedly said 'I don't know why I get so mad. I just do,' at the same time clenching his fists and his teeth followed by a squeal of laughter."

Brad, a thirty-one-year-old loan officer, intended no humor when he confessed that "running lights and speeding are probably the only two major rules that he breaks." With such driving habits, it is likely that aggression will often produce frustration, rather than the other way around. Lena, a hotel manager, was driving while she was being interviewed. At one point in the ride,

> a driver began to run a stop sign in front of us. Lena did not have a stop sign and decided that since she had the right of way, she did not have to stop or even slow down. "It's his problem," was all she had to say. . . . The other driver slammed on his brakes and swerved to the right to avoid hitting us as we went around. Lena said, "What an idiot" and "Hah! I bet he thought I would stop!" And Lena even honked for a lengthy period of time. The

other driver looked completely shocked and clueless as well as amazed at what had just transpired.

In addition to psychological theories of frustration and fear, drivers invoke sociological explanations, pointing to various background factors in standard demographic as well as in culturally distinctive forms. "Machismo" or "testosterone" is blamed, but so also are "women drivers." Bad driving is sometimes attributed to the diminished capacities of the elderly, but carefree youth are also damned. Racial and ethnic identities are blamed, but at one time or another virtually all variations of such identities are cited. As we will see, *some* form of pejorative generalization is inherent in the causal process of becoming pissed off while driving; but that is quite a different matter from taking such background factors at face value as determining forces.

Finally, it is possible that a few aberrant drivers cause all the problematic situations, that the 150 or so subjects in this sample are indeed the impeccable drivers they claim to be, and that they have all had the extraordinarily coincidental bad luck of running across a small core of incorrigibly incompetent motorists. Fortunately the data before us include observational accounts by researchers who conducted their interviews while sitting next to drivers like Lena.

We are left with something of a mystery, not only about how and why people so often get so angry while driving, but also about the kind of causal understanding that could explain these emotional phenomena. It seems that pre-anger background factors, such as frustration at work or gendered driving styles, do not lodge causal forces in the driver, where they wait ready to spring out when the provocation is right. It seems also that no particular configurations of the driving situation create fear, frustration, or other dynamics that always shape the process of becoming pissed off. If we can't look *inside* the actor for reliable explanatory factors, and if we can't look *outside* the actor to identify objective features of the driver's environment that would consistently provoke anger, where *can* we look? We can look closely at the phenomena themselves, and in ways that do not require that we divide "inside" from "outside," "subjective" from "objective" factors, psychology from sociology.

Three lines of inquiry will prove fruitful in this chapter.... First, we will look at the distinctive features of the social interaction of driving, by which I mean the special problems that drivers have in managing their identities as they are perceived by other drivers. Second, we can examine the embodied qualities of the experience of anger which requires that we take seriously the idea of metamorphosis, a sensual transformation in which the body of the person becomes a new vehicle for experience. Third, we must understand how becoming "pissed off" is not simply a "release of tension" or some other negatively defined phenomenon but is a positive effort to construct a new meaning for the situation.... I argue that a distinctive process of interactive interpretation, a specific experience of metamorphosis, and a focused narrative project are the individually necessary and jointly sufficient conditions for becoming pissed off when driving....

1. Driving as Dumb Behavior: The Emotional Provocations of Asymmetrical Interaction

With the exception of some narrow lanes that run through woods, small towns, and countryside, the space that is covered by public roads usually is defined as heading in one of two diametrically opposed directions. The signaling of the direction of travel may be achieved by lines painted on the ground, by arrows displayed on signage at on-ramps, by greenery that divides the land on which pavement is laid, by vacant space that separates pavement held up or hung in the air, or by physical barriers that impede passage from one to the other side of a road. In each case road culture requires drivers to sort themselves into two sets, one they travel "with," the other they travel "against." Once sorted out, drivers relate very peacefully to each other across these opposed moieties. It is a technico-sociological marvel of our civilization that people routinely whiz by each other in massive numbers and at fantastic rates of speed, only very rarely suffering accidents or even insults from those whose lives are headed in precisely opposite directions. Anger at other drivers is very systematically limited to only certain patterns of spatial interrelationship.

If accidents occur most often at intersections, the routine aggravations in driving occur within directional worlds that are more perfectly segregated. On the highway, and on local streets outside of intersections, what is happening among vehicles traveling in the opposite direction usually need not be of immediate concern. Drivers comfortably limit their horizons of perception to lanes traveling in the same rather than the opposite direction. The result is that drivers are most commonly gazing at the rear ends of others' vehicles, a perspective that is not incidentally related to the fact that the most common invective that emerges spontaneously in moments of anger, on L.A. roads at least, is "asshole."

The motorists' pattern of face-to-tail interaction makes for a major distinction with pedestrian passings, which are rich in face-to-face interactions. Exceptional moments of borderline embarrassment, in which people halt and hop around each other, indicate that as a rule, pedestrian passings are negotiated unproblematically. Pedestrians have relatively less reason or opportunity to perceive each other's rear ends, even though, as tortuous tactics indicate, they may have substantial motivations

to observe along those lines.[1] In contrast, drivers have relatively little reason or opportunity to gaze for long at the "faces" of oncoming cars. Even when they look into rearview mirrors to perceive the faces in cars traveling "with" but behind them, drivers readily focus on whether and how much pressure is being placed on their own "tails."

This roughly inverse structure of pedestrian and driving interaction creates roughly inverse forms of personal incompetence. Just because other pedestrians can so readily monitor one's visual perception, one walks in public more or less in the manner of a horse fitted with blinders. In pedestrian passings, the line between a glance and a gaze is morally significant; aware of the social accountability of their vision, pedestrians routinely encumber it.[2] In contrast, drivers are relatively free to look wherever and however they practically can just because their vision is itself relatively invisible to other drivers.

When a person moves from being a pedestrian to being a driver, he or she trades in one dialectical complex of interaction competencies and incompetencies for another. For the same reason that the vision of drivers is relatively unencumbered, the driver's ability to speak and, more generally, to express his or her understanding and intentions to other drivers is severely impaired. The figurative uses of dumbness as a common line of insult among drivers ("idiot," "jerk," "*pendejo*") is an upshot of the exceptional and more literal inarticulateness of motorists in social interaction. In effect, drivers project onto each other, in accusations of idiosyncratic personal incompetence, the systematic incapacity that driving, as a method of going about in public, constructs for all. If the pedestrian is, relative to the driver, made blind, the driver relative to the pedestrian is rendered dumb.[3]

That the social interaction of driving makes drivers dumb is not a matter of an outsider's moral judgment[4] but something that motorists themselves take into account in the elaborate and inventive strategies with which they seek to compensate for the insult that the automobile imposes on their expressive capacities. Through personal inventiveness, the mute character of the automobile is confronted and partially transcended. One driver interviewed for this study keeps a stack of cardboard signs next to her so that she can flash messages of reprimand ("You cut me off, you &*@#%!") and of appreciation ("xxxGod bless!xxx").

For some, the effort to overcome the relatively inexpressive nature of cars begins with a restructuring of the vehicle. Jill, an executive assistant to the vice-president of a construction firm, recalls vividly the original horn in her prior car, a Toyota: "Wimpy. I mean, 'peep, peep.' You couldn't even hear it." Jill's husband delighted her by putting an "air horn" in her Toyota. Now she drives a Mercedes, which "has a *greaat* horn." At a more extravagant level, people may buy a Jeep-like vehicle that will never be driven off of smoothly paved streets but that in any case gives its driver a currently fashionable way of looming large in the sights of others. Drivers of such vehicles, praising the sense of "control" they obtain, often self-consciously enjoy their exceptional resources to project themselves into others' experience.

The aggravating dumbness of driving is exacerbated by the asymmetry of communicative interaction among drivers. Whether stuck in traffic or watching cars freely speed by, each driver has reason to sense that his or her own vivid awareness of other cars is not reciprocated. Shouting at other drivers with one's windows rolled up is a common phenomenon, but not because angry drivers fear violent responses from the object of their aggression. The pattern is common in Sweden as well as in the United States. More fundamentally, people shout in closed cars because the practice re-presents the animating problem, which is the challenge of being effectively appreciated by other drivers about whom one has become all too aware.

Drivers struggle to make communicative interaction more symmetrical. Horns are often insufficient, whether because their use is restricted by local ordinance, because the direction of their intentions can get clouded in a din of collective overuse, or because the target is so well insulated in his or her car and "sound system" that often the sole predictable effect of blowing one's horn is that it will pollute one's own audible environment. An alternative is to adapt the car's lighting system for expressive purposes, as by flashing high beams, but although the appropriate stick may be readily at hand, the driver often will have reason to believe that the message of the flash will not be "read" accurately unless he or she highlights the lighting by projecting it from a specific background, for example by tailgating the target.

Like the use of high beams to send signals, hand gestures also acknowledge the inadequacy of sound as a channel of effective expression. It is common to see a driver attempt to deliver a commentary by first maneuvering around other cars in order to get parallel to an offending driver, and then to launch into some idiosyncratic sign language. For example Carolina, a twenty-four-year-old college student, reports that if another driver has offended her and does not appear to be too intimidating, she will drive alongside and "give a dirty look and wave my hands all over the place with 'what the hell are you doing?' gestures." And Marc, a thirty-one-year-old salesman, employs the device of "shaking his hand in the air when driving by a driver which has made him mad to simulate the motion of masturbation." Marc and his female university student interviewer laughed heartily at this display, which they took as a message to "go fuck yourself."[5]

When used as a means of expression among motorists, headlights tend to be used in a relatively gentle manner. Drivers direct bright headlights at a car ahead in their own side of the road or to an oncoming car on the other side of the road in order to say "Move aside," or "Drop your beams." But when *brake lights* are used to send planned messages, they usually become instruments of perverse intention. Usually employed as devices that unwittingly signal a car is slowing down, brake lights can be strategic devices for, in effect, putting one's rear in another's face. By getting in front of an offending driver and then hitting the brakes unnecessarily, an offended driver literally and figuratively gets back at a driver who blocked an effort to pass. This is a common way of registering a complaint along the lines: you didn't pay attention to me before, but now you certainly will. Used in this manner, brake lights reflect backward in temporal as well as spatial senses, calling attention to an offense that has already been suffered.

At times frantically, offended drivers search the environment in order to find a way of forcing another driver to acknowledge their existence. One small window of opportunity is afforded by the necessity, felt by most if not all drivers, to glance periodically at their rearview mirrors. Tara, a forty-year-old woman, recalled an incident from some years before when she had to brake with all her strength to avoid hitting a car that had suddenly cut her off. When she caught the miscreant glancing at his rearview mirror, she glared at him in order to express her indignation:

> My eyebrows came down and how I wish I could blink him into a tiny little frog, small and ugly. Yeah, I was really frustrated. Then I made sure I pronounced each cursed, angry word clearly so the guy could read them through the rearview mirror.

I have reviewed a few ways that drivers, when becoming angry on the road,

acknowledge the expressive limitations of their vehicles in the actions they take to overcome them. It remains to demonstrate, however, that the relationship between pissed-off driving and the dumbing asymmetry of communication among motorists is causally significant. Is an awareness of this interaction dilemma a necessary condition for the experience of anger? In fact drivers precisely and elaborately appreciate the causal relevance to their anger of asymmetry in their communicative interactions with other drivers. What drivers get mad about is their own dumbness experienced as a sensed inability to get other drivers to take them into account. An emphatic instance was provided by Philip, a twenty-five-year-old rock band musician. He reported that when he is behind someone who is driving slowly and who does not pull over so that he can pass, he will at times "get in front of the person and slow down, to say 'you fucking see me now, bitch!'."

Los Angelenos often disparage other drivers as "unconscious" even though those others are obviously sufficiently conscious to avoid driving off the road. The narcissistic demand in this labeling of others is left implicit; what is essentially disturbing is that the other driver appears to be deaf to one's own concerns. For the angry driver, the disturbance provoked by the apparently impenetrable insulation of other drivers sometime takes on existential dimensions. Jim, a forty-three-year-old realtor who was suffering from a heart condition and a weak real estate market, had just lost a deal because a home buyer had failed to qualify for a loan. A Mercedes approached from his rear and irritated him by speedily changing lanes to pass other cars and then cutting in front of him. Jim remarks: "I get really mad when other drivers weave in and out and cut you off. They think they own the road and that you don't exist."

"Idiot," "unconscious," and similar insults overtly label others as incompetent, but they are the upshot of an energetic sensitivity to one's own incompetence. For all practical purposes, the other's deafness makes oneself dumb. Indeed, there is an irony here that is experienced as a bitter train. The better you are as a driver, in the sense of being dutifully attentive to the movements of other cars, the more you are aware how circumscribed are the attentions of others. Your courtly efforts to accommodate the less competent run up against their failure to see, much less appreciate, what you are trying to do. Conscientiously monitoring others' awareness, superior drivers come to appreciate how, on the road, ignorance is power. Their appreciation of the incompetence of other drivers is at once evidence of their own superior driving competence and an explanation of the frustrating futility of their superiority.

I am arguing that a perception of asymmetrical awareness is a condition of becoming pissed off while driving. Acting as folk sociologists, drivers tacitly analyze the structure of their interaction with other drivers as part of the process of becoming angry with them. When undertaking this quick and dirty social research, drivers cannot easily ask other drivers about their orientations on the road. Instead they commonly use what sociologists call "unobtrusive measures" to infer subjective realities, in particular to characterize others as self-absorbed. Currently, two such measures are car phones and "Diet Coke." Philip, the young rock musician quoted above, bemoans drivers who are

> oblivious when they're in their car. They're always looking for a tape or doing something else rather than driving...[holding] their can of Diet Coke, they are in their own little world.

Other respondents referred disgustedly to drivers who continue past exits with their turn signals flashing on and on.

Some drivers create a characteristic emotional tone by employing a more advanced folk-sociological analysis of interaction asymmetry on the road. Just as sunglasses can be used to build a cool, "tough" image, so the windows of a car can be outfitted to put virtually the whole vehicle in "shades." The result in both cases is to create an aura of mystery rooted in a practical problem for interpretation: the reading of whether and where attentions may be directed becomes a unique problem for the person not sporting shades. Not uncommonly, a party in shades will be perceived as relatively indifferent to others, perhaps even disposed to at least small cruelties.

Because the person in shades does not as readily give off indications of his or her disposition but is presumably unimpaired in detecting the direction of others' gazes, an emotionally provocative potential for an asymmetrical uncertainty is built into street transactions. This became a serious problem for Rudi, a minister's son from Woodland Hills, as he traveled home one midnight on the Hollywood Freeway. After angrily cutting off a car that had cut him off, Rudi found himself surrounded by two cars working together to box in, chase, and fire gunshots at his car. Until almost too late, the tinted windows of the two cars impaired his ability to appreciate that the attentions of both were directed at him, and that their attentions to him were being organized through their attentions to each other.

Notably, the emotional course of this interaction ran close in relationship to its interpretive dynamics. At first believing that another driver was not considering his existence, Rudi was angry about being cut off. Then Rudi became fearful as he realized that he was confronting just the opposite problem, excessive attention to his existence. Drivers in Los Angeles today frequently struggle with defining the line between an oblivious and an overly concerned other, a line that runs on the slippery slope between anger and fear.

The close relationship of interaction asymmetry and anger in driving is revealed in particularly instructive ways when we follow out the emotional ramifications in those instances where the interpretive relationship reverses. It is not uncommon, for example, that a driver who has been angrily honking at a slowly moving, unresponsive car ahead, realizes that the target of his anger has not been ignoring him but has been frustrated by another obstacle further on. Denise, a computer analyst who works in Century City, had been honking at a Land Cruiser, urging the driver to speed up so that she could make a light, when she realized that there was a car in front of him. At this point "she silently fell back into her seat, rolled up the window, wished she could disappear, and mentally cursed herself for being so stupid." What had been humiliation became transformed into shame as Denise realized that she had not in fact been "dumb" in the sense of being unable to get the other driver to take her perspective, but "stupid" in being blind to what the other driver could see.

Embarrassment is the common upshot when one realizes that there is an interpretive asymmetry in the current interaction but that the failure to take the other's perspective is one's own fault alone. Brad, the owner of an export-import business, recalled his growing anger as he was being tailgated on his way to a choir performance:

I could see the headlights glaring in my mirror, so I motioned him to pass by me but he doesn't.... Every single turn I make he's following. I start to think, "Where does this guy live? I mean why does this guy keep following me? Can't he see I'm lost?"...I told my wife, "Why does this stupid ass keep tailgating me?"...Later the guy who drove the car comes up to me and thanks me for leading him to the presentation. I was kind of embarrassed so I just said. "No problem."

In effect, the limited expressive possibility in drivers' social interaction creates an infinite series of ambiguous moments. As a social practice, driving is a kind of endless Rorschach test in which, unless the driver finds interpretive dilemmas fascinating as a subject for study, he or she must impute a taken-for-granted descriptive sense of other drivers' social awareness. It is only by appreciating how driving is a "dumb" way of moving through public space that we can appreciate why the emotional results of motorists' interaction are so routinely appalling.

2. Getting Cut Off: The Metamorphosis of the Angered Body

Within some traditions in sociology, the sole focus of analysis would be on the *interactions* through which anger arises in driving. But getting pissed off while driving is also very much a matter of feeling. Accordingly we must now appreciate a part of social action that is consistently missed by social science: the *sensual* and *aesthetic* dimensions of the experience.

Note first that passengers typically do not have the same emotional experience as drivers. Sitting next to the driver, a passenger may observe the same rudeness, feel frustrated by the same traffic, be startled by the same aggressive conduct on the part of other drivers, but watch with amusement or fear as the driver of his or her own car gets mad. Sprinkled through the interviews in our data set are recollections by interviewer-observers of occasions in which they struggled to calm down their research subjects as the latter responded with frightful ferocity to the "idiots" and "assholes" of the road.

Barry, a fifty-four-year-old attorney practicing in Orange County, is cruising down

Rosecrans Avenue at fifty-five mph in his black Lexus, listening to soft music, with his wife and two others in the car. As he slows to merge into the left-turn lane, he spots a car behind him, "a white Integra with five Asians," that is crossing over the double yellow line in an attempt to enter the left-turn lane before Barry gets there. Angry that "this little shit wouldn't let me in," Barry maneuvers toward the left lane as if he is intent on hitting the other car. The Integra screeches to a stop, and as its driver bolts from his car, Barry stops and rushes out to "confront the confrontation." The passengers are "stunned and startled," not by the Integra but by Barry's rage.

Drivers themselves often realize the contrast between their rage and a passenger's fear. There is a significant clue to the causal contingencies of anger in the fact that drivers' realization of this contrast does not necessarily stem their anger. Ralph, an employee of a Beverly Hills architectural firm, is driving his girlfriend and his brother to Las Vegas. Going seventy on a steep mountain incline, he finds a van pressing from behind with its high beams. When the road gets too narrow for the van to pass, he slows down to piss off its driver. As the van driver succeeds in passing him, he throws Ralph a finger and then cuts in close. Next Ralph uses his high beams on the van, then passes the van and again purposively slows dramatically. Ralph recalls how his girlfriend and brother urged him to calm down, to let it go.

I didn't respond to their comments. I looked at my girlfriend to the right and noticed that she was holding on to the handle on the passenger door. I didn't care though. I didn't care if I was scaring her and my brother. I felt my face really flushed as I kept trying to catch up to the van. As I was driving, I was cussing the guy out at the top of my lungs.

I said things like, "You fucking asshole! Who do you think you are? You don't own the fucking road! I'll show you who owns the fucking road!" Immediately after the incident, I looked at my girlfriend. She was shaking her head in disapproval and told me that my temper is exactly like my father's temper.

There is a crucial difference between the situation of the passenger and that of the driver. Even though both are in the same car, it is only the driver who is cut off. For the driver, being "cut off" is not only a figure of speech. In contrast to the passenger, the driver, in order to drive, must embody and be embodied by the car. The sensual vehicle of the driver's action is fundamentally different from that of the passenger's, because the driver, as part of the praxis of driving, dwells in the car, feeling the bumps on the road as contrast with his or her body not as assaults on the tires, swaying around curves as if the shifting of his or her weight will make a difference in the car's trajectory, loosening and tightening the grip on the steering wheel as a way of interacting with other cars.

Being a passenger is more a matter of being taken around, of hanging on rather than guiding the car through turns, and of orienting oneself to other cars through the driver in the next seat rather than through manipulating the body of the car. Not only are passengers unlikely to share the driver's emotions, but when passengers do get irritated they are more likely to focus on the faults of their own driver than on the drivers of other cars. Note the reference in the following classic complaint about a backseat driver to the very different physical disposition of the passenger-critic. When Ann's husband is her passenger, he often criticizes her. Her interviewer paraphrases her characterization of his attitude:

First she is going too fast, then too slow. Why doesn't she go now? Why didn't she go then? She demonstrates his position as he lies back in the passenger seat, like a lounge chair.

The structuring and the contingencies of the emotions of driver and passenger cannot be explained without taking into account the fact that, although they are only inches from each other and are in essentially the same perceptual position to witness interaction with other cars, their manners of embodying understanding and literally incorporating the scene, are radically different.[6]

Language describing the embodiment of action and the incorporation of personal identity brings us close to the philosophies of Michael Polanyi and Maurice Merleau-Ponty.[7] If we are to explain more satisfactorily the contingencies of the driver's anger we must appreciate how driving requires and occasions a metaphysical merger, an intertwining of the identities of driver and car that generates a distinctive ontology in the form of a person-thing, a humanized car or alternatively, an, automobilized person.[8] If we insist on seeing only human "subjects" on one side of an ontological divide and "objective" conditions or the material circumstances for behavior on the other, we will fail to appreciate fully the difference in the perspectives of driver and passenger, and we will not be able to grasp just what is "cut off" that provokes anger while driving.

With regard to the driver's relationship with other cars, being cut off is a richly varied event. But what all such experiences have in common is a kind of amputation, a loss of a previously engaged, tacit use of the car and a loss of the transcendent body that the driver, in the process of driving, had been taking for granted as naturally available. While nothing happens to his or her physiological body—to that body as a thing described in isolation from its use in context—the driver does not doubt the sensual reality of the fact that *he or she,* i.e., his or her lived or phenomenological body, has

been cut off. By attempting to describe the driver's tacit embodiment of the car, we will prepare the way to understand, in the next section, something that otherwise is very elusive: how becoming angry is a practical project in which the driver attempts to regain a taken-for-granted intertwining with the environment.

The Naturally Transcendent Body of the Driver

What is it that the driver senses so vividly and yet senses in ways so well hidden that intimate companions do not share the sensuality? What the driver senses in anger are transcendent meanings of the moment. From the passenger's side of the car, or when the driver is using discursive reason to talk with an interviewer about the event, only the specific situational meanings of the event are apparent, and they do not justify the anger. Looking narrowly at the socially situated interaction among cars, all that is at stake is:

- as a spatial matter, the necessity for the driver to move one foot a few inches from accelerator to brake;
- on a temporal dimension, the "loss" of a moment's time;
- and from a publicly visible perspective, a change in the relationship of cars, not people's lives.

But emotions are doubly resonant; through his or her emotions a person both attends to the immediate situation and orients to transcendent dimensions of the moment's experience. The feeling, the sensual reality of emotions, *is* this double resonance.

People run into, hit upon, discover or find emotional dynamics in their experience. Like things discovered or found, the significance that an emotion registers is regarded, by the person experiencing it, as already there but previously beyond the boundaries of awareness. Put colloquially, we find ourselves "taken" by emotions. In emotional experience, a person attends corporeally to temporal, spatial, and private meanings that reflect on and transcend whatever he or she is doing at the moment with others. Emotions are a paradoxical kind of turning on the embodied self, a sensual form of self-consciousness that brings into awareness, in the palpably aesthetic medium of the body, commitments that previously were tacitly engaged.

Given the familiar assertion of an opposition between reflection and emotions, it is perhaps ironic to note that, when they are emotional, people are engaged in bringing previously tacit dimensions into their awareness. *But this self-reflection does not take the form of thought.* Drivers usually do not *perceive* themselves being cut off *and then decide* to construct their anger; rather, it is in seeing themselves cut off that they first find themselves angry. What makes the self-conscious nature of emotions difficult to see is that the turn on the self is done sensually and aesthetically, through a kind of living poetry, and not in the form of discursive reason that commentaries about "reflection" have traditionally evoked.

How does becoming angry when driving bring previously tacit, transcendent dimensions of action into vivid corporeal awareness? First of all, driving is itself essentially a means of transcending space, of getting from here to there. When traffic or a "rude" driver cuts one off, the experience is of falling out of a flow and being stuck or held back. In the sense of confinement that anger brings to them, cut-off drivers sense the firmness of the boundary between the overall trajectory of their current trip and the local situation in which they interact with other cars. As cars in traffic start and stop, one responds by inching ahead, starting and stopping, in the process drawing an increasingly thick line describing the bounded nature of one's action. When traffic flows smoothly, if a rude driver cuts in

close, one must fall out of the flow by hitting the brake or at least lifting off of the accelerator, in the process physically pulling oneself out of a previously tacit intertwining of body and machine.

Each driver usually will have no way of appreciating where other drivers are going and why, unless traffic stops completely and drivers exit their cars to converse with each other.[9] Each knows that he or she alone knows how the interaction "here" carries implications for the activities and relationships he or she maintains in some other setting, "there," and that what happens in the interaction with another driver "now" is meaningful with regard to situations "then," that is, with regard to what he or she has lived before and is likely to experience later on. As drivers relate the movements of their cars to each other, each has a necessarily private awareness of the transcendent meanings of his or her actions.

In some of the incidents of becoming angry, drivers are clearly frustrated in their attempts to "get there" and they imagine clear pictures of themselves as they once were or might soon be in other places. Note how anger arises as the following driver situates himself with reference to unpleasant versions of himself that he projects into the future and recalls from the recent past.

Torrential rains in Malibu have slowed traffic to a crawl as Clarence, a tax accountant with a public accounting firm in Santa Monica, bangs his fists on the steering wheel, lights a cigarette, then repeatedly bangs his head against the side window. Aware that he is already late for work and aware that his job performance has recently come under question, Clarence observes a stream of cars moving freely on the shoulder and recalls the ticket he received a week ago for the same maneuver. Observing a police car up in the shoulder up ahead, he moves to block the attempt of a minivan to come off the shoulder into his lane: "Shaking his fists angrily at the minivan, he yelled, 'I am not going to let this fucking bitch in front of me."'

In other experiences of drivers' becoming angry, a spatial rather than a temporal dimension of transcendence is most emphatic. For Dita, talking on a cellular phone as she drives "is a form of therapy" in that it allows her to be in two social places at the same time, interacting with other drivers and with her phone correspondent. If another driver acts rudely, what may be cut off is her ability to remain attentive to her phone call. A set of observational field notes on Francine, a forty-five-year-old travel agent and mother of two, shows how she once became angry in close relationship to her discussion with her daughter-passenger about a dress that she, Francine, had tried on at the mall and was considering buying. Her conversation continued as a white car from the left put on his blinker and moved into her lane. Francine "was not angry, she just slowed down and continued talking about the dress." But as the white car progressively slowed down to well below the speed limit, Francine repeatedly had to hit her brakes.

> Her anger heated up as she glanced at the speedometer and noticed that we were only going forty miles per hour. She stopped talking about that dress she was going to buy and looked over her shoulder to go around the white Camry.

Rude and inconsiderate drivers do not injure only in a symbolic manner, for example by showing disrespect, they strip dimensions from one's social existence, in these cases undermining the drivers' ability to be in two places at once.

As forms of sensuality, emotions render the body a prism, lighting up otherwise invisible, transcendent meanings that in each interaction always pass through the participants. Even for drivers who are not headed toward a pressing engagement and who are focused exclusively on the road, driving may have a series of other temporal and spacial implications that reach beyond and lend emotional significance to particular encounters with other drivers. Driving is a prime field for the study of what Michel de Certeau referred to as the "tactics" of contemporary everyday life.[10] Many people develop what they regard as particularly shrewd ways of moving around society.[11] These include carefully choosing streets that one knows carry little traffic, sneakily cutting across corner gas stations to beat traffic lights, discreetly using another car as a "screen" in order to merge onto a highway, passing through an intersection and brazenly doubling back to avoid the queue in a left-turn lane, and such triumphs of motoring chutzpah as following in the smooth-flowing wake of an ambulance as it cuts through bottled-up traffic. Variations in motoring cunning are endless.

> Eddie keeps his speed between certain levels because to go too slow would put him in an inefficient gear and if he goes too fast "his gas mileage would decrease by 20 percent, due to excess wind resistance." Bob, thirty-seven years old, a drug store employee who drives a recent-model Toyota truck, has his eight-mile round-trip between home and work all worked out. He knows the way the lights normally go, and which lanes to avoid because he could be blocked by "unprotected left turns."

For such shrewd drivers, what is at stake in any given interaction with another car is a trans-situational strategy of which other drivers on the road must be completely unaware. What can be cut off here is an overall game plan and a more or less grand conception of self.

All encounters in social life build their emotional meanings from the juxtaposition between a local situation, one to which the participants collaboratively respond as they construct its sense and boundaries in the "here and now," and the privately known destinations for which the local situation is for each but a way station. Chance meetings on the street, an episode of sexual interaction, an afternoon spent on a crew doing a roofing job, or a meeting of middle managers and lawyers to discuss security concerns at a shopping mall...for each participant what is collectively treated as locally transpiring will have unshared, transcendent implications in the form of sensed relevancies for other encounters in some other time and place. The emotional meanings of everyday life are naturally and necessarily hidden because selves, although they are always presented in forms that are tailored to a social time and place, are always produced by bodies, and what having a body most fundamentally means for a person is that he or she lives an ongoing continuity beyond the social situations passed through in everyday life. Bodies make us mortal in the long run, but until they do they are vehicles of situational immortality, constantly conferring the gift, unwanted or not, of signifying life beyond the deaths of the localized interactions that constitute our mundane social lives.

When a driver gets cut off, what occurs is an instantaneous and exceptionally pristine confrontation, not simply with other drivers but with the existential challenge of interminably working out the relationship between isolated social situations and a transcendent life course. Driving produces conflicts that are at once an unwanted therapeutic challenge, an undesired introduction to the social-psychological structure of everyday life, and a tiresome obligation to try to make sense of one's life.

Who needs this aggravation? Perhaps only drivers who happen to be social psychologists. Most people have other hobbies and occupational concerns. So, as is generally the case with anger, pissed-off drivers are angry that they are angry, that they must give so much importance to working out the relationship between their petty interactions with other drivers and the inescapably compelling themes of their lives.

Because cars are so naturally literal/figurative vehicles for transcendence in spacial and temporal senses, they are ready vehicles for a third dimension of transcendence. Cars as objects, and driving as an activity, are given private meanings that transcend what others—other drivers and the driver's own passengers—can observe. Thus each driver not only does not know where any other driver is going and how long it may be before he or she gets there, but each is unaware of the symbolic meaning that the others may have built into their relationships to their cars. Cars are treated like private living rooms that are driven about in public; secure in their privacy, drivers take for granted that others won't be successful Peeping Toms. Thus Ernie, a used-car salesman at Galpin Ford who lives in the Valley, does not need to change out of his pajamas when he leaves his home at 10:30 P.M. to drive a friend home. As he explains to his wife, "no one's going to see me. I don't have to impress anybody."

Usually, however, what privacy covers is not so much the driver's physical body as the folk philosophy that he or she has developed for his or her car and for driving. What makes driving so richly provocative of emotions is not simply or even primarily that situated interactions with other drivers impede one's progress to a given destination; it is that the sociophenomenological structure of driving interaction crystallizes a challenge common to all of social life. Because the meanings of driving build up from the naturally metaphoric character of the activity, they are especially subtle in their seductive power and doubly hidden, not only from other drivers but from oneself as well. If railroad trips figured prominently in Freud's dreams, narratives of driving play a richly hermeneutic role as contemporary adults dream nightmares of being eternally stalled in traffic, careening around sharp downhill curves while driving family members in a stuffy little car with faulty brakes, or being hauled around by some reckless driver in the company of utter strangers.[12]

When drivers are cut off, their anger may respond to one or both of two possible forms of embodied loss. First, the driver may have to pull out of a previously taken-for-granted corporeal involvement that is specific to the current trip. A given interaction with another driver may interrupt the phone conversation that one is sustaining with a friend, break the flow of strategic maneuvers that had been making the trip a testament to one's extraordinary urban cunning, or require that one remove a hand from lightly stroking a girlfriend's thigh in order to grip a steering wheel tightly.

Second, independent of the driver's machinations as they may be specific to any particular trip, driving a car may symbolize one's overall way of passing through society.[13] The postures and airs in the following examples demonstrate how some drivers habitually intertwine their identities and the bodies of their cars. The crucible that produces the extraordinary emotional power of the driving experience is the routine juxtaposition of immediately situated interaction with other drivers and situationally transcendent meanings of driving. This juxtaposition is a constant in episodes of road rage, even as situational dilemmas and transcendent meanings vary widely from one incident to the next.

Rick, a college student, keeps his 1994 Ford Probe gleaming. It is

> more than just a means to get from point A to point B; I take pride in keeping it looking good, it is a place I go to escape from the pressures of school and work.

Getting stuck in traffic as he is driving from Glendale to the Malibu Sea Lion to celebrate his fiancée's birthday "make it painfully clear that I am not the master of my destiny that I thought I was."

> When it became apparent that the traffic was not going to clear up and that no matter what I did, we were going to be late, I got pissed—I mean REALLY PISSED. I ...basically just lost it in terms of self-control.

Because his car represents a shiny version of his future, traffic turns him to shameful memories of his past. Rick recalled that "my mother drilled it into me as a child that it is bad to be late; it makes you look irresponsible."

If for Rick his car is a pristine body that other drivers threaten to soil, Mark owns the car of Rick's nightmares, but its symbolic meaning is no less capable of generating enraging implications for its owner. Mark's car has 170,000 miles, its wheels are badly out of alignment, and driving it hurts his back. Far from symbolizing that at this stage of his life he is on a rapid trip to a bright future, Mark's car serves him less reliably when it is in motion than when it is functioning as his bedroom. A frequently unemployed roofer who states that he is often underbid on jobs by Mexican illegals, Mark finds that even when he works a forty-hour week he can't pay all of his bills. "My life is more fragile than it's ever been." When other cars cut him off, what they are cutting off often seems to be his last tie to respectable membership in the community. Ugly encounters with other drivers stimulate deep resentments that often take social-class directions. "Sometimes I'll fantasize about running a tailgater off the road or destroying a rich person's car."

The way that a person lives philosophical orientations to his or her car shapes his or her corporeal disposition when driving. Thus when Jill got her Mercedes, it meant "growing up" and being "an adult," which for her means driving cautiously. The "gutless"

Toyota she had before was like driving "the ashtray of the Mercedes, very tinny." The heaviness of the car conveys to her an aspect of stability, which she enhances by braking far in advance of the spot at which she will come to rest and by taking corners slowly enough that the car avoids any tilt. If some "asshole" cuts in front of her, what is cut off is likely to be the faith that she is now secure and immune from the surprises and foolishness that threaten to bring uncertainty into a life.

Cars obviously can be outfitted to reflect the desired personal identities of their drivers with bumper stickers and accessories. But, what is more interesting, some drivers more discreetly *reshape themselves* to fit with the image that they expect the car to project. Brandy, "an attractive thirty-three-year-old Latino from East Los Angeles," is a middle-school teacher's aide who works with children with learning disorders and behavioral problems, work that "requires lots of patience." Interviewed by a female friend, Brandy reports that a " '95 jet-black Jeep Wrangler" is "her pride and joy." She labors elaborately to shape the car, passengers, and herself into a seamless version of self, which the interviewer characterizes as "the Jeep image of fun, adventure, wild youth, and excitement." The car has no radio, because Brandy does not want it to be broken into. On a trip to Tijuana, she parks on the California side of the border and she and her boyfriend walk across because the people there drive "like bats out of hell." The car and her body are mutually altered to create an ongoing, complementary whole. Brandy "would find something to do with herself each time we stopped at a light or slowed down in traffic," such as "smoothing down her hair and turning the mirror to inspect her face." The car elevates its driver, putting her on display, but she refrains from looking into other cars because it would be rude. She "always says that only a certain type of person can own a Jeep, like herself,"

and for that reason she "does not want to be seen in it with thick glasses on," even though, as the condition imposed on her driver's license indicates, she cannot see well without her glasses when she is driving at night.

On returning from a trip to Mexico one evening, the various elements that Brandy had built into her car-body identity came into conflict. When stopped by a CHP officer for speeding, she was given the choice to take a four hundred–dollar ticket, or put on her glasses, or turn the wheel over to her boyfriend-passenger. Not wanting to admit that she fails to wear glasses for the sake of appearance, she allowed him to drive, a choice that subjected her to endless humiliation as the story was told and retold in family and friendship circles....

NOTES

1. Goffman (1963, 87) alludes to what often happens when one is caught employing such tortuous tactics: "when a person takes advantage of another's not looking to look at him, and then finds that the object of his gaze has suddenly turned and caught the illicit looker looking...[t]he individual caught out may then shift his gaze, often with embarrassment and a little shame, or he may carefully act as if he had merely been seen in the moment of observation that is permissible; in either case we see evidence of the propriety that should have been maintained."

2. When gaze is sustained between pedestrians who are facing each other as they approach a passing moment, moral meanings, such as sexual interest or "character contests" (Wolfinger 1995, 335–336, following Goffman 1967a, 239–258) can quickly develop. Goffman refers to pedestrian blinders as "civil inattention." Using an automotive metaphor, Goffman (1963b, 84) describes the required "casting the eyes down as the other passes" as "a kind of 'dimming of lights.' " For the beginnings of a comparative analysis of the

social interaction of pedestrian and vehicular movement, see Goffman 1971, 5–18. On contemporary American inner-city streets, pedestrians must weight the alternative risks of not encumbering their vision enough, in which case they may be seen to emit a suspicious gaze that could be taken as racist (Anderson 1990); and encumbering their vision too much, in which case they become paranoic. There are also now-significant gender-related power struggles over the regulation of gaze in public passings (Gardner 1995).

3. For other aspects of the incompetencies created for their drivers by cars, see McGrane 1994, 170–197. The variations in the structure of the competencies and incompetencies of pedestrians and drivers merit a more elaborate treatment than is justifiable in this volume. Each form of social interaction creates a distinctive ontology, a unique set of touchstones for shaping conduct, for the people who sustain it. The theme of the "embodiment" of social action is currently enjoying great popularity but the term is usually employed on the unjustified assumption that people incorporate different lines of action into constant bodies. Marcel Mauss (1973 [1935]) wrote of the "techniques of the body" in a seminal article in which he introduced the concept of *habitus*. Following his lead, we can search for the bodies that are produced by different technologies, thereby giving sensual and not just symbolic meaning to Goffman's (1967b, 3) directive to study "[n]ot, then, men and their moments. Rather, moments and their men."

4. Compare the concept as used, with no trace of irony, in a psychological study of driving. "Someone has said that a moron makes the best driver. From all the studies we have done, this is not correct. It would be more nearly correct to say that a person of about average intelligence makes the best driver. Apparently the job suits him well and fits his capacity." Lauer 1960, x.

5. The communicative efficacy of such messages depends on the assumption that the gesticulating driver and recipient will share the same symbolic universe, but it is not clear that all intended recipients live in social worlds where such gestures are familiar or recognizable. What is striking is not only that the gesticulators don't care, but that they do care to make an expression whose effective reception they don't care about....

6. The "backseat" driver situation in one respect inverts the interaction asymmetry we have been reviewing, as here the driver's motions are monitored closely and continuously by another who is situated outside of the driver's equally attentive reach. The "backseat" designation, understood as referring to the location of foreground and background regions of consciousness, may be phenomenologically accurate even when applied to a passenger in a front seat. The emotions provoked by the "nagging" imitation of the "backseat driver" may be equally or even more unpleasant than the anger occasioned when one is "cut off" by another driver. But the structure of the displeasure appears to be significantly different when the sense of asymmetrical awareness is a constant awareness of overattentiveness as opposed to a sudden realization of inattentiveness by the other. That drivers tacitly analyze the structure of social interaction to constitute their anger should be verifiable in the responses they make. One customarily "flips off" someone by whom one was "cut off," but one does not usually flip off a backseat driver. For that sort of imitation, the fitting response is a mood of ongoing, numbing rejection, i.e., being sullen, uptight, sarcastic, etc.

7. Polanyi 1966, 1962; Merleau-Ponty 1968.

8. With his development of Mauss's concept of habitus and with phrases like "the intentionless invention of regulated improvisation," Pierre Bourdieu (1990, 57) fights the distinction on a broad front in the history of social thought.

9. This occurs with a certain regularity in some settings, and the emergent emotional tone is instructive. As weekend sojourners return to Mexico City on Sunday afternoons, traffic may stop completely for an hour, and it is

not uncommon for "a one-hour trip" to take five. Leaving their cars, drivers begin making direct contact with each other. They discover common acquaintances, share weekend experiences, and exploit unique interaction possibilities in the common dilemma. Someone pulls an inflated ball from his or her trunk and starts a trans-lane volleyball game. Others build a huge picnic table stretching over half a dozen cars. Strangers may work together to dismantle highway barriers in order to create a shortcut over a flat field. What such events bring out is the fact, usually hidden in the privacy of contemporary lives, that anger emerges from a falling out from community and is curable by the resurrection of community along other lines. Usually, the transcendent project that traffic cuts off is different for each driver. One is on the way to work, another to the market, another to a social event with friends. But for each the current trip is just one of several possible ways of linking an individual life into a communal order. On those rare occasions when everyone happens to be on the same biographical path (in this example, going home; in other examples, "going to the big game"), if a common dilemma develops and drivers are suddenly able to escape the communicative limitations of their automobiles, many motorists will prove ready to produce novel forms of community with enthusiastic creativity.

10. Certeau 1984.
11. Examples of how drivers play "the traffic game" are available in Berger 1993, 53 ff.
12. The railway journey was a powerful stimulant in the nineteenth century. Schivelbusch (1986, 77–78) recalls the sexual significance that Freud attributed to railway travel. Freud commented on dreams of missing a train as "dreams of consolation for another kind of anxiety felt in sleep—the fear of dying," an idea he applies to the dream "of a patient who had lost his father six years earlier" and who dreamed that his father "had been traveling by the night train, which had been derailed." Freud's own dream, known as "Count Thun" or the "revolutionary dream," grow out of an experience with a railway trip and featured

railway experiences in multiple ways (Freud 1965, 241–252). On the prominence of cars and driving in contemporary dreams, see Berger 1993, 18–19.
13. John Brinckerhoff Jackson describes the evolution of the road's meaning. "The Navajo journey is ... everyday existence ruled and protected by rites and precautions. He follows the paths his forebears followed. They lead to places where there are rare and special herbs. They avoid all places associated with death.... [I]n the seventeenth century ... [t]he European metaphorical use of the words *road* or *way* or *path* emphasized the difficulties encountered by the average wayfarer in the course of his or her journey through life.... But over the last century and a half, ... a third interpretation is taking shape: a multitude of roads, each with its own destination, obliges us to choose, to make decisions of our own; and the discourse of planning, of policy in the public realm, increasingly resorts to such road-associated phrases as *crossroads, dead ends, avenues of agreement, gridlock, collision course, impasse* and *bypass.*" Jackson 1994, 203–205.

REFERENCES

Anderson, Elijah. 1990. *Streetwise: Race, Class and Change in an Urban Community.* Chicago: University of Chicago Press.

Berger, K. T. 1993. *Where the Road and the Sky Collide: America through the Eyes of Its Drivers.* New York: Henry Holt.

Bourdieu, Pierre. 1990. *The Logic of Practice.* R. Nice (trans.). Stanford: Stanford University Press.

Certeau, Michel de. 1984. *The Practice of Everyday Life.* Berkeley and Los Angeles: University of California Press.

Freud, Sigmund. 1965. *The Interpretation of Dreams.* New York: Avon.

Gardner, Carol Brooks. 1995. *Passing By: Gender and Public Harassment.* Berkeley and Los Angeles: University of California Press.

Goffman, Erving. 1963. *Behavior in Public Places: Notes on the Social Organization of Gatherings.* New York: Free Press.

———. 1967a. "Where the Action Is." In *Interaction Ritual*, pp. 149–270. Garden City, N.Y.: Anchor Books.

———. 1967b. Introduction to *Interaction Ritual*, 1–3. Garden City, N.Y.: Anchor Books.

———. 1971. *Relations in Public*. New York: Basic Books.

Jackson, John Brinckerhoff. 1994. *A Sense of Time, a Sense of Place*. New Haven: Yale University Press.

Lauer, A. R. 1960. *The Psychology of Driving*. Springfield, Ill.: Charles C. Thomas.

Mauss, Marcel. [1935] 1973. "Techniques of the Body." *Economy and Society* 2:70–88.

McGrane, Bernard. 1994. *The Un-TV and the 10 MPH Car*. Fort Bragg, Calif.: Small Press.

Merleau-Ponty, Maurice. 1968. *The Visible and the Invisible*. Evanston, Ill.: Northwestern University Press.

Polanyi, Michael. 1962. *Personal Knowledge: Towards a Post-critical Philosophy*. Chicago: University of Chicago Press.

———. 1966. *The Tacit Dimension*. Garden City, N.Y.: Doubleday.

Schivelbusch, Wolfgang. 1986. *The Railway Journey: The Industrialization of Time and Space in the 19th Century*. Berkeley and Los Angeles: University of California Press.

Wolfinger, Nicholas. 1995. "Passing Moments: Some Social Dynamics of Pedestrian Interaction." *Contemporary Ethnography* 24:323–340.

16

COLIN JEROLMACK

FEEDING THE PIGEONS: SIDEWALK SOCIABILITY IN GREENWICH VILLAGE

from *The Global Pigeon* (2013)

In this chapter from his study on how animals help to shape the social life of a city, Colin Jerolmack shows how the mundane practice of pigeon feeding can connect pedestrians to sidewalk life and satisfy their desire for public association.

Father Demo Square sits in the heart of Greenwich Village, a triangular brick plot hemmed in by Carmine Street, Bleecker Street, and Sixth Avenue. The plaza, created as a leftover when Sixth Avenue was expanded south in 1925, is named in honor of an Italian pastor who raised money to build the church located just west of the park. As part of a study on interactions in public space, I documented the social life of this park—along with five others—from the spring of 2004 until the fall of 2005. The interactions and setting depicted below were all recorded before extensive renovations, which rendered Father Demo Square inaccessible from 2006 to 2007.

Though only 0.072 acres, the plaza's location in a busy commercial and pedestrian crossroads means that it nourishes the kind of vibrant sidewalk life that urbanist Jane Jacobs, who lived in and wrote about the area, claimed was crucial for fostering a sense of social connectedness in the city.[1] Visitors to the park included many who grabbed a slice from Joe's Pizza or a bagel from Bagels on the Square, delivery-truck drivers and city workers, employees of nearby businesses, tourists poring over their maps, students from New York University, club goers and pub crawlers, and the homeless, among others. The most frequent users of the park during the day were the old, mostly white, lifelong Villagers. Some told me that the few hours they spent there each day served as their primary form of social interaction.

The presence of many park visitors who ate takeout food there, as well as people who specifically came to the park to deposit birdseed and bread, meant that Father Demo Square was also a place that attracted pigeons. Despite the "Do Not Feed the Pigeons" sign, visitors provided the birds with meals all day long. When I spoke with David Gruber, head of a block association whose jurisdiction included the park, he complained about such visitors: "There are some people who come and leave bags of food for these pigeons, and they don't even live in the community." Gruber also complained about homeless people, which he said often slept in the space and could be found passed out drunk in the morning, but he had hopes that the renovated park, which would be fenced and locked at night, would control the homeless population. David was having a harder time trying to figure out how to curb the pigeon population. In a view echoed by the Parks Department and the local councilperson's office, he called the pigeons a nuisance and a health hazard. He explained the pigeons' presence as the product of a few zealous pigeon-lovers that ruined it for everybody else: "It's only a few people that feed the pigeons; 99.999% of people want to see no pigeons in the park. Everybody complains about it."

My observations of everyday park life painted a different picture. I saw that pigeon feeding was a daily routine for at least a half dozen people who came with seed for the birds, and over twice as many who brought bread. Dozens more park users engaged in more casual and spontaneous pigeon feeding every day, preferring to toss their pizza

crust or bagel remains to the birds instead of in the trash. At many moments of the day, pigeons dominated the scene, and many people in the park were engaged with them in some form or another—if not feeding them, then perhaps chasing them (common among children) or photographing them. In fact, human interactions with pigeons seemed to be among the most common "face-to-face" encounters that took place in Father Demo Square.

I was particularly struck by the capacity of pigeons to recognize regular feeders and coax unwitting park visitors into feeding them, behaviors that reflected the birds' adaptation to the demands and opportunities of city living. Biologists have found that pigeons are "able to learn quickly from their interactions with human feeders" on the street and "use this knowledge to maximize the profitability of the urban environment," discriminating between friendly feeders and hostile pedestrians and adopting begging strategies that elicit food from strangers.[2]

While it is obvious what pigeons gain from this synanthropic relationship, this chapter examines the social significance of pigeon feeding. Though the block captain and some municipal authorities framed pigeons as nuisances that impeded people's enjoyment of sidewalk life, I found that pigeon-feeding routines could become part of what Jane Jacobs called the "intricate sidewalk ballet" that enriched pedestrians' experience of the street and satisfied their desire for casual and delimited forms of copresence.[3] It was not uncommon for park visitors to strike up a conversation with a stranger at one moment and then become absorbed in tossing pieces of their meal to pigeons at the next moment. While most sociologists would ignore the human-animal encounter or view it as incommensurable with the social encounter, I saw how both forms of sidewalk interaction offered the solitary pedestrian the simple pleasure of playful, noncommittal association—what classical sociologist Georg Simmel called *sociability*. Pigeons could also instigate spontaneous associations among human strangers by becoming a topic of conversation and a focus of attention. Such interactions reveal how animals can become part of the urban "interaction order," shaping routine sidewalk life.[4] These cross-species encounters also trouble the social psychological axiom that sustained interaction is possible only if participants share a definition of the situation.

Pigeon Feeding

On a mild, sunny November afternoon, I arrived in Father Demo Square around 2:00 p.m. Thirty-two people sat on the benches: some young and some old, some tourists and some locals, some working class in appearance and some in suits. An old white man shuffled through the park, dropping bread as he went but continuing out of the space while looking back to watch 30–35 pigeons swarm the food. This seemed to inspire a Hispanic woman and her daughter, who tossed chips at the pigeons gathered nearby. A middle-aged, disheveled black male shifted his gaze toward about 20 cooing pigeons that gathered expectantly around him. He then tossed some pieces of a bagel to the pigeons and intently watched them consume it, while a young white couple laughed as they watched the birds fight over the food. Two middle-aged white women tossed pieces of bread from their sandwiches to a few pigeons and nonchalantly watched the birds as they continued their conversation. Another older, seemingly homeless black man rummaged through all of the garbage cans and then consumed what he found while breaking off pieces for a dozen pigeons. Two young Hispanic men watched the frenzied activity of the pigeons and laughed, and then began to toss some of their meal to the birds. A second old white man walked through the park and dropped some bread on his way

out, and an old white woman on a bench decided to join in the feeding by tossing some bread from her sandwich.

Then Anna, an old white woman who fed the pigeons every day and whom regulars called the "pigeon lady," took a bag of birdseed out of her purse and dumped some of it on the ground. Well over 50 pigeons flew over to her from surrounding rooftops, cooing loudly and shoving each other as they competed for the food. Anna continued to toss the seed about her, and held some in her hands, which encouraged some of the birds to climb on her body to obtain it. She smiled as a pigeon sat on her knee and another on her shoulder. A white woman stopped to take photos of the spectacle and chatted with Anna. At that point, passersby had stopped to observe, laugh, and take pictures of the event. A black boy, likely in middle school, got up from his bench and raced through the middle of the park, laughing and chasing the birds until they took off in a bunch and circled the plaza. Their simultaneous taking of flight let off loud claps of over 100 wings, and spectators pointed and ducked as the pigeons flew barely over their heads.

I was sitting with a young white woman, Carey, and two old white men, Frank and Jerry, who were regulars at the park. Carey remarked, "It looks like they get fed all day." They laughed as we watched the pigeons try to carry off large pieces of bagels while others attempted to rip it out of their beaks. Frank commented that the pigeons are here to stay because of all the food, and we focused our attention on them as the birds fought it out. In this not unusual five-minute snapshot from an afternoon in the park, out of the 32 people present inside the boundaries of the space, 18 people were directly involved with the pigeons through feeding, chasing, or taking photographs. More people, both those sitting and passersby, were indirectly involved in the action through taking time out from their other activities to watch the interactions.

Though feeding pigeons in New York (and elsewhere) can result in a nuisance citation, it was a routine activity for many visitors to Father Demo Square and other parks I observed around the city. Feeding pigeons also seemed common in the public spaces of many other cities I have visited, from Notre Dame in Paris to the Plaza de Mayo in Buenos Aires. People engage in pigeon feeding with various levels of intensity. Some people feed pigeons while paying little attention to them, or feed them for short durations. Sociologist Erving Goffman would call these "unfocused interactions." But other people achieve "focused interactions"[5] while feeding pigeons, in which they become absorbed in the activity and engage in feeding for an extended period of time. Though there is no absolute boundary between the two, "focused feeding" looks different than "unfocused feeding," and it seems that these two interactive forms tend to function differently as well. Unfocused feeding often helps facilitate associations *among people,* in which pigeons become a resource for conversations and interactions among acquaintances and even strangers. But focused feeding facilitates human associations *with pigeons.* In focused feeding, humans appear to seek these associations as ends in themselves. As a result of sustained attention to the pigeons, humans are rewarded with increasingly complex interactions. In both forms, pigeons—if only for the moment—help satisfy pedestrians' desire for copresence.

Unfocused feeding, in which humans paid little or sporadic attention to the pigeons, often occurred when two or more people were together. On one occasion, a middle-aged black woman and her middle-aged white female companion entered the park with sandwiches and sat down, while a nearby white family of four was feeding about 20 pigeons. After the women had been eating and talking for about two minutes, occasionally looking in the direction of the family, six pigeons slowly approached to within about eight feet of the women, stretching out and cocking their heads sideways. They seemed to expect food. The black woman appeared to notice them first. She ripped several pieces of bread from her sandwich while she returned eye contact to her friend. She then tossed some crumbs one at a time. One pigeon walked ahead of the others, craning its neck just enough to quickly snatch the crumb while maintaining a distance of about three feet from the women. The black woman noticed this from the corner of her eye, and two of the other pigeons advanced and pecked at the crumbs that were closer to the women. Soon, all six pigeons had moved within four feet of the women, and the black woman ripped off and tossed more pieces of bread, appearing to nonchalantly watch them eat with quick glances while she focused most of her eye contact on her friend. However, her friend had noticed the pigeons and also began to tear off and toss portions of her sandwich bread at them.

The women continued their conversation, laughing and discussing a variety of topics such as work and family life. Yet now both women took regular glances over at the pigeons they were feeding. Their actions brought over 5 more pigeons, and a mass of about 30–35 birds began to slowly make their way toward the women and the 11 pigeons already eating there. At this point, the women trained their eyes on the 11 pigeons longer, and they ceased talking to each other but smiled and laughed as they jointly tossed more and more crumbs. They talked about the pigeons to each other, pointing out ones that appeared quite eager or somehow comical in their actions (e.g., cooing loudly). Yet when the larger group of pigeons came within six feet of them, the white woman, and then the black woman, ceased tossing crumbs.

Only when about 25–30 pigeons had left to seek food from other visitors did the women begin the routine again, going back and forth between eye contact with each other and glances at the birds, making small talk that was sprinkled with references to the pigeons, and taking time-outs to focus their eyes on the pigeons. Six or seven minutes had passed, and the pigeons were now coming quite close to the women (less than one foot) to get some food. Yet, when the white woman moved her foot, the pigeons took a short flight away. The birds appeared to stay cautious despite their desire for more food. Again, they returned slowly. From here on out the women maintained an on and off feeding schedule that alternately attracted and then pushed back the pigeons. The women appeared to work to keep a small number of the pigeons interested, and seemed to enjoy their presence, but they also worked to prevent their association from being overwhelmed by the 40–50 pigeons that were currently in the park. After about 15 minutes, the women finished their sandwiches and soon after exited the park.

It appeared that the mere presence of the birds encouraged some people to feed them. It was not quite as simple, however, as copresence. Pigeons worked to bring about this result by "begging." If on statues or lampposts, they swooped to the ground when food appeared. They were often on the ground already, because pigeons, like chickens, are naturally inclined to scavenge for food by pecking the ground—not flowers, trees, and shrubs (which is why they walk rather than hop). Pigeons would move in close, within a range of one to six feet, to the person(s) with food. Moreover, they stretched their necks out and turned their heads sideways so that one of their eyes was clearly directed at the food supply. If people ignored the birds, they often approached even closer, sometimes within inches of one's feet. If no food was forthcoming, they might move away, but often they did so only to double back and try again. In the end, they were remarkably adept at getting the average park visitor to donate scraps from

their meal. Once the food had disappeared, the pigeons backed away.

Feeding episodes often seemed unplanned, and they were also "contagious." There were often lulls where no one was feeding the pigeons, and then as soon as one started, others joined in. Such feeding usually occurred among families and groups. In fact, the women in the episode described above had already observed a family feeding some pigeons before the black woman began to toss her own crumbs. The white family of four, eating pizza, was tossing pieces of crust to the pigeons. The father began the activity, and as a group of about 20 pigeons gathered around, he verbally encouraged his young son and daughter to toss food. He helped them break off the crumbs and throw them, while saying, "Look at the birdies. Feed the birdies." The mother showed her approval, smiling and then grabbing some crust herself to toss to the birds. The children began to laugh, looking back to their parents who reinforced for them (through smiles and continual feeding) that the family as a whole framed this activity as an enjoyable event. All four family members tossed crust and laughed, with the children seemingly delighted to draw the pigeons into their company. The birds became the main involvement of the family, channeling their attention into a communal activity.

Children of varying ages could often be seen stopping by on their way home from school to feed the birds. Groups of adults, including delivery-truck drivers and sanitation workers who took a lunch break there, also incorporated feeding into their routines. Of course, some people fed pigeons and some did not; some who did it focused more attention on the birds than others; and some talked about the pigeons while others did not. The features that were more or less common to these episodes of unfocused feeding were that they were usually spontaneous, tended to occur with two or more associated people, were short in duration (under two minutes) or sporadic, and resulted in a predictable and narrow range of actions on the part of the pigeons. The birds usually stayed several feet away and simply grabbed the food and ran if the feeder did not invest a longer period of uninterrupted time in them (though pigeons habituated quickly, a sudden move could send them off). I seldom saw a large mass of pigeons around casual feeders. Interestingly, the vast majority of unfocused feeding episodes appeared to be instigated by pigeons, which successfully employed begging strategies until they were rewarded.

A key component of unfocused feeding is that pigeons, while brought into interaction with humans, were often incorporated into sociable exchanges that were still largely carried out among people. Significantly, pigeons became resources that facilitated or enhanced associations among humans in this space. There were only brief moments in unfocused feeding that humans directed their full attention to the pigeons. Thus, the presence of pigeons in the park could be a *means* when they acted as a prop employed to instigate interaction among humans. Of course, in the process humans became a means for pigeons in the birds' everyday pursuit of subsistence.

In public places, strangers are often expected to—at most—briefly acknowledge one another and then divert their attention elsewhere. Although strangers may wish to engage in sidewalk interactions, rules of civility dictate that they need an excuse to do so. Erving Goffman observed that dogs are a "classic bridging device" between strangers in public, and studies of urban parks confirm that dogs "facilitate encounters among the previously unacquainted."[6] In public places like Father Demo Square, pigeons too may act as a sort of interactional prop among strangers—in addition to focusing the attention of those already associated.

As I sat in the park one day, Anna the "pigeon lady" was there, engaged in her routine. A white female tourist who had

been wandering by doubled back to witness the pigeons crawling on Anna. After sitting close by and taking some photos, the young woman struck up a conversation with Anna, and they talked for well over 15 minutes. This happened regularly. Indeed, by feeding the pigeons Anna not only obtained their company but also gained the company of strangers she would not otherwise likely interact with. On many occasions, strangers on nearby benches made remarks to one another or struck up sustained conversations based on the pigeon-feeding episodes. Even if people were complaining about the birds, this complaint was often directed to a nearby stranger who was then expected to reciprocate with a response. Such exchanges might last seconds, but occasionally they lasted for over 20 minutes. Once the subject matter of the pigeons had been exhausted, some strangers had worked up enough trust and interest in one another to launch into other subject matters. Other people, however, got drawn into the interactions with the pigeons themselves, seeking these interactions as the ultimate ends of their park visits.

Focused feeding, in which humans engaged in sustained "face-to-face" interaction with pigeons, usually occurred when pigeon feeders were alone, though there were many episodes of its occurrence with pairs of people as well. However, three or more people tended to create an atmosphere in which the pigeons' presence was secondary. One afternoon, I watched an elderly white couple enter the park, the woman pushing the man in a wheelchair. They sat for about three minutes, speaking occasionally to each other as they ate some sandwiches. The woman casually tossed a crumb to a nearby pigeon. This pigeon quickly ate the piece, and the woman then fixed her eyes on it. As about 20 pigeons moved into their proximity, the woman tossed more crumbs to the birds as she smiled and remarked to her companion in Russian. Then he followed her cue, and they continually tossed crumbs as more and more birds gathered around and they maintained their conversation. After about three minutes, over 50 pigeons had crowded around them, cocking and twisting their heads. The couple pointed at the birds and quickened their pace of crumb tossing. In the next minute or so, they entirely ceased their conversation with each other and silently fixed their gazes on the birds gathering about their feet. This continued for about six or seven minutes. The man noticed that some birds approached the base of his wheelchair, so he simply let some crumbs drop right out of his hands. He smiled, and continually monitored the pigeons in his immediate vicinity to decide where to toss his bread next. The pigeons came closer after a couple minutes of constant feeding, willing to go between the legs of the woman to snatch up some crumbs, and she laughed out loud as a few began to jump on the bench and look at her in apparent expectation. The couple appeared completely absorbed, seemingly "lost" in the encounter. It was only when they had run out of food (after about 15 minutes), and the pigeons had moved on to the next feeder, that the couple looked at and spoke to one another. Their smiles faded. Then they looked around quickly, possibly embarrassed, and the woman immediately stood up and wheeled the man out of the park.

I saw this couple feeding the pigeons again three days later, and this time they had purposely brought bread in a bag for the birds. In their previous encounter, they spontaneously and at first casually fed the birds some crumbs, but wound up engaging in a focused interaction. They now returned with a dedicated cache of bread for the pigeons, to ensure a sustained encounter, and they were on their way to becoming regular feeders. Food was an important marker that demonstrated the level of commitment to feeding. Unfocused feeding was not only spontaneous and short lived, but also usually entailed simply breaking off very minor portions of one's bagel, pizza crust, or bread. Many who engaged in focused feeding reserved food just for pigeons, either a separate supply or a generous portion of their own meal. I saw that several apparently homeless men, mostly black, would partake in feeding this way. These men came to the park alone to get food, and after sorting through the garbage cans, they often took a seat and began to eat. It was quite common in this process for some of them to set aside some of the food attained—whether potato chips, noodles, or salad—for the pigeons, tossed on the ground next to the man as he ate, so that it looked as if the pigeons and the man were taking a meal together.

One chilly day I spotted a white male, disheveled and likely in his mid-40s, rummaging through two garbage cans. He found part of a sandwich and some potato chips. He dumped the bag of chips on the ground and then smashed them so that the pigeons could eat them more readily. Then he sat and ate in silence for several minutes, watching the birds. When one came closer to him, he said to it, "Hey little guy," and then he broke off a piece of his sandwich for it. While the man did not smile, he appeared enthused, tossing more bread to the gathering pigeons that now stood in a semicircle around him. He talked to them a bit more: "Here you go"; "Don't fight, there's plenty for everyone." Four pigeons alighted on the bench, and one ate only a few inches from his hand. The man experimented, tossing food closer and closer to him to see how near the pigeons would come for food. When he tried to touch one and it jumped back, he returned to feeding them from a "safe" distance of about six inches. When he finished, after about ten minutes, I introduced myself to him. His name was John, and he told me that he slept by a New York University dorm. John said that he felt sorry for the pigeons and could see how hungry they were, but that he also enjoyed their company and fed them to keep them around.

Many parks have their dedicated pigeon feeders, who come nearly every day with bread or seed especially for the pigeons. While a lot of people who feed pigeons shuttle their attention back and forth between pigeons and other humans, or come to the park and then "discover" the pigeons, these individuals come with the primary intention of feeding the birds. Anna, the elderly white woman mentioned above, was one such person—called the "pigeon lady" by seven or eight regulars of this park. Others abound: in Washington Square there was a middle-aged Hispanic man named Teddy. Near Union Square was an older white woman named Mary. When I met Anna, she was living alone in a nearby walk-up apartment. She complained that all of her old friends from the neighborhood had died or been "put in a home." One time I pointed out some of the people whom I had identified as regulars and asked her about them. Anna seemed to know only one woman, who lived in her building. With her arthritis, getting out of her apartment was a chore. Yet Anna showed up to interact with the pigeons three times a day. While Anna was happy to engage in conversation with humans, she came for the pigeons. It is clear that there was a form of regularity and familiarity in the daily interactions that occurred between the pigeons and Anna, one that I did not see between pigeons and casual feeders.

On an early spring day, Anna walked gingerly into the park with her cane in one hand and bags of food in the other. As usual—for her, but a spectacle to many—the pigeons flew down from the rooftops and walked behind her cooing, following her into the park. Anna carefully lowered herself onto a bench. Anna was 85 years old at the time, and claimed that she had been feeding the pigeons for 31 years. On this day I asked her how she started feeding pigeons, and she replied that everyone asked her that but she really did not know. She said that she just decided to begin feeding them one day

and had since stayed with it. Anna regularly fed the birds seed and chunks of pita bread that she got for free from a Middle Eastern restaurant.

While I had seen pigeons in the park habituate to feeders over time, getting closer and even willing to jump on the bench with humans or stand on their feet, the pigeons displayed an elevated level of "trust" and familiarity with Anna brought about by her regular routines of prolonged feeding. When she got within a block of the park, they followed her. When she neared the bench, some even alighted on her shoulders. When she sat down, they were already beginning to climb on her; and when she fed them, they ate out of her hand. Anna was able to discern certain pigeons that were familiar to her from a pack in which almost all of them looked the same to me. As one pigeon jumped onto her knee, Anna asked me if I had met her friend Spots. She claimed "he" is a good bird, for when he gets enough to eat he leaves. Anna told me that she had three or four "favorites," Spots and Nasty among them. She wondered aloud where Nasty was, expecting him to be here. I asked her if the pigeons have different personalities, and she told me they do. Elaborating, she said that Nasty picks fights with everyone, and that he always tries to get into her pockets. Just then she noticed that Nasty had arrived. The bird flew down and jumped onto her knee to eat out of a plastic bag of seed that she held in her hand, but, sure enough, against her wishes Nasty began to peck in her pockets.

Anna claimed that the birds expected her to come with food, and she as well expected certain pigeons to be there and to interact with her in certain ways. For example, Anna wondered aloud where Nasty was, and she would get more upset when Spots went into her pocket for food than when Nasty did, because Spots was supposed to be the "good" pigeon. Anna saw something in the pigeons that many, including me, missed. She could tell the pigeons apart so that she knew that the same birds were showing up every day, and she would get upset if some went missing. Yet Anna's association with the pigeons went further than this. Based on an established routine, a *relationship* emerged. Anna's feeding habits fostered a unique history with the birds that opened up more interactive possibilities with the pigeons than we have seen with the other feeding episodes. The pigeons *did* recognize Anna from across the street and lined up to wait for her, and Anna could point out certain pigeons and predict with accuracy how they would act and which ones would be willing to sit on her lap. Anna and the pigeons mutually constructed coordinated routines, in which their shared history enabled rather complex and distinctive interactive forms.

Anna's sessions with these birds often lasted for over half an hour; and, like the homeless man John, even if she might have been partially motivated to feed the pigeons so that they did not starve, this motivation seemed at most to serve as a baseline that brought them together. Out of the possibly purposive action of feeding sprung engrossing interactions with far more elaborated forms than those that tended to occur with unfocused feeding. Anna could have simply dumped the food and left the park if she did not seek the association as an end in itself, as some people did (perhaps to avoid a citation). Yet Anna "inefficiently" fed the birds by limiting the amount of food given at one time in order to prolong and expand the parameters of the encounter.

Regular pigeon feeders told me that they found satisfaction in having the birds eat from their hand, and in becoming familiar enough with a group of pigeons that they could discern "regulars." These people did more things with pigeons than casual feeders did, forming associations with greater interactive depth and breadth. Focused feeding almost always happened when feeders were alone. This more easily allowed the feeder to become attuned to the birds' responses, to lose herself in the "flow" of reciprocal interaction. While focused feeding was still common with pairs, any number more than two associated people tended to lead to sporadic and relatively unabsorbed involvement with the pigeons. It seems that the presence of more people threatened to "flood out" the membrane of the human-pigeon encounter by opening up the possibility of distracting "side engrossments" among people.[7] Yet for some people, interacting with pigeons seemed to be an end in itself that provided them with the satisfaction of association, even if it was a more limited form of association than interaction with other humans.

Focused feeding was usually longer in duration (ten or more minutes) and more continuous (uninterrupted) than casual feeding. This fostered more variability in the routines of interaction. Pigeons sometimes emerged as individual personalities, some people talked to them, the pigeons landed on shoulders and ate out of hands, and so forth. Humans experimented with different actions to see what they could "get away with" and still keep the pigeons involved in the encounter. Pigeons and humans were in sync with the actions of the other(s), based on prior history and prolonged interactions. One example is that when Anna lifted her leg, the pigeons did not scurry away the way they did when casual feeders made a similar sudden move. The essential element of focused feeding was that pigeons ceased to be bit players in the background of street scenes; they became the center of attention for humans, who became absorbed in these "focused interactions." To be sure, other humans might still be part of the picture—but often were not. Also, even if interaction with other humans did occur, it was usually sporadic and appeared to be mostly just a slight addition to the interaction context, in the same way that the pigeons often were merely an addition to the interaction context of humans in unfocused feeding.

The experiential difference between focused and unfocused feeding is significant.

The pigeons were there, in the park, an open possibility for anyone to encounter and interact with in a variety of ways. Some ignored them, and some fed them but just as a minor diversion or as a resource for facilitating their socializing with friends or strangers. But in focused feeding, it appears that individuals became engrossed, even "lost," in the associative possibilities of these encounters. Goffman astutely remarked that "solitary playfulness will give way to sociable playfulness when a usable other appears, which, in many cases, can be a member of another species."[8] Pigeons, not just people, can serve as "usable others" for those seeking sidewalk sociability. But how is this interaction coordinated across such a stark human-animal divide?[9]

Asymmetrical Interaction

According to the social psychological paradigm of "symbolic interactionism," sustained interaction depends on participants' ability to mutually negotiate meanings and imaginatively "take the role of the other" so that they can create a shared definition of the situation.[10] This excludes human-animal encounters from the "interaction order" because the absence of language makes symmetrical understandings impossible. Human-animal researchers, however, have demonstrated the depth and complexity of people's everyday interactions with their pet dogs and cats, in which they jointly construct elaborate routines that are marked by bodily communication and attunement to each other's actions. A few scholars have taken this as evidence that humans and their pets *do* share symmetrical understandings of the situation and have some ability to take the role of the other. Clinton Sanders and Leslie Irvine, for example, argue that games like fetch are possible only because both human and dog can read and send signals that symbolize "this is play."[11] But must humans and animals share symbols to interact? This

assumption seems unverifiable. Moreover, while such a theory may help explain how people interact with dogs, it seems that few, if any, would argue that humans and pigeons interact through shared symbols.

An alternative way to understand cross-species interaction is to bracket the collective act and analyze each participant's particular behaviors and strategies. In studying human-dog play, psychologists Robert Mitchell and Nicholas Thompson found that dogs and humans had their own "projects" that they tried to achieve through interaction.[12] For example, a human might have the project of keeping the ball away from the dog, whose project might be to acquire the ball. As long as the flow of the encounters provided both human and dog with sufficient opportunities to pursue their own project, sustained interaction was possible—even if humans were not psychologically engaged in such encounters (e.g., were bored) or were simply trying to give the dog some exercise. This indicates that *compatible projects* are sufficient to produce coordinated interaction, whether shared meanings and goals exist or not. Interacting parties, then, can have different intentions in "successful" interactions and can assign *asymmetrical meanings* to them.[13] This is certainly the case with pigeon feeding.

The behaviors of street pigeons indicated that they had a persistent goal of obtaining food, and they sought out situations in which they could obtain it. This was how humans found pigeons in the park, lurking about and waiting for someone to toss some food on the ground. Further, the pigeons attempted to manipulate the actions of park visitors to ensure the desired result by "begging." People in the park could have any number of projects, but some of them encountered the pigeons in this setting and began feeding them. This may be an example of two purposive projects— pigeons want to eat, and maybe humans want to help nourish these birds. In focused feeding, though, the person centers her attention on the activity. Often, she seeks to elaborate on the interactive possibilities and thus has a more durable encounter. Her project has ceased to be about "just" feeding the birds. Out of this purposive project have arisen additional actions aimed at obtaining playful association and reciprocal interactions with these creatures.

Though the encounters with pigeons followed one basic structure—feeding— humans often performed this task with intentionally "inefficient" moves (e.g., giving one crumb at a time) in order to sustain the flow of the encounter.[14] Interaction took on an ordered, routinized form. Yet people could use the feeding routine as a foundation on which to elaborate and improvise, much as sociable talk among park visitors might consist of "the elaboration of a conversational resource."[15] In focused feeding, humans appeared to become lost in the flow of the encounter; they allowed themselves to be enveloped in these momentary associations. Its reward was its own repetition. And because pigeons—like most animals—were capable of action independent of direct human manipulation, they could also add an enjoyable spice of uncertainty for humans.

Though we may know that pigeons in the park want to eat when they approach us, we can totally disregard their mental states and simply enjoy feeding them. However, "successful" pigeon feeding relies on some amount of monitoring of pigeon habits (e.g., if you walk after pigeons while tossing food, they will run away). Dedicated feeders were able to obtain enhanced satisfaction in the association itself, and their repeated experiences over time resulted in an increased mutual attunement between humans and pigeons that allowed for more elaborated forms of interaction (e.g., the pigeons were no longer afraid when the feeder came near, and sometimes they were quick to eat from her hand or stand on her knee; one could distinguish pigeon "personalities"). There is, then, work involved in achieving

engrossing interactions with pigeons. Compared to, say, dogs, there are fewer possible varieties of interaction. *In form*, however, focused pigeon feeding—like Anna's interactions—still reflects a mutually constructed, relatively complex association.

Feeding pigeons has the potential to be engrossing and meaningful to humans, regardless of how the interaction is experienced by pigeons, because the "projects" or intentions of the two species are compatible with each other—at this moment, in this setting—even as those projects have entirely different aims. However different its intentions, the pigeon still confronts the feeder as an active agent, what philosopher Martin Buber would call a "thou," "a truly *subjective* other whose immediate presence is compelling."[16] The pigeon can initiate and reciprocate action in a number of ways that are neither predetermined nor entirely under the control of people. These traits are present in almost all animals. Yet many of them are not encountered in a city dweller's everyday life, nor do their "projects" play out in ways that would keep them close enough to people to sustain the "face-to-face" interaction possible among humans and pigeons. For example, raccoons in city parks are less likely to open themselves up to such encounters.

Long ago, Georg Simmel observed that even in the midst of instrumental social interactions, there is often an "impulse" to enhance them, to create moments of sheer satisfaction by association.[17] Such sociable play can grow out of the topsoil of purposive action. In the same way, we see that even if one feeds pigeons for the purpose of providing nourishment, from here may grow an "impulse" to elaborate on this here-and-now interaction by introducing interactive forms for no other purpose than to enhance the association. It is this "impulse" to associate as an end in itself, and the fact that the pigeon brings something out of the person that enables both of them to accomplish structures of interaction together, that permits people to experience pigeon feeding as a compelling and fulfilling form of sidewalk sociability.

Sidewalk Sociability and Social Vulnerability

Following Jane Jacobs, urban sociologists have found that noncommittal sidewalk sociability, and even people watching, can mitigate feelings of isolation and foster a sense of connection to the urban social fabric.[18] However, while public spaces provide opportunities for spontaneous interactions, these interactions are not always coveted. Indeed, Jacobs observed that many pedestrians seek to balance a desire for copresence with a demand for privacy. And Goffman noted that, on sidewalks, people from all walks of life are "exposed" to the possibility of being engaged in unwanted interactions with other individuals who, granted the public space they share, have the "right" to initiate encounters that may not be granted in other contexts.[19] An example of this, which I saw many times in Father Demo Square, is when a seemingly homeless person intentionally sits close to a park visitor and initiates a conversation. The visitor, "caught" and not wanting to appear rude, must interact with the homeless person for some duration before it is acceptable to walk away. There is a subtle tension at work, then, when one enters "open regions" such as parks. By putting oneself in a public place, the individual is open to the desirable possibility of engaging in sociable encounters with strangers *and* open to unwanted social entanglements or even social isolation.[20] We are made vulnerable.

Interactions with pigeons took place in this context. Especially if people came to the park alone—as most people who engaged in focused feeding did—they were "open," or "exposed." People often visited the park to take a "time-out" from their instrumental concerns. As Goffman remarked, to avoid appearing strange or conspicuous, unless one engages in people watching, a sort of prop is needed to give the appearance of a "main involvement." Indeed, my observations reveal that people watching may serve as a "legitimate" activity only for a limited duration. Understanding the park visitor in this way, it becomes easy to see how some visitors wound up feeding pigeons. On a basic level, it was something to do that made one appear occupied.

Further, I have almost never seen a pigeon reject food. While this may seem trivial, the fact that it takes such an easily obtainable prop (food) to interact with a pigeon in a way that the person largely controls, and the knowledge beforehand that the pigeons will immediately gather around the person (and maybe even climb on her if one is patient) in the hopes of obtaining more food, assures the individual that it will be quite easy to achieve an association with these creatures. The matter is much less trivial for people who may spend many hours each day in social isolation or experience a sense of marginalization from the larger community, such as some elderly and homeless people. The image of the old, friendless "pigeon lady," an urban archetype reinforced in stories and movies such as *Mary Poppins* and *Home Alone 2*, resonates for a reason. Though I found regular pigeon feeders to be more diverse than the stereotype—including married men, the wealthy, and the middle-aged—they did tend to be older people living alone. Similarly, biologists who studied pigeon feeding in Madrid and Basel described regular feeders as "the lonely, old, disabled—those not accepted in general."[21] Though at first I was surprised to see so many homeless people feeding pigeons, I came to see how the easily secured associations that these episodes afforded could be a powerful lure for those who were generally shunned by people on the sidewalks. Encounters with pigeons ephemerally dissolved their solitude into an experience of "togetherness" with others.

In the process, feeding provided a narrative structure to idle time, as humans instigated behaviors from pigeons (e.g., begging) which in turn required a human response to complete the sequence. Pigeons needed them.

We should shrink from generalizations, though. Perhaps those most eager to feed pigeons were children, who seemed to care less about obeying park rules that forbade the act and who did not yet seem to harbor notions of pigeons as pests. My observations also reveal that casual feeders far outnumbered regular feeders—and those who spontaneously fed pigeons came from all walks of life. The thing that most casual feeders did share was the *social situation of finding themselves alone, and idle, in the park.* In other words, for the moment they experienced the more generalized condition of some of the socially isolated regular feeders, and they responded in kind. Thus, the "impulse" to feed pigeons, which ecologists and nature writers like Edward O. Wilson might construe as the expression of an "innate" psychological desire to commune with other species,[22] may not be so distinct from the impulse to begin chatting with a stranger: they may both be born out of a situational response to solitude in a moment of unstructured time.

The difference between casual and regular feeders was one of degree rather than kind. As I have shown, pigeons could coax unsuspecting park visitors into feeding them. Unfocused feeding readily bled into focused feeding, particularly if a person was alone. And satisfying feeding episodes could beget future encounters. It is easy to see how casual feeders can become regulars. The "career" of a pigeon feeder is not so mysterious or deviant, and her activities and aims may not be so different from other park visitors'.

Pigeons offer possibilities for interaction that newspapers or people watching do not, as Anna's story reveals. Being with pigeons means not being alone. Feeding possesses a "consummatory end-in-itself character,"[23] lending structure and meaning to free time. Outside concerns can be momentarily dissolved; the individual is free to become "lost" in the activity. The satisfaction can precisely be found in investing one's full attention and consciousness into an association in which so little is at stake. Akin to one type of social contact that Jacobs said typified "successful" sidewalk life, pigeons can offer enjoyable, casual associations that penetrate the pedestrian's blasé and reserved public persona while entailing little commitment.[24]

Pigeons are a visible, active part of the street scene. While they may be irrelevant or annoying to some people, to others pigeons provide a ready resource for interaction. They may serve as a prop for associations among people, but they may also become the focus of park visitors' attention. Pigeons play a part in determining this outcome by initiating feeding episodes and sustaining interactions in their quest for food. By virtue of being enmeshed in these relations with people, they can play a prominent role in shaping how people interact in, and experience, urban spaces. The complex interactive routines that regular feeders forge with pigeons challenge the social psychological assumption that coordinated face-to-face encounters require shared symbols. And the sociability that people can achieve through pigeon feeding—especially for solitary pedestrians—demonstrates that mundane encounters with animals can offer opportunities for the kind of informal, bounded forms of copresence that urban sociologists claim enrich people's experience of the sidewalk and combat feelings of social isolation.

Everyday feeding episodes like the ones that I witnessed in Greenwich Village also have material consequences. Pigeons frequent locations where they are fed; if they are fed well, they breed profusely; and because they are rewarded with food for begging, they decrease the time they spend scavenging for food around the city and become more dependent on people. The large number and vast spatial distribution of pigeons, and the problems that such populations may engender, are the direct product of human activity. This socioecological reality indicates how popular pigeon feeding still is, despite its growing stigma.

NOTES

1. Jacobs 1961. Father Demo Square also abuts the blocks where Mitchell Duneier (1999) documented the lives of unhoused book and magazine vendors.
2. Belguermi et al. 2011; see also Weber, Haag, and Durrer 1994.
3. Jacobs 1961, 50.
4. On sociability, see Simmel 1949; on the "interaction order," see Goffman 1983. For those readers versed in "actor network theory," we can think of pigeons as nonhuman "actants" that, like humans, contribute to the orderliness found in this space (see Latour 1988).
5. Goffman 1963, 24.
6. Goffman 1963, 126; Robins, Sanders, and Cahill 1991, 3. Duneier (1999) shows how some of the black street vendors he studied took advantage of this possibility to "entangle" passing white women in conversation that they sought to avoid.
7. On sustaining flow and "play membranes," see Csikszentmihalyi 1975; Goffman 1961.
8. Goffman (1974) 1986, 43.
9. For a more theoretical answer to this question, see Jerolmack 2009.
10. See Blumer 1969; Mead (1934) 1967.
11. Irvine 2004; Sanders 1999; the original statement of this problem comes from Bateson (1956).
12. Mitchell and Thompson 1986, 1990.
13. See Goode 2006; Mechling 1989. The same is true for people; see Fuchs 1989; Garfinkel 1967; Goode 1994; Hendriks 1998.
14. On the role of inefficient gestures in play, see Miller 1973.

15. Watson and Potter 1962; see also Riesman and Watson 1964.
16. Buber 1970; Myers 1998, 82; see also Owens 2007.
17. Simmel 1949.
18. See Anderson 2011; Duneier 1999, 1994; Jacobs 1961; W. H. Whyte 1988.
19. Goffman 1963, 132. Jack Katz (1999, 326) calls such contexts as these, in which he includes places as varied as supermarket checkout lines and highways, areas of "cultural communism." In such locales, "no externally relevant status is routinely useful in the distribution of rights."
20 In his study of relations between unhoused vendors and wealthy neighborhood residents, Duneier (1999) focuses on this tension on the very streets where my fieldwork was carried out.
21. Weber, Haag, and Durrer 1994, 58; see also Humphries 2008, 153–72.
22. Kellert and Wilson 1993; Gibson 2009; Pyle 1993.
23. Goffman 1967, 162.
24. Jacobs 1961, 56; on the "blasé attitude," see Simmel 1971.

REFERENCES

Anderson, Elijah. 2011. *The Cosmopolitan Canopy: Race and Civility in Everyday Life.* New York: W. W. Norton & Co.
Bateson, Gregory. 1956. "The Message, 'This Is Play.'" In *Group Processes.* B. Schaffner (ed.), 145–242. New York: Josiah Macy.
Belguermi, Ahmed, Dalila Bovet, Anouck Pascal, Anne-Caroline Prévot-Julliard, Michel Saint Jalme, Lauriane Rat-Fischer, and Gérard Leboucher. 2011. "Pigeons Discriminate between Human Feeders." *Animal Cognition* 16 (6): 909–914.
Blumer, Herbert. 1969. *Symbolic Interactionism.* Berkeley: University of California Press.
Buber, Martin. 1970. *I and Thou.* W. Kaufman (trans.). New York: Touchstone.
Csikszentmihalyi, Mihaly. 1975. *Beyond Boredom and Anxiety.* San Francisco: Jossey Bass.
Duneier, Mitchell. 1994. *Slim's Table.* Chicago: University of Chicago Press.

———. 1999. *Sidewalk*. New York: Farrar, Straus, & Giroux.

Fuchs, Stephan. 1989. "Second Thoughts on Emergent Interaction Orders." *Sociological Theory* 7 (1): 121–123.

Garfinkel, Harold. 1967. *Studies in Ethnomethodology*. Englewood Cliffs, NJ: Prentice Hall.

Gibson, James William. 2009. *A Reenchanted World: The Quest for a New Kinship with Nature*. New York: Holt.

Goffman, Erving. 1961. "Fun in Games." In *Encounters*, idem, 15–81. Indianapolis, IN: Bobbs-Merrill.

———. 1963. *Behavior in Public Places*. New York: Free Press.

———. 1967. *Interaction Ritual: Essays on Face-to-Face Behavior*. Garden City, NY: Doubleday.

———. (1974) 1986. *Frame Analysis*. Boston: Northeastern University Press.

———. 1983. "The Interaction Order: American Sociological Association, 1982 Presidential Address." *American Sociological Review* 48 (1): 1–17.

Goode, David. 1994. *A World without Words*. Philadelphia: Temple University Press.

———. 2006. *Playing with My Dog, Katie: An Ethnomethodological Study of Canine-Human Interaction*. West Lafayette, IN: Purdue University Press.

Hendriks, Ruud. 1998. "Egg Timers, Human Values, and the Care of Autistic Youths." *Science, Technology, and Human Values* 23 (4): 399–424.

Humphries, Courtney. 2008. *Superdove*. New York: Smithsonian Books.

Irvine, Leslie. 2004. *If You Tame Me*. Philadelphia: Temple University Press.

Jacobs, Jane. 1961. *The Death and Life of Great American Cities*. New York: Modern Library.

Jerolmack, Colin. 2009. "Humans, Animals, and Play: Theorizing Interaction when Intersubjectivity Is Problematic." *Sociological Theory* 27 (4): 371–389.

Katz, Jack. 1999. *How Emotions Work*. Chicago: University of Chicago Press.

Kellert, Stephen R., and Edward O. Wilson (eds.). 1993. *The Biophilia Hypothesis*. Washington, DC: Island Press.

Latour, Bruno. 1988. "Mixing Humans and Nonhumans Together: The Sociology of the Door Closer." *Social Problems* 35 (3): 298–310.

Mead, George Herbert. (1934) 1967. *Mind, Self, and Society*. Chicago: University of Chicago Press.

Mechling, Jay. 1989. " 'Banana Cannon' and Other Folk Traditions between Human and Nonhuman Animals." *Western Folklore* 48 (4): 312–323.

Miller, Stephen. 1973. "Ends, Means, and Gallumphing: Some Leitmotifs of Play." *American Anthropologist* 75 (1): 87–98.

Mitchell, Robert W., and Nicholas S. Thompson. 1986. "Deception in Play between Dogs and People." In *Deception*, edited by R. W. Mitchell and N. S. Thompson (eds.), 193–204. Albany: State University of New York.

———. 1990. "The Effects of Familiarity on Dog-Human Play." *Anthrozoös* 4 (1): 24–43.

Myers, Gene. 1998. *Children and Animals*. Boulder, CO: Westview Press.

Owens, Erica. 2007. "Nonbiological Objects as Actors." *Symbolic Interaction* 30 (4): 567–584.

Pyle, Robert Michael. 1993. *The Thunder Tree: Lessons from an Urban Wildland*. Boston: Houghton Mifflin.

Riesman, David, and Jeanne Watson. 1964. "The Sociability Project: A Chronicle of Frustration and Achievement." In *Sociologists at Work*. P. E. Hammond (ed.), 235–321. New York: Basic Books.

Robins, Douglas M., Clinton R. Sanders, and Spencer E. Cahill. 1991. "Dogs and People: Pet-Facilitated Interaction in a Public Setting." *Journal of Contemporary Ethnography* 20 (1): 3–25.

Sanders, Clinton R. 1999. *Understanding Dogs: Living and Working with Canine Companions*. Philadelphia: Temple University Press.

Simmel. Georg. 1949. "The Sociology of Sociability." *American Journal of Sociology* 55 (3): 254–261.

———. 1971. *On Individuality and Social Forms.* D. L. Levine (ed.). Chicago: University of Chicago Press.

Watson, Jeanne, and Robert J. Potter. 1962. "An Analytic Unit for the Study of Interaction." *Human Relations* 15 (3): 245–263.

Weber, Jacqueline, Daniel Haag, and Heinz Durrer. 1994. "Interaction between Humans and Pigeons." *Anthrozoös* 7 (1): 55–59.

Whyte, William H. 1988. *City: Rediscovering the Center.* New York: Anchor Books.

PART III

RAISING A FAMILY

//

The next section of this reader, "Raising a Family," contains five selections that highlight the connection between families and the context of the urban neighborhoods in which they are embedded. Each of these pieces is based on in-depth knowledge of the community and people under study, and each takes us inside individual families and introduces us to people known by the field-worker for many years.

We begin with an excerpt from Michael Young and Peter Willmott's *Family and Kinship in East London*, a study that in many ways parallels the work of Herbert Gans in part VII. Like Gans, Young and Willmott set out to assess the impact of urban renewal policies. Their field site is the working-class neighborhood of Bethnal Green in London's East End. This area, long known for over-crowding and poor housing conditions, suffered considerable damage during World War II. By the time their research began in the early 1950s, much of the area was slated to be razed, and its residents were to be relocated to modern housing estates. Young and Willmott's original purpose was to study how the lives of these residents were changed by the move. Yet while their initial intent was to follow a "before and after" method to study the effects of housing policy, they soon became fascinated by the extensive network of kinship ties among

working-class residents, which was little understood by social researchers and public policy makers. Their book details the complex web of supportive kinship networks that existed in Bethnal Green, and it documents the destruction of these networks as families were moved into new suburban communities.

In the excerpt presented here, we see how family life encompassed the people of Bethnal Green. Yet, contrary to common belief, such dense kinship ties did not isolate the neighborhood's working-class families from those outside these networks. Instead, as Young and Willmott discovered, family members—cousins, aunts, sisters—became bridges to many people who would otherwise have been strangers. A community bound together by family ties was also tightly connected to the broader society through relatives who provided links to people outside the family. The study was a benchmark in the application of a mixed-method approach to the study of mundane, taken-for-granted aspects of urban life. The authors begin with a memorable walk through the neighborhood with a typical resident to show what these ties mean in practice. Combining detailed field notes on everyday interactions with interview extracts and survey results, the two paint a textured portrait of how the area's community life functions in a very small space.

Carol Stack's classic *All Our Kin* is a work from the 1970s that updates and significantly deepens insight into reciprocity in African-American family life. Stack was responding to growing alarm among policy makers and the media about the rising number of "broken homes," that is, female-headed families, in the black community at the time. Gaining intimate knowledge of the daily life routines of poor black families on public assistance, Stack documented the roles played by large numbers of extended family and friends. What appeared at first to be small, isolated, single-parent families actually turned out to be parts of sprawling kin networks, generally centered around women but involving many men as well.

According to Stack, the men and women she studies "know that the minimal funds they receive from low-paying jobs on welfare do not cover their monthly necessities of life: rent, food, and clothing" (p. 57). At one point, she introduces a poor woman named Ruby Banks and speaks about the daily life of her female-headed family in "the Flats." She demonstrates how the support system of family and friends, built on both mutual exchange and exploitation, enables people to navigate poverty. Stack recognizes that the poor black family is in a precarious position. Yet, rather than viewing family life as the cause of its poverty, she examines its adaptive strategies in the context of the social, political, and economic conditions of Northern ghettos. In later years, as welfare reform cut benefits and moved large numbers of people off the rolls, Stack was to argue that the ability of kin to do the things for each other that had helped them survive for all those years was now in question. "Grandmothers, sisters, and cousins who were once able to offer spontaneous respite care might still have the family system as their primary impulse but could no longer accommodate ten-hour child-care days, when many of them are in the same boat trying to make ends meet."[1]

Our next two readings show urban ethnography's potential to highlight and clarify the distinctive features of family life that are rooted in the urban context of high-poverty neighborhoods. Mary Pattillo's *Black Picket Fences* demonstrates that black middle-class parents trying to raise children in the city must confront obstacles that white middle-class families and those living outside the city do not. This is because segregation and the limited housing options that are available to African Americans make it difficult for black middle-class families to move to neighborhoods physically distant from those in which black poor people live. Therefore, they frequently reside in neighborhoods of "diverse composition," in which children are routinely exposed and sometimes drawn to street-oriented life styles. In addition, most middle-class blacks possess less material wealth than do whites with similar jobs, and they thus retain their class position "by the skin of their teeth." Working constantly to maintain their economic foothold, they are less likely to be able to supervise and monitor their children. As Pattillo discovers, middle-class status does not grant the black middle class the ability to protect their children from the lure of the street or police surveillance, both features of many poor black neighborhoods.

With great literary flair, the next selection illustrates the struggles of poor urban families. Patricia Fernández-Kelly's study of black families in West Baltimore is a sociological portrait based on a decade of careful interaction and observation of parents, children, teachers, and state authorities. Whereas Pattillo focused on middle-class "respectable" people and their efforts to keep a distance from the deviance associated with certain members of the lower classes, Fernández-Kelly depicts how the most desperately poor inner-city parents struggle to keep their children at some remove from the dangers of the street. Unlike the middle-class parents in Pattillo's account, the subjects introduced by Fernández-Kelly do not have the material resources to uphold their moral position. Their efforts to protect their children sometimes even lead to the unintended consequence of landing parents in trouble with authorities. The story of Towanda's relationship with her mother reveals how utterly demoralizing it can be to be a parent in the inner city.

All of these works look at families in the context of dense, often physically small, urban neighborhoods. Nowadays, however, the kin networks and social communities in which people are embedded sometimes transcend spatial boundaries. In the final selection in this section, Joanna Dreby looks at families that are "divided by borders": Mexican immigrants who endeavor to keep families together and coherent despite often being forced to leave children behind in rural Mexico as they struggle to make a living in the urban United States. This is clearly a situation fraught with emotional tension for both parents and children. Having spent time with family members in both Mexico and the United States, Dreby shows the unexpected amount of power and agency that teenagers and even very young children exert in shaping these complicated relationships. This is not something that the children or, in many cases, their parents would or could articulate in a single interview or express in response to a survey. Rather, it is the type of insight that requires long-term ethnographic involvement with people, as well as observation of what they do and what they say as they navigate their daily lives.

NOTE

1. Stack, Carol. "Doing Public Anthropology for Social Justice," Cecil G. Sheps Lecture in Social Justice, University of North Carolina, Chapel Hill, March 28, 2003. Cited in Mitchell Duneier, "On the Legacy of Elliot Liebow and Carol Stack: Context-driven Fieldwork and the Need for Continuous Ethnography," *Focus*, 24:1 (2007), pp. 33–38.

17

MICHAEL YOUNG AND PETER WILLMOTT

KINSHIP AND COMMUNITY

from *Family and Kinship in East London* (1957)

In 1953, Michael Young and Peter Willmott set out to assess the impact of Britain's Labour Party Government's urban renewal policies. They studied a traditional working-class community in a section of East London slated for demolition; they then followed the former residents to the housing estate to which they had been relocated in order to observe how their lives had changed. Though their initial interest was to study the effects of the housing policy, they became fascinated by the extensive network of kinship ties among the working-class residents, which was so little understood by social researchers and public policy makers. Young and Willmott were particularly struck by the role of women in family and community life, as this excerpt shows.

WE have...moved successively outwards from the married couple to the extended family, from the extended family to the kinship network, and from there to certain of the relations between the family and the outside world. We shall now turn from the economic to the social, and consider whether, outside the workplace, people in this particular local community unrelated either by marriage or by blood are related in any other way.

Since family life is so embracing in Bethnal Green, one might perhaps expect it would be all-embracing. The attachment to relatives would then be at the expense of attachment to others. But in practice this is not what seems to happen. Far from the family excluding ties to outsiders, it acts as an important means of promoting them. When a person has relatives in the borough, as most people do, each of these relatives is a go-between with other people in the district.

His brother's friends are his acquaintances, if not his friends; his grandmother's neighbours so well known as almost to be his own. The kindred are, if we understand their function aright, a bridge between the individual and the community: this will be the main theme of the chapter.

The function of the kindred can be understood only when it is realized that long-standing residence is the usual thing. Fifty-three per cent of the people in the general sample were born in Bethnal Green,[1] and over half those not born locally had lived in the borough for more than fifteen years. Most people have therefore had time to get to know plenty of other local inhabitants. They share the same background. The people they see when they go out for a walk are people they played with as children. "I've always known Frank and Barney," said Mr Sykes. "We was kids together. We knew each other from so high. We were all in the same street." They are, the people they went to school with. "It's friendly here," according to Mrs Warner. "You can't hardly ever go out without meeting someone you know. Often it's someone you were at school with." They are the people they knew at the youth club, fellow-members of a teen-age gang, or boxing opponents. They have the associations of a lifetime in common. If they are brought up from childhood with someone, they may not necessarily like him, they certainly "know" him. If they live in the same street for long they cannot help getting to know people whom they see every day, talk to and hear about in endless conversation. Long residence by itself does something to create a sense of community with other people in the district. Even an unmarried orphan would have local acquaintances if he were established in this way. But, unmarried orphans being rare, as a rule a person has relatives also living in the district, and as a result his own range of contacts is greatly enlarged. His relatives are also established. Their play-mates and their school-friends, their work-mates and

their pub-companions, are people whom he knows as well. Likewise, his friends and acquaintances also have their families in the district, so that when he gets to know any individual person, he is also likely to know at least some of his relatives.

The Bethnal Greener is therefore surrounded not only by his own relatives and their acquaintances, but also by his own acquaintances and their relatives. To show what this means in practice, let us accompany one of our informants on an ordinary morning's shopping trip. It lasted about half an hour. As she went along the street, nodding and chatting to this person and that, Mrs Landon commented on the people whom she saw.[2]

(1) MARY COLLINS. "She's a sister of Sally who I worked with at the button place before I got married. My Mum knew her Mum, but I sort of lost touch until one day I found myself sitting next to her in Meath Gardens. We both had the babies with us and so we got talking again. I see quite a lot of Mary now."

(2) ARTHUR JANSEN. "Yes, I knew him before I was married. He worked at our place with his sister and mother. He's married now."

(3) MAVIS BOOT. "That lady there, I know her. She lives down our turning," said Mrs Landon, as she caught sight in the butcher's of a back view of a large woman carrying the usual flat cloth bag. "She's the daughter of one of Mum's old friends. When she died Mum promised to keep an eye on Mavis. She pops in at Mum's every day."

(4) JOAN BATES is serving behind the counter at the baker's. "She used to be a Simpson. She lives in the same street as my sister. My Mum knows her better than me."

(5) SYBIL COOK. "That's a girl I knew at school called Sybil."

(6) KATIE SIMMONS. "She's from the turning, Mum nursed her Mum when she was having Katie."

(7) BETTY SALMON AND HER MOTHER. "They live in the next turning to ours. Betty says she's had nothing but trouble with her daughter since she went to school."

(8) RICHARD FIENBURGH. "That man over there at the corner. He's a sort of relative. He's a brother of my sister's husband. He lives near them."

(9) PATRICK COLLIS. This was a man in an old car parked by the shops. "His mother lives in the turning."

(10) AMY JACOBS is an old and bent woman who turns out to be Mrs Landon's godmother. "Usually it's only when I'm with Mum that we talk."

(11) SADIE LITTLE. This time there was not even a nod. The two women walked straight past each other. "She's quarrelled with my sister so we don't talk to each other."

(12) ALFRED CROSLAND. He is the father of the Katie seen a few minutes before.

(13) VIOLET BELCHER, a tall, thin lady talking to another at the street corner, is an "acquaintance of Mum's. She's got trouble with her inside."

(14) EMMA FRANCE. This was an elderly, very jolly woman, with grey hair and a loud laugh. She engaged Mrs Landon in conversation.
   "How's that other sister of yours?"
   "Lily?"
   "Yes, your Mum told me. She's gone to live in Bow, hasn't she?"
   "She's got a place with her mother-in-law there."
   "She don't like it? No! It never did work and I don't suppose it ever will."
   They both collapsed into laughter at this. Afterwards Mrs Landon explained that Mrs France had been her landlady in the first rooms her Mum had got for her.

That was just one unexceptional shopping trip. "Some days," says Mrs Landon, "you see so many you don't know which to talk to." She kept a record over a week of all the people she saw in the street and whom she considered herself to "know." There were sixty-three people in all, some seen many times and thirty-eight of them relatives of at least one other person out of the sixty-three. Her story showed how she had built up a series of connections with people she had known in school, work, or street, and, even more forcefully, how her mother and other kin acted as a means of communication between herself and the other people in her social world.

Home and Street

We should make it clear that we are talking mainly about what happens *outside* the home. Most people meet their acquaintances in the street, at the market, at the pub, or at work. They do not usually invite them into their own houses.[3] We asked people whether they visited, or were visited by, friends in one or other home at least once a month. "Friend" was here defined as anyone other than a relative. Out of the ninety men and women in the marriage sample, eighty-four exchanged visits with relatives, and only thirty-two with friends. Those exchanging the most visits with relatives also did so with friends; those most sociable inside the family were also the most sociable outside. But the majority neither had nor were guests.

Several people said they had possessed many more friends when they were single. Marriage and children made the difference.

"Since we've had the children I've got no more friends–outside the family I mean."

"I don't see my best friend much. She's married too, and she's always round *her* Mum's like I'm always round mine."

"Since we've had the baby, I've got no men friends—outside the family, that is."

The general attitude was summed up by Mr Jeffreys.

"I've got plenty of friends around here. I've always got on well with people, but I don't invite anyone here. I've got friends at work and friends at sport and friends I have a drink with. I know all the people around here, and I'm not invited into any one else's home either. It doesn't seem right somehow. Your home's your own."

Where every front door opens on to street or staircase, and houses are crowded on top of one another, such an attitude helps to preserve some privacy against the press of people.

This exclusiveness in the home runs alongside an attitude of friendliness to other people living in the same street. Quite often people have themselves lived there for a long time—one out of every ten women and one out of every twenty men in the general sample still live in the street where they were born—and consequently know many of the other residents well. Quite often, too, either they or their neighbours also have relatives in the street who add to the spread of social contacts. If a person gets on bad terms with another person in the street—like Mrs Shipway whose neighbour "started spreading stories about me and told me off for sending my children to Mum's when I go out to work"—she is also on bad terms with her family. "They're all related in this street," said Mr Lamb. "It's awful, you can't talk to anyone in the street about any of the others, but you find it's a relation. You have to be very careful."[4] But if he is careful and keeps on good terms with his neighbours, he is also on good terms with their relatives, and can nod to them in the street, knowing that he will get a response. He only has to stand at his front door to find someone out of his past who is also in his present.

"I suppose people who come here from outside think it's an awful place, but us established ones like it. Here you can just open the door and say hello to everybody."

The streets are known as "turnings," and adjoining ones as "back-doubles." Surrounded by their human associations, the words had a glow to them. "In our turning we," they would say, "do this, that, or the other." "I've lived in this turning for fifty years," said one old man proudly, "and here I intend to stay." The residents of the turning, who usually make up a sort of "village" of 100 to 200 people, have their own places to meet, where few outsiders ever come—practically every turning has its one or two pubs, its two or three shops, and its "bookie's runner." They organize their own parties: nearly every turning had its committee and celebration (and several built wooden stages for the display of local talent) for the Coronation of 1953. Some turnings have little war memorials built on to walls of houses with inscriptions like the following:

R.I.P.
IN LOVING MEMORY OF THE MEN OF
    CYPRUS STREET WHO MADE THE
    GREAT SACRIFICE
1914–1918
J. AMOS, E. AGOMBAR, A. BOARDMAN,
    A. H. COLE . . .

—there follow the names of the other twenty-two soldiers from Cyprus Street. Above it is a smaller plaque to the men killed in 1939–45: "They are marching with their comrades somewhere on the road ahead." Pots and vases of flowers are fixed in a half-circle to the wall; they are renewed regularly by the women of the turning, who make a street collection every Armistice Day.

There is the same kind of feeling in the few small courts still standing where a few houses face each other across a common front-yard. In one of these, the houses are covered from top to bottom with green trellis-work, tiers of window boxes stand out from the trellis, and on one wall is a proliferation of flowers around a war memorial, a Union Jack, and some faded pictures of the Queen. One of the residents told us, with evident satisfaction, that she was born in the same courtyard house that she had lived in for sixty-two years and spoke with slight disparagement of her neighbours: "They're new here—they've only been here eighteen years." She had been shocked to hear that the authorities might he labelling her beloved court a "slum," and was now terrified lest they pull it down.

Robb, whose research was also done in Bethnal Green, cites an even more striking example.

> "One informant who lived in a house that had been occupied by his parents and grandparents stated that he could not remember a new family coming into the street of seventy houses during the previous forty years."[5]

The Villages of the Borough

Sometimes a person's relatives are in the same turning, more often in another nearby turning, and this helps to account for the attachment which people feel to the precinct, as distinct from the street, in which they live. A previous observer remarked:

> There is further location within the borough. People are apt to look for their friends and their club within a close range. The social settlements draw nearly all their members from within a third of a mile, while tradition dictates which way borderline streets face for their social life. The main streets are very real social barriers, and to some residents the Cambridge Heath Road resembles the Grand Ganyon.[6]

In Bethnal Green, the one-time villages which have as elsewhere been physically submerged and their boundaries usually obliterated—Mumford talks of London as a "federation of historic communities"[7]—live on in people's minds. Bow is one, Cambridge Heath another, Old Bethnal Green Road another, the Brick Lane area, once just outside the environs of the City, another. "I reckon it's nice—this part of Bethnal Green I'm talking about," remarked Mr Townsend. "I'm not talking of Brick Lane or that end. Here we're by Victoria Park." "It's all right on this side of the canal," said Mrs Gould, who lives in Bow. "I wouldn't like to live on the other side of the canal. It's different there." Another man, in a letter asking for help in getting another home, wrote "I am not particular where you send me, the farther the better. I do not mind if it is as far as Old Ford as I have left my wife and wish to keep as far away as possible." Old Ford is five minutes' walk from his wife. Other researchers have reported how difficult it was to get people to move even in the war.

> Many stories were told of families who would rather camp in the kitchens of their uninhabitable blitzed houses or sleep in public shelters than accept accommodation in another area of the borough.[8]

When people have to move away from one part of the borough to another, they can appreciate the difference. Mr Gould, when he married, moved away from his parents and went about ten minutes' walk away to live near his wife's parents elsewhere in the borough, in this case in Bow. "I'd like to be back in Bethnal Green," he said, "I would really. In Bethnal Green we have good neighbours, better than those in Bow I can tell you." Mrs Tawney had moved as unwillingly in the other direction.

> "We're both from Bow. We're not very well known around here. We've only lived here since we got married, you see. In Bow you knew everybody, grew up

with everybody, everybody recognized
you. Over here they're a bit on the mob-
bish side—they know you're a stranger
and treat you like one. They cater for you
more in Bow. You like the place where
you're mostly born, don't you?"

People who have moved know that their
old neighbours would still stand by them
if necessary. Mrs Jeffreys told us that in
Ramsgate Street, where she had lived all
her life until she was bombed out in 1944,
even now, over ten years later, "They all
know Edith Jeffreys. Any of them'll give me
a character."

When there is such localism within
the borough it is not surprising that for a
few people places beyond Bethnal Green
are another world. One woman had never
been outside the borough except for an odd
visit to the "Other End," as the West End of
London[9] is known locally. Another never
left the borough except for the usual day-trip
once a year to Southend. Yet another said "I
only went out once when we went to Canvey
just before the war. I felt very strange and
lonely when I went there. I've never been
out of Bethnal Green since except once to
go to Southend for the day." Many of the
most rooted people do not talk about fares
but about "riding fares," and while we do
not know the origin of the term, in context
it sometimes suggested that to pay a fare
to travel anywhere was something outland-
ish and even a little daring. One man said
that his aged mother was in an Old People's
Home "over the water." "Over the water"
meant over the Thames, a mile or two away
in Southwark.

In Bethnal Green the person who says
he "knows everyone" is, of course, exag-
gerating, but pardonably so. He does, with
various degrees of intimacy, know many
people outside (but often through) his family, and it is this which makes it, in the view
of many informants, a "friendly place."
Bethnal Green, or at any rate the precinct,
is, it appears, a community which has

some sense of being one. There is a sense
of community, that is a feeling of solidarity
between people who occupy the common
territory, which springs from the fact that
people and their families have lived there a
long time. We cannot do better than put it in
our informants' own words.

"Well, you're born into it, aren't you?
You grow up here. I don't think I'd like
to live anywhere else. Both my hus-
band and me were born here and have
lived here all our lives."
"You asking me what I think of
Bethnal Green is like asking a coun-
tryman what he thinks of the country.
You understand what I mean? Well,
I've always lived here, I'm contented.
I suppose when you've always lived
here you like it."

The Link through History

The family contributes in another way to
this sense of community, by giving people
a very personal link with its past. People's
parents and sometimes even their grandparents were born in Bethnal Green.

"I was bred and born in Bethnal Green
and my parents and their parents before
them: no, I wouldn't leave Bethnal Green,
I wouldn't take a threepenny bus ride out-
ride Bethnal Green."

In such families local history does not
have to be learnt from books: it is passed on
by word of mouth from parents to children.
Mr Firth probably had not read that Pepys
once came to Bethnal House and had "a fine
merry walk with the ladies alone after dinner in the garden."[10] But he related with a
certain satisfaction that:

"My father used to tell me about the old
days when sheep were grazing where

Victoria Park Gardens are now laid out and Cambridge Heath Road was still fields. At week-ends my father was a keeper at the Burial Ground. It's in Defoe; there's a book on it, father knew all about it."

The past lives on most tellingly in the families of French descent. Almost everyone in Bethnal knows about the Huguenots. The economy stems from the early silk weavers. The love of birds, animals, and flowers, which to this day makes some backyards a glory of bright colour, is said to be due to their influence. The Society for Protestant Refugees from High and Low Normandy still flourishes and serves many local people who could not claim French blood. But in the Huguenot families—and especially those with the French names which still stand out on the electoral rolls—the connexion is a source of special pride.

They rarely have documentary evidence of their ancestry. One local informant not in the sample was exceptional: he brought out an old paper written in somewhat strange French in the year of the Revolution, which as far as could be made out was a petition from a man who was his ancestor beseeching the Governors of the French Hospital in Hackney to employ, and at the same time treat, his granddaughter. Others did not know the details of their genealogies, nor were they even sure of their relationship to other local people of the same name. Mr Michaud thought that some other people were the offspring of his paternal great-uncle, but they were "not quite up to Mum's and Dad's standard." Mr Berthot told us that he had once by accident met a girl who was probably a relative. "Once a girl came up to me at work and said 'You look just like my Dad, what's your name?' It turned out that her name too was Berthot." But though the details were hazy, they did claim to come of Huguenot stock—as one man put it, "My people came over from Lyon with the weavers." For them, and to a lesser extent for other local residents, the fact that their "people" as well as themselves were born in Bethnal Green helps to keep alive a very personal sense of history, and this sense of history reinforces the feeling of attachment (just as it does in a regiment, a university, a trade union, or a political party) to the community and to its inhabitants.

Kinship and Residence: In Conclusion

...In the lives of Bethnal Greeners is kinship all? Is there any room for others than relatives? The answer is tentative. We did not ask in our interviews as closely or systematically about non-relatives as about relatives. But we left with the impression that the kindred, far from being a barrier, are in fact a doorway to the community. Some people do, no doubt, enclose themselves completely within the family; many do not willingly admit any but family to the privacy of their homes; most have no friend who takes pride of place over close relatives. But in general, it seems, relatives do not compete with friends, rather act as intermediaries with them....Each of the relatives in a person's family of origin is a link with yet another family, and so on in a widening network, "each family of marriage being knitted to each family of origin and each family of origin to each family of marriage by a member that they have in common." Our present proposition is that each of the relatives in the families of origin, and indeed in the network as a whole, is a link not only with other families but with people outside the family as well.

In itself this is only a formal proposition, just as the original proposition was formal. To say that there is a "link" (a clumsy metaphorical term, we admit) is not to say anything about its character. We have to inquire what actually happens between the family and the outside world, that is, into the nature of the "Links," just as we have to inquire what actually animates the formal structure of the family. Our belief is that in Bethnal Green the links, with a mother who lives in the next street and hence with her friends, acquaintances, and enemies, are more continuously effective because of the proximity to her and of the length of time for which proximity has existed.

The interaction between length of residence and kinship is therefore the crux of our interpretation. Neither is by itself a sufficient explanation. People in their families of marriage, let us suppose, live for a long period in one district without being related to others. They will establish many common associations through having children at the same schools, through meeting in the same shops, and through travelling on the same trains. But since there are no related families in the locality they will not be able to make use of the kind of social connexion which we have described. People could also, let us suppose, migrate in a caravan of related families. They would then have relatives around them, but these relatives would not be able to introduce them to so many outside the family precisely because none of them would be rooted in the district. Either length of residence or localized kinship does something to create a network of local attachment, but when they are combined, as they are in Bethnal Green, they constitute a much more powerful force than when one exists without the other. Then people have a number of links, or ways of orienting themselves, to the same person: he was at school, he is a relative by marriage, he lives in a well-known neighbourhood. Then people can make use of one or other of their possible approaches to establish a relationship with almost anyone, one might say to get a "bearing" on almost anyone. We only make these distinctions in order to clarify the interpretation. In practice it must be very rare to find long residence without local kinship or local kinship without long residence.

In this old-established district the relatives are a vital means of connecting people with their community. We do not suggest that family is the only doorway to friendship; by taking account of the associations of school and work we have tried to keep a balance between kinship and the rest. Certainly, many friends of whom informants spoke were made by them quite independently, at school, at work, or in the army. But here the family does more than anything else to make the local society a familiar society, filled with people who are not strangers. This has its disadvantages. If you know other people's business, they know yours. Feuds may be all the more bitter for being contained in such small space. But there are advantages too. For many people, familiarity breeds content. Bethnal Greeners are not lonely people: whenever they go for a walk in the street, for a drink in the pub, or for a row on the lake in Victoria Park, they know the faces in the crowd.

NOTES

1. A special analysis of the 1951 Census returns undertaken by the Registrar-General's staff showed that Bethnal Green had a higher proportion of residents born in it than did almost any other London borough.
2. We are indebted for this account to Phyllis Willmott.
3. This has been noticed before, in the course of research in the nearby borough of Greenwich. See Bakke, E. W. *The Unemployed Man,* pp. 153-4.
4. Publicans and shopkeepers also have to be cautious. If they fall out with one person they may lose as customers ten of his relatives as well.
5. Robb, J-H. *Working Class Anti-Semite,* p. 57.
6. Self, P. J. O. "Voluntary Organisations in Bethnal Green," p. 236.
7. Mumford, L. *City Development,* p. 190.
8. Glass, R. and Frenkel, M. "How they live at Bethnal Green," p. 43.

9. Some people regard the West End as an immoral place which good East Londoners should not frequent. In some parts of the East End the last bus at night from the West End was ironically known not so long ago as the "virgin's bus." See Matthews, W. *Cockney Past and Present*, p. 143.

10. Quoted by Rose, M. *The East End of London*, p. 16.

REFERENCES

Bakke, E. W. 1933. *The Unemployed Man*. London: Nisbet.

Glass, R. and Frenkel, M. 1946. "How they Live at Bethnal Green." *Contact: Britain Between West and East*. London: Contact Publications Limited.

Matthews, W. 1938. *Cockney Past and Present*. London: George Routledge & Sons.

Mumford, L. 1946. *City Development*. London: Secker & Warburg.

Robb, J. H. 1954. *Working-Class Anti-Semite*. London: Tavistock Publications.

Rose, M. 1951. *The East End of London*. London: The Cresset Press.

Self, P. J. O. 1945. "Voluntary Organisations in Bethnal Green." In A. F. C. Bourdillon., *Voluntary Social Services: Their Place in the Modern State*. London: Methuen & Co. Ltd.

18

CAROL STACK

SWAPPING: "WHAT GOES ROUND COMES ROUND"

from *All Our Kin* (1974)

In her study of family life among poor African Americans in the early 1970s, Stack shows how networks of family and friends enable people to navigate poverty. Like many observers of the time, Stack sees that the poor black family is in a precarious position. Yet, rather than viewing the pattern of family life as a cause of poverty, she sees it as a strategy for adapting to the context of ghetto life.

Ruby Banks took a cab to visit Virginia Thomas, her baby's aunt, and they swapped some hot corn bread and greens for diapers and milk. In the cab going home Ruby said to me, "I don't believe in putting myself on nobody, but I know I need help every day. You can't get help just by sitting at home, laying around, house-nasty and everything. You got to get up and go out and meet people, because the very day you go out, that first person you meet may be the person that can help you get the things you want. I don't believe in begging, but I believe that people should help one another. I used to wish for lots of things like a living room suite, clothes, nice clothes, stylish clothes—I'm sick of wearing the same pieces. But I can't, I can't help myself because I have my children and I love them and I have my mother and all our kin. Sometimes I don't have a damn dime in my pocket, not a crying penny to get a box of paper diapers, milk, a loaf of bread. But you have to have help from everybody and anybody, so don't turn no one down when they come round for help."

Black families living in The Flats need a steady source of cooperative support to survive. They share with one another because of the urgency of their needs. Alliances between individuals are created around the clock as kin and friends exchange and give and obligate one another. They trade food stamps, rent money, a TV, hats, dice, a car, a nickel here, a cigarette there, food, milk, grits, and children.

Few if any black families living on welfare for the second generation are able to accumulate a surplus of the basic necessities to be able to remove themselves from poverty or from the collective demands of kin. Without the help of kin, fluctuations in the meager flow of available goods could easily destroy a family's ability to survive (Lombardi 1973). Kin and close friends who fall into similar economic crises know that they may share the food, dwelling, and even the few scarce luxuries of those individuals in their kin network. Despite the relatively high cost of rent and food in urban black communities, the collective power within kin-based exchange networks keeps people from going hungry.

As low-skilled workers, the urban poor in The Flats cannot earn sufficient wages and cannot produce goods. Consequently, they cannot legitimately draw desired scarce goods into the community. Welfare benefits which barely provide the necessities of life—a bed, rent, and food—are allocated to households of women and children and are channeled into domestic networks of men, women, and children. All essential resources flow from families into kin networks.

Whether one's source of income is a welfare check or wages from labor, people in The Flats borrow and trade with others in order to obtain daily necessities. The most important form of distribution and exchange of the limited resources available to the poor in The Flats is by means of trading, or what people usually call "swapping." As people swap, the limited supply of finished material goods in the community is perpetually redistributed among networks of kinsmen and throughout the community.

The resources, possessions, and services exchanged between individuals residing in The Flats are intricately interwoven. People exchange various objects generously: new things, treasured items, furniture, cars, goods that are perishable, and services which are exchanged for child care, residence, or shared meals. Individuals enlarge their web of social relations through repetitive and seemingly habitual instances of swapping. Lily Jones, a resident in The Flats, had this to say about swapping. "That's just everyday life, swapping. You not really getting ahead of nobody, you just get better things as they go back and forth."

The Obligation to Give

"Trading" in The Flats generally refers to any object or service offered with the intent of obligating. An object given or traded represents a possession, a pledge, a loan, a trust, a bank account—given on the condition that something will be returned, that the giver can draw on the account, and that the initiator of the trade gains prerogatives in taking what he or she needs from the receiver.

Mauss's (1954) classic interpretation of gift exchange in primitive societies stresses the essence of obligation in gift giving, receiving, and repaying. A gift received is not owned and sometimes can be reclaimed by the initiator of the swap. A person who gives something which the receiver needs or desires, gives under a voluntary guise. But the offering is essentially obligatory, and in The Flats, the obligation to repay carries kin and community sanctions.

An individual's reputation as a potential partner in exchange is created by the opinions other have about him (Bailey 1971). Individuals who fail to reciprocate in swapping relationships are judged harshly. Julia Rose, a twenty-five-year-old mother of three, critically evaluated her cousin Mae's reputation, "If someone who takes things from me ain't giving me anything in return, she can't get nothing else. When someone like that, like my cousin Mae, comes to my house and says, 'Ooo, you should give me that chair, honey. I can use it in my living room, and my old man would just love to sit on it,' well, if she's like my cousin, you don't care what her old man wants, you satisfied with what yours wants. Some people like my cousin don't mind borrowing from anybody, but she don't loan you no money, her clothes, nothing. Well, she ain't shit. She don't believe in helping nobody and lots of folks gossip about her. I'll never give her nothing again. One time I went over there after I had given her all these things and I asked her, 'How about loaning me an outfit to wear?' She told me, 'Girl, I ain't got nothing. I ain't got nothing clean. I just put my clothes in the cleaners, and what I do have you can't wear 'cause it's too small for you.' Well, lots of people talks about someone who acts that way."

Degrees of entanglement among kinsmen and friends involved in networks of exchange differ in kind from casual swapping. Those actively involved in domestic networks swap goods and services on a daily, practically an hourly, basis. Ruby Banks, Magnolia Waters' twenty-three-year-old daughter, portrays her powerful sense of obligation to her mother in her words. "She's my mother and I don't want to turn her down." Ruby has a conflicting sense of obligation and of sacrifice toward her mother and her kinsmen.

"I swap back and forth with my mother's family. She wouldn't want nobody else to know how much I'm doing for her, but hell, that's money out of my pocket. We swap back and forth—food stamps, kids, clothes, money, and everything else. Last month the AFDC people had sent me forty dollars to get a couch. Instead of me getting a couch, I took my money over to Mama's and divided with her. I gave her fifteen dollars of it and went on to wash because my kids didn't have a piece clean. I was washing with my hands and a bar of face soap before the money come. I took all the clothes I had, most of the dirty ones I could find, and washed them. It ran me up to six dollars and

something with the cab that my sister took back home. I was sitting over at the laundry worrying that Mama didn't have nothing to eat. I took a cab over there and gave her ten more dollars. All I had left to my name was ten dollars to pay on my couch, get food, wash, and everything. But I ignored my problems and gave Mama the money I had. She didn't really have nothing after she paid some bills. She was over there black and blue from not eating—stomach growling. The craziest thing was that she wouldn't touch the rent money. I gave the last five dollars out of the rent money. She paid her sister her five and gave me five to get the kids something to eat. I said, 'What about my other ten?,' but she put me off. She paid everybody else and I'm the one who's helping her the most. I could have most everything I needed if I didn't have to divide with my people. But they be just as poor as me, and I don't want to turn them down."

Close kin who have relied upon one another over the years often complain about the sacrifices they have made and the deprivation they have endured for one another. Statements similar to Ruby's were made by men and women describing the sense of obligation and sacrifice they feel toward female kin: their mothers, grandmothers, or "mamas." Commitment to mutual aid among close kin is sometimes characterized as if they were practically "possessed" or controlled by the relationship. Eloise, captured by the incessant demands of her mother, says, "A mother should realize that you have your own life to lead and your own family. You can't come when she calls all the time, although you might want to and feel bad if you can't. I'm all worn out from running from my house to her house like a pinball machine. That's the way I do. I'm doing it 'cause she's my mother and 'cause I don't want to hurt her. Yet, she's killing me."

When Magnolia and Calvin Waters inherited a sum of money, the information spread quickly to every member of their domestic network. Within a month and a half all of the money was absorbed by participants in their network whose demands and needs could not be refused.

The ebb and flow of goods and service among kinsmen is illustrated in the following example of economic and social transactions during one month in 1970 between participants in a kin-based cooperative network in The Flats. As I wrote in my field notes:

Cecil (35) lives in The Flats with his mother Willie Mae, his oldest sister and her two children, and his younger brother. Cecil's younger sister Lily lives with their mother's sister Bessie. Bessie has three children and Lily has two. Cecil and his mother have part-time jobs in a café and Lily's children are on aid. In July of 1970 Cecil and his mother had just put together enough money to cover their rent. Lily paid her utilities, but she did not have enough money to buy food stamps for herself and her children. Cecil and Willie Mae knew that after they paid their rent they would not have any money for food for the family. They helped out Lily by buying her food stamps, and then the two households shared meals together until Willie Mae was paid two weeks later. A week later Lily received her second ADC check and Bessie got some spending money from her boyfriend. They gave some of this money to Cecil and Willie Mae to pay their rent, and gave Willie Mae money to cover her insurance and pay a small sum on a living room suite at the local furniture store. Willie Mae reciprocated later on by buying dresses for Bessie and Lily's daughters and by caring for all the children when Bessie got a temporary job.

The people living in The Flats cannot keep their resources and their needs a secret. Everyone knows who is working, when welfare checks arrive, and when additional resources are available. Members of the middle class in America can cherish privacy concerning their income and resources, but the daily intimacy created by exchange transactions in The Flats ensures that any change in a poor family's resources becomes "news." If a participant in an exchange network acquires a new car, new clothes, or a sum of money, this information is immediately circulated through gossip. People are able to calculate on a weekly basis the total sum of money available to their kin network. This information is necessary to their own solvency and stability.

Social relationships between kin who have consistently traded material and cultural support over the years reveal feelings of both generosity and martyrdom. Long-term social interactions, especially between female kin, sometimes become highly competitive and aggressive. At family gatherings or at a family picnic it is not unusual to see an exaggerated performance by someone, bragging about how much he has done for a particular relative, or boasting that he provided all the food and labor for the picnic himself. The performer often combines statements of his generosity with great claims of sacrifice. In the presence of other kin the performer displays loyalty and superiority to others. Even though these routines come to be expected from some individuals, they cause hurt feelings and prolonged arguments. Everyone wants to create the impression that he is generous and manipulative, but no one wants to admit how much he depends upon others.

The trading of goods and services among the poor in complex industrial societies bears a striking resemblance to patterns of exchange organized around reciprocal gift giving in non-Western societies. The famous examples of reciprocal gift giving first described by Malinowski (1922), Mauss (1925), and Lévi-Strauss (1969) provided a basis for comparison. Patterns of exchange among people living in poverty and reciprocal exchange in cultures lacking a political state are both embedded in well-defined kinship obligations. In each type of social system strategic resources are distributed from a family base to domestic groups, and exchange transactions pervade the whole social-economic life of participants. Neither industrial poor nor participants in nonindustrial economics have the opportunity to control their environment or to acquire a surplus of scarce goods (Dalton 1961; Harris 1971; Lee 1969; Sahlins 1965). In both of these systems a limited supply of goods is perpetually redistributed through the community.

The themes expressed by boasting female performers and gossiping kin and friends resemble themes which have emerged from black myth, fiction, and lore (Abrahams 1963; Dorson 1956, 1958). Conflicting values of trust and distrust, exploitation and friendship, the "trickster" and the "fool," have typically characterized patterns of social interaction between Blacks and Whites; notions of trust and distrust also suffuse interpersonal relations within the black community. These themes become daily utterances between cooperating kinsmen who find themselves trapped in a web of obligations. But the feelings of distrust are more conspicuous among friends than among kin.

Many students of social relations within the black community have concluded that friendships are embedded in an atmosphere of distrust. However, intense exchange behavior would not be possible if distrust predominated over all other attitudes toward personal relations. Distrust is offset by improvisation; an adaptive style of behavior acquired by persons using each situation to control, manipulate, and exploit others. Wherever there are friendships, exploitation possibilities exist (Abrahams 1970, p. 125). Friends exploit one another in the game of swapping, and they expect to be exploited in return. There is a precarious line between acceptable and unacceptable returns on a swap. Individuals risk trusting others because they want to change

their lives. Swapping offers a variety of goods and something to anticipate. Michael Lee, a twenty-eight-year-old Flats resident, talks about his need to trust others. "They say you shouldn't trust nobody, but that's wrong. You have to try to trust somebody, and somebody has to try to trust you, 'cause everybody need help in this world."

A person who gives and obligates a large number of individuals stands a better chance of receiving returns than a person who limits his circle of friends. In addition, repayments from a large number of individuals are returned intermittently: people can anticipate receiving a more-or-less continuous flow of goods. From this perspective, swapping involves both calculation and planning.

Obtaining returns on a trade necessarily takes time. During this process, stable friendships are formed. Individuals attempt to surpass one another's displays of generosity; the extent to which these acts are mutually satisfying determines the duration of friendship bonds. Non-kin who live up to one another's expectations express elaborate vows of friendship and conduct their social relations within the idiom of kinship. Exchange behavior between those friends "going for kin" is identical to exchange behavior between close kin.

The Rhythm of Exchange

"These days you ain't got nothing to be really giving, only to your true friends, but most people trade," Ruby Banks told me. "Trading is a part of everybody's life. When I'm over at a girl friend's house, and I see something I want, I say, 'You gotta give me this; you don't need it no way.' I act the fool with them. If they say no, I need that, then they keep it and give me something else. Whatever I see that I want I usually get. If a friend lets me wear something of theirs, I let them wear something of mine. I even let some of my new clothes out. If my friend has on a new dress that I want, she might tell me to wait till she wear it first and then she'll give it to me, or she might say, well take it on." Exchange transactions are easily formed and create special bonds between friends. They initiate a social relationship and agreed-upon reciprocal obligations (Gouldner 1960; Foster 1963; Sahlins 1965).[1]

Reciprocal obligations last as long as both participants are mutually satisfied. Individuals remain involved in exchange relationships by adequately drawing upon the credit they accumulate with others through swapping. Ruby Banks' description of the swapping relationship that developed between us illustrates this notion. "When I first met you, I didn't know you, did I? But I liked what you had on about the second time you seen me, and you gave it to me. All right, that started us swapping back and forth. You ain't really giving nothing away because everything that goes round comes round in my book. It's just like at stores where people give you credit. They have to trust you to pay them back, and if you pay them you can get more things."

Since an object swapped is offered with the intent of obligating the receiver over a period of time, two individuals rarely simultaneously exchange things. Little or no premium is placed upon immediate compensation; time has to pass before a counter-gift or a series of gifts can be repaid. While waiting for repayments, participants in exchange are compelled to trust one another. As the need arises, reciprocity occurs. Opal Jones described the powerful obligation to give that pervades interpersonal relationships. "My girl friend Alice gave me a dress about a month ago, and last time I went over to her house, she gave me sheets and towels for the kids, 'cause she knew I needed them. Every time I go over there, she always gives me something. When she comes over to my house, I give her whatever she asks for. We might not see each other in two or three months. But if

she comes over after that, and I got something. I give it to her if she want it. If I go over to her house and she got something. I take it—canned goods, food, milk—it don't make no difference.

"My TV's been over to my cousin's house for seven or eight months now. I had a fine couch that she wanted and I gave it to her too. It don't make no difference with me what it is or what I have. I feel free knowing that I done my part in this world. I don't ever expect nothing back right away, but when I've given something to kin or friend, whenever they think about me they'll bring something on around. Even if we don't see each other for two or three months. Soon enough they'll come around and say, 'Come over my house, I got something to give you.' When I get over there and they say, 'You want this?,' if I don't want it my kin will say, 'Well, find something else you like and take it on.'"

When people in The Flats swap goods, a value is placed upon the goods given away, but the value is not determined by the price or market value of the object. Some goods have been acquired through stealing rings, or previous trades, and they cost very little compared to their monetary value. The value of an object given away is based upon its retaining power over the receiver; that is, how much and over how long a time period the giver can expect returns of the gifts. The value of commodities in systems of reciprocal gift giving is characterized by Lévi-Strauss (1969, p. 54), "Goods are not only economic commodities, but vehicles and instruments for realities of another order, such as power, influence, sympathy, status and emotion...."

Gifts exchanged through swapping in The Flats are exchanged at irregular intervals, although sometimes the gifts exchanged are of exactly the same kind. Despite the necessity to exchange, on the average no one is significantly better off. Ruby Banks captured the pendulous rhythm of exchange when she said, "You ain't really giving nothing away because everything that goes round comes round in my book."

These cooperating networks share many goals constituting a group identity—goals so interrelated that the gains and losses of any of them are felt by all participants. The folk model of reciprocity is characterized by recognized and urgent reciprocal dependencies and mutual needs. These dependencies are recognized collectively and carry collective sanctions. Members of second-generation welfare families have calculated the risk of giving. As people say, "The poorer you are, the more likely you are to pay back." This criterion often determines which kin and friends are actively recruited into exchange networks.

Gift exchange is a style of interpersonal relationship by which local coalitions of cooperating kinsmen distinguish themselves from other Blacks—those low-income or working-class Blacks who have access to steady employment. In contrast to the middle-class ethic of individualism and competition, the poor living in The Flats do not turn anyone down when they need help. The cooperative life style and the bonds created by the vast mass of moment-to-moment exchanges constitute an underlying element of black identity in The Flats. This powerful obligation to exchange is a profoundly creative adaptation to poverty.

Social Networks

The most typical way people involve others in their daily domestic lives is by entering with them into an exchange relationship. Through exchange transactions, an individual personally mobilizes others as participants in his social network. Those engaged in reciprocal gift giving are recruited primarily from relatives and from those friends who come to be defined as kin. The process of exchange joins individuals in personal relationships (Boissevain 1966). These interpersonal links effectively define the web of social relationships in The Flats.

Kinsmen and others activated into one another's networks share reciprocal obligations toward one another. They are referred to as "essential kin" in this study.[2] Strings of exchanges which actively link participants in an individual's network define that individual's personal kindred. The personal kindreds...are ego-centered networks. Even the personal kindreds of half siblings differ slightly; each half sibling shares some kin, but relates uniquely to others. Personal kindreds are not a category from which individuals are recruited, but a selection of individuals mobilized for specific ends (Goodenough 1970; Keesing 1966).

In the process of exchange, people become immersed in a domestic web of a large number of kinfolk who can be called upon for help and who can bring others into the network. Domestic networks comprise the network of cooperating kinsmen activated from participants' overlapping personal kindreds. Domestic networks are not ego-centered; several participants in the network can recruit kin and friends to participate in domestic exchanges. Similar to personal kindreds, domestic networks are a selection of individuals mobilized for specific ends and they can be mobilized for extended periods of time.

Many descriptions of black American domestic life by both Blacks and Whites (Frazier 1939; Drake and Cayton 1945; Abrahams 1963; Moynihan 1965; Rainwater 1966) have overlooked the interdependence and cooperation of kinsmen in black communities. The underlying assumptions of these studies seem to imply that female-headed households and illegitimacy are symptomatic of broken homes and family disorganization. These studies fail to account for the great variety of domestic strategies in urban black communities. Whitten and Wolfe (1972, p. 41) suggest that one of the advantages of network analysis is that the researcher can avoid mere categorizing of social systems as "disorganized." The network model can explain a particular web of social relations from several points of view. Throughout this study a network perspective is used to interpret the basis of interpersonal links between those individuals mobilized to solve daily domestic problems.

NOTES

1. Foster's (1963) model of the dyadic contract includes two types of dyadic contractual ties: colleague ties between individuals of approximately equal socio-economic positions and patron-client ties between individuals of unequal social position. The underlying principles of exchange transactions discussed in this chapter approximate features of the dyadic model of colleague ties. According to Foster's model, colleague ties are expressed by repeated exchanges; they are informal and exist as long as participants are satisfied; they are usually of long duration; and exact or perfectly balanced reciprocity between partners is never achieved.

2. "Essential kin" refers to members of the culturally specific system of kinship categories and others who activate and validate their jural rights by helping one another, thereby creating reciprocal obligations toward one another. ... Firth (1970) distinguishes between "effective kin" (those kin with whom one maintains social contact) and "intimate kin" (those kin with whom contact is purposeful, close, and frequent—members of the immediate family circle).

REFERENCES

Abrahams, Roger. 1963. *Deep Down in the Jungle: Negro Narrative Folklore from the Streets of Philadelphia*. Hatboro, Pa.: Folklore Associates.

———. 1970. *Positively Black*. Englewood Cliffs, N.J.: Prentice-Hall.

Bailey, F. G. 1971. *Gifts and Poison: The Politics of Reputation*. New York: Schocken Books.

Boissevain, Jeremy. 1966. "Patronage in Sicily." *Man, Journal of the Royal Anthropological Institute of Great Britain and Ireland* 1 (1): 18–33.

Dalton, George. 1961. "Economic Theory and Primitive Society." *American Anthropologist* 63: 1–25.

Dorson, Richard. 1956. *Negro Folktales in Michigan*. Cambridge, Mass.: Harvard University Press.

———. 1958. *Negro Tales from Pine Bluff, Arkansas, and Calvin, Michigan*. Bloomington: Indiana University Press.

Drake, St. Clair, and Horace R. Cayton. 1945. *Black Metropolis: A Study of Negro Life in a Northern City*. New York: Harcourt, Brace.

Firth, Raymond, Jane Hubert and Anthony Forge. 1970. *Families and Their Relatives: Kinship in a Middle-Class Sector of London*. New York: Humanities Press.

Foster, George. 1963. "The Dyadic Contract in Tzintzuntzan II: Patron-Client Relationships." *American Anthropologist* 65: 1280–1294.

Frazier, E. Franklin. 1939. *The Negro Family in the United States*. Chicago: University of Chicago Press.

Goodenough, Ward H. 1970. *Description and Comparison in Cultural Anthropology*. Chicago: Aldine Publishing Company.

Gouldner, Alvin W. 1960. "The Norm of Reciprocity: A Preliminary Statement." *American Sociological Review* 25: 161–178.

Harris, Marvin. 1971. *Culture, Man, and Nature: An Introduction to General Anthropology*. New York: Thomas Y. Crowell.

Keesing, Roger M. 1966. "Kwaio Kindreds." *Southwestern Journal of Anthropology* 22: 346–355.

Lee, Richard B. 1969. "Kung Bushman Subsistence: An Input-Output Analysis." In *Environment and Culture Behavior: Ecological Studies in Cultural Anthropology*. A. P. Vayda (ed), pp. 47–79. New York: Natural History Press.

Lévi-Strauss, Claude. 1969. *The Elementary Structures of Kinship*. Boston: Beacon Press (first published 1949).

Lombardi, John R. 1973. "Exchange and Survival." Preprint. Boston: Boston University.

Malinowski, Bronislaw. 1922. *Argonauts of the Western Pacific*. New York: Dutton.

Mauss, Marcel. 1925. "Essai sur le don: Forme et raison de l'échange dans les sociétés archaïques." *Année Sociologique*, n.s., I: 30–186.

———. 1954. *The Gift*. New York: The Free Press.

Moynihan, Daniel Patrick. 1965. "The Negro Family: The Case for National Action." Washington, D.C.: U.S. Government Printing Office. Prepared for the Office of Policy Planning and Research of the Department of Labor.

Rainwater, Lee. 1966. "Crucible of Identity: The Negro Lower-Class Family." *Daedalus* 95(2): 172–216.

Sahlins, Marshall D. 1965. "On the Sociology of Primitive Exchange." In *The Relevance of Models for Social Anthropology*. Michael Banton (ed.). A.S.A. Monograph I. London: Tavistock Publications; New York: Praeger.

Whitten, N. E., and Alvin W. Wolfe. 1972. "Network Analysis." In *The Handbook of Social and Cultural Anthropology*. John J. Honigmann (ed.). Chicago: Rand-McNally, in press.

19

MARY PATTILLO

GROWING UP IN GROVELAND

from *Black Picket Fences* (1999)

Black Picket Fences focuses on black middle-class life. Pattillo begins her study by noting that life for the black middle class is much more precarious than for whites with a similar income. The black middle class tends to live in neighborhoods that have higher crime rates, poorer schools, and fewer services than white middle-class neighborhoods have. Drawing on three years of fieldwork in the Groveland neighborhood of Chicago, Pattillo shows how these neighborhood conditions threaten the ability of the black middle class to pass their class status on to future generations. This selection begins to illustrate the challenges faced by parents when raising children in such an environment.

The kin-based branches of the Gibbs family tree spread far and wide in Groveland. The family's trunk—Mr. and Mrs. Gibbs—moved into Groveland in 1961. They raised their six daughters there. Anna Gibbs Morris is one of the three daughters who have chosen to raise their own families in the neighborhood. Last year, Anna Morris's nineteen-year-old daughter, Neisha, had the family's first greatgrandson, Tim Jr. The Morris family represents over thirty-five years in the neighborhood, with four generations, in one square block.

Much has changed since the Gibbs family moved into Groveland. One such change has been an increase in gang activity. Little Tim's father, Tim Ward, Sr., is in a gang, as were many of Neisha Morris's boyfriends before Tim. Drug dealing often goes along with being in gangs. Neisha's mother Anna feels both anger and sadness as she watches Neisha's boyfriends fall prey to the fast life.

I'm so sick of all this shit. 'Cause, you know, Neisha done lost too many friends to all that shit. You know, Neisha just can't take it no more. She lost two boyfriends. And she really took this last one hard. I just hate to see her go through all that. The first one was like her first boyfriend. You know, he was a nice boy. I liked him. But they just be out there doin' they thang. And they shot him. This last one, Sugar, we just buried. You know she had waited about a year after her first boyfriend and she started seeing this boy Sugar. They shot him in the head. He was in a coma for six months. For the past six months we been goin' to visit that boy in the hospital. We all thought he was gon' pull through. And I really took this second one hard. They done lost ten friends already. Close friends too. But still, they still choosin' these little boys who [are] out there like that, I mean, they ain't bad people, but they get caught up in all that stuff sellin' drugs.

The Gibbs family vignette illustrates the permanence of many Groveland families through changing surroundings....Here I elaborate on the local context by focusing on the cohort of adolescents and older youth to which Neisha Morris belongs, and examining the range of resources and exposures of this group.

Contextual particularities of black neighborhoods, even black middle-class neighborhoods, fuel consistent racial disparities in social indicators such as educational attainment and performance, marriage and childbearing, and levels of crime and violence. The impact of the unique middle-class black neighborhood works partly through processes of adolescent socialization. Higher poverty rates in black neighborhoods and in black communities beget greater lifestyle diversity within them. Middle-class black youth grow up with friends from a variety of social backgrounds. As a result, middle-class parents have less control over

the experiences to which their children will be exposed—less than they would in a more homogeneously middle-class setting. While parents do try to control their children's interactions, other avenues continue to be alluring and enticing for their children. This is Anna Morris's dilemma: that her daughter Neisha, after losing ten friends to violence, is still "choosin' these little boys who [are] out there like that...sellin' drugs." While black middle-class youth have a number of resources that smooth the bumps of growing up, they also face unique roadblocks. The possibilities for downward mobility (not to mention violent death) among middle-class black youth as a result of the heterogeneous lifestyles to which they are exposed are reminders of the limited protection that middle-class status provides for African Americans.

Both Street and Decent

Theorizing from his ethnographic research in a number of poor black neighborhoods, Elijah Anderson (1991; 1994) discusses the continuum of lifestyles that exists in such contexts. At the two extremes are "decent" and "street" behaviors. "Decent" families are "loving," "committed to middle-class values," and "willing to sacrifice for their children," whereas the code of the streets revolves around the maintenance of respect, often through violent means (Anderson 1994). "Street" families are especially prevalent (although not the majority) in poor neighborhoods, and there the code of the streets is the dominant mode of public interaction. Although Anderson's categories are related to one's material class status, "street" and "decent" are not fixed attributes of either poor people or middle-class people. Many poor families practice "decent" behaviors despite formidable material obstacles, and the middle class can act in "street" fashion. As Anderson (1991, 375) states, the culture of street families "is characterized by support for and encouragement of an alternative lifestyle that appears highly attractive to many adolescents, regardless of family background."

But Anderson only briefly develops the idea of the malleability of street and decent orientations, and the diversity of behaviors at the individual, familial, and community levels. Families and individuals seem to be either street or decent. While decent parents want their children to be able to navigate the streets, they generally shield their children from street influences, in most cases; according to Anderson, street families produce street children and decent families raise decent children. What I aim to do in my discussion of Groveland youth is develop a much more nuanced picture of families, the choices young people make, and their outcomes. A dynamic intermediate position of balancing street and decent lifestyles is a much more common orientation in Groveland than either fully street or fully decent. While the street/decent dichotomy is useful in some ways, I argue that it is inadequate because, in daily practice, most of the "action" is going on in the middle.

The use of Black English and slang by neighborhood residents of all ages is a good example. Most studies of Black English have focused on its use in poor black communities. But... Black English is also widely used among the children of African American professionals, and even among some of the professionals themselves, especially in casual settings. Language in Groveland constitutes a cultural arena where the significance of race is clear; Black English unites African Americans of different classes. Knowing the latest slang word or peppering stories with curse words symbolically maintains middle-class connections to the streets, especially for youth. For example, Tyson Reed explained that he not only had a different *manner* of speaking with his friends from college and his friends from the neighborhood gang, but he also had a *separate set of topics* to talk about. "You just

gotta know when to speak upon stuff," he advised about the craft of code-switching. But he went on to share how such linguistic maneuvers can also be confusing. "Sometimes now, I be slippin' and be forgettin' who I'm with. Like sometimes I be slippin' when I be with my ghetto-ass friends." Tyson's deliberate code-switching is part of the practice of balancing street and decent orientations that characterizes Groveland youth (and adults).

In black middle-class neighborhoods there are substantial resources to present nonstreet alternatives for young people. At the same time, the streets have a definite appeal to youth traversing the rebellious period of adolescence. And as Anderson (1994, 82) points out, being street-savvy "is literally necessary for operating in public." Black middle-class youth interact with friends who embrace components of both street and decent lifestyles, and neighborhood adults set both street and decent examples. Three Groveland youth—Neisha Morris, Tyson Reed, and Charisse Baker—typify the active negotiation of these two lifestyles within their family, peer, school, and neighborhood contexts. Each of these arenas is nestled within the next, going from the most immediate context of the family to a larger look at the neighborhood. All three young people share similar neighborhood exposures, but their schooling, peer, and home lives are very different.

Neisha Morris (whose family opened this chapter), Tyson Reed, and Charisse Baker are connected through family and friendship ties. Neisha has a first cousin named Ray Gibbs who also grew up in Groveland; both are grandchildren in the four-generation Gibbs clan. Ray Gibbs and Tyson Reed are best friends, played football together at Groveland Park, and went to college together. Charisse Baker is more peripheral to this group, and would probably not recognize the other two young people on a Groveland street, but she does have a weak tie. Neisha's current boyfriend,

Tim Ward, grew up in his grandmother's house two blocks from Charisse's family's home. Tim also played basketball under Charisse's father at the local Catholic school gym. Charisse has a crush on Tim's younger brother—a crush that her father forbids because Tim's younger brother is in and out of jail. Charisse stays informed on the gossip of Tim's relationship with Neisha, although Charisse and Neisha have never met.

Neisha Morris

Neisha's family life can be characterized by the neighborhood-based kin ties described in the first vignette. In addition to her mother's family, Neisha's father also grew up in Groveland, and his family remains in the neighborhood. Neisha's mother, Anna Morris, is a dental assistant, and her father is the supervisor of a South Side park. She has a nine-year-old brother, Nate. Her parents were married for over fifteen years. They recently separated because Neisha's father had a drinking problem. Her father's unpredictable and, according to Neisha, "crazy" behavior played an indirect role in Neisha's getting pregnant at age eighteen. To avoid her father, she moved in with her nineteen-year-old boyfriend, Tim Ward, at his grandmother's home.

> [My father] was too strict on me. That's when I met Tim and I started spending the night with him every night. I got to the point where I felt like Tim took me away from my father, and havin' to come home, and havin' to be bothered with that.

When Neisha got pregnant, she returned to her mother's house, bringing her boyfriend along with her. By that time, Neisha's parents had separated. With Mr. Morris out of the household, Tim's income from selling drugs was a welcome help to pay the bills.

The fact that many black middle-class households are just a few steps away from financial hardship is most apparent when there is a sudden shock like Mr. and Mrs. Morris's separation. Together the Morrises made over $40,000, but the bulk of that income was from Mr. Morris's job as a park supervisor. And, as in most black families, income from their jobs was the only means of support in the Morris household.[1] With Mr. Morris gone, Neisha's mother looked for creative ways to keep the family comfortable.

Neisha's extended family provides both positive supports and examples of negative outcomes. Many of her first cousins who grew up in Groveland run the range of possible current situations. One cousin is in jail in Iowa for assaulting someone who owed him money. Her cousin Ray, after being shot in the stomach, decided to make some changes in his life. He joined his friend Tyson Reed at Grambling State University, a historically black college in Louisiana. Another cousin graduated from college and is a graphic artist for a downtown design firm. Her closest cousin, Kima, has an informal beauty shop in her grandmother's home to support herself and her three-year-old daughter.

Among Neisha's closest girlfriends there is somewhat less diversity. All three are young single mothers like Neisha, searching for career direction.

> My close friends—Libra, she's in college. She goes to Chicago State for nursing. Well, all my friends just had kids. So, Trenique's baby is one. Deshawn is one. And my friend Roxanne, his birthday is Thursday, so he makin' one. So, it's like Trenique didn't finish at Benton High School 'cause she got pregnant. So she went to school and got her GED. So now she in school to do hair, cosmetology school. And Roxanne, she not working either. She just trying to find out really what she wanna do with herself, you know.

As in most friendships, Neisha and her three girlfriends have much in common in addition to being young mothers.[2] The children's fathers are all in the drug business, as is Neisha's boyfriend, Tim. Drug money fills the gaps between what their parents provide, what public aid and food stamps provide, and what they need to support themselves and their children in the style to which they are accustomed.[3] "I can't take care of me and my son off no aid check, not the way he can take care of us," Neisha commented about the discrepancy between public assistance and her standard of living with her boyfriend's support. "It's like I won't have a lot of the stuff I want because my mother has to take care of her and my brother and this house." Yet Neisha knows she cannot fully rely on the unstable income of a drug dealer. "I got to do stuff for myself 'cause that [drug-dealing] lifestyle, you could have it one day and the next day it could be gone."

For the Morris family, drug money is one of the safety nets that support their once middle-income family. Because of Tim's illegal income, Neisha can avoid welfare, although she does receive food stamps. Mrs. Morris does not approve of Tim's business, but she also does not find it reprehensible. Her opinion of drug dealers was not uniformly negative.

> It all depends on that person, what they do. It all depends on the way they carry theyself. Certain of the things they do I don't see them do. See what I'm sayin'? So, what I see of them might be what I like. Maybe what somebody else sees is something different.

Mrs. Morris is content that Neisha's boyfriend does not store drugs in her house, and does his business away from her family. What she sees of Tim—his boyish shyness, the encouragement he gives Neisha to go back to school, and his affection toward his son—is what she likes.

The integration and balancing of street and decent orientations is apparent in the Morris family. Mrs. Morris keeps her garden colorful and her lawn meticulously trimmed. The glass table in her living room never had a smudge on it, an impressive feat with children in the house. The commitment to legal work on the part of Anna Morris, and Tim Sr.'s participation in criminal enterprise (which is also hard work), exist simultaneously. Neisha is an unmarried teen mother, but chooses not to receive welfare. The extra money she might get from public assistance would only add unwanted bureaucratic hassles and stigma to her pot of resources. And, as Mrs. Morris stated in the opening vignette, she abhors the violence that accompanies the drug business. Yet she cannot abandon her daughter, and therefore improvises with various means of keeping the family afloat.

A description of Neisha's schooling similarly depicts the simultaneity of street and decent orientations. Neisha did not attend the local public elementary school. Instead, she was bused to a racially mixed magnet school. "I had some real high scores on my Iowa tests," Neisha remembered. "And they told me to pick another school that I wanted to go to. And that's the school my mother picked, that offered a' enrichment program there." Mrs. Morris was proactive in putting her daughter in a challenging academic environment, a clearly decent strategy to facilitate Neisha's future success. However, young people do not always see the benefits their parents are trying to bestow upon them. Neisha could have continued on to the magnet high school that most of her classmates attended, but she was weary of the long commute and wanted to be with her neighborhood friends. She started at one high school and then transferred to Benton.

Benton High School is in Treelawn, a neighborhood with nearly three times the poverty rate and half the median family income as Groveland.... Benton is not the closest high school to Neisha's house, but the two closer schools have worse gang problems, and one of them in particular is dominated by a rival gang. The Black Mobsters are the dominant gang in Groveland, but they have little clout at the closest two high schools, which is why many Groveland teenagers choose Benton over the closer schools. Even though Benton is designated as a "preparatory academy," so that non-neighborhood students like Neisha must achieve certain standardized test scores to get in, the overall graduation rate there is only 59 percent. Neisha described the mix of students at Benton.

> It's a lotta kids that's strictly into that school, strictly into going to school, all type of activities, honors, this and that. But a lotta people just be there to cut classes all day. Just to go to gym and lunch. And sometimes just come to school and don't even go in the building. And they bring down the school, the whole school. So basically it's half and half.

Neisha did graduate from Benton High, but she was not part of the honors group—not because she was not smart, but because her attentions turned to her friends and to boys.

The examples set by Neisha's family, schoolmates, and neighborhood friends present various roads for Neisha to travel. Both of her parents worked in stable jobs with good incomes. They remained married for fifteen years, until Mrs. Morris could no longer cope with Mr. Morris's drinking. Their home and yard were manicured. Neisha's mother chose a competitive magnet school, but also allowed Neisha to make her own decisions about high school. Of Neisha's neighborhood friends, including her cousins, some went to college and have careers, while others just made it out of high school and have started a family. Many of the young men in Neisha's life are captivated by the fast-money drug

business. All of these situations have been affected by the mix of people who live in Groveland.

Tyson Reed

Tyson Reed was a member of the Black Mobsters in Groveland. The leader of the gang took a special interest in him and Neisha's cousin Ray Gibbs because of their leadership skills. Tyson spent a few years selling drugs and trading guns as a member of the Black Mobsters. Many of his gang friends have, according to his friend Ray, "faded or disappeared." Ray elaborated:

> It's probably three things. Well I should say four things: either in jail, still out here doin' nothin' with theyself, some died and then the other few like us probably trying to do something with theyselves like go to school, or get a job. Just get away.

Tyson and Ray have tried to get away from the gangs and drugs in Groveland by going to Grambling State University together.

Because of the schools Tyson Reed attended, his networks are much more far-reaching than the boundaries of the neighborhood. "You gotta think about it," he instructed.

> I grew up in Groveland, but [I was] always on the West Side. I went to Presley, and kids got bused in to go there, so I knew a lotta people. Then I went to Dayton, kids got bused in to go there. Then I went Down South and went to college, so I had a lotta friends there. Not to mention in between I played football—got a lotta friends—[and] wrestled.

Tyson went to elementary school at Presley Academy, a public magnet school outside of Groveland for which there is a long waiting list. A majority of Presley students perform above national norms on standardized tests. After Presley, Tyson attended Dayton Prep, a public high school in a racially mixed, middle-class neighborhood. While Dayton High School has changed over the years, and it is neither as racially mixed nor as middle class as the neighborhood that surrounds it, it continues to send over 85 percent of its students to four-year colleges, and it is one of the few Chicago public schools to which college admissions officers from elite universities make regular recruiting visits. The list of magnet schools that Tyson attended was the result of his mother's insistence on a good education. Tyson's mother is a high-ranking official in the Chicago public school system. She had just received her Ph.D. a few weeks before I interviewed Tyson, and he proudly showed off her diploma. His mother's own continued schooling illustrates the stress placed on education in the Reed family.

Tyson's immediate family includes his mother and his twin sister. His father has been out of his life since he was a boy. All of what Tyson had to say about his father was filled with intense anger because of his father's absence. "I know where he at, but I don't wanna fuck with him," Tyson snapped. Even though he does not want a relationship with his father, he explicitly recognizes the problems that arise because of absent parents:

> That's a real problem right there with the black community today, with our kids and stuff. People just don't care. I mean, when the kids [are] young really it's the parents' responsibility, well duty, to be around 'em. You know, be around they friends, be around your family or whatever. Matter of fact, outta all my friends, I'll say 90 percent of them either live with their mother or live with their father. Only like 10 percent of my friends live with both of their parents.

From his own experiences, Tyson is convinced that he would not have gotten involved in gangs or drug dealing if his father had been around.[4]

Tyson also harbors anger at his mother for having a boyfriend who seemed to try to take his father's place. At twenty-two years old, Tyson has far from a close relationship with his mother, but he is beginning to realize the advantages he has gained from the kind of education his mother provided for him. He talked about this burgeoning appreciation.

> 'Cause you gotta learn how to appreciate stuff you got. I ain't never really appreciated what my mother used to do for me. Like sending me to Presley and Dayton. I ain't never appreciate that until, until I started to get fucked up a lot, and, you know, I really got on my own. I was like, "Damn, if it wasn't for that I'll be just as dumb as this mufucka over here." You know what I'm saying? Really, when you really think about it, you'on appreciate it till it's too late.

Once Tyson began to appreciate it he started to use it to his advantage. He has just one course to complete to receive his B.A. in criminal justice at Grambling. He has plans to go to law school once he finishes college. In the meantime, he plans to work for the Chicago Board of Education, a job secured through his mother's connections.

Charisse Baker

Because Charisse is the youngest of the three youth, much of her adolescent life is still unfolding. She is sixteen and lives with her mother and younger sister, Deanne, across the street from St. Mary's Catholic Church and School. Charisse's mother is a personnel assistant at a Chicago university, and is taking classes there to get her bachelor's degree. Mr. Baker is a Chicago firefighter. While her father and mother are separated, Charisse sees her father many times a week at the after-school basketball hour that he supervises at St. Mary's gym. He and Charisse's mother are on very good terms, and Charisse has a loving relationship with both parents. Mr. Baker is as active as any parent could be, attending the father/daughter dances at Charisse's high school, never missing a big performance, and visiting his daughters often.

Charisse and her sister are being raised by the neighborhood family in addition to their biological parents. "We [are] real close. Like all our neighbors know us because my dad grew up over here. Since the '60s." Charisse is a third-generation Grovelandite just like Neisha Morris. Her grandparents moved into Groveland with Charisse's then teenage father when the neighborhood first opened to African Americans. Charisse's parents lived in other neighborhoods when they were first married, only to eventually settle back in Groveland a few houses down from Mr. Baker's parents. Now Charisse is benefiting from the friends her family has made over their years of residence in Groveland, especially the members of St. Mary's church, who play the role of surrogate parents. When Charisse was in elementary school at St. Mary's, her late paternal grandmother was the school secretary, and so the Baker girls were always under the watchful eye of their grandmother as well as the staff, who were their grandmother's friends. And in the evenings Charisse's mother would bring her and her sister to choir practice, where they accumulated an ensemble of mothers and fathers.

After St. Mary's elementary school, Charisse went on to St. Agnes Catholic High School for girls, her father's choice. St. Agnes is located in a suburb of Chicago and is a solid, integrated Catholic school where 100 percent of the girls graduate and over 95 percent go on to college. Many of the students come from lower-middle-class

families like the Bakers. Charisse told a story about a recent St. Agnes graduate that illustrated the importance of education at St. Agnes, as well as the economic status of its students.

> I was hearin' about this one girl who went from St. Agnes. She got a full scholarship to Stanford. And she was, you know, she was a minority. She was talkin' about how e'rybody in Stanford drivin' to school with they little Rolls Royce and Corvettes and she was on her little ten-speed. She was like, "That's okay!" She gettin' her education.

The possibility of a Stanford scholarship, as well as the graduation statistics at St. Agnes, make it easy to understand why Charisse's parents chose it over the closer, and free, Benton High School.[5]

Most of Charisse's close friends went to St. Mary's and now go to St. Agnes with her, but her choice of boyfriends shows modest signs of rebellion. From her father's perspective, the mere fact of having boyfriends is rebellious, but Charisse still manages to have a very full social life when it comes to boys. Many of Charisse's male interests are older than she, and irregularly employed—although some are in and out of school. She meets many of them hanging out at the mall. One evening, members of the church's youth choir sat around talking about their relationships. Charisse cooed while talking about her present boyfriend, who had just graduated from high school but did not have a job and was uncertain about his future. But in the middle of that thought, Charisse spontaneously changed her attentions to a new young man that she had just met. "Charisse changes boyfriends like she changes her clothes," her sister joked, indicating the impetuous nature of adolescent relationships.

While these young men are not in gangs or selling drugs, many of them do not seem to share Charisse's strong career goals and diligence in attaining them. Some of them would not gain the approval of her parents. However, this full list of boyfriends has not clouded Charisse's focus. In her always bubbly, fast-talking manner, she declared:

> Okay, I would like to go the University of Illinois in Champaign-Urbana. I would like to major in marketing and I'm considering minoring in communications, because I talk a lot. And once I get a job, I get stable, then I can pursue a relationship. I'd like to get married and I want five kids. 'Cause I love children. I really do. I love children.

Charisse has a clear vision for her life—school, marriage, children. The content and order of these plans subscribe to a very traditional life sequence, perhaps more traditional than anyone ever really follows (Rindfuss, Swicegood, and Rosenfeld 1987). Her parents have made decisions about Charisse's schooling that will prepare her for college, that have instilled in her the Christian values in which they believe, and that have steered her toward a group of like-minded friends.

Yet Charisse's family, friends, and acquaintances are not all angels. "Any of my uncles might be in jail." Charisse responded when asked if she knew anyone in jail. She continued, "I know one uncle I haven't talked to, he could be on parole. And I have a cousin who I know is on parole in Detroit, so he can't see nobody." About her neighbors, Charisse recalled, "I know Harris is in jail. He live around here. You know his brother Big Tim [Neisha's boyfriend]." These relationships show that Charisse is not completely sheltered from a different, perhaps more street-oriented, crowd in either her neighborhood or her family. While Charisse's closest family and friends stress positive behaviors, her larger network provides a more diverse set of experiences and exposures.

Resources and Parental Strategies

Many Groveland parents possess financial, social, and human capital that greatly facilitate parenting, a crucial distinction between them and poor families. All three of these youth—Neisha, Tyson, and Charisse—have familial financial resources that have provided access to private schools, paid for sports equipment and dance lessons, and generated some spending money for movies, the prom, and an occasional trip or vacation. Some of the financial capital of Groveland families goes toward endowing neighborhood institutions. There are thriving local businesses; Groveland Park hosts a full Summer Day Camp and other recreational activities; and many of the churches are well supported. These are the things that money can buy.

The families of these three youth also have important social connections to the work world. Even though Neisha dislikes her father, his job with the Chicago Park District helped her get a summer job. She admitted, "My daddy got a promotion to another park. He's a park supervisor, so I'll probably work at his park, you know, through the summer." Tyson also took advantage of his mother's connections and planned to work for the Chicago Board of Education. And Charisse's younger sister, who was not yet even sixteen years old, spent her summers filing and answering phones in her mother's office, while Charisse worked at a beauty salon owned by a family friend and member of St. Mary's Church.

Finally, Groveland parents have valuable skills and knowledge—human capital acquired through both academic and on-the-job training. Parents impart these resources of information and know-how to their children. Tyson's mother's knowledge about and experience with Chicago public education surely influenced her decision to place her son in magnet schools. The fact that she attended college and graduate school no doubt facilitated Tyson's and his sister's college application process, and Tyson's aspirations for law school. And because of their white-collar employment, both Neisha's and Charisse's mothers work with computers, fax machines, and other high-tech office equipment. Familiarity with such technology is now a prerequisite for future success. Groveland youth are in many ways privileged because of these resources. They enjoy opportunities that their counterparts in poor black neighborhoods do not.

At the same time, Groveland is not far removed from poor neighborhoods where resources are few, and parental strategies run up against the stubborn obstacles of underfunded and understaffed schools, crumbling housing, poor city services, drugs, and violence. The neighborhood is a part of a larger and poorer black community on Chicago's South Side. Groveland residents share many South Side institutions with other neighborhoods. The character of middle-class black neighborhoods and black communities generally increases the options, many of them deleterious, from which middle-class black youth have to choose during the rebellious adolescent period. Even though parents have strategies for raising their children that include steering them in positive directions, they cannot be with their children at all times. Charisse's covert relationships with boys illustrate that fact. Once parental strategies are chosen and enacted, there is inevitably youthful rebellion against those plans. But the shape of this rebellion cannot go too far outside of the options presented in the young person's social and spatial milieu. Some youth emerge from this course unscathed. On the other hand, many find themselves left with a variety of battle scars—gunshot wounds, criminal records, new babies, subpar educations, or one less friend.[6]

Parental strategies are quite recognizable in the life stories of Neisha, Tyson, and Charisse. All three have clear ideas about what their parents do not want for them. In response to the direct question "What do you think your parents definitely don't want for you?" Charisse and her sister answered in agreement: "No drugs. Drug addicts sittin' in a crack house, standin' on the corner tryin' to get high. With three babies! On welfare." Neisha's answer to the same question also stressed self-sufficiency. "[My mother] don't want me to be on [public] aid all of my life." Just as they have similar understanding of what their parents want them to avoid, they also have parallel notions of what their parents positively hope for them. As Charisse put it: "That we be successful in whatever we do. So we ain't constantly callin' them for no money." Neisha expanded on her parents' hopes for her success:

I guess they just want me to really basically go to school, have a nice job, be able to take care of me without depending on somebody else to take care of me, you know. [My mother] want me to have a job and food and enjoy the finer things in life instead of just stayin' around. Like she be sayin' she wish she coulda did this and wish she coulda did that, and I still get all them opportunities. They just want the best for me. Want me to experience more than Second Avenue. You know, more than this right here.

These parental desires are not at all surprising. Most parents, want the best for their children, and prosperity is a key component of parents' "decent" plans.

Groveland parents use explicit strategies to encourage their children's expedient development into self-sufficient adults. Charisse's parents raised her in the Catholic church and school; Neisha took every dance class ever offered at Groveland Park, and she still wants to be a dance instructor, with the full support and urging of both parents; and Tyson's mother used magnet schools to get her son a solid education and steer him toward college. For the most part, these strategies were accepted by each youth, and they developed an interest in these activities apart from their parents' master plans. Yet there were some strategies that did not work, and such disagreements illustrate the different conceptions that young people have from their parents about what their lives should look like. During the rebellious period of adolescence, young people draw from both the street and decent activities available in the neighborhood environment.

Adolescent Rebellion in the Neighborhood Context

Tyson Reed resisted being pushed in the direction his mother had planned for him. He talked about the kind of son his mother wanted him to be.

> Without all the gangbanging. Without knowing the people I know. She really ain't want me to play football. She wanted me to be on the swim team. 'Cause I been swimming since I was like three months old. So I know how to swim real real good. And she would say, "Well why'on't you get on the swim team?" Yeah, awright, that's gay as hell. I mean, when you think about it, it ain't gay, but you thinkin', I'm a male, seventeen, eighteen, nineteen, twenty, whatever. In college, high school. How the hell I look competin', "Oh, I'ma beat you swimmin'." When I can run up and physically hit somebody. You know what I'm sayin'? Or even basketball, you can show your abilities or something. How I look, "Oh, I'm gonna outswim you. I'm faster than you." I mean, even with track, I think it's more manly than swimming.

Tyson dismissed his mother's desire for him to be a studious young man on the swim team with sarcastic obstinacy. His mother's suggestion of swimming as the sport of choice indicated to him that she could not possibly understand the masculine pressures he faced as a young black male. His rebellion was based on common adolescent concerns of gender identity and a tough image.

The absence of Tyson's father compounded his search for a masculine identity, and further fueled the anger toward his mother. In search of male role models and a fellowship of young men, Tyson got "plugged," Chicago slang for joining a gang. According to Tyson's friend, this was not difficult to do. His friend explained the process of becoming a Black Mobster.

> It start off like two or three people'll join a gang, but you hang with them. So you too close to 'em to let somebody beat up on 'em. Somebody mess with them, you in it. So now they look at you as, you know what I'm saying, you with 'em. So now they want you too. But pretty soon you start doing everything they doing. Everything they doing except being plugged. So you just plug. That's when it start.

Tyson's friend's description of getting plugged is a clear illustration that youthful rebellion can go as far as the local options allow. Tyson did not have to search far to get involved in the Black Mobsters and their drug business. There was no elaborate initiation or probationary period. Plugging was as simple as being friends with the boy next door, who was supposedly in a gang, but who himself may have been guilty of the charge only by his association with some other gang-identified friend.[7] The absence of Tyson's father, and then the departure of an uncle to whom he had been close, allowed for Tyson's exploration of delinquent neighborhood networks. His recollection of how he got involved in selling drugs interweaves the search for a male role model and the options offered by the neighborhood.

When I really needed somebody to teach me something, my uncle was there trying to help me. But after he went to college, and I was still in grammar school by myself, it wasn't nothing else to do but go across the street and do what I had to do. Awright, my mama might have a good job, but if my homey [friend] and me go up across the street and he get on and start sellin' drugs, now you honestly think I'ma sit there? That's a form of peer pressure, I know. But you gon' see him make all that money and y'all together. You there anyway, fuck it. You might as well make you some money. That's how I felt about it, you know.

In Tyson's words, the crossroads that he faced are apparent: a young man, feeling directionless because of his father's and uncle's departures, recognizing that his mother has a good job and that that should count for something in his decision. Yet his friends are a strong force at this point in his life (the peer pressure he referred to), and fast money in the era of hundred-dollar-and-up sneakers has an almost irresistible allure. And most important for this focus on neighborhood context and options, just across the street was the short distance Tyson had to travel to make the decision to sell drugs.

In a neighborhood like Groveland, gangs and drug dealing are attractive to these middle-class youth because of the fast money they are supposed to provide. Although, Grovelandites frequently describe the neighborhood as "middle class," being *black* and middle class does not allow for a lot of excess. This was definitely the situation for both Charisse and Neisha, whose families packaged financial resources—sometime illegal ones in the case of Neisha's family—to pay the bills. To get the extra money to buy the newest sneakers or the latest hairstyle, some Groveland youth turn to the Black Mobsters and their drug business. Still, Tyson's professional mother had a high income and an average-sized family on which to spend it. What could possibly be Tyson's rationale? "Your parents give you what you need and sometime they get you what you want," Tyson explained. "But when you sell drugs, *you* get you what you wanted." Tyson's decision to sell drugs despite his family's financial resources was due in part to consumer greed, and in part to the ease of opportunity, which resulted from the diverse neighborhood composition.

The higher poverty rates in black middle-class neighborhoods mean that a nontrivial minority of the families in them will have fewer resources to connect their children to positive activities like dance or swimming, and buy for them the status symbols of contemporary youth consumer culture. For this more disadvantaged portion of the population, the economic attraction to selling drugs is the strongest, and the commitment to decent behaviors is most attenuated (Sampson and Wilson 1995). Middle-class youth—eager to rebel and thrilled by the risks—are often drawn into these orientations. Their parents could provide some luxuries, as Tyson's mother could, but never enough to satisfy the wants of a consumer-minded American adolescent. Many black middle-class youth like Tyson are simultaneously in search of a male peer group and role models, excited by the sheer deviance, and desirous of the flashy material goods that an illegal income can buy. Other youth who are middle class only by the skin of their parents' teeth have clearer economic motives. For all, the opportunity for delinquent rebellion is readily available in Groveland. Tyson did not have to search far to get involved with the "wrong crowd."

Like Tyson's, Neisha's family situation affects the nature of her rebellion, which is in turn circumscribed by the neighborhood milieu. Neisha's parents stayed together for most of her childhood years, provided for her financially, and enrolled her in positive activities, and her extended family continues to give her much love and encouragement. Yet her father's problem with alcohol means that his presence often has negative consequences. When he was still in the household, he was very strict and did not want Neisha on the phone with boys, let alone dating them. Still, Neisha, like Charisse, found a way to have a thriving social life, including boyfriends. Many of the boys Neisha chose, however, have gone a similar route as Tyson. Although Neisha's mother spoke somewhat negatively about her daughter's choice of boyfriends in the opening vignette, she cannot simply forbid Neisha to date them. The reality is more complex than that. Many of Neisha's boyfriends have grown up in Groveland, and Neisha's mother has known many of them for years. She knows where they live. She knows their families. Aside from their seedy involvements, she also knows their friendly, funny, and respectful sides. These longtime neighborhood connections make it difficult to completely sever relationships with the neighborhood delinquents.

For example, Kareem, who holds a leadership position in the Black Mobsters, was one of Neisha's boyfriends before Tim. Kareem, of course, was not *born* a gang member. Before the Black Mobsters, Neisha's mother, aunts, and grandmother all knew Kareem as just another neighborhood kid. Mrs. Morris could not see Kareem and the other young men in the gang as anything but little boys. She said about them, "You know all these little boys, like Kareem and them? I ain't scared of them." How could Mrs. Morris be afraid of Kareem when he had such a humbling crush on her daughter? Neisha described her early neighborhood memories of Kareem, and how they eventually started dating.

Kareem been likin' me for the longest [time], even before he had money. I remember seein' him, he used to be sittin' on some crates over by the store with some ol' raggedy T-shirt on, and his fat just hanging. Well, this was before he had money. He would just keep on talking to me and kept on and kept on. Then, you know, he started makin' money. And I ain't think he even liked me any more. So, you know, I wasn't even thinkin' about it. But then, he just kept tryin' to get my number and shit. Finally, I just gave it to him. And that nigga called me about a hundred times that day. He just kept tryin' to talk to me. The first time we went out he gave me $300. I was like, "What's this for?" But, you know, I really started likin' him. He really real sweet and all.

Kareem is much more than a high-ranking gang member and drug dealer. He is the fat little boy who sat in front of the store, he is "real sweet," and he has been persistent with his attentions toward Neisha. Neisha could undoubtedly find a boy in the neighborhood not affiliated with the Black Mobsters and not selling drugs, but money and power—no matter their source—have always been aphrodisiacs. The neighborhood cycle that fostered Tyson's entrance into the drug business also operates in Neisha's case by shaping her choices of young men to date.

For both Neisha and Tyson, family strategies and circumstances interact with neighborhood options. Parents use strategies to positively direct their children, but onerous family situations can undermine some of these plans and turn young people's thoughts to what else the neighborhood has to offer. The absence of Tyson's father and the frequent cruelty of Neisha's sent them both looking for alternative avenues on which to mature. Because of the diversity of local lifestyles within Groveland, and because street and decent networks are connected at several family and neighborly junctures, it was not difficult for Tyson to get plugged, and for Neisha to be attracted to drug dealers.

Charisse Baker's neighborhood experiences differ in some important ways, although it is more difficult to thoroughly appraise Charisse's choices because she is younger than the other two. A number of factors in Charisse's upbringing converge to provide her parents with considerable control over the choices she can make. Her parents are separated, but her father continues to be a daily and positive presence in her life. And Charisse's intense involvement in the church leaves her little time for much else. Describing how she spends her free time, Charisse joked, "I got a lot of stuff that I have to do at the church. But I don't know if that's considered work or free time?" She listed her involvements in St. Mary's, including the parish pastoral council, youth group, youth council, gospel choir, and the hospitality committee. The extra parenting that she is subject to by church members makes her all the more accountable for her actions.

Charisse's rebellion, like Neisha's, is through boys. And also like Neisha's, her extended family (church and kin) know many of the residents in Groveland—the good and the bad. But unlike Neisha, whose father pushed her away from the family, Charisse and Deanne have a very good relationship with their father. This bond fortifies their conscience when choosing boyfriends and deciding what to do with them. Charisse's sister, Deanne, recalled her father's talk with her about boys.

> I think one good factor is the way my father approached me about boys. He told me when I was like only six or seven. I mean, I was thinkin' 'bout boys but I wasn't goin' to a big long extent or nothing. He sat down, and he was like, "Deanne, boys'll tell you anything to get you in the bed." [She laughs as she remembers her father's words.] I'm thinking that's not true. You know, I'm in second grade. I ain't thinkin' along those lines. He specifically said all boys. He said they'd tell you anything. He was like,

"They'll tell you they love you. They'll tell you anything to get you in the bed." He was like, "Don't do it!" He had that look on his face like if you do it, you in trouble. So, I didn't do it. Later on I found out that all boys aren't bad, but a lot of them are. So I kinda got the hint.

What would happen if either Charisse or her sister were to get pregnant? Charisse answered without hesitation.

> I would run away from home 'cause I think my parents would actually try to kill me. I think my daddy would kill me. I'm not being sarcastic at all. I would run away from home. I would call [my friend] Khadija and say, "Khadija, I gotta go." And I'd be up. And that's all seriousness. That's why I ain't doin' nothin', so I'on get nothin'.

Charisse's good relationship with her parents means that their words stick in her mind. While she tests the boundaries when it comes to boyfriends, she is not inclined to disregard altogether her parents' advice and lessons.

The fact that Charisse's parents have been able to more closely supervise and influence her behavior does not mean that the neighborhood context is unimportant. To the contrary, the church is also a part of the neighborhood context, as are the Catholic school and many of the people who participate in these two institutions. Charisse's family's involvement in the church and school integrates positive family and neighborhood contexts for Charisse. Just as Tyson and Neisha were easily introduced to drug dealers and gang members, Charisse's friends come from families who are paying a premium to send their children to Catholic school. The members of St. Mary's parish include Groveland's state representative, an executive at the Coca Cola Company, an executive assistant at the Urban League, entrepreneurs, teachers, and board members of community organizations. They are examples of success for Charisse to follow. At the same time, Tyson and Neisha also have positive role models in family members and friends who also exemplify hard work and success, and Charisse is by no means sheltered from the neighborhood troublemakers. Charisse knows the neighborhood gang members. She grew up with them just as Neisha did. Some of the young men who play basketball at the church gym under her father's supervision are gang members. Since Mr. Baker grew up in Groveland during the time when the gangs were first forming, he knows many of the founding members as well as the younger cohorts. Mr. Baker's familiarity with the gangs gives Charisse and Deanne a certain feeling of security. Deanne commented, "I want people to know that that's my daddy 'cause I'on wanna be messed with or anything." These associations, and her father's lessons, make Charisse streetwise. Yet within her independence exist the rules and limitations that her parents have set for her guiding her neighborhood relationships.

(Young) Women, (Young) Men, and Families

Neisha and Charisse are teenagers, and Tyson has just passed into his twenties. Their conceptions of sexuality, their personal understandings of gender roles, and their ideas about starting a family are in a crucial stage where what they have observed and learned will soon be translated into their own adult decisions and eventually shape their future. There is a gendered experience of growing up in Groveland. Boys and girls, young men and young women are equal beneficiaries of the resources of their middle-class parents, and so both genders have in front of them similar educational and career options and opportunities. But males and females face very different

"street" temptations in the neighborhood context. The different kinds of street behaviors are themselves gendered....Boys and young men join gangs and sell drugs (as Tyson did for the somewhat gendered reason of wanting a father figure), and girls and young women get pregnant before they are married. Of course the existence of an unwed mother means that there is necessarily an absent father out there somewhere, but this is given less attention than the woman's culpability, and even her moral worth. Still, as the stories of these three youth show, street behaviors exist within a range of other activities, aspirations, and values. Neisha has "decent" plans of getting certified to work for the Chicago Park District, moving out of her mother's house (possibly to the suburbs), and raising her son with Tim Sr. She has seriously reflected on the decision she made to have a child at a relatively young age. She remembered her mother's caution: " 'Havin' this kid is all right, Neisha, but it ain't what you think it's gon' be.' " Contemplating this point, Neisha concluded, "If I woulda known what I knew now, I would have waited." What could easily be labeled as a street behavior—i.e., Neisha's out-of-wedlock motherhood—is not nearly as unidimensional as the popular rendition might suggest.

The same point can be made when dissecting the street and decent labels as applied to certain family forms. Stressful family situations have had an impact on the routes that Neisha, Tyson, and Charisse have taken, and will probably continue to influence the choices they make as adults. Neisha's mother and father stayed married until Neisha was seventeen years old, although her father's drinking problem meant that the Morrises were a two-parent family in name only. On the other hand, Charisse's parents separated when she was in elementary school, but her father is perhaps more involved than most fathers-in-residence. Neisha and Charisse take in their parents' experiences and examples, and their views on marriage reflect those examples. Even though the Bakers' marriage did not work out, we heard Charisse's optimism about marriage fitting neatly in her long-range plan of school, marriage, and then lots of children. Neisha, on the other hand, is more hesitant. "We was just talkin' about that a coupla minutes ago," Neisha reported, referring to a conversation she and Tim Sr. had about getting married. She continued with a skeptical "but."

> But we just both still young. I'm only nineteen, he only twenty. So, I feel like, you know, ain't no rush to get married. You know, you never know what might happen. You know, we cool for how we are now. And if we still together in a few mo' years, then we gon' get married.

Neisha's comments and those of many others in Groveland point to a tolerance and sometimes a preference for flexible family forms. Social scientists are clear on the facts—that two-parent families almost always have more resources to put toward their children's development, and that children from single-parent homes are at higher risk of dropping out of high school, having a teenage birth, and getting in trouble in school or with the law (Garfinkel and McLanahan 1986: McLanahan and Sandefur 1994). But this is a separate question from the family decisions at the local level. Charisse may profess her plans to adhere to the "normative" sequence of family formation, but she also babysits for a best friend who doesn't have a husband, and she is not ashamed of her own fatherless household. The majority of family households in Groveland (57 percent) are headed by a married couple. But this dry demographic does not capture the lived family fluctuations. Both the Bakers and the Morrises are still officially married. Neither couple has undergone a divorce or a legal separation. Mr. Morris moved around the corner to his mother's house, while Mr. Baker moved

about a mile away. Neither husband/father is absolutely absent from the household. Who could say for sure what the response was to the "marital status" question when the census taker came to these homes?

Groveland youth watch these elastic families, growing when a cousin or grandfather moves in and contracting with a husband's or sister's departure. There is no one way to characterize what the youth and adults believe about marriage and families. Words often follow "decent" formulations, but deeds are less dogmatic in their unfolding.[8] Tyson, whose own parents separated when he was very young and who further commented that he had very few models of two-parent families, had mainstream plans for his future family life. "That's why I always said whenever I have some kids or whatever, I'ma stay with one person. I'ma get married one time. And I ain't gon' be trippin'." The test of these beliefs will be his practice. And if his beliefs and his practice contradict one another, is Tyson to be classified as street or decent? Moreover, if "street" connotes some type of dysfunction, then even that label is problematic when applied to non-nuclear families. Mrs. Morris was acting in her children's best interest when she made her husband leave. For her children as well as for her own financial and emotional reasons, she stood by him through years of counseling and periods of sobriety, which were overshadowed by episodes of violence. Her new "female-headed household" status seems quite unlike the dysfunctional connotations of "street." Neisha's out-of-wedlock childbearing may fit more squarely in that category, but even Neisha's situation is affected by family and neighborhood pressures outside her own control. The most important conclusion to draw from these stories is in fact the least satisfying one, because it complicates the neat bipolarity of street and decent, and introduces the multiple realities that families and youth experience that influence their own choices and decisions.

Each of these three youth had some roadblocks along the way, but nevertheless, Tyson will soon graduate from college, Charisse is determined to be successful in business, and Neisha still has aspirations to be a dance instructor and will have much help in raising little Tim. Despite their rebellious forays, their street and decent balancing acts, and the fragility of the collective resources on which they depend, Neisha, Tyson, and Charisse may still be poised to duplicate their parents' middle-class status. While this is true for a good portion of young people growing up in Groveland, there are three important qualifications to such a conclusion.

First, the need to reconcile street and decent lifestyles does not end with adolescence. Adults must also maneuver the neighborhood context, as well as their peer and family relationships. While people may choose their friends, they cannot choose their relatives. Imagine the reunion of Neisha's, Tyson's or Charisse's extended family. The possible stories and gossip— from what cousin is on parole, to which nephew graduated from college, to whose teenage daughter is pregnant, to where a sister landed a new job—run the gamut of street and decent activities. And since for many Grovelandites the extended family is the unit that makes middle-class status possible, it would be unwise for anyone to distance him- or herself from the family, even if remaining close means interacting with some unsavory characters. In all likelihood, Neisha will be able to do well only with the support of her family and the generosity of their resources. So as youth age, there are certain family imperatives, and similar friendship demands, for staying versed in both street and decent ways of life.[9]

Tyson is most explicitly determined not to lose his street edge as he grows older. Even though he is planning for law school, he stays in touch with his neighborhood friends who are still dabbling in drug dealing and maintaining their membership in the Black Mobsters. He is committed to making his future children street-smart as well. "Even if I do become a big-time lawyer, judge, or whatever, e'rybody ain't gon' be able to do that." Tyson reasoned. "So I can always know somebody in the ghetto. I'ma send my kids right over [to their] uncle such-and-such and cousin such-and-such house to let [them] know how it feel if [they] didn't have this." Negotiating street and decent lifestyles is a continuous process for black middle-class individuals embedded in especially heterogeneous neighborhoods, families, and friendship groups.

A second qualification is that a too optimistic reading of these stories disregards the fact that these three young people are the ones who are persevering. This is especially relevant for Tyson, for whom, as a young black male, mere survival has been an accomplishment. The stories of his friends who have "faded or disappeared" would be less sanguine. Neisha, Tyson, and Charisse in many ways represent those who have been or are still being successful in maneuvering their family, peer, school, and neighborhood environments. These young people are still working toward their parents' desires for them of self-sufficiency and happiness. Those who did not succeed now exist only as stories of lost friends and relatives: "Ms. Strong's daughter is on drugs," or "My cousin Ronnie got killed last year." Such reports are indicators of the uniquely perilous road that black middle-class families traverse in raising children.

And finally, the role of other factors in these young people's lives, such as personal agency and family situations, should not be underestimated. Neisha scored high enough on standardized tests to attend a magnet high school, but instead wanted to be closer to her friends, and so attended a less rigorous school. Tyson could have been his mother's angel by staying out of gangs and joining the swim team, but he chose otherwise. Charisse could still choose not to go on to college as her parents have planned for her, in favor of having a baby because she loves children. Without minimizing the importance of individual agency, the neighborhood context exists above and beyond individual and family circumstances. Choices are made within the limits of what options are presented to these young people, and many delinquent options can be realized in Groveland with great ease.

In sum, then, categorizing families as either street families or decent families misses many crucial nuances. The Morris, Reed, and Baker families are all "decent." Each employs specific strategies to guard against street influences. But is Charisse's family more decent than Neisha's because Neisha's father drinks too much, or because Charisse's family regularly attends church? Is Tyson's family more decent than either Neisha's or Charisse's because his mother holds an advanced degree and a professional job? Is Neisha's family the most decent because they have the best-kept yard, prettiest flowers, and cleanest house? Instead of demonstrating mutually exclusive categories, their lives illustrate how street and decent orientations are tangled together—in the neighborhood context, in the same family, and even within the same person. Tyson is, after all, a gangbanger with a college degree (almost). The simultaneous privileges and continuing constraints faced by the black middle class make the intermediate position of balancing street and decent a most common strategy for negotiating a variety of family situations and local and community-wide settings....

NOTES

1. More white families have wealth—both durable and monetary assets—in addition to income, enabling them to get by for longer periods of time when crises hit. Oliver and Shapiro (1995) report that 78.9 percent of black households, compared to only 38.1 percent of white households, are in "precarious-resource" circumstances, meaning that they do not have sufficient net worth or financial assets to survive for three months at the poverty line if there were a crisis that cut off income. Maintaining a middle-class standard of living (as opposed to survival at the poverty level) is even less feasible for many black households.

2. See Merriwether-de Vries, Burton, and Eggeletion (1996, 239) for a discussion of the "peer context" of young mothers. They state, "Embarking on the role of parent limits an adolescent's access to the social world of nonparents because economic and instrumental responsibilities for their offspring frequently preclude the expenditure of precious resources on leisure activities."

3. Edin and Lein (1997, 164) briefly discuss the role of men's illegal income in the survival strategies of poor women. They state, "Chronically unemployed fathers who wanted to maintain their claim on their children were powerfully motivated to engage in any kind of work, including work in the underground economy." The Morris family illustrates that such strategies are also used by middle-class families to maintain their standard of living.

4. Tyson's understanding of how delinquency is related to a concentration of single-parent families is supported by empirical evidence. Single-parent families have fewer economic resources and lack the extra pair of eyes important for monitoring youths (McLanahan and Sandefur 1994; Sampson and Groves 1989; Steinberg 1987).

5. Sending children to Catholic school is a common and successful strategy among African Americans to promote upward mobility (Neal 1997).

6. Sullivan's (1989) comparative research on young males illustrates the importance of the neighborhood context for the shape, content, and duration of youth delinquency. He shows how local employment climates affect the maturing-out process from criminal activity. In the white neighborhood Sullivan studied, young men were able to secure union jobs and desist from crime. In the poor black neighborhood, however, no such alternative to crime existed, and young men participated in

crime into their young adult years. While this chapter does not examine local employment conditions, it does concentrate on the models for and access to deviant pathways provided by the local milieu.

Of course, not all adolescent socialization takes place within neighborhood boundaries. In addition to geographic neighborhoods, there are "neighborhoods of sociability" that also influence youth (Burton, Price-Spratlen, and Spencer 1997). Parents do attempt to structure children's neighborhoods of sociability so that they further their own positive parenting goals. However, to the extent that young people have control over their circle of friends, Groveland youth are likely to befriend youth from a variety of family backgrounds because of the composition of Groveland and the surrounding neighborhoods. For example, the fact that Neisha went to high school in the Treelawn neighborhood, where the poverty rate is nearly triple that in Groveland, indicates the large scalability catchment area for black middle-class youth.

7. In *There Are No Children Here,* Alex Kotlowitz (1991) depicts the uncertainties of gang affiliation. For example, Lafayette and his friends took to writing "4CH" (for the Four Corner Hustlers gang) on their papers and on the walls, but they did not seem to be participating in any other behaviors explicitly associated with the gang. Primarily, they were posturing. Were they *in* a gang or not? Likewise, vague gang-labeling practices doomed one of Lafayette's older friends, Craig, who was shot and killed by agents from the Bureau of Alcohol, Tobacco and Firearms. In the newspaper accounts, Craig was identified as a gang member even though no one in the neighborhood knew anything of such an affiliation. Law-enforcement agents may have a separate set of criteria for gang membership than local residents. This is not to say that there are not initiation rites, or organizational meetings, or rules, by-laws, and mottoes that bind together fellow gang members. Indeed, Grovelandites can easily "read" the color or tilt of someone's hat to

identify gang allegiances, or recognize a seemingly innocent greeting as reserved for gang insiders. The point is that membership can also be very porous, and sometimes impossible to escape if a young person (especially a male) chooses to have friends in a neighborhood where gangs exist.

8. Cultural theorists such as Hannerz (1969) and, later, Swidler (1986) argue that culture is not composed solely of ultimate values, norms, and beliefs, as Kornhauser (1978) would argue. Instead, culture consists of behaviors that are shared within groups, learned by "precept," and modeled in interaction. Hannerz (1969, 183) writes. "As we have seen there is much verbalization of mainstream ideals in the ghetto, even from those who often act ghetto—specifically in direct contradiction of these ideals." He goes on to argue that the definition of culture must be broadened to include these behaviors, because culture is largely situational and arises in response and resistance to social, ecological, economic, and political constraints.

9. Stack (1974) elaborates on the importance of the kin network for women especially. Setting up a self-contained nuclear family severs the extended kin bond and imperils the stability of the extended network. Because the concept of the nuclear family indicates that familial resources are restricted to mother-father-children, the extended family is effectively disconnected from the possible gains made by the member now in a nuclear-family relationship. Furthermore, the person who cuts herself off jeopardizes her own ability to draw on those resources in uncertain times, although the networks often welcome back strays. Stack (1974, 122) summarizes this dilemma. "The life histories of adults show that the attempts by women to set up separate households with their children and husbands, or boyfriends, are short-lived. Lovers fight, jobs are scarce, houses get condemned, and needs for services among kin arise."

Even more relevant, McAdoo (1978) finds that upward mobility for African Americans does not attenuate kin ties and relationships of reciprocal exchange. Essentially, black middle-class individuals often remain connected to their less fortunate family members and friends. These connections across classes, and often across lifestyles, prompt them to have flexible "street" and "decent" orientations.

REFERENCES

Anderson, Elijah. 1991. "Neighborhood Effects on Teenage Pregnancy." Pp. 375–398 in *The Urban Underclass.* Christopher Jencks and Paul E. Peterson, eds. Washington, D.C.: Brookings Institution.

Anderson, Elijah. 1994. "The Code of the Streets." *Atlantic Monthly* 273: 80–94.

Burton, Linda, Townsand Price-Spratlen, and Margaret Beale Spencer. 1997. "On Ways of Thinking about Measuring Neighborhoods: Implications for Studying Context and Developmental Outcomes for Children." In *Neighborhood Poverty: Context and Consequences for Children.* New York: Russell Sage.

Edin, Kathryn, and Laura Lein. 1997. *Making Ends Meet: How Single Mothers Survive Welfare and Low-Wage Work.* New York: Russell Sage.

Garfinkel, Irwin, and Sara S. McLanahan. 1986. *Single Mothers and Their Children: A New American Dilemma.* Washington, D.C.: Urban Institute Press.

Hannerz, Ulf. 1969. *Soulside: Inquiries into Ghetto Culture and Community.* New York: Columbia University Press.

Kornhauser, Ruth. 1978. *Social Sources of Delinquency: An Appraisal of Analytic Models.* Chicago: University of Chicago Press.

Kotlowitz, Alex. 1991. *There Are No Children Here.* New York: Doubleday.

McAdoo, Harriette Pipes. 1978. "Factors Related to Stability in Upwardly Mobile Black Families." *Journal of Marriage and the Family* 40: 761–776.

McLanahan, Sara, and Gary Sandefur. 1994. *Growing Up with a Single Parent: What Hurts,* *What Helps.* Cambridge, Mass.: Harvard University Press.

Merriwether-de Vries, Cynthia, Linda Burton, and LaShawnda Eggeletion. 1996. "Early Parenting and Intergenerational Family Relationships within African American Families." In *Transitions through Adolescence.* Julia Graber, Jeanne Brooks-Gunn, and Anne Peterson (eds.). Mahwah, N.J.: Lawrence Erlbaum Associates.

Neal, Derek. 1997. "The Effects of Catholic Secondary Schooling on Educational Achievement." *Journal of Labor Economics* 15: 98–123.

Oliver, Melvin L., and Thomas M. Shapiro. 1995. *Black Wealth/White Wealth: A New Perspective on Racial Inequality.* New York: Routledge.

Rindfuss, Ronald R., C. Gray Swicegood, and Rachel Rosenfeld. 1987. "Disorder in the Life Course: How Common and Does It Matter?" *American Sociological Review* 52: 785–801.

Sampson, Robert J., and W. B. Groves. 1989. "Community Structure and Crime: Testing Social-Disorganization Theory." *American Journal of Sociology* 94: 774–802.

Sampson, Robert J., and William Julius Wilson. 1995. "Toward a Theory of Race, Crime and Urban Inequality." In *Crime and Inequality*, pp. 37–54. John Hagan and Ruth D. Peterson, (eds.). Stanford: Stanford University Press.

Stack, Carol. 1974. *All Our Kin: Strategies for Survival in a Black Community.* New York: Harper & Row.

Steinberg, Laurence. 1987. "Single Parents, Stepparents, and Susceptibility of Adolescents to Antisocial Peer Pressure." *Child Development* 58: 269–275.

Sullivan, Mercer L. 1989. *"Getting Paid": Youth Crime and Work in the Inner City.* Ithaca, N.Y.: Cornell University Press.

Swidler, Ann. 1986. "Culture in Action: Symbols and Strategies." *American Sociological Review* 51: 273–286.

20

PATRICIA FERNÁNDEZ-KELLY

TOWANDA: MAKING SENSE OF EARLY MOTHERHOOD IN WEST BALTIMORE (2011)

From 1990 to 1997, Patricia Fernández-Kelly conducted participant observation of family life in West Baltimore. Her work highlights how social programs designed to help the poor have unintentionally placed families under surveillance and constrained the ways in which they raise their children, procure work, and become self-sufficient. She argues that children who grow up in this context come to understand their social situations and to define themselves vis-à-vis the state rather than in relation to other institutions, such as the market. This comes across vividly as Fernández-Kelly traces how "Towanda" transitions from a child to an adult in her family and neighborhood context.

Towanda Forrest was twelve years old when I first met her in 1992, a gorgeous woman-child with a grainy inflection and eyes full of dare. She was one of five children born to Lydia Forrest and the second conceived with the man who would eventually become her legitimate husband, James Culver. Towanda's two older brothers had a different father and their birth had taken place much earlier, when Lydia was young and reckless. By the time Towanda came of age, Lydia had emerged as the moral center of her extended family; gone were the days of mayhem and dissipation; towards the end of the 20th century Lydia cultivated dignity.

Towanda's oldest brother named Rueben after his wayward father, and nicknamed Beamy because of his cheerful disposition, was a distant memory. She could not remember him ever living at home; for nearly a decade, he had been locked up after being convicted as an accessory to the murder of a Baltimore cab driver. Once in a while, Lydia would take Towanda with her to visit Beamy at the Jessup Prison—her son, her first born, the child upon whom she had invested so much hope and seen handcuffed, carried away in leg irons as a common criminal.

When she was little, Towanda didn't know enough to tell the difference between prison and the rest of the world. She merely thought that some people, like Beamy, lived in large places where they spoke to visitors through bullet-proof parapets. She remembered putting the palm of her hand against the cold surface of the transparent, dividing shield while Beamy did the same on his side. He had large, strong hands and he always said nice things to her. He was a good brother. When Towanda grew older and understood why Beamy lived away from home, she was first humiliated and then angry. All along, she had been looking up to someone whom no one else respected. From then on, she refused to visit Beamy in prison. By the age of twelve, she could hardly recollect what her half brother looked like. In a desultory, half-resigned tone she told me, "maybe, if I see him in the street, I don't know him, thas jus the way it is."

Next in line was Lorenzo whom the family knew as Weedy. He had been living in Washington, D.C., since Towanda was eight. There he drove a limousine for hire and dealt drugs to supplement his income. His move away from home had been prompted by an altercation with his stepfather, James Culver, whom Weedy despised for many reasons but mainly because James had usurped his place as head of the family. He was an interloper and a drunk, Weedy thought. In passionate contrast, Weedy loved his mother. He visited Baltimore regularly with presents to express his devotion.

The children in Lydia's extended family believed that Weedy owned the limo that he drove and Towanda was no exception. She thought her brother was rich because he brought her gifts and cash. Once he gave her a shiny twenty dollar bill. Towanda kept it for the longest time until she thought about buying a "very fancy make-up set." By the age of six she knew she was attractive and hastened to make the most of her appearance. She had a honey-colored complexion and bold features. Her hair dropped about her shoulders pleated like a mantle.

Felicia, Towanda's older sister, was four years her senior; an obedient, worry-prone girl who worshipped her mother and often took her place looking after the younger children. Even at the age of seven, Felicia had been entrusted with Towanda's care. She bathed her and washed her hair, enthralled by her loveliness all along. Felicia didn't care much for her own looks. She abhorred her short, kinky hair and heavy-set frame. Not able to rely on appearance to be popular, she depended on good behavior at home and at school. People in her circle knew that she could hold her ground—even as a child, she had always been treated as a short adult. She was trustworthy, like her mother, and eager to please. Sometimes she felt invisible but liked it that way; her reward for loneliness was respect. And Felicia had ambition: she hoped, one day, to be a nurse because she was good at taking care of others.

Towanda also had a younger brother, James Jr., known as Mush. He had been born a sinewy child and grew up to be strong and pleasant. He also did well in school. That was until the age of twelve when he was hit by a car while crossing Pennsylvania Avenue. He wasn't killed but suffered concussions that his mother later blamed for the boy's change of temperament. He became belligerent and rebellious, confirming Lydia's newly found conviction, as a Jehovah's Witness, that evil is a real and active force, entering bodies and minds without warning. It was left up to people like Lydia to fight on the side of good, awaiting the Second Coming of Christ, and looking after the fallen angels whose lives Satan was always trying to ruin. Towanda thought differently; she didn't think her younger brother was so much evil as willful. He did what he wanted to do without regard for other people's opinions. In this, Mush was like herself. Towanda was keenly aware of the confusion engulfing youngsters in her crowd but didn't worry about the causes—her main goal was survival.

In addition to her siblings, Towanda thought of Clarise Twigg—who was five years younger and shared her room—as part of the immediate family. Clarise was the daughter of Lydia's crack-addicted niece, Benita, who had been declared in need of assistance by Child Protective Services. Technically, Clarise was Towanda's niece once removed but Towanda thought of her as a sister. Kinship nomenclature in extended families where women become mothers in adolescence assigns all children in the same cohort a similar status and label. Lydia had been appointed as Clarise's guardian and, as a result, the child had become her daughter for all practical purposes. The same was true among the growing number of families in West Baltimore where older women assumed responsibility for grandchildren after their own sons or daughters became parents at an early age. By 1995 more than forty percent of all girls 19 or younger living in Upton and Sandtown-Winchester had given birth to at least one child. With small fluctuations, that trend continued through the first decade of the 21st century. Adolescent pregnancies have been the norm, not the exception, in West Baltimore. Often young mothers are unprepared to care for their children—some are too inexperienced and others, like Benita, Clarise's mother, are impaired by dangerous drugs that consume their time and energy.

Clarise, who thought of Towanda as her older sister, looked up to her in ways that no one else did. The two girls shared the same room in the broken-down house on Goodyear Street that the family inhabited before moving into a low-rise in the projects. As Clarise grew older, she increasingly depended on Towanda to organize her sense of the world. It was Towanda who explained to Clarise who was who in the neighborhood. It was Towanda who shaped Clarise's taste in clothes and eventually told her about boys and sex.

According to her mother, Towanda was tough even as a small child. Lydia could remember the look in her daughter's face when, as a toddler, she confronted parental authority, or was asked to do anything she was unwilling to do. Said the mother, "[Towanda] just stood there, doing nothin, sayin nothin, looking at you like she was all growed up...I jus wanted to slap her face." And Lydia often did, in a futile attempt to bring the girl into compliance. She did not succeed. Towanda always fought back. She was six when her neighbor's seven-year-old son, Davon Price, tried to steal a piece of food from her plate while visiting Lydia's home. Towanda stopped him with a fork. The boy suffered no serious damage but the gesture spoke volumes about Towanda's disposition. Lydia protested the girl's ways but she also respected her. She concluded that it was her daughter's nature to be contrarian. Towanda was strong and clear-minded. She took guff from no one, not even her mother.

It was not surprising therefore that, as she grew older, Towanda became a mighty presence beyond the confines of her modest home. She vividly remembered her first day at the Gilmore Elementary School, its clean corridors and the large bulletin board framed in green crepe paper, featuring signs that read in large yellow letters, WELCOME STUDENTS! It still gave her a thrill, at the age of twelve, to remember her first classroom filled with light and the sound of children ready to learn. "I sometimes wish that day didn't end," she told me wistfully:

> Because it was one of the happiest [days] I ever had. I wasn't afraid; it was good to be out in the world, out of the house. I jus' loved those nice books where we could put numbers and write words. I love

the way they smelled. And the teachers, they was nice. I was only seven but yeah! I wanted to learn so bad...I loved that school.

First impressions gradually faded as Towanda noticed the scrawls in textbooks that had been used before, the indifference shown by some teachers, and the broken gym with its boarded-up door. That was yet to pass but, in the beginning, like most young children, Towanda was filled with expectation. According to her teacher, Paula Robinson, who took an early interest in the girl and remembered her well, "[Towanda] was a pistol. All the other kids wanted either to be near her or really far from her because, if she liked you, she really did, but if you got on her bad side, she could be a force." Towanda agreed:

Right away I knows who need to be my friends. But it's the same everywhere—you start makin friends and that means other people get left out and they get other friends too; so now you have crews that don't like each other. They act nasty to each other. They don't know *much* about each other but they know they don't like each other because they in different groups. So you end up fighting for no reason at all, just because you have different friends. It's crazy but it's real and you learn that right away.

Given her outgoing personality and good looks, Towanda soon became a leader, popular and skillful at bringing people into her sphere of influence, and rejecting others to show her power. At the age of nine, she had her first big fight and, as far as she could tell, her motives had been legitimate:

There are people that just annoy you all the time and Lavinia Thomas was one of those people. She din't know how to behave. She was always out of line, laughing when she shouldn't, mouthing

off all the time. So this one morning she bumped into me, right? And I knows she's not intentional but I still pretend she was, 'cause it was about time she got kicked in the ass for being stupid. So I shoved her back an' she come back to me and we fight. The principal suspended us for a couple of days. When I went back to school, it wasn't the same no more; maybe people thought I was a trouble maker. I started feelin' bad; like I didn't belong.

Then, when Towanda was a sixth grader, her body began to change. She got her first period—a development that filled her with a renewed sense of self—and she grew breasts and hips. Lydia, her mother, was concerned at such a rapid transformation in a child so young. Only yesterday, Towanda had been one more little girl in the neighborhood; now, according to her mother, she looked like "a half-grown mare that needs reining-in real good." Lydia bought Towanda her first brassiere and soon found herself in perpetual conflict with her daughter over what kinds of clothes the girl would be allowed to wear. Typically, Towanda favored garments that displayed her physical assets while her mother tried to conceal them. Such conflicts are common beyond impoverished neighborhoods in American cities and elsewhere in the world but their effects are different from place to place. In neighborhoods like those inhabited by Towanda and her family, there are few resources to buttress adult authority. Children soon learn that mothers lack the wherewithal to impose control given their humble economic and social stature. And so it was that Towanda, smart and pugnacious, began to test limits to her actions, defying Lydia at every step of the way. At first, she felt guilty when yelling back at her mother in bursts of emotion that would leave both of them limp and disgruntled. Eventually, however, feeling gave way to numb habit. Whatever the mother dictated met the daughter's opposition. According to Towanda:

> It's because my mother, she can't understand. She tries to make things right but whas right about our life? My father a drunk, my brother in jail, never enough money to pay for nothing, everybody always screaming. There's never peace. Sometimes, I wish I could just go somewhere far away where I was not myself. I feel bad to say these things but they is true. It would be best if I was someone else.

As Towanda grew older, and home grew more difficult to endure, public spaces offered endless opportunity. Under Lydia's relentless stare, Towanda felt trapped, angry, and guilty. Slamming the front door behind her she could breathe an air of independence; she could step into places where she was not a child anymore but the main protagonist in an unfolding adventure. School became a terrain for sociability where gossip, intrigue, and potential romance vastly outweighed the benefits of formal learning. Towanda may have been poor but she was not stupid; like other children in her circle, she could tell that success through education is a lie when schools have fallen into disrepair; books typically have missing pages, and teachers, perhaps once hopeful and bright, now show hermetic indifference. Few if any in Towanda's circle had completed high school. She knew no one able to hold a better job through the power of education.

By contrast, the street with its variegated landscape of corners and alleys; stoops and doorsteps; parks and playgrounds; presented a platform for experimentation and pleasure. Now thirteen, Towanda attracted more than compliments for her pretty face; boys in the neighborhood went giddy when she walked by. At school, she did not conceal her excitement at being fully female. Sick with jealousy, other girls began to hate her and at least

one of the teachers, Clara Lancy, made plain her contempt for Towanda. She thought the girl was a cockteaser and didn't hesitate to tell her to her face. It was a grossly uneven confrontation—the grownup bullying a young child. But Lancy didn't see it that way; she thought that, by talking straight, she was exercising her right to correct the girl. Her insult paid off, uncharacteristically bringing tears to Towanda's eyes. She knew that some of her peers called her a slut behind her back. Now, the teacher was siding with her enemies. At an age when children in more affluent families are preoccupied with extracurricular activities and athletic pursuits, Towanda was involved in an elemental political struggle defining camps and loyalties. Divisions were clear: her friends were devoted to her, imitating her gestures and manner of dress; by contrast, her opponents tried to find every opportunity to trip her and make her fall. She told me that

> It wasn't like I planned it 'cause I wasn't messin' around with boys or nothing like that but when that bitch [Clara Lancy] call me names, I just decided to show her and the others. You never think a teacher [who's] supposed to set an example would call you names. But she wasn't goin' to make me cry again. No way! It was ok by me if she thought I was a slut. There's no way anyone would call *her* [Lancy] a slut; you know why? Because no man would want to fuck that ugly cow!

It was about the same time, that Towanda began to intensify her confrontations in school as part of an attempt to solidify her top position in the youthful pecking order. When Lucinda Martin, one of her contenders, a girl with a slender body and a filthy mouth, told Towanda that Dionne, the most popular boy in their class, thought she was a ho, Towanda didn't flinch. She stood tall in the school yard chewing gum, looking at her fingernails with a cocked head and a desultory gaze. When Lucinda turned her back and was about to walk away, Towanda leapt forward like a cougar pouncing on a rabbit. She pulled Lucinda's hair, forcing her to the ground and punching her in the face. This brought delight to the gathering crowd until the gym teacher, Mr. Johnson, stopped the fight. Lucinda was bloodied. Towanda was suspended for a week, continuing a troubling trend. That didn't matter to her; she had salvaged her pride and knew that other youngsters admired her for her courage.

With her attention now fully focused on containing anger, responding to insult, and courting favor, Towanda relinquished her last bit of interest in academic subjects. She wrote and read with difficulty and once she confidently stated that New York was the capital of Africa. She wasn't joking. She added and subtracted a little but her knowledge remained rudimentary into adulthood. On the other hand, her warring instincts were superb. Now the center of her social network, she thought of school mostly as a setting for display and competition. Her life was full of trickery and drama. She bargained and made alliances, and soon she began to sample the elements of young adulthood in deprived neighborhoods. At fourteen, she tried her first joint of marihuana. Her homie, Deiondre Garrett, a muscular boy in dreadlocks, sixteen at the time, knew how to get it and where to find the money to pay for it. He was the local procurer, an apprentice of Calvin Cooper, known in the streets as Blackjack. He knew Jamaicans who customarily dumped a variety of controlled substances throughout West Baltimore. Deiondre looked up to Blackjack and from him he obtained small amounts of crack and grass to peddle among his friends and acquaintances. Towanda was one of them.

Before the age of fifteen, Towanda had virtually dropped out of school but not out of sight. She kept up the pretense for the benefit of her mother who still thought that her daughter was headed for Marshall Middle every morning when she left home. Instead, Towanda often met with her crew outside the school to chat and take in the news of the day. Sometimes, she followed Deiondre and the others to a nearby townhouse where the boy lived with an older sister. Because the woman worked long hours at a fast-food place, she was seldom at home. Unbound by the stricture and obligations of school, Towanda found autonomy and status that are seldom available to middle-class youngsters whose lives are overscheduled and tightly regimented. She was imbued with a sense of freedom, which she thought was the mark of adulthood. Now the nodal point in her circle, she exchanged critical bits of information that resulted in the mobilization of scarce resources. She knew, for example, the secrets of kids who didn't speak to one another and could persuade them to combine forces to reach mutually beneficial goals. "It's like this," she explained:

Oscar Miner, you know? The kid who lives at 110 Mosher? He gets money from his granny. Deiondre don't like him 'cause he say [Oscar] is a faggot but I know that's not true, and it don't matter anyway, so I told Deiondre to give a break to Oscar and now Oscar cuts him half of what his grandma gives him every Sunday. I get my piece too.

She needed money to purchase the sorts of clothes that made her into a unique presence in the neighborhood. When she had cash, her favorite point of destination was Mondawmin Mall in Liberty Heights. She could spend hours trying on garments and costume jewelry and imagining where she would wear them if only she was rich. She aspired to have the style that made Tina Turner into an icon. After watching "Born to Win," the film about Turner's tumultuous life, Towanda arrived at two conclusions: one, "men are trouble"; and second, "you can survive if you strong and look good." It was for those reasons that, although Towanda dabbled in the perilous consumption of beer and weed, she kept to herself as far as sex was concerned. She believed that,

> Only fools get pregnant. They be thinking they so smart but they is fools 'cause you don't gain nothing by having a baby, only worries. I tell the other girls. Towanda's smart, she will never get pregnant; never! Just wait and see.

Her friends admired her determination not to fall prey to the lure of the older boys who seemed to want only one thing. Towanda had the skills to keep them interested without giving her young body away.

Within the tight confines of her home, Lydia struggled to keep Towanda out of trouble but her authority had fragile foundations. For one thing, she couldn't keep the girl inside. Crowded and damp, the house offered no refuge from outside dangers, especially during the summer when temperatures reached suffocating levels and youngsters, avid for sociability, took to the streets. Mothers like Lydia fought a constant battle with the nearby playground where children congregated in search of recreation but where older boys sold drugs and negotiated turf control. It was as if the playground was a living force luring away sons and daughters, sucking them in, and spitting them out, transformed. It was an uneven battle in which mothers faced overwhelming odds. Trying to keep a teenager like Towanda at home away from the color and sound of the street was nearly impossible.

Parental authority was also eroded by factors other than the structure of space in the urban ghetto: the brick and mortar of physical context. A negligible status distinction between youngsters and adults erodes the power of the latter. Towanda loved her mother but felt no pride in her. Lydia depended on public assistance and cleaned other people's houses to supplement her paltry income. She suffered from a credibility gap. When competing for the attention of her daughter, she was unable to buttress sensible advice with better assets than those used and controlled by Towanda's peers. The girl felt free and powerful only away from home. When I asked her about her new friends in the neighborhood, she said:

> They's nice kids no matter what mama says. They like me and I like them.
>
> They's cool not like the other people…they don't like me in school, always calling me names. I don't have to take their shit 'cause I can take care of myself and my friends take care of me.

In other words, membership in a youthful social network afforded Towanda protection in an environment bereft of resources. In poor neighborhoods, family integrity and parental authority are threatened on a daily basis by decrepit physical structures, a lack of means to secure children's compliance, and the absence of status distinction between youngsters and adults.

That is not all; an even more paradoxical factor thwarts the attempts of parents to control their sons and daughters: Child Protective Services, the very agency created to protect minors from abuse. Founded on impeccable principles, that agency implements policies often fraught with unexpected consequences typically illustrated by one of several incidents in Towanda Forrest's life. Only weeks after her fourteenth birthday, the girl decided to leave home in the middle of the night to attend a party with her friend, Deiondre. She felt pressure to do so because almost everyone that meant anything to her was planning to go; she just couldn't miss the event. Yet when asked for permission, Lydia resolutely said no, citing concerns about her young daughter's well-being and the reputation of Deiondre and his crew whose dubious record was well known in the neighborhood. Towanda rebutted her mother's objections without success. Lydia held her ground. Towanda then retreated to ponder her options. The picture was clear. She could not miss the party and, given Lydia's unbending position, all she could do was to leave home surreptitiously. Lydia suspected as much—knowing that Towanda was willful and sly, she had been surprised to watch the girl submit so quickly to her authority.

On the evening when the party was scheduled to take place, several things happened in quick succession. Around 9:00 PM Lydia locked up the front door to her small house and waited in the dark living room dozing off, her eyes heavy with exhaustion. More than one hour later, she heard Towanda quietly tiptoeing down the narrow staircase, walking over to the right wall and opening one of the windows that led directly onto the street. The girl straddled the windowsill and was about to touch the sidewalk when her mother, bolting from a corner, dragged her forcibly into the room. Towanda squirmed about, trying to get away from Lydia's grasp but the woman yanked her, slamming her against a wall. She then dashed into the kitchen to fetch a broom and, on her way back, she grabbed Towanda again as she climbed over the windowsill for the second time. Striking her with the broomstick, she chased her all the way upstairs into her bedroom, where Clarise, awakened by the racket was sitting up in her little bed, eyes rounded by surprise and fear.

Towanda fell over crumpled sheets wailing loudly, feeling more rage than pain. In the next room, Felicia and Mush grumbled about the commotion. Lydia retreated without a word. Gradually, the girl's crying diminished and silence befell the home. Worn out, the mother went to bed, expecting to sleep less than six hours. She had planned to leave early the next morning to fit in two house cleanings, one in Towson and the other in downtown Baltimore. But even that small amount of respite was denied to her; the new day had not yet dawned when she was awakened by a loud banging on the door. As she responded, two police cars flashed their lights in the darkened street. One of the two officers in charge informed Lydia that they had received a report of a domestic altercation and possible child abuse. Rushing out of her room and down the stairs, Towanda, still teary eyed, hastened to fill in the details, giving little attention to her stupefied mother who stood nearby in disbelief. By the next evening, the case had been turned over to Child Protective Services and, shortly afterwards, Lydia was confronting a social worker appalled by Towanda's complaints. She was cited with child abuse. A week later, Lydia had to appear in court to explain her behavior and give proof that she was not a danger to her daughter. The girl sat in the front row of the court room, right behind Lydia, chewing gum with a satisfied expression on her young face. She had said she didn't take guff from anyone—not even her mother—and, by God, she had kept her word. For the next twelve months, a social worker visited the family regularly to make sure that Towanda was not maltreated. Filled with frustration, Lydia confided:

> Those peoples [the social workers] they can't tell the difference between child abuse and discipline. It's like they think our kids will listen to us when not even they [the social workers] have respect for us…what could I do [with Towanda]? It was a lot more dangerous for her to be alone at night at that party than for me to chase her around with a broom. And I didn't even bruise her! But they [Child Protective Services] don't see it that way; they think they can come between a mother and her children.

Lydia's sentiments were not isolated. Most of the women that she knew feared and tried to avoid Child Protective Services, whose agents they saw as intruders imposing control and surveillance. "I knows they tryin' to keep children safe, their intentions are good," reflected Lydia, "but the fact is they mess up things more than they improve them." Especially galling was the perception that, because they were poor, women like Lydia were not fit to be parents. When she had a little time to herself, Lydia read the popular tabloids. She was especially fond of *The National Inquirer*. In the pages of such publications, she regularly found the stories of women whose lives appeared to be even more chaotic than her own. But those were celebrities who could pay nannies to take care of their offspring. Most of them averted suspicions of child abuse. By contrast, in poor neighborhoods throughout the nation, the condition of poverty was, and still is, linked to a long list of negative perceptions that include the potential for violence and a diminished ability for competent motherhood.

Lydia's case was emblematic in several ways—in her thoughts and behavior she sought to inspire her family and small community. She had become a Jehovah's Witness as part of an attempt to buttress her position as someone with high moral standards. In the eyes of the world, however, she was little more than an uneducated woman, on welfare for more than a decade, who cleaned houses to supplement her meager income; a woman who countenanced a drunken husband, and possibly abused her children. The two conflicting images—one of a God-fearing mother trying to restore her family; another of a dangerous contaminant to youngsters—aptly sum up a quandary faced by the urban poor in American inner cities.

After Lydia's court hearing, and subsequent to a one-year-long investigation, her name was included in a state-sanctioned list of *alleged* child abusers for seven years, a fact that would soon make it impossible for her to become a teacher's aide.

To secure a job, any job, had been Lydia's goal throughout the full length of the period that she had depended on public assistance. She took resigned pride in the work that she did as a house cleaner but yearned for more. She often wished that she had stayed in school and become a teacher because she felt that she had the temperament to benefit children. In the mid-1990s her aspirations finally dovetailed with changes in welfare policy. Since its inception in 1992, the Clinton administration had made clear its intention to dismantle "welfare as we know it." The rallying cry of government was to get people like Lydia "off welfare rolls and into pay rolls." Critics saw the slogan as a veiled attempt to use welfare mothers as fodder to satisfy public demands for accountability among the poor but women like Lydia were eager to find new lives of dignity by accepting jobs even if those jobs paid low wages.

That was largely the reason why she had risen to attention when one of her friends encouraged her to apply for a position as a teacher's aide at the Gilmore Elementary School. With some difficulty but high hopes, she filled out application forms and submitted them to the school's office of human resources. Some of the teachers knew and liked her. There was a good chance that she would land the position. Only two weeks later her application was declined. Her record showed the blot of *alleged* child abuse. The term was doubly deceptive because, not affirming beyond doubt the commission of a crime, it nonetheless pointed to it as a distinct possibility.

Lydia was in earnest to plead her case before the court of public opinion but it was all for naught. In compliance with the law, she was not eligible for jobs that put her into contact with children. To become a teacher's aide would not have paid more than what Lydia already made as a cleaning woman but her sense of self-worth would have been uplifted. Chasing a rebellious daughter with a broom had put her within the same category as individuals who torture, rape, and kill minors. "There's no winning here," Lydia said dejectedly, "I keep tryin' and tryin' and they's always knockin' me down. You wonder if the government knows what they doin' when they hurt mothers like me."

Then, in 1995, when Towanda was nearing her fifteenth birthday, Lydia fulfilled a long-held dream: to move her family into a low-rise unit within the George Murphy Homes, one of Baltimore's most notorious housing projects (leveled down in 2002 as part of yet another attempt to redistribute poor families in West Baltimore). The transition was auspicious and filled with hope that a break with the past would usher in a new life. As Lydia settled into her new home, she was encouraged to see that Towanda appeared to be changing her ways. She tried to be more helpful at home and was making an effort to resume her studies at Marshall Middle School. Such hopes were short-lived, however. After a few weeks, the girl's behavior began to deteriorate again. A newcomer in the projects, she received far from a hospitable reception from some of the neighbors. She acquired some new friends but not the kind that would encourage her to stay in school. Soon, Lydia started receiving warnings of eviction stemming from Towanda's transgressions. The administration of the publicly subsidized housing complex held the mother responsible for the behavior of her siblings. The girl had been caught breaking curfew and shoplifting. Less than six months after the move to the George Murphy Homes, she was sent to the principal's office, not for the first time, by a dispirited teacher whose class Towanda often disrupted. In frustration, the principal had raised her voice at the girl. Towanda had advanced menacingly towards the woman with a clenched fist. She didn't strike her but the gesture sealed her fate. She was permanently expelled. Sullen but relieved, she returned home and plopped into the sofa of the tiny living room. I asked her whether she realized how difficult she was making life for her family.

I don't mean to be bad. But a girl has to take care of herself; in a 'hood like this you can die if you don't fight for your rights. I wanna make something of myself, you know, to have a family, my own home. I want to be with people that think I'm something.

It was about that time that Towanda met Reggie Brown. He was one of two children born to parents who had been married but divorced when Reggie was ten. His mother, Regina, worked as a clerk at the Motor Vehicle Administration, trying to set a good example for Reggie and his younger sister, Dalia. In the 1940s, her maternal grandfather had migrated from Springfield, South Carolina, to Baltimore. Two generations later, she exemplified the extent to which the code of the street alters the intentions of parents. Like other women in West Baltimore, Regina had seen her two children evolve from enchanting tots into voluble youngsters whose behavior she could not control. She too had been rebellious and filled with desire for a better life. Now in her mid-forties, and afflicted with diabetes, she was completely dedicated to Reggie and Dalia. A devout member of the Bethel AME Church on Druid Hill Avenue, she combined paid work with work as a volunteer in the neighborhood.

Regina remembered her son, as a happy and docile boy. He had grown into a somber adolescent who worried about the well-being of his mother and sister. He thought Regina worked too hard. By the age of sixteen he had dropped out of school and began to make significant contributions to the family's income. He worked part-time jobs but, mostly, he sold drugs. That he did with discretion, never taking unnecessary risks and toning down the taste for exhibitionism that had doomed some of his friends. As a result, he commanded a rare kind of respect.

Reggie had been only nine when he and his friend Manny had gone out seeking to have fun at the local park. On their way, they had stopped at a local store to get a Coke.

As they were leaving, Manny had gingerly taken some cookies from the store's counter. The owner had reported the incident to the police and Manny had been detained. For two weeks, he had been confined to a juvenile center where he had undergone observation before being returned to his anxious mother. That experience had caused an indelible impression on both youngsters, partly because they had seen the same thing happen before—it was not uncommon for the police to pick up boys whom they saw as potential risks for detention and observation. According to Reggie:

> When you little, you don't really know [that] the police are always watching but, then, when you's bigger, you realize everything you do can be turned against you. Manny and me, we was just havin' fun; he didn't mean nothing by taking the cookies…but when you get treated like a criminal, there's no way out, you begin to think of youself as a no-good criminal.

Manny's life was changed by the incident; it strengthened and emboldened him. Filled with rage he formed alliances and became one of the most successful drug runners in West Baltimore. He was only eighteen when he was shot dead by a rival gang.

It was different in Reggie's case. He did not aim to be a gang leader or to make a fortune by selling crack. Mostly, he wanted to be a family man. He felt a sense of responsibility towards his mother and sister. A boy can't become a man without looking out for his own, right? At first, he took part-time jobs in downtown Baltimore. He worked in kitchens, waited on restaurant tables, and swept the floors of several commercial establishments. For his efforts he was paid small sums of money, most of which he gave to his mother. Wanting to earn more, he dropped out of school in the 11th grade hoping to get a full-time job but the sort of position that would have enabled Reggie to support a family was not available to a high-school dropout. It was then, upon realizing his limitations, that Reggie started peddling ice, small plastic bags filled with crack cocaine.

Not lacking talent or drive, Reggie soon became a figure to be reckoned with, an entrepreneur of sorts, and, by the standards of young people in the neighborhood, "a really cool guy." Before the age of eighteen, he had risen to become a local kingpin, always with cash in his pockets. "It's all drug money," Lydia proclaimed in disgust.

By contrast, Towanda, tough and streetsmart, thought that Reggie was about the only boy who might understand her. He too had fought to gain respect and independence. That's why he had dropped out of school and looked for means to help lift the heavy burden that his mother shouldered. He was hard as nails and had honor; kids in the neighborhood looked up to Reggie because he was generous and funny; and he never let the younger children be bullied. Towanda thought that "a boy like Reggie, he looks a bomb, he knows the ins and outs; he knows everything." To be his friend was to hold a firm position in the hierarchy of youthful status. Although she feigned indifference, Towanda was secretly thrilled when Reggie began to show interest in her. They had known each other for most of their young lives but now, in Reggie's eyes, Towanda seemed new and attractive. She had a wild reputation and knew how to dress smart. She had kept other boys at bay and thus presented a challenge. He kept showing up everywhere Towanda went. For hours, he waited for her at Mr. Kim's grocery store, one of the few commercial establishments in the neighborhood, where youngsters often purchased candy. Once, when Towanda was walking down the street with her homies, Reggie came directly at her and blew her a kiss. The girls laughed loudly at the gesture while Towanda cast a disinterested glance in Reggie's direction. For the first time in her turbulent life, Towanda thought that it might be wonderful to have a partner like Reggie Brown.

She was nearing fifteen but, in her imagination, that was not a young age. She had seen life; she was not like those characters on TV family shows that speak in little-girl tones and pretend to be weak so that others take care of them. In Towanda's world you grew up quickly and assumed responsibilities that even some adults might find overpowering. Hadn't she helped find her father when, under the effect of bourbon, he had fallen in the back alley and almost lost his life? She had been only eight when James had to be rushed to the emergency room of Mercy Hospital, and while Lydia stood by his side, Towanda stayed at home, helping Felicia, her older sister. When they ran out of food, it was Towanda who had gone to Kim's store begging to have some cans on credit. Hadn't she taken care of Mush and Clarise when Lydia was out working? Didn't she cater alone to her younger brother after he had the accident on Pennsylvania Avenue? She knew how to cook and clean a house. And she knew how to take care of herself; she wasn't helpless. She wasn't a child. Didn't she have to hold down her turf and earn the respect of kids who carried knives to school?

In other words, although she was very young, Towanda thought of herself as a woman. Poverty, violence, and isolation telescope time in ways not comprehensible to people living in gentler environments. Having resisted the temptations of sex "for a long time," she was now ready to join forces with Reggie Brown:

> He aks'd me to be his woman. Well, you can't trust the men, but to be his woman, eah, he alright...but I wouldn't marry him 'cause men, they wants to be on top and no one's on top of Towanda, not even mama!

Throughout the summer of 1993 Towanda Forrest and Reggie Brown attained a kind of neighborhood notoriety. Their lives were full of turmoil, with quarrels and passionate moments alternating one another. Their romance was watched with interest by other youngsters. After all, Towanda and Reggie were well matched—she was gorgeous and strong; he never lacked money and was loyal to his family.

Many of the girls in Towanda's group had become mothers as early as thirteen. Some in their late teens had two or three children to support, although most of them relied on the help of their own mothers. Many women in the projects were still taking care of their own young children when suddenly confronting the need to shelter grandchildren. Each new arrival became part of the same young generation. Toddlers born to adolescent mothers were to them more like little brothers and sisters than offspring. Grandmothers and sometimes grandfathers saw their families increase assuming central positions and caring for children of widely different ages.

Towanda had been unusual in her determination not to fall prey to motherhood too soon. She wanted her independence but Reggie wanted otherwise. He thought the mark of adult masculinity was a clear demonstration that he could father a child. This is always the condition of masculinity in deprived environments. In lieu of material wealth or access to meaningful levels of education, young people build a reputation with reference to their bodily faculties. A child of one's own is a sign of maturity, a marker of adulthood. To have sex is not mostly about pleasure but about the appropriation of vicarious power. It is like defending turf.

Two months shy of her fifteenth birthday, Towanda was delivered of her first child, a boy named Reggie Shantell Brown. She had pondered the baby's name for several months but, sadly, she couldn't spell it. Towanda was then—and is now—almost illiterate. By the time Reggie Shantell was born she had abandoned school. When I chided her about her earlier resolve not to become pregnant, she retorted, "some things are just meant to be." In the spring of 1996, Towanda was expecting her second child. She was then sixteen.

Shortly after Reggie Shantell was born I found myself engaged in conversation with Lydia Forrest in her small but tidy living room. She was inflamed with Towanda's behavior:

> Them children coming up have no sense; they's always thinking they know better. Towanda, she got an attitude, always got an attitude, I don't know how she came by that attitude!

I was preparing for a barrage of moral righteousness when Lydia's expression changed suddenly. She asked me whether I wanted to see the baby. I certainly did. Like a commander deploying her troops, she raised her voice to call Reggie. "Ma'am," was the courteous response from the second floor. "Bring the baby down!" Obediently, down the stairs came the young man with his son in arms, eyes gleaming with pride.

Moments later I asked Reggie how he felt about the birth of his son:

> It's good, it's good ma'am. And I was there when he was born; right there in the hospital. I 'bout fainted with all the blood and that, but I was there…I sure was there. Now, I have someone to really live for, someone who needs me and who'll look up to me.

I could not help but wonder whether James, Lydia's husband, had felt the same way when his first child was born or whether Reggie would replicate James's defeats in the years to come. Those thoughts were interrupted by the chatter of family members and friends who joined in with admiring expressions. What ensued was a collective demonstration of delight that dissipated any doubt about the extent to which Reggie Shantell was welcome. This was family; this was a reason to party; this was a time to rejoice.

Sitting in a corner, Towanda chewed gum in contentment. Hers was the moment of triumph.

21

JOANNA DREBY

CHILDREN AND POWER DURING SEPARATION

from *Divided by Borders* (2010)

In her book *Divided by Borders*, Joanna Dreby explores the dynamics of "transnational families," in which parents who are working in U.S. cities have children who are being raised—at least in part—by relatives in a rural village in central Mexico. In this excerpt, Dreby shows not only how painful this economically necessary arrangement can be but also how much agency and power even very young children can exert on the adults around them.

Nico was unmistakable in San Ángel for his bleached, spiked hair and for being the youngest hanging around a crowd of older boys. I guessed he was about eleven but learned when I visited his fifth-grade class that he was actually thirteen. On that day, Nico blurted out that his parents lived in the United States, seemingly pleased that I was interested in the experiences of children like himself.

During the week of the town *feria* [a festival of the town's patron saint], Nico was out every night at the rides until late. On the eve of the week's culminating events, Nico was at the rodeo. He and a friend were the youngest groupies hanging around the *jinetes* (cowboys who ride the bulls). I recognized his companion as a local seventh grader. Nico was much quieter than his friend, striking me as a true tagalong. At 1 A.M., I noticed them lying on the unattended trampolines, giggling when they called out catcalls to me in English. Then I saw Nico and his friend at the town dance. In the middle of the crowd they danced wildly to the music, laughing and bumping into each other and an inebriated young man. Shortly thereafter, the boys' older chaperones abandoned them for the company of some ladies. By 3 A.M., Nico was alone, lying on the grass, yawning.

The next afternoon, Nico accompanied a frail old woman to a store downtown. The woman, I learned, was his eighty-three-year-old grandmother, Doña Elizabeth. Later, as we sat in her disarrayed two-room house, Doña Elizabeth told me she recently had had a stroke and had trouble hearing.

> I am the only one to take care of him. He doesn't get along with Flor [a neighbor who helps out]. His oldest brother [an adult] lives down there too, but he doesn't get on with him.... You know, he doesn't really love his parents. I noticed this when they first came back to visit. He was like eight years old. When they came, he didn't want to have anything to do with them. Since then, he doesn't want to talk to them on the phone.... His parents call, but they talk to me. He says he doesn't want to talk to them. He never does. I will call to him and tell him to come to the phone, but he doesn't show up.

When I asked for permission to interview Nico, Doña Elizabeth consented but explained: "He isn't here now. You can find him downtown. He usually goes to watch the volleyball games in the evening and comes back late. During the day he is always down at the river somewhere." Doña Elizabeth, who had been sitting on the floor despite scattered chicken droppings, grew drowsy as we conversed. Our interview ended when she eventually fell asleep.

Before interviewing Nico, I spoke with a number of members of the family who all confirmed that Doña Elizabeth had absolutely no authority over Nico. Nico had been held back three times in school. His teachers described the fifth-grader as a lost cause.

Given his markedly difficult home life, I was not surprised that Nico was resentful of his parents for having left him when they migrated, especially since his other siblings had all joined their parents in Las Vegas. When I asked him what he spoke to them about on the phone, his answer was curt: "I

tell them to send money." This response differed sharply from that of other children, who resisted viewing their relationship with migrant parents as purely an economic one. When I asked Nico for details about his parents, he said, "I don't remember. They left me when I was little," even though his grandmother told me his father was back in February and his mother had come to visit the year before.

Despite being more unruly and outwardly resentful of his parents than others, in many ways Nico's answers to my questions were much like those of other children. Nico told me he did not know why his parents did not come back to Mexico, that he did not want to join them in the United States, and that he wanted them to return to Mexico. Although unsure whether his mother and father love him or whether he loves them, Nico said he felt more affection for his father. Given his general air of ambivalence during the interview, I was surprised at Nico's decisive answer that he would never leave his children to go work in the United States in the future. I asked, "Do you think it is worse for the mom or the dad to go to the United States?" Nico said, "The mom." "Why?" I asked. He answered, "Because...the mom [is different] from the dad.... The dad doesn't do what a mom should do with her child." Like other children, Nico criticized his mother more harshly for her absence than he did his father.

Nico's case was extreme, as he was one of the few children I interviewed who seemed to lack proper care. Yet it illustrates how central children's expectations of parents are to shaping their experiences while parents are away. Above all else, children expect parents to be better able to provide for them by working in the United States. This is what the sociologist Robert C. Smith calls the "immigrant bargain."[1] Although children's assessments of parents' failures or successes as migrants are complicated by gender, children like Nico are disappointed when parents do not live up to this fairly straightforward expectation that children's lives will be better while parents are away. Some, like Nico, lash out their disappointment by acting uncontrollably, especially when it takes longer than parents expect to fulfill their promises. As the journalist Sonia Nazario writes, such disappointment may lead some desperate children to seek out their parents on harrowing journeys of their own to the United States.[2] The emotional costs of migrant parents' failures to live up to their end of the "immigrant bargain" may be greatest for their nonmigrant children.[3]

Expectations of Children

The "immigrant bargain," however, is not one-sided. Nico's parents surely did not anticipate him being so wild while they were away. On the surface, expectations of children seem simple. When asked about his expectations of his children in Mexico, a migrant father explained: "Expectations? Well, that sounds a little weird to me. *De allá pa' acá* [from there to here], yes. I feel like there are quite a lot of expectations of those of us working here. But what do I expect of them? What can I say? That they take care of themselves. That they are good. That they study. That is it." There appears to be an imbalance in expectations, with the burden on migrant parents, who must make something of themselves in the United States to prove that the sacrifice of leaving children in Mexico is worthwhile. At least, this is migrant parents' view.

Yet from the perspective of children of migrants in Mexico, the seemingly minor hopes that children study, take care of themselves, and behave are considerable. Underlying these hopes are parents' expectations that children will understand their reasons for leaving, continue to love and respect parents who are not a part of their lives, and—as they get older—show parents'

sacrifices to be worthwhile by making something of themselves. All of this must be accomplished without the daily support of parents and often while living in relatives' homes. Aspirations for academic achievement are particularly powerful; children's education is a key feature of "intergenerational contracts" between migrant parents and children.[4] Many parents told me that paying for children's schooling justified their absences. Some even planned to retire to Mexico once their children were professionals and could support them through old age.[5] When intergenerational mobility lies at the heart of migrant parents' sacrifices, the expectations of nonmigrant children in Mexican transnational families are exceedingly high.…

Children suffer without their parents, but they are far from powerless in their families. Children's negative experiences give them leverage in negotiating their relationships with the adults in their lives. When parents migrate without their children, the needs of children loom large, symbolically and practically.[6] Children who exhibit disappointment at parental absences increase parents' feelings of insecurity about being away. When children have difficulties in meeting parents' goals of upward mobility through academic achievement, parents may allocate more of the family resources to this end. Children who remain in Mexico have little say in their parents' decisions to migrate, yet they negotiate emotional responses to family separation and its economic ramifications. They have an important role in shaping families' migration patterns.

Unlike parents, whose experiences differ by their gender, children's experiences vary most by their age. Aside from some individual variation, young children, teenagers, and young adults respond to parental absence differently. It is not until children become young adults that their own gender begins to shape their experiences. Because children's life stages affect their reactions, family relationships are dynamic and fluctuate according to children's changing needs.

Young Children

Research suggests that the younger children are at the age of separation from parents, the more deeply they are affected.[7] I find, however, that young children do not describe feeling as distressed by parents' migration as teenagers do.[8] Yet young children have ways of showing that parental absences matter, mostly via different kinds of emotional withholding.

Naming Caregivers and Parents

Five-year-old Marco was not an expert on U.S. migration. When his grandmother mentioned that he was afraid of *gringos*, I called Marco over and asked, "What are *gringos?*" "Police," he answered and ran back to play. Marco also did not know that *el norte* was *Los Estados Unidos* [the United States]. But the young boy demonstrated a clear understanding of his family structure. When I asked whom he lived with, he responded: "mama Carmela" (his grandmother), his "papa Paulo" (his grandfather), and his "tío José" (an uncle). He also said that his mother and father live in *el norte*, and added that he missed them and wanted them to come home.

Doña Carmela, Marco's grandmother, told me that the boy is quite attached to her, since she raised him from infancy. When his parents came to visit two years earlier, he refused to go live with them at their house. "Does he cry for his parents?" I asked.

> No, he doesn't cry for them. Sometimes he cries because he says that I am not his mother. His uncle is always telling him that I am not his mother, that I am his grandmother, and he cries....Sometimes he comes home upset and says he is mad

because they [his uncles] said that I am not his mother. He says I have this many mothers [shows two fingers] and this many fathers [shows two fingers] and this many grandparents [shows three fingers] because he says he has his mother there and me, his father there and his father here. And his grandparents are his fathers' parents and my mother who is still alive.

Among young children, the naming of caregivers—mostly grandmothers—in Mexico as *mamá* or *mami* is common. Yet all of the children I interviewed—even at the young age of five—understood that they have two mothers and, at times, two fathers, even when they call their grandmother mom. None got mixed up in telling me that their "mother" or "father" lived in the United States. They recounted conversations with, and showed me pictures of, their migrant parents, and they often pointed out the gifts migrant parents had sent. Like Marco, most claimed to have multiple mothers and, at times, multiple fathers.

For some children, the naming of caregivers as mothers is due to parents' instruction. Migrant mothers described the sharing of the title of mother as the price of leaving their children. They conceded that children should call caregivers mom, as they are the ones doing the daily care work. At the same time, mothers may feel offended when children do not also recognize them as mothers. One grandmother explained that her daughter told the children to call her *mamá* instead of *abuelita* [grandmother]. But when her daughter called home and spoke to her son, she would say, "Who am I?" and the little boy would answer, "My sister Rosa," after which she would correct him quickly. "No, no, no, I am your *mother.*"

Calling grandmothers *mamá* may simply be a way of expressing the emotional connection children share with caregivers in Mexico, but when children subsequently refuse to call migrant parents *mamá* or *papá*, they signal their lack of attachment to them. Children seem conscious that their use of names can make their mothers feel bad about being away. A migrant mother, Sandra, told me: "When I call, I ask to speak with my daughter, and although they are not talking to me, I overhear a conversation that goes something like this: They say, 'Come, Raquel, your mom is calling.' And she answers, 'Who? Who wants to talk to me?' 'Your mom.' 'Oh, Saaaaaandra,' she says before coming to talk to me on the phone."

According to one grandmother, her granddaughter "has always called her mother by her first name. I can tell that she doesn't really love her. . . . My daughter gets upset and cries to me over the phone. She says that she doesn't love her." Indeed, with migrant mothers I often sensed underlying anxiety around naming. Migrant Nydia, for example, said that four-year-old Kevin calls her mother mom but was quick to explain, "He doesn't deny [that I am] his mother. He knows that I have my place [in his life]." Although biological mothers are willing to share the name of mother with children's primary caregivers, when children pointedly avoid acknowledging their biological parents, migrant mothers feel offended. Naming demarcates the emotional costs of mothers' absences.

Interestingly, naming does not seem to affect migrant fathers in the same way it affects mothers. Although children often said they have two fathers, no migrant fathers reported taking offense at their children's naming practices. The use of names as a sign of affection challenges migrant mothers' investment in a maternal identity as family caregivers.

Acting Indifferent

Young children also express their distress about separation from parents by pretending to be indifferent toward them. Children speak frequently to their migrant parents on the phone, but they often communicate an "out-of-sight out-of-mind mentality" to them. Nydia said, "The only thing that makes me feel badly about my son is when he doesn't want to talk to me." A woman who looked after her nine-year-old nephew after his mother migrated said the boy often refused to talk to his mother on the phone. "I didn't want my sister to think that I was telling him not to talk to her. So sometimes I would trick him to get him to talk to her on the phone. . . . My sister would cry when he didn't want to talk to her."

Children act most indifferent when parents come home to visit.[9] Even when children anxiously await parents' return, once they arrive, children's behavior indicates to parents that migration is not without a price. One mother I met in San Ángel said she was only away from her three children for a year, but when she came back, her five-year-old twins hid from her. "They said, 'since you left, we don't know you anymore.'" Another said that her son spread the rumor that he wasn't going to accept her and her husband when they returned to San Ángel from the United States. "He would tell his uncles that he wasn't going to love us when we came home." Whereas naming is most distressing for mothers, fathers also feel the sting of children's indifference. Two years after Daniel's children went to live with his mother-in-law in Mexico, he explained: "They don't remember me. You don't know what that is. It is hard. They get [me] confused with a brother of mine; they think he is their dad."

It is, of course, understandable that children feel uncomfortable when their parents come home. Children who have grown up without their parents may want their parents to return but may not know how to feel or deal with conflicting emotions once reunited. A mother and grandmother in San Ángel explained how one eleven-year-old girl reacted to her mother's return.

> MOTHER: Well she knew [I was coming], and she was really anxious. She would ask how many days was it until we would arrive.

GRANDMOTHER: Then the car came, and it was outside. So I said to her, "Go, go see your mother." And she said, "No, I don't want to."

MOTHER: But then she came to me, but it was forced, like all of a sudden she was embarrassed and didn't want to come.

Later, the mother explained: "She called me mom ever since I arrived, but she wouldn't get close to me. It is only now [two months later] that she is starting to warm up."

Family members usually described children's feelings of discomfort as temporary. Some researchers have suggested that for young children, distress upon a reunion with parents is typically short-lived.[10] But at age thirty, Paulo still recalled the uneasiness he felt, when his father, Enrique, returned to visit. "When he returned after a lot of time, well, I felt really uncomfortable, as if he was a stranger, for the very reason that we didn't really have a relationship, because I was little when he left." Paulo's father left when he was fourteen, and after three years, when Paulo was seventeen, his father started to visit the family in Mexico annually. Paulo said that although he now gets along with his father, he is still uncomfortable around him. When Paulo visited with his parents, I watched him be outwardly affectionate with his mother yet shy away from his father's company. Children's indifference may have long-term consequences for parent-child relationships.[11]

All of the children I interviewed, even children whose parents left them while they were very young, indicated that their parents were important to them. They commented that they missed their parents, loved them, or wanted them to come home. When young children display indifference to parents, either over the phone or when parents visit, it does not mean that parents are unimportant. Rather by pretending to be indifferent, they express resentment at their powerlessness to affect the migration decisions of their parents, whom they care about deeply.

Parental Authority Disregarded

Young children almost always defer to the authority of their caregivers in Mexico but tend to reject this authority when they become teenagers. Even when parents return, either for temporary visits or more permanently, young children continue to defer to their caregiver's authority during an adjustment period. One grandmother said that when her daughter first came home, her grandchildren were very happy, but it took them a while to adjust to their mother's presence. "At first it was still grandma this and grandma that. Not until now are they leaving me a little and going to their mother." When I asked an eleven-year-old whose parents just returned from the United States, "Who do you ask permission to do things with?" she responded, "I ask my parents for permission only because that is what my grandmother told me I should do."

When parents or single mothers are away, children turn to their grandparents. When fathers are away, children defer to their mother, even when their father visits. As fathers tend to consider themselves the authority figures in Mexican families, children's deference to their mother is often hurtful.[12] Gabriela said that when her husband, Angelo, visits, "the kids always come to me for permission and with their problems. My husband has even commented to them, 'Am I not worth anything here?' Once he told them, 'I am going to leave because you don't respect me.'"

Gabriela's ten-year-old son, Gilberto, demonstrated the way children disregard migrant parents' authority. One day, I asked Gilberto for an interview about having his father home for a visit. He agreed. I explained that first we had to ask his parents for permission. We walked down the street together, and seeing that his parents were not at home, Gilberto went across the street to his grandmother's place to look for them. I lagged behind outside but was close enough to see Gilberto ask his father, sitting just inside the door, where his mother was. Learning that she was at a meeting, Gilberto came back out and said his mother was not around, so we would have to do it later. That evening, Angelo laughed about the incident and explained that this was a common occurrence with all of his four children, especially his eight-year-old son. "He is always playing marbles with his friends on the street. He comes into the house and walks by me looking for his mother to ask if he can go play. I stop him and say, 'What's this, *¿y yo qué?'* What about me?"

Whether intentional or subconscious, overlooking migrant parents signals the importance of the primary caregiver in children's lives. Migrant parents may laugh it off but later shake their heads and wonder, as Angelo did, "what about me"? In effect, ignoring parents' authority underscores the emotional costs of parental absences.

Refusing to Migrate

Many young children resist parents' efforts to reunite the family in the United States, and their parents do not send for children against their will. It is somewhat surprising that more parents do not exert parental authority and send for children regardless of the children's preference, but their unwillingness to do so is consistent with descriptions of minimal-intervention parenting strategies in the Mixtec communities of Oaxaca.[13] Such a regional tendency, however, does not necessarily mean that children in the Mixteca wield greater influence in their families than do children in other parts of Mexico. After all, children felt they had little say over their parents' initial decision to migrate. Instead, I believe parents' reluctance shows that their preoccupation with their children's reactions to separation affords children greater power in shaping family migration decisions than they might have had while living with their parents.

Facing children's resistance to migration, parents typically make elaborate plans to return to Mexico to try to win over their children. One mother, for example, wanted to send for her ten-year-old daughter, which would have cost approximately three thousand dollars. Her daughter said no. "I didn't insist, because she has to make the decision herself." Instead, the mother returned to San Ángel for a three-month visit to convince her daughter to migrate. The visit was much costlier than paying for her daughter's migration, as the mother had no income during this period, had to finance her return to the United States, and—if all went as planned—would pay for the undocumented crossing for both herself and her daughter. Similarly, Zelia went back to San Ángel for her son, Juan Luis. On the last day of her three-week visit, the six-year-old decided that he preferred to stay in Mexico. Zelia returned to the United States without him, having spent nearly three thousand dollars during the short visit.

When young children's emotional withholding makes parents feel bad for being away, parents may make significant efforts to be reunited with their children. This involves substantial costs, given their status as low-wage workers in the United States. In this way, young children's reactions to parents' absences may have significant economic repercussions....

NOTES

1. Smith 2006: 123.
2. Nazario 2006. Indeed, the number of minors illegally crossing the border appears to be rising. In 2002, border patrol officers arrested thirty-five thousand minors attempting to cross the border (Hansen 2003). Between October 1, 2003, and September 30, 2004, more than forty-three thousand minor children were detained while attempting illegal entry (Marizco 2004). Shelters have popped up along border communities to receive captured minors. In places where shelters do not exist, local authorities generally release minors to the streets since

no legal guardians can claim them (Hansen 2003; Marizco 2004; and Nazario 2006).

3. Cati Coe (2008) found that children are more likely to describe feelings of emotional suffering due to family separation during migration than are their parents. Jason Pribilsky (2001) describes children of migrants living in the Ecuadoran Andes as frequently suffering from *nervios,* which is a culturally specific illness with depressive-like symptoms. Jodi Heymann and colleagues (2009) have shown that Mexican children with a caregiver in the United States are more likely to suffer from physical, emotional, and behavioral problems than are children with non-migrant caregivers.

4. Kabeer 2000.

5. Ernesto Castañeda-Tinoco (2006) also writes of Mixteca migrants in Guerrero aspiring to retire in Mexico after investing some years working abroad (see also Massey et al. 1987 and Schmalzbauer 2008).

6. Indeed, along with traditional gender roles, Mexican familism is characterized by the symbolic centrality of children to the family. For more on familism, see Raley, Durden, and Wildsmith 2004; Suárez-Orozco 1995; and Tienda 1980. For more on the centrality of children to mothers and fathers, see Esteinou 2004 and Gutmann 1996.

7. See Woodward, Fergusson, and Belsky 2000.

8. See also Dreby 2007.

9. Leah Schmalzbauer (2004, 2005) has similar findings in her study of Honduran transnational families.

10. Bowlby 1973, as cited in Smith, Lalonde, and Johnson 2004.

11. Research with adult children reminiscing about periods of separation from parents suggests that separation has some long-term effects on their lives. See Arnold 2006; Avila 2008; Olwig 1999; and Smith, Lalonde, and Johnson 2004.

12. On male prerogatives in families, see Esteinou 2004; Melhuus 1996; and Uropesa 1997.

13. Jeffrey Lewis (2000) describes parents in an upper Mixteca community as having a very standoffish approach to child rearing. For regional differences in parenting styles, see Esteinou 2004: 18.

REFERENCES

Arnold, Elaine. 2006. "Separation and Loss through Immigration of African Caribbean Women to the UK." *Attachment and Human Development* 8: 159–174.

Avila, Ernestine M. 2008. "Transnational Motherhood and Fatherhood: Gendered Challenges and Coping." Ph.D. dissertation, Department of Sociology, University of Southern California, Los Angeles.

Castañeda-Tinoco, Ernesto. 2006. "Living in Limbo: The Social Context and Developmental Impact of Migrant Remittances." Master's thesis, Department of Sociology, Columbia University, New York.

Coe, Cati. 2008. "The Structuring of Feeling in Ghanaian Transnational Families." *City and Society* 20: 222–250.

Dreby, Joanna. 2007. "Children and Power in Mexican Transnational Families." *Journal of Marriage and Family* 69: 1050–1064.

Esteinou, Rosario. 2004. "Parenting in Mexican Society." *Marriage and Family Review* 36: 7–29.

Gutmann, Matthew C. 1996. *The Meanings of Macho: Being a Man in Mexico City.* Berkeley and Los Angeles: University of California Press.

Hansen, Gerry. 2003. "Number of Children Crossing U.S.-Mexico Border Rises." *Morning Edition,* National Public Radio, June 23. Retrieved April 27, 2009 (http://www.npr.org/templates/story/story.php?storyId=1307611).

Heymann, Jody, Francisco Flores-Macias, Jeffery A. Hayes, Malinda Kennedy, Claudia Lahaie, and Alison Earle. 2009. "The Impact of Migration on the Well-Being of Transnational Families: New Data from Sending Communities in Mexico." *Community Work and Family* 12: 91–103.

Kabeer, Naila. 2000. "Inter-generational Contracts, Demographic Transitions and the 'Quantity-Quality' Tradeoff: Parents, Children and Investing in the Future." *Journal of International Development* 12: 463–482.

Lewis, Jeffrey. 2000. "The Social Construction of Childhood in a Mixtec Community." Ph.D. dissertation, Department of Education and Sociocultural Studies, University of California, Davis.

Marizco, Michael. 2004. "Smuggling Children." *Arizona Daily Star*, November 21.

Massey, Douglas, Rafael Alarcon, Jorge Durand, and Humberto González. 1987. *Return to Aztlan: The Social Process of International Migration from Western Mexico.* Berkeley and Los Angeles: University of California Press.

Melhuus, Marit. 1996. "Power, Value and the Ambiguous Meanings of Gender." In *Machos, Mistresses, Madonnas: Contesting the Power of Latin American Gender Imagery*, pp. 230–259. M. Melhuus and K. A. Stolen (eds.). London and New York: Verso.

Nazario, Sonia. 2006. *La Travesía de Enrique.* New York: Random House Trade Paperbacks.

Olwig, Karen Fog. 1999. "Narratives of the Children Left Behind: Home and Identity in Globalised Caribbean Families." *Journal of Ethnic and Migration Studies* 25: 267–284.

Oropesa, R.S. 1997. "Development and Marital Power in Mexico." *Social Forces* 75: 1291–1318.

Pribilsky, Jason. 2001. "*Nervios* and 'Modern Childhood': Migration and Shifting Contexts of Child Life in the Ecuadorian Andes." *Childhood* 8: 251–273.

Raley, R. Kelly, T. Elizabeth Durden, and Elizabeth Wildsmith. 2004. "Understanding Mexican American Marriage Patterns Using a Life Course Approach." *Social Science Quarterly* 85: 872–890.

Schmalzbauer, Leah. 2004. "Striving and Surviving: A Daily Life Analysis of Honduran Transnational Families." Ph.D. dissertation, Department of Sociology, Boston College.

———. 2005. "Searching for Wages and Mothering from Afar: The Case of Honduran Transnational Families." *Journal of Marriage and Family* 66: 1317–1331.

———. 2008. "Family Divided: The Class Formation of Honduran Transnational Families." *Global Networks* 8: 329–346.

Smith, Andrea, Richard N. Lalonde, and Simone Johnson. 2004. "Serial Migration and Its Implications for the Parent-Child Relationship: A Retrospective Analysis of the Experiences of the Children of Caribbean Immigrants." *Cultural Diversity and Ethnic Minority Psychology* 10: 107–122.

Smith, Robert C. 2006. *Mexican New York: Transnational Lives of New Immigrants.* Berkeley and Los Angeles: University of California Press.

Suárez-Orozco, Carola, and Marcelo Suárez-Orozco. 1995. *Transformations: Immigration, Family Life, and Achievement Motivation among Latino Adolescents.* Stanford, CA: Stanford University Press.

Tienda, Marta. 1980. "Familism and Structural Assimilation of Mexican Immigrants in the United States." *International Migration Review* 14: 383–408.

Woodward, Lianne, David Ferguson, and Jay Belsky. 2000. "Timing of Parental Separation and Attachment to Parents in Adolescence: Results of a Prospective Study from Birth to Age 16." *Journal of Marriage and Family* 62: 162–174.

PART IV

SCHOOLING AND THE CULTURE OF CONTROL

This section of the reader consists of four selections that are set in urban environments but vary in the ways in which they emphasize this connection. We begin with an excerpt from Paul Willis's *Learning to Labor*. Although this book is best known as a study of working-class white boys, it was written within the multiracial urban context emerging in Britain's industrial West Midland region. Willis's book came along at a time when existing theories of social class were often deterministic, meaning that they claimed that the poor and working classes were trapped by their circumstances, which fully determined their life outcomes. In studying how and why socioeconomic classes tended to reproduce themselves, many analysts of the day drew on the neo-Marxist notion of "false consciousness," that is, the belief that working-class people accept the legitimacy of the dominant class's ideas and institutions even if it is not in their interest to do so. Willis's book was also written at a time when members of the working class could generally depend on employment in factories once they left school.

Learning to Labor shows how working-class students exhibit an implicit understanding that school is not structured to benefit their group (industrial workers) as a whole.

The "lads," as they call themselves, express their understanding that schooling is not designed to better their own conditions. They thus embrace a counter-school culture that valorizes masculinity, manual labor, and nonconformity. The lads set themselves up in opposition to a group of boys who conform to the demands of the teachers. The lads call them the "ear'oles" because they listen passively to what they are told without contributing much or posing any kind of challenge. Far from accepting the idea that the "ear'oles," as better students, deserve better jobs, the lads generally look down on the group and belittle the white-collar futures toward which the members of the other group appear bound. Rejecting the authority of teachers and the school, the lads construct an alternative reality within the school that celebrates group solidarity and devalues educational achievement. These acts of rebellion actually contribute to the "reproduction" of the lads' class position as they discourage the educational achievement necessary for access to better-paying jobs.

As the selection demonstrates, Willis is a consummate observer who melds together his observations of interactions and social situations with direct quotes that illustrate how his subjects define their situation. His book is famous for suggesting that while the actions of working-class youth may be self-destructive in the long run, they are not passive dupes meekly accepting the legitimacy of middle-class authority. Indeed, he shows how the working classes become active agents in their own future subordination, essentially leaving the middle-class jobs to the middle class. Rather than simply focusing on what goes on in the school, he metaphorically follows his lads to the shop floor.

Jay MacLeod's *Ain't No Makin' It* is another highly influential study about social class reproduction set in an American urban housing project at the beginning of the post-industrial era. If Willis's lads came of age in a period when young people could expect to enter working-class jobs, MacLeod's subjects are in school during a period of increasing deindustrialization and unemployment for the urban poor. MacLeod focuses on the lives of two social groups: the Hallway Hangers and the Brothers. The first consists of poor whites and the second of poor blacks. The white Hallway Hangers come from families who have lived in the projects for three generations and have extremely low aspirations. According to MacLeod, they perceive—quite accurately—that they have little chance of upward mobility and thus refuse to embrace the American belief in mobility for all. Their attitude is encouraged by family and friends, who do not want to set them up for disappointment. Through their social lives, they redefine success as loyalty to the group and making money in illegal ways. In contrast, the black Brothers try harder at school because they have aspirations that have not been "leveled." They are more likely to believe in upward mobility and thus accept the American ideology of achievement.

Thanks to this attitude and the then-expanding opportunity structures for African Americans, at least some of the Brothers, MacLeod argues, will be able to enter the stably employed working class. This stands in contrast to the situation of the poor whites, whose attitude toward mobility combined with the decline in the industries that employed their parents (and entered by Willis's lads), make for dim future prospects. MacLeod thus implies that a realistic sense of one's opportunities can be a curse. Although he claims that he is not arguing that poor whites are psychologically worse off than poor blacks, it is hard to escape that conclusion from the evidence he provides. Whereas Willis reveals the connections between his lads and the shop floor, MacLeod demonstrates how the connections between his subjects and the labor market are fraying in the early stages of postindustrialism.

Kathleen Nolan's *Police in the Hallways* is a contemporary study of blacks and Latinos in a Bronx high school, which attempts to update studies such as those by MacLeod and especially Willis in an era of mass incarceration. Based on her fieldwork following students in and out of the schools, Nolan looks at a growing trend in urban school discipline that she claims is an extension of a punitive turn in crime-control policies. Whereas Willis sees student school experiences as being shaped by class differences in the labor market and MacLeod sees attitudes shaped by rising unemployment, Nolan sees school experiences in high-poverty urban neighborhoods being shaped by an increasing likelihood of incarceration. Schools like the one she studies play a role, not so much in the reproduction of a working class, but in the production of a criminalized class. In this selection, she moves between schools and criminal courts. By observing interactions in hallways and classrooms, she shows how small infractions and altercations that would once have led to disciplinary measures in an assistant principal's office may now result in summonses and trials in criminal courts and are thus the first steps toward criminal records and down a school-to-prison pipeline.

The final step in the journey from classroom misbehavior to criminality, stigma, and incarceration is documented by Victor M. Rios's *Punished: Policing the Lives of Black and Latino Boys.* A former gang member himself, Rios follows the lives of several young men in Oakland, California. Like Willis's "lads," these young men rebel against the discipline imposed by school. Unlike their British working-class counterparts, however, the young men that Rios follows have no easy access or clear path to working-class jobs. Instead they find themselves increasingly subject to police and community surveillance, and stigmatized as dangerous "gang bangers" and criminals, a stigma that, ironically, often pushes them deeper into criminal activity and seals them off from noncriminal options.

These pieces demonstrate that though it is popularly believed that schools are vehicles of upward mobility, they are more often structures through which inequality is reproduced. Ethnography shows not simply that this occurs but also how it occurs, in ways that are often varied, complex, and even paradoxical. Read together, these selections highlight the significance of employment, unemployment, and incarceration at different moments in the last half century. They also reveal how urban schools are always an extension of a greater context. As conditions change, however, we need new fieldwork and new theories to illuminate them.

22

PAUL WILLIS

ELEMENTS OF A CULTURE

from *Learning to Labor* (1977)

In *Learning to Labor*, Paul Willis vividly documents how a group of working-class British high school students at Hammertown Boys School create and sustain a subculture that is defined by its opposition to the norms and values of authority, especially school authority. These "lads" work together to devise small ways to resist and defy authority and expectations on a daily basis. They are bound both by their rejection of the school as a "legitimate institution" and by their contempt for "ear'oles" (the more cooperative students).

Opposition to Authority and Rejection of the Conformist

The most basic, obvious and explicit dimension of counter-school culture is entrenched general and personalised opposition to "authority." This feeling is easily verbalised by "the lads" (the self-elected title of those in the counter-school culture).

[In a group discussion on teachers]

JOEY: (...) they're able to punish us. They're bigger than us, they stand for a bigger establishment than we do, like, we're just little and they stand for bigger things, and you try to get your own back. It's, uh, resenting authority I suppose.

EDDIE: The teachers think they're high and mighty 'cos they're teachers, but they're nobody really, they're just ordinary people ain't they?

BILL: Teachers think they're everybody. They are more, they're higher than us, but they think they're a lot higher and they're not.

SPANKSY: Wish we could call them first names and that...think they're God.

PETE: That would be a lot better.

PW: I mean you say they're higher. Do you accept at all that they know better about things?

—

JOEY: Yes, but that doesn't rank them above us, just because they are slightly more intelligent.

BILL: They ought to treat us how they'd like us to treat them.

(...)

JOEY: (...) the way we're subject to their every whim like. They want something doing and we have to sort of do it, 'cos, er, er, we're just, we're under them like. We were with a woman teacher in here, and 'cos we all wear rings and one or two of them bangles, like he's got one on, and out of the blue, like, for no special reason, she says, "take all that off."

PW: Really?

JOEY: Yeah, we says, "One won't come off," she says, "Take yours off as well." I said, "You'll have to chop my finger off first."

PW: Why did she want you to take your rings off?

JOEY: Just a sort of show like. Teachers do this, like all of a sudden they'll make you do your ties up and things like this. You're subject to their every whim like. If they want something done, if you don't think it's right, and you object against it, you're down to Simmondsy [the head], or you get the cane, you get some extra work tonight.

PW: You think of most staff as kind of enemies (...)?

—   Yeah.

—   Yeah.

—   Most of them.

JOEY: It adds a bit of spice to yer life, if you're trying to get him for something he's done to you.

This opposition involves an apparent inversion of the usual values held up by authority. Diligence, deference, respect—these become things which can be read in quite another way.

[In a group discussion]

PW: Evans [the Careers Master] said you were all being very rude (...) you didn't have the politeness to listen to the speaker [during a careers session]. He said why didn't you realise that you were just making the world very rude for when you grow up and God help you when you have kids 'cos they're going to be worse. What did you think of that?

JOEY: They wouldn't. They'll be outspoken. They wouldn't be submissive fucking twits. They'll be outspoken, upstanding sort of people.

SPANKSY: If any of my kids are like this, here, I'll be pleased.

This opposition is expressed mainly as a style. It is lived out in countless small ways which are special to the school institution, instantly recognised by the teachers, and an almost ritualistic part of the daily fabric of life for the kids. Teachers are adept conspiracy theorists. They have to be. It partly explains their devotion to finding out "the truth" from suspected culprits. They live surrounded by conspiracy in its most obvious—though often verbally unexpressed—forms. It can easily become a paranoic conviction of enormous proportions.[1]

As "the lads" enter the classroom or assembly, there are conspiratorial nods to each other saying, "Come and sit here with us for a laff," sidelong glances to check where the teacher is and smirking smiles. Frozen for a moment by a direct command or look, seething movement easily resumes with the kids moving about with that "I'm just passing through, sir" sort of look to get closer to their mates. Stopped again, there is always a ready excuse, "I've got to take my coat off sir," "So and So told me to see him sir." After assembly has started, the kid still marooned from his mates crawls along the banks of the chairs or behind a curtain down the side of the hall, kicking other kids, or trying to dismantle a chair with somebody on it as he passes.

"The lads" specialise in a caged resentment which always stops just short of outright confrontation. Settled in class, as near a group as they can manage, there is a continuous scraping of chairs, a bad tempered "tut-tutting" at the simplest request, and a continuous fidgeting about which explores every permutation of sitting or lying on a chair. During private study, some openly show disdain by apparently trying to go to sleep with their head sideways down on the desk, some have their backs to the desk gazing out of the window, or even vacantly at the wall. There is an aimless air of insubordination ready with spurious justification and impossible to nail down. If someone is sitting on the radiator it is because his trousers are wet from the rain, if someone is drifting across the classroom he is going to get some paper for written work, or if someone is leaving class he is going to empty the rubbish "like he usually does." Comics, newspapers and nudes under half-lifted desks melt into elusive textbooks. A continuous hum of talk flows around injunctions not to, like the inevitable tide over barely dried sand and everywhere there are rolled-back eyeballs and exaggerated mouthings of conspiratorial secrets.

During class teaching a mouthed imaginary dialogue counterpoints the formal instruction: "No, I don't understand, you cunt"; "What you on about, twit?"; "Not fucking likely"; "Can I go home now please?" At the vaguest sexual double meaning giggles and "whoas" come from the back accompanied perhaps by someone masturbating a gigantic penis with rounded hands above his head in compressed lipped lechery. If the secret of the conspiracy is challenged, there are V signs behind the teacher's back, the gunfire of cracked knuckles from the side, and evasive innocence at the front. Attention is focused on ties, rings, shoes, fingers, blots on the desk—anything rather than the teacher's eyes.

In the corridors there is a foot-dragging walk, an overfriendly "hello" or sudden silence as the deputy passes. Derisive or insane laughter erupts which might or might not be about someone who has just passed. It is as demeaning to stop as it is to carry on. There is a way of standing collectively down the sides of the corridor to form an Indian

gauntlet run—though this can never be proved: "We're just waiting for Spanksy, sir."

Of course individual situations differ, and different kinds of teaching style are more or less able to control or suppress this expressive opposition. But the school conformists—or the "ear'oles" for the lads—have a visibly different orientation. It is not so much that they support teachers, rather they support *the idea* of teachers. Having invested something of their own identities in the formal aims of education and support of the school institution—in a certain sense having foregone their own right to have a "laff"—they demand that teachers should at least respect the same authority. There are none like the faithful for reminding the shepherd of his duty.

[In a group discussion with conformists at Hammertown Boys]

GARY: Well, I don't think they'm strict enough now (…) I mean like Mr Gracey, and some of the other teachers, I mean with Groucho, even the first years play him up (…) they [the lads] should be punished like, so they grow up not to be cheeky (…) Some of the others, you can get on with them all right. I mean from the very beginning with Mr Peters everybody was quiet and if you ain't done the work, you had to come back and do it. I mean some of the other teachers, say from the first years, they give you homework, say you didn't do it, they never asked for it, they didn't bother.

It is essentially what appears to be their enthusiasm for, and complicity with, immediate authority which makes the school conformists—or "ear'oles" or "lobes"—the second great target for "the lads." The term "ear'ole" itself connotes the passivity and absurdity of the school conformists for "the lads." It seems that they are always listening, never *doing*: never animated with their own internal life, but formless in rigid reception. The ear is one of the least expressive organs of the human body: it responds to the expressivity of others. It is pasty and easy to render obscene. That is how "the lads" liked to picture those who conformed to the official idea of schooling.

Crucially, "the lads" not only reject but feel *superior* to the "ear'oles." The obvious medium for the enactment of this superiority is that which the "ear'oles" apparently yield—fun, independence and excitement: having a "laff."

[In a group discussion]

> PW: (...) why not be like the ear'oles, why not try and get CSEs?
> —   They don't get any fun, do they?
> DEREK: Cos they'm prats like, one kid he's got on his report now, he's got five As and one B.
> —   —Who's that?
> DEREK: Birchall.
> SPANKSY: I mean, what will they remember of their school life? What will they have to look back on? Sitting in a classroom, sweating their bollocks off, you know, while we've been...I mean look at the things we can look back on, fighting on the Pakis, fighting on the JAs [i.e. Jamaicans]. Some of the things we've done on teachers, it'll be a laff when we look back on it.
> (...)
> PERCE: Like you know, he don't get much fun, well say Spanksy plays about all day, he gets fun. Bannister's there sweating, sweating his bollocks off all day while Spanksy's doing fuck all, and he's enjoying it.
> SPANKSY: In the first and second years I used to be brilliant really. I was in 2A, 3A you know and when I used to get home, I used to lie in bed thinking, "Ah, school tomorrow," you know, I hadn't done that homework, you know..."Got to do it."
> —   Yeah, that's right, that is.
> SPANKSY: But now when I go home, it's quiet, I ain't got nothing to think about,

> I say, "Oh great, school tomorrow, it'll be a laff," you know.
> WILL: You still never fucking come!
> SPANKSY: Who?
> WILL: You.
> [Laughter]
> (...)
> —   You can't imagine...
> —   You can't imagine [inaudible] going into the Plough and saying, "A pint of lager please."
> FRED: You can't imagine Bookley goin' home like with the missus, either, and having a good maul on her.
> —   I can, I've seen him!
> —   He's got a bird, Bookley!
> —   He has.
> FRED: I can't see him getting to grips with her, though, like we do you know.

It was in the sexual realm especially that "the lads" felt their superiority over the "ear'oles." "Coming out of your shell," "losing your timidness" was part of becoming "one of the lads," but it was also the way to "chat up birds" successfully. In an odd way there was a distorted reflection here of the teachers' relationships to the "ear'oles." "The lads" felt that they occupied a similar structural role of superiority and experience, but in a different and more antisocial mode.

[In an individual interview]

> JOEY: We've [the lads] all bin with women and all that (...) we counted it up the other day, how many kids had actually been with women like, how many kids we know been and actually had a shag, and I think it only come to, I think we got up to twenty-four (...) in the fifth year out of a hundred kids, that's a quarter.
> PW: Would you always know though?
> JOEY: Yes I would (...) It gets around you know, the group within ourself, the kids who we know who are sort of semi-ear'oles like...they're a separate group from us and the ear'oles. Kids like Dover, Simms and Willis, and one or

two others like. They all mess about with their own realm, but they're still fucking childish, the way they talk, the way they act like. They can't mek us laff, we can mek them laff, they can fucking get in tears when they watch us sometimes, but it's beyond their powers to mek one of us laff, and then there's us (...) some of them [the semi-ear'oles] have been with women and we know about it like. The ear'oles (...) they've got it all to come. I mean look at Tom Bradley, have you ever noticed him. I've always looked at him and I've thought, Well...we've been through all life's pleasures and all its fucking displeasures, we've been drinking, we've been fighting, we've known frustration, sex, fucking hatred, love and all this lark, yet he's known none of it. He's never been with a woman, he's never been in a pub. We don't know it, we assume it—I dare say he'd come and tell us if he had—but he's never been with a woman, he's never been drinking. I've never known him in a fight. He's not known so many of the emotions as we've had to experience, and he's got it all to come yet.

Joey was an acknowledged group leader, and inclined at times to act the old experienced man of the world. As is clear here, and elsewhere, he is also a lad of considerable insight and expressive power. In one way this might seem to disqualify him as typical of school non-conformist working class lads. However, although Joey may not be *typical* of working class lads, he is certainly representative of them. He lives in a working class neighborhood, is from a large family known as a fighting family whose head is a foundryman. He is to leave school without qualifications and is universally identified by teachers as a troublemaker—the more so that "he has something about him." Though perhaps exaggerated, and though powerfully expressed, the experiences he reports can only come from what he has experienced in the counter-culture. The cultural system he reports on is representative and central, even if he is related to it in a special way.

It is worth noting that, in his own terms and through the mediations of the group, Joey assumes both complete mastery and understanding of the school year and its social landscape. He assumes that information will find its way to "the lads" as the focal point of that landscape. A clear hallmark of "coming out" is the development of this kind of social perspective and evaluative framework. It should also be noted that the alternative standards constructed by "the lads" are recognised by the teachers in a shadowy sort of way—at least in private. There were often admiring comments in the staff room about the apparent sexual prowess of particular individuals from younger teachers, "he's had more than me I can tell you."

Members of the group more conformist to school values do not have the same kind of social map, and nor do they develop an argot for describing other groups. Their response to "the lads" is mostly one of occasional fear, uneasy jealousy and general anxiety lest they be caught in the same disciplinarian net, and frustration that "the lads" prevent the smooth flow of education. Their investment in the formal system and sacrifice of what others enjoy (as well as the degree of fear present) means that the school conformists look to the system's acknowledged leaders, the staff, to deal with transgression rather than attempt to suppress it themselves.

[In a group discussion with conformists at Hammertown Boys]

> BARRY: ...he [one of the teachers] goes on about "Everybody...," you know. I don't like things like that, when they say, "Everybody's...none of you like this, none of you like this, none of you like that. You're all in trouble." They should say, "A few of yer...". Like Mr Peters, he does that, he don't say, "Everybody," just the odd few. That's better, cos some of us are interested (...)

NIGEL: The trouble is when they start getting, you know, playing the teachers up (…) it means that you're losing time, valuable time, teaching time, and that, so it's spoiling it for your, you know, sometimes, I wish they'd just pack up and leave (…)

BARRY: It's better the way they've done it now (…) they've put them all together [CSE groups were not mixed ability groups]. It don't really matter whether they do any work or not… You just get on, get on well now [in the CSE groups], cos if anybody's talking, he tells you to shut up, you know, get on with the work.

PW: (…) have you ever felt that you should try and stop them? (…)

BARRY: I've just never bothered with them (…) now, in the fifth, they should… you know, you don't just go around shouting at people in the classroom, you know, you just talk sensibly. [The teachers] should be more stricter.

Opposition to staff and exclusive distinction from the "ear'oles" is continuously expressed amongst "the lads" in the whole ambience of their behaviour, but it is also made concrete in what we may think of as certain stylistic/symbolic discourses centring on the three great consumer goods supplied by capitalism and seized upon in different ways by the working class for its own purposes: clothes, cigarettes and alcohol. As the most visible, personalized and instantly understood element of resistance to staff and ascendancy over "ear'oles" clothes have great importance to "the lads." The first sign of a lad "coming out" is a fairly rapid change in his clothes and hairstyle. The particular form of this alternative dress is determined by outside influences, especially fashions current in the wider symbolic system of youth culture. At the moment the "lads' look" includes longish well-groomed hair, platform type shoes, wide collared shirt turned over waisted coat or denim jerkin, plus the still

obligatory flared trousers. Whatever the particular form of dress, it is most certainly *not* school uniform, rarely includes a tie (the second best for many heads if uniform cannot be enforced), and exploits colours calculated to give the maximum distinction from institutional drabness and conformity. There is a clear stereotypical notion of what constitutes institutional clothes—Spike, for instance, trying to describe the shape of a collar: "You know, like a teacher's!"

We might note the importance the wider system of commercial youth culture has here in supplying a lexicography of style, with already connoted meanings, which can be adapted by "the lads" to express their own more located meanings. Though much of this style, and the music associated with it, might be accurately described as arising from purely commercial drives and representing no authentic aspirations of its adherents, it should be recognised that the way in which it is taken up and used by the young can have an authenticity and directness of personal expression missing from its original commercial generation.

It is no accident that much of the conflict between staff and students at the moment should take place over dress. To the outsider it might seem fatuous. Concerned staff and involved kids, however, know that it is one of their elected grounds for the struggle over authority. It is one of the current forms of a fight between cultures. It can be resolved, finally, into a question about the legitimacy of school as an institution.

Closely related with the dress style of "the lads" is, of course, the whole question of their personal attractiveness. Wearing smart and modern clothes gives them the chance, at the same time as putting their finger up at the school and differentiating themselves from the "ear'oles", to also make themselves more attractive to the opposite sex. It is a matter of objective fact that "the lads" do go out with girls much more than do any other groups of the same age and that, as we have seen, a good majority of them are sexually experienced.

Sexual attractiveness, its association with maturity, and the prohibition on sexual activity in school is what valorises dress and clothes as something more than an artificial code within which to express an institutional/cultural identity. This double articulation is characteristic of the counter-school culture.

If manner of dress is currently the main apparent cause of argument between staff and kids, smoking follows closely. Again we find another distinguishing characteristic of "the lads" against the "ear'oles." The majority of them smoke and, perhaps more importantly, are *seen* to smoke. The essence of schoolboy smoking is school gate smoking. A great deal of time is typically spent by "the lads" planning their next smoke and "hopping off" lessons "for a quick drag." And if "the lads" delight in smoking and flaunting their impertinence, senior staff at least cannot ignore it. There are usually strict and frequently publicised rules about smoking. If, for this reason, "the lads" are spurred, almost as a matter of honour, to continue public smoking, senior staff are incensed by what they take to be the challenge to their authority. This is especially true when allied to that other great challenge: the lie.

[In a group discussion on recent brushes with staff]

> SPIKE: And we went in, I says "We wasn't smoking," he says (…) and he went really mad. I thought he was going to punch me or summat.
> SPANKSY: "Call me a liar," "I'm not a liar," "Get back then," and we admitted it in the end; we was smoking (…) He was having a fit, he says "Callin' me a liar." We said we warn't smoking, tried to stick to it, but Simmondsy was having a fit.
> SPIKE: He'd actually seen us light up.

Punishment for smoking is automatic as far as senior staff are concerned, and this communicates itself to the kids.

> SPANKSY: Well, he couldn't do a thing [the deputy head], he had to give me three. I like that bloke, I think he does his job well, you know. But I was at the front entrance smoking and Bert comes right behind me. I turns around, been copped, and I went straight to him and had the cane. Monday morning, soon as I got in school, three I had.… You know he couldn't let me off.

Given this fact of life, and in the context of the continuous guerrilla warfare within the school, one of the most telling ways for "the lads" to spot sympathisers, more often simply the weak and "daft," in the enemy camp is to see which teachers, usually the young ones, take no action after an unequivocal sighting of a lighted cigarette.

> FUZZ: I mean Archy, he sees me nearly every morning smoking, coming up by the Padlock, 'cos I'm waiting for me missus, sees me every morning. He ain't never said anything.
> WILL: He said to me in registration—
> PW (INTERRUPTING):   Who's this, Archer?
> WILL: Archy, yeah, he says, "Don't get going up there dinner-time." "What do you mean like, up there?" He says, "Up there, up that way, the vicinity like." I says, "Oh, the Bush," you know, but he's alright, like, we have a laff.

Again, in a very typical conjunction of school-based and outside meanings cigarette smoking for "the lads" is valorised as an act of insurrection before the school by its association with adult values and practices. The adult world, specifically the adult male working class world, is turned to as a source of material for resistance and exclusion.

As well as inducing a nice effect, drinking is undertaken openly because it is the most decisive signal to staff and "ear'oles" that the individual is separate from the school and has a presence in an alternative, superior and more mature mode of social being. Accounts of staff sighting kids in pubs are excitedly recounted with much more relish than mere smoking incidents, and inaction after being "clocked boozing" is even more delicious proof of a traitor/sympathiser/weakling in the school camp than is the blind eye to a lighted "fag." Their perception of this particular matrix of meanings puts some younger and more progressive members of staff in a severe dilemma. Some of them come up with bizarre solutions which remain incomprehensible to "the lads": this incident involves a concerned and progressive young teacher.

[In a group discussion about staff]

DEREK: And Alf says, er, "Alright sir" [on meeting a member of staff in a public house] and he dayn't answer, you know, and he says, "Alright sir?," and he turned around and looked at him like that, see, and er…and he dayn't answer and he says, in the next day, and he says, "I want you Alf," goes to him and he says, "What was you in there last night for?" He says, "I was at a football meeting," he says, "Well don't you think that was like kicking somebody in the teeth?" "No," he says. "What would you feel like if I kicked you in the teeth?" he says. "What do you mean?" he says. "Saying hello like that down there," he says, "what would you expect me to say?" He says, "Well don't speak to me again unless I speak to you first." He says, "Right sir, I won't say hello again," he says, "even if I see you in the drive."

Certainly "the lads" self-consciously understand the symbolic importance of drinking as an act of affiliation with adults and opposition to the school. It is most important to them that the last lunchtime of their last term should be spent in a pub, and that the maximum possible alcohol be consumed. This is the moment when they finally break free from school, the moment to be remembered in future years:

[Individual interview at work]

PW: Why was it important to get pissed on the last day?

SPANKSY: It's a special thing. It only happens once in your life don't it? I mean, you know, on that day we were at school right, you'm school kids, but the next day I was at work, you know what I mean?

PW: Course, you went to work the very next day.

SPANKSY: Yeah, I got drunk, had a sleep, and I went to work (…) if we hadn't've done that you know, we wouldn't've remembered it, we'd've stopped at school [i.e. instead of going to the pub], it'd've been just another day. No, when we did that, we've got something to remember the last day by, we've got something to remember school by.

In the pub there is indeed a very special atmosphere amongst the Hammertown "lads." Spike is expansively explaining that although he had behaved like a "right vicious cunt" sometimes, he really likes his mates and will miss them. Eddie is determined to have eight pints and hold the "record"—and is later "apprehended drunk," in the words of the head, at the school and ingloriously driven home by him. Fuzz is explaining how he had nearly driven Sampson (a teacher) "off his rocker" that morning and had been sent to see the head, "but he wasn't off or anything, he was joking." Most important they are accepted by the publican and other adult customers in the pub, who are buying them drinks and asking them about their future work. At closing time they leave, exchanging the adult promises which they have not yet learned to disbelieve, calling to particular people that they will do their plumbing, bricklaying or whatever.

That they have not quite broken loose, and that staff want to underline this, is shown when "the lads" return to the school late, smelling of alcohol and in some cases quite drunk. In a reminder that the power of the school is backed ultimately by the law and state coercion, the head has called in the police. A policeman is waiting outside the school with the head. This frightens "the lads" and a bizarre scenario develops as they try to dodge the policeman.

[Later in a group discussion]

> WILL: I was walking up the drive [to the school], I was pulling Spike and Spanksy (...) I was trying to get these two alright, you know. Joey saw this copper comin' down the drive (...) I went into the bogs [at the bottom of the drive bounded at the back only by a fence]. I seen the copper, "If he don't see me like, I can jump over the fence and get scot free, like, nobody'll see me, I'll be alright." Then I thought, "Look well if he comes in or summat," so I undone my trousers like I was having a piss, as though I was late or summat. Then Bill come running in. I thought, "Christ," and I climbed over the back fence, went creeping off (...) Simmondsy had seen Bill, he said, "Ah, I want to see you *two*," he says, "You *two*," and I dayn't think you know, I just went walking down.

Eventually "the lads" are rounded up and delivered in an excited state to the head's study, where they are told off roughly by the policeman: "He picked me up and bounced me against the wall"—Spike (I did not see this incident myself). The head subsequently writes to all of their parents threatening to withhold their final testimonials until an apology is received: in the case of Spike he wrote:

> ...your son had obviously been drinking, and his subsequent behavior was generally uncooperative, insolent, and almost

belligerent. He seemed beat on justifying his behaviour and went as far as describing the school as being like Colditz...as is my practice, I wish to give the parents of the boys an opportunity to come and see me before I finally decide what action to take.[2]

Even sympathetic young staff find the incident "surprising," and wondered why "the lads" had not waited until the evening, and then "really done it properly." The point is, of course, that the drinking has to be done at lunchtime, and in defiance of the school. It is not done simply to mark a neutral transition—a mere ritual. It is a decisive rejection and closing off. They have, in some way, finally beaten the school in a way which is beyond the "ear'oles" and nearly unanswerable by staff. It is the transcendence of what they take to be the mature life, the *real* life, over the oppressive adolescence of the school—represented by the behaviour both of the "ear'oles" *and* of the teachers.

Some of the parents of "the lads" share their sons' view of the situation. Certainly none of them take up the head's offer to go and see him.

[In a group discussion]

> WILL: Our mum's kept all the letters, you know, about like the letters Simmondsy's sent [about the drinking]. I says, "What you keeping them for?" She says, "Well, it'll be nice to look back on to, won't it," you know, "show your kids like you know, what a terror you was." I'm keeping 'em, I am.

[Individual interview at work]

> PW: Did your old man understand about having a drink the last day of term?
> SPANKSY: Oh ah (...) he laughed, he said, "Fancy them sending a letter," you know. Joey's father come and had a little laugh about it you know.

No matter what the threats, and the fear of the law, the whole episode is "worth it" to "the lads." It is the most frequently recounted, embellished and exaggerated school episode in the future working situation. It soon becomes part of a personalised folklore. As school uniform and smoking cease to be the most obvious causes of conflict in schools as more liberal regimes develop, we may expect drinking to become the next major area where the battle lines are drawn.

The Informal Group

> On a night we go out on
> the street
> Troubling other people,
> I suppose we're anti-social,
> But we enjoy it.
>
> The older generation
> They don't like our hair,
> Or the clothes we wear
> They seem to love running
> us down,
> I don't know what I would
> do if I didn't have the gang.
>
> (Extract from a poem by Derek
> written in an English class.)

In many respects the opposition we have been looking at can be understood as a classic example of the opposition between the formal and the informal. The school is the zone of the formal. It has a clear structure: the school building, school rules, pedagogic practice, a staff hierarchy with powers ultimately sanctioned—as we have seen in small way—by the state, the pomp and majesty of the law, and the repressive arm of state apparatus, the police. The "ear'oles" invest in this formal structure, and in exchange for some loss in autonomy expect the official guardians to keep the holy rules—often above and beyond their actual call to duty. What is freely sacrificed by the faithful must be taken from the unfaithful.

Counter-school culture is the zone of the informal. It is where the incursive demands of the formal are denied—even if the price is the expression of opposition in style, micro-interactions and non-public discourses. In working class culture generally opposition is frequently marked by a withdrawal into the informal and expressed in its characteristic modes just beyond the reach of "the rule."

Even though there are no public rules, physical structures, recognised hierarchies or institutionalised sanctions in the counter-school culture, it cannot run on air. It must have its own material base, its own infrastructure. This is, of course, the social group. The informal group is the basic unit of this culture, the fundamental and elemental source of its resistance. It locates and makes possible all other elements of the culture, and its presence decisively distinguishes "the lads" from the "ear'oles."

The importance of the group is very clear to members of the counter-school culture.

[In a group discussion]

WILL: (...) we see each other every day, don't we, at school (...)

JOEY: That's it, we've developed certain ways of talking, certain ways of acting, and we developed disregards for Pakis, Jamaicans and all different... for all the scrubs and the fucking ear'oles and all that (...) We're getting to know it now, like we're getting to know all the cracks, like, how to get out of lessons and things, and we know where to have a crafty smoke. You can come over here to the youth wing and do summat, and er'm... all your friends are here, you know, it's sort of what's there, what's always going to be there for the next year, like, and you know you have to come to school today, if you're feeling bad, your mate'll soon cheer yer up like, 'cos you couldn't go without ten minutes in this school, without having a laff at something or other.

PW: Are your mates a really big important thing at school now?
—   Yeah.
—   Yeah.
—   Yeah.
JOEY   They're about the best thing actually.

The essence of being "one of the lads" lies within the group. It is impossible to form a distinctive culture by yourself. You cannot generate fun, atmosphere and a social identity by yourself. Joining the counter-school culture means joining a group and enjoying it means being with the group.

[In a group discussion on being "one of the lads"]

JOEY: (…) when you'm dossing on your own, it's no good, but when you'm dossing with your mates, then you're all together, you're having a laff and it's a doss.
BILL: If you don't do what the others do, you feel out.
FRED: You feel out, yeah, yeah. They sort of, you feel, like, thinking the others are…
WILL: In the second years…
SPANKSY: I can imagine…you know, when I have a day off school, when you come back the next day, and something happened like in the day you've been off, you feel, "Why did I have that day off," you know, "I could have been enjoying myself." You know what I mean? You come back and they're saying, "Oorh, you should have been here yesterday," you know.
WILL: (…) like in the first and second years, you can say er'm…you're a bit of an ear'ole right. Then you want to try what it's like to be er'm…say, one of the boys like, you want to have a taste of

that, not an ear'ole, and so you like the taste of that.

Though informal, such groups nevertheless have rules of a kind which can be described—though they are characteristically framed in contrast to what "rules" are normally taken to mean.

PW: (…) Are there any rules between you lot?
PETE: We just break the other rules.
FUZZ: We ain't got no rules between us though, have we?
(…)
PETE: Changed 'em round.
WILL: We ain't got rules but we do things between us, but we do things that y'know, like er…say, I wouldn't knock off anybody's missus or Joey's missus, and they wouldn't do it to me, y'know what I mean? Things like that or, er…yer give 'im a fag, you expect one back, like, or summat like that.
FRED: T'ain't rules, it's just an understanding really.
WILL: That's it, yes.
PW: (…) What would these understandings be?
WILL: Er…I think, not to…meself, I think there ain't many of us that play up the first or second years, it really is that, but y'know, say if Fred had cum to me and sez, "er…I just got two bob off that second year over there," I'd think, "What a cunt," you know.
(…)
FRED: We're as thick as thieves, that's what they say, stick-together.

There is a universal[3] taboo amongst informal groups on the yielding of incriminating information about others to those with formal power. Informing contravenes the essence of the informal group's nature: the maintenance of oppositional meanings against the penetration of "the rule." The Hammertown lads call it "grassing." Staff call it telling the truth. "Truth" is the formal complement of "grassing." It is only by getting someone to "grass"—forcing them to break the solemnest taboo—that the primacy of the formal organisation can be maintained. No wonder then, that a whole school can be shaken with paroxysms over a major incident and the purge which follows it. It is an atavistic struggle about authority and the legitimacy of authority. The school has to win, and someone, finally, has to "grass": this is one of the ways in which the school itself is reproduced and the faith of the "ear'oles" restored. But whoever has done the "grassing" becomes special, weak and marked. There is a massive retrospective and ongoing re-appraisal amongst "the lads" of the fatal flaw in his personality which had always been immanent but not fully disclosed till now:

[In a group discussion of the infamous "fire extinguisher incident" in which "the lads" took a hydrant out of school and let it off in the local park]

> PW: It's been the biggest incident of the year as it's turned out, hasn't it?
> JOEY: It's been blown up into something fucking terrific. It was just like that [snapping his fingers], a gob in the ocean as far as I'm concerned when we did it, just like smoking round the comer, or going down the shop for some crisps.
> PW: What happened (...)?
> — Webby [on the fringes of the counter-school culture] grassed.
> JOEY: Simmondsy had me on me own and he said, "One of the group owned up and tried to put all the blame on Fuzz." But he'd only had Webby in there.
> SPANKSY: We was smoking out here.
> SPIKE: He's like that, you'd got a fag, hadn't you [to Fuzz].
> SPANKSY: And Webby asks for a drag, so he give Webby the fag. Rogers [a teacher] walked through the door, and

he went like that [demonstrating] and he says. "It ain't mine sir, I'm just holding it for Fuzz."
> WILL: Down the park before, (...) this loose thing, me and Eddie pulled it off, didn't we, me and Eddie, and the parky was coming round like, he was running round, wor'he, so me and Eddie we went round the other side, and just sat there, like you know, two monkeys. And Webby was standing there, and the parky come up to him and says, "Come on, get out. Get out of this park. You'm banned." And he says, he walks past us, me and Eddie, and he says, "I know you warn't there, you was sitting here." And Webby went, "It warn't me, it was...", and he was just about to say summat, warn't he?
> EDDIE: That's it, and I said, "Shhh," and he just about remembered not to grass us.

Membership of the informal group sensitises the individual to the unseen informal dimension of life in general. Whole hinterlands open up of what lies behind the official definition of things. A kind of double capacity develops to register public descriptions and objectives on the one hand, and to look behind them, consider their implications, and work out what will actually happen, on the other. This interpretative ability is felt very often as a kind of maturation, a feeling of becoming "worldliwise," of knowing "how things really work when it comes to it." It supplies the real "insider" knowledge which actually helps you get through the day.

> PW: Do you think you've learnt anything at school, has it changed or moulded your values?
> JOEY: I don't think school does fucking anything to you (...) It never has had much effect on anybody I don't think [after] you've learnt the basics. I mean school, it's fucking four hours a day. But it ain't the teachers who mould you,

it's the fucking kids you meet. You'm only with the teachers 30 per cent of the time in school, the other fucking two-thirds are just talking, fucking pickin' an argument, messing about.

The group also supplies those contacts which allow the individual to build up alternative maps of social reality, it gives the bits and pieces of information for the individual to work out himself what makes things tick. It is basically only through the group that other groups are met, and through them successions of other groups. School groups coalesce and further link up with neighbourhood groups, forming a network for the passing on of distinctive kinds of knowledge and perspectives that progressively place school at a tangent to the overall experience of being a working class teenager in an industrial city. It is the infrastructure of the informal group which makes at all possible a distinctive kind of *class* contact, or class culture, as distinct from the dominant one.

Counter-school culture already has a developed form of unofficial bartering and exchange based on "nicking," "fiddles," and "the foreigner"—a pattern which, of course, emerges much more fully in the adult working class world:

> FUZZ: If, say, somebody was to say something like, "I'm looking, I want a cassette on the cheap like." Right, talk about it, one of us hears about a cassette on the cheap, y'know, kind of do the deal for 'em and then say, "Ah, I'll get you the cassette."

Cultural values and interpretations circulate "illicitly" and informally just as do commodities.

Dossing, Blagging and Wagging

Opposition to the school is principally manifested in the struggle to win symbolic and physical space from the institution and its rules and to defeat its main perceived purpose: to make you "work." Both the winning and the prize—a form of self-direction—profoundly develop informal cultural meanings and practices.... By the time a counter-school culture is fully developed its members have become adept at managing the formal system, and limiting its demands to the absolute minimum. Exploiting the complexity of modern regimes of mixed ability groupings, blocked timetabling and multiple RSLA options, in many cases this minimum is simply the act of registration.[4]

[In a group discussion on the school curriculum]

> JOEY: (...) of a Monday afternoon, we'd have nothing right? Nothing hardly relating to school work, Tuesday afternoon we have swimming and they stick you in a classroom for the rest of the afternoon, Wednesday afternoon you have games and there's only Thursday and Friday afternoon that you work, if you call that work. The last lesson Friday afternoon we used to go and doss, half of us wagged out o' lessons and the other half go into the classroom, sit down and just go to sleep (...)
>
> SPANKSY: (...) Skive this lesson, go up on the bank, have a smoke, and the next lesson go to a teacher who, you know, 'll call the register (...)
>
> BILL: It's easy to go home as well, like him [Eddie]...last Wednesday afternoon, he got his mark and went home (...)
>
> EDDIE: I ain't supposed to be in school this afternoon, I'm supposed to be at college [on a link course where students spend one day a week at college for vocational instruction]
>
> ———
>
> PW: What's the last time you've done some writing?

WILL: When we done some writing?

FUZZ: Oh are, last time was in careers, 'cos I writ "yes" on a piece of paper, that broke me heart.

PW: Why did it break your heart?

FUZZ: I mean to write, 'cos I was going to try and go through the term without writing anything. 'Cos since we've cum back. I ain't dun nothing [it was half way through term].

Truancy is only a very imprecise—even meaningless—measure of rejection of school. This is not only because of the practice of stopping in school for registration before "wagging off" (developed to a fine art amongst "the lads"), but also because it only measures one aspect of what we might more accurately describe as informal student mobility. Some of "the lads" develop the ability of moving about the school at their own will to a remarkable degree. They construct virtually their own day from what is offered by the school. Truancy is only one relatively unimportant and crude variant of this principle of self-direction which ranges across vast chunks of the syllabus and covers many diverse activities: being free out of class, being in class and doing no work, being in the wrong class, roaming the corridors looking for excitement, being asleep in private. The core skill which articulates these possibilities is being able to get out of any given class: the preservation of personal mobility.

[In a group discussion]

PW: But doesn't anybody worry about your not being in their class?

FUZZ: I get a note off the cooks saying I'm helping them (...)

JOHN: You just go up to him [a teacher] and say, "Can I go and do a job." He'll say, "Certainly, by all means," 'cos they want to get rid of you like.

FUZZ: Specially when I ask 'em.

—

PETE: You know the holes in the corridor, I didn't want to go to games, he told me to fetch his keys, so I dropped them down the hole in the corridor, and had to go and get a torch and find them.

For the successful, there can be an embarrassment of riches. It can become difficult to choose between self-organised routes through the day.

WILL: (...) what we been doing, playing cards in this room 'cos we can lock the door.

PW: Which room's this now?

WILL: Resources centre, where we're making the frames [a new stage for the deputy head], s'posed to be.

PW: Oh! You're still making the frames!

WILL: We should have had it finished, we just lie there on top of the frame, playing cards, or trying to get to sleep (...) Well, it gets a bit boring, I'd rather go and sit in the classroom, you know.

PW: What sort of lessons would you think of going into?

WILL: Uh, science, I think, 'cos you can have a laff in there sometimes.

This self-direction and thwarting of formal organisational aims is also an assault on official notions of time. The most arduous task of the deputy head is the construction of the timetables. In large schools, with several options open to the fifth year, everything has to be fitted in with the greatest of care. The first weeks of term are spent in continuous revision, as junior members of staff complain, and particular combinations are shown to be unworkable. Time, like money, is valuable and not to be squandered. Everything has to be ordered into a kind of massive critical path of the school's purpose. Subjects become measured blocks of time in careful relation to each other. Quite as much as the school buildings the institution over time *is* the syllabus. The complex charts on the deputy's wall shows how it works. In theory it is possible to check where every individual is at every moment of the day. But for "the lads" this never seems to work. If one wishes to contact them, it is much more important to know and understand their own rhythms and patterns of movement. These rhythms reject the obvious purposes of the timetable and their implicit notions of time. The common complaint about "the lads" from staff and the "ear'oles" is that they "waste valuable time." Time for "the lads" is not something you carefully husband and thoughtfully spend on the achievement of desired objectives in the future. For "the lads" time is something they want to claim for themselves now as an aspect of their immediate identity and self-direction. Time is used for the preservation of a state—being with "the lads"—not for the achievement of a goal—qualifications.

Of course there is a sense of urgency sometimes, and individuals can see the end of term approaching and the need to get a job. But as far as their culture is concerned time is importantly simply the state of being free from institutional time. Its own time all passes as essentially the same thing, in the same units. It is not planned, and is not counted in loss, or expected exchange.

"Having a Laff"

"Even communists laff" (Joey)

The space won from the school and its rules by the informal group is used for the shaping and development of particular cultural skills principally devoted to "having a laff." The "laff" is a multi-faceted implement of extraordinary importance in the counter-school culture.... The ability to produce it is one of the defining characteristics of being one of "the lads"—"We can make

them laff, they can't make us laff." But it is also used in many other contexts: to defeat boredom and fear, to overcome hardship and problems—as a way out of almost anything. In many respects the "laff" is the privileged instrument of the informal, as the command is of the formal. Certainly "the lads" understand the special importance of the "laff":

[In an individual discussion]

> JOEY: I think fuckin' laffing is the most important thing in fuckin' everything. Nothing ever stops me laffing (...) I remember once, there was me, John, and this other kid, right, and these two kids cum up and bashed me for some fuckin' reason or another. John and this other kid were away, off (...) I tried to give 'em one, but I kept fuckin' coppin' it...so I ran off, and as I ran off, I scooped a handful of fuckin' snow up, and put it right over me face, and I was laffing me bollocks off. They kept saying, "You can't fuckin' laff." I should have been scared but I was fuckin' laffing (...)
>
> PW: What is it about having a laugh, (...) why is it so important?
>
> JOEY: (...) I don't know why I want to laff, I dunno why it's so fuckin' important. It just is (...) I think it's just a good gift, that's all, because you can get out of any situation. If you can laff, if you can make yourself laff, I mean really convincingly, it can get you out of millions of things (...) You'd go fuckin' berserk if you didn't have a laff occasionally.

The school is generally a fertile ground for the "laff." The school importantly develops and shapes the particular ambience of "the lads" distinctive humour.... Many of their pranks and jokes would not mean the same thing or even be funny anywhere else. When a teacher comes into a classroom he is told, "It's alright, sir, the deputy's taking us, you can go. He said you could have the period off." "The lads" stop second and third years around the school and say, "Mr Argyle wants to see you, you'm in trouble I think." Mr Argyle's room is soon choked with worried kids. A new teacher is stopped and told, "I'm new in the school, the head says could you show me around please." The new teacher starts to do just that before the turned away laughs give the game away. As a rumour circulates that the head is checking everyone's handwriting to discover who has defaced plaster in the new block, Fuzz boasts, "The fucker can't check mine, I ain't done none." In a humorous exploration of the crucial point where authority connects with the informal code through the sacred taboo on informing, there is a stream of telltale stories half goading the teacher into playing his formal role more effectively: "Please sir, please sir, Joey's talking/pinching some compasses/picking his nose/killing Percival/having a wank/let your car tyres down."

In a more general sense, the "laff" is part of an irreverent marauding misbehaviour. Like an army of occupation of the unseen, informal dimension "the lads" pour over the countryside in a search for incidents to amuse, subvert and incite. Even strict and well-patrolled formal areas like assembly yield many possibilities in this other mode. During assembly Spanksy empties the side jacket pocket of someone sitting in front of him, and asks ostentatiously "Whose these belong to?" as Joey is clipping jackets to seats, and the others ruin the collective singing:

> JOEY: The chief occupation when we'm all in the hall is playing with all the little clips what holds the chairs together. You take them off and you clip someone's coat to his chair and just wait until he gets up... and you never really listen... you have to be really

discreet like, so as the Clark [the deputy head] won't see yer, call you out, the other teachers don't matter.

(...)

> JOEY: Even on the hymn... when they mek you sing—
> PW: But do they make you sing? I didn't notice many of you singing—
> — I was just standing there, moving my mouth.
> — We've only got one of them books between all our class. We've got one between twenty-five—
> — When we do sing we make a joke of it.
> FUZZ: Sing the wrong verses... So if you're supposed to be singing verse one, you're singing verse three.

[Laughter]

During films in the hall they tie the projector leads into impossible knots, make animal figures or obscene shapes on the screen with their fingers, and gratuitously dig and jab the backs of "ear'oles" in front of them.

As they wander through the park next to the school at lunchtime they switch on the dynamo on the park-keeper's bike, "That'll slow the cunt down a bit." They push and pull everything loose or transportable, empty litterbins and deface signs. Where it looks defenceless private property is also a target:

[In a group discussion on vandalism]

> PETE: Gates!
> JOEY: Gates are the latest crack. Swopping gates over. Get a gate, lift it off, put it on somebody else's.
> BILL: That's what we done. We was going to the ten pin bowling, you know, up by the Brompton Road, there was an 'ouse there for sale. We took the "For Sale" sign out of the one, put it in the next door, then we took the milk carrier from the one, put it next door (...) we took a sort of window box on legs from the porch and stuck that next door. We swapped stacks of things.

SPANKSY: And dustbins! [Laughter]…every night, go in to one garden, tek a dwarf out, and in the end there was a dwarf, a sundial, a bridge, a dwarf fishing, all in this one garden, and there's a big sundial up the road. He got one end of it, I got the other, and carried it all the way and put it in (…)

Outside school visits are a nightmare for staff. For instance, the museum trip. The back seats of the coach are left ominously empty for "the lads" as they arrive late. There is soon a pall of blue smoke at the back of the coach though no red ends are ever visible. When the coach is returned the manager finds all the back seats disfigured with names and doodlings in indelible ink. The head sends the culprits to the garage the next day to clean the coach "for the sake of the reputation of the school."

In the museum "the lads" are a plague of locusts feeding off and blackening out pomp and dignity. In a mock-up Victorian chemist's shop with the clear and prominent injunction "Please do not touch," "the lads" are handling, pushing, pulling, trying, testing and mauling everything in sight. Handfuls of old fashioned cough sweets are removed from the tall jars on the counter, and the high-backed chairs are sat upon and balanced back on their legs "to see how strong they are."

A model village is surrounded and obscured by fifteen backs from a now and for once attentive attendant. Spanksy says with mock alarm, "Oh, look, a tram's crashed" as he gives it a good flick with his finger, and Joey takes one of the carefully prepared and stationed little men, "I've kidnapped one of the citizens."

They get out into the street for a smoke once they can dodge the teacher. Joey is dissecting his little man "to see what's inside" and Spanksy is worrying in case the cough sweets have killed him. They all gather around and point to the sky, "There it is, just above the building," or stare fixedly at the floor, and crack up into laughter when a little

crowd gathers. They stop outside a TV shop, and stare at the woman dressing the window, "Let's all stare at that lady and embarrass her." They succeed and leave. Finally those with some money detach themselves from the rest and go into the pub for a drink where they talk in overloud voices about school, and snigger a bit uncertainly when someone looks at them. When they get back on the coach, late again, the back seats still empty, they are half "grassing each other up" to the young teacher: "There's something wrong with Spanksy, sir, his breath smells." "Eddie's mouth's on fire sir, would you put it out."

Next day, back in school, they are called to the headmaster's study because the coach firm has just rung up, but outside the headmaster's door they cannot decide which offence they are going to "catch it for this time": "Perhaps it's the cough sweets," "Perhaps it's the singing on the coach," "Perhaps it's the boozing," "Perhaps it's for setting fire to the grass in the park," "Perhaps it's for telling the parky to fuck off," "Perhaps it's what we did to the village." They were surprised and relieved to find it was the ink on the seats. Whenever one of "the lads" is called to see the head, his first problem is to mentally list the many things he might be interrogated about, and his second problem to construct a likely tale for all of them. When the formal and the informal intersect, the guilt and confusion in his mind is much greater than the sharper sense of culpability in the head's mind. There is often real surprise at the trivial and marginal nature of the misdemeanour that has "caused all the fuss"— especially in view of the hidden country which could have been uncovered.

Of course "the lads" do not always look to external stimulants or victims for the "laff." Interaction and conversation in the group frequently take the form of "pisstaking." They are very physical and rough with each other, with kicks, punches, karate blows, arm-twisting, kicking, pushing and tripping going on for long periods and directed against particular individuals often almost to the point of tears. The ribbing or "pisstaking" is similarly rough and often directed at the same individuals for the same things. Often this is someone's imagined stupidity. This is ironic in view of "the lads" general rejection of school work, and shows a ghost of conventional values which they would be quick to deny. Though "the lads" usually resist conventional ways of showing their abilities, certainly the ablest like to be thought of as "quick." Certain cultural values, like fast talking and humour, do anyway register in some academic subjects. Joey, for instance, walks a very careful tightrope in English between "laffing" with "the lads" and doing the occasional "brilliant" essay. In certain respects obvious stupidity is penalised more heavily amongst "the lads" than by staff, who "expected nothing better." Very often the topic for the "pisstake" is sexual, though it can be anything—the more personal, sharper and apposite the better. The soul of wit for them is disparaging relevance: the persistent searching out of weakness. It takes some skill and cultural know-how to mount such attacks, and more to resist them:

[A group of "lads" during break-time]

> EDDIE: X gets his missus to hold his prick, while he has a piss. [Laughter]
> WILL: Ask him who wipes his arse. [Laughter]
> SPIKE: The dirty bastard...I bet he changes her fucking rags for her.
> SPANKSY: With his teeth! [More laughter]

[X arrives]

> SPANKSY: Did you have a piss dinnertime?
> BILL: Or a shit?
> SPANKSY: You disgusting little boy...I couldn't do that.
> BILL: Hold on a minute, I want you to hold my cock while I have a piss. [Laughter]

> X: Why am I ...
> WILL (INTERRUPTING):   He don't even know.
> BILL: Does your missus hold your cock for you when you go for a piss?
> X: Who does? [Laughter and interruptions]
> —   You do.
> X: Who?
> —   You.
> X: When?
> SPIKE: You did, you told Joey, Joey told me.

Plans are continually made to play jokes on individuals who are not there: "Let's send him to Coventry when he comes," "Let's laugh at everything he says." "Let's pretend we can't understand and say, 'How do you mean' all the time." Particular individuals can get a reputation and attract constant ribbing for being "dirty," or "as thick as two short planks," or even for always wearing the "same tatty jacket." The language used in the group, especially in the context of derision and the "pisstake," is much rougher than that used by the "ear'oles," full of spat-out swearwords, vigorous use of local dialect and special argot. Talking, at least on their own patch and in their own way, comes very naturally to "the lads":

[In a group discussion on skiving]

> JOEY: (...) You'm always looking out on somebody [when skiving] and you've always got something to talk about...something.
> PW: So what stops you being bored?
> JOEY: Talking, we could talk forever, when we get together, it's talk, talk, talk.

Boredom and Excitement

> PW: What's the opposite of boredom?
> JOEY: Excitement.
> PW: But what's excitement?

JOEY: Defying the law, breaking the law like, drinking like.

SPIKE: Thieving.

SPANKSY: Goin' down the streets.

JOEY: Vandalising (…) that's the opposite of boredom—excitement, defying the law and when you're down The Plough, and you talk to the gaffer, standing by the gaffer, buying drinks and that, knowing that you're 14 and 15 and you're supposed to be 18.

The "laff," talking and marauding misbehaviour are fairly effective but not wholly so in defeating boredom—a boredom increased by their very success at "playing the system."

The particular excitement and kudos of belonging to "the lads," comes from more antisocial practices than these. It is these more extreme activities which mark them off most completely, both from the "ear'oles," and from the school. There is a positive joy in fighting, in causing fights through intimidation, in talking about fighting and about the tactics of the whole fight situation. Many important cultural values are expressed through fighting. Masculine hubris, dramatic display, the solidarity of the group, the importance of quick, clear and not over-moral thought, comes out time and again. Attitudes to "ear'oles" are also expressed clearly and with a surprising degree of precision through physical aggression. Violence and the judgement of violence is the most basic axis of "the lads" ascendance over the conformists, almost in the way that knowledge is for teachers.

In violence there is the fullest if unspecified commitment to a blind or distorted form of revolt. It breaks the conventional tyranny of "the rule." It opposes it with machismo. It is the ultimate way of breaking a flow of meanings which are unsatisfactory, imposed from above, or limited by circumstances. It is one way to make the mundane suddenly *matter*. The usual assumption of the flow of the self from the past to the future is stopped: the dialectic of time is broken. Fights, as accidents and other crises, strand you painfully in "the now." Boredom and petty detail disappear. It really does matter how the next seconds pass. And once experienced, the fear of the fight and the ensuing high as the self safely resumes its journey are addictive. They become permanent possibilities for the alleviation of boredom, and pervasive elements of a masculine style and presence.

JOEY: There's no chivalry or nothing, none of this cobblers you know, it's just…if you'm gonna fight, it's savage fighting anyway, so you might as well go all the way and win it completely by having someone else help ya or by winning by the dirtiest methods you can think of, like poking his eyes out or biting his ear and things like this.

(…)

PW: What do you think, are there kids in the school here that just wouldn't fight?

SPIKE: It gets you mad, like, if you hit somebody and they won't hit you back.

PW: Why?

EDDIE: I hate kids like that.

SPANKSY: Yeah, "I'm not going to hit you, you'm me friend."

PW: Well, what do you think of that attitude?

JOEY: It's all accordin' what you got against him, if it's just a trivial thing, like he give you a kick and he wouldn't fight you when it come to a head, but if he's…really something mean towards you, like, whether he fights back or not, you still pail him.

PW: What do you feel when you're fighting?

JOEY: (…) it's exhilarating, it's like being scared…it's the feeling you get afterwards…I know what I feel when I'm fighting…it's that I've got to kill him, do your utmost best to kill him.

PW: Do you actually feel frightened when you're fighting though?

JOEY: Yeah, I shake before I start fighting, I'm really scared, but once you're actually in there, then you start to co-ordinate your thoughts like, it gets better and better and then, if you'm good enough, you beat the geezer. You get him down on the floor and just jump all over his head.

It should be noted that despite its destructiveness, anti-social nature and apparent irrationality violence is not completely random, or in any sense the absolute overthrow of social order. Even when directed at outside groups (and thereby, of course, helping to define an "in-group") one of the most-important aspects of violence is precisely its social meaning within "the lads'" own culture. It marks the last move in, and final validation of, the informal status system. It regulates a kind of "honour"—displaced, distorted or whatever. The fight is the moment when you are fully tested in the alternative culture. It is disastrous for your informal standing and masculine reputation if you refuse to fight, or perform very amateurishly. Though one of "the lads" is not necessarily expected to pick fights—it is the "hard knock" who does this, a respected though often not much liked figure unlikely to be much of a "laff"—he is certainly expected to fight when insulted or intimidated to be able to "look after himself," to be "no slouch," to stop people "pushing him about."

Amongst the leaders and the most influential—not usually the "hard knocks"—it is the capacity to fight which settles the final pecking order. It is the not often tested ability to fight which valorises status based usually and interestingly on other grounds: masculine presence, being from a "famous" family, being funny, being good at "blagging," extensiveness of informal contacts.

Violence is recognised, however, as a dangerous and unpredictable final adjudication which must not be allowed to get out of hand between peers. Verbal or symbolic violence is to be preferred, and if a real fight becomes unavoidable the normal social controls and settled system of status

and reputation is to be restored as soon as possible.

PW: (…) When was the last fight you had Joey?
JOEY: Two weeks ago…about a week ago, on Monday night, this silly rumour got around. It was daft actually, it shouldn've got around to this geezer that I was going to bash him like and it hadn't come from me, so him not wanting to back down from it, put the word out he was going to have me, we had a fight and we was stopped. I marked him up. He give me a bit of a fat lip, and he dropped the nut on me nose, hurt me nose, hurt me nose here. But I gouged his eye out with my thumb, split his head open, then after they pulled us off, I grabbed him and took him in the corner and I told him there that he knows I wasn't scared of him and that I know I wasn't scared of him, he warn't scared of me, that's an end of it. It was a sort of an…uh…he was from a family, a big family like us, they're nutters, they're fighters the Jones', and…uh…didn't want to start anything between 'em, so I just grabbed him and told him what the strength is like.

In a more general way the ambience of violence with its connotations of masculinity spreads through the whole culture. The physicality of all interactions, the mock pushing and fighting, the showing off in front of girls, the demonstrations of superiority and put-downs of the conformists, all borrow from the grammar of the real fight situation. It is difficult to simulate this style unless one has experienced real violence. The theme of fighting frequently surfaces in official school work—especially now in the era of progressivism and relevance. One of Bill's English essays starts, "We couldn't go Paki bashing with only four," and goes through "I saw his foot sink into his groin" and "kicking the bloke's head in," to "it all went dark" (when the author himself "gets done in"). In the RSLA film option where pupils can make their own short films "the lads" always make stories about bank robberies, muggings and violent chases. Joey gets more worked up than at any time in class during the whole year when he is directing a fight sequence and Spanksy will not challenge his assailant realistically, "Call him out properly, call him out properly, you'd say, 'I'll have you, you fucking bastard' not 'Right, let's fight.'" Later on he is disgusted when Eddie dives on top of somebody to finish a fight. "You wouldn't do that, you'd just kick him, save you getting your clothes dirty."

The perennial themes of symbolic and physical violence, rough presence, and the pressure of a certain kind of masculinity expand and are more clearly expressed amongst "the lads" at night on the street, and particularly at the commercial dance. Even though they are relatively expensive and not so very different from what is supplied at a tenth of the cost at the Youth Club, commercial dances are the preferred leisure pursuit of "the lads." This is basically because there is an edge of danger and competition in the atmosphere and social relations not present at the Youth Club. Commercial provision can be criticised at many levels, not least because of its expense and instrumentalism towards those it caters for. However, it at least responds to its customers' desires, as they are felt, without putting a moral constraint on the way they are expressed. In a sense "the lads" do have a kind of freedom at the commercial dance. Its alienated and exploited form at least leaves them free from the claustrophobia and constriction of irrelevant or oppressive moral imperatives in official leisure organisations. It is possible for indigenous cultural forms to surface and interact without direction from above:

> SPIKE: If there's a bar there, at a dance, it's good.

WILL: Yeah, I think if there's a bar there you have to be more…watch what you're doing, not prat about so much, because some people what's got a bit of ale inside 'em (…) they see like a lot of birds there, and they think, "I'll do a bit of showin' off," and they'll go walkin' round, like hard knocks you know (…) They just pick a fight anywhere.

SPIKE: Billy Everett, kids like 'im, he'll go around somebody'll look at 'im and he'll fucking belt 'im one (…)

PW: How do you start a fight, look at somebody?

SPIKE: No, somebody looks at you.

WILL: That's it, just walk around so somebody would look at you.

SPIKE: Or if you walk past somebody, you deliberately bump into 'em and you swear blind that they nudged you.

PW: So if you're at a dance and you want to avoid a fight, you have to look at your feet all the time do you?

— No.

— Not really.

SPIKE: (…) Look at 'em, and fucking back away.

FUZZ: If you know a lot of people there, you're talkin' to them, you feel safer as well, if you know a lot of people.

WILL: It's OK if you know a lot of people there.

SPIKE: If you go to a dance where you don't know anybody it's rough.

(…)

SPIKE: The atmosphere ain't there [in the school youth wing] there ain't a bar for one. You drink fuckin' fizzy pop, and eat Mars bars all night.

WILL: I think…this club might, if they'd got some new kids we'd never seen before.

SPIKE: It'd be good then.

WILL: It'd be good then, 'cos there'd be some atmosphere and you know, you'd be lookin' at each other, then you'd go back and say, "I don't like that prat, look at the way he's lookin' at us." And there might be something goin' on outside

after...but now you're always gettin'
Jules [the youth leader] walkin' out or
summat, you know.

Evening and weekend activities hold all
the divisions of the school plus others—
sometimes more shadowy, especially if they
involve class differences—further projected
onto clothes, music and physical style. Being
a "lad" in school is also associated with
"being out" at night and developing a social
understanding not only of the school but
also of the neighbourhood, town and streets:

WILL: Classin' it like the modern kids,
right, the kids who dress modern, right.
There's the hard knocks, then there are
those who are quiet (...) but can look
after theirselves, like, dress modern and
hang about with the hard knocks or
summat. Then there's the money givers,
kids who you can blag money off, who'll
buy friendship. Then you get into the
class of the poufs, the nancies (...)

PW: Pouf doesn't mean queer.

WILL: No, it means like ear'oles,
do-gooders, hear no evil, see no evil
(...) I think the hard knocks and that
like reggae, d'you know what I mean,
reggae and soul, they don't listen to
this freaky stuff, then the poufs, the
nancies, they like...the Osmonds,
y'know, Gary Glitter.

PW: (...) weirdos, freaks, hippy types (...)
how do they fit into that, Will?

WILL: Yeah, well, I dunno (...) you find a
lot of these freaks are brainy an'all.

SPIKE: T'aint our scene like (...)

FUZZ: I mean take for instance you go
down The Plough when the disco's on
(...) when there's all the heavy music,
and you see the kids with their hair
long, scruffy clothes (...) jeans and
everything, and you go down on a soul
night, and you see kids with baggy
trousers, you know, spread collar shirts,
you can tell the difference.

(...)

WILL: I think you can feel out of it as
well, 'cos I've been up the Junction,

up town, it's a heavy place, got all the
drugs and everything, and everybody
was dressed really weirdo (...) and I felt
I was out, well, I felt, well, out of it,
you know what I mean, I felt smarter
than the rest, as though I was going to
a wedding, or I was at a wedding, and
they was working on a farm.

It is the wider scope, extra freedom, and
greater opportunities for excitement which
make the evening infinitely preferable to
the day (in school). In some respects the
school is a blank between opportunities for
excitement on the street or at a dance with
your mates, or trying to "make it" with a girl.
In the diaries kept by "the lads," meant to
record "the main things that happen in your
day," only "went to school" (or in Will's case
gigantic brackets) record school, whilst half
a side details events after school, including
the all important "Got home, got changed,
went out." However, although school may
be bracketed out of many of these kids'
lives, this "invisibility" should not lead us
to believe that school is unimportant in the
form of what they do experience....

The pressure to go out at night, to go to a
commercial dance rather than a youth club,
to go to pubs rather than stop in, to buy
modern clothes, smoke, and take girls out—
all these things which were felt to constitute
"what life is really about"—put enormous
financial pressure on "the lads." Shortage of
cash is the single biggest pressure, perhaps
at any rate after school, in their life:

[In an individual discussion]

JOEY: (...) after all, you can't live without
bread, let's face it, fucking money is
the spice of life, money is life. Without
money, you'd fucking die. I mean there's
nothing fucking round here to eat, you
couldn't fucking eat trees, you couldn't
eat bark

All possible contacts in the family and
amongst friends and casual acquaintances

are exploited and the neighbourhood scoured for jobs in small businesses, shops, on milk rounds, as cleaners, key cutters, ice-cream salesmen, and as stackers in supermarkets. Sometimes more than one job is held. Over ten hours work a week is not uncommon. From the fourth form onwards, Spike thinks his work at a linen wholesaler's is more important than school. He gladly takes days and weeks off school to work. He is proud of the money he earns and spends: he even contributes to his parents' gas bill when they've had "a bad week." Joey works with his brother as a painter and decorator during the summer. He regards that as "real" work, and school as some kind of enforced holiday. There is no doubt that this ability to "make out" in the "real world," to handle sometimes quite large cash flows (Spike regularly earns over twenty pounds a week, though the average for the others is something under five pounds) and to deal with adults nearly on their own terms strengthens "the lads" self-confidence and their feeling, at this point anyway, that they "know better" than the school.

There is even a felt sense of superiority to the teachers. They do not know "the way of the world," because they have been in schools or colleges all their lives—"What do they know, telling us…?"…The emerging school culture is both strengthened and directly fed material from what "the lads" take to be the only truly worldliwise source: the working class world of work.

This contact with the world of work, however, is not made for the purposes of cultural edification. It is made within the specific nexus of the need for cash, and responded to and exploited within that nexus. The very manner of approaching the world of work at this stage reproduces one of its characteristic features—the reign of cash. The near universal practice of "fiddling" and "doing foreigners," for instance, comes to "the lads" not as a neutral heritage but as a felt necessity: they need the cash. As Spanksy says, "If you

go out even with just enough money in your pocket for a pint like, you feel different," and it is only the part-time job, and particularly its "fiddles," which offers the extra variable capacity in their world to supply this free cash. This particular form of early exposure to work helps to set the parameters for their later understanding of labour and reward, authority and its balances, and for a particular kind of contained resentment towards those who manage and direct them:

[In a group discussion on part-time work]

SPIKE: (…) it was about eight o'clock in the morning, this was, he's [a butcher] got a telephone, he's got a big bag of ten bobs, and he'd left the two strings over the telephone so that if I touched it, the strings'd come, you know. I opened the bag, got a handful of ten bobs out, zipped it up and just left it. He says, "You've touched this fucking bag, the strings was over the telephone." Well I couldn't say much (…) so he told me to fuck off (…)

WILL: (…) like there was an outside toilet [at a greengrocers where he used to work] but it was all blocked with stinking vegetables and all this, and I used to put 'em [cauliflowers] on top of the cistern, you know (…) he says, I seen 'im counting 'em, and he says, "Uh…there's one missing here." I said "I dunno" (…) He says, "There's one missing here." I says, "There ain't." He says, "There is." I says, "I must have put it in that one, 'ere' have one of 'em," and he dayn't count them, so I was alright. I thought he was laying a trap for me, like, I think it was a Friday night when that happened. The next day (…) I had to have a big fire up the back to burn all the rubbish and that, and I set fire to everything like and all the canal bank. It was like the railway bank like, round the back, it was all dry, bone dry, so I got this cardboard, this piece of cardboard box like that, and I threw it over there and set all the bank on fire to get him back like. And I went walking in, I says, "Is the bank s'posed to be on fire?" [Laughter] He went mad he did. He says, "Was it you?" I says, "No, it must have been the butcher, 'cos they was having a fire." And the fire engines come and everything.

There is some scope for getting money by saving it from dinner money, as well as some possibility for limited extortion from "ear'oles" and younger boys—though "blagging off" first and second formers is not highly regarded. Often the last—and sometimes earlier—resort for getting "money in your pocket" is stealing. Shortage of cash should not be underestimated as the compelling material base for theft. In a very typical articulation of mixed motives, however, "thieving" is also a source of excitement rather like fighting. It puts you at risk, and breaks up the parochialism of the self. "The rule," the daily domination of trivia and the entrapment of the formal are broken for a time. In some way a successful theft challenges and beats authority. A strange sort of freedom—even though it is only a private knowledge—comes from defying the conventions and being rewarded for it. If you are "copped," particular skills in "blagging your way out of it" can be brought to bear, and renewed excitement and satisfaction is obtained if you "get away with it." Sometimes, of course, you do not "get away with it." Two of the Hammertown lads are put on probation for stealing car radios during the research. This is disastrous. Parents are brought into it, official reports written up, and all kinds of unspecified worries about the procedures of the court and the interminable proceedings of bureaucracy turn the original excitement to sickness. This is a moment, again, where the formal wins a decisive and irrevocable victory over the informal. The informal meanings do not survive a direct confrontation. Still, given the near universality of theft amongst "the lads," there are very few convictions for theft. There are many more close scrapes and the dread of "being done" adds extra excitement and an enhanced feeling of sharpness and adroitness when you do "get away with it":

[In a group discussion]

BILL: It's just hopeless round here, there's nothing to do. When you've got money, you know, you can go to a pub and have a drink, but, you know, when you ain't got money, you've either got to stop in or just walk round the streets and none of them are any good really. So you walk around and have a laff.

JOEY: It ain't only that it's enjoyable, it's that it's there and you think you can get away with it...you never think of the risks. You just do it. If there's an opportunity, if the door's open to the warehouse, you'm in there, seeing what you can thieve and then, when you come out like, if you don't get caught immediately, when you come out you'm really happy like.

BILL: 'Cos you've showed the others you can do it, that's one reason.

JOEY: 'Cos you're defying the law again. The law's a big tough authority like and we're just little individuals yet we're getting away with it like.

(...)

FUZZ: (...) we all went up the copper station [for stealing from a sport-shop], he had all our parents in first. Then he had us lot in with our parents and he says, this copper, we was all standing up straight, you know, looks round, he says, "You! How much pocket money do you get?" he says, "would you like someone to pinch that." He says "NO." He says, "Have any of you got anything to say?" "Yes, cunt, let me go" [under his breath]. "You should say, 'Sorry,'" he said, "If anything hadn't've been returned, if a dart had been missing, you'd 'ave 'ad it." Benny Bones had got two air rifles at his house, Steve had got a catapult and a knife, and I'd got two knives at home, and he said, "If anything'd been missing!"

(...)

JOEY: I'd been doing it all night [stealing from handbags], and I was getting drunk and spending the money, and instead of sitting there, doin' it properly, putting your hand down the back of the seat, I lifted the seat up and was kneeling down underneath, getting it out that way, and this bird comes back and says, "What are you doing under there?" I says, "Oh, I just dropped two bob," and then her went on about it, so I just run off like, over the other side of the dance. Her went and told the coppers, and the police sat outside by the bogs. When I went out they just got me into this little cleaning room, and they got me in there and had all me money out. And she'd had four pound pinched, it was a lie really 'cos I'd only pinched three pound, and I'd spent nearly half of it, had a pound on me. If I'd've had four quid on me like, even if it hadn't been hers, I think they'd've done me. I didn't have enough money on me, so they couldn't do me.

Where the target is the school there is a particular heightening of excitement, of challenge to authority, of verve in taking well-calculated risks—and making money as well. Besides being a direct insult to staff, it also puts you absolutely beyond the "ear'oles." They have neither the need for the extra cash, nor the imagination to overcome conventional morality, nor the quickness and smartness to carry through the deed. The school break-in sums up many crucial themes: opposition, excitement, exclusivity, and the drive for cash:

X: I couldn't see how we was going to get copped [when they broke into the school some time previously]. If, you know, I could see how them others [the school had recently been broken

into] was going to get copped, he was, just bust a door down and walked in. There was footmarks all over the place, smashed a window and shit all over the place, and pulling books off....

Y: I mean we had gloves on and before we left his house we even emptied our pockets out to make sure there was nothing identifying. I left all my stuff at his house and he did, we just went then and I had a brown polo neck on, me jeans, gloves, you know, and he had all black things on.

X: All black, polish on my face. [Laughter]

Y: No. We was going to. Weren't we? We got the polish at your house, we was going to, but we thought, no.

PW: Were you nervous when you were doing it?

Y: Yeah.

X: Oh ar. Like this you know [trembling]. 'Cos it's...uh...I've always you know, I've pinched out of people's pockets you know, I've seen two bobs lying about and I've gone, but I've never done anything like that before. I enjoyed it!

Y: And I did, really enjoyed it!

X: And after you know coming down the road we were just in a fit, weren't we? We was that, you know, it was that closely worked out.

Y: And we spent it all up the bleeding Fountain, day'nt we. Getting pissed down the Old Boat.

X: Oh ar...I saved ten bob for the ice rink, remember?

— Yeah.

PW: Why did you want to break into the school rather than anything else?

Y: Got no fucking money (...)

X: We knew the school well and if you try and break in anything else like houses and that, you know, you're not sure if there's anybody in, it's a bit risky, you know what I mean, but the school you know there's nobody sleeping here, you know there's almost no way you can get copped.

Sexism

Two other groups against whom "the lads" exclusivity is defined, and through which their own sense of superiority is enacted, are girls and ethnic minority groups.

Their most nuanced and complex attitudes are reserved for the opposite sex. There is a traditional conflict in their view of women: they are both sexual objects and domestic comforters. In essence this means that whilst women must be sexually attractive, they cannot be sexually experienced.

Certainly desire is clear on the part of "the lads." Lascivious tales of conquest or jokes turning on the passivity of women or on the particular sexual nature of men are regular topics of conversation. Always it is their *own* experience, and not that of the girl or of their shared relationship, which is the focus of the stories. The girls are afforded no particular identity save that of their sexual attraction:

x: I was at this party snogging this bird, and I was rubbing her up and suddenly I felt a hand on my prick, racking me off…I thought, "Fucking hell, we're in here," and tried to put my hand down her knickers, but she stopped me…I thought, "That's funny, her's racking me off but won't let me get down her knickers." Anyway we was walking home and Joe said to me, "How did you get on with that bird, was she racking you off?" I said, "Yeah, how do you know?" He said, "It warn't her, it was me behind you, putting my hand up between your legs!" [Laughter]

y: I can never be bothered [to use contraceptives], I think I must be infertile, the number of times I've fetched inside. I can't be bothered you know…I don't want to pull it out, though sometimes I fetch before. You know, you're struggling with her, fighting, to do it, and you've got her knickers down, and you're just getting it out [giving a demonstration, fumbling at flies with feet apart] and pow! [freezes demonstration] you fetch all over the place, that' terrible that is.

Although they are its object, frank and explicit sexuality is actually denied to women. There is a complex of emotion here. On the one hand, insofar as she is a sex object, a commodity, she is actually diminished by sex; she is literally worthless; she has been romantically and materially partly consumed. To show relish for this diminution is seen as self-destructive. On the other hand, in a half recognition of the human sexuality they have suppressed, there is a fear that once a girl is sexually experienced and has known joy from sex at all, the floodgates of her desire will be opened and she will be completely promiscuous.

y: After you've been with one like, after you've done it like, well they're scrubbers afterwards, they'll go with anyone. I think it's that once they've had it, they want it all the time, no matter who it's with.

Certainly reputations for "easiness"—deserved or not—spread very quickly. "The lads" are after the "easy lay" at dances, though they think twice about being seen to "go out" with them.

The "girlfriend" is a very different category from an "easy lay." She represents the human value that is squandered by promiscuity. She is the loyal domestic partner. She cannot be held to be sexually experienced—or at least not with others. Circulated stories about the sexual adventures of "the missus" are a first-rate challenge to masculinity and pride. They have to be answered in the masculine mode:

[In an individual discussion]

x: He keeps saying things, he went out with me missus before like, and he keeps saying things what I don't like, and y'know like, it gets around…he won't learn his fucking lesson, he

does summat, he sez summat, right,
I bash him for it, he won't hit me back,
he runs off like a little wanker, then he
sez something else (…) he ain't been to
school since Friday (…) when I fuckin'
cop him I'm gonna kill 'im, if I get 'im
on the floor he's fucking dead.

Courtship is a serious affair. The common prolepsis of calling girlfriends "the missus" is no accident amongst "the lads." A whole new range of meanings and connotations come into play during serious courting. Their referent is the home: dependability and domesticity—the opposite of the sexy bird on the scene. If the initial attraction is based on sex, the final settlement is based on a strange denial of sex—a denial principally, of course, of the girl's sexuality for others, but also of sexuality as the dominant feature of their own relationship. Possible promiscuity is held firmly in check by domestic glue:

[In an individual interview]

SPIKE: (…) I've got the right bird,
I've been goin' with her for eighteen
months now. Her's as good as gold.
She wouldn't look at another chap.
She's fucking done well, she's clean.
She loves doing fucking housework.
Trousers I brought yesterday. I took 'em
up last night, and her turned 'em up
for me (…) She's as good as gold and
I wanna get married as soon as I can.

The model for the girlfriend is, of course, the mother and she is fundamentally a model of limitation. Though there is a great deal of affection for "mum," she is definitely accorded an inferior role: "She's a bit thick, like, never knows what I'm on about," "She don't understand this sort of stuff, just me dad." And within the home there is a clear sense that men have a right to be waited on by the mother.

[In an individual interview]

SPANKSY: (…) it shouldn't be done, you
shouldn't need to help yer mother

in the house. You should put your shoes away tidy and hang your coat up, admittedly, but, you know, you shouldn't vacuum and polish and do the beds for her and (…) her housekeeping and that.

The resolution amongst working class girls of the contradiction between being sexually desirable but not sexually experienced leads to behavior which strengthens "the lads" sense of superiority. This resolution takes the form of romanticism readily fed by teenage magazines. It turns upon the "crush," and sublimation of sexual feeling into talk, rumours and message-sending within the protective circle of the informal female group.[5] This is not to say that they never have sex—clearly a good proportion must do—but that the dominant social form of their relationship with boys is to be sexy but in a girlish, latter day courtly love mould which falls short of actual sexual proposition. The clear sexual stimulus which in the first place attracts the boy can thus be reconverted into the respectable values of the home and monogamous submission. If ever the paranoiac thought strikes the boy that, having got the "come on" himself, why shouldn't others, he can be calmed with the thought, "she's not like that, she's soft inside." In this way, still, romanticism brokes the sexual within a patriarchal society. It allows sexual display without sexual promise, being sexy but not sexual.

What "the lads" see of the romantic behavior they have partly conditioned in the girls, however, is a simple sheepishness, weakness and a silly indirectness in social relationships: "saft wenches giggling all the time." Since the girls have abandoned the assertive and the sexual, they leave that ground open to the boys. It is they who take on the drama and initiative, the machismo, of a sexual drive. They have no reservations about making their intentions clear, or of enjoying a form of their sexuality. However, they take it as an aspect of their inherent superiority that they can be frank and direct and unmystified about their desires. The contortions and strange rituals of the girls are seen as part of their girlishness, of their inherent weakness and confusion. Their romanticism is tolerated with a knowing masculinity, which privately feels it knows much more about the world. This sense of masculine pride spreads over into the expressive confidence of the rest of "the lads" culture. It adds a zest to their language, physical and boisterous relations with each other, humiliation of "ear'oles," and even to a particular display style of violence.

The combination of these various factors gives a special tone to interaction between the sexes. "The lads" usually take the initiative in conversation and are the ones who make suggestive comments. The girls respond with giggles and talk amongst themselves. Where girls do make comments they are of the serious, caring or human kind. It is left to "the lads" to make the jokes, the hard comments, the abrasive summations and to create a spectacle to be appreciated by the girls. The girls are clearly dominated, but they collude in their own domination:

[A mixed group talking "by the sheds" at dinner time]

JOAN: We'm all gonna start crying this afternoon, it's the last.
BILL: You've only got two weeks left ain't yer, we'm gonna laugh when we leave (…)
JOAN: I like your jumper.
BILL: You can come inside if yer like!
WILL: Ain't it terrible when you see these old women with bandages round their ankles.
MARY: I ain't got 'em, and I ain't fat.
WILL: I dayn't say you had, I said it was terrible.
BILL: I'm gonna nick Mary's fags and smoke 'em all. [Giggles]
(…)
EDDIE: It's time you lot were back in school, go on. [Giggles and whispering

about someone who "fancies" Eddie.] These wenches don't half talk about you behind your back, me ears are burning. [Loud burp from one of "the lads"]
MAGGIE: Oh, you pig, shut up.
BILL: [Handing cigarettes around] He'are.
MAGGIE: No thanks, I'll have a big one.
BILL: She likes big ones! He's got a big one, ask him, he'll let you have a look.
THE REST: [Singing] He's got a big one, he's got a big one…[Bill takes his coat off]
EDDIE: Have it off.
BILL: [To Mary] Have you ever had it off?
WILL: I've had it off twice today already [Laughter] Do you like having it off? [To Maggie]
MAGGIE: You cheeky sod.
WILL: I mean your coat.

Interestingly, this kind of banter can be used towards the mother but never the father. It takes on a more kindly tone, responding to the domestic rather than the sexual range, but the initiative, force and the tone remain the same:

[In a group discussion of family]

WILL: (…) I just play her up like, I'll be lying there, after I'd just woke up or summat. Her won't be sayin' a thing, and I'll say, "Shurrup," like, "Shurrup, stop talking" (…) Her says to me once, "I think you're mad as a coot," and like once I lit the oven, a gas oven we got. Her was in the kitchen, and I pulled down the oven door like you know to make sure the gas wasn't on, her come in and sez, "What the bloody hell you doin'," I says, "I'm lookin' for me fags." [Laughter] (…) well, I'll just be lying there and say, I've got the radio on, when a good record comes on I'll start jumping about and goin' about makin' mad noises.
PW: What does your mum think?
WILL: Her just sits there, I wouldn't do it in front of our dad.

PW: Why not?

WILL: He'd just, he wouldn't see
no...really, he'd think there was
summat wrong, you know, and uh,
when I ain't seen our mum like, I'll go
home and say, "Give me a kiss, give me
a kiss!"...and her pushes me off, you
know, sayin' "Get off, you daft idiot" (...)
The thing that gets her really mad, say,
you go in to hang your coat up, and I'll
push her into the corner like, and she'll
be trying to get out, and I'll move there,
and she'll go that way, and we'll be like
that [dodging sideways] for about two
minutes and she'll go bloody mad.

Racism

Three distinct groups—Caucasians, Asians
and West Indians—are clearly visible in
most school settings. Though individual
contacts are made, especially in the youth
wing, the ethnic groups are clearly separated by the fourth year. Divisions are, if
anything, more obvious in informal settings. For a period the head of upper school
allows fifth years to use form rooms for
"friendship groups" during break time.
This is yet another, this time defensive and
accommodating, variant of the continuous
if subtle struggle to contain opposition. Its
results, however, demonstrate for us what
are the clear informal patterns of racial culture beneath and sometimes obscured by
the official structures of the school.

> HEAD OF UPPER SCHOOL: We have got
> the Martins (Bill), Croft (Joey), Rustin,
> Roberts (Will), Peterson (Eddie),
> Jeffs (Fuzz) and Barnes (Spike) in
> the European room. Buckner, Grant,
> Samuels, Spence in the West Indian
> room and Singh, Rajit and co in the
> Asiatic room. So much for integration!
> There are three distinct rooms. You
> go into the white room and you will
> probably sit down and have a cup of tea
> made. You go into the Indian room and

they are all playing cards and they are
jabbering to each other, and then you
go into the West Indian room and they
are all dancing to records. In the West
Indian room they are sort of stamping
around, twisting.

From the point of view of "the lads" the
separation is certainly experienced as rejection of others. There is frequent verbal, if
not actual, violence shown to "the fuckin'
wogs," or the "bastard pakis." The mere fact
of different colour can be enough to justify
an attack or intimidation. A clear demarca-
tion between groups and a derogatory view
of other racial types is simply assumed as
the basis for this and other action: it is a
daily form of knowledge in use.

> SPANKSY: We had a go at the Jamaicans,
> 'cos you know, we outnumbered
> them. We dayn't want to fight them
> when they was all together. We
> outnumbered them.
> SPIKE: They was all there though.
> SPANKSY: They was all there, but half of
> them walked off dayn't they, there was
> only a couple left. About four of us got
> this one.
> JOEY: Not one of us was marked...that
> was really super.

Racial identity for "the lads" supplants
individual identity so that stories to friends
concern not "this kid," but "this wog." At
Hammertown Boys there is an increasing
and worrying tension between the ethnic
groups, particularly the Caucasians and the
Asians, which sometimes flares up into violence. The deputy head then gets everyone
into the hall and lectures them, but this
only suppresses the immediate expression
of dislike:

[In a group discussion on recent distur-
bances at the school]

> JOEY: He [the deputy in the hall after an
> incident] even started talking about the

Israeli war at one stage, "This is how war starts. . . . Pack it in."

PW: (...) was he convincing you a bit?

JOEY: He was just talking, we were just listening thinking, "Right you black bastard, next time you start, we'll have you"—which we will.

This curiously self-righteous readiness to express and act on dislike is reinforced by what "the lads" take to be a basically collusive attitude of staff—no matter what the public statements. This is perhaps even an unconscious effect and certainly where racism exists amongst staff it is much less virulent than that in the counter-school culture. There is, however, by and large much less sympathy and rapport between (a massively white) staff and ethnic minorities than between staff and whites. In an almost automatic cultural reflex minorities are seen as strange and less civilised—not "tea," but "jabbering to each other" and "stamping around." Certainly it is quite explicit that many senior staff associate the mass immigration of the 1960s with the break up of the "order and quietness" of the 1950s and of what is seen more and more retrospectively as their peaceful, successful schools. Both "lads" and staff do share, therefore, a sense in their different ways of resentment for the disconcerting intruder. For racism amongst "the lads" it provides a double support for hostile attitudes. The informal was, for once, backed up by at least the ghost of the formal.

The racism in the counter-school culture is structured by reified though somewhat differentiated stereotypes. Asians come off worst and are often the target for petty intimidation, small pestering attacks, and the physical and symbolic jabbing at weak or unprotected points in which "the lads" specialise. Asians are seen both as alien, "smelly" and probably "unclean," and as sharing some of the most disliked "ear'ole" characteristics. They are doubly disliked for

the contradictory way in which they seem simultaneously to be both further off, and closer to received English cultural models. They are interlopers who do not know their station and try to take that which is not rightfully theirs but which is anyway disliked and discredited on other grounds.

West Indians come off somewhat better at the hands of "the lads." Although they are identifiably "foreign," sometimes "smelly" and probably "dirty" and all "the rest," they at least fit into the cultural topography a little more consistently. Their lack of conformist achievement is seen as more appropriate to their low status, and aspects of their own oppositional, masculine and aggressive culture chime with that of "the lads." There is some limited interaction, between males at any rate, on the grounds of shared cultural interests in "going out," reputation, dancing, soul, R and B, and reggae. The combination of racial dislike with some shared cultural interests meets, however, with most tension in the area of sexual relations where "the lads" feel direct sexual rivalry and jealousy as well as a general sense of suspicion of male West Indian sexual intentions and practices—ironic, of course, in the light of their own frankly instrumental and exploitative attitudes. "The lads" feel, however, barely consciously and in an inarticulate way, that they are bound, at least in the serious stage of "courting," by some unwritten rules of de-sexualisation and monogamy which are not respected in West Indian culture.

To the elements of an enviable style and dubious treatment of women in the stereotype is added finally a notion of the alleged stupidity of West Indians. "The lads" have their own notions of what constitutes "sharpness" and "nous" and the most common butt outside their own circles of denunciations and jokes turning on its opposite, "thickness," are the West Indians. For the "ear'oles" there is at least a degree of ambiguity about such charges, but "wogs" can be safely and deprecatingly seen as "stupid," "thick as pudding," "bone-headed." This range of prejudice is real and virulent and potentially explosive in the sexual arena but in some important senses more comfortable for "the lads" than the register of prejudice felt for Asians.

NOTES

1. It is now recognised that some teachers retained on school teaching staffs are seriously disturbed and that this is a growing problem. See, for instance, J. Lawrence, "Control experiment," *The Guardian*, 18 March 1975.
2. Spike's letter of apology is carefully pitched to maintain his own dignity as well as to secure his leaving certificate: "I would like you to accept my sincere apologies.... The school *itself* has nothing to resemble 'Colditz' in any way whatsoever.... I realise what I have done, which might I add I find stupid now, *but at the time not so stupid,* so I am now prepared to face the consequence which you see fit" (my italics).
3. A recent piece of research on Dartington, the progressive private school in the West of England, claims that its children did not have a taboo on informing. This is extremely unusual and is explained (in that piece of research) by the way in which informal groups and the anti-school culture are inhibited by the exceptional unity, openness and democratic organisation of the school (reported in *The Guardian*, 1 January 1976).
4. It has been widely claimed that streaming, traditional subject-based curriculum planning, exams and general achievement orientation are likely to be conducive to the emergence of anti-school or semi-delinquent groups amongst the lower forms.

    In Hammertown Boys it was quite clear that oppositional groups had emerged under streaming by the end of the third year. However, after mixed ability grouping was introduced at the beginning of the fourth year, the counter-school groups developed and hardened in exactly the same fashion as may have been expected under streaming. Furthermore, it was by no means only the least able who were involved in the counter-school group. Some of its really central members were highly articulate, clear-sighted, assertive, and able to across a wide range of activities. They had decided that, for them and at that stage, the life of "the lads" offered more than the conventional road. Although continued streaming may have had a reinforcing effect on those of low ability in the "ghetto" form with the orthodox effects we have been led to expect, we should also be aware that de-streaming can lead to a creative social mix which is developmental, not only for the overall social system of the school, but also, and in particular, for its informal, radical and oppositional wing. And those verging towards the anti-school perspective were, if anything, aided by the new forms of mixed ability groupings, topic centred teaching, student centred teaching and the obvious confusion caused by the high number of group changes during the course of the day, compounded in particular by the sheer number of RSLA options open to the pupils—on other counts, of course, a desirable thing. See D. H. Hargreaves, *Social Relations in the Secondary School*, RKP, 1957; M. D. Shipman, *Sociology of the School*, Longman, 1968; and R. King, *School Organisation and Pupil Involvement*, RKP, 1973.
5. The field work in the main case study was focused on boys in a single sex school. There was a "twinned" girls' school next door, however, and "the lads" often chatted with groups of girls in the park at lunchtime. Angela Macrobbie first suggested to me the pivotal role of romanticism in the experience of working class girls.

REFERENCES

Lawrence, J. 1975. "Control experiment." *The Guardian* (18 March).

Hargreaves, D. H. 1957. *Social Relations in a Secondary School*. London: Routledge and Kegan Paul Ltd.

King, R. 1973. *School Organisation and Pupil Involvement*. London: Routledge and Kegan Paul Ltd.

Shipman, M. D. 1968. *Sociology of the School*. London: Longmans.

23

JAY MACLEOD

LEVELED ASPIRATIONS: SOCIAL REPRODUCTION TAKES ITS TOLL

from *Ain't No Makin' It* (1987)

MacLeod spent more than three years studying two groups of youths in a Boston public housing project: the white "Hallway Hangers" and a group of African Americans he calls "the Brothers." MacLeod attempts to understand how school, family, the peer group, race, and the labor market work to shape the diverging aspirations and beliefs about achievement he finds between the two groups.

...That many boys in both groups do not even aspire to middle-class jobs is a powerful indication of how class equality is reproduced in American society. These youths' prospects for socioeconomic advancement are doomed before they even get started; most of the boys do not even get a foothold on the ladder of social mobility. In this chapter, the task before us is to illuminate in as much detail and depth as possible the process of social reproduction as it is lived by the Hallway Hangers and the Brothers.

The regulation of aspirations is perhaps the most significant of all the mechanisms contributing to social reproduction; however, aspirations themselves are largely a function of structural mechanisms that should be considered when possible. Mention already has been made of the effects of tracking and the school's valuation of the cultural capital of the upper classes, both of which influence aspirations but also have independent effects on reproducing class structure. An additional and essential component of social reproduction is the process by which individuals in a stratified social order come to accept their own position and the inequalities of the social order as legitimate.

Whereas force and coercion often have ensured the cohesion of societies and the maintenance of oppressive relationships, ideology is more important in fulfilling this function in contemporary America. In particular, the achievement ideology is a powerful force in the legitimation of inequality and, ultimately, in social reproduction. In short, this ideology maintains that individual merit and achievement are the fair and equitable sources of inequality in American society. If merit is the basis for the distribution of rewards, then members of the lower classes attribute their subordinate position in the social order to personal deficiencies. In this way, inequality is legitimated.[1] ...

In contemporary America, the educational system, by sorting students according to ostensibly meritocratic criteria, plays a crucial role in the legitimation of inequality. Because the school deals in the currency of academic credentials, its role in the reproduction of inequality is obscured. Students believe that they succeed or fail in school on the basis of merit. By internalizing the blame for failure, students lose their self-esteem and then accept their eventual placement in low-status jobs as the natural outcome of their own shortcomings. If individuals are convinced that they are responsible for their low position in society, then criticism of the social order by the subordinate classes is deflected. The process of social reproduction goes on, unscrutinized and unchallenged.

If this legitimation function is working, then members of the lower classes will suffer from low self-esteem, which originally was developed in the school and then carried into later life to reconcile them to their position. In gauging the degree to which lower-class individuals accept the social order and their position in it as legitimate, we must determine whether they attribute their inferior social position to personal inadequacy or to external forces as well.

The Hallway Hangers: Internalizing Probabilities, Rescuing Self-Esteem

According to Bourdieu, the aspirations of the Hallway Hangers should reflect their objective probabilities for upward mobility. Immersed as they are in their social universe at the bottom of the class structure, their subjective hopes should be as modest as their objective chances are slim. Indeed, this is the case. The Hallway Hangers view their prospects for substantial upward mobility as very remote, which accounts for their low occupational aspirations. Drawing on the experiences of their families, and on their own encounters with the job market, the boys' appraisals of the possibility for social upgrading often preclude the formation of any aspirations at all. Moreover, the available evidence indicates that the boys' parents do not intercede significantly in their children's aspiration formation. In general, the parents of the Hallway Hangers have little influence in their sons' lives. Like most parents, they want the best for their children, but if Stoney's mother is any indication, they also are hesitant to encourage excessively high aspirations in their sons for fear of setting them up for disappointment.

Although the families of the Hallway Hangers have a pervasive influence on their aspirations, so have their own work experiences. All the Hallway Hangers have held summertime employment since they have been of working age. Apart from Steve, they are searching for full-time work. In their struggles to find meaningful, stable employment, all have been thwarted. Invariably, once they think they finally have found a decent job, the opportunity falls through. This type of firsthand experience on the job market further deflates any illusions they might have had about the openness of the opportunity structure. When a boy searches in vain for work that pays seventy-five cents more than minimum wage, his estimation of the prospects for significant upward mobility is bound to be low.

In addition to family and work, school has an important, if less direct, influence on aspirations. Because the school devalues the cultural capital of the Hallway Hangers, their chances for academic success are diminished substantially. Although the Hallway Hangers do not see the intricacies of this process taking place, half have remarked that students from "higher" social backgrounds have a better chance to do well in school. The Hallway Hangers have seen their older siblings fail in school; they see their friends fail as well. Even their Clarendon Heights peers who try to succeed in school meet with only modest success; for verification of this the Hallway Hangers need only look to the Brothers. Thus, the Hallway Hangers question their own capacity to perform well in school, a view that informs their assessment of the chances for social mobility.

Of more importance is the Hallway Hangers' belief that performance in school is of only tangential importance in securing a job. They challenge the widely held notion that success in school translates into success on the job market. But if they feel that schooling will not boost them up the ladder of social mobility, what will? In essence, the Hallway Hangers see a ladder with no rungs on it, or at least none they can reach. They believe that the educational system cannot deliver on its promise of upward social mobility for those who perform well in school. Thus, in part, their leveled aspirations reflect their feeling that schooling is incapable of doing much for them.

In concentrating on this point, however, it is easy to miss some of the intraschool processes that affect the aspirations of the Hallway Hangers. The school is distinctive not for what it does but for what it fails to do.

Lincoln School officials are aware of the process of social reproduction (although they would not conceptualize it in these terms). Bruce Davis, a young, enthusiastic, and dedicated guidance counselor in the Occupational Education Program, acknowledges social reproduction as a simple fact of life.

> BD: These kids [those enrolled in the Oc. Ed. Program] go directly into hard jobs. They're generally from homes where people are laborers. I mean, kids who go to college are from families whose parents went to college. That's how it works, it seems to me. That's where these kids are coming from; they're geared to manual labor jobs, like their brothers, sisters, fathers, uncles, whatever—mothers, like the jobs they have.

Rather than attempting to use the resources of the school to mitigate this process, school officials seem content to let it unfold unhindered. The Oc. Ed. Program, for example, is designed to prepare its students for the rigors of manual work.

> BD: We constantly stress to the kids that they have to be responsible, reliable, and dependable, that they can't be a screw-off. Really, we're just trying to make the kids accountable for themselves. Y'know, most of these kids won't go to college. When they leave here, they can't sleep 'til eleven and then get up and go to three classes. They've really got to be disciplined. They're going to be right out there working. In Oc. Ed, that's really what we're all about. We're trying to simulate a work experience, make class just like a job. It's not just their competency that matters; to be a good worker, your willingness to cooperate, your attitude, is so important.

Bowles and Gintis's argument that working-class students are socialized for working-class jobs and that the social relations of school mirror those of the workplace hardly could be better substantiated.

My point here is not that the school, consciously or unconsciously, levels the aspirations of some students but that it accepts and exacerbates already existing differences in aspirations. By requiring the Hallway Hangers, as eighth graders, to choose their educational program, the school solidifies what is often a vaguely felt and ill-defined preference for manual work or a desire simply to be with one's friends into a definite commitment to a future in manual work. The decision is essentially their own, and it makes a good deal of sense considering that experience in a trade ostensibly will be of some advantage in a difficult job market. Slick's decision to enter the Oc. Ed. Program, despite his high level of achievement in grammar school, typifies the quandary of these boys. Very few middle-class students with decent grades would select a vocational program, but Slick felt the need to do so in order to improve his chances of getting work after graduation.

Although the boys chose their various programs, there are grounds for skepticism about the degree to which this was a completely uncoerced choice. James Rosenbaum, in his 1976 study of a working-class high school, found that guidance counselors and teachers applied subtle and not-so-subtle techniques to channel students into particular tracks and keep them there, sometimes against the students' wishes. But the school officials did this in such a manner that both the youngsters and their parents believed it was a free choice.[2]

Lincoln High School boasts a more liberal educational philosophy than that of Rosenbaum's school, so we hardly can extrapolate his findings to Lincoln High. Nevertheless, in response to a question concerning the process by which students choose their program, Wallace responded, "Oh, that's done for them in grammar school." Sensing that I had picked up on

the "for them," she hastily went on to say that it is a process that initially involves a conference between the eighth-grade counselor and the student as well as parents. "According to however they performed in grammar school, the counselor will come up with a suggested schedule and send it home for approval. Of course, the parent can disagree and pick other courses."

Resolution of the extent to which this is a decision of self-selection requires detailed ethnographic data on the transition from grammar school to Lincoln High, without which we must stop short of Rosenbaum's conclusion that the school exacerbates and actually creates inequality by its discriminatory tracking procedures. There is no doubt, however, that the school, by requiring that such choices be made at a young age, reinforces existing differences in aspirations.

In trying to understand the impact of family, work, and schooling on the aspirations of the Hallway Hangers, Bourdieu's theory that the habitus engenders aspirations that reflect objective probabilities seems accurate. According to Bourdieu and Passeron:

> The structure of the objective chances of social upgrading according to class of origin and, more precisely, the structure of the chances of upgrading through education, conditions agents' dispositions towards education and towards upgrading through education—dispositions which in turn play a determining role in defining the likelihood of entering education, adhering to its norms and succeeding in it, hence the likelihood of social upgrading.[3]

But the concept of the internalization of objective probabilities, because it limits the scope for human agency and creativity, has little explanatory value when we consider the influence of the peer group on the Hallway Hangers. This is a serious deficiency because according to our ethnographic sketch the peer group, especially for the Hallway Hangers, is of primary importance in these boys' lives.

In a country in which success is largely measured by income and occupational status, the Hallway Hangers have a problem. Unemployed, living in public housing, at the very bottom of the socioeconomic spectrum, they are regarded as failures, both by others and, at least to some extent, by themselves, a phenomenon Sennett and Cobb document for working-class people in general in *The Hidden Injuries of Class*.[4] The Hallway Hangers have been enrolled in programs that are designed for "fuck-ups" (as Mike of the Brothers put it), have been placed in the lowest educational tracks, and have received failing grades; all these constitute part of the emotional attack the boys suffer in school. The Hallway Hangers may have little of their self-esteem tied up in school, but, as Scully argues, they cannot help but feel "a judgment of academic inferiority cast upon them, be it by teachers, classmates, or their seemingly objective computerized report card."[5] The subculture of the Hallway Hangers must be understood as an attempt by its members to insulate themselves from these negative judgments and to provide a context in which some semblance of self-respect and dignity can be maintained.

To characterize the subculture of the Hallway Hangers as a defense mechanism against these onslaughts to their self-esteem, however, would be incomplete. Scully argues that most student countercultures have both defensive and independent features;[6] studies by Sennett and Cobb, Stinchcombe, and Willis verify this duality. The Hallway Hangers, like Willis's lads, have their own distinct set of values. These values are indigenous to the working class; they do not arise simply in opposition to the school. The Hallway Hangers' valuation of physical toughness, emotional resiliency, quick-wittedness, masculinity, loyalty, and group solidarity points to a subculture with its own norms, which are passed on from the older to the younger boys. Frankie describes how the subculture of the Hallway Hangers is learned and passed on.

(in a group interview)

> FRANKIE: We were all brought up, all we seen is our older brothers and that gettin' into trouble and goin' to jail and all that shit. Y'know, seeing people—brothers and friends and shit—dying right in front of your face. You seen all the drugs, Jay. Well, this place used to be a thousand times worse than it is now. We grew up, it was all our older brothers doing this. We seen many fucking drugs, all the drinking. They fucking go; that group's gone. The next group came. It's our brothers that are a little older, y'know, twenty-something years old. They started doing crime. And when you're young, you look up to people. You have a person, everybody has a person they look up to. And he's doing this, he's drinking, he's doing that, he's doing drugs, he's ripping off people. Y'know, he's making good fucking money, and it looks like he's doing good, y'know? So bang. Now it's our turn. We're here. What we gonna do when all we seen is fuckin' drugs, alcohol, fighting, this and that, no one going to school?

By providing a realm in which to be bad and tough are the main criteria for respect, the peer group of the Hallway Hangers reverses conventional cultural norms. Like almost all subcultures, however, the Hallway Hangers cannot escape the dominant culture's definitions of success. No matter how strong and insular the group, contact with the dominant culture, especially through school and work, is inevitable. Listening to the Hallway Hangers describe their descent through the school's programs, one detects a sense of shame, despite all their bravado. For Frankie to report that he finally found work, but as a temporary employee with the city's sanitation department as a garbage collector, clearly involved quite a swallowing of pride.

This inability on the part of a subculture to shelter itself completely from the dominant culture's values and norms has been documented widely; Willis's lads are pained by teachers' insults; the children Sennett and Cobb describe as having developed their own "badges of dignity" still have much of their sense of self-worth tied up in academic performance and teacher approval; and, the inside world of black streetcorner men who congregate at Tally's Corner in Elliot Liebow's study "is no more impervious to the values, sentiments and beliefs of the larger society than it is to the blue welfare checks or to the agents of the larger society, such as the policeman, the police informer, the case worker, and the landlord."[7]

Despite the fact that the Hallway Hangers' subculture affords its members only partial protection from the negative judgments of the dominant culture, it does provide a setting wherein a person can salvage some self-respect. The Hallway Hangers, who have developed alternative criteria for success, understand their situation in a way that defends their status; they manage to see themselves differently from the way the rest of society sees them. This is not entirely a self-protective psychological inversion; their ways of understanding their situation also are real. The Hallway Hangers are not living a fantasy. The world of the street exists—it is the unfortunate underside of the American economic system, the inevitable shadow accompanying a society that is not as open as it advertises. Moreover, the Hallway Hangers *are* physically hard, emotionally durable, and boldly enterprising. Those of us who are supposed to be succeeding by conventional standards need only venture into their world for the briefest moment to feel as though our badges of success are about as substantive and "real"

in that environment as the emperor's new clothes.

The subculture of the Hallway Hangers is at odds with the dominant culture. The path to conventional success leads in one direction; the path to a redefined success lies in another. A boy cannot tread both paths simultaneously; orthodox success demands achievement in school, a feat that can be accomplished only by respecting the authority of teachers, which is inconsistent with the Hallway Hangers' alternative value scheme. All the current members of the Hallway Hangers have chosen, more or less definitively, to tread the path to a redefined success. (It should be remembered, however, that this choice is not an altogether free one; the Hallway Hangers see the path to conventional success as blocked by numerous obstacles.) Nevertheless, some do choose the path to conventional achievement; Billy, who expects to attend college next year, is being studied carefully by the Hallway Hangers as a testament to what they may have passed up.

The decision to break away from the group and pursue conventional success is not just a matter of individual calculation, however. More complicated forces are at work, forces that strain the individualistic orientation of American society. The solidarity of the Hallway Hangers is very strong. We have seen, for example, that the sense of cohesion and bonds of loyalty are such that Slick would not leave Shorty at the scene of a crime, preferring to be arrested himself. These communitarian values act to restrain individual Hallway Hangers from breaking away from the group and trying to "make it" conventionally. Slick, for example, scores very well on standardized tests, attended Latin Academy for a year, and is very articulate. Despite class-based barriers to success, he had a relatively good chance of "making it." But Slick also demonstrates the strongest sense of loyalty to the group. In a group interview, for example, he commented, as the rest of the group nodded their heads in agreement, that "money is secondary to friendship; I think friendship is more important than money." Jinks realizes that this loyalty can constrain individuals from striving for upward social mobility.

(in an individual interview)

> JM: Do you have anything else to add about kids' attitudes down here?
>
> JINKS: I'd say everyone more or less has the same attitudes towards school: fuck it. Except the bookworms—people who just don't hang around outside and drink, get high, who sit at home— they're the ones who get the education.
>
> JM: And they just decided for themselves?
>
> JINKS: Yup.
>
> JM: So why don't more people decide that way?
>
> JINKS: Y'know what it is, Jay? We all don't break away because we're too tight. Our friends are important to us. Fuck it. If we can't make it together, fuck it. Fuck it all.

One of the forces operating to keep the Hallway Hangers from striking out on their own is the realization that there is little chance of their making it as a group, and to leave the others behind is to violate the code of loyalty. Recall how Slick contrasts the Hallway Hangers and the "rich little boys from the suburbs." "How do you think they got rich? By fucking people over. We don't do that to each other. We're too fucking tight. We're a group. We don't think like them. We think for all of us." This group loyalty rests on some very strong communitarian values and vaguely parallels an affirmation of class solidarity over individual interests, a point to which I shall return.

With respect to the influence of the peer group on social reproduction, there are some complicated processes at work that Bourdieu's theory fails to capture. Conceptually "flat," the model Bourdieu

develops with Passeron struggles to account for the resistance and nonconformity characteristic of the Hallway Hangers' subculture. To some extent, membership in the subculture of the Hallway Hangers tends to level one's aspirations. Although influenced by the definitions of the dominant culture, the value scheme of the peer group devalues conventional success; the norm among the Hallway Hangers is low aspirations. This ethos, passed down from older to younger boys, is a powerful force on the individual. In addition to the general climate of the peer group, there is a tendency among the Hallway Hangers to resist raised aspirations because to act on them would involve breaking one's ties and leaving the group, a transgression of the code of loyalty.

It is possible to examine the workings of the process of legitimation as it applies to the Hallway Hangers. We have seen that their self-esteem is relatively resilient to poor academic performance, for little of each boy's sense of self is invested in the school. In addition, the peer group subculture affords the Hallway Hangers additional protection for their self-esteem and alternative ways of generating self-esteem through the value system of the group. Although failure in school is psychologically debilitating for the Hallway Hangers in some ways, their self-esteem is partially buttressed from the assaults of the educational system.

If legitimation were functioning smoothly, the Hallway Hangers, in addition to low self-esteem, would internalize their failure and point only to personal inadequacy as the cause of their plight. But such is not the case; the Hallway Hangers realize that internal and external factors contribute to their low social position. Although they do blame themselves to some degree for their failure, they also recognize external barriers to success.

When the Hallway Hangers talk, one almost can feel the struggle being waged in their minds between the tenets of the achievement ideology and the lessons distilled from their own experiences. This tension produces a deep-seated ambivalence. At times the boys are prone to take full responsibility for their dismal social status, but on other occasions they blame external obstacles to their social advancement. Boo-Boo reproaches himself at the beginning of an interview ("I just screwed up") but later maintains that boys from a middle-class neighborhood have an advantage when it comes to achieving social and economic prosperity. Other boys hold a similarly dichotomous outlook.

CHRIS: I guess I just don't have what it takes.
(in a separate interview)
CHRIS: We don't get a fair shake and shit.

FRANKIE: We're all just fucking burnouts.... We never did good anyways.... We've just fucked up.
(in the same interview)
FRANKIE: If I had the fucking money to start out with, like some of these fucking rich kids, I'd be a millionaire. Fucking right, I would be.

SHORTY: I'd go in there, and I'd try my hardest to do the work, right? I'd get a lot of problems wrong cuz I never had the brains much, really, right? That's what's keepin' me back.
(in a different interview)
SHORTY: Hey, you can't get no education around here unless if you're fucking rich, y'know? You can't get no education.... And you can't get a job once they find out where you come from. "You come from Clarendon Heights? Oh, shit. It's them kids again."

The Hallway Hangers see through parts of the achievement ideology, but at some level they accept the aspersions it casts on lower-class individuals, including themselves. However, although the Hallway Hangers do not escape emotional injury, neither does the social order emerge unscathed. In the eyes of the Hallway Hangers the opportunity structure is not open, a view that prevents them from accepting their position and the inequalities of the social order as completely legitimate.

Although the legitimation of inequality could be working more efficiently with respect to the Hallway Hangers, the whole process is not ready to collapse. Like those of the lads in Willis's study, these boys' insights into the true workings of the system are only partial, and often vague and ill-defined at that. Moreover, although they are cognizant of external barriers to success, the Hallway Hangers raise no fundamental challenge to the fairness or efficacy of the system as a whole. For the most part, in the absence of any systematic critique of capitalism, the Hallway Hangers simply are plagued by a sense of unfairness and the uneasy conviction that the rules of the contest are biased against them. Thus, there is a discrepancy between their strongly felt conviction that they are getting "the short end of the stick" and their inability to understand fully how this is so.

They conveniently fill this gap with racism. The Hallway Hangers seem to believe that if they are stuck with the short end of the stick, it must be because the "niggers" have the long end. Their feelings of impotence, frustration, and anger are subsumed in their hatred of blacks and in their conviction that their own plight somehow has been exacerbated, if not caused, by the alleged economic and social advancement of black Americans. Recall how Shorty attributed his brother's unemployment to the "spics and niggers." Frankie and Smitty account for their predicament with one reason.

SMITTY: All the fuckin' niggers are getting the jobs.
FRANKIE: Fuckin' right. That's why we're hanging here now with empty pockets.

Affirmative action affords the Hallway Hangers a handy explanation for their own demise. Slick, despite his perceptiveness, succumbs to the same misunderstanding. Although his decision to quit school was undoubtedly the result of many factors, Slick insists that he dropped out of school solely because of supposed favoritism toward black students at Lincoln High. In a different interview, Slick begins by accusing the school of class-based prejudice but muddles the issue by suddenly bringing blacks into the discussion: "They favor all them fucking rich kids at that school. All the rich people. They fucking baby 'em. They baby all the fucking niggers up there."

This confusion between class bias and alleged reverse racial discrimination is symptomatic of the Hallway Hangers' outlook. By directing their resentment at affirmative action and those who benefit from it, the Hallway Hangers can spare themselves blame, but then the social order also is spared any serious scrutiny. In Willis's terms, racism is a serious "limitation" on the cultural outlook of the Hallway Hangers. Just as the lads' reversal of the usual valuation of mental versus manual labor prevents them from seeing their placement into dead-end, low-paying jobs as a form of class domination, so does the Hallway Hangers' racism obscure reality.

Thus, the Hallway Hangers harbor contradictory and ambivalent beliefs about the legitimacy of their social position. Their identification of class-based barriers to success and their impression that the deck is unfairly stacked against them, insights that could catalyze the development of a radical political consciousness, are derailed by their racism. On the one hand, the Hallway Hangers puncture the individualistic orientation of American society by their adoption of communitarian values to the point where a realization that the entire group cannot "make it" prevents individuals from striving for conventional success—a point

of view that runs in the same direction as a class logic. But on the other hand, the Hallway Hangers support some politically conservative values and leaders. The prevalence of this type of dual, contradictory consciousness, embodying both progressive, counterhegemonic insights and reactionary, distorting beliefs, is discussed at length by Antonio Gramsci.[8] More recently, Michael Mann has argued convincingly that ambivalence about social beliefs leads to "pragmatic acceptance" of the social order rather than complete acceptance of it as legitimate.[9]

It is instructive to compare in detail this analysis of the Hallway Hangers with Willis's depiction of how social reproduction takes place for the lads in his study. The Hallway Hangers, as residents of public housing, are from a lower social stratum than the lads, who are from stable working-class families. Moreover, the British working class, with its long history, organized trade unions, and progressive political party, has developed an identity, pride, and class consciousness that are lacking in the United States. Despite these differences, substantial similarities in the way each peer group experiences the process of social reproduction warrant a comparison.

Willis argues that the lads' rejection of the achievement ideology and of the values and norms of the educational system is based on some key insights into the situation of their class under capitalism. However, the crucial element in the process of social reproduction—placement into manual labor jobs—is experienced by the lads as an act of independence and self-election, not a form of oppression. Because of the value placed on machismo in the wider working-class culture, which the lads appropriate for their own, they choose to enter the bottom of the occupational structure. At the root of social reproduction for the lads is the cultural inversion by which manual labor, equated with the social superiority of masculinity, is valued over white-collar work, which is associated with the inferior status of femininity.

Whereas the lads reject school because it has no bearing on the manual labor jobs they intend to pursue, the Hallway Hangers reject school for different reasons. For the lads, the seeds of leveled aspirations, and hence social reproduction, lie in their cultural affirmation of manual labor. Like the lads, the Hallway Hangers place a heavy premium on masculinity; their emphasis on being cool, tough, streetwise—in a word, bad—indicates the prevalence of machismo in their cultural outlook. Nevertheless, this emphasis on masculinity seldom is linked with distaste for white-collar work. The subculture of the Hallway Hangers contains no systematic bias toward manual work; their depressed aspirations result from a look into the future that sees stagnation at the bottom of the occupational structure as almost inevitable. The Hallway Hangers' outlook is more pessimistic than that held by the lads; there is no room on the job market for independence, election, or even choice. Thus, the Hallway Hangers reconcile themselves to taking whatever job they can get. Given this resignation, their belief that education can do little for them, and their assessment of the costs of educational success, the Hallway Hangers reject the institution of school. Although they do not experience unemployment or entry into low-level jobs as acts of triumph but rather as depressing facts of lower-class life, neither do the Hallway Hangers incriminate the social order as entirely unjust. In both cases the structure of class relations is reproduced, largely through the regulation of aspirations, but the processes through which it happens for the lads and the Hallway Hangers vary. The lads' sexism keeps them from decrying class domination; the racism of the Hallway Hangers serves the same purpose.

It is difficult to conceptualize the process of social reproduction when it is depicted in general terms. To facilitate our understanding of how the aspirations of the Hallway Hangers are leveled, I now describe the mechanisms associated with social reproduction as they affect Jinks. By looking at his experiences, the processes we have been discussing can be rendered concrete.

According to one of his friends, Jinks was an A student in his freshman year. At first, he worked hard and conformed to the rules of the school, but during his sophomore year, he started to weigh the costs and benefits of attendance and hard work. Every morning, he would socialize with the rest of the boys at Pop's for about fifteen minutes, maybe smoke a joint, and then head to class. "Hey, man, what the fuck? Sit down and smoke another bone. Whaddya wanna go to school for? You like them teachers better than us?" After leaving the group to comments like this, in class his mind would wander back to his friends sitting in Pop's, getting high, relaxing. He would think about his brother who dropped out of school at the age of sixteen and had a union job at the shipyards. He would think about another brother who had graduated the year before and joined the navy, and about his oldest brother, who was dead. He would think about the older boys at the Heights, some graduates of high school, some dropouts—all unemployed or in lousy jobs. Gradually, Jinks's attitude toward school started to change.

JINKS: I started hanging around, getting high, just not bother going to school…started hanging down Pop's. Cutting, getting high.

JM: What were the reasons behind that? Why'd you start going down to Pop's?

JINKS: Friends, friends.…I'd go to my classes and meet them at lunch, but when I was with 'em, I'd say, "The hell with it. I ain't even going." Besides, I didn't really care to try in school.…You ain't got a chance of getting a good job, even with a high school diploma. You gotta go on to college, get your Masters and shit like that to get a good paying job that you can live comfortably on. So if you're not planning on going to college, I think it's a waste of time.

By his junior year, Jinks attended school only sporadically, and when he did go to class, he was often drunk or high, a necessity if he was to "listen to the teachers talk their shit."

Faced with the need for income to pay for, among other things, his weekly ounce of marijuana, Jinks began to deal drugs on a small scale, stopping only after a close call with the police. After four months of searching and waiting, Jinks landed a job and began working in the afternoons, attending school for a few hours each day. Convinced that school was doing him little good and faced with the opportunity to work full-time, Jinks quit school, only to be laid off shortly thereafter. Although his parents wanted him to finish school, Jinks downplays their influence on him: "They want me to graduate from high school, but I ain't gonna. They'll be mad at me for a week or two, but that's life."

Now that he is out of school, out of work, and out of money, Jinks does not have much to which he can look forward. Nevertheless, he is not as "down and out" as we might think. He has plenty of time for his friends and accepts his predicament placidly, with thorough disrespect neither for the system nor for himself. The situation is, after all, not much different than he had expected.

The Brothers: Internalizing Failure, Shorn of Self-Esteem

If the mechanisms by which the Hallway Hangers and lads end up in dead-end jobs are somewhat different, the process of social reproduction as it operates with respect to the Brothers presents an even sharper contrast. Applied to the Brothers,

Bourdieu's concept of the internalization of objective probabilities does not ring true. Undoubtedly, the Brothers do internalize their chances of "making it," and this calculation certainly moderates their aspirations. Yet, their view of the probabilities for social advancement is informed not only by the objective opportunity structure but also by their parents' hopes for their future and the achievement ideology of the school. In this sense, there is no such thing as the internalization of objective probabilities, for all perceptions of the opportunity structure necessarily are subjective and influenced by a host of intervening factors. The actual habitus of the Brothers is much more complex than Bourdieu and Passeron would have us believe. A theory stressing a correspondence between aspirations and opportunity cannot explain the excessive ambitions of the Brothers because it underestimates the achievement ideology's capacity to mystify structural constraints and encourage high aspirations. The Hallway Hangers reject the achievement ideology, but the situation for the Brothers is quite different.

Like the Hallway Hangers, the Brothers come from families in which their parents either hold jobs that are at the bottom of the occupational structure or are unable to find work at all. An important difference, however, is that, with the exception of Derek, all the Brothers are either the oldest male sibling in the family or have older brothers and sisters who attend college. Thus, the Brothers are not faced with a picture of nearly uniform failure in school. In addition, the parents of the Brothers actually encourage high aspirations in their children, as a tool to motivate them to achieve in school and perhaps as a projection of thwarted ambitions. Thus, from their families, the Brothers take away a contradictory outlook. On the one hand, they see that hard work on the part of their parents has not gotten them very far, an implicit indictment of the openness of the opportunity structure, but on the other hand, they are encouraged by these same people to have high hopes for the future.

For the Brothers, work is an exclusively summertime affair; only Juan is on the job market full-time. Thus, their experience on the labor market is very limited, and that experience has been sheltered from the rigors and uncertainties of finding work. Most of these boys have been enrolled almost exclusively in federal summer youth employment programs and only have had to fill out an application form to be placed in a summer job. Whereas the more extensive contact of the Hallway Hangers with the world of work tends to level their aspirations, a comparable process has not taken place for the Brothers—at least not yet.

The Brothers' peer group does not tend to level their hopes for the future. Because the Brothers do not comprise a distinctive subculture but rather accept the norms and values of the dominant culture and strive to embody them, their peer group does not provide them with a redefinition of success. The Brothers are achievement oriented, prize accomplishments in school and obedience to the law, and measure success as does the rest of society. The ethos of their group encourages high aspirations and reinforces behavior that contributes to the realization of their goals.

The Brothers unconditionally accept the school's achievement ideology, a step that requires a belief in equality of opportunity and the efficacy of schooling. But at the same time that their aspirations tend to rise because of their faith in these precepts, the Brothers are being prepared psychologically for jobs at the bottom of the occupational structure. In low educational tracks and the recipients of poor grades, the Brothers struggle in school. They blame themselves for their mediocre academic performances because they are unaware of the discriminatory influences of tracking, the school's partiality toward the cultural capital of the upper classes, the self-fulfilling

consequences of teachers' expectations, and other forms of class-based educational selection. Conditioned by the achievement ideology to think that good jobs require high academic attainment, the Brothers may temper their high aspirations, believing not that the institution of school and the job market have failed them, but that they have failed themselves.

For most of the Brothers, this "cooling-out" process, documented by Burton Clark in his study of a community college,[10] will not be completed until they actually graduate from high school and are face to face with the job market. Armed with a high school diploma and a good disciplinary record, the Brothers will have a better chance to land suitable jobs than the Hallway Hangers do, but the Brothers' opportunities still will be quite limited. Juan, the only Brother to have graduated, already has begun to "cool out."

Juan, who left high school with a diploma and a skill (he spent 1,500 hours in school learning culinary arts), has lowered his aspirations significantly after six months of unemployment. Although he previously expressed distaste for a job in auto mechanics because of its association with dirty manual work, Juan now hopes to find work in precisely that area. We can expect many of the Brothers to undergo a similar reorientation after graduation.

From the description of the Brothers' experiences in school it seems clear that the legitimation of inequality is working smoothly for them. In general, the Brothers, without the protection of a peer group with a distinctive subculture, suffer from low self-esteem as a result of their academic performances. In addition, they do not acknowledge the existence of external barriers to their success in school and instead blame themselves for their mediocre performance. We can expect that the same will be true for what may turn out to be their low occupational status.

Whereas the Hallway Hangers are analogous to Willis's lads, the Brothers are closer to the ear'oles. Although our picture is complicated by the variable of ethnicity, the Brothers' experiences illuminate the process of social reproduction as it is undergone by conformist lower-class youth, a subject into which Willis does not delve. Reflecting their acceptance of the achievement ideology and the concomitant notion that all those who are capable can get ahead on their own merits, the Brothers have developed significant ambitions. Relative to the depressed aspirations of the Hallway Hangers, the middle-class aspirations of the Brothers attest to their belief that they are involved in a fair competition. If they fail to get ahead, they will probably attribute their social and economic fate to their own incapabilities, to their own lack of merit.

But we cannot be sure. Will the Brothers and the ear'oles become disillusioned with themselves when they are "cooled out," or will their disillusion encompass the social order as well? This issue demands a longitudinal study spanning a number of years, without which no definite pronouncements are possible. I suspect that although some cynicism about the openness of American society will result, the achievement ideology has been internalized so deeply by the Brothers that their subsequent "careers" will be interpreted in its light. Moreover, if one of the Brothers should be lucky enough to "make it," those that do not will be all the more likely to blame themselves. Far from contradicting the social reproduction perspective, the limited social mobility that does take place in liberal democracies plays a crucial role in the legitimation of inequality. ("If Billy can make it, why can't I? The problem must reside in me.") This "controlled mobility" encourages working-class self-reproach and goes a long way toward explaining why in the United States working-class students with Super's outlook far outnumber those with Jinks's perspective and why in Britain there are more ear'oles than lads.

When Super switched from the Occupational Education Program to House C in the regular academic program, he was placed in the lowest educational tracks for nearly all his subjects because of his low academic performance in grammar school and the fact that switching into the classes in the middle of the semester would have been difficult for him academically. Now in his sophomore year, Super still is enrolled in the "basic" tracks and maintains a high D average.

Super aspires to professional or middle-class work, which reflects his parents' insistence that Super aim for a white-collar job, the premium his peer group places on conventional success, his minimal contact with the job market, and the achievement ideology of the school. Within the course of a year he variously expressed hopes of becoming a doctor, a businessman, or a computer specialist. Reconciling these aspirations with his academic performance is a difficult exercise for Super. At the same time that he affirms the achievement ideology ("It's easy to do anything as long as you set your mind to it") and his own effort ("I swear, I'll be tryin' real hard in school"), Super admits that his performance is lacking ("I just can't seem to do it"). The only explanation left for him is that his own abilities are not up to par, a conclusion that Super accepts, despite its implications for his sense of self-worth. Every lower-class student who internalizes the achievement ideology but struggles in school finds himself or herself in this dilemma. Moreover, the way is clear for lower-class students again to attribute their failure to personal inadequacies when they find themselves in a low-status job. The feeling is a harsh one, but the American school system and the structure of class relations demand that it be borne by many. That Super and the other Brothers feel it strongly is evidence that the legitimation function of the school and the larger process of social reproduction are at work.

If schooling is the training ground at which students are prepared to participate in the race for the jobs of wealth and prestige, the Brothers are being cheated. Told over and over again that the race is a fair one and led to believe that they are given as much attention during the training as anyone, the Brothers step to the starting line for what they see as an equitable race. When the starter's gun goes off and they stumble over the first few hurdles while others streak ahead, they will in all likelihood blame only themselves and struggle to keep going.

The Hallway Hangers see that the race is unfair. They reject official declarations of equity and drop out of the training sessions, convinced that their results will be unsatisfactory no matter how hard they train. They expect to do poorly, and even those who might stand a chance stay back with their friends when the race starts. Instead of banding together, however, and demanding that a fair race be held, the Hallway Hangers never really question the race's rules and simply accept their plight.

This leaves us with an important question: How can the same race be viewed so differently? Why is it that the entrants who have racial as well as class-based hurdles to overcome are the ones who see no hurdles at all?

The Sources of Variation

Although the distinctive processes of social reproduction that have been detailed previously make internal sense, what accounts for the variance between them? What factors contribute to the fundamental incongruity between the two peer groups in the first place? Why is the influence of the family so different for the two peer groups? Why are their experiences in school so dissimilar?

To answer these questions, we must move to a deeper level of analysis that is centered on the role of the achievement ideology. The Hallway Hangers reject this ideology; the Brothers accept it. It is at this point that

their paths diverge and the groups experience the process of social reproduction in different ways.

The achievement ideology runs counter to the grain of all these boys' experiences. Neither the residents of their neighborhood nor the members of their families have "made it." In a housing project plagued by unemployment and crime, we might expect both groups of boys to question the existence of equality of opportunity, yet only the Hallway Hangers do so. Of course, they have their own experiences on the job market to which they can point, but this explanation is only of limited value because in most instances they have dismissed the ideology even before experiencing the job market firsthand. The question remains: Why do the Hallway Hangers dismiss the achievement ideology while the Brothers accept it?

The Hallway Hangers reject the achievement ideology because most of them are white. Whereas poor blacks have racial discrimination to which they can point as a cause of their family's poverty, for the Hallway Hangers to accept the achievement ideology is to admit that their parents are lazy or stupid or both. Thus, the achievement ideology not only runs counter to the experiences of the Hallway Hangers, but is also a more serious assault on their self-esteem. Acceptance of the ideology on the part of the Brothers does not necessarily involve such harsh implications, for they can point to racial prejudice to explain their parents' defeats. The severe emotional toll that belief in the achievement ideology exacts on poor whites relative to poor blacks explains why the Hallway Hangers dismiss the ideology while the Brothers validate it.[11]

The Brothers believe the achievement ideology to be an accurate depiction of the opportunity structure as it exists in the United States today because they perceive the racial situation to be substantially different for them than it was for their parents. Whereas their parents were barred from lunch counters and disqualified from the competition before it began, the Brothers see themselves in entirely different circumstances. Mokey's mother, for example, in commenting on Mokey's chances of "making it," says, "I feel Mokey has a equal chance to [be successful], regardless of money or color. That's a chance I never had." ... Indeed, it is amazing how often the Brothers affirm the openness of the opportunity structure. Presumably encouraged by perceived gains made in the past two decades, the Brothers seem to believe that equality of opportunity exists today as it did not in their parents' time. This view allows them to accept the achievement ideology without simultaneously indicting their parents. Because the Brothers fully expect to "make it" themselves, embracing the achievement ideology involves little assault on their self-esteem.

This belief that the situation for blacks has improved in the United States also explains why the parents of the Brothers encourage high aspirations in their children while the Hallway Hangers' parents do not. Believing the situation that contributed to their own condition to have changed, the Brothers' parents are convinced that their children have a better chance of "making it" and see no danger in encouraging lofty aspirations. The Hallway Hangers' parents, in contrast, believe that the deck is stacked against their children as it was against them and are wary of supporting unrealistically high aspirations.

Quantitative studies on the generation of ambition have produced equivocal results about whether blacks have higher aspirations than whites from the same socioeconomic background. In general, more recent studies indicate higher aspiration levels for blacks, while those utilizing data from the 1960s and early 1970s find that whites maintain higher aspirations than blacks. The only issue on which there is a consensus among quantitative practitioners is that the aspiration levels of blacks seem to have risen during the past ten to fifteen years,[12] a finding consistent with the attitudes of the Brothers and their families.

A number of factors can account for the increased aspirations of blacks. Because black youths perceive a change in the opportunity structure their parents faced (a change that may or may not have occurred to the degree perceived), they may feel that affirmative action has reduced the occupational handicap of color and that discrimination in employment has abated. Or it may be that the incontrovertible gains of the civil rights movement (e.g., affirmation of basic political and civil rights for blacks, an end to legal Jim Crow segregation, the emergence of black leaders on the national stage) have imbued many blacks with a general sense of progress and improvement that has affected their occupational aspirations. Or political mobilization itself may have created feelings of efficacy and resistance to being "cooled out" that have led to the higher aspirations. To the extent that the civil rights movement was about aspirations and dreams and a refusal to be reduced to hopelessness, blacks may feel that diminutive aspirations are somehow a form of surrender and a betrayal of past gains.

The divergence between how the Brothers and Hallway Hangers react to the achievement ideology is not entirely racial.... Many of the Hallway Hangers and their families have lived in low-income housing projects for a long period of time, and some have been on public assistance for as many as three generations. This extended duration of tenancy in public housing cannot help but contribute to a feeling of hopelessness and stagnation on the part of the Hallway Hangers. With family histories dominated by failure, the Hallway Hangers' cynicism about the openness of the opportunity structure and their rejection of the achievement ideology are understandable.

The Brothers' situation is quite different. Their families have lived in public housing, on average, for less than half the time the Hallway Hangers' families have. The Brothers' families also have resided in the Clarendon Heights neighborhood for a substantially shorter period of time. Many of the families see their move to the neighborhood as a step up in social status; some families came from worse projects in the area, others from tenement flats in the black ghetto. Moreover, some of the Brothers' parents (Super's, James's, Mokey's) have moved up from the south, bringing with them a sense of optimism and hope about making a fresh start, feelings that have not yet turned into bitterness. For those families that have come to the United States from the West Indies in the past twelve years (Craig's, Juan's), this buoyancy is even stronger. Like the optimism felt by turn-of-the-century immigrants despite their wretched living conditions and the massive barriers to success that they faced, the Brothers' outlook encompasses a sense of improved life chances. Although at the bottom of the social ladder, the Brothers feel that they are part of a collective upward social trajectory, a belief that is conducive to acceptance of the achievement ideology.

Another factor that bears on the Hallway Hangers' rejection of the achievement ideology and the Brothers' acceptance of it is the way in which these peer groups define themselves in relation to one another. The character of the Brothers' peer group is in some measure a reaction to distinctive attributes of the Hallway Hangers. Thus, we can understand, in part, the Brothers' aversion to drugs and alcohol and their general orientation toward achievement as a response to the Hallway Hangers' excessive drinking, use of drugs, and general rejection of the standards and values of the dominant culture. As Super remarks pointing at a group of the Hallway Hangers loitering in doorway #13, "As long as I don't end up like *that.*" Having moved into a predominantly white neighborhood that is generally unfriendly toward blacks and having been taunted and abused by a group of disaffected, mostly white boys, the Brothers react by disassociating themselves completely from the Hallway Hangers and by pursuing a distinctly different path—one that leads to success as it is conventionally defined.

For these and other reasons, the Brothers are not representative of poor black teenagers generally. One might discover black peer groups with a similar ethos in other lower-class, predominantly white communities, but if one ventures into any black ghetto, one finds an abundance of black youths hanging in doorways who are pessimistic about the future and cynical about the openness of American society. These youths have formed subcultures with values similar to those of the Hallway Hangers and present a marked contrast to the Brothers in outlook and behavior....

To view the general orientation of the Brothers' peer group as a mere reaction to that of the Hallway Hangers would be a vast oversimplification that fails to account for both the complexity of their reaction to the situation in which they find themselves and their powers of social discernment. We have seen that the Hallway Hangers see through the achievement ideology, not so much because of greater insight into the workings of the system but because of the assault this ideology makes on their self-esteem. The Brothers' acceptance of the ideology and their own individualistic orientations toward achievement are not entirely uncritical. The Brothers are not ideological dupes. They make their own partial "penetrations"[13] into their economic condition, and these insights inform their actions.

The Brothers' decision to "go for it," to work hard in school in pursuit of a decent job, makes a good deal of sense in view of the Hallway Hangers' decision to opt out of the competition. With the number of "good" jobs fixed, one's objective chances increase as individuals remove themselves from contention. Thus the bipolarity between the Hallway Hangers and the Brothers should not surprise us. In deciding whether to purchase a raffle ticket, the wily individual takes note of how many others are buying them, conscious that the fewer sold, the more sense it makes to purchase one. Lower-class individuals generally do not have a good chance of "making it," but as one social group eschews the contest, others see it in their interest to vie seriously. Where we have a group like the Hallway Hangers, it is only natural that we have a group with the outlook of the Brothers. Willis notes a similar logic in *Learning to Labor:* "The ear'oles' conformism...takes on a more rational appearance when judged against the self-disqualification of the lads."[14]

The Brothers' orientation toward individual achievement is even more understandable when we consider affirmative action measures. Although a far cry from what is needed to ameliorate racial injustice in the United States, affirmative action for minorities does increase the Brothers' objective chances of securing stable employment. There is, of course, no analogous measure offered to the lower classes as a whole to mitigate class injustice in the United States, so the anger of the white working class about affirmative action should not surprise us. The perception among whites in Clarendon Heights is that blacks now have an advantage on the job market. There may even be a measure of support for this view among blacks. Chris, for example, believes that although the white boys will face unemployment, his fate could be different: "Watch when I go for a job for the city or something: I'll get it. They'll say, 'Minority—you got the job.'" The Brothers' decision to "buy into" the system also seems to be based on the understanding that, all other things being equal, affirmative action can give them an advantage over their white lower-class peers on the labor market....

There are then, a number of factors that contribute to the dissimilarity between the Brothers and the Hallway Hangers. The Brothers, who have moved to the northeastern United States within the last

generation and recently have moved into public housing, see themselves on a social upswing. This ambiance of ascension is intensified by their impression that racial injustice has been curtailed in the past two decades, thereby making the opportunity structure they face more pliant than the one their parents encountered. The Hallway Hangers have no such grounds for optimism, having been left behind when much of the white working class moved to the suburbs. Whereas Clarendon Heights seems a step up for the Brothers' families, the Hallway Hangers believe they cannot slide much lower. Hailing from families who have resided in the projects for many years, some in Clarendon Heights for three generations, the Hallway Hangers feel that little has changed and consequently are despondent about their own futures. We also might point to variances in the families of the two groups as a source of their divergent outlooks. The Brothers' family members, especially their older siblings, have achieved a slightly higher status in terms of educational and occupational achievement than have the Hallway Hangers' family members.

Although all these factors contribute to the optimism of the Brothers and the pessimism of the Hallway Hangers, they do not in themselves account for the wide disparity between the two groups, nor do they explain the distinctive subculture of the Hallway Hangers. This oppositional culture partially shelters the Hallway Hangers from the abnegations of the dominant society, the negative judgments they sustain as poor members of an ostensibly open society. The Brothers are pained by these appraisals, too, of course, but the achievement ideology represents a more potent assault on the Hallway Hangers because as white youths they can point to no extenuating circumstances to account for their poverty. The subculture of the Hallway Hangers is in part a response to the stigma they feel as poor, white Americans. Finally, the differences between the two groups seem to be amplified by their tendencies to define themselves in relation (i.e., in opposition) to one another.

Where are these two paths likely to lead? In all probability, the Brothers will be better off than the Hallway Hangers. With a high school diploma, a positive attitude, and a disciplined readiness for the rigors of the workplace, the Brothers should be capable of landing steady jobs. An individual or two may work his way into a professional or managerial occupation, and a few might slide into a state of chronic unemployment, but the odds are that most of the Brothers will end up members of the stable working class, generally employed in jobs that are toward the bottom of the occupational ladder but that afford some security.

The Hallway Hangers probably will end up quite differently. Dependent on alcohol or drugs or both, disaffected and rebellious, and without qualifications in a credential-based job market, the Hallway Hangers generally will end up as Slick predicts: "They're not gonna be more than janitors or, y'know, goin' by every day tryin' to get a buck." An alcoholic himself, who becomes more despondent every day that he remains unemployed, Slick may well meet the same fate, despite his exceptional intelligence and articulate nature.

Of course, the Hallway Hangers do not deny that upward social mobility is possible. Their rejection of school was based not on the premise that they could not succeed but on the premise that the prospects for limited social mobility did not warrant the attempt, given the costs involved in the try. This is a calculation they all now have come to question. Having experienced life on the streets without a job, the Hallway Hangers generally indicate that if they had it to do over again, they would apply themselves in school.

> JM: Would you do anything different if you could do it over again?

(all in separate interviews)

> BOO-BOO: Yeah, lots. Wouldn't screw up in school as bad as I did, wouldn't get high with my friends as much.

> CHRIS: I dunno, man, wouldn't fuck up in school. I guess I shoulda learned to live with their shit. It's just the way I am. Like, if I decide, if I say I'm not going to do something, I don't give a fuck what they do to me. I'm not going to do it. That's just the way I am. I guess that's what's gonna fuck me over in the long run.

> FRANKIE: Yeah, definitely. I wouldn't have fucked up as much. I coulda been a—I fucked it up for myself, maybe. Maybe I woulda tried going to school more. But still, I don't think I woulda come out much better. So, y'know, just fuckin' bein' less rude to people, truthfully.

> STEVE: Yeah, I'd make sure I got more credits my freshman year. I only got five fucking credits, man. That's rough to fuckin' jump back on and shit. It's a bitch.

> JINKS: I'd probably get more interested in school, but it's too late now.

Almost any price would be worth paying to avoid the pain and misery of hopelessness at such a young age.

NOTES

1. Maureen Anne Scully, "Coping with Meritocracy" (Thesis, Harvard College, 1982), p. 6.
2. James Rosenbaum, *Making Inequality* (New York: Wylie and Sons, 1976).
3. Pierre Bourdieu and Jean-Claude Passeron, *Reproduction in Education, Society, and Culture* (London; Sage, 1977), p. 156.
4. Richard Sennett and Jonathan Cobb, *The Hidden Injuries of Class* (New York: Vintage Books, 1972)
5. Scully, "Coping with Meritocracy," p. 83.
6. Ibid., p. 85.

7. Elliot Liebow, *Tally's Corner* (Boston: Little, Brown, 1967), p. 209.
8. Antonio Gramsci, *Selections from Prison Notebooks* (London: Lawrence and Wishart, 1971).
9. Michael Mann, "The Social Cohesion of Liberal Democracy," *American Sociological Review* 35 (June 1970): 423–439.
10. Burton Clark, "The 'Cooling Out' Function in Higher Education," *American Journal of Sociology* 65 (1960): 576–596.
11. I am not arguing that blacks living in poverty are psychologically better off than their white counterparts. Given the internalized effects of racism on blacks, such is clearly not the case. It is only in considering the effect of the achievement ideology alone that I am making a comparative statement about the emotional suffering of poor blacks and poor whites.
12. Kenneth I. Spenner and David L. Featherman, "Achievement Ambitions," *Annual Review of Sociology* 4 (1978): 388.
13. The term, of course, is borrowed from Willis, who first directed my attention to the penetrations of the Brothers after reading a draft of the book.
14. Paul Willis, *Learning to Labor* (Aldershot: Gower, 1977), p. 148.

REFERENCES

Bourdieu, Pierre. 1977. "Cultural Reproduction and Social Reproduction." In *Power and Ideology in Education*. Jerome Karabel and A. H. Halsey (eds.). New York: Oxford University Press.

Bourdieu, Pierre, and Jean-Claude Passeron. 1977. *Reproduction in Education, Society, and Culture*. London: Sage.

Bowles, Samuel, and Herbert Gintis. 1976. *Schooling in Capitalist America*. New York: Basic Books.

Clark, Burton. 1960. "The 'Cooling-Out' Function in Higher Education." *American Journal of Sociology* 65: 576–596.

Gramsci, Antonio. 1971. *Selections from Prison Notebooks*. London: Lawrence and Wishart.

Liebow, Elliot. *Tally's Corner*. Boston: Little, Brown.

Mann, Michael. 1970. "The Social Cohesion of Liberal Democracy." *American Sociological Review* 35 (June): 423–439.

Rosenbaum, James E. 1976. *Making Inequality*. New York: Wylie and Sons.

Scully, Maureen Anne. 1982. "Coping with Meritocracy." Thesis, Harvard College.

Sennett, Richard, and Jonathan Cobb. 1972. *The Hidden Injuries of Class*. New York: Vintage Books.

Spenner, Kenneth I., and David L. Featherman. 1978. "Achievement Ambitions." *Annual Review of Sociology* 4: 373–420.

Stinchcombe, Arthur L. 1964. *Rebellion in a High School*. Chicago: Quadrangle Books.

Willis, Paul. 1977. *Learning to Labor*. Aldershot: Gower.

24

KATHLEEN NOLAN

INSTITUTING THE CULTURE OF CONTROL: DISCIPLINARY PRACTICES AND ORDER MAINTENANCE

from *Police in the Hallways* (2011)

In this piece, Kathleen Nolan documents the pervasive roles that control and discipline have come to play in shaping the daily life experiences of urban youth. Drawing on a year of fieldwork in one public high school in the Bronx, her experience teaching in a similarly situated public school in the area, and her decade living in the neighborhood, her book shows that for some schools in the inner city, order maintenance has become their central mission.

Although a variety of policies and practices were part of the culture of control inside Urban Public High School (UPHS), the most central was the systematic use of order-maintenance-style policing. This included law-enforcement officials' patrolling of the hallways, the use of criminal-procedural-level strategies,¹ and the pervasive threats of summonses and arrest, which together led to three essential consequences. First, the heavy policing of students on a daily basis and an official policy of police intervention for minor school infractions led to the criminalization of misbehavior. In fact, frequently the police intervention itself triggered the behavior that was ultimately considered criminal. Second, disciplinary incidents that could have been considered violations of the law but had once been handled internally by educators, such as fighting, came to be defined as serious crimes and were often handled through police intervention, summonses, and the arrests of students. Third, as school discipline merged with an ideology of street policing, the boundaries between once-separate domains—the school, the street, and institutions of the criminal-justice system—became blurred. As David Garland suggests, as crime-control responsibilities move beyond the boundaries of the criminal-justice system, institutions of civil society, such as the urban public school, assume explicit roles in the larger societal project of the penal management of marginalized, low-income youth of color.[2]

What Does "Disorderly" Mean, Anyway? The Policing of Misbehavior and the Criminalization of Disrespect

How did the new disciplinary plan work in actual practice? One way to find out was to look carefully at the kinds of acts that became defined in everyday practice as the appropriate domain for police action. With this question in mind, I undertook a systematic examination of the school occurrence reports for the 2004–2005 year [the years in which Nolan conducted her fieldwork]. During this time at least 113 summonses and 58 youth referrals were meted out and more than 50 arrests were recorded, 221 occurrences in total.[3] My careful examination of the reports led to one striking finding: 52 percent of the offenses were for "disorderly conduct." Given that so many students were charged with this offense, it was important to examine the actual behaviors that led to it. My experiences at UPHS shed light on the definitional process, from the initial interaction between police and students that led to the charge of disorderly conduct, to the hours students spent in court.

It was late September. I was standing in the office of the assistant principal of school safety, Juarez. I was there to pick up an ID card that had been made for me. Only the secretary, the aide, and I were present. The quiet morning lull of office work was broken suddenly when three police officers escorted two handcuffed boys into the office. For me, the experience was still new. I had not yet grown accustomed to the scene, and it seemed jarringly out of place in a school. The boys were forcibly pushed down into two chairs. Two more police officers entered the room, which suddenly felt much smaller. Their anger was palpable. The secretary and the aide did not seem fazed. The aide began to print out information on the two students. One was nineteen years old. "He needs to go to the precinct," one of the officers said.

The five officers stepped to one side of the room near the door to confer. This strange moment of waiting and conferring I would see again and again over time. They appeared to be making decisions on the fly. The secretary continued to work. The aide quietly said to me, "Your card won't be ready until tomorrow," cuing me to leave.

"I'm watching this," I said.

"I don't think you have permission."

"I have the principal's," I assured her.

The two young men were talking to each other. The older one whispered, "They're beasts," referring to the officers. Their chairs were about three feet apart. They leaned close to each other with their cuffed wrists behind their backs and continued to complain in low voices about the treatment they had received. I later learned that they were brothers—Terrell and James. The older one claimed that he had come to the defense of his younger sibling. The occurrence report, which I obtained later, described the incident like this:

Two male students were arrested by PO [police officer] —— of the XX pct for Disorderly Conduct and Resisting Arrest. One student refused to provide identification. They were both disorderly and disrespectful when stopped. Parental contact unsuccessful. Suspensions are pending.

One of the officers glanced at me. I felt very conspicuous. More angry words were exchanged between the boys and the officers as they waited for the police van. I pretended not to notice. Finally, my awkwardness got the better of me and I left the room. Just then Assistant Principal Juarez came rushing in. He was a smallish, well-dressed Dominican man with a charming disposition and a mild manner. But at that moment he was not happy and, like the mood in his office, he had transformed. From just outside the doorway, I heard his stern voice shouting, "I know what I'm doing.... If you don't like it, leave! I can't have all these people in my office. Get out!"

"Okay, okay," one of the officers said. "We'll step outside."

I walked toward the side entrance of the building where I predicted the boys would be taken out. A few moments later, the police escorted them past me out to the police van. Juarez followed. He looked at me as he passed and said, "Sometimes we don't always see things the same way."

Although the tension between the school administrator and the police was evident, what struck me most about the incident was how it confused me. I could not understand why the boys were arrested. What had they been caught doing? It was the beginning of the school year, and I had not quite figured out the process by which small disciplinary matters escalated into police matters.

The story continued two months later, on a cold November morning, when I arrived at the Bronx Criminal Court House at 8:30. Unbeknown to me, it was the day that Terrell and James were to appear before the judge. I was there to meet Carlos, who had also received a summons at school for disorderly conduct. The courthouse was an immense stone building that extended the length of a block. A wide, shallow set of steps led up to the main entrance on 161st Street, a busy commercial strip with several government buildings in the vicinity. I figured Carlos would be late, as he found it difficult to make it to school before 10:00 AM, so I waited on the corner of 161st and Sheridan, propped against some scaffolding, and began to read.

Periodically, I looked up from my book to scan for Carlos. The streets were alive with morning shoppers, vendors, and people starting out for the day. By 9:00, the line into the courthouse extended along the front of the building and wrapped around the corner where I was standing. It was made up predominantly of young men, but there were women too, many alone, some with mothers and small children, a few with older men. Some people had arrived in pairs, others by themselves, some in suits, others in baggy jeans and do-rags. Virtually all were black or Latino/a, except for one recognizably white woman, scantily clad, with a haggard face and teased hair dyed platinum blond. The line had a calm energy and was sprinkled with small pink papers clutched in people's gloved hands.

At 9:45, I felt a light squeeze on the back of my arm. I turned to see Carlos's impish smile and large almond-shaped eyes looking up at me. He told me he got them from his Peruvian father. ("But don't tell anyone. My mom is Puerto Rican, so I just tell people I'm Puerto Rican," he said half jokingly one day during one of our first talks.) He was dressed in his typical style—extremely baggy clothes that made his small frame appear even smaller, a do-rag, and his favorite Yankees baseball cap.

Carlos apologized for being late as we walked toward the entrance. There was no longer a line to join. Carlos assured me that the last time he was at court, he wasn't called into the courtroom until after 10:00. I realized then that he was unaware that names were called in the order people arrived at the courthouse and handed in their summonses. Submitting a summons after 10 AM assured us a long day!

As we entered the courthouse, we were directed toward different lines to pass through the metal detectors. I was still uncomfortable with the process. I felt somehow exposed standing with my arms stretched out, the officer guiding the hand-held scanner over the contours of my body. We couldn't figure out why I kept beeping. At last, I found Carlos slipping his belt back through its loops. We had stood like that before, but still I was embarrassed and diverted my eyes.

"I hate that process," I said.

"Imagine how the girls at school feel doing that every day," he responded in a quiet voice.

Carlos handed in his summons at the window, and we slid into one of the long rows of benches arranged like church pews facing the large double doors into the courtroom. We sat for hours, intermittently in easy silence and casual conversation. We talked about our favorite movies and musicians, school, family, his urban childhood memories and my suburban ones. I showed him the book I was reading—a book about homeless men. "I don't understand how people become homeless," Carlos said. (Later in the year, his mother would take in his uncle for a couple of months while he was in transition.)

We bumped into Terrell and chatted briefly. Like Carlos, he and his brother James had received summonses for disorderly conduct. Carlos knew Terrell from the neighborhood. I recognized him from that late September day in Juarez's office. He smiled warmly and said, "I know you. You're the lady writing a book or something."

At some point during our wait, I asked Carlos, "So, how did you end up getting this summons, again?" He explained how a police officer had found him in the hallway of the school after the bell had rung. It was going into fourth period and Carlos was on his way to lunch. Carlos claimed that the stairwell was too crowded, so he decided to take another route, but the bell rang before he was able to work his way through the building to the cafeteria. Carlos believed that the police officer had disrespected him by demanding to see his ID and refusing to listen to an explanation for why he had been in the hallway when he wasn't supposed to be. As with so many students in

similar situations, Carlos decided not to cooperate, because he did not believe he had done anything wrong, so the officer cuffed him, brought him to the detention room, and gave him a summons for disorderly conduct.

It was after 1:30 in the afternoon when we returned from a lunch break. The court officer shouted out another round of names. Finally, we heard, "Carlos Mendoza!"

We went through the double doors and quietly took seats in another set of benches. About twenty people inside the small courtroom were waiting to see the judge, most of whom had received summonses evidently in the streets of their own neighborhoods. Terrell and his brother were already inside. They smiled at us. The officer bellowed out the names of the offenders and their offenses.

"Jose Rodriguez, public urination.... Fifty dollars. Can you pay it today?" The lawyer mumbled something. Jose did not have the money that day.

"Hector Media, open bottle, twelve-ounce Budweiser, and public urination...."

"Thomas Jones, disorderly conduct." A young black man from another Bronx high school presented himself before the judge. "What high school do you go to?" the judge asked from behind his large wooden desk on a high perch.

On that particular day, the judge decided he wanted to see the schoolboys on another day with a parent. Of the four in the room, none was accompanied by a parent that day. This was not always how a judge handled such cases. On another of my visits to court, with Duane, the judge took a different approach. Instead of requesting to meet with parents, he made a tired attempt to engage each offender.

"Duane Gordon, disorderly conduct!" the officer called out. I scooted over to give Duane room to pass.

The judge seemed confused by the charge of disorderly conduct. "So, what did you do?" he asked.

"Disorderly conduct," the lawyer replied as if that would clarify things.

The small judge, in his early sixties with thick, round glasses, was growing irritable. "Whatever you did, just don't do it again. Dismissed," he said with a slight sigh. As the courtroom doors closed behind Duane and me, we looked at each other and giggled at the judge's reaction.

But on that November afternoon, the judge's request to see a parent worried Carlos. He hadn't experienced this strategy. He asked me if I thought he'd be locked up. I said, "No, I think he just wants to speak to your mother." And I hoped that was really the case. (The next month we learned that that indeed was the case. Carlos missed another day of school and his mother, a counselor in a group home for developmentally disabled adults, missed a day of work to attend court and hear the judge rehash why her son needed to behave in school.)

After checking out the movie listings at the Concourse Plaza across the street, we walked along 161st Street toward the subway. Carlos was not his playful self; he was still worried about having to return to court with his mother, so we walked in silence. As we stepped off the curb at the Grand Concourse, he asked, "What does 'disorderly' mean, anyway?"

Given the ambiguity surrounding the events that led to police interventions, Carlos's question was not easily answered. In the context of UPHS, what *did* "disorderly" mean? I wondered. In his case, it referred to the acts of being in the hallway after the bell had rung, refusing to hand over his ID in an attempt to get a security agent to listen to his explanation, and arguing when the security agent refused to listen. Likewise, the arrests of and summonses given to Terrell and James arose from their being in the hallway when they were not supposed to be there. But how did the breaking of a school rule escalate so quickly into a police matter resulting in the issuance of a court summons?

When I first arrived at UPHS, I did not quite understand the behaviors that would lead to an arrest or summons for disorderly conduct. I remember asking one day in the deans' office, "What was that student arrested for?" The answer I received was resisting arrest. I persisted. "But why was he arrested in the first place?" The dean with whom I was conversing gave me a confused look and after a moment conceded, "Oh, I don't know. I wasn't there."

I began to explore the issue and learned from my examination of the occurrence reports that generally there were two types of behavior labeled disorderly conduct: altercations between students (total number: 45 out of about 110, covering twenty-two separate incidents); and students' insubordination during an exchange with an adult, usually involving the refusal to show identification (total number: 65).[4] So the refusal to show ID was landing all of these kids in front of a judge? It was hard to believe, but several individuals I interviewed gave similar accounts. One dean explained that students cut classes and hung out in the hallways, wearing hats and do-rags and fooling around. Then, when they were approached by security, they acted in an inappropriate manner. They wouldn't give up their IDs, they wouldn't go to class, and they just refused to do what they were told. Then they were brought downstairs (to the deans' office) and given a summons. It was the same process Carlos told me about, except that the story was now told from the perspective of an adult who was tired of students not being where they were supposed to be and disrespecting police officers.

An examination of the occurrence reports submitted by the deans helps to provide an understanding of what often transpired between a student and a school safety agent or officer leading up to an arrest or summons for disorderly conduct.[5] We see from the samples I quote here that the reports also reveal the interplay between an institutional demand for respect and the culture of penal control—one feeding the other.

(September 22, 2004) Sarah Watkins was issued a summons by PO —— of the XX pct for misbehaving.

(October 4, 2004) A male student Jonathan Walker was arrested by PO —— of the XX pct for insubordination. Jonathan refused to show ID to Officer ——.

(October 15, 2004) A male student was issued a summons by School Safety Task Force for Insubordination. He refused to identify himself. When SSA's [school safety agents] continued to ask him for identification he became irate. A suspension is pending.

(October 29, 2004) A male student was arrested by SSA —— and transported to the XX [precinct] for Disorderly Conduct and Resisting Arrest. He was observed with glazed eyes and an odor. It was suspected that he might be under the influence of a controlled substance. He was being escorted to the office when he became irate and resisted authority. A suspension is pending.

(November 5, 2004) A male student was issued a summons by PO —— of the XX pct for Disorderly Conduct and insubordination. He refused to show ID and was cursing at staff members. PO —— also arrested the student for an outstanding warrant.

(November 10, 2004) A male student was issued a summons by SSA —— for Disorderly Conduct. He refused to show ID and became irate and disorderly. A suspension is pending.

(November 23, 2004) A male student was issued a summons by PO —— of the Task Force for Disorderly Conduct. He was asked for his ID by an SSA, but he refused. A suspension is pending.

(December 17, 2004) A male student was issued a YD [youth referral] by PO —— of the School Safety Task Force for Insubordination. He refused to ID himself and was found loitering in the hall more than once. A suspension is pending.

(December 17, 2004) A female student was issued a YD for Disorderly Conduct by PO —— of the XX pct. She refused to present identification when asked to do so. A suspension is pending.

(December 23, 2004) A male student was issued a summons by PO —— of the XX pct for Disorderly Conduct. He refused to produce ID and became verbally abusive toward the officer. A suspension is pending.

(January 19, 2005) Two male students, Donald and Steven was issued a Summons by PO —— of the XX pct for Disorderly Conduct. They refused to show ID when asked by the officers. A suspension is pending.

(February 11, 2005) A female student was issued a YD by PO —— of the XX for Disorderly Conduct. She refused to show identification and cursed out a Dean. A suspension is pending.

(February 14, 2005) A male student was issued a summons by PO —— of the School Safety Task Force for Insubordination. He was being uncooperative towards a police officer and refused to show his identification. Student Quinton Willis, was found on the 3rd floor stairwell with a female student. PO —— approached Quinton and requested his ID card. Quinton claimed he didn't have one and became very defiant and insubordinate towards the police officer. Quinton was taken downstairs to the dean's office and was issued a summons.

(March 3, 2005) A male student was issued a summons by PO —— of the XX pct for Disorderly Conduct. He was asked to stop by PO —— and became irate and uncontrollable. He had to be restrained. A suspension is pending. At the time of occurrence, defendant was asked to stop and present ID, refused and became verbally abusive to PO —— and did public alarm and disturbance on the 3rd floor.

(March 21, 2005) A male student was issued a YD by PO —— of the XX pct for Disorderly Conduct. He was verbally abusive towards the PO's and he refused to comply with their instructions. A suspension is pending. Student was insubordinate and verbally abusive.

(March 30, 2005) A male student was issued a YD by PO —— of the School Safety Task Force for Insubordination. He was insubordinate with SSAs and PD. A suspension is pending. Shane Tompkins attempted to enter the student cafeteria and was told to go to class. Shane became uncooperative to school safety agent —— and SSA —— requested for assistance. PO —— approached Dean —— and SSA ——. Shane was told to leave but became belligerent and insubordinate to PO ——.

(March 31, 2005) A female student was issued a YD by PO —— of the XX pct for Disorderly Conduct. She was insubordinate towards a female SSA —— and used profanity towards her. A suspension is pending. Student was insubordinate to SSA —— and used abusive language when given a directive.

(April 6, 2005) A female student was issued a summons by PO —— of the XX pct for Disorderly Conduct. She refused to show identification and she verbally abused SSA ——. Suspension is pending.

(April 6, 2005) A female student was issued a YD by PO —— of the XX pct for Disorderly Conduct. She was approached by PO —— and was disrespectful and used inappropriate language towards him. A suspension is pending.

(May 25, 2005) A male student was issued a summons by PO —— of the XX pct for Disorderly Conduct. He refused to obey the directions of officers and became verbally abusive. A suspension is pending. Student Marcus Brown was issued a C-Summons for disorderly conduct by NYPD. He refused to follow directions and was verbally disrespectful.

(May 25, 2005) A male student was issued a YD by PO —— of the XX pct for Disorderly Conduct. During scanning he refused to follow directives and punched the glass in the door causing injury to his hand. EMS transported [student] to the hospital. A suspension is pending. Student Juan Garcia was defiant with Dean —— and SSA agents —— and —— when asked to take off his "Doo-Rag" and step into the vestibule before entering school. After several minutes of insubordination and defiant behavior, Juan punched through the glass of the lobby door, injuring his hand. He was issued a YD and taken to —— Hospital as a result.

Each of these incidents began with a student breaking a school rule defined by the Department of Education rather than the law. Sarah Watkins was misbehaving; Juan Garcia refused to follow directions during scanning; Shane Tompkins attempted to enter the cafeteria when it was not his assigned lunch period. In a number of incidents, although the rule was not explicitly stated in the report, students may have been in the hallways or stairwell when classes were in session, were possibly spotted in an unlikely part of the building, or perhaps were wearing a hat. In fact, none of these behaviors was a matter that warranted a police intervention; in most cases, the inciting behavior is listed in the 2004 DOE Discipline Code as a level-one infraction—the least serious type of offense. An incident usually escalated into a police matter when a student refused to hand over his or her ID card. But even this, "failing to provide school officials with proper identification," was considered a level-one infraction.[6]

Sometimes the inciting moment came when a security agent grabbed a student or pulled the student's hat off his or her head and the student "became irate" or even reacted physically. These were the types of scenarios that I observed and that were commonly reported to me by students but were not documented in occurrence reports. It became particularly palpable for me, though, one day while I was walking down the hallway at the tail end of the change of periods and a security agent, whose attention was diverted toward two students on the other side of him, suddenly swung his arm up in front of my chest and grabbed my shoulder, thinking I was a student. When he turned and saw a rather stunned adult, he apologized profusely: "I'm so sorry, miss, I thought you were one of the kids." Despite his apology, I was left feeling a little unsettled, knowing that at least this security agent considered it acceptable to grab students.

According to the language in the occurrence reports, the issuance of a summons or an arrest for disorderly conduct appeared to be justified in the eyes of law-enforcement officials and deans by a student's display of "irate," "insubordinate," "disrespectful," "uncooperative," or "uncontrollable" behavior. None of the occurrence reports provided any sort of explanation of the student's behavior. There was an implicit assumption that students' irate behavior was completely unprovoked or, in any case, inappropriate, and warranted punishment not only through the school system but also through the criminal- (or juvenile-) justice system.

Several police officers explained to me that a summons was "no big deal." It simply indicated a "violation of the law" and was "virtually no different than receiving a traffic ticket." However, it *was* different, in several important ways. For one thing, when students received a summons in school for disorderly conduct, they had to appear in criminal court, not transit court. The criminal-court experience was markedly different from the traffic-court experience, where there were no escorted handcuffed individuals on display, no officers yelling out people's offenses, no standing before a judge, and no wondering whether this would be the time the judge would say, "Enough. It's time this kid does some time."

When students received summonses and got arrested during situations that began with the breaking of a school rule, the behaviors they displayed for which an officer issued a summons often came only *after* the officer or agent confronted the student. Yet no one asked, at least in official terms, why a student had become disorderly or what it actually meant. Order had become top priority, and "disrespect" was not tolerated within the emerging culture of control.

Violations of the Law: The Predominance of Law-and-Order Practices

At UPHS, 56 percent of all student actions that resulted in a summons, youth referral, or arrest might be subject to criminal-procedural-level strategies in other contexts. In most cases, they would be considered violations of the law (a lesser offense than a misdemeanor) or actual misdemeanors, and in a very small number of cases,[7] the behaviors might be considered felony offenses. The vast majority of these latter incidents involved fighting, weapon possession, or drug possession and, therefore, were punishable by law. Nevertheless, several questions arose for me regarding the efficacy and fairness of arrests and summonses in these cases.

My questions stemmed, first, from the disproportionately high levels of surveillance to which students at UPHS were subjected. Second, I observed that criminal-procedural-level strategies tended to overshadow the use of positive (as opposed to punitive) educational strategies to reduce drug sales and participation in violence. In fact, even when positive strategies, such as counseling, were used, they were auxiliary strategies. The criminal-justice-oriented strategies were the ones that came to define a given incident as a crime.

Finally, particularly in the case of fighting, there was considerable subjectivity in determining whether a behavior was actually a violation of the law. This subjectivity might be explained, in part, by how school personnel contested policing practices and preferred to use their own strategies whenever possible. But, at the same time, minor physical altercations were often defined as criminal acts, and a penal logic tended to eclipse both the efforts toward and the use of more positive or transformative strategies for the reduction of violence and crime, such as peer mediation, comprehensive student-directed antiviolence initiatives, or massive antidrug campaigns.

Drug and Weapon Possession

Inside a school like UPHS, where students had become the subjects of high surveillance and heavy policing, the actions that often resulted in arrest or the issuance of a summons were often not ones that would have been detected in any other circumstance. According to occurrence reports, drug-possession violations, for example, were almost always discovered during the morning scanning ritual, and, in a few instances, controlled substances were found on students during body searches conducted after a student "disrespected" a law-enforcement official during a routine interaction. In other circumstances, say, on the street or in a park or in a typical suburban high school, the police would not have the authority to search a child who did not elicit any suspicion.

Like summonses for drug possession, virtually all summonses for weapons possession were given out at scanning, as students entered the building. In these incidents, the dual impact of zero tolerance and order maintenance became most evident. Many school personnel, for example, regarded the practices around weapons possession as problematic, because students who intended to use weapons in schools were often not the ones getting caught with weapons during scanning. The principal explained: "If a child goes through scanning with a box cutter, it's because they really had no intention of doing anything with it. And I would say [this is true] 99 percent of the time, because otherwise the child would try to hide the blade. There's many ways of hiding a blade very easily to come through scanning."

Many reports in the last decade have presented long lists of absurd arrests made for weapon possession under the national policy of zero tolerance, such as a young child getting suspended for pointing a chicken strip at a classmate as if it were a gun.[8] At UPHS, no report was quite so absurd; in most cases the instrument in question clearly qualified as a weapon. Twenty-four summonses for weapon possession were given out during the school year for the following: five knives, six box cutters, seven razor blades, two cans of mace, one can of pepper spray, one metal pick, and one unspecified weapon. Some may have been carried with the intent to harm someone. However, it was commonly accepted among administrators, deans, and officers that such weapons were carried most often because they were instruments students used at work or for other nonviolent tasks (for example, one of the seven razors was found in a girl's book bag; she claimed that she used it to do her hair), or because they offered students a sense of protection as they walked through their neighborhoods (for example, the mace and pepper spray—common defensive measures against rape—were found on girls). Alvarez lamented,

> There's that zero tolerance in terms of bringing weapons into the building, which I agree with. You know, honestly, however, those policies do not see the young lady or the young man who works for a living to help support the family who has to go into the stock room and open boxes and put them on the shelves, goes

home late every day, puts the box cutter in his pocket, forgets about it, comes the next day into school, and the child has to be arrested, suspended, because you have to follow the policy. So that is a very difficult situation for any administrator to be in, to have a child who actually comes to school, who actually does the work, who's doing fairly well, and then you have to arrest the child and suspend him.

None of the incidents involving drugs led to a student referral into a drug-treatment or education program. Students carrying weapons into school were not invited into an antiviolence program and certainly not a self-defense class; nor were the reasons for their having a weapon explored by counselors or administrators in any systematic way. There was also no systemic effort to provide possible alternatives for students, such as tutoring, career counseling, or job training to set them on alternative paths. There were some services provided at the school through the SPARK program,[9] the guidance counselors' office, and the deans' office, but such interventions reached a relatively small percentage of the population and occurred more through the tenacious work of individuals than through any institutionally supported efforts.

Physical Altercations

It is difficult to make definitive claims about the ways in which incidents of violence were handled in the school based on an examination of occurrence reports. On the one hand, I found that not all physical acts of violence were criminalized, despite the fact that there might have been some justification for doing so. On the other hand, there sometimes appeared to be excessively punitive responses to minor physical altercations. According to the occurrence reports, there were forty-one incidents of physical altercations during the school year

for which eighty-two students were either arrested or given a summons or youth referral.[10] Of these, fifty-six students received summonses or youth referrals for disorderly conduct. In the remaining cases, students were either charged with assault or the charge was unspecified. Additionally, the reports revealed that there were at least twenty-seven incidents of fighting or other forms of violence in which the police were not involved.

Among the incidents that led to the use of criminal-procedural-level strategies, there was significant variation in the level of severity. Several reports simply indicated that "students were involved in physical altercation." Some were a little more specific, stating something like, "Two girls were fighting in the hallway," or "The verbal argument led to a physical altercation." One report indicated that four students received youth referrals for disorderly conduct for a verbal altercation that "almost led to a physical altercation." Others seemed to indicate a more serious situation. For example, one report described an altercation between six boys that "led to riotous conditions."

There are numerous explanations for the subjectivity that is revealed in these data, including whether or not an incident was gang related and the dissimilarity in students' disciplinary records. Additionally, the inconsistent responses to violence, in part, were due to the persistent efforts of some administrators and deans to contest the use of criminal-procedural-level strategies and to emphasize the use of their own strategies, such as peer mediation and counseling. Nevertheless, minor incidents, even a few that, according to occurrence reports, involved only verbal altercations, sometimes resulted in the use of criminal-procedural-level strategies.

There is another possible reason for the inconsistent use of criminal-procedural-level strategies as a response to violence: the behaviors of students *after* an incident took place. Students appeared to be at risk of receiving a summons when they displayed anger or were unable to calm themselves after an emotionally charged altercation, especially when they appeared to think the intervening officers or school officials treated them unnecessarily harshly. In these cases, it seemed that students received summonses as an outcome of their "disorderly" behavior after a physical altercation, rather than for their participation in it. Occurrence reports did not indicate this specifically, but on several occasions I observed confrontations between students and law enforcement officials that occurred after a student was "picked up" for fighting where it appeared that the summons was an outcome of the student's conflict with law enforcement (or school personnel).

The Ubiquity of the Threat

The actual number of arrests and summonses issued over the entire school year may not seem excessive to some, considering the total number of students in the school,[11] the length of my study (a full school year), and the nature of urban youth violence and crime. However, the culture of control was not simply a by-product of the use of summonses, arrests, and other criminal-procedural-level strategies; as these policies and practices went into effect, it seemed that a law-and-order discourse emerged within the school, and the use of *threats* of summonses and arrest became commonplace. These threats played a significant role in the establishment of a culture of control in the school.

On several occasions, after altercations took place or when students were brought to B-40 as a result of a confrontation with a law-enforcement official or teacher, I observed students' being questioned. When a student did not present him- or herself in a calm and "respectful" manner, the adult—a dean or officer—would often threaten the student with arrest and

a summons, and at times the police would make good on their threat. Typically, these moments would entail heated exchanges between students and school personnel or officers. For example, on a number of occasions I heard both security agents and school personnel say things like, "Keep it up and you'll get a summons," or, "Do you want to get arrested? Calm down."

Even when threats were made as warnings by well-meaning educators who actually wanted to prevent an arrest, the threats ultimately reinforced the culture of control. Threats attempted to squelch dissent. They strengthened the culture of control in that they appeared to grow out of the belief that students had given up their rights in the moment when they broke a school rule or lost control of their emotions. After such an incident, a student was at risk of being handcuffed, charged with breaking the law, and summoned to criminal court if he or she did not quickly become calm and respectful. A brief exchange I witnessed exemplifies this attitude. A student who had been in a fight sat at a desk in the deans' office. It did not appear that the police were set to arrest the other students who had taken part in the fight. They were nowhere in sight. To no one in particular, the student in the office made barely audible comments declaring that he had rights and complained about the way the incident had been handled. A dean admonished him, "Be quiet. You've already abdicated all your rights. The more you say, the more trouble you'll be in. Keep it up and you know what will happen."

Summonses Inside and Out

One morning during spring break, my phone rang while I was getting ready to meet Carlos. It was Officer Bowen from Transit. "Do you know Carlos Mendoza?" he asked.

"Yes," I said and waited for his reason for calling me, although I already realized that Carlos must have been picked up on his way to meet me. The officer told me that Carlos had used his school-issued MetroCard to ride the subway on a nonschool day. The officer needed me to verify Carlos's identity, because Carlos did not have identification on him. (In such circumstances, individuals are brought to a precinct house until their identities are verified. Youth, in particular, are subjected to this process, as they are less likely than adults to have ID with them.)

I explained that Carlos may have thought he was on a school-related excursion to meet me, a researcher. But my explanation came too late and was not relevant to the officer. Carlos was issued a summons for fare evasion, which meant a $65 fine and yet another one-hour trip to Brooklyn transit court and a day of missing school. I had just been to transit court with him a few months earlier. (Unlike criminal court, there were no handheld scanners or bellowing proclamations of people's offenses in transit court—just a large room full of young black and Latino/a men and women and a long set of cashier windows.)

This was a typical experience of many of the students at UPHS that I met. It was not just at school that students received summonses. They accumulated them around school, in their neighborhoods, and in the subway stations. One day in early October, sitting in the detention room with Duane and a group of his friends, I asked them about this. They all had received a number of summonses both inside and outside school. One of the boys, Evan, in response to my question, pulled a crumpled wad of six slips out of his pocket. He smiled sheepishly and explained, "I have to hide them from my father."

But it was not just students frequenting the detention room who were accumulating summonses. Most of the students I interviewed had received at least one summons at some point within the previous year. Kalif, an articulate junior whom I met in the school leadership office, received a summons for

fare evasion one night when he used his school MetroCard to return to school after official hours to pick up something he had forgotten. Another student, David, got one for walking through a park after closing hours and another one for loitering in front of the school. One student claimed to have gotten a summons for smoking. Many others reported getting summonses outdoors for loitering, jumping the subway turnstile, disorderly conduct, or littering.

"What kinds of summonses are kids getting outside of school?" I asked eighteen-year-old Wanda.

"Okay, if, like, say I'm on 149th and Grand Concourse; I'm waiting for the number 2 train to come. This happened to me. I spit my gum out on the platform. The cop was, like, 'Excuse me, did you just spit your gum out on the platform?' And, you know, I'm not going to lie, because obviously he seen me. I was, like, 'Yes.' He gave me a sixty-dollar ticket."

"For littering?"

"For littering," Wanda confirms. "I was, like, *a piece of gum*! For a thirty-cent gum I'm gonna get a sixty-dollar fine?"

Later in our discussion, Wanda pointed out that, like many of the students I interviewed, she avoided going outside at the end of the month, because she believed that the police had a quota of summonses to fill. I asked her to explain. She said, "The quota is when the police officers have to give a certain amount of people tickets at the end of the month, and if they don't meet that, they get in trouble."

"So, they're looking for students to . . ."

"Basically," Wanda explained, "and that's when kids don't mouth off to the cops at the end of the month, because they know better."

"Interesting. You think that's a pretty standard thing? Kids know?" (In fact, I had already been informed by an officer that it was not an actual NYPD policy, but officers conceded to me that some cops did need to bolster their numbers and tended to look for kids to give summonses to at times.)

Wanda replied, "Yeah, kids know. Like, right now, from last week till this week, I haven't been outside."

"Why is outside...?"

"It's not that I'm scared to go outside, I just don't want to get a ticket, because them tickets add up, and, plus, if you don't pay the tickets, they come looking for you." And indeed they do. Young people who do not appear in court are eventually found and hauled down to the precinct in handcuffs. I even noted a few instances when students with unanswered summonses were tracked down and pulled out of their classes. Sometimes police caught up with youngsters when they received additional summonses, because their names were already in the police database. On one occasion, Carlos spent almost twenty-four hours in a jail cell when he was picked up for sneaking into a movie theater, and unbeknown to him, there was a warrant out for his arrest for a summons he had received and forgotten about. Upon leaving jail, he was sentenced to one day of community service and fined $95.

Thus, given that the young people in my study were receiving summonses inside and outside school, school-based policing interacted with street policing, creating an intensified level of penal control over their lives. A summons received in school could come back to haunt them in a movie theater, and a summons received on the street could lead to getting pulled out of class.

Penal Control in the Lives of Excluded Urban Youth

...I have attempted to show how school disciplinary policies and practices— namely, order maintenance, along with zero tolerance—have the effect of criminalizing noncriminal behavior. My goal was to demonstrate how policies and practices shape school culture, and, more specifically, how order maintenance and the threats that are doled out within the current framework foster a culture of control. Additionally, I have detailed how the students at UPHS were subjected to the same policing strategies around the school and in their neighborhoods. The use of order-maintenance policing in so many of the public domains through which urban youth traverse appears to create situations where they are routinely being confronted by police officers and accumulating court summonses—and if they are not actually getting summonses, they are keenly aware of the possibility of getting them, as Wanda explained. These findings highlight that, although the oft-used metaphor of the school-to-prison pipeline is helpful (and real), the lived experience of many students at UPHS can be better understood through a nuanced description of daily life rather than the pipeline metaphor.[12] Despite a valuable body of scholarly literature on the subject, not all students in these schools are going to prison.[13] In fact, the majority will not likely spend significant time behind bars. To gain sufficient understanding of the everyday life experience of students at the school, it is useful to highlight a more mundane but pervasive phenomenon: how the lives of impoverished urban students are managed by a complex interpenetration of systems. The school, where they are by law required to spend most of their day, becomes an auxiliary to the criminal-justice system. These findings show that urban youth get subjected to levels of surveillance and repression that are not the same as long-term incarceration, but nonetheless, as the school merges with an ideology of street policing, the courts, and even the prison, a particular culture of penal control becomes an aspect of everyday life at school and beyond.

NOTES

1. "Criminal-procedural-level strategies" was a term used by officers to distinguish their own approaches from the approaches used by educators for dealing with discipline problems. Such strategies include body searches, handcuffing, interrogating, arrests, and the issuance of court summonses.
2. Garland, *Culture of Control*, 124–129.
3. According to aggregate data reported by the police department, which appear on the school report card (see New York City Department of Education, School Report Cards), 240 incidents led to police action (arrest or summons). The discrepancy may exist because deans may not have written up all incidents. This possibility is supported by the fact that there were at least two police incidents that I was aware of that took place inside the school for which I did not find occurrence reports. It is also possible that school personnel did not write up incidents that took place outside the school despite their being considered school-related matters.
4. There were three more summonses issued for disorderly conduct for unspecified reasons. In the case of physical altercations, there were other incidents in which it was not clear whether students received summonses for disorderly conduct, assault, or harassment. In cases where students received summonses for "misbehaving" or "insubordination," I included these in the "disorderly conduct" category.
5. Statements are quoted verbatim and in their entirety. Only names were changed, to pseudonyms.
6. New York City Department of Education, *New York City School Discipline Code*, 10.
7. On the School Report Card for the 2004–2005 school year (New York City Department of Education), the number of "crimes against persons" in the "major crimes" category was eight. Occurrence reports offer no information as to the classification of criminal offenses, and information as to what these crimes were is unavailable. From the data I did collect, however, it appears likely that these incidents were gang-related fistfights or assaults. Although there was documentation for several incidents of weapon possession, only one occurrence report indicated the use of a weapon during a fight. In this incident, a female student hit another student in the head with a combination lock. The offender was arrested for assault. Another report indicated that a student was transported to a hospital.
8. American Bar Association, *ABA Zero Tolerance Report*.
9. SPARK is a program that provides services related to the social aspects of schooling. SPARK staff counsel students and engage them in discussions on the consequences of risky behavior.
10. In some cases, only one student received a summons. During other incidents, as many as six students received summonses.
11. The total population of UPHS was about 3,000. The total number of police actions (arrests, summonses, and youth referrals) was 240, according to police records. There were occurrence reports for 221 of these actions.
12. Brown, *Derailed* and *Education on Lockdown*.
13. American Bar Association, *ABA Zero Tolerance Report*; Brown, *Derailed* and *Education on Lockdown*; and Ziedenberg, Brooks, and Shiraldi, *School House Hype*.

REFERENCES

American Bar Association. 2001. *ABA Zero Tolerance Report*. Washington, D.C.: American Bar Association (February).

Brown, Judith. 2003 *Derailed: The Schoolhouse to Jailhouse Track*. Washington, D.C.: Advancement Project.

————. 2005. *Education on Lockdown: The Schoolhouse to Jailhouse Track*. Washington, D.C.: Advancement Project.

Garland, David. 2001. *The Culture of Control: Crime and Social Order in Contemporary Society*. Chicago: University of Chicago Press.

New York City Department of Education. 2004. *New York City School Discipline Code*.

New York: New York City Department of Education.

————. School Report Cards, 2004–2005. http://schools.nyc.gov/daa/SchoolReports/ (accessed September 18, 2006).

Ziedenberg, Jason, Kim Brooks, and Vincent Shiraldi. 2000. *School House Hype: Two Years Later*. Washington, D.C.: Justice Policy Institute (April).

25

VICTOR M. RIOS

THE LABELING HYPE: COMING OF AGE IN THE ERA OF MASS INCARCERATION

from *Punished* (2011)

In his book, the sociologist Victor M. Rios (himself a former gang member) follows the lives of several young men from Oakland as they become involved in criminal activity. In this excerpt, he explores how one young man, "Tyrell," copes with various formal and informal forces, including school, that label him as a potential criminal—a label that he himself eventually accepts.

Tyrell, a Black youth, and Jose, a Latino youth, both sixteen years old, sat on a splintered wood bench at the bus stop on the corner of 35th and International, in front of Hernandez Meat Market. Right above them, a pig and the head of a cow, painted on the meat-market wall, stared straight down at them. A street sign, adjacent to the bus stop, read, "All activity on this block is being recorded." I leaned back on the sign, as I observed and listened to Tyrell and Jose. They looked around: Jose stared at people in cars, while Tyrell looked at a group of four teenage Black boys walking across the street.

I was shadowing Tyrell and Jose as they made their way home from school. Tyrell lived close to 65th Avenue; and Jose, past 80th Avenue. They were having a conversation about their principal. "Man! Mr. Schwartz is an asshole! He be on one, man [gets crazy]!" Tyrell told Jose. Jose rubbed his head and replied, "Dude just called the police on me today." When I asked why, he answered, "'Cause he said I was threatening him. But all I did was tell him that if he called the police, they had nothing on me.... He said, 'Oh, yeah, all right. Let's see.' And then he called them." Jose dug into the baggy black jeans' pocket that sat close to his knee and handed me a yellow citation given to him by the police officer. At the top it read, "Notice to Appear," with the number 0188546XX. In the middle was Jose's violation: "CPC 647 Dist. Peace." "Dude [police officer] came by and just started writing me a ticket. He said he would arrest me, but he had some other shit to do."

"What did you do?" I asked.

"Shit, disturbed the peace at school.... I talked back to the principal. That's what I get."

Tyrell responded, "Homey, that's nothing. You should see all the times they've stopped me for little shit, like looking at them crazy or walking down the street."

During three years of observations I counted forty-two citations imposed on the boys. Loitering, disturbing the peace, drinking in public, not wearing a properly fitted bicycle helmet, and violating curfew were among the violations they received citations for. Minor citations for "little shit" played a crucial role in pipelining many of the young men in this study deeper into the criminal justice system. Some of the boys missed their court dates; others appeared in court but could not pay their citations. This led to warrants for arrest or probation. Warrants and probationary status marked the young men for further criminalization. Police, school personnel, and probation officers would graduate the boys to a new level of policing and harassment. Being on probation, for instance, meant that the boys could be stopped, searched, or reported, at any given moment. Probation status provided the youth control complex a carte blanche in its endeavor to stigmatize, punish, and exclude young people. When a young person is on probation, he is left with few

rights; he can be stopped and searched for no reason, and he can be arrested for non-criminal transgressions such as hanging out with his friends or walking in the wrong part of the neighborhood....

[L]abeling is not just a process whereby schools, police, probation officers, and families stigmatize the boys, and, in turn, their delinquency persists or increases.[1] In the era of mass incarceration, labeling is also a process by which agencies of social control further stigmatize and mark the boys in response to their original label.[2] This in turn creates a vicious cycle that multiplies the boys' experiences with criminalization, what I call a labeling hype. I found that the boys in this study felt outcast, shamed, and unaccepted, sometimes leading them to a sense of hopelessness and a "deviant self-concept."[3] In addition, I also found that the young men were caught in a spiral of punitive responses imposed by institutions which labeled them as deviant. Being labeled or marked for minor transgressions would place the boys at risk for being granted additional, more serious labels.

Institutions became involved in a spiral of criminalization that began with informal, trivial labels, such as "This kid comes from a bad family and is at-risk." This label alone would sometimes lead to more detrimental labels, such as "This kid is delinquent, and he is a risk." Criminologist Paul Hirschfield argues that labels have little impact on the individual identities of marginalized black males, but they have a big effect on young people's social mobility. He posits that "mass criminalization" is responsible for "social exclusion" and "diminished social expectations."[4] In the era of mass incarceration, labeling not only generates criminality; it also perpetuates criminalization.

Previous studies in urban ethnography have done an exceptional job at describing blocked opportunity and its consequences.[5] However, criminalization as a system that contributes to this blocked opportunity has yet to be analyzed. This system had such an extensive influence on the lives of the boys in this study that many of them were criminalized even when they were victims of crime. Criminalization became internalized by many of the boys, even leading some to believe that they did not deserve protection from the police. Tyrell's . . . [life story] shows the process by which young men come of age in Oakland being labeled as deviant and eventually being treated like criminals. In this respect, [he is] representative of many of the other boys in this study. . . .

The bus arrived. Tyrell and Jose changed their conversation about police and citations. Tyrell asked me, "So you still wanna go to the Ville?" I told him I did. The "Ville" was a low-income housing project located on 66th Avenue and International. Tyrell spent most of his childhood there. Although he had recently moved out, he hung out there every day with his friends, in an alley that residents refer to as "Death Alley." We got on the bus and remained silent, observing the twenty or so other teenagers sardined inside. Tyrell and I got off the bus and silently nodded to Jose, who remained on the bus heading further down International. When we arrived at the Ville, I asked Tyrell to give me a tour, from his perspective, and tell me about growing up in this environment.

Tyrell's Too Tall

Since the late 1980s, the Ville housing project has been notorious for its crime rate.[6] Famous former residents include Felix Mitchell, who established one of the most influential crack-cocaine gang empires in the country there during the '80s. Mitchell was killed in prison in 1986, but he is still a legend in this community. The 1991 film *New Jack City* used Mitchell's life as the basis for one of its main characters, Nino Brown. Tyrell and his friends still talk about Mitchell; "Mitchell was a true G

[gangster]. . . . He is like the only role model we got," said Tyrell. This statement is indicative of the lack of programs in schools or in the community, which could have exposed young people to professional and college-educated role models.

The Ville, notorious for its drug trafficking and violence, consisted of rows and rows of two-story, shoebox-shaped apartment buildings, with metal window and door gates—the epitome of West Coast housing projects. The new two-tone light-beige and pink paint and fancy geometric trim on the top of some of the recently remodeled buildings belied the bullet holes in apartment windows, the homemade tin-foil crack pipes laying on the lawns, and the dire poverty of little kids fighting to ride the only neighborhood bike. The city had recently demolished similar buildings down the street and in their place developed modern townhouse-style projects, shaped like squares, with attractive geometrical rooftops and three-tone light-beige, yellow, and green paint jobs. These new housing developments were juxtaposed with drug dealers standing at the corner, with middle-aged crack addicts pacing about in desperation and the bloody street fights that constantly took place in the Ville. The millions of dollars spent on physical upgrades could not bandage the persistence of violence, crime, and criminalization that could only be transformed by implementing programs which could change the social order and social control of the neighborhood, not just its physical appearance.[7] If certain social contexts breed criminality, then certain social contexts breed criminalization. The cycle of crime and violence cannot be addressed by changing the appearance of a place and incarcerating its denizens; we must start by changing the social contexts that provide actors the resources for partaking in specific behaviors and by transforming the ways in which we perceive and treat—criminalize or incorporate—these populations.

As we walked around the Ville, Tyrell pointed to different locations that ignited his memory; where he first got high, where he first witnessed a murder in Death Alley, and where the police brutalized him for the very first time. Tyrell looked at me when we got to "Death Alley," an alley that residents understood as a space where deadly violence was a regular presence, and asked, "What do you want to know?" The space seemed to spark a desire in Tyrell to share his story. We sat on a giant piece of broken concrete which was used to form a retaining wall between the alley and a now-abandoned house.

Tyrell was raised by his father, John. According to Tyrell, his mother had left them for a man who made a good living selling crack. "She told my dad, 'You ain't shit, can't even get a job,' so she bounced." Soon after, she became addicted to crack. According to Tyrell, his mother's boyfriend was also a crack user and passed the addiction on to her. Tyrell's mother showed up sporadically, asking him and his grandmother for money to support her addiction. "She smokes so much crack, she calls herself 'Bubbles,'" Tyrell told me. On another day, when I was hanging out with Tyrell in Death Alley, where he and his friends would convene every afternoon, Tyrell's mother came around the corner. She asked him, "Have you seen Mo?" Tyrell nodded, looking embarrassed. She asked me for money, and I told her I would give Tyrell some money on her behalf. She thanked me for what she perceived as my helping her son and walked off, through an alley onto an adjacent block. This situation was not unique to Tyrell: eighteen of the boys in the study reported having at least one parent who had problems with drugs or alcohol.

Tyrell was homeless for part of his childhood, sleeping in cars, shelters, crack houses, and in the parking lot of the Ville. In Tyrell's account, the housing authority did not want to provide his father housing. "Because he was not a woman...they told

him that he had no reason for not having a job." Tyrell's dad was a mechanic but could not find work at the time:

He worked on other people's cars, but they were broke too. They gave him five, ten dollars, but he couldn't pay rent with this. So we ended up at other people's houses or in our car most of the time....One day a crack head [addict] told us she was moving back to Atlanta. She said that we could live in her apartment if we wanted, but we had to pay rent. This is when we got our own place. I was hella happy knowing that I would have my own place. That's crazy, I was happy, 'cause I was gonna live in the projects....It was hella fun living there.

Despite the surrounding violence, drug abuse, and poverty—as well as the consequential trauma, homelessness, and hunger—Tyrell remembers having a fun childhood. His father taught him about being respectful to others and obeying the law no matter how poor they were. "Pops wouldn't steal from nobody. He would rather starve than steal," Tyrell told me. John attempted to keep Tyrell sheltered from the effects of poverty; sometimes it worked. John taught him that some police officers were good and encouraged him to be the cop when he played cops and robbers. By the second or third grade, all his friends made fun of him for playing the cop. By then, most of his peers believed that the police were a negative force in the community, but Tyrell still believed that police had the power to "take the bad people away from the Ville."

Despite not having the resources to provide "proper" parenting, such as help with homework or money for school trips or work clothes, the majority of the boys' parents attempted to instill positive values in their children, even if some of them did not have a standard definition of mainstream values. Often, parents became desperate in their failed attempts to guide their children. This led some parents to ask probation, police, or school officials to teach them strategies for parenting their children. As these institutions advised desperate individuals on how to parent their children, they passed on their punitive approaches to treating deviant and delinquent behavior. In a sense, they taught parents how to criminalize their own children....

In fourth grade, an older Tyrell and his homies would walk a few miles to the Oakland Coliseum, located two miles from the Ville, when the Oakland Athletics or Oakland Raiders played games. "We would walk like twenty blocks to the Coliseum to watch the games. They wouldn't let us in, so we stood outside on the very top and looked through the cracks between the fence. The guys [players] were this little [he measures about an inch with his thumb and index finger], but we still got to see 'em, they hit a homerun." Police chased Tyrell and his friends off the Coliseum grounds. He could not understand why they were so aggressive toward him, when he was "just trying to watch a game." According to Tyrell, police threatened him and his friends with arrest if they continued to loiter at the Coliseum.

By the sixth grade, Tyrell felt that he could no longer exist outside the violence that defined the Ville. "Sixth grade is where it all went down. Cops started beating on me, fools [peers] started getting hyphy [crazy] with me. I had to get into, um, lots of fights," Tyrell said. He told me that his height contributed to his forced entry into street life. In the sixth grade, Tyrell was the tallest student in school. He remembered going into class on the first day of sixth grade, and his teacher, Mrs. Turpin, would not stop staring at him. Tyrell became bothered and asked her, "What you lookin' at?" She used his comment as a lesson to the class that everyone was to respect the teacher. She kicked him out of class and told the principal she was "threatened" by Tyrell. Twenty-two of the boys reported feeling as if their teachers were scared of them.

Tyrell believes that the teacher was not the only person who saw him as a threat, because of his height, when he was younger. In his account, because he looked like a man by age twelve, he also became a target of constant police surveillance and random checks for drugs or criminal suspicions:

The five-o [police] stopped me all the time. They checked me for drugs and guns most of the time. At first I was scared and told them I was only twelve. They didn't believe me and kept asking me where I was hiding the drugs. That made me hella mad 'cause I wasn't slanging [selling drugs] or anything. On mama's [I promise] I wasn't slanging. I said, fuck it. So a few months later I started selling weed.

Tyrell's perspective was that he could not control his height, physical appearance, or the perceptions that others had of him. The one thing he could control was making the choice to sell drugs to support himself. Tyrell's decision to sell drugs is representative of the patterns that I found among all the boys during their first arrest. They chose to commit a crime, consciously calculating the potential risk of arrest and incarceration. Many of the boys came to this assessment after believing that they had no other choice, that they had nothing to lose.

In my observations, I noticed that Tyrell had a compelling presence. Police officers whom he had never encountered before targeted Tyrell more often than the other Black and Latino youths I hung out with. Over the course of three years, I watched or heard from Tyrell about being stopped by police twenty-one times, more than any other youth in this study. Most of the time, these stops ended with just a short conversation. But sometimes, police officers seemed threatened by Tyrell, and they either handcuffed him, pulled a gun on him, or put him in the patrol car.

Meanwhile, according to Tyrell, his father increasingly took his stress and anger out on Tyrell. John grew frustrated at his inability to find a steady job. Despite his charisma and exceptional mechanic skills, he could not find regular work. He was only able to find employment in the local informal economy: poor local residents would bring their cars to him for repairs but were not able to pay enough for him to make a living. In the Ville, no matter what time of day, I always saw John working on someone's car. He was always cheerful and joked around with everyone in the neighborhood. While John had all the characteristics of a supportive father, his lack of economic resources led Tyrell to realize that he would have to "hustle" for his own money:

> I told him I had a little money, and he knew where I got it from. He got hella mad and beat me down. He told me he did not want me selling that shit. I told him it was only weed, but he didn't care. He told me that I would end up selling crack. I think he didn't want me to start smoking that....I stopped selling it for a while, but we both were broke. This is when I started selling at school again but just didn't tell him.

In Tyrell's worldview, he made a conscious choice to commit crime within the context of the limited resources available to him and the vilification he encountered at school and with police. To the extent that material resources became scarce, and he became constructed as a deviant, he calculated that his only choice was to sell drugs. His father's inability to provide for him, and the stigma that school officials and police officers imposed on him, left Tyrell feeling trapped. In this constricted location, Tyrell's options were few, and one of the only lucrative options available at the time was to sell drugs. He dropped out of school and dedicated himself to making money on the streets. Breaking the law was his decision, yet his hand was largely forced by overdetermined structural conditions. In Tyrell's perspective, poverty and criminalization "pushed" him into selling drugs, but he also consciously took this "jump," knowing that this was one of the only ways he could make some money.[8]

Tyrell had agency to decide whether he would commit crime or not. But a system of punitive social control established a context for Tyrell in which he felt disconnected from his community, stigmatized, and socially outcast, leading him to see criminality as almost inevitable. As such, Tyrell was punished into believing something external to his sense of self: that he was a criminal, that he had nothing at stake, and that he "might as well handle business"— sell drugs and victimize others—since he has "nothing to lose." All the young men in this study believed that they were inherently criminal; their interactions with the world around them had led them to internalize a foreign concept, that criminality was part of their persona. Tyrell, like many other marginalized youth, experienced a life-course process in which he was systematically punished into believing that he had nothing to lose. In the context of punitive social control, some marginalized boys are fostered by punishment, at every stage in their development, encountering a social world that, in their account, treats them as suspects and criminals.

Although I was not present during the boys' various stages of childhood development, the three years I spent in the field taught me that their perceptions of a punitive social order were rational and reasonable. One only needs to spend a few hours with marginalized young people in their everyday settings to realize how much they are policed, stigmatized, and treated differently from other citizens. Their stories were corroborated by observations of similar events that took place during my time in the field....

Tyrell Gets Marked

Eventually...Tyrell became marked as [a criminal]. When Tyrell was fourteen, he was caught with an ounce of marijuana and spent three weeks in juvenile hall. When he returned home after release, his father attempted to beat him. Tyrell fought back, wrestling his father to the ground. After the fight, his father disregarded him, saying that if Tyrell thought he was a man, he should take care of himself. He refused to speak to Tyrell for weeks at a time, and, as a consequence, their relationship more or less shifted to that of roommates: "I do my own thing, and he does his own thing. He can't say shit to me anymore, and I don't trip off of him."

The combination of stigma at school, harassment from police on the street, and Tyrell's resentment of his defunct relationship with his father may have led him to develop the attitude to "not give a fuck." In Tyrell's frame of reference, the implications of breaking the law were imposed on him daily. In such situations, getting incarcerated might begin to feel like a viable option. The irony of Tyrell's mentality was that the stress of being criminalized in the neighborhood led him to believe that juvenile hall might serve as an escape. In some sense, he was willing to trade one punitive community for another: "In juvy," Tyrell explained, "at least if I follow the rules, I'll be left alone."[9] When incarcerated, Tyrell could predict when he would be treated punitively: if he broke the rules. On the street, however, even if he followed the rules, he felt he would still be punished. For Tyrell and many of the boys, detention facilities became preferred social contexts because they provided structure, discipline, and predictability—rare attributes in the punitive context of the streets. Although the boys did not want to be incarcerated, detention facilities were the only spaces where they felt that they could predict cause and effect. Tyrell described it this way: "If I do my program,

then I know I will be straight [good]....If I don't follow directions, then I'll be stuck." We can make sense of why many young people who decide to violate their probation or parole do so, to seek shelter from a punitive social order, a youth control complex, that to many is worse than being incarcerated.

Hypercriminalization creates conditions in which young people actually seek more predictable, albeit more restrictive, forms of punishment. Many of the boys talked about liking the structure of incarceration because it dictated a clear set of rules. In the community, police, probation officers, schools, businesses, and families were perceived as unpredictable; the youths reported frustration with not knowing when their teachers, parents, or police would criminalize them.

Compelled to become a man on his own, to act and maneuver as an adult, and to take responsibility for himself, Tyrell faced the wrath of peer violence and police oppression. By the time he was fifteen, Tyrell became a bona-fide target for police. The police could pick him out easily because of his height, and they harassed him every time they saw him: "Man, they wouldn't stop messing with me. One day I pushed a cop, and he fell. They grabbed me and whooped my ass. They beat me so bad that they let me go. They felt bad for me. I have a scar here and here [he points to two small scars on his scalp and forehead]." Instead of dealing drugs in fear of being arrested again, Tyrell chose a different specialization. He went to the drug dealers in the neighborhood and offered to collect from people who owed them money. The drug dealers began paying him to recover debts. With this work Tyrell became extremely violent, as he recovered amounts owed that ranged from ten to five hundred dollars:

I had to send the message that I was not fucking around, so I ran into a crack head that owed my nigga [friend] some money. I grabbed his ass and whooped him so hard he's been limping ever since....That was all I had to do. Most of the time people paid me what they owed. One day, though, I had to whoop some fool's ass. I hit him on the leg with a golf club, so they charged me with aggravated assault and assault with a deadly weapon, but they dropped the deadly weapon charge. I still did three months in juvy.

At sixteen, Tyrell was placed on two years' probation. He was also placed on electronic monitoring (EM) as a condition of his release. EM is a program that probation officers use to keep track of juvenile offenders. A black, square-shaped device, about the size of a large cellular phone, is strapped around the youth's ankle. Whenever Tyrell went over a few hundred feet from his house, the device would send a message to his probation officer. The probation officer then could arrest him for violating probation. In the beginning, Tyrell was arrested and held for two days for going outside his area limit. Afterward, however, he got the hang of the monitoring device and completed his six-month program:

> I did it, but it was hecka hard. I couldn't leave home, and then that shit started itching me all the time. [He shows me his leg, scarred from the scratching.] My boys thought that shit was tight [appealing], but I told them it wasn't cool at all. They would come visit me and kick it at my house, since I couldn't go anywhere. We set up shop [a hangout space] there and just chilled there until they let me off.

Tyrell and his friends were confined to a small apartment because of his requirement to remain at home. The consequence of the electronic monitoring device was that it created a new "kick-it spot" for the boys in Tyrell's apartment building. This new hangout concentrated a large group of delinquent boys in a private space where they became invisible. The possibility of their receiving support or services from adults in the public sphere who wanted to help them was now diminished. Yet Tyrell and his friends believed this to be a safe haven from the criminalizing interactions they endured in the public sphere: suspicion in stores, automatic searches by police and probation officers, denial of employment for having a criminal record, and stigma imposed by school authorities and other adults....

NOTES

1. See Ageton and Delbert (1974); Becker (1963); and Hepburn (1977).
2. See Dodge (1983) and Lebel (2008).
3. Matsueda (1992).
4. Hirschfield (2008).
5. See Anderson (1990); Bourgois (1995); Horowitz (1983); Sánchez-Jankowski (1991); Venkatesh (2006); Vigil (1988).
6. In March 2009, a twenty-six-year old Black male killed four police officers, just a few miles from this neighborhood. The day before, two blocks from where the murders happened, I had been interviewing Black and Latino boys about their experiences with the police. The day after, I returned to ask them about their perspectives on the killings. In a nutshell, the youths believed that their lives were not valued as much as police lives. A few weeks prior to the police murders, an unarmed fifteen-year-old boy had been killed by police in the same area. Police had earned themselves a reputation as a violent occupying army among the boys, and some of the boys therefore perceived their deaths as justice.
7. Herbert Gans (1962) and Claude Fischer (1976) have found that despite ecological change, social organization remains the same in urban settings.
8. Payne (2008) has developed a "sites of resiliency" theory, in which he argues that the streets organize meaning for street-oriented youths around feeling safe, secure, and fulfilled. Young people engage in behaviors which will make them feel this way. These behaviors are often seen as criminal and oppositional. However, Payne argues, street-oriented youths are not oppositional;

they are actually attempting to accomplish a mainstream lifestyle with marginal resources.

    MacLeod (1995) argues that inner-city Black men are neither victims nor victimizers. Instead, they live in a context in which committing crime can be seductive, but at the same time there is very little choice but to commit the act. Young people are both agents and subjects. Covington (1995) has warned researchers about explanations that attempt to explain crime committed by racialized groups. She urges researchers to understand that cultural and structural theories of crime have often assumed that all poor Blacks are at risk of committing crime, when in reality only a small number of poor Blacks commit crime. The problem, she contends, is that Black crime has almost always been measured in relation to White crime. Covington reminds us that poor Black criminals have more in common with poor White criminals than they do with other poor Blacks.

9. Sociologists John Hagen and Bill McCarthy (1997) have found that the combination of negative experiences at home and in the community can lead young people to embrace criminality: "Family based experiences of shame and rejection can interact with state-sponsored criminal stigma to provoke what.... labeling theory referred to as secondary deviance—that is, the criminal behavior that follows sanctioning" (p. 183).

REFERENCES

Ageton, Suzanne, and Elliot Delbert. 1974. "The Effect of Legal Processing on Delinquent Orientation." *Social Problems* 22:87–100.

Anderson, Elijah. 1990. *Streetwise: Race, Class, Change in an Urban Community.* Chicago: University of Chicago Press.

Becker, Howard. 1963. *Outsiders: Studies in the Sociology of Deviance.* New York: Free Press.

Bourgois, Philippe. 1995. *In Search of Respect: Selling Crack in El Barrio.* New York: Cambridge University Press.

Covington, Jeannette. 1995. "Racial Classification in Criminology: The Reproduction of Racialized Crime." *Sociological Forum* 10:547–568.

Dodge, Kenneth. 1983. "Behavioral Antecedents of Peer Social Status." *Child Development* 54:1386–1399.

Fischer, Claude S. 1976. *The Urban Experience.* San Diego, CA: Harcourt Brace Jovanovich.

Gans, Herbert J. 1962. *The Urban Villagers: Group and Class in the Life of Italian-Americans.* New York: Free Press.

Hagan, John, and Bill McCarthy. 1997. *Mean Streets: Youth Crime and Homeless.* New York: Cambridge University Press.

Hepburn, J. R. 1977. "The Impact of Police Intervention upon Juvenile Delinquents." *Criminology* 15:235–262.

Hirschfield, Paul. 2008. "The Declining Significance of Delinquent Labels in Disadvantaged Urban Communities." *Sociological Forum* 23 (3).

Horowitz, Ruth. 1983. *Honor and the American Dream: Culture and Identity in a Chicano Community.* New Brunswick, NJ: Rutgers University Press.

Lebel, Thomas P. 2008. "Perceptions of and Responses to Stigma." *Sociology Compass* 2 (2): 409–432.

MacLeod, Jay. 1995. *Ain't No Makin' It: Aspirations and Attainment in a Low-Income Neighborhood.* Boulder, CO: Westview.

Matsueda, Ross. 1992. "Reflected Appraisal, Parental Labeling, and Delinquency: Specifying a Symbolic Interactionist Theory." *American Journal of Sociology* 97:1577–1611.

Payne, Yasser A. 2008. "'Street Life' as a Site of Resiliency: How Street Life–Oriented Black Men Frame Opportunity in the United States." *Journal of Black Psychology* 34 (1): 3–31.

Sánchez-Jankowski, Martín. 1991. *Islands in the Street: Gangs and American Urban Society.* Berkeley: University of California Press.

Venkatesh, Sudhir Alladi. 2006. *Off the Books: The Underground Economy of the Urban Poor.* Cambridge, MA: Harvard University Press.

Vigil, James Diego. 1988. *Barrio Gangs: Street Life and Identity in Southern California.* Austin: University of Texas Press.

PART V

GETTING PAID

//

One of the most fruitful lines of research in urban ethnography focuses on work, particularly on the experiences of people in largely invisible occupations that are taken for granted. From the 1920s to the 1940s, the Chicago School looked at a wide variety of mundane and low-profile jobs, from the homeless street peddler to the taxi-dancer to the Chinese laundryman. In later years, ethnographers continued this tradition, studying unemployed streetcorner men, fast-food workers, and doormen. In all these cases, close analyses of the workers' situations from the inside revealed a group of people who have frequently been misunderstood.

The first selection about the lives of hobos illustrates this point. Most people who had seen such homeless men—"bums," as they were usually called—living on the main stem of West Madison Street in Chicago imagined them as groups of idle people. In his 1923 study, Nels Anderson demonstrates that the typical hobo "is a worker," and though he does not labor steadily, he "earns most of the money he spends." This distinction is only the beginning, however. Through a careful analysis of the hobo's work, Anderson points out the difference between tramps who work as dishwashers, porters, and night clerks and those who have turned "getting by" into an art. It is to the latter that he devotes most of his attention, for appearances can be deceptive to the outside observer. Peddlers on West

Madison Street, for example, are frequently beggars. This is not readily obvious, though, because the license to sell shoelaces and pencils provides them with a "moral prop." A set of crucial distinctions exists among these men. The able-bodied who beg are "beneath contempt." Other distinctions exist as well, such as the one between peddling and "street faking" (approaching crowds or individuals with some sought-after good), which takes greater initiative and is a more elaborate kind of hustle. Thanks only to such careful fieldwork is Anderson able to discover that within the ranks of these discredited beggars and peddlers lies a system of "ranking and worth" and that no group is without some status.

The second selection, also a classic from the Chicago School of Sociology, shifts the focus from men to women. In it, Paul Cressey takes the reader into the taxi-dance hall, a popular institution in Chicago and many American cities during the 1920s. Taxi-dancers were usually white women of Polish, Irish, Italian, or Jewish descent who danced with lonely men for several cents per dance. They tended to come from conventional homes but were seeking to escape their dissatisfaction with neighborhood, work, or friends. The world of the taxi-dance hall provided easy money and excitement, especially for a new girl who suddenly found herself popular with customers bored with the ones who had worked there longer.

The men who frequented these clubs were mostly immigrants, mainly Filipino, who were part of a migration flow that did not include many women. Taxi-dance halls allowed them to develop intimate connections that otherwise they may not have had. When women first came to the clubs, they often chose not to dance with these so-called Oriental men. Their racial prejudices led them to focus their attention on white men instead. But once the immigrants' presence in the hall became normal and the rush for their affections subsided, it became gradually more acceptable for the women to affiliate with Filipino men. This marked the beginning of a process of readjustment that in some cases led down a road to prostitution in the black ghettos. At each stage, the women briefly experienced higher status in their new environments. But once this moment expired, they came to realize that in order to survive they had to move on to a new "lower" world to earn a living. It was such processes— or "life cycles" as they were known—that the Chicago School became best known for documenting. Its studies showed how people could start out with conventional frames of reference and then pursue a legitimate alternative that ended up being the first step on a road to utter degradation. Such processes of personal change occurred through continuous interactions in a social context.

The next selection looks at the lives of Chicago's Chinese laundrymen, a group more ubiquitous than that of the taxi-dancers yet full of experiences unknown to the average person. During the heyday of the Chicago School, these laundrymen could be seen throughout the city. Like Paul Cressey, who tied the lives of the Filipino men in the dance halls to immigration law, Paul Siu analyzed the social isolation of Chinese migrants who arrived in America under the Chinese Exclusion Act, which severely restricted their

numbers. In response to these constraints, many men migrated to the U.S. alone, leaving their wives and families behind in China. As a result, vast numbers of Chinese men ended up without female companionship in the U.S. The men's isolation was exacerbated by the fact that they lived by themselves, often in the back of tiny laundromats scattered throughout the city. Unlike immigrants who lived in "Chinatown" and returned to it each night, the laundryman dwelt among strangers. He had few if any coworkers, and, isolated by barriers of language and racial prejudice, could interact with customers and neighbors only in passing. The selection we have chosen highlights those few opportunities these men had to break from such isolation.

After these early pieces spanning the first decades of American sociology from the 1920s to the late 1940s, we skip ahead to the mid-1960s, when Elliot Liebow published *Tally's Corner*. This book is not as much about work and dead-end jobs as it is about the inevitable conclusion of such jobs once people have "come to terms with themselves and the world they live in." Liebow takes his readers into the social world of a group of black men in their twenties and thirties to explain why they seem so different from middle-class white Americans with regard to the priority they place on holding down jobs and their commitment to their children, wives, lovers, and friends. The central dialogue of the book revolves around the idea that poverty is transmitted from generation to generation through culture. Though Liebow is trained as an anthropologist, we see in his work the influence of the sociologists Howard S. Becker and Erving Goffman, who brought the concerns of symbolic interactionism to social science in a very prominent way. Liebow's emphasis on roles, the "definition of the situation," the presentation of self, acting, concealment, and the vulnerability of the self in social life and group life are central to his account. Like the taxi-dancer who constantly adjusts her continuously diminished expectations, the streetcorner man begins with high hopes of differing from his father and older brothers, only to experience the same failures they did. Over time, he takes refuge in the small group on the corner "where a shadow system of values constructed out of public fictions serves to accommodate just such men as he, permitting them to be men once again provided they do not look too closely at one another's credentials" (p. 213).

Katherine Newman's *No Shame in My Game* updates many of these issues within the more recent urban context of the 1990s. This work was the product of team ethnography in which the key part of the research project—participating and observing—was delegated to assistants. The strengths and advantages of this kind of work, which are mainly that it is a strategy for dealing with issues of generalizability, are often overlooked. Relying on a team of graduate students from Columbia University who worked in various fast-food restaurants, observed a select number of workers' family lives, and interviewed hundreds more, Newman succeeded in surveying a large sample of respondents and covering more ground than any individual ethnographer could. Research of this sort lies somewhere between a survey and individual ethnography. Although in certain respects it functions like a survey of a large group of people, it also allows for more wide-ranging and open-ended questions, which traditional surveys are unable to cope with or code.

To understand how fast-food jobs were experienced by workers, members of Newman's research team spent four months putting on crew uniforms and working behind the counters of fast-food restaurants. "Day in and day out," they worked the french-fry machines, prepared burgers and shakes, and engaged "in the daily banter that makes a boring job palatable" (p. 36). What they observed was that, unlike Liebow's subjects in another era, these fast-food workers could come to terms with their situation without accepting the inevitability of a life on the corner. Yet in doing so, they had to overcome the stigma associated with fast-food jobs. Newman shows how powerful these put-downs can be as well as the extent to which workers will go to avoid them. Just as the street corner is a refuge for failure, so too fellow workers and managers create an atmosphere that offers a defense against character assassination and even creates an honored identity.

Peter Bearman's *Doormen* is a highly original study that stands at the place where the traditions of participant observation meet team ethnography and even survey research. Bearman resided for many years in a doorman building on the Upper West Side of New York, and his experiences as a resident sensitized him to research questions that might not have been evident to someone without that experience. Working with his undergraduate class at Columbia University, he created a research team that distributed surveys, conducted interviews, and observed the social life of lobbies. The result was a brilliant work of microsociology built around a series of puzzles that focused on the apparently minor interactions between tenants and doormen over days, weeks, and years. For example, when Bearman spoke to doormen, he discovered that they typically told him two inconsistent things. On the one hand, they would describe their jobs as "very stressful," but on the other they would say that their work was mindless and boring. "Not a single doorman escapes this seemingly strange problem" (p. 67), writes Bearman. This inconsistency mapped on to how tenants perceived their doormen. Why is it that the doormen appear to be sitting around doing very little so much of the time yet are always so busy whenever their help is needed? To help explain this phenomenon, Bearman looked at the way time unfolds over the course of the day and argued that the doorman-resident relationship is a special kind of problem faced by all client-server systems that experience uneven flow and congestion at certain times. What is distinctive is that the doorman sees his client many times per day and every request made of him is for something so minor that it is hard for the tenant to comprehend why the need is not met—especially when the doorman seems to be doing nothing for so much of the day.

Like *Doormen*, Tamara Mose Brown's *Raising Brooklyn* focuses on a very old occupation, albeit one that has become increasingly common in recent decades: the child-care worker. Set in contemporary Brooklyn, a borough to which many privileged whites have migrated, the author studies the relations between Caribbean nannies and their upper middle-class employers, as well as the community that the workers have created among themselves. Brown, who identifies herself as mixed race and who grew up in a Trinidadian immigrant household in Canada, was a relatively new mother when she took her two toddlers to the same parks in which the nannies hung out. She planted herself on the park benches and in this way spent three years getting to know this population. Although nannies have been around at least as long as doormen, Brown takes her subjects into the contemporary era by showing how the Internet and cell-phone technology have become woven into their daily experiences. Like Siu's laundrymen, the child-care workers labor under conditions that appear, at first, extremely isolating. They usually work in their employers' homes. For much of the day they are alone with small children and have little contact with other adults. Brown, however, shows how they work hard at creating a community that provides camaraderie, support, and information about the job

and at the same time helps establish labor standards. New technology has facilitated this because it grants the workers more freedom and makes them feel less lonely. On the other hand, it has also left them more constrained. In the selection we have chosen, Brown shows how cell phones are deployed by nannies to create community. She also demonstrates how the Internet and cell phones are used by employers to keep tabs on their employees and achieve a new form of power through surveillance.

There are work sites where even the most dedicated ethnographer cannot follow or observe his informants. In *The Stickup Kids*, Randol Contreras traces the careers of a crew of drug robbers, former drug dealers, who, in the face of a declining drug market, have turned to the dangerous if lucrative business of robbing other drug dealers. These are brutal crimes, often involving torture and betrayal, that do not allow an observer—even one well accepted by the robbery gang—to "tag along" and watch. In documenting the social rules that govern these robberies, Contreras relies on stories the robbers have told him after the fact. How does he know that they are not simply telling tales and bragging? While there is no way he can be completely sure, his confidence in his account stems from the hours he spent with the robbery crew over many years and from his conversations about the same events with different people, alone and in groups, in various settings. Contreras is also careful not to report details of any particular robbery that he cannot verify and that, if he did, might be used as evidence against his informants. Instead, he presents a chilling composite account of how and why the robberies generally go the way they do.

Contreras's long association with the robbers treads the line between ethnography and memoir. As he reveals in his book, he grew up with some of his informants in a poor Dominican-American neighborhood in the Bronx at the height of the crack epidemic. Like many young men in the neighborhood, he was drawn to the money and excitement of drug dealing. Like most of them, he never actually made much money in "the game." Indeed, he notes that it was probably his utter failure as a criminal that started him on the path to college and graduate school. By contrast, the men in the drug crew were among the successful few—at least for a time. Their prowess in the drug game, which Contreras once admired, eventually led them to prison, however, and to becoming both perpetrators and victims of horrendous violence. Most likely, only someone like Contreras, who "had history" with these men, could have gained their trust in order to be able to write such a riveting account. Though perhaps the ultimate "insider" ethnography, Contreras's book underscores both the advantages and limitations of being an insider, and it also documents his own struggle with the realization that once he had taken up the analytical role of ethnographer, he could no longer be a true "insider"—even among people he had known most of his life.

26

NELS ANDERSON

"GETTING BY" IN HOBOHEMIA

from *The Hobo* (1923)

Nels Anderson's *The Hobo* was among the first participant observation studies to come out of the Chicago School. Nowadays we often think of early twentieth-century "hobos" as homeless people. Yet, unlike much of today's homeless population, the migratory laborers Anderson wrote about had lives that were defined as much by their participation in the labor force as by their exclusion from it. Anderson knew this world well, having grown up in hobo settlements and done "hobo work" before entering graduate school. In this selection, Anderson details the multiple ways in which hobo men earn money to make ends meet or, as they say, "get by."

A man who is conservative can live in Hobohemia on a dollar a day. If he is not too fastidious he can live for sixty cents, including a bed every night. Sleeping in a ten-cent "flop" and sticking to coffee and rolls, he can get along for fifty cents. Old men who do not move around much will live a long time on "coffee-an'," which they can get at the average restaurant for a nickel. The man who is reduced to "coffee-an'," however, has touched bedrock.

An old beggar who lingers about the Olive Branch Mission on South Desplaines Street claims that if he were guaranteed forty cents a day he could get on nicely. This would give him a bed every night and, as he says, a good bed is sometimes better than a meal.

The daily routine of this old man's life rarely takes him beyond the limits of a single block. On the south side of Madison Street, between 62 Desplaines Street and the Transedes Hotel, he is at home. All else is, for him, the open sea. When he ventures beyond the limits of this area into outlying territory he plans the trip the day before.

There are perhaps a hundred old men on South State and West Madison streets whose interests and ambitions have shrunk, to the same unvarying routine and the same narrow limits.[1]

Every man who enters Hobohemia is struggling to live above the "coffee-an'" level, and the various devices that are employed in accomplishing this are often ingenious. This business of wringing from chance source enough money each day to supply one's insistent wants is known on the "stem" as "getting by." "Getting by" may mean anything from putting in a few hours a day at the most casual labor to picking a pocket or purloining an overcoat. It includes working at odd jobs, peddling small articles, street faking, "putting over" old and new forms of grafts, "working" the folks at home, "white collar" begging, stealing, and "jack rolling."

Working at Odd Jobs

In spite of all that has been said to the contrary, the hobo is a worker. He is not a steady worker but he earns most of the money he spends. There are migratory casual workers, who spend three or four months each year in a Chicago lodging-house, who never look to the public for assistance. They know how much money they will need to tide them over the winter, and they have learned to spread it thin to make it reach. Casual in their work, they are conservative in their spending.

There are others who are never able to save anything. No matter how much they bring to town they soon spend it. For these the odd job is the likeliest means of livelihood. In a city like Chicago there are almost always opportunities for men who are content to take small jobs. Every restaurant must have dishwashers and waiters. Every

hotel needs porters; every saloon or pool hall employs men to do odd jobs. Petty as these jobs are and little as they pay, men not only take but seek them. One man who has been twenty years on West Madison Street is working as night clerk in a lodging-house; another does janitor work at nights and loafs day-time; still another has been for some time a potato peeler in a Madison Street restaurant.

Men who spurn steady jobs in favor of petty ones with pay every night sometimes do so because they hate to leave the street. Often it is because they are not properly clad or have no money to pay their way.

Peddling a Device for "Getting By"

In the eyes of the law, peddling in Chicago, at least, is not begging.[2] Nevertheless much of the peddling in the streets is merely legalized begging. Usually the articles offered for sale are cheap wares which are disposed of for whatever "you care to give." Not infrequently the buyer gives four times what the article is worth. There are hundreds of cripples in Chicago who gain a livelihood by selling pencils or shoestrings. Many of these are homeless men. Pencils bought for thirty-five cents a dozen retail for a dime, or whatever the purchaser cares to tax himself. A peddler's license is a protection against the police and serves as a moral prop to the beggar.

A peddler of shoestrings and pencils usually measures his success by the number of sales made in which no change is asked. He expects to be overpaid. Sometimes he persuades himself he is entitled to be overpaid. The business of "getting by" by "touching hearts" is usually spoken of as "work." A peddler who works the North Side will say: "I didn't work yesterday; the day before I made three dollars and eighty-five cents." This man considers himself a *real* cripple, because he has locomotor ataxia. He is incensed when he meets a one-armed peddler, because a man with one arm is not a real cripple. Real cripples should have first consideration. An able-bodied man who begs when broke is beneath contempt. That is "panhandling" and an able-bodied "panhandler" is always considered despicable.

Many peddlers live in Hobohemian hotels, and spend their leisure on the "stem." When they go to "work" they take a car. Some of them have regular stands. Not infrequently a peddler will assume to monopolize a position in front of a church or near the entrance of a factory where girls go and come. Beggars have a liberal fund of knowledge about pay days. They know the factories where the workers, when they have money, are "good."

Street Faking

The chief difference between peddling and street faking is one of method. The peddler appeals to the individual; the faker appeals to the crowd. The faker is a salesman. He "pulls" a stunt or makes a speech to attract the crowd. The peddler is more than often a beggar. It requires considerably more initiative and force to play the rôle of a street faker than to peddle.

Almost any time of the day at some street corner of the "stem" one may see a faker with a crowd around him. His wares consist perhaps of combination sets of cuff buttons and collar buttons, or some other such "line." Success depends upon the novelty of the article offered. A new line of goods is much sought after and a good street faker changes his line from time to time. Many fakers are homeless men. Numbers of the citizens of Hobohemia have tried their hand at some time or other at this kind of salesmanship. Those who are able to "put it over" generally stay with the work.

Peddling jewelry is one old device for getting money, but it is not too old to succeed. There are men who carry with them cheap rings or watches which they sell by approaching the prospective buyers individually. Sometimes they gather a crowd around them but that rarely succeeds as well as when they work quietly. A faker may sit beside a man in a park or approach him on the street and proffer a ring or watch or pair of eyeglasses for sale cheap, on the grounds that he is broke. Sometimes he will pretend that he found the article and would like to get a little money for it. Often he will tell of some sentiment connected with an article that he is trying to dispose of. A man may have a ring that his mother gave him and he will only part with it on condition that he might have the privilege of redeeming it later. If he thought he could not redeem it he would rather starve than part with it, etc. Hobos are often the victims as well as the perpetrators of these fakes.

Grafts Old and New

Few of these tricks are new but none of them are so old that they do not yield some return. They probably owe their long life to the proverbial identity of fundamental human nature wherever it is found.

One of the most ancient and universal forms of deception is the fake disease. In Hobohemia a pretended affliction is called "jiggers" or "bugs."

4. L. J. appealed to the Jewish Charities with a letter signed by a doctor in a hospital in Hot Springs saying that he had treated L. J. who was suffering from syphilis and that his eyes were affected and he would "undoubtedly go blind." It was learned later that this letter was a forgery as were other credentials that the man carried. He had been in a hospital and had been treated for a venereal disease. While there he familiarized himself enough with the terminology of the

disease so that he could talk with some intelligence about his case. He would say with conviction, "I know I'm going blind before long." It further developed that he had been exploiting charity organizations in several cities. Before his entry upon this deception it was learned that he had earned a prison record.

An ancient ruse is to feign to be deaf and dumb. A man who played "deaf-and-dumb" worked restaurants, drug stores, groceries, and other places of business. He would enter the places and stand with cap in hand. Never would he change the expression of his face, regardless of what was said or done. When spoken to he would point to his ears and mouth until he received some money, and then he would bow. If there was a chance of getting something, he would never leave a place unless he was in danger of being thrown out. An investigator followed him for two hours before he learned he was neither deaf nor dumb. Three months later he met the same man working the same graft in another part of the city.

"The hat trick," as it is sometimes called, is a popular means of "getting by." On a Sunday, a holiday, or indeed any evening, the streets of Hobohemia are likely to be enlivened by men who have a message, haranguing the crowds. They may be selling papers or books on the proletarian movement. In any case, most of them terminate their speeches by passing the hat. Few speakers spend their eloquence on the audiences of Hobohemia without asking something in return. It must not be assumed that these men are all insincere. Many of them are, but most of them are in the "game" for the money it yields. One of these orators is conspicuous because his stock in trade is a confession that he is not like the other speakers. He admits that he is out for bed and board. He will talk on any subject, will permit himself to be laughed at, and jollied by the crowd, but when he passes the hat he usually gets enough for another day's board.

The missions attract men who are religious primarily for profit. Many who are really sincere find it more profitable to be on the Lord's side. Nearly every mission has a corps of men who perform the "hat trick" by going from house to house begging old clothes or cash or whatever the people care to give. The collector's conscience is the only check on the amount of money taken in. Some missions divide all cash collections with the solicitors. Sometimes the collector gets as much as fifty cents on the dollar.

The exploitation of children is as old as the history of vagrancy. Even the tramp has learned that on the road boys may be used to get money. A boy can beg better than an older man, and frequently men will chum with boys for the advantages such companionships give them. Boys who are new on the road are often willing to be exploited by a veteran in exchange for the things they can learn from him.

"Working the Folks"

There is a type of tramp who lives on his bad reputation. He may have been sent away for the sake of the family, or have fled for safety, or he may have gone voluntarily to start life anew. Seldom does he succeed, but family pride stands between him and his return. He capitalizes the fact that his family does not want him to return.

Such a man resides on South State Street. He comes from a good family but his relatives do not care to have him about. He is fat and greasy and dirty; he seems to have no opinions of his own; is always getting into people's way and making himself disagreeable by his effort to be sociable. His relatives pay him four dollars a week to stay in Chicago. On that amount, with what he can earn, he is able to live.[3]

Another man raises funds now and then when he is broke by writing or telegraphing that he is thinking about returning home. His return means trouble. His requests for assistance are a kind of blackmail levied on the family.[4]

"White Collar" Begging

Most interesting among the beggars is the man, the well-dressed and able-bodied individual, who begs on the strength of his affiliations. These are the men who make a specialty of exploiting their membership in fraternal organizations. Labor unions are very much imposed upon by men who carry paid-up cards but who are temporarily "down." The organizations as such are not appealed to as much as individual members. It is hard for a union man who is working to turn away a brother who shows that he is in good standing with the organization.

Of late the "ex-service-man" story has been a good means of getting consideration, and the American Legion buttons have been worked to the limit. Most of the men who wear parts of a uniform or other insignia indicative of military service have really seen service and many have seen action, but a great many of them have heard more than they have seen.

There are men who make a specialty of "working" the charity organizations. Some of them are so adept that they know beforehand what they will be asked and have a stereotyped response for every stereotyped question. These men know a surprising amount about the inside workings of the charitable agencies and they generously hand on their information to their successor. They usually know, for example, what material aid may be had from each organization. A typical case is that of Brown.

5. Brown had not been in Chicago an hour until he had located the chief organizations to which he might go for help. He knew that he could check his bag at the Y.M.C.A. He learned

where to go for a bath, where to get clean clothes, how to get a shave and haircut and he actually succeeded in getting some money from the United Charities. He was able to "flop" in a bed even though he came to town without money late in the afternoon; whereas many other men in the same position would have been forced to "carry the banner." He knew about the charity organizations in all the cities he had visited from the Atlantic to the Pacific. After his case was traced it was learned that he told about the same story wherever he went and that he was known in organizations in all the cities to which he referred. He is 27 years old and has been living for the most part in institutions or at the expense of organizations since he was 13.

6. Another case is that of P. S., a Jewish boy who made his way between New York and Chicago three times and received accommodation at the Jewish charity associations in nearly every big city on his road between here and New York. He is a mental case and goes to the Charities because of a sense of helplessness. Since the last contact with him that the Chicago Jewish charities have had he has learned to get over the country with a little more confidence but he never fails to hunt up the welfare organization as soon as he comes to town. He was last heard of in California.

Borrowing and Begging

Nearly every homeless man "goes broke" at times. Some of them do not feel that a trip to town has been a success if they return to the job with money in their pockets. On the other hand, they do not feel that they have had their money's worth unless they remain in town a week or two after they have "blown in." As they linger they face the problem of living. They may have friends but that is unusual. The homeless man used to get advances from the saloon keeper with whom he spent his money. Such loans were often faithfully made good, but they were just as often "beat." Prohibition has put an end to that kind of philanthropy.

Many of the men who visit the city intermittently loaf and work by turns. These men often beg but they do not remain at it long, perhaps a day or so, or until disgust seizes them. Often when they beg they are drunk or "rum-dum." As soon as they are sober they quit. Sometimes they succeed in attaching themselves to a friend who has just arrived with a "roll." But living at the expense of another migrant quickly palls. Soon they will be found scanning the "boards" for free shipment to another job. They disappear from the streets for a season. As soon as they get a "stake," however, they will be seen again treating the boys and swapping stories on the "main stem"; if not in Chicago, then in some other city. It is the life.

The more interesting types are those who live continuously in the city and are broke most of the time. Some of them have reduced the problem of "getting by" to an art. The tramp who only occasionally goes "broke" may try to imitate these types but he soon tires of the game and goes to work. The chief classes of beggars are the "panhandlers" and the "moochers."

The "panhandler" can sometimes extract from the pockets of others what amounts to large sums of money. Some "panhandlers" are able to beg from ten to twenty dollars a day. The "panhandler" is a beggar who knows how to beg without loss of dignity. He is not docile and fawning. He appeals in a frank, open manner and usually "comes away with the goods." The "moocher" begs for nickels and dimes. He is an amateur. He goes to the back door of a house or hotel and asks for a sandwich. His appeal is to pity.

The antagonisms between beggars and peddlers are very keen. The man who carries a permit to peddle has no respect for the individual who merely begs. Nevertheless, some peddlers, when business is slow, themselves turn beggars. On the other hand, the man who begs professes to consider himself far more respectable than the peddler who uses his license as an excuse to get money. This is the language and opinion of a professional: "Good begging is far more honorable than bad peddling and most of this shoestring and lead pencil peddling is bad. I am not going to beat around the bush. I am not going to do any of this petty grafting to get enough to live on."[5] These antagonisms are evidence of a struggle for status. When a peddler denounces the beggars he is trying to justify himself. His philosophy, like most philosophies, is an attempt to justify his vocation. The same is true of plain beggars. Most of them are able to justify their means of "getting by."

Stealing

Hobos are not clever enough to be first-class crooks nor daring enough to be classed as criminals. Yet most of them will steal something to eat. There are men who are peculiarly expert at stealing food from back-door steps—pies or cakes that have been set out to cool, for example. There are men who wander about the residential areas, in order to steal from back doors. Some men follow the milkman as he goes from door to door delivering milk and cream, in order to steal a bottle when the opportunity offers. A quart of milk makes an excellent breakfast.

Stealing becomes serious when men break into stores and box cars. It is not what they take but what they spoil that does the damage. This is the chief complaint of the railroad against the tramp. In the country the tramp is often destructive to the orchards he visits. He will shake down more fruit than he can possibly use and dig up a dozen hills of potatoes to get enough for a "mulligan."

"Jack Rolling"

"Jack rolling" may be anything from picking a man's pocket in a crowd to robbing him while he is drunk or asleep. On every "stem" there are a goodly number of men who occasionally or continually "roll" their fellow-tramps. Nearly every migrant who makes periodical trips to the city after having saved his earnings for three or four months can tell of at least one encounter with the "jack roller." Scarcely a day goes by on Madison Street but some man is relieved of a "stake" by some "jack" who will, perhaps, come around later and join in denouncing men who will rob a workingman.

The average hobo is often indiscreet with his money, and especially so when he is drunk. He often displays it, even scatters it at times. This is a great temptation to men who have been living "close to their bellies" for months. As unpopular as the "jack roller" is among the tramps there are few who would overlook an opportunity to take a few dollars from a "drunk," seeing that he was in possession of money that someone else was bound to take sooner or later.

7. An investigator became acquainted with two men who were jack rollers who operated on Madison Street west of Halsted. They were well dressed for the "street" though not so well groomed as to be conspicuous. The investigator pretended to them that he had just spent ninety days in the jail in Salt Lake City for "rolling" a drunk. They had no sympathy for a man who would get drunk and wallow in the gutter. "He's not entitled to have any money." Neither of these men drank but they "chased women" and one of them played the races. Neither had any scruples against taking money from a drunken or sleeping man. They were able to justify themselves as easily as the peddlers and beggars do. Said one of them, "Everybody is eating on everybody he can get at, and they don't care where they bite. Believe me, as long as I can play safe I'm going to get mine."

"Getting By" in Winter

During the cold winter months the problem of "getting by" becomes serious. In the spring, summer, and fall hobos can sleep in the parks, in vacant houses, on the docks, in box cars, or in any other place where they may curl up and pass a few hours in slumber without fear of disturbance. But finding "flops" in winter usually engages the best effort a "bo" can muster. Besides food and shelter, the hobo must manage in some way to secure winter clothing. Above all he needs shelter, and shelter for the man without money is not easy to find in the city.

The best scouting qualities the average man can command are needed to get along in winter. There are many places to sleep and loaf during the day, but the good places are invariably crowded. For sleeping quarters police stations, railroad depots, doorways, mission floors, and even poolrooms are pressed into service. It is not uncommon for men who cannot find a warm place to sleep to walk the streets all night. This practice of walking the streets all night, snatching a wink of sleep here and a little rest there, is termed, in the parlance of the road, "carrying the banner." He who "carries the banner" during the night usually tries to snatch a bit of sleep during the day in places he does not have access to in the night time. He may go into the missions, but in cold weather the missions are crowded. They are crowded with men who sit for hours in a stupor between sleeping and waking. In almost every mission on the "stem" there are attendants known as "bouncers," whose duties during the meetings are to shake and harass men who have lost themselves in slumber.

Lodging-houses are also imposed upon by men who have no money to pay for a bed but who loaf in the lobbies during the day. Most lodging-houses make an effort to keep men out who are not guests. Fear is instilled into their hearts by occasionally calling the police to clear the lobbies of loafers. All who dare spend their leisure time in the public library, but the average tramp, unkempt and unclean from a night on the street, cannot muster sufficient courage to enter a public library.

The missions and other charity organizations play an important part in supplying the cold-weather wants of the tramp. They usually make it a point to get on hand at the beginning of winter a large supply of overcoats, or "bennies," and other clothes that are either sold at moderate prices or are given away. Such clothes are usually solicited from the public, and the men on the "stem" believe that they are entitled to them. Hence each man makes an effort to get what he feels is coming to him. When winter comes they begin to bestir themselves and concoct schemes for securing the desired amount of clothing to keep out the cold. During the winter time many of these men will submit to being "converted" in order to get food and shelter.

Competition between homeless men in winter is keen. Food is scarce, jobs are less plentiful, people are less generous, and there are more men begging. Many of the short-job men become beggars and a large number of those who are able to peddle during the summer likewise enter the ranks of the beggars. As beggars multiply, the housewife is less generous with the man at the back door, the man on the street also hardens his heart, and the police are called on for protection.

8. "Fat" is a very efficient "panhandler." He does not always "panhandle" but works when the opportunities present and the weather permits. He gets his money from men on the street, but he does most of his begging in winter when he cannot get the courage to leave town. He can beg for three or four hours and obtain about three dollars in that time. He only "panhandles" when his money is gone. He has a good personality and appeals for help in a frank, open manner giving no hard-luck story. He says that he is a workingman temporarily down and that he is trying to get some money to leave town. He does not work the same street every day. He keeps sober.

He has no moral scruples against begging, nor against work. He works and works well when circumstances force him to it. He doesn't feel mean when out begging or "stemming." He looks upon it as a legitimate business and better than stealing, and so long as the situation is such he might as well make the best of it. He seldom "panhandles" in summer.

He has an interesting philosophy. He calculates that according to the law of averages out of each hundred persons he begs, a certain number will turn him down, a certain number will "bawl him out," a certain number will give him advice, and a certain number will give him something, and his earnings will average about three dollars. So he goes at the job with vigor each time in order to get it over as soon as possible. "You get to expect about so much police interference and so much opposition from the people, and you get more of this in winter than in summer, but that is the case in whatever line you go into."

"Fat" works and begs as the notion strikes him but he does less begging in summer and less work in winter. If he doesn't like one city he goes to another. Last winter (1921–22) he was in Chicago, not because he likes Chicago but because he happened to be here.

The Game of "Getting By"

"Getting by" is a game not without its elements of fascination. The man who "panhandles" is getting a compensation that is not wholly measured by the nickels and dimes he accumulates. Even the peddler of shoestrings likes to think of "good days" when he is able to surpass himself. It matters not by what means "the down-and-out" gets his living; he manages to find a certain satisfaction in the game. The necessity of "putting it over" has its own compensations.

No group in Hobohemia is wholly without status. In every group there are classes. In jail grand larceny is a distinction as against petit larceny. In Hobohemia men are judged by the methods they use to "get by." Begging, faking, and the various other devices for gaining a livelihood serve to classify these men among themselves. It matters not where a man belongs, somewhere he has a place and that place defines him to himself and to his group. No matter what means an individual employs to get a living he struggles to retain some shred of self-respect. Even the outcast from home and society places a high value upon his family name.

> 9. S. R. is an Englishman fifteen years in this country. When he came to the United States to earn a "stake" he left his wife in England. His intention was to save enough money to send for her. He came here partly to overcome his love for alcohol but he found as much drink here and it was as accessible. He earned "big money" as a bricklayer but he never saved any. He became ashamed of himself after a year or two and ceased to write to his wife. That is, he had other interests here.
>
> Today he is a physical wreck. He is paralyzed on one side and he is also suffering from tuberculosis brought on by injudicious exposure and drink. He told his story but asked that his real name, which he told, should not be used. For, he said, "I am the only one who has ever disgraced that name."

Several old men on West Madison Street are living on mere pittances but are too proud to go to the poorhouse. They much prefer to take their chances with other mendicants. They want to play the game to the end. As long as they are able to totter about the street and hold out their hands they feel that they are holding their own. To go to an institution would mean that they had given up. Dependent as they are and as pitiful as they look, they still have enough self-respect to resent the thought of complete surrender.

In the game of "getting by" the homeless man is practically sure sooner or later to lose his economic independence. At any time (except perhaps in periods of prolonged unemployment), only a small proportion of homeless men are grafters, beggars, fakers, or petty criminals. Yet, all the time, the migratory casual workers are living from hand to mouth, always perilously near the margin of dependence. Consequently, few homeless men have not been temporary dependents, and great numbers of them must in time become permanent dependents.

This process of personal degradation of the migratory casual worker from economic independence to pauperism is only an aspect of the play of economic forces in modern industrial society. Seasonal industries, business cycles, alternate periods of employment and of unemployment, the casualization of industry, have created this great industrial reserve army of homeless, foot-loose men which concentrates in periods of slack employment, as winter, in strategic centers of transportation, our largest cities. They must live; the majority of them are indispensable in the present competitive organization of industry; agencies and persons moved by religious and philanthropic impulses will continue to alleviate their condition; and yet their concentration in increasing numbers in winter in certain areas of our large cities cannot be regarded otherwise than as a menace. The policy of allowing the migratory casual laborer to "get by" is, however, easier and cheaper at the moment, even if the prevention of the economic deterioration and personal degradation of the homeless men would, in the long run, make for social efficiency and national economy.

NOTES

1. See Document 18.
2. The mayor's office issued about 6,000 free permits in 1922 to peddle from house to house (not from wagon or cart), from basket or other receptacle, only for a period of sixty days.
3. Unpublished Document 111.
4. Unpublished Document 112.
5. Unpublished Document 113.

27

PAUL CRESSEY

THE LIFE-CYCLE OF THE TAXI-DANCER

from *The Taxi-Dance Hall* (1932)

This is a classic study of 1920s taxi-dance halls, which were places where lonely men could go to dance with partners for a fee. Most of the patrons were immigrants who did not have enough women of their own nationalities in the United States. In this excerpt, the author shows the career of a dancer as she becomes immersed in the social world of the halls and is gradually transformed by the conditions she encounters. The selection shows how a relatively innocent woman could end up as a prostitute a few years later.

A generation ago the young girl who broke with her home and neighborhood and set out alone upon the high roads of adventure had little opportunity to do other than sink, almost immediately, into some form of prostitution. But today many legitimate avenues are open to her, and, if she adopts an unconventional mode of life, many intermediate stages precede actual prostitution. The girl may organize her life in terms of an intermediate stage and never become a prostitute. The life of the taxi-dancer is one of these intermediate stages, and, like prostitution, it is an employment which can be of only short duration. The career of a taxi-dancer ends in her late twenties. It is a source of income only for the interim between later adolescence and marriage. Many young women use the taxi-dance hall in this way. Others use it to provide for themselves during the interlude between marital ventures. Still others—married women—use it as a source of additional funds and, not infrequently, as a diversion from monotonous married lives.

All this exists today because, as never before in our mobile cities, it is possible for young people to lead dual lives, with little probability of detection. Thus the young woman may "get in" and "out" of prostitution with a facility and rapidity which renders ineffective the traditional forms of social control. Likewise the taxi-dancer, if she so desires, has a greater opportunity than ever before afforded to such a girl to "come back" and again fit into conventional society.

Many girls, however, do not satisfactorily readjust themselves to conventional life. A part of the explanation may be that they are the more unstable and improvident ones, who naturally would be unable to extricate themselves from any exigency in which they might find themselves. More important, it would seem, is the fact that in this little isolated world of taxi-dance halls, the young woman may very soon come to accept without great resistance the standards of life and the activities of those with whom she is inevitably associated. The impersonal sanction of numbers ("everybody does it") seems quite effective in inducing the immature young woman to change radically the personal standards inculcated by her family.

In the following instance, May Ferguson, a young woman of twenty-four, cut all connections with her relatives and friends in Rogers Park and, for a time, lived intensely the life revolving around the taxi-dance hall. Her reactions to the critical question of "dating" and marrying an Oriental reflect the effectiveness of this social world in making possible a complete change in the activities and personal standards of a young woman of middle-class American society.

> It's strange how my attitudes toward the mixing of the races has changed and then changed back again in a little over a year. Two years ago I would have shuddered at the thought of dancing with a Chinaman or a Filipino and hated them just about as much as I did a "nigger." Then I learned that Dick had been unfaithful to me, and I wanted to get away from everything, everybody. For a while I didn't care what happened.

> When I first started in the dance hall on the West Side everything was exciting and thrilling. The only thing that bothered me was to have to dance with the Filipinos and the Chinamen. The first time one danced with me it almost made me sick. But after I'd been dancing there two months I even came to think it was all right to go out with Filipinos. You see, everybody else was doing it, and it seemed all right. But I never got so I would go out with a Chinaman.

> I didn't really think of marrying a Filipino until I met Mariano. He seemed different. I thought he was really going to school. He always treated me in a perfectly gentlemanly way, and I thought he was better than other Filipinos. For a time I let myself think seriously of marrying him, but down deep I knew I could never marry a Filipino. One thing I could never get straightened out was the question of the children. What would they be? They'd be neither Filipinos nor Americans.

> Soon after, Mariano and I broke up, and I never was serious with any other Filipino.... Then I quit the dance hall, and went back to live my old life on the North Side.

> Just a few weeks ago, after I'd been away from the West Side for nearly a year, I was talking with some friends. They were telling about a chop-suey proprietor who had married a white woman. For some reason that made me mad, and I started in telling what I thought of anyone who would marry a "Chink." Then all of a sudden I stopped and bit my lip.... I had just realized that only the year before I was seriously considering marrying a Filipino, who was even darker than a Chinaman. And now, just a few months later, I had all the hatred toward them that I had before I went out on the West Side.[1]

I. The Taxi-Dancer's Life-Cycle Fundamentally Retrogressive

For those young women who do not "get out" of the dance-hall life while still relatively new to it there appear to be rather definite and regular stages of regression which eventually lead to some form of prostitution. It may be noted also that the "lower" the level reached by the girl, the more difficult is her re-entrance into conventional society. These stages in their life-cycle appear, on careful inspection, to be so regular and almost inevitable for those who persist in taxi-dancing that in its generalized aspects this life-cycle may be considered valuable for prediction.

The hypothesis is here suggested, with a view toward further verification, that the taxi-dancer, starting with an initial dissatisfaction in her home situation, tends to go through a series of cycles of a regressive character, i.e., the latter part of each cycle involving a continual loss of status in a given group, and the initial part of a succeeding cycle indicating a regaining of status in a new but usually lower group than the preceding ones. This cyclical theory of the taxi-dancer's life is simply a graphic way of conceiving of the difficulties of maintaining status over any span of years in a social world of the type found in the taxi-dance hall.

A very important aspect of the hypothesis has to do with the higher status granted the girl by each group during the initial period in each cycle. Finding herself losing favor in one social world, the taxi-dancer "moves on" to the group with which, in the natural course of her life, she has recently been brought most vitally in contact. This may involve a movement from one taxi-dance hall to another, perhaps one of lower standing; and again, it may in the later stages mean a trend toward other social worlds to which the life in the taxi-dance hall is frequently but a threshold. As a "new girl" in a new group, she is accorded a satisfactory status, and in the novelty of the situation she finds new excitement. Thus begins a new cycle in the girl's life. After a time, however, she is no longer a "new girl" and finds herself losing caste in favor of younger and still newer girls. Her decline in any particular social world may be rapid or slow, depending upon the personality, ingenuity, and character of the individual girl, but in any case a gradual decline in status in any such dance hall seems almost inevitable.

Every girl reaches, in time, a point of relative stability. In the ruthless sorting-out process continually going on, the taxi-dancers are certain to find their "level," at which each girl in her own way, and with the personality and techniques she has available, will be able—if she so desires—to maintain herself for at least a few years on a fairly stable equilibrium. In some cases this point may not be reached for some time, and the girl may rush through the earlier stages, eventually reaching an equilibrium at a "low" stage. Others may attain a satisfactory adjustment upon a relatively "high" plane.

The initial position of status accorded the "new girl" in the taxi-dance hall and the later struggle to maintain that status is indicated in the following case of Wanda, a young girl of Polish parentage, who subsequently married a Filipino youth whom she had met in the dance hall. This case also reveals the way in which the girl's scheme of life may be completely altered through a brief sojourn in the world of the taxi-dance hall.

> Wanda, American-born but of Polish parents, at fifteen was doing fairly good work at school. But suddenly, with the consent of her parents she secured work in a cigar factory, telling her employer that she was eighteen. Shortly after she left home, and no trace of her was found until four months later, when she was found married to a young Filipino. He said his wife told him that she was nineteen and that he had no reason to doubt her. Wanda met him in the

taxi-dance hall in which she had been employed. They had known each other only a month before their marriage.

According to Wanda's story, she left the cigar factory because the work was monotonous. All day long she wrapped cigars until after a month she could endure it no longer. Through a friend in the factory she secured employment in the dance hall, dignified by the name of a "dancing school for men."...Wanda was rather embarrassed at first at the prospect of dancing with so many strange men, but before the end of the first evening she found herself thoroughly enjoying it and turned in more tickets than any other girl on the floor. She began to look forward to the evenings in the dance hall; she "got a thrill" from meeting so many new people.

Her popularity continued for several evenings, much to the annoyance of the other girl employees. But one night one of her steady partners tried to "get fresh." Wanda left him in the middle of the floor. Her partner complained to the management, and that evening Wanda got a "terrible bawling out." She was made to understand that she was hired for the purpose of entertaining, not insulting the patrons. If she didn't like it, she could leave. But she didn't want to leave. She had been having too good a time, and so she agreed to be more compliant.

But her clientèle began to fall off. She learned that several of the other girls, jealous of her success, were circulating tales that she was a "bad sport" and a prude. To rectify this Wanda resorted to the wiles of the other girls; she rouged heavily, darkened her eyes, and shortened her skirts. Again she achieved popularity, also the other girls grew more tolerant of her.

One evening she danced with Louis, a Filipino. His peculiar accent intrigued her, and she accepted an invitation to supper. Their friendship grew. He told her of his childhood on his native islands, and she confided her growing dislike for the dance hall. They agreed that they would like to "settle down," and so one evening Wanda "resigned" and they drove to Indiana and were married.[2]

In the whole gamut of cycles through which the taxi-dancer tends to go, at least four may be suggested. The first cycle involves the girl's dissatisfaction with the type of life associated with the home and neighborhood. This may come about largely through a growing consciousness of economic lack in the family, through a thwarting of the desire for a type of masculine contacts which the home or the neighborhood fails to offer, through a sense of insufficient prestige in the home and the community, or through a loss of status due to the girl's supposed transgression of the established moral code. At all events, the girl, finding her way sooner or later to the taxi-dance hall, secures therein a satisfaction of certain wishes previously unfulfilled.

Here she at first finds an enhanced prestige accorded her—even though by a world which her family and her neighborhood would adjudge as lower than their own. Thus begins a second cycle for the girl. As a novice in the taxi-dance hall she is at first "rushed," and enjoys the thrill of being very popular. But after a time she ceases to be a novitiate and must make a deliberate effort to maintain her status. If she fails and is no longer able to secure sufficient patronage exclusively from the white group, she comes eventually to accept the romantic attentions of Filipinos and other Orientals.

Thus begins a third cycle for the girl, at the beginning of which she experiences a new prestige accorded her by the Oriental group. Here, again, a girl may continue to "get by" with the group with which she has become associated, being consistently accorded a degree of status which to her is satisfying. But such are the hazards of maintaining standing in this social world that if she accepts the attentions of too many Orientals she is adjudged "common" by them, and thus again loses caste.

A failure to make satisfactory adjustment in the world of Orientals may bring the girl to a fourth cycle, which is begun when she centers her interests upon the social world which in Chicago has been associated with the "black and tan" cabarets. She usually comes into contact with these groups through her association with Orientals. With the Negroes she again achieves temporarily the prestige accorded the novitiate. But here, too, she is doomed to a decline in status, and this seems very frequently to lead to prostitution in the Black Belt.

As has been said, the evidence to support this theory of retrogressive cycles is not conclusive, and the suggestion is offered merely as a hypothesis for further study. Yet the data which are at hand seem to be suggestive. Consider first the case of Florence Klepka, a girl born and raised in Chicago, whose mother and stepfather are of Dutch ancestry. This case has value in that it reveals the conditions under which the girl was reared in her home. It is not a "perfect" case for the reason that in every instance the girl does not gravitate toward a group held in lower esteem. But in no case is there a trend toward a higher social group, and throughout the girl's life there is an unmistakable trend toward a lower estate. It likewise suggests the tendency of the girl to attempt to solve her personal and social problems by "moving on" to a new group and into a new social world.

In the case under consideration dissatisfaction with the home is manifest very early, for at the age of thirteen years the girl has already developed the habit of running away, which the mother seems to have been unable to alter. This no doubt is a way of escaping from an environment which is at least quite unsatisfactory. Lying, too, which came to be chronic with her, was also merely a means for adjusting to a disagreeable situation. Her contacts outside the home very probably caused her to become ashamed of it, and to want to prevent her friends, both boys and girls, from knowing of her home conditions. Such a situation encourages a girl's break with her home, even though, as in this case, she has parents who are willing to support her. She then goes through a cycle of experiences associated with her employment in a South State Street "men only" show. She subsequently passes on to another cycle, centering in the North Clark Street "Rialto." Finally she gets into the world of the taxi-dance hall, thus starting a new cycle of experiences. These three cycles, while quite distinct one from the other, involving as they do different social worlds in each case, cannot be said arbitrarily to be lower or higher than one another. All can be said, however, to be retrogressive in character, the girl descending as "low" as she permits herself, and subsequently extricating herself and focusing her activities upon a different group. This case, furthermore, reveals very clearly the "white cycle" and the "Filipino cycle" through which the girl retrogressively passes.

> Florence Klepka when nineteen years of age was reported by a policewoman to be living at a cheap Loop hotel under the name of Mrs. Bok, and taking part in a "men only" burlesque show on South State Street. She was reported to be hanging around corners at all hours of the night with sailors and recruiting officers, and was seen in restaurants at 2:30 and 3:00 A.M. The mother wanted the girl to return home and keep away from bad company.
>
> Between 1920 and 1924 she is known to have frequented South State Street and for a time to have lived with a man she met there, by whom she had a child. Florence claims to have been involved in several raids

of prohibition agents on saloons and cabarets on South State Street and South Wabash Avenue.

Later her center of activities was transferred from the South State Street "main stem" to the North Clark Street "Rialto." Here she entered the cabaret life along the street. She lived in the notorious hotels and rooming-houses of the vicinity, and is reported to have lived at different times by clandestine prostitution and by several unstable alliances.

During the winter of 1925 she entered a taxi-dance hall where she met certain young Italians and Greeks, with whom she associated for a time. She was subsequently discharged by the management when the kind of life she was leading became too well known.

In the fall of 1925 Florence's center of activities shifted to the Near West Side, where she continued in a new taxi-dance hall. Her career there was essentially the same as elsewhere. At first she made a very creditable impression, but later became notorious because of her extensive and unguarded promiscuity. Finally she became so notorious that patrons did not want to be seen dancing with her and she was discharged.

She shifted her activities back to a taxi-dance hall on the Lower North Side, where she allied herself wholly with the Filipinos and with the girls associated with them. In 1926 she virtually abandoned all efforts to make a living through taxi-dancing. She had become "common" to the Filipino group as well as to the white. Thence she shifted her activities to the Filipino clubhouse, where she met many men, establishing different relationships with them. Now she has come to be known as a "bum." On some occasions she was reported to have visited the rooming-houses occupied by

Filipinos, going from room to room soliciting.[3]

The following case is one in which the girl ran through the whole gamut of experiences until she reached a low level of prostitution. It might be stated here that this case shows, in fact, the steps by which a certain number of girls quickly become prostitutes in the Black Belt.

Tiny was a Polish girl whose parents lived on the Northwest Side. When she was about sixteen she married a young man from the same neighborhood. She later left him, claiming non-support and entered a taxi-dance hall, where she was for a time quite popular. At first she would not dance with Filipinos if she could avoid it. Sometime later, however, when she had come to regard them as a lucrative source for income she became very interested in several. They frequently escorted her to "black and tan" cabarets and in this way she made contacts with young Negroes.

The Filipinos, very conscious of their anomalous racial position in this country, would tolerate no such conduct on the part of any girls with whom they associated. They immediately deserted her, leaving her in the cabaret. In this way began her activities in the South Side Black Belt, where she subsequently became known as an independent prostitute, carrying on her business chiefly with Negroes and Chinese. Occasionally she seeks to return to the taxi-dance halls and to other Filipino activities, but there are always those who remember her and warn the others that she has already "gone African."[4]

The theory of the retrogressive life-cycles, while only a hypothesis, can perhaps be seen best through a reference to the typical experiences of taxi-dancers before and after entering these resorts. These experiences seem so frequently to have common elements in them and to follow such a regular sequence of typical experiences that they can be conceived as a "behavior sequence." In any event it is clear that a better perspective can be gained by classifying these experiences and arranging them chronologically. Some of the characteristic experiences, fortunate and unfortunate, which befall the taxi-dancer can be seen in the following.

2. Distracting and Disorganizing Experiences before Entering the Taxi-Dance Hall

It is clear...from many of the life-history excerpts that the typical taxi-dancer, even though young in point of years, is not inexperienced. Most taxi-dancers have had varied experiences, both occupationally and sexually. They have engaged in a variety of occupations, usually of the unskilled type, such as waitress, factory operative, or salesgirl. Their experiences often include at least one marriage, usually unsuccessful and characterized by considerable infidelity on both sides, resulting in separation or divorce. In most cases there seems to be, in addition, a background of intense family conflict.

When the girl enters the taxi-dance hall she usually has already broken with many of the stable community groups, such as her family and church. Usually, she also has failed to find conventional ways of satisfying certain dominant interests, such as her need for friendship and affection, for status, and for excitement. Nor does she have a well-defined standard of conduct or a goal in life toward which she may work. The taxi-dancer enters her vocation already somewhat disorganized, often feeling herself in conflict with conventional society.

3. The Initial Period of Uncertainty and Distrust

The initial experiences of the taxi-dancer are so similar that it is possible to perceive a fundamental sequence in the girl's affiliation with the establishment and its personnel. With few exceptions, the primary factor attracting the girl to the establishment is the possibility of making money in an easier way than she otherwise could. A young taxi-dancer without training of any kind frequently earns as much as thirty-five or forty dollars a week. But the economic interest is paralleled by an interest in the "thrill" and excitement of the dance hall. Yet the strangeness and uncertainty of the situation, coupled with an antagonism or disgust for the conduct of certain taxi-dancers, may cause many new taxi-dancers to remain aloof. Also, detached as she often is from the neighborhood and family groups in which she was reared, she is very slow to confide in other girls whom she meets in the dance hall. Except perhaps for a trusted girl friend, the novice in the dance hall remains for a time a detached figure, associating only casually with the taxi-dancers.

Many of the young girls who attempt a career in the taxi-dance hall drop out during the first few weeks.[5] Either they are not able to attract sufficient patronage or they are antagonized by the practices seen about the establishment. Likewise, to many taxi-dancers their work in the dance hall is purely a segmental activity, engaged in primarily to supplement an insufficient income earned as clerical office-workers, clerks in department stores, or at light industry and in laundries.

4. Thrills of Early Success: The Romantic Period

The successful novices among the taxi-dancers, however, very soon overcome any hesitancy they may have and throw themselves whole-heartedly into the life revolving about the establishment. Courted intensively and sought after in a manner seldom experienced in more conventional life, the "new girl" comes to enjoy immensely these new thrills and satisfactions. A host of new men, many of them attractive, some of them strange and fascinating, present themselves and bid for her favor. She is escorted to expensive night clubs where she is served in a manner which, according to her conception, befits only the socially elect.

Out of it she very quickly gains an enhanced conception of herself. The Polish girl from "back of the yards" is metamorphosed into a "dancing instructress," and frequently acquires a new name comparable to her new station in life. The following list, while disguised,[6] nevertheless distinguishes in a true manner the characteristic original and "professional" names, respectively, of certain Chicago taxi-dancers. These new names reveal the girl's new conception of herself and suggest the ideals and aspirations by which her life is ordered.

Real Name	"Professional" Name
Christina Stranski	DeLoris Glenn
Agnes Gretin	Lorine Boyle
Marie Boris	Billye Hart
Florence Klepka	Anita Costello
Louise Lorenz	Bobby LeMann
Sophie Zelinski	Gwendolyn Llewellen
Alma Heisler	Helene de Valle
Pearl Babcock	Melba DeMay
Eleanor Hedman	Gloria Garden
Anna Prasenski	Althea LeMar
Mary Bulonowski	LaBelle Shelley
Gertrude Pressley	Betty Lucrece
Alice Borden	Wanda Wang
Mary Maranowski	Jean Jouette

With this new conception of herself the girl enters a series of romantic experiences, in which every consideration is sacrificed for the free play of the romantic impulse.

I don't know what there is about the dance hall, but I never had so many serious "cases" in such a short time as I had those few months I was on the West Side. I was always getting a flame over this fellow or that one. If it wasn't a Filipino it was a good-looking young Italian or even a Greek. I never have been able to understand what got into me. There was always someone I was crazy about.[7]

When still a "new girl" in the hall, the successful taxi-dancer does not have to give any thought to the problem of inducing patrons to dance with her. She is yet a "new girl"—often with an attractive youthful naiveté—and is sought after by many patrons.

5. "Getting the Dances"—The Veteran Taxi-Dancer's Problem

As the taxi-dancer becomes an accepted member of the dance-hall personnel and, unconsciously, has come to acquire in it a certain rôle, the problem of "getting the dances" becomes a more pressing one. While she may remain a popular girl with a certain group of patrons, many others have abandoned her for other new and more interesting taxi-dancers. As her pay check dwindles, she begins deliberately to use certain techniques to attract dance partners. At the same time the girl has become more aware of her standing with her co-workers. They, in turn, demand certain standards of performance from her. In response to their ridicule, jeers, and laughter, she complies with their expectations, changes her mode of dressing, of acting, and of thinking, and gradually becomes accepted into the little group of women who set the mode in the world of the taxi-dance hall. Through these contacts the novitiate gradually learns the techniques for being a successful taxi-dancer.

6. Learning the Taxi-Dancer's Techniques

These techniques are often very simple in character. One of the first considerations is the question of the type of dressing and "make-up" most advantageous in the dance hall.

> "Say," Lila said to me, "why don't you blondine your hair? You know, all the Filipinos go for blondes.
>
> "I'm afraid you won't go so big. You are too quiet and don't fix yourself up enough. And those earrings! Why the hell, if you're going to wear them, don't you get some that aren't so big and don't look so much like they came from the 10-cent store?
>
> "Of all the goofy ideas of make-up— you have the world beat! You come over to my house tomorrow and I'll fix you up before we go to the dance. One bottle of peroxide will do it. Your hair ain't so dark anyway. And then we'll put a hem in your dress and make it tighter. You aren't such a bad looker. Your shape ain't bad, but you don't know how to show it."[8]

Likewise, another device for interesting patrons is "dancing fast and peppy," and "acting peppy" when waiting for dances.

> It pays to dance close and fast. Act like you're just full of pep. When I'm waiting for dances I walk along the side acting like I'm full of the Old Nick. Sometimes I feel just the opposite, but I couldn't afford to show my real feelings or I wouldn't get the dances.[9]

There is also the ruse by which the girl, who believes that a patron does not recognize her, represents herself to him as a novice with the hope that she will thereby secure more dances with him. The pretended promise of a late night engagement is also used to induce patrons to continue dancing. In this way the patron is kept in a mood for spending money until the dénouement, at the close of the evening's dancing, when the girl informs him that she has made "other arrangements."

A somewhat more complex technique involves the playing of the racial prejudices against each other. Especially with such incompatible groups as Filipinos and race-conscious white Americans, the shrewder taxi-dancer may devise a plan by which she utilizes the racial attitudes of both groups for her own financial advantage.

> I noticed a rather attractive young woman of medium build, standing on the side lines beside a Filipino. As she saw me looking at her, her eyes glanced down obliquely toward him in a manner which seemed to indicate that she at least despised the rather dark-skinned youth with whom she had just been conversing. This seemed a new and interesting affection. As she moved away from the Filipino I approached her and began conversation.
>
> "Apparently you don't like your sun-browned friend," I commented. "Well, no!" she replied, hesitatingly. "You see he's a Filipino." "But you should worry about that," I countered. "The Flips [Filipinos] treat a girl better and will spend more money on her than the other fellows." She hesitated a moment and then said in mock concern, "But they're not white!"
>
> Late in the evening, after she had seen me in friendly conversation with several Filipinos, this same girl approached and offered the following explanation of her conduct:
>
> "I don't know whether you know, but I'm engaged to marry the Filipino you saw me talking to. I just acted the way I did about him to get you

to dance with me. When I saw you looking at us, I decided I'd have to pretend I didn't like him, so that you would give me some tickets....Most of the white fellows won't dance with me if they learn I go out all the time with Flips. So I say something against them when I'm with white fellows just so they'll give me more dances....

"Even if I do go out with Filipinos, it doesn't pay to dance all the time with them. If I dance all the time with Filipinos I've got to dance with many different ones. If a girl dances with too many Flips they think she's common, so they won't keep on coming to her for dances....I've got to dance with some good-looking white fellows once in a while so the Filipinos will keep on dancing with me."[10]

Other techniques have to do with the exploitation of a patron after the taxi-dancer leaves the dance hall with him. Here again the "sex game" enters the situation. In some instances the devices may be quite simple; in other cases more elaborate.

I've only been in the dance halls a month, but I already know how to be a success. I make $30 a week at the hall and figure on making some on the side.

The first thing in being a successful "gold-digger" is to choose the right fellow. He can be of any age, but he's got to be one who ain't wise. The new ones at the halls are best but sometimes the old ones are all right, too. Some "fish" don't learn very fast, you know. The first impression I have to make is that I'm an innocent little girl in hard circumstances. Then when a fellow asks for a date I tell him how hard up I am and that I'd like to go but just can't afford to take time away from the hall.

Then I get the idea across that I'll go out if he'll pay me what I'd earn at the dance hall. When he asks how much that is, I make it more than I would earn actually if I stayed....I always insist on getting the money before I go out. The first thing is to get a fellow to take me to a café, and after I get a good meal off of him, I invent some way of getting away. One way is to ask him to excuse me for a moment, pretending to go to a telephone or to the rest room, and then I slip out the door when he isn't looking.

But if there is only one door and the fellow can see me leaving, I go to the phone and call up an older girl who lives where I do. I tell her where I am and for her to come down and get me. Then she comes in, accidentally like, and pretends she is my aunt who is supposed to take care of me. She threatens to call the police to arrest the man who is trying to make her niece a bad girl. And the fellow is glad enough to let me go....When she comes down to help me that way I always pay her taxi bill and split with her fifty-fifty on the rake-off.

Of course, I can work that only a few times, but "there's one born every minute" and a lot of them come to these halls. They're such easy "carp" I figure that if they hang around long enough somebody's bound to knock them off. I need the money more than the others, and I might just as well be the one to "fish" them.[11]

7. Discovering a Profitable Dance-Hall Personality; Types among the Taxi-Dancers

Out of the commercial rivalry among the taxi-dancers, certain rather definitely understood "roles" develop, by which different girls have discovered they can commercialize most efficiently their personal charm. Each of these rôles has its own activities, its own patterns of behavior, its own individual techniques, its own standards, and its own scheme of life.

The highest type among these dance-hall rôles is that of the so-called "nice girl." The "nice girl" is the one who possesses sufficient charm, physical attractiveness, and vivacity to secure dances without transgressing the conventional standards of propriety. She may never accept dates from patrons, or may not even frequent a hall where she is expected to dance with Filipinos and other Orientals. She plays the part of the entirely virtuous girl.

> Gwendolyn Costello, as she styles herself, is the "belle" of one of the taxi-dance halls in the Loop, where she has danced for over three years. She is a vivacious girl with a coquettish—almost roguish—manner. She is a graceful dancer, and can follow successfully any kind of dancing. In addition, she has what is called a "good line." Although she looks as though she were eighteen she is probably every bit of twenty-four. She is very popular with the patrons, especially with the men between twenty-five and forty. On busy nights at the establishment she is never inactive except on her own volition. Most of the men—new and old patrons—appear to like her but she is known never to accept dates from anyone met in the hall. For most of the men who dance with her she remains as much of a mystery at the end of a year's contact as she was the first evening.[12]

While the motive toward exploitation may be found in the case of the "nice girl," it is more prominent in the case of the "smart girl." The girl of this type accepts exploitation as the order of the day and frankly sets out to utilize her attractiveness for all the material gain which can be realized therefrom. "Fishing" and the "sex game" become for these girls the accepted ways of earning a living; and prestige is accorded to the one who is cleverest in gaining the most.

Among the more immoral young women can be distinguished a third type, the "never-miss girl." She is the type who is known by the more initiated patrons to be quite affectionate. Sometimes to other taxi-dancers she may represent herself as successfully "fishing" her men friends. But to her masculine acquaintances she presents an entirely different picture. The girl of this type may occasionally have a little retinue of men who have special "rôles" or functions in her life. Toward each she has a certain romantic interest, though even with her it is sometimes coupled with a unique sense of objectivity and detachment.

> I know men are all deceitful, but still I can't get along without them. It used to be that one man at a time was enough, but now since I'm married I've got to have several.... Now take right now! I have "Frenchy" and "Toughy" and Jimmy, and Buddy, and Al. Now "Frenchy" is a good-looking little Frenchman who knows how to make love. When I'm in low spirits and want somebody to cheer me up, I go to the phone and give him a ring. An hour with him and I'm "sitting on the top of the world." But that's all he's good for. And the worst of it is, I know he doesn't mean it—except for the moment.
>
> Now "Toughy," as I call him, comes from South Chicago. He's a bad boy. He's liable to do almost anything. I guess that's what makes him so interesting. Once in a while "Toughy" comes up and takes me out, but only for one night. Then there is Jimmy. He was my husband's cousin who sometimes interests me; I don't know why. I'm "out" with him now, because of the way he treated me, but he still

owes me some money he promised to loan me.

Buddy is the fellow I go to talk things over when I'm in some difficulty. He's a friend to call on when I need help. But that's all. Then there is Al. Al is a tall, slender fellow, good-looking, about twenty-eight years old. He's as safe as the old family horse.... He's got a big car and drives me around wherever I want to go.[13]

Always fearful lest she become notorious and thus no longer able to secure dance patronage, yet desirous of having what she chooses to consider a "good time," the taxi-dancer of this type is torn between the double dilemma of respectability with decreasing income and the greater hazard of becoming notorious and thus unemployable at legitimate dancing in the taxi-dance halls.

For the young woman whose character is held in question, or who for some reason cannot measure up to the requirements for the other types, there is yet one opportunity to continue in some taxi-dance halls, if she will but join the fourth class of taxi-dancers—those who engage in sensual dancing. The older, more sophisticated women, the more homely girls, and others not especially superior in beauty, ability in dancing, and who, for one reason or another, do not wish to date patrons, constitute this fourth class.

For the girl who adopts this way of "getting along," financial hazards are considerably reduced. In the other rôles the girl is insecure, always exposed to the vicissitudes of dance-hall popularity, always uncertain of her income. But after once adapting herself to sensual dancing her income becomes more regular and more secure. Every week means that she can earn a certain amount in the dance hall, irrespective of the rise and fall of her personal fortunes outside the establishment. It is also unnecessary for her to engage in coquetry and cajolery to secure patronage.

I used to have to worry about getting my dances. Sometimes I'd make money and sometimes I wouldn't do so well, but the landlady wanted her money just the same.... Now I know if I come up here for so long I'll have so much money when I get through. Before I'd waste all my time looking for dances.

It's a lot easier, too. Before I had to "kid" the fellows along all the time. Now I don't have to worry. The fellows come without being kidded. I've never had to wait long for a dance in months.[14]

The contact of the patrons with the taxi-dancer who practices sensual dancing is almost invariably impersonal and utilitarian. Romance, even of the type found among other taxi-dancers, seldom develops between patron and girl meeting on the basis of sensuality. A cold, impersonal bargaining interest identical with prostitution characterizes these contacts. In the dance hall this type of taxi-dancer functions as a utility for her patrons.

While these rôles are rather distinct at any given time, competition among the dancers, as well as the arrival of new girls, makes for continual readjustment among them. The taxi-dancer who formerly was the belle of the dance hall is forced either to work harder for her laurels or to engage in less desirable practices, i.e., accept a new and lower rôle for herself.

8. "Moving On": Seeing the United States Via Taxi-Dancing

When the life and activities in the taxi-dance halls of a certain city begin to pall, the taxi-dancer may travel to another city where she can secure similar employment. She will find in almost every large city[15] taxi-dance halls, all essentially alike. Once adjusted to the life, she can easily make her way in any taxi-dance hall. Another stimulus toward movement from city to city is her constant association with people who are in the habit of moving about frequently. She catches the spirit and also wants to "see the country." Among veteran taxi-dancers it is not uncommon to find girls who have been to both the Pacific and the Atlantic coasts, making their way about the country through their earnings in the taxi-dance halls. Such a story as the following is not at all uncommon.

> I've been all over the country because of these halls. My home's Chicago, but I've been in New York, New Orleans, Kansas City, Seattle, and Los Angeles. There are dance halls like this in all these cities—sometimes they work it a little different, but they're the same kind of places.
>
> Everywhere I went, though, I'd meet somebody I'd known somewhere else. In New York I saw some Flips [Filipinos] I used to know here in Chicago. When I was in Los Angeles I met a girl that used to be out on the West Side. The other night I met a Flip here I used to know out in Seattle. It's a small world, after all.[16]

At present there is a tendency for taxi-dancers of the Middle West to migrate eastward toward New York. The stages in this migration often include Kansas City or St. Louis, then Chicago, and finally New York. One Chicago investigator, when visiting a certain taxi-dance hall in New York, discovered in one evening twelve taxi-dancers who were known by him to have been previously in Chicago taxi-dance halls.

The future of this new type of feminine migration is uncertain. These young taxi-dancers, with their good incomes, the relative ease with which they can quickly secure employment in taxi-dance halls in other cities, have become a mobile group of a new variety. They have gained a freedom of movement and a ready source for a legitimate income beyond the conception of any previous generation of girls.

NOTES

1. Case No. 11.
2. Reported by a Chicago social worker.
3. Compiled from Juvenile Protective Association case records and from information supplied by three men who had known of her activities in three different social worlds.
4. Compiled from information supplied by two persons well acquainted with the young woman.
5. It has been estimated that more than half of the girls who attempt a career in the taxi-dance hall drop out during the first weeks.
6. All of the real and the "professional" names given below have been carefully altered.
7. Case No. 11.
8. Jane Logan, *Chicago Daily Times,* February 1, 1930.
9. Case No. 15.
10. Report of an investigator.
11. Case No. 15.
12. Records of an investigator.
13. Case No. 10.
14. Case No. 9.
15. It is commonly understood among social workers that the taxi-dance hall in some guise is to be found now in most cities of five hundred thousand population or more.
16. Case No. 6.

28

PAUL C. P. SIU

THE LAUNDRYMAN'S SOCIAL WORLD

from *The Chinese Laundryman* (1953)

Harsh immigration laws placed restrictions on the number of Chinese allowed to migrate to the United States in the nineteenth and early twentieth centuries. As a result, men often migrated alone, leaving behind their families. In the U.S., these men frequently took up residence in cities like Chicago where they worked in small laundromats across the city. Siu, whose research was conducted in the 1930s, documents the isolation that these men, who slept in the tiny shops where they worked, experienced from their fellow Chinese. In this excerpt we see the exception to their daily routine as they go to Chinatown and engage in leisure activities on weekends when their shops are closed.

In the American neighborhood, the Chinese laundry is a "Chinatown." Whatever contacts the laundryman has with the general public tend to be impersonal and commercial. His position is upon the symbiotic level of the community life. To his customers and other acquaintances, he is a thing and a stereotype. Only to his fellow Chinese is he a person. His relations with relatives and friends tend to be intimate and spontaneous. In company among themselves, laundrymen are free from lack of poise and race consciousness. The situation is similar, no doubt, in the cases of other minorities as well as the Jew, of whom Dr. Wirth writes:

Within the inner circle of his own tribal group, he received that appreciation, sympathy, and understanding which the larger world could not offer. In his own community, which was based upon the solidarity of the families that composed it, he was a person with status, as over against his formal position in the world outside. His fellow-Jew and the members of his family to whom he was tied by tradition and common beliefs, strengthened him in his respect for and appreciation of the values of his own group, which were strangely different from the alien society in which for the time being he lived.[1]

The social world of the Chinese laundryman is located between his quaint laundry shop and his racial Chinatown. Within this social world, people share common interests and conventional understandings; their relation is mutual and genuine, especially among members of the inner circle.

It is not that the laundryman is cut off from social contacts with non-Chinese, but rather a situation under which he can hardly unite "in his relations primary and secondary contacts."[2] The laundryman is not, to be sure, a marginal man. Rather, he is a sojourner, an individual who clings to the heritage of his own ethnic group and lives in isolation.

For the Chinese laundryman, to be able to speak English is something extra rather than necessary. It is not that he does not want to learn. He has, in fact, no time, no chance, and no facility for learning. He has not the incentive to learn English.

"In this sort of menial labor," one says, "I can get along speaking only 'yes' and 'no.' "

"If I knew how to speak and read English," says another, "I wouldn't have remained a washerman."

The majority of Chinese laundrymen speak pidgin English. Some talk so brokenly that their customers can only guess at what they are saying.

In leisure time and social events, the Chinese have a world of their own which is based upon the social solidarity of the families, the clans, and the kinship system. The American red-letter days sometimes are observed but with Chinese meanings converted to them.

1. Leisure-Time Activities

The problem of recreation for the Chinese laundryman is crucial. The world outside of his laundry is cold and strange. He strolls down the street with a lonely heart and a desire to get excitement after a week of strenuous labor. He seems to have no definite idea where to go for it. Going to a motion picture show is the most popular American recreation, but for a Chinese laundryman it is more of a way to kill time.

> INTERVIEWER: This cinema is so close by here, do you go to see a show often?
>
> C. M.: Once in a long time, seldom. On the week days, we have no time. Only Saturday afternoon and Sunday are free. But then people like to go to Chinatown and somewhere else.
>
> L. M.: You don't understand the talking—I seldom go. So far I have seen movies only twice.
>
> F. M.: I used to like movies very much. I went every day when I was not working, four years ago. A cousin of ours and I went to see a show every day because we had nothing else to do. Now, I don't care to see a picture unless I have nowhere to go.
>
> INTERVIEWER: C. L. goes to a show almost every Sunday.
>
> C. L.: Well, that's because I don't care to go down to Chinatown, and I can't sleep all day long Sunday.
>
> L. M.: Why don't you like to go to Chinatown?
>
> C. L.: Just too lazy, that's all. We used to have a club there, but now, if I go down there, I have no place to hang around. What is the use to travel so far to go down there for nothing.
>
> L. M.: Come! Let's go down to Chinatown after lunch.

Laundrymen from different laundries visit each other when they are free.

A social gathering usually takes place in Mr. Laundryman's shop Saturday afternoon. But the party seldom lasts long. Unless they sit down and play ma-jong, as some of them do, the meeting would be adjourned after a big dinner. Then they want to go out for recreation. Where? To Chinatown probably.

Sept. 17, 1938; 5:30 p.m.:

MOY: "Oh! You come just on time—a good dinner for you this evening."

I found Wai, the man who owns a laundry in the neighborhood, another middle-aged man, and a little boy about five years old there, besides Moy's partner and a helper. The man was introduced to me as a younger brother of Moy's partner. The boy is a son of their cousin who is a storekeeper in Chinatown. The brother used to be in partnership with them in this place. He sold his share to his brother and Moy and went to Detroit. Bringing the son of their cousin, he visited his brother and clansman and brought with him two big live lobsters.

Wai, a frequent visitor from the neighborhood, was invited and he helped as a cook.

As soon as the dinner was ready, all sat down to plenty of food, fried lobsters, four other dishes of meat, several vegetables, beer, and Chinese liquor.

At the table, people were talking mostly about China's war with Japan.

After dinner, H. M., a young boy of seventeen, an apprentice in the laundry, was sent over to a store to buy several bottles of Coca-Cola.

Before the brother left, Moy was trying to make him take back the money he paid for the lobsters. The brother, playing sentiment, too, was reluctant to accept his cousin's offer.

"You are not making good these days," said Moy. "Take it. Come on! Take just two dollars, please! If you

have caught eight or nine spots [in the lottery ticket], that's different. You can treat us then...."

"It is worth less than two dollars," returned the brother. "Oh, don't do this."

"Oh, yes! You take this or I'll....Please!" Moy insisted.

"No! I don't like to...." The brother was rather stubborn too.

"Then I have to put it into your pocket. You...."

"Oh! Would you keep quiet...."

"You come to visit us from out of town, we ought to treat you. You need the money for carfare...."

After a five-minute struggle, the brother finally accepted the money. He put the money into his pocket. Then he said he had to go to meet an appointment. Soon after the brother left. Moy took the boy home.

The other two members of the laundry had to remain in the laundry. They would not go any place until tomorrow—Sunday.

A social gathering of this sort represents a situation where primary group relationships and control are observable. With father and son, uncle and nephew, brothers, and other relatives present, the Old World sentiments and taboos tend to be maintained. An essential characteristic of such a type of gathering is the absence of talk about sex. This is due to the presence of members of different generations of a primary group. A large percentage of Chinese laundries in the city consist of relationships of this type. Like the family, it comes to have a control function on the conduct of its individual members. Persons working in a laundry with this type of relationship are subjected to the influence of a set of Old World sentiments and taboos. When the members are by themselves, their conversations are not only under the control of the Old World moral sentiments and taboos, but also tend to be rigid and dull. Chinese elders maintain, in certain culturally defined way, personal distance from their junior members in order to keep their reverence. To respect the old, on the other hand, is a virtue of youth, and is still observed in this type of primary group relationship in the Chinese laundry.

In contrast, there is a second type of Chinese laundry where sex is the dominant subject of interest in the daily leisure-time conversation. The people involved in such a group tend not to be related to one another. They may be cousins or clansmen, but are somewhat demoralized. Each member in such a group is more or less free; each minds his own business so far as his duty as a workingman in the laundry is concerned. The sex mores and taboos observed in the first type of laundry are out of the question here because of the absence of the venerable elder. The role of such a person in the group is due not so much to his age as to his status in the group. The absence of such a person may release the group from taboos, as shown in the following case:

> Members of the laundry:
> Chan Ming-lung, 40.
> Chan Ming-hong, 44 [partner of Minglung].
> Chan Sai-kong, 55 [clansman—employed].
> Fong Fook, 60 [unemployed friend of the partners].

MING-LUNG: Have you a girl for us? Introduce us to some of the girls. You must know many. [Ming-lung was operating the mangle while Ming-hong and Sai-kong ironed shirts, when the observer walked in. After ten minutes of exchange of greetings and about news of the war, Ming-lung suddenly changed to another subject.]

OBSERVER: I was thinking that you might get me a girl instead. I understand some prostitutes come to laundry shops, soliciting business. Any of them come to your place?

MING-HONG: Not in this neighborhood. I don't know why. [Admitted in a later interview girls did call.]

MING-LUNG: Sure, some girls [customers] come in here all the time, but they don't even talk to us.

MING-HONG: How about the office girl across the street? Does she like Chinese? [The girl was mentioned because they knew that the observer had business connections with the store across the street.]

OBSERVER: I don't know. Why don't you send old Mr. Fong Fook over to find out?

MING-LUNG: Yes, go ahead, Old Fook, go over. Ask if she likes Chinese. Go ahead.

FONG FOOK: Del-ka-ma! Go you to die.

MING-LUNG: Del-ka-ma! I told him to bring Sue, and he has never kept his promise. He said she is his daughter. Sue is his daughter, and she is pretty. Oh, I don't believe him [*laugh*].

FONG FOOK: Del-ka-ma! Go you to die. [*Qu si la*].

MING-LUNG: *Chot-chow!* [literally, "stupid as a pig"]. Is not it bad enough that she goes with black devils [Negroes]. Would you rather let the black devils have her. What about us Chinese?

MING-HONG: Del-ka-ma! She always goes to the dancing hall at Thirty-fourth Street, dancing with black devils. Both of the sisters do the same thing. This other one's name is Kitty, isn't it? You know them, don't you? [To observer, and observer happened to know who they were talking about. Sue and Kitty are two Chinese girls related to Fong Fook.]

OBSERVER: Yes, I know them. They are daughters of Fong Sun-yuin.

MING-LUNG: They are now living at.... Their father has a chop suey house in the neighborhood. Go and find them and bring them here, you, will you please [to Fong Fook]?

MING-HONG: Sue is better; I heard she is very hot....

MING-LUNG: Always like to be fucked. Black devil's "big thing." Del-ka-ma! Hers must be broken already!

MING-HONG: Oh! No [*laugh*].

FONG FOOK: Del-ka-ma! She has gotten a job on the stage. She wants to think of you. She doesn't even know you.

MING-LUNG: I don't know her! What are you talking about? I have fucked her so many times that she likes me well and you dare to say I don't know her.... You go and ask her, chot-chow [*laugh*].

FONG FOOK: Del-ka-ma! Damn liar! This what the Americans say, "Damn liar."

MING-LUNG: If you don't believe me, go and ask her.

FONG FOOK: Go you to die.

MING-LUNG: Go you to die, Old Fook. She is your daughter. You must be crazy.

FONG FOOK: She is your daughter. How do you like it?

MING-LUNG: All I want is to get her and sleep with her—daughter or no daughter. Del-ka-ma, he says he has a wife, a white woman, and a young, beautiful daughter called Sue-hing.

OBSERVER: Is that true, Old Fook?

FONG FOOK: Del-ka-ma, no, no more daughter—they are married.

MING-HONG: He wants to keep his daughter for his own use—such a kind of kai doi! [*laughter*].

MING-LUNG: Gets his own daughter-in-law, too, such a kind of kai doi!

FONG FOOK: You, you go to die—all of you.

OBSERVER: I don't believe what they say, Old Fook, but can you get them girls really?

FONG FOOK: They have girls; they have both black and white girls.

MING-LUNG: Oh, I had a black one here the other day. Good, very good. She is half white and half black. Just hot and tight enough and good water, too. Gave her a couple of dollars and I had her the whole night long. Since I don't have Chinese girl and white girl, black one is better than nothing, see. The only difference is that of her skin, but I don't care. So long as she has a hole, it is all right.

OBSERVER: Are you telling me the truth?

MING-LUNG: Yes, that is the truth.

OBSERVER: Is that true, Ming-hong?

MING-HONG: That's true [*laughter*].

OBSERVER: What do you do Sunday, usually?

MING-HONG: Well, go down to the park and try to look around and see if there are any wild chickens.

MING-LUNG: Want to catch some and bring them home. Good? See, see this table here. We had entertained many girls right here with drinks. Make them drink first, see, until they get drunk, then begin to have affair with her. You come around Saturday or Sunday. If you have no girl to bring us, let us go out to look for some. It is easy if you have a car. You just drive around in the West Side. Just pick them up at the street corner. I have done this before when I had the car. They came in and took a ride [*pause*]—but I dared not do it though. Just gave them a ride for a while and brought them home. Some of those Polish girls in the West Side—it's easy.

OBSERVER: How long ago did you do that?

MING-LUNG: Oh, several years ago—soon after I came from Detroit. It was very romantic that time, looking for girls always. See, see here, I smoked a pipe too. Some of the girls prefer a pipe smoker for a sweetheart. So I began to smoke a pipe. I still keep some of my old tobacco. Here, do you want to try it? It is good tobacco, expensive.

OBSERVER: How many times did you pick up girls in the West Side? [*smoking*].

MING-LUNG: Several times. Dared not to do it that time. Some of them were too young. They were only fourteen or fifteen. Some were old enough. It is worse today; it's different. Make friends with them—buy them some gifts, see; that's what all women like. After you become well acquainted with her, she would be yours. Some may want to marry you, can't tell. But I don't know enough English—it is best to be able to talk to her well.... That's my trouble. Fong Fook, you bring Sue to me, I can at least speak Chinese to her.

FONG FOOK: Del-ka-ma! Again. You go to die.

SAI-KONG: She does not speak Chinese, though.

MING-HONG: Yes, they don't even speak Chinese; they speak English, even at home. These American-born girls.

MING-LUNG: Is that so? Well, they must be able to speak a little at least. They are Chinese, after all.

The Chinese laundryman, like other homeless beings, is especially fond of sex jokes and stories. This case is interesting not merely because of the unreserved sex utterances in their gossip, but the picture of their sex adjustment in an isolated situation. Jokes and gossip essentially are more or less the character of amusement between long working hours. It may or may not be related to actual experience. The language above is rather rough because of the presence of Fong Fook, an out-clan member, who volunteers his help in exchange for board and perhaps a few dollars for "carfare." The partners have no respect for Fong Fook, partly because of the latter's personality, and partly because of his dependency, his out-clan affiliation in spite of his old age. He had to be ridiculed and made fun of. There are many old men in different laundries who are not full-time workers; they are given room and board with the laundryman because they have no place to live; they are usually clansmen and kinsmen of the laundrymen. An aged uncle, for instance, may move to his nephew's laundry shop to spend his retirement years. The accommodation usually is mutual and expected. To help the

uncle, or to get rid of him, the nephew may want to send the old man home to China at his own expense. Sometimes a group of friends and relatives may get together to contribute enough money for the old man's homeward trip.

The partners, if there is no discord among them, usually talk while they are working. They may make jokes about each other, or may tell stories and tales on various subjects. Sex and gambling are usually favorite subjects if there is no elder man present. Other subjects are war and politics, particularly politics in China.

In Chinatown, the laundrymen regularly visit each other in one or two places Sunday afternoon. They crowd around the room, some sitting down and some standing up, each of them contributing news and views on world politics, on personal occurrences during the week, on friends and relatives, and on their laundry business. In this way, most of them spend their Sunday afternoon. Every Sunday, the same group of people meet and discuss the same subjects. When one has talked enough in one place, he goes to another place. He stays for a while and makes a few more remarks then walks out to the street around Wentworth and Cermak Road. On the sidewalk he may meet a fellow laundryman and they chat for a few more minutes; one will probably ask the other: "How is the business this week?" The answer would be either, "The same as usual," or "Good, pretty good," or "Poor, very poor," or "Less business [or more business] than last week." If they have no important matter to discuss, they will soon separate. If it is dinner time, he may gather some of his relatives and friends for dinner in one of the eleven restaurants in Chinatown. In the restaurant, on every Sunday evening, the laundrymen dine together. These are the busiest hours of the week for the restaurant. At different tables in the dining room, the most interesting phenomenon can be observed in the grouping of the diners. Dining with him are very likely his clansmen. One can identify the surnames of the men at each of the tables, if one knows them; for instance, at this table are members of the Moy clan, and at another are members of the clan of Chan, and so on.

2. Social Events

The laundryman seldom goes to visit parks, museums, and other public and educational institutions in the community. Occasionally, he goes to a motion picture show and window shopping in the Loop. If he is young and ambitious, he may attend one of the eight Sunday Schools in which English and Bible lessons are taught. Wherever he may have been, he does not forget to pay a visit to Chinatown where he feels more at home, where he shops for daily necessities and attends to business matters, and, above all, where he is recognized as a person, enjoying a life of primary relations where sentiments and attitudes are warm, intimate, and spontaneous.

The social events the Chinese laundryman shares with fellow Chinese are festivals, rites, and ceremonies. The cultural life of China is rich in festivals, but only a few are sufficiently transplanted to the New World. Those which have been transplanted, moreover, are subjected to modification due to American circumstances. Perhaps the most persistently observed festivals are the New Year celebration (lunar year) and the so-called "Commencement of the Year"— the Spring Festival [*Chun Jie*].

For the Chinese immigrants, Spring Festival is a traditional annual social get-together for a banquet. It is usually planned for soon after the New Year. All members of the social circle are supposed to join for a hearty dinner of the most elaborate art of Chinese cookery. Due to the peculiarity of its secular function, and the elasticity of its time limit, it is possible for every family, every clan, every store, and every chop suey house and laundry shop to have a

Spring Festival social get together. Perhaps most characteristic is the Spring Festival of the clan. Each clan chooses the date convenient to all, including the married daughters and their husbands and children. If it is a small clan, the banquet may be held in the clan house. The food is either prepared in the house or ordered to be brought in from the restaurant. Larger clans may have to make arrangements with a restaurant in Chinatown so that the whole dining room or a section of it may be occupied by the special party. When the participants arrive, they are all like a big family. The adult males and the family units all contribute a small sum of money as the so-called "oil and light fee" to the clan house. Sometimes, in case of conflict, one person may have to be present at two banquets in the same evening.

The banquet is usually followed by speeches and messages from elder men and celebrities of the clan, and of the community, too, on some occasions.

> In the midst of this beautiful spring season, the Gee Tak Kung Saw [*Zhide Sande Gongsuo*] (a combined clan association) of Chicago, for the purpose of celebrating the birth of its ancestor, the ancient venerable Duke Ham Fo (a historical ancestor), held a social gathering in its clan house last Sunday.
>
> At 5:00 p.m., a banquet was held in Wah Ying Restaurant and guests and brethren of the clan and their families came together with high satisfaction and delight. The party occupied twenty-odd tables.
>
> Amidst the banquet, eldermen Wu Chi-ten and Yong Hui-fong held their cups up and drank to the health and luck of all, and people drank together, wishing each other the same. Then Chi-ten, the toastmaster of the meeting, began to announce the purpose of the evening. He went on telling the story of the origin of Wu, Chow, Tsui, Yang fraternity. He stated that the four

clans were offspring of King of Tai [ancient Duke Ham Fo]. At the beginning, the surname was Ku and the different offspring of King of Tai were later awarded titles, and from then on the four names were used according to the titles. The history of the clan can be traced back for centuries. He urged his brethren to hold and to keep the old virtues of *yen* [*ren*] (kind) and *jen* [*ren*] (unselfish) for the good of all.

Following are the speeches and messages of the guests. They were introduced as Mr. Lee Kong-lam, chairman of the National Consolidated Benevolent Association (C.C.B.A.); Mr. Chan Kong-fong, president, Oak Chun Kung Saw [*Duqing Gongsuo*] (another combined clan association); Mr. Yen Sai-jen, chairman, Yen Shee Kung Shaw [*Zhensi Gongsuo*] (a clan association); and their messages were generally of greeting about the Spring Festival and the necessity for co-operation between different organizations in Chinatown. Each time after these good speeches, there was loud applause.

At last elderman Chow Yee-fen gave thanks to those who came to honor the meeting. Both guests and members of the clan fully enjoyed the meeting and it adjourned about 7:00 P.M. Later in the evening there was Chinese music and opera melodies for entertainment in the clan house. The celebration lasted until 12:30 after midnight.[3]

The laundryman seldom closes his laundry shop to attend any social function; to suit him best, any meeting has to be on Sunday. So the Sunday crowd in Chinatown is largely a laundrymen's crowd; the chop suey worker would not be free on Sunday, because that would be his busiest day. To celebrate the Spring Festival as well as any other social get-together, the laundryman may join as member or as guest. He may be an elder man of the clan and venerable guest of the family, store, and other voluntary associations in Chinatown. His social activities, therefore, are more or less tied up with his personality, his prestige, and above all, his success.

I have been too busy lately; after one or two weeks I'll have more time to attend this matter. You know, we Chinese have Spring Festival following the New Year holiday. Once a year, they want to have something to do.

I was appointed secretary of our clan and manager of our clan woi [loan committee]. This coming Sunday, there will be a banquet, Spring Festival. They asked me to let you know, you be sure to come, too.

There will be two banquets for me this coming Sunday. Kung Wah Yuen is inviting me, too. They are conflicting with ours. They didn't know perhaps our clan would have our own Spring Festival this coming Sunday.

For the last two weeks, there were banquets, banquets, every Sunday. Bing-lung had his last Saturday evening. His son called several times, asking us to go to eat. We are far less busy here in America at this season. You probably remember that in the native village, at this season, every family has its own festival, taking turns for the whole month. With a grand-family as big as ours, I used to attend one banquet every day for nearly a month, getting sick and tired of eating meat, meat and fish, every day, every day— too much of it.

But I like the way we have our Spring Festival here, though. Once a week, a big dinner is very nice. Last week was at Toy-wah's [a cousin]. He is the fellow who is fond of cooking. He cooked the best *doong qua chung* [*dong gua zhong*] (a special pot of wintermelon soup) that I have tasted for a long time.

Next week, we will have a banquet here in this place. There will be about ten coming. This place is limited in space; we cannot have more. Several years ago, we once had more than ten, though. Bing-lung brought his nephew and the nephew's six children. We had to put them all at one table, all the children, I mean, that small table in that corner.

Please come. We will have something you like. It will not be as good cooking as that from the restaurant, but Sing-yang [a partner] is a very good cook. Sing-yang has already called Chinatown, ordering a big capon. And we hope to have "doong qua duck" too. We got *yin wou* [bird nest] already sometime ago.

I am the secretary of our clan organization this year. I want to tender my resignation this Sunday when they are together. I have been on it for the last two years. It is quite a responsibility; keeping the accounts and taking the money is quite a little job. I would like to have some one else do it this year. I recommended Sing-yang last year, but they thought Sing-yang is gambling now and then. Cousin Chung-shih and Big Brother Chung-ying [the chairman] urged me to continue for another year. They said I have good handwriting and insisted I take it. You know, the trouble is that very few of us know how to write [Chinese].

The laundryman's leisure-time activities seem to take place between the laundry and Chinatown. Chinatown is the social center; the laundry shop is his home. He may like to entertain guests at his laundry. Guests, after all, are people of his social circle. If he wants to have a birthday party, for instance, he can either entertain friends and relatives in a restaurant or at his laundry. A feast in the restaurant is more formal and expensive.

Such a celebration is likely to be given by a relative in his honor; particularly by a son, son-in-law, or nephew. Men over sixty may expect birthday celebrations given by junior members of their immediate family. Usually the laundryman prefers to cook in his laundry shop because getting dinner is something of a play activity, to say nothing about saving money. When he is not working, he must have something to do to occupy his time. The best time for a dinner with invited guests would be Saturday or Sunday. On his actual birthday he has to work without celebration. The dinner has to be postponed until Saturday or Sunday.

December 13, 1938: Chan Sang sent three dollars to Ann, daughter of his cousin, and a letter which read:

Dear Ann:

I am sending you three dollars; it is my Christmas present for you. I have not the time to look for something you may like. In fact, I don't know what you like. So I send the money, hoping you will use the money to get what you want.

This coming Saturday will be my birthday. I shall prepare a special dinner here in my laundry. I am expecting you and your brothers and sister. You can take a cab; I shall take care of the fare. Come earlier, for the dinner will probably be ready about six o'clock.

Uncle Sang

December 17, 1938: It was a busy day for Chan Sang. He got up at five-thirty in the morning and began to cook the dinner....

Finally, about four-thirty, the young guests arrived. They didn't take a cab as Chan told them in the letter. They brought one dozen of oranges. It was a birthday gift. "You bring fruit, too! Your mother told you to bring this!"

The dinner was ready at six-thirty. Chan Sang sent Chan Ming over to the chop suey restaurant in the next block to get some of the people over to eat. Soon Chan Ming returned: "They are too busy at this hour; they can't come over."

Chan Sang then took over to the chop suey house one-fourth of the cooked capon and some roast pork himself. He soon returned to join the party. Besides the children, there were five adults. Eight of us finally sat down and began to eat. It lasted us three-quarters of an hour. There was the best kind of Chinese wine—*ng ka pe* [*wujiapi*].

After the dinner, Chan Sang took all the children home to Chinatown in a cab.

January 4, 1931: One of the relatives in Chinatown was going to give a birthday party. Aunt Sun-lan reminded Chan Ming to invite Chan Sang last Sunday. Chan Ming was telling Chan Sang that both of them were invited and Chan Sang would be the guest of honor.

"Are you sure that she wanted me to the dinner?"

"Most certainly," answered Chan Ming. "If you don't believe me, ask Ling-po."

"Yes, I heard that she asked him to invite you," said Chan Ling-po.

"All right."

The next day, Chan Sang went down to Chinatown. He walked into a Chinese grocery store. He ordered a six-pound live chicken and one dozen oranges. He told the clerk to wrap it up with red paper because it was for a birthday present.

He took the package over to his relative, Aunt Sun-lan's house, and the old lady met him at the door.

"Aunty, this is a little something from me, for this evening."

"Oh, Brother Sang!" exclaimed Aunt Sun-lan, "you shouldn't have done that. All I want is that you come to dinner. As you spend so much money, I dare not invite you the next time. Uncle Teh-hing left me five dollars and said a dinner should be prepared. So I thought I would ask some of our cousins together. I told Brother Ming to remind you, too. But you shouldn't have done this! I don't want to make you spend the money."

"That's all right."

"Thank you! Oh, thank you, Brother Sang! And you be sure to come back Sunday."

"If I am late or don't show up, don't wait for me," replied Chan Sang. "I don't feel good these few days."

Chan Sang can be regarded as a typical character in the social life of the Chinese laundryman in America. He is usually very generous in spending money for social purposes. His inner social circle are composed of members of his clan and kin. The clansmen and kinsmen are his guests and he is their guest. Some of the distant relatives with whom he may not have anything to do in China, in America become much closer to him. This is the case between Aunt Sun-lan and Chan Sang. In China, they are members of different villages, and, in celebrating a birthday of Aunt Sun-lan's husband, Chan Sang would never have participated. In America, Chan Sang's relation with Aunt Sun-lan becomes closer. It produces a new social solidarity. A person with such sentiments and attitudes is fighting for status in the inner social circle. If he is not recognized in the circle as expected, he may be very indignant. The feeling of T. C. in the following case is a good illustration.

A birth ceremony was held last Sunday for Moy Wing's second grandchild.... In another store, several relatives and neighbors of the family were talking about it.

K. L.: Moy Wing's second grandson's birthday ceremony is today. Are you invited, T. C.?

T. C.: No! I don't know anything about it.

C. C.: Why? Your partner is invited—both of you are related to them.

T. C.: How can I ask them to invite me! *Del* (fuck)! I don't care.

S. T.: You can't blame them. You have been in their place, haven't you? I heard only those who gave presents to the baby are invited. Many of us know them, but we haven't given the baby presents. So I, too, am not invited. They don't invite you because they are afraid you will spend money.

K. L.: I am glad I am not invited. I am different from you, T. C. If they invite me I would have to spend at least three dollars. If I have three dollars, I can have all I can eat in any of the restaurants, too. You shouldn't be mad.

T. C.: Who's mad?...I don't care if my partner is invited. We two are in the same laundry, but he is invited and not me.

S. T.: But Ah Chung [father of the baby] may be looking for you, T. C. He may not have a chance to find you at all.

C. C.: I tell you, since I know they have a baby, I wouldn't want to go to visit their place. I don't care to spend money for a present. If I visit the place, it is not nice not to give any present. So I avoid going to their place this two weeks. I would wait until it is over. If I happen to see the baby, I then can give it a dollar or so for candy money.

S. T.: I don't know a thing. I just won't go to their place. I don't feel bad not to be invited. When their first grandson had its birthday ceremony, I made a present of three dollars. There was no dinner the last time. Instead of a dinner gathering, a cooked chicken and roasted pork cutlets were distributed to each giver. I don't know why it is a dinner this time.

C. C.: Well, they are having quite a few guests. You can count who will be there this evening. The son-in-law, the son-in-law's brother's family, Moy Wing's cousins, Hsin-hing, Kwong-sun, and Moy Jak. With so many persons, it will take three tables.

T. C. left the place without saying anything more; he looked not pleased at all. And S. T. said:

"T. C. is a strange fellow. He doesn't feel happy if he is not invited."

"That's funny," responded C. C., "He doesn't care if he has to spend ten dollars—he would feel better. Such a silly fellow."

In spite of the indifferent remarks in the conversation, the issue in this case seems to be clear: the expectation of being included in a given circle is defined by clan and kin relationship. As both belong to the same clan, T. C. thinks that since his partner is invited to the party, he should be invited also. Whether the incident is a misunderstanding between T. C. and the family is another question. The case is interesting to illustrate the character of the inner circle of the laundryman's social world. It is essentially based on the clan and kin system; it is a social world of relatives. The laundryman seldom establishes primary contacts with people other than his own clansmen. In his social world, individuals with the same surnames are by virtue of this his *hing doi* [*xiongdi*] (brethren); individuals related to him or to his immediate family by marriage are *chan-chieh* [*qingqi*] (relatives by marriage); and individuals from the same native district are *hiang-le* [*xiangli*] (neighbors). He is bound up with these people not only in social activities but also in business ventures.

3. New Social Activities

The Chinese laundryman, although having either vague or superficial ideas about American holidays and other social activities, often takes part in some of the American institutional activities as a chance to get some extra satisfaction. Christmas, for example: the Chinese laundryman, to a certain extent, observes it, but with a different meaning. So Christmas is called Winter Festival [Dong Jie], which is an annual affair of ancestor worship comparable to Christmas because it comes shortly before the New Year. He observes Christmas by sending presents to some of his relatives and friends. To his customers he usually gives Chinese tea, li-chi nuts, silk, and chinaware. The presents are handed to every customer as the latter calls for his laundry. Unlike the ordinary Christmas gifts, the laundryman seldom wraps the packages with Christmas paper; the packages are not even named for the receivers, because the giver does not even know the names of his customers. In case he does know the name, to wrap it properly and enclose a card in the proper form is sometimes beyond his ability. He may not have the time to bother about it, anyway.

> Every year we spend at least forty dollars, buying tea and li-chi nuts for our customers. It is once a year and the Americans regard it as their biggest day of the year. We don't feel good if we have nothing to give them. In this way, we feel good and they feel good, too, see.
>
> No, very few of our customers ask for it. It is always we pass it out and they take it.
>
> Yes, we pay special attention to some of our best customers. We have one family that does about five to six dollars' business with us every week. So we buy some Chinese tea, some li-chi nuts, and a pair of vases for them. We have another good customer, a widow

and a young daughter. Every time she brings laundry, it must be a big bundle. So we got something for her and something for her daughter, too. We have about a dozen of such good customers.

The present, it seems, is essentially given with an economic motive, but not entirely without a human touch. Christmas may not mean the same thing to him as it does to Christians, but it is a celebration; Chinese love festivals by heritage. He gets satisfaction thinking that his customer would appreciate the present. Under some special condition, in order to feel better, the present becomes almost necessary to the laundryman for his customer. The celebration of the Christmas holiday in this fashion is not at all uniform. In certain neighborhoods where customers usually are of a poorer type and the business relationship is more or less on an impersonal basis, the laundryman may not feel it necessary to give presents to his customers. This is the case in some of the Negro areas. It is by no means without exception; Chinese laundries in the so-called "Black Belt" do distribute tea and li-chi nuts at Christmas time. A laundryman with poor business in a white neighborhood may not feel it necessary to give, also. There are also laundries where only good customers receive gifts.

> Well, some places just pass it out to everybody. We found it is not necessary to do it. We buy something only for our good customers, those give us much more business. This is merely to express our thought of gratitude for their patronage.

Occasionally the laundryman's customers repay him with presents which he does not expect. It is also an interesting practice that laundrymen exchange greeting cards among themselves. On many occasions, gifts are bought for children of friends and relatives—once a year as an expression of human sentiment.

As an old Chinese proverb says: "Getting in the village, follow its customs; going down the river, follow its current," [*ruxiang suisu chushui suibo*] the Chinese laundryman observes Thanksgiving Day; he calls it *Fu-Qai-Chih* [*Huoji Jie*] (Turkey Festival).

> "Just eat it once a year," Chan Sing remarked while he held a big piece of turkey meat between his chop sticks. "It is a good thing—just like our Chinese festivals. Since we are in this country, we like to eat turkey, too, although it is not our own custom."
>
> I told him Thanksgiving was not merely eating turkey. "Well," he said, "if the American give thanks for their good life—but only Chinese Christians believe in God...."
>
> "Whenever the Americans have a holiday, they can really enjoy it. They have family and relatives and friends, men and women, boys and girls. They have lots of places to go. A holiday means something to them. That means to have a real good time. What can a Chinese immigrant do? Nothing. He can only go down to Chinatown. A holiday is just like any other day. That means some of the gamblers lose more money on the gambling tables.
>
> "Americans are different. They have parties at home, with friends and relatives. They enjoy some good music and have some fun together. We can have the same thing in China, yes, but not here.
>
> "Eat turkey does not mean anything, since everybody eats turkey today; we, too, eat it, that's all."

This is how some of these lonely men eat turkey at Thanksgiving. It is nothing more than something different to eat. The following case, however, shows that laundrymen, too, get their friends and relatives together and celebrate the holiday with social meaning:

> In the Charlie Moy laundry a twenty-five-pound turkey is roasted besides preparing other Chinese dishes. Soon three men arrive, and two more are expected. Another half hour of waiting, the expected guests still did not show up. The sixteen-year-old boy got on his bicycle and rode away. About twenty minutes later the lad came back alone.
>
> "Granduncle T. K. is still too busy," said the boy. "He did not think he could come."
>
> "In that case," said his father, "you had better bring some turkey over to him. Here I cut a piece. It takes you only ten minutes. And on your way, you might as well drop in to see Lo Loh [Old Loh]. If he is still home in his laundry, ask him to come to eat turkey."
>
> Hurriedly, the boy again went out on his bicycle. When he came home again, everybody sat down to eat and drink heartily.
>
> "Eat! Eat as much as you can!" F. M. urged everybody. "After dinner, we will go down to Chinatown. Maybe there will be another turkey dinner." He was mentioning some places where he could be invited if he showed up in time.
>
> "Really turkey is not as good as chicken," said H. M., "but if Americans eat it, we, too, can have some. It is only once a year for this festival, that's all. It is a big day, American big day. But Americans don't have so much to eat as Chinese do in our festivals."

An additional chance of a social get-together, the abundance of food in a feast, and the "once a year" attitude give one a feeling that the laundryman is celebrating a Chinese festival to one familiar with the folk life in the Chinese village. The psychology of it is that the laundryman misses his Old World Festivals. Eating turkey on Thanksgiving Day means to him something of a substitute. To be sure, both on Christmas and on Thanksgiving Day he can close his laundry shop for a holiday because his customers are celebrating and would not come for their laundry. On the days of Chinese festivals, however, he is too busy to celebrate or has actually forgotten all about them. He participates in some American institutional activities because he is just as human as the others. He is bound to have a different interpretation of the event.

NOTES

1. Louis Wirth, *The Ghetto* (Chicago: University of Chicago Press, 1928), p. 26.
2. R. E. Park and E. W. Burgess, *Introduction to the Science of Sociology*, 2nd ed. (Chicago: University of Chicago Press, 1924), p. 286.
3. *San Ming Morning News*, March 17, 1937.

REFERENCES

Park R. E. and E. W. Burgess. 1924. *Introduction to the Science of Sociology*. 2nd ed. Chicago: University of Chicago Press.

Wirth, Louis. 1928. *The Ghetto*. Chicago: University of Chicago Press.

29

ELLIOT LIEBOW

MEN AND JOBS

from *Tally's Corner* (1967)

In *Tally's Corner*, Elliot Liebow shows how a group of mainly unemployed men living in Washington D.C. think and feel about their life situation. On the basis of nine months of participating in and observing their lives, Liebow tries to explain in this excerpt why the men place such a low value on the jobs that are available to them.

A pickup truck drives slowly down the street. The truck stops as it comes abreast of a man sitting on a cast-iron porch and the white driver calls out, asking if the man wants a day's work. The man shakes his head and the truck moves on up the block, stopping again whenever idling men come within calling distance of the driver. At the Carry-out corner, five men debate the question briefly and shake their heads no to the truck. The truck turns the corner and repeats the same performance up the next street. In the distance, one can see one man, then another, climb into the back of the truck and sit down. In starts and stops, the truck finally disappears.

What is it we have witnessed here? A labor scavenger rebuffed by his would-be prey? Lazy, irresponsible men turning down an honest day's pay for an honest day's work? Or a more complex phenomenon marking the intersection of economic forces, social values, and individual states of mind and body?

Let us look again at the driver of the truck. He has been able to recruit only two or three men from each twenty or fifty he contacts. To him, it is clear that the others simply do not choose to work. Singly or in groups, belly-empty or belly-full, sullen or gregarious, drunk or sober, they confirm what he has read, heard and knows from his own experience: these men wouldn't take a job if it were handed to them on a platter.[1]

Quite apart from the question of whether or not this is true of some of the men he sees on the street, it is clearly not true of all of them. If it were, he would not have come here in the first place; or having come, he would have left with an empty truck. It is not even true of most of them, for most of the men he sees on the street this weekday morning do, in fact, have jobs. But since, at the moment, they are neither working nor sleeping, and since they hate the depressing room or apartment they live in, or because there is nothing to do there,[2] or because they want to get away from their wives or anyone else living there, they are out on the street, indistinguishable from those who do not have jobs or do not want them. Some, like Boley, a member of a trash-collection crew in a suburban housing development, work Saturdays and are off on this weekday. Some, like Sweets, work nights cleaning up middle-class trash, dirt, dishes, and garbage, and mopping the floors of the office buildings, hotels, restaurants, toilets, and other public places dirtied during the day. Some men work for retail businesses such as liquor stores which do not begin the day until ten o'clock. Some laborers, like Tally, have already come back from the job because the ground was too wet for pick and shovel or because the weather was too cold for pouring concrete. Other employed men stayed off the job today for personal reasons: Clarence to go to a funeral at eleven this morning and Sea Cat to answer a subpoena as a witness in a criminal proceeding.

Also on the street, unwitting contributors to the impression taken away by the truck driver, are the halt and the lame. The man on the cast-iron steps strokes one gnarled arthritic hand with the other and says he doesn't know whether or not he'll live long enough to be eligible for Social Security. He pauses, then adds matter-of-factly, "Most times, I don't care whether I do or don't." Stoopy's left leg was polio-withered in childhood. Raymond, who looks as if he could tear out a fire hydrant, coughs up blood if he bends or moves suddenly. The quiet man who hangs out in front of the Saratoga apartments has a steel hook strapped onto his left elbow. And had the man in the truck been able to look into the wine-clouded eyes of the man in the green cap, he would have realized that the man did not even understand he was being offered a day's work.

Others, having had jobs and been laid off, are drawing unemployment compensation (up to $44 per week) and have nothing to gain by accepting work which pays little more than this and frequently less.

Still others, like Bumdoodle the numbers man, are working hard at illegal ways of making money, hustlers who are on the street to turn a dollar any way they can: buying and selling sex, liquor, narcotics, stolen goods, or anything else that turns up.

Only a handful remains unaccounted for. There is Tonk, who cannot bring himself to take a job away from the corner, because, according to the other men, he suspects his wife will be unfaithful if given the opportunity. There is Stanton, who has not reported to work for four days now, not since Bernice disappeared. He bought a brand new knife against her return. She had done this twice before, he said, but not for so long and not without warning, and he had forgiven her. But this time, "I ain't got it in me to forgive her again." His rage and shame are there for all to see as he paces the Carry-out and the corner, day and night, hoping to catch a glimpse of her.

And finally, there are those like Arthur, able-bodied men who have no visible means of support, legal or illegal, who neither have jobs nor want them. The truck driver, among others, believes the Arthurs to be representative of all the men he sees idling on the street during his own working hours. They are not, but they cannot be dismissed simply because they are a small minority. It is not enough to explain them away as being lazy or irresponsible or both because an able-bodied man with responsibilities who refuses work is, by the truck driver's definition, lazy and irresponsible. Such an answer begs the question. It is descriptive of the facts; it does not explain them.

Moreover, despite their small numbers, the don't-work-and-don't-want-to-work minority is especially significant because they represent the strongest and clearest expression of those values and attitudes associated with making a living which, to varying degrees, are found throughout the streetcorner world. These men differ from the others in degree rather than in kind, the principal difference being that they are carrying out the implications of their values and experiences to their logical, inevitable conclusions. In this sense, the others have yet to come to terms with themselves and the world they live in.

Putting aside, for the moment, what the men say and feel, and looking at what they actually do and the choices they make, getting a job, keeping a job, and doing well at it is clearly of low priority. Arthur will not take a job at all. Leroy is supposed to be on his job at 4:00 P.M. but it is already 4:10 and he still cannot bring himself to leave the free games he has accumulated on the pinball machine in the Carry-out. Tonk started a construction job on Wednesday, worked Thursday and Friday, then didn't go back again. On the same kind of job, Sea Cat quit in the second week. Sweets had been working three months as a busboy in a restaurant, then quit without notice, not sure himself why he did so. A real estate agent, saying he was more interested in getting the job done than in the cost, asked Richard to give him an estimate on repairing and painting the inside of a house, but Richard, after looking over the job, somehow never got around to submitting an estimate. During one period, Tonk would not leave the corner to take a job because his wife might prove unfaithful; Stanton would not take a job because his woman had been unfaithful.

Thus, the man-job relationship is a tenuous one. At any given moment, a job may occupy a relatively low position on the streetcorner scale of real values. Getting a job may be subordinated to relations with women or to other non-job considerations;

the commitment to a job one already has is frequently shallow and tentative.

The reasons are many. Some are objective and reside principally in the job; some are subjective and reside principally in the man. The line between them, however, is not a clear one. Behind the man's refusal to take a job or his decision to quit one is not a simple impulse or value choice but a complex combination of assessments of objective reality on the one hand, and values, attitudes, and beliefs drawn from different levels of his experience on the other.

Objective economic considerations are frequently a controlling factor in a man's refusal to take a job. How much the job pays is a crucial question but seldom asked. He knows how much it pays. Working as a stock clerk, a delivery boy, or even behind the counter of liquor stores, drug stores, and other retail businesses pays one dollar an hour. So, too, do most busboy, car-wash, janitorial, and other jobs available to him. Some jobs, such as dishwasher, may dip as low as eighty cents an hour and others, such as elevator operator or work in a junk yard, may offer $1.15 or $1.25. Take-home pay for jobs such as these ranges from $35 to $50 a week, but a take-home pay of over $45 for a five-day week is the exception rather than the rule.

One of the principal advantages of these kinds of jobs is that they offer fairly regular work. Most of them involve essential services and are therefore somewhat less responsive to business conditions than are some higher paying, less menial jobs. Most of them are also inside jobs not dependent on the weather, as are construction jobs and other higher-paying outside work.

Another seemingly important advantage of working in hotels, restaurants, office and apartment buildings and retail establishments is that they frequently offer an opportunity for stealing on the job. But stealing can be a two-edged sword. Apart from increasing the cost of the goods or services to the general public, a less obvious result is that the practice usually acts as a depressant on the employee's own wage level. Owners of small retail establishments and other employers frequently anticipate employee stealing and adjust the wage rate accordingly. Tonk's employer explained why he was paying Tonk $35 for a 55–60 hour workweek. These men will all steal, he said. Although he keeps close watch on Tonk, he estimates that Tonk steals from $35 to $40 a week.[3] What he steals, when added to his regular earnings, brings his take-home pay to $70 or $75 per week. The employer said he did not mind this because Tonk is worth that much to the business. But if he were to pay Tonk outright the full value of his labor, Tonk would still be stealing $35–$40 per week and this, he said, the business simply would not support.

This wage arrangement, with stealing built-in, was satisfactory to both parties, with each one independently expressing his satisfaction. Such a wage-theft system, however, is not as balanced and equitable as it appears. Since the wage level rests on the premise that the employee will steal the unpaid value of his labor, the man who does not steal on the job is penalized. And furthermore, even if he does not steal, no one would believe him; the employer and others believe he steals because the system presumes it.

Nor is the man who steals, as he is expected to, as well off as he believes himself to be. The employer may occasionally close his eyes to the worker's stealing but not often and not for long. He is, after all, a businessman and cannot always find it within himself to let a man steal from him, even if the man is stealing his own wages. Moreover, it is only by keeping close watch on the worker that the employer can control how much is stolen and thereby protect himself against the employee's stealing more than he is worth. From this viewpoint, then, the employer is not in wage theft collusion with the employee. In the case of Tonk, for instance, the employer was not

actively abetting the theft. His estimate of how much Tonk was stealing was based on what he thought Tonk was able to steal despite his own best efforts to prevent him from stealing anything at all. Were he to have caught Tonk in the act of stealing, he would, of course, have fired him from the job and perhaps called the police as well. Thus, in an actual if not in a legal sense, all the elements of entrapment are present. The employer knowingly provides the conditions which entice (force) the employee to steal the unpaid value of his labor, but at the same time he punishes him for theft if he catches him doing so.

Other consequences of the wage-theft system are even more damaging to the employee. Let us, for argument's sake, say that Tonk is in no danger of entrapment; that his employer is willing to wink at the stealing and that Tonk, for his part, is perfectly willing to earn a little, steal a little. Let us say, too, that he is paid $35 a week and allowed to steal $35. His money income—as measured by the goods and services he can purchase with it—is, of course, $70. But not all of his income is available to him for all purposes. He cannot draw on what he steals to build his self-respect or to measure his self-worth. For this, he can draw only on his earnings—the amount given him publicly and voluntarily in exchange for his labor. His "respect" and "self-worth" income remains at $35—only half that of the man who also receives $70 but all of it in the form of wages. His earnings publicly measure the worth of his labor to his employer, and they are important to others and to himself in taking the measure of his worth as a man.[4]

With or without stealing, and quite apart from any interior processes going on in the man who refuses such a job or quits it casually and without apparent reason, the objective fact is that menial jobs in retailing or in the service trades simply do not pay enough to support a man and his family. This is not to say that the worker is underpaid; this may or may not be true. Whether he is or not, the plain fact is that, in such a job, he cannot make a living. Nor can he take much comfort in the fact that these jobs tend to offer more regular, steadier work. If he cannot live on the $45 or $50 he makes in one week, the longer he works, the longer he cannot live on what he makes.[5]

Construction work, even for unskilled laborers, usually pays better, with the hourly rate ranging from $1.50 to $2.60 an hour.[6] Importantly, too, good references, a good driving record, a tenth grade (or any high school) education, previous experience, the ability to "bring police clearance with you" are not normally required of laborers as they frequently are for some of the jobs in retailing or in the service trades.

Construction work, however, has its own objective disadvantages. It is, first of all, seasonal work for the great bulk of the laborers, beginning early in the spring and tapering off as winter weather sets in.[7] And even during the season the work is frequently irregular. Early or late in the season, snow or temperatures too low for concrete frequently sends the laborers back home, and during late spring or summer, a heavy rain on Tuesday or Wednesday, leaving a lot of water and mud behind it, can mean a two or three day work-week for the pick-and-shovel men and other unskilled laborers.[8]

The elements are not the only hazard. As the project moves from one construction stage to another, laborers—usually without warning—are laid off, sometimes permanently or sometimes for weeks at a time. The more fortunate or the better workers are told periodically to "take a walk for two, three days."

Both getting the construction job and getting to it are also relatively more difficult than is the case for the menial jobs in retailing and the service trades. Job competition is always fierce. In the city, the large construction projects are unionized. One has to have ready cash to get into the union to become eligible to work on these projects

and, being eligible, one has to find an opening. Unless one "knows somebody," say a foreman or a laborer who knows the day before that they are going to take on new men in the morning, this can be a difficult and disheartening search.

Many of the nonunion jobs are in suburban Maryland or Virginia. The newspaper ads say, "Report ready to work to the trailer at the intersection of Rte. 11 and Old Bridge Rd., Bunston, Virginia (or Maryland)," but this location may be ten, fifteen, or even twenty-five miles from the Carry-out. Public transportation would require two or more hours to get there, if it services the area at all. Without access to a car or to a car-pool arrangement, it is not worthwhile reading the ad. So the men do not. Jobs such as these are usually filled by word of mouth information, beginning with someone who knows someone or who is himself working there and looking for a paying rider. Furthermore, nonunion jobs in outlying areas tend to be smaller projects of relatively short duration and to pay somewhat less than scale.

Still another objective factor is the work itself. For some men, whether the job be digging, mixing mortar, pushing a wheelbarrow, unloading materials, carrying and placing steel rods for reinforcing concrete, or building or laying concrete forms, the work is simply too hard. Men such as Tally and Wee Tom can make such work look like child's play; some of the older work-hardened men, such as Budder and Stanton, can do it too, although not without showing unmistakable signs of strain and weariness at the end of the workday. But those who lack the robustness of a Tally or the time-inured immunity of a Budder must either forego jobs such as these or pay a heavy toll to keep them. For Leroy, in his early twenties, almost six feet tall but weighing under 140 pounds, it would be as difficult to push a loaded wheelbarrow, or to unload and stack 96-pound bags of cement all day long, as it would be for Stoopy with his withered leg.

Heavy, backbreaking labor of the kind that used to be regularly associated with bull gangs or concrete gangs is no longer characteristic of laboring jobs, especially those with the larger, well-equipped construction companies. Brute strength is still required from time to time, as on smaller jobs where it is not economical to bring in heavy equipment or where the small, undercapitalized contractor has none to bring in. In many cases, however, the conveyor belt has replaced the wheelbarrow or the Georgia buggy, mechanized forklifts have eliminated heavy, manual lifting, and a variety of digging machines have replaced the pick and shovel. The result is fewer jobs for unskilled laborers and, in many cases, a work speed-up for those who do have jobs. Machines now set the pace formerly set by men. Formerly, a laborer pushed a wheelbarrow of wet cement to a particular spot, dumped it, and returned for another load. Another laborer, in hip boots, pushed the wet concrete around with a shovel or a hoe, getting it roughly level in preparation for the skilled finishers. He had relatively small loads to contend with and had only to keep up with the men pushing the wheelbarrows. Now, the job for the man pushing the wheelbarrow is gone and the wet concrete comes rushing down a chute at the man in the hip boots who must "spread it quick or drown."

Men who have been running an elevator, washing dishes, or "pulling trash" cannot easily move into laboring jobs. They lack the basic skills for "unskilled" construction labor, familiarity with tools and materials, and tricks of the trade without which hard jobs are made harder. Previously unused or untrained muscles rebel in pain against the new and insistent demands made upon them, seriously compromising the man's performance and testing his willingness to see the job through.

A healthy, sturdy, active man of good intelligence requires from two to four weeks to break in on a construction job.[9] Even if he is willing somehow to bull his way through the first few weeks, it frequently happens that his foreman or the craftsman he services with materials and general assistance is not willing to wait that long for him to get into condition or to learn at a glance the difference in size between a rough $2'' \times 8''$ and a finished $2'' \times 10''$. The foreman and the craftsman are themselves "under the gun" and cannot "carry" the man when other men, who are already used to the work and who know the tools and materials, are lined up to take the job.

Sea Cat was "healthy, sturdy, active and of good intelligence." When a judge gave him six weeks in which to pay his wife $200 in back child-support payments, he left his grocery-store job in order to take a higher-paying job as a laborer, arranged for him by a foreman friend. During the first week the weather was bad and he worked only Wednesday and Friday, cursing the elements all the while for cheating him out of the money he could have made. The second week, the weather was fair but he quit at the end of the fourth day, saying frankly that the work was too hard for him. He went back to his job at the grocery store and took a second job working nights as a dishwasher in a restaurant,[10] earning little if any more at the two jobs than he would have earned as a laborer, and keeping at both of them until he had paid off his debts.

Tonk did not last as long as Sea Cat. No one made any predictions when he got a job in a parking lot, but when the men on the corner learned he was to start on a road construction job, estimates of how long he would last ranged from one to three weeks. Wednesday was his first day. He spent that evening and night at home. He did the same on Thursday. He worked Friday and spent Friday evening and part of Saturday draped over the mailbox on the corner. Sunday afternoon, Tonk decided he was not going to report on the job the next morning. He explained that after working three days, he knew enough about the job to know that it was too hard for him. He knew he wouldn't be able to keep up and he'd just as soon quit now as get fired later.

Logan was a tall, two-hundred-pound man in his late twenties. His back used to hurt him only on the job, he said, but now he can't straighten up for increasingly longer periods of time. He said he had traced this to the awkward walk he was forced to adopt by the loaded wheelbarrows which pull him down into a half-stoop. He's going to quit, he said, as soon as he can find another job. If he can't find one real soon, he guesses he'll quit anyway. It's not worth it, having to walk bent over and leaning to one side.

Sometimes, the strain and effort is greater than the man is willing to admit, even to himself. In the early summer of 1963, Richard was rooming at Nancy's place. His wife and children were "in the country" (his grandmother's home in Carolina), waiting for him to save up enough money so that he could bring them back to Washington and start over again after a disastrous attempt to "make it" in Philadelphia. Richard had gotten a job with a fence company in Virginia. It paid $1.60 an hour. The first few evenings, when he came home from work, he looked ill from exhaustion and the heat. Stanton said Richard would have to quit, "he's too small [thin] for that kind of work." Richard said he was doing O.K. and would stick with the job.

At Nancy's one night, when Richard had been working about two weeks, Nancy and three or four others were sitting around talking, drinking, and listening to music. Someone asked Nancy when was Richard going to bring his wife and children up from the country. Nancy said she didn't know, but it probably depended on how long it would take him to save up enough money. She said she didn't think he could stay with the fence job much longer. This morning, she said, the man Richard rode to work with knocked on the door and Richard didn't answer. She looked in his room. Richard was still asleep.

Nancy tried to shake him awake. "No more digging!" Richard cried out. "No more digging! I can't do no more God-damn digging!" When Nancy finally managed to wake him, he dressed quickly and went to work.

Richard stayed on the job two more weeks, then suddenly quit, ostensibly because his pay check was three dollars less than what he thought it should have been.

In summary of objective job considerations, then, the most important fact is that a man who is able and willing to work cannot earn enough money to support himself, his wife, and one or more children. A man's chances for working regularly are good only if he is willing to work for less than he can live on, and sometimes not even then. On some jobs, the wage rate is deceptively higher than on others, but the higher the wage rate, the more difficult it is to get the job, and the less the job security. Higher-paying construction work tends to be seasonal and, during the season, the amount of work available is highly sensitive to business and weather conditions and to the changing requirements of individual projects.[11] Moreover, high-paying construction jobs are frequently beyond the physical capacity of some of the men, and some of the low-paying jobs are scaled down even lower in accordance with the self-fulfilling assumption that the man will steal part of his wages on the job.[12]

Bernard assesses the objective job situation dispassionately over a cup of coffee, sometimes poking at the coffee with his spoon, sometimes staring at it as if, like a crystal ball, it holds tomorrow's secrets. He is twenty-seven years old. He and the woman with whom he lives have a baby son, and she has another child by another man. Bernard does odd jobs—mostly painting— but here it is the end of January, and his last job was with the Post Office during the Christmas mail rush. He would like postal work as a steady job, he says. It pays well (about $2.00 an hour) but he has twice failed the Post Office examination (he graduated from a Washington high school) and has given up the idea as an impractical one. He is supposed to see a man tonight about a job as a parking attendant for a large apartment house. The man told him to bring his birth certificate and driver's license, but his license was suspended because of a backlog of unpaid traffic fines. A friend promised to lend him some money this evening. If he gets it, he will pay the fines tomorrow morning and have his license reinstated. He hopes the man with the job will wait till tomorrow night.

A "security job" is what he really wants, he said. He would like to save up money for a taxicab. (But having twice failed the postal examination and having a bad driving record as well, it is highly doubtful that he could meet the qualifications or pass the written test.) That would be "a good life." He can always get a job in a restaurant or as a clerk in a drugstore but they don't pay enough, he said. He needs to take home at least $50 to $55 a week. He thinks he can get that much driving a truck somewhere... Sometimes he wishes he had stayed in the army... A security job, that's what he wants most of all, a real security job ...

When we look at what the men bring to the job rather than at what the job offers the men, it is essential to keep in mind that we are not looking at men who come to the job fresh, just out of school perhaps, and newly prepared to undertake the task of making a living, or from another job where they earned a living and are prepared to do the same on this job. Each man comes to the job with a long job history characterized by his not being able to support himself and his family. Each man carries this knowledge, born of his experience, with him. He comes to the job flat and stale, wearied by the sameness of it all, convinced of his own incompetence, terrified of responsibility—of being tested still again and found wanting. Possible exceptions are the younger men not yet, or just, married. They suspect all this but have yet to have it confirmed by repeated personal experience over time. But those who are or have been married know it well. It is the experience of the individual and the group; of their fathers and probably their sons. Convinced of their inadequacies, not only do they not seek out those few better-paying jobs which test their resources, but they actively avoid them, gravitating in a mass to the menial, routine jobs which offer no challenge—and therefore pose no threat—to the already diminished images they have of themselves.

Thus Richard does not follow through on the real estate agent's offer. He is afraid to do on his own—minor plastering, replacing broken windows, other minor repairs, and painting—exactly what he had been doing for months on a piecework basis under someone else (and which provided him with a solid base from which to derive a cost estimate).

Richard once offered an important clue to what may have gone on in his mind when the job offer was made. We were in the Carry-out, at a time when he was looking for work. He was talking about the kind of jobs available to him.

> I graduated from high school [Baltimore] but I don't know anything. I'm dumb. Most of the time I don't even say I graduated, 'cause then somebody asks me a question and I can't answer it, and they think I was lying about graduating.... They graduated me but I didn't know anything. I had lousy grades but I guess they wanted to get rid of me.
>
> I was at Margaret's house the other night and her little sister asked me to help her with her homework. She showed me some fractions and I knew right away I couldn't do them. I was ashamed so I told her I had to go to the bathroom.

And so it must have been surely, with the real estate agent's offer. Convinced that "I'm dumb...I don't know anything," he "knew right away" he couldn't do it, despite the fact that he had been doing just this sort of work all along.

Thus, the man's low self-esteem generates a fear of being tested and prevents him from accepting a job with responsibilities or, once on a job, from staying with it if responsibilities are thrust on him, even if the wages are commensurately higher. Richard refuses such a job, Leroy leaves one, and another man, given more responsibility and more pay, knows he will fail and proceeds to do so, proving he was right about himself all along. The self-fulfilling prophecy is everywhere at work. In a hallway, Stanton, Tonk, and Boley are passing a bottle around. Stanton recalls the time he was in the service. Everything was fine until he attained the rank of corporal. He worried about everything he did then. Was he doing the right thing? Was he doing it well? When would they discover their mistake and take his stripes (and extra pay) away? When he finally lost his stripes, everything was all right again.

Lethargy, disinterest, and general apathy on the job, so often reported by employers, has its streetcorner counterpart. The men do not ordinarily talk about their jobs or ask one another about them.[13] Although most of the men know who is or is not working at any given time, they may or may not know what particular job an individual man has. There is no overt interest in job specifics as they relate to this or that person, in large part perhaps because the specifics are not especially relevant. To know that a man is working is to know approximately how much he makes and to know as much as one needs or wants to know about how he makes it. After all, how much difference does it make to know whether a man is pushing a mop and pulling trash in an apartment house, a restaurant, or an office building, or delivering groceries, drugs, or liquor, or, if he's a laborer, whether he's pushing a wheelbarrow, mixing mortar, or digging a hole. So much does one job look like every other that there is little to choose between them. In large part, the job market consists of a narrow range of nondescript chores calling for nondistinctive, undifferentiated, unskilled labor. "A job is a job."

A crucial factor in the streetcorner man's lack of job commitment is the overall value he places on the job. *For his part, the streetcorner man puts no lower value on the job than does the larger society around him.* He knows the social value of the job by the amount of money the employer is willing to pay him for doing it. In a real sense, every pay day, he counts in dollars and cents the value placed on the job by society at large. He is no more (and frequently less) ready to quit and look for another job than his employer is ready to fire him and look for another man. Neither the streetcorner man who performs these jobs nor the society which requires him to perform them assesses the job as one "worth doing and worth doing well." Both employee and employer are contemptuous of the job. The employee shows his contempt by his reluctance to accept it or keep it, the employer by paying less than is required to support a family.[14] Nor does the low-wage job offer prestige, respect, interesting work, opportunity for learning or advancement, or any other compensation. With few exceptions, jobs filled by the streetcorner men are at the bottom of the employment ladder in every respect, from wage level to prestige. Typically, they are hard, dirty, uninteresting, and underpaid. The rest of society (whatever its ideal values regarding the dignity of labor) holds the job of the dishwasher or janitor or unskilled laborer in low esteem if not outright contempt.[15] So does the streetcorner man. He cannot do otherwise. He cannot draw from a job those social values which other people do not put into it.[16]

Only occasionally does spontaneous conversation touch on these matters directly. Talk about jobs is usually limited to isolated statements of intention, such as "I think I'll get me another gig [job]," "I'm going to look for a construction job when the weather breaks," or "I'm going to quit. I can't take no more of his shit." Job assessments typically consist of nothing more than a noncommittal shrug and "It's O.K." or "It's a job."

One reason for the relative absence of talk about one's job is, as suggested earlier, that the sameness of job experiences does not bear reiteration. Another and more important reason is the emptiness of the job experience itself. The man sees middle-class occupations as a primary source of prestige, pride, and self-respect; his own job affords him none of these. To think about his job is to see himself as others see him, to remind him of just where he stands in this society.[17] And because society's criteria for placement are generally the same as his own, to talk about his job can trigger a flush of shame and a deep, almost physical ache to change places with someone, almost anyone, else.[18] The desire to be a person in his own right, to be noticed by the world he lives in, is shared by each of the men on the streetcorner. Whether they articulate this desire (as Tally does below) or not, one can see them position themselves to catch the attention of their fellows in much the same way as plants bend or stretch to catch the sunlight.[19]

Tally and I were in the Carry-out. It was summer, Tally's peak earning season as a cement finisher, a semiskilled job a cut or so above that of the unskilled laborer. His take-home pay during these weeks was well over a hundred dollars—"a lot of bread." But for Tally, who no longer had a family to support, bread was not enough.

"You know that boy came in last night? That Black Moozlem? That's what I ought to be doing. I ought to be in his place."

"What do you mean?"

"Dressed nice, going to [night] school, got a good job."

"He's no better off than you, Tally. You make more than he does."

"It's not the money. [Pause] It's position, I guess. He's got position. When he finish school he gonna be a supervisor. People respect him. . . . Thinking about people with position and education gives me a feeling right here [pressing his fingers into the pit of his stomach]."

"You're educated, too. You have a skill, a trade. You're a cement finisher. You can make a building, pour a sidewalk."

"That's different. Look, can anybody do what you're doing? Can anybody just come up and do your job? Well, in one week I can teach you cement finishing. You won't be as good as me 'cause you won't have the experience but you'll be a cement finisher. That's what I mean. Anybody can do what I'm doing and that's what gives me this feeling. [Long pause] Suppose I like this girl. I go over to her house and I meet her father. He starts talking about what he done today. He talks about operating on somebody and sewing them up and about surgery. I know he's a doctor 'cause of the way he talks. Then she starts talking about what she did. Maybe she's a boss or a supervisor. Maybe she's a lawyer and her father says to me, 'And what do you do, Mr. Jackson?' [Pause] You remember at the courthouse, Lonny's trial? You and the lawyer was talking in the hall? You remember? I just stood there listening. I didn't say a word. You know why? 'Cause I didn't even know what you was talking about. That's happened to me a lot."

"Hell, you're nothing special. That happens to everybody. Nobody knows everything. One man is a doctor, so he talks about surgery. Another man is a teacher, so he talks about books. But doctors and teachers don't know anything about concrete. You're a cement finisher and that's your specialty."

"Maybe so, but when was the last time you saw anybody standing around talking about concrete?"

The streetcorner man wants to be a person in his own right, to be noticed, to be taken account of, but in this respect, as well as in meeting his money needs, his job fails him. The job and the man are even. The job fails the man and the man fails the job.

Furthermore, the man does not have any reasonable expectation that, however bad it is, his job will lead to better things. Menial jobs are not, by and large, the starting point of a track system which leads to even better jobs for those who are able and willing to do them. The busboy or dishwasher in a restaurant is not on a job track which, if negotiated skillfully, leads to chef or manager of the restaurant. The busboy or dishwasher who works hard becomes, simply, a hard-working busboy or dishwasher. Neither hard work nor perseverance can conceivably carry the janitor to a sit-down job in the office building he cleans up. And it is the apprentice who becomes the journeyman electrician, plumber, steam fitter, or bricklayer, not the common unskilled Negro laborer.

Thus, the job is not a stepping stone to something better. It is a dead end. It promises to deliver no more tomorrow, next month, or next year than it does today.

Delivering little, and promising no more, the job is "no big thing." The man appears to treat the job in a cavalier fashion, working and not working as the spirit moves him, as if all that matters is the immediate satisfaction of his present appetites, the surrender to present moods, and the indulgence of whims with no thought for the cost, the consequences, the future. To the middle-class observer, this behavior reflects a "present-time orientation"—an "inability to defer gratification." It is this "present-time" orientation—as against the "future orientation" of the middle-class person—that "explains" to the outsider why Leroy chooses to spend the day at the Carry-out rather than report

to work; why Richard, who was paid Friday, was drunk Saturday and Sunday and penniless Monday; why Sweets quit his job today because the boss looked at him "funny" yesterday.

But from the inside looking out, what appears as a "present-time" orientation to the outside observer is, to the man experiencing it, as much a future orientation as that of his middle-class counterpart.[20] The difference between the two men lies not so much in their different orientations to time as in their different orientations to future time or, more specifically, to their different futures.[21]

The future orientation of the middle-class person presumes, among other things, a surplus of resources to be invested in the future and a belief that the future will be sufficiently stable both to justify his investment (money in a bank, time and effort in a job, investment of himself in marriage and family, etc.) and to permit the consumption of his investment at a time, place, and manner of his own choosing and to his greater satisfaction. But the streetcorner man lives in a sea of want. He does not, as a rule, have a surplus of resources, either economic or psychological. Gratification of hunger and the desire for simple creature comforts cannot be long deferred. Neither can support for one's flagging self-esteem. Living on the edge of both economic and psychological subsistence, the streetcorner man is obliged to expend all his resources on maintaining himself from moment to moment.[22]

As for the future, the young streetcorner man has a fairly good picture of it. In Richard or Sea Cat or Arthur he can see himself in his middle twenties; he can look at Tally to see himself at thirty, at Wee Tom to see himself in his middle thirties, and at Budder and Stanton to see himself in his forties. It is a future in which everything is uncertain except the ultimate destruction of his hopes and the eventual realization of his fears. The most he can reasonably look forward to is that these things do not come too soon. Thus, when Richard squanders a week's pay in two days it is not because, like an animal or a child, he is "present-time oriented," unaware of or unconcerned with his future. He does so precisely because he is aware of the future and the hopelessness of it all.

Sometimes this kind of response appears as a conscious, explicit choice. Richard had had a violent argument with his wife. He said he was going to leave her and the children, that he had had enough of everything and could not take any more, and he chased her out of the house. His chest still heaving, he leaned back against the wall in the hallway of his basement apartment.

> "I've been scuffling for five years," he said. "I've been scuffling for five years from morning till night. And my kids still don't have anything, my wife don't have anything, and I don't have anything.
>
> "There," he said, gesturing down the hall to a bed, a sofa, a couple of chairs and a television set, all shabby, some broken. "There's everything I have and I'm having trouble holding onto that."
>
> Leroy came in, presumably to petition Richard on behalf of Richard's wife, who was sitting outside on the steps, afraid to come in. Leroy started to say something but Richard cut him short.
>
> "Look, Leroy, don't give me any of that action. You and me are entirely different people. Maybe I look like a boy and maybe I act like a boy sometimes but I got a man's mind. You and me don't want the same things out of life. Maybe some of the same, but you don't care how long you have to wait for yours and I—want—mine—right—now."[23]

Thus, apparent present-time concerns with consumption and indulgences—material and emotional—reflect a future-time orientation. "I want mine right now" is ultimately a cry of despair, a direct response to the future as he sees it.[24]

In many instances, it is precisely the streetcorner man's orientation to the future—but to a future loaded with "trouble"—which not only leads to a greater emphasis on present concerns ("I want mine right now") but also contributes importantly to the instability of employment, family, and friend relationships, and to the general transient quality of daily life.

Let me give some concrete examples. One day, after Tally had gotten paid, he gave me four twenty-dollar bills and asked me to keep them for him. Three days later he asked me for the money. I returned it and asked why he did not put his money in a bank. He said that the banks close at two o'clock. I argued that there were four or more banks within a two-block radius of where he was working at the time and that he could easily get to any one of them on his lunch hour. "No, man," he said, "you don't understand. They close at two o'clock and they closed Saturday and Sunday. Suppose I get into trouble and I got to make it [leave]. Me get out of town, and everything I got in the world layin' up in that bank? No good! No good!"

In another instance, Leroy and his girl friend were discussing "trouble." Leroy was trying to decide how best to go about getting his hands on some "long green" (a lot of money), and his girl friend cautioned him about "trouble." Leroy sneered at this, saying he had had "trouble" all his life and wasn't afraid of a little more. "Anyway," he said, "I'm famous for leaving town."[25]

Thus, the constant awareness of a future loaded with "trouble" results in a constant readiness to leave, to "make it," to "get out of town," and discourages the man from sinking roots into the world he lives in.[26] Just as it discourages him from putting money in the bank, so it discourages him from committing himself to a job, especially one whose payoff lies in the promise of future rewards rather than in the present. In the same way, it discourages him from deep and lasting commitments to family and friends or to any other persons, places, or things, since such commitments could hold him hostage, limiting his freedom of movement and thereby compromising his security which lies in that freedom.

What lies behind the response to the driver of the pickup truck, then, is a complex combination of attitudes and assessments. The streetcorner man is under continuous assault by his job experiences and job fears. His experiences and fears feed on one another. The kind of job he can get—and frequently only after fighting for it, if then—steadily confirms his fears, depresses his self-confidence and self-esteem until finally, terrified of an opportunity even if one presents itself, he stands defeated by his experiences, his belief in his own self-worth destroyed and his fears a confirmed reality.

NOTES

1. By different methods, perhaps, some social scientists have also located the problem in the men themselves, in their unwillingness or lack of desire to work: "To improve the underprivileged worker's performance, one must help him to learn *to want*...higher social goals for himself and his children....The problem of changing the work habits and motivation of [lower class] people...is a problem of changing the goals, the ambitions, and the level of cultural and occupational aspiration of the underprivileged worker." (Emphasis in original.) Allison Davis, "The Motivation of the Underprivileged Worker," p. 90.

2. The comparison of sitting at home alone with being in jail is commonplace.

3. Exactly the same estimate as the one made by Tonk himself. On the basis of personal knowledge of the stealing routine employed by Tonk, however, I suspect the actual amount is considerably smaller.

4. Some public credit may accrue to the clever thief but not respect.

5. It might be profitable to compare, as Howard S. Becker suggests, gross aspects of income and housing costs in this particular area with those reported by Herbert Gans for the low-income working class in Boston's West End. In 1958, Gans reports, median income for the West Enders was just under $70 a week, a level considerably higher than that enjoyed by the people in the Carry-out neighborhood five years later. Gans himself rented a six-room apartment in the West End for $46 a month, about $10 more than the going rate for long-time residents. In the Carry-out neighborhood, rooms that could accommodate more than a cot and a miniature dresser—that is, rooms that qualified for family living—rented for $12 to $22 a week. Ignoring differences that really can't be ignored—the privacy and self-contained efficiency of the multi-room apartment as against the fragmented, public living of the rooming-house "apartment," with a public toilet on a floor always different from the one your room is on (no matter, it probably doesn't work, anyway)—and assuming comparable states of disrepair, the West Enders were paying $6 or $7 a month for a room that cost the Carry-outers at least $50 a month, and frequently more. Looking at housing costs as a percentage of income—and again ignoring what cannot be ignored: that what goes by the name of "housing" in the two areas is not at all the same thing—the median income West Ender could get a six-room apartment for about 12 percent of his income, while his 1963 Carry-out counterpart, with a weekly income of $60 (to choose a figure from the upper end of the income range), often paid 20–33 percent of his income for one room. See Herbert J. Gans, *The Urban Villagers*, pp. 10–13.

6. The higher amount is 1962 union scale for building laborers. According to the Wage Agreement Contract for Heavy Construction Laborers (Washington, D.C., and vicinity) covering the period from May 1, 1963 to April 30, 1966, minimum hourly wage for heavy construction laborers was to go from $2.75

(May 1963) by annual increments to $2.92, effective November 1, 1965.

7. "Open-sky" work, such as building overpasses, highways, etc., in which the workers and materials are directly exposed to the elements, traditionally begins in March and ends around Thanksgiving. The same is true for much of the street repair work and the laying of sewer, electric, gas, and telephone lines by the city and public utilities, all important employers of laborers. Between Thanksgiving and March they retain only skeleton crews selected from their best, most reliable men.

8. In a recent year, the crime rate in Washington for the month of August jumped 18 percent over the preceding month. A veteran police officer explained the increase to David L. Bazelon, Chief Judge, U.S. Court of Appeals for the District of Columbia. "It's quite simple.... You see, August was a very wet month.... These people wait on the street corner each morning around 6:00 or 6:30 for a truck to pick them up and take them to a construction site. If it's raining, that truck doesn't come, and the men are going to be idle that day. If the bad weather keeps up for three days...we know we are going to have trouble on our hands—and sure enough, there invariably follows a rash of purse-snatchings, house-breakings and the like.... These people have to eat like the rest of us, you know." David L. Bazelon, Address to the Federal Bar Association, p. 3.

9. Estimate of Mr. Francis Greenfield, President of the International Hod Carriers, Building and Common Laborers' District Council of Washington, D.C., and Vicinity. I am indebted to Mr. Greenfield for several points in these paragraphs dealing with construction laborers.

10. Not a sinecure, even by streetcorner standards.

11. The overall result is that, in the long run, a Negro laborer's earnings are not substantially greater—and may be less—than those of the busboy, janitor, or stock clerk. Herman P. Miller, for example, reports that in 1960, 40 percent of all jobs held by Negro men were as laborers or in the service trades. The average annual wage for nonwhite nonfarm laborers was $2,400. The average earning of nonwhite service workers was $2,500 (*Rich Man, Poor Man.*, p. 90). Francis Greenfield estimates that in the Washington vicinity, the 1965 earnings of the union laborer who works whenever work is available will be about $3,200. Even this figure is high for the man on the streetcorner. Union men in heavy construction are the aristocrats of the laborers. Casual day labor and jobs with small firms in the building and construction trades, or with firms in other industries, pay considerably less.

12. For an excellent discussion of the self-fulfilling assumption (or prophecy) as a social force, see "The Self-Fulfilling Prophecy," Ch. XI, in Robert K. Merton's *Social Theory and Social Structure.*

13. This stands in dramatic contrast to the leisure-time conversation of stable, working-class men. For the coal miners (of Ashton, England), for example, "the topic [of conversation] which surpasses all others in frequency is work—the difficulties which have been encountered in the day's shift, the way in which a particular task was accomplished, and so on." Josephine Klein, *Samples from English Cultures,* Vol. I, p. 88.

14. It is important to remember that the employer is not entirely a free agent. Subject to the constraints of the larger society, he acts for the larger society as well as for himself. Child labor laws, safety and sanitation regulations, minimum wage scales in some employment areas, and other constraints, are already on the books; other control mechanisms, such as a guaranteed annual wage, are to be had for the voting.

15. See, for example, the U.S. Bureau of the Census, *Methodology and Scores of Socioeconomic Status.* The assignment of the lowest SES ratings to men who hold such jobs is not peculiar to our own society. A low SES rating for "the shoeshine boy or garbage man seems to be true for all [industrial] countries." Alex Inkeles, "Industrial Man," p. 8.

16. That the streetcorner man downgrades manual labor should occasion no surprise. Merton points out that "the American stigmatization of manual labor...*has been found to hold rather uniformly in all social classes*" (emphasis in original; *Social Theory and Social Structure*, p. 145). That he finds no satisfaction in such work should also occasion no surprise: "[There is] a clear positive correlation between the over-all status of occupations and the experience of satisfaction in them." Inkeles, "Industrial Man," p. 12.

17. "[In our society] a man's work is one of the things by which he is judged, and certainly one of the more significant things by which he judges himself....A man's work is one of the more important parts of his social identity, of his self; indeed, of his fate in the one life he has to live." Everett C. Hughes, *Men and Their Work*, pp. 42–43.

18. Noting that lower-class persons "are constantly exposed to evidence of their own irrelevance," Lee Rainwater spells out still another way in which the poor are poor: "The identity problems of lower class persons make the soul-searching of middle class adolescents and adults seem rather like a kind of conspicuous consumption of psychic riches" ("Work and Identity in the Lower Class," p. 3).

19. Sea Cat cuts his pants legs off at the calf and puts a fringe on the raggedy edges. Tonk breaks his "shades" and continues to wear the horn-rimmed frames minus the lenses. Richard cultivates a distinctive manner of speech. Lonny gives himself a birthday party. And so on.

20. Taking a somewhat different point of view, S. M. Miller and Frank Riessman suggest that "the entire concept of deferred gratification may be inappropriate to understanding the essence of workers' lives" ("The Working Class Subculture: A New View," p. 87).

21. This sentence is a paraphrase of a statement made by Marvin Cline at a 1965 colloquium at the Mental Health Study Center, National Institute of Mental Health.

22. And if, for the moment, he does sometimes have more money than he chooses to spend or more food than he wants to eat, he is pressed to spend the money and eat the food anyway since his friends, neighbors, kinsmen, or acquaintances will beg or borrow whatever surplus he has or, failing this, they may steal it. In one extreme case, one of the men admitted taking the last of a woman's surplus food allotment after she had explained that, with four children, she could not spare any food. The prospect that consumer soft goods not consumed by oneself will be consumed by someone else may be related to the way in which portable consumer durable goods, such as watches, radios, television sets, or phonographs, are sometimes looked at as a form of savings. When Shirley was on welfare, she regularly took her television set out of pawn when she got her monthly check. Not so much to watch it, she explained, as to have something to fall back on when her money runs out toward the end of the month. For her and others, the television set or the phonograph is her savings, the pawnshop is where she banks her savings, and the pawn ticket is her bankbook.

23. This was no simple rationalization for irresponsibility. Richard had indeed "been scuffling for five years" trying to keep his family going. Until shortly after this episode, Richard was known and respected as one of the hardest-working men on the street. Richard had said, only a couple of months earlier, "I figure you got to get out there and try. You got to try before you can get anything." His wife Shirley confirmed that he had always tried. "If things get tough, with me I'll get all worried. But Richard get worried, he don't want me to see him worried....He *will* get out there. He's shoveled snow, picked beans, and he's done some of everything....He's not ashamed to get out there and get us something to eat." At the time of the episode reported above, Leroy was just starting marriage and raising a family. He and Richard were not, as Richard thought, "entirely different people." Leroy had just not learned, by personal experience over time, what Richard had learned. But within two years Leroy's marriage had broken up and he was talking and acting like Richard. "He just let go completely," said one of the men on the street.

24. There is no mystically intrinsic connection between "present-time" orientation and lower-class persons. Whenever people of whatever class have been uncertain, skeptical, or downright pessimistic about the future, "I want mine right now" has been one of the characteristic responses, although it is usually couched in more delicate terms: e.g., Omar Khayyam's "Take the cash and let the credit go," or Horace's *"Carpe diem."* In wartime, especially, all classes tend to slough off conventional restraints on sexual and other behavior (i.e., become less able or less willing to defer gratification). And when inflation threatens, darkening the fiscal future, persons who formerly husbanded their resources with commendable restraint almost stampede one another rushing to spend their money. Similarly, it seems that future-time orientation tends to collapse toward the present when persons are in pain or under stress. The point here is that, the label notwithstanding, (what passes for) present-time orientation appears to be a situation-specific phenomenon rather than a part of the standard psychic equipment of Cognitive Lower Class Man.

25. And proceeded to do just that the following year when "trouble"—in this case, a grand jury indictment, a pile of debts, and a violent separation from his wife and children—appeared again.

26. For a discussion of "trouble" as a focal concern of lower-class culture, see Walter Miller, "Lower Class Culture as a Generating Milieu of Gang Delinquency," pp. 7, 8.

REFERENCES

Bazelon, David L. 1963. *Address to the Federal Bar Association, National Press Club*, Washington, D.C. (April 30). (Mimeographed)

Becker, Howard S. 1958. "Problems of Inference and Proof in Participant-Observation." *American Sociological Review*, 23 (6): 652–660.

Davis, Allison. 1946. "The Motivation of the Underprivileged Worker." In *Industry and Society*. William F. Whyte (ed.). New York: McGraw-Hill.

Gans, Herbert J. 1962. *The Urban Villagers*. New York: The Free Press of Glencoe.

Hughes, Everett C. 1958. *Men and Their Work*. Glencoe: The Free Press.

Inkeles, Alex. 1960. "Industrial Man." *American Journal of Sociology* 66 (1), 1–31.

Klein, Josephine. 1965. *Samples from English Cultures*. 2 vols. London: Routledge and Kegan Paul.

Merton, Robert K. 1957. *Social Theory and Social Structure*. Rev. ed. Glencoe: The Free Press.

Miller, Herman P. 1964. *Rich Man, Poor Man*. New York: Crowell.

Miller, S. M., and Frank Riessman. 1961. "The Working Class Subculture: A New View." *Social Problems* 9 (1): 86–97.

Miller, Walter B. 1958. "Lower Class Culture as a Generating Milieu of Delinquency." *Journal of Social Issues*, 14 (3): 5–19.

Rainwater, Lee. 1965. "Work and Identity in the Lower Class." Paper prepared for Washington University Conference on Planning for the Quality of Urban Life. (April). (Mimeographed)

——.Forthcoming. "Work and Identity in the Lower Class. 1969." In *Planning for a Nation of Cities*. Sam Bass Warner (ed.). Cambridge: MIT Press.

U.S. Bureau of the Census. 1963. *Methodology and Scores of Socioeconomic Status*. Working Paper No. 15. Washington, D.C..

30

KATHERINE S. NEWMAN

NO SHAME IN (THIS) GAME

from *No Shame in My Game* (1999)

Katherine Newman's team of researchers spent roughly four months working in four fast-food restaurants in Harlem that she calls "Burger Barns." Combining this firsthand experience with a year's observation of twelve workers and interviews with hundreds more, Newman draws a vivid portrait of their lives. In this selection, she shows the stigma and jealousy that many young people who decide to take such jobs must overcome.

In the early 1990s, the McDonald's Corporation launched a television ad campaign featuring a young black man named Calvin, who was portrayed sitting atop a Brooklyn stoop in his Golden Arches uniform while his friends down on the sidewalk passed by, giving him a hard time about holding down a "McJob." After brushing off their teasing with good humor, Calvin is approached furtively by one young black man who asks, *sotto voce,* whether Calvin might help him get a job too. He allows that he could use some earnings and that despite the ragging he has just given Calvin, he thinks the uniform is really pretty cool—or at least that having a job is pretty cool.

Every fast food worker we interviewed for this book knew the Calvin series by heart: Calvin on the job, Calvin in the streets, Calvin helping an elderly woman cross the street on his way to work, Calvin getting promoted to management. And they knew what McDonald's was trying to communicate to young people by producing the series in the first place: that the stigma clings to fast food jobs, that it can be overcome, and that even your best friends will come to admire you if you stick with it—after they've finished dissing you in public.

Americans have always been committed to the moral maxim that work defines the person. We carry around in our heads a rough tally that tells us what kinds of jobs are worthy of respect and what kinds are to be disdained, a pyramid organized by the income a job carries, the sort of credentials it takes to secure a particular position, the qualities of an occupation's incumbents—and we use this system of stratification (ruthlessly at times) to boost the status of some and humiliate others. This penchant for ranking by occupation is more pervasive in the United States than in other societies, where there are different ways of evaluating the personal worth of individuals. In these societies, coming from a "good family" counts heavily in the calculus of social standing. Here in America, there is no other metric that matters as much as the kind of job you hold.

Given our tradition of equating moral value with employment, it stands to reason that the most profound dividing line in our culture is that separating the working person from the unemployed.[1] Only after this canyon has been crossed do we begin to make the finer gradations that distinguish white-collar worker from blue-collar worker, CEO from secretary. We attribute a whole host of moral virtues—self-discipline, personal responsibility, maturity—to those who have found and kept a job, almost any job, and dismiss those who haven't as slothful or irresponsible.

We inhabit an unforgiving culture that is blind to the many reasons why some people cross that employment barrier and others are left behind. While we may remember, for a time, that unemployment rates are high, or that particular industries have downsized millions of workers right out of a job, or that racial barriers or negative attitudes toward teenagers make it harder to get a job at some times and for some people, in the end American culture wipes these background truths out in favor of a simpler dichotomy: the worthy and the unworthy, the working stiff and the lazy sloth.

These days, our puritanical attitudes owe some of their force to the resentment the employed bear toward the taxes they must pay to support those who cannot earn on their own. But it has deeper cultural dimensions. From the earliest beginnings of the nation, work has been the *sine qua non* of membership in this society. Adults who work are full-fledged citizens in the truest sense of the term—complete participants in the social world that is most highly valued. No other dimension of life—community, family, religion, voluntary organizations—qualifies Americans for this designation of citizen in the same way.

We express this view in a variety of ways in our social policies. Virtually all our benefits (especially health care but including unemployment insurance, life insurance, child care tax credits, etc.) are provided through the employment system. In Western Europe this is often not the case: health care is provided directly through the tax system and benefits come to people who are political "citizens" whether they work or not. In the United States, however, those outside the employment system are categorized as unworthy and made to feel it by excluding them from these systems of support. To varying degrees, we "take care" of the socially excluded by creating stigmatized categories for their benefits—welfare and Medicaid being prime examples. Yet we never confuse the approved, acceptable Americans with the undeserving, and we underscore the difference by separating them into different bureaucratic worlds.

For those on the positive side of the divide, those who work for a living, the rewards are far greater than a paycheck. The employed enter a social world in which their identities as mainstream Americans are shaped, structured, and reinforced. The workplace is the main institutional setting in which individuals become part of the collective American enterprise that lies at the heart of our culture: the market. We are so divided in other domains—race, geography, family organization, gender roles, and the like—that common ground along almost any other lines is difficult to achieve. Indeed, only in wartime do Americans tend to cleave to their national origins as a major feature of their self-concept. The French, by contrast, are French whether they work or not. But for our more diverse and divided society, participation in the world of work is the most powerful source of social integration.

It is in the workplace that we are most likely to mix with those who come from different backgrounds, are under the greatest pressure to subordinate individual idiosyncrasy to the requirements of an organization, and are called upon to contribute to goals that eclipse the personal. All workers have these experiences in common; even as segregation constrains the real mix of workers, conformity is expected to a greater degree for people who work in some kinds of jobs than in others, and the organizational goals to which they must subscribe are often elusive, unreachable, or at odds with personal desire.

The creation of an identity as a worker is never achieved by individuals moving along some preordained path. It is a transformation worked by organizations, firms, supervisors, fellow workers, and the whole long search that leads from the desire to find a job to the end point of landing one. This is a particularly dramatic transformation for ghetto youth and adults, for they face a difficult job market, high hurdles in convincing employers to take a chance on them, and relatively poor rewards—from a financial point of view—for their successes. But the crafting of an identity is an important developmental process for them, just as it is for their more privileged counterparts.

Powerful forces work to exclude minorities from full participation in American society. From a school system that provides a substandard education for millions of inner city kids, to an employment system rife with discrimination, to a housing market that segregates minority families, there is almost no truth to the notion that we all begin from the same starting line. Precisely because this is the case, blasting one's way through the job barrier and starting down that road of acquiring a common identity as a mainstream worker is of the greatest importance for the young. It may be one of the few available pipelines into the core of American society, and the one with the greatest payoff, symbolic and material.

The Social Costs of Accepting Low-Wage Work

Even though we honor the gainfully employed over the unemployed, all jobs are not created equal. Fast food jobs, in particular, are notoriously stigmatized and denigrated. "McJob" has become a common epithet for work without much redeeming value. The reasons for this are worth studying, for the minority workers who figure in this book have a mountain of stigma to overcome if they are to maintain their self-respect. Indeed, the organizational culture they join when they finally land a job at Burger Barn is instrumental in generating conditions and experiences that challenge a worker's self-esteem.[2]

As Robin Leidner has argued,[3] fast food jobs epitomize the assembly-line structure of de-skilled service positions: they are highly routinized and appear to the casual observer to be entirely lacking in discretion—almost military in their scripted nature. The symbolic capital of these assembly-line jobs can be measured in negative numbers. They represent the opposite of the autonomous entrepreneur who is lionized in the popular culture, from *Business Week* to hip-hop.

Burger Barn workers are told that they must, at whatever cost to their own dignity, defer to the public. Customers can be unreasonably demanding, rude, even insulting, and workers must count backwards from a hundred in an effort to stifle their outrage. Servicing the customer with a smile pleases management because making money depends on keeping the clientele happy, but it can be an exercise in humiliation for teenagers. It is hard for them to refrain from reading this public nastiness as another instance of society's low estimation of their worth. But they soon realize that if they want to hold on to their minimum-wage jobs, they have to tolerate comments that would almost certainly provoke a fistfight outside the workplace.

It is well known among ghetto customers that crew members have to put up with whatever verbal abuse comes across the counter. That knowledge occasionally prompts nasty exchanges designed explicitly to anger the worker, to push him or her to retaliate verbally. Testing those limits is a favorite pastime of teenage customers in particular, for this may be the one opportunity they have to put a peer on the defensive in a public setting, knowing that there is little the victim can do in return.

It is bad enough to be on the receiving end of this kind of abuse from adults, especially white adults, for that has its own significance along race lines. It is even worse to have to accept it from minority peers, for there is much more personal honor at stake, more pride to be lost, and an audience whose opinion matters more. This, no doubt, is why harassment is a continual problem for fast food workers in Harlem. It burns. Their age-mates, with plenty of anger bottled up for all kinds of reasons extraneous to the restaurant experience, find counterparts working the cash register convenient targets for venting.

Roberta is a five-year veteran of Burger Barn who has worked her way up to management. A formidable African-American woman, Roberta has always prided herself on her ability to make it on her own. Most of her customers have been perfectly pleasant; many have been longtime repeat visitors to her restaurant. But Roberta has also encountered many who radiate disrespect.

Could you describe some of the people who came into the store during your shift?

The customers? Well, I had alcoholics, derelicts. People that are aggravated with life. I've had people that don't even have jobs curse me out. I've dealt with all kinds. Sometimes it would get to me. If a person yelled out [in front of] a lobby full of people... "Bitch, that's why you work at [Burger Barn]," I would say [to myself], "I'm probably making more than you and your mother." It hurts when people don't even know what you're making and they say those things. Especially in Harlem, they do that to you. They call you all types of names and everything.

Natasha is younger than Roberta and less practiced at these confrontations. But she has had to contend with them nevertheless, especially from customers her age who at least claim to be higher up the status hierarchy. Though she tries, Natasha can't always control her temper and respond the way the firm wants her to.

It's hard dealing with the public. There are good things, like old people. They sweet. But the younger people around my age are always snotty. Think they better than you because they not working at [Burger Barn]. They probably work at something better than you.

How do you deal with rude or unfriendly customers?

They told us that we just suppose to walk to the back and ignore it, but when they in your face like that, you get so upset that you have to say something....I got threatened with a gun one time. 'Cause this customer had threw a piece of straw paper in the back and told me to pick it up like I'm a dog. I said, "No." And he cursed at me. I cursed at him back, and he was like, "Yeah, next time you won't have nothing to say when I come back with my gun and shoot your ass." Oh, excuse me.

Ianna, who had just turned sixteen the summer she found her first job at Burger Barn, has had many of the same kinds of problems Natasha complains of. The customers who are rude to her are just looking for a place to vent their anger about things that have nothing to do with buying lunch. Ianna recognizes that this kind of thing could happen in any restaurant, but believes it is a special problem in Harlem, for ghetto residents have more to be angry about and fewer accessible targets. So cashiers in fast food shops become prime victims.

> What I hate about [Burger Barn] is the customers, well, some of them that I can't stand....I don't want to stereotype Harlem...but since I only worked in Harlem that's all I can speak for. Some people have a chip on their shoulders....Most of the people that come into the restaurant are black. Most of them have a lot of kids. It's in the ghetto. Maybe, you know, they are depressed about their lifestyles or whatever else that is going on in their lives and they just...I don't know. They just are like, urff! And no matter what you do you cannot please them. I'm not supposed to say anything to the customer, but that's not like me. I have a mouth and I don't take no short from nobody. I don't care who it is, don't take anybody's crap.

Despite this bravado, Ianna knows well that to use her mouth is to risk her job. She has had to work hard to find ways to cope with this frustration that don't get her in trouble with management.

> I don't say stuff to people most of the time. Mostly I just look at them like they stupid. Because my mother always told

me that as long as you don't say nothin' to nobody, you can't never get in trouble. If you look at them stupid, what are they going to do? If you roll your eyes at somebody like that, I mean, that's really nothing [compared to]...cursing at them. Most of the time I try to walk away.

As Ianna observes, there is enough free-floating fury in Harlem to keep a steady supply of customer antagonism coming the way of service employees every day of their work lives. The problem is constant enough to warrant official company policies on how crew members should respond to insults, on what managers should do to help, on the evasive tactics that will work best to quell an ugly situation without losing the business. Management tries to minimize the likelihood of incidents by placing girls on the registers rather than boys, in the apparent belief that young women attract less abuse and find it easier to quash their anger than young men.

Burger Barn does what it can to contend with these problems in the workplace. But the neighborhood is beyond their reach, and there, too, fast food workers are often met with ridicule from the people they grew up with. They have to learn to defend themselves against criticism that they have lowered themselves by taking these jobs, criticism from people they have known all their lives. As Stephanie explains, here too she leans on the divide between the worker and the do-nothing:

> People I hang out with, they know me since I was little. We all grew up together. When they see me comin', they laugh and say, "Here come Calvin, here come Calvin sister." I just laugh and keep on going. I say, "You're crazy. But that's okay 'cause I got a job and you all standing out here on the corner." Or I say, "This is my job, it's legal." Something like that. That Calvin commercial show you that even though his friends tease him he just

brushed them off, then he got a higher position. Then you see how they change toward him.

Tiffany, also a teen worker in a central Harlem Burger Barn, thinks she knows why kids in her community who don't work give her such a hard time. They don't want her to succeed because if no one is "making it," then no one needs to feel bad about failing. But if someone claws her way up and it looks as if she has a chance to escape the syndrome of failure, it implies that everyone could, in theory, do so as well. The teasing, a thinly veiled attempt to enforce conformity, is designed to drag would-be success stories back into the fold.

> What you will find in any situation, more so in the black community, is that if you are in the community and you try to excel, you will get ridicule from your own peers. It's like the "crab down" syndrome.... If you put a bunch of crabs in a big bucket and one crab tries to get out, what do you think the other crabs would do now? According to my thinking, they should pull 'em up or push 'em or help 'em get out. But the crabs pull him back in the barrel. That's just an analogy for what happens in the community a lot.

Keeping everyone down protects against that creeping sense of despair which comes from believing things could be otherwise for oneself.

Swallowing ridicule would be a hardship for almost anyone in this culture, but it is particularly hard on minority youth in the inner city. They have already logged four or five years' worth of interracial and cross-class friction by the time they get behind a Burger Barn cash register. More likely than not, they have also learned from peers that self-respecting people don't allow themselves to be "dissed" without striking back. Yet this is precisely what they must do if they are going to survive in the workplace.

This is one of the main reasons why these jobs carry such a powerful stigma in American popular culture: they fly in the face of a national attraction to autonomy, independence, and the individual's "right" to respond in kind when dignity is threatened. In ghetto communities, this stigma is even more powerful because—ironically—it is in these enclaves that this mainstream value of independence is most vigorously elaborated and embellished. Film characters, rap stars, and local idols base their claim to notoriety on standing above the crowd, going their own way, being free of the ties that bind ordinary mortals. There are white parallels, to be sure, but this is a powerful genre of icons in the black community, not because it is a disconnected subculture but because it is an intensified version of a perfectly recognizable American middle-class and working-class fixation.

It is therefore noteworthy that thousands upon thousands of minority teens, young adults, and even middle-aged adults line up for jobs that will subject them, at least potentially, to a kind of character assassination. They do so not because they start the job-seeking process with a different set of values, one that can withstand society's contempt for fast food workers. They take these jobs because in so many inner-city communities, there is nothing better in the offing. In general, they have already tried to get better jobs and have failed, landing at the door of Burger Barn as a last resort.

Social stigma has other sources besides the constraints of enforced deference. Money and mobility matter as well. Fast food jobs are invariably minimum-wage positions.[4] Salaries rise very little over time, even for first-line management. In ghetto areas, where jobs are scarce and the supply of would-be workers chasing them is relatively large, downward pressure on wages keeps these jobs right down at the bottom of the wage scale.[5]

The public perception (fueled by knowledge of wage conditions) is that there is very little potential for improvement in status or responsibility either. Even though there are Horatio Algers in this industry, there are no myths to prop up a more glorified image. As a result, the epithet "McJob" develops out of the perception that fast food workers are not likely to end up in a prestigious job as a general manager or restaurant owner; they are going to spend their whole lives flipping burgers.

As it happens, this is only half true. The fast food industry is actually very good about internal promotion. Workplace management is nearly always recruited from the ranks of entry-level workers. Carefully planned training programs make it possible for employees to move up, to acquire transferable skills, and to at least take a shot at entrepreneurial ownership. McDonald's, for example, is proud of the fact that half of its board of directors started out as crew members. One couldn't say as much for the rest of the nation's Fortune 500 firms.

However, the vast majority never even get close to management. The typical entry-level worker passes through his or her job in short order, with an industry-average job tenure of less than six months. Since this is an average, it suggests that a large number of employees are there and gone in a matter of weeks. It is this pattern, a planned operation built around low skills and high turnover, that has given fast food jobs such a bad name. In order for the industry to keep functioning with such an unstable labor force, the jobs themselves must be broken down so that each step can be learned, at least at a rudimentary level, in a very short time. A vicious circle develops in which low wages are attached to low skills, encouraging high departure rates. Hence, although it is quite possible to rise above the fray and make a very respectable living as a general manager overseeing a restaurant, most crew members remain at the entry level and leave too soon to see much upward movement. Observing this pattern on such a large scale—in practically every town and city in the country—Americans naturally conclude that one can't get anywhere in a job like this, that there is no real future in it, and that anyone with more "on the ball" wouldn't be caught dead working behind the counter....

The stigma also stems from the low social status of the people who hold these jobs: minorities, teenagers, immigrants who often speak halting English, those with little education, and (increasingly in affluent communities afflicted with labor shortages) the elderly. To the extent that the prestige of a job refracts the social characteristics of its average incumbents, fast food jobs are hobbled by the perception that people with better choices would never purposely opt for a "McJob."... Entry-level jobs of this kind are undeserving of this scorn: more skill, discretion, and responsibility are locked up in a fast food job than is apparent to the public. But this truth hardly matters where public perception is concerned. There is no quicker way to indicate that a person is barely deserving of notice than to point out he or she holds a "chump change" job at Kentucky Fried Chicken or Burger King. We "know" this is the case just by looking at the age, skin color, or educational credentials of the people already on the job: the tautology has a staying power that even the smartest public relations campaign cannot shake.

Ghetto youth are particularly sensitive to the status degradation entailed in stigmatized employment. As Elijah Anderson (in *Streetwise*, University of Chicago Press, 1990) and others have pointed out, a high premium is placed on independence, autonomy, and respect among minority youth in inner-city communities—particularly by young men. No small amount of mayhem is committed every year in the name of injured pride. Hence jobs that routinely demand displays of deference force those who hold them to violate "macho" behavior codes that are central to the definition of teen culture. There are, therefore, considerable social risks involved in seeking a fast food job in the first place, one that the employees and job-seekers are keenly aware of from the very beginning of their search for employment.

It is hard to know the extent to which this stigma discourages young people in places like central Harlem from knocking on the door of a fast food restaurant. It is clear that the other choices aren't much better and that necessity drives thousands, if not millions, of teens and older job-seekers to ignore the stigma or learn to live with it. But no one enters the central Harlem job market without having to face this gauntlet.

Tiffany started working in the underground economy bagging groceries when she was little more than ten years old because her mother was having trouble supporting the family, "checks weren't coming in," and there was "really a need for food." She graduated to summer youth by the time she was fourteen, but two years later she needed a "real" job that would last beyond the summer, so she set about looking—everywhere. As a young black teenager, she quickly discovered there wasn't a great deal open to her. Tiffany ended up at Burger Barn in the Bronx, a restaurant two blocks from her house and close enough to her high school to make after-school hours feasible.

> The first Burger Barn I worked at was because nobody else would take me. It was a last resort. I didn't want to go to [Burger Barn]. You flip burgers. People would laugh at you. In high school, I didn't wanna be in that kind of environment. But lo and behold, after everything else failed, Martin Paints, other jobs, [Burger Barn] was welcoming me with open arms. So I started working there.

Tiffany moved to Harlem when she finished high school, and found she couldn't commute back to the Bronx. Still sensitive to the stigma attaching to her old job, she tried her luck at moving up, out of the fast food business and into a service job with more of a "white-collar" flavor; she looked everywhere for a position in stores where the jobs are free of hamburger grease and hot oil for french fries, stores where clerks don't wear aprons or hairnets. Despite her best efforts, nothing panned out.

> I'm looking at Lerners and Plymouth [clothing stores] and going to all these stores, but nothing is coming through. But [Burger Barn] was waitin' for me because I had two years of experience by then.

The new Burger Barn franchise was right in the middle of Harlem, not far from the room she rents over a storefront church, and it had the additional appeal of being "a black-owned business," something that mattered to Tiffany in terms of the "more cultural reasons why [she] decided to work there." She was glad to land a job, but worried that her high school diploma couldn't take her any farther than this entry-level position. It didn't augur well for the future.

William followed a similar pathway to Burger Barn, graduating from summer youth jobs in the middle of high school and looking for something that would help pay for his books and carfare. The Department of Labor gave him a referral to Burger Barn, but he was reluctant at first to pursue it.

> To go there and work for [Burger Barn], that was one of those real cloak-and-dagger kinds of things. You'll be coming out [and your friends say], "Yo, where you going?" You be, "I'm going, don't worry about where I'm going." And you see your friends coming [to the restaurant] and see you working there and now you be, "No, the whole [housing] project gonna know I work in [Burger Barn]." It's not something I personally proclaim with pride and stuff.... If you

are a crew member, you really aren't shit there.... You got nothing there, no benefits, nothing. It was like that [when I was younger] and it's like that now.

William tried every subterfuge he could think of to conceal his job from the kids he knew. He kept his uniform in a bag and put it on in the back of the restaurant so that it would never be visible on the street. He made up fake jobs to explain to his friends where his spending money was coming from. He took circuitous routes to the Barn and hid back by the gigantic freezer when he spotted a friend coming in. The last thing William wanted was to be publicly identified as a shift worker at Burger Barn.

In this he was much like the other teen and young adult workers we encountered. They are very sensitive to stigma, to challenges to their status, and by taking low-wage jobs of this kind they have made themselves vulnerable to exactly the kind of insults they most fear. But the fact is that they do take these risks and, in time, latch on to other "narratives" that undergird their legitimacy.

Breaking the Stigma

One of the chief challenges facing an organization like Burger Barn involves taking people who have come to it on the defensive and turn them into workers who appear at least on the surface to enjoy their work. Customers have choices; they can vote with their feet. If ordering french fries at Burger Barn requires them to put up with rudeness or indifference from the person who takes their order, they can easily cross the street to a competitor the next time. It is clearly in the company's interest to find ways to turn the situation around. Ideally, from the industry's viewpoint, it would be best if the whole reputation of these jobs could be reversed. This is what McDonald's had in mind when it launched the Calvin series. But for all the reasons outlined earlier..., this probably

won't come to pass, since the conditions that give rise to the stigma in the first place—low wages, high turnover, enforced deference— are not likely to change. Beyond publicizing the opportunities that are within reach, much of which falls on deaf ears, there is little the industry can do to rehabilitate its workers in the eyes of the public and thereby reduce the tension across the counter.

Yet behind the scenes, managers and workers and peers working together in restaurant crews do build a moral defense of their work. They call upon timeless American values to undergird their respectability. Pointing to the essential virtues of the gainfully employed, Burger Barn workers align themselves with the great mass of men and women who work for a living. "We are like them," they declare, and in so doing they separate themselves from the people in their midst who are not employed. And they have plenty of experience of individuals who don't work, often including members of their own families. They see beggars come around the restaurants looking for handouts every day; fast-talkers who walk into Burger Barn hoping for free food; agemates who prefer to deal drugs. In general, these low-wage workers are far less forgiving, far less tolerant, of these "losers" than are many liberal writers. Since they hold hard, poorly paid jobs, people like Kyesha or Jamal see little reason why anyone else ought to get a free ride. What the indigent should do is to follow their example: get a job, any job.

Ianna is an articulate case in point. She has had to confront the social degradation that comes from holding a "low job" and has developed a tough hide in response. Her dignity is underwritten by the critique she has absorbed about the "welfare-dependent":

> I'm not ashamed because I have a job. Most people don't, and I'm proud of myself that I decided to get up and do something at an early age. So as I look at it, I'm not on welfare. I'm doing something.

I'm not knocking welfare, but I know people that are on it that can get up and work. There's nothing wrong with them. And they just choose not to.... They don't really need to be on [welfare]. They just want it because they can get away with it. I don't think it's right, because that's my tax dollars going for somebody who is lazy, who don't wanna get up. I can see if a woman had three children, her husband left her, and she don't have no job 'cause she was a housewife. Okay. But after a while, you know, welfare will send you to school. Be a nurse assistant, a home attendant, something!

Even if you were on welfare, it should be like, you see all these dirty streets we have? Why can't they go out and sweep the streets, clean up the parks? I mean, there is so much stuff that needs to be done in this city. They can do that and give them their money. Not just sit home and not do anything.

Patricia, a mother of five children in her late thirties, has worked at Burger Barn for five years. She moved up to New York from Tennessee after her husband walked out on her, hoping to find more job opportunities than were available in the rural South. It took a long time for Patty to get on her feet; during the time she was really desperate, she turned to the welfare system to put food on the table. Eventually she broke free of her heavy-handed caseworker and landed her Burger Barn job. Given this background, one imagines Patty would be tolerant of AFDC recipients. After all, she has been there. Not so. Having finally taken the hard road to a real job, she sees no reason why anyone else should have an easier ride.

There's so much in this city; it's always hiring. It may not be what you want. It may not be the pay you want. But you will always get a job. If I can work at Burger Barn all week and come home tired and

then have to deal with the kids and all of that, and be happy with one twenty-five a week, so can you. Why would I give quarters [to bums on the street]? My quarter is tax-free money for you! No way.

Or, in a variation on the same theme, Larry reminds us that any job is better than no job. The kids who dare to hard-time Larry get nothing but a cold shoulder in return, because he knows deep down that he has something they don't have: work for which he gets paid.

I don't care what other people think. You know, I just do not care. I have a job, you know. It's my job. You ain't puttin' no food on my table; you ain't puttin' no clothes on my back. I will walk tall with my Burger Barn uniform on. Be proud of it, you know.

Danielle is a little less confident, and allows that she doesn't advertise the nature of her job by wearing her uniform on the street. But she agrees with Larry that what is most important is that you work at all. What a person does for a living is less critical than willingness and ability to find and keep a job of any kind.

Regardless of what kind of work you do, you still can be respected. Ain't saying I'm ashamed of my job, but I wouldn't walk down the street wearing the uniform.... Guys know you work there will say, "Hi, Burger Barn." I ain't gonna lie and say I'm not ashamed, period. But I'm proud that I'm working. You know, my daughter's father ... used to grab pigs and clean pigs all day. But he was respected for his job. I respected him because he worked, regardless of what kind of work it was. He got laid off a better job, and that was the only job he could find at the time. So he took it, and I respect him for that. Anybody who could work any kind of job should be respected. Because they was getting that money honestly. They don't have to go out there and get it illegal.

These conservative views trade on a sentiment shared by the working poor and the working class: work equals dignity and no one deserves a free ride. Of course, this means more coming from people who have stood on their feet for eight or nine hours at a stretch for the minimum wage. Virtually all they have to show for their trouble is the self-respect that comes from being on the right side of the chasm that separates the deserving (read "working") and the undeserving (read "nonworking") poor.

Other retorts to status insults are possible as well. Flaunting financial independence often provides a way of lashing back at acquaintances who deride young workers for taking jobs at Burger Barn. Brian, born in Jamaica but raised in some of Harlem's tougher neighborhoods, knows that his peers don't think much of his job. "They would just make fun," he says. "'Ah, you flipping burgers. You gettin' paid four twenty-five.' They'd go snickering down the street." But it wasn't long after Brian started working that he piled up some serious money, and everyone around him knew it.

> What I did was make Sam [the general manager] save my money for me. Then I got the best of clothes and the best sneakers with my own money. Then I added two chains. Then [my friends] were like, "Where you selling drugs at?" and I'm like, "The same place you said making fun of me, flipping burgers. That's where I'm getting my money from. Now, where are you getting yours from?" They couldn't answer.

Media attention given to the glamour of the drug trade suggests that it is an attractive magnet for kids who need money. But the young adults we met in Harlem are frightened of the drug lords and want to stay as far away from their business as possible.

They know too many people who are dead, in jail, or permanently disabled from the ravages of drugs. Kyesha explained:

> People like to down me, like this job wasn't anything, like it was a low job. Like selling drugs was better than working at fast foods. But I was like, "Nah." I never went that way, toward drugs, so I'm just gonna stick to what I do. Now they locked up, and I don't think I'm gonna get locked up for selling hamburgers and french fries!

If you aren't willing to join the underground economy, where are you going to get the money to dress yourself, go out on the town, and do the other things teens throughout the middle class do on Mom and Dad's sufferance? Harlem families cannot provide it. That leaves the youth themselves to earn the cash to support their lifestyle, a primary force pushing them to find jobs. A young man like Brian can remain a player in the local social scene by supporting his consumer needs with a job. He takes no small amount of pleasure outdoing his friends on style grounds they value as much as he does.

It might be comforting to believe that these hardworking, low-wage workers were, from the very beginning, different from their nonworking counterparts, equipped somehow to withstand the gauntlet of criticism that comes their way when they start out on the bottom of the labor market. It would be comforting because we would then be able to sort the admirable poor (who recognize the fundamental value of work and are willing to ignore stigma) from the rest (who collapse in the face of peer pressure and therefore prefer to go on the dole). This is simplistic. Burger Barn workers of all ages and colors have been the butt of jokes and the target of ridicule. Some, like Jamal, claim they don't care what other people think, but when you get to know them personally, they will admit that it took a long time, a lot of swallowed pride, to build up this confidence. The sting of public criticism did get to them.

How, then, did they manage to develop the backbone it takes to stay the course in a stigmatized job? How do ghetto residents develop the rejoinders that make it possible to recapture their dignity in the face of social disapproval? To some degree, they can call on widely accepted American values that honor working people, values that "float" in the culture at large.[6] But this is not enough to construct a positive identity when the reminders of low status—coming from customers, friends, and the media—are relentless. Something stronger is required: a workplace culture that actively functions to overcome the negatives by reinforcing the value of the work ethic. Managers and veteran employees play a critical role in the reinforcement process. Together they create a cocoonlike atmosphere in the back of the restaurant where they counsel new workers distressed by bad-mouthing.

Kimberly, a twenty-year-old African-American woman, began working at Burger Barn when she was sixteen and discovered firsthand how her "friends" would turn on her for taking a low-wage job. Fortunately, she found a good friend at work who steadied her with a piece of advice:

> Say it's a job. You are making money. Right? Don't care what nobody say. You know? If they don't like it, too bad. They sitting on the corner doing what they are doing. You got to work making money. You know? Don't bother with what anybody has to say about it.

Kim's friend and adviser, a Burger Barn veteran who had long since come to terms with the insults of his peers, called upon a general status hierarchy that places the working above the nonworking as a bulwark against the slights. The advice Kim gleaned from her friend and her manager made a big difference in helping her to see that she deserves her dignity.

> Kids come in here...they don't have enough money. I'll be like, "You don't have enough money; you can't get [the food you ordered]." One night this little boy came in there and cursed me out. He [said], "That's why you are working at [Burger Barn]. You can't get a better job...." I was upset and everything. I started crying. [My manager] was like, "Kim, don't bother with him. I'm saying, *you got a job.* You know. It is a *job.*"

Immigrants who have taken jobs in central Harlem are particularly in need of a defense against character assassination, because they are targets for the ire of African-Americans who resent their presence in a community with an insufficient number of jobs to go around. Ana, a native of Ecuador, had a very difficult time when she first began working as a hostess at Burger Barn. A pretty, petite nineteen-year-old, she was selected for the job because she has a sparkle and vivaciousness that any restaurant manager would want customers to see. But some of her more antagonistic black customers seemed to see her as an archetype: the immigrant who barely speaks a word of English and snaps up a job they may have tried to get themselves. Without the support of her bilingual Latino manager, she would not have been able to pull herself together and get on with the work.

> I wasn't sent to the grill or the fries [where you don't need to communicate with customers]. I was sent to the cash register, even though the managers knew I couldn't speak English. That was only one week after my arrival in the U.S.! So I wasn't feeling very well at all. Black people were cursing me out, saying I shouldn't have that job. Thank God, three weeks later I met a manager who was Puerto Rican. He was my salvation. He told me, "Ana, it's not that bad." He'd speak to me in English, even though he knows Spanish. He'd tell me, "Don't cry. Dry off those tears. You'll be all right, you'll make it." So he encouraged me like no other person in that Burger Barn, especially when the customers would curse at me for not

knowing English. He gave me courage, and after that it went much better.

Among the things this manager taught Ana was that she should never listen to people who give her a hard time about holding a job at Burger Barn. Having been a white-collar clerical worker in her native country, Ana was unhappy that she had slipped down the status hierarchy—and she still is. She was grateful to have a way to earn money, and her family was desperate for her contribution. But when customers insulted her, insinuating that someone who spoke limited English was barely worthy of notice, she turned to management for help. And she found it in the form of fellow Latino bosses who told her to hold her head up because she was, after all, working, while her critics, on the whole, were not.

With this moral armor in hand, Burger Barn workers often take the process of carving an honored identity one step further: they argue their jobs have hidden virtues that make them more valuable than most people credit. Tiffany decided in the end that there was more substance to her job than she initially believed:

> When I got in there, I realized it's not what people think. It's a lot more to it than flipping burgers. It's a real system of business. That's when I really got to see a big corporation at play. I mean, one part of it, the foundation of it. Cashiers. The store, how it's run. Production of food, crew workers, service. Things of that nature. That's when I really got into it and understood a lot more.

Americans tend to think of values as embedded in individuals, transmitted through families, and occasionally reinforced by media images or role models. We tend not to focus on the powerful contribution that institutions and organizations make to the creation and sustenance of beliefs. Yet it is clear that the workplace itself is a major force in the creation of a "rebuttal

culture" among these workers. Without this haven of the fellow-stigmatized, it would be very hard for Burger Barn employees to retain their dignity. With this support, however, they are able to hold their heads up, not by defining themselves as separate from society, but by calling upon their commonality with the rest of the working world.

This is but one of the reasons why exclusion from the society of the employed is such a devastating source of social isolation. We could hand people money, as various guaranteed-income plans of the past thirty years have suggested. But we can't hand out honor. Honor comes from participation in this central setting in our culture and from the positive identity it confers.

Roosevelt understood this during the Great Depression and responded with the creation of thousands of publicly funded jobs designed to put people to work building the national parks, the railway stations, the great highways that crisscross the country, and the murals that decorate public walls from San Francisco to New York. Social scientists studying the unemployed in the 1930s showed that people who held WPA jobs were far happier and healthier than those who were on the dole, even when their incomes did not differ significantly.[7] WPA workers had their dignity in the midst of poverty; those on the dole were vilified and could not justify their existence or find an effective cultural rationale for the support they received.

This historical example has its powerful parallels in the present. Joining the workforce is a fundamental, transformative experience that moves people across barriers of subculture, race, gender, and class. It never completely eradicates these differences, and in some divisive settings, it may even reinforce consciousness of them—through glass ceilings, discriminatory promotion policies, and the like. But even in places where pernicious distinctions are maintained, there is another, overarching identity competing with forms that stress difference: a common bond within the organization and across the nation of fellow workers. This is what makes getting a job so much more than a means to a financial end.

NOTES

1. There are further shades of gray below the line of the employed that distinguish those who are searching for jobs and those that have accepted their fate as nonworkers, with the latter suffering the greatest stigma of all. To signal a total lack of interest in work is to place oneself outside the pale of the morally worthy altogether.

2. The application of efficient, deskilled, routinized work by corporate organizations was made famous through Frederick Taylor's system of scientific management, in which meaningful decision-making is deliberately withdrawn from workers and given over to a small number of managers. Each worker, whose performance is easily supervised and evaluated, repeatedly performs a limited number of well-defined tasks, resulting in very uniform products. Social critics have written extensively on the toll such practices take on workers in manufacturing and clerical bureaucracies. But fast food workers, as well as others in the service sector, are required to interact directly with customers, and in very particular ways, even when customers fail to play by the rules. Counter employees are asked to display warm, sincere smiles whether or not such expressions are authentic. Thus demands to subordinate themselves to the work process extend even further into their on-the-job behavior and self-presentation. Firms rarely achieve exact compliance with these requirements; in fact, workers, both individually and collectively, almost always undermine such efforts in all sorts of ways. But good line managers know that regulating workers' appearance, attitudes, and conduct in the name of proper customer service involves workers' most basic means of self-expression and their profound private feelings, which they are asked to actively deny or suppress on a daily basis. Robin Leidner, *Fast Food, Fast Talk Service Work and the Routinization of Everyday Life* (University of California Press, 1990), is an

incisive study of the social negotiations made among managers, workers, and customers at McDonald's, and how these negotiations shape roles, strategies, and identities at the workplace. See also Arlie Hochschild, *The Managed Heart: Commercialization of Human Feeling* (University of California Press, 1983), which explores the nature of "emotional" labor through an analysis of flight attendants and bill collectors, both of whom are expected to engage in deep acting so as to change the status of their customers (in opposite directions).

3. Leidner, *Fast Food, Fast Talk*.

4. In areas experiencing exceptionally tight labor markets—including much of the midwest in the late 1990s—wages for these jobs are climbing above the minimum-wage line.

5. The steepest increases in inner-city poverty took place in the 1970s as a result of rising joblessness and declining wages, which continue today. Aside from housing and educational policies that contributed to these results, there are a host of interdependent economic reasons for these trends: a shift in demand toward higher-educated workers in higher-wage industries, massive industrial restructuring that was especially pernicious in the urban northeast and midwest, and the increasing suburbanization of employment, taking jobs from downtown to metropolitan peripheries. See William Julius Wilson, *When Work Disappears* (Knopf, 1996). America's inner cities have such incredibly impoverished job bases that they are almost always characterized by slack labor markets. Only when the labor supply outside ghetto walls has tightened down to almost impossible levels do we begin to see this tide lift inner-city boats. Eventually employers do turn to the workers who are low on their preference queues, as we learned in the 1980s during the Massachusetts miracle. See Richard E. Freeman, "Employment and Earnings of Disadvantaged Young Men in a Labor Shortage Economy," and Paul Osterman, "Gains from Growth? The Impact of Full Employment on Poverty in Boston," both in Christopher Jencks and Paul E. Peterson, eds., *The Urban Underclass* (Brookings Institution, 1991). These analyses

show not only that tight labor markets help the employment opportunities in our inner cities but also that the people who live there take full advantage of these opportunities when they arise. These conditions are, sadly, rare and generally short-lived. This is one of the many reasons why increasing the minimum wage is so important. Significant increases in the minimum wage could theoretically lead to raising some employment displacement, especially among youth. One of the reasons for the introduction of the minimum wage in the late 1930s was to lower youth competition for jobs. See Paul Osterman, *Getting Started* (MIT Press, 1980). In an analysis of youth labor markets of the 1970s, Osterman argues that while the minimum wage has modest negative effects on youth employment, it is not a major structural source of youth unemployment. But it is difficult to see how already lean retail firms, such as fast food establishments, could do much more to cut the numbers of front-line employees. What is more, only 15% of minimum-wage earners are teens; 39% are the sole earners in their households; 1994 data, U.S. Department of Labor, "Making Work Pay: The Case for Raising the Minimum Wage" (press release, October 2, 1995). The real value of the minimum wage declined sharply throughout the 1980s (it became so low, in fact, that states began to legislate their own minimum wages that were higher than the federal minimum); this alone was a major factor in the increasing wage inequality at the bottom of the U.S. income distribution, especially for women. See John DiNardo, Nicole M. Fortin, and Thomas Lemieux, "Labor Market Institutions and the Distribution of Wages, 1973–1992: A Semiparametric Approach," *Econometrica* 64, no. 5 (September 1996), pp. 1001–1044. John DiNardo and Thomas Lemieux, "Diverging Male Wage Inequality in the United States and Canada, 1981–1988: Do Institutions Explain the Difference?" *Industrial and Labor Relations Review*, 50, no. 4 (July 1997), pp. 629–651, finds that unions and changes in minimum wages account for two-thirds of the differential growth in male wage inequality between the United States

and Canada. The new minimum-wage hike (to $5.15 in September 1997), brought the purchasing power of the minimum up to a level that is still 14% lower than the minimum wage of 1979. In time we will see whether these increases lead to reduced turnover and heightened productivity in firms that have trouble holding on to good employees, offsetting higher payroll costs. See Chris Tilly, *Half a Job: Bad and Good Part-Time Jobs in a Changing Labor Market* (Temple University Press, 1996), p. 181. A now famous examination of the effects of a number of state and federal minimum-wage hikes that took place from 1989 to 1992, David Card and Alan B. Krueger, *Myth and Measurement: The New Economics of the Minimum Wage* (Princeton University Press, 1995), finds that, contrary to what economics textbook models predict, these recent increases did not reduce employment and sometimes had modest positive effects. One of Card and Krueger's main empirical studies considers employment in the fast food industry before and after New Jersey advanced its minimum wage in 1992. They conducted surveys of over 400 restaurants in New Jersey and neighboring eastern Pennsylvania before and after the increase, and found that employment in New Jersey was not negatively affected by the wage hike. Indeed, they learned that employment in New Jersey expanded. In fact, employment growth in New Jersey was higher at those restaurants that had to raise their wages to comply with the law than at those that were already paying more than the new minimum. While Card and Krueger, among others, note that the benefits of a minimum wage are not targeted directly at the poor (workers from nonpoor families also work at minimum-wage jobs), workers who earn the minimum or slightly more than the minimum are disproportionately drawn from families in the lower portion of the earnings distribution. "Minimum-wage earners are primarily women (57.9%), have full-time jobs (47.2%) or work between 20 and 35 hours weekly (33.3%), are disproportionately black (15%) or Hispanic (13.8%), and are concentrated in the low-wage retail sector (44.3%)." Lawrence Mishel, Jared

Bernstein, and Edith Rasell, "Who Wins with a Higher Minimum Wage" (Economic Policy Institute Briefing Paper, 1995), p. 1.

6. The fact that Harlem residents rejected for these jobs hold these values is some evidence for the preexisting nature of this mind-set—although these rejects had already piled up work experience, which may have contributed to the sharpening of this alternative critique.

7. Scholars and critics acknowledged many problems and inefficiencies in the WPA's function as a relief agency, but emphasized the psychological superiority of paid work over direct relief. See E. Wight Bakke, *The Unemployed Worker: A Study of the Task of Making a Living Without a Job* (Yale University Press, 1940). For history and analysis of the WPA and other work relief programs of the New Deal, see Michael B. Katz, *In the Shadow of the Poorhouse: A Social History of Welfare in America* (Basic Books, 1986); and Nancy E. Rose, *Put to Work: Relief Programs in the Great Depression* (Monthly Review Press, 1994). Political writer Mickey Kaus writes frequently on the stigma of welfare and the need for a WPA-like jobs program. See, for example, Mickey Kaus, *The End of Equality* (Basic Books, 1992).

REFERENCES

Card, David and Alan B. Krueger. *Myth and Measurement: The New Economics of the Minimum Wage.* 1995. Princeton: Princeton University Press.

Kaus, Mickey. 1992. *The End of Equality.* New York: Basic Books.

DiNardo, John, Nicole M. Fortin, and Thomas Lemieux. 1996. "Labor Market Institutions and the Distribution of Wages, 1973–1992: A Semiparametric Approach" *Econometrica* 64 (5): 1001–1044.

DiNardo, John, and Thomas Lemieux . 1997. "Diverging Male Wage Inequality in the United States and Canada, 1981–1988: Do Institutions Explain the Difference?"

Industrial and Labor Relations Review 50 (4): 629–651.

Freeman, Richard E. 1991. "Employment and Earnings of Disadvantaged Young Men in a Labor Shortage Economy." In *The Urban Underclass.* Christopher Jencks and Paul E. Peterson (eds.). Washington D.C.: The Brookings Institution.

Hackbarth, Alexa. 2003. "Vanity, Thy Name Is Metrosexual: D.C.'s Dating Scene Gets a Lot Prettier." *Washington Post* (November 17): C10.

Hochschild, Arlie. 1983. *The Managed Heart: Commercialization of Human Feeling.* Berkeley-Los Angeles: University of California Press.

Katz, Michael B. 1986. *In the Shadow of the Poorhouse: A Social History of Welfare in America.* New York: Basic Books , 1986.

Leidner, Robin. 1990. *Fast Food, Fast Talk Service Work and the Routinization of Everyday Life.* Berkeley-Los Angeles: University of California Press.

Mishel, Lawrence, Jared Bernstein, and Edith Rasell. 1995. "Who Wins with a Higher Minimum Wage." Economic Policy Institute Briefing Paper.

Osterman, Paul. 1980. *Getting Started.* Cambridge: MIT Press.

Osterman, Paul. 1991. "Gains from Growth? The Impact of Full Employment on Poverty in Boston." In *The Urban Underclass.* Christopher Jencks and Paul E. Peterson (eds.). Washington D.C.: The Brookings Institution.

Rose, Nancy E. 1994. *Put to Work: Relief Programs in the Great Depression.* New York: Monthly Review Press.

Tilly, Chris. 1996. *Half a Job: Bad and Good Part-Time Jobs in a Changing Labor Market.* Philadelphia: Temple University Press.

U.S. Department of Labor. 1995. "Making Work Pay: The Case for Raising the Minimum Wage." Press release (October 2).

Wight Bakke, E. 1940. *The Unemployed Worker: A Study of the Task of Making a Living Without a Job.* New Haven: Yale University Press.

Wilson, William Julius. 1996. *When Work Disappears: The World of the New Urban Poor.* New York: Knopf.

31

PETER BEARMAN

SERVING TIME

from *Doormen* (2005)

In this mixed-method study that includes observation, interviews, and survey techniques, Peter Bearman studies New York City's doormen. In this selection, he addresses the puzzle of why doormen frequently appear to be doing nothing, yet are seemingly too busy to attend to tenants at moments when they most need their assistance.

Up on the Upper West Side, it is four in the afternoon on a beautiful early spring day. Doormen are standing in front of their buildings. Across the street, kids play in the park, their parents or nannies sitting on benches talking, one supposes, about this and that. Joggers and dog walkers and bicyclists pass by. Back in front of the buildings, nothing appears to be happening. A couple of doormen have left their posts and traversed the seventy-five feet or so that separates them, meeting in the middle. They converse, often looking back at their door. One or two smoke a cigarette. There is a constant awareness of danger. But the danger comes not from potential criminals, but from supervisors who may appear at any moment from one of the buildings where they live. So conversations tend to be short,

just a minute or two. And then the doormen return to their posts. Every five minutes or so, at one of the buildings, someone comes in. As they approach the building, they adjust their tempo subtly to allow the doorman to open the door for them. Always the doorman will greet them, and sometimes one can observe a short conversation. "It's beautiful out today, huh?" is the typical starter for these conversations. If it were cold, a friendly "Bundle up" could be heard. Whatever the weather, there is always something (generic) to say.

Sometimes tenants can be seen leaving the buildings. When the doormen are outside, most tenants manage to open the door by themselves, but every so often, one will wait for service. Suddenly at one building, there is a flurry of activity. An old couple arrives into the lobby from the elevator, waiting to exit. A cab shows up. The mailman arrives; the dry cleaner's truck appears. For a few seconds, everyone is jammed up by the door. Abram (the doorman) lets the old couple exit, and the mailman enters and heads for the mailboxes in the rear. Abram takes the dry cleaning and brings it inside. The cab has to wait since the lobby is active. He barely glances at it.

The cab has discharged a family with shopping bags. Quickly shift focus and consider their experience. They struggle to bring the bags to the door, now shut behind them as Abram logs the dry cleaning in the back room. By the time he returns, they have used their key, entered the building, and called the elevator. When they left two hours earlier, he had been sitting quietly in the lobby reading the *Post*. It's odd, they think: whenever we need him, he is unavailable. Later, after putting the groceries away, they leave the building to take a walk in the park. It is 4:30, and the doorman is preparing to leave. He is talking with his neighbor from down the street who clocked out a few minutes early. Left behind in the lobby is Rickie, who works the swing shift. Having just changed, he is now foraging through the drawer to see what he can read. The elevator lands on the first floor, and the family walks toward the door. Rickie starts to get up, but the kids are faster and already at the door. He greets the family and talks about the weather. They all agree it is a beautiful day, which it is.

For Rickie, the swing shift runs until 1:00 A.M. It has been a quiet night; most of the tenants have stayed at home. A few take-out orders from a Chinese restaurant have arrived and some videos have been delivered. Rickie sent one video delivery directly to one apartment, but held on to the videos for another, instead calling the tenants on the house phone to tell them that their videos had arrived. Shortly after, a small man came down to collect them. The casual observer would have been puzzled by Rickie's behavior—why does he block direct deliveries from one company but allow the other to go right up? One tenant is having a small party. Rickie recognizes some of the guests. They have come before and he sends them up without calling. Other visitors arrive and Rickie asks them where they are going. Without asking the tenants, he sends one young man up to the thirteenth floor and then quickly calls the apartment he is heading to, warning them. The couple heading to 2G is asked to wait until he confirms that there is someone expecting them. As they go up, he moves toward the stairs to confirm that they have stopped on the second floor.

Around 9:30, the elevator comes down to the first floor and Amanda gets out. She looks like she is going out for a run. Rickie greets her and asks how she is doing. He notes that it is late for a run and advises her to "be careful out there." She meanders over to the bench by the window and plops down. She asks about his day. They talk about the weather and the neighborhood. She tells him that the tenant in 6F is planning to move out. Amanda helps pass the time; every now and then, someone comes in or leaves. These exiting and entering tenants almost always say hi, although a few walk by in silence. And for the most part, Amanda talks to them as well. Just before 11:00, Amanda looks at her watch and apparently realizes that she lost the chance to go out. She gets back on the elevator and returns to her apartment. Later Rickie says that this happens at least once a week with her. And there are others who talk too much as well. Listening is part of the job, but most people don't think Rickie is working when he talks. So far that evening, more than a handful of tenants saw him seemingly doing nothing all night. And that is their usual experience. Yet once again, at the same time, when they most need him, he is often busy. The tenants find this puzzling. We can observe something else, perhaps equally puzzling: Rickie treats similar problems differently throughout the evening. Some guests are forced to wait, while others are allowed immediate access. In some cases, he calls tenants so that they can come pick up their videos, whereas others have them delivered directly to their door. There appears to be no rhyme or reason to his selective provision of service. How can we explain these different patterns of behavior? And why do they matter?

This chapter is concerned with the daily experience of tenants and doormen as they negotiate the seemingly minor interactions they have during the course of a day, interactions that occur in the context of the course of a year, and typically over the course of many years. Most tenants in most buildings know their doorman by name. Many have watched him grow older. They typically know a little about his family. But they generally know little else. They do not know what kind of food he eats, the last movie he saw at home, his drinking habits, his friends, or his relatives. In contrast, Rickie—and the other doormen—have watched their tenants for years. He knows their names. If they have kids, he has watched them grow. He knows when they come home, what they do at night, the movies they watch, and what kinds of foods they eat. He knows if they drink. He knows when one of them is having an affair, is in trouble, and when one of their friends is in town. He likely knows their relatives by sight. And he knows their preferences (in large part because he has helped develop them). Do they want to be called when a friend comes? Do they want to have their movies left downstairs and if so, why? He knows which ones have movies left downstairs because they want to avoid having to tip the kid who brought the movies and which have the movies left downstairs because they are renting porno and don't want to take the chance that the kid who delivers the movies will know that and embarrass them. Do they want to be

greeted each time they see him, or just the first few times? If asked, any doorman will tell you that it is their job to know all this stuff though few doormen will tell you anything at all that they do know about specific tenants in their buildings.

Doormen bridge and sustain the border between the inside and outside of a building. They work in the same buildings for years on end, serving the same tenants in the same small ways. It is the constancy of their relationship with the same people, the "smallness" of the services that they repeatedly provide, and the irregularity of the comings and goings that define their day and generate the specific phenomenological condition that structures and gives rise to their experience. In relationships that reproduce themselves daily and traverse years, there is a constant dance where tenants and doormen jointly manage the affairs of the lobby. In this chapter, I focus on one aspect of this management process, the management of activity and time. I consider one of the most visible contradictions of the lobby, the tension between inactivity and boredom and intense activity and stress, seen from both the perspective of doormen and tenants.

When considering the management of time, a central feature of the work experience is the fact that doormen describe their jobs as both boring and stressful. Not a single doorman escapes this seemingly strange problem. I discuss the sources of this contradiction and show that it is a generic problem for server-client systems. While all server-client systems give rise to periods of congestion (and stress) and idleness (and boredom), the peculiar relationship between doormen as servers and tenants as clients leads to a unique set of issues and problems that provides a skein for the daily construction of the lobby as an interactive environment. Before focusing on the deep problem, let's clear away the simple quantitative material, the nuts and bolts of the job, in terms of tasks done.

What Tasks Do Doormen Actually Do?

One idea is that doormen are personal butlers who serve their tenants whatever their requests may be at the moment the requests are made. Typically, this view is held by people, if at all, who have not encountered doormen. But in describing their jobs, some doormen provide this as the essential model. As Isaac says, for example:

> Well, more or less, our job is to make the tenants' lives easier so that they don't have to lift a finger. And that's really our job. So more or less, whatever they need, that's what we do. We accommodate them.

More strongly many doormen think that their tenants are completely useless and unable to help themselves. In responding to a question about why he thinks people live in doormen buildings, Bob says:

> Why do they need us, because they can't do it themselves. That's the only thing I know. The things we do here, I can do them myself, know what I mean? Opening the door for someone I can do myself. Carry a bag, what the hell, take a package. They can't do it, they got the money, they can afford it.

Even if they do lots of things, there are many things that doormen do not do for their tenants. Likewise, some things that tenants would like their doormen to do for them create problems for other tenants, so doormen cannot easily satisfy all of their clients at the same time. This aside, doormen have many tasks and it is possible to describe the nuts and bolts of the job with reference to a generic task list.

Here, then, are the nuts and bolts. The typical observation of a doorman finds him just standing at the door or sitting at a desk in the front lobby. At any given minute, this is in fact what doormen are doing. While most of their time is spent at the door or in the lobby, and most of that time is seemingly idle time, doormen typically do much more each day than hold the door for tenants and their visitors. In this section, I consider what work tasks doormen have, and how these tasks vary by shift and neighborhood. The goal is simple description in quantitative terms, as background. As the bottom row of table 31.1 shows, virtually all doormen greet visitors (92.6%), sign for packages (88.7%), announce visitors (89.7%), and provide security (90.2%). More than half of all doormen report that they call taxis (69.6%), keep public areas of the building clean (63.2%), shovel snow (56.9%), and deliver packages to their tenants (52.9%). Roughly one-third of all doormen are responsible for delivering mail (35.8%), maintaining outdoor areas in front of their building (39.7%), delivering newspapers (32.4%), operating elevators (33.3%), and helping with minor maintenance duties in their tenants' apartments (33.3%). Significantly fewer doormen are responsible for parking tenants' cars (9.8%), removing trash (20.1%), or other activities (not shown), such as gardening (6.7%) and checking IDs (6.7%).

The balance of table 31.1 reports the distribution of these activities by shift. While any twenty-four-hour day has potentially only three non-overlapping eight-hour shifts, some doormen regularly work different shifts (half-swing or half-night, for example). Only 5% of the doormen we interviewed solely worked a night shift (12–7 A.M.); of those who did work nights, most alternated between the swing and night shifts. So typically, when doormen consider their jobs, they tend to summarize across the multiple shifts that they may work. Against this background, which could lead to a blurring of distinctions between shifts, I consider how shift structures tasks in relation to the overall distribution of work tasks. With this possible caveat in mind, one can see from table 31.1 that the shifts

TABLE 31.1. Shifts by Tasks

Shifts	Greet visitors	Call taxis	Deliver newspapers	Deliver mail	Park cars	Sign for packages	Shovel snow	Keep public areas clean	Remove tenants' trash	Maintain outdoor public areas	Announce visitors	Provide security	Minor maintenance duties	Operate elevator	Deliver packages to tenants
Day N = 57	51 89.5%	43 75.4%	19 33.3%	23 40.4%	4 7.0%	50 87.7%	32 56.1%	31 54.4%	11 19.3%	21 36.8%	50 87.7%	50 87.7%	17 29.8%	18 31.6%	31 54.4%
Swing N = 95	92 96.8%	63 66.3%	30 31.6%	28 29.5%	9 9.5%	86 90.5%	51 53.7%	56 58.9%	18 18.9%	36 37.9%	87 91.6%	84 88.4%	31 32.6%	32 33.7%	48 50.5%
Night N = 10	10 100%	7 70.0%	4 40.0%	2 20.0%	3 30.0%	7 70.0%	7 70.0%	8 80.0%	3 30.0%	2 20.0%	9 90.0%	10 100%	4 40.0%	2 20.0%	4 40.0%
Multiple N = 42	36 85.7%	29 69.0%	13 31.0%	20 47.6%	4 9.5%	39 92.9%	26 61.9%	34 81.0%	9 21.4%	22 52.4%	37 88.1%	40 95.2%	16 38.1%	16 38.1%	25 59.5%
Total N = 204	189 92.6%	142 69.6%	66 32.4%	73 35.8%	20 9.8%	181 88.7%	116 56.9%	129 63.2%	41 20.1%	81 39.7%	183 89.7%	184 90.2%	68 33.3%	68 33.3%	108 52.9%

are remarkably similar in terms of the tasks that doormen do. Whatever it is that doormen do, their official tasks do not seem to vary by shift. As Peter, a doorman who alternatively works the day and swing shifts on the East Side, says:

> What would be an average day? We come in; we do the book. Log in; get rid of what we don't need. Receive packages, dry cleaning, sort mail, and food deliveries. We coordinate food deliveries; we coordinate workmen, handymen. We direct the handyman and the superintendent to problem areas in the building. We receive complaints and we direct it to the handyman. We have to announce everybody and be aware of everybody who comes in the building. And we have to be aware of danger—we're responsible for the lobby and the inside area. That's basically our duty. That's a basic day. Everything else in between is the usual stuff. That'd be the basic coming in, logging in. Logging packages, deliveries, dry cleaning, sorting the mail, greeting tenants, getting taxis, coordinating, making sure everything's functioning. That's basically our job.

In response to the same question, "What about shifts? Do they matter in terms of what you do?" Nicolai says:

> No, not really. Swing I read more after 8:00. I got more deliveries for food— pizza and Chinese food—I got the trash to collect from downstairs and sort, nights I take the trash out to the street, but swing shift you just get it ready. I got the dry cleaning and packages to log out when people come back from work. Nights get pretty boring sometimes, that's all. After 2:00 I sit back with my feet in the air; then early the papers come, I got the *Post*, the *Times*, the *Journal*, all to mark apt. 14c and 13A, like that. I clean the lobby and get ready for the next day.

Which suggests that if the tasks do not officially vary—the door has to be attentive, log in when logging is required, keep track of things, and so on—the feeling of each shift varies quite a bit when broken down by the flow of time. Swing frees up after 8:00 P.M., relative to the crush of activity at the start of the shift, whereas the night gets slow after 2:00 A.M., with only sporadic activity, such as when the morning papers are delivered. And with flow variation, relationships to others and satisfaction with one's schedule and opportunities for promotion also vary. Those on the day shift are more likely to be very satisfied with their schedule, their relationships, and the promotion possibilities; those who work on the swing and night shift less so. These relationships are observed in tables 31.2, 31.3, and 31.4, where I consider shift worked and satisfaction with people, work schedule, and promotion opportunities.

Neighborhood Effects?

Tasks do vary somewhat by neighborhood, however, although rarely significantly. Here I just focus on the Upper East Side, East Side, West Side, Midtown, and downtown, which are the simple socio-spatial regions

TABLE 31.2. Shifts by Satisfaction with Contact with Other People

Shift	Very satisfied	Satisfied	Less satisfied	Not satisfied	Total
Day	24 (41.4%)	25 (43.1%)	6 (10.3%)	3 (5.2%)	58 (100%)
Swing	30 (31.6%)	54 (56.8%)	5 (5.3%)	6 (6.3%)	95 (100%)
Night	2 (18.2%)	8 (72.7%)	1 (9.1%)	0	11 (100%)
Multiple	11 (26.2%)	26 (61.9%)	3 (7.1%)	2 (4.8%)	42 (100%)
Total	67 (32.5%)	113 (54.9%)	15 (7.3%)	11 (5.3%)	206 (100%)

TABLE 31.3. Shifts by Satisfaction with Work Schedule

Shift	Very satisfied	Satisfied	Less satisfied	Not satisfied	Total
Day	26 (45.6%)	19 (33.3%)	6 (10.5%)	6 (10.5%)	57 (100%)
Swing	18 (18.4%)	49 (50.0%)	17 (17.3%)	14 (14.3%)	98 (100%)
Night	1 (10.0%)	4 (40.0%)	8 (30.0%)	2 (20.0%)	10 (100%)
Multiple	6 (15.0%)	19 (47.5%)	9 (22.5%)	6 (15.0%)	40 (100%)
Total	51 (24.9%)	91 (44.4%)	35 (17.1%)	28 (13.7%)	205 (100%)

TABLE 31.4. Shifts by Satisfaction with Opportunity for Promotion

Shift	Very satisfied	Satisfied	Less satisfied	Not satisfied	Total
Day	7 (14.9%)	11 (23.4%)	6 (12.8%)	23 (48.9%)	47 (100%)
Swing	5 (5.8%)	26 (30.2%)	22 (25.6%)	33 (38.4%)	86 (100%)
Night	0	3 (33.3%)	3 (33.3%)	3 (33.3%)	9 (100%)
Multiple	3 (8.1%)	16 (43.2%)	8 (21.6%)	10 (27.0%)	37 (100%)
Total	15 (8.4%)	56 (31.3%)	39 (21.8%)	69 (38.5%)	179 (100%)

of the city. Table 31.5 reports how tasks vary across these neighborhoods. As expected, the differences across neighborhoods appear most clearly for less frequent tasks. Still, even across all of the more common activities, doormen on the Upper East Side do more than other doormen. Likewise, across all of the less frequent activities, doormen working in Midtown do less, in some instances significantly less than all other doormen. And in general, keeping with New York City stereotypes and their experience, Upper East Side doormen always do more and Midtown doormen always do less. But across all of the possible comparisons, most of the differences are not statistically significant—doormen pretty much do the same kinds of things (formally at any rate) wherever they work.

This does not mean that there are no neighborhood effects, or at least discussion about neighborhood effects. In comparing experiences working as a doorman on the East Side to the West Side, one doorman remarks:

It's better over here [West Side]. The people in this building are real people. They have jobs, so they know what it's like to be a worker. So they treat you better. When I am busy, they understand and wait. On the East Side, everybody thinks they have something special.

Canseco echoes this sentiment as well:

Well, personally, I say it's harder to work on the East Side. Because they, the tenants on the East Side, are more demanding and I mean this is a strictly straight A of a class A building. And it's hard. I mean you really got to pay attention. You got to be alert. There is no playing around. You know what I mean. You have to be serious.

But, as with many other things, this seems just as likely a simple stereotype, since other doormen with similar experiences (working in different buildings) report exactly the opposite; for example, Carmen, now on the East Side—having moved up from a large building in Midtown—says about his new clients:

They're a better sort of people in this building. Some of my friends say that

TABLE 3–5. Neighborhoods (Workplace Zip Codes) by Tasks

Neighborhood	Greet visitors	Call taxis	Deliver newspapers	Deliver mail	Park cars	Sign for packages	Shovel snow	Keep public areas clean	Remove tenants' trash	Maintain outdoor public areas	Announce visitors	Provide security	Minor maintenance duties	Operate elevator	Deliver packages to tenants
Downtown N = 17	14 82.4%	7 41.2%	4 23.5%	4 23.5%	2 11.8%	13 76.5%	8 47.1%	7 41.2%	3 17.6%	4 23.5%	14 82.4%	17 100%	5 29.4%	3 17.6%	4 23.5%
Midtown N = 11	8 72.7%	5 45.5%	2 18.2%	3 27.3%	0	9 81.0%	3 27.3%	6 54.5%	1 9.1%	2 18.2%	8 72.7%	9 81.8%	2 18.2%	1 9.1%	2 18.2%
East Side N = 39	39 100%	32 82.1%	3 7.7%	8 20.5%	3 7.7%	38 97.4%	20 51.3%	28 71.8%	5 12.8%	14 35.9%	38 97.4%	35 89.7%	13 33.3%	4 10.3%	19 48.7%
Upper East Side N = 80	78 97.5%	70 87.5%	41 51.3%	37 46.3%	9 11.3%	72 90.0%	54 67.5%	52 65.0%	22 27.5%	34 42.5%	75 93.8%	75 93.8%	28 35.0%	37 46.3%	48 60.0%
Upper West Side N = 60	53 88.3%	28 46.7%	17 28.3%	21 35.0%	7 11.7%	52 86.7%	31 51.7%	37 61.7%	10 16.7%	27 45.0%	51 85.0%	51 85.0%	20 33.3%	23 38.3%	37 61.7%
Total N = 207	192 92.8%	142 68.6%	67 32.4%	73 35.3%	21 10.1%	184 88.9%	116 56.0%	130 62.8%	41 19.8%	81 39.1%	186 89.9%	187 90.3%	68 32.9%	68 32.9%	110 53.1%

people here [on the East Side] are snobby, but that is not accurate. They are proper. And that means that they treat you right. The better, the higher-quality people don't look down on doormen, and the lower-quality generally have hang-ups about them, their personal inferiority complexes, so they try to make up by putting somebody else down.[1]

In short, sides of town make less difference in tenants-doorman interaction than social class distance—approximated by city side, but only partially.

Boredom

Still, all things considered, neither shift nor neighborhood plays as much of a role in structuring activities as one might have expected. While doormen certainly have many more tasks as part of their daily job description on the Upper East Side, they are just as likely to report boredom and inactivity as those in other neighborhoods are. Nor are they more likely to report stress. All doormen, wherever they work and across all shifts, describe their jobs as alternating between periods of sheer boredom and intense activity. Consider, for example, John, a doorman working on the West Side, who in describing his routine day says:

Something like this, busy then quiet, then busy, see like now I'm able to interview, other times I couldn't even say hello to you because I'm so busy. I got people coming in with groceries, delivery boys as you can see, it gets hectic and then like now, look, dies out.

In a similar vein, Eric describes the same alternation of activity and boredom, although here he distinguishes between busy (Saturday) and deadly (Sunday) days.

Well, it depends on what shift you work on. I work the relief man. I got two shifts: four to twelve and midnight to eight. And usually four to twelve is pretty busy because people go in and out. Going out to movies, dinner, and all that. People don't cook for nothing here. So they go out to dinner and everything, and I get busy, back and forth.... Sundays are the worst days. Every hour it feels like three [from lack of anything to do].

For long periods of the day, doormen often have absolutely nothing to do. And they are often bored. As Eamon says, in response to a question asking him to describe a routine day:[2]

Boring, very boring. Between one person coming in to the next person coming in is quite long. Sometimes it could be a half hour, fifteen minutes, and they want you to be standing at attention or something when they do come.

Mario expands on the theme:

I come here, I smoke a cigarette about every twenty minutes. I read the newspaper every day, I read whatever is under the counter. At 8 P.M., I take my dinner break. Sometimes my friends come by and we talk and hang out. I have to buzz the deliverymen in and ask the tenants if they want to come down or want them to come up. That is about it.

And Felix describes his job in similar terms:

Well, this shift here is really boring. And it's just four to twelve, so most of the people are just coming home. So what I usually do is help them with packages or take the groceries in. The hardest part of this job is just trying to stay awake. That'll be the hardest part. You'll see. You could be here twenty minutes and not have one person come in. So it kind of drags at night. I just got to watch the door and not try to do anything extracurricular. No reading or telephone, they kind of want you standing like a statue at the door. The job doesn't take too much.

Stress

But boredom is only half of the story doormen tell. The other half is about stress. The same doormen who in one part of the interview describe their job as deadly simultaneously report high levels of stress and responsibility. Consider Pedro, who in answer to a question about his least favorite part of the job, says:

> What do I like the least? The stress, it's very stressful. I have been here quite awhile, it's a stressful, stressful job, and it can get really very stressful. If you don't know what you are doing on the door, you could really screw up.

Similarly, Laran describes his routine day as stressful and busy:

> The routine during the day is a lot of work...and it is taxable. Sometimes the busiest hours can be when the mail comes in, packages come in, and the laundry comes in. Chinese guys are trying to sneak into the building putting menus up, which is a constant problem. There are people, businesses in the buildings, they have messengers who come and go, tenants give you things for somebody to pick up. They give you messages, everything they talk about, and also this kind of stuff can be very simple, but all this may come out and you have maybe five to seven to twelve things all at once, and they all think they are number one.

The "Chinese guys" problem, which sounds absurd, is a frequent lament. All the buildings have posted signs saying. "No Menus," but this doesn't really seem to derail the serious. As Tom, a doorman for the past twenty-one years on the East Side, says (note how he finds himself at risk when he is getting a car!):

> Twenty-one years... I don't know how the Chinese man, the Chinese people, the Chinese guys from the restaurant, how they sneak into this place and put menus under each door. That's what beats me. They'll watch you, you know, I think. They sneak up, when you go to get a car from somebody, the guys run in. But he's hiding somewhere in the bushes. It's the strangest thing I ever think about happening.

Radzac, working on the Upper East Side in a cooperative building with a lot of turnover in tenants, describes his day:

> You've really got to make sure that no one goes up unannounced or who's not welcome there. And we've got security cameras on the back door, so you've got to sort of keep your eye on that door. You've got people coming in as someone's leaving; you have to worry about logging in packages. UPS will come with fifty boxes and you have to keep logging them in while you're dispatching a handyman to go to an apartment or taking service orders over the phone, like, "Oh, my bathtub leaks," so you've got to sit here entering it into the book. Then you've got to log and enter all of the stuff, for all the repairmen, the workers, who come in here. And so on and so forth. You've got to put stickers out on boxes so tenants come home and know they have a package. You know, it's a lot of responsibility; it's not an easy thing to do. You're answering phones, you've got walkie-talkies, the intercom is ringing at the same time, you've got fifteen people lined up for packages, you've got delivery

people there. I mean, sometimes it's like, "Leave me alone!"

The problem that needs to be explained is how it is possible for the same job to be experienced as both boring and stressful. Can other jobs be similarly described and if so, which ones and why? One obvious comparison is to other jobs in the service industry, flight attendants on transatlantic flights, bartenders and wait staff, wedding planners, security personnel at airports, and hot dog sellers in the park all come to mind as people whose jobs are experienced in bursts of idleness and intensity. Making sense of this experience—from the upperside-model view—is the focus of the next section.

Queues and Congestion

Why are doormen bored from lack of activity and stressed out about too much to do at the same time? The answer comes from a strange source—people working on problems of traffic flow at airports, on switching networks for telephone and electric service, and on organizing optimal server networks for high-demand, high-sensitivity computer systems that cannot afford breakdowns—operations research, in short. There is a long and distinguished tradition of scholarship arising from operations research that is concerned with congestion, queuing, and waiting. While there has been considerable recent progress in modeling dynamic serving systems (mainly through complex simulation, a direction first seriously attacked by Leonard Klienrock), for our purposes the early classical work is the most germane. Here, the introductory text by D. R. Cox and Walter Smith (1961) provides an easily accessible starting point.[3]

Within reasonable bounds, servers are designed to efficiently handle mean client flow over some period of time. In the grocery store, one does not expect to have only one checkout lane operating between 4 and 7 P.M., and, likewise, one does not expect to see eight cashiers working between 2 and 4 A.M. If firms have too many servers to handle routine mean flow, they are wasting money. On the other hand, if there are too few servers, they are unable to process normal client demand. So firms try to find the right number of servers for the typical flow, defined technically as "mean client flow over some period of time, T." But while the "mean client flow over some period of time, T," will be closest to the observed number, on average, for any given period of time, T, the actual observed flow will vary. Some periods will be characterized by light client flow, others by heavy flow. Systems designed for mean flow will at some points be naturally swamped, while at other times, naturally idle.

If this was the only problem, client-flow variation around the mean, server systems would be impossible to calibrate perfectly but the complications would be relatively few, certainly not sufficient to give rise to a subfield of mathematical theory—the theory of queues. The real problem, well known in operations research, is that given any degree of irregularity in the arrival of clients and variability in the time taken to serve a client, server-client systems (where servers could be anything from clerks at counters to runways for airplanes) will induce congestion.

First, consider just the problem posed by variability in arrival time. Define arrival time as the moment a client (customer, plane, message, etc.) enters the system. This could be a phone number dialed, a tenant coming downstairs to take a taxi, a Chinese food delivery, someone arriving at the door, and so on. What kind of model best predicts the arrival time of the next client? Unless there are pre-allocated schedules for arrivals (appointments every fifteen minutes, as with the doctor, or takeoffs every four minutes for runways, for example), the simplest, and also most likely to be accurate, model would simply predict that the probability of an element arriving is random across time. More complicated models exist, of course. But they tend to exacerbate the situation produced by a random arrival model, as we will see.

Arrivals

Assume that on average there are N events in a specific period of time, T—which could be a minute, an hour, or a day, whatever is a socially defined interval for the system in question. In our case, we would think in terms of eight-hour shifts. If event arrivals are random with respect to time, then the probability of an event arrival is simply T/N. Imagine a simple case of N = 100 events, arriving over a single shift broken up into 100 little time periods (for an eight-hour shift, this would be 8 × 60 minutes = 480 minutes/100 or an event roughly every 5 minutes). Life would be simple if events took less than five minutes to complete and each event arrived evenly spaced out every five minutes or so. A single server could handle them day after day, if human, without stress or boredom.

But life is not so simple. Ignoring the second deep problem of variability of time taken to complete an event, just consider the timing of the events across the 100 five-minute sections of the day. Some periods of the day are empty, and others are dense with events. This pattern of sparseness and density is natural. It comes from the fact that the probability of a client arrival is independent of the arrival of other clients. The chance that an event will arrive is the same across all remaining moments in time. And naturally if arrivals "don't care" about time (which is the meaning of independence), they will come as they please. And this means that, probabilistically, they will tend to bunch up in some periods. If they bunch up in some periods, other periods will not have any events in them.

When arrivals bunch up, congestion occurs. When congestion takes place, doormen are stressed out. When clients don't arrive, servers are idle and doormen feel bored. It is as simple as that.

Independent, then, of the time it takes to service a request, the simple distribution of client arrivals will generate congestion at some periods and idleness at others. If all clients are the same, they can be pretty much scheduled at will; thereby organizing server systems to avoid congestion. This is the case, for example, with mailbox collection. The postal service treats each location as similar and sets up a collection schedule that maximizes the number of boxes that can be serviced (emptied) once or twice in a single day. Most assembly processes work in the same way. For example, similar jars (as clients) travel down an assembly line at fixed intervals awaiting tops (as servers) to be placed on them. But these simple cases for operations research specialists involve instances where events are scheduled, when clients are homogeneous, and where there is no variability in the time taken to serve a customer. They are rare.

The first problem is that in social contexts, like the lobby, clients come with different needs. Some take seconds to satisfy, others much longer. The sources of variability in time taken to serve a customer are countless. Just to pick a familiar example, consider what occurs at the grocery store. Everybody comes to the store to buy groceries, so at one level it seems that service time ought to be pretty fixed. But obviously it is not. One source of variability in service time (here, checking through the cashier) is the number of items in the grocery cart—which has motivated stores to create express lines for shoppers with just a handful of items. But even ignoring item volume, the possibilities for delay are seemingly limitless. Most of us have had the unfortunate experience of standing behind a customer who painfully counts pennies to be "helpful" and give exact change. Likewise, the shopper whose cart contains canned items with scannable prices will be faster than the shopper whose cart contains exotic fresh vegetables and herbs that the cashier has to look up and enter a code number.

There is no reason to believe that variability in service time can be completely anticipated. In the grocery store, people whose shopping carts contain only cans arrive at the stores at the same time as people who only buy exotic vegetables. In the lobby, difficult deliveries or difficult guests don't arrive only when the staff is free. Because people arrive in the lobby (or the store) with different needs, there is enormous variability in service time; and this means that some clients will have to wait in queues some of the time.

Coupled with variability in arrival time, the consequence of this kind of variability is that servers will be extremely busy at some times, and that clients will have to wait in lines. Even short unanticipated delays can cause congestion for some period down the queue. If congestion is systematically too severe, additional servers can be added (more clerks, another doorman, an additional dentist for the practice, a new runway for small planes, etc.). But unless enormous redundancy is built into the server system, at some moment more than one customer will arrive at the point of service at the same time or when the server is busy, and all but one of them will need to queue up and wait their turn. Waiting is the first consequence of dynamic service systems. If people are forced to wait too long, or if their experience is that they routinely have to wait, deep client dissatisfaction is an obvious second-level consequence.[4] From the client perspective—that is, for those who are routinely forced to queue up—it may be the only important one. But that is not exactly true. There are multiple views that need to be considered, and these views bring to light a set of other consequences that are equally important.

Priority of Service

For those who serve, congestion generates dilemmas and decisions. The dilemmas center on priority of service, what is known in operations research as the "queue discipline"—or the method by which a customer is selected for service out of those who are in waiting. Who, or what kinds of demands, should be acted on first? How should priority be allocated? At what point, if ever, do individuals fall out of queue? Decisions have to be made in order to enact priority schemes. Nor do priority schemes really provide solutions to congestion problems. As we shall see, even with priority systems, ranking allocation of server time to activities or individuals, there will always be, unless enormous redundancy is built in, instances in which clients with the same priority compete for the same limited attention of servers. Even more complicated are cases in which competing legitimate demands to priority are built into a single server system. Both of these situations induce congestion dilemmas and heighten employee perception of stress.

Consider, for example, the typical airline response to plane cancellations. Imagine a system in which three planes are flying from city A to city B on a single day, and where airlines are competing for runway server space that is completely allocated. If the first flight of the day is delayed, the runway remains idle during the time it could otherwise be used. Flights next in line cannot leave early, since they have to wait until their scheduled departure—so as to ensure that ticket holders get on board. Delayed flights need to be scheduled, but when? There are two simple rules. They pick up the next free slot, resulting in what could be a long delay if the runways are completely booked, or they hold their place in queue once they are ready to fly and delay subsequent planes.

For delays in this scenario, all things being equal, airports follow the second alternative and adhere to the first come, first served queue discipline. Strangely, if the flight is canceled, the airlines behave differently with respect to clients. They could follow the simple first come, first served discipline by placing seat holders on the first flight onto the second, bumping the latter to the third, and delaying those on the third flight until a new plane is brought in. This seems the most natural thing to do. This is, after all, the same discipline that the airports follow with delays. And it is what we expect from dentists and doctors. If the 9:30 appointment runs late at the dentist office and the dentist is not free until 10:30 (thereby missing the 10:00 A.M. appointment), s/he would never consider first seeing the 10:30 patient and skipping the 10:00 until some other free time at the end of the day. The burden of the lengthy first appointment is passed on as delay all down the line.

Obviously, some competing principles are in play. And equally obvious, there are industry norms that govern client expectation of treatment from servers. Airlines cannot easily bump individuals from seats on scheduled flights. But they can pass on delay. They don't because by localizing delay for one group of travelers (those unfortunate few who have their flight canceled), they minimize widespread client annoyance. Of course, this also helps them score better marks on the statistic that they jointly agree to adhere to in advertising their service proportion of flights delayed. But why don't doctors and dentists do the same thing, that is, "burn" some clients, keeping the rest on schedule? Why is it that they don't make a similar claim: Ninety percent of our patients are seen on time!

Airport controllers know something else about their clients, and this helps them make decisions about enforcement of the first come, first served queue discipline. They know the size of the plane, the number of passengers it is carrying, the congestion status of the receiving airport, the number of passengers on the plane who have subsequent connections to make, and

the airline it is "employed by." If the airline has a hub at the airport, if the plane is large, if capacity is full, if most passengers will miss connections, and if the receiving airport is congested, the first come, first served queue discipline is easily sacrificed for getting a higher-priority plane off the ground. Some planes are clearly more important than others. But when they are equal, the airport adheres to the first come, first served discipline. This is because airports jointly agree to advertise their service with respect to volume of landings and takeoffs per hour. Volume is insensitive to specific planes. Passing on the delay does not detract from volume, so airports are happy to do it.

Dentists don't have such a luxury. They have no foundation from which they can prioritize clients, except for emergencies, since all clients are equal. The homophily principal operates here as well: dentists get patients mainly through referral. People refer people who are similar to them; consequently, most patients at most practices share the same social status. Dentists cannot, therefore, make strategic decisions about which patients to burn very easily.[5] Nor do cashiers at grocery stores have the luxury of deciding whom to serve first. All clients arrive equal, whatever they are buying. On the other hand, sales clerks at fancy department stores can make guesses about expected purchase volume and allocate attention to customers who seem likely to make substantial contributions to their monthly sales record.

Queue Discipline in the Lobby

Doormen are stuck in the middle, somewhere between clerks in high-status retail shops and dentists. For doormen, one line of argument insists that all clients are equal, or at least that all tenants are equal. This is the dental model, net of emergencies. Another line of argument insists that delivery people, who have schedules to keep, FedEx carriers who need a signature, and Chinese food deliverers with food quickly getting cold deserve quick attention. This is the high-end clerk model—some clients have queue priority. Certainly, delivery people are not happy about waiting for service, and they have the capacity to exert some structural power over residents and doormen.[6] Serving delivery people first carries some risk since waiting for service is not a skill that the people for whom the doorman works—the building tenants—have either. Typically, they are people who in other walks of life make others wait for service. So a final line of argument is that not all tenants are equal. And the reality is that some tenants appear to the doormen to be either more demanding or more important than other tenants. This is in fact the case. But it is not advertised.

Against this confusing background, if everyone arrives at the same time, the doorman has to respond in crisis mode. Decisions have to be made about priority. Some clients cannot be immediately served. If four events arrive at the same time, three have to wait. It is a simple reality. And throughout, congestion is likely to become worse. This is because arrivals arrive without respect to queues. So they are as likely to arrive when the doorman is busy as when he is free. This experience of managing the competing demands of clients induces stress. The experience of stress is heightened because unlike our relationship with cashiers at stores or even our dentist, tenants and doormen are stuck together in long iterative sequences of service, often stretching out for years. The repetition of small tasks for tenants, who are both socially distant and close at the same time, creates additional problems for doormen. They cannot prioritize their tenants' demands by ignoring a food or dry-cleaning

delivery, since the materials brought to the building are going to another tenant. Consequently, while they have to enforce queue discipline, they cannot easily commit to the specific priority scheme they adopt. The schemes are constantly changing in relation to the specific tenants who need service.

Doormen face problems of enforcing queue discipline since clients with different priority are likely to arrive at the same time. While Peter was being interviewed, for example, a Chinese food delivery arrived at the door. Many doormen allocate food deliveries high priority in the queue, since delays result in cold food and unhappy tenants. Delays also keep outsiders in the lobby, and this is something doormen do not want, since they have to attend to the outsider during his or her sojourn. In this case, though, the food was brought to the wrong address. After the mistake was taken care of, Peter said:

> She [the individual who ordered the food] is not in this building and telephoned someone somewhere outside. It was 9530 instead of 5530 [phone numbers], so this lady is telling me, "What are you talking about? I didn't order any Chinese food." That is another thing that always happens. They will screw up in a restaurant, so when you come here, you call the wrong person. They get angry with you because you called them and it is not for them. I didn't screw up—they screwed up. You see it gets so crazy, and one thing in this job is you can't panic. You could when it gets busy, have five guys standing here with all deliveries, the phone will be ringing, you will have a cab pull up, you know it will get really hectic. Most buildings have two doormen. Now I do the job of like two or three guys. I handle the street and whatever deliveries come in; I'm constantly running around, unless it's slow like this.

Continuing, he describes how he enforces queue discipline when clients pile up on one another at the same time. First come, first served rules are quickly violated; the inside of the building is managed first, then the outside, unless…the client is an old lady!

> I have the experience; another guy will be like, "What do I do?" The phone will be ringing, a cab will pull up, groceries coming in, Chinese food, and you['re] like, "Well, what do I do first?" But I got it down; I know what to do first. The cab will have to wait because I have no business in the street, anyway, my objective is right here. It can get so hectic, believe me, you wouldn't be able to handle it. You don't have the experience. It can get so crazy, but I'm used to it already; I mean, it's a piece of cake. You know what I mean? In other words, I'll concentrate on the most important thing first, if I see an old lady pull up in a cab, actually I'm going to help her first before I help the kid.

Eamon describes his attempts at enforcing queue discipline with clients who are often difficult to control. Here the situation is radically different from airplanes queuing on runways or patients in a dental clinic. Instead of passive clients waiting to be served, doormen often contend with active clients content to serve themselves, if they think it is needed.

> You try to line up things, and sometimes some people just want to jump out of the line and do it on their own. So then they complicate it for you because you have to slow that person down or you have to stop that person running into the building because he can't just run into the building. First you are going to have to find out that he is running and then you have to find out why. So in the meantime, he slows you down because there are other

people also, and they may come before him, and until you get them answered to their situation, you can get involved in four or five other things. So you try and keep it in order, what I want, keep it fair.

It is not always possible to line things up neatly and keep them ordered, especially when the things lined up are people with their own programs and expectations. In all of these cases, doormen try to solve problems posed by congestion that are exacerbated by simultaneous arrivals of clients, who from competing first principles demand to be served first. In some cases, the demands are illegitimate. In others, the problem of competing legitimate demands is quite common. Whether they are illegitimate or legitimate does not really change the experience for the doormen, since they still have to manage the stress of trying to accomplish too many things at once. Nor does their self-understanding of the job always provide great assistance in making decisions about how to proceed, although it helps eliminate one class of events as competing for priority—visitors and guests.

The Guest Problem

…Most doormen report that the first priority is to provide security. Fundamentally, this involves managing the relationship between the inside and the outside of the building. Strangers who arrive with a clear function—delivering food, laundry—can be screened quickly. Most doormen see the same delivery people day in and day out, so the screen can be as quick as a glance. On the other hand, those strangers who arrive without a clear function need to be screened more carefully. The screening takes time, but it is critically important, for a primary risk that doormen face is that someone they allow into the building breaches security. While exceptionally rare, if such an event were to occur, the doorman could easily lose his job. Doormen have strong reasons, then, to be naturally suspicious. As a general rule, if a stranger claims to need to visit a tenant, the tenant has to be contacted and the legitimacy of the visit confirmed. Some tenants prefer such contact. Others find it intrusive and want their guests to be allowed to visit them without having to be screened and then announced at the door. Doormen have to know which tenants have which preference, and consequently, for some, they need to make decisions about who to let in without screening on the spot, a decision based on the appearance and demeanor of the visitor.

Ironically, the tenants most concerned about their safety and most likely, therefore, to insist that their visitors are screened are the least likely to have visitors whose appearance (to the doormen or other tenants) might generate suspicion. Such ironies are common in many settings. For example, those most concerned about contracting AIDS are those who are at the least risk (since their concern translates into behaviors that would protect them from HIV acquisition). Likewise, those most concerned about being mugged are the least likely to put themselves in situations (dark lonely streets late at night, the subway after 2:00 A.M., and so on) where mugging is most likely. Since the least traditional tenants are the most likely to prefer less intrusion and the most likely to have less traditional visitors who don't "look so good," doormen have to rely on instinct as they confront the decision whether or not to call the tenant, and the decision has to be a snap decision. They need to read the signals that the visitor emits very quickly, in terms of the specific person he or she is claiming to visit.

It is widely reputed that doormen are less likely to admit blacks to a building than they are to admit whites. The real test of this hypothesis would be an audit study, but the sense is widespread enough to try to understand how such a situation could arise. Because doormen are recruited from within ethnic networks, they are less likely

to be black than expected by chance. While not necessarily overtly racist, the fact that doormen tend to be white creates the possibility that they systematically make access to their buildings harder for blacks than for whites. This is the simplest explanation. It is also the least likely. More likely is the idea that others perceive this to be the case, simply because doormen are exercising the preferences that their tenants have as well as making snap decisions where tenant preferences do not provide sufficient guidance. That the former exercise (doing what tenants want) is purely innocent is not the case, however, since doormen work to shape their tenants' preferences when they can. Jacob describes one such situation in detail:

> You also adjust your work to the personal requirement of the client. I'll give you an example, one tenant, a couple of them—it's not one—a couple of them [are] extremely strict. They want exactly that you call up; if they say "yes," they can go up [based on] who that person is, then you can let that person enter. But then there are other tenants who are very upset if you [call them; they say,] "Don't bother me—just let them up!" Now you notice, let's say two different people come and you stop one, ask where he is going, to find out if he can go to the strict person...so he has to stay there. In the meantime, [here] comes another person who's going to a different apartment where they don't want you to wait and they don't want you to bother—"Just let him in."...I would just let him up. Think about the guys who come five times a day to the same apartment: you don't have to ask; you have to send him up. Now, when you send this guy up...the first person [says,] "How come you didn't...How come you stopped me?"
>
> I had a situation where one asshole thought because her color—her skin

color is...that was a black person—that's why I let the other person in and it has nothing to do [with it], and I told her, "Because the other person is going to a different apartment and the tenant in that apartment [has] different ways, different requirements for the doorman." He wants me to work with him in a particular way and the person knew I couldn't force him to work, that's why. [So, the second person said,] "NO, I'M GOING IN." "No, you are not going in even if I have to stop you, take you from the building, you are not going to go up." You know, you go through this kind of stuff, sometimes you have to be hardcore, maybe any visitor, there are people, no, they are going to here and maybe you are going to there. They are not going to go into the building, so I will stop the elevator. I will put my hand into the door....[T]he point is that you have the rules, and you also know how tenants want it. So you find the rights within the rules [that] you will adjust to that client, to the person.

Here, the consolidation of race and tenant preferences (and perhaps the doorman's preferences as well) serves to block access to minorities, while appearing to provide unfettered access to white visitors. The collective cognitive experience—intended by none—will be one of inequality. In this case, Jacob follows his tenant's preference. It so happens that the tenant with the strict call policy invited a black friend over who happened to arrive at the same time that a tenant with an open-access policy had a white friend arrive. The opposite outcome is equally likely, but the racial context within which guests interpret actions ensures that this alternative scenario will not be imbued with the same meaning or even recounted later in an equivalent way. Queuing dynamics make such congestion events likely. The

black guest was not discriminated against, but it appears as if she was. If these events happen repeatedly, the collective experience is one of discrimination, even if each micro-event has a non-discriminatory foundation.

Because the risks to other tenants and to their job are considered high should a criminal enter the building, one would think that doormen would simply always call tenants to check on visitors. But the real risk of malfeasance is low, and the one guaranteed thing that doormen confront is the constancy of contact with tenants. Doormen have to see their tenants every day—and they have to be attentive to their needs and wishes. It is this attentiveness that allows them to construe their jobs as professional—that is, as involving the capacity to make substantive distinctions. Of course, it is not easy to stick to a formal system, for example, constantly screening visitors, when one knows that this is not what their tenant wants. Nor is it professional. Only when doormen work to rule, that is, come to define their relationship with tenants as an employee-employer relationship (as versus a client-server relationship), do they stick to formal systems. An irony is that working to rule, by sacrificing their claim to professional status, generates formally fair treatment but yields substantively irrational outcomes.

Tenants are always the clients, no matter how old, cranky, or experienced in the role (e.g., with fixed preferences) they are. So doormen cannot easily burn one tenant for another. This means that some priority systems will not work. At the same time, doormen cannot afford to burn other service providers, since most service providers, from the local restaurant to national postal services (UPS, FedEx, U.S. mail, etc.) preserve route integrity by sending the same people out on the same route day after day. Consequently, doormen develop long-term relationships with their servers, and they cannot afford to alienate them. Against this constraint, the first clients to get the cold

TABLE 31.6. Shifts by How Many of Tenants' Visitors Do You Like

Shift	All	Most	Some	Few	None	Total
Day	16 (28.6%)	20 (35.7%)	15 (26.8%)	3 (5.4%)	2 (3.6%)	56 (100%)
Swing	28 (28.6%)	39 (39.8%)	23 (23.5%)	7 (7.1%)	1 (1.0%)	98 (100%)
Night	3 (30.0%)	2 (20.0%)	2 (20.0%)	3 (30.0%)	0	10 (100%)
Multiple	11 (26.8%)	16 (39.0%)	10 (24.4%)	4 (9.8%)	0	41 (100%)
Total	58 (28.3%)	77 (37.6%)	50 (24.4%)	17 (8.3%)	3 (1.5%)	205 (100%)

shoulder when work gets stressful are visitors. As Rajah says:

> The other doormen...they earn a lot, but they [have] a double standard. When they are not tenants, they are not nice to them. Why, because they do not live here. The tenants...excuse my words...they [the other doormen] kiss [the tenants'] ass. I am not like that....I am like that the whole year round. I am nice, to everyone.

Because they are more likely to burn tenants' visitors (even the more regular guests) than tenants or delivery people, it is not surprising to discover that of all the people they come into contact with in an average day, visitors are the least liked. Whereas over 80% of doormen report liking all or most of their tenants, far fewer report liking their tenants' guests. Compared to supervisors, delivery people, coworkers, and maintenance workers, guests receive the "lowest" approval rating, even considering that a non-trivial proportion of doormen actively dislike their supervisors. The relationship between liking tenants' guests and shifts is also of some interest, reported in table 31.6. It is easier to burn people you don't like. No doubt, the fact that guests feel ignored by doormen contributes to behaviors on their part (walking in, being rude) that later come to provide the justification for the burn. This is an example of a self-fulfilling prophecy, where sets of beliefs about outcomes shape behaviors that induce the outcome initially believed in.[7]

It makes sense that guests are the least likely to be liked of all people whom doormen interact with. They come only occasionally, and they have little motivation to be polite. If unknown, they must be treated with suspicion and the legitimacy of their visit ascertained. And they are vulnerable. Unable to independently discover whether or not their host is in, they are at the mercy of doormen, who can rationalize slow service by reference to security concerns. And this is why many tenants try to circumvent the doorman by insisting that their visitors be allowed to pass without a security check. Here, there is a duality difficult to escape. On the one hand, the special request allows the doorman to assume a professional role, where professional is defined by the particular treatment of others. On the other hand, by making a special request of this nature, tenants further reduce the opportunity for their doorman to demonstrate that he is doing his job. Consequently, they are more likely than others to perceive him as idle or unhelpful at precisely the moments that service is required.

Tenant Perceptions

It is not uncommon for tenants to talk about their doormen. In fact, since they see them each time they come home, or at least expect to see them each time they come home, who was on the door and what they were or were not doing are routine topics of conversation. This is true even if the tenants claim to not really care at all. Lori, for example, notices:

> At night the doorman is not as available. Occasionally the door will be locked and you need to key yourself in because he is taking a break or getting food. I am not really sure what he is doing. During the day there is someone consistently there, but at nighttime, especially late at night, like around the hours of seven to nine. I am not really sure what they are doing. It does not bother me. Like I said, I do not need someone to open the door for me. I do not mind having to let myself in, but I just wonder, "What are they doing? Why are they not there for like a two-hour period of time?" I come home and he is not there. And then one of my roommates will come home and she will mention something to me about the doorman not being there. And I'll just be, "Well where the heck are they?"

Tenants talk about their doormen with their partner, and if they have no partner, they will talk about them with their friends and neighbors. The talk frequently turns on a mix of wonder and complaint. Tenants wonder where the doormen are when they are not on the door. And they wonder why their doorman never seems to be around....They wonder what they do during their shift, since most of the time they seem to be doing absolutely nothing. And, of course, all of these seemingly innocent thoughts veil complaints about the apparent mismatch between presence and service. As noted above, the mismatch is driven by the stochastic nature of the work experience—the fact that clients can and do arrive with heterogeneous problems all at once, so as often as not when an individual needs them, they are busy.

The fact that Lori misses her doorman between seven and nine has more to do with the scheduling of the dinner hour than congestion per se, but the fact of congestion implies a second consequence that is of equal import. Doormen will be idle much of the time. In fact, they are likely to be idle most of their shift unless they are assigned (as they often are) to other tasks only indirectly associated with their main job—for example, polishing brass in the lobby. And so, most of the time where tenants see their doorman, the doorman appears to have nothing to do.

The deepest irony is that tenants are most likely to observe doormen either when they have absolutely nothing to do or when they are extremely busy. In the first case, they can only conclude that the doormen don't really do anything. In the second case, they are likely to feel slighted because their position in the queue was "not respected" and conclude that the doormen are "doing nothing" or "inattentive to their specific needs." A critical element of the job of being a doorman involves changing these perceptions. Oddly, in operations research, little thought seems to be given to understanding how servers shape clients. In sociology, by contrast, there is much interest in considering how server systems shape client behavior, for example, in workplace and laboratory studies. For those interested in the dynamics of professionalization, however, little attention has been paid to how claims to professional status shape client preferences and thus mitigate (by inducing distinction in client preferences) potential congestion.

The problem that doormen face with respect to tenant perception is especially vivid because doormen as servers are in a different relationship to their tenants as clients than, for example, airlines are to their clients. Whereas airlines can burn specific individuals scheduled on a specific flight by not passing on the delay to the aggregate group of travelers, doormen do not have such a luxury. If they are burned, passengers may not return to the airline, it is true, but if all airlines do the same thing, which they do, passengers will eventually find their way back. The problem that doormen have is that their clients will return, whether they burn them or not. And they will return right away. Worst of all, when they do return, because most of the time doormen have nothing to do besides their job getting the door, watching the door, securing the lobby, and so on—the client is likely to observe them doing "nothing," thereby vividly reminding them of the previous "injustice."

There are a few things that doormen can do to shift tenant perceptions. These can be considered "coping mechanisms" insofar as they are things that doormen do to cope with server problems. The simplest thing is to try to manage the overall perception of the tenant by being attentive. This can involve the simplest of interactions—saying "Good morning"—or can stretch over into overtly obsequious service. Whether tenants want it or not, doormen will greet them when they come in and out. As Peter says:

> That is [a] second part of the job, be nice. You must not be downtrodden to people; you have to be bold and nice, and tell them, "Good morning," "Good afternoon," "Good evening," whatever; regardless of how many times they come in here, that's what you have to say— "Good evening"—every time. You have one man comes here five times a day, that's what you have to say. One man tells me, he says, "You don't have to tell me good morning." I say, "Well, that's my job, I'm sorry." That's what it takes [for] me to do.

When they are not otherwise engaged, doormen will thus proactively initiate contact with their tenants and try to engage them in conversation—usually about the weather, but also about the day that they will have, the building, or the traffic. And most doormen report that most of their tenants are more than happy to talk. So doormen initiate these conversations, whether they really enjoy it or not. As noted above, the most common topic is the weather. On a daily basis, more than 70% of the doormen report talking about the weather with their tenants. Most doormen spend so much time talking about the weather that they make sure they have the latest information before starting their shift. Angel says:

> The first thing I do, I am not even at work, I'm just getting ready for work at home. I turn on the weather station and I listen to the forecasts for the day, the week, whatever I can. That way I get to work and I can say, "It's going to rain this afternoon, but clear up at night," or whatever the news is. So that's my first job. It's pretty lame when the doorman doesn't know the weather, or if he doesn't know if a certain person is home.

Or more bluntly, Richie says:

> I keep good track of the weather, the time, the traffic, everything. So when you're going out, you call me and say, "Hey, how's the traffic?" It's the little things like that. For example, we are not supposed to carry radios, but I always carry my little Bloomberger, which just tells me what I need to know. I think it's fucked up for someone to ask a doorman, "You know if it's going to rain today?" and the doorman say[s], "I don't know." I mean, you've got to know the fucking weather. Some of these other guys are fucking lazy, like they won't even stick their fucking head outside so they know if it's raining or not; if you are going to be a doorman, you have to know what it's [the weather] going to do and what it's doing now.

Second on the topic parade is sports (68.8%). More than half of our doormen report daily conversations with tenants on both building matters and current events. After September 11, doormen, like all others in the city, talked constantly about the World Trade Center, the victims, and the fate of the city. Doormen can talk about some kinds of contemporary events, but not all. The weather, news, traffic, and the state of the building provide generic elements of quick conversation that are stripped of content with respect to the revelation of personal views but signal an availability to be of service. In contrast, some topics are off the hit parade; under this rubric can be found the bigger issues of the day—politics, religion, cultural values, and so on. Tenants utilize the conversation openings provided by doormen in turn to ask for favors, to inform their doorman that they are expecting a package, dry cleaning, and whatnot. By initiating conversation when they are idle, doormen connect with tenants that they know will, sooner or later, discover them too busy to help. In this sense, the idle conversation of the lobby serves both as a depository, but more critically, as a signaling device, operating on tenants to shift their perception from "doing nothing" to "available for service." Doormen successful in effecting such switches have only to discipline tenants into developing preferences for specific services. This is more difficult.

Too Much Talk

The problem with appearing ready to serve as a strategic deployment against the perception of idleness is that at times the conversation that ensues is onerous and a distraction from other aspects of the job. As Hans says about overly voluble tenants, "Outside [i.e., as a projection, not outside the building] we can be friendly and talk, but we have to do our job first." Likewise, Felix describes unwanted contact with his tenants as "intense at times. People do get on my nerves. The hardest thing is trying not to show them that you are getting bothered."

In some instances, tenants spend long periods talking to doormen. More typical on the swing or night shift than the day shift, doormen recognize that they are not really being asked to "talk, but to just listen." They often see themselves as unpaid

psychotherapists. Elbert describes one situation, of many:

> [A tenant asked if she could just stay with me], if I don't mind that she would stay right here and just talking to me because she has to spill her guts to somebody because it's craziness what happened to her, and then you listen and you let them talk, and if they trust you with problems of their personal life, it can be helpful, like a psychologist, I guess…you let them talk, and listen. And it, and it's fine sometimes, so they may be with you for a few hours.

About one old man who has no friends in the building, Billy says:

> I tell him to come down and talk to me if he is lonely and just wants to shoot the breeze, that I don't have much to say but that I am a good listener. So he comes down once or twice a shift and we talk a few minutes.

In some cases, routine small talk creates priority problems when events that need attention do arise. Tenants arriving with groceries may find their doorman engaged in conversation and consequently unable to get to the door; and doormen who use conversation to signal availability often feel unable to extricate themselves just when they want to. As Radzac says:

> See, like now, I'm talking to you about sports or something and this one comes in and I have to give her a wink or something just to tell her, "This one talks a lot; I'm going to be right there." So it's like all the time I'm saying one thing to you and another to her.

These winks can become encoded into specific relationships that tenants have with doormen. One tenant describes how, because he speaks Spanish with one of his doormen, they have developed a code largely inaccessible to other tenants. Using a reference to the TV show *Naked City*, which ends, "There are eight million stories in the Naked City. This has been one of them," his doorman says, "Another story [in Spanish]," when Richard sees him trapped in one of many long conversations. Such "special relationships" that doormen have with their tenants are not unique, although they are experienced as unique by the tenants, who tend to believe that their doormen are especially close to them, not thinking necessarily that they must be close to others as well. The successful doorman develops such special relationships with most of his tenants. The perception that doormen have special relationships extends beyond the relationship. Tenants in buildings where their doormen have worked for many years almost invariably feel that their building is unique. They are thus surprised to find that this is the case in most buildings. That tenants who talk with doormen feel that their relationship is special says something about the capacity of doormen to project closeness, despite the status differences that are always present. . . .

More Movement and Less Talk

The problem is that talk is cheap, as the saying goes. On average, though, neither small talk nor in-depth conversation with a few needy tenants is sufficient to counter by itself tenant perceptions that their doormen have too little do to or that they ignore them when tenants need them. To shift these perceptions, doormen generate services that they can do for tenants in their free time. They may appear to jump up to hand them their laundry, take an extra trip up the elevator to personally deliver a package, or rush outside to watch their tenants' car to make sure that when

parked in front of the building, it will not receive a ticket. These small services are a constant feature of the workday for most doormen. Doormen do not articulate that they engage in these services to change tenant perceptions. Rather, they talk in terms of providing professional service. However articulated, these services often tend to go unnoticed by tenants, who perceive them as either building policy or simply the way that their doorman is (except around Christmas, when the prevailing rhetoric shifts to allow tenants to interpret small services as non-normative and motivated by the upcoming bonus). Even outside the Christmas season, the provision of small extra service is not always successful. Overtly obsequious service may backfire in some cases. Donald, for example, reports how in one case he "heard one of the tenants speak to another tenant, and I guess maybe I was too polite or something, she said, 'It's like having an English butler working here.'"

In describing what other doormen do, some doormen adopt a cynical attitude. Atzan describes coworkers in his building in relatively uncharitable terms:

> Certain doormen do certain different things for tenants also. Go the extra mile. You know, feed the plants, feed the cats, walk the dogs, wash windows. You'd be surprised what some of these doormen do just to make that extra dollar. It's a hustle, everything's a hustle, and this is one of them.

As noted above, this is a view that most tenants share on the approach of the Christmas season, when tenants read doorman behavior as bonus seeking. Doormen, on the other hand, report little seasonal change in their behavior. They are wrong; their behavior does change. But tenants are also wrong. Doorman behavior (increased attentiveness) changes not as an explicit attempt to bolster the bonus but because of very subtle structural changes in the temporality of work. As the holiday season nears, the pace and intensity of work increases. In the weeks before Christmas, the volume of packages increases, and even a slight change in the number of packages received for any given day creates new queuing problems for doormen. And longer queues make it more likely that they will be busy when tenants need something. Therefore, doormen are likely to compensate as best they can when they are free, so they take the time to deliver the packages, greet tenants when they enter the lobby, and initiate conversation. Many tenants perceive this as a rather obvious attempt to bolster their bonus. In contrast, the doormen see this additional service as necessary to compensate for the busy times of the day.... .

Service and talk are the simplest strategies that doormen employ to shift tenant perceptions that they both do nothing and are unhelpful when needed. In reality, doormen cannot control the flow of events that enter the lobby, and so they are bound, like any server system, to be unable to serve everyone at the same time. This fact creates stress, since they have to make quick decisions about who to serve—and the priority schemes that they utilize will make some tenants unhappy. If they were always busy, tenants could become disciplined into adjusting to a first come, first served model, assuming that the door—like the pizza parlor, the grocery store, and the dentist's office—will get to clients when it is their turn. But because doormen are often seen without anything to do, tenants become frustrated that they are not available when they need them. The main "weapon" that doormen have to counter negative perceptions that arise from a misreading of the nature of the server system they are embedded in is to shape client preferences.

Grocery stores, dentists, airports, and other server systems also experiment with shaping preferences. For example, airlines develop systems for rewarding frequent

fliers with shorter queues, and grocery stores induce different shopping patterns by linking specific servers to the number of items purchased. Consumers of those services make choices about their own behaviors based on the incentive structures provided by the server systems. In the absence of express lanes, people are less likely to purchase just one or two items in the grocery store. Since the average cost of each item in a small (less than ten-item) cart is higher than in a large cart, stores create incentives to attract small cart shoppers. These incentives, over time, shift purchasing behaviors.

In the same way, doormen try to develop over time their tenants' specific preferences for services. If they are successful, they gain some control over the temporality of their day; while they do not necessarily reduce stress, they do lay the groundwork for a claim of professional status. And this proves exceptionally important in the management of the lobby. Not all doormen are successful and some strategies fail. Shaping tenant preferences requires that doormen distinguish tenants on multiple dimensions. If doormen fail to distinguish tenants—that is, induce distinction—they can only treat them as equivalents, who are therefore subject to the presence (or absence) of the same formal rules. Thus, failure is first and foremost associated with a commitment to universalism and unwillingness to be particularistic with respect to conversation, service, greetings, and attention. In this sense, doormen who work to rule will fail. Another way to say this is that doormen must in relation to tenants renounce being an employee and claim professional status. The obvious tension is that, rhetorically, one aspect of professionalism entails a commitment to universalism. For example, doctors should treat all persons, whatever their capacity to pay for services. Likewise, one would consider lawyers who do a bad job for some kinds of people (those who cannot pay, those whom they do not like, etc.) unprofessional.

But this is simply a rhetorical structure, for the salient indicator of professionalism is the capacity to act substantively against the demands of blind formal application of rules. Doormen commit to the professional norm to serve, but this commitment entails inducing differences among tenants so as to serve them better.[8] When doormen fail to differentiate across tenants, they are likely to develop negative attitudes toward them. This is often followed by exit, for doormen who seek protection from discretion must work to rule, an experience deeply frustrating for both tenants and doormen.

Induction of Distinction from the Little Things

When guests arrive, doormen can hold them in the lobby and phone up to the apartment for confirmation that the guests are invited. Alternatively, doorman can send the guests on their way, phoning as soon as they step into the elevator. Or they can just send them up unannounced. When packages arrive, doormen can hold them in the back, bring them up, phone ahead, or keep them at the front desk. Videos can travel upstairs with or without warning or be held at the front desk. If cars come early to pick tenants up, doormen can call up to tell the tenant that their car has arrived or wait until the scheduled time for departure before calling. Dry cleaning can be laid out in public or stored in the back. When children come down to play, doormen can watch them or let them be. If while the parents are gone their teenagers had a party, the doorman can tell the parents or not. These small things and hundreds of others should seemingly be inconsequential. And in most instances they are. But they need not be. If unexpected guests are announced over the phone while they are downstairs, tenants who don't feel like socializing with them are caught at home and could feel trapped by the unexpected visit. Better for some would be prior warning that Mr. X and Ms. Y were

on their way up. Tenants may want to avoid tipping their delivery person; if so, doormen might hold food and videos until after the delivery. Some parents may want the doormen to watch their children when they are playing out front; others may find that intrusive. The doormen do not care which preferences their tenants have, only that they have preferences and they know what they are. If tenants do not have preferences, doormen help them acquire them. As Tito, who works on the swing shift in a small building on the Upper East Side, says:

> Right away. I try to ask what they want. Should I call after I send people up or before? What about their kids' friends? Do they just go up, or do I call? Relatives, people they always want to see, the whole works. If they don't care, I tell them some people I call up, others want them to go straight. If they don't know what they want, then I tell them what I like. For me, if I never seen the people before, I call up when they are in the elevator. If I know them and they come a lot, I call when they are in the lobby so they don't have to go up. But this is their choice, see. I get them to make a choice.

Training tenants to have preferences is interactive. Doormen may bring packages up to tenants and ask, "Would you rather I just held it for you downstairs?" Likewise, if kids come down to play, the doormen may call up to the apartment and say, "Hi, Mrs. X, this is the front desk. It's no problem for me to keep an eye on the kids. You want me to make sure they don't get off the sidewalk?" Repeatedly, doormen will work to find just that mix of services that tenants want. When they find it, they stick to it, often reminding the tenants that this is in fact what they want. As Bob says:

> I always say, "I got your package safe in the back just the way you want it." I want them to know I am thinking about them.

Not leaving their package around on the front table 'cause they don't want others looking at it or whatever.

These little tricks of the trade provide the framework for inducing tenants to have and communicate preferences. The induction of distinction across tenants is important not because it provides better service—most of the distinctions are trivial enough to be within tenants' zone of indifference—but because it provides a solution to the management of time in the lobby. Or more precisely, because it begins to solve some of the problems associated with the experience of time—of too much and too little to do, and tenant perceptions thereof.

Overview

People do not often find themselves thinking or talking about all the people whose job it is to think deeply about how many people to put to work in some specific way in order to sufficiently provide for one service or another without creating too much redundancy. But there are a lot of those people and they are all trained in operations research. In operations research, such problems are commonplace and certainly complicated enough, once the possibility that the structure of service systems will shape client preferences is established.[9] One reason these problems are so difficult is that people are not so easily divided up. If a doorman is a little too busy and the busy period is random across the shift he works (rather than bunched in such a way as to allow hiring a part-time assistant), the only solution is to build in excess redundancy by hiring another doorman. Because employees are expensive, managers of server systems try to minimize the number of servers at work at any one time. This impacts the doorman's

world, for doormen, like other service providers, struggle with the simple fact that clients arrive sporadically and with heterogeneous needs. This creates moments of intense activity and long periods of boredom and inactivity. But here ends the comparison to most other server systems, for the doorman's clients appear and reappear constantly. It is the clients who are the inescapable aspect of the doorman's daily work life. Because their needs are generally small, tenants often cannot understand why they are not met, especially since they see their doorman doing nothing most of the time. At the same time, while an enormous social gulf separates doormen from tenants, tenants are by virtue of the smallness of the services provided and the constancy of interaction very close to their doormen. This closeness is in part produced by doormen, who work to induce preferences for services and interactions with their tenants as part of their claim to professional status. But the closeness is also simply a product of the intense scrutiny that comes with serving as a border between the inside and the outside of the building. No tenant can escape for long without his or her preferences for friends, foods, movies, wines, and other services being noticed and recorded, and if absent, induced....

NOTES

1. This sentiment could arise, though, because as Bob (a doorman on the West Side) says, "When you wait on rich people, you start to become a snob yourself."
2. Midway through five quotes, the reader may be feeling bored by the repetition of sentiment. Books are, as Sudhir Venkatesh tells me, not like movies, where directors can shape audience mood, since readers, unlike filmgoers, can just skip sections when the going gets slow. I take the chance here because the experience of boredom is

so pronounced that it is difficult to convey without, in some sense, boring the reader.

3. Klienrock et al., *Communication Nets;* Klienrock et al., *Queuing Systems;* Cox and Smith et al., *Queues.*

4. In many systems where congestion dynamics are common, clients may have multiple strategies at their disposal. To use Hirschman's terms, in *Exit, Voice, Loyalty,* they can exit, express voice, or remain loyal. Passengers on airplanes are not allowed the exit option while the flight is in the air, but they can select another airline for their next flight. Drinkers can always find a bar less busy if the place gets too crowded. But tenants have few realistic exit options. Consequently, they either complain (voice) or express loyalty....The typical tenant response is loyalty.

5. They can, of course, make decisions on the basis of treatment need, sacrificing routine care for emergency treatment. And they can differentially see patients whose treatment regime involves a long process that is temporally sensitive. But these are changes to the priority service rule that operate on the margins. Readers with dentist phobia who may feel that they are doing others a favor by making appointments and then canceling them at the last moment, with excuses that make undergraduates whose grandmothers die at an impossible rate just around exam period look creative, should continue to feel bad, since dentists, like airplanes, typically assume cancellations (the rate varies by practice) and so overbook.

6. Doorman cannot easily justify serving delivery people before clients without recourse to the rhetoric of security. If they do not justify priority service to delivery people on the basis of security, they have to try to claim that serving delivery people first is a contribution to the collective good. After all, one could argue, each tenant would prefer that the other tenants waited so that their Chinese food would arrive hot. But, as with all collective goods, each tenant cares little about the temperature of their neighbor's food and would prefer to be served first, all things being equal.

7. The most famous self-fulfilling prophecy in the sociological literature is the Pygmalion in the classroom study, described in Rosenthal and Jacobson, *Pygmalion in the Classroom.* Here, teachers were told that some students would experience an intellectual blossoming in the subsequent year on the basis of a new assessment test. But the test was simply a standard IQ test, and students were allocated to experimental and control groups at random. Not surprisingly, those students expected to have a blossoming increased overall IQ by more than thirty points in grades 1–3. Teacher expectations about the blossoming led them to attend to students differently. More disturbing than IQ gains—which reveals much about the plasticity of IQ—were teachers' subjective assessments of students, as curious, troublesome, difficult, and so on. Teachers subsequently rated previous high achievers who were not identified as bloomers as disruptive, needy, and troublesome. These students internalized the negative sentiments and began to become less attached to school.

8. This brings to light a more general problem.... Is it the case that in all interacting social systems—especially those characterized by formal hierarchy—particularism in practice will emerge as a key "coping" strategy? This is certainly the case, for example, in graduate student training, even in the presence of unions. Without pronouncing from on high, one can safely say that where possible, humans will work hard to preserve substantive rationality through the exercise of discretion. The willingness and capacity to exercise judgment is at the same time a key element of professional status.

9. This possibility was considered previously. A simple example is that small-item lanes in grocery stores shape client behavior insofar as they strive, if close, to stay under the ten- or fifteen-item limit for the express lane. For doormen, known congestion at some times

of the day, perhaps when the mail carrier is scheduled to arrive, may motivate tenants to report their problems either earlier or later in the day.

REFERENCES

Cox, D. R., Walter L. Smith et al. 1961. *Queues.* London: Methuen.

Hirschman, Albert. 1972. *Exit, Voice, Loyalty: Responses to Declines in Firms, Organizations, and States.* Cambridge, MA: Harvard University Press.

Kleinrock, Leonard, and Richard Gail. 1996. *Queueing Systems: Problems and Solutions.* New York: Wiley.

Kleinrock, Leonard, and Karreman Mathematics Research Collection. 1964. *Communication Nets: Stochastic Message Flow and Delay.* New York: McGraw-Hill.

———. *Queueing Systems.* 1975. New York: Wiley.

Rosenthal, Robert, and Lenore Jacobson. 1968. *Pygmalion in the Classroom: Teacher Expectation and Pupils' Intellectual Development.* New York: Rinehart and Winston.

32

TAMARA MOSE BROWN

MOBILITY FOR THE NONMOBILE: CELL PHONES, TECHNOLOGY, AND CHILDCARE

from *Raising Brooklyn* (2011)

In her book *Raising Brooklyn,* Tamara Mose Brown reports on her three years of hanging out with Caribbean child-care workers. She explains in this selection the significance that cell phones have taken in the daily lives of these women, including their relationships with their employers.

Cell Phones

I first came to realize that West Indian childcare providers relied heavily on their cell phones when I gained entry into their social group.[1] I knew that I had achieved this status when Rachel, from St. Lucia, began calling me to arrange a meeting place with her and the rest of the sitters I had come to know either in the park or at storytime in the public library. They were no longer waiting to see if I was around at the park; instead they would seek me out by calling while en route to a particular location to see if I would be joining them. At this point, and after reading several field notes, I noticed that almost all childcare providers had a cell phone, something that our technological generation has now taken for granted as a symbol of middle-class and socially networked status.

Sitters used cell phones to combat isolation at work and maintain their personal social networks.[2] ... Using cell phones, they could organize playdates, plan to meet at the public library for storytime, or simply arrange to meet and run errands together. Rachel told me that "all the babysitters carry cell phones," and Carla affirmed, "Oh yeah, all the time. That's what we use [it] for—playdates or you want to go to this park. Especially me and Jennie, we rack up some minutes."

The childcare providers used cell phones in other ways as well. Some were obvious: to call family members back in the islands or in New York, pay bills and transact other business, and stay in contact with employers. Some were not as obvious: the childcare providers were able to socially exclude others from their conversations even in their immediate presence as well as decide whom to interact with over the cell phone through caller identification. In a related vein, I also observed how cell phone users created more restricted social spaces in a public park through their language use and body position while on the phone. This, combined with the fact that many sitters called "back home" from a cell phone during the workday to stay in touch with family members and old friends, helped me explore how the providers might use cell phones to preserve West Indian culture and combat isolation in the workplace while at the same time excluding others.

Parallel Management of Work and Family

The cell phone was important not only to the West Indian providers whom I studied but also the employers of these women, especially the mothers.... The cell phone is in a way similar to the washing machine in its pseudoliberatory effect. Just as the washing machine was seen as cutting down the amount of time needed to wash clothes when in fact it made it possible for women to do more washing and general housework, cell phones, by extending the ability to work from any location at any time, have subjected the mothers of babysitters' charges parallel shifts on which home and work duties can be carried out simultaneously.[3]

West Indian childcare providers similarly carried out overlapping parallel shifts by using the cell phone to contact their own children, either in the United States or back in their homeland, while working in public places, where writing a note or calling on a land line might not be appropriate or possible.

For employers, the parallel management of work and family duties took a variety of forms. One provider, Brenda, told me, "She [the mother, who is a schoolteacher] only calls me if she wants me to do something for her. That's when she'll call me. Like Easter time, now last week, she called me to boil some eggs for her classroom..."

Unsure whether what I had just heard was correct, I asked, "You had to boil the eggs for her classroom work that she has to do?"

"Boil the eggs. She called me and asked me to boil the eggs for her classroom. And she came and picked it up and went back to school." Brenda made it clear from the roll of her eyes that she did not feel she should have to do a task that was part of her employer's teaching job and went beyond the childcare duties originally stipulated in Brenda's job description. The employer managed to provide services for her own job (in this case the Easter activity of decorating eggs) while exploiting Brenda in the process.

Mobile phones have redefined not only employers' workplaces but also the organization of domestic space.[4] Because of the parallel shift, which involves managing home and work responsibilities simultaneously, employers view the accessibility of their childcare provider as a crucial requirement of the job. Some employers go so far as making cell phone access mandatory and state that if need be they will get the provider a cell phone, with certain restrictions on its use. Brenda spoke candidly about these restrictions when I asked how often her employers called during the workday.

"Sometimes, twice, three times, four times for the day," she said.

I asked her, "Was it more in the beginning?"

"First of all they gave me a cell phone when I just started to work. And then he said, the husband said to me, 'Oh, we're giving you that cell phone, but it's only for us to call you.'"

Since I knew that the employer was aware that Brenda had children of her own, I asked Brenda, "So no one else could be in touch with you?"

"I couldn't call my kids from off it," she replied.

For West Indian childcare providers, the possession of a cell phone that made them constantly accessible to their employers but that they could not use on their own behalf equated to a loss of control in their daily routine, but for female employers especially this arrangement was a means of existing "in their [employers'] domestic and work worlds simultaneously."[5] The employer was able to use what Rakow and Navarro have called "remote mothering" techniques, or parenting from a distance, often in public contexts where she would be perceived by other parents, her own family, and others (perhaps co-workers) as being constantly available, through the phone calls, to her children, family, and childcare provider.[6] Providers themselves used remote mothering with their own children. In the field, both employers and employees used cell phones to ensure that children had eaten their food, taken a nap, done their homework, had a successful music, dance, or art lesson, and more generally were behaving properly.

Carla's employer made checking in on the cell phone about her child's behavior a top priority. In a conversation with me about the reasons why her employer called on the cell phone, Carla explained how the employer attempted to pull information throughout the day to determine whether to come home: "She likes to ask what

mood her son is in because her son…I'm not there, but from what I've heard from her and the other sitter, like he'll yell and run around on the floor and act the fool. You know, he thinks she [the mother] did something, you know or whatever. So she always calls every, like, every hour or so to see [imitating the mother] 'What mood is he in? Where is he? How is he doing?' And if I say good…I realize now that if I say, 'Oh yeah, he's in a great mood,' she comes in [meaning home] earlier. So he's always in a great mood." We both laughed. "Regardless of what he's doing?" I asked. Carla continued while pretending to speak to the employer over the cell phone: "Yeah, he's in a great mood, he's outside playing, he's having fun." She then resumed her regular speaking voice after her fooling performance to say, "Regardless of what mood he's in, come home and deal with him yourself…I'm gone." Fielding constant calls from employers who are "checking in" tends to be overlooked as one of the challenges that many childcare providers face.

Several of the sitters I studied had children and families of their own here in New York and in the islands from which they came, and they used the cell phones to handle family responsibilities as much as their employers did. Cell phones, by making it possible for users to be in contact at all times, do not require "nearness as a defining element" and allow for considerable flexibility in connecting with others even over great distances.[7] It is in this context that I place West Indian childcare providers' use of the mobile phone to call their family and friends in the Caribbean.

Calling Back Home

…While the West Indian childcare providers in my study mentioned some of the disadvantages to having a cell phone,…most enjoyed using cell phones to stay in constant touch with relatives and friends in the Caribbean.

When I asked Brenda how often she used her cell phone to call people back home in Grenada, she responded, "Oh Lord, some-times it's bad....Sometimes I run up my phone bill like two hundred, three hundred or something dollars. But this morning, I texted everybody."

Interested in how she used the text messaging function on the cell phone, I repeated, "You texted them?"

"Yes, I texted them to wish them Happy Easter. So I texted everybody, and everybody call me back saying, 'I don't know how to use the text.' I taught them how to do it, so they text me back most the time. I call often," Brenda replied.

"Like every day, would you say?"

"No, maybe twice a week."

"And whom do you talk to back home?"

"Talk to my cousins, my nieces, I have a friend and I talk to him all the time."

Speaking on the cell phone to family and friends was common among the providers, though some of them limited their phone use for this purpose. Rachel, for example, found comfort in knowing that she could keep in contact with her father in St. Lucia, who would give her the latest gossip on friends back home: "Did you hear that this one did this?" But she preferred not to call her dad on her cell phone because he liked so much to keep her up to date on events in St. Lucia that he would speak for too long and raise her phone bill. Likewise, some preferred to use their home land line because their employers paid for the cell phone and they did not feel comfort-able using it to make personal calls when someone else was paying the bill. Jennie told me that when she called her friends and family in Grenada she used her home phone because "I want to feel comfort-able and be able to talk for like an hour." She also said she didn't like other sitters to have her cell phone number: "I don't give too many sitters the phone [number],

but the mother says, 'You can, you can,' so yes, I can give it to sitters who want to contact me for playdates." Carol owned her cell phone but commented, "I don't be on the cell like them other girls...my ears get tired." She even requested no long distance on it because she preferred to pay two dollars for a phone card for fifty-four minutes worth of time to call back home to Trinidad and speak with her husband twice a week.

Cell Phones and the Construction of Representational Space

West Indian childcare providers who used cell phones in public constructed represen-tational space in a variety of ways....For instance, I saw [them] use cell phones while pacing back and forth with strollers to block off areas of the benches that surrounded the open park spaces from other public park users and, in addition, leave diaper bags on a nearby bench to indicate that they were using that space. Sometimes ten to fifteen such strollers and bags were placed along an entire side of the public park benches while the sitters were either using their cell phones or talking with one another while watching their charges.

I remember one morning seeing the strategy of physical self-isolation used by a West Indian babysitter who was sitting down at one of the picnic tables inside a large open park space. Her hair was shoul-der length, black and relaxed straight, with a slim headband pulling the hair away from her face. She wore dark denim pants, a blouse, and a heavy, knitted black sweater. I almost never saw this woman talk to oth-ers in the park, except for other West Indian childcare providers. She sat quietly as she did most mornings and used her cell phone to pay the bills that were stacked in her checkbook—the only time I had ever seen her use the cell phone. This routine of sit-ting by herself to make personal calls on her cell phone was her way of creating a private space within a public place. She indicated through her low tone, limited eye contact, and "bench-sitting" position that, like most individuals who are handling private financial matters, she did not want other people to intrude.

"Cell-yell" was not seen as commonly as the opposite, what I am tempted to call "cell-murmur." West Indian childcare providers typically did not want others to hear their private conversations with family or employers. They considered it insulting to other West Indians to boast about planned trips back to the homeland, since not everyone could afford to take such trips, or about other matters that would be seen to be of no concern to others. Often sitters did not want to fully disclose details about their relationships with their employers to other babysitters. Some tended to communicate to other babysitters that their working relationship was open, honest, and relaxed, though I actually overheard conversations in which the employer was dictating certain directions to the babysitter that would have made the babysitter feel disrespected in front of her peer group. Childcare providers would hide their true working relationships by speaking softly through their cell phones, although I was able to capture some discussions by sitting close enough during my observations. On the other hand, some childcare providers spoke quietly on their cell phones so as to not appear too "friendly" with employers whom they actually did like working for. There seemed to be an unwritten rule among some childcare providers that you shouldn't "like" your employer (when someone spoke positively about her employer, the providers became quiet and did not engage in further conversation, perhaps because of skepticism or denial that someone could possibly have a decent employer), so a provider would speak badly about her employer in public parks but then joke around with her

employer on the cell phone. Other sitters spoke negatively about their employers in the parks and then said some of the most wonderful things about them to me in private. The ambivalence-charged social relations between employer and employee were evidenced through cell phone conversations.

Quiet cell phone use followed not only the West Indian cultural prescription that one should never boast about what one has or what one is doing and that one should maintain a good working relationship with the employers in private but also the belief, in many Caribbean cultures, that speaking in a low tone shows self-control and proper public conduct. Raising one's voice in public would be considered improper and a lack of "brought-upcy" (manners), so providers were careful to monitor their phone behavior in public places. This influenced childcare practices in that the self-control exercised by these women made them more successful as providers in the eyes of those observing their behavior (meaning other providers and possibly other people who used public spaces).

Who Pays the Cell Phone Bill?

All of the West Indian childcare providers I interviewed agreed that the employer should be responsible for paying some, if not all, of the cell phone bills, since a cell phone was now considered a crucial tool for the work of childcare providers. Moreover, cell phones that were used during the workday came with so many restrictions, such as limited free minutes, that some providers would refuse to answer their cell phones even when they knew it was the employer who was trying to contact them. Most providers agreed that the employer had every right to know what was going on during the day with their child, but not at the expense of the babysitter.

Brenda told me that the mother of the children in her care had told her not to use the home phone line anymore: "I used to answer their house phone, and she [the mother] stopped me from answering the house phone." When I asked why, she responded: "I think one day what happened was that I had the bigger one when he was a baby and somebody left a message on the phone and I forgot to tell her. So she was like, 'Don't answer the phone, let the answering machine pick up.' So what I do now—sometimes they would be calling and I know they're calling and I wouldn't answer the phone. I would run away from the phone, I wouldn't answer it. And then they would be calling me on my cell phone and I shut it off! And then when they come they say, 'I was trying to get you.' And I was like, well, I don't know…I didn't want to answer my phone, you know. I pay my cell phone bill, I pay all my bills."

Who paid the cell phone bill was a common concern among West Indian providers. They stated that they did not necessarily have enough money to pay for their cell phone bills, especially when the parents called frequently or, in the case of emergencies, when providers were out with their charges and needed to call the parents. The Trinidadian babysitter Irene was in this position after her youngest daughter dropped her personal cell phone in the fish tank. After going without a cell phone for some time, Irene finally told her employers that they needed to purchase her a cell phone for work. She said, "I'm always at doctor's appointments…somewhere with the kids [and] need to call car service in case of [an] emergency. In every job that I've had, they would get me a cell phone whether I had a cell phone or not.…Even if you have your own cell phone and they want to pay some of the bill, then that's fine. If you have your own cell phone, that doesn't have nothing to do with them [the employers] because if you're taking their kids out or anything, the cell phone is always good because of emergency."

Irene now had two cell phone plans and two phones, one that she shared with her husband and one that she shared with the employer.[8] She still called the latter phone "her phone," although the plan her employer had given her had limited minutes. Irene stated that she tried not to go over the minutes. She made some personal calls on the phone shared with the employer but did "try to use it just for them [the employers].…I don't like to put personal stuff in work."

Darlene, on the other hand, did not "believe in" owning a cell phone unless the employer was paying for it, although she admitted she had been looking into it. She recognized with some amusement that if all cell phone plans actually offered the same features, such as free long distance or unlimited text messaging, the companies would all go bankrupt. She said she thought that cell phones were taking over the way babysitters did their work, but she made it clear who should be responsible for the purchase of cell phones for childcare providers: "I've never purchased a cell phone myself.…I've been in jobs where they give you a cell phone with the strictest understanding that it's only to be used for work purposes.…I see the way some people are with the cell phone, they've got the thing stuck to their ear every time you look at them.…People [employers] say, 'Do you have a cell phone?' and I say, 'No, I don't.' 'Okay, we'll give you a cell phone.' And I've heard people went on the interview and the person asked if they had a cell phone, and she said, 'No,' and they said, 'Well, you've got to get a cell phone before you start this job.' They wanted the worker to pay for the cell phone. Now that to me is a job you don't want." As this story suggests, the cell phone has provoked a small social transformation in that ownership of one now determines, in some quarters, whether someone should or should not get a job.

The cell phone could also bring about another transformation: it could close the gap between public and private domains of communication in the employer-employee relationship, as when employers demanded access to employees' own personal cell phone numbers. Darlene became bothered when she talked about workers losing their jobs for refusing to go along with the employer on this, but she also admitted, "I blame the workers to a certain extent because if I [were to] have a cell phone, I don't see what business my cell phone has to do with my job, it's my cell phone." Darlene did not believe that a childcare provider should have to get a cell phone as a prerequisite for a job. Instead, she felt that the employer should provide it.

Concerned for that parent out there who desperately wanted to check in with his or her childcare provider, I asked, "What if the parents want to get in touch with you?" Darlene responded, "I have no problem with that, just give me a cell phone. If you want me to use my cell phone, you should be contributing to the costs. To me, you've got a nerve, I'm paying the bills, you probably aren't giving me enough money as it is anyway, and you've got the nerve demanding that I give you my cell phone number for you to use up my minutes? What am I, a Charlie [a dick]? Why would I agree to that? And if you're going to make those demands, then this isn't the job for me." Though I felt that Darlene was right to insist that she shouldn't have to pay for a cell phone to communicate with her employer, I was not fully convinced that childcare providers could be so selective about their employers that they could resist this demand.

Unlike Darlene, Grace, who also worked for Domestic Workers United, had recently become the owner of her own cell phone, a birthday gift from her cousin. But she didn't let her employers know this. "I had a lot of slack [sic] for not having a cell phone.... I didn't see the need for a cell phone...not to say that it's not a worthwhile tool. I'm just not one of those people. So I had one and I didn't even know the

number...and I start giving out the number to a few people and stuff like that, but...the last job I had, I didn't get one. But when I got mine, I didn't tell them, I didn't give them the number.... If she [the mother] wants to be calling me on my number, she has to be paying me. She has to be contributing."

Very much like Darlene, Grace believed that an employer who wanted to "control" a babysitter's movements throughout the day via cell phone calls had to pay for the privilege. Both Darlene's and Grace's statements expressed not only some hostility or resentment but also a consciousness that a phone was a private and personal possession that should be respected as such throughout the workday. Grace continued, "She can get a phone and put me on her plan and it's just for her business. When I leave, I leave it at her house.... But if she wants it, she's going to have to pay. You can't let these people get the better of you...but if you feel you need to know every step I make, you give me a cell phone."

Victoria expressed the same view, that if the employer had access to her private cell phone she should contribute monetarily to its use, but she noted some advantages to having a cell phone as well: "It was my personal cell phone. So I definitely felt at times that maybe that they should be paying for it because the amount of time I spent talking on it during the day—which most people don't use their cell phones too much during the day—definitely it was substantial. It was definitely substantial. But, you know, I guess at other times it was positive to have a cell phone. You know, it's certainly good for making the playdates and all that kind of stuff, and finding out where mom is when she's not home on time and all of those things."

The advances in cell phone technology have made these phones accessible to almost everyone, with prices decreasing annually for the simplest phone and calling plans becoming more diverse. But it was still the consensus among West Indian providers that employers should pay for the cell phone if it was a requirement of the job position and that the person who was paying for the phone should allow the employer to have access to it only if the employer paid for the privilege—thereby defining the limits of the job and, in essence, the power relation.

Surveillance: Parent Blogs, Nanny-Cams, and Stroller License Plates

While many sitters gained primary employment through word-of-mouth networking, virtual technology had become a significant resource for many sitters. One day when some of the sitters came to my house for a playdate, Debbie asked me to submit a post for her on a babysitter Web site because she would be looking for a new job in spring 2007. Taylor, the two-year-old Debbie cared for, would be staying home with her father, who was retiring and therefore wouldn't need hired childcare services any longer. There are several "parent blogs" on the Internet where parents and babysitters can post their needs for childcare or their employment availability. I asked several sitters if this was a regular means of getting a job as a sitter or nanny. They all said yes. They told me that sometimes the employers themselves helped sitters find new employment by posting an announcement of their availability accompanied by a reference. But a drawback to this new way of finding work was that several sitters did not have Internet access at home and therefore either did not know how to navigate the Internet or could not access it without paying a fee at an Internet café, which might charge up to a dollar a minute. Although the public library had computer access, sitters did not use it for this feature since they were watching small children when they were at the library. Moreover, providers reframed the library

specifically as a play space; they did not view it as a place for books for their own use or Internet access.

The Internet is increasingly being used for surveillance of nannies, as are cell phones and other technological devices. A search of LexisNexis for articles in northeastern newspapers on this topic revealed that surveillance is one of employers' main uses of cell phones. Further, "nanny-cams," small cameras that can be creatively installed in various ornaments around the home, are being used to "keep an eye" on what the childcare provider is doing when the employer is not at home. The term *nanny-cam* alone is disturbing because it implies that among all the possible uses of spy cameras in the home, the surveillance of nannies is the most needed. Some companies even advertise themselves as "nanny surveillance companies" to play on the insecurities of parents with a new babysitter.[9] While these devices have indeed allowed some employers to monitor and ultimately "catch" their babysitters in some act of deviance, they are simultaneously a way to ensure that when the babysitter is in the private household she is continually under the employer's control. Childcare providers may feel that surveillance tactics diminish their self-esteem and autonomy—though sometimes they find ways to get around them. Darlene told me that her employer had recounted to her a conversation with a friend who had just had a nanny-cam for the sitter surreptitiously installed in an ornament. Darlene's employer told Darlene that she had simply laughed and said to the friend, "Darlene would never go for that, she'd figure it out in a second."

West Indian sitters, remaining a predominant choice for many Brooklyn families, still face some of the harshest criticism from the very people who employ them. This criticism is now posted on the Internet. Erynn Esposito, a community organizer and documentarian, informed me that Park Slope parents posting at sites on Yahoo Groups had gone to great lengths to "ensure the safety of their children" by reporting and discussing their observations about nannies online. One Yahoo Web site chat room even featured a comment thread in which parents graded "nannies" by race; "West Indian sitters were at the bottom and Tibetan women were rated #1." Apparently this "grading system" had begun when one parent told another that she had seen her West Indian sitter use physical means to discipline a child and wanted to get the sitter fired. Not all parents went along with the idea of grading sitters in this way. Some commenters stated that this type of discussion was completely racist, and one woman who employed a West Indian babysitter (not the sitter who had disciplined the child) remarked that it "makes me so upset that you are looking at my sitter with this racist eye while they are with my child."

When I asked Darlene about her take on such a grading system, she responded that West Indian women had been doing domestic work for many years in New York and had worked so many babysitting jobs that "they know what they're worth....They know what they should or shouldn't do, and they have higher standards than someone who recently came in and are more placid...more agreeable...because you have some people that if they can take advantage of you they think you're wonderful, but if they cannot take advantage of you then you're not that wonderful." Darlene was saying here that newer immigrants to the city might not be as demanding as West Indians who had a history of work in New York and understood their value to employers. West Indian childcare providers might thus demand more in terms of their work's worth, and employers would see this as a generalizable trait—that West Indian providers were too demanding and not as "good" as the newcomers. Whether the newer immigrant Tibetan childcare providers were indeed more easily manipulated could not be confirmed. However, Darlene's

conclusions were based on her experiences working for Domestic Workers United with a variety of ethnic and immigrant groups involved in domestic service.

A Grenadian provider, Tricia, whom I met at Carroll Park in June 2005 told me that some of the parents on this very Web site had reported that "the West Indian sitters are taking the white children to Jay Street [Fulton Mall, a mainly black ethnic enclave and shopping center] and they [the parents] disapprove." She was very upset by the comments made by these parents who were judging the responsibility level of babysitters in their everyday work. These comments also raise the question, Why was it so terrible for West Indian sitters to want to go to a shopping area that had mainly black clientele? No one ever questioned white parents' taking their children to white neighborhoods to shop. And why was the race of the neighborhood the first characteristic invoked to explain this disapproval? Maybe most parents saw certain gentrified neighborhoods as public spaces that were more "private," whereas they saw "ethnic" neighborhoods as "too public" and hence "unsafe." Some parents implied their greater comfort in "white" spaces in blog entries that expressed an unwarranted uneasiness with spaces such as Fulton Mall or the Flatbush area, which were inhabited predominantly by black Caribbeans. But what about the comfort level of babysitters who went out with the children in their care? Perhaps the babysitters were going there for even more rudimentary reasons than the comfort of contact with their own culture: the purchase prices of everyday items at the Fulton Mall were lower than those found in most of the neighborhoods where these babysitters worked.

Yet another means of doing surveillance on nannies through the Internet was reported in 2006 in a *New York Times* article called "Spying on Nanny." According to the article, a former New York City prosecutor had created a Web site offering parents a small license plate for their child's stroller for $50. I never came across anyone who used these license plates, but according to the article parents can "affix the plate to their child's stroller, [and] any 'concerned citizen' with access to the Internet can file an anonymous report on the nanny pushing the stroller so parents know where their children have been."[10]

Such new forms of surveillance through the Internet undermine the already strained relationship between employer and employee by playing up the fears that most parents already have when their children are under the care of another. They are becoming a concern for babysitters and parents alike because they show how easily individuals' privacy can be invaded by strangers.

Even the movement arts studio owner Victoria found that the surveillance of babysitters on the Internet could be damaging. Though she admittedly benefited from the advertising that she did online, she stated that the Internet was "probably more negative than positive" because it allowed information to spread "like wildfire" and because "I think that people are very willing to say things in that environment that they would never say to somebody in person." She noted that it was "easier," more comfortable, for employers to engage in surveillance through the various forms of technology than to confront an employee about what she might be doing incorrectly.

One of the more famous Web sites that supports Internet surveillance is "I Saw Your Nanny" (isawyournanny.com). Margaret Nelson and Anita Ilta Gary's book about the surveillance that contemporary families encounter has a chapter on this Web site based on a twenty-two-week analysis of over two hundred nanny sightings and over a thousand comments. Nelson and Gary found that 77 percent of the nannies identified on the Web site were marked either by race or ethnicity explicitly or by some other code of ethnicity, such as "speaks Spanish"

or "attractive dark skinned, black hair nanny."[11] The children under care were far less likely to be identified by race or ethnic background, but when they were, 78 percent were identified as white. Indicators of class status were also used, such as descriptions of a bag that the nanny was carrying or descriptions of the nanny's clothing.[12] Class distinctions were also made in postings that suggested that if the nanny was shopping at a "nice" store she had to be shopping on behalf of her employer, whereas if she was shopping at a "lower-status" store she had to be making a purchase for herself. This became relevant in my research when the appropriateness of the nanny's location, such as the Fulton Mall, came up in a posting.

Though both parents and nannies could use this site, and though it was generally the nanny who was demonized in multiple ways, parents, particularly mothers (as the blog's founder and editor admitted), could also be "outed" as neglectful and thus publicly shamed.[13] If a neighbor was in the park and recognized a child in a nanny's care, he or she sometimes used the comments page to speak to the child's mother in patronizing tones, suggesting that the mother should be home with her child since children were vulnerable at such a young age. The mother would then become a public target for the community's criticism. She might feel obliged to explain the situation or defend the nanny on the Web site, or, even worse, to the neighbor if the neighbor identified him- or herself. This form of surveillance through blogs emphasized an "us-versus-them" dialogue (between employers and nannies, between other parents and nannies, and between parents themselves), thus stirring up conflicts and divisions between the parties engaged in the work of childcare and mothering that took place on everyone's behalf.

Most childcare providers do not search and comment on such Web sites, yet they learn about them through other providers or through other parents who tell them about recent comments. Gentrified Brooklyn is a prime site for postings, since its public spaces, bounded by residential neighborhoods and commercial streets, and its high population of "creative class" workers with flexible schedules who can be out and about in such spaces throughout the day just as the childcare providers are, offer many opportunities to closely observe the behaviors of others. The Web sites give posters the impression that they are part of a community that values this form of surveillance, and while this is true given the popularity of such sites and the many postings that come from the gentrified Brooklyn neighborhoods that I researched, it also demonstrates how the virtual community differs from the physical community. The like-mindedness of blog contributors encourages a kind of social identity different from that constructed in a physical community. In the physical space of a community people are as likely to say things to each other, but they are far less harsh than if they have an open and supposedly anonymous forum such as the Internet. In other words, in the physical community people will reflect on the consequences of their words more than if they are using an anonymous forum.…

The comfort that employers derive from Internet-facilitated surveillance and that employees derive from being able to connect with others by cell phone should not be overlooked. The frequent use of both cell phones and the Internet by providers and their employers has meaning for both parties. This meaning can be as simple as the ability to reach out to family members abroad and locally, or to other providers in the work communities, but the meaning can be deeper. Cell phones and the Internet make it easier to avoid confrontations with family members or with employees. They can also be tools of subordination through the various surveillance tactics that are being used to control public behavior. For all these reasons, the use of such new technologies

is an ongoing topic of study. The more features become available—the iPhone's new video recording option, Skype's free video conferencing feature—the more complicated the issues of surveillance and networking become.

Digital technologies are a necessary part of how people do their work in the twenty-first century. As both employees' and employers' use of these technologies makes evident, they have become uniquely interwoven into the family dynamic: while making it easier for employees to contact their family members and friends, including those outside the country, they have also increased control over employees' public behavior through surveillance. Whether or not people want to believe that technology should play such a large role in everyday life, the Internet and cell phones have become integrated into our daily experiences. Therefore, it is important for both childcare providers and their employers to understand how people adapt to such technologies and to reach some form of consensus as to how they should be used throughout the workday. The flexible nature of childcare requires continual dialogue between employers and employees to negotiate ever-changing boundaries while respecting the autonomy of workers and the needs of employers.

NOTES

1. This reliance was further evidenced by the fact that several providers could be seen wearing cell phone earpieces for most of the day while walking about the neighborhoods they worked in.
2. Katriel (1999); Lee Humphreys (2005).
3. Hochschild and Machung (1989) were the first to discuss the phenomenon of parallel shifts within the home and at work.
4. Gumpert and Drucker (1998).
5. Rakow and Navarro (1993).
6. Remote mothering has been discussed in Rakow and Navarro (1993) and Leung and Wei (2000).

7. Gumpert and Drucker (1998).
8. Cell phone sharing plans allow two or more people to access a shared number of minutes with a single bill, which is typically paid by the employer.
9. Hollander (1998).
10. McLaughlin and Kraus (2006).
11. Nelson and Garey (2009:113).
12. See Nelson and Garey (2009) for more details about how nannies are constructed as characters on the I Saw Your Nanny Web site and how these constructions give meaning to the behaviors being posted.
13. See Nelson and Garey (2009) for a comment analysis on how parents who work from home compare to parents who work outside the home and how this affects their decision to defend their nanny.

REFERENCES

Gumpert, Gary, and Susan J. Drucker. 1998. "The Mediated Home in the Global Village." Communication Research 25 (4): 422–438.
Hochschild, Arlie Russell, and Anne Machung. 1989. The Second Shift: Working Parents and the Revolution at Home. New York: Penguin Books.
Hollander, Ricki. 1998. "Spy or Wary Eye? Nannies on Camera." Christian Science Monitor, May 1.
Humphreys, Lee. 2005. "Social Topography in a Wireless Era: The Negotiation of Public and Private Space." Journal of Technical Writing and Communication 35 (4): 367–384.
Katriel, Tamar. 1999. "Rethinking the Terms of Social Interaction." Research on Language and Social Interaction 32 (1–2): 95–102.
Leung, Louis, and Wei Ran. 2000. "More Than Just Talk on the Move: Uses and Gratifications of the Cellular Phone." Journalism and Mass Communication Quarterly 77 (2): 308–320.
McLaughlin, Emma, and Nicola Kraus. 2006. "Spying on Nanny." New York Times, November 19.
Nelson, Margaret K., and Anita Ilta Garey. 2009. Who's Watching? Daily Practices of Surveillance among Contemporary Families. Nashville: Vanderbilt University Press.
Rakow, Lana F., and Vija Navarro. 1993. "Remote Mothering and the Parallel Shift: Women Meet the Cellular Phone." Critical Studies in Mass Communication 10 (2): 144–157.

33

RANDOL CONTRERAS

GETTING THE SHIT

from *The Stickup Kids* (2013)

Randol Contreras studied a crew of "stickup kids"—former New York drug dealers who, in the face of a declining drug market, have turned to robbing other drug dealers. These men operate in a world of betrayal, deceit, and often sickening violence. Yet even here there are rules and social expectations. In this passage, Contreras shows what happens when the robbers gain access to a drug dealer's apartment, determined to get him to divulge the location of his "stash" of drugs and cash—information that he is equally determined to withhold.

The Violence

After getting inside the apartment, the drug robbery is dizzying and explosive; the furious search for people, in the bedroom, in the closet, behind the door, *get everybody, get everybody*; the demands to know if anyone else is inside, anywhere inside, *don't lie, don't lie*; the punches to the jaw, the kicks to the stomach, *don't move, don't move.*

And after subduing the dealers, robbers begin the questioning.

Let us pause.

That is what drug robbers often got, silence. Or if a dealer responds, it is to plead ignorance, to cry foul, to beg mercy, to insist on being left alone. This is why, more often than not, drug robberies get bloody and grimy, with robbers resorting to torture. For instance, when I asked Gus about why he cut off the dealer's earlobe, he provided a glimpse into how drug robbers transitioned into torture.

"You tell them, 'Look, I'ma ask you what you do. If you don't tell me what I wanna know, I'ma cut your ear.' So, when you tell 'em that shit, you gotta do it. Or they gonna wanna start fuckin' with you, 'Ah, this nigga's bullshit. He told me he was gonna cut my ear off and he didn't cut it.' So, I asked him what he had on 145th Street and Broadway. He said that he doesn't know.

I didn't even ask him again. I just cut his earlobe off. But I mean, that was like the second option. That's not the first. Like, we let them know that we will do something to them. But we don't go straight into that. 'Cause if we ask you, and you tell us, everything goes down right. You just saved a lot of trouble."

As for torture, the setting often shaped the process. Apart from a gun, drug robbers rarely carried torture tools, instead using everyday household items to do violence. If a knife is nearby, they might slice off fingers. If an electrical appliance is nearby, they might electrocute. And if a hammer is nearby, they might hammer fingers, legs, or heads—or anything until the dealer gives up the goods.

For instance, Tukee, in a rare criminal admission, described an incident where a frustrated robber found a torture tool in the kitchen. "One time, there was this dude [dealer]," explained Tukee, "who just ain't want to talk. This dude I was with was like, 'Fuck this.' He went to the kitchen, got this big ass knife, came back, was like, 'Look, tell us where the shit's at, or I'ma cut your finger off.' The dude didn't say nothing. 'A'ight.' [We] put his hands on the table, held that shit…Shaaa! Chopped off one of his fingers, like the tip of it off. The nigga [dealer] started screamin', blood was shootin' out of that shit [finger]. My boy was like, 'You better talk or I'ma cut all your fingers off.' The nigga [dealer] looked down, saw the little part of his finger on the table, then he started talkin'. If he just would'a told us from the get-go, he woulda still had his finger. Stupid motherfucka."

Lalo, a drug robber who sometimes came to the block to learn of potential scores, also described the use of household items for torture. "We had the guy in the bathtub," Lalo explained, in Spanish, "and we were hitting him with the gun so much that his head was swollen. But damn, the guy kept sayin' he didn't know anything. I grabbed a bottle of Clorox and told him, 'Let's see

if you talk. If you don't talk, *maricón,* I'm going to pour this Clorox into your eyes. You want to go blind?' Then the guy was like, 'That's not right, I don't even have anything.' And I poured it into his eyes. And real quick he started saying, 'Stop! That's it, stop!' Ha-ha. The bottle was empty [now], but he didn't know that. I was like, 'Talk or I'll keep going. You're going to go blind, cocksucker.' And he told us everything."

However, the most profound torture tool is the iron. The iron is often the savior for drug robbers, and if they find one in a dealer's apartment, it's all over: after heating the iron, robbers place it against a dealer's flesh, which produces immediate results. "The worst torture is an iron," Pablo explained. "You gonna give up everything. You gonna give up even your own mother. Because from what I seen, the worst feeling is an iron burnin' your back up, kid. I haven't met a man that could take the iron, ha-ha. And usually these guys, where they got their stuff [drugs] like in a house—they got TVs, sofas, beds…they gotta make it look like a house, in case Five-O [police] comes, or the super[intendent] comes to fix something. And most of the time they chill in them. So they got to have an iron. You don't even have to bring one."

Thus, the iron, in the drug robber's world, is legend. It resurfaced in successful robbery tales as the technique that would always turn the tables on a dealer. Gus provided such an account, where he and others interrogated and beat a dealer in the living room. After the dealer refused to talk, Gus went into a bedroom closet, found an iron, and confronted the dealer.

"So, boom, I had the iron in front of the nigga's face," Gus said. "I was like, 'Yo, just tell me where the shit is at. If you don't tell us, I'ma fuckin' burn your ass.' He ain't say nothing. So I told my boy to put duct tape over his mouth 'cause I knew the nigga was gonna be screamin', I didn't want nobody to hear that shit. We take everything off, his shirt, everything, bro. And while we doin' all this, we got the iron like heatin' up, gettin' that shit hot. Soon as it got real hot, I put that shit on his back. Shaaaa! Nigga was screamin', bro. Screamin', screamin'. But you couldn't hear him that much 'cause of the duct tape. I took the iron off and saw this big ass red mark turnin' like purple, bro. I was like, 'Fuck it.' I put that shit on him again. Nigga couldn't take that shit, bro. These niggas [the other robbers] had to hold him down, he was movin' so much. I took the iron off and waited a while. When I saw that he like calmed down. I took the duct tape off [his mouth], and asked him again to tell us where the shit is at. Right there he told us."

There were many more torture tactics—like heating an uncoiled metal hanger wire on a stove and then placing it in a dealer's ear. But again, the torture mostly depends on the circumstance: if a dealer is dragged into a bathtub to avoid bloodying the floor, the robbers may fill the tub with water, which makes electrocution an option. If a dealer happens to be ironing clothes when he is subdued, burning becomes an option. In short, drug robbers use their imagination with household items to make a dealer surrender the goods.

Hardheadedness

So far we see that dealers often refuse to give up the drugs or cash despite facing torture. A simple reason explains a dealer's hardheadedness, or resistance:[1] the consignment system. In the drug world, dealers often receive drugs on consignment, a system where suppliers provide drugs on credit and wait for dealers to sell the drugs to get paid.[2] However, it is a dreadful credit system: no legal recourse exists and it works within a capitalist frame.

For instance, let's say that a kilo of cocaine has a retail value of twenty thousand dollars. A dealer receiving the kilo on credit and selling it keeps a thousand dollars (profit) and returns the remaining nineteen thousand dollars to the supplier. The deal is done. Likewise, a dealer receiving ten kilos on credit and selling them keeps a profit of ten thousand dollars (one thousand for each kilo) and returns one hundred and ninety thousand dollars to the supplier (nineteen thousand dollars for each kilo). Again, the deal is done.

However, if robbers steal the ten kilos of cocaine from that dealer, not only does the dealer lose a profit of ten thousand dollars, but the supplier loses one hundred and ninety thousand dollars. And if a sneaky dealer lies, says he was robbed, then he can earn a lot of money. After selling the "robbed" product, the dealer can earn up to the entire retail value as profit, two hundred thousand dollars. *Diablo, 'mano!*

But there is a chance that the dealer's supplier needs that sum to pay his own provider. There is a chance that, despite having enough disposable cash, the supplier does not want to absorb the loss. And there is a chance that the supplier holds the dealer accountable, not caring whether the robbery tale is true or not. To drug dealers, robbery tales are suspect, regarded as *pura mierda*. It is not unheard of for drug dealers to try to escape payments through cries of having been "stuck up." But typically, a dealer eventually pays—through selling drugs for several months with no profit, through broken limbs, bruised bodies, or, sometimes, through lost lives. *Muerte, papa.*

One night, Sylvio talked about why drug dealers resist drug robbers during a stickup. "Depending on who's the supplier, they take more than half [of the drugs] on consignment. So let's say you have five hundred thousand worth of material. It's more than likely not all yours. It's the Colombians' or the Mexicans' or whoever. They wouldn't buy that stickup line like it was something normal. They would think you fuckin' with them. And those are not people you would really want to fuck with. Regular common street thugs, you can handle. These guys, they don't take no shit."

"You're sayin' they won't believe you?" I asked.

"No, they won't believe you at all. They want their money, that's it. Or you gotta pay with something else."

"Like, have you heard of stories?"

"Yeah, I heard of stories, you know, guys comin' by, and they say they got stuck up and these guys all of sudden they disappear. You never hear from them again. So I wonder what happened to them. Some of it's true [that they get robbed]. Some of them they just take all of it on consignment, five hundred, three hundred thousand dollars and they just go to [the] Dominican Republic, go wherever they from, Jamaica, and that's it. You know, this is what the guys that own the material [drugs] are worried about."

So even in the face of a gun barrel pressed against their temple, or a heated iron waiting to be placed on their back, drug dealers are courageously stubborn. The potential consequences are enough to keep them from giving up their drugs and cash.

Gus provided an example. He told me of a job he had recently gotten as an enforcer for some upper-level Puerto Rican drug dealers. These men had supplied a dealer with forty kilos of cocaine—a million dollars worth of drugs—on consignment. The dealer later claimed that he was arrested by police, who then released him and kept the drugs. The Puerto Rican dealers did not believe him. So they paid Gus and his old prison-mate twenty thousand dollars to get information out of the dealer. The duo then held the dealer hostage in a basement. They tortured him for three days.

"I had bought a little welding torch," Gus recalled. "So I was askin' him, I was like, 'Look, this is what's happening. These people want their money or they want their drugs. You decide if you gonna give it to me or not. Don't worry about it. I got all night.' And when I'm talkin' to him, I'm fuckin' with the torch, you know, lightin' it and everything. Yo, kid, I started burnin' this nigga just a little bit, you know, just passin'

the flames, burnin' his hairs, fuckin' with him, smackin' him. Nigga won't talk. I start burnin' him for real. I'm puttin holes in his chest. The nigga passed out on me twice, put it like that. I had to hose him down with a water hose in the basement, twice.

"I told him, 'Look, these people givin' me a hundred thousand dollars to do this to you. If you pay me, I'll stop. I don't got nothing to do with what you owe them.' He was like, 'Yeah, I know that this is your job. And you're doing a good job.' He was tellin' me that shit, ha-ha. He was like, '*Tu 'ta 'ciendo un buen trabajo*. But I don't got no money.'"

"So, what they made us do after they found out that he ain't have no money or nothing on him, they made us tell him to call his wife in [the] Dominican Republic and sign [off] like all his property. I'm tellin' you, his house is worth like eight million in pesos... he had a business that's worth like seven million [pesos]... I mean, all his shit was worth mad money. And he had to sign all that shit over to them."

Gus' account also showed why a dealer might endure horrible torture even if he knew he was going to give in eventually. Because if a dealer claims that vicious robbers robbed him, but has not a bruise or scratch, then a supplier might think that the robbery tale is a lie. *Pura mierda*. No puffed-up eye, no swollen jaw, no burn marks on the back—*yup, he took the shit*. A dealer, then, might undergo torture to have a good explanation for the missing goods.

Drug robbers understand a dealer's resistance. But they also need the goods. So, after drug robbers question a dealer, the next step is torture. However, a problem emerges— deciding on length and intensity. To succeed, drug robbers must not quit when dealers hold out. Otherwise, they won't profit. As Jack Katz notes, robbers need "a true hardheadedness,"[3] or stubbornness, to complete a robbery.

But, again a dealer could be just as hardheaded, showing a dangerous commitment to keeping the drugs and cash.

For a victimized dealer, life after a rob-bery—always running, always owing, always dodging death—might be worse than experiencing immediate pain. So the robbery could turn into what sociologist Erving Goffman called a "character con-test,"[4] an emotional contest between robber and dealer. If a dealer demonstrates resolve through severe pain, then a robber must intensify the torture. However, a robber must check his emotions.

The dealer cannot not die.

Playing by the Rules: *No Lo Maten*

To understand why drug robbers must avoid killing, we should briefly return to the end of the robbery that started the chapter. After a night of torture—of beating and kicking and electrocution—the dealer had not sur-rendered the whereabouts of the drugs and cash. Gus decided to grab the dealer's keys and go to the drug stash apartment. "I just didn't want to deal with this nigga," Gus recalled, " 'cause we was gonna end up killin' him."

Overall, it had become an ordeal to con-tinue torturing without receiving informa-tion. The crew even insisted to the dealer that they knew he sold drugs and where he lived. They just needed exact information on the whereabouts of his drug and money stash. The crew, though, already knew that he kept about three hundred grams of her-oin and forty-eight thousand dollars in cash in his small, rented room. But how?

Like most drug robberies, this one began through betrayal. The dealer's partner, who had inside details, provided information to the crew. And after getting the drugs and cash, the crew planned to split the profits with the partner. Then the partner would pretend astonishment at the dealer's loss. *What happened? Who did this? They took what?*

But if the robbers held inside informa-tion—if they knew the exact location of the drugs and cash—then why did they torture rather than grab the apartment keys from the start?

There are rules to this game. As in a boxing match or a gang rumble, the drug robbers and traitorous partner established guidelines to reduce physical and emotional loss. One rule is that drug robbers must pre-tend ignorance of the drugs' location. This protects the betraying partner from a victim who later suspects foul play. Because if rob-bers went straight to the stash—the loose floor tile, the hidden sneaker box, the small tear in the sofa cushion—without jump-ing any hurdles, then they clearly received inside information. Sensing treachery, a dealer might seek retaliation against a partner.

"Because his friend was the one that told us where everything is at," Gus explained. "So, the only people that know where that shit is at are the ones that work there. So, we have to make him tell us where that shit is at 'cause then he was gonna suspect everybody that knows about this shit—he's gonna think, 'It's me, the other kid that works with me, and my man that I brought up here one time.' So, you know, I had to make him tell us where it was at."

Neno, this time in English, con-curred: "Like the person who gives me the job could tell me where it's [the drugs] at exactly. You know, 'The nigga got the shit under the bed.' Sometimes they tell you exactly where it's at, but you can't take it like that 'cause then they could get in trouble, you feel me? So you have to do it the right way. 'Cause if I go and get your drugs with-out you tellin' me nothing, then you gonna be like, 'Who said something? I ain't say nothing. It's my drugs.'"

Another rule in most drug robberies is *No lo maten.* Do not kill him. Despite the betrayal, a partner wants the dealer to stay alive. Often, they establish strong friend-ships with co-workers; they eat in familiar ethnic restaurants; drink and dance in night-clubs; talk and joke on the streets; and compare notes on the cars, clothes, and women they bought, either for friendly competition or a good laugh. In other words, dealers create strong bonds.

But business is business. Money supersedes all. The name of the game is high profits at whatever cost.[5] And dealers understand this, which is why they use guns to keep the money-grubbing sharks at bay. And setting up a partner? That's part of the game.

Yet betraying partners often show concern. They order robbers not to kill their partner, a sign of some humanity.[6] So robbers might beat them repeatedly with their fists, bloodying and bruising faces; they might burn them with an iron, creating bumpy, pockmarked scars; they might chop off fingers and slice off ears, laming and stigmatizing them for life—but *no lo maten*. Maim him, scar him, but *no lo maten*. Break him, shatter him, but *no lo maten*.

No. Lo. Maten.

For instance, Topi explained how betraying partners gave a green light to torture, but warned to stop short of a killing. "They always say to not kill the guy [dealer]," Topi said, in Spanish. "Because they are friends, you know. They look for ass [women] together, smoke weed together...they're friends. Like one time, this guy told me. 'You could do what you need to do because the guy [the victim] is a lion. If you let him, he'll eat you alive. But he's my buddy. Do what you need to do. But don't kill him. You're going to have to hit him a lot, but don't go over [the line]. Do not kill him.'"

This rule created a problem for Gus, David, and the others in the robbery described at the beginning of the chapter. After torturing the dealer and receiving no confession, the crew moved toward more life-threatening harm. At one point, Jonah struck the dealer repeatedly across the face and the blindfold came off. The dealer stared into Jonah's face.

Angry, Jonah yelled, *"Si, si! Mírame la cara! Mírame la cara bien, mama huevo, que yo se que te voy a matar!* (Yes, yes! Look at my face! Look at my face well, cocksucker, because I know I'm going to kill you!)

But they could not kill the man.

"The guy that gave this [robbery] to us is his friend," David explained, in Spanish. "And he told us, 'If you are going to hurt him, hurt him. But try not to do too much shit to him. *No la maten.'"*

NOTES

1. Jack Katz uses this term to describe a necessary trait for successful robbers. Here, I borrow it in reverse: as a trait drug dealers need to keep their drugs and cash from robbers. [Katz, *Seductions of Crime: Moral and Sensual Attractions of Doing Evil* (New York: Basic Books, 1988)].

2. For an overview of drug-selling systems, see George F. Rengert, *The Geography of Illegal Drugs* (Boulder, Colo.: Westview Press, 1996).

3. Katz, Seductions, p. 194.

4. Erving Goffman, *Interaction Rituals: Essays on Face-to-Face Behavior* (New York: Doubleday, 1967).

5. [Timothy] Black, *When a Heart Turns Rock Solid: The Lives of Three Puerto Rican Brothers on and off the Streets* (New York: Pantheon Books, 2009).

6. Randall Collins, personal communication.

REFERENCES

Black, Timothy. 2009. *When a Heart Turns Rock Solid: The Lives of Three Puerto Rican Brothers on and off the Streets*. New York: Pantheon Books.

Goffman, Erving. 1967. *Interaction Rituals: Essays on Face-to-Face Behavior*. New York: Doubleday.

Katz, Jack. 1988. *Seductions of Crime: Moral and Sensual Attractions of Doing Evil*. New York: Basic Books.

Rengert, George F. 1996. *The Geography of Illegal Drugs*. Boulder, Colo.: Westview Press.

PART VI

PLAYING TOGETHER: THE SERIOUS SIDE OF RECREATION AND LEISURE

Cities are more than places in which people work and sleep. They are also places of sociability, play, recreation, entertainment, and the creation of culture. In this section we show how urban ethnographers have engaged aspects of everyday life that go beyond work and residence. The pieces that follow demonstrate how seriously urban dwellers take these activities, even when they are defined as fun. They also reveal how ostensibly frivolous activities can reflect the most serious issues at stake. Generally there are two, sometimes overlapping, ways in which this occurs. On the one hand, recreational activities highlight distinctions between in-groups and out-groups ("us" and "them"), some of which preexist these activities while others are created as a consequence of the activities themselves. On the other hand, recreation and play often reflect the desire for recognition and respect.

Consider the case of the bowling matches between college boys and corner boys in William Foote Whyte's *Street Corner Society*, a 1943 classic about an Italian-American neighborhood in Boston's North End. Whyte moved into the community while he was

a Junior Fellow at Harvard, lived with an Italian-American family, and came to know a full range of people in the area. One of the most famous parts of the book is his description of the bowling matches between and among groups of working-class young men and their college-attending peers. Bowling became an outlet for highlighting group and status differences among the groups. By keeping careful track of both individual and group bowling scores, Whyte concluded that the scores of both the "corner boys" and the "college boys" depended on whether they bowled individually or as a group. Sometimes a person who bowled well on his own did much worse when bowling with others, especially if his self-confidence was undermined by fellow bowlers. Whyte therefore claimed that a close connection usually existed between social position and bowling score. This begs the reader to question whether people's positions in the group were determined by their bowling ability or whether their scores were actually a result of their positions.

Howard S. Becker's "The Professional Dance Musician and His Audience" is another classic ethnographic study that builds on leisure-time spaces in the city and those who work in them. Becker was a professional dance-band musician, who in the years after World War II supported himself in graduate school by playing in nightclubs and for dances. He came to see how he and his fellow musicians divided up the world into "hip folks" (jazz musicians and the small number of jazz aficionados who shared their musical tastes) and "squares" (those who made up most of their audiences). For the musicians and others in the jazz world, the "squares" were musically ignorant and responsible for making the musicians play commercial works that they found boring and that challenged their self-image as authentic artists rather than mere entertainers. Becker identifies countervailing pressures on them to be creative (and to see themselves as creative) on the one hand, and to "sell out" by appeasing those who actually "pay the bills," on the other. This leads to a series of interactions on the dance floor that give rise to subtle and explicit pressures on the musicians to self-segregate themselves from the audience. The musicians look down on the audience, yet they also crave their approval—a situation that is tense and in some ways quite sad.

Becker's article was researched in the late 1940s, and the interactions he documents take place at the height of the "bebop" revolution that changed both the sound and the social role of jazz in American cultural life. This was a period in which modern jazz was growing more distinct and separate from American popular music as bebop musicians pushed the harmonic and rhythmic envelope to create music that was more complex and challenging. Younger musicians often affected an uncompromising avant-garde pose, and they criticized their elders for giving in to audience demands for humor and entertainment. Yet though this cultural moment has been written about extensively by music critics and historians, it is usually seen as

the story of a small group of leading musical innovators. Becker reminds us that the struggle to produce "art"—and perhaps to create distance from the "squares"—took place in a much larger cultural context. As already noted, good ethnography can, over time, turn into great social history. In this case, the ethnographer gives us a new angle on a familiar cultural moment. Instead of seeing this movement from the viewpoint of a handful of leading actors in well-known venues, we see it as it played out among thousands of itinerant musicians and their listeners in small clubs and banquet halls across the country.

After these two studies, we move on to a series of more recent pieces, beginning with Loïc Wacquant's instant classic, *Body and Soul*, a study of the Woodlawn boxing gym in a poor black community on Chicago's South Side. In order to write about this population, Wacquant apprenticed for three years as a boxer and fought in the annual Golden Gloves tournament for amateurs. His boldness and commitment, as well as his sociological analysis of the construction of the "pugilistic habitus" mark the book as a memorable study. In this excerpt, readers will also be interested in the way that he takes them into a fight night to show the relations among boxers, coaches, and spectators. Much like Becker's study of jazz musicians, Wacquant finds that boxers experience a certain disrespect for many in the audience who do not really understand their craft and are merely looking for brutality and a knockout. In this piece, he demonstrates how an ethnographer recovers his subjects' categories for understanding action. Thus, the boxing world classifies boxers as "journeymen" (true professionals who will fight anyone even if they cannot win), "bums" (those who are less talented and disciplined), and "divers" (people who participate in a match for the money and lose on purpose in the early rounds). Wacquant's piece is highly reflexive, revealing the nature of his rapport with his subjects and showing how, through that rapport, he gained the perspective necessary to depict their group life in intimate detail.

Having started with bowling and moved on to boxing, the next piece in this section is an excerpt from Sherri Grasmuck's *Protecting Home: Class, Race, and Masculinity in Boys' Baseball*. This is a work of participant observation in the tradition of those who have lived their lives around an activity and come to realize the value of doing a sociological study about it. Grasmuck was a "baseball mom," the wife of a coach, and a commissioner at Fairmont Sports Association, an organization that went back generations before her own children came of age in the community. A long-standing working-class area with a proud local baseball tradition, Fairmount had begun to "gentrify" as upper middle-class families such as the Grasmucks began moving in and raising children. The baseball league became a prism through which to see the tensions arising between middle-class newcomers and working-class old-timers on the ball field. Grasmuck's study underscores the importance of voluntary neighborhood organizations, as well as the tensions between working-class baseball enthusiasts, for whom the league is often an all-consuming activity, and their new upper middle-class neighbors, for whom baseball is "just a game."

In Amy Best's *Fast Cars, Cool Rides*, the reader is taken into the car scene at Freedom High School, a low-income school in San Jose, California, populated mainly by first-generation Chinese-, Vietnamese-, Indian-, and Mexican-American students. Best studies a group of young, mostly Asian-American men who race and customize cars. They support their expensive hobby through low-wage, low-status work in fast-food restaurants, big-box stores, theme parks, and other minimum-wage jobs. While they do not have the same resources to pump into their hobby as middle-class kids do, they still invest enough in their cars to

center their lives and identity around street racing. This enables them to create their own subculture and define group boundaries between whites, Latinos, and Asians, which, in turn, allows them to create their own cohesive social world. In this activity, they seek recognition, respect, and the "intense sensation" of driving very fast. The youths generally race light, imported cars, often Hondas and Toyotas, and they define themselves against the "American kids" who tend to race larger, U.S.-manufactured "muscle" cars, such as Ford Mustangs. High school students in San Jose try to gain recognition through racing—by making their cars louder and flashier—and establishing a masculine identity in a world that increasingly values brains over brawn. By participating in this world and surviving its risks, they gain subcultural capital and achieve a visibility lacking in their other everyday interactions.

Our next selection by Reuben May and Kenneth Chaplin highlights the ways in which leisure time can be competitive or even humiliating. The African-American men whose lives they describe in their study of nightlife in downtown Athens, Georgia, are attempting to achieve the same kind of recognition and fun as their white counterparts who line up outside trendy nightclubs. African Americans are excluded from these clubs, however, because, according to club bouncers, they are dressed in a "hip-hop" style and do not wear garments that accord with the dress code established by the white owners of the businesses. At least, that is what they are told at the door. May and Chaplin observe many white people leaving the clubs dressed in precisely the same types of garments as worn by the black patrons who had been rejected. However, their account also highlights an aspect of discrimination that is perhaps more evident in everyday life than in controlled experiments, for they find that while many blacks are indeed excluded from the club, those who do dress "appropriately" and learn to "crack the code" tend to be let in. Yet though blacks are not completely excluded from the clubs, they are consistently held to a clearly different, probably higher, standard of dress and affect. The memorable irony of this article is that the clothing worn by the excluded blacks is associated with the hip-hop culture that produces the music and dance styles featured in the clubs. The clubs, in other words, do not want the black people who come there "dressed the part." This is not merely pointed out by the authors but is perceived as an aspect of their humiliation by the subjects. At the same time, May and Chaplin show how this double standard eventually becomes accepted as legitimate by those blacks who have learned to "crack the code" and are regularly admitted to the club.

Our next selection revisits some of the themes raised by May and Chaplin's study but embeds them in the context of a city's political economy. David Grazian's *On the Make* is a study of nightclub and bar interactions as experienced by his students at the University of Pennsylvania. Grazian claims that elites—club owners, entrepreneurs, and city government officials—manipulate everyday urban experiences, which the people who go out at night largely take for granted. Though this world is constructed by businessmen and their allies for the sake of profit, Grazian does not portray the people who go to clubs and bars as mere victims of capitalism but as people with their own goals and plans. Their experiences are structured and manipulated in ways that they may or may not be aware of. Yet they are not really naive dupes in a confidence game; instead, they are willing participants in the creation of a nightlife scene. Viewing nightlife as a kind of sporting ritual, his subjects approach it as a high-stakes game. Indeed, like the young people depicted in May's study, the often-underage undergraduates in Grazian's study begin the evening with anxiety over whether or not they will successfully score the first goal in the game: admission into clubs. To get past the velvet rope, young women dress with exposed cleavage, and young men dress with a "metrosexual" style. In doing so they help create the atmosphere the club owners are trying to maintain. Grazian's work highlights the way that sociology can move from the macro to the micro level and demonstrates how people respond to structural conditions. Looking at how individuals interact with one another as they move through space, and the ways in which their identities get implicated in these interactions, he reveals how people come to feel about themselves and others based on those interactions. "Going out," Grazian reminds us, is a collective activity as the nightlife game is nearly always played in groups.

Our final selection, Jooyoung Lee's "Battlin' on the Corner," brings us back to the black ghetto, this time in South Central Los Angeles, where we see many of the same themes. Here too social life and fun ultimately revolve around the desires for recognition and respect. In this ghetto, the people who meet to have fun are rappers, and they come to perform in groups known as ciphers, which form spontaneously and can last from a few minutes to an hour. What Lee shows is that even "play" must be actively constructed as such or else it may quickly degenerate into conflict and even violence. This "play" occurs through ritualized cues and signals during the raps. Looking carefully at how participants make transitions to their peers' performances, or how they handle situations in which one person appears to be "hoggin' the microphone," Lee shows how the rappers actively remind each other that, even in this highly competitive situation, they are "just playing." This becomes most evident as staged "battles" escalate into agitated moments for the participants, who nevertheless pretend that they are "not catching feelings" in order to sustain a sense that they are all engaged in play. Through video technology, Lee is able to show how play is an ongoing collective accomplishment, something understood as well by his participants as it is by the sociologist who reconstructs it. Without their interaction, desire for recognition and respect on the corner can lead to showdowns, and even minor slights can turn into serious confrontations.

34

WILLIAM FOOTE WHYTE

BOWLING AND SOCIAL RANKING

from *Street Corner Society* (1943)

In the 1930s, William Foote Whyte lived for three years in a Boston slum that he called Cornerville. In the excerpt here, he shows how the social standing of a young man influences his bowling performance even though some might think that it would raise his social standing within the group. The article illustrates the social psychology of performance in playful situations.

One evening in October, 1937, Doc scheduled a bowling match against the Italian Community Club, which was composed largely of college men who held their meetings every two weeks in the Norton Street Settlement House. The club was designed to be an organization of well-educated and superior men, although Doc was a member, and Angelo, Lou, and Fred of the Nortons had been voted in upon his recommendation. The other Nortons felt that the club was "high-toned," and around the corner it was known as the "Boys' Junior League." They were a little flattered that members of their group could mix with such a club, but their opinion was formed largely from the personalities of Chick Morelli, the president, and Tony Cardio, another prominent member, both of whom they considered snobbish and conceited. Consequently, the Nortons took this match very seriously.

Doc was captain of the Nortons. He selected Long John, Frank, Joe, and Tommy for his team. Danny and Mike were not bowling in this period. Chick and Tony led the Community Club team.

Feeling ran high. The Nortons shouted at the club bowlers and made all sorts of noises to upset their concentration. The club members were in high spirits when they gained an early lead but had little to say as the Nortons pulled ahead to win by a wide margin.

After the match I asked Frank and Joe if there was any team that they would have been more eager to beat. They said that if they could pick out their favorite victims, they would choose Chick Morelli, Tony Cardio, Joe Cardio (Tony's brother), Mario Testa, and Hector Marto. These last three had all belonged to the Sunset Dramatic Club.

Frank and Joe said that they had nothing against the other three men on the Community Club team but that the boys had been anxious to beat that team in order to put Chick and Tony "in their places." Significantly, Frank and Joe did not select their favorite victims on the basis of bowling ability. The five were good bowlers, but that was not the deciding factor in the choice. It was their social positions and ambitions that were the objects of attack, and it was that which made victory over the Community Club so satisfying.

Lou Danaro and Fred Mackey had cheered for the club. Although they were club members, the boys felt that this did not excuse them. Danny said: "You're a couple of traitors—Benedict Arnolds.... You're with the boys—and then you go against them.... Go on, I don't want your support."

Fred and Lou fell between the two groups and therefore had to face this problem of divided allegiance. Doc's position on the corner was so definitely established that no one even considered the possibility of his choosing to bowl for the Community Club against the Nortons.

This was the only match between the two teams that ever took place. The corner boys were satisfied with their victory, and the club did not seek a return match. Tony Cardio objected to the way in which the Nortons had tried to upset the concentration of his team and said it was no fun to bowl against such poor sports. There were, however, clashes with individual members of the club. One night in November, Doc, Frank Donelli, Joe Dodge, and I were bowling when Chick Morelli and Lou Danaro came in together. We agreed to have two three-man teams, and Chick and Doc chose sides. Chick chose Lou and me. The match was fairly even at first, but Doc put his team far ahead with a brilliant third string. Toward the end of this string, Chick was sitting next to Joe Dodge and mumbling at him, "You're a lousy bum.... You're a no-good bowler."

Joe said nothing until Chick had repeated his remarks several times. Then Joe got up and fired back at Chick, "You're a conceited ———! I feel like taking a wallop at you. I never knew anybody was as conceited as you.... You're a conceited ———!"

Doc stood between them to prevent a fight. Chick said nothing, and Doc managed to get the six of us quietly into the elevator. Joe was not satisfied, and he said to me in a loud voice: "Somebody is going to straighten him out some day. Somebody will have to wallop him to knock some of that conceit out of him."

When we were outside the building, Lou walked away with Chick, and the rest of us went into Jennings' Cafeteria for "coffee-ands." We discussed Chick:

> DOC: It's lucky you didn't hit him. They'd be after you for manslaughter. You're too strong for the kid.
> JOE: All right. But when somebody's too tough for me, I don't fool around.... He shouldn't fool around me.... If he's gonna say them things, he should smile when he says them. But I think he really meant it.
> DOC: The poor guy, so many fellows want to wallop him—and he knows it.
> FRANK: I liked him all right until the other night. We went to the Metropolitan Ballroom.... He didn't mingle in at all. He just lay down on a couch like he wanted to be petted. He wasn't sociable at all.

After driving Chick home, Lou joined us in Jennings'. He said that Chick felt very bad about the incident and didn't know what it was that made people want to hit him.

Lou added: "I know he didn't mean it that way. He's really a swell kid when you get to know him. There's only one thing I don't like about him." Then he told about a time when Chick had started an argument with a dance-hall attendant on some technicality involved in the regulations of the hall. Lou commented: "He was just trying to show how intelligent he was."

A few days later, when Joe's anger had subsided, Doc persuaded him to apologize.

Doc did not defend Chick for friendship's sake. Nor was it because they worked together in the Community Club. In the club Doc led a faction generally hostile to Chick, and he himself was often critical of the manner in which Chick sought to run the organization. But Doc had friends in both groups. He did not like to see the groups at odds with each other. Though friendship between the Nortons and Chick was impossible, it was Doc's function to see that diplomatic relations were maintained.

The Community Club match served to arouse enthusiasm for bowling among the Nortons. Previously the boys had bowled sporadically and often in other groups, but now for the first time bowling became a regular part of their social routine. Long John, Alec, Joe Dodge, and Frank Bonelli bowled several nights a week throughout the winter. Others bowled on frequent occasions, and all the bowlers appeared at the alleys at least one night a week.

A high score at candlepins requires several spares or strikes. Since a strike rarely occurs except when the first ball hits the kingpin properly within a fraction of an inch, and none of the boys had such precise aim, strikes were considered matters of luck, although a good bowler was expected to score them more often than a poor one. A bowler was judged according to his ability to get spares, to "pick" the pins that remained on the alley after his first ball.

There are many mental hazards connected with bowling. In any sport there are critical moments when a player needs the steadiest nerves if he is to "come through"; but, in those that involve team play and fairly continuous action, the player can sometimes lose himself in the heat of the contest and get by the critical points before he has a chance to "tighten up." If he is competing on a five-man team, the bowler must wait a long time for his turn at the alleys, and he has plenty of time to brood over his mistakes. When a man is facing ten pins, he can throw the ball quite casually. But when only one pin remains standing, and his opponents are shouting, "He can't pick it," the pressure is on, and there is a tendency to "tighten up" and lose control.

When a bowler is confident that he can make a difficult shot, the chances are that he will make it or come exceedingly close. When he is not confident, he will miss. A bowler is confident because he has made similar shots in the past and is accustomed to making good scores. But that is not all. He is also confident because his fellows, whether for him or against him, believe that he can make the shot. If they do not believe in him, the bowler has their adverse opinion as well as his own uncertainty to fight against. When that is said, it becomes necessary to consider a man's relation to his fellows in examining his bowling record.

In the winter and spring of 1937–38 bowling was the most significant social activity for the Nortons. Saturday night's intra-clique and individual matches became the climax of the week's events. During the week the boys discussed what had happened the previous Saturday night and what would happen on the coming Saturday night. A man's performance was subject to continual evaluation and criticism. There was, therefore, a close connection between a man's bowling and his position in the group.

The team used against the Community Club had consisted of two men (Doc and Long John) who ranked high and three men (Joe Dodge, Frank Bonelli, and Tommy) who had a low standing. When bowling became a fixed group activity, the Nortons' team evolved along different lines. Danny joined the Saturday-night crowd and rapidly made a place for himself. He performed very well and picked Doc as his favorite opponent. There was a good-natured rivalry between them. In individual competition Danny usually won, although his average in the group matches was no better than that of Doc's. After the Community Club match, when Doc selected a team to represent the Nortons against other corner gangs and clubs, he chose Danny, Long John, and himself, leaving two vacancies on the five-man team. At this time, Mike, who had never been a good bowler, was just beginning to bowl regularly and had not established his reputation. Significantly enough, the vacancies were not filled from the ranks of the clique. On Saturday nights the boys had been bowling with Chris Teludo, Nutsy's older cousin, and Mark Ciampa, a man who associated with them only at the bowling alleys. Both men were popular and were first-class bowlers. They were chosen by Doc, with the agreement of Danny and Long John, to bowl for the Nortons. It was only when a member of the regular team was absent that one of the followers in the clique was called in, and on such occasions he never distinguished himself.

The followers were not content with being substitutes. They claimed that they had not been given an opportunity to prove their ability. One Saturday night in February, 1938, Mike organized an intraclique match. His team was made up of Chris Teludo, Doc, Long John, himself, and me. Danny was sick at the time, and I was put in to substitute for him. Frank, Alec, Joe, Lou, and Tommy made up the other team. Interest in this match was more intense than in the ordinary "choose-up" matches, but the followers bowled poorly and never had a chance.

After this one encounter the followers were recognized as the second team and never again challenged the team of Doc, Danny, Long John, Mark, and Chris.

Instead, they took to individual efforts to better their positions.

On his athletic ability alone, Frank should have been an excellent bowler. His ball-playing had won him positions on semiprofessional teams and a promise—though unfulfilled—of a job on a minor-league team. And it was not lack of practice that held him back, for, along with Alec and Joe Dodge, he bowled more frequently than Doc, Danny, or Mike. During the winter of 1937–38 Frank occupied a particularly subordinate position in the group. He spent his time with Alec in the pastry shop owned by Alec's uncle, and, since he had little employment throughout the winter, he became dependent upon Alec for a large part of the expenses of his participation in group activities. Frank fell to the bottom of the group. His financial dependence preyed upon his mind. While he sometimes bowled well, he was never a serious threat to break into the first team.

Some events of June, 1937, cast additional light upon Frank's position. Mike organized a baseball team of some of the Nortons to play against a younger group of Norton Street corner boys. On the basis of his record, Frank was considered the best player on either team, yet he made a miserable showing. He said to me: "I can't seem to play ball when I'm playing with fellows I know, like that bunch. I do much better when I'm playing for the Stanley A.C. against some team in Dexter, Westland, or out of town." Accustomed to filling an inferior position, Frank was unable to star even in his favorite sport when he was competing against members of his own group.

One evening I heard Alec boasting to Long John that the way he was bowling he could take on every man on the first team and lick them all. Long John dismissed the challenge with these words: "You think you could beat us, but, under pressure, you die!"

Alec objected vehemently, yet he recognized the prevailing group opinion of his bowling. He made the highest single score of the season, and he frequently excelled during the week when he bowled with Frank, Long John, Joe Dodge, and me, but on Saturday nights, when the group was all assembled, his performance was quite different. Shortly after this conversation Alec had several chances to prove himself, but each time it was "an off night," and he failed.

Carl, Joe, Lou, and Fred were never good enough to gain any recognition. Tommy was recognized as a first-class bowler, but he did most of his bowling with a younger group.

One of the best guides to the bowling standing of the members was furnished by a match held toward the end of April, 1938. Doc had an idea that we should climax the season with an individual competition among the members of the clique. He persuaded the owner of the alleys to contribute ten dollars in prize money to be divided among the three highest scorers. It was decided that only those who had bowled regularly should be eligible, and on this basis Lou, Fred, and Tommy were eliminated.

Interest in this contest ran high. The probable performances of the various bowlers were widely discussed. Doc, Danny, and Long John each listed his predictions. They were unanimous in conceding the first five places to themselves, Mark Ciampa, and Chris Teludo, although they differed in predicting the order among the first five. The next two positions were generally conceded to Mike and to me. All the ratings gave Joe Dodge last position, and Alec, Frank, and Carl were ranked close to the bottom.

The followers made no such lists, but Alec let it be known that he intended to show the boys something. Joe Dodge was annoyed to discover that he was the unanimous choice to finish last and argued that he was going to win.

When Chris Teludo did not appear for the match, the field was narrowed to ten. After the first four boxes, Alec was leading by several pins. He turned to Doc and said, "I'm out to get you boys tonight." But then he began to miss, and, as mistake followed

mistake, he stopped trying. Between turns, he went out for drinks, so that he became flushed and unsteady on his feet. He threw the ball carelessly, pretending that he was not interested in the competition. His collapse was sudden and complete; in the space of a few boxes he dropped from first to last place.

The bowlers finished in the following order:

1. Whyte	6. Joe
2. Danny	7. Mark
3. Doc	8. Carl
4. Long John	9. Frank
5. Mike	10. Alec

There were only two upsets in the contest, according to the predictions made by Doc, Danny, and Long John: Mark bowled very poorly and I won. However, it is important to note that neither Mark nor I fitted neatly into either part of the clique. Mark associated with the boys only at the bowling alleys and had no recognized status in the group. Although I was on good terms with all the boys, I was closer to the leaders than to the followers, since Doc was my particular friend. If Mark and I are left out of consideration, the performances were almost exactly what the leaders expected and the followers feared they would be. Danny, Doc, Long John, and Mike were bunched together at the top. Joe Dodge did better than was expected of him, but even he could not break through the solid ranks of the leadership.

Several days later Doc and Long John discussed the match with me.

> LONG JOHN: I only wanted to be sure that Alec or Joe Dodge didn't win. That wouldn't have been right.
> DOC: That's right. We didn't want to make it tough for you, because we all liked you, and the other fellows did too. If somebody had tried to make it tough

for you, we would have protected you.... If Joe Dodge or Alec had been out in front, it would have been different. We would have talked them out of it. We would have made plenty of noise. We would have been really vicious....

I asked Doc what would have happened if Alec or Joe had won.

They wouldn't have known how to take it. That's why we were out to beat them. If they had won, there would have been a lot of noise. Plenty of arguments. We would have called it lucky—things like that. We would have tried to get them in another match and then ruin them. We would have to put them in their places.

Every corner boy expects to be heckled as he bowls, but the heckling can take various forms. While I had moved ahead as early as the end of the second string, I was subjected only to good-natured kidding. The leaders watched me with mingled surprise and amusement; in a very real sense, I was permitted to win.

Even so, my victory required certain adjustments. I was hailed jocularly as "the Champ" or even as "the Cheese Champ." Rather than accept this designation, I pressed my claim for recognition. Doc arranged to have me bowl a match against Long John. If I won, I should have the right to challenge Doc or Danny. The four of us went to the alleys together. Urged on by Doc and Danny, Long John won a decisive victory. I made no further challenges.

Alec was only temporarily crushed by his defeat. For a few days he was not seen on the corner, but then he returned and sought to re-establish himself. When the boys went bowling, he challenged Long John to an individual match and defeated him. Alec began to talk once more. Again he challenged Long John to a match, and again he

defeated him. When bowling was resumed in the fall, Long John became Alec's favorite opponent, and for some time Alec nearly always came out ahead. He gloated. Long John explained: "He seems to have the Indian sign on me." And that is the way these incidents were interpreted by others—simply as a queer quirk of the game.

It is significant that, in making his challenge, Alec selected Long John instead of Doc, Danny, or Mike. It was not that Long John's bowling ability was uncertain. His average was about the same as that of Doc or Danny and better than that of Mike. As a member of the top group but not a leader in his own right, it was his social position that was vulnerable.

When Long John and Alec acted outside the group situation, it became possible for Alec to win. Long John was still considered the dependable man in a team match, and that was more important in relation to a man's standing in the group. Nevertheless, the leaders felt that Alec should not be defeating Long John and tried to reverse the situation. As Doc told me:

Alec isn't so aggressive these days. I steamed up at the way he was going after Long John, and I blasted him.... Then I talked to Long John. John is an introvert. He broods over things, and sometimes he feels inferior. He can't be aggressive like Alec, and when Alec tells him how he can always beat him, Long John gets to think that Alec is the better bowler.... I talked to him. I made him see that he should bowl better than Alec. I persuaded him that he was really the better bowler.... Now you watch them the next time out. I'll bet Long John will ruin him.

The next time Long John did defeat Alec. He was not able to do it every time, but they became so evenly matched that Alec lost interest in such competition.

The records of the season 1937–38 show a very close correspondence between social position and bowling performance. This developed because bowling became the primary social activity of the group. It became the main vehicle whereby the individual could maintain, gain, or lose prestige.

Bowling scores did not fall automatically into this pattern. There were certain customary ways of behaving which exerted pressure upon the individuals. Chief among these were the manner of choosing sides and the verbal attacks the members directed against one another.

Generally, two men chose sides in order to divide the group into two five-man teams. The choosers were often, but not always, among the best bowlers. If they were evenly matched, two poor bowlers frequently did the choosing, but in all cases the process was essentially the same. Each one tried to select the best bowler among those who were still unchosen. When more than ten men were present, choice was limited to the first ten to arrive, so that even a poor bowler would be chosen if he came early. It was the order of choice which was important. Sides were chosen several times each Saturday night, and in this way a man was constantly reminded of the value placed upon his ability by his fellows and of the sort of performance expected of him.

Of course, personal preferences entered into the selection of bowlers, but if a man chose a team of poor bowlers just because they were his closest friends, he pleased no one, least of all his team mates. It was the custom among the Nortons to have the losing team pay for the string bowled by the winners. As a rule, this small stake did not play an important role in the bowling, but no one liked to pay without the compensating enjoyment of a closely contested string. For this reason the selections by good bowlers or by poor bowlers coincided very closely. It became generally understood which men should be among the first chosen in order to make for an interesting match.

When Doc, Danny, Long John, or Mike bowled on opposing sides, they kidded one another good-naturedly. Good scores were expected of them, and bad scores were accounted for by bad luck or temporary lapses of form. When a follower threatened to better his position, the remarks took quite a different form. The boys shouted at him that he was lucky, that he was "bowling over his head." The effort was made to persuade him that he should not be bowling as well as he was, that a good performance was abnormal for him. This type of verbal attack was very important in keeping the members "in their places." It was used particularly by the followers so that, in effect, they were trying to keep one another down. While Long John, one of the most frequent targets for such attacks, responded in kind, Doc, Danny, and Mike seldom used this weapon. However, the leaders would have met a real threat on the part of Alec or Joe by such psychological pressures.

The origination of group action is another factor in the situation. The Community Club match really inaugurated bowling as a group activity, and that match was arranged by Doc. Group activities are originated by the men with highest standing in the group, and it is natural for a man to encourage an activity in which he excels and discourage one in which he does not excel. However, this cannot explain Mike's performance, for he had never bowled well before Saturday night at the alleys became a fixture for the Nortons.

The standing of the men in the eyes of other groups also contributed toward maintaining social differentiation within the group. In the season of 1938–39 Doc began keeping the scores of each man every Saturday night so that the Nortons' team could be selected strictly according to the averages of the bowlers, and there could be no accusation of favoritism. One afternoon when we were talking about bowling performances, I asked Doc and Danny what would happen if five members of the second team should make better averages than the first team bowlers. Would they then become the first team? Danny said:

> Suppose they did beat us, and the San Marcos would come up and want a match with us. We'd tell them, those fellows are really the first team, but the San Marcos would say, "We don't want to bowl them, we want to bowl you." We would say, "All right, you want to bowl Doc's team?" and we would bowl them.

Doc added:

> I want you to understand, Bill, we're conducting this according to democratic principles. It's the others who won't let us be democratic.

35

HOWARD S. BECKER

THE PROFESSIONAL DANCE MUSICIAN AND HIS AUDIENCE (1951)

One might think that recreational spaces such as dance halls are places in which patrons and musicians simply have a good time. But Howard S. Becker demonstrates that musicians come to resent the very people whose presence pays their salary. They see their fans as "squares" whose requests for popular songs annoy them. By contrast they view themselves as hip, and so they self-segregate and try to have as little as possible to do with their audience.

The service occupations are, in general, distinguished by the fact that the worker in them comes into more or less direct and personal contact with the ultimate consumer of the product of his work, the client for whom he performs the service. Consequently, the client is able to direct or attempt to direct the worker at his task and to apply sanctions of various kinds, ranging from informal pressure to the withdrawal of his patronage and the conferring of it on some other of the many people who perform the service.

This contact brings together a person whose full-time activity is centered around the occupation and whose self is to some degree deeply involved in it and another person whose relation to it is much more casual, and it may be inevitable that the two should have widely varying pictures of the way in which the occupational service should be performed. It seems characteristic of such occupations that their members consider the client unable to judge the proper worth of the service and resent bitterly any attempt on his part to exercise control over the work. A good deal of conflict and hostility arises as a result, and methods of defense against outside interference become a preoccupation of the members.

The present paper outlines the dimensions of such an occupational dilemma as observed among professional dance musicians in a large American city. This occupation presents an extremely favorable situation for studying such phenomena, since in it the problem is, to a greater degree than in many occupations, frankly faced and openly discussed. Musicians feel that the only music worth playing is what they call "jazz," a term which can be defined only as that music which is produced without reference to the demands of outsiders. Yet they must endure unceasing interference with their playing by employer and audience. The most distressing problem in the career of the average musician is the necessity of choosing between conventional success and his "artistic" standards. In order to achieve success he finds it necessary to "go commercial," that is, to play in accord with the wishes of the nonmusicians for whom he works; in so doing he sacrifices the respect of other musicians and thus, in most cases, his self-respect. If he remains true to his standards, he is doomed to failure in the larger society. Musicians classify themselves according to the degree to which they give in to outsiders; the continuum ranges from the extreme "jazz" musician to the "commercial" musician.[1]

The discussion will center around the following points: (1) the conceptions which musicians have of themselves and of the nonmusicians for whom they work and the conflict they feel to be inherent in this relation, (2) the basic consensus underlying the reactions of both commercial and jazz musicians to this conflict, and (3) feelings of isolation and the segregating of themselves from audience and community. The analysis is based on materials gathered during eighteen months of interviewing and participant observation. My research was disclosed to few people. In general, I was accepted as just another young piano player by most of the men from whom this material was gathered. The bulk of the material comes from younger men, but enough

contact was made with other musicians to permit the analysis of basic occupational problems.

I. Musician and "Square"

The whole system of beliefs about what musicians are and what audiences are is summed up in a word used by musicians to refer to outsiders—"square." It is used as a noun and as an adjective, denoting both a kind of person and a quality of behavior and objects. The term refers to the kind of person who is the opposite of all the musician is, or should be, and a way of thinking, feeling, and behaving (with its expression in material objects) which is the opposite of that valued by musicians.

The musician is conceived of by the professional group as an artist who possesses a mysterious artistic gift setting him apart from all other people. Possessing this gift, he should be free from control by outsiders who lack it. The gift is something which cannot be acquired through education; the outsider, therefore, can never become a member of the group. A trombone player said, "You can't teach a guy to have a beat. Either he's got one or he hasn't. If he hasn't got it, you can't teach it to him."

The musician feels that under no circumstances should any outsider be allowed to tell him what to play or how to play it. In fact, the strongest element in the colleague code is the prohibition against a musician criticizing or in any other way trying to put pressure on another musician in the actual playing situation "on the job." Where not even a colleague is permitted to influence the work, it is unthinkable that an outsider should be allowed to do so.

This attitude is generalized into a feeling that musicians are completely different from and better than other kinds of people and accordingly ought not to be subject to the control of outsiders in any branch of life, particularly in their artistic activity. The feeling of being a different kind of person who leads a different kind of life is deep-seated, as the following remarks indicate:

> I'm telling you, musicians are different than other people. They talk different, they act different, they look different. They're just not like other people, that's all.... You know it's hard to get out of the music business because you feel so different from others.
>
> Musicians live an exotic life, like in a jungle or something. They start out, they're just ordinary kids from small towns—but once they get into that life they change. It's like a jungle, except that their jungle is a hot, crowded bus. You live that kind of life long enough, you just get to be completely different.
>
> Being a musician was great, I'll never regret it. I'll understand things that squares never will.

An extreme of this view is the belief that only musicians are sensitive and unconventional enough to be able to give real sexual satisfaction to a woman.

Feeling their difference strongly, musicians likewise believe that beings such as they are under no obligation to follow the conventional behavior of the squares. From the idea that no one can tell a musician how to play it follows logically that no one can tell a musician how to do anything. Accordingly, behavior which flouts conventional social norms is greatly admired. Stories reveal this admiration for highly individual, spontaneous, "devil-may-care" activities; many of the most noted jazzmen are renowned as "characters," and their exploits are widely recounted. For example, one well-known jazzman is noted for having jumped on a policeman's horse standing in front of the night club in which he worked and ridden it away. The ordinary musician likes to tell stories of unconventional things he has done:

> We played the dance and after the job was over we packed up to get back in this old bus and make it back to Detroit. A little way out of town the car just refused to go. There was plenty of gas; it just wouldn't run. These guys all climbed out and stood around griping. All of a sudden, somebody said, "Let's set it on fire!" So someone got some gas out of the tank and sprinkled it around, touching a match to it and whoosh, it just went up in smoke. What an experience! The car burning up and all these guys standing around hollering and clapping their hands. It was really something.

This is more than idiosyncrasy; it is a primary occupational value, as indicated by the following observation of a young musician: "You know, the biggest heroes in the music business are the biggest characters. The crazier a guy acts, the greater he is, the more everyone likes him."

As they do not wish to be forced to live in terms of social conventions, so musicians do not attempt to force these conventions on others. For example, a musician declared that ethnic discrimination is wrong, since every person is entitled to act and believe as he wants to:

> S———, I don't believe in any discrimination like that. People are people, whether they're Dagos or Jews or Irishmen or Polacks or what. Only big squares care what religion they are. It don't mean a f———ing thing to me. Every person's entitled to believe his own way, that's the way I feel about it. Of course, I never go to church myself, but I don't hold it against anybody who does. It's all right if you like that sort of thing.

The same musician classified a friend's sex behavior as wrong, yet defended the individual's right to decide what is right and wrong for himself: "Eddie f———s around too much; he's gonna kill himself or else get killed by some broad. And he's got a nice wife too. He shouldn't treat her like that. But what the f———, that's his business. If that's the way he wants to live, if he's happy that way, then that's the way he oughta do." Musicians will tolerate quite extraordinary behavior in a fellow-musician without making any attempt to punish or restrain. In the following incident the uncontrolled behavior of a drummer loses a job for an orchestra; yet, angry as they are, they lend him money and refrain from punishing him in any way. It would be a breach of custom were anyone to reprimand him.

> JERRY: When we got up there, the first thing that happened was that all his drums didn't show up. So the owner drives all around trying to find some drums for him and then the owner smashes a fender while he was doing it. So I knew right away that we were off to a good start. And Jack! Man, the boss is an old Dago, you know, no bulls——— about him, he runs a gambling joint; he don't take any s——— from anyone. So he says to Jack, "What are you gonna do without drums?" Jack says, "Be cool, daddio, everything'll be real gone, you know." I thought the old guy would blow his top. What a way to talk to the boss. Boy, he turned around, there was fire in his eye. I knew we wouldn't last after that. He says to me, "Is that drummer all there?" I said, "I don't know, I never saw him before today." And we just got finished telling him we'd been playing together six months. So that helped, too. Of course, when Jack started playing, that was the end. So loud! And he don't play a beat at all. All he uses the bass drum for is accents. What kind of drumming

is that? Otherwise, it was a good little outfit.... It was a good job. We could have been there forever.... Well, after we played a couple of sets, the boss told us we were through.

> BECKER: What happened after you got fired?

> JERRY: The boss gave us twenty apiece and told us to go home. So it cost us seventeen dollars for transportation up and back, we made three bucks on the job. Of course, we saw plenty of trees. Three bucks, hell, we didn't even make that. We loaned Jack seven or eight.

The musician thus views himself and his colleagues as people with a special gift which makes them different from non-musicians and not subject to their control, either in musical performance or in ordinary social behavior.

The square, on the other hand, lacks this special gift and any understanding of the music or way of life of those who possess it. The square is thought of as an ignorant, intolerant person who is to be feared, since he produces the pressures forcing the musician to play inartistically. The musicians' difficulty lies in the fact that the square is in a position to get his way: if he does not like the kind of music played, he does not pay to hear it a second time.

Not understanding music, the square judges music by standards which are foreign to musicians and not respected by them. A "commercial" saxophonist observed sarcastically:

> It doesn't make any difference what we play, the way we do it. It's so simple that anyone who's been playing longer than a month could handle it. Jack plays a chorus on piano or something, then saxes or something, all unison. It's very easy. But the people don't care. As long as they can hear the drum they're all right. They hear the drum, then they know to put their right foot in front of their left foot

and their left foot in front of their right foot. Then if they can hear the melody to whistle to, they're happy. What more could they want?

The following conversation illustrates the same attitude:

> JOE: You'd get off the stand and walk down the aisle, somebody'd say, "Young man, I like your orchestra very much." Just because you played soft and the tenorman doubled fiddle or something like that, the squares liked it....
> DICK: It was like that when I worked at the M—— Club. All the kids that I went to high school with used to come out and dig the band.... That was one of the worst bands I ever worked on and they all thought it was wonderful.
> JOE: Oh, well, they're just a bunch of squares anyhow.

"Squareness" is felt to penetrate every aspect of the square's behavior just as its opposite, "hipness" is evident in everything the musician does. The square seems to do everything wrong and is laughable and ludicrous. Musicians derive a good deal of amusement from sitting in a corner and watching the squares. Everyone has stories to tell about the laughable antics of squares. One man went so far as to suggest that the musicians should change places with the people sitting at the bar of the tavern he worked in; he claimed that they were funnier and more entertaining than he could possibly be. Every item of dress, speech, and behavior which differs from that of the musician is taken as new evidence of the inherent insensitivity and ignorance of the square. Since musicians have an esoteric culture these evidences are many and serve only to fortify their conviction that musicians and squares are two different kinds of people.

But the square is feared as well, since he is thought of as the ultimate source of "commercial" pressure. It is the square's ignorance of music that compels the musician to play what he considers bad music in order to be successful.

> BECKER: How do you feel about the people you play for, the audience?
> DAVE: They're a drag.
> BECKER: Why do you say that?
> DAVE: Well, if you're working on a commercial band, they like it and so you have to play more corn. If you're working on a good band, then they don't like it, and that's a drag. If you're working on a good band and they like it, then that's a drag, too. You hate them anyway, because you know that they don't know what it's all about. They're just a big drag.

This last statement reveals that even those who attempt to avoid being square are still considered so, because they still lack the proper understanding, which only a musician can have—"they don't know what it's all about." The "jazz fan" is thus respected no more than other squares. His liking for jazz is without understanding and he acts just like the other squares; he will request songs and try to influence the musician's playing, just as other squares do.

The musician thus sees himself as a creative artist who should be free from outside control, a person different from and better than those outsiders he calls squares who understand neither his music nor his way of life and yet because of whom he must perform in a manner contrary to his professional ideals.

II. Reactions to the Conflict

We will now consider the attitudes of "commercial" and "jazz" musicians toward the audience, noting both the variation in attitude and the basic consensus underlying the two sets of feelings. Two themes run through this conflict: (1) the desire of the musician to live in terms of the creative principle, and (2) the recognition of many forces influencing him to abandon that principle. The jazzman tends to emphasize the first, the commercial musician the second; but both recognize and feel the force of each of these guiding influences. Common to the attitudes of both kinds of musician is an intense contempt for and dislike of the square audience whose fault it is that musicians must "go commercial" in order to succeed.

The commercial musician, though he conceives of the audience as squares, chooses to sacrifice self-respect and the respect of other musicians (the rewards of artistic behavior) for the more substantial rewards of steady work, higher income, and the prestige enjoyed by the man who "goes commercial." One commercial musician commented:

> They've got a nice class of people out here, too. Of course, they're squares, I'm not trying to deny that. Sure, they're a bunch of f——ing squares, but who the f—— pays the bills? They pay 'em, so you gotta play what they want. I mean, what the s——, you can't make a living if you don't play for the squares. How many f——ing people you think aren't squares? Out of a hundred people you'd be lucky if 15 per cent weren't squares. I mean, maybe professional people—doctors, lawyers, like that—they might not be square, but the average person is just a big f——ing square. Of course, show people aren't like that. But outside of show people and professional people, everybody's a f——ing square.[2] They don't know anything.
>
> I'll tell you. This is something I learned about three years ago. If you want to make any money you gotta please the squares. They're the ones that pay the bills, and you gotta play for them. A good musician can't get a

f——ing job. You gotta play a bunch of s——. But what the f——, let's face it. I want to live good. I want to make some money; I want a car, you know. How long can you fight it?... .

> Don't get me wrong. If you can make money playing jazz, great. But how many guys can do it?...If you can play jazz, great, like I said. But if you're on a bad f——ing job, there's no sense fighting it, you gotta be commercial. I mean, the squares are paying your salary, so you might as well get used to it, they're the ones you gotta please.

It is to be noted that the speaker admits it is more "respectable" to be independent of the squares, and expresses contempt for the audience, whose squareness is made responsible for the whole situation.

These men phrase the problem primarily in economic terms: "I mean, s——, if you're playing for a bunch of squares you're playing for a bunch of squares. What the f——are you gonna do? You can't push it down their throats. Well, I suppose you can make 'em eat it, but after all, they *are* paying you."

The jazzman feels the need to satisfy the audience just as strongly, although maintaining that one should not give in to it. Jazzmen, like others, appreciate steady jobs and good jobs and know that they must satisfy the audience to get them, as the following conversation between two young jazzmen illustrates:

> CHARLIE: There aren't any jobs where you can blow jazz. You have to play rumbas and pops[3] and everything. You can't get anywhere blowing jazz. Man, I don't want to scuffle all my life.
> EDDIE: Well, you want to enjoy yourself, don't you? You won't be happy playing commercial. You know that.
> CHARLIE: I guess there's just no way for a cat to be happy. 'Cause it sure is a

drag blowing commercial, but it's an awful drag not ever doing anything and playing jazz.

EDDIE: Jesus, why can't you be successful playing jazz?... I mean, you could have a great little outfit and still play arrangements, but good ones, you know.

CHARLIE: You could never get a job for a band like that.

EDDIE: Well, you could have a sexy little bitch to stand up in front and sing and shake her ass at the bears.[4] Then you could get a job. And you could still play great when she wasn't singing.

CHARLIE: Well, wasn't that what Q———'s band was like? Did you enjoy that? Did you like the way she sang?

EDDIE: No, man, but we played jazz, you know.

CHARLIE: Did you like the kind of jazz you were playing? It was kind of commercial, wasn't it?

EDDIE: Yeah, but it could have been great.

CHARLIE: Yeah, if it had been great, you wouldn't have kept on working. I guess we'll always just be unhappy. It's just the way things are. You'll always be drug[5] with yourself.... There'll never be any kind of a really great job for a musician.

In addition to the pressure to please the audience which emanates from the musician's desire to maximize salary and income, there are more immediate pressures. It is often difficult to maintain an independent attitude. For example:

I worked an Italian wedding on the Southwest Side last night with Johnny Ponzi. We played about half an hour, doing the special arrangements they use, which are pretty uncommercial. Then an old Italian fellow (the father-in-law of the groom, as we later found out) began hollering, "Play some polkas, play some Italian music. Ah, you stink,

you're lousy." Johnny always tries to avoid the inevitable on these wedding jobs, putting off playing the folk music as long as he can. I said, "Man, why don't we play some of that stuff now and get it over with?" Tom said, "I'm afraid if we start doing that we'll be doing it all night." Johnny said, "Look, Howard, the groom is a real great guy. He told us to play anything we want and not to pay any attention to what the people say, so don't worry about it...."

The old fellow kept hollering and pretty soon the groom came up and said, "Listen, fellows. I know you don't want to play any of that s—— and I don't want you to, but that's my father-in-law, see. The only thing is, I don't want to embarrass my wife for him, so play some Dago music to keep him quiet, will yuh?" Johnny looked around at us and made a gesture of resignation.

He said, "All right, let's play the *Beer Barrel Polka*." Tom said, "Oh s——! Here we go." We played it and then we played an Italian dance, the *Tarentelle*.

Sometimes the employer applies pressure which makes even an uncompromising jazzman give in, at least for the duration of the job:

I was playing solo for one night over at the Y—— on ——rd St. What a drag! The second set, I was playing *Sunny Side,* I played the melody for one chorus, then I played a little jazz. All of a sudden the boss leaned over the side of the bar and hollered, "I'll kiss your ass if anybody in this place knows what tune you're playing!" And everybody in the place heard him, too. What a big square! What could I do? I didn't say anything, just kept playing. Sure was a drag.

Somewhat inconsistently, the musician wants to feel that he is reaching the audience and that they are getting some enjoyment from his work, and this leads him to give in to audience demands. One man said:

> I enjoy playing more when there's someone to play for. You kind of feel like there isn't much purpose in playing if there's nobody there to hear you. I mean, after all, that's what music's for—for people to hear and get enjoyment from. That's why I don't mind playing corny too much. If anyone enjoys it, then I kind of get a kick out of it. I guess I'm kind of a ham. But I like to make people happy that way.

This statement is somewhat extreme; but most musicians feel it strongly enough to want to avoid the active dislike of the audience: "That's why I like to work with Tommy. At least when you get off the stand, everybody in the place doesn't hate you. It's a drag to work under conditions like that, where everybody in the place just hates the whole band."

III. Isolation and Self-Segregation

Musicians are hostile to their audiences, being afraid that they must sacrifice their artistic standards to the squares. They exhibit certain patterns of behavior and belief which may be viewed as adjustments to this situation; they will be referred to here as "isolation" and "self-segregation" and are expressed in the actual playing situation and in participation in the social intercourse of the larger community. The primary function of this behavior is to protect the musician from the interference of the square audience and, by extension, of the conventional society.

The musician is, as a rule, spatially isolated from the audience, being placed on a platform which, being inaccessible to them, provides a physical barrier that prevents any direct interaction. This isolation is welcomed because the audience, being made up of squares, is felt to be potentially dangerous. The musicians fear that direct contact with the audience can lead only to interference with the musical performance. Therefore, it is safer to be isolated and have nothing to do with them. Once, where such physical isolation was not provided, a player commented:

> Another thing about weddings, man. You're right down on the floor, right in the middle of the people. You can't get away from them. It's different if you're playing a dance or in a bar. In a dance-hall you're up on a stage where they can't get at you. The same thing in a cocktail lounge, you're up behind the bar. But a wedding—man, you're right in the middle of them.

Musicians, lacking the usually provided physical barriers, often improvise their own and effectively segregate themselves from their audience.

> I had a Jewish wedding job for Sunday night.... When I arrived, the rest of the boys were already there. The wedding had taken place late, so that the people were just beginning to eat. We decided, after I had conferred with the groom, to play during dinner. We set up in a far corner of the hall. Jerry pulled the piano around so that it blocked off a small space, which was thus separated from the rest of the people. Tony set up his drums in this space, and Jerry and Johnny stood there while we played. I wanted to move the piano so that the boys could stand out in front of it and be next to the audience, but Jerry said, half-jokingly, "No, man. I have to have some protection from the squares." So we left things as they were....

Jerry had moved around in front of the piano but, again half-humorously, had put two chairs in front of him, which separated him from the audience. When a couple took the chairs to sit on, Jerry set two more in their place. Johnny said, "Man, why don't we sit on those chairs?" Jerry said, "No, man. Just leave them there. That's my barricade to protect me from the squares."

Many musicians almost reflexively avoid establishing contact with members of the audience. When walking among them, they habitually avoid meeting the eyes of squares for fear that this will establish some relationship on the basis of which the square will then request songs or in some other way attempt to influence the musical performance. Some extend their behavior to their ordinary social activity, outside of professional situations. A certain amount of this is inevitable, since the conditions of work—late hours, great geographic mobility, and so on—make social participation outside of the professional group difficult. If one works while others sleep, it is difficult to have ordinary social intercourse with them. This was cited by a musician who had left the profession, in partial explanation of his action: "And it's great to work regular hours, too, where you can see people instead of having to go to work every night." Some younger musicians complain that the hours of work make it hard for them to establish contacts with "nice" girls, since they preclude the conventional date.

But much of this behavior develops out of the hostility toward squares. The attitude is seen in its extreme among the "X—— Avenue Boys," a clique of extreme jazzmen who reject the American culture *in toto*. The quality of their feeling toward the outside world is indicated by one man's private title for his theme song: "If You Don't Like My Queer Ways You Can Kiss My F———ing

Ass." The ethnic makeup of the group indicated further that their adoption of these extreme artistic and social attitudes was part of a total rejection of conventional American society. With few exceptions the men came from older, more fully assimilated national groups: Irish, Scandinavian, German, and English. Further, many of them were reputed to come from wealthy families and the higher social classes. In short, their rejection of commercialism in music and squares in social life was part of the casting aside of the total American culture by men who could enjoy privileged status but who were unable to achieve a satisfactory personal adjustment within it.[6]

Every interest of this group emphasized their isolation from the standards and interests of the conventional society. They associated almost exclusively with other musicians and girls who sang or danced in night clubs in the North Clark Street area of Chicago and had little or no contact with the conventional world. They were described politically thus: "They hate this form of government anyway and think it's real bad." They were unremittingly critical of both business and labor, disillusioned with the economic structure, and completely cynical about the political process and contemporary political parties. Religion and marriage were rejected completely, as were American popular and serious culture, and their reading was confined solely to the more esoteric *avant garde* writers and philosophers. In art and symphonic music they were interested also in only the most esoteric developments. In every case they were quick to point out that their interests were not those of the conventional society and that they were thereby differentiated from it. It is reasonable to assume that the primary function of these interests was to make this differentiation unmistakably clear.

Although isolation and self-segregation found their most extreme development among the "X—— Avenue Boys," they were manifested by less deviant musicians as well. The feeling of being isolated from the rest of the society was often quite strong; the following conversation, which took place between two young jazzmen, illustrates two reactions to the sense of isolation.

> EDDIE: You know, man, I hate people. I can't stand to be around squares. They drag me so much I just can't stand them.
> CHARLIE: You shouldn't be like that, man. Don't let them drag you. Just laugh at them. That's what I do. Just laugh at everything they do. That's the only way you'll be able to stand it.

A young Jewish musician, who definitely identified himself with the Jewish community, nevertheless felt this professional isolation strongly enough to make the following statements.

> You know, a little knowledge is a dangerous thing. That's what happened to me when I first started playing. I just felt like I knew too much. I sort of saw, or felt, that all my friends from the neighborhood were real square and stupid....
>
> You know, it's funny. When you sit on that stand up there, you feel so different from others. Like I can even understand how Gentiles feel toward Jews. You see these people come up and they look Jewish, or they have a little bit of an accent or something, and they ask for a rumba or some damn thing like that, and I just feel, "What damn squares, these Jews," just like I was a goy myself. That's what I mean when I say you learn too much being a musician. I mean, you see so many things and get such a broad outlook on life that the average person just doesn't have.

On another occasion the same man remarked:

> DICK: You know, since I've been out of work I've actually gotten so that I can talk to some of these guys in the neighborhood.
> BECKER: You mean you had trouble talking to them before?
> DICK: Well, I'd just stand around and not know what to say. It still sobers me up to talk to those guys. Everything they say seems real silly and uninteresting.

The process of self-segregation is evident in certain symbolic expressions, particularly in the use of an occupational slang which readily identifies the man who can use it properly as someone who is not square and as quickly reveals as an outsider the person who uses it incorrectly or not at all. Some words have grown up to refer to unique professional problems and attitudes of musicians, typical of them being the term "square." Such words enable musicians to discuss problems and activities for which ordinary language provides no adequate terminology. There are, however, many words which are merely substitutes for the more common expressions without adding any new meaning. For example, the following are synonyms for money: "loot," "gold," "geetz," and "bread." Jobs are referred to as "gigs." There are innumerable synonyms for marijuana, the most common being "gauge," "pot," "charge," "tea," and "s——."[7]

The function of such behavior is pointed out by a young musician who was quitting the business:

> I'm glad I'm getting out of the business, though. I'm getting sick of being around musicians. There's so much ritual and ceremony junk. They have to talk a special language, dress different, and wear a different kind of glasses. And it just

doesn't mean a damn thing except "we're different."

IV. Conclusion

This paper has explored certain dimensions of the relationship between dance musicians and their audience, emphasizing the hostility which arises out of the interaction of professional and layman in the working situation. Attention has also been paid to the way in which musicians feel themselves isolated from the larger society and how they maintain that isolation through various modes of self-segregation.

It may be suggested that similar conflicts are to be found in other service occupations and that research in such areas could profitably focus on such matters as the professional's conception of his client, the manner in which the client impinges on (or, from the professional's point of view, interferes with) his work, the effects of such conflicts on professional organization, with particular reference to the defensive tactics employed by the profession, and the relation of such dilemmas to the individual's participation in the life of the larger society.

NOTES

1. A full discussion of this situation may be found in the complete study on which this paper is based: Howard S. Becker, "The Professional Dance Musician in Chicago" (unpublished M.A. thesis, Department of Sociology, University of Chicago, 1949).
2. Most musicians would not admit these exceptions.
3. Popular songs.
4. Synonym for "squares."
5. Unhappy.
6. Professor David Riesman first called my attention to these implications of the data.
7. These words will probably be out of date soon after this is written; some already are. They change as musicians feel that they have gained currency among outsiders.

REFERENCE

Becker, Howard S. 1949. "The Professional Dance Musician in Chicago." Unpublished M.A. thesis, Department of Sociology, University of Chicago.

36

LOÏC WACQUANT

FIGHT NIGHT AT
STUDIO 104

from Body & Soul (2004)

Loïc Wacquant's *Body and Soul* is "carnal ethnography" of the fabrication of the boxer in the black American ghetto, based on a three-year apprenticeship of the craft in a gym on Chicago's South Side ghetto. In this selection, Wacquant takes us backstage of a run-of-the-mill "boxing card" headlined by one of his gym mates, Curtis Strong. He displays the enmeshment of the Sweet Science with black working-class sociability; maps out the basic types and strategies of prizefighters; and spotlights the interplay of interest and honor, constraint and desire, self-delusion and collective belief that propels boxers as they navigate the fistic economy. He also gives us glimpses of the subtle and ambivalent relation between the observer and the observed.

Welcome to Studio 104

We zip down the Dan Ryan Expressway until we hit 104th Street, then head east on Torrance Avenue to pull in two blocks down, at the end of the street, at a long, red brick, barnlike building nestled between a junkyard ("Bill's Used Auto Parts"), an industrial brewery, and a vacant lot bordered by abandoned railroad tracks. This is Studio 104 (pronounced "One-o-four"), a tavern and nightclub located for some thirty years in this declining working-class neighborhood isolated from the rest of the city, at the far end of the South Side.

I discovered this joint last month on the occasion of an outdoor card organized by its owner, the famed Lowhouse, a notorious gangster who, it is rumored, uses the fight nights held in the parking lot of his establishment to launder the monies drawn from the various illegal rackets he runs.[1] In point of fact, [head coach] DeeDee had warned me to be discreet with my tape recorder because the hoods who turf there could get the idea that I was an undercover cop or an FBI agent. I understood that the Woodlawn coach wasn't kidding when, several days after this card, [Matchmaker] Jack

Cowen came back to the subject during a conversation in the gym. "Louie better be more careful with his tape recorder, with all the dealers who hang out down there. If he walks around with his recorder like that, one of these days we might find a dead body on the other side of those railroad tracks." Here is a description of the place, as recorded in my field notebook following my first visit.

Studio 104 is a place for business, entertainment, and sociability specific to the African-American working class. It exudes a distinctive atmosphere: jovial, quasi-familial, and furiously "black." You come to this tavern not only to drink, feast, and dance but also and above all to mingle with friends and to "conversate" for hours among regulars.[2] You watch sports championships there, you celebrate birthdays there, you have bachelor parties there, you drown your sorrows and parade your joys there to the rhythm of the music, dance parties, and would-be erotic shows (wet T-shirt competitions, "sexy legs" contests, and assorted striptease gigs). The establishment and the neighborhood and its residents live in osmosis, as testified by the bevy of pickup trucks buzzing around it at the end of the day. On your way out, shy kids are handing out colored flyers announcing Fourth of July picnics thrown by local politicians and cards printed by the district's black representative (recently implicated by one of his secretaries in a murky sexual harassment case).

HEAR YOUR
CONGRESSMAN: GUS SAVAGE
10TH ANNUAL REPORT, STATUS OF
DEMOCRACY ON
INDEPENDENCE DAY!
(PENDING LEGISLATION)
JULY 4TH 1 P.M.,
KICKAPOO WOODS, 146TH AND
HALSTED

Clusters of roving young men and burly guys are ambling at the back of the parking lot where the ring has been set up, straight as ramrods, proud to the point of looking a touch threatening in their gaudy sweatsuits and caps with snakeskin visors, their chests heavily loaded with chains and gold medallions. The girls who accompany them—unescorted female spectators are far and few—are hypersexualized, made up and dressed provocatively, often seductive and always fleshly; short skirts, plunging necklines, and glamorous hairdos are a must. ([Manager] Jeb Garney is aroused by it all and loudly bemoans not being twenty years younger.) People are happy to be there, to see each other and to be seen, to exchange greetings and full-bellied laughter. Among the crowd are all the regulars at these events, trainers, old-timers, and aficionados of the Sweet science. A good number of the city's pro boxers come to size up possible rivals or simply to be admired, like "Jazzy" James Flowers, who is sauntering among the crowd decked out in his Illinois middleweight championship belt (as well as the stitches he earned along with it).

People mosey back and forth between the parking lot and the bar, knocking back drinks in generous quantities. Beer is flowing freely in spite of the high prices charged for consumables: $1.50 for a plastic cup of Old Style or a hot dog, a dollar for a can of soda, 50 cents for a bag of chips, and 25 cents for a glass of water. The bar alone is worth a visit: it's fifty feet long, with a magnificent gold-framed mirror running along one side, a giant color TV at one end, bathrooms on either side, and eight round tables surrounded by red Naugahyde armchairs in the middle of the room; in a corner stands a mock basketball backboard where customers can shoot hoops for 25 cents. Outside, people follow the fights distractedly, unless they personally know the boxer in action, in which case fanatical excitement erupts: frenetic applause, wild vociferations, yelling and shouting, high-pitched whistling, hooting, and howls of raucous laughter. Whether timid beginners or seasoned professionals, people noisily support the boxers from the area as a matter of local (and racial) patriotism. Kayos are always much appreciated, as is courage in adversity—the quality that practitioners of the

Manly art call "heart." But that's about it: this isn't a crowd of connoisseurs, far from it. The vast majority of the spectators at these shows has no knowledge of boxing at all and is therefore incapable of appreciating the fights on a technical and tactical level. Practitioners of the Sweet science, and particularly the trainers, commonly consider them to be "squares" who can be made to swallow anything, much the way jazz musicians view the audiences at the clubs they play.

"They Squares"

GENE [sixty-nine years old, head trainer at the Fuller Park gym]: The people who come to these shows, they squares. They jus' come in [in a tone heavy with derision], *they jus' get a kick outa seein' somebody kick somebody's ass*, know what I'm talkin' about? They don't come out—they don't know, well lotta people don't even know what they lookin' at.

LOUIE: Isn't it kinda depressing that you spend so much time perfecting that skill and people can't really appreciate it?

GENE: As long as they payin' the money...They don't know the difference, all they doin' is they see somebody gettin' they butt beat, they pay their ticket [his voice turns into a high-pitched whistle with incredulousness], *some people like dat*, you know peoples are like that!

LOUIE: It doesn't get on your nerves sometimes?

GENE: I been doin' it, seein' it for so long, it goes in *this* ear an' out the other ear, I don't even pay no attention [laughs]...Lotta don't understand [the fight] because they *never understand it*, they jus' *talk* about boxing, but they jus' don't, it's nothin' but talk.

The fact that the fights are taking place outdoors adds much to the appeal of the scene. The "card girls" who strut around in the ring between rounds to the great delight of the crowd, two tall, brazen black women turned out in minuscule bikinis that leave nothing to the imagination, are enticing to the point of whoreishness. The private security staff, comprised of three big, easygoing black policemen moonlighting off their job, take care of preventing any incidents and keep gatecrashers to a trickle. But they can't do much about the two dozen Mexicans watching the fight for free leaning up against the wall of their yellow frame house directly adjoining the parking lot.

We drop [coach] DeeDee off at the front door of the club, where Jeb Garney has been champing at the bit, wondering if we haven't gotten lost on the way. (As usual, he's dressed like a bum, in spite of the fact that he's rich in the millions from his racing dog kennels and his ranches.) Curtis, who addresses his manager with a deference that is painful to watch—"*Mister Garney*, please close the door, please, thank you sir"—hands him three blue tunics with "Curtis Strong" embroidered on them. Garney also finds that there's a little something missing: "We should have had them put on a gold stripe for each win."

The employees of the restaurant are raising a big blue tarp to cut off the parking lot from the street so that passersby won't have a free view of the ring. They have a terrible time getting it raised on its poles owing to the strong wind that keeps inflating it like a sail every time they lift it up. We run into [gym rat and photographer] Kitchen, with his sempiternal camera strapped across his chest. He presses Curtis to let him take pictures of his fight. Curtis recommends that he first check with Jeb Garney since he's the one who holds the purse strings. Kitchen would rather get Curtis's approval so as to put moral pressure later on his manager to buy the maximum number of pictures, but the Woodlawn boxer slips away. An enormous black limousine, sparkling with luxury, is parked in front of the door of the club, its three rows of seats spread out over ten yards behind tinted windows. Curtis whispers to me, a big smile lighting his face, "Pretty soon *it's gonna be my turn to be ridin' in one of those,*

Louie, you watch." I just hope that he'll pick me up hitchhiking when that day comes....

I glance at the official program for the event and find out that Little Keith, who has achieved four wins in five fights, will be facing an opponent who isn't exactly a titan of the ring, with a record of zero wins for thirteen bouts. As for Jeff Hannah [a boxer brought in from Indiana to face Curtis], he's run up 18 wins, 21 losses, and a draw. In other words, he's a solid "journeyman," seasoned but on a downhill slide for a while, who from now on will serve as a stepping-stone for boxers on the rise like Curtis. (This kind of disparity, which might seem shocking at first, is not at all anomalous: it is by pairing them up with notably weaker opponents that a promoter gives local pugilists, especially those to whom he might be linked by an exclusive contract, which is the case between Jack Cowen and Curtis, a decisive advantage, if not a guarantee of victory—a surprise is always possible inside the ropes, as we will soon discover.)[3]

Instead of changing clothes in a van parked on the lot in the midst of which sits the ring, as they did for last month's card, the fighters have a dressing room inside the club at their disposal this time. If you can call it a dressing room, that is: since Curtis is the headliner, the boxers from Woodlawn have been allotted a storeroom behind the ticket window at the entrance to the nightclub. A room ten by thirteen feet, separated from the ticket booth by a blue curtain and encumbered with folded metal tables and chairs, cardboard boxes of Bacardi, piles of mops, cartons filled with various objects (ashtrays, knickknacks, coffee filters, aprons, kitchen utensils), a reel for a garden hose, two dismantled red wooden minibars, two broken popcorn machines, and four big stacks of posters vaunting Studio 104's weekly festivities: "Sexy Leg Contests," "Happy Hours," and the usual "Ladies' Nights." As we struggle to fit all of us into this cramped space, DeeDee asks the guys who aren't putting on the gloves tonight to make room and leave. We unfold three metal chairs as best we

can for Keith, Curtis, and Jeb Garney. As for DeeDee, he sits on a tall barstool (ideal for his knees, which balk at bending) and right away gets busy wrapping Keith's hands, since he will box first. Rolls of gauze, adhesive tape, scissors. Keith's gaze clouds over with apprehension. Meanwhile, the other boxers are changing in the adjoining dance hall next to the main bar, in full sight of the customers who are chatting and drinking away, leaning on one of the three counters.

Curtis whispers to me with an air of mystery, "C'mon, Louie, come with me." He just wants me to go with him to the bathroom, which is pretty scuzzy, with malodorous toilets surrounded by pools of urine. He disappears into one of the stalls, from which he continues to "conversate" with me while defecating with loud noise. "I really needed to take a shit. Ooooh! [sound of a cascade of farts] all that gas!...So Louie, *doesn't all this all make you esscited? Dontchya wish you was fightin' pro?"* Yes, it's exciting, no question, but in order to fight with professionals, I would first have to have the requisite skills. It's true that with Curtis on the night's bill, there's electricity in the air. He looks serene, not at all anxious and shifty as he had been these last few days in the gym with his supposed arm injuries.[4] The hardest days are those preceding the bout; then, when the moment to fight approaches, Curtis gets his self-confidence back. He knows that he's going to climb into the ring, where he can express his talent as an "entertainer": once he's in the squared circle, he's in his element, "at the office" or "at home," as pugilists are fond of saying.[5]

"I Always Wanteda be an Entertainer"

[Curtis Strong, 23 years old, Illinois Junior Lightweight Champion]

It's *very important* to be a performer. One day, I thin' I was 'bout thirteen, I wan'ed be a *singer.* Me an' my brothers an' them, they didn' wanna sing. I use to always grab them, you know, from out the kitchen, they be by the fidgerator, I grab them [in an excited, giddy voice], "Come on, I got these steps I wantyall to see 'em." We go in the bedroom an' be rehearsin' these steps, but they always got *tired*, they tired out fas', they didn'—I guess they jus' didn' really git in to the entertainmen' part like I did: I always wanteda be an entertainer, it played a big par' in my life.

Lookin' at television, *Michael Jackson:* you know [murmuring in awe], seein' him, how he was jus'— how he *blossom like a flower* an' stuff, throughout the crowd, the public y'know. I jus' wan' to be a entertainer when I'm in the ring, I feel like I got to be at my bes', you know, t'perform to my bes'. I know if I'm at my bes', an' he [my opponent] at his bes', *somebody gotta be winnin', right?* An' the crow' gonna look at the guy that's winnin'. So if I'm in my bes', I can git the crow' underdivided [!] attention instead of tellin' them [in a muffled voice], "Sit down an' listen! Look at me!" You know, I git up there an' do my thin' an' everybody rootin' for…[lowering his voice even more for greater dramatic effect] *Curtis Strong.*

Back in the storeroom that's serving as the dressing room for the evening. Shoptalk…

On the program of tonight's card is a pro who's just starting out from Tinley Park, the neighborhood of Craig "Gator" Bodznianowski (a very popular local pug who fights in spite of having had his foot amputated after a motorcycle accident and who bought himself a fitness and weightlifting gym in that small white working-class burg with his earnings in the ring). An entire busload of guys from his gym are there to cheer him on. Which leaves Curtis puzzled. "How they get *all those white guys to come out all the way to d'South Side* like that, DeeDee?" DeeDee concedes that the black community doesn't support its own boxers at all, no

doubt due to lack of income. In response to which OB (O'Bannon's nickname) maintains that Curtis is the one bringing in most of the crowd tonight: "You're drawin', *you got a name* in Chicago." And then, without further warning, the three of them launch into a verbal joust about the differences between blacks and whites: the mailman starts off by tossing out "But I ain't colored, I never picked no cotton, never owned a mule," and the others instantly follow suit.[6] All the stereotypes about blacks are canvassed, from slavery to the ghetto. "That's what you should be gettin' on your tape, Louie," OB chuckles. To my great chagrin, I didn't catch this chunk of rhetorical bravura on tape and I wouldn't venture to try to transcribe it from memory!

Curtis's brothers come to greet him one by one: Derrick preening as the ultimate male, Lamont playing the part of the shy one, Bernard with his shaved head and spacey demeanor. They are followed by a half-dozen of his buddies who wish him good luck for his fight. Curtis asks OB if he isn't afraid of losing Steve Cokeley (a young hopeful from the club that the mailman sponsors) as he earlier lost Cliff, his pet boxer.

> OB: I ain't worried. As long as he's in the gym, got somebody to look out for him [with a pronounced nod toward DeeDee].
> CURTIS: But that's what I mean, 'cuz he ain't been in the gym that much…You were really taking care of Cliff, too, always askin' him if he need any money and stuff.
> OB: Oh, but Cliff, he was my son. The things I did for him, *my God* [rolling his eyes]…I went to get him at the gym and drove him back home every night. Found him a job, got his wife a job…

The mustachioed mailman goes on to insist that if Curtis succeeds in the ring, "it's because *you got a strong woman behind you,* that's what make the difference." Eddie interrupts them to get Curtis's attention: "Your dad's here at the door, you wanna see him?" Glacial silence—Curtis's father abandoned him when he was little, him and his seven brothers and sisters, and never expressed the slightest interest in him until his career in the ring started to take shape. Curtis darkens suddenly: "No, tell him no, *I don't wanna see nobody till after the fight.*" OB avers that Curtis should talk to him, for you don't brush your father aside like that. "And why should I? *You* can see him if you want." DeeDee intercedes in favor of his protégé: "An' he should see 'im for what? What they gonna be doin', uh, lookin' and gapin'? You don' need that now." Curtis swiftly takes refuge behind the authority of his coach: "Tell him DeeDee don't want nobody in d'dressing room right now." Besides, DeeDee is asking all the latest arrivals to clear the premises because we're literally stepping on each other, between Garney, Curtis, Keith, Eddie *[cornerman]*, Strickland (who has put on his "Curtis Strong" tunic and will officiate as the third cornerman tonight), Anthony, and Maurice. The latter is holed up in the dressing room for fear that the security guards for the night club will find him: he snuck in and doesn't have the money to pay for his ticket; if they throw him out, he'll miss the fights and will have to cool his heels outside until the end of the evening.

[My sparring buddy] Ashante and Liz have just arrived. I ask DeeDee for a ticket from Curtis's quota; it's the last one. I go slip it to the Doc, who's pacing outside the door with Fanette. They haven't missed anything, since the fights, which were scheduled for seven, won't start until eight. Back in the mock dressing room, Ashante is pumping Curtis and Keith up for battle. Curtis catches me scribbling in my field notebook—I decided to take detailed handwritten notes rather than just tape them this time (so as not to risk arousing the suspicions of the bar employees with my recorder). "What you writin'?" We stare at each other intensely, I stay mum. After several seconds of stunned silence, we burst out at the same time with a long laugh. Curtis strikes a blow: "You know what? Some day *you gonna commit suicide,* Louie, 'cuz *you write too much.* What you say, DeeDee? People're gonna be wonderin' (in a worried

little voice) 'What happen to Louie?' but *we* know why, yeah, we know why."

What a strange prophecy! After two years among them, my buddies from the gym are still surprised to see me functioning in my capacity as a sociologist. It's something that is never taken for granted, even if they've gotten accustomed to seeing me walking around with my tape recorder in hand, and now pretend to be irritated by my questions only for show. Eddie leans over me to murmur discreetly: "When you write your book. Louie, ten years from now, I'monna be your technical advisor, okay?"

The young cream-colored guy that Jack didn't want to hire to fight this morning at the weigh-in ceremony comes around to hand out gloves to us—used pairs, which is against the state regulation that stipulates that brand-new gloves must be used for all official fights. We grope about in his big duffle bag for a pair the right size for Curtis. The tension is imperceptibly, slowly but surely, mounting in the storage-dressing room. We talk less and less loudly. Our gestures are more restrained. We take care not to demand anything of the two boxers who are readying themselves....

During this hourlong wait, Curtis wards off his mounting anxiety by teasing me. When he sees me get out my tape recorder, he slips in slyly, as if in confidence: "Shhhh! C'mon now, *everybody say some curse words Louie got his tape on,* ha, ha, ha!" DeeDee takes advantage of the opportunity to comment ironically again about the fact that the hoodlums from the area are going to bump me if they ever catch me recording in the tavern. To which I retort: "But before that happens, I'll give them a taste of my mean left hook." DeeDee, in a very dead earnest tone: "An' they'll whup you to death." I counter him with one of his trademark tirades: "Then I'll tell them: 'Careful, I'm DeeDee Armour's main man, you better not touch me: *he controls some killers.*'" The old coach nods without piping a word. All these jokes and banter serve to stave off fear and to curb the tension that is gradually inching up.

"They full of butterflies"

A comment by LeRoy Murphy, a boxer from Fuller Park and former holder of the world light heavyweight title:

I know what it takes to get in that ring an' *every time I got in that boxin' ring I was scared*, everytime I climbed in the ring, everytime I put my hands up, I was nervous. Didn't nobody know but me, that be a little thing that you keep inside your own self, an' that's how I was....I was always nervous two, three days before the fight. I get up in the mornin' run, go an' get a workout, light workout, eat breakfast, an' I come back an' I watch cable, I watch videos, like that, I don't go out the room. I'd start eatin' small portions then 'cause I feel nervous, my stomach feel nervous an' I'll try to—usually after the weigh-in I feel better....The afternoon of the fight I never slept, *noooo*. Guys, before the fight they don't sleep, they lay there an' rest but they full of *butterflies*, they be scared, every fighter, even [Muhammad] Ali admitted he was scared when he fought an' I like that: when you're not afraid, somethin' wrong wid' you. Everytime I got in the ring, I was afraid.

Pitiful Preliminaries

The opponents for the Chicago boxers finish getting ready in the barroom which holds the dance floor. They are changing in silence, with slow and deliberate gestures, their clothes and equipment (handwraps, gloves, cups, shorts, and robes) tossed over the back of a chair. Jeff Hannah is sitting absentmindedly on a table, legs dangling; he laces up his boots while chatting in a low voice with his father, head down, as if to better cut himself off from an environment that he senses is hostile. He knows that he is the sacrificial victim being served up to the local hopeful, in front of an audience already rooting for his opponent and judges who won't cut him any slack, and thus that he has every chance of losing his bout. This is the common lot of "opponents" on the circuit: their only chance of winning in their rival's "backyard" is to knock him out. Lots of things must be going on in his head and in his body—where I wouldn't want to be, tonight or tomorrow.

As I'm coming out of the bar, I run into Liz, who kisses me lustily. Eddie grabs me by the shoulder, laughing, like a cop arresting an outlaw: "Come on, Louie, that's enough, stop it, she's gonna make you soft if she keep kissin' you like that, I already warned you 'bout that! You ain't gonna be ready for your next fight."[8] The makeshift spotlights clamped to the metal poles stuck in the four corners of the ring light up. The show is about to begin. Everyone sits where they can—there's no reserved seating or VIP section at ringside for an event of this caliber. For once they skip the national anthem to launch straight into the customary introduction of the officials, judges, referees, and timekeeper by a corpulent, bearded announcer in a black tuxedo jacket:

Ladies and Gentlemen, *welcome to Studio One-O-Four*, here on Chicago's beautiful Southeast Side! The boxing contests on your program are sanctioned by, and under the supervision of, the Professional Boxing and Wrestling Board of Illinois, the Department of Professional Regulation, Mister Gordon Bookman, chairman of the Board, Mister Nick Kerasiotis, executive secretary, and Mister Frank Lira, supervisor of athletics. This is Rising Star Promotions.[9] Your officials are judges Bill Lerch, Gino Rodriguez, and Stanley Berg, timekeeper Joe Mauriello, and your referees Tim Adams and Pete Podgorski.

O'Bannon has settled down in the front row with Michonne, behind the red corner. Liz, Fanette, and the Doc are sitting over in the next row, with Curtis's family, Anthony, and Ashante. Jack is standing up in the aisle, keeping an eye on things. [Cutman] Laury Myers isn't around, an indication that he didn't manage to get himself hired for the night. It's Little Keith who's boxing in the opening bout, as the slanting light heralds the end of the day. His manager, the dapper Elijah (owner of a chain of dry cleaners in the ghetto), is teamed up with DeeDee and Eddie in the corner. His opponent, a short, potbellied black pug from Milwaukee with very rudimentary skills, is clearly eager for one thing only: to "lie down" and go home with his "paycheck." Keith has barely enough time to graze him with a couple of rights to the body before the guy throws himself to the canvas a first time, then a second, as Keith and the referee look on in frustration. The referee urges him to fight, but nothing doing: when the Woodlawn boxer lands a weakish combination, the tub of lard from Milwaukee crumbles like a pile of rubble and fakes a kayo. The referee kneels at his side and sharply rebukes him and then, seeing that his remonstrances are to no avail, takes his mouthguard out of his mouth and sends him back to his corner. This guy is not just a bum but a genuine "diver" and I wonder if he's going to get paid—the judges have the authority to take away the purse of a boxer who refuses to fight, and the brotherhood of pugilists severely reproves of those who publicly fail to uphold its warrior ethos this way. Elijah and Eddie crowd around Keith and raise his arms as a sign of victory, to a combination of whistles and applause from the crowd. It's not very convincing but we're happy for him just the same.

Matchmaker Jack Cowen: Journeymen, Bums, and Divers

JACK COWEN: A *journeyman* is a fellow that, in all likelihood, will never be a champion but he's capable of fighting almost anyone and will win on a given day and may lose on a given day. Because they will win once a while and make money. And put up a good fight if they're capable.

I'm not talking about somebody who's just a *diver* and who's gonna go here and get knocked out in the first round and then show up someplace else and get knocked out in the first round again. I'm not talking about those—those are *bums*, that's something that really has no place in boxing although they seem to succeed.

LOUIE: They have no place in boxing and yet there's quite a few of them around...

JACK: They... I shouldn't say no place because, obviously, there's always a place. You have guys, beginners, starting out, who need poor opponents to go ahead and see what they can do, to get confidence and test themselves: maybe they prove to be no better than the bums themselves after you get them in there—you don't know!

I do a quick count of the audience, which is about 80 percent male and ethnically mixed, with a slight preponderance of whites and Latinos: at most 300 people at the start of the event and about 450 at the end, not including the forty-odd Mexicans crowded against the wall of the house next to the parking lot (after an fruitless attempt, the manager of Studio 104 gave up trying to stretch a tarp in front of the house, to Ashante's great discontent, who insists that they be made to pay even if they're sitting in their own yard). This is about half the number necessary for the promoters to cover expenses.[10] And it's less colorful than last time: the burly toughs who control the various illicit rackets in this part of the South Side didn't turn out in numbers tonight, a weeknight, and the wind blowing in gusts cools things off quite a bit.

The opening bout wasn't a pretty sight, but the second fight is pathetic to the point of becoming comical. It pits two "bums" of the first order against each other: a big flabby white guy from Tinley Park swathed in lard (his lower belly bulges out his trunks so far that you might think he's pregnant) against an older black pug from Milwaukee sporting a powder puff of red hair that gives him a wildly effeminate look. It's all too obvious that the latter never "smelled a glove" before tonight: incapable of putting up his guard correctly, he throws his fists with the backs of his hands in front, as if offering a bouquet of flowers, then flees away on tip-toe with his derriere to his opponent! As his only defense, he does his best to derail his opponent's blows by stretching his wiry arms out in front of him and swings them from left to right with a jerky vacillating movement that makes him look like a sort of human windshield wiper. You would think these are two big numskulls playing at boxing—except that they're both terrified at finding themselves in a ring. Every time the referee calls for them to "break," they lift their fists to the sky in concert, as if performing an incantation, and suspend hostilities with a relief so palpable that it's embarrassing.

The audience is chortling and derisively egging the two fighters on with exaggerated encouragement: "Throw your bomb!" "Come on, champ!" They figure that the white guy from Tinley Park, who is beefier and occasionally manages to land a few halfway decent-looking punches, is going to win (besides, he did win his first two fights whereas his opponent is making his pro debut). But the old pug with the powder-puff hair is getting bolder and his comical tap-tap is growing more accurate, while his rival is tiring visibly. By the third round, the crowd is siding openly with the black "bum," who was clearly served up as "feed" for his opponent, as the saying goes. The sympathy of the audience isn't just racial: the bloke from

Milwaukee quite simply doesn't belong in a ring. But when, by sheer accident, he catches his opponent with a sharp right to the chin, the unexpected intrudes: the big flabby white guy rolls onto his back, tries to get up, staggers around, displays a series of distorted facial expressions that mingle surprise and suffering, then crumples to his knees again, powerless to command his legs. It's a surprise kayo! Consternation in the section where the whites from Tinley Park who came to support their buddy are massed; hilarious jubilation among the rest of the audience. Ashante and Eddie are laughing their heads off, nearly rolling on the ground. And Kitchen is delighted because he managed to slip onto the ring as cornerman for the winner, which will earn him a few bucks.

"I'm like someone buying and selling stock"

The only son of a Jewish family that immigrated from Russia in the 1920s, Jack has been immersed in the pugilistic milieu for nearly half a century. When he was little, his father, who owned a chain of dry cleaners, took him to the fight cards held in the Chicago of the Golden Age, when the legendary Jewish fighters were shining their last lights in the ring and the Chicago Stadium vied with Madison Square Garden for the title of Mecca of the Manly Art. This is how he met DeeDee, and got to know the main local boxing figures while he was still a kid. "My father was somewhat of a fight fan. He took me to a boxing show when I was about eleven years old and I was fascinated with it, and, I implored him to continue taking me to fights, which he did on a fairly regular basis. Once I got old enough to go myself, I went to the fights at every opportunity, which there was quite a few opportunities in those days." Jack put on the gloves briefly at the neighborhood YMCA and competed in a few amateur bouts, but without much success or consequence. No matter: his precocious and intensive exposure to the Sweet Science enabled him to develop a deft pugilistic judgment.

After graduating from college, Jack took over the management of the family laundry business and started up another business manufacturing cosmetics. To fill up his spare time, he and a childhood friend got into producing music-hall shows. "It was a sideline for me, the music. It was the kinda thing that we would run maybe six-eight-ten shows a year. We made money, generally speaking. But it was hard and trends in music were changing, it became tougher and tougher. (He winces.) The bands were all of the sudden beginning to demand very, very high dollars, where you had to have probably eighty percent capacity in order to break even. And ultimately the places that we were running them got torn down, the picture was changing, the type of music was changing, the moneys were changing. And so we just walked away from that and wanted to do something together. And my buddy's a boxing fan and I suggested boxing and, I said 'Well hey! Let's get us a a fighter.' And we did. And from there I managed fighters, this is back in 1957."

For two decades, Jack would simultaneously run his dry-cleaning business and manage a small stable of fighters. And when the transformations of the pugilistic economy – the drying up of vocations and the disappearance of neighborhood clubs, the deskilling of managers, the contraction of the local market, and the nationalization of commercialization circuits – revealed the pressing need for a middleman capable of compensating for the withering away of traditional networks, Jack was well placed to launch himself into matchmaking. "A lot of the people that have fighters are just there, they sit and wait and hope that nobody asks their fighters to fight someone. And I was more aggressive and built up numbers and built up acquaintanceships and such, traveling with the fighters continually, and established relationships. Some of the

relationships I have with the promoters and other agents, it all goes back fifteen-twenty years, even longer in a couple of cases." After two years of tryout, Jack decided in 1977 to liquidate his dry-cleaning assets and to become a matchmaker fulltime. HIs subsequent success has earned him a quasi-monopoly in supplying fighters for the greater Chicago area today.

Jack Cowen's main activity consists of 'filling the card' of the boxing events of the region by recruiting suitable opponents for the star boxer headlining the card and setting up the preliminary matches, called the 'undercard." He sometimes takes charge of the material organization of the event: the ring, production, concession stands for drinks and hot dogs, ticketing and advertising. Jack produces about three hundred fights a year in the Midwest in this way, in addition to the matches he negotiates as an agent for the boxers whose services he rents out on the national and international markets. (With his Florida colleague Johnny Boz, Jack exports several dozen mediocre fighters to France and Italy every year, where they serve as stepping-stones for the rising stars and marquee boxers of the Old World. He also officiates as a representative of Cedric Kushner Promotions, one of the major players in the global pugilistic economy, for which he signs up-and-coming boxers from Illinois. Finally, he is the co-owner of the Chicago Golden Glove franchise and his wife – who is African American – manages two boxers with his advice.

Concretely, Jack's work day is divided up into endless haggling on the telephone with managers, promoters, and other agents (he makes several dozen calls between six and eleven every morning), making the rounds of the city gyms in the afternoon to keep abreast of the condition and availability of the local pugilists, then a new batch of negotiations by fax and telephone in the evening. He spends six weeks of the year "on the road" to attend cards for which he supplied fighters in neighboring states and abroad: it is vital that he go in person in order to judge de visu the quality of the boxers, the venue, the audience, and the trustworthiness of the organizers and other parties involved.

The search for and pairing of boxers takes place according to an interactive and cascading process, each deal leading to the next as a function of the desiderata and needs of the various parties. "It's like a shopping list: I'm looking for this and that and something else or we have things that match and (he frowns slightly) the economics of the fight make sense. Like' we're not going to bring a fighter from the island of Tonga for a four-rounder in Gary, Indiana...I'm calling people, people are calling me. It's a network. It's a number of people that are agents for fighters in addition to being matchmakers and, or promoters as I am. And they are booking for people in other areas. It's an ongoing thing. You're always talking to people about something. Sometimes you can get through the morning with nothing in the world working. And then, two or three phone calls, you've made two or three matches some place and you've picked up a thousand dollars... So that's really what I'm doing: I"m sitting at home, I'm almost like someone buying or selling stock, if you will. Or perhaps a bookie taking bets on horses. I have people that have needs, you have people that have needs, and we try to match it up to make sense."

A matchmaker must to take into account three series of constraints in putting together a "card." He must first abide by the bureaucratic rules stipulated by the Boxing Commission of the state concerned (which is hardly onerous, given their extreme laxity). He must then make sure that the fights are economically viable, even profitable, by staying within the budget allotted to him by the promoter who hired him. Last, insofar as possible, he must "pair up" the boxers so as to produce matches that are enjoyable to watch and relatively balanced, while at the same time giving an edge to the boxers to whom he has ties. The requisite qualities for doing all this are a sound sense of organization and good bookkeeping skills, the capacity to cross social and racial lines with ease, and a good "pugilistic eye" to determine with acuity and accuracy the worth, style, and professionalism of the boxers hired. These are qualities that Jack acquired, respectively, from his experience as an entrepreneur in the laundry business, from his ethnic origin and family trajectory, and from his precocious and prolonged contact with the Manly Art. "I was in the dry-cleaning business and in the cosmetics business, and I took up boxing on the side and it got out of hand. You can get into boxing easily but you can't get out. Once you're in it, you're in it. [He smiles calmly.] Not a problem, I'm happy. I like the activity, I like bein' involved in the thing, I get a big kick out of it, it's still fun after all the years; I'll do it forever."

NOTES

1. A well-placed informant whom I had asked if it would be interesting for me to meet Lowhouse had answered abruptly: "That guy is a criminal, he's an ignoramus, you won't get anything out of him. I would not advise you to interview him, you'd be wasting your time. He's crude, suspicious...And the guys that hang around his tavern are dangerous. For him, the fights are just a business: he gives money to someone to organize them and that's about it he doesn't give a damn and doesn't know anything about boxing. Besides, he'd never agree to be interviewed."

2. On the key role played by these establishments in the reproduction of the expressive sociability of the black American community, see the fine book by Michael J. Bell. *The World from Brown's Lounge: An Ethnography of Black Middle-Class Play* (Urbana: University of Illinois Press, 1983).

3. This is how a manager or promoter "builds" a boxer, by "feeding" him inferior opponents until he has a record that will allow him to

seek televised bouts for which the purses become sizeable.

4. During the last two weeks leading up to the fight, Curtis complained repeatedly of a mysterious dysfunction in his shoulder that would suddenly make his arm seize up. This was a way of attracting the attention of his trainer (and, indirectly, of his manager) to his disastrous financial situation, a situation that the Studio 104 card would not suffice to resolve.

5. This attraction for the stage is not exclusive to boxers: bodily crafts and a sense of performance occupy an epicentral place in the urban society of black Americans, from music to religion to sports, comedy, and politics. See Loïc Wacquant, "From Charisma to Persona: On Boxing and Social Being," in *The Charisma of Sport and Race* (Berkeley: Doreen B. Townsend Center for the Humanities, Occasional Papers n. 8. 1996), pp. 21–37.

6. On the role of verbal jousts and the importance of the art of speaking well in urban African-American culture and sociability (of which rap is the most recent avatar in the commercial sphere), consult Roger D. Abrahams, *Down in the Jungle: Negro Narrative Folklore from the Streets of Philadelphia* (New York: de Gruyter, 1963) and Thomas Kochman, *Rappin' and Stylin' Out: Communication in Urban Black America* (Urbana: University of Illinois Press, 1972).

7. Trainers never miss a chance to remind their charges, even if under cover of a joke, of the commandment of the professional catechism of "sacrifice" which stipulates that the boxer shall strictly limit all erotic contact so as not to risk dulling this instrument for virile battle that is his body; Loïc Wacquant. "The Prizefighter's Three Bodies," *Ethnos* 63, 3 (November 1998): 325–352.

8. Rising Star Promotions is merely a local front for Cedric Kushner (via Jack Cowen), one of four major promoters who then shared the national market, the others being Don King Promotions, Top Rank, Inc. (Bob Arum's company), and Main Events (managed by rock concert promoter Shelly Finkel and trainer-manager Lou Duva).

9. The resulting deficit is absorbed by the managers who make the initial layout of funds to put together the event so as to keep their boxers active and to enable them to lengthen their records. At this level of the pugilistic market, the only person who makes any financial hay from the enterprise is the matchmaker, since he invests nothing out-of-pocket and takes a commission as middleman off the top, a share of the boxers' purses (10 percent), and a fixed fee for running the production of the card. Wacquant, "A Flesh Peddler at Work," pp. 23–30.

10. This is a concrete illustration of the structural dilemma with which every matchmaker finds himself confronted due to the very nature of his activity: when fight go well, people credit the boxers and their entourage and he fades into the woodwork; in the opposite case, it is he who is the target of all the unhappiness and recriminations, such that he becomes everywhere "the most unpopular man in the city," as the famous matchmaker Teddy Brenner notes in his autobiography. Teddy Brenner and Brian Nagler, *Only the Ring Was Square* (Englewood Cliffs, N.J.: Prentice-Hall, 1981), p. 22.

REFERENCES

Abrahams, Roger D. 1963. *Down in the Jungle: Negro Narrative Folklore from the Streets of Philadelphia*. New York: de Gruyter.

Bell, Michael J. 1983. *The World from Brown's Lounge: An Ethnography of Black Middle-Class Play*. Urbana: University of Illinois Press.

Brenner, Teddy and Brian, Nagler. 1981. *Only the Ring Was Square*. Englewood Cliffs, N.J.: Prentice-Hall.

Kochman, Thomas. 1972. *Rappin' and Stylin' Out: Communication in Urban Black America*. Urbana: University of Illinois Press.

Wacquant, Loïc. 1996. "From Charisma to Persona: On Boxing and Social Being." In *The Charisma of Sport and Race*, pp. 21-37. Berkeley: Doreen B. Townsend Center for the Humanities, Occasional Papers n. 8.

Wacquant, Loïc. 1998. "The Prizefighter's Three Bodies." *Ethnos* 63 (3): 325–352.

37

SHERRI GRASMUCK

THE CLUBHOUSE AND CLASS CULTURES: "BRINGING THE INFIELD IN"

from *Protecting Home* (2005)

For more than ten years, Sherri Grasmuck was involved in the Fairmount Sports Association, a youth baseball league in the Fairmount neighborhood of Philadelphia. During this time her role shifted from being a baseball mom to the wife of a coach, even a commissioner—with each of these roles giving her different insights. The neighborhood itself had undergone profound racial and class transitions during the last thirty years. Working-class, white Fairmount families initially saw their middle-class counterparts flee the area, only to be replaced by black and Puerto Rican families, who, in turn, were replaced by more affluent white professional gentrifiers. As the white middle class moved out, the white working class was forced to accept black and Puerto Rican players if it wished to preserve the league. Then, in the late 1990s, the league had to learn how to accept and integrate the new, upper middle-class population. It is the management of these transitions that forms the subject of *Protecting Home*.

In 1995, a middle-aged newcomer named Howard took it upon himself to run for an office in the normally uncontested election of the FSA board of directors. A businessman who lived outside the neighborhood, Howard had coached his son's seven-to-nine team at FSA for three years prior to the election. His son, who attended a secular private school in Center City, as did many of the newcomers' children, was a relatively strong player among the younger boys. Howard, with long, hippy-like grey hair, typically dressed in baggy khaki shorts and a polo shirt. Although he had an easy-going, personable coaching style, old-timers often complained that he was unfocused and spacey in his approach to tasks. Beyond coaching, Howard contributed in unusual ways to the organization by devoting himself to maintaining the large fields of grass in the early hours of the weekends. His heavy time contribution was welcomed. But because something about his social style irritated many Fairmount old-timers, he was never accepted as an insider.

Howard loved the league but had numerous complaints about the way newcomers were treated. He decided to lobby other newcomer parents and coaches to come out and support his candidacy as an officer against a Fairmount old-timer who, although formerly active, Howard felt no longer did much beyond sit in the clubhouse. But some insiders felt that the years of service this Fairmounter had put in entitled him to a regular presence in the clubhouse, and making him a board member guaranteed that. Howard's newcomer challenge was resisted by a rapid counter-defense and display of neighborhood solidarity. Sandy, one of the most experienced Fairmount coaches, and someone who had grown up in the neighborhood and played ball as a boy in FSA, recounted the tale, often gossiped about on the bleachers, of this aborted challenge.

> There was a campaign a couple of years ago to try to take over, to push Howard Gold as vice president. We were ready for this for years, but it never happened. Three years ago, it happened....[On election night] I noticed early on that lots of people were coming in to vote. They come in to push to take over the leadership..."the yuppies," we call

them....They hadn't been around long. All of a sudden they wanted to get active coming in the door. Howard showed up late to vote. But he definitely was involved. He's very sneaky, Howard is. And I knew it. The election was from seven to ten. At 7:15, I said we're going to have to make a move here. He [our guy] is going to lose. The normal thirty votes wouldn't cut it this time....[Laughing] I got on the phone. I drove a van around picking people up on the corners to get them to vote....I was driving around the neighborhood. "How old are you? Are you eighteen? Get in the van." "How old are you? Get in the van." Out the door people were voting, all of a sudden. Usually the total votes is thirty or forty....Over 100 voted, because of this movement to get Howard Gold in....Howard got an unbelievable amount of votes. But I got everybody out. I made sure a guy who worked here for years, I made sure he was the winner....I think we proved the point that we can get as many votes as we need to make sure our guy gets vice president or president.

This move to resist a newcomer challenge to FSA leadership was swift and effective. No such newcomer challenge occurred again, at least for the next nine years. The defense reflected a deep sense of entitlement to decision-making on the part of the Fairmounters. The conversation makes clear the extent to which the categories of "neighborhood guys" and "yuppies" were part of insider FSA consciousness and the very effective way neighborhood solidarity could be tapped to thwart an overt attempt by newcomers to gain organizational control.

If it is remarkable that the racial integration that characterized the ball association over several decades occurred relatively smoothly given the history of racial conflict in this neighborhood, it is equally remarkable that class came to trump race by the 1980s as the principal social boundary—a transition that carried over onto the baseball field. This is because the white professionals started appearing at the ball field in the late 1980s with agendas that did not match neatly those of the old-timers. So, by the mid-1990s, tensions at the baseball field centered on divisions between old-timer Fairmounters and the newcomer professionals who periodically tested the boundaries of power at the clubhouse and found them firm. If newcomers were not given the benefit of the doubt concerning leadership in the association, it was because many Fairmounters already had a stockpile of resentments toward the new professionals, based on earlier neighborhood encounters. Besides, FSA leaders held onto their influence by holding the boundaries firm.

Class Resentments in the Neighborhood

Fairmounters' feelings of resentment toward newcomers to their neighborhood often lurked just below the surface. Tensions were related not just to the conspicuously more affluent lifestyles of some of the new professionals, with their capacity to purchase homes at skyrocketing prices, but to a social style that Fairmounters perceived as condescending and pushy. Newcomers were overly eager to change things they didn't understand; worse yet, they were perceived as contributing to a fading sense of community.

The village-like feel of the neighborhood had diminished with the arrival of the newcomers. Fairmounters blamed this on the tendency of the newcomers to have fewer children, and to send those children mostly to private, non-neighborhood schools, which minimized local mixing. An elderly Fairmounter, who hung out regularly in the local Vietnam memorial park, the oldest such park in the nation, told me, "[Before the professionals moved in] there was a lot of kids around. But people only have dogs

and cats now. They don't have no children anymore. They don't raise kids. We got a lady up here has two, no, three dogs and cats and won't come down here [outside in the park] at all." Frannie, a seventy-plus-year-old Fairmounter whose family members had attended the same Catholic grade school since the late 1880s, voiced a similar critique of newcomers' lack of integration with locals:

Yeah, and these people who are moving around here now, these couples they don't have children. They might have one, but when they have it, when the child is four years old, the first thing you know, he doesn't go to our school. He either takes a bus and goes to private school, or they move. We've had a lot of people...and we can always call the shots...."Oh, they'll be moving soon." If they do stay, they have the private bus pick up the child and the kids usually don't mix with the rest of the kids....They don't let them to come out and mix. You know what I mean? They're almost like house-tutored.

He then related the lack of neighborhood solidarity and local responsibility on the part of the newcomers to their focus on their work lives.

Well, the only time they join a group is if they have a child they want to get on a baseball team or something like that. Because we have these town watches and we can't get anybody. We have the same handful of people who do it all the time. We can't get nobody else. And I don't think it's that they are antisocial. It's that they are so busy paying their bills really....We had a house up here sold for over $300,000. You believe that? Years ago, you could have bought the whole block for that! A young couple bought it. I don't think either one of them is thirty. Now you know, they got to really work to pay that. You're not going to see too much of them. It's not that they are bad people.

They're good people. They are lawyers and doctors, all money people.

Fairmounters who had gained economically from the neighborhood transformation tended to see gentrification more favorably. One Fairmounter who owned a small neighborhood shop stressed this: "The changes have been good. Good for me, the business here.... People moved out. A lot of them thought they were bettering themselves too. It's not like they were pushed out. They made more money. My oldest sister bought a house for $58,000 sold it for $110,000, made $62,000 in two years, and moved out. Another example of people raking it up." Another Fairmounter woman, Patty, who also felt positively about the newcomers, nonetheless also stressed their lack of commitment to the neighborhood, local schools, or social networks.

> It's nicer but less neighborhood than it was here before. I hear stories [from her husband who grew up in Fairmount] about having twenty-thirty kids on a block. You didn't have to go anywhere to play, just Pannock, Swain Streets. Now, there are fewer kids and such a variety of kids: They all go to different schools. Private kids, public kids, now Waldron, Masterman, St. Frannies school. Wow! But we like that. All the children get to know all variety of children; whether Catholic, Jewish, Greek, black, white. Pretty good mix of kids. But it drives me nuts how some come and everything is wonderful. Oh they love it, love it. And then, they're gone when the kid is five for schools in the suburbs.

Wally, a longtime Spring Garden resident, offered a harsher critique of the new professionals based on their instrumental approach to relationships with people. Their greater affluence had brought more economic stability to the neighborhood but had weakened the connections within the community, because of the tendency of newcomers to form friendships based on business or economic interests outside local space. "I tend to find that, with the gentrification, there is a different group of people who live in the neighborhood now. I guess what you could call Fairmount or Spring Garden is now made up predominantly of professional people or people with higher incomes. And friendships, although they'll have friendships with people close to them, maybe a block over or two blocks over, most of their friendships form around either business contacts or professional contacts. And that's where the main thrust of their friends and their social activity, through business contacts, is."

Some residents saw the divisions between Fairmounters and newcomers as nothing more than the latest version of the class divisions that had existed in the old neighborhood. One Fairmounter remembered the tensions during his youth between the more securely employed Fairmounters and their poorer neighbors. The Fairmounters currently feeling rejected (including himself) were the ones whose families had formerly done the rejecting.

> I used to kid my mother before she died. She'd say, "It's not the same. People [newcomers] are not as friendly." I said to her, "Mom, all you used to do is sit on the step and talk about other Fairmounters. Like, 'There's Joe Schmoe. He's drunk again,' or 'His kid's a little pain in the ass.'"... I mean, they [Fairmounters] will tell you, "Well, our people moved out," or "I don't know these new people." Well, I say, "Have you tried to know them? Have you just resented them moving in or have you went across the street?" My wife and I try. But still, there's just some new people here who, apparently, I don't say they don't *like* us, but we're not their style.

Indeed, some Fairmounters felt less negatively about the exodus of some of their neighbors precisely because it was selective and "solved" some of the internal class divisions that had historically existed. Jessie, a longtime resident of Fairmount, explained it this way: "My parents' home cost $6,000. Twenty years later, we sold it for $76,000. The property values, it brings new people in. [Pause] I think it's been good for the neighborhood, myself. I mean, it's gotten rid of a lot of garbage. Because they see dollar signs, and they're out the door, and we say, 'Oh good! We got rid of that family.' And it kind of gives you... it's like looking out and seeing some new taste." Jessie's home business brought her into regular contact with many new professionals and their children, and her attitude toward the newcomers had softened over time. In particular, she pointed to their parenting styles as preferable to some she saw among Fairmount families:

> In the beginning the neighborhood people were angry. The new people didn't really do anything. It's just that you are in our neighborhood basically. But I think it's kind of like acceptable now. I mean, now I look at it like, oh good, they'll fix up, they'll do that. It's good for the neighborhood. They are family oriented, which is a good thing. A lot of these people, years ago, I mean the fathers at the bar and da da da. And these new people are more family oriented with their children. And that's a good thing for the kids. You know, a lot of the kids who might just be hangin' corners would play with the kids who have a family atmosphere. They can see the other side of the coin, so to speak. I think it is good for some children. I mean, it wouldn't affect me whether they lived here or not. But for some of the children who don't have that type of family background, I think it is good for them, they can see other kids, play with them.

But the more gracious view of newcomer professionals apparent in Jessie's comment was frequently undermined, both in this interview and in subsequent conversations with her, by other resentments she held toward the newcomers. For example, several years later when she and I were down at the ball field discussing my recent decision to take my son out of his private Quaker school and the fact that he had never identified with the culture of that school, she blurted out, "I'm with him. I hate every one of those yuppie parents from that school. I work for 'em, but you gotta make a buck somehow!" Despite the obvious irony, she intended this as a statement of solidarity with me. It was a complex moment. As I drank in her words of comfort, I also realized she was probably talking about some of my friends. Still, we found space to bond over our shared resentments.

Fairmounter irritations did not always lie dormant beneath the surface. They were not accustomed to being pushed around by outsiders, at least not in their own neighborhood. Another comment from Jessie illustrates the direct manner in which she confronted pushiness and indiscretion on the part of newcomers: "When a newcomer comes in, I feel like I have seniority. Don't come and tell me you want to make big changes. They [two new neighbors] moved in and said, 'We'd like to get permit parking.' And I said, 'You know what, Neil, you and your wife better go back in the house. There is no permit parking around here, Hon. I'm not paying the city another dime for parking. Not one more penny. You see this block. You're just one vote. So don't even bring it up.' [We both laughed.] It is like, 'Newcomers, you have no seniority!'"

How did the newcomers take all of this? Understanding their responses depends in part on also understanding their social backgrounds and attitudes. Gentrification doesn't happen uniformly. There are phases to the process, phases often identified with different social actors who arrive in new neighborhoods with different sets of motivations, and there are different consequences for traditional residents.[1] Merely knowing that gentrification means that new affluent residents move into modest or marginal neighborhoods is not sufficient to understand the impact of the process on those neighborhoods. It is worth briefly considering what kind of middle-class people choose to live in urban areas like Fairmount and Spring Garden and how they might differ from their middle-class counterparts who prefer the suburbs. After all, most affluent movers facing restructuring American cities continue to choose the suburbs over the central cities.[2] Compared to this suburban backdrop, the gentrifiers are only a "modest urban demographic blip."[3]

Gentrification and the New Cultural Class

The rise of a new middle class of professional and managerial workers in postindustrial societies has drawn considerable attention from scholars over the past several decades.[4] Central to this discussion has been the question of how this "new class" is divided and the implications of these divisions for politics, social inequality, economic development, and urban life.[5] Some theorists have linked this broader debate about the new middle class to gentrification and patterns of urban change similar to the transformation that occurred in the Fairmount and Spring Garden area after the 1970s. For example, Ley ascribes a distinct geographic identity to a specific cadre among the new middle class, a group he calls "the cultural new class," consisting of social and cultural professionals. This sector is concentrated in central areas of large metropolitan areas and is identified with left-liberal politics. For example, in gentrifying neighborhoods within Toronto, Montreal, and Vancouver, the cultural new class challenged conservative urban growth coalitions and supported oppositional reform regimes in city government.[6]

The most liberal sector within the new middle class consists of those in social and cultural fields, such as academics, social scientists, architects, lawyers, and professionals who work outside the private and corporate sector.[7] These metropolitan professionals are also more committed to racial integration, more in favor of government spending on social programs, and more likely to consist of dual-career families compared to their other middle-class counterparts.[8] For our purposes, the relevance of this broader scholarly discussion is that, beyond the economic issues of gentrification, there is often something cultural and political behind the forces of gentrification that may contribute autonomously, or paradoxically, to local economic transformations.[9]

The new professionals who moved into the Spring Garden and Fairmount areas, and eventually entered the neighborhood baseball space, fit quite closely the above description of the new cultural class associated with gentrification in other places. The newcomer coaches and parents I interviewed came almost exclusively from this sector of the middle class. Almost all of the twenty newcomer coach and parent interviewees held professional jobs in governmental, educational, or legal services unconnected to the corporate sector. Almost half of them were educators—teachers, principals, and professors. When describing their motivations for moving to this area of the city, newcomers often spoke of their preference for the cultural lifestyle of the city, and specifically cited the diversity of the city as a plus. Their attitudes are similar to the "diversity seekers" described by Goode and Schneider in Olney, another changing Philadelphia neighborhood.[10] Many had working-class parents who helped them achieve upward mobility through educational advancement, and they remained positive toward, and emotionally comfortable with, the social style of many of the Fairmounters. While Fairmounters might see them as sometimes condescending and distant, the new professionals who chose to live in an inner-city neighborhood like Fairmount often did so as a vote against suburban lifestyle precisely because of its homogenous, predominantly white culture. They often held liberal social views and welcomed, within limits, the economic and ethnic diversity around them. As one professor who had two sons in the league expressed it, "I guess because I'm a teacher and come from a working-class family, I am very sympathetic to what working-class people are like—even though I don't want to go back. I mean, I worked like hell to escape it, and I'm glad I did. But I'm very sympathetic to Fairmounters. It is easier in some respects for me, dealing with professionals. They're better educated. I understand the neighborhoods they're coming from and their priorities and stuff. But one of the reasons I really like Fairmont is because it is this little sociological melting pot." Another newcomer mother, who had originally moved to Spring Garden as a single woman and spent twenty years slowly renovating her home, described how relieved she was to be raising children in the city rather than the suburbs. "I feel like my kids already live a pretty sheltered existence. They go to a [private] school where things are pretty easy for them, and they don't confront the things there that they might in another setting. And so, there's more reality here, and on the baseball field." Indeed, this group's identity was as likely to be posited in opposition to their professional counterparts in the suburbs than in opposition to their more working-class Fairmount neighbors. In short, many newcomers liked the Fairmounters more than the Fairmounters liked them.

Some, from the first wave of professionals who entered Spring Garden, were worried by the 1990s that the very diversity that had attracted them in the first place was slipping away. One professional couple, a public interest lawyer and a pediatrician, moved to the Spring Garden area in 1967, had worked hard in the early 1970s to defeat local real estate developers who were

urging city officials to end scattered-site public housing in the area,[11] and had also fought in the early 1980s for the establishment of a shelter run for and by homeless people in a church at Spring Garden and 20th Street. Yet, by the middle of the 1990s, they bemoaned the rapid "upscaling" of the neighborhood as it began to attract not just comfortable professionals like themselves, but residents of considerable wealth and political influence.

While Fairmounters saw newcomers as uninterested in local friendships and community affairs, newcomers sometimes felt that their participation was not welcome. They saw themselves as the ones being excluded from neighborhood social life. One medical doctor described his treatment by the locals in the ten years since moving to a block in Fairmount filled with residents who had grown up together. "You have to be related to Fairmounters before they talk to you." Marsha, a forty-year-old lawyer who had moved into Spring Garden thirteen years before, described the distance as a social wall between Fairmounters and newcomers that was inevitable and mutually imposed. But rather than begrudge Fairmounters their tendency to exclude people like her, she linked it to a rational way of sharing resources and eyed their sense of community longingly, from a distance:

> I think something that I envy about the Fairmount people, that I don't know that we have at our socioeconomic level quite as much, because people at our level tend to be more self-sufficient....More affluent people have more resources available to them because of their financial situation or because of their intellectual ability. They can draw from other places. Whereas, I think when you get down to that level, people don't have many resources, and they actually draw from each other constantly. So there is this real tight-knit community that I am clearly not a part of, and I envy that. And I couldn't

get in. I don't belong in. It would never work. I realize that, 'cause even the times that I've tried, we can only go so far and just, the door shuts. But I absolutely think it's two-way. So I envy that, that close-knit thing. And I kind of enjoy that in the summer [at the ball field], 'cause I get a piece of it. But we definitely don't have it otherwise.

Marsha's mostly positive attitude about the neighborhood is fairly typical of new-comers and reflects the partiality of partici-pants' understandings; she gets only a piece of it. Choosing to live in the city did not mean that they wanted an intensive neighborhood social life. Fairmounters' suspicions were on target here. The newcomers were some-what aware that old-timers were not enthu-siastic about their arrival, but they wore the cool reception lightly on their shoulders, for their deeper interests and investments were often in spaces beyond the neighborhood.

The apprehensions between Fairmounters and new professionals operated in the neigh-borhood mostly as undercurrents. But they surfaced in more overt ways at the ballpark, the symbolic center of neighborhood iden-tity and culture. The two groups essentially wanted different things, not only from neigh-borhood life but also from baseball.

Baseball and Belonging

Stylistic differences between newcomers and Fairmounters surfaced on the bleach-ers, in the dugouts, and on the ball field. But the differences were most visible in the social distance between the clubhouse, controlled by old-timer Fairmounters, and the rest of the field. Although who sat on the bleachers, and who coached, changed a great deal at FSA as the neigh-borhood changed (between the 1980s and 2000), not that much changed in the club-house. It was as if a kind of membrane surrounded the clubhouse that protected insider Fairmounters from too much out-side interference. The clubhouse became like a family living room, with lots of kin-folk who came and went. The newcomers were unexpected dinner guests. They were invited in and tolerated, but not embraced as kin. From time to time, someone at dinner would do something rude by fam-ily norms, and when this happened it was usually a newcomer who did it. As guests, the newcomers never felt completely wel-come or comfortable, and they were never sure why. This was because the only way to feel comfortable was to become part of the family, to move in. Some "crossovers" did this and were eventually adopted as dis-tant kin. But most newcomers didn't want strong ties or time-intensive visits. They had too many other dinners to attend, too many other sports to play, and they couldn't really even stay for dessert. And mostly this suited everybody just fine. But there were occasional sparks.

In order to understand how some of the neighborhood tensions played out at the ballpark, it is important to first under-stand the formal structure of Fairmount Sports Association (FSA) and the critical role voluntary labor always played in its survival. FSA had, since its beginnings, depended on the labor of men who were very rooted, physically and socially, in their community. It evolved from an informal club with loosely organized teams in the 1960s to a formal organization recognized by the City of Philadelphia in the 1990s, with bylaws, elected officers, and support from community development grants. Its transition from informal recreation to a formal sports league paralleled trends in youth recreation across America,[12] a shift from pickup games involving few adults to scheduled encounters mediated and controlled by adults. But despite the shift toward a more formal organization, FSA had always survived because of the time and labor contributed by neighborhood adults.

Those three decades of neighborhood support created for Fairmounters a deep sense of entitlement to organizational leadership and decision-making about the baseball league and the way baseball was to be played. Local tradition held that long-term labor and participation constituted the only legitimate road to influence within the league. From the mid-1980s on, most new professionals entering FSA approached the space with only a vague sense of how its residents had sustained baseball for three decades. They also often came from work experiences where they were in charge and made autonomous decisions. In general, they were accustomed to wielding social influence. Their suggestions for how the organization might be improved upon, which came almost immediately, went over like a lead balloon.

It would be a surprise to most of the newcomers entering the organization in the 1990s to learn that FSA leadership at this time was actually the third generation of FSA leaders.... The first group, whom I call "the purists," founded the club, secured the right to play in the current field across from the Philadelphia Museum of Art with their sit-ins, and managed the league from 1961 to 1975. They were strictly baseball. They walked to the field just before games, played, and then went home. They prohibited drinking on the field and they resisted any suggestions for making the space more agreeable to adult spectators. The second generation, in control from 1976 to 1985, oversaw the league during the neighborhood's gentrification, opened the league to the first wave of newcomers to the neighborhood, introduced girls' softball, and received the first middle-class blacks into the league. This new generation of leaders was younger at the time of their takeover than the founders had been when they started the association. They were *not* strictly baseball. Adult socializing

and beer-drinking became a regular feature of the space. This was also the group that secured city approval for the construction of the clubhouse, concession stand, and staff room. This building became the organizational headquarters, the site for player registration, league planning, and socializing after games. The third generation of FSA leaders emerged in the mid-1980s and remained in charge through the early 2000s. Many in this third generation had played ball as boys with the coaches of the first generation of FSA leaders and spoke of them with reverence. They had then come up through the ranks; many of them had been coaching since their late adolescent years. They oversaw the construction of the clubhouse, ushered in a large wave of parents and children of color, and confronted real and imagined organizational challenges to their leadership from the newcomers, whose relative numbers had grown. The ball field had been a core part of the childhood of this third generation. Their parents and their parents' friends had kept it going. It was their birthright. They were in charge here. Their social identities seemed more tied to this baseball space than to their world of work, where they more typically received orders rather than gave them. In my interviews with some of the Fairmount men, I was often surprised at the depth of emotions that surfaced as they discussed the overall meaning of their involvement in the league. During one week of interviews, three different Fairmount men I interviewed separately cried over a baseball memory. I began to wonder if something about me made men cry. One FSA leader, Shawn, a sales representative at a machine supply company, whose father had been one of the first-generation coaches, teared up three different times during our interview as he described his feelings about the league:

Yeah, I mean I love the game. I grew up with it. Well, since I was ten.... It's always something. I always tell Jill [his wife], it's the only thing that I'm good at. Only thing, I said, you know, I've got my job, I've got this, I've got that, but...there's just something about baseball that...it's hard to say....[He pauses as his eyes water.] I can talk to people about it, and I can listen to other coaches, but it's something that I know what I'm talking about, and I know that I'm right. You know? I'll always take in other knowledge, so I feel that I can carry a conversation with anyone. I mean, like politics....A conversation with politics is like, "OK, yeah...Clinton's an okay President." But I can't hold that conversation. But if I have a baseball conversation with virtually anyone, I feel like I can stay in that conversation and hold my weight. With baseball I know what I'm doing.

Participation in baseball was a centerpiece of the Fairmount identity of these men. Two different Fairmounters I interviewed used the phrase "Baseball is all we had." It contributed to feelings of social worth and to a sense of place. Yes, they needed newcomer children to fill the dugouts and help fill out the league to a viable size. But as the relative numbers of newcomers increased, Fairmounters became uneasy. Such large numbers put their control of this birthright at risk. It became increasingly important over time to take steps to ensure control. Someone from the second generation of FSA leaders described the third generation as the group that "circled the wagon against the yuppies."

The Baseball Club and Unequal Participation

How did the organization that needed defending operate? The formal organization of FSA consists of a president and nine officers (vice president, secretary, treasurer,

field maintenance manager, kitchen manager, equipment manager, purchasing agent, and umpire commissioner). These members constitute the deep insiders of the organization. There is a formal election every September for these positions; the elections are normally uncontested. Typically, very few parents turn out to vote. In addition to the officers, there is an advisory board that formally consists of the seven or so commissioners of the boys' and girls' divisions, from T-ball to the thirteen-to-fifteen-year-olds, although the president or other officers sometimes nominate supplementary floating members. This means that the size of the board has varied—sometimes more expansive, sometimes strictly the cluster of commissioners and officers. Below each commissioner are the clusters of coaches for each age group, six or seven for the boys' divisions and three to five for the girls. These constituted the positions of power within the organization.

What comes with this power? For one thing, an immense amount of work. As a tax-exempt voluntary organization, FSA depends on donated time to keep the operation afloat. A myriad of tasks are required to launch and sustain a season. Along with maintaining two well-manicured fields and keeping the concession stand stocked and staffed, in early spring FSA volunteers send out registration materials to the families of potential players, order and repair equipment, set up the batting cage, negotiate with the city to deliver dirt, plow the infield, set up the fences, and dig up and reset pitching mounds and base paths when needed. Then the regular seasonal tasks begin, including: staffing the office during sign-ups, recruiting the forty or so coach-managers for the teams (that is, convincing working adults to devote several hundreds of hours during a season to the job), organizing the drafting of teams, ordering the uniforms for every team, recruiting commercial sponsors from the neighborhood to support teams financially, managing the finances of the organization, maintaining the park grounds throughout the entire season, stocking the kitchen and concession area with all the supplies needed to provide hot dogs, hamburgers, and other tasty, non-nutritious food for the four active months of the season, monitoring the kitchen support of inexperienced parent volunteers, filling in when parents fail to show up for their allotted hours of kitchen or field duty in order to keep the immaculately clean concession stand open and functional five evenings a week and all day on Saturdays and Sundays throughout the entire four months of the season, recruiting the volunteer umpires, filling in when umpires don't show, recruiting paid umpires for the playoffs, developing scheduling grids that fit forty teams, each playing approximately fifteen games, onto two fields, redoing the scheduling grids after periods of rain, fending off streams of questions from confused parents regarding changes in the schedules, and listening to complaints from parents about coaches, rules, schedules, and umpires.

Who did all this work? Volunteers did, but in very unequal degrees. Based on my interviews with strategic FSA leaders and coach-managers,[13] I estimated the different degrees of involvement of the 100 or so most active volunteers keeping the organization running over the 2000 season. Table 37.1 illustrates five levels of volunteer participation. At the highest level, there was an inner core of three volunteers, all Fairmounters, who spend most of their waking hours outside of work at the clubhouse, maintaining an almost constant presence. These three men spent an average of fifty-three hours a week for five months of the year, and many unaccounted hours during the winter months, ordering equipment, maintaining the clubhouse and fields, and hanging out at the clubhouse. All three have been associated with the organization for more than two decades. A second level of support is provided by about six core supporters, also Fairmounters, who spend an average of twenty-six hours a week managing a team (sometimes multiple teams), umpiring other games, and supporting the general activities of the clubhouse. A third level of support comes from approximately twelve "super head coaches," who, beyond spending twenty hours a week coaching a

TABLE 37.1. Estimates of the market value of the seasonal contribution of unpaid volunteers at fairmount sports association by level of support

Levels of Support/Positions	Hours per Week	Months per Year	Hours per Season/ Person[a]	Hours per Season/Group	Cost of Seasonal Labor[b] ($6/hour)	Cost of Seasonal Labor[b] ($10/hour)
3 Core Insiders	53	3	1166	3498	22,667	$37,778
6 Core Supporters	26	5	572	3432	22,239	$37,065
12 Super Coaches	20	5	440	5280	34,216	$57,024
30 Head-Coaches	20	4	352	10,550	68,428	$114,048
60 Assistant Coaches	10	4	176	10,560	68,428	$114,049
Total 111				33,330	$215,976	$359,963

[a]Hours per season is calculated by multiplying hours per week by 4.4 weeks per month by months per season.
[b]Dividing the total hours of seasonal support for all groups (33,330) by the 111 individuals who make up these five levels of support, we arrive at the per capita hours of labor for this entire group: 300 hours per season. The minimum seasonal labor cost is estimated on the basis of paying a $6.00 minimum wage plus 8 percent for FICA and Social Security contribution. This is an extremely conservative way of calculating this, as none of these adult volunteers are earning minimum wage on the labor market. The second estimate uses a $10.00 hourly wage plus the 8 percent FICA and Social Security contribution.

Source: Project Data, Grasmuck

team, provide additional support before and after the season in getting the fields ready, and often fill in as umpires during the season. Among this group are also a few Fairmount women who either coach softball or support FSA administratively. Although Fairmounters also predominate in this third group, there are several newcomers accepted here as well. These three levels constitute the "deep insiders."

Next, there are thirty other head coaches, the "fourth level," who support FSA by coaching one team. They spend approximately twenty hours a week during the four-month season on the practices and games of their teams. These head coaches typically restrict their contributions to the managing of their teams, although they may help out from time to time on odd jobs around the clubhouse. While historically, head coaches at FSA were exclusively long-time residents of Fairmount, the proportion of newcomers in coaching positions began to grow in the early 1990s and by the end of the decade the ratio was equal.[14] However, few, if any, newcomers had entered the ranks of head coaches of the older divisions or of the higher-status traveling teams. Finally, at the fifth level, the head coaches rely on the contributions of assistant coaches, minimally two per team, who help manage the practices, keep score, or coach first or third base. The devotion of assistant coaches varies greatly, but a fairly reliable one spends approximately ten hours a week during the four-month season. In summary, about 111 adults devote approximately 33,330 hours of labor a season.

After those hundred-plus adults (the organizational leaders down to the assistant coaches), there is a huge drop-off in the amount of time that others, principally parents, devote to the organization. FSA expects the parents of the approximately 500 households, in addition to paying the eighty dollar inscription fee, to provide four hours of kitchen, field, or bathroom duty during the season. Parents may pay an additional fifty dollars to be exempt from those four hours of work. It is almost always newcomers who take this "I'll-pay-rather-than-work" option.[15] Although most parents are aware that there are many volunteers who contribute more time than they do, few are aware of the amount of time the core volunteers devote.

Think of the organization, then, as a set of concentric circles moving out from a small inner core of Fairmounters who played baseball in the neighborhood and have spent thousands of hours of their adult leisure time at the clubhouse and the field over the past several decades, to a larger, middle group of Fairmount core supporters who have also been affiliated with the organization in most cases since their childhoods and continue to devote hundreds of hours of time each season to FSA. Next we have larger groups of manager-coaches and their assistant coaches who, by the year 2000, consisted of about half old-time Fairmounters and half newcomers who joined FSA more recently, as parents, after they moved into the neighborhood, or who came from nearby areas. Beyond these layers of deep insiders, middle-level supporters, and head coaches, we have the outer group of parent supporters who sign up their children, bring them to practices, attend games, and devote one afternoon or morning in the season to helping out, with varying degrees of devotion and regularity. This outer group has been divided about equally since the year 1998 between parents coming from Fairmount/Spring Garden and those from outside the neighborhood.[16]

The gap in the amount of time dedicated to maintaining FSA by the inner core of volunteers, whose participation ranges from ten to fifty-three hours every week of the season (or an average of 300 hours each season per "activist"), and the outer circle of regular parents, who contribute only four hours once during a season, is a source of significant resentment on the part of insiders in the organization. The cost of these community services, if they were to be contracted on the labor market rather than provided by volunteers, would be staggering. If the community had paid its one-hundred-plus volunteers just minimum wage for their services in 1998, it would have cost over $200,000 for that one season. If paid something closer to a more realistic wage, say ten dollars an hour, the labor costs would have risen to $359,968 for the year. It is not hard to imagine the feelings of those who put in these kinds of hours when confronted with complaints and suggestions for change from affluent strangers who devote only four hours a season, and sometimes fail to do even that.

Wanting Different Things from Baseball

The different degrees of involvement in FSA became a central locus of tensions between old-timers and newcomers in FSA—tensions...already established in the neighborhood. But time devoted to the organization was just one symbolic issue that divided them. Just as Fairmounters complained that newcomers had weak ties to the neighborhood and engaged in little local mixing, held instrumental views of friendship, and offered minimal community support, they saw newcomers approach the baseball organization in a similar manner—for the instrumental needs of their individual children and not as a neighborhood treasure that needed nurturing. Many newcomers were oblivious to this resentment. Others countered with their own complaints about Fairmounters' coolness to outsiders, about unfair access to insider information about teams and opportunities, and about the adult-centered, competitive way Fairmounters ran an organization for children.

Neighborhood Coaches versus Father Coaches

The Fairmount tradition established in the 1960s of neighborhood men volunteering to coach baseball, whether or not they had a son in the league, continued in a modified way for decades. In the 1990s, many teams in FSA were still associated with a Fairmounter coach who "kept his team" year after year. That is, a particular man would coach the Rangers, or the Angels, in the seven-to-nine age division year after year. Teams came to be identified as "The Padres—John's team," or "The Grays—Bob's team." For example, one Fairmounter coach named Jerry coached the Angels for seven years. He had had his son on his team at one time, but he continued to coach the seven-to-nine team after his son moved on. For many old-timers, then, while kids changed each year, the coach stayed the same and to a large extent the reference group stayed the same—namely, other coaches and the old neighborhood. As a result, the coach would build a reputation (for better or worse) with his team, and each new crop of boys represented the potential to help or hurt this reputation. Most newcomer coaches, on the other hand, were father-coaches and often, unlike Fairmounters, coached their sons in other sports, such as soccer. Their reference group was more their own son, and other players and parents on the team, rather than spectators outside this small group. Thus, newcomer coaches spent more time addressing targeted parents and players than on socializing beyond their specific games. They were less likely to stay with the same team or the same age division over time and more likely to move up in age division as their sons did. They almost never coached or maintained contact with the organization beyond the playing careers of their children. Therefore they established less identification with a particular team and less investment with the organization beyond their team.

Why were Fairmounters more willing to agree to coach a team without a son on it, or long after their son had moved up?[17] This pattern of "neighborhood coaches" versus "father coaches" represents a crucial difference in viewpoint concerning the organization between Fairmounters and newcomers; indeed, it reflects different motivations for coaching and joining the organization. We may think of this as different kinds of investments. One is more of an investment in the community or the neighborhood, and the other is more an investment in a life-stage of parenting. This pattern was true at all levels of the organization throughout the 1990s, from T-ballers to the sixteen-year-old traveling team.

These patterns were evident in two teams we followed in the first year of the ethnography, the Angels and the Senators. The Angels were coached by a Fairmounter named Jerry, a manual laborer who also worked side jobs painting houses. This was Jerry's seventh year coaching the Angels but he had coached in years prior to that for other teams when his older children had played. Jerry had nothing to do with the nearby soccer organization. The second team, the Senators, was coached by a lawyer, Kyle, who had coached his son's baseball team at Fairmont for three years and also coached in the parallel soccer organization. Kyle did not live in Fairmount, but in a nearby neighborhood.

Jerry often greeted friends at the field, talking or joking about the performance of his team. He also spent time in the clubhouse and drank beer with other Fairmounters on the weekends between and after games. After he agreed to have Josh, my research assistant (who had grown up nearby in another baseball neighborhood), shadow his team and help with practices, he expected that this meant sharing social time as well, and he generously extended to Josh several invitations to join in Friday-night hanging out at the clubhouse. In contrast, Kyle did little of this. In general Kyle talked less than Jerry to anyone outside of the team, and when he did talk, it was directed to the players and/or parents. Jerry's wife was also very involved with the league, winning an award at the end of the season for her all-around contributions to FSA. Kyle was divorced, and his ex-wife's involvement with the organization was restricted to game attendance. She seemed to know relatively few people in the organization and she was largely unknown to the old-timers.

This practice of equating a team with a coach puts the focus more on the coach and how he is doing, rather than on the kids' performance, at least in the eyes of the reference group of friends. Thus, it is quite common at the field to hear someone ask, "How is Dan's team doing this year?" or "How are the Angels this year?" Associating a team with a coach also provides structural pressures that increase competition, by creating a strong identification of a particular coach with the team and the team's win-loss record and division standings. It can also heighten the attachment of the coach's ego to the team's performance. Even Fairmounter coaches who ignored these pressures and minded the boys and their needs as a top priority received regular commentary about their "career record" in the league. For example, one coach, a Fairmounter, is legendary in the league for having won the championship five times, once every other year for nine years, with his seven-to-nine team, the Rangers.

Many times over the years, I observed the tendency of Fairmounter coaches to meet and greet friends during their coached games. Fairmounter coaches were more likely, for example, to stand either along the third base line or near the dugout talking with friends or other buddies who were coaching other teams. It became clear that many Fairmounter coaches felt they were being observed and perhaps judged by peers and neighborhood friends. Thus, the pressure for these coaches to have a winning team comes from the commentary of their buddies in the neighborhood about how well their team is doing. This predisposes these coaches to think about their teams as much, or more, through friends' eyes as through their players' eyes or through the eyes of the parents of their immediate teams. All the insider interest in the outcome of games at Fairmount made some Fairmounter coaches see as their reference group other coaches in the league, and friends and long-time families of the neighborhood. Most of these Fairmount coaches had numerous relatives in the organization—brothers, sons, sisters, wives, and in-laws—who served as coaches and organizational officers in FSA. These Fairmount insiders hung out socially in the FSA office on weekends, relaxed after hours and on weekend nights under the large sycamore tree adjacent to the ball field, and regularly attended social events sponsored by FSA, such as "casino night," when a rented bus would take insiders and Fairmounter friends and relatives to Atlantic City.

One year after one of the traveling teams won the final game of the citywide championship, the first such victory in the thirty years of the organization, I was selling hot dogs in the concession stand along with the sister of the winning coach, Billy, a six-foot, three inch old-timer, as he entered the kitchen upon arriving from across town. She asked him in a whisper, "Have you called Mommy yet to tell her?" Surprisingly, he reported that he had already done so, apparently within minutes of having completed the game. This was an indication both of how tuned in his mother was to his performance, and of the importance he placed on her knowing immediately. It seemed inconceivable that the newcomer coaches, with mothers far removed from the neighborhood, indeed, perhaps from the city, would make such a call. Moreover, historically it was common for the wives of some male coaches to also have girls' softball teams. Thus there was a complicated network of local contacts, with cousins,

in-laws, husbands, and wives from a relatively small number of families holding a considerable proportion of the strategic positions in the organization.

The different ways coaches related to the organization and the divisions between neighborhood coaches and father coaches had a parallel in the form of teams that Fairmount insiders favored and teams that needed to be beaten—the "clubhouse teams" versus the "yuppie teams." After a few years in the league, I noticed how, during certain defining games (like the playoffs or a game that would clinch a team's position in the standings) the size of the crowds gathered behind the two teams would be very lopsided. Behind the team with a Fairmount head coach, a large crowd would congregate, many of whom were not parents of players but simply neighborhood folks who had come out to root either for this coach or for boys they knew on the team. In contrast, if the opposing team was headed by a newcomer coach, the crowd, even for championship games, was typically smaller. I also began to realize that the teams with Fairmount coaches typically also had a large proportion of Fairmount kids on them. Similarly, the newcomer coaches had a large number of newcomer kids on their teams.

The frequent turnout of Fairmounters for teams on which they had no children was a collective endorsement by Fairmounters of their community. Rarely, if ever, did I see large collections of newcomer parents gather at games in which they did not have a child playing. They seemed to have no such group identity or loyalties. I preferred for my son to be on the Fairmount teams, and so did he. They were more exciting. The crowds were bigger. I learned more about the nuances of the game in these contexts. The conversations with team parents behind the dugout, or in the bleachers, were more frequently about the nuances of the game and less about schools, colleges, or work—common topics among the professional parents. Sometimes, a newcomer parent would come alone to see the team their child had been on before leaving for summer camp, in order to report to the child at camp. But typically, their interest in the outcome of games not involving their child did not extend this far. What this meant was that, if a newcomer coach entered the championship series against a Fairmounter coach, the newcomer team could expect only a small cluster of parents from that team (and even at championships this did not mean all parents), whereas behind the Fairmount team, referred to by some as the "clubhouse team," almost the entire neighborhood might be seated.

My Community versus My Boy

Part of the intensity Fairmounters felt about the outcomes of games and championships stemmed from their definition of baseball as the only sport, perhaps even the only social activity that mattered. As one regular umpire for FSA told me, "Fairmount is 'strictly baseball.' The people who run the building, who control Fairmount sports, are from the neighborhood, and their main interest is baseball or has been baseball up until the last two years when they introduced basketball." Once, as I was working kitchen duty, a Fairmount leader chatting with me shared his frustration that the local soccer league, run almost exclusively by newcomers, had scheduled their "opening day" on the same day as FSA's "closing day." He mumbled something about their lack of respect or willingness to coordinate things, but laughed as he finished off the conversation with, "Besides, is soccer really a sport?" Another Fairmounter coach complained that newcomers' over-involvement in multiple leisure activities and other sports translated into making each a "jack of all trades and master of none." Citing their "general lack of baseball talent," he said,

The quality of the ballplayers is much weaker now, because of the yuppies moving in. It used to be hard-working, neighborhood people. Every kid was a good player. Now we have people from all over the city, and the talent is worn so thin. Old-fashioned, neighborhood people are better ball players.... They played more often. You played with your friends, and they played baseball.... They weren't involved with soccer, and Hebrew school on Saturdays, and all those other things. A bunch of people are involved now. The quality of play is down now too.

In interviews with FSA insiders, some complained that newcomers used the league as a day care service, dropping their kids off at practice or games and coming back later to pick them up. They viewed this as particularly a problem with newcomer parents. In part, this is because when it happened with a Fairmounter child, they often knew where the child lived and what other adults were friends with the child and felt less worried if something happened to the child. With the newcomer kids, they didn't have this same sense of security, as expressed in this comment from one of the organization's officers: "We had a kid badly hurt here last season. There was no relative of his in a 20-mile radius."

One set of tensions that arose over the issue of scheduling practices and games relates to the different nature of the ties the boys and their parents have to the neighborhood. Fairmounter coaches seemed to take a more organic approach to the neighborhood, assuming, for example, that people would be around and available for games and practices. To them, it was less important to give much advance notice for games and practices. Fairmount boys were also more organically tied to networks in the neighborhood, like the local Catholic school. The former practice in Fairmount of scheduling sign-ups on several Saturday evenings in February, for a season that began several months later, presented no problem for a community that communicated relatively effectively through word-of-mouth or through the schools. Once the season began Fairmount boys were likely to be around for practices and games, and were unlikely to leave town for expensive sleep-over camps. If their parents were not at the field, chances were that someone else there knew them and could tend to them or walk them home. Everyone they knew was deeply tuned into the cycle of the season and understood the need for the juggling of games after rainouts, or for rescheduling games when there were conflicts with traveling team schedules or with the scheduled games of the local Catholic school, where many Fairmounter boys also played. No such accommodations were made, however, for the activities of non-Catholic schools. This became a major source of irritation to newcomers who were not in the loop of information. Fairmounters sometimes referred disparagingly to newcomer parents as "the summer-camp crowd," a reference to their tendency to disappear during the playoffs in July. This became such a problem that FSA added a question to the signup sheets about plans for summer camp, so coaches could take this into account as they drafted players. One Fairmount mother advocated putting all "summer campers" on the same team, so that their team would self-destruct at playoff time and not "mess up the playoffs for the rest of us." The summer camp issue was a hot-button issue, in part, because it dramatically symbolized the inequalities among the children. While it was never discussed in terms of "who can afford to send them and who can't," the judgment about whether leaving for camp before finishing out the season was fair or unfair was colored by how natural going to overnight camp for a month at the age of ten or eleven seemed to the one doing the judging. One Fairmount mother told me she considered this practice a form of child abuse. After

years of having the playoffs disrupted by the exodus of middle-class kids, FSA leaders required that parents specify on their registration if the child was camp-bound. This information in the top right corner of the registration form, almost a certified stamp of "yuppie kid," then weighed into considerations during the draft, somewhat alleviating the problem. But the perception that Fairmounters could be counted on to commit for the season and that newcomers were as likely to turn to other competing interests rattled many old-timers. An old-timer who had held numerous positions in the league over a twenty-year period put it this way:

Sometimes newcomer parents are uncooperative with what you are trying to do, or insensitive or just ignorant with what you are trying to do. And they place their activities and their kids' activities over the commitment to the team.... You had a critical game situation, and if they had to go down the shore they just went down the shore.... If the commitment that you make in the beginning doesn't pay off, and you have the opportunity to leave legitimately, then leave. Or don't sign up again next year, if it didn't work out. If you signed up for nine weeks of baseball, or fifteen weeks of baseball, see it through to the end. No matter if you're the best player on the team who feels unsatisfied because everybody else stinks, or you're the best player on the team. This is something that happens in life. You don't always have these chances to move around.... But I see parents who see things not work out, and they just say, "Okay, hell with it." I think they're sending the wrong message. 'Cause what they're telling the kid is, "You can just shop around, and if this works for you, great, take advantage of it. But if this doesn't work out, then hell with it and hell with them." Fairmounter parents have a different mentality, more stick to it once you make a commitment.

Newcomers sometimes countered that insider favoritism determined how rules were applied, that FSA leaders, for example, cancelled and rescheduled games according to the needs of the high-status traveling teams on which many of the sons of the Fairmount leadership played. It was easy to stick to your FSA commitments when schedules were juggled with *your* competing activities taken into account. There was truth to this claim. In fact, to avoid conflicts for Catholic school players, the entire season's schedule of FSA games was not finalized until the schedule for the Catholic league, in which many Fairmounter boys also played, was established. Thus what looked like "strong commitment" from Fairmounter boys could as easily be interpreted as "participation made easy."

Newcomer kids were also less tied to neighborhood networks, more tied to networks that extended beyond the neighborhood, less familiar and less legitimate to Fairmounter coaches. This put them at a disadvantage sometimes, when information about practices circulated informally among Fairmount boys at the local Catholic school. Moreover, the general social trend in America toward increasingly complex social schedules for children, with few available hours of unplanned leisure, is especially marked among more affluent families.[18] Baseball was typically only one of a number of sports played by newcomer boys and was less likely to be ranked by them as their favorite than it was for Fairmounter boys. Just as Fairmounter parents chafed at the professional classes' inability to make the games and questioned their commitment to the league, professional parents often grumbled over short notice for practices or schedule changes and the difficulty of juggling complex schedules. Last minute changes to schedules in lives this tightly

scheduled set off fits. As one newcomer father complained:

I tell you, there's a group of people, three or four people, that seem to make the decision about when games are played and how games are played and when the playoffs are played. And then, their decisions aren't always logical. It's based on what's always been, or what's easiest for them, and not based on what's good for all the kids. Like when the playoffs games start, whether people might have vacations, might have other things to do in the summer. No concern for things like that. You really can't talk to them either. You really can't change it....They just don't—they're not open to change, and they don't want to hear from you.

There were also frequent accusations of conflicts of interest against the Fairmounters. There was the fact that Fairmount commissioners, for example, were sometimes also head coaches of a team in the same division. So if a conflict erupted in a game with this coach/commissioner there was no independent party to which an appeal could be made. As another example, each year, tradition has it that the head coach of the championship team orders a personalized Fairmount jacket for Trophy Day for every member of his team who is willing to pay for it. One year, when a team of one of the commissioners was defeated in the championship, he and his team nonetheless ordered and received team jackets with "division champions" sewed on them. Never before had a first-place team which had gone on to lose the championship ordered such an honor for itself. During another season, a middle-class newcomer who lived outside Fairmount, but whose son had played at FSA for five years, exploded one weekend when he heard that the commissioner had cancelled his son's playoff game on a Friday, the day before the game. This father had rearranged weekend plans for the beach in order to be there, only to find out that the commissioner had cancelled it. It seemed that the opposing team (on which the commissioner's son played) did not have enough players, because they were all down at the shore! "I'm sick of this stuff. It happens all the time. I'm sick of those traveling teams too. And don't tell me it is just a few people, 'cause it is Fairmount. The league lets this happen." Newcomers also complained when a coach of one team served as an umpire for a game between two other teams in his own division in which the outcome would significantly impact the umpire's team's standing. Others grumbled about the umpires favoring "clubhouse teams" in which the boys of FSA officers played. Yet, finding newcomer volunteer umpires was difficult, either because many didn't feel competent to umpire or because they were unwilling to volunteer. FSA was therefore forced to draw, from deep within its own internal ranks, individuals who, conflict of interest or not, were more willing to come forward, stand in the often smothering heat, wear heavy equipment, and weather parental insults and grumblings about judgment calls.

An African American newcomer described the central divisions in FSA as being not about race, but about insiders versus strangers. Nonetheless, he explained how the insider culture sometimes fueled race suspicions:

> I think it is not so much race. It's about a group of people who may have grown up together, socialized together. They played in the league as youngsters, and they socialize as adults in the same circles, and they've kind of kept that circle closed. If you're not initially a part of that group, then either you will not feel comfortable in joining that group or there will be discussions or decisions made, or whatever, within that small circle at different

times. And pretty much that's what the organization is about....And I'll give you a great example. Last year my son had a really successful year, lots of home runs, plus he was pretty good all around. They started a travel team, basically a ten-year-old travel team. But they had a number of kids who were younger than ten on it, some were just turning nine or whatever, but we were never invited to try out for the team. When we inquired as to what the procedure was, we were told that the kids had to try out. What tryouts? Those folks who were in that inner circle would be privy to that; so their kids would typically have the opportunity to try out and ultimately make the team....And I could have easily concluded that maybe they didn't want African American boys on the team, maybe they were afraid we would push their kids out from the elite status on the team. One could conclude that there was some racial motivation there, as some other parents did.

A white newcomer mother implied that there was a higher bar for newcomers, black or white, on the traveling teams: "If you are not a Fairmounter, your kid has to be three times as good to get selected for their travel teams." One Fairmounter leader agreed that talent was not the only criterion for selecting which children would "go travel" because with that honor sometimes came a trip to Cooperstown. "We're gonna select kids whose parents have been helping out all this time and deserve some recognition for that. Not just someone who rolls up new this year with a little talent." Men who were putting in hundreds of hours of labor to umpire, coach, administer, or work as commissioner had become accustomed to the prevailing sense that, without them, the league couldn't exist. They merited certain kinds of payoffs, perquisites. Judgment calls were part of their rights, a compensation for the drudgery they put in daily during the season. Misunderstandings came because most newcomers took the requirement of four hours of labor at face value. Even though there was a lot of passive resistance about completing that duty, once it was paid, they expected equal treatment and information in exchange. They were usually unaware that additional labor contributions could translate into more consideration for their children.

Social activities sponsored by FSA that were unrelated to baseball marked another boundary between the clubhouse and the outsiders. Newcomers rarely participated in these outings and were often entirely unaware that they existed. Sometimes these activities involved a group of Fairmounters going to see a minor league baseball game together in Reading or Camden or renting a bus to go as a group to Atlantic City for the evening. One newcomer mother, whose son played ball at FSA for six years, put it this way: "I've never been invited to those events and don't know how you get invited. I've just seen the bus driving away." A professional father, when asked about his participation in these FSA-sponsored events, reflected on his peculiar position of being rather engaged with the organization but outside it at the same time. "Well, I have never been specifically invited [to social events]. I feel that I am not, well—There's the typical Fairmount members, and I'm a newcomer. I'm a newcomer, a professional. And a large part of those people, I feel that we don't have a lot in common. And I feel that they don't want to get to know me, and I'm not sure that I want to get to know them. So I feel there's some sort of social gap or something between us." Once my husband asked Brian, one of the FSA leaders, about an upcoming trip to the casinos be had heard about, thinking that a few of the parents on his team might be interested.

JOHN: Are there any flyers or anything I could hand out to my team?

BRIAN: No.
JOHN: 'Cause some of the parents on my team might want to go.
BRIAN: Aren't they all yuppies?
JOHN: No, you're thinking of me. My team isn't.

They both laughed, but no flyers were forthcoming.

The boundary between those who attended such events and those who didn't was not merely between Fairmounters and newcomers. It only appeared that way to newcomers. In reality most Fairmounter parents did not participate either. These were social activities for the Fairmounters most deeply involved in the day-to-day work of holding together the organization: the inner circle of FSA staff, their family members, and their friends. But the tightness of this group, and the visibility of some of their socializing, underscored newcomers' feelings of being on the outside. It also explained why even many Fairmounter parents did not consider themselves insiders.

To get a feel for this sensibility, I asked all the parents I interviewed if they considered themselves to be insiders, outsiders, or something else. Not surprisingly, none of the newcomer parents I interviewed described themselves as insiders. They were about equally divided between those who described themselves as outsiders and those who answered "something else." Here are some typical self descriptions of newcomers:

—I consider myself an outsider who knows what's going on and is aware of a lot of stuff. I follow all the gossip and hang out there a lot. So I'm not directly involved with them, but I'm not an outsider either.
—I'm an outsider, but a friendly outsider.
—Absolutely 100% outsider.
—A far outsider.
—I'm something else, in the middle. To be an outsider means you don't feel comfortable there. And I feel perfectly

comfortably down there but certainly not an insider.

While none of the Fairmounter parents described themselves as pure outsiders, the majority also did not consider themselves to be insiders. This was because they too perceived a divide between the clubhouse and the rest of the organization. More typically, Fairmounters thought of themselves as "something else," as expressed in this sample of their answers:

—Something else. First I was an insider, and then I was an outsider. And now I'm something else. That's how I want it. Plenty of people have been pushed out down there. That's usually how they end up getting out. Why? The clique just decides.

—I feel like I'm in between. Why? There are lots of politics involved in FSA. I don't like politics. I like to see everything positive. If I see any negativity, I stay away. I umped for about seven years, umping and that's it. I went down, umped the game, and said "hi" and "goodbye." I lived in the neighborhood and umped but still wasn't an insider. There's a kind of exclusion.

—We're kind of caught in the middle, 'cause we're not real Fairmounters. But we're not outsiders either. My husband grew up here, but he's an attorney now, that kind of thing. You know, he can talk to them, but he's not them.

—On the outside, right up against the window, but I don't want on the inside. [Laughter] I like it on the outside. I really do. There are some I like down there, but some are obnoxious. I want no part. I could be if I wanted. If I said, "Oh, I'll come down and work the kitchen every night," they'd say, "Oh sure Jessie." But no thanks.

This last comment is especially telling in that she indicates, in contrast to the opinion of many newcomers, that there was one sure-fire way for a woman to become accepted as a newcomer: to donate long hours at the concession stand. There is some truth to this claim, especially when we consider the case of the only African American newcomer parent I ever saw accepted as an apparent insider. Sometime around 2002, this young mother could be seen sitting in the circle of chairs under the sycamore trees where FSA leadership watched games, regularly selling hot dogs at the concession stand, and joining insider barbecues after games. As one newcomer board member described it, "She is amazing to me. She just walked in, started helping with whatever she saw going on, ignored all raised eyebrows, and years later, she was in."

The Catholic Imagination and Local Accountability

There was something of the "Catholic imagination" that informed the tight cultural feel of the baseball club. Andrew Greeley, a sociologist of religion, argues that the Catholic religious imagination shapes the social lives of practicing and lapsed Catholics in subtle ways that often distinguish them from non-Catholics.[19] An ordered community, close ties among neighbors, and an emphasis on layers of hierarchy or authority flow from this religious sensibility. We have already seen how Fairmounters lamented the weak social ties of newcomers to the neighborhood. Similarly, Fairmounters at FSA, who were overwhelmingly Catholic,[20] often complained about the individualistic, self-serving way that newcomers approached the organization. One Fairmounter who had grown up in the neighborhood, attended college, and achieved success as a professional saw himself as seated right in the middle between the two groups. But he emphasized that central to "the problem" at FSA was the individualism of the professionals and their instrumental approach to the league.

I think they're more selfish to a degree. I don't say completely, because I have met some really outstanding people.... It just seems to be a trait that you notice with a lot more professional people. Maybe they're more goal-oriented, so a lot of secondary issues don't mean anything to them.... They also don't have any real connection to the neighborhood, or don't consider themselves Fairmount.... It's not a problem for them to use the organization to their benefit like they would use any other organization.... "Look, I paid my money. You got me down here doing kitchen duty and field maintenance. I'll do what I want." This isn't a big thing for them. I would say, it would seem to be a trend you would see in more professional people.... Maybe they had more opportunities to do other things. They have more choices than those who live up in Fairmount.... Fairmounters, on the other hand, aren't that way.... They make a commitment.... They follow through.... The culture in Fairmount, you don't quit teams.... You follow through.... If you don't like it after it's [the season] done, then you don't come back.... I think that trait is more apparent with people who grow up in Fairmount or have a Fairmount mentality.

This judgment, that the new professionals were in it for themselves, was highlighted one year when FSA leaders discovered that two newcomer head coaches had used private connections with city officials to secure permits to use one of the practice fields in Fairmount Park for their own teams and had not offered to share the opportunity democratically with the entire organization. Finding a good place to practice would put any coach at an advantage since, often times, the practice fields were hard to come by. One of the coaches had secured the permit as an individual, but the other had used FSA's name, heightening the general condemnation. The permit was angrily reclaimed by

FSA in the name of equal access. Yet, ironically, and consistent with the newcomer complaint of insider advantage, after it was taken away from these newcomer coaches, only selected coaches, mostly Fairmounters, were informed of the availability of the new practice field.

Ironically, while newcomers often felt powerless and shut out from real influence in decision making, or even from understanding the logic of many decisions, some Fairmounters felt that newcomers often got more of what they wanted in the organization because they were less constrained by the opinions of their neighbors in pushing for their kids' interests. The Fairmounters' deeper connections to the neighborhood sometimes operated to make *them* feel more constrained in FSA and less able to "get their way" than newcomers, for fear of alienating old friends and neighbors they saw regularly in church and at school. In short, Fairmounters viewed newcomers as shameless lobbyists for their children's individual interests. This accusation is reminiscent of the way middle-class parents often use their educational credentials to intervene with teachers and principals to secure institutional advantages for their children at the expense of working-class children, whose parents are more reluctant to interfere with teachers' judgments.[21] A Fairmounter named Jessie grew agitated as she described this pattern:

Most of them who are down on this ball field are my age, a couple years older than me. We've grown up together. We formed that league more or less together. So you watch what you say to each other. New people don't have that same relationship, and they really don't care what they say. And they say what they want. And you know what? They're probably better off, because their kids play where they want to play.... They always get what they want. That's the best part. Because I could kick myself in the ass all the time. I'm thinking, look where their kids are playing, you know? My kid's screwed [laughter] all the time…because I'm afraid this one won't talk to me, or that one won't talk to me, if I complain because you've grown up all your life together. You just have a different bond. The new people in the neighborhood don't have a problem with saying anything. I'm not a big one for someone from the outside coming in and telling me how to do something after all these years of sweating blood and all this stuff you put into this organization, and that is something that happens. You get the yuppies coming in, and they are being very vocal because they don't know you from Adam. If you are an outsider, you can run your mouth and get more action, whereas I won't run my mouth. But that tends to make like bad blood 'cause you're like, "Wait a minute, I've been here for twenty years sweepin' floors, picking up dirt. [laughs] Who the hell are you?"

In her view the "bonded social capital"[22] of the neighborhood could inhibit insiders as much as it might provide an advantage. The degree to which longtime residence worked as a form of social control that disadvantaged old-timers was echoed by another Fairmounter parent: "If you do something to offend somebody, they are going to remember it.…And it might take five, ten, fifteen years before they forget.…Like I was saying, the argument I had with that other coach.…It's still in existence.…And it's been ten years! And when I see him to this day, a cold stare.…And we grew up together! And it will be that way till we're dead I guess."

There was also the problem of some newcomers who acted too independently once they were given some responsibility. They seemed to have less sense of the hierarchy of the organization than did the Catholic Fairmounters, less awareness of its subtle requirements for deference to leaders. If a

newcomer was permitted to manage a team, or to serve as commissioner for one of the divisions, this didn't mean that he shouldn't run most of his decisions by the leadership on a regular basis. To do otherwise would be considered disrespectful. But as Sennett puts it, "respect is an expressive performance" that requires an artful use of words and gestures that convince others that you mean it.[23] Not all newcomers, even with the best of intentions, found the right words and gestures of respect. One old-timer described the dilemma many newcomers faced (and I had the distinct impression his example referred to my husband's brief stint as commissioner) in searching for the proper deference:

Sometimes the newcomers feel, they're made to feel, as intruders. They're not that warmly received. If you don't say or do the right thing, or behave right at the beginning, in the right manner, you can isolate yourself. It's very easy to say the wrong thing. You're not even aware that you're saying the wrong thing.…[As an example] maybe being too independent, by not letting the front office know what you were about. It's funny, even though you might be the commissioner of the league, it's prudent to run it past the office. Say to them, "You know, this situation happened. Here, this is what I'm going to do." And then listen and see what their reaction is. Their reaction in most cases is, "Yeah, do that then," or "Let's do it that way. That's right. It's the right thing to do."…You really get advice. You can sense if it's not a good idea with the front office. You think it's a good idea, but you can sense that they're not happy with it. Then you can try it another way. Or you should just drop it. I found, not to act too independently, and let them find out later. Although 90 percent of the time they would have agreed, but without advice, it sort of strains the relationship.…[People who don't do it] they find out when it's too late, after they get yelled at, or after they don't get what they want, or they were overruled....But you're never told this. You're expected to do it. And it's what, if you're from Fairmont, it's what you're expected to do. And you wouldn't think of doing it otherwise. If you're from Fairmont, why would you even think of it? Know what I'm saying? So the contradiction is, if you're not from Fairmont you don't know what you should be doing.

Hierarchical Communalism versus Child-Centered Individualism

If Fairmounters saw newcomers as individualistic and not community minded enough, newcomers would counter that at least theirs was a child-centered individualism. The sharpest newcomer critique related to newcomers' view that FSA prioritized adult socializing over children's interests. While Fairmounters might devote lots of time to the organization, they argued, a good amount of that time was devoted to hanging out in the clubhouse and drinking beer, which set a bad example for the kids. The clubhouse has a keg refrigerator so that cold beer is always on tap. Insiders have only to grab a plastic cup, pull down a lever, and fill up. One black middle-class father elaborated this critique this way: "If I had a pet peeve [with the ball club], it would be the consumption of alcohol on the premises. I'm not sure if there's a legal issue there, but I think it was poor, it was in real bad taste when you have adults drinking alcohol when there's lots of kids....But I understand it kind of has some history to it. These are people in the neighborhood that kind of grew up together and socializing. I just think because the product is children that we have to adjust our behavior when we're in their presence. So that's what

I probably liked the least, the alcohol, and how the parents come down hard on their kids." Another newcomer father, whose son had played in the league for more than eight years, went further: "At FSA, there's drinkers and non-drinkers. I see alcohol as the major problem in the Fairmount Sports Association. The amount consumed by the coaches, amounts consumed in the clubhouse....And sometimes I think that it's an organization, not for the kids but, for the parents, so that the parents, whoever the people in the organization are, will have a place to hang out, drink beer, and be with their buddies....Yeah. A social club for the coaches and parents and not so much for the kids."

Once, when a pediatrician whose son had played in FSA for years found out that my husband had agreed to serve as commissioner one year, he asked me, "Hey, now that he is commissioner, is he gonna start hangin' at the clubhouse drinking until 3:00 in the morning?" The aloof treatment of newcomers fueled the suspicions of some, that little more than drinking was going on in there, that it was a subsidized, inner-city country club for insiders. One Fairmounter coach revealed his awareness of this external critique when he said, "'The clique' they call us. We're the clique. And it's the clique versus the newcomers. It's like the Hatfields and the McCoys. It's been going on forever....But it took a lot of work to be involved in that clique. Sign up to do something, and then you'll know what is going on."

The complaint that FSA was adult-centered went beyond discomfort with beer-drinking in the clubhouse. Actually, many newcomers thought that drinking beer in the staff office and using the clubhouse year round as a hang-out place was perfectly acceptable, even appropriate compensation for the hours they spent holding the organization together. When newcomers said that the organization wasn't enough about children they usually had in mind an emphasis on winning games, winning championships, and winning in the city-wide league. Among the parents I interviewed, it was disproportionately newcomers who felt FSA leaned excessively in the competitive direction and who longed for more emphasis on individual instruction of players. In contrast, Fairmounter parents tended to see the organization as more balanced, with an appropriate balance of emphasis between teaching skills and winning games.[24] Typical among newcomer parents were these comments from one father. "At FSA they are very much playing games to win, very competitive. This is one of the things I don't like. See, certain kids are not going to get a base hit because the coach just teaches them to bunt, so he can win the game. They learn to bunt but should be learning to hit and [then they would] have a slightly better chance to get on base than by [just] bunting. I prefer to teach kids how to play baseball and not how to win. But when games are not competitive it's not as much fun to watch, maybe not so much fun for kids. Still, I would have less emphasis on playoffs, so there's not so much emphasis on winning." Another newcomer father described FSA as "less instructional and more about winning" and related it to the need of coaches to have bragging rights in the neighborhood. This argument relates back to the issue of "clubhouse teams" versus the newcomer teams. Baseball as a central element of the Fairmount neighborhood's identity meant that losing a game, especially for a "clubhouse team," took on added significance. The association of particular teams with insiders focused energy on the importance of winning to prove something to some other group of adults. Many newcomers thought that that other group of adults was them. One black professional father who lived in Center City and had spent years in FSA with his children believed that, with the arrival of significant numbers of players of color, the need to win at FSA had intensified.

I think Fairmount stresses competition more than instruction. . . . Here's the whole thing. Let me see if I can express it. You have this new dynamic of all of these black kids in the league now. It happened. But the league is still controlled by a small group of white people who have been there for a long time. I think the parents have been feeling that, and this is something that black people feel anyway, which is, when we come in, we can come in, but we'll never be able to control it. And, um, I think many parents felt that when it came down to winning, these white coaches who are involved in the league will win at all costs, thus to show that they're still in control of their knowledge, that they know more. . . . The winning carries over to more than just we *win*, but I'm still, *we're* still, in *control* of this thing. We *have* to be here because we know the most about this game. We're not gonna have coaches coming from outside of the league who know more than we do because, although that may be the case, people may know as much, but if you look at the result, the result was that we won, and we obviously won because we know more.

Beyond how parents judged the competitive nature of the organization as a whole, I wanted to know how they differed as individuals in their approaches to competitive games. To understand this, I presented all the parents I interviewed with the following scenario involving a boys' game in the ten-to-twelve division:

I'd like to ask you to consider the following game scenario and tell me what you think the coach should do: It is the bottom of the last inning of the game. Your son's team is ahead by one run. They are in the field and already have two outs. The other team has runners on second and third, and their clean-up hitter is up to bat. What should the coach of your son's team do?

If the parent was confused about the implied dilemma of the scenario (an expression of lack of baseball knowledge), they were probed as to whether the coach should intentionally walk the batter, since the tying and winning runs were on base, and let the pitcher confront a weaker hitter. There was a pronounced clustering around the different answers to this question. Fairmounter parents almost universally (nine of ten) endorsed the more competitive, "intentional walk" position. Newcomers were more divided, but more (seven of eleven) favored the pitch-to-the-batter solution. Moreover, the justifications for their distinct answers were often emphatic. To see these contrasting sensibilities, consider this selection of typical justifications offered by Fairmounter parents for the intentional walk:

—Fairmounter father: Sure you walk him automatically.... If your pitcher's not better than their hitter, you walk him, and you go to next guy and put pressure on him.... In ten-to-twelve, you still walk him because the fifth hitter will be more intimidated than the fourth hitter would. It's baseball, that's the way you would do it. [When probed about alternative response] If you moved to high school, what would your high school coach tell you to do? Walk him. That's baseball. The knowledge of the game is, in order to win you put the pressure on the weak link. The weak link becomes the fifth batter.... It's not a matter of man against man; it's a matter of position against position.
—Fairmounter father: Automatic walk. It's a beautiful game between both teams, but it's close, and you don't want to lose that game, not like that. I'll take a chance and go after the next guy. We'll get the fifth batter at the plate.
—Fairmounter father who also coached: Walk 'em. Definitely. As long as

I know my pitcher can throw strikes, no ifs, ands, or buts [laughs when probed about the alternative]. It's just simple good baseball.... I wouldn't be a good coach, if I didn't do whatever I could to make the team, to put 'em in a position to win.
—Fairmount mother: I would walk him. Load up the bases then go with your fifth batter. [When probed about alternative answer] Do you want to win? Everybody always does this thing. "Well, it's for fun." Jump rope's fun. [Laughter] Yeah, jump rope. I hate it when they say that: "It's for fun." Because if it was just for fun, there would be no score. There is a score. There's an object here. Somebody's got to win. Somebody's got to lose. I think they would be better off teaching the children, you know: "Win some, lose some, blah, blah, blah." I can't stand when they do that—the confidence thing. "He has to build his confidence." But it's an important game! You have to win it. It's strictly the game.
—Fairmount mother: Walk. Yeah. I learned that from the real baseball.... Yeah, I'm out to win. We're just trying to do the best that we can to win. Of course, I would get mad if it was the opposite. [Laughter]

In contrast, here is a sample of newcomer parents' rationales for letting pitchers confront the clean-up batter:

—Newcomer father: Pitch to him instead of walking. Why? It's an instructional league—even though you're playing the game to win. I just don't think it's fair to the batter at that level and the team. I mean, it's a legitimate move. I just feel, at that level it should be about the kids not the coaches.
—Newcomer father: If it was in the regular season, I would pitch to him. See if my pitcher can face the situation. Let him get their best hitter, to build their confidence. But if it was a championship, I might intentionally walk
—Newcomer father: I don't get it. [After an explanation of the dilemma] Oh, pitch to

him. I'd have confidence in my pitcher and let him have the out.

—Newcomer father: I would encourage the pitcher to do his best to throw strikes. No, an intentional walk would not be my first choice. If the game is on the line, we're gonna either win it or lose it. You're gonna play to win, so take chances—it's an opportunity for a guy to come up after, chances are as good as with the fourth batter.

—Newcomer mother: I probably would not do an intentional walk, but it is an acceptable strategy, I wouldn't find anything wrong with a coach who would walk, but I probably wouldn't. I'm a shoot-from-the-hip kind of person.

—Newcomer mother: I've learned that, in baseball strategy you should walk the clean-up hitter, especially at the higher level. But in little league, let him swing. 'Cause it's little kids, not the major leagues. They should be able to have the experience of batting in a pressure situation. He's in a clean-up spot. When my son was on a bad team last year, they walked him all the time. He was so frustrated and built up a lot of anger because he couldn't swing the bat. He was putting up with all these errors of others and come his turn, if they didn't walk him, the umpire was calling a ball or strike that wasn't.

One black newcomer parent, in contrast to these other newcomer positions, did vote for the walk position. But in discussing her logic, she went on to oppose organized youth sports in general, precisely because of the need to follow the strategic logic of the game rules. "I think he should walk him. If you're playing the game, you're playing to win. You should walk him. But that's why I'm not sold on youth sports, per se. If you're playing the game, you're playing the game. If you want to just hit and have fun, then let kids hit and have fun. But if you're playing organized sports, then it's

like playing checkers. What is the objective of checkers? To win, and you have rules. The same thing with baseball and any other sport. As soon as you organize, that's what happens.... Unfortunately, in our society, we over-organize. When I was growing up, we formalized our own teams, made up our own rules. We didn't have the parents there. We didn't have all this hoopla. There wasn't the pressure then. But the minute you make it baseball, you make it the real game. You make it organized. You have teams, parents, everything, and then it becomes the real game, the real pressure, and you have to deal with it. I think we have organized baseball too soon. Most of them are not ready for that kind of pressure."

One Fairmounter father challenged the assumption behind my question, that this was a matter of individual choice and not a matter of group culture. He had coached for many years in FSA's past and stressed how important the overall culture of the league was for signaling what coaches should do. "It doesn't matter what I want to do. It matters what the other coaches are doing. More than half the coaches and parents out there will say, 'Walk 'em.' They want competitive ball. So if that is the case, I'm a sucker if I give my pitcher a chance against their number four, but my number four gets walked every other inning." His point is important and underscores the way frustrations arise when individuals try to introduce less competitive approaches into a setting where more competitive approaches dominate.

The differences in the way Fairmounters and newcomers related both to the neighborhood, as described above, and to the league reflected a competing set of cultural values related to individual responsibility, group solidarity, and how best to promote children's interests.[25] The different orientations toward the community could be described as hierarchical communalism versus child-centered individualism. While there was a range of opinion about most of these concerns within the two groups, when differences did appear they often took this form. Fairmounters, on the one hand, regularly brought up resentments about the way newcomers used the organization narrowly for the benefit of their own children, without appropriate levels of support, or deference, to the needs of the broader group and its leadership—much like their approach to the neighborhood. Brett Williams describes the metropolitan vision of professional newcomers in a gentrifying neighborhood of Washington, D.C., as one riddled with contradictions: "they want a diverse community but they want the best for their children as well." Their quest for variety and for maximum advantage for their children distanced them from local life and from the less affluent residents whose "passions for texture" created human connections in local space and kept street life and the community nourished, despite the stigma of doing so. Although the Fairmount old-timers are different from the poorer "renters" of William's neighborhood, their criticism of newcomers' lack of care for the space beyond the fleeting experience of their children's games is similar. In response, newcomers to FSA complained that their interests were ignored, that Fairmounters too often listened only to other Fairmounters and ran the organization to benefit themselves and their adult friends, with concern for children running a distant second. But newcomers' critique of Fairmounters was less intense than the Fairmounter critique of them; in part this is because the space meant less to them.

Segmented Understandings

Despite the emphasis in this discussion on the divisions and tensions between and among Fairmounters and newcomers, there were also many understandings and feelings of connection forged across these groups. Indeed, the cross-class sympathies may even have been stronger than some of the tensions between the deep insiders and newcomers. After all, you had to be somewhat "in the know" with the organization to even notice some of the divisions. Most importantly, many newcomers cherished being a part of FSA, despite its warts and their somewhat marginal position. But the emerging empathies wove themselves across the space in a segmented manner, similar to the uneven and segmented way racial understandings happened at FSA. In the words of one newcomer, "We represent some of the outsiders. But I think the mixture of kids here is terrific. I'm not aware of any tensions. I think it's one of the few places where kids of different colors, different ethnicities, and different socioeconomic incomes come together for a common purpose in this city. It's wonderful."

The loyalty of newcomers to FSA was tested at one point by the emergence of another baseball organization run predominantly by upper-middle-class professionals. A small group of dissatisfied newcomers whose children played at FSA but who lived mostly outside the neighborhood, in Center City, rebelled against FSA by leaving and starting an alternative baseball organization in a nearby area referred to as Taney. The goal, presumably, was to create a club that they would control and run in a manner more consistent with their needs. This would be a club run in a less competitive fashion than FSA, with more baseball instruction for the kids, and with clinics offering coaches more professional training. There would be no separate softball divisions; girls would play hardball with the boys. Because of the smaller numbers of children at Taney, they only fielded teams through the age of twelve. Once their children reached thirteen, some parents returned to FSA to finish out the thirteen-to-fifteen division. Others who had started at Taney also moved over at this point.

There was an enormous amount of discussion at FSA over the years about what the Taney "breakaway" meant, what it promised to deliver, and the reality of what it did deliver. Occasionally, when a Fairmount–newcomer conflict would erupt, the escape value of Taney would be pointed to, such as the time a Fairmount staff member shouted to my husband, who had complained about the practice schedule, "And if you don't like it, you can always go to Taney." But others acknowledged that there might be a difference between the professionals who opted to be at Taney and those who preferred FSA. As one old-timer saw it, "A lot of them, see, they wanted their own league down at Taney. The ones with problems, they left. They were not used to taking orders, or whatever it is they want for their kids—their girls to play on boys' teams. The ones that are staying here at FSA, they like the guys who run it all right. So they're okay."

A very common theme among newcomer professionals at Fairmount was their preference for the diversity of FSA over the class homogeneity of Taney. Common among the reasons for the loyalty to FSA was an affinity for the working-class style of the league as something emotionally familiar to many, either from their own parents or from their own childhoods. One newcomer, who actually lived in the Taney area but had spent a decade at FSA, explained his preference:

I like the feel of it [FSA].... In a time when the world has changed so drastically, it's a lot like when I played as a kid.... Some of the people's values are still in the '50s as well. But when Taney started, it was not even a consideration for us to go over there. I just felt like, where I grew up was fairly working-class, and I really appreciated that looking back. And this feels a lot like that. It was real people in a particular kind of way. And at a time where it's very easy to be in an environment where there is not a lot of diversity...Taney, it just didn't have quite the same feel at the time when it was being started. It was much more a very white, upper-middle-class

organization. The people of Fairmount have their flaws. The people of Taney have their flaws. We all have our flaws. I was just more comfortable with the people at Fairmount and their flaws. The people at Taney were just all too familiar to me. We felt that, for our kids, Fairmount was an opportunity to meet real Philadelphia kids who they would grow up with, and know, and, in some ways, sort of bond with. And should they decide that some day, as adults, that they are going to live in Philadelphia, these are probably kids they will come across.

A professor who knew many of the Taney people explained why he felt unsympathetic to their revolt:

They felt like it [FSA] was a closed shop. They felt like there were sets of rules for the insiders of Fairmount, like their suggestions weren't considered. In fact, in certain instances, they felt that their efforts were being undermined. Things like miscommunication in terms of, say, the availability of times for the practice field. They basically felt persecuted. I would say they were a little paranoid. But I wouldn't say it was totally without merit. Though in some ways, I think it was an extreme reaction. And I happen to know some of the people. At least a couple of them were pretty high-powered people who basically weren't used to being told that you have to work your way up in this organization. You take a very high-powered businessperson or lawyer from a big law firm, he isn't going to want to hear, "Come on down at 6:30 or 7:00 Sunday morning, and pick up trash, and take the field." They sort of saw themselves as executive decision-makers. And that was the part where I was much more sympathetic to the people of Fairmount who spent twenty-five or thirty years building this organization, and didn't need some fancy guy to come in and tell them, "This is the way you should be doing it."

Some newcomers at FSA had experienced both leagues and concluded that Taney had its own distinct set of problems, including serious internal political conflicts and a less than organic approach to baseball.

My son had played at Taney before we came to FSA, a terrible experience. Everybody had said Taney was more low-key—but for us, a terrible experience.... Taney is run by a whole different group, people with graduate degrees and major business people. So I would say there's no improvement there—as many problems there as here.... My husband's view is that a lot of Taney people can't play sports, so they want a league where their kids can win. They can't easily win here. It's really critical for them. They don't look like they played sports, clearly weren't athletic. At least, in Fairmount you have people who played sports and know what baseball is. They really know how to play, may still be playing. I like that, even with its negative stuff—it's not take baseball.

Other challenged the claim that Taney's middle-class league really offered a less competitive approach to baseball for its children. "These leagues are all the same. When they say Taney is more instructional, it's not true. I would stand up in court and say that. I've seen two attorneys up at Taney battle it out, rolling on the ground in the dirt."

Regardless of the truth value of these claims about Taney, the point is that many newcomers at FSA perceived themselves as making a conscious choice to be part of Fairmount and to work toward community understanding, despite its challenges. Over time, some even felt defensive on behalf of the Fairmounters, who were sometimes ruthlessly critiqued by the Taney people,

even more so than by the professional discontents within FSA:

What I don't like about Taney is the precious, special, upper-middle-class nature of the people there. I didn't really know about them until these people started coming back to Fairmount from there. They started at Fairmount and then went off when Taney was founded, a mass of them. First year, all they could do was bitch and moan about how terrible Fairmount was and how wonderful Taney had been, and now they had to come back and deal with lug heads in the clubhouse— just their lack of understanding of what Fairmount was about.... I thought the Taney people just kind of lacked a whole perspective about the class nature of their conflict, the rights and wrongs.

The sympathies that emerged across class and racial lines at FSA were especially apparent in encounters the ball club had with the outside world, such as in traveling team championships played in remote neighborhoods of the city and suburbs. Professional parents at FSA were sometimes surprised to learn that suburban teams viewed Fairmount in an undifferentiated way, as a low-class, inner-city team. The generalized apprehension of suburbanites for anything inside the city translated into nervousness about even neighborhoods as affluent as Spring Garden had become. This external judgment stimulated community loyalty. I remember feeling this acutely one year, as my son's twelve-and-under traveling team faced an extremely affluent suburban team. Our team was about one-third boys of color and their team was all white. Neighborhood men and women had driven more than an hour to see this important Fairmount game, many with no child on the team. After watching the Council Rock parents leave their BMWs and slick SUVs in the immense parking lot behind their practice field, I saw the Fairmounter adults line up behind our dugout. Seeing this crowd of adult Fairmounters outside our neighborhood, all of us looking particularly ragtag compared to the well-dressed suburban parents we faced, I could feel our "insider/newcomer" problem slip away. As the game proceeded, many Fairmounters shouted out nonstop encouraging comments to each of the Fairmount players. Although some were still strangers to me, they called to my son by name. They also called out the names of our black catcher and third baseman in a raucous, public testimony of solidarity for the community we sometimes achieved.

Although Fairmounters had many complaints about newcomers' individualism, some also recognized the importance of contributions made by professionals who were strategically placed in the city. Newcomers were sometimes generous in tapping their networks and resources to provide a different kind of financial support, one that was more lucrative than "booster day," where ballplayers knocked on neighborhood doors with FSA cups asking for donations. (My son calls this "kids' begging day.") As one FSA staffer acknowledged, "Yes, and they're [the newcomers] able to get us sponsored money, where in the past, we used to knock on doors. Now they just email each other, and it's here. That really helps. So it's less work for the twelve people most involved. It's less work because, they can call two friends and a check comes in the mail. It's beautiful." While receiving checks in the mail might produce more revenue, knocking on doors builds community support for the field and connects the baseball children with locals who might not have children in the league. It was this combination of both orientations, reaching inward to capitalize on community solidarity and reaching outward for inclusion and external support, that built on the strengths of the two worlds of Fairmounters and newcomer professionals.

A few strategic professionals also played an important behind-the-scenes role when FSA faced its most serious external threat in decades. Thirty years after Fairmount men defended their right to use the park ground as a baseball field with informal sit-ins, the field again came under threat from city agencies in the form of a Parkway development plan. The plan slated the baseball fields for mid-rise residential development. There was a sustained email campaign on the part of Fairmounters and newcomers in opposition to this plan. But significantly, Kyle, a professional who had coached at FSA for years, happened to work at the Philadelphia City Planning Commission, which formally responded to the Parkway plan of the Central Philadelphia Development Corporation. Although FSA leadership did not especially appreciate Kyle as a coach, Kyle was, nonetheless, a lover of the space and its history. He wrote the first draft of the Planning Commission's report:

> For many families in the Fairmount neighborhood, Fairmount Park's Von Colln Fields, known to those who use them as the Fairmount Fields, are the heart and soul of their closely knit community. The Center City District's concept to displace this neighborhood facility in order to reap a "higher, better and more profitable" use of city parkland is misguided for a number of reasons. For one, the idea of selling public parkland for commercial and residential development is an abhorrent precedent. The Von Colln Fields were created by the City for the neighborhood not on an interim basis until a better deal came along, but as a long-term commitment to provide a much needed public amenity to a densely compacted urban neighborhood. The recreational opportunities and visual openness of this wonderful piece of City parkland should not be for sale to the highest bidder.

The Fairmount Park Commission would *never consider selling or building on Pastorius Park in Chestnut Hill or Rittenhouse Square in Center City*, or any piece of its magnificent park system that serves the City so well.

The Center City District's myopic suggestion that this site can simply be replaced with a recreation facility somewhere to the south is a cynical attempt to deflect the serious nature of its assault on the residents of the Fairmount neighborhood. Moving the ball fields south of the Parkway would mean that the many children who use the fields would have to cross Parkway traffic to get to their baseball games and soccer practices. Replacing the open space that affords a grand view of the skyline to all who come to the fields with mid-rise apartment buildings would rob this important City neighborhood of a tremendous and unique asset, one that gives value to their properties and enjoyment to their lives. Is the residential character and livability of the Fairmount neighborhood to be sacrificed for the benefit of the hospitality industry in Center City?[26] (italics mine)

Although this draft was toned down in the final report, it is striking that part of Kyle's defense of the baseball space was class-based, namely equating Fairmount's right to claim "its" park as a baseball field with the right of two of the most affluent neighborhoods in the city to maintain the traditional use of their prestigious parks. So while different cultural orientations divided some Fairmounters from some newcomers within FSA, important cross-class ties of solidarity coexisted, in the form of segmented understandings, more than the organizational gatekeepers acknowledged.

The fact that many working-class people live in an obviously unequal social world doesn't mean that they judge themselves, or others, in terms of the hierarchy of class or economic status. Michèle Lamont found that blue-collar workers and lower-status white-collar workers evaluated themselves and others more in terms of the quality of their interpersonal relationships. They also often articulated a moral critique of "people above" whom they judged as lacking warmth, having domineering styles, and dedicated to a fast-track ambition that impoverished social encounters. Something similar was behind the judgments of Fairmounters about what was problematic in professional newcomers' approach to the organization. But in the case of FSA we have a localized, neighborhood expression of this negative moral assessment of the more affluent. The fact that the encounter occurred in a space historically nourished by Fairmounters, and on terrain where their baseball expertise should matter, even to professionals accustomed to ordering others around at work, further aggravated the general cultural grievance of these Middle Americans against the more educated upper middle class. The external hierarchy of work life was temporarily reversed in this space and hence maintaining locals' control over it was particularly important. Understandings were forged but control was non-negotiable.

If you were a baseball coach and your team was in the field and faced a very close baseball game where any run scored mattered greatly, with a runner on third and less than two outs, you might opt to bring the infield in. Then on a ground ball you would have the chance to get an out at the plate and prevent the opposing team from scoring. It is a time-honored defensive strategy because it diminishes the chance of a ground ball becoming an RBI. But it also comes with a certain amount of risk, since the range of ground balls your team could field would be smaller than usual. You "bring the infield in" typically when you are winning or tied and the game is in the late innings. It is an aggressive defensive strategy to win the game. Fairmounter insiders who controlled FSA for decades did something like this in defending their baseball space as new professionals entered; they brought their infield in. They vigilantly and successfully protected their control of the organization, its leadership, and its social style. They monitored closely any newcomer moves that revealed a trace of autonomy or independence and made sure no unproven, inappropriately assertive types got any unnecessary runs.

NOTES

1. See Frank F. DeGiovanni, "Patterns of Change in Housing Market Activity in Revitalizing Neighborhoods," *Journal of the American Planning Association* 49 (1983): 22–39; Jason Hackworth, "Post-recession Gentrification in New York City," *Urban Affairs Review* 37, no. 6 (2002): 813–843; Gary Bridge, "Gentrification, Class, and Residence: A Reappraisal." *Environment & Planning D: Society & Space* 12, no. 3 (1994): 31–51.

2. See P. Dreier, J. Mollenkopf, and T. Swanstrom, *Place Matters: Metropolities for the Twenty-first Century* (Lawrence: University Press of Kansas, 2001), 100.

3. See John Logan and Harvey Molotch, *Urban Fortunes: The Political Economy of Place* (Berkeley: University of California Press, 1987), 287.

4. See Alvin Gouldner. *The Future of Intellectuals and the Rise of the New Class* (New York: Seabury Press, 1979); E. O. Wright and B. Martin, "The Transformation of the American Class Structure, 1960–1989," *American Journal of Sociology* 93 (1987): 1–29; S. Lash and J. Urry. *The End of Organized Capitalism* (Cambridge: Polity Press, 1987).

5. See M. Savage, P. Dickens, and T. Fielding, "Some Social and Political Implications of the Contemporary Fragmentation of the 'Service Class' in Britain," *International Journal of Urban and Regional Research* 12 (1988): 455–476; J. Ehrenreich and B. Ehrenreich, "The Professional-Managerial Class," in P. Walker, ed., *Between Labor and Capital* (Boston: South End Press, 1979), 5–45.

6. David Ley, "Gentrification and the Politics of the New Middle Class," *Environment and Planning D: Society and Space* 12 (1994): 53–74.

7. S. Brint, "New Class and Cumulative Trend Explanations of the Liberal Political Attitudes of Professionals," *American Journal of Sociology* 90 (1984): 30–71.

8. T. Butler and C. Hamnett, "Gentrification, Class, and Gender: Some Comments on Warde's 'Gentrification as Consumption,'" *Environment and Planning D: Society and Space* 22 (1994): 477–493. See L. Bondi, "Gender, Class and Gentrification: Enriching the Debate," *Environment and Planning D: Society and Space* 17 (1999): 261–282, for a review of literature on the role of gender as well as class factors involved in gentrification.

9. N. Smith's *The New Urban Frontier: Gentrification and the Revanchist City* (New York: Routledge & Kegan Paul, 1996) provides a comprehensive review of the literature on gentrification in the 1980s and 1990s, organized in terms of consumption and production side explanations. It is widely recognized that the arrival of "the gentry" in marginal housing markets produces a series of chain reactions, often leading to the displacement of lower-income native residents, as happened to Puerto Ricans in Spring Garden. More recently, scholars have turned their attention to the political and cultural impact of gentrification. See David Ley, *The New Middle Class and the Remaking of the Central City* (Oxford: Oxford University Press, 1996); and J. Betancur, "The Politics of Gentrifications: The Case of West Town in Chicago," *Urban Affairs Review* 37, no. 6 (2002): 780–814. Also, J. Caulfield, in "'Gentrification' and Desire" (*Canadian Review of Sociology and Anthropology* 26, no. 4 [1989]: 617–632), has examined the way gentrification in Canadian cities involves a paradoxical outcome, initially

a reflection of a cultural "emancipatory drive" by those critical of current city-building trying to establish new ways of urban social interaction only to be undermined by a "culture industry" led by modern property entrepreneurs, those who sell not just housing but commoditized lifestyles (626). See also S. R. Prince. "Changing Places: Race, Class, and Belonging in the "New' Harlem," *Urban Anthropology & Studies of Cultural Systems & World Economic Development* 31, no. 1 (2002): 5–35; A Ramos-Zayas, "Racializing the 'Invisible' Race: Latino Constructions of 'White Culture' and Whiteness in Chicago," *Urban Anthropology* 30, no. 4 (2001): 341–360; and see Joseph Barry and John Derevlany, eds., *Yuppies Invade My House at Dinnertime* (Hoboken, N.J.: Big River Publishing, 1987), for a hilarious account of the cultural conflict behind gentrification as reflected in letters to the local newspaper. Eli Anderson, in *Street Wise: Race, Class, and Change in an Urban Community* (Chicago: University of Chicago Press, 1990), also documented phases in the process of gentrification, from old-timer Villagers, to ex-counter-culture types, both relatively positive toward racial diversity in their neighborhoods, to the latter arrival of "the yuppies," younger professionals, mostly childless, who appear to favor a more homogeneous community and are more uncomfortable with diversity.

10. See Judith Goode and Jo Anne Schneider, *Reshaping Ethnic and Racial Relations in Philadelphia:Immigrants in a Divided City* (Philadelphia: Temple University Press, 1994).

11. They explained how they lost this battle by pointing to a critical moment in the process of gentrification in the area. A meeting between neighborhood residents, dominated by several real estate developers, and city officials from the Redevelopment Authority and Philadelphia Housing Authority occurred in a church at the corner of Mt. Vernon and 22nd Street. At this meeting an explicit agreement was negotiated that there would be no scattered-site, public housing in Spring Garden beyond 21st Street. This

resident claimed that this was a defining moment for the area. "Before then it was great; there were Hispanics playing dominos outside, bongo drums playing. But after that meeting, gentrification took off like crazy. The developers felt secure and poured money into their houses and then prices soared."

12. See Jay Coakley, "Organized Sport Programs for Children: Are They Worth the Effort?" in Jay Coakley, ed., *Sport in Society: Issues and Controversies* (St. Louis: Times Mirror/Mosby, 1980), 87–112.

13. In FSA head coaches are referred to as "managers." They both coach and manage the team. FSA leadership selects the head coaches, but the head coaches select their assistant coaches, who may be a friend of theirs or may come from the ranks of parents. In the text, I sometimes use the phrase "manager-coach" and sometimes "head coach." Strategic FSA leaders estimated the intensity of the work contributions of the most active volunteers, and the twenty coach-managers provided estimates of the time they spent during the season on coaching and other support activities.

14. By 1997, the ratio of newcomer managers to Fairmounter managers in both the seven-to-nine and the ten-to-twelve divisions was even. From that point on, newcomers came to dominate in numbers, hovering around 60 percent for the next several years.

15. In addition to the registration fee, the hidden cost of joining the organization is really about $150, since on top of the registration players are expected to come with a glove and cleats. These expenses insure that relatively few poor families from the surrounding areas can afford entrance.

16. Based on the registration forms (contact sheets) for the 187 families who signed boys up to play in either the seven-to-nine or the ten-to-twelve division of FSA in 1998, 46 percent were from Fairmount/Spring Garden, and 54 percent came from nearby areas (26 percent from Center City, 16 percent from West Philadelphia, and 12 percent from other areas). Project data collected by author.

17. Between 1996 and 1999, 65 percent of Fairmounter head coaches agreed to take a team when they had no son playing in the division. By comparison, only 20 percent of the newcomer head coaches coached a team on which their son did not play over this same period. After 1998, newcomers came to dominate in numbers, hovering around 60 percent of head coaches over the next several years. This ushered in an increase in "father coaches," since newcomers typically coached only when they had a son on the team, unlike their Fairmounter counterparts.

18. See Annette Lareau, *Unequal Childhoods: Class, Race, and Family Life* (Berkeley: University of California Press, 2003).

19. See Andrew Greeley, *The Catholic Imagination* (Berkeley: University of California Press, 2000), 137. Greeley's argument about the Catholic imagination is not merely a theoretical argument based on doctrine. He presents empirical evidence for a persistent, distinctively Catholic social orientation related to the sacredness of place or local, community ties and hierarchical structures in the community.

20. All of the Fairmounter parents I interviewed were Catholic, but none of the newcomer parents were. The eleven newcomer parents were equally divided between Protestants, Jews, and those who claimed no religious affiliation.

21. See A. Lareau, *Home Advantage: Social Class and Parental Intervention in Elementary Education* (Lanham, Md.: Rowman & Littlefield Publishers, 1958).
Brett Williams, in *Upscaling Downtown: Stalled Gentrification in Washington.D.C.* (Ithaca, N.Y.: Cornell University Press, 1989), explored the implications for communities of this same tendency of middle-class parents to scout externally for social opportunities that maximize advantage for their children and in the process weaken the fiber of local communities.

22. See Robert Putnam, *Bowling Alone: The Collapse and Revival of American Community* (New York: Simon and Schuster, 2000).

23. Richard Sennett, *Respect in a World of Inequality* (New York: Norton, 2003), 207.

24. Seven of the ten newcomer parents described FSA as stressing competition (playing games to win) over instruction (teaching individual and team skills), whereas only two of the ten Fairmounters described the ball club as relatively competitive. Most Fairmounters sow FSA as appropriately balancing competition with instruction.

25. Some of the differences at FSA between Fairmount parents and newcomer parents correspond to findings by Geoffrey Watson, in "Games, Socialization and Parental Values: Social Class Differences in Parental Evaluation of Little League Baseball" (*International Review of Sport Sociology* 9: 17–48), who compared parents in a middle-class Little League program with parents in a working-class league and evaluated their children's experiences. Middle-class parents tended to view the games more as social events, whereas working-class parents saw them as primarily athletic events, as a "means," and therefore exhibited much more emotional involvement in game interactions and game decision making. Working-class parents also put more stress on the importance of children learning to respond to authority or to conform to highly structured social conditions. One can see why, once parents with such different expectations around the game come together in a shared space like the FSA, their different expectations might be translated into judgments by newcomers that Fairmounters are "too competitive," or judgments by Fairmounters that newcomers don't take the overall game seriously enough, or conform to the logic of the game, or for that matter, have the need to conform to a coach's authority or whims.

26. This was the wording of the original draft produced by the Philadelphia City Planning Commission, reduced and edited for the final version ("City Planning Commission Comments on the Central Philadelphia Development Corporation Parkway Plan," 2000, 6–7, unpublished memo).

REFERENCES

Anderson, Elijah. 1990. *Streetwise: Race, Class, and Change in an Urban Community.* Chicago: University of Chicago Press.

Barry, Joseph, and John Derevlany, eds. 1987. *Yuppies Invade My House at Dinnertime.* Hoboken, N.J.: Big River Publishing.

Betancur, John J. 2002. "The Politics of Gentrification: The Case of West Town in Chicago." *Urban Affairs Review* 37 (6): 780–814.

Bondi, Liz. 1999. "Gender, Class and Gentrification: Enriching the Debate." *Environment and Planning D: Society and Space* 17: 261–282.

Bridge, Gary. 1994. "Gentrification, Class, and Residence: A Reappraisal." *Environment & Planning D: Society & Space* 12 (1): 31–51.

Brint, S. 1984. "New Class and Cumulative Trend Explanations of the Liberal Political Attitudes of Professionals." *American Journal of Sociology* 90: 30–71.

Butler, Tim, and Chris Hamnett. 1994. "Gentrification, Class, and Gender: Some Comments on Warde's 'Gentrification as Consumption.'" *Environment and Planning D: Society and Space* 12: 477–493.

Caufield, Jon. 1989. "'Gentrification' and Desire." *Canadian Review of Sociology and Anthropology* 26 (4): 617–632.

City Planning Commission. 2000. "Comments on the Central Philadelphia Development Corporation Parkway Plan." Unpublished memo. 6–7.

Coakely, Jay J. 1990. *Sport in Society: Issues and Controversies.* 4th edition. St. Louis, Mo.: Mosby.

DeGiovanni, Frank F. 1983. "Patterns of Change in Housing Market Activity in Revitalizing Neighborhoods." *Journal of the American Planning Association* 49: 22–39.

Dreier, Peter, John Mollenkopf, and Todd Swanstrom. 2001. *Place Matters: Metropolitics for the Twenty-first Century.* Lawrence: University Press of Kansas.

Ehrenreich, J., and Barbara Ehrenreich. 1979. "The Professional-Managerial Class." In P. Walker, ed., *Between Labor and Capital.* Boston: South End Press. 5–45.

Goode, Judith, and Jo Anne Schneider. 1994. *Reshaping Ethnic and Racial Relations in Philadelphia: Immigrants in a Divided City.* Philadelphia: Temple University Press.

Gouldner, Alvin. 1979. *The Future of Intellectuals and the Rise of the New Class.* New York: Seabury Press.

Greeley, Andrew M. 2000. *The Catholic Imagination.* Berkeley: University of California Press.

Hackworth, Jason. 2002. "Post-recession Gentrification in New York City." *Urban Affairs Review* 37 (6): 815–843.

Lamont, Michèle. 1999. "Above 'People Above'? Status and Worth among White and Black Workers." In *The Cultural Territories of Race: Black and White Boundaries.* Michèle Lamont (ed.). Chicago: University of Chicago Press. 127–150.

Lareau, Annette. 1989. *Home Advantage: Social Class and Parental Intervention in Elementary Education.* Lanham, Md.: Rowman & Littlefield Publishers.

———. 2003. *Unequal Childhoods: Class, Race, and Family Life.* Berkeley: University of California Press.

Ley, David. 1994. "Gentrification and the Politics of the New Middle Class." *Environment and Planning D: Society and Space* 12: 53–74.

———. 1996. *The New Middle Class and the Remaking of the Central City.* Cambridge: Oxford University Press.

Logan, John, and Harvey Molotch. 1987. *Urban Fortunes: The Political Economy of Place.* Berkeley: University of California Press.

Prince, Sabiyha Robin. 2002. "Changing Places: Race, Class, and Belonging in the 'New' Harlem." *Urban Anthropology & Studies of Cultural Systems & World Economic Development* 31 (1): 5–35.

Putnam, Robert D. 2000. *Bowling Alone: The Collapse and Revival of American Community.* New York: Simon and Schuster.

Ramos-Zayas, Ana. 2001. "Racializing the 'Invisible' Race: Latino Constructions of 'White Culture' and Whiteness in Chicago." *Urban Anthropology* 30 (1): 341–380.

Savage, M., P. Dickens, and T. Fielding. 1988. "Some Social and Political Implications of the Contemporary Fragmentation of the 'Service Class' in Britain." *International Journal of Urban and Regional Research* 12: 455–476.

Sennett, Richard. 2003. *Respect in a World of Inequality*. New York: Norton.

Smith, N. 1996. *The New Urban Frontier: Gentrification and the Revanchist City*. New York: Routledge & Kegan Paul.

Watson, Geoffrey. 1974. "Games, Socialization and Parental Values: Social Class Differences in Parental Evaluation of Little League Baseball." *International Review of Sport Sociology* 9: 17–48.

Williams, Brett. 1988. *Upscaling Downtown: Stalled Gentrification in Washington, D.C.* Ithaca, N.Y.: Cornell University Press.

Wright, E. O., and B. Martin. 1987. "The Transformation of the American Class Structure, 1960–1980." *American Journal of Sociology* 93: 1–29.

38

AMY L. BEST

RACE-ING MEN: BOYS, RISK, AND THE POLITICS OF RACE

from *Fast Cars, Cool Rides* (2006)

For five years, Amy Best participated in and observed the social world of young Latino, Asian, and white high school students who race cars on the streets of San Jose, California. In this selection, she shows how their lives revolve around their cars and how their intense focus on racing helps them achieve recognition in a world in which they feel otherwise invisible.

On a warm Tuesday morning at Freedom High School, I find myself at "auto shop" class. The room is cavernous and full of the sort of clutter one would expect to find at an actual mechanic's garage: soiled rags blackened by oil and grease strewn throughout the room, a small mountain of safety glasses in one corner, a dust-covered windshield in another, rows of tires stacked like doughnuts, metal cabinets spilling over with an assortment of tools. I spend much of my morning moving between the groups of boys who are scattered throughout the room before making my way over to a small huddle of boys working on a Honda CRX, a beat-up car that officially belongs to the auto shop. Right now they are working on

recharging the car's battery, since it won't start. Moments before, two of the boys, Justin and David, had pushed the CRX over beside a much newer Honda Civic parked in the car lot a few feet from the car bays. The Civic is painted a purplish-blue and is equipped with a sleek body kit and shiny chrome rims. Its frame rests much lower to the ground than any stock Honda, but just enough above the shiny rims to still be "street legal." I ask the group whose car it is and a tall South Asian boy whom I come to know as Shrini offers up, "Mine." Don, who is sitting in the driver's seat of the CRX, his hands firmly placed on the steering wheel, sticks his head out the car's window to ask if I like it, which causes the group to erupt into laughter. "You can buy it if you want," Shrini tells me with a more serious tone. I ask him why he's selling it. He explains he wants to get a Subaru STi, which is much faster. Tim, a classmate, has a Subaru, the very one Shrini hopes to get after he unloads this car. Nearly all agree Tim's is the fastest car in school. And they should know. These boys and a string of others are "racers," a tag they use to distinguish themselves from the "cruisers," "lowriders," "gang-bangers,"[1] and the endless variety of other "subcultural" groups of boys at their school.[2]

Shrini's car is an automatic, a point he reluctantly offers only after I ask. Though his car has undergone some changes to the body, there have been no performance upgrades. Right now, the car doesn't run fast enough, and since it is automatic, it is unlikely it ever will. A slow car confers little status to its owner among the street racers, especially if its exterior has been customized to look fast. Such a look eventually discredits racers, attaching to them what is arguably the worst sort of shame. Speed, driver skill, and a willingness to take risks behind the wheel are what matter most in the world of street and organized racing. A slow car, no matter its appearance, provides little opportunity to demonstrate any of these virtues.

This band of boys race imports: Honda Civics and Accords, Nissans and Acura Integras, all cars imported from Japan, where a vibrant and parallel racing scene has also emerged.[3] They are part of what has been called "the Import Car Scene," which originated in southern California in the early 1990s but has spread north to San Jose and San Francisco and east beyond California. The import scene in southern California and in San Jose is dominated by Asian and Asian American young men in their teens and twenties.[4]

These young men are all Asian, first- and second-generation Chinese, Indian, and Vietnamese mostly, with exceptions

like Daniel, who is Mexican. And they are students at Freedom High School, one of a handful of "low-income schools" in San Jose that has an overrepresentation of immigrants and kids of color and is also underserved in terms of both academic resources and avenues of upward mobility. The kids make up a loosely organized group of small crews that know each other mostly by the cars they drive.

Most in this group at Freedom High School own used cars, almost all purchased for less than $5,000 and almost all having anywhere between 100,000 and 150,000 miles already logged before the new owners get behind the wheel. Justin, who drives an emerald green Acura, bought his car for a clean $3,500 almost four months ago and currently has 127,000 miles logged on the odometer. For most in the group, these low-priced cars serve as templates for a series of costly modifications that in the end can more than double the initial cost of the car. Body kits, lowered suspensions, engine upgrades, multimedia systems, and altered exhaust systems make up a multibillion-dollar industry of aftermarket car parts, an industry largely supported by these young men and others like them who on weekend nights gather in the early hours of the morning in abandoned industrial zones and business parks to see whose car will outdrive all the others.

How do they afford these expensive car modifications? For a small number of young men tied to the import car scene, parents finance these indulgences, but not for these boys. Long hours stocking shelves, slinging burgers, punching cash register keys, and mopping floors provide just enough disposable income for them to gain access to this dizzying world of pulleys and bbk's, h-pipes, adjustable struts, sway bars, intercooler kits, and injectors called alternately "moding" or "tuning." They spend hours surfing the Web in search of a deal, special struts for $100 each on eBay, for example, and are proud of their ability to know a good deal when they see one. Few in the group drive new cars because they can not afford them, but others in the import car scene do. The middle- and upper-middle-class Asian American young men from Orange County, California in Victoria Namkung's 2004 study of Asian American youth culture and the import car scene all appeared to drive new cars, spending upwards of $25,000 when including the initial cost of the car and the upgrades. Many of the young men in Namkung's study came from far more affluent families than the boys at Freedom High School and were already in college, with a lot more of their own disposable income than these high schoolers. Within the broader import scene in San Jose, this is also the case.

For this group of high school boys, life revolves around their cars and racing. Economic constraint keeps them from funneling the same kind of cash into their cars that upper-income and older kids do, but it doesn't prevent them from putting whatever money they do have into "running" their cars. Thuy Vo, who drives a customized Honda Civic hatchback, works at Great America, a local theme park where many youth work the rides in exchange for baseline wages.[5] *All* his money, he tells me, goes to transforming his car's engine and exterior. So far he has installed a sway bar, which enables him to better handle turns at high speeds, and a new exhaust. He has shaved his door handles and removed the windshield wipers. In their place he has sprayed "Rain Off" on the windshield, a commercial product which is supposed to repel the rain. The car has been lowered several inches, the "H" that normally resides on the car's hood has been removed, and the back lights have been replaced. These exterior changes enable Thuy Vo to achieve what he considers "a cleaner look." I heard many of these import racers describe a "clean look" as a car's ideal. In many ways, this clean look achieves "an aesthetic of speed." With its sleek streamlining, its

center of gravity bugging the road, the car visually appears to look fast and not "frumpy" and "rumpled" like the standard stock Civic hatchback or, worse, a lumbering American giant like a Dodge or Chevy. Beyond these changes, his car has been painted "egg-shell white," a custom color, and he has installed red car seats, new "racing" seat belts, a new steering wheel, a red racing stripe, and red and gold rims, which he painted himself to resemble from a distance a very expensive set of rims he admits he can not afford. Thuy Vo, like a number of these boys, uses auto shop to make as many of these modifications to his car as is possible given the limited resources of the school (sometimes at the expense of completing the official class projects assigned by Mr. O'Malley, the auto shop teacher). On the weekends, Thuy Vo, along with the others in his crew, travels to meeting spots to race against other imports. During the week, he spends his time outside work and school driving around malls, local streets in the neighborhood and sometimes Santa Clara Street in the hope that his car will be recognized, especially now that he has all but finished customizing it.[6] Thuy Vo's car, which was always parked just outside the car bays despite a school policy that restricts students from parking in that specific school lot, was the subject of much discussion among the students, racers and nonracers alike, in the three other classes I observed. On one occasion, two boys came by to take digital pictures of the car. When I asked Don, one of the students, about the picture taking, he explained, "See, we see cars as artistic, like artwork....Taking pictures is a way to show appreciation for the car and the work that has gone into it." On another occasion, I overheard one of the boys from a class remark to another, "Daammmn, I see that car everywhere." Thuy Vo has gained what he had hoped to achieve, a much-sought-after visibility for his individual style and a collectively recognized one through his car.

Imports versus American Muscle

Thuy Vo, Don, Shrini, Vicrum, and Justin, along with other boys who participate in the import car scene, distinguish themselves from another group of racers, those who have declared a devout allegiance to American Muscle, Ford and Chevy drivers who at Freedom High School represent at best a handful of boys. (Among the four auto shop classes I observed only one boy, Jeff, identified himself with American Muscle. He drove a 1966 Chevelle that he was restoring with his father.)[7] Since the 1950s, American Muscle has stood at the center of the "illegal" street and "legal" organized car racing and hot-rodding scenes. However, in the past decade, the flourishing import scene has given hot rodders a run for their money. Writing on the cultural relevance of the import car scene in southern California, Victoria Namkung has argued that "the growing import racing scene has unquestionably changed the automotive industry and altered the dynamics of the vibrant car culture.... Import racing has propelled a historically invisible ethnic group onto center stage of the previously Anglo-dominated consumer market and culture."[8] Many would agree that the ascendance of import racing and import racers in the commercial world and the world of car enthusiasts has subverted the longstanding rivalry between Chevy and Ford, replacing it with a new one—a rivalry between domestics and imports. Two different value systems organize the domestic and import scenes. Within the world of American Muscle, having a car that is either "fast," "loud," or "big," a car with "hog power," that is, translates into what the late French scholar Pierre Bourdieu, writing on the social practices that produce social distinctions and symbolic boundaries, called "symbolic capital."[9]

A car's muscle is not celebrated among participants in the import scene, where far less emphasis is placed on horsepower or having a large engine. Quick, lightweight cars reign over the import scene. Acuras and Hondas are regarded as superior to Mustangs, the reigning modern American muscle car. They are low cost and lightweight, and their more powerful Honda engines (like the Prelude's) can be dropped easily into the car. The more powerful engine in a lightweight car can make the car very fast, particularly if it also has a nitrous oxide boost (usually called NOS by insiders to this world). The boys from Freedom High School swear to me that such a Honda could outrun a 4.6- or 5.0-liter Mustang in a second. This claim, of course, is met by howling protestations by those who align themselves with American Muscle, like Kenny and Tom, who both currently drive modified Mustangs and are part of the same crew. When I ask if they ever race against the imports, they are sure to let me know theirs is the superior car, working hard to convince me that it could barely be considered a "fair" race. "It's not worth it," Tom says with a firm shake of his head. "If you call it racing," Kenny, smirking, adds. "Their car's really slow; my car's really fast."

By all accounts, the car racing scene, made up of these so-called street racers, is "big" in San Jose. This despite increasing efforts by Bay Area police to dampen these underground activities. In June 2001, fifty officers from a South Bay task force discovered 247 cars at one of the business parks during a bust of an illegal street race, which led to nineteen cars being seized and fourteen arrests, according to the *San Francisco Chronicle*.[10] San Jose is not distinct in this regard. Street racing is popular in a lot of places where the boundaries between urban and suburban life are blurry, where cars can traverse long stretches of empty (and not-so-empty) road. Imports and American muscle serve as the two pivotal points around which this scene, fluid in its form, membership, rituals and rules, codes and conduct, coalesces. These two groups regularly gather in the same meeting places, but import racers and domestics race primarily against cars of the same kind; every once in a while, they go head to head. The groups are largely ethnically split. "You got your Asian rice rockets. Honda Civics that are souped up, got their Na's, their flo masters and stuff. So, you have that and Latinos, Mexicans, with their old-school muscle cars," JP, an Anglo kid and self-described racer who drives a Chevy, explains. Melissa, who as a young woman resides at the periphery of these overlapping scenes, echoes JP's remarks: "Trust me, if you go out there and look, you'll see a complete difference between a Vietnamese car and a white person's car. I feel like I'm being racist, but I'm not.... Asian cars, they'll always do a body kit. And that's why they call them Rice Rockets. Because their cars sound a lot different than.... they do something different with their mufflers and their intakes." These groups have become increasingly antagonistic as loyalists to American Muscle have attempted to reassert their dominance over the car racing scene.

Formally and informally, the racing scene operates as a space of competition and antagonism, where racers regularly challenge other racers. Respect and recognition are extended to those who can "step up" and "hold their own" against those already recognized as the most skilled drivers with the fastest cars. Impromptu street racing is also common among those whose cars can compete, and a shared code of communication, the revving of an engine at a stop light or a quick nod to the rival driver, signals a willingness to race. Suffice it to say, not to engage is to lose face. "You'll be at a stop light and guys pull up and you know they antagonize, you race. If a guy comes up and challenges you, then you race him," explains Trevor, who also drives a modified Mustang. "Even if I don't race him, you have to respond in some type of way. If you're not going to race, then you bark at him and how

you bark at him is by revving your engine, just to let him know, you know, I'm not scared but at a different time."

Street racing and car customizing are activities shared among men—a set of social practices and relations from which young men work to construct and articulate coherent narratives that solidify a sense of being men. It is this heightened sense of competition that fortifies the enduring link between cars and masculinity. Perhaps this helps to explain why high-level risk-taking assumes such significance for these young men; the level of risk one is willing to take becomes the means to set oneself apart from other men.

Risky Business: Boys Who Race

AB: Um, what's the fastest you've ever driven?

KENNY: One hundred forty-two miles an hour.

AB: Really, on a highway?

KENNY: Uh-huh, on the freeway.

AB: Um, what, was it, like late at night, or?

KENNY: Yeah, it was coming home from those races you were talking about.

AB: Oh, my gosh. Did you have people in the car?

KENNY: Four people.

AB: Were you scared?

KENNY: Yeah.

AB: Well, describe what it's like. I mean, I've never driven that fast.

KENNY: It's a rush, it's like crazy, like.

AB: Well, how do you feel?

KENNY: Calm, I feel really calm when I do it, like I don't know, it just feels like you're flying or something. Yeah, it feels like you're floating across the road.

Daring, danger, and peril reside at the center of this competitive world of racing.[11] These boys travel to forbidden territories, abandoned industrial zones, in search of a profound "experience" that will enable them to transcend the shackles of time and place, to step outside the self as they step into the flow, to engage risk and defeat it. They race to *feel* the intense sensation, difficult to describe in words, that provides the means to anchor themselves within a physical world where one's existence is known because it is felt.[12] Their desire to do so at times almost overwhelms them. These boys talk incessantly about the rush they gain from racing, of being in the flow, the "high" they get from being at the edge, almost losing control and somehow finding their way back. "It is all about the rush," I hear over and over from this group of boys and others who race. The source of the rush? Testing themselves against themselves and against others, since displays of danger and daring are the principal means to gain respect and recognition. Perhaps that is why, when not racing, they spend hours with others in their crew reliving stories of near-peril, sharing what the adolescent psychologist Cynthia Lightfoot regards as "risk narratives."[13] These narratives make up these boys' "storyworlds," where their reality is constructed as much as it is expressed, through which they gain recognition and visibility. The auto shop is a particularly strategic space in this regard, since it provides opportunity to talk about cars, risk, danger, and peril of all sorts, and talk they do. The boys spend much of their time rehashing details of past races, whose car outdrove whose. Talk about speed, how fast they drive, and the fastest they have ever driven is regularly interjected into conversation as they debate what counts as "sick" driving, celebrating those who are willing to do "crazy shit." Their stories serve to signify a life lived at the edge. I hear countless stories of driving that seem to provide opportunity for these young men to flaunt, above all else, their own driving skill, since they did, after all, live to tell the tale. "I used to race people on the freeway 'cause this car it always attracts people that want to race me so I always end

up racing," Olie, a young man, explains. "Sundays are really good days for when guys are out like older, like little thirty-years-olds in their Corvettes or whatever who want to race. I'm down, I'm okay. 'Cause I'm really good at maneuvering through traffic, and I make really crazy moves and stuff." On another morning, boys trickle into class, settling into their seats as they talk about the events of the past weekend. I overhear two of the boys rehash the race that occurred between two other boys in the class. This is interrupted by John, another student, also a racer, who begins to recount to Mr. O'Malley his race at Sacramento raceway over the weekend with a friend. He flips through an auto parts magazine, describing how the rear axle and the drive shaft broke on his friend's Camano SS as a large number of the students now listen in. I am suddenly reminded of Daniel telling me last week how he had blown up the engine of his Civic in a race the weekend before. Beyond this, I hear countless stories of driving on bald tires, stripped struts, and ever-thinning brake pads that seemed to be a way to affirm their participation in a world of risk.[14]

I hear several stories of tickets, like the story George, who drives a Jetta, told me one morning during class, as the two of us watched Rich sand down one of the side panels on his white pickup truck. Last month, George was racing down the road neck and neck with Rich. As the two lanes of the road merged into one, George pulled ahead of Rich. Neither noticed the cop car parked in the side street. The race resulted in a $400 fine for George, since his car was in the lead; Rich barely escaped. Speeding tickets, especially tickets issued for "exhibition speed" and "reckless driving," which carry hefty fines, are badges of courage and-bravery, since such violations provide evidence of a life lived on the edge. I talk to David as he measures the tire pressure of one of the cars as several hover around passing the time.

"I have a Civic at home," he tells me, but he is not allowed to drive it since he has a suspended license, he says as he chuckles to himself. When I ask why, he responds, "Reckless driving." He and another guy were "just fooling around" in a parking lot. He says earnestly, "We weren't even racing," but the cops stopped them and checked their car "because they think we do drugs." This resulted in a $1,500 ticket and a suspended license, which won't be returned until some ten months hence. Strangely, he seems only slightly upset by this turn of events. Perhaps it is because he has simply resigned himself to the fact. Or perhaps it is because this has become a good story to tell, a story that secures his rightful place as a man among men.

Cops are important to the storyworlds these boys construct, since their presence helps to define racing as a risk activity that involves more than just the obvious physical risks taken for driving at breakneck speeds. Cops serve as reminders of the boys' willingness to put their life at risk in other ways. These young men risk arrest, tickets, fines, possible jail time, and the disruption of their futures. In short, they are willing to risk it all. I can't help wondering if taking such significant risks is a way to remain in control of their lives. This is a group whose lives are largely defined by a set of circumstances that are beyond their control. As low-income kids with few secure or promising avenues available to them, their futures beyond high school remain largely uncertain.[15] These risk narratives, which construct their reality as much as express it, seem to be a way to manage, if not control, the uncertainty of their future. Within their storyworlds, what lies ahead rests squarely within their own hands. They are the narrators of their own lives, and if they mess up they have only themselves to hold responsible. This is after all the model of the autonomous, self-determining individual to which many Americans aspire and upon which masculine status rests.

The Need for Speed: Masculinity and Performance Vehicles

Cars have long served as objects for men to position themselves in terms of masculinity, enabling an elaborated performance of the masculine: But the relationship these young men forge between cars and being masculine is far from uncomplicated, rather, it is fraught with messy contradictions and struggle. To understand the nature of this struggle, which is the subject of the rest of this chapter, requires an understanding of the world in which boys are becoming men. The sociologist Michael Kimmel, among other scholars, has argued that modern masculinity is in crisis, its foundation rapidly crumbling as the traditional anchors of manhood recede in importance or become all but impossible to obtain.[16] Financial independence is increasingly an empty pursuit, since most young men will be unable to provide for themselves, let alone for others, if they are to continue to reside in communities like San Jose. Outside the realm of sports, physical competence, a traditional marker of masculinity, carries little occupational prestige in a world organized around the exchange of information, not displays of muscle.[17] In an increasingly posttraditional world, where social roles (e.g., being the breadwinner) are less likely to serve as guides for action and identity formation, young men inevitably will face an existential crisis.[18] Their participation in the world of cars and car racing provides a space to manage the existential dilemmas of masculinity, where these young men work to construct and sometimes repair a set of boundaries through which masculine power is reasserted.

These boys invest in fast cars and this fast scene as they traverse a changing world in search of recognition, visibility, and respect when the traditional ways to gain respect as men are unavailable. They also confront other problems because their struggle to become men occurs in a context where masculinity is increasingly transparent as a social construct. (Consider, for example, the ways masculinity is increasingly parodied and satirized in the popular media.) In a so-called postmodern world of hyperreality, where there is no original, no "real," behind the imitation but only other imitations, as Baudrillard has argued, the struggle to gain recognition as masculine requires a far more nuanced and subtle performance to be believable.[19] Against a masculinity that reveals itself to others as a fake, as a performance, these boys struggle to be "authentically men."

Perhaps this explains why boys are increasingly called upon to monitor their own masculinity, to demonstrate a self-awareness that the performance of the masculine self is after all a performance. "I think, um, there's always some internalized pressures to drive a certain way in terms of my gender. There seems to be some expectation to drive fast and live and do everything fast," Richard, one particularly insightful twenty-year-old, remarked. "Like every time I see my little rearview mirror and I see people trailing behind me and I think oh maybe I should go faster…I feel those pressures."

These young men must be convincing as men not only for an ever-increasing group of skeptics and ironists but also to themselves.[20] Identity formation today occurs in a context where "the self is seen as a reflexive project for which the individual is responsible."[21] In a media-saturated culture where images and parodies of men are profuse, men are increasingly expected to be reflective about their manhood. Hypermasculine men are ones who are "unreflective about manhood." They are seen as not self-actualized and thus not in control of themselves.[22]

The shifting ground on which these "reflective masculinities" are mapped has consequences for understanding the struggle for masculinity of these young men who participate in the car-racing scene. Racers walk a thin line because the car-racing scene is often regarded as

a hypermasculine space to outsiders (this given its ties to white working-class masculine culture).[23] This point is clearly illustrated in the following conversation with two young men who stand outside the car-racing scene. Here they link cars and "macho" as they attempt to present themselves as authentically masculine against macho men, men who are largely regarded as imposters.

ROBERT: I think it's kind of a macho thing to like, I don't know, I've heard people like, I can drive when I'm drunk and like, oh you can't do it? So it's just…

AB: What do you think about that, the whole macho thing?

ROBERT: Stupid.

mitch: I don't know, I'm not a macho person, so I'm not going to try and play it off.

AB: So what defines like a macho person?

MITCH: Someone with flows and big subwoofers in the cars and—

ROBERT: Yeah.

AB: Well, I was going to ask actually because you had said earlier that you were not the type to do all that stuff to your car and um, and…

ROBERT: A sound system might be different because I really like music, but I'm not going to, like, put a lift on my car, get big twenty-inch wheels or whatever. What some people do to their car, like what they put into it, is so amazing.

MITCH: That's what the parking lot's [at school] like. It's like a battle between who has the loudest bass on their car or…

AB: Really?

MITCH: Yeah.

ROBERT: Or, who…

MITCH: The loudest engine.

AB: What do you think about that?

ROBERT: I think it's silly, yeah. I like to watch people, like while you're spinning out your tires, so you'll have to be like, you know, spending three hundred dollars on new tires like, you know, five months earlier than I am.

Young men today parody others and themselves for performances of masculinity that are too obviously fakes. This is perhaps especially apparent around cars because they have long been associated with masculinity and also provide ground for competition. A number of these boys sought to expose the ways some men use their cars as a status means to "get" women, lest they be accused of doing precisely that themselves. Trying to explain why he has such disdain for car cruising, Aldo offers, "I don't know, like, guys being dogged, you know trying to say, 'What's up baby?' you know, 'What's your number?'" Scott explains why he was not into "one of those big macho cars." "Why bother? I have nothing to show off." This young man saw having a "big macho car" as a feeble attempt "to get into somebody's pants." For Olie, talk about cars becomes a space to parody himself, perhaps before someone else does. "I was just pulling into the movie theater like I thought I was really cool 'cause I was with a girl and stuff. Yeah, you know what I'm saying and I didn't see one of those cement blocks and I was like, oh shit."[24]

Many young men today, whether racers or not, distance themselves from "macho"—the hypermasculine "straw man" as they solidify their own identities as authentic men. But their reflections and parodies fall short of actually subverting the privilege accorded to them by the mere fact that they are men. To the contrary, this kind of talk is central to reaffirming the power of masculinity that ultimately establishes, regulates, and sometimes rewards these young men.

Trevor, an African American young man who did not get his license until he was twenty-one, reveals, "I was ashamed of it [not having a license]. Ah man, you know, my girl drives me around. My friends kind of let me hear about it a lot. It's something you have to swallow and get on with life." Trevor now has a black Ford Mustang GT, a car with considerable power, especially following various engine modifications. Explaining why he chose to modify the engine, he remarked with a surprising frankness, "It makes it louder, meaner and tougher.... Like I said, some guys they pull up and they want to show off and they rev their cars, you know, and if you can't, you know, you feel embarrassed, stupid, so you got to get that." This sense of struggle to achieve masculinity by debasing and discrediting other men is well illustrated in the following example drawn from one of the countless electronic bulletin boards organized around street racing. The following posts represent an ongoing conversation, occurring over several days, about the meaning of a "real" racer.[25]

Malachi #1:

I've been in the game since '94. Not that duration is important, but for the last 9 years I've eaten, slept, dreamed and worked for going faster. My driving is always being examined and my mechanical skills are always improving. The name racer always sounded stupid to me, but it's what I am. Who here is a real racer? Post up and tell me why. *Do not post if your just gonna list the parts you bought, and why your euro style taillights were a performance upgrade.*[26]

Green Goblin #2 is the first to respond, offering the following:

A racer is a one who races. I drive a Ford Explorer, but I've raced other SUVs. I know it isn't the fastest vehicle on the road, and I don't act like it is, but it IS at least faster than a lot of other SUVs. I don't go around places saying "I am a racer" but I have raced others in the past and I still do, so therefore, I am a racer.

This is followed by a series of messages. The conversation rapidly becomes hostile, with repeated attempts by these men to distance themselves from and to debase other young men as they talk about their own relationship to cars.[27] They position themselves against a particular group of racers who are recognized as "all show and no go," the aforementioned "ricers."

Abcd 123 #3:

I see what you're getting at. I have a few friends like that. Some keep at it for more power, some keep at it, but for more speed. I don't consider myself a real racer. Maybe back in the day, I would drag anything that moved. Cars weren't as powerful, and the police was not an issue. There was more emphasis on being able to cut through traffic than actual horsepower, since mods were unheard off.

SL porn series #4:

I've been racing since 94 also back in high school. I guess I caught the bug from when pops was a kid. He raced anything from lola's old chevy station wagon, his triple deuce, GTO, Sting ray, Vet, his Suburban. We always BS about comparing apples vs oranges as no replacement to displacement. etc....He's a strong vette follower and a supervisor mechanic for PG&E. He's a real racer from drag to autoX, to go carts, to road courses. He's pretty impressed with imports and he also likes driving my turbo hatch I do it for fun and not to be trendy. I've dragged charged buicks, Pop's C5, and a lot of Hondas. I respect anybody that races and works on their cars. *I do it for sport. Unlike most ricers these boys who drive to be trendy and be "noticed." Peace!*

Sleeper #5:

Street...well that's just full of posers...it would be so easy for me to claim something that any car obviously does do...but it happens at the scene all the time (we usually call them ricers or idiots). I do push my car to the limits on the way back roads...if I have to drive 2 hours to find a remote spot, I will...with minimal risk to me, my car and more importantly others who wish not to be involved. I also, usually don't take anyone with me...the main reason is that most of the people in my town are all talk and I don't trust the abilities of other drivers. I do accept the risks and have no problem taking tickets if I'm doing something wrong...cops usually respect that too. I accept responsibility for my mistakes.

Lt. What? #6:

Fake racer. I pretend to drive my cars. They really drive themselves, they're the real racer.

Another thing, you ignorant prick, if you're going to talk shit in your sig, you might want to spell check. I'm sure you'll respond saying I don't know anything short the english language, much the same as engines, and 'your are' is proper english.

Lastly, did you really need to include a setup for your little rib at Nick? I'm sure only one with your intellect could put together that the comment in YOUR sig was FROM you. Thank you for labeling it for us mere mortals. *Eat a dick, bitch.*

333racer #7:

however i need to bring up another point, for all those people who proclaim they are "real" street racers. i find that term to be absolute BS true you may be racing on the streets, but i noticed that all those who were from back in the day they don't admit to racing on the streets and many more are actually ashamed to say they do. i think that the term street racer has turned into a trendy little label to make people feel like they are important. real racers know the importance of keeping the racing secret.

Runner #8:

> Let's not get into what is racing and what is not. I really don't like to drag now. I road race exclusively. I will drag once in a while though, I haven't for few years though.
>
> I wrench, I don't really like to. But when it's my ass on the line, I gotta know my car will be there for me. I don't trust anyone. I've been screwed. No one will care like I do. I've only bought one aftermarket body panel in my life, a Spoon CF lip for my old EG. I drive a WRX now. It's ugly and fast as fock. Not done yet, it's being built as a well rounded car. Suspension/Brakes/Power-Driving skill. That's all that matters to me. No euro tails, no Z3 gills, no supra headlights, no lighted washer nozels and no 15 year old on my hood! But the WRX will have some nicer panels in the end.
>
> *I remember when the scene was pure. When all we wanted to do was go faster. I sold my civic because I was tired of being associated with scum. Too harsh? Stop doing ghetto shit to the car, get rid of the euro tail lights.*

These young men draw on the language of purity and pollution, what the anthropologist Mary Douglas regards as central to the hierarchical distinctions groups invoke as they draw distinct moral boundaries between us and them. In the words of Runner #8, "I remember when the scene was pure."[28] These writers/racers define the boundaries clearly: "real" racers modify the

performance of their cars, and "fakers" make modifications for aesthetic appeal.[29] In this sense, gender tropes are clearly in play as examples of display are linked to feminine activity. In their struggle to be recognized as real racers, these young men distance themselves from feminine practices of paying too much attention to the body (car body or otherwise), since the car body can be seen as a metaphor for the physical body. Spending too much time "primping" is decidedly unmasculine....This can be seen primarily in the recurring challenge to needless and gratuitous display that emerges beginning in the first instance with Malachi: *"Do not post if your just gonna list the parts you bought, and why your euro style tailights were a performance upgrade."* At several points, driving skill is privileged over aesthetic changes as they draw lines between those who are rightful insiders and those who are outsiders—those who are men and those who are not.

I also witnessed attempts to draw distinctions between real racers and fakers in the auto shop class: On one occasion, a group of import racers, Ping, Brad, and Vicrum, are at work on Ping's Civic hatchback. They are planning to attach a black lip to the bottom. Other kids hover around watching them as they work to figure how precisely they are to attach this lip. As I look on, I ask why they want to attach the lip to the car, and one of the guys, the only nonimport racer in the group, responds with noted sarcasm, "To make it *look* lower," as he chuckles to himself before walking off. A few moments later, another nonimport racer approaches, asking the group at work sarcastically, "Does it make it faster?" Interestingly, though these young men are questioned about the types of modifications they are doing, because they are doing the work themselves, they are not discredited as "half men." As SL porn series #4 remarked in his post, "I respect anybody that races and works on their cars."

In this competitive context, having knowledge about car parts and how cars work serves as a key cultural resource affirming one's status within the group, solidifying a hierarchy of respect, and serving as a basis of exclusivity.[30] Boys who pay someone else to customize or modify their cars accrue less status than those boys who are able to work on their cars themselves, because they are seen as imposters.[31] This explains why a car that is fast but has only limited visual appeal is often regarded as a "work in progress," which enables its owner to claim respect. A primed hood, for example, becomes a way to announce that this car is being worked on by oneself. As a useful point of comparison, consider my earlier comments about Shrini's car, which had significant visual appeal but no speed. Shrini was actively trying to sell this car, lest he be discredited as "all show and no go."[32] Having to pay someone to fix and modify one's car can also serve to discredit a racer. It is in this sense that knowledge of car parts and cars themselves communicates what Sarah Thornton has termed "subcultural capital," a type of capital that structures an alternative hierarchy by which people vie for status—a social good that can be bestowed only by others and not awarded by oneself.[33]

American Muscle and Talking Trash

The comments posted on the bulletin boards that defined racers who focus on exterior changes rather than performance upgrades as "ricers" is quite telling.[34] As SL porn series #4 remarked in his post, "most ricers these days who drive to be trendy and be noticed." Runner #8 comments, "I remember when the scene was pure. When all we wanted to do was go faster. I sold my Civic because I was tired of being associated with scum. Too harsh? Stop doing ghetto shit to the car, get rid of the euro tail lights." Sleep #5 writes, "Street...well that's just full of posers...it would be so easy for me to claim something that my car obviously does do...but it happens at the scene all the time (we usually call them ricers or idiots)." Within the world of car racing, the term *ricer* or *rice rocket* is used interchangeably with the term "import." Ricers and rice rockets are Hondas, Nissans, and Acuras. Fords and Chevys are never called rice rockets.

The condemnation of "ricers" was widespread on these message boards and elsewhere. The following rap, entitled "The Ricer Anthem," appeared on one of the message boards where import and domestic racers routinely post messages, debate the merits of different cars, and constitute the moral and cultural perimeters of the racing world.

The Ricer Anthem

> Hi! My name is (who?)...my name is (what)...my name is (stretches)...Rice Burner!
> Hi Kids, do you like 5 inch tips?
> Wanna see me stick chrome fender flares over each of my Konigs?
> Wanna follow me and do exactly as I did?
> Try NAWS and get your motor fucked up worse than my life is?
> My brain's dead weight, I'm trying to get my head on straight
> But I can't figure out which sticker to put on my license plate.
> And the mechanic says "Rice burner you's a crack head" "Nu-uh" "Then why's your car dead man it's wasted"
> Well since age 9 I've wanted an SI so I could put chrome 18s on it and make it run 16.9's.
> Got pissed off and ripped all my Honda emblems off.
> And replaced them with "R" badges so people know I'm not soft.
> I smoke a big bowl of chronic, and lay in my lawn
> For longer then it took me to put my altezzas on.

"Come here bastard" "Dude, wait a
minute that a viper dawg!!"
I don't give a fuck, I'll just fly by and put
my hazards on!!!

After this anthem was posted on the message board, a number of writers posted
replies, including jdanger, who wrote,
"This rice burner anthem, it says exactly
what needs to be said. Ricer burners want
to look performance but can't perform.
I would rather have performance than
looks." Another wrote, "all show and no go,
that's rice."

The distinction between an authentic
racer, somebody who is focused on power,
speed, and skill, and a "poser" is presented
through racialized metaphors that align
cars and aesthetics with particular ethnic or racial groups. This rivalry might
be explained by the fact that these car
scenes are ethnically organized. American
Muscle continues to be dominated largely
by Anglos, while the import scene is predominantly Asian. Recall also my earlier
comments that American Muscle's hegemony in the racing world has been challenged in recent years as imports have
posed a legitimate threat that must be
taken seriously. American Muscle racers
have managed this threat through attempts
to discredit imports and import racers
and by physically and discursively distancing themselves from this group. I repeatedly listened to young Anglo, Mexican,
and African American men aligned with
domestics denounce any association with
the import car scene, the cars, rice rockets,
and the drivers, known as "ricers." "Yeah,
I'm not into the car scene where they all
like rice rockets," seventeen-year-old Cesar
explains. Jorge echoes Cesar: "Rice rockets the small, you know, Hondas, I don't
like 'em. Honda. Civics souped up, stereotypically Asian....I have no respect
for imports...they give them too much
credit...for what they've done and if it
wasn't for I guess the American cars you've

got bigger muscle cars...they wouldn't be
around. And they still have to give respect
to those cars 'cause you know who you're
messing with and who you're not messing
with [laughing]." Even within the group
of import racers, the distinction between
ricer and racer was clearly drawn. Brad
tells me, "To hot rodders and cruisers
we're all ricers in the [import] racer community." But to Brad and his friends, there
is a difference between an import racer
and a ricer. In the words of the sociologist
Erving Goffman, they "stratify their own,"
a common enough strategy among those
who must routinely manage a stigmatized
identity.[35] Brad and his friends distance
themselves from those racers who make
"excessive" exterior changes (pointing out
some of the cars in the lot that are "ricers"
or "border-on-ricers") as they struggle to
maintain legitimacy within this world of
risk and competition.

This condemning talk directed at import
racers and the racial logic upon which it
rests is also visible in a conversation that
occurred during one of the focus group
interviews at Weston High School. While
this was a racially mixed group of kids,
importantly, no Asian kids were present in
this group. As was the case in other focus
groups, the young men dominated the conversation. In this particular focus group,
one of the boys, JP, an Anglo kid and the
oldest in the group, initiated much of the
dialogue.

JP: I don't like imports.
AB: You don't like imports, how come?
JP: I just don't.
ab: So what do you like then, like what's
kind of...
JP: Oh no, I have, I respect them, I don't
say anything about them at all,
I just...
AB: It's just not your style?
JP: Like them, they don't like muscle
cars, and then they actually do go and
talk crap about muscle cars.

AB: Who's they?

ADAM: I know.

JP: Imports.

ADAM: Asian people.

JP: If you think about it, you go buy a $20,000 car okay, it might have some advantages like air conditioning, CD player, and all that, but then you get a car for half the price, an American one, and it ends up out running all those cars, for half that price, and you put, you work that other half of the money into your car, and then you have a machine... it's crazy.

ADAM: What you call them is you call them imports and domestics, me and him both drive domestics, so that's Chevy, Ford, all those, those are domestics.

JP: And then you got your imports, which is like Honda, your Integra.

ADAM: Your Acuras.

TOM: Integra.

JP: All that crap is imports and that's the ones you hear nnneeeennneeeee goin' down the street, and stuff like... See, I just like domestic cars a lot better, and like lowriders, they're cool, but I hate, why are you going to do that to an American car? I hate that, because when you see all them lowriders doing all their hydraulics.

JP starts out talking about cars but ends up talking about the drivers, too. Ricers are no longer cars but people, Asians, as he attempts to denounce imports and import racers. Racial tropes are mobilized as JP defines the values of this cultural scene. Asians are constructed as the outsiders—the others against which he and other hot rodders solidify their identities as men. This is further illustrated by additional comments he makes in the course of the focus group. He draws specifically on the emergent stereotype of Asians as "bad drivers" as he again attempts to discredit not simply the import scene but an entire racial group.

JP: I think Chinese shouldn't really drive because they don't even really know how to drive.

CYNTHIA: Oh my God.

AB: Who?

ADAM: Asian people.

JP: No actually a lot of Asians.

AB: So why do you think that?

JP: [imitating a Chinese accent] Ohhhh, oh, you son of bitch you wreck my car.[laughter from the group]

AB: Well, what about American-born Asians?

JP: Then they get out and they start yelling at you for parking your car.

AB: What do other folks think? So, is this like all Asian folks, like Asian born folks or...

JP: They can't see.[Laughter again from the group]

AB: [referring to a comment by AS] Well, okay, well, he just said that your comment was racist.

TOM: No, actually Asian people are very good at racing, like I know lots of guys...

AB: [referring to DH] You just said it's because they are rich?

DH: 'Cause they always have nice cars.

AB: So are there any Asian kids that go to this school?

TH: A lot.

AB: so, well, what do you think about that? So what if there was an Asian person sitting here right now, would you be saying the same thing, or...

CJ: Maybe.AM: I don't think so.

AB: You don't think so.

CC: I don't think so.

CJ: But, I mean they can't drive, seriously, they can't drive, they drive piece of shit cars, sounds like a goddamn mouse through your house. It's like come on now, get a real car. I don't like the ones that make so damn, so much noise, like the, the ones they call "rice rockets."

The idea that Asians can't drive also emerged in auto shop class. On one occasion, a group of us are gathered around Brad's red Civic hatchback. He is balancing what are horribly bald tires. The group of young Asian men around the car is talking about another car on the lot whose fender has a deep and sizable scratch, and Sean, one of the Asian boys, remarks, as he explains the scrape, "He can't drive. He's Asian." Incredulous, Daniel, the only Mexican boy who hangs around with the import racers, responds, "Daaammmnnn, and you're Asian." To this Sean retorts, "Yeah, I can't drive, I can admit it," as the group collapses in laughter.

Interpreted one way, this comment reflects the psychosocial dynamics of racial dominance, revealing a pattern of internalized oppression, what Paulo Friere has called "horizontal violence." After all, this statement is articulated by a young Asian man and is met with laughter by other young Asian men and in this sense reflects what Goffman called "identity ambivalence." But, interpreted another way, this comment about Asian drivers in the context of this largely Asian, all-male group is a way to manage the enduring stereotypes, what Patricia Hill Collins refers to as "controlling images," used to discredit them as less than men and thus to justify their subordination. These boys know that JP is not alone in his condemnation of the import car scene or of Asians. By preemptively making the charge, they can control the joke themselves. In various ways, these young men are engaged in what Goffman regarded as interactional strategies to manage the stigma of race as they attempt to preserve a sense of being men in a context of an intense competition over the symbolic resources that define masculinity.

This point is also illustrated in another instance. One early evening I am driving across town to a restaurant for dinner, and I pull up behind a Honda Civic at a stop light; it is an older model of the very car I have, but, unlike mine, its suspension has been lowered, and while my muffler is barely audible, its exhaust buzzes each time

the driver, a young Asian guy with short black hair shaped into small spikes, taps his foot on the accelerator. As I sit waiting for the light to turn green, I inspect this car, curious about its driver, who he is and where he's going. I notice that just above the car's back bumper is written in white script *"Got Rice?"* Within moments the light turns green, and the small vehicle idling in front of me is gone; its rear lights fade as the distance between us grows. I am left in its wake. I imagine a scenario where this car is racing against another on a highway or empty street; it pulls ahead, leaving its rival behind, with a derisive *Got Rice? Got Rice?*, all the more powerful as the last word, is loaded with intention and mocking, a means to invert and convert the pejorative meaning of *ricer*.[36] It is a call to war, an attempt to inflame the animosity that inspired the term in the first place and to subvert the hegemony of American Muscle.

The sociologist Paul Connolly argues that young men express deep racial animus in situations of tense competition, though they might not in other situations. Certainly car racing is a space of hypercompetition, since the activity is not only organized around winners and losers but emerges as a terrain of claims to dominance and superiority. Imports and domestics are locked in a battle over not simply whose cars are faster but also what constitutes the basis of legitimate masculinity for these young men coming of age in a posttraditional society. Because many import drivers are Asian, this struggle over dominance is largely directed toward Asian men and reflects the historical legacy of anti-Asian, nativist rhetoric.

Racial constructions are routinely used to work out deep anxieties about masculinity, to define who is authentically masculine and who is not. The sociologist R. W. Connell's understanding of race and what he calls "hegemonic masculinity," defined in part by invisible whiteness and reliance on the hypermasculinization of black men and the hyperfeminization of Asian men, is useful for making sense of these exchanges among young men who participate in the car-racing scene.[37] Asian import racers as a group, who have historically been feminized, get discredited in this car world as others actively (re)feminize them. The sociologist Yen Le Espirtu has argued, "Asian American men have been excluded from white-based cultural potions of the masculine," noting that Asian American men are regularly depicted in the media as "impotent eunuchs" and emasculated "model minorities."[38]

The feminization of Asian men is achieved in two specific ways. First, by arguing Asians can't drive, detractors position Asian men outside a masculine world of skill, risk, and competence. Similar arguments about women drivers also once served as justification to keep women off the road.[39] Second, the cars of Asian import drivers are feminized as "rice rockets," cars with gratuitous display. Consider the comments of jdanger: "I hope you guys see where I am coming from. These little jap cars are nothing but the nastiest, dumbest girl in school with plastic surgery."

One might also consider the possibility that attempts to discredit import racers as ricers through a critique of gratuitous display is also part of an intense backlash against Asians and Asian immigrants in post-1965 America. Changes in immigrant policy in the mid-1960s led to an influx of immigrant groups in the 1980s and 1990s, a time of eroding economic opportunity as hundreds of thousands of manufacturing jobs were lost in the United States. A number of scholars and activists have identified a heightened anti-Asian, anti-immigrant sentiment in California and nationally in the context of economic uncertainty.[40] The charge of gratuitous display against "ricers" appears to be tied to nativist critiques of conspicuous consumption directed at Asians and Asian Americans that grows from the perception that they are claiming too large of a piece of the proverbial pie,

thereby displacing other groups competing for employment and housing opportunities.[41] A deep racial animus against upwardly mobile Asians is present in JP's focus group where all Asians are defined as "being rich." Indeed, this has served as the very basis of the model-minority myth that continues to target Asians as interlopers.[42]

A larger narrative is at work here that reflects deepening inequalities and conflict in an increasingly global world marked by ever-growing economic and social polarization. The rise of distinct ethnically based car scenes and the emerging rivalry between domestics and (Asian) imports are consequences of a changing, competitive global world order where the perception that "Americans" must continually reassert their supremacy in the face of unwarranted attacks by outsiders and foreigners is intense and pervasive. Consider these comments, posted on another message board by jdanger:

> You guys that LOVE imports can say all you want about how they're cool and stuff, but they still will be little jap cars. You can say NOS this and turbo that, but nothing is gonna beat American Muscle. I know maybe some American companies are manufacturing in other countries but they still make better cars than Honda, acura and all the other jap brands. I do want to ask you one question…why fix up little crappy 4 bangers when you can fix up a muscle car and get at least twice the power?

Posted comments of this kind often become the source of disagreement but seem to reflect longstanding anti-Asian ideas that led to a century of reactionary policies, panics, and sentiments against Asians and Asian countries, from the Immigration Exclusion Acts of the 1800s and 1900s, directed at Chinese immigrants and others, to the Japanese internment camps during World War II, to the "Buy American" movements that emerged in the 1970s and 1980s as U.S. multinationals halted production in the United States and relocated to other countries with cheaper labor and fewer environmental restrictions while U.S. laborers (many of whom were white union men) lost their jobs. Even some of the racers, though failing to see the broader historical context that has given rise to the anti-Asian sentiments that lurk beneath the anti-import rhetoric, recognize the narrow Americanism that is operating. Consider the following post, written by "Nissan Fan":

> If you were a true car fan you would see past all the "American Pride in Our Cars" shit who the fuck cares what country it came from look at the car not at the country…just because you hopped on the bandwagon of biased Yankee car lovers does not mean that Japanese cars suck…P.S. jdanger what your saying is very stereotypical.

LancasterWannaBE wrote, "I don't understand why there's always so much fuss about tuning Japanese cars. Last time I looked there were also many Jettas on the road— and guess what, they're imports too. I never hear anyone complaining about someone else tuning an Audi." The sociologist Lillian Rubin (2004) has argued that anti-immigrant sentiments are often articulated by white working-class men because they are the ones who have lost the most and who are increasingly vulnerable in a postindustrial America.[43]

Brave Men in a Brave New World: Global Masculinities

At the center of this competitive and antagonist world, where what you know serves to define where you are and where the level of risk you're willing to take is the measure of a man, is an ongoing and often heated rivalry between domestics and imports: Hondas against Mustangs, "Ricers" against "American Muscle." A quick car versus a powerful one. Asian versus Anglo. Who are the better drivers? Who has the fastest cars? Who can beat whom? Young men who participate in this world spend hours debating these points as clear and distinct lines are firmly etched. I have argued that this struggle, because it is organized to position Anglos and Asians at odds, is racialized. By this I mean that racist ideologies that have long suppressed and oppressed Asian men are used as a way to reaffirm white masculinities.

Phrases like *rice rockets, ricers,* and *riced out* operate as code words, allowing kids to talk about race, to participate in racial discourses, to express a deep racial animus, and to uphold a veiled racism that is taken as something else. All the kids I interviewed were familiar with these phrases and could use them easily. What stands behind these racial repertoires are young men's struggle for masculinity in a context where the traditional measures of being a man are increasingly out of their reach. For young men of color perhaps this has always been so. But for young white men who align themselves with American Muscle, many of whom are working class and have experienced a loss of status as they confront eroding job opportunities and as those jobs that remain open to them in the service economy are defined as women's work, they struggle to reassert their dominance in other ways. In this instance, it is through the symbolic work of distinction. As Sarah Thornton has argued in her writing about the social logic of subcultural capital, "Distinctions are never just assertions of equal distance; they usually entail some claim to authority and presume the inferiority of others."[44] Masculine identity construction for these young men occurs within a play of global and racial forces. Cars reveal some of the complexities that surround the process of becoming men and the role of symbolic boundaries.

An interesting parallel can be drawn between the work young men do on their cars and the work young women do on their bodies as both prepare to participate in spaces where the car rules. Boys work on their cars as a way to work on their masculinity, just as girls work on their bodies as a way to work on their femininity. Both converge in these car spaces, where boys' cars are presented for display much in the same way as girls' bodies are, that is, for boys to see. One might conclude that in these spaces, boys rule as much as cars do. Yet, one also wonders whether girls realize the time and energy boys direct towards fashioning their cars. Certainly, there are times when it exceeds the work young women do in fashioning their bodies.

In these spaces where boys and girls cruise "together but apart"[45] and where boys race against themselves and each other, young people search for recognition and visibility, for connection and belonging. They travel into these spaces where cars rule, where pleasure, desire, power, and struggle converge, to experience an intensity of emotion as they construct, play with, puzzle over, and defend who they are.

NOTES

1. These are terms used widely by youth in San Jose. Concern about "gangs" in San Jose, specifically the Nortenos and Surenos, are frequently articulated in the context of school, youth, and community life. Additionally, there are several "gang prevention" programs in the wider county. However, what actually constitutes a gang has been the subject of much popular and academic debate. I do not address this debate here, but I do resist reifying this contentious term.

2. I hesitate to use the term *subcultural* given the increasing questioning over the value of this term in understanding the social practices that define the experiences of youth in an increasingly global context. The term *subcultural* originates with the "Birmingham School" of cultural studies and signifies youth groups formed in and against the

"host" culture. *Subculture* was used to signify oppositional class-based groups (usually working-class young men) who engage in a sort of cultural and class warfare through style politics. In the past several decades, scholars studying youth culture have identified three problematic points arising from "subcultural studies": class reductionism; the romantic construction of these youth groups; and the limits of aesthetic forms of resistance in a context of rapid market appropriation and cooptation that have led to a reevaluation of this term. For a more comprehensive discussion see Muggleton and Weinzierl (2003).

3. In this sense, the import car scene has a transnational dimension.

4. Namkung (2004).

5. Mike, a bicultural Filipino..., also worked at Great America while in high school. And while he travels within the same loosely extended group of import racers, he is an upper-income kid. He attended a prestigious private high school in the area, and his parents, both professional workers, own several homes in northern California. The import car-racing scene appears to be a scene where young men develop loosely formed ties across economic groups. In this instance, being Asian as much as having an interest in imports seems to serve as the basis of their social ties. Victoria Namkung (2004) has argued that the import scene reflects attempts to construct a pan-Asian identity among Vietnamese, Filipinos, Japanese, Chinese, and South Asian youth largely on the basis of their exclusion from "mainstream" or the dominant Anglo youth culture broadly and the hot-rodding car culture specifically. Signs of a pan-Asian identity are clearly visible in this research.

6. Some car racers cruise in the absence of a race. But there are fairly distinct lines between the racers and the cruisers. If there is nothing else to do, racers sometimes cruise, though they generally talk about this activity with some disdain. Cruisers attend races every once in a while but not routinely and usually do so as spectators, not racers.

Tino told me that he did not race because he enjoyed the collective experience of cruising. In his words, you get to spend time with "your homies," but when you race, "you're alone." Most of the time racers in these semi-organized races in business parks do not have passengers in their cars when they actually race. While the boundaries between these two groups are sometimes fluid and allow some level of boundary crossing, when it comes to "identity talk," cruisers and racers draw distinct lines between their groups.

7. This has much to do with the racial-ethnic composition of the school itself. A majority of the students are Asian or Latino. Hot rodding continues to have a predominately Anglo membership.

8. Namkung (2004): 160.

9. For example, twenty-year-old Melissa explains that her boyfriend, Jake, who aligns himself with American Muscle, "will park next to the lowest car to make his truck look bigger.... Jake will not park next to [trails off] he'll park next to a truck that he knows will make it look stupid. Like he'll park next to the truck that's smaller than his. He'll park next to like a '87 Blazer that's got a 3-inch lift and big tires and he'll park where his car looks bigger."

10. *San Francisco Chronicle*, June 12, 2001, available at www.sfgate.com.

11. The car-racing scene shares particular sensibilities with the underground graffiti world that MacDonald (2001) depicted as "an illegal confine where danger, opposition and the exclusion of women is used to nourish, amplify, and salvage notions of masculinity" (149).

12. McDonald (1999) sees the search for intensity and visibility as central to the project of self-creation in the context of what Zygmunt Bauman (2000) calls "liquid modernity," a period of late modernity that emerged in the late 1970s and was defined by flow and movement, rather than the stability and stasis that are associated with "solid modernity." Drawing from their insights, I see racing as an attempt to disassociate from the self on

the one hand and an attempt to know the self through intense sensation on the other. It is as if the racer steps outside himself in order to step back in at some other point of entry. In some ways, I conceptualize the structure of the self along the lines of how George Herbert Mead conceptualized the self as made up of its component parts, the "I," the part of the self in action, and the "Me," the reflective self that allows for an awareness of self and also social control.

13. See Lightfoot (1997).

14. Bearing witness to dangerous scenarios and crazy situations is also central to constructing their world as a world of danger, daring, and peril. One morning I learned that Jason, who now drives a green Jetta, had originally had a Mustang until it was stolen, right out of the parking lot at school during fourth period. I responded with visible shock, since I was amazed that a car could be stolen from a high school parking lot. I could tell he still found the whole thing slightly bewildering. His was not the last nor the first story I heard about stolen cars. The boys seemed able to easily recall stories of theft in the neighborhoods where they live around the school, which is partly a function of their living in low-income neighborhoods. Thuy Vo, on another morning, showed me where someone tried to jimmy the lock on his Civic. His car had been parked outside his house in the driveway when this had happened (during the day, no less).

15. In talking with these boys and others in the class, I consciously directed the conversations toward future plans. I had the opportunity to speak with almost all of the 125 or so students in the four classes I observed. Only a handful (fewer than five) intended to move on to four-year colleges. Among this handful, all were in advanced placement classes and had decided to take this class to be either more "well-rounded" or because they saw the class as an easy "A." A much larger group planned to move on to community colleges or technical schools, where they hoped to gain career skills in graphic design or as auto technicians. About half of the racers

with whom I spent the majority of my time planned to move on to community colleges because they weren't quite sure what else there was to do. A few talked about moving on to community college because it was a more affordable alternative to a four-year school. None (among this group of racers) talked about plans to move on to a four-year college after community college. All assumed they would continue with the jobs they currently held. It is likely that some in this group will move on to four-year colleges eventually, but this clearly was not on their immediate horizon.

16. Blackshaw (2003); Kimmel (1997); Horrocks (1994).

17. The declining significance of physical strength to masculine dominance in the Western world might also help to explain the proliferation of images of "ass-kicking" women in popular culture, from *Buffy, the Vampire Slayer,* to the new *Charlie's Angels,* to the Quentin Tarantino film *Kill Bill I* and *II,* in which the female protagonist wreaks utter havoc (against a large group of Asian men in one instance) in her search for revenge.

18. See Anthony Giddens's (1991) discussion in "Ontological Security and Existential Anxiety."

19. See Baudrillard (2000) for a discussion of hyperreality and simulacra.

20. Vered Vinitzky-Seroussi (1998) makes a related point in her investigation of high school reunions. She examines how people manage the discrepancy between their biographical self and their social self, their past self and their present self, arguing that ultimately the most important audience for the performance of self is the self. This is a key point that Goffman (1959, 1963), in his investigations of impression management and the performance and presentation of the self, overlooked. I also argue that convincing the self of one's performance of self is especially important in the context of late modernity, given Anthony Giddens's arguments about the increased pressure to generate identity in a "reflexive" mode. In the posttraditional, demodernized period that characterizes late modernity,

people are disengaged from social roles. Social roles have been replaced by a new individualism marked by the rise of anxiety and uncertainty as traditional anchors of identity become less secure. This has given rise to the idea of the self as a project for improvement, according to Giddens. See Giddens's (1991) discussion in "The Trajectory of the Self."

21. Giddens (1991): 75. Perhaps this explains why the feminist movements and the men's movement of the 1970s were able to publicly scrutinize masculinity in ways that were impossible at other historical moments.

22. The hypermasculine is increasingly antithetical to celebrated forms of masculinity, what R. W. Connell (1987, 1995) would regard as hegemonic masculinity because it is seen as inauthentic and unreflective.

23. The ultimate hypermasculine social type is almost always in the image of a white working-class guy. He can usually be seen drinking cans of domestic beer, wearing flannel, his belly spilling over his jeans, espousing reactionary racist rhetoric. His wife, worn and beaten, is relegated to the kitchen, lest she be the subject of his wrath.

24. One might regard these acts and actions as "gender strategies," a term sociologist Arlie Hochschild uses to talk about the ways men attempt to solve the problem of achieving masculinity. See Hochschild (1989).

25. These passages posted to the bulletin boards appear as they appeared on the bulletin boards. I did not change typographical or grammatical errors.

26. I have placed in italics those portions of the text that I identify as particularly important to this masculine struggle.

27. See Goffman's (1963) classic examination of the interactional work involved in managing discredited and discreditable identities.

28. There is also a logic operating here about cultural boundaries and status hierarchies that is similar to the logic elites use to prevent the popularizing and massification of cultural practices. Presumably the scene was pure when it was restricted to those in the know.

The opening or broadening of racer culture is seen to have spoiled or polluted the activity. See for example Lamont and Fournier (1992).

29. I draw here on boundary theory, which has explored the production and reproduction of social inequalities through the use of symbolic boundaries and status distinctions. Boundary theory often emphasizes the informal practices that constitute cultural boundaries, seeing these as central to the formation of cultural hierarchies. A particular emphasis has been placed on the connection between what Bourdieu first called "cultural capital," referring to types of "high-status" knowledge, and the reproduction of social and economic inequality. See Bourdieu (1977, 1984), Lamont (1992, 1999), Lamont and Fournier (1992). See DiMaggio (1982) for an examination of boundary distinctions and cultural capital in schooling. See Lareau (2003) for an examination of the distinctive class-based parenting logics that produce different kinds of cultural capital. See Carter (2003) for a discussion of dominant and nondominant forms of cultural capital (specifically black cultural capital) in educational contexts. See Vallas (2000) for an application of boundary theory to work organizations. Vallas explores the distinction between mental and manual labor and its role in creating new forms of social inequality at work as new technologies increasingly organize the workplace.

30. Boundary theory is particularly applicable to understanding the complex and subtle distinctions these young men draw between posers and fakes. "Symbolic capital" and "cultural capital" are both useful concepts here. See Bourdieu (1977, 1984); Vallas (2000). The refined knowledge about cars, car parts, and car engines held by many of these young men operates as a type of "cultural capital" that confers status on the knower, just as "symbolic capital," having a particular kind of car with particular kinds of modifications, confers prestige or status on or discredits the car owner.

31. Somewhere along the way, I realized that my ability to pass in this world as a woman who looks more like their teachers than like them is entirely dependent on the fact that my questions became an occasion for them to demonstrate their knowledge about cars. I found myself in situation after situation listening attentively to the breadth and depth of their knowledge about cars and car parts, which these boys were eager to share. Many of these young men relished the opportunity to reach me about this world of which they are so thoroughly a part.

32. These young men are engaged in a struggle over the relevance of what R. W. Connell has referred to as hegemonic masculinity. In a traditional Gramscian sense of hegemony, allegiance to this masculine construct is achieved largely through the consent of men, many of whom gain very little from this social arrangement, since it depends upon various subordinated forms of masculinity. For Connell (1987, 1995), the production of masculinity exists within a hierarchical order, so that some forms of masculinity are deployed to debase and discredit men. As Connell reminds us, it is the interplay among varying modes of masculinity that helps sustain a patriarchal social order, and thus active attempts at debasing and discrediting others are critical to masculine dominance. Relating to my points earlier, I argue that a hypermasculine type is one example of a subordinated masculinity that is used to gain men's allegiance to a hierarchy of masculinities and to a dominant type. For Connell, there is no hegemonic femininity that corresponds to a hegemonic masculinity, although a hierarchy of femininities is in operation. Forms of femininity, although always defined by their relation to hegemonic masculinity, uphold dominant masculine forms in varying degrees. He identifies "emphasized femininity" as a dominant form of femininity that works to secure masculine power, but he also recognizes that other forms of femininity subordinate to emphasized femininity threaten masculine dominance. See also Diaz (2002); Horowitz (2001); Mac An Ghaill (1994); Messner (1992); Meyer (2001); Shackleford (2001) for discussion of

masculine identity construction in the context of social struggle.

33. There is a very large body of sociological literature that examines the social mechanics of status arising from Weber's work on status as a social good, but I see little reason to rehearse that here.

34. Thuy Vo's car discussed earlier in the chapter, though admired by many as "artwork," was also referred to as a "ricer" by some of the racers.

35. Goffman (1963): 107.

36. There is also a clear play on the meaning that circulates in commodity culture. I am reminded of the cleverly conceived and wildly successful marketing campaign "Got Milk?" launched by the American Dairy Association, specifically targeting would-be young milk drinkers, that has appeared in a host of magazines for young readers, from *Rolling Stone* to *Seventeen*. The inscription *Got Rice?* as much as it reveals something about the racial order young people occupy, also provides clues about youths' immersion in a consumer world.

37. The import car culture emerged as a distinctly Asian American male youth culture within a broader context of hyperfeminization of Asian men. Cars became central to constructing masculine identity for young Asian men who had otherwise been excluded from the muscle car culture of the 1970s and 1980s, since cars are codified as masculine. Yet many of these Asian young men, as they forged alternative masculinities through the import car-racing scene, came to reject a "brutish" mode of masculinity epitomized in the muscle car of the 1970s and 1980s, distancing themselves from a masculinity rooted in white working-class culture, a form traditionally defined by one's physical strength and skill in working with one's hands (e.g., mechanics).

38. See Espiritu (1997): 90. See also Kondo (1998) and David Henry Hwang's *M. Butterfly*.

39. See O'Connell (1998).

40. During the conversation, as Brad talked, one of the guys, joking, said, "I am ricer." I was struck by how he embraced this. I raised the point of *ricer* being an anti-Asian slur,

and the group fell silent. No one challenged me. While I cannot be sure if they too saw all this hubbub as expressing the anti-Asian and anti-immigrant nativist attacks that have intensified in post-9/11 America, they didn't attempt to teach me or correct me as they had at other times.

41. See Espiritu (1997); Rubin (2004); Wu (2002).

42. Within the context of Silicon Valley's economy, where Asian professionals play active roles in the tech sectors, the perception that Asian men on H1B visas are stealing jobs from skilled professional "American" workers (i.e., computer programmers and engineers) is widespread, fueled especially by the economic downtown that began in 2000. Thousands of professional workers were laid off as the tech bubble burst, among them were many South and Central Asians and Asian Americans. See also for historical discussions of this Anti-Asian pattern Takaki (1989); Nomura et al. (1989); Wu (2002).

43. Rubin (2004) argues that, although upper-middle-class whites have benefited from the influx of documented and undocumented immigrants because they provide a cheap source of domestic labor for the upper classes, the willingness of immigrants to work for cheap wages undercuts the demands for solid wages made by working-class unions. This point is also made by Fine and Weis (1998) in their examination of the eroding opportunities for young white working-class men who are part of the much maligned Generation X and in Weis's (1990) investigation of white working-class high-schoolers in deindustrialized Buffalo.

44. Thornton (1997): 201.

45. "Together but apart" is a statement Thorne (1993) used to describe the gender realities of elementary school playgrounds.

REFERENCES

Baudrillard, J. 2000. "The Ideological Genesis of Needs." *The Consumer Society Reader.*

J. Schor and D. B. Holt (eds.). New York: New Press.

Bauman, Z. 2000. *Liquid Modernity*. Cambridge: Polity Press.

Blackshaw, T. 2003. *Leisure Life: Myth, Masculinity, and Modernity*. London: Routledge.

Bourdieu, P. 1984. *Distinction: A Social Critique of the Judgment of Taste*. Cambridge, MA: Harvard University Press.

Bourdieu, P. 1977. *Outline of a Theory of Practice*. Cambridge: Cambridge University Press.

Carter, P. 2003. " 'Black' Cultural Capital, Status Positioning, and Schooling Conflicts for Low-Income African American Youth." *Social Problems* 50(1): 136–155.

Collins, P. H. 1990. *Black Feminist Thought: Knowledge, Consciousness and The Politics of Empowerment*. New York: Routledge.

Connell, R. W. 1995. *Masculinities*. Berkeley: University of California Press.

Connell, R. W. 1987. *Gender and Power: Society, the Person and Sexual Politics*. Stanford: Stanford University Press.

Connolly, P. 1998. *Racism, Gender Identities and Young Children: Social Relations in a Multi-Ethnic, Inner-City Primary School*. London: Routledge.

DiMaggio, P. 1982. "Cultural Capital and School Success: The Impact of Status Culture Participation on the Grades of U.S. High School Students." *American Sociological Review* 47 (April): 189–201.

Diaz, V. 2002. " 'Fight Boys, 'til the Last': Island-style Football and the Remasculinization of the Indigeneity in the Militarized American Pacific Islands." *Pacific Diaspora*, ed. Paul Spickard, Joanne Rondilla, and Debbie Hippolite Wright. Honolulu: University of Hawaii Press.

Douglas, M. 1966. *Purity and Danger: An Analysis of Concepts of Pollution and Purity*. London: Routledge & Kegan Paul.

Espiritu, Y. L. 1997. *Asian American Women and Men: Labor, Laws and Love*. Thousand Oaks, CA: Sage.

Fine, M., and L. Weis. 1998. *The Unknown City: The Lives of Poor and Working-Class Young Adults*. Boston: Beacon Press.

Giddens, A. 1991. *Modernity and Self-Identity: Self and Society in the Late Modern Age*. Stanford: Stanford University Press.

Goffman, E. 1967. *Interaction Ritual: Essays on Face-to-Face Behavior*. New York: Pantheon.

Goffman, E. 1963. *Stigma: Notes on the Management of Spoiled Identity*. New York: Simon & Schuster.

Goffman, E. 1959. *The Presentation of Self in Everyday Life*. New York: Doubleday.

Hochschild, A. 1989. *The Second Shift*. New York: Avon.

Horowitz, R. 2001. *Boys and Their Toys? Masculinity, Class, and Technology in America*. New York: Routledge.

Horrocks, R. 1994. *Masculinity in Crisis: Myths, Fantasies and Realities*. New York: St. Martin's Press.

Kimmel, M. 1997. "The Contemporary 'Crisis' of Masculinity in Historical Perspective." *The Making of Masculinities: The New Men's Studies*, ed. H. Brod. Boston: Allen & Unwin.

Kondo, D. 1998. *About Face: Performing Race in Fashion and Theater*. New York: Routledge.

Lamont, M. (ed.) 1999. *The Cultural Territories of Race: Black and White Boundaries*. Chicago: University of Chicago Press.

Lamont, M. 1992. *Money, Morals, and Manners: The Culture of the French and American Upper Middle Classes*. Chicago: University of Chicago Press.

Lamont, M., and M. Fournier. 1992. *Cultivating Differences: Symbolic Boundaries and the Making of Inequality*. Chicago: University of Chicago Press.

Lareau, A. 2003. *Unequal Childhoods: Class, Race, and Family Life*. Berkeley: University of California Press.

Lightfoot, C. 1997. *The Culture of Adolescent Risk-Taking*. New York: Guilford Press.

Mac An Ghaill, M. 1994. *The Making of Men: Masculinities, Sexualities and Schooling*. Buckingham, UK: Open University Press.

Macdonald, N. 2001. *The Graffiti Subculture: Youth, Masculinity and Identity*. London: Palgrave Macmillan.

McDonald, K. 1999. *Struggle for Subjectivity: Identity, Action and Youth Experience*. Cambridge: Cambridge University Press.

Mead, G. H. 1934. *Mind, Self & Society: From the Standpoint of a Social Behaviorist*. Chicago: University of Chicago Press.

Messner, M. 1992. *Power at Play: Sports and the Problem of Masculinity*. Boston: Beacon Press.

Meyer, S. 2001. "Work, Play, and Power: Masculine Culture on the Automotive Shop Floor, 1930–1960." In *Boys and Their Toys? Masculinity, Class, and Technology in America*. Roger Horowitz (ed.). New York: Routledge.

Muggleton, D., and R. Weinzierl (eds.). 2003. *The Post-Subcultures Reader*. Oxford: Berg.

Namkung, V. 2004. "Reinventing the Wheel: Import Car Racing in Southern California." *Asian American Youth: Culture, Identity, and Ethnicity*, ed. Jennifer Lee and Min Zhou. New York: Routledge.

Nomura, G., R. Endo, S. Sumida, and R. Leong (eds.). 1989. *Frontiers of Asian American Studies: Writing, Research and Commentary*. Pullman: Washington State University Press.

O'Connell, S. 1998. *The Car in British Society: Class, Gender and Motoring, 1896–1939*. Manchester: Manchester University Press.

Rubin, L. 2004. *Families on the Fault Line: America's Working Class Speaks about the Family, the Economy and Race and Ethnicity*. New York: HarperCollins.

Shackleford, B. 2001. "Masculinity, the Auto Racing Fraternity, and the Technological Sublime: The Pit Stop as a Celebration of Social Roles." In *Boys and Their Toys? Masculinity, Class, and Technology in America,*. Roger Horowitz (ed.). New York: Routledge.

Takaki, R. 1989. *Strangers from a Different Shore: A History of Asian Americans*. Boston: Little, Brown.

Thorne, B. 1993. *Gender Play: Girls and Boys in School*. New Brunswick, NJ: Rutgers University Press.

Thornton, S. 1997. "The Social Logic of Subcultural Capital." *The Subcultures Reader*. Ken Gelder and Sarah Thornton (ed.). London: Routledge.

Vallas, S. 2000. "Symbolic Boundaries and the New Division of Labor: Engineers, Workers and the Restructuring of Factory Life." *Social Stratification and Mobility* 18: 3–37.

Vinitzky-Seroussi, V. 1998. *After Pomp and Circumstance: High School Reunion as an Autobiographical Occasion*. Chicago: University of Chicago Press.

Weis, L. 1990. *Working Class without Work: High School Students in a Deindustrializing Economy*. New York: Routledge.

Wu, F. 2002. *Yellow: Race in America beyond Black and White*. New York: Basic Books.

39

REUBEN A. BUFORD MAY AND KENNETH SEAN CHAPLIN

CRACKING THE CODE: RACE, CLASS, AND ACCESS TO NIGHTCLUBS IN URBAN AMERICA (2008)

Reuben May and Kenneth Chaplin did their participant observation in the nightclubs of the college town Athens, Georgia. They use their position as observers to show how anti-black discrimination unfolds in Athens nightlife and how it is experienced by black men in the scene.

Urban sociologists have long considered the interesting ways individuals in cities negotiate public space.... Some... have introduced race as an important consideration for the evaluation of strangers—i.e., the anonymous other—in urban public space. Most notably, Anderson (1990) considers how the presence of black males influences the ways in which individuals negotiate urban public space. Anderson is particularly concerned with how white urban residents, who may occasionally encounter black males on the urban streets, determine the intent of the anonymous black male. Understanding the intent of the anonymous black male, who has been generally characterized as a predatory criminal (for a description see Duneier 1992; Pain 2001), takes on special significance when fluid spatial boundaries permit heterogeneous groups to move in and out of the same social space. Despite rich alternative depictions of black males and their lives (e.g., see Duneier 1992, 1999; Anderson 1999; Venkatesh 2000; May 2001a; Wacquant 2004; Young Jr. 2004), the prevailing public view of young black males is that they are engaged in an oppositional culture which takes criminal activity and violence as its main dictates (Anderson 1999).

One strategy that those who negotiate public space use when frequently encountering young black males in the public streets is to absorb the "vocabulary and expressions of the street" and learn the meaning of certain styles of dress (Anderson 1990, p. 231). For instance, city dwellers often use appearance—including clothing styles—to evaluate the presence of others within a setting. They base their evaluations on the kind of individuals they expect to see in particular social spaces (Lofland 1973; Lofland 1998; Simmel [1903] 1971). Thus, styles of dress, embedded with symbolic clues about social identity, become cultural mandates for action (Lamont and Molar 2002). Given negative perceptions of young black males and the symbolic meanings associated with certain styles of dress, it is important to examine the use of dress codes for controlling access in urban settings.

While many passersby perceive nightclubs as urban public spaces accessible to all, these spaces are in fact privately owned with restricted access. Owners may limit access to individuals who meet specific criteria (May 2001a). In practice most nightclubs are semi-public spaces where access is granted to anonymous individuals who demonstrate the willingness to comply with formal or informal rules for access (May 2001a; Anderson 1978; Bell 1983; Oldenburg 1997). In some nightclubs, for instance, dress codes are used to limit or grant access to individuals. The interpretation of these dress codes for those black males denied access within racially heterogeneous places presents a problematic.

In this paper we explore the context of the downtown nightlife in Athens, Georgia, as a threshold of public and semi-public space in which individuals negotiate dress codes, race, and class. Since black males are disproportionately affected by nightclub dress codes in this context, we focus on their responses. First, we examine the responses

of those black males rejected from nightclubs for dress code infractions. The majority of these black males propose that race is the most significant factor for being rejected from the nightclubs. Second, we briefly contrast these responses to the general experiences of black males who were granted access to the nightclubs. For these black males race was less salient in their general experiences. We argue that there is a fluid relationship between race and class that influences black males' responses and experiences in this context.

We conclude that the nuanced reality of lived racial and class experiences for many young black males problematize the narrow interpretation of what we call a *black cultural essence*. The idea of a *black cultural essence* is suggested in the work of Gwaltney (1980) who argues that blacks, despite being located in various social class positions, share a core black culture because they share a racialized social experience. Steele (1989) has suggested that such a presumption of a shared black culture is rooted in the goals of the civil rights movement that sought to bond blacks together as victims of racism by selecting lower class blacks' lives as representative of blacks' experiences more generally. Thus, being black became contrary to being middle class....

...We attempt to demonstrate how dress codes used at the threshold of public and semi-public space help to illuminate the limits of a *black cultural essence* for various black participants in downtown nightlife. We suggest that some black males are able to *crack the code*. By *crack the code* we mean that an individual has a requisite understanding of the nuances of dress in this context based upon their own class socialization. It is an implicit and explicit set of skills regarding the creation of a "respectable" appearance in Athens nightclubs and society more broadly. The ability and desire to *crack the code* is an important concept for explaining the cultural nexus of race and class. We use this idea to expose how urban styles of dress that have long been associated with being black, are in fact a matter of class sensibility for those young men who *crack the code*.

...We wish to note that dress codes for women and their enforcement are important, but given the complexity of gender and the limited space we have to discuss race and class, we focus our analysis only on men....

Dress Codes

Dress codes are standards of clothing attire employed by a variety of institutions to regulate what individuals wear in particular settings.... Such codes are a means for institutions to establish status, order, and control with minimal conflict. In general, individuals recognize the authority of signs like, "No Shoes, No Shirt, No Service" or "Coat and Tie Required." Although some individuals, because of their social status, may occasionally violate these codes without reprimand, the guidelines tell us who may make use of particular social spaces and how they should be dressed. Beyond their general use as a means of social control, dress codes are also embedded with cultural expectations about taste as reflected in style.

...Individuals and groups select styles of dress "on the basis of their perceptions of their own identities and lifestyles" (Crane 2000, p. 15). Thus, ways of dressing become ways for the wearer to send cultural messages about who they are to those who are assessing styles. Such is the case for black males selecting hip-hop styles of dress.

Styles of Dress and Race

Styles of dress embody cultural cues that help individuals sort out where others belong. As Bourdieu (1984) argues these styles are embedded in tastes as strong

indicators of one's consumption patterns. Particular objects of consumption are encoded with cues that have "meaning and interest only for someone who possess the cultural competence, that is, the code into which it is encoded" (Bourdieu 1984, p. 2). Individuals' tastes are guided by their habitus, which "organizes practices and the perception of practices" (Bourdieu 1984, p. 170). The selection of particular styles then becomes a sort of cultural identity embedded with indicators for both the wearer and those viewing the attire. As Lieberson (2000) demonstrates, individuals evaluate others according to their choice of styles.

The interpretation of particular choices of clothing style by those outside of the cultural milieu poses problems when race is involved. Pattillo-McCoy (1999), in her discussion of oppositional styles of dress associated with gangsta rap, makes this point. She suggests that whites' "stylistic displays are less harshly sanctioned relative to the surveillance of black youth who follow the same fashions" (Pattillo-McCoy 1999, p. 118). The importance of such variance in surveillance is that "the race of the wearer affects the degree to which certain styles are criminalized" (p. 119). Pattillo-McCoy's point is particularly germane when discussing clothing styles that are associated with young black males in urban areas. Those clothing styles, absent a viewer's intimate knowledge of those black males passing on the streets, become a proxy by which others attribute criminal intent to black males (Anderson 1990; Duneier 1992, 1999).

Fashionable among many young urban blacks today are the clothing styles associated with hip-hop culture—a culture that grew out of poor, young black and Latinos' artistic articulations (see, e.g., Rose 1994). These articulations are much like the subcultures of resistance identified among punk rockers (e.g., see Hebdige [1979] 1994), working class "lads" from Britain (see Willis 1981), and Puerto Rican drug dealers in the barrio (see

Bourgois [1996] 2003). In this hip-hop culture, athletic jerseys, baggy jeans, oversized plain white T-shirts, sweat-bands, do-rags (polyester head wraps), "wife beaters" ("tank tops"), and thick gold chains are worn as a means of representing one's identification with that culture. These clothing styles are typically adopted by young, black males in urban areas. Although these clothing styles have made considerable inroads into mainstream consumer culture, they continue to be emphasized internally and externally as a way for blacks to represent a collective black identity (Lamont and Molnar 2001). Interestingly, these styles of dress are the very styles regulated by dress codes in several of the nightclubs in downtown Athens.

Method and Data

We collected the data for this paper using participant observation.... Reuben May—an African American male—collected data from the summer of 2002 to the summer of 2005. He regularly conducted observations in downtown Athens on Thursday, Friday, and Saturday nights between 9:00 PM and 3:00 AM. He wore casual dress, typically a collared, buttoned down or polo style shirt, blue jeans or khaki pants, gym shoes or sandals, and a baseball cap.

May's observations were focused on interpersonal intentions on the streets, in the nightclubs, and at late night eateries. He supplemented these observations with "on the street" conversations with strangers, young men he knew from playing basketball at the local gym, university administrators who occasionally sampled early evening nightlife, and students and former students he would encounter during his late night observational periods.[1] The subjects covered in the conversations varied widely, but the primary research focus was on understanding how individuals negotiated public space with others in downtown Athens.

For most of the time in the field, May recorded scant notes on a small note pad in the seclusion of nightclub restrooms and then wrote more extensive fieldnotes shortly thereafter. In addition to his formal data collection, he also reflected upon informal observations that he had gleaned prior to the launching of the formal project on nightlife in downtown Athens. These observations were made from 1996 to 2002 because he has always been "drawn to the crowds, the clamor, the drinking, the lights, and the overall social interaction" of nightlife (May 2003, p. 443).

Reuben May and Kenneth Chaplin met in the field where they both discovered a mutual interest in the kinds of activities and social phenomena happening in downtown Athens. At the invitation of May, Chaplin—also an African American mate—joined the project and conducted formal data collection for about four months in the spring and summer of 2005. He too made observations on street corners, in nightclubs, and late night eateries. Because he was a graduate student, he also encountered people from the university with whom he had pre-existing relationships. He conducted informal interviews with other graduate students, people he knew from around the university, and complete strangers who were patronizing downtown Athens. He completed notes about his interactions and observations upon his return home each evening. In addition to his formal data collection, he made informal observations of the downtown party scene from 2002 to 2005. Thus, not only is our analysis informed by our three years of combined field research, but also by our twelve years of combined informal observation.[2]

... Our specific focus on dress codes is the result of coding our fieldnotes and discovering numerous instances in which dress codes influenced the use of downtown social space. Furthermore, over the course of the research we had to more purposely consider how our master status as black men meant that our own styles of dress would come under scrutiny at the thresholds of public and semi-public space.

During the spring and summer of 2005 we collected fieldnotes simultaneously. At that time we used a collaborative ethnography approach as outlined by May and Pattillo-McCoy (2000). Essentially, we entered the field separately, interacted both jointly and individually with other participants, and collected and recorded our fieldnotes independent of one another. Our separately recorded fieldnotes produced a larger body of data—from which we could draw on to describe and understand life in the social setting—than if we had been lone ethnographers (May and Pattillo-McCoy 2000). We garnered our fieldnotes on visits to downtown Athens each week on Thursday, Friday, and Saturday evenings and nights.... .

The Setting: Downtown Athens and Night Club Dress Codes

Athens is located in the Northeast region of Georgia, approximately 70 miles east of Atlanta. It is known regionally among southeastern US college students because it is a big-time college town and home to the University of Georgia (UGA) Bulldawgs. Indeed the university is a major drawing force for Athens. It is annually ranked as one of the top party schools in the country and has a rich tradition.... UGA and the city of Athens have an entwined social history based on geography, cherished social associations, and the personal interactions that have occurred between the local Athenian community and the University population over several decades.

Athens has a population of approximately 100,000 residents (US Census Bureau, 2000). When the local colleges and universities in the Athens area are in full session, an additional 40,000 students populate the town. The average age of the residents in Athens is 25. The ratio of male to female population is approximately 49,000 men to 51,000 women. Sixty-five percent of the residents identify as White, 27% as African American, 3% as Asian, and 5% as other (US Census Bureau 2000).

According to the 2004 UGA Fact Book, the student population is about 32,500 students—25,000 who are undergraduates. Most of the UGA students come from the northeast Atlanta area (Cobb County, Fulton County, Dekalb County, Gwinnell County, and Clarke County), and approximately 84% of the students identify as White, 5.5% as foreign nationals, 5.5% as African American, 1.5% as Latino, and 3.5% as other.[4] These demographics significantly affect the interactions and relationships among the local Athenians and the University students in shared social spaces such as downtown Athens.

Downtown Athens, a social hub, is about 21 square blocks. There are approximately 220 businesses, 50 bars—four of them with dance floors—and 40 restaurants. Residential communities on the east, north, and west sides border downtown. To the south stands the University of Georgia. All around the downtown area there is a mixture of student housing, loft apartments, and pockets of subsidized government housing. At nighttime students are commonly seen walking in large groups in well-lit areas because most students are aware of the "dangerous urban pockets" where criminal activity and poverty exist. Despite these dangerous urban pockets, Athens' reputation as a college party town prevails.

The local black population once thought of downtown Athens, with its "hick music," "rock and roll," "drunk white people," and "Bulldawg fans," as a place exclusively for whites. Yet the nightclubs' gradual shift to hip-hop and pop music has drawn more blacks to the area. These local black Athenians are the sons and daughters of blacks who work in various service and manufacturing sectors in Athens. Often, many of the black males that visit the downtown area are from the low-income areas immediately surrounding downtown. Many college students perceive these black males as the anonymous black males—those who are commonly identified in the media as criminal—who are a threat to the social sanctity of downtown Athens. This perceived threat has resulted in increased police patrols, a "no cruising" law, the university admonishing its students to use greater caution in the area, and surveillance cameras positioned on various street corners in downtown.

Black males that stand outside the corner nightclubs clad in the latest hip-hop gear are perceived to pose the greatest threat to those patrons that move from nightclub to nightclub. The clothing styles worn by the young black males have been associated with a violent counter culture (see Hebdige [1979] (1994) for an analysis of other subcultures perceived as violent). The nightclub owners' implementation of dress codes coincided with the increased visibility and presence of young black males.

Most of the dress codes in downtown Athens began appearing in 2002. Their appearance coincided with the closing of the only downtown late night dance club, The Bounce (all names are pseudonyms), designated by the local black population as a place to go out and have a good time. The Bounce had provided a cultural milieu where blacks could share in the dress styles, dance, and interactions associated with hip-hop. When this club which attracted both the local and college black population closed, its patrons sought entertainment in some of the downtown area bars and clubs that played a mixture of music that included hip-hop. Although other nightclubs had regular black patrons, the closing of The Bounce brought greater numbers of blacks to other downtown clubs. This is the context for the dress code implementation.

The dress codes in downtown Athens convey to potential patrons which clothing attire might be grounds for being denied access. They are posted at seven nightclubs that play a considerable amount of hip-hop music: River Run Tap, The Corral, Figaro's, Kilpatrick's, Insignia, Ernie's Cove, and Club Connections. Although these nightclubs have explicit dress codes, some of the other bars may have dress codes but they are not posted because these bars do not play hip-hop music and do not attract patrons who have adopted the style of dress associated with young black males and urban hip-hop culture. Some items restricted by dress codes vary by bar, but the following is a generalized list of garments and accessories consistently prohibited at the seven nightclubs: All athletic jerseys, plain white T-shirts, sleeveless shirts ("wife beaters" or "tank tops"), blue jean shorts, sweat pants, loose or baggy clothes, do-rags, caps turned (other than forward or backward), sweat bands, or large jewelry chains (necklaces). While the list of items is explicit, some of the descriptions leave room for a variety of interpretations. For instance, what constitutes baggy clothes to one individual might constitute "loose fit" to another. In addition to those generalized descriptions of clothing, the dress codes typically end with a phrase like, "We have the right to refuse anyone," "Clothes must fit the atmosphere," or "Any clothes deemed inappropriate."

Some nightclubs have neatly typed, plastic coated signs on plain white paper. The prohibited clothes are listed in regular twelve-point font. Most patrons entering the bars fail to see the listed dress codes because the loud music and flashing lights gleaned from right near the door offer a distraction. These dress codes, however, become fully visible when an infraction is noted by a bouncer who then points to the sign hanging on the wall a few feet from the doorway of the nightclub.

At one bar, River Run Tap, the sign placement of the dress code is inconspicuous.

It is located at the base of an iron gate surrounding the patio of the bar. There is an interesting phrasing of the prohibited jewelry listed on this dark green, type written, plastic coated sign. In addition to listing the other prohibited items, the sign reads. "…absolutely no Mr. T starter kits."[5] The use of the "no Mr. T starter kits" phrase on a professionally printed dress code sign makes light of the serious nature with which some patrons view race as part of the cultural biases of the dress codes.

It is within the context of nightclubs that play hip-hop music and where whites frequent that dress codes are most consistently enforced.…

Interpretive Responses of Rejected Black Males

The dress codes employed by the nightclubs have particular meaning to various individuals who use the bars. The underlying theme for the black males rejected from nightclubs is that the dress codes were put in place by white bar owners in response to the presence of black males, in short, the black males believe the dress codes are racist. This belief is further evidenced by the fact that the black patrons fail to understand why their particular taste in clothing is subject to dress codes, when from a stylistic standpoint, a white T-shirt or an athletic jersey conveys similar social status as the colored cotton T-shirts or polo style shirts worn by white males.

Furthermore, if one were to consider the cost of clothing, according to the black males, they would discover that some of the black males' clothing is more expensive than clothing worn by the typical white male. Indeed, in our own investigation we discovered that the average cost of the authentic athletic jerseys worn by some of the black males was between $100–$300, whereas the polo style shirts, such as Izod

and Ralph Lauren, worn by the white males cost between $50–$80. Still, the dress codes are enforced against only the types of clothing frequently worn by black males. This fact leaves many black patrons believing that the dress codes are directed against blacks. For instance, Joe, an undergraduate senior from UGA, responds to being rejected from Figaro's. He is from a largely black metropolitan area in central Georgia. May, the first author, knew him from informal interactions in the student union.[6]

I had been standing on the corner just after 12:00 AM. The crowd had swelled. It was warm out and folks were dressed in shorts and short sleeves all about. I watched as Joe attempted to enter Figaro's wearing a red collarless shirt, blue jean shorts, and white tennis shoes. The bouncer, a white male, motioned to Joe's shorts. Joe turned around frustrated without even talking and walked toward the corner where a group of black males had gathered. I was standing in front of the group wearing what Chaplin and I call "all access" gear. I had on a yellow, collared, buttoned down, short sleeve shirt, khaki shorts and sandals. The group of black males standing just behind me wearing an assortment of hip-hop clothes. When Joe looked up and saw me I said, "What's up man?"

He looked frustrated, "Nothing, man." We shook hands as he continued. "They're tripping over at Figaro's."

"What do you mean?" I asked.

"They wouldn't let me in with blue jean shorts," Joe said. "You know a lot of places have their guideline, you know, the dress code. But to me it just seems like it's to exclude blacks from coming in," he said.

"Why does it seem like that?" I asked.

"The dress code policy or whatever is basically, no jean shorts, no athletic wear, no jewelry, no excessive jewelry. Anything that's like, in reference to the hip-hop culture is excluded. You know what I'm saying, it's excluded from downtown but at the same time they wanna play all the hip-hop music, you know what I'm saying. But they don't want black people in the club. It's like a contradiction. They can play the music, but we can't dress the part. You know."

Joe observes that there is an apparent contradiction in the use of dress codes in the downtown nightclubs. According to Joe, club owners wish to play the music that originates from urban blacks, but yet they do not accept urban styles of dress that are closely associated with blacks. To Joe, this is a direct way to limit blacks' access to the social spaces that play hip-hop music.

There are many instances that appear consistent with Joe's assessment that the dress codes are about race. For instance in Chaplin's fieldnote two black males whom he did not know are rejected for dress code violations.

It was around 11:00 PM and I was standing near the door of Figaro's just observing the people passing and cantering the club. Two black males walked up and Ron, a white bouncer, refused access to them. One black male was wearing long baggy, blue sweat shorts, a large royal blue T-shirt, a do-rag, baseball cap, and gym shoes.
I went up to the black male and asked him. "Ain't you going in?"
He said, "I can't. They said I had to have khaki shorts to get in."
The other black male with him decided not to go in because his friend could not get in.
They both looked frustrated as if to convey a taken-for-granted sense of, "you know what this is about."

In this instance the black males were being rejected for dress code violations. From an objective standpoint the young men's dress did not fit the requirements for access to the nightclub. Yet, both of the black males looked at one mother and Chaplin as if to convey a universally understood idea that black men are under greater scrutiny than others. To them, they were being rejected for more than just their lack of meeting a dress code. As Chaplin continues with the interchange, he garners evidence that would suggest that the men's nonverbal cues indicating frustration for being rejected because they were black were in fact merited.

About the time that I was asking them about going in I noticed two white males leaving through the other door of the bar. The two white males were both wearing polo styled golf-shirts. One was wearing his hat backwards, and the other no hat. Both of them were wearing blue jean shorts. One had dark blue jeans and the other light blue jeans.

Perhaps if the black males had seen the white patrons exiting they might have asserted with more confidence the idea that they were victims of racial discrimination. Irrespective of such confirmations, explicit proof is not necessary for black males to assert that they have experienced an instance of racial discrimination.

During the same evening Chaplin observed two additional black males, also not known by him, that were rejected at Figaro's. These black males provide their perspective about the dress codes and what those codes mean to them.

A few minutes later two additional black males walked up to Figaro's. One was wearing a sweatband around his head, and the other was wearing a do-rag. I asked them after they were talking with the bouncer, "Dog, they not gonna let you in?"

He said, "Uh naw. You know, I ain't tryin' to go in. You know what I'm saying. This is white folks town. I'm from Atlanta, you know. This is their town. You have to play by their rules. I ain't even trying to sweat that shit tonight."

The patron's explicit reference to Athens as "white folks' town" suggests that he has accepted downtown Athens as a public space for whites. Given this context, the patron chooses not to "sweat it" or engage in confrontation about the dress code because such confrontation would be useless for gaining access.

For those black male patrons rejected at the door for dress code violations, there is a heightened degree of humiliation and frustration associated with being rejected. These emotions are heightened when those black males rejected witness that white males are given access even when their clothing does not fit the dress code. For instance, in May's fieldnote below Harry recounts being humiliated and frustrated by being rejected when he saw that others, who apparently did not meet the dress code requirement, were given access. Harry is from a small town in west Georgia and grew up in a low-income area of that town. He became acquainted with May as a student in May's class several years prior. Harry shares his recollection of the previous night's events while standing with May on the corner in front of Kilpatrick's, The Corral, and Figaro's.

I stood on the corner talking to Harry about hanging out last night. He told me that he had come out and gone around to different nightclubs, but that he was wearing blue jean shorts and couldn't get in. He said, "I got so frustrated yesterday man. Shit, these bouncers wouldn't let me in. I had some blue jean shorts, and I had been to a couple of places—Kilpatrick's, The Corral, and Figaro's. I couldn't get in the other places so when I finally got to Figaro's and they wouldn't let me in,

I was like, 'Man, this is it. I'm tired of this shit.' I was so frustrated that I stood right by the door counting the white boys they let in. They must have let about six white boys in with blue jean shorts. I was like fuck and I just left."

For Harry, the dress code enforcement is clearly about race. His experiences throughout the previous night made him particularly frustrated by the fact that some white males were given access when they were also wearing blue jean shorts. Without intimate knowledge of why these white males had been accepted given their dress code infraction, Harry was left taking their admittance as prima facie evidence that dress codes were specifically enforced against black males.

While black males' claims that dress codes are being enforced in a racially discriminatory manner might seem unfounded to some viewers of the dress code, these complaints occur within a broader context in which blacks must evaluate everyday slights that deal both implicitly and explicitly with race (e.g., see Feagin 1991; Feagin and Sikes 1994; May 2001a, b). Thus, the black males' adamant claims that they are being rejected on the basis of race are legitimate given their overall experiences with race.

Despite these examples of black males being rejected from nightclubs, there are black males who do gain access. The presence of these black males within the nightclubs raises an interesting question: If the dress codes are strictly about race as some black males interpret, then how is the presence of black males within the nightclubs to be explained? . . .

Experiences of Black Males Granted Access

The groups of black males standing out front of nightclubs clad in their hip-hop gear provide visual evidence that the dress codes are enforced against styles of dress typically associated with black males and hip-hop culture. These black males generally protest to one another arguing that the nightclub owners are racist. Still, many black males frequent the nightclubs that some have suggested are racially discriminatory in granting access. As one might suppose, those black males who have gained access to the nightclubs have chosen styles of dress that are inconsistent with hip-hop dress. These black males are dressed like their middle-class white counterparts who have chosen polo style shirts, khaki pants or shorts, flip flops, or other articles of clothing associated with middle-class college students. Furthermore, these patrons typically view the dress codes as the prerogative of owners who have the power to make the decisions about who comes into the club.

Typical comments made by these black patrons are like those made by Derrick. Derrick is a regular patron to nightclubs in Athens that use dress codes. He also speaks as a person who frequents all-black nightclubs in Atlanta where there are also dress codes implemented by black nightclub owners and enforced by black bouncers. He once commented to May about the dress codes, "The nightclubs are not racist. It's just insurance against letting the wrong kind of people in. You know, the kind of people that start fights and stuff."

Terrell, another regular to downtown Athens nightclubs with dress codes views the use of dress codes somewhat differently. He also attends UGA and had previously been rejected from nightclubs because he enjoys wearing clothes that are part of the hip-hop style of dress. He said, "They might have come up with dress codes that target clothes worn mostly by minorities, but if you wanna get in, you gotta confront. You gotta put on your collared, buttoned down shirts. That's reasonable." For Terrell, it matters little whether the nightclub owners are motivated by race because the owners have not asked the patrons to meet an unachievable criterion.

Terrell has exhibited the ability to *crack the code* by using an implicit and explicit set of skills regarding the creation of a "respectable" appearance in downtown Athens. First, for one to *crack the code* they must demonstrate the ability to perceive the nature of the dress codes. They must appreciate the taste sensibilities of the nightclub owners who are creating, implementing, and having dress codes enforced. Or rather than appreciate these taste requirements, they must be willing to discard the implicit notion that they as black men, are the sum of what they wear. In reality this is the central tension between those who gain access and those who do not....

Discussion and Conclusion

Dress codes are used in the downtown nightclubs to indicate which individuals will be admitted to engage in the nightclub activity. These dress codes are presented as objective standards of dress. Yet, their implementation, enforcement, and interpretation are based on subjective meanings and understandings for those who enforce the dress codes and those subjected to dress code enforcement....We have been concerned with the responses of black males who are disproportionately represented among those individuals rejected from nightclubs. We have cast their responses in contrast to the experiences of these black males who have gained access to the nightclubs. It is in our analysis of black males' responses and experiences with the enforcement of dress codes that we have located the complexity of race and class....

Race is a key characteristic for how individuals relate to others. It is the basis upon which individuals reject or accept others in particular contexts. There are few contemporary examples in which race is viewed with greater importance than in the evaluation of black males in urban public space.

As indicated in other urban ethnographies, black males are typically viewed as predatory criminals (see discussions in Duneier 1992, 1999; Pattillo-McCoy 1999; Anderson 1999; Venkatesh 2000). This notion, affirmed by negative racial stereotypes of black males in the media, reinforces black males as a threat (May 2001 a, b). Given this, it is easy to see how partygoers to downtown Athens might regard the presence of black males within that urban public space. Furthermore, it is reasonable to surmise why nightclub owners created the dress codes if the presence of black males, as represented by those who wear hip-hop clothing, was presumed to negatively impact their business ventures. Additionally, given the possible attitudes of partygoers and nightclub owners, it is easy to see why those black males rejected from nightclubs view this rejection as a matter of race.

The implementation of dress codes, surveillance cameras, and no cruising laws correspond with our own observations of increased use of downtown public space by blacks. These policy changes provide the context for concluding that race is the impetus for increased social control. Indeed, we observe that this idea is consistent with the interpretations of those black males rejected from nightclubs. But if those black males who are rejected because of race are correct, then how do other black males get inside? Perhaps those black males who evaluate the enforcement of dress codes as solely about race fail to consider how a social class sensibility, as reflected in nuanced taste in clothing, may affect their ability to gain access.

We suggest…that class in the context of downtown Athens most frequently manifests as a matter of taste. One assumption regarding class differences is that those individuals from middle-class backgrounds share tastes quite different from those of the lower class.[7] These subtleties of taste are conveyed both implicitly and explicitly and are made sharper though a variety of

institutions that reflect one's social class experience (Bourdieu 1984; Lieberson 2000). Thus, the styles of dress that one chooses are a manifestation of their social class background. For the black males who wear hip-hop clothing—generally associated with the black urban poor—they are knowingly or unknowingly subjecting themselves to nightclub dress code enforcement. Thus, their rejection from the nightclubs in downtown Athens is based on the evaluation of both race and class.

Such evaluation is complicated by the prevalence of black middle-class youth who adopt the hip-hop clothing styles associated with the "street" identity of the lower class. Like the cultural omnivores identified by Peterson and Kern (1996), these black middle-class youths become samplers of cultural styles originating with the black urban poor. Perhaps this phenomenon can be explained by the close proximity to which the black middle-class lives to its lower-class kindred (Pattillo-McCoy 1999). These communities become places where the nuances of race and class are hybridized through taste. According to Pattillo-McCoy (1999) this creates a dynamic where "every generation of black youth has been influenced by some form (and usually many forms of ghetto-based cultural production)" (p. 120). An additional explanation for black middle-class youths' adoption of these styles could be related to an "increasingly ubiquitous mass media" that has "introduced the aesthetic tastes of different segments of the population to each other" (Peterson and Kern 1996, p. 905). Thus, black middle-class youths may have appropriated their styles from the mass media presentation of hip-hop culture.

Irrespective of the source, the black middle-class youths' adoption of these clothing styles problematizes the presences of black males in urban public space. Some onlookers are left wondering whether those wearing, for instance, athletic jerseys are part of the black middle class whose members are generally regarded as civil, or the black urban poor whose members are generally regarded as predatory criminals. Indeed, the conclusions drawn by observers in the city matter. A miscounting of the cultural cues being conveyed can be merely embarrassing or have detrimental consequences for both the assessor and the assessed (Anderson 1999; Pattillo-McCoy 1999; Venkatesh 2000). Yet, in most everyday occurrences a reading of such cultural cues is only important for access to particular social spaces.

We...found in the context of downtown Athens that there are some black males who recognize the cultural cues of style associated with middle-class sensibilities. They are able to *crack the code* because they exercise a sense of taste that includes the acceptability of dress commonly associated with that of the broader middle class. They have learned, as a basic part of their socialization, that athletic jerseys might help them identify with their black urban kindred, but clothes like polo shirts and khakis are necessary clothing to indicate tastes to others. Thus, when these patrons are asked to give up their athletic jerseys, white T-shirts, do-rags, or other clothing associated with hip-hop culture, they do not perceive it as an attack on their racial identity. Rather, they regard this request as a matter of taste and not a matter of race.

Alternatively, black males who refuse to relinquish hip-hop styles of dress to gain access to the nightclubs seem to subscribe to a constraining notion of a *black cultural essence*. That is, for instance, the belief that being black is defined by a very specific cultural taste in dress. Thus, to relinquish these styles of dress is to conform to "white" standards. In this instance, clothing styles such as do-rags, athletic jerseys, sweat bands, tank tops, and blue jean shorts become essential identity markers for what it means to be black. Given the internal and external emphasis placed on such items

as being part of a collective black identity (Lamont and Molnar 2001), it is easy to see why giving up one's style of dress is like giving up one's *black cultural essence*.

Yet such definitions restrict individuals' complex lifestyles to conceptions of race that are grounded in a lower class experience that historically had been related to a majority of the black population. Thus, the nuanced reality of lived class experiences for many blacks today is lost in contexts where race is interpreted to equal class by a variety of observers (see also Jackson 2001). Ultimately, the tension between race, class, and taste problematizes the idea of a *black cultural essence*....

NOTES

1. Downtown Athens is a social space used predominantly by college-age patrons, but occasionally May would encounter older university administrators or other professors in the area. These patrons usually departed downtown before the 12:00 AM hour and typically patronized only restaurants or drinking establishments that targeted more mature patrons. For a more detailed description of May's encounters with other patrons and his discussion of how he negotiated multiple identities see May (2003).

2. We note that although our analysis is based primarily on the data gathered by May, this paper is developed through the synthesis of our ideas derived from our discussions and written communications about black males' responses to the dress codes.

3. Population & Demographics (2000), Athens-Clarke County Information (Electronic Version). Retrieved May 20, 2005, from the US Census Bureau (Electronic Version) at http://factfinder.census.gov.

4. *The University of Georgia 2004 Fact Book* (Electronic Version), retrieved May 24, 2005, from http://www.oir.uga.edu/factbks.htm.

5. The Mr. T notation makes reference to a black actor who is most known for his role

as Sgt. Bosco Albert, "B.A." (Bad Attitude), Baracus, in the 1980s television series *The "A" Team*. On the show Mr. T played the role of a gruff, hyper-masculine, aggressive member of a military Special Forces Unit. Mr. T demonstrated irrational phobias and contributed little to the intellectual process of planning an attack. During his public appearances Mr. T wore several large gold chains around his neck. Thus, the sign indicating "no Mr. T. starter kits" suggests that patrons may not be permitted in the nightclub if they have a single gold chain that is presented to be a beginning to subsequent gold chains.

Although it might seem that this generation of partygoers might be unfamiliar with Mr. T, their knowledge of such entertainers and television programs from the 1980s is based on the constant replay of television programs, music, and videos from this time. The themes and actors from the 1980s are re-appropriated by these college viewers. In fact, there were several 80s music theme parties held in downtown Athens. We observed at these parties that college students collectively sang the lyrics to songs that were popular before the college students had been born.

6. It is important to note that given the under-representation of African American male professors at most universities, they are highly sought after by black students to participate on panels, act as mentors, and for general advice. Thus, May had come into contact with many African American students from his general campus involvement. Indeed, these relationships sometimes become over extended and have been cited by senior faculty as additional responsibilities that typically hinder junior faculty from attaining tenure.

7. Here we use the nuanced notion of class based on John Jackson's (2001) conceptualization of class. Jackson indicates that class "is not just education or occupation, income or wealth, but lifestyles—skills and cultural practices—that distinguish and determine classes" (p. 63).

REFERENCES

Anderson, E. 1978. *A Place on the Corner.* Chicago: University of Chicago Press.

Anderson, E. 1990. *Streetwise: Race, Class, and Change in an Urban Community.* Chicago: University of Chicago Press.

Anderson, E. 1999. *Code of the Street: Decency, Violence, and the Moral Life of the Inner City.* New York: Norton.

Bell, M. J. 1983. *The World from Brown's Lounge: An Ethnography of Black Middle-class Play.* Urbana: University of Illinois Press.

Bourdieu, P. 1984. *Distinction: A Social Critique of the Judgment of Taste.* Cambridge, MA: Harvard University Press (translated by Richard Nice).

Bourgois, P. 2006 [1996]. *In Search of Respect: Selling Crack in El Barrio.* New York: Cambridge University Press.

Crane, D. 2000. *Fashion and its Social Agendas: Class, Gender, and Identity in Clothing.* Chicago: University of Chicago Press.

Duneier, M. 1992. *Slim's Table: Race, Respectability, and Masculinity.* Chicago: University of Chicago Press.

Duneier, M. 1999. *Sidewalk.* New York: Farrar, Straus and Giroux.

Feagin, J. 1991. "The Continuing Significance of Race: Antiblack Discrimination in Public Places." *American Sociological Review*, 56: 101–116.

Feagin, J. & Sikes, M. 1994. *Living with Racism: The Black Middle Class Experience.* Boston: Beacon Press.

Gwaltney, J. L. 1980. *Drylongso: A Self-portrait of Black America.* New York: Random House.

Hebdige, D. 1994 [1979]. *Subculture: The Meaning of Style.* New York: Routledge.

Jackson, J. L. 2001. *Harlemworld: Doing Race and Class in Contemporary America.* Chicago: University of Chicago Press.

Lamont, M. & Molnar, V. 2001. "How Blacks Use Consumption to Shape their Collective Identity: Evidence from Marketing Specialists." *Journal of Consumer Culture*, 1: 31–45.

Lamont, M. & Molnar, V. 2002. "The Study of Boundaries in the Social Science." *Annual Review of Sociology* 28: 167–195.

Lieberson, S. 2000. *Matter of Taste: How Names, Fashions, and Culture Change*. New Haven, CT: Yale University Press.

Lofland, L. H. 1973. *A World of Strangers: Order and Action in Urban Public Space*. New York: Basic Books.

Lofland, L. H. 1998. *The Public Realm: Exploring the City's Quintessential Social Territory*. Hawthorne, NY: Aldine de Gruyter.

May, R. A. B. & Pattillo-McCoy, M. 2000. "Do You See What I See: Examining a Collaborative Ethnography." *Qualitative Inquiry* 6: 65–87, March.

May, R. A. B. 2001a. *Talking at Trena's: Everyday Conversation at an African American Tavern*. New York: New York University Press.

May, R. A. B. 2001b. "The Sid Cartwright Incident and More: An African American Male's Interpretive Narrative of Interracial Encounters at the University of Chicago." *Studies in Symbolic Interaction* 24: 75–100.

May, R. A. B. 2003. "'Flirting with Boundaries': A Professor's Narrative Tale Contemplating Research of the Wild Side." *Qualitative Inquiry* 9: 442–465.

Oldenburg, R. 1997. *The Great Good Place*. New York: Marlowe & Co.

Pain, R. 2001. "Gender Race, Age and Fear in the City." *Urban Studies* 38: 899–913.

Pattillo-McCoy, M. 1999. *Black Picket Fences: Privilege and Peril among the Black Middle Class*. Chicago: University of Chicago Press.

Peterson, R. & Kern, R. 1996 "Changing Highbrow Taste: From Snob to Omnivore." *American Sociological Review* 61: 900–907.

Population & Demographics. (2000). Athens-Clarke County Information (Electronic Version). Retrieved May 20, 2005, from http://censtats.census.gov/data/GA/1701303436.pdf from the 2000 US from the US Census Bureau (Electronic Version) retrieved from http://factfinder.census.gov.

Rose, T. 1994. *Black Noise: Rap Music and Black Culture in Contemporary America*. Hanover, NH: Wesleyan University Press.

Simmel, G. 1971 [1903]. The Metropolis and Mental Life. In *On Individuality and Social Forms*. D. Levine (ed.). Chicago: University of Chicago Press.

Steele, S. 1989. "On Being Black and Middle Class." *The Best American Essays*. G. Wolff (ed.) New York: Ticknor & Fields.

Venkatesh, S. 2000. *American Project: The Rise and Fall of a Modern Ghetto*. Cambridge, MA: Harvard University Press.

Wacquant, L. J. D. 2004. *Body & Soul: Notebooks of an Apprentice Boxer*. New York: Oxford University Press.

Willis, P. 1981. *Learning to Labor: How Working Class Kids Get Working Class Jobs*. New York: Columbia University Press.

Young Jr., A. 2004. *The Minds of Marginalized Black Men: Making Sense of Mobility, Opportunity, and Future Life Chances*. Princeton, NJ: Princeton University Press.

40

DAVID GRAZIAN

WINNING BAR: NIGHTLIFE AS A SPORTING RITUAL

from On the Make (2008)

David Grazian asked his undergraduate students at the University of Pennsylvania to take field notes about their experiences out on the town in Philadelphia. Supplementing their eight hundred submissions with his own observations and interviews, Grazian reveals how the night is socially constructed. A hustle created by nightclub owners and real-estate developers, nightlife is maintained by individual patrons, especially males, who view their efforts to meet women as a sporting ritual.

... Cultural producers manufacture and promote the nightlife of the city and its glamour by relying on the art of the hustle and its many techniques, including the staging of restaurant and nightclub interiors, the scripting of interactions with customers, the exploitation of attractive women workers, the engineering of creative publicity and editorial placement, and the employment of reality-based marketing schemes. Of course, it would be naive to assume that all consumers blindly fall for these dodgy gambits. Many diners and nightclub patrons are sufficiently wary of the emotion work performed by bartenders and servers, and critical of the sexist procedures used for hiring cocktail waitresses and hostesses. Others are quick to point out the inconsistencies in menu pricing and food preparation, and easily recognize the staged artifice of Pod, Morimoto, and similarly theatrical Starr restaurants and their copycats.

However, just as movie buffs willfully ignore the well-known realities of film production (elaborate scripting and blocking of actors, use of stuntmen and body doubles, multiple takes, computer-generated imagery, sound effects editing) in order to blissfully enjoy their popcorn thrills at the cineplex, nightlife consumers often find that it is also in their best interests to suspend disbelief—all the better to enjoy the excitement of urban glamour, no matter how contrived. More cynical consumers take pleasure in gleefully deconstructing the more transparent gimmickry employed in local hot spots—Barclay Prime's White Castle–inspired Kobe beef mini-hamburgers, or "sliders"; Alma de Cuba's Chocolate Cigar (an almond cake wrapped in chocolate mousse, dusted with chocolate, and served with *dulce de leche* ice cream); Continental Mid-Town's peanut-butter-and-jelly-sandwich cookies—while ironists playfully plunge headfirst into such silliness, lapping at the trough with a wink and knowing smile.

Young consumers experience a variety of contradictory emotions upon discovering the hustle of urban nightlife. Certainly, some club-hoppers (particularly those who are underage) approach Old City's exclusive velvet-roped nightclubs with wide-eyed awe and anxious desperation. They wonder, *How will I ever get in? Can I afford the steep cover charge? Will I get served once I gain admittance? Is this where the city's most beautiful people rendezvous, and am I hot enough to be included in their company?*

Yet in the face of anxiety, plenty of young men and women respond to the exclusionary world of urban nightlife as if it presented a challenge worth subduing. Consequently, they turn their entire evenings into a series of *sporting* rituals, or cultural scripts oriented around competitive gamesmanship and strategic interaction. Negotiating nightlife scenes drives young people to engage in sporting rituals that incorporate the skills of the hustler and the confidence artist. They include the art of imposture through fashion, grooming, and style, and the performance of social status through effective techniques of role performance and theatricality. These sporting rituals demand a reliance on trusted confederates when approaching strangers. They additionally require the targeted deployment of physical dominance and dexterous wit necessary

for buttering up bouncers and bartenders, tactfully sliding through crowds, slipping in and out of conversations, and disarming the most protective of souls. The anonymity of the urban metropolis makes these sporting rituals possible for young people to perform in public, and in some instances may even require them as a condition for participating in the nightlife of the city in the first place.

The sporting ritual represents a kind of hustle designed for negotiating the city at night, and younger people enduring the rocky transition from adolescence to adulthood perform such hustles with varying degrees of skill, and all under tremendous pressure to avoid embarrassing themselves in front of their peers. These sporting rituals include *the masquerade, the girl hunt,* and *winning bar,* and illuminate how young people experience urban nightlife as a rite of passage. The city's downtown entertainment zones—along with their many restaurants, nightclubs, and cocktail lounges—represent an upscale playground where affluent young adults prepare for the postadolescent life by learning, practicing, and refining a set of nocturnal selves and high-status cultural competencies. This playground provides the theatrical backdrop where these young people perform the art of the hustle before an audience of anonymous strangers.

The Masquerade of Urban Nightlife

For most affluent young women, urban nightlife almost always presents opportunities for masquerade. It begins with the everyday strategies of impression management required by contemporary gender norms and ideals of feminine beauty and sexual attractiveness. As Simone de Beauvoir observes in *The Second Sex*, a woman endures many burdens, not the least of which is the expectation that she will exert great effort to adorn herself in her "evening costume" so that she is "disguised as a woman," just as Erving Goffman describes the arduous performance aspects of playing a woman as a "pose," as "a mask of manner." Both remind as that femininity itself is an accomplished performance, and its success requires a great deal of strenuous training, preparation, and expressive control.[1]

Abigail, a nineteen-year-old sophomore, describes her own laborious preparations for an evening at Tangerine by listing off the endless catalog of activities and accessories necessary to pull off such a production:

> I undergo the usual one-hour getting-ready ritual of showering, ironing my hair, and applying my makeup, which all takes a combined thirty minutes. The rest of my time is spent pondering over the most important question of the evening: "What am I going to wear?" After trying on about five pairs of jeans, all Sevens and Diesels but varying slightly in shades of washed-out-ness and having rips in slightly different places, I finally decide on my lightest Sevens. Then I spend the rest of the time accessorizing the outfit with a hot pink belt and fun earrings.... After frantically running around my room collecting my belongings for the evening (the usual—wallet, cell phone, keys, gum, mints, lip gloss, lip liner, and any other makeup that I can squeeze into my undersized but fashionably overpriced Christian Dior handbag), I'm finally ready to go. "Oh shit, what jacket should I take?" I throw about six jackets off my coat rack, [my boyfriend] grabs my long, black, puffy one, and we're out the door.[2]

While women's daywear is notably varied in style, formality, and level of androgyny (particularly on university campuses, where both male and female students commonly wear sweatpants, flip-flops, and baseball caps to class), downtown nightclubs and upscale restaurants demand a more precisely gendered uniformity in fashion.[3] In keeping with those structured tastes and expectations, college women model themselves at night according to high-status feminine norms as expressed through brand-name fashion and celebrity style. While exceptions obviously prevail (as they inevitably do), the standard nightlife attire for women typically consists of "premium" or "luxury" designer denim jeans (currently represented by labels such as Seven, Diesel, and Dolce & Gabbana), dark revealing tops, and impossibly high-heeled shoes.[4] As Cynthia, a twenty-year-old sophomore, remarks on her preparations for dining at Tangerine: "I knew this place was really trendy, so I wanted to dress the part. That includes Seven jeans, a James Perse off-the-shoulder black shirt, and of course stilettos. I knew it was going to be an older crowd, and I didn't want to look like a college student."

The ubiquity of stiletto-heeled shoes among affluent young women merits special attention. In her 1963 exposé "I Was a Playboy Bunny," Gloria Steinem reports on the footwear policy of the New York Playboy Club, a source of Steinem's permanent scars from her employment—including the half-size enlargement of her feet. As her club's wardrobe mistress demanded, "Make sure you get three-inch heels. You'll get demerits, you wear 'em any lower."[5] Decades later in a turnaround that must fill every second-wave feminist with dread, stilettos regained popularity in the 1990s when British designer Manolo Blahnik's oppressive mules were worn by (and relentlessly photographed on) notables from Madonna to Princess Diana and television characters from *Sex and the City, Absolutely Fabulous*, and even the animated sitcom *The Simpsons*.[6] Today high-heeled stilettos once again serve as a common piece of sexual armor in the arsenal of women's nightlife fashions, even among managers. In spite of the protests of some young women—"I don't like wearing heels; I feel uncomfortable; I feel like I am going to fall or something"—others argue that the exaggerated heel size gives a much-desired height augmentation to short women who want to literally level the playing field of the city's nightspots. Speaking in a focus group of sophomores, Cory remarks, "I am just really short...I am five two. People always look down on me. Heels just give me a little help in this department....I just really need the height. Most of my guy friends are six foot two-ish and most of my girlfriends are at least five five—at home most of my girlfriends are five seven; five five—so I definitely need height just to catch up to them, for that reason alone."

Another group of sophomore women led by Lauren, a college senior, associate the erotic properties of the pencil-thin high-heeled shoes with their own coming-of-age: "To me it's mood altering, almost. I feel like stilettos are kind of symbolic of sexuality. Like when I was ten, I was *not* wearing stiletto heels. I distinctly remember what my first pair of stilettos looked like, and I was so happy to have those things it was unreal."

"I think you walk a different way, too."

"Yeah, exactly."

"When you say you walk a different way, what do you mean?" asks Lauren, the group leader.

"It changes, you feel a little more confident."

"I guess part of it is just the way the heel is shaped—you have to walk a certain way when you wear them."

"Otherwise you look like a goofball."

"They make you focus a little bit more on how you are walking than just walking around in flats."

"And like when you are wearing a skirt with stilettos, it makes your legs look better and longer. It's kind of like a confidence booster in a way."

Just as they do with shoes and clothing, young women describe their cosmetic preparations for the masquerade of urban nightlife in strategic terms as well. According to Deborah, a twenty-year-old junior:

Since Continental is a very trendy Stephen Starr restaurant with an average patron age between twenty-five and thirty-five, I had to make myself look older through hair styling and makeup. I applied a white base eye shadow, a light pink shade to the middle of the eyelid, and a dark charcoal shadow at the base of the eyelid. I was taught this makeup trick by my older cousin, who says this is a professional technique used to make the eyes look larger. I straightened my hair with a flat iron and a blow dryer and flipped under the ends of my hair to create an older, more sophisticated look.

In addition to expressing a highly strategic orientation toward her presentation of self, Deborah's remarks are notable for two reasons. First, her confidence in the aforementioned "makeup trick" relies on the merit she attributes to the "professional" (whether real or imagined) basis of the technique and the folk wisdom of her "older" cousin: both suggestive of the authority she invests in adult status (relative to her age and life experience) as an objective measure of one's expertise in the area of gendered impression management.

Moreover, Deborah's attempt at forging a "more sophisticated look" suggests a feminine performance of upper-class status. Like gender, the dramatization of social class requires the accomplishment of a related set of styles, gestures, and behaviors considered culturally appropriate to a given status category and recognized as such in public.[7] Just as young women desire to exude maturity and adult sexuality, and often succeed in spite of their young age and otherwise adolescent appearance in less formal contexts, the enactment of elite class status as a wholly contrived presentation of self is hardly limited to those who hold such lofty positions, as becomes readily apparent in depictions of confidence artists from Patricia Highsmith's *The Talented Mr. Ripley* to reality TV's *Joe Millionaire.*[8]

Still, for the uninitiated, a performance of high-status savoir faire can come off with varying degrees of success. According to Eve, a twenty-year-old junior with plans to dine at Alma de Cuba, attempting such a role without the requisite cultural capital necessary to pull off such a caper presents an array of anxiety-producing challenges:

> During the day on Friday, I couldn't stop thinking about what I was going to wear. I had never been to a place like this before, and no one I knew had ever gone, so I didn't know what would or would not be appropriate. I finally decided that I would wear an aquamarine wool/silk turtleneck, a short, brown tweed-patterned skirt, nude stockings, and brown slingbacks. I had showered earlier that day and straightened my hair, so I only really needed to shower my body, not my hair. After I got out of the shower and dressed, I re-straightened my hair and put on makeup.[9] I wore my hair down, and my makeup was relatively the same as it usually is when I go out, except I wore my lipstick slightly darker (for a more grown-up look). Unfortunately, I did not have a pair of nude tights, so my boyfriend and I had to quickly go to CVS to pick a pair up before we went to the restaurant. I was dashing around and getting strange looks from people as I put them on in the car....
>
> As we were walking up Walnut Street, I could barely keep my shoes on my feet, literally! Because they were slingbacks, they couldn't grip anything because I was wearing stockings. I started to feel like people were looking at me, I started to doubt my "sophisticated" style that night. The

streets were crowded with young adults, and I was feeling like a kid. I shook it off and we finally made it to the restaurant.

For young people undergoing what has become in recent decades an elongated transition to adulthood, adopting a grown-up style is always an inherently risky proposition. This is particularity the case when such an appropriation includes a so-called "sophisticated" wardrobe of short skirts, stockings, and slingbacks borrowed from the glamour-drenched divas and dating games portrayed on popular television shows like *Sex and the City* and *Ally McBeal*, women's fashion magazines from *Vogue* to *Cosmopolitan*, and cheeky chick-lit titles such as Lauren Weisberger's *The Devil Wears Prada* and Plum Sykes's *Bergdorf Blondes.*[10] For Frida—a Chinese-Swedish sophomore going to Red Sky, an upscale restaurant and nightclub in Old City—role-playing represents a self-conscious process of negotiation in which one inevitably settles for seeming at least a little out of place:

> The clientele was definitely older than my nineteen years, and I felt like a little kid playing grown-up. The few men at the bar were wearing slacks and button-down shirts, while the even fewer women wore either dress pants or nice jeans with heels and a nice shirt. No sneakers to be found anywhere. Sophia and I were definitely overdressed for this bar.... We were both wearing cocktail dresses, but I decided that that was better than being underdressed and the youngest person there.

Both Eve and Frida describe the sensation of feeling "like a little kid" even when donning slingbacks or a cocktail dress. In these instances, such attire wears more like a Halloween costume than a well-worn outfit. In fact, for young people "playing grown-up" often involves the contradictory demonstration of juvenile inexperience in a world of adult expectations.[11] Once Abigail (the nineteen-year-old sophomore) and her friends arrive at Tangerine, they attempt to conceal their display of an inappropriate yet all too conventional adolescent faux pas:

> I chose my typical apple martini, never veering from what is an excellent drink choice. I then realized I had gum in my mouth, which is most certainly not a surprise, and had to figure out the most discreet, polite method of disposing of it. [My friends] revealed that they also had gum in their months, and I volunteered to have everyone spit their gum in my hand so that I would have an excuse to [visit] the bathrooms. Okay, so maybe this wasn't the most discreet, polite method, but it worked.

For some young women, the challenge of contriving a more mature appearance is purely expressive and rooted in a desire to achieve a heightened sense of adult sexuality and social status. Strategies of impression management among Penn women range from donning push-up bras to indulging in elective nose reshaping and breast augmentation surgery.[12] But for others, particularly those underage, full-fledged participation in the nightlife of the city additionally requires that they successfully masquerade as twenty-one-year-olds. According to one female student, "I hope that when I go to a bar, people can't recognize me as underage, so maybe that is one thing about when you dress up to go out—I try to be older. When you are going downtown, you want to look older, present yourself as older than you are."[13]

Young women describe a variety of strategies for pulling off such an imposture. Some express the challenge as one of face-work at the moment of interaction with a doorman or bartender. According to Kristen, a junior: "Don't waste a lot of time—act like you belong inside, and not like you are a little child trying to sneak through the doors." Young women also

gain encouragement from their abilities to choose an appropriately "grown-up" cocktail (they cite cranberry vodkas and sour-apple martinis as no-no's), calmly order, and graciously tip their bartender without giving themselves away.

Many young women will additionally manipulate their appearance in order to appear older, whether by laboriously straightening their hair, applying makeup (but not too much makeup, they insist, or else they might look like a "clown"), or wearing expensive designer clothes. In some ways, the effort itself makes them feel more grown-up and conveys to outsiders an expertise in self-presentation, although as Felicia, a sophomore, observes, "You don't want to look like you are trying too hard." Since so many undergraduates rely on counterfeit identification to gain entry into bars and nightclubs, some dedicate their time not only to masquerading as older women, but specifically as the older women depicted in the photographs on their fake IDs. According to Sharon, "With my ID, the girl that's on my ID has long blond hair. So I always make sure my hair is down, and so I at least look like her." To ease this transformation of self, many young women appropriate the driver's license of an older sister or other closely related look-alike. (The familial tie also makes it easier to remember the name and address on the ID, just in case the bouncers quiz them.)

For others, the challenge of the masquerade is interpreted more explicitly as one of sexual display. Just as when wearing cosmetics, upon choosing their nighttime apparel, young women must walk the narrowest of tightropes in their attempts to dress in sexually attractive attire without coming across as stereotypically "trashy" or "cheap" in public according to middle- and upper-class norms of propriety.[14] Nevertheless, for underage nightlife consumers, access remains a paramount concern, which often encourages pandering to the sexist expectations and discretions of male bouncers and security guards. According to Carol, a sophomore, "I've actually noticed that the way I am dressed sometimes makes a difference. Like one night I went out wearing a T-shirt and jeans and a blazer—definitely a cute outfit—but my cleavage was not *out* in any way, and I got denied twice using an ID that I always get in with. And then on other nights, it's like not even a problem when the boobs are out." Felicia acknowledges the persistence of this sad state of affairs: "If you are wearing a low-cut shirt, you have a much easier time getting in. It's true—sometimes they won't look at your ID as much....Lower-cut shirts, higher skirts, higher heels..." Or as Mandy, a junior, remarks of many male nightclub bouncers, "Show a little skin and be a little flirty, and then they don't care."

Male Vanity and Metrosexuality

If these young women unfortunately seem to conform to a stereotype of the urban female as overly concerned with her appearance, they hardly differ much from their heterosexual male counterparts. Just as Abigail, the nineteen-year-old sophomore, juggles multiple pairs of Sevens and Diesels, Ryan, an upperclassman, describes his hierarchy of dungarees suitable for eveningwear: "I have different levels of jeans. I have expensive jeans that I'll basically just save for the nights when I go downtown that I won't ever wear around [campus]." Bill, a twenty-year-old sophomore, challenges typical assumptions about the carefree slovenliness of the modern straight man:

After my shower, I headed back to my room to change, and as is often the case, I tried on four pairs of pants and five button-down shirts before selecting my "choice" outfit. My choice of clothing was determined by the following: Before even attending Denim [a Rittenhouse Square nightclub], I was under the impression

that it was one of Philadelphia's premier social scenes. I went with a blue, yellow, and green Burberry button-down shirt, gray flat-front pants from Express Men's, a lucky pair of Hawaiian shirt-style boxers, and black Prada shoes.

Like similarly aged women, a weekend night on the town presents itself to young men as a kind of masquerade as well. By dressing up "without the glasses" and in a "messier, higher, and spikier" hairstyle, Evan, a straight twenty-four-year-old senior, jokes that his expensive attire and application of fashionable facial products suggests a transformation of self that makes him "feel like Clark Kent and Superman":

I showered and put on my gray Diesel jeans and white long-sleeve undershirt. Over my long-sleeve shirt, I chose to wear my stone-gray and navy blue–trim Asics T-shirt, that says "Onitsuka Tiger Japan" on the front. I put on my contacts and unscrewed my orange peel molding crème hair product—controlled messiness, with the front part of my hair really high and spiky. I slid on my retro ACG Nikes and went back to the bathroom for the final touch. Which cologne? Dolce & Gabbana, or Creed?[15]

Affluent young men prepare for their evenings out by crafting a highly stylized and tirelessly groomed performance of sexuality, in this case one deemed attractive to young heterosexual women.[16] According to Tyler, a nineteen-year-old sophomore:

When I go out, I love meeting new people, especially those of the opposite sex. With this in mind, I take pride in getting ready before I go out. I try to wear certain clothes and scents that are palatable to females. This process includes taking a shower, putting on deodorant, aftershave lotion, cologne, and my "clubbing clothes," which are comprised of jeans and a dark collared shirt. The process of getting ready usually takes anywhere between ten and twenty-five minutes.

Tyler is confident that his preparations are well worth the trouble: "Back at the club I was very thankful that I spent a good amount of time getting ready because there were some very good-looking women." But even as men rely on some of the same exact strategies of impression management as women, they try to distance themselves from what have traditionally been considered feminine grooming activities.[17] For instance, since dressing up is not necessarily compatible with conventional visions of masculinity, men will often expend much effort to contrive a "devil-may-care" look, as if their appearance requires no preparation at all. According to Sammy, an eighteen-year-old freshman:

> I showered, gelled my hair, applied deodorant and cologne, and gargled Listerine: the next step was getting dressed. I am not nearly a trendy guy; however, I do recognize that my attire reflects my personality and image to some extent, so I am careful when deciding what to wear. I picked out a recently purchased long-sleeve, button-down Tommy Hilfiger shirt and a pair of khaki pants. I had a white T-shirt underneath, and I left the top button open, giving me the desired "I don't care how I look" image.

Edward, a twenty-year-old sophomore, cynically describes his preparations for a night of club hopping with his friend Jordan by emphasizing the strategies of impression management necessary to pull off such a feat, apologizing each step of the way:

> Jordan and I go way back. He is the kind of kid whose insecurities manifest in him trying to make himself as trendy and fashionable as possible. He is what is commonly referred to

as "metrosexual." Jordan was wearing designer jeans with strategically placed tears and some burgundy shirt that looked like a hybrid silk-and-velvet material. All this was topped off with a strategically placed wristband (which I refused to let him wear). Judging by Jordan, he dressed for the club in a manner that made him look as wealthy, hip, and attractive as possible from the assets he had.

> Upon critiquing Jordan I realized I fell into the same category. I also tried to make myself look as nice as possible with the limited wardrobe I had. I wore a pseudo-designer shirt, jeans (that I stole when I worked for Abercrombie), and a pair of nice black shoes....Our dressing styles represented a microcosm of male American men trying to ingratiate themselves to a more affluent lifestyle and social group. It didn't so much concern us that we were becoming part of a stereotype, because in the end you have to dress this way if you want to get laid. I hadn't hooked up with a girl in a couple of weeks, and I needed to break my slump (the next girl you hook up with is commonly referred to as a "slump-bust" in my social circle). So I was willing to dress in whatever manner would facilitate in hooking up.[18]

In his strategic preparations for meeting women in the city at night, Edward only tentatively embraces what he refers to as the slickly stylized guise of a so-called "metrosexual" since it contradicts his vision of an appropriately *hetero*sexual masculine performance. As reported in the *Washington Post* a metrosexual "is a straight man who styles his hair using three different products (and actually calls them 'products'), loves clothes and the very act of shopping for them, and describes himself as sensitive and romantic. In other words, he is a man who seems stereotypically gay except when it comes in sexual orientation."[19] At the very least, Edward is willing to forgo a more rugged, detached performance of manhood in exchange for success at "hooking up," for him the ultimate expression of masculinity, particularly as filtered through the collective expectation of his collegiate peer network.[20]

Gay men are often stereotyped as being more concerned with body image and fashion sensibility than their heterosexual brethren and certainly many internalize these social expectations. According to Bradley, a gay nineteen-year-old freshmen:

> My night began at 10:30 P.M. on Wednesday when my friends came over to my room…but my preparations for my evening began before that. Earlier that night I had gone to the gym to work out. I knew that if I wanted to look like anything close to all those guys that look perfectly toned and like they just stepped out of the gym, I would need to lift some weights before I went to Woody's [a downtown gay bar]. With the intense obsession with body image that is rampant in the gay community, I often feel the pressure to have that "perfect body" or something close to it if I want to pick up a guy when I go out. I got back from the gym at 10:00 P.M. and took a shower. After meticulously picking out what I was going to wear and trying it on for my next-door neighbors, I was ready.

However, while women and gay men are generally stereotyped as being more concerned with fashion and grooming than their straight male counterparts, their habits are not as different as one might suspect. In fact, the metrosexual look is fairly common among straight and gay affluent young men, just as a wide range of men have popularized other formerly gay signals (such as wearing earrings in both ears). In my one-on-one interview with Miles, a gay junior who is also a member of a traditional campus fraternity, he revealed that straight male students wear designer jeans as often as women and gay men, and similarly take their time preening for a night out:

> It's surprising how pretty fraternity boys are, in terms of how much time they take to get ready. I mean, having lived in the house, I definitely know they take just as long as I do. So it's not related to sexual orientation at all—or maybe it is, and they are all just repressed. But they wear the same stuff.…They definitely wear "designer." Not like "designer" in the sense of high-end designer, like Dolce & Gabbana or one of those fashion houses, but better than mall stores—in between the two. Especially at a place like Penn, where people seem to be much more conspicuously consuming what they wear, where everything is a parade, the guys definitely do wear very expensive clothes out. And not all of them, certainly, but a lot of them, and certainly the ones who are of that scene, the hip scene, the cool scene, because if you know where to go, you also know what to wear, right?
>
> All of them spend a significant amount of time getting ready, and certainly go through nearly the same steps. I will say that I am probably more conscious of it than they are, in terms of my appearance and how I look. I definitely feel much more aware of that than they do, in my mind. But at the same time, they have all the same stuff—most of it is, in fact, nicer. They are all Easterners, so I guess they are accustomed to that whole thing, but they do the same thing with the face washes, and the creams, and the hair gel.…But anyway, when they get dressed, I think they are actually very similar to women in terms of the stereotype. They will pick out several outfits.…I don't know who trains single straight men to behave in the way that they do, and then also to cover up for it. But they definitely

do…even in our bathroom. It's weird in our apartment: whereas my stuff is all out, theirs is all put away, like it can't be seen, especially the high-end stuff. I mean, the stuff where they spent like $40 on some face wash and that gets put away.…And they don't really talk about it, except to like say, "Look, I am like you, Miles, it's like I'm gay—I'm using face lotion."

Many men (straight *and* gay) explicitly identify their elaborate preparations as overtly feminine and thus socially stigmatized to the point where they obligate themselves to defend their decision on the basis of their sexual pursuits.[21] As Jay, a twenty-one-year-old junior, reports:

It was to be a good, long night of partying, starting with dinner and ending with dancing. I got ready for the night in my usual way. I took my normal twenty-minute shower to start, and then tried on several outfits before deciding on a nice pair of jeans with a button-down shirt and aviator glasses to top it off. I put on my trusty old sport deodorant along with Polo Blue cologne (the ladies love this stuff) and a little wax-based hair stuff to keep my hair lively throughout the night. I brushed my teeth, tied up my shoes, grabbed my jacket, and headed out with two of my roommates. Some may call my grooming habits feminine, but hey, how are you supposed to attract women looking and smelling like a slob?

John, a twenty-one-year-old sophomore preparing for an expedition to Club 27, an Old City dance club, is similarly defensive while explaining his elaborate strategies of impression management:

I use Coconut shampoo, a particular favorite of one of my closest lady friends. I then pull out the razor and shave from my chest down past the mid-region. (It just looks better and feels smoother—don't judge me.) I shave my face, put on some mild aftershave and two sprays of Cool Water cologne, and brush my teeth. I perform all of these minor tasks with the future goal in mind of bringing back a girl, or multiple girls if I play my cards right. I run back to my room and put on the dark blue Banana Republic shirt along with my boot-fit blue jeans to accentuate my eyes.

Likewise, according to Jake, a twenty-three-year-old senior on his way to Finnigan's Wake, an Irish-themed bar, on a Friday night:

I started my evening off around 7:30 P.M. by showering and shaving and picking out my finest Abercrombie size small shirt that I could squeeze into. (My normal shirt size is a large to an extra large.) It's a bad fashion habit of mine—buying shirts that probably would have fit me when I was in third grade—but it's always good to look as buff as possible when you're going cruising for girls downtown. I always catch crap from my friends for this, but at the end of the night with a couple of new phone numbers in my phone, I don't seem to mind.

The Pregame Show

After these cosmetic preparations for the night out have been made, young men and women commonly hunker down for the collective ritual known among American college students as "pregaming." Harry, an eighteen-year-old freshman, explains:

Given that this was a Tuesday night. I would not be accompanied by my usual cast of characters.…That didn't stop my other friends from drinking with us before leaving in what has become a sacred ritual, known as pregaming." Pregaming consists of drinking with

your boys so that you don't have to purchase as many drinks while you are out
to feel the desired buzz. On top of being
cost-efficient, the actual event of pregaming can get any group ready and excited
to go out.

Students usually describe pregaming as an
economical and efficient method of getting
drunk on shots of bottom-shelf vodka, cans
of Keystone Light, cardboard boxes of Franzia
white zinfandel, and all other varieties of bar-
gain-basement booze before going out into
the city. Although colleges and universities
have been cracking down on pregaming over
the last several years, students continue to
work around such measures.[22] Once again,
according to Edward, age twenty:

> Jordan and I wanted to drink before we
> went out for three reasons. First, we are
> broke college students. Money is at a pre-
> mium. So we wanted to drink alcohol in
> my dorm where it is cheap, as opposed
> to buying one beer for the price of five
> at the club. Second, drinking lowers your
> level of inhibition.... When I go out at
> night, I am typically a lot more affable,
> approachable, and charismatic. Alcohol
> facilitates my transformation into a more
> gregarious person. Last, we had an hour
> to kill before we were going to leave.
> Drinking seemed like a fun way to pass
> the time.

Edward defends pregaming for its utility: the ritual provides an efficient means of
getting drunk *cheaply*, in order to offset the
costs of drinking downtown; insures that
one is drunk *prior* to going out in public,
thereby decreasing their inhibitions; and
offers a convenient means of *stalling* the
more formal proceedings in order to hit the
downtown scene at an optimally exciting
time. Yet I would argue that something also
is going on as well. For many young people,
partying downtown may prove anxiety-producing since it entails the risks that come
with breaking the law (at least for underage drinkers); negotiating the city at night
and its anonymous world of strangers; and
handling the stress generated by meeting
new people, particularly potential sexual or
romantic partners.[23]

Shown in this light, the goals of pregaming make a lot more sense. If interacting
in public ordinarily fosters anxiety among
young people, then some students may
imagine that alcohol provides the liquid
courage to relieve them of their nervousness. But more importantly, the pregame
provides young people with a ritual of solidarity designed to engineer cohesion within
their peer group, in order to mentally prepare them to negotiate the human traffic of
city nightclubs and bars, just as players on
an athletic team might warm up together
before a sporting contest. In the company of
their friends, they are able to build up their
confidence; the alcohol may start the party
early, but ultimately it is the *sociability* of the
gathering itself that lowers the anxiety associated with the challenges surrounding the
experience of urban nightlife.[24]

For this reason, young people often
structure the pregame around a series of
competitive drinking rituals that while
evidently designed for the efficient delivery of excessive amounts of alcohol to the
brain, also function as machines for generating camaraderie and collective unity
among participants, even as their behavior
becomes increasingly slovenly and antisocial. Some students engage in racing contests by "shotgunning" cans of beer, while
others join in a decidedly dangerous Power
Hour in which contestants chug a shot of
beer per minute for one solid hour—often
in sync with customized music mixes that
flip songs every minute. (An extended version of this vomit-inducing game called
Century Club requires drinking a shot per
minute for one hundred minutes.)[25] Other
contests turn common parlor games into
alcohol-soaked competitions, such as Beer
Pong and Beirut (both variants on table

tennis), Quarters (in which players bounce coins into a shot glass), or Kings (played with a regulation deck of playing cards). According to Thomas, a twenty-one-year-old African American junior, even informal coed drinking involves an organized pattern of action—lined-up cocktails, familiar toasts, and the use of nicknames geared to express intimacy among partners in crime as they nervously await the pressures of city at night.

> I don't enjoy the club scene very much—I am too shy to approach strangers on the dance floor, and I don't like to pay the cover charges just to be a wallflower.... Knowing that I normally don't go to the clubs, [my friends] begin to plead with me to go. I only consent because another one of my housemates is going, so I will have a wingman once they start dancing by themselves.... I am contemplating not going, but Jason convinces me that going to the club and having a good time is exactly what the doctor ordered. So, it is on to Phase Two of my preparty activities—relaxing the nerves with a little alcohol.
>
> I pour out the correct number of shots of either the cheap vodka or the equally cheap rum, and line them up on the table. Everyone grabs their shot glass and waits for a toast to be offered. The first toast is a silly sorority saying: "This is to being single, seeing double, and sleeping triple!" It elicits lots of happy cheers from Johanna and her girlfriends, while Chris, Reefer, and I just down our shots.... Whenever we start drinking, we start using each other's nicknames. So as we continue to pound four or five shots, Jason becomes "Reefer," Chris becomes "Belly" or "Macho Man Savage," and I become "B. Jizzle," or "Jizz" for short (and it is a long story how I got that nickname that has absolutely nothing to do with what it sounds like it does).

Winning Bar

...Upon arriving at their destinations for the evening, young men...rely on a series of strategies for gaining entry to entertainment venues in the face of legal and emergent barriers and for negotiating the confrontational human traffic of excessively crowded public places. Just like adults, young people do not always enact these strategies in a self-conscious manner, and their tactics are usually less successful than originally anticipated. Nevertheless, the anonymity and competitiveness among strangers in the city makes the implementation of at least *some* types of strategic action both desirable and necessary for participation in scenes of urban nightlife, at least for these consumers.

Of course, these methods for achieving entry vary in degree of craftiness and sophistication. At the lower end of the spectrum, Edward, the twenty-year-old sophomore, describes what he refers to as his "'hot girl' strategy":

> Dominic persuaded us that there were the most girls at Finnigan's Wake. He dropped us off there. Much to Jordan's chagrin, it was time to test out if his ID would work.... I was permitted in, but Jordan was not.... The battle was lost, but the war was still to be won. We walked the block and a half to Tiki Bob's Cantina. This time we were fortunate enough to walk behind one really attractive girl and her two friends. The bouncer almost let us in because he thought we were with the girl. But she was quick to dispel that myth, and we were sent outside again. Seeing that beautiful girls seemed to have more clout with bouncers than bad fake IDs, we decided to find some girls before we tried our luck at the next establishment.[26]

Jam-packed queues of eager would-be patrons signal a nightclub's fashionableness and exclusivity, which is why half-crowded establishments artificially burnish their desirability by preventing customers from entry under false pretenses. As these audiences wait in vain behind velvet ropes, the gathering queue showcases the club's inflated popularity to sidewalk passersby. Moreover, the extended wait increases anxiety among nightlife revelers, who impatiently wonder if they will ever get to the head of the queue to eventually gain the admittance they crave. Similarly, in his comparison of police techniques and confidence games, criminologist Richard A. Leo reveals how detectives purposely make their suspects stew in a secluded interrogation room for fifteen minutes before joining them, with the goals of augmenting their anticipation and anxiety level while simultaneously persuading them of their insignificance to the proceedings at hand.[27] Joey, an eighteen-year-old freshman, emphasizes the challenge of achieving entry to Red Sky while waiting on a queue of young warriors with stone faces but nervous bellies:

> Once in front of the club, no matter if you were mad at someone or not, no one really communicates with each other. I looked around and saw each kid I had come with—each of them was peering around and checking out the whole situation outside the club. Most of them had this mature and stern look on their face. I believe they were trying to look older so that they would get into the club. Everyone always gets a little nervous before getting into a club, and so no one really talks, just a lot of fidgeting. You always think that you're the only one that won't get in, and then what are you going to do?
>
> I could see that each person was worrying only about himself and whether his/her fake ID would work. While the line moved up, we finally reached the front door. I witnessed a number of people try to make small talk with the bouncers running the club, really just trying to get in good with them. The bouncers looked stereotypically Italian and muscular, with gold chains and slicked-back hair. A couple of kids got laughs out of the bouncers and were let in. I tried to listen to what they were saying in the hope I could figure out something clever to say, but it's almost as if I froze. I couldn't think of anything quick-witted, so I figured I would try my usual—look cool and try not to stand out—which usually worked for me. I made sure not to look the bouncer right in the eye. I moved quickly into the club, but the bouncer stopped me and asked me my date of birth and my street address. I quickly rattled them off with perfection. I then said a couple of things in Italian because I am now enrolled in Italian 120 at Penn. I lied and told him that my dad is Italian and is from Milan. He didn't say anything but looked down at me, and let me go. He said in my ear, "Don't drink too much, buddy." I didn't respond and walked straight into the club, and gave a huge sigh of relief.

American nightlife establishments are caught in a bind as they are legally prohibited from serving affluent college students younger than twenty-one years of age—the very customers who possess the sort of disposable incomes, lack of familial and occupational responsibilities, and flexible waking hours that encourage unrestrained spending on excessively indulgent drinking, thereby contributing to heightened bar revenues. Given that according to the University of Pennsylvania's Office of Health Education, 37 percent of Penn students (not including abstainers) enjoyed the majority of their alcohol consumption in bars and restaurants in 2001–02 (whereas only 17 percent of students did so in fraternity and sorority houses), it would appear that—at least in Philadelphia—local drinking establishments often turn a blind eye to underage drinking.[28] During [a] Barclay Prime staff meeting…one of the managers explained why university students in particular may occasionally be given preferential treatment at expensive restaurants as well as shady nightclubs in Philadelphia:

> While we are on beverage, just some clarification here. As we get more popular, Starr Restaurant Organization restaurants are a draw to specifically University of Pennsylvania students. We need to be aware of our responsibility, legally, to not serve underage guests. My experience often has been that when someone tries to present a fake ID or get drinks, that sometimes we get indignant—we forget that we were once under twenty-one or used to get carded. *They may not be of age to drink now, tonight, but at some point they will, so we want to treat them courteously.*

Yet despite the potential revenue represented by affluent and spendthrift youth, service employees throughout the city share near-universal disdain for Penn students. As is common among college populations enmeshed in typical town-gown animosities of this sort, Penn students find themselves consistently singled out as an undesirable class of consumers assumed to be crippled by a combination of clumsy naïveté and upper-class snobbery. According to Jason, who recently tended bar at a restaurant just off the university campus:

> They are assholes. They are! They are elitist.…. The problem is, and I guess it comes with the Ivy League territory—they feel like they are above us, especially waiters. Waiters are there to serve, and yeah, they are, but you don't have to be an asshole about it, and they are very *good* at being assholes about it.… Penn people, they are socially retarded. They don't know how to act. That's the biggest indicator: they don't know how to act. It's like

being in that environment is so alien that they act out of place.… It's like if you are not Ivy League they don't know how to deal with you because that's their world, and I guess some of it is being eighteen and being at an Ivy League school thinking, somewhat rightly so, "Oh, I am better than these people."[29]

Of course, Penn undergraduates are not necessarily distinguishable on sight from affluent students attending other local elite colleges and universities like Swarthmore, Haverford, and Villanova. (In this manner, the Penn student unfairly emerges as an imaginary boogeyman, stereotyped as characteristic of all obnoxious collegiate behavior in Philadelphia.) Consequently, when bouncers admit students of *any* university into their venues, they frequently treat them with condescension, even those of legal drinking age. Drew, a twenty-one-year-old junior, observes, "One club we went by, 32 Degrees, had a cover charge and it was past 1 A.M. already. We told the guy we weren't going to pay for less than an hour of being in there, and he said something about how 'we should go home then and play our Nintendo.'"

Remarks like these only add to the nervousness of college students attempting to gain entry to popular nightspots. Moreover, many nightclubs in the city enforce a prohibitive dress code that forbids clothing popularized by young black men but celebrated as a staple of global youth culture—long T-shirts, tank tops, baggy pants, athletic attire. For instance, at Tiki Bob's Cantina, a nightclub on the outskirts of Old City, their dress code, one employee revealed, "No Timberland boots, no jerseys, no hats, no sweats…*no ghetto*." Given that young people representative of almost all races, ethnicities, and class backgrounds wear these kinds of clothes on a regular basis, such policies grant club bouncers and security guards a great deal of discretion when denying admittance to young patrons on the basis of appearance.

In and when young men actually do gain admittance to a bar or nightclub, next they must maneuver their way through drunken crowds to place their order at the bar. This endeavor often entails bumping into strangers and their precariously balanced cocktails along the way, only to be rebuffed by a busy bartender who cherry-picks his customers based on their recent tipping histories. As Jason explains, "I bought two drinks the other night, and it came to $14. I gave the bartender a twenty, and I told her, 'Keep it.' It was the right thing to do. Number one, if I want anything else, that bartender is coming back. Because when you get tipped well, you pay attention upfront. You can even lower your tip ratio as the night wears on—as long as you have that upfront hit, that's what the bartender is going to pay most attention to."

I ask Jason, "When you are a bartender, do the tips keep you..."

"Attentive? Yes, if I know I am getting money, damn straight—whatever you want is going to be like *that*, even if I have to hop over other people."

For this reason, *all* newly arrived anonymous customers suffer a long wait for service during crowded weekend evenings at downtown bars and nightclubs, particularly university students whose reputation for being stingy (or more likely inexperienced) tippers precedes them. In the midst of this idle waiting, the defensiveness displayed by young men at this crucial stage of the evening cannot be underestimated. This is particularly the case when they are in the company of a desirable female companion, as illustrated by Allan, a nineteen-year-old sophomore, attempting to remain composed while ordering liquor illegally at Tangerine:

> Our waitress had not made it to our table, and we became suspicious. Was she ignoring us because we looked young, and hoping we would get the hint and leave? Were we not Tangerine caliber? Or maybe she was just busy? We discussed the possibilities and remained steadfast in our positions. Finally, Cassandra informed as that she would be our waitress for the night. I was thinking, "No shit," because she was the only waitress in the room. She asked us what we wanted to drink, and we asked her for a menu. We were reluctant to send her away, fearing she would take another twenty minutes to come back, but she was speedy this time. We had our fake IDs ready and were hopeful that they would work.
>
> Eliza decided to order the house drink, the "Tangerine" (ingredients consist of tangerine puree, vanilla vodka, and a splash of club soda). I asked for a dry martini, assuming they had a house gin to make it with. I ordered a martini in order to look cool, and I ordered it dry because I wanted to look like I knew what I was talking about. "Vodka, or gin?" she wanted to know. I chose gin. She inquired, "What kind?" I chose Bombay. She replied, "Bombay, or Bombay Sapphire?" I asked her if I said Bombay Sapphire, because if I didn't, I probably meant Bombay. She asked, "With olives?" I wanted to wring her neck! This bitch! This stupid bitch is treating me like a fucking idiot! I know what a fucking martini is! I said, "Yes." What she assumed is that I knew nothing about alcohol. What she did not know is that I have my bartending license and knew perfectly well that unless specified, martinis come with gin, not vodka. I also knew that I should take this question as a condescending insult, unless I was just being analytical, and she was the one who did not know what she was talking about...fucking idiot.

Losing his cool, Allan dramatizes what should otherwise seem to be an easily forgettable encounter by interpreting, the server's behavior as deeply patronizing—although as I was informed by Allison, the cock-tail waitress at Tangerine, management requires *all* employees to follow the same inquisitive script when taking martini orders. "Gin or vodka? Up or on the rocks? Olives or a twist?" Allan's internalization of this imaginary drama with Cassandra soon snowballs to include his fellow patrons:

> There was a couple who looked our age.... They sat symmetrical to us and reminded me of us. Diagonal sat five Indian males and one girl. They were dressed like they had just come from a club and were abnormally loud. By the bar some new couples stood. They paced about, and all looked like they owned the place. Black pants seemed to be a requirement, as did greasy hair with frosted tips. The bar posse was having a group discussion, while us "tables" kept amongst ourselves.
>
> Were they cooler then we were? Probably. Everyone seemed to be confident and purposeful, and their purpose was to win. To win the game of—*bar*. I told this to Eliza.... We decided that *bar* is a game that people at Tangerine play. Each person tries to sit with their legs crossed the longest, be the most attractive, and sip their drink the sexiest. Eliza and I were los-ing, as we were still waiting for our drinks—she for her Tangerine, and I for my dry martini made with gin, not vodka, branded with Bombay, not Bombay Sapphire, garnished with olives.

The irritation that emerges from Allan's perceived competitiveness among his fellow strangers for situational status is palpable as he later reports, "We wanted to talk to people but were intimidated by their drive to win *bar*. So instead we just continued to chat with each other." Yet this is a familiar trepi-dation among strangers in close physical proximity to one another in upscale public

settings, and a reason why nightclub cus-tomers typically do not converse with one another across groups of friends even when excited by the charged atmosphere provided by the pleasure of their collective company. Patrons thrive on the social energy gener-ated within crowded public spaces, but only if the nuisance of undesirable face-to-face encounters does not shatter the illusion of invulnerability provided by their vaguely bounded interpersonal comfort zones—as Allan yet again illustrates:

> Eliza began to tell me the story of her first love, and I got bored. I remembered that I had wanted to rub my fingers through the beaded curtain to my side, and I did this. The guy who was part of the couple that reminded me of us also did this. We both sat listening to our partners talk, and let the cold small beads massage our hands. I was perfectly happy and never wanted to part with the beads. I began to compete with the other person finger-ing the beads, and I was winning. I was making the curtain wave more and was gentler with the beads at the same time. My bead nemesis gave up and stopped playing with the beads. So did I.

The choice of terms here—"competing" for beads with a "nemesis"—is laughably hyperbolic yet provocative. Is Allan's goal to become King of the Beads, to win at bar? Allan wants to reign victorious, but he is doubtful. "I felt honored to be a part of such a seemingly high-class group of people. I felt elite. I felt like I could afford $10 drinks and become a regular at Tangerine, and one day maybe even win bar! But in my heart I knew this was not true."

In fact, the competition inherent in win-ning bar can become so heated that large clusters of men will direct such rivalries inward as close friends compete among themselves by trying to one-up each other for the smallest of hierarchical status gains. According to Allison:

Most of the time when I get a group of guys, they are all trying to outdo themselves in some way. If someone gets a Jack and Coke, the next guy is getting whiskey on the rocks with a *splash* of Coke. Then the next guy is getting a Manhattan, on the rocks. And the next guy is just getting straight whiskey or bourbon on the rocks. Stuff like that. Or someone orders an Amstel Light. Well, the next guy has got to have a Heineken; the next guy's got to have a Stella Artois; and the next guy's gona have a Fin du Monde [a Belgian-style ale brewed in Quebec]. He's never had it before; he doesn't know what to expect—he doesn't know how to pour it. It's a mess because he'll start pouring it and then it'll start foaming out.[30]

Sometimes the combativeness among male patrons grows decidedly more impassioned. This particularly occurs among strangers engaged in ambiguous and confusing encounters rooted in testosterone-fueled competitiveness and a desire for risky action, as symbolized through interpersonal confrontations with strangers in public.[31] According to Karl, a twenty-two-year-old senior attending a sorority-sponsored party at Plough and the Stars, a popular Old City bar and restaurant:

There were tables scattered around the large floor, but most people were standing since it was fairly crowded. I attempted to move up toward the bar with my friend, but apparently during this voyage I kept bumping into a girl behind me. This was a complete accident, which I think was quite clear, but her boyfriend (or whatever he was) got upset that I was "knockin' his girl." I apologized to the girl, but in so doing went to touch her arm as I was apologizing. This seemingly benign gesture got the boyfriend even more heated, so he pushed me a little and suggested that I "keep walkin'" and warned me not to "touch his girl no more." Rather perplexed by this encounter, I did.

Hollywood films feature plentiful barroom brawl scenes, but in real life bar fighting occurs with much less frequency than one might otherwise predict. There are a few reasons for this. First, alcohol-related violence tends to be concentrated within specific neighborhoods, types of establishments, and bar environments. In several studies a number of environmental variables have been correlated with barroom aggression, including crowd density, the presence of competitive games (e.g., billiards, pool, darts) and illegal activity, poor ventilation, smoky air quality, high noise level, dirtiness, hot temperatures, and a preponderance of male employees, particularly bouncers.[32]

Additionally, as sociologist Randall Collins argues in his book *Violent Interaction*, a very low percentage (typically 15 percent or less) of almost any population known for violent behavior—soldiers, police officers, bar brawlers—actually carries out that violence. Although men who do engage in bar fighting and carousing might desire to perform masculinity through physicality, they often only begin fights in public settings in which there is a greater chance the fight will be broken up before it spirals out of control beyond the first punches; perhaps for this reason barroom aggression rarely escalates into incidents involving significant physical injury. Moreover, the emotional energy required to jump-start a bar brawl quickly dissipates after the fight concludes—making it highly unlikely that a second fight will come off in the same bar later in the evening.[33]

Perhaps because of this latter set of reasons, the moments of conflict that do emerge in nightclub settings tend to reveal abrupt yet flighty displays of aggression and bravado during moments featuring highly ambiguous signaling among male participants: a spill of the drink or gentle shove against one's arm in a crowded pub; a barely stolen glance at another man's girlfriend across a poorly lit dance floor; an oblivious cutting of a restroom queue. These moments of ambiguity typically occur in high-traffic areas of nightclubs and bars where opportunities for physical interaction are most likely to occur (whether accidentally or intentionally), such as dance floors, gaming and service bar areas, entrances and exits, parking lots, and sidewalks alongside venue doors.[34] Given the density of potential targets of aggression as well as available audience members, these crowded spaces conveniently provide enterprising young men with the opportunity to dazzle friends and onlookers by displaying situational dominance against a genuinely startled victim, all as a self-conscious performance. According to Sid, an upperclassman describing a particular evening out, "I mean, there were no actual fights or whatnot, but so many times I think things would come down to people, usually guys, trying to impress girls....I would see guys pushing—you know, because it's crowded—to get a drink, and if a guy pushes a guy the wrong way and it's one of those types of guys who decides he is going to make a scene and draw attention to himself, he'll like, first of all, make sure there are girls around before he does it, like 'Hey man, come on, what are you doing?' and a shove or a shoulder or something. Those are things that I see the most of—things that (in my mind anyway) it's pure trying to be macho and impress people."

Male nightlife patrons commonly antagonize one another in drunken bouts of competitive braggadocio in which the sources of these contests are generally devoid of substance, often farcically so. On the crowded streets of Old City on a Thursday night, Nancy, a twenty-one-year-old Chinese senior, reports on such an encounter, laden with empty threats and overblown bluster:

> We were rounding the corner to go to Plough and the Stars, when Brian tried to change the subject and said that he was planning to go to Atlantic City on Saturday. We were passing a group of maybe ten people. They were mostly white except for one Asian male....Brian walked by, saying, "I wanna go to A.C.,"

and the Asian person, drunk, overheard and butted into the conversation, yelling to his friends, "Hey, they want to go to A.C. They think they're going to win some money." We were rounding the corner, and Brian kind of nodded and moved the drunken person out of his way. Maybe seven feet ahead, we felt water hit our feet. The Asian fellow was mad that Brian ignored his comment and flung the water from his water bottle at us. We turned back surprised; his group of friends was holding him back. My other friend James kept on saying, "Ain't that some shit?! He was such a wuss. If I wanted to hit someone with water, I would have walked straight up to them and thrown that water at them, to not miss. I wanna hit him so bad. If I wasn't here, and was anywhere else but here, I would have socked him!" That group ended up catching up to us. The Asian fellow with his four white friends kept asking us about A.C.

Typically these kinds of incidents speedily deflate into a soft whimper rather than all-out fisticuffs, and frequently the violence that opponents *do* inflict is of a purely symbolic nature—a kind of chest beating performed after the dramatic confrontation has safely played itself out. According to J.J., a senior discussing bar fighting with his fraternity brothers, "The only time I did have a fight with a bouncer, I was at the Irish Pub on Chestnut Street and they had a tank of something at the door and I was really drunk with a bunch of my friends, and I tried to steal it....It was like a gas tank, a nitrogen tank. It was heavy, but I was with a couple of my friends and we were all really drunk....We tried to steal it, and the bouncer accosted us and was basically very threatening—threatened to break my arms, et cetera, or call the police. Of course, we ran away, came back, and took a piss on the door."

Much literature on urban violence suggests that the desire for physical confrontation with strangers and its attendant heroics often emerges out of the peer influence generated by interpersonal dynamics within small groups, whether college pranksters, inner-city youth gangs, or even networks of male friends residing in middle-class suburban areas.[35] But often young men desiring the risky action provided by open confrontation in public spaces may do so despite (and perhaps in some instances *because of*) the more risk-averse orientations of the group majority. According to Julian, another upperclassman:

> I have a few friends who can be real sloppy. Like they get beer muscles a little bit. I mean it doesn't come out all the time, but like every once in a while we'll have a little incident or something and just for, I guess, for no reason other than to just try to be funny and humorous and impress some people, they'll start with somebody.... They'll just say something usually just mocking someone else in the room or something, and they'll say it loud. I mean, it's never really gotten to the point where there has been a huge, crazy, physical altercation or whatever. And usually the rest of us that are there will just be like, "Shut up, you're being an asshole, just relax."

There are good reasons why risk-averse group members might frown upon the confrontational behavior of a fellow member: his aggressiveness may mistakenly signal to other groups of men spoiling for a brawl that his *entire group* is interested in pursuing the initiation of violence, thus making his friends collectively susceptible to attack. In the event that the pugnacious group member does find himself amidst physical conflict, conventional codes of honor among American men may require his friends to protect him from harm and perhaps join in the fray themselves. In fact, it is common during barroom incidents for participants to change roles from conciliator to aggressor as conflicts progress—or quickly *devolve,* as is generally the case.[36]

The Pickup as a Sporting Ritual

While every romantic comedy may suggest otherwise, the challenges of meeting total strangers in public—even on a platonic basis—can be insurmountable, particularly as young adults age into their late twenties and beyond. As Avram Hornik, a local bar and nightclub owner in his thirties, observes: "It's not appropriate [to approach strangers], even in a public space. Some people walk up and say, 'Hi, my name is Joe,' and it's out of the blue—walks up and introduces himself to people. *Five* percent of people can pull that off—you have to be the right person.... If you go to a wedding, you can pretty much walk up to anyone and say, 'Hi, how are you? I am a friend of the groom.' At a bar you really can't—you don't know why that person is there, so you may not be able to do that. Or you have to be able to do it in a subtle way, where you get a signal whether or not it's appropriate or inappropriate. So some people are good at it; some people aren't.... In general, at this age I have established who my friends are and who aren't. When I go out, I am not looking for another best friend."

Jason agrees. "I think it's a bigger problem than the bar scene. I mean, we are so compartmentalized in our lives that we don't know how to meet people.... And how quickly do you want to get personal with people? I think that's a big impediment to meeting people. How much do you want to give up about yourself with somebody you just met at a bar?"

"In what kinds of circumstances do strangers talk to each other in bars and nightclubs?" I ask.

"All right, the most common is the guy hitting on the girl, to varying degrees of success. I guess if you add a little alcohol, people will loosen up a little bit. But then, *how do you go about it?* If you are attracted to someone, how do you open that up? As a bartender, they've got to come to you, so you instantly have the opening. But if you are on the other side of the bar, it's a lot harder.

"I think that everybody's got a comfort zone. Adding alcohol will stretch your comfort zone, but only so far. Approaching anyone you don't know is a fairly tough proposition. Just like cold-calling, it's tough. It's hard—you've got to have some kind of connection, some kind of connecting point. Especially with these larger places, people go out in their crowds as insulation, to look like they know everybody, ever though they don't know *anybody*. So you are still being seen, and you are seen being social, but you are talking to the same eight people that you always talk to. But to everybody else looking...nobody knows if you have known each other for a long time, or if you have just met."

In a context in which the expectations of meeting singles are significantly greater than the average nightclubber's actual potential to do so, rituals of deception and guile often appeal to even the most otherwise upstanding of individuals, especially considering how little is actually at stake. For instance, according to an unpublished paper by economists at MIT and the University of Chicago, Internet daters regularly lie about their physical appearance. Less than 1 percent of both men and women describe themselves as having "less than average looks"; men report heights that are one inch taller than the national average, while women underreport their weight (compared to the national average) by a difference of twenty pounds for women in the 30–39 and 40–49 age ranges; and women are far more likely to identify their hair color as blond or auburn than are men. As Jennifer Egan reports in the *New York Times Magazine*, "Most online daters have at least one cranky tale of meeting a date who was shorter or fatter or balder or generally less comely than advertised. Small lies may even be advisable, by dropping a year or two off her age, a 40-year-old woman will appear in many more men's searches, and the same is true for a man shorter than 5-foot-11 who inflates his height even slightly."[37]

In the face-to-face dating world of pickup bars, these measures are difficult to fake (except for natural hair color, of course); however, singles still find a wealth of personal characteristics about which to exaggerate, including age and occupational status. While conversing with other patrons, underage men sneaking into bars will create an identity for themselves in order to appear old enough to legally gain entry and pass as equals among older and more nature customers.

"I just tell them I am in graduate school or something," explains one male student. "I just graduated from Penn or something like that. Something modest, so they don't ask me something like, "Oh, I am a ———, too!' and ask me some question. So I usually try to keep it pretty simple." In other instances when faced with an older pool of strangers, affluent college men will falsely claim to be investment bankers, as revealed in a discussion among a focus group of fraternity brothers.

"I definitely did that once, down at Alma de Cuba. I was there with another fraternity and two of my other friends: we talked amongst each other, and we came up with a storyline that we were investment bankers at Commerce Bank. And we proceeded to talk to these four girls and they believed every part of it. It was pretty funny."

"Why did you choose that story? What were you trying to get out of it? What made it funny? What made it work?" his fraternity brother (and my research assistant) Andrew asks.

"We were all in suits, so we figured it might as well be something business-related and...I don't know, they asked us what bank we worked for, we hadn't really come up with much of it, and my friend just said 'Commerce Bank' randomly, which is pretty funny, and we just went with it.

"As far as posing, I was in Georgia for spring break and I met this woman who was working as a nurse, and I told her that I work for Merck. I thought that she would find it interesting, and women generally tend to sleep with older men anyway, who are a couple years older, like three to four years older. So I've done that only once."

"And it was to actually sleep with her, ideally?"

"It was to sleep with her. It was over spring break, and it was to basically get laid."

"Did it work?"

"It worked, yeah."

"Have you been with other guys…[who have] posed as people who they are not?"

"Oh yeah, some of my fraternity brothers were at a club downtown down in Florida, and some of them were investment bankers, and I think that particular person uses that ruse pretty often."

"Why does he use the ruse? How does he go about using it? Are there support roles or is it just him out there as an investment banker?"

"He does it, I think, because that is probably what he is going to become when he graduates, and he likes the whole sexiness of the job. And there are support roles, usually some other fraternity brothers will come and persuade the fine young lady that he is actually an I-banker."

"So it's generally to get the girl in the end?"

"Yes."

On less frequent but likely more memorable occasions, physically robust college men will try to pass themselves off as professional athletes. According to one male undergraduate:

A couple of my friends, they were down in Florida for spring break and they said they played for the Eagles, and this girl totally believed them…and the other guys, the smaller guys were their agents and stuff, and they totally had this girl going.…Just because I think they found her kind of naive, and they are big guys, like three hundred pounds, two-ninety. So they thought it would be funny to make stuff up to see if she believed it.…She just kept buying them drinks. It was weird. You would think that professional athletes would be paying for the girl's drinks.…They just wanted to make up a story that was funny.

Many young men are single-minded in their heterosexual stalking of women as a sporting ritual and employ a philosophy of strategic gamesmanship to enliven their pursuit. Brian, a nineteen-year-old Caban sophomore, refers to the game as a *girl hunt*:

Whether I would get any girl's phone number or not, the main purpose for going out was to try to get with hot girls. That was our goal every night we went out to frat parties on campus, and we all knew it, even though we seldom mention that aspect of going out. *It was implicitly known that tonight, and every night out, was a girl hunt.* Tonight we were taking that goal to Philadelphia's nightlife. In the meanwhile, we would have fun drinking, dancing, and joking around [emphasis added].

Young men consistently remark on the girl hunt as a strategic and competitive goal of going out, and some discuss their attempts to successfully interact with women (while besting their male rivals) as if explaining the relationship between predators and their prey. According to Joey, the freshman who talked his way into Red Sky:

Once I reached the dance floor, the first thing I noticed was that a few guys were hanging out on the perimeter with their eyes each on a specific girl. I watched the guys from a distance before going over to Jessica's area. I wanted to see if anybody was looking at Jessica. *I saw a guy make a circle around the girl he was interested in. It reminded me of how a shark might move around its prey.* I realized that I often do the same thing. I focused my attention on a pair of girls dancing together. I witnessed a guy circling around them until he made his move and came up behind one of the girls, trying to grind her from behind. She didn't push him away, so I figured she either knew him or actually liked it. I preferred to believe that they didn't know each other. I don't know if I could have done that with someone I didn't know at all. I hate getting rejected, especially when I haven't even had one drink. I thought about the fact, though, that it may be better to approach a girl on the dance floor from the rear, since you don't have to worry about her looking in your face and pushing you away. I figured I was going to try that tactic with Jessica. I circled around her and gave her a couple of looks from the front. I came up behind her and started dancing wildly. I was really just having fun imitating the guy I had just seen. I was hoping he wasn't watching me, thinking that I could possibly get a fist in my jaw if he really knew what I was doing. Jessica and I started dancing and moving to every beat and every word. We were having so much fun. It was amazing [emphasis added].

Of course, the city at night also provides an opportunity for young women to employ strategic cunning in their own sexual pursuits. For both men and women, a successful encounter with a member of the desired sex may not evolve into romance or physical intimacy (not is this necessarily preferable by either party), but their ability to reduce the social distance between themselves and a *potential* sex partner (no matter how remote its realization might be) can at the very least provide confirmation that one has successfully performed a recognizably desirable gender and sexual role in public.[38] In addition, as young women discover the high-ranking prestige attached to the performance of feminine sexuality in public, they learn to exploit its situational advantages in the context of urban nightlife. Vanessa, a twenty-year-old sophomore, acknowledges the privileges granted to attractive women at World Fusion, a bar and restaurant:

There was an immense crowd of people trying to get drinks, so I pushed through and stood in between two guys who both looked around twenty-one. Riley handed me her credit card to start a tab. The guys next to me seemed annoyed because they were standing there for a while for the bartender, but the fully tattooed bartender with a shaved head saw me right when I squeezed through and asked me what I wanted. It seems like the male bartenders love to serve the females first because they enjoy flirting with them.

As Vanessa's remarks suggest, young women may not initially recognize the distinctive social value attached to the public display of feminine sexuality (or describe it in these terms). However, after repeat encounters they will likely begin to appreciate the *consequences* of this valuation, as signified by solicitous bar service in crowded lounges, attention from male passersby, envy from female onlookers, and so forth. During subsequent encounters, they may choose to rely on specific strategies of interaction designed to capitalize on the rewards associated with its elaborated performance, particularly by flirting with male service staff. As Shannon, a junior, observes, "When it comes to getting in bars and getting cheap or free drinks, totally.... Because yeah, it's not like the bartender really thinks you are going to go home with him, but he enjoys the flirting so he'll come to you more." According to Aimee, a nineteen-year-old freshman at Marmont, a bar and lounge:

A thirty-something sleazeball trying to look about twenty-three with spiky black hair immediately started talking to Amber... and buys us both a Blondie and a Leetini [both designer cocktails mixed with vanilla-flavored vodka and pineapple juice]. It is then that I realized how easy it is in the bar scene being a girl, compared to [our friends] John, Larry, and Christopher, who were unsuccessfully eying the older professional chicks.... "Hey, missy, what's next?" the muscled bartender breaks my nebulous night-dream. I notice his yellowish tinted eyes and let my hand linger as I leave him my crumpled-up ten-dollar bill in exchange for a shot of Stoli Razberi. This little economic incentive and splash of flirting insures a night full of quicker drinks and casual conversations.

As young women, particularly those transitioning from adolescence to adulthood, gradually develop confidence in bars, nightclubs, and lounges, they become more skillful in engineering interaction rituals with male strangers that allow them to trade on their performance of feminine sexuality in exchange for free or discounted cocktails, and potentially desirous attention from good-looking, upper-class men. Along with her girlfriends at Alma de Cuba, Tracy, a twenty-one-year-old senior, strategically positions herself to attract a group of young professionals:

Being the girls that we are, we automatically comb the scene for cute guys to talk to or to buy us more drinks! After five minutes of making eye contact with a group of guys, we are eventually approached. They are young professionals who work downtown and are definitely a little older than us. After introducing ourselves, we innocently flirt back and forth. Their names are Andrew, Jack, and Mike. They are pretty sure of themselves, a little on the cocky side. Not really my type, but nice guys nonetheless. They, too, seem to be wearing the "official" going-out dress code for guys: dark pants and a button-down shirt. We are asked the usual questions: "Where are you from? What are you studying? Where else have you been tonight? Do you want another drink?" They buy us a round of drinks, and at this point everyone is feeling pretty good.

For these young women, flirting is a game played for cocktails and compliments, a sporting ritual that serves as its own kind of urban hustle. Of course, women may enthusiastically enter such contests only to find their male opponents hopelessly exhausting, boring, creepy, and occasionally dangerous, and in these instances they develop strategies of mild deception in order to tactfully exit such interaction rivals with grace. Just as men are highly strategic in their approach to meeting potential sexual partners, Tracy's account suggests that women must become equally savvy in handling these encounters as well.

Although I am not attracted to any of them, we trade cell phone numbers. The guys push for us to come with them to Twenty Manning, another bar down the street. They are meeting up with some other friends there. We decline the offer, knowing that none of us are really interested in pursuing them past this conversation or locale. So we tell them we are going to stay longer at Alma de Cuba, but tell them we will call them if we decide to leave anytime soon. We know that's a lie and they probably do too, but it's a nice way to close the night with them. We smile and thank them for the drinks and conversation, and wave good-bye as they leave.

To be sure, the discomfort produced by these strategic games of interaction often disagrees with young men and women alike. According to a female sophomore, "Sometimes I do feel a little guilty....I wouldn't let someone keep buying me drinks if I were totally not interested in them, because they would get the wrong idea." And as Joey himself admits in his frustration, "Often when I walk over to a girl that I want to talk to, I get a little insecure if she doesn't acknowledge me right away but continues her conversation with her friends. The first notice of a girl that you want to say 'hi' to can be weird, because you don't know if you should wait for them to come to you or actually walk past the other people and go straight to her. It seems like everything is a game."

In the end, the emphasis on strategies of gamesmanship and the presentation of a nocturnal self among young singles likely *prevents* them from meeting one another despite their best efforts to dress and impress. As Jason reminds us of the hustle of urban nightlife, "You get into costume and you go out, and it's kind of looked down upon if you *don't* in some places. There are places where it's cool to just be you, and go and hang out, and there are places where you are expected to be *more*. And I think it's the expectation of being *more* that actually may prevent people from talking to each other.... Because *you* are not more than *you*. You are playing this role, but that's the *only* place that you play the role. It's not necessarily a role you are comfortable in.

"That's the problem. When you go out you make it like a 'big night,' you are becoming somebody that's a little further away from you, which makes it harder to socialize—because you are *not* you. Because you are being the thing you *created*, not being yourself."

NOTES

1. Simone de Beauvoir, *The Second Sex*, ed. and trans. H. M. Parshley (1952) (New York Vintage, 1989), 532: Erving Goffman, *The Presentation of Self in Everyday Life* (Garden City, NY: Anchor Books, 1959), 57–58; Candace West and Don H. Zimmerman, "Doing Gender," *Gender & Society* 1 (1987):125–151.

2. While excerpts taken from my student-written accounts have been mildly edited for spelling, punctuation, and (in extreme cases only) grammar to ensure readability, I have otherwise attempted to present them as unadulterated as possible. All students' names have been changed to protect their identity.

3. On the androgynous quality of much of contemporary women's fashion, see Fred Davis, *Fashion, Culture, and Identity* (Chicago: University of Chicago Press, 1992).

4. Premium designer jeans have spiked up dramatically in popularity and price since the late 1990s; see Guy Trebay, "Who Pays $600 for Jeans?" *New York Times* April 21, 2005.

5. Gloria Steinem, "I Was a Playboy Bunny," in *Outrageous Acts and Everyday Rebellions* (New York: Plume, 1983), 37, 58.

6. Housewife Marge Simpson wore a pair of Blahnik's mules in a 1991 episode of *The Simpsons*.

7. Erving Goffman, "Symbols of Class Status," *British Journal of Sociology* 2 (1951): 294–304; Pierre Bourdieu, *Distinction: A Social Critique of the Judgment of Taste*, trans. Richard Nice (Cambridge, MA: Harvard University Press, 1984); Candace West and Sarah Fenstermaker, "Doing Difference," *Gender & Society* 9 (1995): 8–37.

8. Patricia Highsmith, *The Talented Mr. Ripley* (1955) (New York Everyman's Library, 1999). Of course, the reverse is also true insofar as affluent youth sometimes attempt to present themselves in working-class attire and demeanor as a means of performing authenticity, subcultural style, or proletarian chic; see Ned Polsky, *Hustlers, Beats, and Others* (Garden City, NY: Anchor, 1969): Dick Hebdige, *Subculture: The Meaning of Style* (London: Routledge, 1979); and David Grazian, *Blue Chicago: The Search for Authenticity in Urban Blues Clubs* (Chicago: University of Chicago Press, 2003).

9. As black scholars argue, straightened hair and other European hair textures and styles conform to dominant conventions of high-status feminine beauty, which may explain why hair straightening represents such a popular strategy among young women (both black and white) in their nightlife preparations. On the racial polities surrounding women's hair, see Kathy Russel, Midge Wilson, and Ronald Hall, *The Color Complex: The Politics of Skin Color among African Americans* (New York: Anchor, 1993), 81–93; Kobena Mercer, "Black Hair/Style Politics," in *The Subcultures Reader*, ed. Ken Gelder and Sarah Thornton (London: Routledge, 1997), 420–435; Patricia Hill Collins, *Black Feminist Thought: Knowledge, Consciousness, and the Politics of Empowerment*, 2nd ed. (New York: Routledge, 2000), 89; and Ayana D. Byrd and Lori L. Tharps, *Hair Story: Untangling the Roots of Black Hair in America* (New York: St. Martin's Press, 2001).

10. Lauren Weisberger, *The Devil Wears Prada* (New York: Broadway Books, 2003); Plum Sykes, *Bergdorf Blondes* (New York: Hyperion,

2004). On the iconic representations of contemporary feminine fashion displayed in television programs such as *See and the City* and *Ally McBeal*, see Maureen Dowd, *Are Men Necessary?: When Sexes Collide* (New York: Putnam, 2005).

11. Gary Alan Fine, "Adolescence as Cultural Toolkit: High School Debate and the Repertoires of Childhood and Adulthood," *Sociological Quarterly* 45 (2004): 1–20.

12. According to the American Society of Plastic Surgeons, American doctors performed 10.2 million cosmetic plastic surgery procedures in 2005; breast augmentation and nose reshaping surgeries were included among the top five procedures performed, along with liposuction, tummy tuck, and eyelid surgery.

13. Despite university policy and the laws of Pennsylvania, many of my undergraduates under the age of twenty-one used fake IDs to gain access to bars and nightclubs in the city, and consequently drank alcohol illegally while conducting the nightlife participation required by the assignment for my course.... While I rely on their reports in the book, please note that I did not condone such behavior, and in subsequent semesters underage students have been explicitly advised by me not to consume alcohol for purposes of the assignment, while students twenty-one and older have been advised not to drink to excess.

14. Laura Grindstaff, *The Money Shot: Trash, Class and the Making of TV Talk Shows* (Chicago: University of Chicago Press, 2002), explores how these class-based stereotypes are reproduced through popular culture.

15. Perhaps unsurprisingly, these represent high-end grooming products; according to 2006 figures, most varieties of Creed men's cologne cost $90 an ounce.

16. On the uniform among undergraduate students at elite American colleges, see Paul Fussell, "Uniformity in American Higher Learning," in *Uniforms: Why We Are What We Wear* (Boston: Houghton Mifflin, 2002), 136–139.

17. Of course, this so-called "feminized" behavior has long been associated with masculinity for centuries, and only in the modern period have women (and gay men) taken over this role in Western culture.

18. In the misogynist world of professional baseball, a "slump-buster" refers to an undesirable woman with whom a ball player superstitiously has sex in order to break a batting slump or losing streak; see Jose Canseco, *Juiced: Wild Times, Rampant 'Roids, Smash Hits, and How Baseball Got Big* (New York: Regan Books, 2005), 95–96.

19. Alexa Hackbarth, "Vanity, Thy Name Is Metrosexual: D.C.'s Dating Scene Gets a Lot Prettier," *Washington Post*, November 17, 2003, C10. The term is problematic insofar as it solidifies a monolithic and essentialist vision of what both homosexual and heterosexual men ought to be like, yet correctly emphasizes the contemporary blurring of fashion boundaries between affluent gay and straight men; see David Colman, "Gay or Straight? Hard to Tell," *New York Times*, June 19, 2005.

20. "Hooking up" is an ambiguous term referring to a range of possible sexual encounters (including kissing, genital stimulation, oral sex, and vaginal or anal intercourse) that take place on a casual basis among participants who may (or may not necessarily) be involved in a traditional romantic relationship. On the sexual rituals surrounding "hooking up" among college students, see Kathleen A. Bogle, *From Dating to Hooking Up: The Emergence of a New Sexual Script* (Ph. D. diss., University of Delaware, 2004); Paula England and Reuben J. Thomas, "The Decline of the Date and the Rise of the College Hook Up," in *Families in Transition*, 14th ed., ed. Arlene S. Skolnick and Jerome H. Skolnick (Boston: Allyn and Bacon, 2006). In his ethnographic work on inner-city neighborhoods, Elijah Anderson, in "Sex Codes and Family Life among Poor Inner-City Youths," *Annals of the American Academy of Political and Social Science* 501 (1989): 59–78; *Streetwise: Race, Class, and Change in an Urban Community* (Chicago: University of Chicago Press, 1990); and *Code of the Street: Decency, Violence, and the Moral Life of the Inner City* (New York: Norton, 1999), documents how sex codes among youth evolve in a context of peer pressure in which young black males "run their game" by women in the pursuit of in-group stams, a finding that can be generalized to explain the sexual behavior of other youth populations as well.

21. Some gay men associate their elaborate preparations with femininity (and thus stigmatized) as well. According to Landon, a twenty-two-year-old senior, "Gay preparation can be as bad as a sorority girl sometimes. Yeesh."

22. Marcella Bombardieri, "Colleges Crack Down on Preparty Drinking: Schools Target Underage Binging," *Boston Globe*, April 9, 2006.

23. In his preparations for the pregame, Edward expresses his anxieties over making an illegal alcohol purchase as a twenty-year-old:

The first we did was go to Campus Pizza to buy some beer. Granted, neither of us are twenty-one. On our walk over, we played "odds-evens" (each person puts out either one or two fingers: if the total is what you called, odds or evens, you lose) to see who would have to risk their fake ID to buy the beer. I lost, so I had to buy the beer. The clerk sold me the beer, but told me he would never sell to me again with the ID I used. He said this partially because it was not me on the ID, and partially because it had expired.

24. The pregaming ritual mimics similar activities associated with adult-oriented socializing, including professional football game tailgate parties and pre-theater cocktail parties.

25. During the 2000–01 academic year, the University of Pennsylvania's drinking rate— as measured by the proportion of students who reported imbibing at least four (for women) or five (for men) alcoholic drinks on a single occasion at least once in the two weeks prior to the study—was 49 percent and pregaming rituals such as the Power Hour are inevitably a likely contributor. See "Data Review—Undergraduate Alcohol and Other Drug Use at Penn," Office of Health Education, University of Pennsylvania; http.//www.vpul.upenn.edu/alcohol.

26. In these kinds of status-challenging moments, affluent young men sometimes resort to unlawful sidewalk behaviors such as urinating in public. As Edward confesses:

First we had to find a place to pee. We obviously were not welcome in the club to use their bathroom. There was even a security standing guard in the parking lot. Jordan showed on a brilliant maneuver (or at least I thought so). Stand by a bush with a cell phone by your ear as you go. This makes you completely incognito to any security because they think you're just making a call.

The propensity for this type of unapologetic antisocial behavior among adolescent men and young adults likely contributes to the current moral outrage and spirited public scorn against underage binge drinking in the United States. Still, the fact that affluent young men regularly urinate in public while intoxicated, while homeless men face public harassment and the possibility of arrest for committing the same misdemeanor, speaks to society's double standard concerning the treatment of the poor versus their well-off counterparts in the city at night. On the similar propensities for homeless black men and wealthier whites to urinate in public (while facing radically different consequences for such behavior), see Mitchell Duneier, *Sidewalk* (New York: Farrar, Straus and Giroux, 1999), 186.

27. Richard A. Leo, "Miranda's Revenge: Police Interrogation as a Confidence Game," *Law & Society Review* 30 (1996): 271.

28. For these and other relevant data on student drinking, see Office of Health Education, University of Pennsylvania; http://www.vpul.upenn.edu/alcohol.

29. Also see Kristen Henri, "Penn in the Neck," *Philadelphia Weekly*, May 10, 2006, 55.

30. According to linguistics professor Deborah Tannen, *You Just Don't Understand: Women and Men in Conversation* (New York: William Morrow, 1990), 24–25, social norms of communication among men dictate that even everyday interactions ought to be understood as contests of one-upmanship, as "negotiations in which people try to achieve and maintain the upper hand if they can."

31. In his essay "Where the Action Is," Erving Goffman, *Interaction Ritual: Essays on Face-to-Face Interaction* (New York: Pantheon, 1967), examines a range of risk-taking activities, including gambling, stickups, and surfing.

32. Kathryn Graham, Linda La Rocque, Rhoda
Yetman, T. James Ross, and Enrico Guistra,
"Aggression and Barroom Environments,"
Journal of Studies on Alcohol 41 (1890): 277–
292; Kathryn Graham and Ross Homel,
"Creating Safer Bars," in *Alcohol: Minimising
the Harm*, ed. Martin Plant, Eric Single, and
Tim Stockwell (London: Free Association
Books, 1997); Brian M. Quigley, Kenneth E.
Leonard, and Lorraine Collins, "Characteristics
of Violent Bars and Bar Patrons," *Journal of
Studies on Alcohol* 64 (2003):765–772. Rather
than assume that the presence of bouncers
serves as a cause of violent barroom behavior,
it could very easily be the case that venues
known for violent activity simply tend to hire
more bouncers due to security concerns.

33. Randall Collins, *Violent
Interaction: A Microsociological Theory*
(Princeton, NJ: Princeton University Press,
2007); Graham et al., "Aggression and
Barroom Environments."

34. Kathryn Graham and Samantha Well,
"Aggression among Adults in the Social
Context of the Bar," *Addiction Research and
Theory* 9 (2001): 204.

35. Jack Katz, *Seductions of Crime: Moral
and Sensual Attractions in Doing Evil*
(New York: Basic Books, 1988); Anderson,
Code of the Street; Curtis Jackson-Jacobs,
"Taking a Beating: The Narrative Gratifications
of Fighting as an Underdog," in *Cultural
Criminology Unleashed*, ed. K. J. Hayward, Jeff
Ferell, Wayne Morrison, and Mike Presdee
(London: Glasshouse Press, 2004).

36. Graham and Wells, "Aggression among
Young Adults," 201.

37. Guenter Hitsch, Ali Hortacsu, and Dan Ariely,
"What Makes You Click? An Empirical Analysis
of Online Dating," unpublished ms., University
of California, Santa Cruz, 2004, 9, 10; Jennifer
Egan, "Love in the Time of No Time," *New York
Times Magazine,* November 23, 2003.

38. Erving Goffman, "The Arrangement Between
the Sexes," *Theory and Society* 4 (1977): 301–331.
As suggested by my use of non-gender-specific
language here, I extend Goffman's discussion
of instigated courtship rituals to apply to
both men *and* women of heterosexual *and*

homosexual persuasions, whereas Goffman's
somewhat dated article emphasizes public
interactions initiated by straight men.

REFERENCES

Anderson, Elijah. 1999. *Code of the Street:
Decency, Violence and the Moral Life of the
Inner City.* New York: Norton 1999.
Anderson, Elijah. 1989. "Sex Codes and Family
Life among Poor Inner-City Youths" *Annals
of the American Academy of Political and
Social Science.* 501: 59–78.
Anderson, Elijah. 1990. *Streetwise: Race, Class,
and Change in an Urban Community.*
Chicago: University of Chicago Press.
Bogle, Kathleen A. 2004. "From Dating to
Hooking Up: The Emergence of a New
Sexual Script." Ph. D. dissertation,
University of Delaware.
Bombardieri, Marcella. 2006. "Colleges Crack
Down on Preparty Drinking: Schools Target
Underage Binging." *Boston Globe* (April 9).
Bourdieu, Pierre. 1984. *Distinction: A Social
Critique of the Judgment of Taste.* Richard Nice
(trans.). Cambridge, MA: Harvard University
Press.
Byrd, Ayana D. Lori L. Tharps. 2001. *Hair
Story: Untangling the Roots of Black Hair in
America.* New York: St. Martin's Press.
Collins, Randall. 2007. *Violent Interaction:
A Microsociological Theory.* Princeton,
NJ: Princeton University Press.
Davis, Fred. 1992. *Fashion, Culture, and Identity.*
Chicago: University of Chicago Press.
Duneier, Mitchell. 1999. *Sidewalk.* New
York: Farrar, Straus and Giroux.
Egan, Jennifer. "2003. Love in the Time of No Time."
New York Times Magazine (November 23).
Canseco, Jose. 2005. *Juiced: Wild Times, Rampant
'Roids, Smash Hits, and How Baseball Got
Big.* New York: Regan Books.
Colman, David. 2005. "Gay or Straight? Hard to
Tell." *New York Times* (June 19).
De Beauvoir Simone. 1989 [1952]. *The Second
Sex.* H. M. Parshley (ed. and trans). New
York: Vintage.
Dowd, Maureen. 2005. *Are Men Necessary?: When
Sexes Collide.* New York: Putnam.

England, Paula and Reuben J. Thomas. 2006. "The Decline of the Date and the Rise of the College Hook Up." In *Families in Transition*. 14th ed. Arlene S. Skolnick and Jerome H. Skolnick (eds.). Boston: Allyn and Bacon.

Erving Goffman. 1959. *The Presentation of Self in Everyday Life*. Garden City, NY: Anchor Books.

Fine, Gary Alan. 2004. "Adolescence as Cultural Toolkit: High School Debate and the Repertoires of Childhood and Adulthood." *Sociological Quarterly*. 45: 1–20.

Fussell, Paul. 2002. "Uniformity in American Higher Learning." In *Uniforms: Why We Are What We Wear*. Boston: Houghton Mifflin.

Goffman, Erving. "Symbols of Class Status." *British Journal of Sociology* 2 (1951): 294–304.

Goffman, Erving. 1967. "Where the Action Is." In *Interaction Ritual: Essays on Face-to-Face Interaction*. New York: Pantheon.

Goffman, Erving. 1977. "The Arrangement Between the Sexes." *Theory and Society*. 4: 301–331.

Graham, Kathryn, Linda La Rocque, Rhoda Yetman, T. James Ross, and Enrico Guistra. 1980. "Aggression and Barroom Environments." *Journal of Studies on Alcohol* 41: 277–292.

Graham, Kathryn and Ross Homel. 1997. "Creating Safer Bars." In *Alcohol: Minimising the Harm*. Martin Plant, Eric Single, and Tim Stockwell (eds.). London: Free Association Books.

Graham, Kathryn and Samantha Well. 2001. "Aggression among Adults in the Social Context of the Bar." *Addiction Research and Theory* 9.

Grazian, David. 2003. *Blue Chicago: The Search for Authenticity in Urban Blues Clubs*. Chicago: University of Chicago Press.

Grindstaff, Laura. 2002. *The Money Shot: Trash, Class and the Making of TV Talk Shows*. Chicago: University of Chicago Press.

Hebdige, Dick. 1979. *Subculture: The Meaning of Style*. London: Routledge.

Henri, Kristen. 2006. "Penn in the Neck." *Philadelphia Weekly* (May 10).

Highsmith, Patricia. 1999 [1955]. *The Talented Mr. Ripley*. New York: Everyman's Library.

Hill Collins, Patricia. 2000. *Black Feminist Thought: Knowledge, Consciousness, and the Politics of Empowerment*. 2nd ed. New York: Routledge.

Hitsch, Guenter, Ali, Hortacsu, and Dan Ariely. 2004. "What Makes You Click? An Empirical Analysis of Online Dating." Unpublished manuscript. University of California, Santa Cruz.

Jackson-Jacobs, Curtis. 2004. "Taking a Beating: The Narrative Gratifications of Fighting as an Underdog." In *Cultural Criminology Unleashed*. K. J. Hayward, Jeff Ferell, Wayne Morrison, and Mike Presdee (eds.). London: Glasshouse Press.

Katz, Jack. 1988. Seductions of Crime: Moral and Sensual Attractions in Doing Evil. New York: Basic Books.

Kobena, Mercer. 1997. "Black Hair/Style Politics." In *The Subcultures Reader*, pp. 420-435. Ken Gelder and Sarah Thornton (eds.). London: Routledge.

Leo, Richard A. 1996. "Miranda's Revenge: Police Interrogation as a Confidence Game." *Law & Society Review* 30.

Office of Health Education, University of Pennsylvania. "Data Review—Undergraduate Alcohol and Other Drug Use at Penn." http.//www.vpul.upenn.edu/alcohol.

Polsky, Ned. 1969. *Hustlers, Beats, and Others*. Garden City, NY: Anchor.

Quigley, Brian M., Kenneth E. Leonard and Lorraine Collins. 2003. "Characteristics of Violent Bars and Bar Patrons." *Journal of Studies on Alcohol* 64: 765–772.

Russel, Kathy, Midge Wilson, and Ronald Hall. 1993. *The Color Complex: The Politics of Skin Color among African Americans*. New York: Anchor.

Steinem, Gloria. 1983. "I Was a Playboy Bunny." In *Outrageous Acts and Everyday Rebellions*. New York: Plume.

Sykes, Plum. 2004. *You Just Don't Understand: Women and Men in Conversation*. New York: William Morrow.

Trebay, Guy. 2005. "Who Pays $600 for Jeans?" *New York Times* (April 21).

Weisberger, Lauren. 2003. *The Devil Wears Prada*. New York: Broadway Books.

West, Candace and Don H. Zimmerman. 1987. "Doing Gender." *Gender & Society* 1: 125–151.

West, Candace and Sarah Fenstermaker. 1995. "Doing Difference." *Gender & Society* 9: 8–37.

41

JOOYOUNG LEE

BATTLIN' ON THE CORNER: TECHNIQUES FOR SUSTAINING PLAY (2009)

In this study of streetcorner rap "battles" in South Central Los Angeles, Jooyoung Lee draws on four years of observation and interviews to show how men seek recognition and respect through their songs. The social order of apparently playful moments always turns out to be precarious, but participants are constantly attuned to how to make repairs. Lee examines in detail how the rappers play, how they understand what they are doing, and how order prevails when a passerby might reasonably think that violence is about to occur.

It is 2 A.M., and like most early Friday mornings, there is crowd of young African American men rapping on the corner of 43rd Place and Leimert Boulevard in South Central Los Angeles. Nocando [No-can-do] and "Lil Duce" are standing face to face in the middle of a circle of 20 peers. Lil Duce, who is a member of a local street gang, is trying to ignore a flurry of "punchlines" coming from Nocando; at one point, he plugs his ears with his index fingers and beings humming loudly to show that he is not interested in batting Nocando. This does not deter Nocando, who sips from a 40-ounce bottle of Old English malt liquor before dissing Lil Duce: "You get stamped on yo' couch! You wanna go against this? Cuz I'm so relentless, you're feminine—you have ho intentions! Don't pretend, bitch!" Onlookers start cheering and laughing after these lines, which seems to further aggravate Lil Duce.

After weathering a couple more insults, Lil Duce flips around to face Nocando and yells back, "You can't fuck with me, my nigga, I'm telling you, I'm so professional! Calm down, slow down, don't be tryin' to talk all loud!" He becomes angrier and louder with each line: "You a bitch nigga, dog, you wanna fuck with me? I knock yo' fuckin' brains out!" Lil Duce then quickly throws off his jacket, moves closer to Nocando, and punches his open hand a few inches away from Nocando's face—as if he is preparing to fight. Onlookers are no longer laughing; there is an eerie silence as everyone waits to see what is going to happen next.

Still smiling, Nocando takes another sip from his drink before responding back: "You don't wanna stand in the place, you punch me right now, you probably break your hand on my face!" Everyone standing around the battle starts laughing. The crowd looks relieved when Nocando responds with punchlines instead of challenging Lil Duce to a fight. Although he still seems annoyed, Lil Duce's anger seems to have passed; he slips his jacket back on and stands with his arms crossed, waiting for his chance to respond to Nocando. For the next few minutes, both Nocando and Lil Duce take turns dissing each other in front of onlooking peers. After they stop battling, both give each other "daps"—a local handshake and hug—and share a few laughs about comments that each made about the other.

This paper draws from ethnographic observations, in-depth interviews with regulars, and several hours of video recordings to describe how inner-city men sustain the playfulness of street corner rap "battles" (lyrical duels) in South Central Los Angeles. I show that individuals use battles as playful ways of resolving perceived disrespect that emerges in group rap "ciphers," which are group rap sessions on the corner. Although participants provoke each other with ritual insults, they use cues to collaboratively construct the shared understanding that "this is play." The person who offends the other participant uses various cues to signal, "I was just playing" and should not be taken seriously; the offended party, meanwhile, answers with their own cues to say, "I'm not taking you seriously," or in local terms, "I'm not catchin' feelings." However, although these battles begin as play, they can become "more than play." Indeed, participants

battle each other with ritual insults that have the power to provoke strong feelings of rage in opponents, arousing emotions which can propel individuals into "bluster" and violence (cf. Collins 2008; Katz 1988; Luckenbill 1977). Sensing that one or both participants have broken frame, onlookers step in between individuals, tell jokes, and use other techniques to interrupt escalating tensions....

Hanging Out on the Corner

For close to four years, I have conducted ethnographic fieldwork in Leimert Park, a public park located along Crenshaw Boulevard in South Central Los Angeles. In 2000, 93 percent of Leimert Park's population self-identified as black or African American. During the week, patrons from all over South Central visit soul food restaurants, music festivals, barbershops, weekend drum circles, African art stores, jazz venues, and coffee shops in Leimert Park.

The data for this paper were collected on the street corner outside of KAOS Network, a community center in Leimert Park. Founded by independent filmmaker and community activist Ben Caldwell, KAOS Network hosts after-school programs, computer literacy classes, capoeira practice, and other youth-oriented activities (Caldwell 1993). In 1995, KAOS Network began hosting "Project Blowed," Los Angeles's longest running hip hop "open mic." Every Thursday night young men and a few women (most of whom are African Americans between the ages of 18 to 26) come together, hang out, and rap at Project Blowed (Lee forthcoming b; Morgan 2002). Some perform "writtens" (prewritten songs) inside the club. Meanwhile, others rap in ciphers and battles on the street corner outside of KAOS Network (Lee forthcoming a). On any given Thursday, there are between 20 and 100 participants hanging out and rapping on this corner. Unlike the premeditated writtens individuals perform inside of KAOS Network, participants "freestyle" (improvise) their raps on the corner....

Battlin' to Resolve Disrespect in the Cipher

Regulars hang out and rap in ciphers, spontaneously forming group rap sessions on the corner. Typically, ciphers consist of 3 to 10 rappers standing around in a circle and taking turns rapping with each other. Onlookers gather around those rapping in the middle. Over the course of the night, different participants enter and exit the cipher. While some ciphers may last five minutes, others can go on for a couple hours at a time.

Each participant in the cipher raps until someone else is ready to rap. The person who wants to rap uses verbal cues (e.g., "yo," "yeah," "listen," and "uh") to signal to the person currently rapping that they want to get "on stage," Meanwhile, the person being interrupted will finish their next line before getting "off stage." Here is an example of a routine transition in the rap cipher. In this instance, Big Flossy, SS, and CP were rapping together on the corner, next to CP's car. Both Big Flossy and CP use different verbal cues to transition on stage:

> SS: I ain't talkin' centers in the paint, gettin' dumped o[n like guards].
> BF: [Yo you can] say I'ma gangsta without the coup, I'm a have to sock this nigga when I get out the booth, niggas ain't knowin' dog, you be missin' a tooth I'm a straight up[ga]ngsta now take[th] e pr[oof].
> CP: [uh] [yo] [lis]ten, they ain't fuckin' wit the Westside resident, steppin' in the scene with a high price neck-a-lace...

Big Flossy says "yo" to signal to SS that he is going to start rapping. Like clockwork, SS

stops rapping and allows Big Flossy to have his turn. In the next transition, CP uses three consecutive cues ("uh," "yo," and "listen") to transition into his rap. Recognizing these cues, Big Flossy stops rapping and allows CP to have the stage.

Although most transitions occur smoothly, there are also transitions that do not go smoothly and in which participants feel disrespected by each other. When these situations happen, participants call each other out to rap battles, which are competitive verbal duels in which individuals take turns boasting about themselves *and* dissing their opponent. The call outs that participants use are similar to "hoo ridin'," "hittin' up," and other verbal provocations inner-city men use to stage fights (cf. Anderson 1999; Garot 2006, 2007), but are also distinct because they are delivered in rap form, a sign that they want to stage a battle.

Cut Offs

First, battles begin when a participant interprets another person's attempt to start rapping as an unwarranted and disrespectful "cut off." Unlike routine transitions, which occur seamlessly, individuals become visibly annoyed, agitated, and openly hostile to another person during a cut off. In the following example, SS, Big Flossy, Flawliss, and T3 are rapping with each other in a cipher. At one point during the cipher, T3 tries to transition on stage before SS is ready to stop rapping. SS becomes visibly upset at T3's attempt to rap and breaks frame by calling him out to a battle (see Figure 41.1):

> SS: You want bricks I give to you right now, I pay the rent, you can see me...(frame 1)
> T3: ...See me on the scene, yes, I'm T3...[SS becomes visibly annoyed, squinting his eyes and gritting his teeth at T3, who is standing to my left, not picture in the frame.] (frame 2)

FIGURE 41.1. Feeling Cut Off 1. SS raps. 2. SS feels cut off by T3. 3. SS disses T3. 4. SS simulates violence against T3.

SS: Ay nigga! You better call rounds nigga! Before you speak, you better calm down nigga! (frame 3). [SS's voice grows louder.] "I'm a hustla, fuck I'll move the weight, nigga I pop that 8(mm)[1] right your face!" [As he says this, he holds his hand out and pretends to shoot a (now) embarrassed T3 in the face.] (frame 4)

This example illustrates how SS breaks frame shortly after T3 starts rapping (frame 2). SS's facial expression and the content of his rap change when this happens. He moves from rapping to others in the cipher (frame 1), to "calling out" T3 (frames 2 and 3), to simulating violence against T3 (frame 4).

All 25 of my interviewees described cut offs as the most common way battles begin on the corner.[2] Their accounts reveal a common experience of feeling underestimated, overlooked, and not taken seriously by one's peers in the cipher. For example, "Flawliss," an unabashedly heavyset, 26-year old African American male, compares feeling "cut off" in the cipher to feeling cut off and overlooked in other parts of his everyday life:

Say I'm about to spit [rap], and say I spit like 4 bars [lines], and some dude jumps in and starts rapping loud. I feel like I didn't get to say what the fuck I was about to say, ya know? It was my turn, fairly, and he cut me off—like some kid cutting you off at lunch and shit, when you're in high school—"What the fuck you doing? I'm right here, homey!" (laughs) . . . so then that causes beef [tension] because I feel disrespected. So now, I'ma say something!

Inner-city men experience cut offs as premature and unwarranted interruptions in their rapping. Cut offs transform an individual's experience of a social situation, much like feeling cut off in other social situations. Like Jack Katz's (1999) analysis of feeling cut off while driving in Los Angeles, Flawliss's account highlights the connections between feeling cut off in the "here and now" and previous experiences of feeling cut off in other times and places. In the case of the battle, feeling cut off can transform a light-hearted group rap cipher into a competitive battle between two individuals.

Mic Hoggin'

Participants also start battles when they feel that someone else is "hoggin' the mic," a local term for not giving others a chance to rap in the cipher. The "mic hog" literally hogs or monopolizes on stage time in the cipher. Like overly precocious students who answer every question just to hear themselves talk, mic hogs annoy their peers who also want a chance to rap. In this next case, "Cane" becomes frustrated with Flawliss, who continues rapping despite his repeated attempts to get on stage. Flawliss is in the middle of his rap when Cane tries to enter the cipher:

> Cane leans forward into the cipher and starts rapping, "I leave a nigga depressed…" Flawliss, however, does not stop rapping, Cane grimaces toward CP, who's standing across from him. He waits for a few more moments and starts rapping again; this time both Flawliss and Cane rap at the same time. After about 10 seconds where both are rapping at the same time, Cane stops and looks over at CP again and starts grumbling about Flawliss, "C'mon I'm not even trying to battle, open it up!" Flawliss stops rapping a few moments later, after which time Cane starts dissing Flawliss, "But see, everybody trying to spit some hot shit, but this nigga [points at Flawliss] always wants control the topics!"

After repeated failed attempts to transition into his rap, Cane calls out Flawliss for "mic hoggin'." Cane raps, "this nigga [Flawliss] always wanna control the topics!" Cane's comment, "C'mon I'm not even trying to battle," shows that he feels disrespected by Flawliss's insistence to stay on stage, and more generally illustrates how regulars view mic hoggin' as a warrant to battle. In short, there is a tacit belief among participants that people *should* share the stage with others—battling, then, is a locally accepted way of addressing mic hogs.

There are subtle differences between feeling cut off and feeling that someone is mic hoggin'. First there is a temporal difference. Unlike the cut off, in which individuals experience disrespect in one particular moment, mic hoggin' is an offense that accumulates over a period of time. In the above example, Cane becomes increasingly frustrated with Flawliss after repeated failed attempts to start rapping; this is different from feeling cut off, which individuals experience in one highly charged moment. Second, individuals feel cut off *in the act* of rapping, whereas people feel like they are not getting a fair chance to rap when they accuse someone of mic hoggin'. Thus, while feeling cut off is about not getting to finish what one has started, accusing someone of mic hoggin' is motivated by not getting a chance to start at all.…

Framing the Battle as Play

Although participants stage battles to playfully resolve moments of disrespect in ciphers, some escalate into more than play. Indeed, throughout the course of the battle individuals say things about each other that have the power to embarrass, humiliate, and deeply offend their opponent—all of which can because precursors to violence (cf. Katz 1988; Luckenbill 1977). While most regulars view hoo ridin' and explicit gang references as "off limits," each person brings a different set of expectations concerning which comments are "fair game" and which are not. For example, some regulars describe how comments about family members and other loved ones are off limits.[3] While hanging out on the corner, June One, a 24-year-old mixed race male rapper from Inglewood, told me, "I'm a pretty mild mannered guy and you can say what you will, know what I'm sayin'?" I ask, "When is someone crossing the line?" June One smirks, "Maaaaan, if somebody talk bad about my mama, then it's on some *other* shit, know what I mean?" Others like Flawliss, however, are open to any and all disses because, "hip hop is a competitive sport, na mean? Niggas actin' all sensitive and shit when somebody makes fun of them. SO!? This is battlin'; it ain't like you tryin' to make friends and shit." In short, there is a degree of risk and uncertainly in battles that further demonstrates the need for clear and unambiguous cues that this is play.[4] . . .

The shared understanding that this is play is an ongoing accomplishment.[5] In the following case, a small crowd of onlookers gather around Flawless and Nocando, two of the most well-respected battle rappers on the black. At different points in the battle, both laugh at comments that their opponent makes about them—an emotional sign that they are not catching feelings and thus understand the battle as play:

> FLAWLISS: C'mon mang, you don't really want it with me, c'mon you're like a half, I'm a hundred emcees! [Nocanda and surrounding audience members erupt into laughter after this line.] That's whole a big diff, a whole big stiff, and your hair is happy, that's a whole big stiff! Nigga you so small, I make yo body get lift! [Nocando laughs along with this line, acknowledging that Flawliss "got him."]
>
> NOCANDO: Aww, you suck dick, the only hundred you are, are McNuggets, kick buckets! [Flawliss' eyes light up after this line. He and several other onlookers laugh aloud after Nocando says this line.]

In other instance, participants catch themselves in the process of becoming angry and use emotional and embodied cues to show that they are not catching feelings. For example, on another night, Nocando battled "Machine Gun Man," a member of a grassroots political group organized against police brutality. At one point in the battle, Machine Gun Man became visibly upset by Nocando's belittling remarks about his political beliefs and participation in community organizing. However, in the midst of becoming enraged, Machine Gun Man started smiling and offered daps to Nocando, two signs that he was not catching feelings:

> NOCANDO: Eh, eh! Eh, you're livin' in hell, you say that shit to the pigs and they'll leave you in jail, fuck you in the ass when they twistin' your tail! [A couple onlookers laugh aloud after hearing this.]
>
> MGM: "WHAT!?" [He becomes visibly enraged by this comment, his nostrils flare up, he makes a snarling noise, starts gritting his teeth, and points his index finger at Nocando.]
>
> NOCANDO: . . . But say what to a lug, cuz it's over, with this raw shit, and we both sober, high off shit, I got the rhyme wrong bitch, you wanna find yo miss. [Onlookers start stirring and wait to see if MGM is going to start a fight with Nocando. However, within a few seconds, the anger dissipates from MGM's face and he starts laughing.]
>
> MGM: [Now smiling] . . . I got you! I got you! I got you! I got you! [While saying this he and Nocando give each other daps.]

Much like comments about someone's physical appearance, material possessions, or family members, disparaging remarks about an opponent's political beliefs can also provoke strong feelings between participants. Nocando's remarks provoke temporary feelings of rage in Machine

Gun Man—it is literally written on his face. However, instead of breaking frame, Machine Gun Man starts smiling, laughing, and announces "I got you!" to show that he has a rebuttal for Nocando, and that he is still in the play frame of the battle.

Both participants may understand the battle as play in the beginning of the battle, but may have very different understandings of the battle after a later exchange. In the following example, Big Flossy and Goldie are battling next to Big Flossy's truck. There is a small audience (between 10 and 12 people) standing around watching them. Big Flossy and Goldie use cues throughout the battle to sustain the playfulness of the battle (see Figure 41.2):

> BIG FLOSSY: . . . Stop it my nigga, you don't carry pounds (of drugs)! You don't got money, you don't got no dope! You ain't got no bitches, you got no hope! (frame 1) [Onlookers start laughing after hearing this line.] "You need to stop it man, see when you scream—wait, your lips are ashy, anybody got Vaseline?" [Big Flossy points to Goldie's mouth as he says this. Goldie, meanwhile, covers his mouth and begins laughing along with onlookers after this remark.] (frame 2) See man, dog, you on the wrong team, killer, you know that ain't gold, that's silver! Cubic zirconius (sic), that's fake diamonds, but I'ma give you a dap for tryin'!" [While saying this last line, he extends his fist for a dap.] (frame 3)

Later in the same battle, Goldie is having trouble maintaining the attention of onlookers. He is not projecting his voice clearly and seems to be losing confidence in himself. Instead of responding to Goldie, and further humiliating him, Big Flossy offers Goldie daps to symbolize a peaceful end to the battle (see Figure 41.3):

> GOLDIE: *inaudible lyrics* [Onlookers begin stirring and seem disinterested in Goldie, who is not projecting his voice.]

> BIG FLOSSY: C'mon, OG. [Big Flossy waves his hands for Goldie to "bring it" and taps Goldie's arm.] (frame 1)
> GOLDIE: (*inaudible lyrics*) [Goldie still does not project his voice and onlookers are quickly losing interest.]
> BIG FLOSSY: [laughing playfully] You're fallin' dude, you gotta come hard, c'mon!" (frame 5) [At this point, it feels like Goldie keeps rapping because he doesn't want to stop and hand Big Flossy the victory outright.]
> BIG FLOSSY: It's all good, it's all good. [Big Flossy offers Goldie daps; he and Goldie "hug it out."] (frame 6)

These examples reveal the ongoing work participants do to sustain the battle as play. Instead of taking Big Flossy's disses seriously, Goldie laughs *with* Big Flossy, and thus shows that he is not catching feelings (frame 2). From there, Big Flossy offers Goldie daps to symbolize that he is just playing and does not intend to seriously offend Goldie (frame 3). Sensing that Goldie is "falling off" and cannot compete with him (frames 4 and 5), Big Flossy calls an end to the battle. Rather than allow Goldie to keep rapping, which might further damage Goldie's local reputation as a rapper, Big Flossy effectively ends the battle by hugging it out with Goldie (frame 6).

Although participants stage the battle as play, there is work required to keep it that way. To do this, participants use different techniques to show that they are just playing *and* that they are not catching feelings throughout the battle.

Onlooker's Interventions in Battles

In close to four years of fieldwork, I witnessed seven battles escalate into bluster, the interactional stage in which individuals make pointed and aggressive gestures to either get into violence or intimidate their opponent to back down from violence

FIGURE 41.2. Laughing and Dapping. 1. BP disses G. 2. G laughs with BF. 3. BF offers G daps.

(Collins 2008).[6] Although I cannot determine with certainty if participants *really* wanted to use violence in these situations (which is not the point of this paper), or if they were bluffing and created the outward appearance of rage to get their opponent to back down, I can show how onlookers mobilized to sustain the playful character of these exchanges. This section describes different ways onlookers defuse battles that appear to be headed toward violence.

At a basic level, onlookers intervene when participants are not sharing the stage with each other. This helps preserve the playful frame and cooperative structure rap of battles, and distinguishes them from yelling matches, hoo ridin', "woofin'," and other aggressive verbal provocations to violence on the streets (cf. Anderson 1978; Garot 2006, 2007). In this example, Raz calls out CP. At first, both take turns dissing each other in rap form. However, in the second round, Raz continues rapping *over* CP.

When this happens, several audience members remind Raz that battles have a "one at a time" rule in effect (see Figure 41.4):

> CP: I fuck this nigga [pointing at Raz] up like booze and dope do. [Grabbing his chain.] This chain be the same thing I use to choke you! Listen. nigga... (frame 1)
>
> RAZ: You ain't chokin' shit. Only thing you chokin' on is a big ass... (frame 2)
>
> ONLOOKERS: One at a time! [A group of onlookers hold up their index fingers to signal "1" and yell at Raz, who now looks slightly embarrassed and stops rapping on a dime, allowing CP to have the rest of his turn.] (frame 3)

Although there is no official end to a battle, most battles end when participants and onlookers feel that there is a clear winner. In some situations, both participants and onlookers will openly say, "It's over" or

FIGURE 41.3. Hugging It Out. 4. BF: "Bring it" gesture. 5. BF: "You're fallin'…". 6. BF and G "hug it out".

"That's a wrap!" to mark the end of a battle. However, there are battles that persist past their natural conclusion. These are precarious situations because the person who is losing the battle may resort to personal attacks and pointed threats if they feel that they have no other means of winning or saving face. Onlookers monitor the overall rhythm of the battle and pay particular attention to changes in the body language and overall demeanor of participants. In the following example, G-Wiz steps in between CP and Raz, who have stopped rapping and are inching closer together—signs that they have broken frame and may be nearing violence. From there, Flawliss uses a self-effacing line to start his rap; this transforms the battle back into a group cipher, but also defuses tensions in the battle (see Figure 41.5):

> CP: You just got "ate up"[7] by two
> niggas here!

RAZ: Ate up, nigga!? [CP and Raz inch closer together and start pushing each other lightly.] (frame 1)

GW: [Shaking his head in disbelief. He steps down from the curb and jumps in between CP and Raz, prying them apart.] (frame 2) Y'all niggas is hoggin' the mic! Y'all niggas is hoggin' the mic! [Turns to Raz.] You keep, you keep repeatin' the same sentence. Y'all niggas is time out! Time out! (frame 3)

CP: Ay! Blame this nigga. [Points his finger a Raz, as a way of saying, "It's *his* fault."]

FLAWLISS: *Time out, time out,* let Flawliss's fat ass rip a thyme now! (frame 4)

This example illustrates different ways onlookers collaboratively defuse tensions in battles. G-Wiz separates CP and Raz when they start yelling and lightly pushing each other, which are signs that they are breaking frame and nearing violence (frames 1 and 2). Moreover, instead of singling out a lone culprit, G-Wiz blames both CP and Raz for hoggin' the mic and for breaking frame. This allow both participants to walk away from the battle without losing face.[8] And, finally, Flawliss helps transform the heated battle into a cipher by rapping; moreover, he defuses tensions by making a self-deprecating remark about himself: "Time out, time out, let Flawliss's fatass rip a rhyme now" (frame 4).[9]

Onlookers also try to reason with participants who break frame and threaten to use violence. In this next case, CP upsets "Skrills" in a battle. Moments later, Skrills stops rapping and, announces that he will "knock CP out." In rhyme form, the same comment would not raise concerns among onlookers, since disses in battles are often more obscene, aggressive, and offensive. Indeed, one of the characteristic features of verbal duels is that participants exchange "wondrously obscene" comments with each other (Goffman 1974:49–50). However, as a spoken statement, such threats are taken seriously by onlookers. To defuse the situation, Black Soultan jumps in and makes light of the situation, and dismisses CP's behavior:

> Skrills becomes noticeably upset at CP's last remark and looks like he wants to fight: "Nigga, I got one hand (the other is in a cast) and I'll knock yo ass out!"
> CP responds [in rap form]: "See when they battle, some niggas wanna take it further…"
> Skrills is still unhappy about CP's comments: "C'mon stop playing all that fake shit, *I'll knock yo ass out.*"
> CP begins to walk away from Skrills, when Black Soultan steps in the middle of the battle and begins joking and reasoning with Skrills: "We a little older now, I'm 30! He's 19, 20, you know how you was when you were that age…high…just spittin' whatever comes to mind, you know we too old for that shit! [nervous laugh]. Skrills seems skeptical of

Black Soultan at first, but then nods in agreement with Black Soultan.

There are a couple of ways that Black Soultan defuses tension in the battle. First, he steps in between CP and Skrills, which interrupts the light touching and pushing that precedes fighting.[10] Second, Black Soultan reasons *with* Skrills and asks him to excuse CP's immaturity. By saying, "You know how you was when you were that age…" and "you know we too old for that shit!" Black Soultan interrupts Skrills's escalation into rage and violence; he appeals to Skrills by saying that he "knows better" and is above getting upset at CP, who is younger and not as experienced.

Hoo Ridin' and Flashing Heat: When Blustering Nearly Turns Violent

Many regulars remember a near fatal shooting that emerged from a battle several years before I became a regular on the corner. According to "Cash," a 28-year old African American male who has been a regular on the corner for the past eight years, the battle started as a playful dispute between participants and escalated into "niggas throwin' up gang signs" (hoo ridin') after one participant made disparaging remarks about the other's religious ties to Islam:

> My nigga, "C-Note," starts clownin' this Muslim nigga. I heard these niggas was throwin' up gang signs and shit. They got all heated for a cool minute, and the next thing I know, I hear gun shots—like 3 or 4 of them. I ran to my car and took off, and then heard from my nigga, C-Note, that he got shot in the stomach by that Muslim nigga!

This event and other accounts from the corner are sobering reminders that battles *can* lead to violence. Regulars remember this instance and are especially weary of

FIGURE 41.4. Audience Intervention: One at a Time!. 1. CP: This chain be the same thing.... 2. R interrupts CP. 3. Audience: One at a time!.

battles that escalate into hoo ridin'—a type of verbal provocation gang members use to challenge each other on the streets (cf. Garot 2006, 2007). Unlike aggressive yelling, pushing, and other types of blustering, hoo ridin' sets up a series of violent moves to follow. Individuals who hoo ride are not only insulting their opponent, but also drawing upon a scripted type of challenge that sets up violent encounters on the inner-city streets (cf. Garot 2006, 2007). In the following example, 'Spyda,' a 26-year old African American male, gets into a heated battle with "Chavy," a Latino male in his twenties, who escalates the battle by hoo ridin' and using "nigga" in a disaffiliative way:

Chavy, a Latino male and Spyda are batting each other next to a phone booth on the corner. The onlooking crowd of about 20 erupts into laughter after Spyda calls Chavy a "lag." Chavy seems particularly

embarrassed by this and starts hoo ridin' on Spyda, "Nigga! Where you from!?" Spyda, who was laughing along with others, quickly becomes serious. He fires back, "Don't say Nigga again! You can diss me on whatever you want, but remember where you at, homey!" There are some murmurs among onlookers, who wait to see how Chavy is going to respond. Instead of apologizing or downplaying his comment, he reasserts his question, this time a little louder than previously, "I *said*, nigga where you from!?" Spyda is fuming now and while walking back to his car, he announces, "Nigga, I'ma show you where I'm from!" He opens the passenger door of his car, reaches into the glove compartment, and pulls out a black .9mm handgun. He cocks the gun once and walks back over to Chavy. Onlookers start to scatter at this point. Spyda holds the gun up and points it at Chavy's face. Spyda continues, "Now

FIGURE 41.5. Audience Intervention: Time Out. 1. CP and R light pushing. 2. GW separates CP and R. 3. GW: Time out. 4. Flawliss starts rapping.

what's up!? You ain't sayin' nothin' now!" A temple of Chavy's friends grab him by the arm and drag him away from Spyda.

Although this situation did not result in a shooting, regulars were quick to reprimand Spyda for his action. A few minutes after the commotion died down, a few of Spyda's friends scolded him for pulling his "heat." Spyda listened attentively, but also defended his side of the story, and eventually admitted to others that he was not *really* planning to pop (shoot) Chavy.

There are important clues from this interaction that expand my analysis. First, Chavy breaks frame and proceeds to hoo ride on Spyda, an interactional technique that transforms an already confrontational battle into more than play. Unlike other kinds of bluster, aggressive interactions over a person's gang affiliation have less room for negotiation; they are scripted ways of getting into

violence on the streets. Second, Chavy further offends Spyda when he uses the word nigga in a disaffiliative way. Although a few nonblack regulars use the term "nigga" while casually hanging out or rapping with black regulars, used in this context, nigga is a disaffiliative word that can further escalate already tense moments in a battle. Third and finally, Spyda establishes an ultimatum that Chavy transgresses. After Chavy yells, "Nigga, where you from!?" the first time, Spyda cautions him to *not* say something like that again. This does not deter Chavy, however, who defiantly repeats himself, further undermining Spyda's moral authority. This ratchets the tension even closer to violence, since Spyda would lose face if he did not respond in like form to Chavy.

...Onlookers sustain the playfulness of battles by enforcing limits. In some cases, onlookers discipline rowdy and unruly participants who do not allow their opponent to have a turn. These moves preserve a basic level of cooperation in the battle, which further distinguishes battles from yelling matches, hoo ridin', and other aggressive face-to-face interactions. In other situations, onlookers step in between participants who look like they are ready to fight. Onlookers look for light pushing, shouting, and other signs that participants have broken frame and may be nearing violence. Lastly, onlookers also tell jokes or start rapping to defuse tensions in the battle. These moves interrupt the escalation of violence by lightening the mood and deflecting attention away from people who are blustering; in other words, onlookers stifle escalations into violence by taking away a potential audience from those trying to use violence....

Conclusion

The line between play and violence is a precarious one.... Although participants begin with the shared understanding that the battle is meant to be play, this does not guarantee that the battle will remain that way. Clear and unambiguous cues that participants see the battle as play help thwart possible escalations into bluster and violence. These cues, however, do not always work. Ritual insults appear in a flash, and can unexpectedly arouse emotions that propel individuals into new and more serious interactional frames. When this happens, onlookers employ a variety of techniques to defuse tensions. Subtle changes in a participant's body language, posture, and overall orientation to the interaction are cuds for onlookers to tell jokes, step between participants, and create other diversions to defuse escalating tensions; these are ways onlookers enforce limits.

Although the subtle smiles, laughter, and daps emerge in street corner battles,

they point toward more general interactional techniques individuals use to maintain the playful meanings of interaction. To develop a more robust grounded theory of play-sustaining techniques, further studies should examine what is common and what is distinctive about how people sustain the playfulness of different social interactions. While I cannot include a comprehensive review of such interactions, I can allude to some fruitful examples for future research. For example, it is common for groups of men to engage in light-hearted banter, debate, and repartee with each other at parties and other social gatherings. At some point in the interaction, somebody may make an off-handed comment that offends another person in the group. Remarks about politics, religion, sexual orientation, or other sensitive topics have the power to offend and escalate tensions. To help sustain the playful and light-hearted manner of this situation, the individual who said the comment may smile, wink, or make self-effacing remarks (e.g., "I'm an idiot! Don't listen to me!") to defuse tension. Meanwhile, the person who took offense to these comments may laugh off the comment as "no big deal," or use some symbolic gesture (e.g., smiles, winks, shakes hand) to downplay the seriousness of the other person's remark.

Onlookers may also help defuse escalating tension in the above example. For example, a neutral party in this interaction may tell jokes, invite others into a communal ritual (e.g., "I think it's time for another round of drinks!"), or redirect the conservation toward something that emphasizes commonality between participants (e.g., "The music at this party is really lame, eh?"). Although these moves are different in form, they are similar in function to those that onlookers use in tense street rap battles. Moreover, onlookers in these situations pay careful attention to the body language and overall orientation that different people have toward each other. Subtle changes in demeanor may signal a change in frame that warrants intervention. Thus, laughter, smiles, winks and other playful gestures are not simply descriptive details of interaction. They are more fundamental parts of how interaction works. Future research should compare the different play sustaining cues groups use to organize interactions with each other.

NOTES

1. An "8" refers to an .8 mm handgun, much like a "9" refers to a .9 mm handgun.
2. Theoretical insights from CA describe how individuals prefer conversations that are affiliative and orderly. Conversely, prolonged moments of overlap create tensions between interlocutors [cf. Sacks, Schlegloff, and Jefferson 1974].
3. All 25 of my respondents described comments about another person's racial authenticity, class standing, sexual prowess (or lack thereof), and masculinity as fair game.
4. Hughes and Short, Jr. (2005) find that fun and recreational activities like "playing the dozens" and "horsing around" often lead to more serious kinds of violence among youth gang members. Moreover, they highlight the "fluid and uncertain boundaries between acceptable behavior and more direct challenges to status" within activities that begin as fun or recreation (Hughes and Short Jr. 2005:64).
5. Garfinkel (1967) pioneered studies that demonstrate how social interactions are ongoing accomplishments between individuals.
6. Collins (2008:347) describes the multiple social functions of blustering: "It is an expression of pointed threat, anger directed at an immediate opponent. It may be the first step in the fight, a move to intimidate, to force the opponent to waver, to gain an

advantage, an opportunity in which to strike. But bluster can also be a move that forestalls and substitutes for violence." There are also different kinds of blustering. For instance, "hoo ridin'" (also known as "hittining up") is a verbal strategy inner-city gang members use to provoke and intimidate potential rivals on the street (cf. Garot 2006, 2007). Typically, hoo ridin' involves some combination of representing or extolling one's gang over the other person's gang, followed by aggressive challenges to fight.

7. Regulars have various local terms for when someone loses a battle. In addition to saying someone "got ate up," regulars also say someone "got served," "got burned," and "got murked."
8. Phillips and Cooney (2005:336) show how individuals can walk away from a near conflictual situation without losing face when a third party intervenes with a "settlement."
9. Francis (1994) examines how people use humor to defuse tensions within an interaction.
10. Jackson-Jacobs (2006) analyzes the different ways individuals get into fights with each other. His research illustrates the need for more up-close and situated studies on getting into violence.

REFERENCES

Anderson, Elijah. 1978. *A Place on the Corner.* Chicago: University of Chicago Press.
———. 1999. *Code of the Street: Decency, Violence, and the Moral Life of the Inner City.* New York: Delta.
Caldwell, Ben. 1993. "Kaos at Ground Zero: Vitleo. Teleconferencing, and Community Networks." *Leonardo* 26(5):421–422.
Collins, Randall. 2008. *Violence: A Microsociological Theory.* Princeton, NJ: Princeton University Press.
Francis, Linda. 1994. "Laughter, The Best Mediation: Humor as Emotion Management in Interaction." *Symbolic Interaction* 17(2):147–163.

Garfinkel, Harold. 1967. *Studies in Ethnomethodology.* Englewood Cliffs, NJ: Prentice-Hall.

Garot, Robert. 2006. "Inner-City Teens and Face-Work: Avoiding Violence and Maintaining Honor." In *A Cultural Approach to Interpersonal Communication: Essential Readings*, pp. 294–317. Lella Monaghan and Jane Goodman (eds.). Cambridge, UK: Blackwell Press.

———. 2007. "Where You From!" *Journal of Contemporary Ethnography* 36(1):50–84.

Goffman, Erving. 1974. *Frame Analysis: An Essay on the Organization of Experience.* Cambridge, MA: Harvard University Press.

Hughes, Lorine and James Short, Jr. 2003. "Disputes Involving Youth Street Gang Members: Micro-Social Contexts." *Criminology* 43(1):43–76.

Jackson-Jacobs, Curtis. 2006. *"Tough Crowd: An Ethnographic Study of Fighting."* Ph.D. dissertation, Department of Sociology, University of California, Los Angeles. Los Angeles, CA.

Katz, Jack. 1988. *Seductions of Crime: The Moral and Sensual Attractions in Doing Evil.* New York: Basic Books.

———. 1999. *How Emotions Work.* Chicago: University of Chicago Press.

Lee, Jooyoung. Forthcoming a. "Escaping Embarrassment: Face-Work in the Rap Cipher." *Social Psychology Quarterly.*

———. Forthcoming b. "Open Mic: Professionalizing the Rap Career." *Ethnography.*

Luckenbill. David. 1977. "Criminal Homicide Is a Situated Transaction." *Social Problems* 25(2):176–186.

Morgan, Marcyliena. 2002. *Language, Discourse, and Power in African American Culture.* Cambridge, UK: Cambridge University Press.

Phillips, Scott and Mark Cooney. 2005. "Aiding Peace, Abetting Violence: Third Parties and the Management of Conflict." *American Sociological Review* 70:334–354.

Sacks, Harvey, Emanuel A. Schegloff, and Gail Jefferson. 1974. "A Simplest Systematics for the Organization of Turn-Taking for Conversation." *Language* 50(4):696–735.

U. S. Census Bureau. 2001. "California Census 2000 Summary File 1." Retrieved June 8, 2009 (http://www.census.gov/census2000/states/ca.html).

PART VII

"BUT DOES IT HAVE A POINT?" ETHNOGRAPHY AND SOCIAL POLICY

E thnography is often thought of as largely descriptive, yet it can also lead to prescriptions for social action. The next section of the reader features selections that make a more explicit connection between urban life and public policy. Illuminating the intended and unintended consequences of social policy, these studies use ethnography to reveal how momentous changes are experienced, perceived, and defined by those directly impacted on the ground.

Herbert Gans's study of the urban redevelopment of Boston's West End is one example. In the late 1950s, at the height of the era of "urban renewal," Gans moved into a working-class community that had been targeted for destruction by political and business figures. These elites wanted to replace the shabby but well-situated neighborhood with a new hospital and high-rent buildings that would generate tax revenue and spur further downtown development. In his ethnography, Gans shows the many ways in which the people of the community thought about and defined their neighborhood and viewed the redevelopment process. In the excerpt presented here, he highlights how policy makers were able to carry out this

major urban development—destroying an area that many residents deeply valued—with scarcely any protest from the people in the community. It is extremely difficult to understand the residents' apparent inertia without knowing how they perceived the situation as it unfolded. Because Gans was there, he offers an explanation grounded in the way the residents understood their role in the community as well as their efficacy in the society in general.

William Kornblum's "Working the Deuce" highlights other themes in the way that urban ethnography engages with public policy. Written at a time when New York City's real-estate developers were actively working to sanitize the Times Square area of pornography, gambling, and drug dealing, Kornblum tried to get to know the people who were to be displaced from that community. He concluded (correctly as it turned out) that these people would not go away but would simply migrate to other parts of the city. Kornblum's article also shows how one may develop a better understanding of how policy might play out by speaking to people who are often believed to be incapable of creating their own meaning out of the situation. The drug dealers make him understand that when the area is upscaled, their best customers will become more numerous, and that their incentive to remain in the area will therefore actually increase. Finally, Kornblum's essay illustrates ethnography's potential to portray the people impacted by larger policies as living, breathing human beings, while not losing sight of the larger forces and their impact on human lives. While he shows a number of characters involved in scams and hustles on the street, he never forgets the "real con artists"—the real-estate developers—who, he concludes, are implicated in the greatest hustle of all: the assurance that upscaling is the way to solve social problems.

The next article, Terry Williams's "Letter from a Crackhouse," is an intimate portrait of the social world of an apartment where drug users come and go. Set on a run-down corner of New York City's Washington Heights neighborhood, the apartment is where "regulars" come to use drugs and have sex. Williams claims that his subjects have ended up in this place because of complex forces ranging from the deinstitutionalization of the mentally ill to increases in homelessness and unemployment. Nevertheless, he seems well aware that his advantage lies not in providing explanations or relating how crack use became an epidemic but in accumulating as many facts as possible in order to present a sociological portrait of an otherwise invisible social world, showing in intimate detail how it works. Williams introduces us to the crackhouse's local language and unique way of life. He ends by stating that his subjects want to get off crack and that they do not believe that drug legalization is the solution to their woes. All the same, he never tells the reader what he thinks. Like Jacob Riis in *How the Other Half Lives*, he appears

motivated by the belief that exposing how people live will make it much harder for policy makers and citizens to ignore human suffering. Yet, unlike Riis, Williams is interested in showing how the subjects make sense of their own world rather than in providing a description based on reports made by the police or other authorities.

The next selection in this section, Kathryn Edin and Christopher Jencks's "Welfare," is yet another memorable effort at fact finding within worlds to which policy makers have little access. Writing in response to the widespread American belief that single mothers on welfare should be pushed off the rolls into full-time work, Edin and Jencks set out to find out more about the social situation of these largely invisible women. Why were they not working? How did they make ends meet? Edin obtained introductions to welfare recipients, developed a rapport with them, and then asked them basic questions about their budgets. The data she obtained on their sources of income and how they spent that money reveal the importance of residence in determining an individual's ability to make ends meet without outside assistance. As she discovered, those who chose not to live in the most dangerous public housing paid much higher rents on the private market and lived far away from buses and trains—thus increasing their costs for transportation. Their decision—one that probably most Americans would make—led to their need for more money than the welfare office could provide. The women thus ended up supplementing their income with a variety of sources that usually went unreported to the welfare office. Edin and Jencks also used the interviews to reflect on why many welfare mothers chose not to work when jobs were offered to them. They discovered that the amount of money mothers would earn from working was less than the combined income they derived from welfare and off-the-books employment and financial support. Edin and Jencks's interviews with welfare recipients in the Chicago area thus illuminated a social situation that was largely unknown to policy makers who lacked such facts. Because working mothers pay for housing, medical care, child care, transportation, and taxes, they must have incomes that are amply above the poverty level in order to make ends meet.

The next selection, "Missing the Connection," once again demonstrates the potential of urban ethnography to enter into a dialogue with policy makers. During the past few decades, one of the most popular explanations for urban poverty has been the "spatial mismatch hypothesis," according to which geographic distance from manufacturing jobs is seen as a cause of inner-city unemployment. Following this logic, policy makers often work to bring industry and businesses to poor neighborhoods with the belief that they will open up job opportunities to local residents. Prior to the study conducted by Philip Kasinitz and Jan Rosenberg, however, few researchers had spoken to employers to find out how this policy works in a community context. Kasinitz and Rosenberg met with forty-eight firms in the Red Hook section of Brooklyn, New York. They show that bringing businesses to poor ghetto neighborhoods does not necessarily change employment prospects for locals. Here was an area in which a considerable number of unskilled jobs were located within walking distance of a large public housing project with perennially high unemployment. Yet local residents rarely got the jobs already located in their own neighborhood! Focusing on the role of social networks and unions, as well as discrimination against the locals, Kasinitz and Rosenberg provide a more complex understanding of the problems facing low-income job seekers than that suggested by simple geographic explanations.

We conclude this section with a recent study of the criminal justice system's impact on a Philadelphia ghetto. Since the early 1990s, harsh US drug laws have led to the imprisonment of unprecedented numbers of poor black men, mainly for drug offenses. Alice Goffman moved into an intensely policed, poor black neighborhood in order to understand the impact that mass incarceration was having on the everyday life of these communities. She discovered that in today's ghetto many warrants are issued for small offenses, such as failing to pay court fees, failing a urine test after drug treatment, or missing a court date. Becoming part of the everyday life of a group of young men known as the 6th Street Boys, she found that in their case, activities, relations, and localities that others relied on to maintain decent and respectable identities had been transformed into a system that authorities used to locate, arrest, and confine them. For these "wanted" individuals, interactions with the police and courts were not the only danger that they faced. Even simple activities such as showing up for work, going to the hospital, spending time in public, or interacting with family members could pose risk. Instead of a safe place to sleep, eat, and find acceptance and support, a mother's home was transformed into a "last known address," one of the first places where the police would look for someone. Close relatives, friends, neighbors, and even the mothers of their children become potential informants. Mass incarceration thus proved to have devastating effects not only on those who were eventually incarcerated but also on all the other people in their lives and indeed their entire community. Goffman reveals what few judges or politicians could not have realized without conducting careful fieldwork, namely, the unintended consequences of their policies on the social fabric of poor families and communities.

42

HERBERT J. GANS

THE DESTRUCTION OF BOSTON'S WEST END

from *The Urban Villagers* (1962)

In the late 1950s, Herbert Gans moved to the West End of Boston, a white working-class community that had been targeted for clearance by city and federal authorities. In this selection, he tells the history of that destruction, and he explains why there was so little protest or resistance from community residents.

The idea for redeveloping Boston's West End dates back to the turn of the century, when the area was already known as a densely occupied low-income neighborhood. In the late 1930s, Nathan Straus, one of the founders of the public housing movement in America, visited the West End and suggested that the entire area be cleared and replaced with public housing. Although his advice was not heeded, the creation of the federal slum clearance program after World War II did lead the Boston Planning Board to suggest that the West End, together with the North and South Ends, were ripe for clearance. In 1950, the Boston Housing Authority applied to the federal government for preliminary planning funds to study the West End, but work proceeded slowly, and it was not until April 1953 that the decision to redevelop the West End was announced officially.

At about that time, the first stirrings of protest were heard from the West End. A small group of young West Enders organized the Save the West End Committee, and with the help of a Beacon Hill resident who had opposed other city modernization schemes in the past, they carried on several years of opposition to the project.

The Committee received little overt support from the rest of the West Enders, and its opposition did not significantly interrupt the city's planning. Soon after federal and local approval of the plan was obtained, the project was opened to bidders. The private developer chosen for the new West End proposed a 2400-unit complex of elevator apartment buildings—and a handful of townhouses—to be rented for about $45 a room, a figure that placed the project firmly in the luxury housing category. The plans were presented at a public hearing in April 1957 and approved by the City Council and the Mayor three months later.

In October 1957, the Redevelopment Authority commissioners held an informal hearing in the West End regarding the scheme they were taking over from the Housing Authority. Two hundred people from the West End attended this hearing, most of them strongly opposed to the redevelopment. According to one of the commissioners with whom I later spoke, his group was impressed with the protest. But after "a lot of soul-searching," the commissioners concluded that the process had gone too far to be reversed. In January 1958, the city and the federal government signed the contract that would require the latter to pay two-thirds and the former, one-third of the cost of purchasing the land, relocating the present residents, and clearing the site for the redeveloper.

Surveyors started to come into the West End at that time, and in February 1958, a site office was set up to handle relocation surveys and other procedures for relocation and clearance. The city took official title to the land under the power of eminent domain during the last week in April, thus marking the beginning of actual redevelopment and relocation.

When schools closed for the year in June 1958—some of them never to reopen—West Enders began to move out in large numbers. The exodus continued throughout 1958, and by November of that year, 1200 of the 2700 households had departed. After a slowdown during the winter, the moveouts resumed in spring 1959; by the summer of 1959,

the West End was emptying rapidly. As the Redevelopment Authority began to tear down buildings as soon as they had become vacant, this encouraged the departure of people in neighboring structures. Thus the relocation process, which had been expected to take three to four years, was completed after little more than eighteen months. By the summer of 1960, only rubble remained where two years ago had lived more than 7000 people. Meanwhile, foundations were being laid for the first of the new apartment buildings, and in January 1962, the initial residents of the new West End started to move in.

The City's Reasons for Redevelopment

There were many reasons for the city to redevelop the West End. Boston is a poor city, and the departure of middle-class residents and industry for the suburbs has left it with an oversupply of tax-exempt institutions and low-income areas that yield little for the municipal coffers. Through the federal redevelopment program, the city fathers hoped to replace some of the low-yield areas with high-rent buildings that would bring in additional municipal income. Moreover, they believed that a shiny new redevelopment project would cleanse its aged, tenement-dominated skyline, and increase the morale of private and public investors. This in turn would supposedly lead to a spiral of further private rebuilding in the city.

The West End was thought to be particularly suitable for redevelopment. Because of its central location adjacent to Beacon Hill and near the downtown shopping area, real estate men had long felt that the area was "ripe" for higher—and more profitable—uses. The long block fronting on the Charles River was considered attractive for luxury housing. Some businessmen believed that the decline of the downtown shopping district could be ended by housing "quality shoppers" on its fringes. Moreover, Massachusetts General Hospital was expanding rapidly, and its trustees had long been unhappy about being surrounded by low-income neighbors.

The business community and the city's newspapers were favorably inclined, as were the political leaders of the city outside the West End. And even the West End protest seemed muted. Some years earlier, when it had been proposed to clear the North End, the citizens and the political leaders of that area had raised such an outcry that the project was immediately shelved. But the local politicians in the West End were too few and too powerless for their protests to be heeded. Nor could the West Enders themselves make their voices heard. The Save the West End Committee's protest was noted, but as the group's membership was small, the Committee, in effect, had no political influence. Moreover, the local settlement houses and other caretaking agencies all approved of the redevelopment, partly because their lay leaders were drawn from the Boston business community, and partly because the staffs of these agencies felt that the fortunes of the West Enders would be thereby improved. The Catholic Archdiocese, whose local church was to be saved for architectural reasons, also gave its blessing.

Finally, all of Boston was convinced that the West End was a slum that ought to be torn down not only for the sake of the city but also for the good of its own residents. This belief was supported by the general appearance of the area, by studies that had been made in the West End by public and private agencies, and by stories that appeared in the press. In 1957, for example a popular Boston columnist could wildly exaggerate both past and present conditions in the area to claim that:

> The West End is today definitely a slum area. In fact it has always been....It

gradually degenerated into a rooming-house section and then went from bad to worse....Around the turn of the century...every conceivable sort of vice that makes for a slum flourished....That was nearly sixty years ago. Any change since has slowly slid towards the worse.[1]

After calling the area a cesspool, the columnist urged his readers to "come back in ten years, and you won't know the reborn city."[2]

The West Enders' Perception of the Redevelopment Process

To the West Enders, the many years between the announcement that the area would be redeveloped and the actual clearing of their neighborhood appeared quite differently than it did to the city and its officials. No one with whom I talked was quite sure when the West Enders had first heard about the plans for redeveloping their neighborhood. The Planning Board's recommendation in 1949 had been made public, of course, and the press had also carried stories of the preliminary planning studies that had begun in 1951. At that time, the residents were opposed to the redevelopment, but did not feel themselves sufficiently threatened to be alarmed.

The initial announcement, however, did have some more important consequences. During the postwar era, the West End—like most other inner-city districts—had begun to lose some of its recently married couples to the suburbs. The announcement itself undoubtedly spurred additional moves, and it seems also to have discouraged other people from moving into the West End. Whatever the causes, the vacancy rate in the area began to climb, especially in buildings owned by absentee landlords, who then began to have a change of heart about the redevelopment. Eventually, in fact, they became its most fervent adherents, and in later years urged the city and federal government to hasten the process, because they were losing money on vacant apartments that they could no longer rent.

Tenants, and resident owners whose buildings were still occupied, were almost unanimously opposed to the redevelopment. Some of the tenants in the most dilapidated structures were hopeful that government action would provide them with better places to live. But the vast majority of West Enders had no desire to leave. They were content to live in the West End, and were willing to overlook some of its physical defects in comparison with its many social advantages. Those who had been born there cited the traditional belief that "the place you're born is where you want to die." Even criticism of the area would sometimes be stilled by the remark, "never disparage a place in which you've grown up." Many of the people who had left the West End at marriage would come back occasionally—if only to shop—and one man whose family had left the area shortly after his birth twenty years earlier insisted that "you always come back to the place of your childhood."

Most people were not very explicit at that time about their feelings toward the area. Because the West End still existed, and because they had never known anything else, they could not estimate how its disappearance might affect them.[3] "What's so good about the West End? We're used to it," was one quite typical comment. Subsequently, however, I heard more anguished remarks that indicated how important the area and its people were to the speaker. In December 1957, the day after the federal government gave the city the go-ahead, one young Italian man said:

I wish the world would end tonight   I wish they'd tear the whole damn town down, damn scab town.... I'm going to

be lost without the West End. Where the hell can I go?

Another West Ender told me: "It isn't right to scatter the community to all four winds. It pulls the heart out of a guy to lose all his friends." Shortly before the taking, a barber in his early sixties ended a discussion of death that was going on in the shop with these comments:

I'm not afraid to die, but I don't want to. But if they tear the West End down and we are all scattered from all the people I know and that know me, and they wouldn't know where I was, I wouldn't want to die and people not know it.

Perhaps because most people were opposed to the redevelopment, they could not quite believe that it would happen. Over the years, they began to realize that the redevelopment plans were in earnest, but they were—and remained—skeptical that the plans would ever be implemented. Even on the day of the taking, the person just quoted told me: "I don't believe it; I won't believe it till it happens. I'll wait till I get my notice.... You'll see, they'll start at the lower end, and they'll never come up here."

There were several reasons for the West Enders' skepticism. First, they had considerable difficulty in understanding the complicated parade of preliminary and final approvals, or the tortuous process by which the plans moved back and forth between the Housing Authority, the City Council, the Mayor, the State Housing Board, and the federal Housing and Home Finance Agency. Instead of realizing that each approval was one step in a tested and finite administrative procedure, the West Enders saw it as merely another decision in a seemingly purposeless, erratic, and infinite series. Thus, when the federal housing agency did give its final approval in the winter of 1957, most West Enders did not understand that this was the last step in the process. They recalled that the same agency had approved it several times before, without any visible result. Thus, they felt certain that there would be more meetings, and more decisions, and that twenty-five years later, the West End would still be there.

Their failure to understand the process can be traced back partly to the poor information that they received from the press and the city agencies. The latter, assuming that West Enders understood the nature of the process, did not attempt to describe it in sufficient detail. Moreover, city officials did not see that to West Enders, all government agencies were pretty much the same, and that notions of city-state-federal relationships were strange to them. The West Enders in turn paid little attention to the press releases, and were more receptive to distorted facts and the many rumors that they could hear from friends and neighbors.

Moreover, they noted that official announcements were vague about when things would begin to happen in the West End. If estimates were given, they were usually wrong.

Nor could West Enders really conceive of the possibility that the area would be torn down. They had watched the demolition of parts of the North End for the Central Artery—the city's expressway system—and while they disapproved, they realized that a highway was of public benefit and could not be opposed. But the idea that the city could clear the West End, and then turn the land over to a private builder for luxury apartments seemed unbelievable.

Their skepticism turned to incredulity when the city awarded the redevelopment. The idea that a private builder could build apartments then estimated to rent for $40 to $50 a room—more than they were paying for five- and six-room apartments—was hard to believe. And that the government could encourage this venture seemed incomprehensible except as a result of political corruption, the exchange of bribes,

and the cutting in of politicians on future profits.[4] As one West Ender among many pointed out:

> The whole thing is a steal, taking the area away from the people, and giving it to some guys who had paid off everyone else.... It is just someone making money at our expense. There are many areas lots worse than this one. Look at [the Mayor], a city clerk once, and now he's rich enough to buy up Boston itself. Yes, just a city clerk and look at him now.

Thereafter, all of the steps in the process were interpreted as attempts to scare the West Enders out of the area, so that the values of the buildings would be reduced and the private developers could buy them more cheaply. But even then, people were skeptical that this scheme would come to fruition, partially because it was so immoral. Many West Enders argued that only in Russia could the government deprive citizens of their property in such a dictatorial manner.

Also, West Enders found it hard to think far ahead. Even if they could admit to themselves that the area might eventually be "thrown down"—as they put it—it was still difficult to think about what might happen years hence, especially in the absence of incontrovertible evidence. As already noted, official announcements and newspaper stories generally were not accepted as evidence; people had to see more concrete examples of the city's plans before they would believe that the city was in earnest. For example, the registered letters, which the Redevelopment Authority sent to all West Enders indicating that it had taken over the area, were less persuasive than the announcement that, as of May 1958, rents were to be paid not to landlords but to the city's relocation office. Only when people saw their neighbors—and especially their landlords—going to that office to pay their rents did all of them realize that the end had come. Conversely, a few weeks earlier, when the announcement of the taking was imminent, West Enders were much cheered by the city's repaving of streets immediately outside the project area and by the gas company's installation of more modern gas meters in West End apartments. These were concrete actions that could be taken as evidence, especially since they seemed to prove what West Enders wanted to believe—that nothing was going to happen—and were considered much more reliable than official announcements or news stories.[5] And finally, of course, West Enders simply denied the possibility of redevelopment because they did not want it to happen. They were content to live in the West End, and could not imagine living elsewhere, or going about the city looking for "rooms."

As a result, life in the West End went on as always, with relatively little overt concern about the redevelopment and even less public discussion of it. On the days following the announcement of another decision in the process, people would talk about it heatedly, but then it would be forgotten again until the next announcement. There had been so many announcements, and so many meetings, and nothing ever seemed to happen afterward. Surely it would be safe—and easy—to assume that nothing would ever happen.

Social agencies knew, of course, that the area would be redeveloped, and were not in doubt over the outcome of the long process. This knowledge, the gradual reduction in the number of their clients, and the appearance of some of the lower-class newcomers, sapped their morale. Although most of the agencies and their staffs were in favor of the redevelopment, they were also sorry to see the neighborhood torn down and its residents dispersed. They did not voice their feelings in public, but at the annual board meeting of one of the settlement houses, the staff put on a skit about the redevelopment that reflected its ambivalence toward the destruction of the West End. The caretakers

also tried, with little success, to prepare the West Enders for what was about to happen. Some of them urged the redevelopment agency to improve its relocation procedures, but by then it was too late.

The best illustration of the lack of impact of the redevelopment process on the West Enders was the failure of the Save the West End Committee to attract their overt support, and the absence of other forms of protest. As noted earlier, the Committee came into being in 1956, when a handful of West Enders met with a local civic and political leader who had long been interested in the West End. An upper-class Bostonian, he helped to build the park, pool, and boating area along the banks of the Charles River and had participated in other improvement projects since the 1930s.[6] He promised to support the group politically and financially, and, with his help, the Committee rented a vacant store in the area. Over the years, it held a number of meetings, spoke at public hearings, published pamphlets and leaflets, went to Washington to try to overturn the decision, and eventually took its case to the courts. The Committee sought, of course, to enroll the neighborhood in its work, but attracted only a small—although loyal—group of members, who kept up a steady barrage of protest over the years. Not until the very end, however, did they gain a wider audience.

One of the major obstacles to the Committee's effectiveness in its own neighborhood was its outside leadership. Although many West Enders had heard of the civic leader who helped to guide the Committee, they knew also that he lived outside the area, and, that however strong his sympathy, he was in class, ethnic background, and culture not one of their own. Nor was he at ease among the West Enders. While he identified with the neighborhood, he often seemed to feel more strongly about the facilities on the riverbank—which were of little interest to the West Enders— than about the tenement streets and their occupants.

Moreover, the other active members—and the people who originally asked for his guidance—were neither typical West Enders nor the kinds of people who could enroll them. Among the most active were an Italian writer and an artist, a young Jewish professional, a single Polish woman, and a number of elderly ladies who lived in the Charlesbank Homes. While some of them did have leadership ability, almost all of them were in one way or another marginal to their own ethnic groups in the West End. Thus, they could not attract these groups to their cause.

This inability had nothing to do with the Committee's point of view, for that was based on the beliefs shared widely by a majority of West Enders: That the redevelopment was motivated by political chicanery and individual greed; that government actions to scare the West Enders into leaving stemmed from sympathy or collusion with the builders; and that until definite proof was available, there was no reason to believe the West End would actually be torn down.

The Committee, however, did not develop a program that would require West Enders as a whole to take action. Its pamphlets and speeches expressed the same indignation and incredulity felt by all, but it did not ask them to act, other than to come to meetings, help the Committee in its mailings, and stay in the West End.

Yet all of these considerations for the Committee's lack of success in gaining active neighborhood support paled before the most important one: the inability of the West Enders to organize in their own behalf. Indeed, other causes were only effects of that basic inability. Had the West Enders flocked to meetings in larger numbers, the leadership would probably have gone to someone whom the residents would have followed. As it was, they watched the activities of the Committee with passive sympathy. Some were suspicious: they argued that the Committee consisted of people who had been left out when the graft was distributed;

that the leadership was Communist; and that an officer of the Committee who was Jewish was related to one of the developers. The majority, however, did agree with all that the Committee claimed, and shared its anger. But even then, they could not break out of the peer group society and organize in common cause. It was impossible to fight city hall; this was a function of the local politician. If he failed, what else was there to do?

Action-seeking West Enders would have relished a march on City Hall to do violence to the officials principally associated with the redevelopment, but the act of joining with neighbors to work together for halting the redevelopment was inconceivable. At the meetings at which West Enders spoke, they spoke as individuals, about their own individual cases. The local politicians who appeared at these meetings spoke *to* the West Enders rather than *for* them; they convinced the audience of their own opposition to the redevelopment, and tried to display themselves as loyal representatives of the West End. But they too were unable—and perhaps unwilling—to organize an effective protest movement.

Even the resident leaders of the Committee—notably those of Italian background—were ill at ease about guiding a protest group that called for citizen participation. They realized that their Beacon Hill supporter could not attract the West Enders, but they were also skeptical as to their own ability to rally them. In addition, they were ambivalent about their personal involvement. They were able to make speeches and to share their anger with an audience, but other activities came less easily. Being a leader without any proof of results, spending time away from family and friends or from second jobs and other individual pursuits was difficult. When Committee members were asked to carry out the routine tasks of organization, and failed to come through—as was often the case—the leaders who gave the orders resented having to carry out these tasks themselves. They were hurt that they should give up their own free time, and extend themselves for the group if no one else did and if there was no reward for such self-deprivation. Thus, the Committee itself was constantly split by bickering, by people withdrawing from activity when no support was forthcoming, and by individuals offering new solutions and making speeches to each other when more prosaic activity was called for.

The leaders were also hampered by lack of information. The politicians claimed—with some justification—that since they were opposed to the project, they had not been kept properly informed by redevelopment officials. Also, they and the leaders of the Committee were unable to deal properly with what information was available. Like most other West Enders, they believed that the project's fate was in the hands of one individual, the Mayor, and that it could be overturned simply by persuading him of its immorality. As unable as the rest of the West Enders to follow the series of steps that led to the final taking of the land, some of them believed until the last moment that the redevelopment would never take place. They accepted the rumors that swept the area like everyone else, and could not detach themselves sufficiently from their neighbors to look objectively at the doings of the outside world. Thus, none of the prerequisites or minutiae of organizational activity came easily to the Committee leaders. Much of the time, only their anger at the outrage they felt was being perpetrated against themselves and their neighbors kept them going.

The truth was, that for a group unaccustomed to organizational activity, saving the West End was an overwhelming, and perhaps impossible, task. Indeed, there was relatively little the Committee could do. The decision to redevelop the West End had been made early in the decade, and it had received the blessings of the city's decisive business leaders and politicians. The West End's local politicians all opposed the

redevelopment, but were powerless. Nor did the West End have other attributes of power, such as those displayed by the neighboring North End. This area had a larger population and a much larger business community—some of it politically influential. Most important, the North End was the center—and symbol—of Italian life in Boston. Its destruction thus would have been a threat—or at least an insult—to every Italian voter in Boston, and the city's politicians simply could not afford to alienate this increasingly influential vote. Conversely, although the Italians were also the largest group in the West End, they were not in the majority. And because they had attained a plurality only comparatively recently, the area had never really been considered an Italian neighborhood. Thus, it is doubtful whether even a unanimous turnout in opposition by the West Enders would have been sufficient to set in motion the difficult process of reversing years of work by local and federal agencies and giving up the large federal grant that financed the clearance of the area.

Redevelopment: The Last Days of the West End

With every decision, the more knowing West Enders began to realize that the days of the area were numbered. When the state gave its approval in October 1957, and the federal government signed the final contracts in January 1958, the die was cast. Even then, many West Enders were still not sure that these steps would lead to action. Conflicting signs appeared to confuse those who were looking for concrete evidence. Surveyors were sent by the city to map the area, but as noted before, the repaving of streets leading into the project area gave some people hope that another decision that would spare the neighborhood would soon be forthcoming. Other surveyors came to interview the residents, to find out where they wished to be relocated, and how much rent they could afford. Some people refused to answer; a few threw out the interviewers; but the majority answered, and then discounted the significance of the questionnaire.

Thus, in the spring of 1958, life went on pretty much as before. There were fewer businesses than had started the winter, and others were threatening to shut. A barber, who had closed his shop at the age of eighty-four, died shortly afterward, and many people felt his death had been caused by the redevelopment "scare." But otherwise, the routine prevailed. Housewives prepared for Passover or Easter, and gave their apartments the traditional spring cleaning.

On April 22, 1958, stories began to appear in the city papers that letters would be sent to the West Enders any day, announcing the taking of the land and the beginning of redevelopment. Only the week before, one of my neighbors had insisted, "They're still arguing about something; it might be five years yet." Another was thinking that nothing at all might happen, and that he would find a first-floor apartment in the area, and fix it up properly. Even the newspaper stories had relatively little impact. Many people did not read the papers regularly, and heard about it from neighbors. "It's just another attempt to scare us," said one; "I'm not frightened by the article. We'll wait till we see something." One of the local politicians was among those not yet convinced.

On April 25, all West Enders received registered letters from the Redevelopment Authority announcing the taking, explaining that rent was to be paid to the city from now on, and pointing out the procedures involved in relocation. But as the letters were written in the traditionally formal language of official agencies, I doubt seriously that many West Enders read them through to the end. There could be no doubt now, however, that the West End was coming down. Even so, the real impact of the decision did not come until about a week later, when the May rent payments were due at the relocation office. The idea of no longer paying rent to the landlord and of taking it to a city office was the concrete evidence West Enders needed to accept the redevelopment of their neighborhood.

The first reaction was a feeling of relief that the suspense was over, and that hopes would no longer be raised or lowered by contradictory evidence. For some people, the news was a real shock. But most West Enders were not overly excited. They now accepted what they had known or suspected all along, and what they should have realized earlier. For many years, they had considered the possibility of the neighborhood's destruction, and even if they had rejected the idea each time, the periodic reappearance of the threat had left a residue of belief. What they had denied so fervently before, they could now accept more easily.

The shock was softened by other conditions. One was the inevitability of the event. "Underneath we are all upset, but what can we do?" asked one West Ender. Another mitigating factor was the traditional resignation toward the behavior of the outside world. Because West Enders had always expected the worst from this world, the redevelopment was just another in a long series of deprivations and outrages. Since the city had estimated that relocation would take three years, some felt they could remain in the West End for a considerable time yet.

Finally, there were many who still did not accept the facts, and looked for even more concrete evidence. As one lady put it, "We won't believe it until we see something; we'll find out when something happens." Others found solace in the belief that the taking was illegal because the city could not charge rent under eminent domain and they had not paid the landlords for their property when they took it. One of my neighbors argued that there had been no taking: "They didn't even give the landlords a dollar. I won't believe it until I see something come down." Another neighbor pointed out that the only people who had started to move were nurses and transient middle-class residents in the area; the real West Enders were staying put.

The notices also drew people closer together, and offered them some opportunity for feelings of revenge against the landlords. A Holy Name picnic, which took place as scheduled two days after the notices came, attracted an overflow crowd. A few days later, one of my neighbors remarked, "Everyone is more friendly, like old times: why couldn't it be like that before?" Tenants who felt that they had been mistreated by their landlords were glad that the latter would now be paying rent like everyone else. Some landlords raised the rents that relatives were paying at the last moment, in the hope of increasing the value of their buildings, and other tenants were pleased at the discomfort this caused. There was some feeling of relief that one no longer needed to be polite to landlords. As one neighbor said, "Now we can have some parties; we don't have to worry about the landlord anymore." But tenants also felt sorry for the "good" landlords and the resident owners, whose properties had been taken by the city without immediate payments.

Since the city had now become the landlord and had promised to keep the buildings in good condition, some West Enders thus made demands on the city to make those repairs the landlords had neglected. The people who were angriest sought more direct forms of revenge, and found it by withholding rent payments. After the first week in May, only half the people had paid their rent to the city. At the end of the year, however, the relocation office reported that only about 150 households had actually withheld rent monies for any length of time.

In the weeks immediately following the taking, the area's anger caused the Save the West End Committee to experience an energetic but short-lived renaissance. Right after the announcement, the Committee scheduled a mother's march on City Hall, a form of protest that had worked well for the

West End some decades earlier when the neighborhood had still been predominantly Jewish. But, as no one except the leaders of the march appeared at the appointed time, it had to be cancelled. One of the Italian men explained that they would not allow their women to take part in such forms of public display.

Then, in the week after the taking, the Committee underwent a change of leadership. A young Jewish student, who had been an inactive member of the group, suddenly became interested following the announcement—spurred on considerably by the anger of his family that had now lost its store and livelihood. Since the Committee's original area leaders had lost hope, he was asked if he wanted to take over. Thereupon, he formulated an eleven-point program, which included an appeal not to pay rent and not to move out; a march on City Hall to see the Mayor; and a scheme for rehabilitating the area with the monies being paid to the city as rents. A public meeting was called for May 5, about ten days after the taking, and over two hundred people—the largest crowd ever to attend a Committee meeting—showed up. They listened enthusiastically to an area politician urge the people not to move, and somewhat less so to the student's eleven-point program. But for some, the meeting restored the hope that the area might still be spared.

This hope—fantastic as it seemed—was based on the previously mentioned assumption that the redevelopment had been planned and executed by the Mayor, and that if he could be persuaded to change his mind, the West End might be saved. Immediately after the meeting, however, plans for implementing the program foundered over the question of how to persuade the Mayor. The philosophy student, a pacifist, and a follower of Gandhi's principles of civil disobedience, urged people to be kind and loving to their enemies, and to persuade the Mayor through nonviolent methods. Even at the public meeting, this proposal had been received with grumbling. At a long strategy session afterward, the old leaders of the Committee, and some other West Enders who had stayed behind—all Italians—disagreed strongly. "The Mayor is a thief," they said, "and how can you trust a thief or respect him?" Some suggested a one-hundred-car caravan to City Hall that would threaten the Mayor with violence if he did not call off the redevelopment.

Because the student would not agree to demonstrations of violence and the others refused to follow his approach, the Committee was virtually stymied. Nevertheless, another meeting was called for the following week, and notices were posted in the West End, proclaiming that there was still hope:

> For five years, and once in every three months, they have been announcing, in big headlines, that the West End would fall and that we would be cast forth from our homes before the dawn of another season. These were lies, for we're still here, and we're not moving.

Again the meeting drew over two hundred people, but the local politician who had been the main speaker the week before did not come as he had promised, and the West Enders felt that they had been deserted. Again, they did not respond to the student's appeal for a Gandhian approach, and by now it was evident that he would not be accepted as a leader. Moreover, the laws about incitement to riot made it impossible for any of the speakers to urge nonpayment of rent, leaving West Enders no other way of expressing their anger. Although another meeting was held the subsequent week, the audience was smaller, and by the end of the month, people began to think about moving.

As buildings began to empty, the remaining tenants were loath to remain in them, and even those who had planned to stay to the bitter end began to leave. People were afraid of being alone, of being the last in the house and thus isolated from the group. Then, unknown teenagers began to roam through semideserted buildings, using them for nocturnal parties, setting fires, and vandalizing wherever they could. The families still remaining in these buildings became fearful and moved more quickly than they had intended. The empty structures were torn down as soon as the last tenant left, and the resulting noise and dirt encouraged people in adjacent buildings to move also. Consequently, the West End was emptied in little more than eighteen months after the official taking of the land.

I was told that before the West End was totally cleared—and even afterward—West Enders would come back on weekends to walk through the old neighborhood and the rubble-strewn streets.[7] The last time I saw the area, it had been completely leveled except for the buildings that had been marked for preservation. A museum of Yankee artifacts and the library—now closed—remained at one corner, the Hospital at another. The Catholic church—where services were still being held for parishioners living on the Back of Beacon Hill—stood in lonely isolation in the center of the cleared area. The Hospital had graded some of the adjacent property for temporary parking, and at a far corner, fronting on the river, the first of the new buildings were going up. The cleared area looked very tiny, and it was hard to imagine that more than 20,000 people had once lived there.

NOTES

This chapter is abridged from "The Redevelopment of the West End" in *The Urban Villagers: Group and Class in the Life of Italian Americans*, written by Herbert J. Gans. 1962. New York, NY: The Free Press. It appears in Gans, Herbert J. *Making Sense of America:Sociological Analyses and Essays*. 1999. New York, NY: Rowman and Littlefield.

1. Bill Cunningham, "Two Project to Alter Boston," *Boston Herald,* November 17, 1957.

2. *Ibid.*
3. For a more detailed discussion of the West Enders' reactions, see Marc Fried and Peggy Gleicher, "Some Sources of Residential Satisfaction in an Urban 'Slum,'" *Journal of the American Institute of Planners* 27 (1961): 305–315; and Marc Fried, "Grieving for a Lost Home," in *The Urban Condition*, ed. Leonard J. Duhl (New York: Basic Books, 1963), 151–171.
4. I heard from several disparate sources that one of the city councilors had asked for a sizable "campaign contribution" in exchange for a favorable vote on the redevelopment. Since his vote was not needed, he did not get the money. Eventually, he voted for it anyway.
5. These feelings even affected me. Although I knew enough about redevelopment procedures to realize that the process was moving toward its inevitable climax, I was opposed to the redevelopment, and hoped it would not take place. Since I was not in touch with city officials, occasionally I would begin to share the West Enders' beliefs that "our children will still be here when they break it up," and wondered whether the rumors that the project had collapsed might not be true. It

is thus understandable that West Enders, who knew much less about the process, and could not call city officials to get the facts, would hold these beliefs more stubbornly.
6. His father had been a founder of the public playground movement in the United States; and his relatives, who included all of the famous names of Boston's aristocracy, had helped to build the West End settlement houses. They also supported the charities and social welfare agencies that served the area and the larger community.
7. I left the West End in May 1958 to begin my already scheduled study of Levittown, New Jersey.

REFERENCES

Cunningham, Bill. 1957. "Two Project to Alter Boston." *Boston Herald* (November 17).

Fried, Marc and Peggy Gleicher. 1961. "Some Sources of Residential Satisfaction in an Urban 'Slum.'" *Journal of the American Institute of Planners* 27: 305–315.

Fried, Marc. 1963. "Grieving for a Lost Home." In *The Urban Condition*, pp. 151–171. Leonard J. Duhl (ed.). New York: Basic Books.

43

WILLIAM KORNBLUM

WORKING THE DEUCE (1988)

West 42nd Street in Times Square, New York City, was known to its regulars as "the Deuce." In the late 1980s, plans were made to redevelop this area in an effort to rid it of vice as well as well as to increase employment and property values. In this selection, William Kornblum introduces the people who are to be displaced by redevelopment. He argues that until jobs are created for them, their activities will simply go underground or move elsewhere.

Once again, a mood of reform has come to lower Times Square. New York City's Public Development Corporation and New York State's Urban Development Corporation are moving ahead with plans to raze much of the West Forty-second Street corridor between Broadway and Eighth Avenue. This will be done in the interests of driving sin out of the area and, of course, increasing local employment and taxation yield.

As an Urban Development Corporation report notes:

> Forty-second Street between Seventh and Eighth Avenues stands out more than any other as a symbol of the area's glitter and tarnish, and it is the blighted conditions

on that block today that have given rise to the 42nd Street Development Project.

The two development corporations propose to take property from the owners of theaters and small commercial buildings on the street and to assemble all of these smaller parcels into the largest midtown development site since the construction of Rockefeller Center. A smaller, wealthier, and more entrepreneurial group of investors will be invited to replace the existing middle-scale property owners, since, in the words of the Urban Development Corporation, prior efforts to check blight and clean up the area have failed "in attracting the private sector investment to an area that has seen no new construction for over a half century." The state hopes to bring a new order of scale to West Forty-second Street, establishing economic institutions that benefit an entirely new cast of players, generate a great deal more public revenue, and scrape clean once and for all some of the most valuable real estate in Manhattan.

There is nothing new about this reform impulse. "The Deuce," as West Forty-second Street is known to its regulars, has been a zone of moral ambiguity for over sixty years. Prohibition and the movie craze of the 1920s transformed the street from a theater-and-nightclub district to a flashier but seedier neighborhood of movie houses during the 1920s and 1930s. Crusades against burlesque closed the street's last outlets for live music and comedy in 1937. The armed forces' attempts to declare the street off limits to soldiers and sailors during World War II only increased its attraction as a place for cheap eats and cheap thrills. During the 1960s the street became known as the haunt of midnight cowboys, hustlers, and others who lurked around the edges of the world of commercial sex and drugs. Malcolm X wrote of his experiences there with hustles and petty con games, as did Claude Brown in *Manchild in the Promised Land*. By the 1970s, West Forty-second Street and lower Times Square had acquired the reputation of being a moral combat zone dominated by a black and Hispanic underclass, and that remains its dominant image now.

So the street is seen by most New Yorkers as a place of despair, depravity, illness, and danger. A great majority of them believe that drugs and pornography have changed the temper of the area for the worse. And as observers like me check the life of the street it does seem at times to be dominated by a sadder, meaner, more desperate cast of street characters than was true in earlier periods of its history. Sadder: Malcolm X described a successful pimp named Cadillac who strutted the Deuce in the 1950s and 1960s. His

"ladies" worked the bars of Eighth Avenue and kept him in furs. But by 1978, when I first met him, Cadillac was a dying old man, an alcoholic who circulated in a world of tottering bottle gangs and slept with other homeless people in alleys where the bright lights do not reach. And meaner, too: in a recent novel Andrew Vachss has a character say about one of the turfs surrounding West Forty-second Street:

> I got to Bryant Park around nine-thirty. This little plot of greenery located behind the Public Library is supposed to enhance the citizens' cultural enjoyment of their surroundings. Maybe it did once—now it's an open-air market for heroin, cocaine, hashish, pills, knives, handguns—anything you might need to destroy yourself or someone else. There's a zoning law in effect, though—if you want to have sex with a juvenile runaway from Boston or Minneapolis, or to buy a nine-year-old boy for the night, you have to go a few blocks further west.

This is not a true portrait of the West Forty-second Street area. It describes but one of the social worlds New Yorkers have created and sustained in lower Times Square. The area has its dark sides, no question about it, but there are other worlds and other markets there, too, many of them underground but in no way as grimy and menacing as Vachss's portrait might suggest.

Lower Times Square is an entertainment zone, first of all: a place for booze, sex, gambling, drugs, and a hundred other expensive and inexpensive thrills. That West Forty-second Street is, among its other identities, an area of street hustles and shady transactions is hardly a new development. Over fifty years ago Damon Runyon wrote about the touts and horseplayers and crapshooters and bootleggers and street characters of all kinds who gave the Bright Light Zone its character in a wide-open time of jazz and nightclubs.

Runyon's Times Square seemed a whimsical place. Its regulars were people of the street with colorful nicknames like the Big Nig, the Lemon Drop Kid, Dark Dolores, Nathan Detroit, and Good Time Charlie. It was not all whimsy, of course. In "The Brain Goes Home," for example, we learn of an attempted rubout in which "Daffy Jack, who is considered a very good shiv artist, aims at the Brain's heart, but misses it by a couple of inches, leaving the Brain with a very bad cut in his side which calls for some stitching." So Runyon's world was edged with vengeance and violence, but it was clearly not the grimy, desperate place the authorities now imagine themselves to be cleaning up.

Yet in many ways the Deuce is still like the neighborhood Damon Runyon knew. It remains, at least for now, a place where an amazing array of social currents mix according to a special chemistry. It is in many respects a community, a world with its own cultures, tribal ways, and unique markets. There are legitimate businesses on the street, of course—theaters, restaurants, shops, offices. But its public spaces are home to a world of dealers, players, hustlers, touts, and con men, and all the rest of those who find ways to work the street.

The question no one seems to have addressed is: What will happen to these people and the trades they ply if the Deuce is redeveloped? They are part of a thriving underground market that serves customers throughout the city, and the most anyone can expect from a moral cleanup is that some of those people and some of those trades will be swept to other parts of Manhattan, thereby creating problems elsewhere. The most troubled street populations, the indigent and homeless, will probably be pushed out, especially as more of the old hotels give way to redevelopment. But a large number of the players who now work the street's underground markets will remain, and some will even thrive on the business new patrons bring.

Let me introduce some of the characters who operate the underground economy of Times Square. Joe Regensberg, for example, a figure Runyon would have known, liked, and understood.

Last year Joe's friends dedicated in his name a lovely stained-glass window in their small fur-trades synagogue, which stands a few short blocks below West Forty-second Street in the fur district. For over thirty years old Joe, a wiry, streetwise "vonce," was a respected moneylender, paper buyer, and sometime bookmaker. (*Vonce,* the Yiddish word for "flea" or "louse," is used to refer to someone who is small, quick, and hard to pin down.) His apartment on nearby Park Avenue was filled with goods given in partial payment of stale debts. A man with no children of his own but deeply attached to his extended family, Joe was discreet to a fault in his dealings on the street and rarely called attention to himself—although he often made his entrance at weddings and bar mitzvahs with two gorgeous Hungarian fur models on his arm, and on family occasions might hire a stretch limousine to carry him, his models, and his matronly sisters out to affairs on Long Island.

Joe made enough money in his fur-coat business by the end of the 1930s to quit sewing pelts, but he continued working out of a storefront on Seventh Avenue between Thirty-seventh and Thirty-eighth streets. To his friends and landsmen of the fur trade he was known as a "shylock." He lent short-term cash, usually at 25 percent interest, so his friends could buy pelts. And when friends wanted to place a bet as well, they often came to Joe—whereupon he would usually send a runner up to the Off-Track Betting parlor on Forty-second and Broadway to lay off on the bet as a hedge against unexpected losses. Joe calculated that about 15 percent of his loans were no good, but his remedy was simply to cut the person off. There was no violence within the boundaries of that community, and smart people remained there because to go outside to the wise-guy loan sharks could endanger one's health.

In good weather Joe would amble up to Forty-second Street himself. He remembered when the Off-Track Betting office had been the Old King Cole Room of the famous Knickerbocker Hotel. George M. Cohan and Enrico Caruso were among its most famous patrons; the great Caruso had sung "The Star-Spangled Banner" from its balcony at the end of the First World War. The building remains, but the famous Forty-second Street watering hole and artists' hangout never made it past Prohibition. The ground-floor betting room is now crowded by down-and-out men with nothing but time on their hands and by office workers hurrying to place a bet and get back to work.

One day three years ago, on his way back from the Off-Track Betting parlor, Joe went into his favorite cigar store on the ground floor of a fur-trade building, and was caught in a holdup. Three stickup men with guns pushed Joe to the ground. "Go ahead," he cried. "Shoot an old man. What good am I to you with no money?" They dragged Joe into the freight elevator and sent him up to the top floor, grabbing about three hundred dollars in cash from the trembling cigar-store clerk. A security guard found Joe on the top floor of the building unable to get up. His hip was broken.

Before Joe would let the guard call an ambulance, he tipped him and made him call three cronies from the street. While the police were downstairs questioning the clerk, Joe's friends wrote him checks for the fifteen thousand dollars cash he was carrying in his pocket. They also took his star-sapphire ring and his wallet and left him with enough cash to pay the private ambulance, which they immediately called to take him directly to a private hospital. This was a scenario they had rehearsed many times around their favorite table at Dubrow's, an old cafeteria now closed and subdivided.

Taking the holdup as a bad omen and as another sign of the changes occurring in the garment district, Joe gave the "business" to his cousin Bunny Ripkin. Bunny was not so lucky: a few months later he was robbed and shot by the same threesome. By this time, though, Joe was convalescing in the old Valencia Hotel in La Jolla, California, far away from the mean street. The heavy plaster ceiling of his hotel room came down on his head one night, and not long after that insult Joe died. The moneylenders in the fur trade just below West Forty-second Street are much more careful about doing their business in public now, but they haven't gone away and won't. It would be hard to imagine the fur trade without them.

Meet Al Davis, another regular on the street—a figure who would have been quite unfamiliar to Runyon. Al is a twenty-six-year-old Afro-American and native New Yorker who has been selling marijuana along Forty-second Street for eight years. In a good week, if the weather holds, he can gross over a thousand dollars in cash. He has a group of younger hustlers whom he supplies with loose joints and nickel (five-dollar) or dime (ten-dollar) bags. Bryant Park is Al's central market and business headquarters, but *his* Bryant Park is not at all like Andrew Vaschss's. Al depends on its relative safety and orderliness, for most of his customers are looking for a reliable dealer and an atmosphere of calm. Periodic police sweeps can make the park a bit risky at times, but the storm passes quickly; and when there is too much heat, the marketplace can easily shift to other malls or public areas nearby.

Al thinks the restoration of West Forty-second Street will only increase his business. "The police think we only sell whak, you know, beat goods to kids going to the movies," he laughs, "so when the cheap movies are gone they think the market will go. But the real trade is with office workers and garment workers during the day and just after work. They like to smoke a joint or two. It makes the work less boring. No, the problem with this business is getting beat by my own kids, and competition from the Puerto Ricans and from the ones who do sell phony goods. They make it hard to do business. It wears me down sometimes and I don't know how much longer I can stay in it, but really it's what I do best."

Clifford Geertz's account of the Middle Eastern pasar economy in *Peddlers and Princes* describes the soft drug markets of West Forty-second Street as well as anything one might read. As in the Middle East, the competition in the street drug market between the seller and the buyer is just as fierce as it is between different sellers. Phony goods are sold everywhere, and customers must be streetwise not to be taken. They must know the dealers, as many do, or must be adept at reading the dealing situation. If a customer shows signs of inexperience or fear of the police, the dealer can use those clues to treat the deal not as a sale but as the opportunity for a short con. "Let's go, my man," he may whisper, while throwing furtive glances over his shoulders, "we can't stand here all day." The flustered customer becomes an easy mark, and he is quite unlikely to seek satisfaction once he realizes he has been beaten.

Street hustlers do not usually read anthropologists like Clifford Geertz or sociologists like the late Erving Goffman, but an outsider who would know the ways of the Deuce would be wise to do so. Goffman's "Normal Appearances" is a brilliant exegesis of the tricks and dodges used by street actors who wish to appear "normal" or who manipulate perceptions of normality while engaged in simple swindling.

The members of this three-card monte team illustrate Goffman's essay almost perfectly. Jerry, his "lady" Maria, and their running buddies of the moment, Pickles and Stash, are crack heads and petty grifters. They work the midtown neighborhoods of Manhattan. Depending on where they think the heat is least likely to be out in force, and on when there should be extra money on the street—especially Fridays and Saturdays—you may find them in Times Square. Their favorite hustle is the monte game. It is fast and increasingly risky, but a good team can often make big scores.

The team is racially integrated, which helps in its work quite a bit. Jerry and Pickles are black, Maria is a light-skinned NeoRican (New York–born Puerto Rican), and Stash is from Czechoslovakia. The men met while doing time at Rikers Island where Jerry taught them the monte game. Pickles and Stash are the "slides." Maria is the "shill." Jerry, the "slinger," sets up the box and throws the cards. The slides are usually posted at either end of the short block where Jerry places his box and starts his pitch. Their job is to look nonchalant and unsuspicious while they "eyeball the street to make the man"—that is, they must recognize undercover police officers in their various street disguises. At the signal, "Slide easy," Jerry will kick over his box and "slide"—simply walk away—which is why one sees so many empty boxes sitting on Times Square sidewalks. If the cry is "Slide hard," Jerry knows the man is about to bust his crew and he runs, tearing up his cards as he flies.

Maria must be a convincing gambler. She appears to win more often than she loses until a real "vic" (victim) comes along to join the game. If there is more than one team working the block, the groups can share slides and add more shills, bringing customers on faster. Jerry and Maria have a signal system which allows her to know where the winning card is at all times. To entice the victim she will often place a bet on the wrong card. Jerry then takes her money and asks the prospect to point to one of the two remaining cards. If the guess is correct, Jerry turns the card up before any money is bet, showing the victim that in theory, at least, he or she can win. If the victim has pointed to the wrong card, Jerry asks for a bet, and also exhorts Maria to put new money down on the same bet; and if the victim seems especially sure of the bet, the two will attempt to increase the stakes before Jerry turns the cards over and takes the money.

Little con games like three-card monte, a variation on the shell-and-pea game, were around in Runyon's time and well before that. In the monte game the dealer pays even money when the victim guesses the correct color of one of two or three cards. Were this a fair game of chance, as society defines fairness, a two-to-one payoff to the gambler would ensure the house an enormous steady profit, while permitting the players to feel they have a reasonable chance of winning. But the monte team does not have the time to simply milk the public steadily, as the licensed casinos are allowed to do. Indeed, if the monte dealer had the leisure to be fair, his rakeoff would be far more exorbitant than anything found at the casinos. But this is a fast hustle, conducted on the run, and the odds of winning are as close to zero as one can get. Why then do so many people who think they are smart allow themselves to be fleeced on the street?

The slinger shows the victim the cards as he moves them around. "Follow the red, my man, just leave back the black, easy to play, you win I pay." The risk seems reduced and the "bet" is perceived as a sure thing. "I don't holler," Jerry intones, "I pays dollar for dollar." Instead of asking why the monte man is giving such lousy odds, or even why he would want to show a suspicious stranger the cards at all, the prospect becomes convinced he or she can follow the card and beat the game, which also means beating the monte man's hands. It is a sleight-of-hand game, a charade which, like professional wrestling, depends on the desire of customers to suspend their disbelief. The monte dealer shows the victim a card in his hand and appears to throw it on the box, face down, but there is another card concealed behind the first. He can drop it at will without making the deception evident. Jerry's hands and cards and mouth,

and especially his eyes, are forever moving, checking the scene, watching the shill for cues, listening for sounds, pocketing the money, soothing the vic ("cooling off the mark," as Goffman called it).

> The name
> of this game is the
> gypsy twist.
> Sometimes you see it;
> sometimes you miss.
>   Red, red
> rooster head,
>   Choose the red,
> take home the bread.
>   Choose the black,
> I'll pick up the
> slack.
>   Minnie the Mo is
> a git-down Ho.
>   Choose the red
> cause I got mo.

It is a hustle requiring time to practice, the kind of time one has in prison. The game is played under intense pressure, for most customers lose what cash they are willing to risk in less than three bets—at which point the crew may choose to slide suddenly, pretending to be on the run from the police, which leaves the befuddled victim with little time to gather his wits and look for help. At any point during the scene when the slinger senses a suspicious person in the crowd, he will either just stop the game or slide off to another location. So when the monte players claim, as I once heard Jerry do, that "We took a rabbi for three thousand dollars," one can be fairly confident that the story is true, or at least a close approximation. They are boasting about the size of the score, of course, but they are also bragging that they took someone—referred to as a rabbi only because he wore a yarmulke—whose people tend to think of themselves as good with numbers and wise on the street.

Changes in the ecology of the street brought on by new building development or increased police pressure may scatter the street games and street markets, but only briefly. When the heat is on the commercial sex industry, as is the case right now, it is momentarily displaced to other neighborhoods or forced underground. The live sex markets in the Forty-second Street area have been diminished of late by crackdowns and new buildings, but that only serves as an invitation to transvestites, streetwalkers, male prostitutes, and all manner of pimps and procurers to move into the area. For many in the industry, Times Square remains the organizational base. Carol the Fluffer, for example, is a strong woman, which means in the vernacular of the trade that she is not squeamish about doing the most unconventional sex acts before live audiences. For a fee she will smoke a cigarette with her vagina or flap her breasts in a customer's face or more. (There are agents in the Forty-second Street and Times Square area who book her and hundreds of other women in her trade for shows all over the East Coast as well as for parts in porn movies, a side of the sex industry which remains dominated by organized crime.) Carol got into prostitution and petty drug dealing years ago in her home town. Once in New York she worked her way free of pimps by gravitating toward pornographic movie sets and live sex shows, where she often works as a fluffer. The fluffer's job is to make sure that the male performers go on before the cameras with an erection. She "fluffs him up"—a job not found in the *Dictionary of Occupational Titles.*

Although the area around West Forty-second Street and Eighth Avenue is commonly perceived as a haven for street prostitution, the business is actually better conducted nearer the big hotels where out-of-town businessmen congregate or in quiet side streets near bars and nightclubs. This is especially true since the casinos in Atlantic City opened; many of New York's street hookers and their pimps migrated there to work the easier crowds. Now most of the prostitution in the Forty-second Street area is conducted by transvestites or young male prostitutes known as "chickens"—whose "tricks," naturally, are known as "chicken hawks." But a few veterans still look for "tunnel tricks," for car or truck drivers who will hire them for a ride to New Jersey under the Hudson River. And, in the meantime, the shows that employ the likes of Carol move further and further away.

So what will happen to the people who occupy this special social world when massive renewal takes place? The biggest hustle of all is the developer's assurance that "upscaling" is the way to solve a social problem. It only solves the developer's problem. The Deuce may be darkened a bit as a result of gentrification, but the underground markets will continue to flourish nearby, and, far more ominously, our failure as a society to create jobs for the unskilled and homes for the indigent is likely to add new and younger faces to those hustling scenes. The hungry and homeless and ill—the refuse of society—can temporarily be swept away, but they simply pile up elsewhere when urban plans neglect their plight. And the opportunity for profit will continue to attract the street players—prosperous ones like Joe the Shylock and, at his best, Cadillac the Pimp; and marginal ones like Al the Dealer, Jerry the Slinger, and Carol the Fluffer—all of whom are playing parts in a large and important economy. They will not go away either.

44

TERRY WILLIAMS

LETTER FROM A CRACKHOUSE (1991)

At the height of the crack cocaine epidemic in New York City in the late 1980s and early 1990s, Terry Williams spent three years observing the social life of crackhouses. In this brief piece about a single location north of Harlem, he introduces the crackhouse's unique culture as well as its central characters and their despair.

Washington Heights lies just to the north of Harlem, between 155th and Dyckman Street. Through the years, it has been transformed from an elegant brownstone outpost of the upper classes to a refuge for successive generations of tired and poor folks yearning to breathe free. Today the neighborhood is a complex mosaic of newly arrived Dominicans, Ecuadorans, Koreans, and West Indians, overlaying the remaining earlier generations of Jews and Italians, a few of whose shops—fish stores and pizzerias—linger.

Tonight, I am standing in front of a five-story faded brownstone with green copper arches. Sitting between Leona's Discount House and Perfumery and Victor's Travel Agency, there is not much to distinguish it from hundreds of similar buildings in the neighborhood. Residents recognize it only by subtle signs: the jammed door, the furtive glances of white suburban buyers, the quick steps, the pocket-plunging users hiding their recently purchased cocaine packets, the unshaven lookouts with sunken eyes. It is a crackhouse.

I have spent a lot of time in the last three years in and out of crackhouses like this one, discovering a culture far different from what I imagined or what most people might expect from reading the daily press. A crackhouse is not, generally speaking, a marketplace but a home. It is not primarily a place where cocaine is sold, but where it is used. Most of the many crackhouses I have visited do not allow selling. Those that do are usually still in transition: former "crack spots" (retail sales operations) in the process of becoming true crackhouses. The typical crackhouse is created by an ex-cocaine dealer or his girlfriend. Crackhouse operators have descended from occasional cocaine use to heavy abuse. Enthralled to the drug, they can no longer deal resourcefully or profitably; setting up crackhousekeeping, they turn from primarily selling cocaine to primarily consuming it.

Crack, oddly enough, is not the drug of choice in most crackhouses. Most of the time, crackhouse habituals smoke freebase cocaine instead. Both base and crack are cocaine with the hydrochloride boiled away, but crack is usually pre-cooked and mixed with other chemicals, while base is not. Other drugs are represented as well: Cocaine sniffers mingle freely with freebasers, needle shooters, and marijuana smokers.

Tonight, as usual, many crackheads hide in the outside stairwells. Like sentinels they stand to the left and to the right, wearing jeans and half-laced sneakers. Staring blankly they wait for a buyer to beg from, a stranger to steer, a scaleboy (who manages day-to-day drug selling operations) to run an errand for, a friend to whom to complain. On a given night between ten and twenty people come to the crackhouse. Some are just visiting from out of town or stopping by on the way home from a party. But each crackhouse has its regulars, who live in the house and in many ways form a family.

Since the late 1970s there have been lots of new arrivals on the street: the mentally ill, the undomiciled, drug dealers, mendicants, and addicts. Many of these young men, women, and children, castoffs from the above-ground economy, become vassals of the vast underground multinational cocaine industry. By some estimates as many as 150,000 people in New York may be working in the cocaine trade on a daily basis. Some are selling. Others act as runners, stash catchers (who stand behind the building and are thrown bags of drugs in the event of a police raid), steerers (who steer buyers to places where drugs are sold), and spotters (who keep watch and alert dealers of approaching police). Some are lookouts for the cocaine and crack-spot operators, pulling in thirty dollars, two meals, and a gram of crack for a 12-hour shift. Others pace crack-spot halls searching for specks of crack a hapless consumer may have dropped. But many or most are volunteer lookouts, hangers-on waiting to seize upon any opportunity that will reward them with enough crack to continue what one devotee calls "pleasurable suicide."

By the early Eighties, the fashionable sniffing culture which made a home for itself in after-hours clubs was dying out, and a new freebasing culture emerged in its place. Coca leaf cultivation in Bolivia, Peru, and Colombia exploded from 220,000 acres in 1980 to over 520,000 acres in 1988. The price of a kilo dropped from $50,000 in 1980 to roughly $12,000 today. Crack, packaged in small quantities and selling for as little as $2, offered a new chance to expand the market to a new class of consumer: the persistently poor. As the price plummeted, so did the social class of its users: Cocaine addiction moved from the glamour professions to the street.

By 1984, cocaine users were firmly ensconced in "basing galleries," or what later came to be called crackhouses. The frequenters of crackhouses were, by and large, of a different class than those who haunted after-hours clubs, which were designed to meet the needs of the largely upper- and upper-middle-class sniffers who first popularized cocaine use in this country. Addiction knows no class boundaries, but those who can command resources are rarely found in the confines of a ghetto crackhouse, an institution that emerged to meet the needs of poor addicts.

Inside the brownstone now, the stench is immediately recognizable: human odors mixed with garbage, crack freebase, musty halls, and unwashed floors. The entry hall retains signs of its former elegance: The marble floors are braided with yellow and red designs woven down the long hallway. From the ceiling light fixtures, gargoyles look down with their mouths wide open. Only two sculpted faces remain, however; the other fixtures have been replaced by cheap lightshades. Scattered about are vials, stems of glass, and broken lighters. It is three in the morning.

In the darkened hallway leading to the crackhouse, which properly speaking, is a single apartment in this building, I see two women standing against the wall lighting up a pipe. "You're losing it, you're losing it," the tall one with the hoarse voice mumbles, meaning the lighter is too hot and the crack is burning too fast to inhale. "Let's go inside," the other says.

The interior is not much to look at. A set of stark, neglected rooms provide a minimalist sensory arena for guests and family. The doors are always open to a steady mix of people: men and women, Latino and Asian, black and white—but more than half of its regulars are women under 25. Women do not run crackhouses, but they do play a key role in crackhouse culture.

Everybody is here to get high. The center of attention is a small glass vessel, known as a shaker, in which small particles of cocaine are mixed with baking soda and water. Once mixed and dried, the cocaine particles turn into a "rock," a hardened smokable mass. Preparing the drug is an aesthetic experience. Ritual is used to focus attention, to help strip the mind of outside concerns so total absorption can take place.

Those around the table sit with a glass pipe in each hand—"the devil's dick," one woman calls it, "because the more you smoke the more you want." They place a small pebble in the mouth of the pipe and inhale deeply.

Reactions to crack cocaine use vary. Some people become active, moving about the room, touching people and things. They rise slowly, retreat to a favorite location, a chair, a room, a corner spot—depending on whether they are interested in sex or just conversation. Others freeze momentarily in static poses, their eyes closed, trying to see "Scotty."

The crackhouse has a language all its own, much of which, oddly enough, has been transported from the old television show *Star Trek*. A search for new drugs, for example, is known as a "mission" (as in "Its five-year mission: To boldly go where no man has gone before"). And the characteristic cocaine high goes by the name of the Enterprise's chief engineer ("Beam me up, Scotty"). They speak about him intimately, in matter-of-fact tones, lending a surrealistic quality to the conversation. "The first time I met Scotty," or "when I fell in love with Scotty," or "when Scotty fell in love with me," are typical crackhouse utterances.

The smoke and despair are everywhere. Ambient smoke penetrates my skin, covering my clothing, rushing in through the pores. The place is so full of odors competing for the olfactory senses: marijuana, tobacco, sulfur matches, butane torches. The night rituals have begun: the cooking, the smoking, and the compulsive sex. As for the despair, all here know that the she-wolf, crack cocaine, is insatiable. The more she devours, the more she seeks to devour.

In case you have been wondering why I am here, I am an ethnographer. My profession is probing urban nocturnal subcultures that thrive far from the sunlit mainstream. Tonight, my Virgil is Headache, the street name of a Jewish man who turned to cocaine. Headache, who introduced me to the Washington Heights crack scene, is 46, short, and powerfully built. His hair is streaked with gray. He has cauliflower ears and a Kirk Douglas dimple. Born into a family of wealthy merchants, he graduated from college, married, and became a salesman. He bought real estate in Harlem and began using cocaine and procuring it for his wealthy downtown friends. To avoid being an absentee landowner, he says, Headache moved into this Washington Heights apartment. Eventually he started freebasing with his girlfriend, an imposing West Indian woman named Joan. His apartment became a crackhouse.

My Beatrice is a Puerto Rican woman named Monica. At 23, Monica is one of the crackhouse regulars, a woman with little means, large lips, and elegant vulgarity. She struts, talking constantly, pressing others to respond. Her blouse is open at the top, to tease. It is Monica who gives me precise instructions about how to navigate the many passageways where crack and women cohabit. Headache, like Virgil, could only take me so far, I need to know about the women, and Monica takes the lead.

"There ain't but two kinds of women out here," she says, lighting up her glass stem. "And that's touchers and buffers." The crack scene, she tells me, is the half-world of the touchers (women seeking affection) and the buffers (women who give oral sex). Both are looking to exchange their sexual labor for the pleasures of cocaine.

There are the nontouchers too, those who refuse to be touched because they have been touched too much. But it is the buffers that attract the regulars to the household, and thus keep the crackhouse together. "Most of the girls will give a bj, if they know the guy will give them something to smoke for the night," Monica says, lighting her pipe for the third time.

As in any household, there are certain instrumental relationships that keep the crackhouse from exploding into pure chaos. Headache is a worker, Monica is a buffer. He brings in money to keep crack in the pipe and food on the table. She keeps people coming into the house. When Headache's money runs out, Monica can trade sex for crack.

Three principal activities take up time and give cohesion to life in the crackhouse: missions, which bring in the cocaine; work (both regular and irregular jobs), which bring in the money to buy food and cocaine; and sex. Sex is the chief currency of the crackhouse. The crackhouse regulars here tonight have various sources of funds: Joan works odd jobs and occasionally delivers cocaine to middle-class clients. Headache works as a messenger on Wall Street; Tiger gets Social Security; Venus steals. But sex is the great final resource that both attracts people to the crackhouse and sustains their life there. When there is no money, sex will buy cocaine.

Crackhouse roles are structured to keep the high going continuously with only brief periods of depleted supply. As in any household, people share, lest no one share with them. Violating the sharing rule would almost certainly shatter the fragile peace in the edgy, nervous world of the crackhouse.

As in any household, the air is thick with suppressed feuds and petty jealousies. Tiger and Liz and Sonneman, for example, think Headache is too soft on Joan: "She has a tendency to take control and to take advantage of him."

Joan has a different point of view.

"Yesterday," Joan states angrily, "he beat the f— outta me. And he did it because I didn't wanna hear f—ing Spanish music." The fight which precipitated this unusual outburst of profanity from Joan was caused by her rivalry with Liz. Liz likes Spanish music and Joan does not, or at least not when Headache is getting too much attention from Liz. When Joan complained, Headache hit her. When so much cocaine is coursing through the system, the threat of violence is always there.

At last, the supply of crack is depleted. The last smoky spiral ascends to the ceiling. It is time to get more. Time to go on a mission. One of the younger women volunteers: "I'll try my luck tonight. Anybody got any money?"

The search is on, the thirst is growing. The dance will continue tonight and tomorrow, and compulsively on into the unknown but easily guessed future, not only here but also in hundreds of other crackhouses throughout the five boroughs.

A few habituals will be rescued by family or friends. But for many the union with cocaine will be sundered only by death: from AIDS, from chronic self-neglect, from street violence. Sometimes I ask crackhouse residents whether they think the drug should be legal. Every person I asked said no.

The crackhouse is a world about which we know far too little, so we do too little. Many who made their way into the crackhouse do not seem to know or understand how they got there. Many of those I met in the crack culture want to escape reality, but just as many want to escape crack.

45

KATHRYN EDIN AND CHRISTOPHER JENCKS

WELFARE

from *Rethinking Social Policy* (1992)

In this selection, Kathryn Edin and Christopher Jencks try to solve a basic puzzle that has long perplexed policy makers: why do some women on welfare choose not to work, and how do they make ends meet? By talking directly to welfare recipients and analyzing their budgets, they make some surprising discoveries.

How Welfare Mothers Survive in Illinois

When we began studying the Illinois welfare system in 1988, Aid to Families with Dependent Children (AFDC) paid a single mother with one child and no outside income $250 per month. She also got $149 per month in food stamps, plus a Medicaid card that entitled her to free medical care and prescription drugs. Since food stamps are virtually the same as cash, a mother with one child ended up with $399 a month, or roughly $4800 per year. Her annual income (including food stamps) rose to $6700 if she had two children, $7900 if she had three, and $9300 if she had four. These benefit levels were 60 to 75 percent of the federal poverty line.

To see how families got by on so little money, Edin conducted intensive interviews with twenty-five welfare families in Cook County (which includes both Chicago and its nearby suburbs) during 1988 and with another twenty-five early in 1990. Previous experience suggested that if she simply drew a random sample of welfare recipients, went to their homes, and asked them to describe their income and expenditures, she would get a lot of refusals, a lot of evasion, and a lot of budgets that did not include enough income to cover the family's expenditures. She therefore took a different tack, asking acquaintances who knew welfare recipients in different capacities to introduce her to one or two recipients and tell them she was trustworthy.[1] All but nine of the fifty-nine mothers she contacted in this way agreed to be interviewed.[2]

Cook County is obviously not representative of the nation as a whole. Its AFDC benefit levels are close to the national average, but rents in Chicago, while lower than in New York or Los Angeles, are higher than in most small cities. Cook County probably has more subsidized housing than most smaller metropolitan areas, but much of this housing is extremely dangerous and many welfare mothers are unwilling to live in it.[3]

Because Edin used personal contacts to locate her sample, she could not make it perfectly representative of Cook County, and she did not try to do so.[4] Since 77 percent of Cook County recipients are black, she had to oversample white recipients in order to get enough whites for racial comparisons. Her final sample was 46 percent African American, 38 percent European, 10 percent Latin American, and 6 percent Asian. National figures are quite similar.[5] Because Edin oversampled whites, she also oversampled the Chicago suburbs relative to the city.[6] In order to maximize her chances of finding recipients who lived on what they got from the welfare department, she drew 44 percent of her sample from subsidized housing. In the nation as a whole, only 18 percent of all recipients live in subsidized housing.[7] Oversampling recipients in subsidized housing reduces the discrepancy between the rents her mothers paid and the rent that the average American welfare mother pays.

Not one of Edin's fifty mothers claimed that she lived exclusively on her welfare check, and only two even came close.[8] In this respect Edin's mothers are…much like welfare mothers in larger national samples. But unlike the welfare mothers interviewed in national surveys, almost all of Edin's mothers reported enough income, both legal and illegal, to cover their expenses.[9] Every single mother supplemented her check in some way, either by doing unreported work, by getting money from friends and relatives, or by persuading someone else to pay a lot of her expenses.

Not one of these fifty mothers reported all her extra income to the welfare department, and only four reported any of it. Not reporting outside income is illegal, but the chances of being caught are low. Furthermore, even if a recipient is caught, she cannot be cut off the rolls or prosecuted for fraud unless the state can show that she *intended* to break the law, which it seldom can. A recipient who gets caught cheating is supposed to repay her excess benefits, but so long as she remains on welfare, the state can reduce her monthly check only by 10 percent.[10]

Once we look at these mothers' monthly budgets, it is easy to see why they all supplemented their AFDC checks. Unless a welfare mother lived in subsidized housing, her check was seldom enough to pay even her rent and utility bills, much less her other expenses. Edin interviewed twenty-eight mothers who lived in unsubsidized housing. (Seventeen had their own apartments, while eleven shared an apartment with another adult.) These twenty-eight mothers' AFDC checks averaged $327 per month. They paid an average of $364 a month for rent, gas (the principal source of heat in Chicago), and electricity. On the average, therefore, rent and utilities cost them $37 more than AFDC provided.

The twenty-two mothers who lived in subsidized housing were in a much better position. They got an average of $320 a month from AFDC and spent only $123 on rent and utilities. This left them with $197 in cash to get through the month. None managed on this amount, but they came closer than mothers in private housing.

Where did the money go? Almost all welfare mothers get food stamps, but very few can feed their family for an entire month on stamps alone. Edin's fifty mothers received stamps worth $14 per person per week. They spent about $18 per person per week on food. Their families averaged just over three members, so they needed about $50 in cash during an average month for groceries. For the sample as a whole, cash expenditures on food, rent, gas, and electricity averaged $314 a month. Since the average recipient got only $324 a month in cash from the welfare department, she had only $10 left for other expenses.

Welfare mothers are not miracle workers. Like everyone else, they must pay for clothing, laundry, cleaning supplies, school supplies, transportation, furniture, appliances, and so on. Edin's welfare mothers spent only a third of what the average midwestern mother spent on items of this kind. Nonetheless, by the end of the month expenses other than food, rent, and utilities had cost the average mother $351.[11] Almost all this money came from unreported income.

...Only 58 percent of [the mother's] income came from food stamps and AFDC. Of the remaining 42 percent, just over half came from absent fathers, boyfriends, parents, siblings, and student loans, while just under half came from unreported work of various kinds. Seven mothers held regular jobs under another name, earning an average of $5 an hour. Twenty-two worked part time at off-the-books jobs such as bartending, catering, babysitting, and sewing, earning an average of $3 an hour. Four sold marijuana, but even they earned only $3 to $5 an hour. A fifth sold crack as well as marijuana and earned something like $10 an hour, but she was murdered soon after Edin interviewed her, apparently because she had not repaid her supplier. The only mothers who earned a lot on an hourly basis were the five who worked occasionally as prostitutes. They earned something like $40 an hour.

How Well Do Chicago Welfare Mothers Live?

Edin's welfare families averaged just over three members.[12] Those who lived in private housing reported total incomes, including both cash and food, stamps, averaging $940 a month. Those who lived in subsidized housing reported total incomes averaging $840 a month, but if we allow for the fact that their housing subsidies saved them about $240 a month, their cash-equivalent incomes averaged about $1080 a month.[13] Taken together, therefore, Edin's fifty mothers were consuming goods and services worth at least $1000 a month.[14]

The federal poverty line for a family of three was only $9435 when Edin started interviewing in 1988 and was no more than $10,000 when the finished her interviewing early in 1990. Since Edin's mothers were consuming goods and services worth an average of $12,000 a year, relatively few of them were poor by the federal standard. The federal poverty line is not a very good benchmark, however, because it is not based on the cost of the goods and services that poor people really consume. It is merely an arbitrary line, drawn in 1964 so as to divide the richest four fifths of the population from the poorest one fifth.[15]

Public-opinion surveys show that the average American now thinks a family needs an income well above the official poverty line to escape from poverty. In 1989, the Gallup survey asked 3511 American adults the following question: "People who have income below a certain level can be considered poor. That level is called the 'poverty line.' What amount of weekly income would you use as a poverty line for a family of four (husband, wife, and two children) in this community?" Respondents' answers averaged $303 a week

($15,700 a year) which was 24 percent higher than the official poverty line for a family of four ($12,675). Respondents in cities of one million or more set the figure about 12 percent higher, at about $17,600 a year.[16]

Most of Edin's mothers lived in families of two or three, so they presumably needed less than $17,600 a year to escape poverty. How much less is unclear. The official poverty line for a family of three is 22 percent less than that for a family of four. But when survey researchers have asked the public how much money families of different sizes need to maintain any given standard of living, the answers do not vary much by size. The best available evidence suggests that the public would probably set the poverty threshold for a family of three only 8 or 9 percent below the threshold for a family of four.[17] In a city the size of Chicago, therefore, the public would probably set the poverty line for a family of three at about $16,000. For a family of two, the figure would probably be about $14,400. Using this standard, all but one of Edin's fifty welfare families was poor.

Another way of characterizing Chicago welfare recipients' standard of living is to ask how many lacked the material comforts that most Americans regard as necessities. It is hard to answer this question precisely, but Edin's judgment was that forty-four of her fifty mothers lacked at least some of the things most Americans take for granted. One of the six mothers who seemed relatively comfortable had recently received $7000 from an insurance company after being hit by a car. Another worked full time caring for Alzheimer's patients, earning $8 an hour. A third had an unusually generous rent subsidy and supplemented her income by stealing large quantities of meat from grocery stores. A fourth headed a large family of Asian refugees and had two grown sons who lived elsewhere but covertly paid the rent on the family's $600-a-month apartment. A fifth mother had a live-in boyfriend who held a steady job as a bus driver.

The sixth was the sample's only successful drug dealer, who also held a regular job under an assumed name and lived with her mother. Not even these six families lived especially well, but they were not deprived by conventional standards.

The remaining forty-four families did without things that almost everyone regards as essential. Half lived in very bad neighborhoods. Half lived in badly run-down apartments, where the heat and hot water were frequently out of order, the roof leaked, plaster was falling off the walls, or windows fitted so badly that the wind blew through the apartment in the winter. One in four did without a telephone, and one in three reported spending nothing whatever on entertainment. Many said their food budgets were too tight for fresh fruit or vegetables. Only two of the Chicago residents had a working automobile. (Nine of the thirteen suburbanites had automobiles, since they lived in areas without public transportation.)

It is true that all fifty families had color television sets, and that a quarter had video recorders—"extravagances" that often offend intellectuals who rely on books for entertainment. But because both TV sets and video recorders last a long time, they cost only a few dollars a month. Since they provided both the mothers and their children with cheap entertainment, the mothers were willing to forgo almost any other comfort (such as reliable hot water or fresh vegetables) to ensure that they had a working television. Without one, their lives would have been extraordinarily bleak.

These mothers also bought a few other things that would raise conservative eyebrows. More than half occasionally rented a video tape or took the children to McDonald's for dinner. More than half used cigarettes or alcohol. Three spent $20 to $40 a month on the lottery. From an economic viewpoint, however, these luxuries were of minor importance. Taken together, they accounted for only 6 percent of the sample's total expenditures.

More important than these small extravagances, at least from an economic viewpoint, was the fact that half these welfare mothers were unwilling to live in Chicago's worst neighborhoods. If we set aside those in public housing, mothers who lived in very bad neighborhoods paid $180 to $265 a month in rent, whereas those who lived in average neighborhoods usually paid $325 to $425 a month. Mothers who lived in average neighborhoods could therefore have cut their monthly expenditures by something like $150 if they had moved to bad neighborhoods. It is important to remember, however, that bad neighborhoods are not just run-down, dirty, and short on amenities. They are also dangerous. White, Asian, and Mexican welfare mothers are particularly reluctant to live in these neighborhoods, which are overwhelmingly black. But some black mothers also paid higher rent to live in better neighborhoods.

Most of the Chicago residents could have cut their expenses even further if they had been willing to move into one of Chicago's large public housing projects, such as Cabrini Green or Robert Taylor Homes. But living in "the projects"—and especially exposing their children to this environment—was an appalling prospect to all the whites and Asians whom Edin interviewed and to many of the blacks. These mothers were willing to do almost anything to avoid such a fate.....

How Much Must a Welfare Mother Earn to Be Better Off?

In Edin's sample, welfare families consumed goods and services worth an average of at least $12,000 a year.[18] If these women had worked in legitimate jobs, our estimates suggest that they would have needed an additional $800 for medical bills, $300 for clothing, $500 for transportation, and $1200 for childcare.[19] They would therefore have needed $14,800 in cash, food stamps, and housing subsidies to maintain their current standard of living. When we add in taxes, the total rises to about $16,000 a year.[20] Interestingly, the Gallup survey suggests that the public would also have set the poverty threshold for these mothers at about $16,000.

A woman who worked thirty-five hours a week and was unemployed 10 percent of the time would have to earn almost $10 an hour to make $16,000 a year. By current American standards, $10 an hour is a lot of money. The average wage for all nonagricultural workers in the United States, male and female, skilled and unskilled, was only $9.66 in 1989.[21]

We can recast these calculations in a slightly different way by asking how many hours a week Edin's welfare mothers would have to work in order to earn $16,000. If they earned $6 an hour, which is a bit more than those with regular jobs actually earned, they would have to work 2667 hours a year. If they worked every week and took no vacation, they would have to put in fifty-one hours a week (50 percent more than the average American works) to maintain their current standard of living. If they were unemployed 10 percent of the time, they would have to put in fifty-seven hours during the weeks they worked.

These calculations lead inexorably to one conclusion. An unskilled single mother cannot expect to support herself and her children in today's labor market *either* by working *or* by collecting welfare. If she wants to make ends meet, she must get help from her parents, her boyfriend, the absent father, or the government. This help can take many forms: child-support payments, housing subsidies, food stamps, AFDC benefits, Medicaid, or sharing a residence. But without some kind of help, she cannot make ends meet.

If we make the plausible assumption that a single mother in Chicago can earn $5 an hour, work thirty-five hours a week, and expect to work forty-seven weeks a year, we can expect her to earn $8225 before taxes. That means she needs Medicaid, food stamps, housing subsidies, childcare subsidies, and child-support payments worth another $7000 to maintain the same modest standard of living as Edin's mothers. At present, her best hope of getting that much money is to collect AFDC and to work without telling the welfare department. If we want her to work more and cheat less, we need policy changes that make this practical....

Can Welfare Benefits Be Raised?

The traditional liberal response to single mothers' economic problems has been to push for higher AFDC benefits. In our view this is a mistake. The only politically viable strategy for significantly improving the economic position of single mothers and their children over the next generation, we would argue, is to concentrate on helping those who work at low-wage jobs.

American liberals have a habit of trying to help the neediest. Because AFDC benefits have always been low, welfare mothers look like the neediest of the needy. As a result, liberals have fought hard to help welfare recipients, while largely ignoring single mothers with low-wage jobs. Welfare recipients have always gotten Medicaid, for example, while equally impoverished working mothers seldom have.

Legislators' failure to help single mothers with low-wage jobs has turned the American welfare system into a political and moral disaster. To begin with, it has made "welfare" synonymous with helping people who do nothing to help themselves. In addition, it has created a system in which unskilled single mothers cannot improve their situation by working harder—a situation that violates deeply held American ideals cutting across all partisan divisions. Such a system will never have many political supporters, even among hard-core liberals. If we try

to prop it up, we will fail. Welfare benefits will remain low, single mothers will remain poor, and we will turn another generation of recipients into welfare cheaters.

By now most liberal legislators have accepted the conservative view that we should encourage single mothers to work. This shift reflects a pervasive change in public attitudes toward working mothers. Even affluent mothers are now going out to work in unprecedented numbers. This change has made it increasingly difficult to argue, as liberals once did, that single mothers should have a right to stay home with their children at the taxpayer's expense. Most Americans now see becoming a full-time homemaker not as a right or a necessity but a luxury. Few see any reason why they should pay higher taxes in order to make this luxury available to the poor.

In today's political climate, the only convincing argument for paying poor mothers to stay home would be that having a full-time mother at home helps children escape from poverty. This was a plausible claim in the 1950s, when most Americans saw working mothers as child abusers. Now, when more than half of all married mothers work, the idea that they are doing their children irreparable damage is less popular. It is also incompatible with the evidence. Comparisons between children whose mothers do and don't work offer little support for the idea that staying home does children much good. Some studies show benefits, some show costs, and most show no effect at all. If working outside the home does harm a mother's children, the effect is too small to be of much social importance.[22]

Defenders of welfare can still argue, of course, that it is cheaper to pay unskilled women to care for their children than to provide their children with high-quality daycare at public expense. For very young children, this argument is correct. As a result, almost everyone who has thought about the problem agrees that we need some variant of welfare for single mothers with infants. But once children are toilet-trained, they require less attention. From a strictly economic viewpoint, it seldom makes sense to pay mothers to stay home with young children, especially after they enter kindergarten.

If a mother does not have a God-given right to stay home with her children, if paying her to do so does not make economic sense, and if it does not do her children much good, the case for welfare collapses. At the moment, most liberal legislators still assume that welfare mothers are needier than single mothers with jobs, so they feel some moral obligation to improve welfare benefits. But…most northern states provide welfare packages as generous as those that employers offer unskilled workers. The moral case for helping welfare mothers rather than working mothers therefore rests on a factual mistake. As the number of working mothers increases, the political case for helping them will become ever more compelling. Eventually, liberal legislators will figure this out.

Strategies for Helping Single Mothers Who Work

Most legislators, both liberal and conservative, already agree that we should try to make work pay for single mothers. Conservatives want to do this by cutting welfare benefits, while liberals want to increase the benefits of work. Thus far, liberal attempts to make work more rewarding have taken three forms: job training, raising the minimum wage, and tougher enforcement of absent fathers' child-support obligations. Each of these strategies helps single mothers who work, but even if we pushed each strategy to its limits we would not solve single working mothers' economic problems.

Job training. As we have seen, even universal job training would probably not raise the average welfare mother's potential earnings by more than $1000 or $2000.

Minimum wage. The minimum wage rose to $4.25 in 1991. Yet even if every welfare mother could find steady work at $4.25 an hour, her expected earnings would be less than $8000 a year. If we make realistic assumptions about unemployment rates, the figure would be more like $7000.

If we wanted to ensure that every employed single mother could support herself and two children from her earnings alone, we would have needed a minimum wage of at least $9 an hour in 1988. Political difficulties aside, raising the minimum wage to $9 an hour would be an economic disaster. Most American communities already have more unskilled workers than unskilled jobs. Anything that raises the cost of hiring unskilled workers will further reduce demand for their services. If McDonald's had to pay its workers $9 an hour, a Big Mac would cost twice what it now costs, and more working people would make their lunches at home, reducing the number of fast-food jobs. Like-wise, if manufacturers had to pay unskilled workers $9 an hour, they would buy more machines to replace unskilled workers and would move more plants overseas, where unskilled workers are cheaper and often more reliable. This is not a promising way of solving single mothers' problems.

Child support. Better child-support enforcement makes work more attractive because the law allows a working mother to keep whatever the absent father contributes. A welfare mother, in contrast, can keep only the first $50 of the father's monthly contribution. The more the father pays, therefore, the bigger the advantage to the mother of working rather than collecting welfare.

But the absent fathers of children on welfare are mostly young, poorly educated, and poorly paid. Furthermore, judges and legislators seldom expect absent fathers to allocate more than 30 percent of their income to their children. As a result, their support payments seldom amount to much, even when they make them. Under the widely used "Wisconsin standard," for example, the typical absent father would have owed only $2000 in 1987.[23] Since many absent fathers now pay nothing at all and many others pay only part of what they owe, collecting even $2000 would represent a substantial improvement over the present situation. But a big-city mother with two children who got $2000 from an absent father would still need about $13,000 from other sources to make ends meet. Relatively few single mothers will be able to earn that much in the near future.

Liberals clearly need a new strategy for helping single mothers. In trying to formulate such a strategy they can afford to be flexible about details so long as they keep in mind three basic principles:

- Urban families with children can seldom make ends meet on incomes below the poverty line. Any policy that pretends families can somehow "make do" on the sums that welfare currently gives them is a fraud and will force welfare recipients to engage in fraud. If mothers work, they will need incomes substantially above the poverty line, since they have to pay for medical care, childcare, transportation, and taxes.
- Single mothers without higher education can seldom earn enough to support themselves and their families. This will remain true even if we raise the minimum wage to $5 or $6 an hour, get more welfare mothers to return to school, and provide more and better job training.
- While child-support enforcement can help single mothers with low-wage jobs make ends meet, such mothers also need direct help from the public treasury.

Broadly speaking, there are two ways of using public funds to help single mothers who work: we can modify the existing welfare system so it helps those who work, or we can gradually create a separate system of government-financed "fringe benefits" for all working men and women. Modifying the existing welfare system would be cheaper, at least in the short run. In the long run, however, a program of fringe benefits for all working families would win more political support, be more just, and do more good.

Transforming AFDC

The simplest way of helping single mothers who work is to let all single mothers collect AFDC, regardless of how much outside income they get. This approach would, in effect, convert AFDC into a child-support system for single mothers. Instead of seeing welfare as a program that ought to provide single mothers with a decent standard of living but doesn't, we would redefine it as a program that ought to provide a single mother with enough income so she can make ends meet if she also works, gets child support, or gets help from her boyfriend or family. This is the way welfare recipients already look at the program. By making their behavior legal, we would encourage their efforts at self-help instead of discouraging them.

If all single mothers were eligible for AFDC, the cost of AFDC in fiscal 1990 would have been about $35 billion instead of $20 billion.[24] Instead of accounting for roughly 0.5 percent of all personal income, AFDC would have accounted for almost 1 percent. Allowing all single mothers to collect AFDC would have at least three benefits. First, more single mothers would work in the official economy, where jobs usually provide more valuable experience and pay better than the off-the-books jobs that most welfare mothers now take. Second, single mothers would no longer have to choose between keeping their families together and breaking the law (though some would, no doubt, continue to lie about their living arrangements). Third, material hardship would decline among single mothers, and it would decline most among those who now obey the law and work in low-wage jobs.

Despite these advantages, making AFDC available to all single mothers is politically impossible. Setting aside the income tax, AFDC is America's least popular government program. Few politicians would want their name associated with a proposal that doubled the number of welfare recipients, even if the proposal also changed the meaning of being on welfare. Furthermore, if we eliminated restrictions on welfare recipients' outside income, legislators would soon cut welfare benefits, leaving single mothers unable to make ends meet even if they worked. Single mothers are a relatively small, unorganized, and unpopular group. A program aimed exclusively at them will never be generous.

Helping All Parents with Low-Wage Jobs

Given these political difficulties, liberals should probably follow Daniel Patrick Moynihan's advice to Richard Nixon on race and subject welfare to a protracted period of benign neglect. Instead of trying to reform a system that has resisted reform for as long as it has existed, liberals should try to construct a new system that concentrates on helping all parents who work in low-wage jobs. Rewarding work is consistent with current American values. And trying to help low-wage workers with families is consistent with widespread legislative concern about the current condition of children.

Fringe benefits for low-wage parents also seem a natural response to the steady decline in unskilled workers' purchasing power over the past generation. The average male worker's real earnings have hardly changed over the past two decades, but the real wages of the least educated have fallen, while the real wages of the best educated have risen. A national effort to help those at the bottom could, we suspect, win widespread support from the Democrats' traditional constituency.

In shaping a program of fringe benefits for working Americans, we should focus on workers who are trying to support children. Some obvious possibilities would be to:

- Provide extra cash to parents who work at low-wage jobs by increasing the Earned Income Tax Credit. We should also make the credit larger for families with more children.[25]
- Provide tax credits for childcare expenses if all the adults in a family have full-time jobs. Single mothers would get these credits if they worked. Two-parent families would get them if both parents worked.
- Allow all workers to buy Medicaid coverage for themselves and their family for, say, 5 percent of their earnings. (Or better yet, provide universal health insurance with premiums tied to income.)
- Give all parents who work a tax credit for housing expenses equivalent to the average value of a Section 8 housing certificate (or perhaps equivalent to what we now give the average homeowner).
- Provide mortgage subsidies for working parents who buy homes in low-income neighborhoods, helping to stabilize these neighborhoods.

Because Americans have such a strong prejudice against taxation, such benefits may have to decline as family income rises, but our goal should be to ensure that every working parent gets some benefit from every program. Except for medical care, however, none of these benefits should be defined as a universal right. They should be defined as rewards for work, as social security is. In America, social-welfare policy cannot afford to be seen as offering the indolent something for nothing.

If programs of this kind existed today, the great majority of welfare mothers would seek regular employment. Even in what passes for a full-employment economy, however, there are many communities in which unskilled women cannot find steady work. When the economy goes into recession, as it periodically does, such communities become more numerous. In areas where unemployment exceeds, say, 6 percent we should guarantee single mothers either a low-wage public-service job or paid job training. These positions should provide the fringe benefits we have already described.

Even in tight labor markets there will also be some single mothers whom nobody wants to hire. Some of these women ought to qualify for disability benefits. The remainder should stay in the existing AFDC system. But if we really made work pay for single mothers, the welfare rolls would shrink dramatically.

A program for making low-wage work economically attractive could win broad political support. Perhaps more important, it could retain such support over time, because it would be seen as reinforcing rather than subverting the work ethic. We cannot create such a system overnight. Indeed, we probably cannot create it in a decade. But what liberals need most today is not a program they can get through Congress next year. They need an agenda worth pursuing over the long run. The creation of an economic system that allows unskilled workers to support their families through some combination of wages and government benefits could and should be a central element in any such agenda.

NOTES

1. Edin also promised all her recipients anonymity and recorded the interviews using fictitious names.

2. Edin actually contacted sixty mothers, but we dropped one of them because she cared for her children only two days a week.

3. We were not able to obtain data on the proportion of Cook County AFDC recipients in subsidized housing, so our judgment about the availability of subsidized housing is impressionistic. We discuss comparative housing costs in more detail later.

4. Edin's method almost inevitably oversamples welfare recipients with a lot of friends and undersamples short-term recipients. For a more detailed description of the way in which the initial sample of twenty-five was drawn, see Kathryn Edin, "There's a Lot of Month Left at the End of the Money: How Welfare Recipients in Chicago Make Ends Meet," Ph.D. diss. (Department of Sociology, Northwestern University, 1989).

5. According to the Illinois Department of Public Aid, Cook County recipients are 77 percent black and 10 percent non-Hispanic white. In the nation as a whole, recipients are roughly 40 percent black and 39 percent non-Hispanic white. U.S. House of Representatives, Committee on Ways and Means, "Background Material and Data on Programs within the Jurisdiction of the Committee on Ways and Means" (Washington: U.S. Government Printing Office, 1989), p. 564.

6. Roughly 17 percent of Cook County recipients live in the suburbs, compared to 26 percent of Edin's recipients.

7. In the nation as a whole, 9 percent of all AFDC recipients lived in public housing in 1987, while another 9 percent lived in other forms of subsidized housing ("Background Material and Data on Programs within the Jurisdiction of the Committee on Ways and Means," 1989, p. 564). In Edin's sample, 20 percent lived in public housing, and 24 percent lived in other forms of subsidized housing. Almost all the mothers in public housing lived in Chicago's two largest projects (Cabrini Green and Robert Taylor Homes). All but one of the twelve mothers in other forms of subsidized housing lived in the suburbs.

8. The two mothers who came close to living on their checks ran deficits of $26 and $54 a month. A third teenage mother ran a cash surplus because she lived with her own mother, who paid her rent, utilities, and groceries. This allowed the teenager to use most of her $250 AFDC check for personal expenses. She saved the balance (about $60 a month) in order to attend college. The value of the food, rent, and utilities this

teenage recipient received from her mother substantially exceeded her monthly savings, so without her mother's help she would have had a deficit.

9. When national surveys ask welfare mothers about their income and expenses, most mothers report spending far more than they take in. Economists have traditionally explained such puzzles by arguing that the families in question were only temporarily poor and were either drawing down their savings or borrowing against future income. (The classic formulation of this argument is Milton Friedman, *A Theory of the Consumption Function,* Princeton University Press, 1957.) This explanation of excess consumption among low-income families makes sense when applied to farmers or small businessmen who have had a bad year. It does not make much sense for welfare mothers, since mothers with savings are not eligible for welfare and very few have access to long-term credit. Only two of Edin's respondents had sufficient assets to support expenditures in excess of income for more than a month or two. (Both had received insurance settlements after going on welfare.) None had significant debts other than student loans, which they (and we) treated as ordinary income. A few had bought furniture or appliances on time, but they (and we) treated these as equivalent to renting the item in question.

Edin's respondents reported substantial month-to-month income fluctuations, which they dealt with by small-scale saving and borrowing. To eliminate this source of noise, Edin asked about "average" monthly income and expenditures. Using this approach, most respondents' estimates of their monthly income and expenditure came very close to balancing. A few respondents reported average monthly income significantly higher than their average expenditure. Since only one respondent reported saving anything, we infer that most respondents with "surplus" income were overestimating their income, underestimating their expenditures, or both. (Such optimism is common at all income levels.) For the sample as a whole, monthly income (including food stamps but no other in-kind income) exceeded expenditure by an average of 4.8 percent.

10. If a recipient has not repaid her excess benefits by the time she leaves the rolls, she must in theory make a lump-sum repayment.

11. To estimate the average midwestern family's expenditure on items other than food, shelter, and utilities in 1988–1990, we used data from the Consumer Expenditure Survey for the first quarter of 1989 (see U.S. Bureau of Labor Statistics, "Consumer Expenditure Survey: Quarterly Data from the Interview Survey," Report 784, 1990, table 4). Since welfare mothers get Medicaid, we excluded health-care expenditures from the comparison. Edin's fifty mothers reported cash expenditures averaging $664 a month, of which $50 went for food, $203 for rent, $30 for gas, $30 for electricity, and $13 for health care. That left $339 for everything else. The average midwestern family spent $1022 a month on items other than food, shelter, utilities, and health care.

12. The AFDC recipient unit—usually the mother and those of her children under eighteen—averaged 3.14 in Edin's sample, which is almost exactly the national average. The recipient unit is often smaller than the household, which may include the recipient's mother, a girlfriend, a boyfriend, an unreported husband, or grown children. Most mothers saw themselves as financially separate entities within their household and described budgets that covered only themselves and their children. When this was not the case, Edin had to make somewhat arbitrary allocations.

13. The monetary value of housing subsidies is a vexed question. If all the subsidized housing in which Edin's welfare mothers lived were rented at its market value, the ten apartments in public housing projects would rent for less than the twenty-eight unsubsidized apartments, while the twelve subsidized units in private buildings (eleven of which were in the suburbs) would rent for considerably more than the unsubsidized private units. Averaging over all subsidized units, their

market value was probably not very different from that of the unsubsidized units. We therefore estimated the market value of the subsidy by calculating the difference between what subsidized and unsubsidized tenants paid for rent and utilities ($240 a month). The actual cost to the taxpayer is undoubtedly higher than this.

14. When Edin estimated the value of all noncash income, including all gifts provided by relatives and boyfriends, the fifty mothers' total income rose another $100 a month, to $1126. This estimate is conservative, in the sense that Edin tried to err on the low side when valuing gifts.

15. For details on how the original line was constructed, see Mollie Orshansky, "Counting the Poor: Another Look at the Poverty Profile," *Social Security Bulletin*, 28 (January 1965), 3–29.

16. The Gallup results are reported in William O'Hare, Taynia Mann, Kathryn Porter, and Robert Greenstein, *Real Life Poverty in America: Where the American Public Would Set the Poverty Line* (Washington: Center on Budget and Policy Priorities, 1990). Families with incomes below $10,000 set the line somewhat lower than more affluent families. The published Gallup data suggest that poor families in cities of one million or more would probably set the poverty line for a family of four at about $16,000 (in 1989 dollars).

17. Lee Rainwater, in *What Money Buys* (New York: Basic Books, 1974), showed that survey respondents' estimates of how much money it took to achieve a given standard of living ("not poor," "getting along," "comfortable") all had about the same elasticity with respect to family size, regardless of which adjective he used to define the level of living. The elasticity of the poverty line with respect to family size was 0.29. The poverty threshold for a family of three should therefore be about $(3/4)^{.29} = 92$ percent of that for a family of four, while the threshold for a family of two should be $(2/4)^{.29} = 82$ percent of that for a family of four. Averaging across all five of

the living levels that Rainwater investigated, the elasticity of respondents' estimates with respect to family size averaged 0.32. Since differences between living levels appear to be random, one could argue for using this figure rather than 0.29. In that case the poverty line for a family of three would be 91 percent of that for a family of four, and the line for a family of two would be 80 percent of that for a family of four.

18. This estimate ignores goods and services provided by parents, boyfriends, and other private parties but includes food stamps and housing subsidies, as well as cash transfers from private parties.

19. ...The estimate for childcare assumes that 60 percent of welfare mothers would have to pay for childcare if they worked and would pay the same amount that working single mothers now pay.... The estimate for transportation assumes that mothers use public transportation. Many must buy cars, but the cost of a car cannot be treated solely as a work-related expense.

20. The Committee on Ways and Means ("Background Material," 1989, p. 536) estimates the net tax burden on a single mother earning $15,000 at $1676.

21. *Economic Report of the President, 1990*, p. 344.

22. For a review of this literature, see Cheryl Hayes and Sheila Kamerman, eds., *Children of Working Parents: Experiences and Outcomes* (Washington: National Academy Press, 1983).

23. See Michalopoulos and Garfinkel, "Reducing Welfare Dependence and Poverty of Single Mothers by Means of Earnings and Child Support," table 1. The "Wisconsin standard" sets the absent father's obligation at 17 percent of his gross income for one child, 25 percent for two children, 29 percent for three, and 31 percent for four.

24. In 1988 there were 12.9 million children under eighteen living in female-headed families. Of the 7.33 million children receiving AFDC, roughly $8.6 percent or 6.49 million lived in single parent families (Committee on Ways and Means. "Background Material," 1989, pp. 559, 563). Making all children in female-headed families

eligible for AFDC would, therefore, raise the number of children on the rolls by roughly $(12.9 - 6.5)/7.33 = 87$ percent.

We expected to spend about $15.2 billion on AFDC for single mothers and their children in fiscal 1990. Had all female-headed families been eligible, and had the new recipients been distributed among states in the same way as existing recipients, costs would have risen by about $13.7 billion. The actual figure would probably be lower than this rough estimate, because the takeup rate among single mothers is currently lower in low-benefit states, so growth would be concentrated in those states. Making AFDC taxable, as we should if we made it available to all single mothers, would slightly reduce its cost. Allowing AFDC recipients to keep their earnings would also raise their money incomes, reducing their food-stamp entitlements somewhat. In theory, making eligibility depend entirely on marital status should also lower administrative costs.

25. Congress took a significant step in this direction as part of the deficit-reduction package passed in October 1990.

REFERENCES

Michalopoulos, Charles and Irwin Garfinkel. 1989. *Reducing the Welfare Dependence and Poverty of Single Mothers by Means of Earnings and Child Support: Wishful Thinking and Realistic Possibility.* No. 89. University of Wisconsin-Madison, Institute for Research on Poverty.

Office of Planning and Research, U.S. Department of Labor. 1965. The Negro Family: The Case for National Action. Washington, D.C. U.S. Government Printing Office. Popularly known as "The Moynihan Report."

46

PHILIP KASINITZ AND JAN ROSENBERG

MISSING THE CONNECTION: SOCIAL ISOLATION AND EMPLOYMENT ON THE BROOKLYN WATERFRONT (1996)

Many policy makers believe that bringing industry and business to poor neighborhoods will open up job opportunities for neighborhood residents. In this selection, Philip Kasinitz and Jan Rosenberg look at a Brooklyn community with an abundance of jobs and ask why poor people do not get jobs located in their own neighborhood.

The spatial concentration of urban poverty and the social and cultural tendencies presumed to accompany it are widely considered to be among the gravest problems now facing U.S. cities. This "hyperghettoization," to borrow Wacquant's (1995) term, is said to be marked by the erosion of the material foundations of the traditional ghetto, the decline of local social institutions, and a striking geographic, economic, and social isolation of the urban poor. The literature points to the persistent high levels of joblessness among inner city residents as both a cause and effect of these processes. In this paper we will present a case study of employment patterns in a neighborhood of concentrated poverty where most residents live in public housing. However, unlike most poor neighborhoods this area is also home to a declining but nonetheless still active core of industrial facilities and blue-collar employment. Despite this proximity local people rarely hold local jobs, leading us to ask: Why do poor people not get the jobs that are located in their own communities?

In *The Truly Disadvantaged,* William Julius Wilson argues that one characteristic that makes contemporary urban poverty distinct is the "social isolation" of the ghetto poor. This isolation is defined as a "lack of contact or of sustained interaction with individuals and institutions that represent mainstream society" (Wilson 1987:60) and is presumed to be most intense for people living in places where poverty has become more concentrated. Wacquant and Wilson (1989) refine this notion with their discussion of "social capital," a term Portes would later define as "the capacity of individuals to command scarce resources by virtue of their membership in networks or broader social structures" (Portes 1995:12; see also Coleman 1988), Drawing on Pierre Bourdieu's ideas about social capital formation, Wacquant and Wilson argue that the amount of social capital in a group, specifically in this case a geographic urban community, may become depleted as more advantaged members leave. With the loss of these "ambassadors," communities of the poor become increasingly socially isolated. This problem would seem to be most acute for members of minority groups who are already at some social distance from the mainstream.

To this, Fernandez (1990) adds the question of personal networks: Do the social relationships in which a poor person is embedded facilitate or inhibit useful contacts with the broader society, such as access to employment? Social isolation may be further compounded by critical mass effects that occur when the number of poor people in a given locale overwhelms

the capacity of formal and informal institutions to cope with poverty. Finally Massey and Denton (1993), who challenge the causal significance of middle-class flight from poor neighborhoods, suggest that in predominantly Black areas it is racial segregation that drives out investment and limits employment opportunities (see also Massey and Eggers 1990).

All of this work implicitly or explicitly emphasizes the role of spatial location. In a dramatic shift from much of the poverty research of the 1960s, those who emphasize the role of social structure and those who emphasize the behavioral attributes of the poor have taken to using geographic units of analysis. To be a member of Rickett and Sawhill's (1988) "underclass," Wilson's (1987) "socially isolated poor," or of Jargowsky and Bane's (1990) "ghetto poor" it is not necessary that one be poor but rather that one lives in a place where a large portion of the population is poor.[1] On the whole this seems a welcome recognition of the importance of neighborhoods in shaping employment opportunities and broader life chances. Yet while most contemporary observers conclude that "neighborhood effects" play a real and important role in the perpetuation of poverty, there is little consensus as to exactly what these effects are and how they work (see Huang and Attewell 1993; Ellwood 1992; Crane 1991; Rosenbaum and Popkin 1991; Case and Katz 1991; Mayer and Jencks 1989; Tienda 1989).

Take for example the debate over the "spatial mismatch" hypothesis. In 1968 John Kain first suggested that the lack of access of inner city Blacks to jobs—in particular to manufacturing jobs—was at least in part due to the increased distance between those jobs and the inner city areas in which most poor Blacks lived. This notion of a spatial mismatch has been elaborated by some (Kasarda 1989) and questioned by others (e.g., Ellwood 1986; Fainstein 1987). The most exhaustive review of the literature on this question found the evidence to be inconclusive (Jencks and Mayer 1990). Yet throughout this debate those who insist on the importance of location and those who discount it have tended to define spatial factors very narrowly, focusing primarily on the physical distance between the places poor people live and the location of entry-level jobs. Yet as Wilson reminds us:

> even in those situations where job vacancies become available in an industry near or within an inner city neighborhood, workers who live outside the inner city may find out about these vacancies sooner than those who live near the industry because the latter are not tied into the job network. (Wilson 1987:60)

Even if it can be shown that the spatial concentration of poverty contributes to keeping the poor poor, it does not necessarily follow that living closer to middle-class people is beneficial (see for examples Gans 1990, 1995). Further, the location of prosperous neighborhoods very near poor ones is no guarantee of "spill over" effects (positive or negative), particularly if social custom, racial hostility, or even physical barriers limit contact between residents of adjacent areas (see Anderson 1990; Kasinitz 1988).

The recent geographic turn in poverty research has important policy implications. Aid to "communities" and "community-based" programs usually assume that geographic location implies community, which is in turn grounded in economic activity. Both of these assumptions are problematic. Sviridoff, for example, urges that social policy should support economic development only in those neighborhoods that have functioning social organizations, particularly community development corporations (Sviridoff 1994). Even more skeptical about the value of community, Lemann advocates policies focused on "people not places"—that is, traditional social services

to individuals—rather than neighborhood economic development (Lemann 1994). The concept of "empowerment zones"—a favorite Republican policy proposal in its earlier incarnation as "Enterprise Zones," now taken up by Democrats as well—assumes that bringing business into an area will help the job prospects of poor people who live there (see Kasinitz and Rosenberg 1993).

The following case study raises questions about this assumption. Our research points instead to the critical importance of social networks that functionally bypass and actively exclude local residents from local jobs. Our study further indicates that racial discrimination and the stigma attached to the local area may actually discourage neighborhood employers from hiring local residents.

Red Hook: The Setting

The Red Hook section of Brooklyn is a neighborhood of approximately 13,500 located on a peninsula in the New York Harbor. While the name Red Hook was once used to refer to a larger section of the Brooklyn waterfront, today it is used almost exclusively to describe the area cut off from the rest of the borough by a confluence of highways and the toll plaza for a large tunnel. It is a mixed-use area, where people live in close proximity to a declining but still significant number of blue-collar jobs. Red Hook is close to several middle-class neighborhoods. It is also near the lower Manhattan financial district, and the twin towers of the World Trade Center dominate the skyline.

Despite this central location, residents perceive themselves as isolated.[2] This is most obvious at the physical level. Red Hook is surrounded on three sides by water and cut off from the rest of Brooklyn by highways. As one resident puts it, "You don't come through Red Hook to go anywhere." Crossing highways makes entrance to the neighborhood difficult on foot or by car. A "two fare zone" (i.e., an area requiring a bus ride to reach the subway), the area is underserved by mass transportation, and the most common route to the subway requires sprinting across a six-lane highway, underneath an elevated expressway, and then walking three blocks through a predominantly Italian neighborhood that many members of Red Hook's Black and Hispanic majority view, not without cause, as hostile territory.

The area has seen considerable housing abandonment and "white flight" in recent decades. Red Hook's official population fell from more than 22,000 in 1950 to just more than 11,000 in 1990, although the Housing Authority estimates that approximately 2,500 additional people are unofficially living "doubled up" in the Red Hook Houses public housing project. As Table 46.1 indicates, about half of the residents live below the poverty level. When asked to describe their neighborhood, residents frequently start by listing services and facilities that are no longer there. Today Red Hook has only a few stores, although a large discount supermarket opened in 1991. It has no pharmacies, no movie theaters, and only one legal bar, although a number of ostensibly private clubs actually function as taverns and pool halls. There are a number of restaurants but most cater primarily to area workers rather than residents and close up tight by 4 P.M. There are two Chinese take-out restaurants

that dispense meals from behind bullet proof Plexiglas. There are no banks, although there are several check-cashing services—increasingly the banks of the poor. There are also a growing number of private car services in the area, as even in this least automotive of U.S. cities, private automobile use has increased as much for reasons of safety as convenience. Concern for security is a dominant force shaping the streetscape. The roof of the windowless branch of the public library is ringed with razor wire.

First settled in colonial days, by the time of the Civil War Red Hook was a busy neighborhood of wharves, homes, and warehouses. By the mid-1900s the area was predominantly Italian, but it was also home to the remnants of older Irish and Scandinavian communities as well as Brooklyn's first Puerto Rican enclave. These groups shared a dependence on the waterfront industries. Dock workers in particular formed strong community bonds, and the often volatile activity of their union was a central feature of the neighborhood's political life (Defazio 1985; Kimmeldorf 1988). As recently as 30 years ago Red Hook was perhaps the quintessential "tough" working-class neighborhood, the locale for Arthur Miller's *A View From the Bridge* and Hubert Selby's *Last Exit to Brooklyn*. Yet it was also a springboard from which a large number of people joined the middle-class.

TABLE 46.1. Demographic characteristics, 1990

	Total Population	Race				% Below Poverty	% Fem. Headed Hshlds
		White	Black	Hispanic	Other		
Red Hook	11,071	8%	49%	41%	1%	46%	69%
"The Back"	2,922	29%	13%	57%	1%	38%	51%
Public Housing	8,149	1%	63%	35%	1%	49%	75%
New York City	7,371,282	44%	26%	24%	7%	16%	36%

Note: "Hispanic" refers to a category of origin where the possible responses include white non-Hispanic, Black non-Hispanic, other non-Hispanic, white Hispanic, Black Hispanic, other Hispanic. In this table "Hispanic" includes any response of "Hispanic" regardless of race.
Source: 1990 U.S. Census.

Today most area residents live in the Red Hook Houses. One of the largest housing projects in New York, Red Hook Houses opened in 1939 and consists mainly of six-story buildings with open courtyards and pedestrian malls. A model of early public housing design (see Mumford 1940; Plunz 1990), it physically resembles middle-class developments like New York's Stuyvesant Town more than notorious high-rise public housing projects like St. Louis' Pruitt-Igoe or Chicago's Robert Taylor Homes. As in most New York public housing projects, the population is highly stable: In 1990 the mean length of tenancy was just slightly under 16 years.[3] Yet as Table 46.1 indicates, the Red Hook Houses is a very poor place, and in 1989 54 percent of the households received public assistance income. It is also a dangerous place. Gunfire is common and a constant concern for project residents.

The part of Red Hook outside the project, locally known as "the Back," has lost population steadily since the early 1960s. The remaining residents provide an interesting contrast to the population of the projects. Many are also poor: In 1989 38 percent of their households were below the poverty level. However, families in the Back had a far wider range of incomes, with a number of relatively prosperous working-class families remaining and a handful of middle-class "pioneers" arriving recently. The proportions of female-headed households and families on public assistance (35.7 percent) were significantly lower than in the project, although still quite high. The 1990 unemployment rate (14.3 percent) was lower than in the project (26.7 percent). Although minorities are the majority in both areas, in 1990 the projects were 63 percent Black and 35 percent Hispanic, whereas the Back was predominantly Hispanic (57 percent) with a considerable non-Hispanic white minority (29 percent). As Table 46.2 indicates, the Back has higher labor force participation

than the project, particularly for men. Workers from the Back are twice as likely to work in the traditional blue-collar manufacturing and construction industries. In both the Back and the projects, however, blue-collar employment has declined dramatically in recent decades.[4]

The people in the Back—unlike people in the projects—also retain the image of themselves as tied to industrial employment, and with that comes a sharp sense of betrayal. "Our parents worked in these shipyards," one woman complains, "and now these jobs go to people from Jersey, Pennsylvania, whatever. It ain't fair." This contributes to the general feeling of being left behind. There is a strong division of opinion about the Brooklyn Local of the International Longshoremen's Association (ILA), a union with a long reputation for "taking care of the neighborhood." Some see the ILA as shirking this responsibility while others remain loyal to the union. At the time of this study one high-ranking ILA official owned a home in the area and had a reputation for helping out with financial trouble or when local young people had brushes with the law. But with most waterfront jobs unavailable, his ability to "deliver" was quite limited.

Employment in Red Hook

Red Hook has high and persistent levels of unemployment and poverty. While these problems are worse for public housing residents than for those outside the projects, and worse for Blacks and Hispanics than for whites, lack of access to jobs is perceived as a problem by all groups in the neighborhood. While there are a substantial number of private-sector jobs in this one small area, local residents rarely hold these jobs. The question, clearly, is why?

While there is a large literature on employment practices in general and Black male unemployment in particular, there has

TABLE 46.2   Red hook selected occupation and industry characteristics, 1990 (as a percentage of employed persons)

	Persons 16 years and over	Labor force participation		Employed Persons	Industry	
		Male	Female		Construction	Manufacturing
Red Hook	7,377	60%	35%	2,574	6%	11%
"The Back"	2,105	72%	40%	1,014	8%	16%
Public Housing	5,272	54%	33%	1,560	4%	8%
New York City	5,858,104	71%	54%	3,284,198	4%	11%

Source: 1990 U.S. Census.

been relatively little work that asks employers "who do you hire and for what reasons?" The most notable exception is the work of Kirschenman and Neckerman (1991) and Neckerman and Kirschenman (1991). In many ways, although our methods are different, our findings closely parallel theirs. To a considerable degree Red Hook residents, and particularly Black, male, public housing residents, are excluded from Red Hook jobs for reasons of discrimination: both negative discrimination against local residents and positive discrimination in favor of other groups. Further, the discrimination against local residents is multifaceted, including a combination of racial, class, and locational preferences (what Kirschenman and Neckerman term "address" discrimination), fear of crime, and a general hostility to the local environment on the part of employers (see also Paugam 1991). This is aggravated by residents' general lack of social embeddedness, which leaves them outside of the networks by which local jobs are filled. Despite their physical proximity to employment, Red Hook residents, particularly those from the projects, often lack the "weak ties" that Granovetter (1973) suggests are so important in shaping the employment patterns of middle-class people.

Unlike most inner city areas, Red Hook remains an industrial neighborhood. Of the approximately 3,600 private-sector jobs in the area at the time of our survey, the majority are blue-collar. These include jobs in the maritime industries, woodworking, construction contracting, light manufacturing, warehouses, and New York's fast-growing solid waste transfer industry. The various factors that keep most local residents from getting these jobs are closely intertwined, and it is difficult in a qualitative case study to determine the relative causal significance of each. However, our research suggests the key role that social connections to networks play in the employment process—both for Red Hook residents and for non-residents who hold jobs in the area.

It could be true, as Mead's (1986) work implies, that many local people are simply not interested in low-wage work. However, when a discount supermarket chain announced its intention to open a store in the area in early 1991, it was instantly besieged by more than 300 applicants—two thirds of them Red Hook residents—for minimum-wage jobs. Our survey of these applicants (admittedly a self-selected group) revealed some striking patterns. The overwhelming majority said they were willing to take virtually any job in the area. Housing project residents, even those with considerable job experience, seem more connected to service-sector jobs than to manufacturing. By contrast, applicants from the Back were far more acquainted with traditional blue-collar work. This was true even for applicants with similar levels of education (for similar findings in other New York neighborhoods, see Sullivan 1989).

On the other hand, applicants from the projects and the Back *both* tend to have highly unstable job histories. This seems to be related to both a propensity to leave jobs (reasons frequently cited include disagreements with bosses and "lack of respect" shown by bosses and co-workers) and to the chronic instability of the low-wage job market. Many have experience with temporary work, day labor, lay offs, and job loss due to company closing.

Some Red Hook job applicants were uninterested in jobs that would take them out of the neighborhood. This coincides with the experience of recruiters for job training programs who report great problems in retaining Red Hook youth in programs in other areas. This is not altogether surprising—the area is a "two fare zone," and coming back to it at night is dangerous. There is also a striking lack of the minimal credentials needed for even many unskilled jobs. For example, in an area that employs many truck drivers, only 9 percent of the 300 job applicants had driver's licenses.

People in the projects and the Back also differed greatly on what types of jobs they wanted. This is particularly true for men. In the Back physical work remains associated with masculinity. As a white, 22-year-old, high school drop-out—out of work but with considerable experience in non-unionized contracting jobs—puts it:

> Hey, I always find a job. You know, construction, demolition, whatever...I can't sit behind a desk. I mean that's OK for girls, you know, but not for me. If I had to do like you do, sit behind a desk all day, I'd fuckin' die.

An Hispanic 25-year-old with a history of warehouse jobs puts it more simply:

> I need hard work. Men's work.

African American men, particularly from the projects, were far less concerned with traditional sex roles in labor, and were generally drawn to white-collar work. They expressed interest in "learning computers," working in offices, and even in acquiring secretarial training. However, these same men frequently came to the employment office with presentational styles that were not conducive to white-collar employment. This could be seen as an example of social isolation and a lack of cultural capital, i.e., lack of knowledge of correct interview costume; or as resistance—an unwillingness to "play white" (see Fordham and Ogbu 1986). It should be noted, however, that the presentational style of these men did not differ dramatically from that of the white and Hispanic youth from the Back. At the same time, such "inappropriate" dress and presentation-of-self poses considerably greater problems for those seeking office positions than it does for men seeking blue-collar work.

Women from the projects often have an easier time finding clerical work, although the small number of clerical positions in the industrial area necessitates long commutes to low-paying jobs that frequently conflict with child care responsibilities. Many local women work for temporary employment agencies, and a number report preferring such situations. These agencies are more flexible in their demands, and the women believe themselves less likely to encounter prejudice in a temporary position.

Many local men do want industrial jobs. So why aren't they hired in local industry? To investigate this question we conducted a series of in-depth interviews with local employers. Using a list of local firms compiled by the Local Development Corporation (LDC), we sampled all of the 19 firms that employed 40 people or more and drew a 10 percent random sample of all others, producing an overall sample of 48 firms. Of these, 7 were no longer in business or otherwise not eligible. Of the 41 remaining we completed 34 interviews, and 7 refused to be interviewed.[5] Open-ended interviews were conducted with the owner or the person in charge of hiring at their places of work. Interviews ranged from 30 to 90 minutes. Of the 32 private-sector employers, 13 (41 percent) employed at least one Red Hook resident at the time of the interview, although 18 (56 percent) reported that they had employed at least one Red Hook resident at one time. In most cases, however only one or two local residents were employed at any one time, and most of these residents were local whites from the Back. Three small firms reported that the majority of their employees were Red Hook residents: one that hired primarily local whites and two that employed local Blacks and Latinos. None of these firms employed more than 40 persons.

This sampling method missed two key sources of employment for people in the project. Only two not-for-profit or governmental agencies showed up in our sample because, for most, headquarters were elsewhere. We therefore cluster sampled three additional work sites: two day care agencies and a public school. All five had employed Red Hook residents in the past and four of the five did so at the time of the interview. In all four cases this included project residents. This is made all the more interesting by the fact that all of these agencies use far more rationalized hiring procedures. All used formal applications and four of the five required state or other licensing procedures, educational requirements, fingerprints, and criminal background checks, Nevertheless, to the extent they could control who they hired, employers at these agencies expressed a preference for local residents.[6]

We discovered that the LDC list missed most small retailers. We supplemented our survey with short interviews with the 27 retail establishments that actually face the projects. We were able to contact 23 of these, which employ 70 people. Only 7 of these employ Red Hook residents, 12 full-time and 3 part-time employees. Only one, a local barber shop, is owned by a Red Hook resident, which also is the only small retailer that regularly employs local Blacks.

"It's Who You Know": Networking, Sponsoring, and "Vouching"

There are a variety of mechanisms, formal and informal, by which blue-collar jobs are filled on the Brooklyn waterfront. However, from the highest to the lowest skilled positions, few Red Hook employers report that finding workers constitutes a significant problem. Despite Red Hook's inaccessible location, in the current slack blue-collar labor market, both skilled and unskilled jobs are easily filled. While employers tended to be quite vocal about what they liked about doing business in Red Hook (cheap rents, waterfront access, proximity to Manhattan) and what they did not (crime), access to labor was never listed as an important factor.

In the case of many of the highest paying local jobs, employers actually have little choice in who they hire. Longshoremen are assigned to jobs by their union, not the employer. After the news that they had received a large contract was reported in the press, a local shipyard was besieged with applications, but virtually all of the jobs were guaranteed to unionized workers laid off from previous positions across the East Coast. Contractors are often obliged to inform craft unions of available jobs before advertising them. In some craft industries, union agreements oblige a contractor to hire a certain number of union members from the local in the area where the job is located.

In such cases residential location may once have played a role in who gets jobs, but it is residential location in the past rather than the present. Shipyard workers and longshoremen may have lived in the neighborhood once but generally no longer do. In these industries new workers are not recruited from Red Hook, or anywhere else for that matter: There are no new workers. While the wages of the waterfront workers have increased dramatically over the last few decades, deindustrialization and automation have decreased their numbers. The rationalization of the stevedoring industry and the introduction of the guaranteed annual wage in 1966 made it no longer necessary for longshoremen to live near the docks, and no new longshoremen have been hired in the port of New York since 1972. Other high paying blue-collar jobs are filled not on the basis of where workers live, but where their relatives lived a generation ago. For example, a large contractor hires carpenters from a union hiring hall near Red Hook. Many members of this "father and son" local live in the distant suburbs. Yet they have first crack at Red Hook jobs, in part because their fathers, uncles, or grandfathers once lived near the waterfront.

Most local jobs, however, are in lower paying industries. Yet here, too, there are many examples of "positive discrimination" that advantage non-local job seekers. The primary quality most employers report they are looking for in an unskilled position is reliability; they contend that the best way to find steady, reliable employees is by personal referral. Thus Red Hook industries typically hire primarily on the basis of referrals, often from the current workers. An oil transportation company, which recruits its barge workers from as far away as the Gulf Coast (they work on a one-month-on, one-month-off basis) explains: "Basically it is all word of mouth now. We don't advertise at all."

In this case promotion also was largely based on referrals from within:

> Right now we have probably four or five guys that have licenses to steer a boat, but we don't have openings so they are just deck hands. So we gradually break them in... They will just observe the area and how the work is done, and when somebody speaks for them, then we will move them into a full-time position. Interviewer: Speaks for them? When somebody is willing to put in the time to take them on their watch. Because the captain has to, there is extra time involved.

A contractor who must hire his craftsmen through the union, but hires his own clerical workers notes:

> I call a lot of the GCs (general contractors), and they all have girls working for them. And I say to them "Do you know of anyone that needs a job?" And they say "Oh, I have a cousin, I have a friend." And I do take the time and interview everybody.

The owner of a recycling center says:

> We hire almost entirely by word of mouth. I have a couple of guys who brought in almost everybody, all the unskilled anyway. They bring in their friend, their cousin, their uncle, whatever. I have had maybe five guys come in off the street and only two or three have worked out even for a short time. We have a formal application, but it's really only for record keeping purposes.

This preference for referrals is even stronger among employers who do hire from the local area. A small carpentry shop, which has hired locals including Blacks from the Red Hook Houses notes:

> If you have somebody who is good and they recommend somebody, then you generally think that they're good. Now we have a guy who we took who came out from three years in jail. We would have never taken him without a recommendation.

A warehouse owner concurs:

> When we are in hiring mode and looking for people we often times hire people who come in off the street. But most of the time (they) will know some of the employees here and they'll mention a name and we'll check them out with our employees.

Hiring "off the street" is rare, however, even in the lowest paying jobs. A commercial baker notes:

> We'll give anyone who walks in off the street an application. Likelihood of their being hired is slim, because we don't know them...We don't tend to just take people off the street because I've had a lot of bad experiences. That's true of all ethnic groups including white Americans...it doesn't matter.

Most private-sector employers report little need to run ads for workers in newspapers, although contractors often do so to fulfill the mandates of city or state contracts. Most Red Hook businesses report that they would simply not consider hiring someone who walked in off the street, and several stated the belief that local Blacks who did occasionally come in looking for work were probably "casing" the business for a robbery.

The reliance on referrals and the reluctance to hire from newspaper ads or "off the streets" often amounts to reliance on ethnic networks. This was no surprise in small retail businesses, which are usually family run and almost always employ members of a particular ethnic group. Korean, Chinese, Arab, and Dominican retailers all hired co-ethnics exclusively. Yet many larger businesses also hire through ethnic networks, and sometimes the employers are actually only peripherally aware of how the process works. One large contractor reports that more than half of his workers are immigrants from Spain who travel to Red Hook from Jersey City and Newark, New Jersey (a journey of more than an hour by car and longer by public transportation). "They all know each other over there, I guess, and when they hear we have an opening, somebody just shows up." Other employers have very specific notions about the ethnicity and gender of the people they would like to hire, such as the low-wage factory owner who told the employment service at the Local Development Corporation to send him "only Hispanic women." In such cases discrimination may be circumscribed by what the employer thinks he can afford. An employer with a Latin American workforce that commutes through the five boroughs notes:

> (Our workforce has) always been Spanish (sic) mainly, because that is the workforce that is out there. Generally in any kind of manufacturing—look, we're not talking $20 an hour manufacturing here. We're talking $8, $10 an hour manufacturing and the people willing to do the work—it's largely the Spanish community. They tend to be the ones to seek these jobs out.

This employer was not sure exactly how most of his "Spanish" workers (they actually came from a variety of non–Puerto Rican Latino backgrounds) heard about jobs. So long as his current employees kept providing him with a reliable supply of workers, he did not care.

Sometimes ethnicity will also be a reason for positive discrimination beyond referrals. A warehouse manager explains:

> See there's a general perception amongst employers that Irish immigrants, Polish, and Mexicans are the latest desirable employees. There's a friend of mine who is a carpenter and...(he says) that all the Mexican guys he's come in contact with are incredibly good workers. You hear that enough times and then if a Mexican guy came here for work I'd probably hire him based on that.

No such reputation is attached to local Blacks and Puerto Ricans. In fact people who do have good experience hiring local Blacks and Puerto Ricans almost inevitably report this as a happy exception, rather than a basis for positive generalizations.

There is a large literature on the role of social networks in job placement (see, for examples Waters, forthcoming; Montgomery 1994; Bowes 1987; Jackall 1978; Kornblum 1974; Granovetter 1974). Social networks fill at least three functions in the labor market. At the most basic level, networks provide specific job information: i.e., where and when a specific opening is going to occur and the best way of obtaining the position. Second, job networks often provide direct sponsorship. In this case a current employee directly "vouches for" the new employee. If the new employee works out, this will reflect positively on the "sponsor." If the employee does not work out it may reflect badly on the sponsor and reduce his ability to sponsor workers in the future. Finally networks provide role models of successful employees and transmit general information about how to function successfully in certain jobs.

When we think of depletion of cultural capital in the ghetto, we usually mean the loss of this last function. Indeed, Anderson's ethnographic account of the "old heads"—the steadily employed adult Black men and women who provided general lessons on correct adult behavior, practical information, and job skills—points to the importance of networks in transmitting this sort of cultural capital (Anderson 1990). In Red Hook the authority and resources of the "old heads" have been shrinking, as the number of young people to be helped has grown.[7] With fewer local people employed in blue-collar industries, there are fewer opportunities to sponsor young people. In the public-sector jobs where today's female old heads are concentrated, sponsorship is limited by bureaucratic regulations and requirements. Thus today's old heads have less authority in part because they simply have less to give than in times past, and the rewards of following their example so obviously pale in comparison to the "crazy money" of the drug business. Further, the increasing violence and incivility of life in Red Hook has made "straightening out" neighborhood youth a dubious (and dangerous) proposition. Many Red Hook adults are now afraid of local young people and are less likely to fill the old head role.

Yet the lack of access to local jobs also points to the importance of the other functions of social networks. Red Hook residents simply do not hear about openings, which are rarely advertised. When they do, they usually lack a sponsor on the job. These problems are most acute for residents of the project, but they are also increasingly perceived by young people in the Back, where the remaining job networks are tied to declining industries. The old heads in both the projects and the Back also recall that in the 1960s and '70s their connections with labor unions and political machines afforded opportunities for sponsorship that are no longer available.

Finally, the social changes that have affected Red Hook have limited people's ability to build effective job networks. In many ways the social spaces in which networks can be formed have been sharply constricted by the pervasive fear of violence. The two tenants' associations and the two local parents' associations have only a handful of regular members, all middle-aged and older, and all report difficulty in getting anyone to attend meetings at night. A number of churches have left the area in recent years, and those that remain have curtailed their activities. Even the number of informal meeting spaces has decreased: There is one barber shop where 20 years ago there were three; one legal bar (catering only to white customers) where once there were several catering to various groups. The social spaces that remain tend to be sharply segregated by age; the local recreational center serves children during the day but is the turf of some of the area's toughest teenagers at night, and few adults now venture there. Throughout the neighborhood, but particularly in the project, many adults avoid teenagers, a situation hardly conducive to effective sponsorship. Indeed the project's more relatively affluent members often seek to assure their own safety by minimizing time spent in public (for a similar case, see Merry 1982).

As a result, the social networks of local residents are not only limited but are increasingly one dimensional and lacking in what Boissevian (1979) calls "multiplexity"; Red Hook residents lack opportunities to form links with a wide variety of people. With fewer residents in the labor force, the amount and variety of job information declines. As public life has constricted, social ties are increasingly made in private, i.e., with people of similar interests. The resulting social networks are more homogeneous and less useful in a dynamic

labor market (see also Fernandez-Kelly and Schauffler 1994).

Race, Place, and Crime: Location-Based Discrimination

In contrast to the employers interviewed by Neckerman and Kirschenman (1991), many of whom articulated strong racial preferences, most Red Hook employers were reluctant to discuss the role of race in their hiring decisions and were anxious to make clear that they do not practice racial discrimination. A salt distributor, for example, reports pride in a largely Black workforce, although all but one of these workers are from far outside the area. The oil distributor mentioned earlier also reports "absolutely no problems" with the Blacks in his workforce: immigrants from Honduras and an African supervisor. In general Black immigrants were favored over Black natives, and non–Puerto Rican Latinos over Puerto Ricans (both are important distinctions in New York). But employers rarely articulated anti-Black attitudes.

However few employers show any hesitation about expressing "locality" discrimination against residents of the Red Hook Houses. In some cases there was a general dislike for hiring people who lived too near work, precisely because it was "too convenient." For some employers local employees meant that the complicated lives of the poor could spill out into the workplace.

> We have drawn people from the Red Hook area for a number of jobs and we haven't had particularly good experiences. It's interesting that the thing that seems to be the problem is that people feel almost too close to home. They tend to want to go home for lunch and stay

there…They tend to have a fair number of visitors. Sometimes children, spouses, boyfriends, and girlfriends come in to visit them…We've found that sometimes that can be very disruptive.

More often, however, the focus of locality discrimination is the fear of crime. An employer with a large facility on the waterfront pointed with pride to his Black, West Indian team of security guards (commuters from central Brooklyn and Queens) but scoffed at the idea of hiring local African Americans: "What, the bums hanging around outside? You want me to hire the guys who are trying to rob me?"

Another recycler responded to our attempt at subtly raising the question of hiring Red Hook Houses residents:

Look. I know what you're driving at. Let me save you some time. Do I hire people from the projects? I have had, maybe, five people come in here over the years. I gave one or two a shot. And they didn't last a day. Mostly they gave me the impression that they were just looking around so they could come back for their "real job," at night.

This notion—that any local Black or Puerto Rican who came looking for a job without a referral probably had criminal intent—came up several times during the interviews.

Concern about crime is by no means unreasonable. Crime is rampant in the area and businesses are frequent targets. Most of the Red Hook employers report some experience with pilferage and many have had employees mugged. Thus, it would be unfair to dismiss these concerns as simple euphemisms for racism. It remains true, however, that for many employers there is a strong mental association between local Blacks and crime.

Further, for many private sector employers the neighborhood is seen as a hostile environment to be kept at bay. They have adopted a visible fortress mentality. Firms frequently do not post signs, and steel reinforced doors and blacked out windows are common. In one case it took the interviewers half an hour to find the entrance to a manufacturing firm, which was two flights up an exterior metal stair case, behind an unmarked steel door pock marked with bullet holes. Frequently negative feelings about the area are transferred to the residents:

We see junkies, we see prostitutes standing outside, and I wouldn't hire someone who lived in that. The projects have a very strong stigma attached. It's not just a matter of race. I don't discriminate. I'd be very upset if one of my people did. But naturally you distrust somebody who comes from a place like that. It's unfortunate, because there are probably lots of good people who live there…I mean look, we had a case out here just about a year ago. When I came into work there were 30 cop cars, right out in front of my place. There was a machine gunning going on. My god, you know, do you want to hire someone who comes out of that!

Finally, even some employers who do employ ghetto residents still discriminate against Red Hook residents. One moving-company owner who employs primarily Black men on a day-by-day basis, explains that he prefers to hire men from out of the area. Men from the neighborhood, he explained, would come under pressure from friends to help them steal. Men from similar backgrounds but from distant neighborhoods would be under less such pressure.

Jencks (1992) argues that while many contemporary employers are willing to hire Blacks who culturally resemble whites, there continues to be a strong "distaste for ghetto culture" and a reluctance to hire "assertive workers from an alien culture they don't understand" (Jencks 1992:128–129). Yet this is not "culture" in the sense that we usually use the term: Mexican "culture," for example, is not widely admired in the United States. While a few Red Hook employers expressed something like an admiration for the "values" of their ethnic employees, others indulged in crude ethnic stereotypes about their immigrant workers. What is generally admired are a few perceived attributes: punctuality, reliability, willingness to work hard and to be a pliable labor force. Further, while employers may resent the assertive style of young Blacks and Puerto Ricans, the often confrontational blue-collar male culture of many of the Red Hook employers is clearly not lacking in assertiveness.

Thus Red Hook residents, particularly those from the housing project, are excluded from many Red Hook jobs on the basis of positive discrimination in favor of those better connected to hiring networks, and negative discrimination on the basis of race, address, fear of criminality, and the employer's preconceptions about their work habits.

Who Does Hire "Locals"?

Occasionally most local employers do hire someone from the area, and a few hire a significant number of Red Hook residents. In the private sector these tend to be those paying the lowest wages and offering the least stable jobs. Some of these firms hire on a daily basis, and at least one still uses the old-fashioned "shape up," in which men line up in the morning hoping to be picked for a day's work. They lay people off frequently and sometimes pay below minimum wage (a fact employers were surprisingly candid about). They often see hiring locals as a last resort. "At these wages who else am I going to get?" says one manufacturer. Yet even model employers practice

selection procedures that lock many project residents out of the job market. One small woodworking shop owner frequently hires local residents, Black and Hispanic, men and women, including people from training programs and even parolees. He does not, however, hire people older than in their mid-twenties. He explains that the wages he can afford are only appropriate for a "young guy," who can learn a lot in a business like his and then move on. An older person willing to work for such wages, however, either has less work experience than the employer believes he should for his age, or is unusually desperate. Both are signs, the employer believes, that the individual is going to be trouble.

In other cases, such as the large local supermarket, a large, young, mostly minimum-wage labor force from the neighborhood was absolutely necessary for business. Here the employer assumed that the majority of workers would not last out the year. Nor was he entirely unhappy about this: Turnover was less costly than raises he was required to pay for workers who lasted long enough to join the union. Few did last.

There are other reasons that a few companies prefer local workers. The convergence of ideas about race, residential location, and crime generally appears to have a greater impact on male employment. Several industrial employers reported good experiences in hiring women from the Red Hook Houses for clerical positions:

I prefer to hire local women for the inside jobs. It's tough to get someone from outside the area to come back here. It's a two fare zone, you really need a car. And it's a pretty rough area, so it's good to have someone who knows the place. We really don't pay that much, and given their choice, most women would prefer to work in New York (Manhattan) where they can at least go out to lunch or something. So it makes more sense for someone who is back here already.

Yet this employer does not generally hire male locals for blue-collar positions: "The men, they can be a problem."

Another important exception occurred when the Local Development Corporation began a job referral service aimed at connecting local workers with local jobs. While at first their success was limited, and mostly concentrated among women and very low-wage jobs for young people, the agency repeatedly tried to place adult Black men in industrial and construction jobs. Eventually a few local construction contractors who needed minorities to fill the affirmative action requirements of city contracts, agreed to take on a few laborers from the LDC pool and reported that the workers had "basically worked out." The contractors, however, did not decide that they should start recruiting in the Red Hook Houses. They generally credited the considerable screening done by the LDC for the successful experience.

Significantly, four out of the five not-for-profit, public-sector and social service employers we surveyed did hire large numbers of people from the Red Hook Houses. In all of these situations, having employees who were "part of the community" was seen as a significant plus. These agencies made considerable use of the local labor pool despite far greater procedural restrictions on who could be hired. This may help to explain preference for more rationalized (and theoretically less discriminatory) hiring procedures that some African American job seekers reported.

It is likely, however, that local Blacks do better in non-profit and governmental employment because that is where their connections, their "weak ties" are. These ties reflect both the huge expansion in Black public-sector employment over the last 30 years and the fact that local Blacks come into contact with (and thus have opportunity to build ties with) local public-sector agencies in their role as clients. This is sometimes true even in jobs with considerable educational requirements. For example, many school aides and paraprofessionals in the local schools were originally parent activists who acquired minimum credentials (usually the GED—the high school General Equivalency Diploma) to become school aides at the urging of a principal or the Parents Association leaders. After becoming aides, many enrolled in programs sponsored by the teacher's union, which allowed them to acquire further educational credentials and become paraprofessionals. A few eventually obtain a bachelor's degree and become teachers. Similarly, local women who became active in "Great Society" programs and the welfare rights movement in the late 1960s now run several of the local child care facilities, although in this case many have capitalized on this upward mobility by moving out of the neighborhood.

However, these opportunities clearly remain limited for the less well-educated applicants. In Red Hook, government and non-profit jobs are overwhelmingly traditionally female jobs, and even the least skilled of them—such as day care workers—involve complex credential procedures, although good connections may help. Finally, it should be noted that the "client route" of establishing connections does not have an easy equivalent in industrial employment, where the bulk of Red Hook jobs are.[8]

Conclusions

As in any case study, one must be cautious in generalizing. Some aspects of Red Hook's history are unusual, and this research was conducted at a time of high local unemployment: A tighter labor market might have led to different results. Nevertheless, the study does point out how the social isolation of poor communities may limit access to even those employment opportunities that may appear the most available. It also raises questions about the wisdom of assuming that locating jobs in the inner city will benefit inner city residents.

At one level, social isolation is, in effect, a lack of social resources. One of those resources clearly is "cultural capital," but another, just as important, is social embeddedness. One thing we know is that among the most important resources one can have in the job market is friends or kin that can help you. This is true throughout the labor force, but it is most clearly true in private-sector blue-collar employment where bureaucratic hiring procedures are less developed than in white-collar and public-sector employment.

To the extent that friendship and ethnic networks often correspond to residential location, and to the extent that neighborhoods function as conduits through which information flows, residential location is important to our understanding isolation from employment. Nevertheless, Red Hook demonstrates that geography is not the only factor in this process. Simply locating low-skilled jobs near where poor people live is no guarantee that they will have access to those jobs. Further, there are many aspects of life in poor communities that may limit the "multiplexity" of the social ties and diminish the mix of "strong" and "weak ties" central to maintaining effective social networks.

Thus, this study calls into question many of the assumptions behind economic development strategies based on geographically targeted tax incentives. In Red Hook there is little reason to expect that an expansion of local business activity would have a dramatic effect on the employment patterns of local residents. Empowerment Zones, if not accompanied by considerable local hiring requirements, will not address this problem. Red Hook employers would like the tax breaks, but there is no reason to assume that if Red Hook businesses expanded they would use more local labor, particularly if the overall labor market remained loose. Currently fashionable "job readiness programs" that seek to instill missing items of cultural capital—such as appropriate interview attire or saying "ask" instead of "ax"—may have some utility for entry-level white-collar workers (although educational requirements effectively exclude many ghetto residents from such jobs); but they seem unlikely to make any difference in blue-collar employment patterns.

On a more optimistic note, it may be possible to create substitute referral networks. The success of the handful of African American Red Hook residents placed in industrial settings by the local development corporation is mildly encouraging in this regard. In part this may have been because these workers, who were screened by the LDC, were, in fact, better employees than the average Red Hook resident. But the main reason that employers were willing to "give them a chance" in the first place was that the employers trusted the LDC and took their reference seriously. Whether that sort of approach could be replicated on a larger scale is, of course, a matter of speculation.

Finally, while racial discrimination continues to be a factor in limiting poor people's access to unskilled jobs, it is one of a number of interrelated factors that contributes to the isolation of the poor. In Red Hook, being a member of a stigmatized race, living in a stigmatized place, and not having a sufficient diversity of social connections all come together to block residents' access to jobs, even—perhaps particularly—to those jobs located virtually on their door steps.

NOTES

1. Or in the case of Ricketts and Sawhill, where a large number of people exhibit certain behavioral characteristics.

2. Some area residents actually use the term "social isolation" to describe their situation. We do not know whether this indicates the wide diffusion of Wilson's ideas or whether they arrived at the term independently.

3. The average tenancy for New York City Housing Authority projects is 15.2 years.
4. In 1960 manufacturing accounted for 41 percent of all employment in the projects and 40 percent in the Back.
5. A response rate of 70.8 percent, or 83 percent of those eligible.
6. Of the 32 private-sector interview subjects, 30 were white, one was Chinese, and one was Latino. Of the five public-sector subjects, three were Black, one was white, and one was Latino.
7. Although we take the term "old heads" from Anderson (1990), it is commonly used in much the same way in Red Hook.
8. There is a potential equivalent in retailing. However, here local applicants run up against perhaps the strongest ethnic networks of all, particularly in small retailing.

REFERENCES

Anderson, Elijah. 1990. *Streetwise: Race, Class and Change in an Urban Community*. Chicago, Ill.: University of Chicago Press.

Boissevian, R. 1979. "Network Analysis: A Reappraisal." *Current Anthropology* 20:392–394.

Bowes, Lee. 1987. *No One Need Apply*. Cambridge, Mass.: Harvard Business School.

Case, Anne C., and Lawrence F. Katz. 1991. "The Company You Keep: The Effects of Family and Neighborhood on Disadvantaged Youths." National Bureau of Economic Research; Cambridge, Mass. Working Paper No. 3705.

Coleman, James. 1988. "Social Capital and the Creation of Human Capital." *American Journal of Sociology*, 94, Supplement: S95–S120.

Crane, Jonathan. 1991. "The Epidemic Theory of Ghettos and Neighborhood Effects on Dropping Out and Teenage Childbearing." *American Journal of Sociology* 96:1226–1259.

Defazio, William. 1985. *Longshoremen*. South Hadley, Mass.: Bergin and Garvey.

Ellwood, David T. 1986. "The Spatial Mismatch Hypothesis: Are There Teenage Jobs Missing in the Ghetto?" In *The Black Youth Employment Crisis*, pp. 147–185. Richard Freeman and Harry S. Holzer (eds.). Chicago, Ill.: University of Chicago Press.

———. 1992. "Mr. Wilson's Neighborhoods? Review of Neighborhood Effects." Paper presented to the SSRC Conference of the Urban Underclass. University of Michigan, Ann Arbor, June.

Fainstein, Norman. 1987. "The Underclass/ Mismatch Hypothesis as an Explanation for Black Economic Deprivation." *Politics and Society* 15:403–452.

Fernandez, Roberto. 1990. "Social Isolation and the Underclass." Paper presented at the Chicago Urban Poverty and Family Life Conference.

Fernandez-Kelly, M. Patricia, and Richard Schauffler. 1994. "Divided Fates: Immigrant Children in a Restructured Economy." *International Migration Review* 8:662–689.

Fordham, Signithia, and John Ogbu. 1986. "Black Student's School Success: Coping with the Burden of 'Acting White'." *The Urban Review* 18:176–205.

Gans, Herbert. 1990. "Deconstructing the Underclass: The Term's Dangers as a Planning Concept." *Journal of the American Planning Association* 177:271–277.

———. 1995. *The War against the Poor: The Underclass and Antipoverty Policy*. New York: Basic.

Granovetter, Mark. 1973. "The Strength of Weak Ties." *American Journal of Sociology* 78:1360–1380.

———. 1974. *Getting a Job: A Study of Contacts and Careers*. Cambridge, Mass.: Harvard University Press.

Huang, Qi, and Paul Attewell. 1993. "Testing Theories of the Underclass." Unpublished paper, Department of Sociology, the Graduate Center, City University of New York.

Jackall, Robert. 1978. *Workers in a Labyrinth: Jobs and Survival in a Bank Bureaucracy*. Montclair, N.J.: Allanheld.

Jargowsky, Paul A., and Mary Jo Bane. 1990. "Ghetto Poverty: Basic Questions." In *Inner*

City Poverty in the United States, pp. 16–67. Laurence E. Lynn and Michael McGeary (eds.). Washington, D.C.: National Academy Press.

Jencks, Christopher. 1992. *Rethinking Social Policy: Race, Poverty and the Underclass*. Cambridge, Mass.: Harvard University Press.

Jencks, Christopher, and Susan Mayer. 1990. "Residential Segregation, Job Proximity and Black Job Opportunities." In *Inner City Poverty in the United States*, pp. 187–222. Laurence Lynn and Michael McGeary (eds.). Washington, D.C.: National Academy Press.

Kain, John. 1968. "Housing Segregation, Negro Employment and Metropolitan Decentralization." *Quarterly Journal of Economics* 26:110–130.

Kasarda, John. 1989. "Urban Industrial Transition and the Underclass." The Annals of the American Academy of Political and Social Sciences, January.

Kasinitz, Philip. 1988. "The Gentrification of Boerum Hill: Neighborhood Change and Conflicts over Definitions." *Qualitative Sociology* 11:163–182.

Kasinitz, Philip, and Jan Rosenberg. 1993. "Why Enterprize Zones Won't Work." *The City Journal* 3:63–71.

Kimmeldorf, Howard. 1988. *Reds or Rackets?* Berkeley: University of California Press.

Kirschenman, Joleen, and Kathryn Neckerman. 1991. " 'We'd love to hire them but...': The Meaning of Race to Employers." In *The Urban Underclass*, pp. 203–232. Christopher Jencks and Paul E. Peterson (eds.). Washington, D.C.: Brookings.

Kornblum, William. 1974. *Blue Collar Community*. Chicago, Ill.; University of Chicago Press.

Lemann, Nicholas. 1994. "The Myth of Community Development." *The New York Times Magazine*, January 9.

Massey, Douglas, and Nancy Denton. 1993. *American Apartheid: Segregation and the Making of the Underclass*. Cambridge, Mass.: Harvard University Press.

Massey, Douglas, and Mitchell Eggers. 1990. "The Ecology of Inequality: Minorities and the Concentration of Poverty, 1970–1980." *American Journal of Sociology* 95:1153–1188.

Mayer, Susan, and Christopher Jencks. 1989. "Growing Up in Poor Neighborhoods: How Much Does It Matter?" *Science* 243:1441–1445.

Mead, Lawrence. 1986. *Beyond Entitlement: The Social Obligations of Citizenship*. New York: Free Press.

Merry, Sally Engle. 1982. *Urban Danger: Life in a Neighborhood of Strangers*. Philadelphia: Temple University Press.

Montgomery, James D. 1994. "Weak Ties, Employment and Inequality: An Equilibrium Analysis." *American Journal of Sociology* 99:1212–1226.

Mumford, Lewis. 1940. "A Versailles for the Masses." *The New Yorker* 16:40–41.

Neckerman, Kathryn, and Joleen Kirschenman. 1991. "Hiring Strategies, Racial Bias and Inner-city Workers." *Social Problems* 38:433–447.

Paugam, Serge. 1991. *La Disqualification Sociale: Essai sur la Nouvelle Pauvre*. Paris: Presses de Universitaires de France.

Plunz, Richard. 1990. *A History of Housing in New York City*. New York: Columbia University Press.

Portes, Alejandro. 1995. "Economic Sociology and the Sociology of Immigration: A Conceptual Overview." In *The Economic Sociology of Immigration*, pp. 1–41. Alejandro Portes (ed.). New York: Russell Sage Foundation.

Ricketts, Errol, and Isabel Sawhill. 1988. "Defining and Measuring the Underclass." *Journal of Policy Analysis and Management* 7:316–325.

Rosenbaum, James E., and Susan Popkin. 1991. "Employment and Earnings of Low-income Blacks Who Move to Middle Class Suburbs." In *The Urban Underclass*, pp. 342–356. Christopher Jencks and Paul E. Pederson (eds.). Washington, D.C.: The Brookings Institute.

Sullivan, Mercer. 1989. *Getting Paid: Youth Crime and Work in the Inner City*. Ithaca, N.Y.: Cornell University Press.

Sviridoff, Mitchell. 1994. "The Seeds of Urban Revival." *The Public Interest* (Winter): 82–103.

Tienda, Marta. 1989. "Poor People and Poor Places: Deciphering Neighborhood Effects on Behavioral Outcomes." Research Report of the Population Studies Center, University of Michigan, No. 89–166.

Wacquant, Loïc J. D. 1995 [1989]. "The Ghetto, the State and the New Capitalist Economy." In *Metropolis: Center and Symbol of Our Time*, pp. 418–449. Philip Kasinitz (ed.). New York: New York University Press.

Wacquant, Loïc J. D., and William J. Wilson. 1989. "The Cost of Racial and Class Exclusion in the Inner City." *Annals of the American Academy of Political Science*, January:8–25.

Waters, Mary C. Forthcoming. *Black Like Who?* Berkeley: University of California Press.

Wilson, William J. 1987. *The Truly Disadvantaged*. Chicago, Ill.: University of Chicago Press.

47

ALICE GOFFMAN

ON THE RUN: WANTED MEN IN A PHILADELPHIA GHETTO (2009)

Over a six-year period, Alice Goffman hung out with a group of young black males she called the "6th Street Boys". Writing in the late 2000s, in an era when rising imprisonment was concentrated in poor black communities, she introduces us to a group of men who are "on the run" from the criminal justice system.

The number of people incarcerated in the United States has grown seven times over the past 40 years, and this growth has been concentrated among Black men with little education (Garland 2001; Western 2006). For Black men in recent birth cohorts, the experience of incarceration is now typical: 30 percent of those with only high school diplomas have been to prison, and 60 percent of those who did not finish high school have prison records by their mid-30s (Pettit and Western 2004). One in four Black children born in 1990 had a father imprisoned (Wildeman 2009). Such "mass imprisonment" (Garland 2001) transmits social and economic disadvantage, to be sure. African American former felons face significant discrimination in the labor market, as well as health costs, obstacles to housing, and large-scale disenfranchisement (Hammett, Harmon, and Rhodes 2002; Pager 2007; Rubenstein and Mukamal 2002; Uggen and Manza 2002; Western 2006). Moreover, imprisoned and formerly imprisoned men have difficulties participating in sustained ways in the lives of their families (see Nurse 2002; Western, Lopoo, and McLanahan 2004). Their partners and children consequently become socially and economically disadvantaged in the process (for reviews, see Comfort 2007; Hagan and Dinovitzer 1999).[1]

Expansions in incarceration have been accompanied by increases in policing and supervision in poor communities. While the police were scarcely present in the ghetto decades ago, today, police helicopters can regularly be heard overhead, cameras now monitor people on the streets, and large numbers of young men—including many who have never been convicted of felonies—have pending cases in the criminal courts, are on probation, released on bail, issued low-level warrants, and are routinely chased, searched, questioned, and arrested by the police. How does this affect daily life in poor Black communities? Unfortunately, we know little in this regard. Indeed, much of the research literature, which relies on statistical data, field experiments, or interviews, most often centers on the consequences of going to prison. Although ethnographic accounts should arguably capture what enhanced policing and supervision has meant for the dynamics of daily life in poor minority communities, most ethnographies were written before the criminal justice system became such a prevalent institution in the lives of the poor (see, e.g., Anderson 1978; Liebow 1967; Stack 1974).[2]

This article, building on prior work pertaining to the urban poor, as well as broader conceptions of power in the modern era (e.g., Foucault 1979), draws on six years of fieldwork with a group of poor African American young men in Philadelphia. In doing so, it offers an extended ethnographic look at life in the policed and surveilled ghetto that has taken shape in the era of mass imprisonment. As the findings reveal, the dealings these young men have with the police, the courts, and the probation and parole board grant them an illegal or semi-legal status and instill an overriding fear of capture. Suspicious even of those closest to them, young men cultivate unpredictability or altogether avoid institutions, places, and relations on which they formerly relied. Yet because being wanted is understood to be deeply constraining, it can, within the context of limited opportunity, serve as an excuse for obligations that may have gone

unfulfilled anyway. The result is a complex interactive system in which ghetto residents become caught in constraining legal entanglements while simultaneously calling on the criminal justice system to achieve a measure of power over one another in their daily lives.

The Urban Poor and Policing

Ethnographic accounts of poor urban communities have long included descriptions of people who commit serious crimes, stand trial, go to jail, or find themselves on the run from the police (see, e.g., Anderson 1978; Liebow 1967). Until recently, these people comprised only a small group of criminals in a neighborhood: most residents of poor Black communities did not interact much with the authorities. Before the 1990s, in fact, the ghetto was frequently described as nearly abandoned by law enforcement.

Anderson (1978:2), writing about street-corner men in Chicago in the early 1970s (he devotes a whole chapter to hoodlums), reports that "the police glance over and slow down, but they seldom stop and do anything. Ordinarily they casually move on, leaving the street-corner men to settle their own differences." Venkatesh's (2008) description of the Chicago projects some 20 years later depicts a similar scene, noting that police simply do not come when called. Instead, gang leaders step in and maintain an informal, de facto system of justice with the help of project leaders and a few neighborhood cops. In *Crackhouse,* Williams (1992:84) likewise describes how, in New York during the late 1980s and early 1990s at the peak of the crack boom, police typically did not disturb open air crack sales:

> The police have firm knowledge about selling spots, but they usually ignore the spots until community pressure builds to a level that forces them to take

action.... For the most part, the police stay away.... One night I watched a police car, with lights flashing, move down this street past hundreds of buyers, runners, touts, and dealers marching by continually making exchanges. Over the car's loudspeaker an officer kept saying, "Move on off the block everybody. This is the police." The buyers and sellers paid no attention.

Times, however, have changed. The past few decades have seen the war on crime, the war on drugs, a blossoming of federal and state police agencies and bureaus, steeper sentencing laws, and a near unified endorsement of "zero-tolerance" policies from police and civic leaders (Beckett 1997; Simon 2007). The number of police officers per capita increased dramatically in the second half of the twentieth century in cities across the United States (Reiss 1992). In 2006, more than 14 million people were arrested and charged with a criminal offense in the United States, and more than five million people were under probation or parole supervision (Glaze and Bonzear 2006; U.S. Department of Justice 2007).

In Philadelphia—my field site—the number of police officers increased by 69 percent between 1960 and 2000, from 2.76 officers for every 1,000 citizens to 4.66 officers.[3] The Philadelphia Adult Probation and Parole Department supervised more than 60,000 people in 2006. These people paid the city more than 10 million dollars in restitution, fines, court costs, and supervisory fees that year. In Philadelphia, 12,000 people violated the terms of their probation or parole and were issued warrants for their arrest (Philadelphia Adult Probation and Parole Department 2007). Even more people were issued bench warrants for missing court or for unpaid court fees, or arrest warrants for failure to turn themselves in for a crime. Such surveillance, policing, and supervision raise important sociological questions about the role of the state in managing poverty and maintaining racial inequality (Wacquant 2001). They also raise questions about the nature and consequences of modern surveillance and power.

Foucault (1979) suggested that the modern era would increasingly be characterized by surveillance and that state monitoring of citizens would become increasingly complete. Building on ethnographic insights, my conclusions highlight ways in which contemporary surveillance may indeed be taking the forms Foucault described in his analysis of panoptic power. Yet my conclusions also suggest that the consequences of such surveillance for everyday life may differ from those envisioned by Foucault. Rather than encouraging self-monitoring, the forms of supervision and policing found in the neighborhood I observed foster a climate of fear and suspicion in which people are pressured to inform on one another. Young men do not live as well-disciplined subjects, but as suspects and fugitives, with the daily fear of confinement.

Fieldwork, the 6th Street Boys, and Neighborhood Context

When I was an undergraduate at the University of Pennsylvania, I tutored a high school student, Aisha (names of people and streets are fictitious). I began to get to know some of her friends and neighbors, and in the fall of 2002 I moved into an apartment in the poor to working-class Black neighborhood in which she lived. At this point, Aisha's mother had begun referring to me as her "other daughter" and Aisha and I became "sisters" (Anderson 1978; Stack 1974). When Aisha's cousin Ronny, age 15, came home from a juvenile detention center, Aisha and 1 started hanging out with him in a neighborhood about 10 minutes away called 6th Street. Ronny introduced me to Mike, who was 21, a year older than I was. When Mike's best friend

Chuck, age 18, came home from county jail, we began hanging out with him too.

When I first started spending time with Ronny and Mike on 6th Street, their neighbors and relatives remarked on my whiteness and asked me to account for my presence. Ronny introduced me as Aisha's "sister," and I mentioned that I lived nearby. After a few months, Mike decided to "take me under his wing" and began referring to me as "sis." Bit by bit, other young men in the group started introducing me to others as their cousin or as a "homie" who "goes way back."

The five blocks known as 6th Street are 93 percent Black, according to a survey of residents that Chuck and I conducted in 2007. At the busiest intersection, men and boys stand outside offering bootleg CDs and DVDs, stolen goods, and food to drivers and passersby. The main commercial street includes a bullet-proofed Chinese food store selling fried chicken wings, "loosie" cigarettes, condoms, baby food, and glassines for smoking crack. The street also includes a check-cashing store, hair dresser, payday loan store, Crown Fried Chicken restaurant, and a pawnshop. On the next block, a Puerto Rican family runs a corner grocery.

Of the 217 households surveyed, roughly one fourth received housing vouchers. In all but two households, members reported receiving some type of government assistance in the past three years. The neighborhood also contains many people who make their living as teachers, bus drivers, parole officers, health care workers, and so on. Aisha's neighbors commonly referred to the area of 6th Street as "nice and quiet," and a place they would move if they had enough money.

Chuck, Mike, and Ronny were part of a loose group of about 15 young men who grew up around 6th Street and were joined by the fact that they were, for the most part, unemployed and trying to make it outside of the formal economy. They occasionally referred to their group as "the 6th Street Boys" when distinguishing themselves from other street-corner groups, and five of them had "6th Street" tattooed on their arms. Among the 15 young men, eight were 18 or 19 years old when I met them, four were in their early 20s, and one was age 23. Ronny was 14 and Reggie was 15. Six years later, Mike was the only one to have graduated from high school. Alex worked steadily in his father's heating and air-conditioning repair shop, and four others occasionally found seasonal construction jobs or low-skilled jobs at places like Taco Bell and McDonald's. By 2002, the crack trade was in decline, as it was in other parts of the country (Jacobs 1999). Seven of the young men worked intermittently as low-level crack dealers; others sold marijuana, Wet (PCP and/or embalming fluid), or pills like Xanax. Some of the men occasionally made money by robbing other drug dealers. One earned his keep by exotic dancing and offering sex to women.

All but two of the young men lived with female relatives, although about half got evicted and slept on other people's couches or on the streets for months or years at a time. Anthony slept in an abandoned truck on 6th Street for most of the time I knew him, although Chuck later let him sleep in his basement or got the women he was seeing to let Anthony sleep on the floor when Chuck spent the night.

Between January 2002 and August 2003, I conducted intensive observation "on the block," spending most of my waking hours hanging out on Chuck's back porch steps, or along the alley way between his block and Mike's block, or on the corner across from the convenience store. In the colder months, we were usually indoors at Chuck's and a few other houses in the area. I also went along to lawyers' offices, court, the probation and parole office, the hospital, and local bars and parties. By 2004, some of the young men were in county jails and state prisons; for the next four years I spent between two and six days a week on 6th

Street and roughly one day a week visiting members of the group in jail and prison. I also kept in touch by phone and through letters.

The young men agreed to let me take field notes for the purpose of one day publishing the material, but I generally did not ask direct questions and most of what is contained here comes from observations I made or conversations I heard.[4] Over the course of this research I also interviewed two lawyers, a district attorney, three probation officers, two police officers, and a federal district court judge.

On Being Wanted

By 2002, curfews were established around 6th Street for those under age 18 and video cameras had been placed on major streets. During the first year and a half of fieldwork, I watched the police stop pedestrians or people in cars, search them, run their names to see if any warrants came up, ask them to come in for questioning, or make an arrest at least once a day, with five exceptions. I watched the police break down doors, search houses, and question, arrest, or chase suspects through houses 52 times. Police helicopters circled overhead and beamed search lights onto local streets nine times. I noted blocks taped off and traffic redirected as police searched for evidence or "secured a crime scene" 17 times. I watched the police punch, choke, kick, stomp on, or beat young men with night sticks 14 times during this first year and a half.

Children learn at an early age to watch out for the police and to prepare to run. The first week I spent on 6th Street, I saw two boys, 5 and 7 years old, play a game of chase in which one assumed the role of the cop who must run after the other. When the "cop" caught up to the other child, he pushed him down and cuffed him with imaginary handcuffs. He patted the other child down and felt in his pockets, asking if he had warrants or was carrying a gun

or any drugs. The child then took a quarter out of the other child's pocket, laughing and yelling, "I'm seizing that!" In the following months, I saw children give up running and simply stick their hands behind their backs, as if in handcuffs, or push their bodies up against a car, or lie flat on the ground and put their hands over their head. The children yelled, "I'm going to lock you up! I'm going to lock you up, and you ain't never coming home." I once saw a 6-year-old child pull another child's pants down and try to do a "cavity search."

When Chuck, Mike, and Steve assembled outside, the first topic of the day was frequently who had been taken into custody the night before and who had outrun the cops and gotten away. They discussed how the police identified and located the person, what the charges were likely to be, what physical harm had been done to the man as he was caught and arrested, and what property the police had taken and what had been wrecked or lost during the chase.

People with warrants out for their arrest for failure to turn themselves in when accused of a crime understand that the police may employ a number of strategies in attempting to locate them. In an interview, two police officers explained that when they are looking for a suspect, they access Social Security records, court records, hospital admission records, electric and gas bills, and employment records. They visit a suspect's "usual haunts" (e.g., his home, his workplace, and his street corner) at the times he is likely to be there, threatening his family or friends with arrest, particularly when they have their own lower-level warrants or are on probation or have a pending court case. The police also use a sophisticated computer mapping program that tracks people who have warrants or are on probation, parole, or released on bail. The police round up these potential informants and threaten them with jail time if they do not provide information about the suspect they are looking for.

In the 6th Street neighborhood, a person was occasionally "on the run" because he was a suspect in a shooting or robbery, but most people around 6th Street had warrants out for far more minor infractions. In the survey that Chuck and I conducted in 2007, of the 217 households that make up the 6th Street neighborhood, we found 308 men between the ages of 18 and 30 in residence.[5] Of these men, 144 reported that they had a warrant issued for their arrest because of either delinquencies with court fines and fees or for failure to appear for a court date within the past three years. Also within the past three years, warrants had been issued to 119 men for technical violations of their probation or parole (e.g., drinking or breaking curfew).[6]

Young men worried that they would be picked up by the police and taken into custody even when they did not have a warrant out for their arrest. Those on probation or parole, on house arrest, and who were going through a trial expressed concern that they would soon be picked up and taken into custody for some violation that would "come up in the system." Even those with no pending legal action expressed concern that the police might "find some reason to hold them" because of what they had done, who or what they knew, or what they carried on their person. In this sense, being "on the run" covers a range of circumstances. I use the term to mean anyone whose claim to a life outside of confinement is not secure or legitimate and who may be taken into custody if they encounter the authorities. People "on the run" make a concerted effort to thwart their discovery and apprehension, as Chuck, age 19, concisely put it in speaking to his 12-year-old brother:

> You hear the law coming, you merk on [run away from] them niggas. You don't be having time to think okay, what do I got on me, what they going to want from me. No, you hear them coming, that's it, you gone, period. Because whoever they

looking for, even if it's not you, nine times out of ten they'll probably book you.

Police, jail, and court language permeates general conversation. Young men refer to their girlfriends as "Co-Ds" (codefendants) and speak of "catching a case" (to be arrested and charged with a crime) when accused of some wrong by their friends and family. "Call List," the term for the phone numbers of family and friends one is allowed to call from prison or jail, becomes the term for one's close friends.

One way to understand the quantity and quality of young men's legal entanglements is to look at nine members of the group during one month. In December 2003, Anthony, who was 22 years old and homeless, had a bench warrant out for his arrest because he had not paid $173 in court fees for a case that had ended the year before. He had spent nine of the previous 12 months in jail awaiting the decision. Later in the month, two neighbors who knew that Anthony had this bench warrant called the police and got him arrested because they said he had stolen three pairs of shoes from them. Shawn, a 21-year-old exotic dancer, was in county jail awaiting trial for selling crack, a charge that would ultimately be dismissed. Chuck, age 18, had a warrant because he had not paid $225 in court fees that were due a few weeks after his case for assault was dismissed. He spent almost his entire senior year of high school in county jail awaiting trial on this case.

Reggie, then age 16, and his neighbor Randy, age 19, had detainers out for violating the terms of their probation, Randy for drinking and Reggie for testing positive for marijuana (called "hot piss"). Alex, age 22, was serving a probation sentence, and Steve, age 19, was under house arrest awaiting the completion of a trial for possession of drugs. Ronny, age 16, was in a juvenile detention facility, and Mike, age 21, was in county jail awaiting trial.

Between 2002 and 2007, Mike spent about three and a half years in jail or prison.

Out of the 139 weeks that he was not incarcerated, he spent 87 weeks on probation or parole for five overlapping sentences. He spent 35 weeks with a warrant out for his arrest, and in total had 10 warrants issued on him. Mike had at least 51 court appearances over this five-year period, 47 of which I attended.

The fact that some young men may be taken into custody if they encounter the authorities is a background expectation of everyday interaction in this community. It is a starting principle, central to understanding young men's relations to family and friends, as well as the reciprocal lines of action between them.

Paths to Prison and Strategies of Evasion

Once a man finds that he may be stopped by the police and taken into custody, he discovers that people, places, and relations he formerly relied on, and that are integral to maintaining a respectable identity, get redefined as paths to confinement. I am concerned here with the kinds of relations, localities, and activities that threaten a wanted man's freedom, with the techniques he commonly employs to reduce these risks, and with some of the contingencies associated with these techniques.

Hospitals and Jobs

Alex and his girlfriend, Donna, both age 22, drove to the hospital for the birth of their son. I got there a few hours after the baby was born, in time to see two police officers come into the room and arrest Alex. He had violated his parole a few months before by drinking alcohol and had a warrant out for his arrest. As an officer handcuffed him, Donna screamed and cried, and as they walked Alex away she got out of the bed and grabbed hold of him, moaning, "Please

don't take him away. Please I'll take him down there myself tomorrow I swear, just let him stay with me tonight." The officers told me they had come to the hospital with a shooting victim who was in custody and, as was their custom, ran the names of the men on the visitors list. Alex came up as having a warrant out for a parole violation, so they arrested him along with two other men on the delivery room floor.

After Alex was arrested, other young men expressed hesitation to go to the hospital when their babies were born. Soon after Chuck turned 21, his girlfriend, age 22, was due with their second child. Chuck told her that he would go to the hospital, even though he had a detainer out for a probation violation for breaking curfew. Chuck stayed with her until she was driven to the hospital, but at the final moment he said she should go ahead without him and that he would come soon. He sat with me later and discussed the situation. As we spoke, his girlfriend called his cell phone repeatedly, and he would mute the sound after a ring and stare at her picture as it came up on the screen each time. He said:

> I told her I was on my way. She mad as shit I ain't there. I can hear her right now. She going to be like, "You broke your promise." I'm not trying to go out like Alex [get arrested], though. You feel me?

Alex spent a year back upstate on the parole violation. Just after his son's first birthday he was re-released on parole, with another year left to complete it. He resumed work at his father's heating and air-conditioning repair shop, stopped smoking marijuana, and typically came home before his curfew. Three weeks before Alex was due to complete his parole sentence, he was on his way home from 6th Street when a man with a hooded sweatshirt covering his face stepped quickly out from behind the side of a store and walked Alex, with a gun in his back, into the alley. Alex said the man took his money and pistol-whipped him three times, then grabbed the back of his head and smashed his face into a concrete wall.

Alex called Mike and me to come pick him up. When we arrived, Alex was searching on the ground for the three teeth that had fallen out, and the blood from his face and mouth was streaming down his white T-shirt and onto his pants and boots. His jaw and nose were swollen and looked as if they might be broken. I pleaded with him to go to the hospital. He refused, saying that his parole officer might hear of it and serve him a violation for being out past curfew, for fighting, for drinking, or any other number of infractions.

That night, Alex called his cousin who was studying to be a nurse's assistant to come stitch up his face. In the morning, he repeated his refusal to avail himself of medical care:

> All the bullshit I done been through [to finish his parole sentence], it's like, I'm not just going to check into emergency and there come the cops asking me all types of questions and writing my information down and before you know it I'm back in there [in prison]. Even if they not there for me some of them probably going to recognize me then they going to come over, run my shit [run a check on his name].....I ain't supposed to be up there [his parole terms forbade him to be near 6th Street, where he was injured]; I can't be out at no two o'clock [his curfew was ten]. Plus they might still got that little jawn [warrant] on me in Bucks County [for court fees he did not pay at the end of a trial two years earlier]. I don't want them running my name, and then I got to go to court or I get locked back up.

Alex later found out that the man who beat him had mistaken him for his brother, who had apparently robbed him the week before. Alex's jaw still bothers him and he

now speaks with a kind of muffled lisp, but he did not go back to prison. Alex was the only member of the group to successfully complete a probation or parole sentence during the six years I spent there.

Like hospitals, places of employment become dangerous for people with a warrant. Soon after Mike, age 24, was released on parole to a halfway house, he got a job through an old friend who managed a Taco Bell. Mike refused to return to the halfway house in time for curfew one night, saying he could not spend another night cooped up with a bunch of men like he was still in jail. He slept at his girlfriend's house, and in the morning found that he had been issued a violation and would likely be sent back to prison, pending the judge's decision. Mike said he wasn't coming back and they were going to have to catch him. Two parole officers arrested him the next day as he was leaving the Taco Bell. He spent a year back upstate for this violation.

A man with a warrant can get arrested on the job even if the police are not specifically searching for him. Chuck, who started working at the local McDonald's when he was 19, was issued a probation violation for driving a car (his driving privileges had been revoked as part of his probation sentence). Although he had a warrant, Chuck kept working, saying that if the police came he would simply run out the back door.

A couple of weeks later, an old employee got into a fight with three other employees, and the police shut down the McDonald's while they questioned witnesses and looked for the women who had been fighting. When the fight began, Chuck was in the storeroom talking on the phone with his girlfriend. He came out, he said, and saw six police officers staring at him. At this point he called and asked me to come and pick up his house keys, fairly certain he would be taken into custody. When I got there he was driving away in the back of the police car.

The Police and the Courts

Like going to work or to hospitals, using the police and the courts was risky. After Mike completed a year in prison he was released on parole to a halfway house. When his mother went on vacation, he invited a man he met in prison to her house to play video games. The next day Mike, Chuck, and I went back and found his mother's stereo, DVD player, and two televisions were gone. A neighbor told as he had seen the man taking these things out of the house in the early morning.

Mike called the police and gave them a description of the man. When we returned to the block, Reggie and Steve admonished Mike about the risks he had taken:

> REGGIE: And you on parole! You done got home like a day ago! Why the fuck you calling the law for? You lucky they ain't just grab [arrest] both of you.
>
> STEVE: Put it this way: They ain't come grab you like you ain't violate shit, they ain't find no other jawns [warrants] in the computer. Dude ain't pop no fly shit [accused Mike of some crime in an attempt to reduce his own charges], but simple fact is you filed a statement, you know what I'm saying, gave them niggas your government [real name]. Now they got your mom's address in the file as your last known [address], so the next time they come looking for you they not just going to your uncle's, they definitely going to be through there [his mother's house].

Mike returned to the halfway house a few days later and discovered that the guards were conducting alcohol tests. He left before they could test him, assuming he would test positive and spend another year upstate for the violation. Three days later the police found him at his mother's house and took him into custody. He mentioned that he thought their knowledge of his new address must have come from the time he reported the robbery.

Using the courts was no less dangerous. Chuck, age 22, was working in construction. He had been arguing with his children's mother for some months, and she stopped allowing him to see their two daughters, ages one-and-a-half and six months. Chuck decided to take her to court to file for partial custody. At the time, Chuck was also sending $35 a month to the city toward payment on tickets he had received for driving without a license or registration; he hoped to get into good standing and become qualified to apply for a driver's license. The judge said that if he did not meet his payments on time every month, he would issue a bench warrant for his arrest,[7] and Chuck could work off the traffic tickets he owed in county jail (fines and fees can be deducted for every day spent in custody).

Five months into his case for partial custody in family court, Chuck lost his job working construction and stopped making the $35 payments to the city for the traffic tickets. He was unable to discover whether he had been issued a warrant. Chuck went to court for the child custody case anyway the next month, and when the children's mother said he was a drug dealer and not fit to get partial custody of their children, the judge ran his name in the database to see if any warrants came up. They did not. Walking out of the courthouse, Chuck said to me and his mother:

> I wanted to run, but it was no way I was getting out of there—it was too many cops and guards. But my shit came back clean, so I guess if they is going to give me a warrant for the tickets they ain't get around to it yet.

The judge ruled in Chuck's favor, and he was granted visitation on Sundays at a court-supervised daycare site. These visits, Chuck said, made him anxious: "Every time I walk in the door I wonder, like, is it today? Are they going to come grab me, like, right out of the daycare? I can just see [my daughter's] face, like, 'Daddy, where you going?'" After a month, Chuck was allowed to go to the mother's house on the weekends and pick up his daughters. Chuck appeared thrilled with these visits because he could see his children without having to interact with the courts and risk being taken into custody for any warrant that might come up.

While people on probation or parole may make tentative use of the police and the courts, men with warrants typically stay away. During the first year and a half I spent on 6th Street, I noted 24 instances in which members of the group contacted the police when they were injured, robbed, or threatened. These men were either in good standing with the courts or had no pending legal constraints. I did not observe any person with a warrant call the police or voluntarily make use of the courts during the six years I spent there. Indeed, young men with warrants seemed to see the authorities only as a threat to their safety. This has two important implications.

First, steering clear of the police means that wanted men tend not to use the ordinary resources of the law to protect themselves from crimes perpetrated against them. This can lead a person to become the target of those who are looking for someone to rob.

Ned, age 43, and his long-time girlfriend Jean, age 46, lived on Mike's block. Jean was a heavy crack user, although Chuck noted, "she can handle her drugs," meaning she was able to maintain both a household and her addiction. Ned was unemployed and occasionally hosted "dollar parties" (house parties with a dollar entrance fee and with drinks, food, and games that all cost a dollar) for extra money and engaged in petty fraud, such as stealing checks out of the mail and stealing credit cards. Their primary income came from taking in foster children.

Jason lived on Chuck's block and sold marijuana with his younger brother. In January of 2003, the police stopped Jason on a dirt bike and arrested him for receiving stolen property (they said the bike came up stolen in California four years earlier). Jason did not appear for court and was issued a bench warrant.

Around this time, Ned and Jean discovered they might be kicked out of their house because they owed property taxes to the city. Jean called Jason, telling him to come to the house because she had some gossip concerning his longtime love interest. According to Jason, when he arrived on the porch steps, Jean's nephew robbed him at gunpoint. That night, Jean acknowledged to me that she would take this money and pay some of their bills owed to the city. Reggie later remarked that Jason should have known not to go to Ned and Jean's house: as the only man on the block with a warrant out for his arrest at the time, he was vulnerable to violence or robbery because he could not call the police.

Second, wanted people's inability to turn to the police when harmed can lead young men to use violence to protect themselves or to get back at others. Black (1983) argues that some crimes can be understood as people taking matters into their own hands, that is, punishing people whom they consider to have committed a crime. This kind of self-help crime is typically carried out when the police and the courts are unavailable (in this case, because people have warrants out for their arrest and may be held in custody if they contact the authorities).

One winter morning, Chuck, Mike, and I were at a diner having breakfast to celebrate the fact that Mike had not been taken into custody after his court appearance earlier that morning. Chuck's mother called to tell him that his car had been firebombed outside her house and that fire trucks were putting it out. According to Chuck, the man who set fire to his car was someone who had given him drugs to sell on credit, under the arrangement that Chuck would pay him once he had sold the drugs. Chuck had not been able to pay because the police had taken the money out of his pockets when they searched him earlier that week. This was the first car that Chuck had ever purchased legally, a '94 Bonneville he had bought the week before for $400 from a used-car lot in northeast Philadelphia. Chuck was silent for the rest of the meal, and as we walked to Mike's car the said:

> This shit is nutty, man. What the fuck I'm supposed to do, go to the cops? "Um, excuse me officer, I think boy done blown up my whip [car]." He going to run my name and shit, now he see I got a warrant on me; next thing you know my Black ass locked the fuck up, you feel me? *I'm* locked up because a nigga firebombed my whip. What the fuck. I'm supposed to let niggas take advantage?

Chuck and Mike discussed whether it was better for Chuck to take matters into his own hands or to do nothing (referred to as "letting it ride" or "taking an L" [loss]). Doing nothing had the benefit of not placing him in more legal trouble, but, as they both noted, "letting it ride" set them up to be taken advantage of by people who understood them to be "sweet."

A few days later, Chuck drove over to 8th Street with Mike and Steve and shot at the young man whom he believed was responsible for blowing up his car. Although no one was injured, a neighbor reported the incident and the police put out a body warrant for Chuck's arrest for attempted murder.

Labeling theory suggests that those accorded a deviant status come to engage in deviance because of being labeled as such (Becker 1963; Lemert 1951). This phenomenon is known as "secondary deviance" (Lemert 1951:75). Declining to engage authorities when there may be concrete reasons for doing so should be considered in this context. Young men's hesitation to go to the police or to make use of the courts when they are wronged, because of concern they will be arrested, means they became the targets of theft and violence because

it is assumed they will not press charges. With the police out of reach, men then resort to more violence as a strategy to settle disputes.

Family and Friends

Like going to the hospital or using the police and the courts, even more intimate relations—friends, family, and romantic partners—may pose a threat and thus have to be avoided or at least carefully navigated. My observations of Alex made this all too clear. When I met Alex, age 21, he was on parole and living with his girlfriend Donna. Alex had recently gotten a job at his father's heating and air-conditioning repair shop. After work, he usually went to see his friends from 6th Street, and occasionally he would stay on the block drinking and talking until late at night.

Donna and Alex frequently argued over what time he came home and his drunken condition. In these fights, I observed that Donna would threaten to call his parole officer and say that Alex was in violation if Alex did not return home at a reasonable hour. Donna also threatened to call the parole officer and tell him that Alex was out past curfew or associating with known criminals if he cheated on her, or if he did not contribute enough of his money to the household. Because Alex was paroled to Donna's apartment, she could also threaten to call the parole office and say that she no longer wanted Alex to live with her. If this were to happen, she explained to me, Alex would be placed in a halfway house.

In the early morning after a party, Mike and I drove Alex back to Donna's apartment. She was waiting on the step for him:

> DONNA: Where the fuck you been at?
> ALEX: Don't worry about it.
> DONNA: You must don't want to live here no more.
> ALEX: Come on, Don. Stop playing.

DONNA: Matter of fact I'll give you the choice [between prison or a halfway house].

ALEX: Come on, Don.

DONNA: Uhn-uhn, you not staying here no more. I'm about to call your P.O. now, so you better make up your mind where you going to go.

ALEX: I'm tired, man, come on, open the door.

DONNA: Nigga, the next time I'm laying in the bed by myself that's a wrap [that's the end].

Later that day, Donna called me and listed a number of reasons why she needed to threaten Alex:

I can't let that nigga get locked up for some dumb shit like he gets caught for a DUI or he gets stopped in a Johnny [a stolen car] or some shit. What the fuck I'm supposed to do? Let that nigga roam free? And then next thing you know he locked up and I'm stuck here by myself with Omar talking about "Where Daddy at?"

Donna stopped short of calling the police on Alex and seemed to see her threats as necessary efforts at social control. This use of the criminal justice system as threat can be seen as parallel to the way in which single mothers threaten to turn fathers over to child-support authorities if they do not contribute money informally (Edin and Lein 1997). I also witnessed women go a step further and call the police on their boyfriends or kin to punish them or get back at them.

Mike and Marie's relationship witnessed just such a tension. They had a son when they were seniors in high school and a daughter two years later. When Mike and Marie were 22, and their children were 1 and 3 years old, Mike began openly seeing another woman, Tara. Mike claimed that he and Marie had broken up and he could do as he wished, but Marie did not agree to this split and maintained they were still together and that he was in fact cheating. ("He don't be telling me we not together when he laying in the bed with me!") Mike provoked expressions of jealousy (called "stunting") as he began riding past Marie's block with Tara on the back of his ATV motorbike. Marie seemed infuriated at the insult of her children's father riding through her block with another woman for all of her family and neighbors to see, and she told him that he could no longer visit their two children. Mike and Marie spent many hours on the phone arguing over this. Mike would plead with her to let him see the children and she would explain that he would have to end things with Tara first.

Tara said she wanted to fight Marie and almost did so one afternoon. Marie stood outside her house, with six relatives in back of her, waving a baseball bat and shouting, "Get your kids, bitch. I got mine!" (Meaning that she had more claim to Mike than Tara did because they shared two children.) One of Tara's girlfriends and I held her back while she took off her earrings and screamed, "I got your bitch, bitch!" and "I'm going to beat the shit out this fat bitch."

One afternoon when Mike was sitting on a neighbor's steps, a squad car pulled up and two police officers arrested him. He had a bench warrant out for missing a court date. He said later that he never even thought to run, assuming the police were there to pick up the men standing next to him who had recently robbed a convenience store. As Mike sat in the police car, Marie talked at him through the window in a loud voice:

You not just going to dog [publicly cheat on or humiliate] me! Who the fuck he think he dealing with? Let that nigga sit for a minute [stay in jail for a while]. Don't let me catch that bitch up there either [coming to visit him in jail].

Although Marie did call the cops and get Mike taken into custody that day, she was the first person to visit him in county jail after he got out of quarantine and she continued to visit him (sometimes wearing a "Free Mike" T-shirt) throughout his year-long trial. On the day of his sentencing, she appeared in the courtroom in a low-cut top with a large new tattoo of his name on her chest.

I also observed women use the police and the courts as a form of direct retaliation. Michelle, age 16, lived with her aunt on 6th Street. When Michelle started showing, she claimed that Reggie (who was 17 at the time) was the father. Reggie denied he had gotten her pregnant, and when Michelle said she wanted an abortion, he refused to help pay for it. Michelle's aunt declared that she and her niece were cutting off their relationship with Reggie and that he was no longer welcome in their house. Michelle threatened to have Reggie beaten up by various young men she was involved with. Reggie typically stood on the corner only two houses away from where they lived, and this became a frequent verbal conflict.

Around the same time, a newcomer to the block and to the group shot and killed a man from 4th Street during a dice game. The slain man's associates ("his boys") began driving up and down 6th Street and shooting at Reggie, Chuck, and Steve. On one of these occasions, Reggie fired two shots back as their car sped away; these bullets hit Michelle's house, breaking the glass in the front windows and lodging in the living room walls. Although the bullets did not hit anyone, Michelle was home, and called her aunt, who called the police. She told them that Reggie had shot at her niece, and the police put out a body warrant for his arrest for attempted murder.

After five weeks, the police found Reggie hiding in a shed and took him into custody. Reggie's mother and his brother Chuck tried to talk Michelle and her aunt out of showing up in court so that the charges would be dropped and Reggie could come home.[8]

From jail, Reggie called his mother and me repeatedly to discuss the situation. Once when we were both on the line he said:

> REGGIE: The bitch [Michelle's aunt] know I wasn't shooting at them. She know we going through it right now [are in the middle of a series of shootouts with men from another block]. Why I'm going to shoot at two females that live on my block? She know I wasn't shooting at them.
>
> MOTHER: What you need to do is call her up and apologize [for not taking responsibility for her niece's pregnancy].
>
> REGGIE: True, true.

Reggie did apologize and spread the word that he was responsible for making Michelle pregnant. Michelle and her aunt did not show up at three consecutive court dates, and after six months the case for attempted murder was dropped and Reggie came home. Michelle's aunt seemed pleased with this result:

> You not just going to get my niece pregnant, then you talking about it's not yours, you know what I'm saying? Fuck out of here, no....I mean, I wasn't trying to see that nigga sit for an attempt [get convicted of attempted murder], but he needed to sit for a little while. He got what he needed to get. He had some time to sit and think about his actions, you dig me? He done got what he needed to get.

While family members, partners, or friends of a wanted man occasionally call the police on him to control his behavior or to punish him for a perceived wrong, close kin or girlfriends also link young men to the police because the police compel them to do so. It is common practice for the police to put pressure on friends, girlfriends, and family members to provide information, particularly when these people have their own warrants, are serving probation or parole, or have a pending trial. Family members and friends who are not themselves caught up in the justice system may be threatened with eviction or with having their children taken away if they do not provide information about the young men in their lives.

Reggie, age 17, was stopped by the police for "loitering" on the corner and allowed the police to search him. When the police officer discovered three small bags of crack in the lining of his jeans, Reggie started running. The cops lost him in the chase, and an arrest warrant was issued for possession of drugs with intent to distribute.

Reggie told me that the police raided his house the next night at 3:00 A.M. He left through the back door and ran through the alley before they could catch him. The officers came back the next night, breaking open the front door (which remains broken and unlocked to this day), and ordered Reggie's younger brother and his grandfather to lie facedown on the floor with their hands on their heads while they searched the house. An officer promised Reggie's mother that if she gave up her son, they would not tell Reggie she had betrayed him. If she did not give Reggie up, he said he would call child protective services and have her younger son taken away because the house was infested with roaches, covered in cat shit, and unfit to live in.

I was present two nights later when the police raided the house for the third time. An officer mentioned they were lucky the family owned the house: if it was a Section 8 building they could be immediately evicted for endangering their neighbors and harboring a fugitive. (Indeed, I had seen this happen recently to two other families.) The police found a gun upstairs that Reggie's mother could not produce a permit for; they cuffed her and took her to the police station. When her youngest son and I picked her up that afternoon, she said they told her she would be charged for the gun unless she told them where to find Reggie.

Reggie's mother begged him to turn himself in, but Reggie refused. His grandfather, who owned the house, told Reggie's mother that he would no longer allow her to live there with her kids if she continued to hide her son from the police:

> This ain't no damn carnival. I don't care who he is, I'm not letting nobody run through this house with the cops chasing him, breaking shit, spilling shit, waking me up out of my sleep. I'm not with the late night screaming and running. I open my eyes and I see a nigga hopping over my bed trying to crawl out the window. Hell no! Like I told Reggie, if the law run up in here one more time I be done had a stroke. Reggie is a grown-ass man [he was 17]. He ain't hiding out in my damn house. We going to fuck around and wind up in jail with this shit. They keep coming they going to find some reason to book my Black ass.

Reggie's grandfather began calling the police when he saw Reggie in the house, and Reggie's mother told him that he could no longer stay there. For two months, Reggie lived in an abandoned Buick LeSabre parked in a nearby alleyway. Reggie's mother said she missed her son and felt she had betrayed him by abandoning him, even though she had not turned him in to the police. When the police finally took Reggie into custody, she expressed relief:

> Well, at least he don't have to look over his shoulder anymore, always worried that the law was going to come to the house. He was getting real sick of sleeping in the car. It was getting cold outside, you know, and plus Reggie is a big boy and his neck was all cramped up [from sleeping in the car]....And he used to come to the back like: "Ma, make me a plate," and then he'd come back in 20 minutes and I'd pass him the food from out the window.

Whether a man's friends, relatives, or girlfriend link him to the authorities because the police pressure them to do so or because they leverage his wanted status to get back at him or punish him, he comes to see those closest to him as potential informants. Mike and Chuck once discussed how they stood the highest chance of "getting booked" because of their friends and relatives' attempts to "set them up." Mike noted:

> Nine times out of ten, you getting locked up because somebody called the cops, somebody snitching. That's why, like, if you get a call from your girl like, "Yo, where you at, can you come through the block at a certain time," that's a red flag, you feel me? That's when you start to think like, "Okay, what do she got waiting for me?"

I observed wanted men try to reduce the chance of their intimates informing by cultivating secrecy and unpredictability. Chuck and Reggie referred to this strategy as "dipping and dodging" or "ducking in and out." Chuck, age 20, remarked:

> The night is really, like, the best time to do whatever you got to do. If I want to go see my mizz [mother], see my girl, come through the block and holla at [say hello to] my boys I can't be out in broad day. I got to move like a shadow, you know, duck in and out, you thought you saw me, then bam, I'm out before you even could see what I was wearing or where I was going.

When Steve, age 19, had a bench warrant out for failure to appear in court, he was determined, he said, never to go back to jail. He slept in a number of houses, not staying more than a few nights in any one place. On the phone, he would lie to his family members, girlfriend, and fellow block members about where he was staying and where he

planned to go next. If he got a ride to where he was sleeping, he requested to be dropped off a few blocks away, and then waited until the car was out of sight before walking inside. For six months, nobody on the block seemed to know where Steve was sleeping.

Cultivating unpredictability helps wanted men reduce the risk of friends and family informing on them. In fact, maintaining a secret and unpredictable routine decreases the chance of arrest by many of the other paths discussed previously. It is easier for the police to find a person through his last known address if he comes home at around the same time to the same house every day. Finding a person at work is easier if he works a regular shift in the same place every day. Cultivating secrecy and unpredictability, then, serve as a general strategy to avoid confinement.

Being Wanted as a Means of Accounting

Once a man is wanted, maintaining a stable routine, being with his partner and family, going to work, and using the police may link him to the authorities and lead to his confinement. Yet when wanted men (or social analysts) imply that being wanted is the root cause of their inability to lead "respectable" lives, they are stretching: long before the rise in imprisonment, urban ethnographers described the distrust that Black people felt toward the police and one another, and the difficulties poor Black men faced in finding work and participating in the lives of their families (Anderson 1999; Cayton and Drake [1945] 1993; Du Bois [1899] 1996; Duneier 1999; Edin and Lein 1997; Liebow 1967; Newman 1999; Stack 1974). While legal entanglements may exacerbate these difficulties, being wanted also serves as a way to save face and to explain inadequacies.

Liebow (1967:116) wrote that the unemployed men he spent time with accounted for their failures with "the theory of manly flaws." For example, instead of admitting that their marriages failed because they could not support their spouses, they explained that they were *too manly* to be good husbands—they could not stop cheating, or drinking, or staying out late. For the young men of 6th Street, being "on the run" takes the place of, or at least works in concert with, the "manly flaws" described by Liebow as a means to retain self respect in the face of failure.

Mike, age 21, had a bench warrant out because he did not show up to court for a hearing in a drug possession case. During this time, he was not making what he considered to be decent money selling drugs, and he had been unable to pay his son's Catholic school fees for more than a month. Parents' Day at his son's school that year was a Thanksgiving fair, and Mike had been talking about the day for weeks. The night before the fair, Mike agreed to pick up his children's mother, Marie, and go to the school around 10:00 the next morning.

The next morning, Marie began calling Mike's cell phone at 8:30. She called around 13 times between 8:30 and 9:30. I asked Mike why he did not pick up and he said that it was not safe to go, considering the warrant. At noon, he finally answered her call. By then the fair was almost over and Marie had caught the bus back and forth herself. She was yelling so loudly that Steve, Chuck, and I could hear her voice through the phone:

What the fuck good are you on the streets if you can't even come to your son's fair? Why I got to do everything myself—take him to school, pick him up from school, take him to the doctor…And you on some "I'm falling back. I'm laying low. I can't be up at no school. I can't do this I can't do that." What the fuck I'm supposed to tell your son: "Michael, Daddy can't come to the fair today because the cops is looking for him and we don't want

him to get booked." Is that what you want me to say?

Mike called her some names and hung up. Before going back to sleep, he mentioned what a "dumb-ass" she was:

Do she want me to get locked up? How I'm going to be there for my kids if I'm locked up? She don't be thinking, like, she don't have to look over her shoulder, you know what I'm saying. She be forgetting I can't just do whatever I want, go wherever I want.

Mike seemed convinced that going to the fair would put him at risk, and at the time I believed this to be the reason he stayed home. But a few months later, although he was still wanted for the same bench warrant, he attended a parent–teacher conference.

ALICE: I thought you didn't want to go up there. Remember Marie was mad as shit the other time you didn't go.

MIKE: I'm cool now because I just paid the school fees. I ain't want dude to come at my neck [get angry], like, "Where the money at? Why you ain't pay?" I wasn't trying [didn't want] to hear that bullshit.

From this, I gathered that Mike had not gone to Parents' Day earlier in the year at least in part because he had not paid the school fees and did not want to confront the school's administration. Once he paid the bill, he proudly attended the next event, a parent–teacher conference. The warrant provided him with a way to avoid going to Parents' Day without admitting that he did not want to go because he could not pay the school fees.

Warrants also serve as an important explanation for not having a job. Steve had a warrant out for a few weeks when he was 21, and repeatedly mentioned how he could not get work because of this warrant:

If I had a whip [car] I'd go get me a job up King of Prussia [a mall in a neighboring county] or whatever. But I can't work nowhere in Philly. That's where niggas be fucking up. You remember when Jason was at McDonald's? He was like, "No, they [the police] ain't going to see me, I'm working in the back." But you can't always be back there, like sometimes they put you at the counter, like if somebody don't show up, you know what I mean? How long he worked there before they [the police] came and got him? Like a week. They was like, "Um, can I get a large fry and your hands on the counter because your Black ass is booked!" And he tried to run like shit, too, but they was outside the jawn [the restaurant] four deep [four police officers were outside] just waiting for him to try that shit.

Although Steve now and then invoked his warrant as an explanation for his unemployment, the fact was that Steve did not secure a job during the six years I knew him, including the times when he did not have a warrant.

James, age 18, moved with his aunt to 6th Street, and after a while became Reggie's "young-boy." Like the other guys, he talked about his court cases or mentioned that he had to go see his probation officer.

Steve, Mike, Chuck, and I were sitting on Chuck's back-porch steps one afternoon when Reggie drove up the alley way and announced: "Yo, the boy James he clean, dog! He ain't got no warrant, no detainer, nothing. He don't even got like a parking ticket in his name."

Reggie told us he had just been to James's mother's house across town, and she had complained to him that James had not yet found a job. James's mother informed Reggie that James had no pending cases, no warrants or detainers or anything "in the system that would hold him" and so should have no problem finding employment.

When Reggie finished explaining this to us, Mike continued the conversation:

> MIKE: What happened to that case he caught? Damn that was a little minute ago [a while ago].
> CHUCK: I think he spanked that jawn [the case was dropped].
> REGGIE: I wish I would get my shit [warrant] lifted. I'd be bam, on my J-O [job], bam, on my A-P [apartment], bam, go right to the bank, like, "Yeah, motherfucker, check my shit, man. Run that shit. My shit is clean, dog. Let me get that account." I be done got my elbow [driver's license] and everything.

Reggie explained how his wanted status blocks him from getting jobs, using banks, obtaining a driver's license, and renting an apartment. Yet the things that Reggie thought a "clean" person should do were not things that Reggie himself did when he was in good standing with the authorities over the course of the years that I knew him. Nor were they things that most of the other men on the block did. Alex, Mike, and Chuck looked for jobs when they did not have warrants out for their arrest, but others, like Reggie and Steve, did not. None of them obtained a valid driver's license during the six years I knew them.[9] Only Mike secured his own apartment during this time, and he kept it for only three months. To my knowledge, none of the men established a bank account.

Being wanted serves as an excuse for a wide variety of unfulfilled obligations and expectations. At the same time, it is perhaps only because being wanted is in fact a constraining condition that it works so well as a means of accounting for failure. Having a warrant may not be the reason why Steve, for example, did not look for work, but it was a fact that police officers did go to a man's place of work to arrest him, and that some of the men experienced this first-hand. In the context of their ongoing struggles, what they said amounted to reasonable "half-truths" (Liebow 1967) that could account for their failures, both in their own minds and in the minds of others who had come to see their own lives in similar terms.

Discussion

The presence of the criminal justice system in the lives of the poor cannot simply be measured by the number of people sent to prison or the number who return home with felony convictions. Systems of policing and supervision that accompanied the rise in imprisonment have fostered a climate of fear and suspicion in poor communities—a climate in which family members and friends are pressured to inform on one another and young men live as suspects and fugitives with the daily fear of confinement.

Young men who are wanted by the police find that activities, relations, and localities that others rely on to maintain a decent and respectable identity are transformed into a system that the authorities make use of to arrest and confine them. The police and the courts become dangerous to interact with, as does showing up to work or going to places like hospitals. Instead of a safe place to sleep, eat, and find acceptance and support, mothers' homes are transformed into a "last known address," one of the first places the police will look for them. Close relatives, friends, and neighbors become potential informants.

One strategy for coping with these risks is to avoid dangerous places, people, and interactions entirely. A young man thus does not attend the birth of his child, nor seek medical help when he is badly beaten. He avoids the police and the courts, even if it means using violence when he is injured or becoming the target of others who are looking for someone to rob. A second strategy is to cultivate unpredictability—to remain secretive and to "dip and dodge."

To ensure that those close to him will not inform on him, a young man comes and goes in irregular and unpredictable ways, remaining elusive and untrusting, sleeping in different beds, and deceiving those close to him about his whereabouts and plans. If a man exhausts these possibilities and gets taken into custody, he may try to avoid jail time by informing on the people he knows.

Whatever the strategy, a man finds that as long as he is at risk of confinement, staying out of prison and participating in institutions like family, work, and friendship become contradictory goals; doing one reduces his chance of achieving the other. Staying out of jail becomes aligned not with upstanding, respectable action, but with being an even shadier character.

Family members and romantic partners experience considerable hardship because of their association with men who are being sought or supervised by the state. Specifically, I found that family members living with a relative or boyfriend with a warrant out for his arrest are caught between three difficult lines of action: allowing him to stay in their homes and placing their own safety and security in jeopardy, casting him out, or betraying him by turning him in to the police.

It is possible that issuing warrants to a large group of young men for minor probation violations or delinquencies with court fees, while straining family life and making it difficult for men to find and keep a job, also serves to discourage them from committing crime. Although this article notes some instances of warrants potentially encouraging crime (e.g., by keeping men from participating in the formal labor market or by leading men with warrants to become the target of robbers), I cannot speculate as to the net effect of such policies on crime or violence. The data presented here merely suggest that current policies in Philadelphia grant a sizable group of people—before they are convicted of crimes and after they have served a sentence—an illegal or semilegal status, and that this status makes it difficult for them to interact with legitimate institutions without being arrested and sent to jail.

More surprisingly, the system of low-level warrants and court supervision has the unintended consequence of becoming a resource for women and relatives who, possessing more legal legitimacy, can use it to control their partners and kin. Girlfriends, neighbors, and family members threaten to call the police on young men to "keep them in line," and occasionally they call the police or get a man arrested as payback for some perceived wrong. Young men also turn their wanted status into a resource by using it to account for shortcomings or failures that may have occurred anyway. Because being wanted is understood by 6th Street residents to be deeply constraining, young men with little income, education, or job prospects can call on their wanted status to save face and to assuage the guilt of failing as a father, romantic partner, or employed person.

Contemporary theories of social stratification and political sociology argue that the criminal justice system has become a vehicle for passing on disadvantage (Western 2006) and "an instrument for the management of dispossessed and dishonored groups" (Wacquant 2001:95). The findings presented here confirm these important theses, but my fieldwork also suggests that those so managed are hardly hapless victims, immobilized in webs of control. Instead, men and women on 6th Street evade and resist the authorities, at times calling on the state for their own purposes, to make claims for themselves as honorable people, and to exercise power over one another....

NOTES

1. Although this body of research points overwhelmingly to the detrimental effects of incarceration and its aftermath, this picture is complicated by close-up accounts of prisoners and their families. Comfort (2008) shows how women visiting incarcerated spouses find that the prison's regulations in some ways enhance their relationships. As romantic partners, inmates contrast favorably to "free men."

2. Ethnographies of ghetto life published more recently rely on fieldwork conducted in the 1980s and early 1990s, before the change in policing practices and crime laws took their full effect (see, e.g., Anderson 1999; Bourgois 1995; Venkatesh 2006; Wacquant 2004; for exceptions, see Jacobs 1999; LeBlanc 2003).

3. Data on the number of police officers in Philadelphia is taken from the Federal Bureau of Investigation, Uniform Crime Reports (1960 through 2000). Population estimates of Philadelphia are taken from the U.S. Bureau of the Census.

4. I use quotes when I wrote down what people said as they spoke (by typing it directly onto a laptop or by using a cell phone text message). I omit the quotes when I noted what people said after an event or conversation, and I paraphrase when I wrote down what people said at the end of the day in my field notes. Since I did not use a tape recorder, even the speech in quotes should be taken only as a close approximation.

5. I counted men who lived in a house for three days a week or more (by their own estimates and in some cases, my knowledge) as members of the household. I included men who were absent because they were in the military, at job training programs (like JobCorp), or away in jail, prison, drug rehab centers, or halfway houses, if they expected to return to the house and had been living in the house before they went away.

6. These violations are not the same as the "disorderly conduct" that became the focus of "quality of life" policing in places like New York during the 1990s. "Quality of life" policing arrests people for minor offenses like urinating in public, jumping turnstyles, or public drinking (Duneier 1999). The young men in this study were initially arrested for more serious offenses such as drug offenses,

and then were served warrants when they failed to show up for court dates during the pretrial and trial, to pay court fees at the end of the cases, or to follow the dictates of probation and parole sentences they were issued after or instead of completing time in jail or prison.

7. In Philadelphia, the courts can issue an arrest warrant if a person fails to pay fines for traffic violations or misses a court date in regard to these violations. A person can also be imprisoned for failing to pay moving violation fines (Philadelphia County, 33 Pa.B. Doc. No. 2745 and Pa.B. Doc. No. 03-1110).

8. This is a fairly common thing to do. Some people get others arrested simply to extort money from them, which they request in exchange for not showing up as a witness at the ensuing trial.

9. Obtaining a driver's license requires a birth certificate or passport, a Social Security card, and two proofs of residence. Obtaining these items, in turn, requires identification and processing fees. One must undergo a physical exam by a doctor, pay for and pass a written permit test, and locate an insured and registered car with which to take the driving test. Because men drove without proper documentation, they got tickets, which had to be paid before they could begin the application process.

REFERENCES

Anderson, Elijah. 1978. *A Place on the Corner.* Chicago, IL: University of Chicago Press.
———. 1999. *Code of the Street.* New York: W. W. Norton.
Becker, Howard. 1963. *Outsiders.* New York: Free Press.
Beckett, Katherine. 1997. *Making Crime Pay.* New York: Oxford University Press.
Black, Donald. 1983. "Crime as Social Control." *American Sociological Review* 48(1):32–45.
Bourgois, Philippe. 1995. *In Search of Respect.* New York: Cambridge University Press.
Cayton, Horace and St. Clair Drake. [1945] 1993. *Black Metropolis.* Chicago, IL: University of Chicago Press.
Comfort, Megan. 2007. "Punishment Beyond the Legal Offender." *Annual Review of Law and Social Science* 3:271–296.
———. 2008. *Doing Time Together.* Chicago, IL: University of Chicago Press.
Du Bois, W. E. B. [1899] 1996. *The Philadelphia Negro.* Philadelphia, PA: University of Pennsylvania Press.
Duneier, Mitchell. 1999. *Sidewalk.* New York: Farrar, Straus and Giroux.
Edin, Kathryn and Laura Lein. 1997. *Making Ends Meet.* New York: Russell Sage Foundation.
Foucault, Michel. 1979. *Discipline and Punish.* New York: Vintage.
Garland, David. 2001. "Introduction: The Meaning of Mass Imprisonment." *Mass Imprisonment: Social Causes and Consequences,* pp. 1–3. D. Garland (ed.). London, UK: Sage.
Glaze, Lauren and Thomas Bonzear. 2006. "Probation and Parole in the United States, 2005." *Bureau of Justice Statistics Bulletin.* U.S. Department of Justice, NCJ 215091. Retrieved March 2009 (http://www.ojp.usdoj.gov/bjs/pub/pdf/ppus05.pdf).
Hagan, John and Ronit Dinovitzer. 1999. "Collateral Consequences of Imprisonment for Children, Communities, and Prisoners." *Crime and Justice* 26:121–162.
Hammett, Theodore M., Mary P. Harmon, and William Rhodes. 2002. "The Burden of Infectious Disease among Inmates of and Releasees from U.S. Correctional Facilities, 1997." *American Journal of Public Health* 92(11):1789–1794.
Jacobs, Bruce. 1999. *Dealing Crack.* Boston, MA: Northeastern University Press.
LeBlanc, Adrian Nicole. 2003. *Random Family.* New York: Scribner.
Lemert, Edwin. 1951. *Social Pathology: A Systematic Approach to the Theory of Sociopathic Behavior.* New York: McGraw-Hill Book Company.
Liebow, Elliot. 1967. *Tally's Corner.* Boston, MA: Little, Brown.
Newman, Katherine. 1999. *No Shame in My Game.* New York: Vintage and Russell Sage.
Nurse, Anne. 2002. *Fatherhood Arrested,* Nashville, TN: Vanderbilt University Press.

Pager, Devah. 2007. *Marked: Race, Crime, and Finding Work in an Era of Mass Incarceration*. Chicago, IL: *University of Chicago Press*.

Pettit, Becky and Bruce Western. 2004. "Mass Imprisonment and the Life-Course: Race and Class Inequality in U.S. Incarceration." *American Sociological Review* 69:151–169.

Philadelphia Adult Probation and Parole Department. 2007. *2006 Annual Report*. Retrieved March 2009 (http://fjd.phila.gov/pdf/report/2006appd.pdf).

Reiss, Albert J. 1992. "Police Organization in the 20th Century." *Crime and Justice* 15:51–97.

Rubenstein, Gwen and Debbie Mukamal. 2002. "Welfare and Housing-Denial of Benefits to Drug Offenders." In *Invisible Punishment: The Collateral Consequences of Mass Imprisonment*, pp. 37–49. M. Mauer and M. Chesney-Lind (eds.). New York: New Press.

Simon, Jonathan. 2007. *Governing through Crime*. New York: Oxford University Press.

Stack, Carol. 1974. *All Our Kin*. New York: Harper Colophon Books.

Uggen, Chris and Jeff Manza. 2002. "Democratic Contradiction? Political Consequences of Felon Disenfranchisement in the United States." *American Sociological Review* 67(6):777–803.

United States Department of Justice, Federal Bureau of Investigation. September 2007. *Crime in the United States, 2006*. Retrieved March 2, 2009 (http://www.fbi.gov/uer/cius2006/arrests/).

Venkatesh, Sudhir. 2006. *Off the Books*. Cambridge, MA: Harvard University Press.

———. 2008. *Gang Leader for a Day*. New York: Penguin Press.

Wacquant, Loïc. 2001. "Deadly Symbiosis: When Ghetto and Prison Meet and Mesh." *Punishment & Society* 3(1):95–133.

———. 2004. *Body and Soul*. New York: Oxford University Press.

Western, Bruce. 2006. *Punishment and Inequality in America*. New York: Russell Sage Foundation.

Western, Bruce, Leonard Lopoo, and Sara McLanahan. 2004. "Incarceration and the Bonds between Parents in Fragile Families." In *Imprisoning America*, pp. 21–45. M. Patillo, D. Weiman, and B. Western (eds.). New York: Russell Sage Foundation.

Wildeman, Christopher. 2009. "Parental Imprisonment, the Prison Boom, and the Concentration of Childhood Disadvantage." *Demography* 46:265–280.

Williams, Terry. 1992. *Crackhouse*. Reading, MA: Addison Wesley.

PART VIII

ETHNOGRAPHERS AND THEIR SUBJECTS

//

In selecting the readings for this volume we generally avoided accounts that seemed to us either overly focused on the experiences of the ethnographers themselves or "how-tos" for the field of urban ethnography. There are a number of reasons for this. First, the audience for urban ethnography is, and should be, far larger than merely the practitioners and aspiring practitioners of the craft. It is our hope that the insights provided by this volume will be of value to social scientists and future social scientists (no matter what their methodological preferences are) as well as to general readers who are interested in the nature of modern urban life.

For those who already do this sort of work or who plan to do it in the future, we also feel that there is probably more value in reading examples of the wide variety of ways in which ethnography has actually been done rather than instructional readings on how it should be done. Ethnography is one of those things that can be learned, but it is questionable whether it can be taught. (Because we, the three editors of this volume, make part of our living by teaching it, we are well aware of the paradoxical position in which this statement places us. So be it.). A good teacher can, of course, provide exercises and advice on how to write field notes, how to conduct unstructured interviews, and how to collect, keep track of, and analyze data. There are already many fine books on these more technical "how-to" aspects of urban ethnography.[1] However, knowing how to make sense of the many, sometimes contradictory things the ethnographer encounters is perhaps something that is learned only through doing. One thing, however, that can help the aspiring ethnographer learn his or her craft is reading and critiquing examples of how other ethnographers have done their work; we hope that the readings in this volume will allow people to do just that.

The other reason why we have generally avoided works that are mainly about the experience of the ethnographic research process lies in the danger (and there are many) that such works can shift focus from the people or places under study to the observer. Of course, at some point most ethnographers do write about themselves—both how they did the work and who they are. Readers naturally want to know *who* the people making these observations are and why anyone should trust their inevitably subjective account. How did they come to know the people they write about, and what has been the nature of the relationship between writer and subject? It is extremely important to take into account the "standpoint" of the observer when reading this kind of social scientific research. The reader has probably noticed that as the history of urban ethnography progressed the pieces presented in this volume have become more self-consciously reflexive. Early and mid-twentieth-century urban ethnographers were often preoccupied with establishing their work as social *science*, in order to differentiate what they did from those who wrote journalism or literature. In doing so, they sometimes adopted a detached stance that seemed to assert that their "results" were replicable—that any competently trained observer would come to more or less the same conclusions. Of course, this is never really true. The best of early urban ethnographic research is usually shaped by insights gleaned in part from the observer's autobiography even if he or she is reluctant to share this fact.

Over time, ethnographers have become more and more open about describing their research and writing process, their relationships with their informants, and the role that their own social position— their "standpoint"—has played in shaping their work. In our judgment, however, this reflexive turn has sometimes led to the opposite problem: a kind of self-reflexive paralysis, a reluctance to make judgments, and even a retreat into "auto-ethnography." Self-reflection, taken too far, can easily become self-absorption. The reflexive turn in ethnographic work since the 1970s has been enormously valuable to the extent to which it has sensitized researchers and readers to the role that people's values, biases, and standpoints play in framing perceptions of "the other." Yet, taken to extremes, this approach can shift the focus to the inner life and struggles of the ethnographer. There are many philosophical reasons to question such an approach, but we reject it for a simpler one. As ethnographers ourselves, we regretfully report that our own inner lives are just not all that interesting. Certainly our own struggle to make sense of the worlds we observe and to figure out how we know what we think we know is relevant for the reader's assessment of our work, and we have all written about it when we think it is important to do so. But generally speaking, the process of how we do our work is probably the least interesting thing about it.

There is another danger in putting the spotlight too much on the ethnographer. If the writer is talented enough, if his or her inner life *is* interesting enough, the story of how the work is done can become entirely too easy a narrative for readers to identify with. Often middle-class readers are better able to identify with the ethnographer than with her or his informants. Thus, if the ethnographer occupies too much of the center stage in his or her account, the result may become a traveler's tale or an adventure saga; the story of the middle-class observer, a person who may be much like the reader, who goes forth on a risky adventure among strange and different people, facing great challenges and coming back to tell the tale. In the process, the people written about can become more, not less, exotic—exactly the opposite of what we feel ethnography should do.

There is, however, one aspect of the ethnographic process that is so central to the enterprise that we did feel it was important to include readings that address it. That is the relationship between the ethnographer and her or his informants. This is something that readers are usually curious about, with good reason. It is also among the hardest things for ethnographers to write about, although the readings in this final section provide some wonderful examples of how it can be done well.

What should this relationship be like? There are no hard and fast rules. How could there be, as it is a relationship between human beings that usually lasts for years, sometimes long after the official "research" period has ended. Where is the line between being a researcher, a collaborator, or simply a friend? How does that relationship change once it has been committed to the page for all to see? Informants often give ethnographers huge amounts of their time, their hospitality, and access to many aspects of their lives. What sorts of reciprocity are implied in this relationship? And how do these bonds shape or limit the story that ends up being told?

There are many different notions of how to manage such relationships. Herbert Gans, for example, has famously told generations of students (Kasinitz among them) that their role was to be "friendly but not friends" to the people they study. For him, a certain amount of distance was important in order to avoid feeling the need to present people—people who have often been extraordinarily generous to the researcher— in the best possible light. Others take a different view, seeing their role as giving "voice" to people who may have less ability to make their own voices heard. In recent years it has become common practice to present ethnographic writing to the key informants before publication. This clearly has practical value. Informants can often sharpen the analysis as well as spot factual errors and misunderstandings that no one else would be able to catch. But this raises the question of whose work ethnography is and to what extent informants have the right to see themselves presented in a way that they would prefer. Precisely because ethnography is more than simply conducting interviews, it is often important for the researcher to report things that the informant may not be aware of or is unable or unwilling to articulate. In the end, we feel that the ethnographer owes the informant more than mere service as a megaphone; he or she must also bring his or her critical judgment to the situation. The greatest and often only recompense the

ethnographer can give the informant is to try, to the extent of his or her limited abilities, to get the story right.

Often the relationship between the ethnographer and a key informant is an ongoing dialogue. Sometimes the informant becomes a teacher or mentor, "showing the ropes" to the ethnographer, who takes on the role of a sort of apprentice (for examples of this sort of relationship, see Loïc Wacquant's work on boxing or William F. Whyte's work on bowling, both excerpted in Part VI). Yet once the work is committed to paper it is the ethnographer who assumes authority. There is an inevitable power imbalance implicit in the fact that (usually) only one participant in what was a two-way conversation will be doing the writing and presenting it to the world. This problematic situation is made more complicated when (as is usually the case) there are class, ethnic, racial, or gender and power differences between the ethnographer and the people being studied. In some cases these obviously unequal power dynamics have led social scientists to conclude that only members of a given social group can understand and thus should be writing about their own group—for example, only African Americans should study African Americans or only women should write about women. Yet, while there are clear advantages in bringing "insider" knowledge to an ethnographic project, the notion that only "insiders" should study members of a group (or at least of a "subaltern" group) begs the obvious question: who is an insider and what are the boundaries of the group? Can a middle-class African American study poor African Americans? Can younger women write about older women? And who gets to decide which are the most relevant group boundaries? This line of thinking clearly leads to a sort of infinite regression that would ultimately make most ethnographic work impossible. Furthermore, as Georg Simmel observed long ago, there are real advantages to the view of the outsider. Often it is "the stranger" who can grasp things about a social situation that insiders cannot see or will not discuss.[2]

The chapters in this final section are all examples of how ethnographers have tried to think about and navigate their relationships with their informants. Barbara Myerhoff studied the lives of Jewish senior citizens in Venice Beach, California, the same neighborhood studied during a later time frame by Andrew Deener in Part I. While Myerhoff was much younger than her informants, and was therefore, in some regards, an outsider, she noted in her book that she was writing about a group of people—elderly Jews—to which she hoped eventually to belong. Sadly this was not to happen. The anthropologist and filmmaker died of cancer at fifty in 1985. Yet her work shows both the advantages and the limitations of her "semi-insider" status, as well as the problems caused by the fact that her informants saw her as too much like their own children.

By contrast, Philippe Bourgois presents us with the dilemmas faced by an outsider—a young, white, well-educated man—entering the insular and often violent world of Puerto Rican crack dealers in New York's East Harlem. Bourgois is keenly aware of how his racial and class position shapes the manner in which his informants see him. Yet he also demonstrates how such boundaries, which at first seem utterly insurmountable, can be overcome.

What is it like to see the relationship from the informant's perspective? Hakim Hasan, a former street vendor and a key informant for Mitchell Duneier's *Sidewalk*, discusses how the relationship looks from the "data's" point of view. In writing his own afterword for Duneier's ethnography, Hasan breaks the stereotypes of the voiceless subaltern informant and the college-educated researcher, and he reveals instead much about his own intellectual partnership and his occasional disagreements with the researcher.

Sudhir Venkatesh looks back after twenty years on his experience doing ethnography among gang members in Chicago's Robert Taylor Homes Public Housing project as a graduate student. Like Bourgois, Venkatesh, a young, middle-class Californian, could hardly have been more of an "outsider" in this setting (For more of an "insider's" ethnographic view on similar populations, see Rios in Part IV and Contreras in Part V). Yet, as Venkatesh has noted, his situation is somewhat different in that, as a dark-skinned South Asian, his informants often do not know how to classify him along racial lines—there was no place for one such as him in the racial schema with which they mapped the people of their world. For this reason he became something of a human Rorschach test on which they imposed their ideas about his assumed racial identity.

Finally Annette Lareau describes, with notable honesty, the reactions of her informants to the way they were portrayed in her classic study about social class and child-rearing in greater Philadelphia, *Unequal Childhoods*. Lareau clearly did not let her subjects censor her. She presents them as she saw them, well aware that they would not always agree with her assessment. At the same time, she is frank about the sense of betrayal felt by her informants and about the pain this has clearly cost her.

NOTES

1. See, for example, *Writing Ethnographic Fieldnotes* (Emerson, Fretz, and Shaw 2011), *Learning from Strangers* (Weiss 1995), and *Analyzing Social Settings* (Lofland, Snow, Anderson, and Lofland 2005), among others.

2. See "The Stranger" (Simmel 1950).

REFERENCES

Emerson, Robert, Rachel Fretz, and Linda Shaw. 2011. *Writing Ethnographic Fieldnotes.* 2nd ed. Chicago: University of Chicago Press.

Lofland, John, David Snow, Leon Anderson, and Lyn Lofland. 2005. *Analyzing Social Settings.* 4th ed. Independence, Ky.: Wadsworth Publishing.

Simmel, Georg. 1950. "The Stranger." In *The Sociology of Georg Simmel*, pp. 402–408. Kurt H. Wolff (ed.). Glencoe, Ill.: Free Press.

Weiss, Robert. 1995. *Learning from Strangers.* New York: Free Press.

48

BARBARA MYERHOFF

"SO WHAT DO YOU WANT FROM US HERE?"

from *Number Our Days* (1979)

For four years, Barbara Myerhoff spent time at a Jewish senior-citizen center near the boardwalk in the Venice neighborhood of Los Angeles. In this selection, Myerhoff discusses the difficulties she experienced as a participant observer as she tried to learn about their lives. Her presence was often a reminder to her subjects of their own children who did not visit and of their own failure to pass on their heritage to them.

Every morning I wake up in pain. I wiggle my toes. Good. They still obey. I open my eyes. Good. I can see. Everything hurts but I get dressed. I walk down to the ocean. Good. It's still there. Now my day can start. About tomorrow I never know. After all, I'm eighty-nine. I can't live forever.

Death and the ocean are protagonists in Basha's life. They provide points of orientation, comforting in their certitude. One visible, the other invisible, neither hostile nor friendly, they accompany her as she walks down the boardwalk to the Aliyah Senior Citizens' Center.

Basha wants to remain independent above all. Her life at the beach depends on her ability to perform a minimum number of basic tasks. She must shop and cook, dress herself, care for her body and her one-room apartment, walk, take the bus to the market and the doctor, be able to make a telephone call in case of emergency. Her arthritic hands have a difficult time with the buttons on her dress. Some days her fingers ache and swell so that she cannot fit them into the holes of the telephone dial. Her hands shake as she puts in her eyedrops for glaucoma. Fortunately, she no longer has to give herself injections for her diabetes.

Now it is controlled by pills, if she is careful about what she eats. In the neighborhood there are no large markets within walking distance. She must take the bus to shop. The bus steps are very high and sometimes the driver objects when she tries to bring her little wheeled cart aboard. A small boy whom she has befriended and occasionally pays often waits for her at the bus stop to help her up. When she cannot bring her cart onto the bus or isn't helped up the steps, she must walk to the market. Then shopping takes the better part of the day and exhausts her. Her feet, thank God, give her less trouble since she figured out how to cut and sew a pair of cloth shoes so as to leave room for her callouses and bunions.

Basha's daughter calls her once a week and worries about her mother living alone and in a deteriorated neighborhood. "Don't worry about me, darling. This morning I put the garbage in the oven and the bagels in the trash. But I'm feeling fine." Basha enjoys teasing her daughter whose distant concern she finds somewhat embarrassing. "She says to me, 'Mamaleh, you're sweet but you're so *stupid.*' What else could a mother expect from a daughter who is a lawyer?" The statement conveys Basha's simultaneous pride and grief in having produced an educated, successful child whose very accomplishments drastically separate her from her mother. The daughter has often invited Basha to come and live with her, but she refuses.

What would I do with myself there in her big house, alone all day, when the children are at work? No one to talk to. No place to walk. Nobody talks Yiddish. My daughter's husband doesn't like my cooking, so I can't even help with meals. Who needs an old lady around, somebody else for my daughter to take care of? They don't keep the house warm like I like it. When I go to the bathroom at night, I'm afraid to flush. I shouldn't wake anybody up. Here I have lived for thirty-one years.

I have my friends. I have the fresh air. Always there are people to talk to on the benches. I can go to the Center whenever I like and always there's something doing there. As long as I can manage for myself, I'll stay here.

Managing means three things: taking care of herself, stretching her monthly pension of three hundred and twenty dollars to cover expenses, and filling her time in ways that have meaning for her. The first two are increasingly hard and she knows that they are battles she will eventually lose. But her free time does not weigh on her. She is never bored and rarely depressed. In many ways, life is not different from before. She has never been well-off, and she never expected things to be easy. When asked if she is happy, she shrugs and laughs. "Happiness by me is a hot cup of tea on a cold day. When you don't get a broken leg, you could call yourself happy."

Basha, like many of the three hundred or so elderly members of the Aliyah Center, was born and spent much of her childhood in one of the small, predominately Jewish, Yiddish-speaking villages known as *shtetls*, located within the Pale of Settlement of Czarist Russia, an area to which almost half the world's Jewish population was confined in the nineteenth century.[1] Desperately poor, regularly terrorized by outbreaks of anti-Semitism initiated by government officials and surrounding peasants, shtetl life was precarious. Yet a rich, highly developed culture flourished in these encapsulated settlements, based on a shared sacred religious history, common customs and beliefs, and two languages—Hebrew for prayer and Yiddish for daily life. A folk culture, *Yiddishkeit*, reached its fluorescence there, and though it continues in various places in the world today by comparison these are dim and fading expressions of it. When times worsened, it often seemed that Eastern Europe social life intensified proportionately. Internal ties deepened, and the people drew sustenance and courage from each other, their religion, and their community. For many, life became unbearable under the increasingly reactionary regime of Czar Alexander II. The pogroms of 1881–1882, accompanied by severe economic and legal restrictions, drove out the more desperate and daring of the Jews. Soon they were leaving the shtetls and the cities in droves. The exodus of Jews from Eastern Europe swelled rapidly until by the turn of the century, hundreds of thousands were emigrating, the majority to seek freedom and opportunity in the New World.

Basha dresses simply but with care. The purchase of each item of clothing is a major decision. It must last, should be modest and appropriate to her age, but gay and up-to-date. And, of course, it can't be too costly. Basha is not quite five feet tall. She is a sturdy boat of a woman—wide, strong of frame, and heavily corseted. She navigates her great monobosom before her, supported by broad hips and thin, severely bowed legs, their shape the heritage of her malnourished childhood. Like most of the people who belong to the Aliyah Center, her early life in Eastern Europe was characterized by relentless poverty.

Basha dresses for the cold, even though she is now living in Southern California, wearing a babushka under a red sun hat, a sweater under her heavy coat. She moves down the boardwalk steadily, paying attention to the placement of her feet. A fall is common and dangerous for the elderly. A fractured hip can mean permanent disability, loss of autonomy, and removal from the community to a convalescent or old age home. Basha seats herself on a bench in front of the Center and waits for friends. Her feet are spread apart, well-planted, as if growing up from the cement. Even sitting quite still, there is an air of determination about her. She will withstand attacks by anti-Semites, Cossacks, Nazis, historical enemies whom she conquers by outliving. She defies time and weather (though it is not cold here). So she might have sat a century ago, before a small pyramid of potatoes of herring in the marketplace of the Polish town where she was born. Patient, resolute, she is a survivor.

Not all the Center women are steady boats like Basha. Some, like Faegl, are leaves, so delicate, dry, and vulnerable that it seems at any moment they might be whisked away by a strong gust. And one day, a sudden wind did knock Faegl to the ground. Others like Gita, are birds, small and sharp-tongued. Quick, witty, vain, flirtatious, they are very fond of singing and dancing. They once were and will always be pretty girls. This is one of their survival strategies. Boats, leaves, or birds, at first their faces look alike. Individual features are blurred by dentures, heavy bifocals, and webs of wrinkles. The men are not so easy to categorize. As a group, they are quieter, more uniform, less immediately outstanding except for the few who are distinctive individuals, clearly distinguishable as leaders.

As the morning wears on, the benches fill. Benches are attached back to back, one side facing the ocean, one side the boardwalk. The people on the ocean side swivel around to face their friends, the boardwalk, and the Center.

Bench behavior is highly stylized. The half-dozen or so benches immediately to the north and south of the Center are the territory of the members, segregated by sex and conversation topic. The men's benches are devoted to abstract, ideological concerns—philosophical debate, politics, religion, and economics. The women's benches are given more to talk about immediate, personal matters—children, food, health, neighbors, love affairs, scandals, and "managing." Men and women talk about Israel and its welfare, about being a Jew and about Center politics. On the benches, reputations are made and broken, controversies explored, leaders selected, factions formed and dissolved.

Here is the outdoor dimension of Center life, like a village plaza, a focus of protracted, intense sociability.

The surrounding scene rarely penetrates the invisible, pulsing membrane of the Center community. The old people are too absorbed in their own talk to attend the setting. Surfers, sunbathers, children, dogs, bicyclists, winos, hippies, voyeurs, photographers, panhandlers, artists, junkies, roller skaters, peddlers, and police are omnipresent all year round. Every social class, age, race, and sexual preference is represented. Jesus cults, Hare Krishna parades, sidewalk preachers jostle steel bands and itinerant musicians. As colorful and flamboyant as the scene is by day, it is as dangerous by night. Muggings, theft, rape, harassment, and occasional murders make it a perilous neighborhood for the old people after dark.

Farther up the boardwalk other elderly Jews stake out, their territory on benches and picnic tables used for chess, pinochle, poker, and Mah-Jongg. The Center members do not regard them as "serious" or "cultured" people while they, in turn, consider the Center elderly too political or religious, too inclined to be "joiners," for their taste. Still other old Jews periodically appear on the boardwalk selling Marxist periodicals, Socialist tracts, collecting money for Mexican laborers, circulating petitions to abolish capital punishment. For them, the Center people are too politically conservative. All the elderly Jews in the neighborhood are Eastern European in origin. All are multilingual. Hebrew is brought out for punctuating debates with definitive learned points, usually by the men. Russian or Polish are more used for songs, stories, poems, and reminiscences. But Yiddish binds these diverse people together, the beloved *mama-loshen*[2] of their childhood. It is Yiddish that is used for the most emotional discussions. Despite their ideological differences, most of these people know each

other well, having lived here at the beach for two and three decades.

Signs of what was once a much larger, more complete Yiddish ghetto remain along the boardwalk. Two storefront synagogues are left, where only a few years ago there were a dozen. There is a delicatessen and a Jewish bakery. Before there were many kosher butcher stores and little markets. Only three Jewish board-and-care homes and four large hotels are left to house the elderly. The four thousand or so elderly Jews in the neighborhood must find accommodations in small, rented rooms and apartments within walking distance of the Center. A belt, roughly five miles long and a mile wide, constitutes the limits of the effective community of these Eastern European immigrants, nearly all of whom are now in their middle eighties and up. Several special organizations in the area meet some of their present needs—a secular senior citizen club operated by the city, an outreach city- and state-funded social service center, a women's private political-cultural club, a hot-meals-for-the-elderly service held at a local school. At the edge of the community, still within walking distance of the Center, are several expensive apartments and board-and-care homes (known as "residential facilities"); these accommodate the handful of members who are relatively well-off.

A decade ago, census figures suggest that as many as ten thousand elderly Eastern European Jews lived in the neighborhood. Then Yiddish culture flourished. Groups such as the Workmen's Circle, Emma Lazarus Club, women's philanthropic and religious organizations, various Zionist and Socialist groups were plentiful. Poetry and discussion groups often met in people's homes. There was a dance hall and a choral society. Then, it was said that the community had "the *schonste*[3] Yiddishkeit outside of New York." Around thirty years ago, Jews from all over the country began to immigrate to the beach community, particularly those with health problems and newly retired. Seeking a benign climate, fellow Jews, and moderately priced housing, they brought their savings and small pensions and came to live near the ocean. Collective life was and still is especially intense in this community because there is no automobile traffic on the boardwalk. Here is a place where people may meet, gather, talk, and stroll, simple but basic and precious activities that the elderly in particular can enjoy here all year round.

In the late 1950s, an urban development program resulted in the displacement of between four and six thousand of these senior citizens in a very short period. It was a devastating blow to the culture. "A second Holocaust," Basha called it. "It destroyed our shtetl life all over again."[4] Soon after the urban development project began, a marina was constructed at the southern end of the boardwalk. Property values soared. Older people could not pay taxes and many lost their homes. Rents quadrupled. Old hotels and apartments were torn down, and housing became the single most serious problem for the elderly who desperately wanted to remain in the area. While several thousand have managed to hang on, no new members are moving into the area because of the housing problem. Their Yiddish world, built up over a thirty-year period, is dying and complete extinction is imminent. Perhaps it will last another five or at the most ten years. Whenever a Center member leaves, everyone is acutely aware that there will be no replacements. The sense of cultural doom coincides with awareness of approaching individual death. "When I go out of here; it will be in a box or to the old folks' home. I couldn't say which is worse," Basha said. "We've only got a few more years here, all of us. It would be good if we could stay till the end. We had a protest march the other day, when they took down the old Miramar Hotel. I made up a sign. It said, 'Let my people stay.'"

Yet the community is not a dreary place and the Center members not a depressed group. The sense of doom, by some miraculous process, functions to heighten and animate their life. Every moment matters. There is no time for deception, trivia, or decorum. Life at the Center is passionate, almost melodramatic. Inside, ordinary concerns and mundane interchanges are strangely intense, quickly heating to outburst. The emotional urgency often seems to have little to do with content. This caldronlike quality is perhaps due to the elders' proximity to death and the realization that their remaining days are few. They want to be seen and heard from, before it is too late. Fiercely, they compete with each other for limited supplies of time and attention. Perhaps it is due to the members' extreme dependence on each other; though strongly attached, they are ambivalent about living so closely with others brought into contact with them more by circumstance than choice. Perhaps it is because these elderly people enjoy the strong flood of energy and adrenaline released in intense interactions, assuring them that they are still alive and active.

In spite of its isolation, the beach community is well-known in the city, primarily because of its ethnic distinctiveness and longevity. It is small, stable, cohesive, delimited, and homogeneous in terms of the people's cultural and historical background, an urban ghetto—closed, encapsulated, and self-contained. Relations between the older beach citizens and the broader urban and Jewish worlds are attenuated and episodic. Periodically, various charitable organizations and synagogues offer the Center services and aid, for it is well-known that the majority of old people are isolated and living on small, fixed incomes, below national poverty levels. But Center folk are not easy people to help. Pride and autonomy among them are passions. They see themselves as givers, not takers, and devote enormous effort toward supporting others more needy than they, particularly in Israel. These elders, with few exceptions, are cut off from their family and children. From time to time, relatives visit them or take them back to their homes for holidays or to spend the night, but on a day-to-day basis, the old people effectively are on their own. They miss their family but cherish their independence.

As the numbers of such people shrink and the neighborhood changes, the Aliyah Center becomes more and more important to its members. Sponsored by a city-wide philanthropic Jewish organization, it is maintained as a day center that emphasizes "secular Judaism." Officially, about three hundred members pay dues of six dollars a year, but these figures do not reflect the actual importance of the Center to the community. Many more use it than join, and they use it all day, every day. The Center is more halfway house than voluntary association, making it possible for hundreds of people to continue living alone in the open community, despite their physical and economic difficulties. Daily hot meals are provided there, and continuous diverse programs are offered—cultural events, discussions, classes of all kinds, along with social affairs, religious ceremonies, celebrations of life crises, anniversaries, birthdays, memorials, and occasional weddings. The gamut of political and social processes found in larger societies are well-developed in Center life. Here is an entire, though miniature, society, a Blakeian "world in a grain of sand," the setting for an intricate and rich culture, made up of bits and pieces of people's common history.

Center culture is in some respects thin and fragile, but its very existence must be seen as a major accomplishment, emerging spontaneously as a result of two conditions that characterize the members: continuities between past and present circumstance, and social isolation. Several marked similarities existed between the circumstances of members' childhood and old age. They had grown up in small, intimate Jewish communities, cohesive, ethnocentric, surrounded by indifferent and often hostile outsiders. Previously, in Eastern Europe, they had been marginal people, even pariahs, as they were now. They had strong early training in resourcefulness and opportunities to develop sound survival strategies. Then, as now, they had been poor, politically impotent, and physically insecure. Then, as now, they turned to each other and their shared Yiddishkeit for sustenance, constituting what Irving Howe has called a "ragged kingdom of the spirit."[5] It was not a great shock for these people to find themselves once more in difficult circumstances, for they had never given up their conviction that life was a struggle, that gains entailed losses, that joy and sorrow were inseparable. They knew how to pinch pennies, how to make do, and how to pay attention to those worse off than they and thereby feel useful and needed. They had come to America seeking another life and found that it, too, provided some fulfillments, some disappointments. And thus, they were now not demoralized or helpless.

Their culture was able to emerge as fully as it did because of the elders' isolation from family and the outside world, ironically, the very condition that causes them much grief. Yet, by this separation, they were freed to find their own way, just as their children had been. Now they could indulge their passion for things of the past, enjoy Yiddishkeit without fear of being stigmatized as "not American." With little concern for public opinion, with only each other for company, they revitalized selected features of their common history to meet their present needs, adding and amending it without concern for consistency, priority, or "authenticity." It had taken three decades for this culture to develop to its present state of complexity, now a truly organic, if occasionally disorderly and illogical amalgam of forms and sentiments, memories and wishes, rotating around a few stable, strong symbols and premises. Claude Lévi-Strauss had used the word *bricolage*[6] to describe the process through which myths are constructed in preliterate societies. Odds and ends, fragments offered up by chance or the environment—almost anything will do— are taken up by a group and incorporated into a tale, used by a people to explain themselves and their world. No intrinsic order or system has dictated the materials employed. In such an inelegant fashion does the *bricoleur* or handyman meet his needs.

Center culture was such a work of bricolage. Robust and impudently eclectic, it shifted and stretched to meet immediate needs—private, collective, secular, and sacred. Thus, when a Center Yiddish History class graduated, a unique ceremony was designed that pasted together the local event with an analogous, historical counterpart, thereby enlarging and authenticating the improvised, contemporary affair. And the traditional Sabbath ceremony was rearranged to allow as many people as possible to participate—making speeches, singing songs, reading poems, taking into account the members' acute need for visibility and attention. Among them, two or even three women instead of one were required to light the Sabbath candles—one singing the blessing in Hebrew, one in Yiddish, one putting the match to the wick. Similarly, Center folk redefined the secular New Year's Eve, holding their dance a full day and a half before the conventional date, since this made it possible for them to get home before dark and to hire their favorite musicians at lower rates. These improvisations were entirely authentic. Somehow midday December 30 became the real New Year's Eve and the later, public celebration seemed unconvincing by comparison. In all this, no explicit plan or internal integration could be detected. Cultures are, after all, collective, untidy assemblages, authenticated by belief and agreement, focused only in crisis, systematized after the fact. Like a quilt, Center life was made up of many small pieces sewn together by necessity, intended to be serviceable and to last. It was sufficient for the people's remaining years.

The vitality and flexibility of the Center culture was especially impressive in view of the organization's meager budget. Enough money was available only to pay for a few programs and the salary of the director, Abe, who had devoted himself to these elderly people for fourteen years. Sometimes he was a surrogate son, sometimes a worrying, scolding, protecting parent to them. Thirty years younger than most members, Abe was a second-generation American, from the same background as they. A social worker by training, he watched over the elders' health, listened to their complaints, mediated their quarrels, teased and dominated them when they lost heart, and defended them against external threats, insisting to them and the outside world that they survive. Without his dedication, it was unlikely that they would have been able to continue for so long and so well, living alone into advanced old age in an open, inhospitable setting.

I sat on the benches outside the Center and thought about how strange it was to be back in the neighborhood where sixteen years before I had lived and for a time had been a social worker with elderly citizens on public relief. Then the area was known as "Oshini Beach." The word *shini* still made me cringe. As a child I had been taunted with it. Like many second-generation Americans, I wasn't sure what being a Jew meant. When I was a child our family had avoided the words *Jew* and *Yid*. We were confused and embarrassed about our background. In public we lowered our voices when referring to "our people" or "one of us." My grandparents had also emigrated from an Eastern European shtetl as young people. Like so many of the Center folk, they, too, wanted their children to be Americans above all and were ashamed of being "greenhorns." They spoke to my parents in Yiddish and were answered in English. None of the children or grand-children in the family received any religious education, yet they carried a strong if ambivalent identity as Jews. This identity took the form of fierce pride and defensiveness during the Holocaust but even then did not result in any of us developing a clear conception of how to live in terms of our ethnic membership.

I had made no conscious decision to explore my roots or clarify the meaning of my origins. I was one of several anthropologists at the University of Southern California engaged in an examination of Ethnicity and Aging. At first I planned to study elderly Chicanos, since I had previously done fieldwork in Mexico. But in the early 1970s in urban America, ethnic groups were not welcoming curious outsiders, and people I approached kept asking me, "Why work with us? Why don't you study your own kind?" This was a new idea to me. I had not been trained for such a project. Anthropologists conventionally investigate exotic, remote, preliterate societies. But such groups are increasingly unavailable and often inhospitable. As a result, more and more anthropologists are finding themselves working at home these days. Inevitably, this creates problems with objectivity and identification, and I anticipated that I, too, would have my share of them if I studied the Center folk. But perhaps there would be advantages. There was no way that I could have anticipated the great impact of the study on my life, nor its duration. I intended to spend a year with them. In fact, I was with them continuously for two years (1973–1974, 1975–1976) and periodically for two more. In the begriming, I spent a great deal of time agonizing about how to label what I was doing—was it anthropology or a personal quest? I never fully resolved the question. I used many conventional anthropological methods and asked many typical questions, but when I had finished, I found

my descriptions did not resemble most anthropological writings. Still, the results of the study would certainly have been different had I not been an anthropologist by training.

Sitting in the sun and contemplating the passing parade on the boardwalk that morning in 1973, I wondered how I should begin this study. At eleven-thirty the beaches began to empty as old people entered the Center for a "Hot Kosher Meal—Nutritious—65¢," then a new program provided by state and private funds. Inside there was barely enough room to accommodate between 100 and 150 people who regularly ate there. The Center was only a simple shabby hall, the size of a small school auditorium, empty except for a tiny stage at one end with a kitchen behind it, and a little area partitioned off at the other end, used for a library and office. The front window was entirely covered by hand-lettered signs in Yiddish and English announcing current events:

> TODAY AT 2:00
> Jewish History Class.—Teacher, Clara Shapiro.
> *VERY EDUCATIONAL.*
> SUNDAY AT 1:00
> SPECIAL EVENT: FILMS ON ISRAEL
> *Refreshments. Come. Enjoy.*
> MONDAY AT 3:00
> Gerontology Class.—Teacher, Sy Greenberg.
> *Informative. Bring Your Questions.*
> TUESDAY AT 10:00
> Rabbi Cohen Talks On Succoth.
> *Beautiful and enlightening.*

Over the front door hung another hand-made sign, written and painted by one of the members: "To the extent that here at the Center we are able to be ourselves and to that extent self feels good to us." The walls were adorned with pictures of assorted Yiddish writers, scholars, and Zionists. Two large colored photographs of the Western Wall in Jerusalem and of

Golda Meir hung above a bust of Moshe Dayan. Seniors' arts and crafts were displayed in a glass case. Their paintings and drawings hung along one wall, depicting shtetl scenes and household activities associated with sacred rituals—the lighting of the Sabbath candles, the housewife baking the Sabbath loaf, a father teaching his children their religious lessons, and the like. Portraits of rabbis, tailors, scholars hung there, too, along with symbols of Jewish festivals and holidays—a papier-mâché *dreidel,* and cardboard *menorah, a shofar.*[7] A large, wooden Star of David illuminated by a string of Christmas tree lights was prominently displayed. Framed certificates of commendation and thanks from Israeli recipients of the elders' donations hung alongside photographs of kibbutzim children to whom the Center elders had contributed support. The wall opposite bore a collective self-portrait in the form of a room-length mural, designed and painted by the members, portraying their common journey from the past to the present in several colorful, strong, and simple scenes: a picture of a boatload of immigrants arriving at Ellis Island, a shtetl marketplace, a New York street scene, a shtetl street scene, and a group of picketers bearing signs, "Better Conditions First," "We Shall Fight for Our Rights," "Power and Justice for the People," and one that simply said, "Protest Treatment." The last sequence rendered the elders at present, seated on benches along the boardwalk and celebrating the Sabbath inside the Center. Over the small stage, the line from the Old Testament was lettered, "Behold How Good It Is for Brethren to Dwell Together in Unity," and opposite, a prominent placard that read, "Cast Me Not Out in My Old Age But Let Me Live Each Day as a New Life." More than decoration, these visual displays were the people's icons, constituting a symbolic depiction—the group's commentary on itself—by reference to its sources of identity, in particular, its common history. This use of symbols pointed to a community that was highly conscious of itself and its own distinctive ideology.

I followed the crowd inside and sat at the back of the warm, noisy room redolent with odors of fish and chicken soup, wondering how to introduce myself. It was decided for me. A woman sat down next to me who I soon learned was Basha. In a leisurely fashion, she appraised me. Uncomfortable, I smiled and said hello.

"You are not hungry?" she asked.
"No, thank you, I'm not," I answered.
"So, what brings you here?"
"I'm from the University of Southern California. I'm looking for a place to study how older Jews live in the city."
At the word *university,* she moved closer and nodded approvingly. "Are you Jewish?" she asked.
"Yes, I am."
"Are you married?" she persisted.
"Yes."
"You got children?"
"Yes, two boys, four and eight," I answered.
"Are you teaching them to be Jews?"
"I'm trying."
"So what do you want with us here?" asked Basha.
"Well, I want to understand your life, find out what it's like to be older and Jewish, what makes Jews different from other older people, if anything. I'm an anthropologist and we usually study people's cultures and societies. I think I would like to learn about this culture."
"And what will you do for us?" she asked me.
"I could teach a class in something people here are interested in—how older people live in other places, perhaps."
"Are you qualified to do this?" Basha shot me a suspicious glance.
"I have a Ph.D. and have taught in the university for a number of years, so I suppose I am qualified."

"You are a professor then? A little bit of a thing like you?" To my relief, she chuckled amiably. Perhaps I had passed my first rite of entrance into the group.

"Faegl, Faegl, come here!" Basha shouted to a friend across the room. Faegl picked her way neatly over to where we were sitting. She was wiry and slight as Basha was heavy and grand. "Faegl, sit down. Faegl, this here is——What did you say your name was? Barbara? This is Barbara. She is a professor and wants to study us. What do you think of that?"

"Why not? I wouldn't object. She could learn a lot. Are you Jewish?" Faegl leaned past Basha and carefully peered at me over her bifocals.

Basha accurately recited my qualifications and family characteristics. Faegl wasted no time. She moved over to sit next to me and began her interrogation.

"So you are an anthropologist. Then you study people's origins, yes? Tell me, is it true that human beings began in Africa once upon a time?"

"Many scholars think so," I answered.

"Ha! And once upon a time this country belonged to the Indians. That's right?" she went on.

"Yes, certainly," I answered.

"Now a lot of people don't think it's right that we took away from them the country just because we were stronger, yes?"

"Yes." I was growing wary, sensing an entrapment.

Faegl continued systematically. "So this business about putting all the Arabs out of Israel because we said we had our origins there, maybe that's not right either? It is not so simple, is it?"

"No, no. Certainly it is not simple," I answered.

"So Bashaleh, what do you say now?" Faegl asked her. "She's a professor and she says maybe it's not right. Like I told you, even from the Arabs we can't take away the land."

Basha looked at me closely while Faegl waited.

"You don't believe in *Eretz Yisroel?*"[8] she asked me. "You are some kind of anti-Semite?"

Faegl rescued me. "Basha! You think everyone who isn't a Zionist is an anti-Semite? Shame on you. You used to be an internationalist. You used to have beliefs."

Their argument had grown loud enough to attract attention. Abe, the director, came over to see what was going on. Again, Basha introduced me. I asked him about the possibility of doing my study here. He was non-committal but friendly and after the lunch, we walked along the boardwalk together. He was exceptionally well-informed about the changes in the neighborhood during the last decade and a half. He seemed to know everyone on the streets, not only the elderly. But when he spoke of them, his voice was thick with affection, and anger at their being neglected. He evidently knew all the members, where they lived, how much money they had, where their families were, their state of mind and health, on an hour-by-hour basis. Abe was a naturally gifted sociologist and he had a remarkable memory. Because of these qualities, and his lengthy association with the area and its people, he proved to be an invaluable source of insight and information throughout the work I did there. In the course of our walk and talk, he filled me in on the background characteristics of most Center members.

Nearly all came from poor families, he explained. Their fathers were craftsmen, traders, peddlers, and middlemen, and their mothers worked, too, despite numerous children. The shtetl of their childhood was still very much a presence among them. They remembered it with intense affection and nostalgia in spite of its terrible hardships. Self-regulating, highly stratified, valuing religious education and study even above wealth and family connections, the shtetl Jews had held themselves apart from the surrounding illiterate peasantry; but by the end of the nineteenth century, these communities were being rent apart by internal as well as external forces. The new movements sweeping that part of the world—communism, Zionism, the international trade union movement—the secularization and concern with worldly matters known as the Haskala[9] began to pull young people away from shtetl customs. Youth were growing impatient with their parents' strict religious orthodoxy, conservatism, and fatalism. Immigration to the New World swelled until around the turn of the century nearly everyone had a relative in America, someone who could help one start a new life.

Most Center folk had come to America as children or young adults, settling first in the urban industrial centers of the East Coast. They worked there as petty merchants, retailers, wage workers, and artisans and went to night school to learn English. They married people like themselves and dedicated the next twenty years of their lives to their children's education. It generally took American immigrant groups three generations or so to accomplish what these people achieved in one; as a result, they were dubbed, "The one-generation proletariat." Professors, scientists, musicians, industrialists were the children of peddlers, craftsmen, and laborers. But the cost of such a rapid ascent was the development of strong social and cultural barriers between the Old World parents and New World children. They had jettisoned much of their Yiddish practices and beliefs, for it seemed to them that, as one writer puts it, "a clean break with religion...was the best and surest way of becoming an American."[10]

"You know, these people may seem unique to you, but there are others like them all over the country—Pittsburgh, New York, Florida," Abe explained to me. "They're a proud bunch. No wonder. Look what they've lived through. You gotta be strong to survive what they have. Something in them, something about their background must have given them tremendous courage

and independence. We don't know what that 'something' really is. It would be good if you could find out. You don't have long, because they'll be gone soon. And when they go, there's nobody else. The sixty- and even seventy-year-olds who were born here, they're nothing like that. So if you really want to do this study, you had better get going."

For the next four years I was to be involved with these people, as an anthropologist, doing fieldwork, as a friend, and sometimes as a family member. When Josele Masada decided that I looked like his mother and told everyone I was his long-missing granddaughter, Barbarinka, no one was certain what to make of this, for boundaries between his memories, dreams, and the present were often blurred. Did he "really" think there was a biological bond between us, was this a wish, a metaphor, a great compliment? Since no one was certain of Masada's notion, our relationship could neither be affirmed nor denied, and it remained a puzzle to everyone, including me. I was right in expecting that my closeness to the subject would be both troublesome and advantageous, but there was no way I could have anticipated what the specific struggles and compensations would be.

The anthropologist engages in peculiar work. He or she tries to understand a different culture to the point of finding it to be intelligible, regardless of how strange it seems in comparison with one's own background. This is accomplished by attempting to experience the new culture from within, living in it for a time as a member, all the while maintaining sufficient detachment to observe and analyze it with some objectivity. This peculiar posture—being inside and outside at the same time—is called participant-observation. It is a fruitful paradox, one that has allowed anthropologists to find sense and purpose within a society's seemingly illogical and arbitrary customs and beliefs.[11] This assumption of the natives' viewpoint, so to speak, is a means of knowing others through oneself, a professional technique that can be mastered fairly easily in the study of very different peoples. Working with one's own society, and more specifically, those of one's own ethnic and familial heritage, is perilous, and much more difficult. Yet it has a certain validity and value not available in other circumstances. Identifying with the "Other"—Indians, Chicanos, if one is Anglo, blacks if one is white, males if one is female—is an act of imagination, a means for discovering what one is not and will never be. Identifying with what one is now and will be someday is quite a different process.

In working among the elderly—also, I suspect, among the very young—an exceptionally important part of one's information is derived from nonverbal communication and identification, this because the bodily state is such a large determinant of well-being for the growing and declining organism. At various times, I consciously tried to heighten my awareness of the physical feeling state of the elderly by wearing stiff garden gloves to perform ordinary tasks, taking off my glasses and plugging my ears, slowing down my movements and sometimes by wearing the heaviest shoes I could find to the Center. Walking a few blocks to the day-old bakery in this condition became an unimaginably exhilarating achievement. Once by accident I stumbled slightly. The flash of actual terror I experienced was shocking. From the close watching of the elderly it seems I had acquired their assiduous need to avoid falling, though of course, to one my age in good health such a minor accident presents no real danger. This recognition occurred after I had been watching two very old women walk down the alley with great concentration, arms tightly linked, navigating impediments in slow-motion movements that were perfectly coordinated and mutually supportive. So great was their concern

with balance they might have been walking a high wire.

The work with the very old people at the Center was not the first time I had employed this imaginative identification as a source of information. Years before, in doing fieldwork with the Huichol Indians of Mexico, I had had similar experiences.[12] However much I learned from that was limited by the fact that I would never really be a Huichol Indian. But I would be a little old Jewish lady one day; thus, it was essential for me to learn what that condition was like, in all its particulars. As a society, we are increasingly cut off from the elderly. We do not have them in the midst of our daily lives, and consequently have no regular access to models of successful old age. How can we then do anything but dread the coming of age? I consider myself very fortunate in having had, through this work, an opportunity to anticipate, rehearse, and contemplate my own future. This has given a temporal integration to my life that seems to me an essential ingredient in the work of maturing.

I *see* old people now in a new way, as part of me, not "they." Most normal, relatively sensitive people identify naturally with children. They remember what it was like to have been a child themselves and as a result *see* children—are aware of them as a part of life, appreciative of their specific needs, rights, and characteristics. But in our culture today, we do not have this same natural attentiveness to and empathy with the elderly, in part because they are not among us, and no doubt they are not among us because we don't want to recognize the inevitability of our own future decline and dependence. An insidious circularity has developed—ignorance, based in part on denial of our future, leading to fear and rejection of the elderly, engendering guilt that is often expressed as neglect or mistreatment, then more guilt, avoidance, and ignorance; agism is characterized by the same self-fulfilling processes that operate in racism. Our anxiety about the future is guaranteed by our own behavior, assuring that our worst unspoken, unspeakable fear will be realized: Our children will treat us as we treat our parents.

As usual, Basha had a *myseh*[13] on the subject, told to her by her grandmother. Paraphrased, it went as follows:

Once there was a rich man who decided he would give all his money to his son as soon as the boy was grown instead of following the custom of making the boy wait till the father's death to inherit. He did this, but soon the son began to neglect his elderly father, and one day the son put him out of the house. The old man left and came back many years later. He saw his little grandson playing outside the house and told the child who he was. "Fetch me a cloak, child," he said, "because I am cold and poor." The little boy rummaged in the attic for an old cloak and was cutting it in half when his father came in. "What are you doing, child?" he asked. "Father, I am going to give half of the cloak to my grandfather and keep the other half for you, for the time when I am grown up and you have grown old."

What the Center people taught me went beyond knowledge about old age. In addition they provided a model of an alternative life-style, built on values in many ways antithetical to those commonly esteemed by contemporary Americans. The usual markers of success were anathema to them—wealth, power, physical beauty, youth, mobility, security, social status—all were out of the question. Lacking hope for change, improvement, without a future, they had devised a counterworld, inventing their own version of what made "the good life." It was built on their veneration for their religious and cultural membership and it was full of meaning, intensity, and consciousness. This they had managed

on their own, creating a nearly invisible, run-down, tiny world, containing a major lesson for any who would attend it. It was not the first time that an anthropologist had found in obscure, unworldly folk a message of wide applicability for the larger outside society.

It was especially their passion for meaning that appealed to me so deeply; this the Center folk valued above happiness or comfort. Their history and religion provided them with ample raw material for enacting their celebratory attitude toward their lives. "It's good to be a Jew. It's hard to be a Jew. What else is new?" laughed Basha when contemplating the pros and cons of her contemporary situation and past history. The word *Jew* in this context served as a metaphor for being human. She used it the same way other people might have said, "That's what life is like." Basha shared with others in the Center an acute sense of dignity, irony, and stoicism, and these were enormously helpful to her in meeting the challenges of her present life, and so, too, the recognition maintained since her early shtetl experience—that a sense of humor is redeeming and ultimately one must face being alone. Among the Center people life was highly ritualized, and their penchant for ceremony and symbol was aided by Judaism's particular richness in these domains. Drawing on their cultural background, Center people were able to elevate mundane affairs, bringing to each moment a heightened consciousness that rendered suffering and scarcity explicable, and because explicable, bearable. Most of these people had developed some conceptual framework in terms of which their afflictions become comprehensible. This was particularly evident late one Friday afternoon not long ago, when following the Center's celebration to welcome the Sabbath, I lingered to walk along the ocean front with Josele and Nathan. I left them talking on a bench in front of the Center, somewhat uneasily, because I had noticed a young woman familiar in the neighborhood, pacing back and forth, evidently hallucinating, ranting wildly to herself. Just as I was about to pull away, I glanced at the rearview mirror of my car and was shocked to see her attacking the two old men. She had thrown over a huge garbage can next to the bench where they sat. Josele had shouted at her and waved his cane to try to shoo her away. She had seized the cane and thrown him to the ground. He rolled about helplessly, trying to cover his face as she beat him about the head with his cane. As I ran toward them, I heard her yell, "Dirty Jew, fuck you, I'm going to kill you, dirty Jew!" I couldn't wrest the deadly flailing cane from her, but shouting for help, I managed to draw her away from Josele by enticing her to chase me down the boardwalk. Bystanders seized and held her before she got to me. Someone had helped Josele onto the bench. He was bleeding from the mouth and nose and there was a purple lump over one eye the size of a tennis ball. I insisted that Josele wait for the police and paramedics. He didn't want to. "I got no use for police," he said. "What could they do with this poor crazy girl? Nothing. Could they make my poor head stop hurting? Police don't know from these things.

"Today is not the first time I got beat up. When I was only a boy I was already a revolutionary, working for justice, that's all I cared about. Then the Cossacks threw me to the ground and beat me up with clubs yelling all the time like this girl, 'Dirty Jew.' So what has changed? As long as these things happen, I know my work is not finished. Now I go home. I don't keep the Sabbath with prayers. I got my own ways." He chuckled, heaved himself up from the bench, and picked up his cane. "On Fridays the cats on my street get extra rations. Since we got no more beggars in America, we got to do the best we can with what we have." He limped off down the alley.

Being so rooted in their Judaism helped the old people in their struggles and celebrations. They were sufficiently comfortable with it to improvise upon it and adapt it freely as needed, for small requirements and large. Basha exemplified this when she described her dinner preparations. She ate alone in her tiny room. Over an electric hot plate, she cooked her chicken foot stew (chicken feet were free at the supermarket). Before eating, she spread a white linen handkerchief over the oilcloth covering the table, saying:

> This my mother taught me to do. No matter how poor, we would eat off clean white linen, and say the prayers before touching anything to the mouth. And so I do it still. Whenever I sit down, I eat with God, my mother, and all the Jews who are doing these same things even if I can't see them.

Such a meal is a feast, superior to fine fare hastily eaten, without ceremony, attention, or significance. I wondered if Basha's daughter knew how to dine so splendidly. Because of such things, I came to see the Center elderly as in possession of the philosophers' stone—that universally sought, ever-elusive treasure, harboring the secret that would teach us how to transmute base metals into pure gold. The stone, like the bluebird's feather of happiness, is said to be overlooked precisely because it is so close to us, hidden in the dust at our feet.

Alongside death and the ocean, a third invisible protagonist was present among Center members—guilt. These people were a distinctive breed, survivors all. A group selected to endure many times over, living considerably beyond the norm, they were biologically elite. And they were also psychologically and socially special. Unlike most of their siblings, cousins, and parents, they had found the courage and vision to break with family, home, and community to better their own and their unborn children's lot. Because of their decision to leave

Eastern Europe, they had escaped extinction; virtually all who remained behind perished in the Holocaust. Subsequent courageous choices and sacrifices had allowed them to realize their most cherished ambitions—providing education and freedom for their children. In the course of their history, these people had demonstrated their capacity for survival many times over; they were determined, and resourceful beyond the norm.

But one's own survival, when loved ones are being destroyed, is not experienced as a simple triumph or stroke of good luck, as the literature coming out of Hiroshima and Hitler's Europe demonstrates so clearly. It is an extremely problematic condition, often arousing the most severe, even crippling anguish, "survivor's guilt."[14] The Center people were survivors twice over, once due to their escape by emigration from the unnatural ravages of the Holocaust, and again later by living into extreme old age, surviving their peers, family, and often children. That the more recent losses were the natural, inevitable results of the mere passage of time did not necessarily make them more bearable. These elderly men and women, like all those who cry out in moments of extreme pain, asked, "Why me, O Lord," requesting explanation, not for their affliction but for their escape. Thus do victims and survivors alike petition the gods to know the sense behind their destiny. "How do I deserve this? In what ways am I better or worse than those who perished?" There is evidence that suggests it may be universal for survivors of mass destruction to believe that the best die, that by merely being alive, one is guilty, that somehow others died in one's stead. It must be said even when it is self-evident, that survivor's guilt is often irrational, an expression of humanity's metaphysical passion for morality and order. Survivor's guilt, as well as a reality, is a metaphor, referring to that sense of intermingled destinies that denies impotence,

solitariness, and the irrelevance of each of us for the others. These elderly Jews were not, strictly speaking, survivors of the Holocaust, for by emigrating they had escaped. Still, they participated in the Holocaust with intensity and depth, and most spoke of it as though it had been their own experience as well as that of the families and peers they left behind. Although they had not actually been through it, they were much more than spectators, and they asked themselves many of the same questions and manifested many of the same characteristics noted among actual survivors. They searched their consciences often and with severity, and held themselves responsible for the fates of those who had not survived. This guilt was not "realistic," for as nearly as I could determine every person I met had strained him or herself utterly, exhausting all the human and material resources they could mobilize to bring their families to safety in America, as soon as possible. Still they wondered what more they might have done. Still, they tormented themselves with questions about why things had turned out as they had. Faegl described her struggle to bring her parents and younger sister to America. For two years she had nearly starved herself to scrape up money for their passage. Her parents came but the sister would not. They did not stay long—they missed the younger daughter too much and returned to Poland. All were killed in Auschwitz. "How can I account for this?" Faegl closed her eyes and wrung her hands when she talked of it. "Were my parents killed because they loved their child so dearly? Was I saved because I didn't love them enough to go back with them?"

The need to reiterate here the irrationality of survivor's guilt comes from the ever-present tendency to blame victims for their fate.[15] To find them in some way responsible for what happened—by their alleged collusion, passivity, weakness, cowardice, selfishness, or denial, as well as more venal attributes—is reassuring. It tells us that people get what they deserve, that they have power over themselves, that the universe is predictable, so that if we are strong and attentive we can avoid the victim's conduct and assure our own safety. "It can't happen to me," comforts onlookers but not survivors themselves. They know by what slender threads their lives are distinguished from those who died; they do not see in themselves soothing virtues or special merits that make their survival inevitable or right. They know how easily it could have happened to them; to these people complacency is forever lost.

Survivor's guilt can be crippling, but among these elderly people it was not. Instead it served as a transformative agent that made it impossible for them to lead the unexamined life. Life for these elderly was many different things: gift, relentless struggle, challenge, a curse, and all the shadings in between. But it was never taken for granted. Above all, it contributed to their passion for meaning.[16] It is common for survivors to attempt to re-create an orderly universe, one that can be found somehow to be sensible; despite the brutality of the concentration camps, inmates during internment and afterward pursued and seized upon any evidence of sense and justice in the world. Meaningless accidents, chaos, and inexplicability are more insupportable than suffering and cruelty. Survivors have a heightened desire for interpretation, for finding the comprehensible elements in their experiences. Says psychiatrist Robert Jay Lifton, who has documented the psychology of survivors of Hiroshima as well as the Holocaust, "...Any experience of survival—whether of large disaster or intimate personal loss...involves a journey to the edge of the world of the living." What he calls the formulative effort—the search for meaning—is the survivor's means of return from that edge.[17] Then it was not merely these elders' proximity to their own deaths

that so enlivened them—rather it was due to their survival of loved ones, the guilt and responsibility this generated, and the subsequent necessity for understanding what had brought about the destruction of their people and their natal world. These were what turned them so strongly toward the symbolic life.

Survivorhood accounted for other, positive features among them. It validated their values. In foiling enemies determined to destroy them, by merely outliving them, they demonstrated that they were indeed Chosen People. And survivorhood also caused them to intensify their dedication to social justice; they not only sought evidence of morality in a shattered, disordered world, but also worked to establish it. Such activity—"collecting justice" Lifton calls it—is common among survivors, and of course these people's traditions had always emphasized it. Their sense of responsibility for the welfare of others was the transformation of survival guilt into conscience, another commonplace among those who live despite others' efforts to destroy them, as historian Terence Des Pres observes.[18] Their philanthropic activities, the construction of a symbolic universe made out of the long past, the quest for meaning, and their concern for human dignity—all were signal traits in Center life, accentuated by the survival experience.

In the beginning phases of my work with the elderly I too suffered severe pangs of guilt. It took many forms and floated about, settling on different issues at different times. At first it focused on questions concerning my competence in the task I was embarking upon. Did I know enough Judaica? Did I know enough Yiddish? Was I too young? Was I too emotionally involved? Should I be working for the old people's welfare instead of studying them? and the like. In the course of a conversation with Shmuel, a very learned man who was to become one of my principal informants, I confessed my fears about not being able to do justice to the materials he was giving me. There was so much I did not understand. As usual, he was severe but not unfair in his response.

> You don't understand. How could you expect to understand? You ask me all these things, but you know nothing. You don't know Yiddish. You don't know Hebrew. You don't know Aramaic. You don't know Russian and not Polish. You have not set your eyes on any part of the place we lived in. How can you expect to understand?

I agreed with him and was terribly discouraged. For a while, I stopped to study Yiddish, then realized that I was taking too much time out of the fieldwork. It was wasteful in view of the Center people's fluency in English. I also spent some time studying Jewish law and history, but the subjects were overwhelmingly complex, needing lifetimes of devotion to achieve more than a superficial understanding. I decided to try to follow the old people's leads in deciding what to study, learning as much as I could from them. I would enter these fields of knowledge in an *ad hoc* fashion, letting the elders point out what I needed to know as the work progressed rather than plowing into it systematically or for its own sake.

Resolving the question of my right to do the work did not free me from the inner and outer taunts. Many of the Center people continued to "make" me feel guilty. After greeting me warmly, Basha would often ask. "Never mind these other things you all the time ask about. Tell me, who's with your children?" Men and women alike would admire a new skirt or dress I wore, then turn over my hem for inspection. Nathan remarked, "For a lady professor, you don't do so good with a needle." When I stayed away too long, they scolded and snubbed me. When I was not completely fair (and sometimes even when I was) in the distribution of attention, I paid dearly for it. The old people were genuinely proud of me, generous, and affectionate, but at times their resentment spilled over. My presence was a continual reminder of many painful facts: that it should have been their own children there listening to their stories; that I had combined family and a career, opportunities that the women had longed for and never been allowed. And, too, that I knew so little of their background suggested to them that they had failed to transmit to future generations any but fragments of their cherished past. I felt guilty about invading their privacy, for however much I explained my publication intentions, I knew our conversations sometimes crossed the invisible line from informed disclosure to inadvertent confidence. Diffuse and even irrational guilt plagued me until I had to laugh at myself. I had become a tasteless ethnic joke, paralyzed by Jewish guilt: about my relative youth and strength, about having a future where they did not, about my ability to come and go as I chose while they had to await my visits and my convenience, when I relished food that I knew they could not digest, when I slept soundly through the night warmed by my husband's body, knowing the old people were sleeping alone in cold rooms. (In some African tribes, all the elderly are loaned a child for warmth and companionship at night.)

I considered quitting. It was unbearable to abide the countless ways in which the Center people used guilt, often unconsciously, intending not to hurt but only to make themselves feel potent. But after a time I accepted the fact that one cannot be "made" guilty. One volunteers. The arousal of guilt is what I have called "a strategy of intimacy," one of many used by the Center old people. Useless among strangers, it is based on interdependence and connectedness. The bright side of guilt is that it is an expression of a sense of responsibility for another's well-being. When I realized that, I became resigned and even grateful about my responses to my subjects.

I had been with these people for almost two years when I hit on what seemed the most significant component of my complex feelings about them. I chanced to read a comment by Isaac Bashevis Singer in one of his novels about survivors. A single statement of his suddenly clarified matters for me. In reference to his own difficulties in writing about victims he remarked, "Although I did not have the privilege of going through the Hitler holocaust...."[19] Yes, it was that feeling that they were set apart from the rest of us and hallowed by their suffering. Paradoxically they were the privileged ones for having, lived on our behalf through what was in one sense our common fate. How, then, could anyone look at them dispassionately? How could I feel anything but awe and appreciation for their mere presence? In view of their proximity to mass destruction, it was indecent to ask more of them than that they be alive and in good spirits. But they were more than their sufferings; too great an appreciation on my part was a disservice and falsification, ultimately disrespectful. I wanted my people to be loved and admired as a result of my study, for in addition to being survivors, they were presently poor and maltreated. I wanted to protect them, even from my responses. But finally I accepted the necessity for sacrificing that desire. A reverential, protective attitude would allow the reader to distance him- or herself from them. The elders' accomplishments were important precisely because they were not heroes or saints, indeed this was one reason why they and the life they created were so colorful and appealing. Their flamboyance, humor, tendency to self-parody and self criticism, their reaches for dignity and integrity, their occasional failures and lapses into foolishness, selfishness, and unkindness were part of what contributed to their success as survivors. My work would have to be a full-length portrait, light and darkness with more shading than sharp lines. Since neutrality was impossible and idealization undesirable, I settled on striving for

balance. If these people emerged as real in their entire human range and variety, arousing admiration and disappointment, laughter and tears, hope and despair, I would be satisfied. My admiration for and gratitude to them must be evident. In the end the only acceptable answer I could find to the question "Am I qualified to write this book?" was that my membership and my affection were my qualifications. When I judge these people, I judge myself.

The amount and variety of information accumulated in a field of study is overwhelming. There is no definite or correct solution to the problem of what to include, how to cut up the pie of social reality, when precisely to leave or stop. Often there is little clarity as to whom to include as "members," what to talk about with those who are. The deliberate avoidance of preconceptions is likely to result in the best fieldwork, allowing the group or subject to dictate the form the description ultimately takes. But always there is a high degree of arbitrariness involved. Choices must be made and they are extremely difficult, primarily because of what and who must be omitted. In this case, these methodological dilemmas were especially troublesome. Nearly everyone at the Center wanted to be included, feeling so strongly as they did the wish to be recorded and remembered.

In this work I decided to concentrate on the Center, its internal affairs, and its most active members as much as possible. This eliminated the nonjoiners, the marginal individuals, the majority of people living in the neighborhood and, accordingly, limited the generalizations that I could make in the end. I decided not to compare the Center elders with others. I felt the Center people and their generation were sufficiently unique to warrant most of my time. The choice favored depth over breadth, tight focus rather than representativeness. My interpretation, therefore, must be read as pertaining to these particular people at a given period of time – how much they have in common with others must be determined by someone else.

Of the three hundred Center members, I met and talked with about half, though I observed all at one time or another during the years of the study. Of these, I knew personally, and interviewed and spent most of my time with thirty-six. I tape recorded extensive interviews with these, ranging from two to sixteen hours, visited nearly all in their homes, took trips with them from time to time outside the neighborhood – to doctors, social workers, shopping, funerals, visiting their friends in old age homes and hospitals, and often following my subjects to convalescent homes and hospitals; I went to many funerals and memorial services. Apart from these excursions and my interviews with outsiders who knew Center people well – teachers, rabbis, local politicians, volunteers – I concentrated on the Center and its external extensions, the benches, boardwalk, and hotel and apartment lobbies where they congregated.

As often happens, I established a particularly strong and gratifying attachment to one individual, and also as often happens, in addition to being particularly knowledgeable and articulate about the community, this person was also an outsider. "Shmuel the Filosofe," he was called, and in a very significant way he was my teacher, critic, and guide. To him alone, a complete chapter is devoted (chapter two), and his voice is heard throughout the book. I have included my own voice in his chapter, for it proved impossible to expunge. His statements and retorts did not make sense without that, for he was directing his commentary to me. That is not the only place I have included my words and reactions. For a long time I resisted this. I wanted to focus on the Center, not myself, but it became clear that what was being written was from my eyes, with my personality, biases, history, and sensibility, and it seemed dishonest to exclude that, thereby giving an impression of greater objectivity and authority than I believed in.

As often as possible I have included verbatim materials, heavily edited and selected, inevitably, but sufficient to allow the reader some degree of direct participation. I have tried to allow many individuals to emerge in their fullness and distinctiveness rather than presenting a completely generalized picture of group life without reference to the living breathing people who comprise it, and who are in the end the only reality. In the interest of economy and privacy, I have combined several of the minor characters who appear on these pages, though most would have preferred to have been identified. Wherever possible I have altered identifying biographical features that seemed insignificant. All verbatim statements are presented as they were given, usually taken from tape recordings. Major figures are disguised as much as possible but uncombined. Events reported are actual occurrences, subjectively witnessed and interpreted by me.

The always complex problem of assuring privacy to one's subjects was made more difficult in this study because of the production of a documentary film on which I collaborated with Lynne Littman toward the end of research. Also called *Number Our Days,* it was based on my fieldwork at the Center.[20] We were not at all sure that the film would cross the ethnic barrier, and were surprised when it was widely viewed and enthusiastically received. To our great satisfaction, it brough the elderly concrete benefits in many forms – unsolicited funds, attention and favors from strangers and friends, and above all, visibility, which they so long for. But it made effective disguise of the Center and its director impossible. Nevertheless, privacy for individuals could be preserved, and so I have changed all names of people and groups mentioned here, this to allow myself freedom to record some of the unflattering things I saw there, as much as possible to prevent the elderly from recognizing themselves and each other, to save them and their children any embarrassment that might accrue. Certainly, I did not want to cause the old people pain that could be avoided, nor did I wish to jeopardize my welcome among them.

Several conscious decisions distinguished the film from the book. The film, Lynne Littman and I agreed, should focus on people's survival strategies, their resourcefulness and courage, emotional vitality, their bold and often joyous use of religion in their response to aging and adversity. Deliberately we glossed the troubles and antagonisms within the organization and among people. The film could do what the book should not do - serve to repay them for some of what they had given me.

The format of this book is designed to meet several purposes. In addition to wanting to speak within it as a participant, and wishing to preserve particular indivduals, I wanted to render the elders' speech. Many verbatim statements are included; the most extensive of these are called "*bobbe-myseh*," or grandmothers' tales, speeches and exchanges between people that occurred in a "Living History" class, which I will describe shortly. The bobbe-myseh were drawn from miles of tape, intended to convey the texture of the speech, people's characteristic thought, and interaction style. It was Shmuel, the critic and philosopher, who dubbed these stories and exchanges "bobbe-myseh." He found them inelegant and rambling. Sometimes they build to a significant point about Center people's beliefs and experiences, but even so, these are much embedded in "trivia." Seldom grand, occasionally self-serving, always vital and original, it was inconceivable to leave them out.

The middle section of the book (chapters three through six) is given to four situationally specific episodes, social or socio-cultural dramas as anthropologist Victor Turner has called such events.[21] These are public occasions wherein a significant crisis emerges and is resolved. Usually an orderly sequence of stages occurs. The drama begins when a threat to collective life is perceived. Often this happens when someone in the group violates an important rule or custom. The mechanisms that operate to contain or dispel conflict fail and the difficulty spreads, drawing in more and more members until it constitutes a genuine crisis. Some mending, some action that restores order and redresses the violation is called for, and this occurs in the third stage. The last part, the conclusion, achieves an equilibrium and often is accompanied by a realignment of social relationships where dissident factions or individuals are reintegrated into the group. The final stage of the sequence is often accomplished through symbolic displays of unity or ritual performances that affirm members' widest or most basic beliefs. This model perfectly suits the developments in two of the chapters (four and five). The other two episodes (chapters three and six) revolve around crises more of belief than social relations. They follow the same sequences as those set forth by Turner, but there is a significant difference in the redressive work they accomplish. No social rearrangements are accomplished, rather redress consists solely of the performance of the group's shared and unquestionable truths, made unquestionable by being performed. As such, these dramas are religion-in-the-making, for in them the Center people are agreeing upon and making authoritative the essential ideas that define them. In these dramas they develop their collective identity, their interpretations of their world, themselves, and their values. As well as being social dramas, the events are definitional-ceremonies, performances of identity, sanctified to the level of myth.

It was not an accident that the performamce of definitional-ceremonies often occurred among Center people. Always, self and society are known—the subjects themselves and to the witnessing audience—through enactments. Rituals and ceremonies are cultural mirrors, opportunities for presenting collective knowledge.[22] Like all mirrors, these reflections are not always accurate. They may also alter images, sometimes distorting, sometimes disguising various features, and for various reasons. More like myths than photographs, nevertheless they were the means the Center people employed to "see" themselves. Because their invisibility was so exceedingly painful to them, and they struggled to find opportunities to appear in the world, thus assuing themselves that indeed they existed. No natural audience in the form of progeny or a younger generation was recording their existence. No one would remain after they died to "bear witness" for them. They had to serve as their own witness and audience in these dramas. Enacted beliefs have a capacity for arousing belief that mere statements do not. "Doing is believing," hence ritual and ceremony generate conviction when reason and thought may fail.[23] And Judaism is particularly highly developed in the area of ritual. Center folk had tradition and ample source materials to work with here.

The character of Center social life was distinctively tumultuous and dramatic. In part this was due to the tensions arising from contradictions within their ideology, most conspicuously, betewen their Zionism and internationalism, their agnosticism and Judaism, their identification with modern American society and the Eastern European past. All cultures are ridden with internal inconsistencies, but they do not generally produce the kind of social disorganization so evident at the center. More troublesome than the inconsistencies in their beliefs were certain paradoxes or structural conflicts that disrupted solidarity and prevented their society from developing the stability it otherwise might have. Three paradoxes were particularly evident: First was people's need for passionate experiences, in opposition to their desire for dignity and harmony. Second, people had extreme need for each other socially and psychologically, with no corresponding material, economic need; this resulted in a peculiar imbalance that generated much strain and confusion. Finally, Center elders required witnesses to

their past and present life and turned to each other for this, though it is a role properly filled by the succeeding generation. Lacking suitable heirs to their traditions and stories, they were forced to use peers who, they realized, would perish along with them, and thus could not assure the preservation of what they had witnessed. Center people were tightly bound to each other, but in a web of relations that never fully coalesced into the firm, clear shapes typical of many social organizations.

Let me return now to a discussion of the Living History classes, for in these a private process was unfolded, parallel to the public processes revealed in the socio-culutral dramas. Center people, like so many of the elderly, were very fond of reminiscing and storytelling, eager to be heard from, eager to relate parts of their life history. More afraid of oblivion than pain or death, they always caught opportunities to become visible. Narrative activity among them was intense and relentless. Age and proximity to death segmented the Jewish predilection for verbal expression. In their stories they witnessed themselves, and thus knew who they were, serving as subject and object at once. They narrated themselves perpetually, in the form of keeping notes, journals, writing poems and reflections spontaneously, and also telling their stories to whoever would listen. Their histories were not devoted to marking their successes or unusual merits. Rather they were efforts at ordering, sorting, explaining—rendering coherent their long life, finding integrating ideas and characteristics that helped them know themselves as the same person over time, despite great ruptures and shifts. No doubt their emigrant experience and the loss of their original culture made them even more prone to seek continuity and coherence. Survivors, it is often noted, are strongly impelled to serve as witnesses to what has been lost. Often these materials were idealized and sentimentalized.[24] Despite its poverty and oppression, shtetl life was often described as a golden age in comparison with much of the present, which was found lacking. But in recounting the past, they kept that early life alive, weaving it into their present. Freud suggests that completion of the mourning process requires the survivor to develop a new reality that no longer includes what has been lost.[25] Judging from experience of the Center elderly, full recovery from mourning may do the very opposite—preserving what has been lost, restoring it to life by incorporation into the present; Center culture was built around just such a revitalization of the past.

I was eager to respond to Center people's desires to tell me their stories and puzzled as to how to find the means and the time to listen to as many as possible. Abe was helpful here, too. He suggested that I offer a class in the Center where people could assemble for recounting their life history. We pondered the subject together and decided it should be called "Living History." Such a class would provide a forum in which a stable group of people could reminisce and sort out their individual and collective memories, for themselves, each other, and for a written record of some sort. People would have an opportunity to bring in their writings, poems, and the like, and read them to the group, an activity they enjoyed greatly and found few opportunities for in the Center's crowded schedule. They might bring in photographs, letters, and any materials they wished to have included. The class was to be the creation of another arena of visibility and performance, an unstructured and unpressured opportunity for the elders to receive attention. The class would also provide a suitable means for me to gain entree into the community. Abe would help me get started, he said. He thought it would work, especially if I brought refreshments. But, he warned me, I would have to be careful not to let the sessions take on the appearance of group therapy. If people thought they were expected to publicly discuss their problems and share very private, painful materials, they would be reluctant. I agreed with that. But, I wondered, would people be willing to tell me, a stranger, their life history, and would they be inhibited if I tried to tape record the sessions?

Abe and I sat on a bench talking about the class in the early days of my work. Basha came out of the Center and Abe called to her, "Basha, how would you like to have the professor make a book from your life?" Basha did not hesitate. "You got a pencil? You want to get it down right. I begin with my childhood in Poland. Tell me if I go too fast. Naturally, it's a long story."

The following month, classes began. I was prepared with cookies, tea, coffee, tape recorder, and two-dozen notebooks and pencils for people who would be willing to use them at home. Abe had made a sign for the window: "New Center Class: Living History. Come and tell your story. Help teach our Professor Barbara about the beautiful life of the elderly. Tuesdays at 10." For five months we met in the little room over the Center that had recently been converted into a library, then we met again after the summer for another four months. It was light and pleasant upstairs, and quiet. But the stairs were too hard for many people and eventually the classes had to be moved to the noisy hall below. That was just as well because the upstairs room still carried the taint of therapy, having been used for that by a social worker previously. Those seen walking up were in danger of being labeled "crazies." It was used, too, for political discussions by the left-wing intellectuals, the "linkies,"[26] and others were wary of being associated with them. But we overcame these associations and met happily for two hours each week. I asked people to speak in English, or if they used Yiddish to keep it short and provide a translation, to ease the problems in transcribing the tapes. I promised everyone an opportunity to speak each week, however briefly, and insisted everyone listen to each other with a minimum of interrupting. This was very difficult for the old people and only after many weeks of meeting were they certain enough that they would have a chance to talk to manage to hold back their offerings. They—and I—used the tape recorder to good purpose. Pleading that the typist could never work with tapes in which everyone spoke at once, I turned the machine off when they tried to shout each other down. As gently as I could, I took the microphone away from anyone who went on too long. When I told them that in transcribing the notes, their names would be changed, they were disappointed. Everyone wanted to leave a personal statement, wanted to be identified with an enduring record, some indication of what had happened to them, what they believed, that they had been here.

At first a half-dozen people came, but after the word spread that there were no political fights and no insistence on public disclosure of personal matters, more attended. Soon a core of about twenty people had formed and they came faithfully. Cynics and onlookers wandered in and out from time to time. Those who would not or could not listen to the others were naturally discouraged and in time the discussions were fairly orderly. In this setting, people heard and saw one another in a new way—as they had not previously. Neighbors and *lansleit*[27] who had known each other for decades learned things never before revealed. Listening was not these people's custom. They yearned desperately for an audience, but for many reasons it was very difficult to allow others center stage. Coherence in the discussions suffered when people were required to speak strictly in turn. But only this format gave them enough trust to wait. I spoke as little as possible, occasionally focusing the topic or asking questions. Generally a common theme emerged and clustered loosely around a set of broad topics: memories of the Old World, the meaning of Being a Jew, being old, and life in America today. The people referred to me as "the teacher" and

they liked the concept and model of a class and learning, but it was soon clear that they were the teachers and I, surrogate grandchild, was the student. I was deeply moved and saddened when people blessed me for merely listening.

The longer the classes lasted, the more people had to say. They stimulated one another's memories. And they validated certain images, values, accomplishments, subtle and grand, that made their histories subject to comprehension and approval. Suffering, failure, and disappointments came into the discussion, too, and were woven, incorporated, into their accounts. The work they were doing was not a cosmetic operation; it was the search for pattern and continuity amid the accidental features of their life. Always in these stories, they sought evidence that they were still the same people now that they had once been, however transformed. The sense of constancy and recognizability, the integrity of the person over time was their essential quest. In the process they created personal myths, saying not that it had all been worthwhile, neither that it had not.[28] Truth and completeness of accounts were never at issue in this work, and no one questioned private or shared pasts. As people brought in more of the deep memories, they also brought in dreams, wishes, and questions about ultimate concerns, often profanely interlarded with daily, trivial matters, woven into the always pungent, swift, funny, cutting interchanges among them.

I loved these classes and the style of the exchanges and stories. Shmuel was right to call them grandmothers' tales, for they were the kind of rambling, bubbling, unfocused, running comments that a bobbe might tell her grandchildren without putting down her dough or her sewing. Too busy to stop and shape a tale with grace and art, but too alive to imagination and verbal expression to be silent, so she might weave a kitchen tale that despite its crude surface, came from and went to a deep place. This was

"Domestic Religion," as Rachel once called it, and its roots were in the heart and bones and genes.

Hitting on a format that allowed for storytelling was a fortunate accident. When we began the sessions, there was no way I could have anticipated the significance of these exchanges. In time it became clear that storytelling was a passion among these people, absolutely central to their culture. Even Shmuel, who disdained the Living History classes, had great respect and affection for the art of narration. Once when we were taping part of his life story, he stopped to explain why it was so important that we record his history correctly, in terms of events and with just the right attitude. He first acquired his taste and regard for stories from the "wonder rebbes," Hasidic rabbis who visited his shtetl from time to time.[29]

"Oh, the stories they would tell us, full of wisdom, full of humor. It was immense. These rebbes could speak to you in such a way that it stays with you all your life. They understood the simple people who lived in these little towns. They learned from somewhere, I don't know from where, how to put into the Bible and the Talmud a life you could never imagine. They could put you directly in touch with Abraham, Jacob, Isaac, and the God of Jacob. The rebbes knew how to put things in terms of spirits and demons, and into the most ordinary events they would bring out mysterious and wondrous things. All of us, little boys by the dozen, would follow them when they came into the town. You could always tell them by the chalk on their caftans, this they carried to mark around them a circle of chalk that would keep out the spirits. My father did not approve of me listening to them, but I would sneak out whenever I could, because what they brought you was absolutely magic. This experience was developing in me a great respect for telling stories. This is why it is important to get just the right attitude and just the right words for a story. You should get everything just right

because no matter how pleasant, it is a serious thing you are doing."

The Center people who came to the Living History classes were increasingly pleased with the storytelling sessions. Here is Rachel's comment on the class toward the end of our meetings:

All these speeches we are making reminded me of a picture I have from many years ago, when we were still in Russia. My brother had been gone already two years in America. I can see my mother like it is before me, engraved in my head. A small house she goes out of, in wintertime, going every morning in the snow to the post office, wrapped up in a shawl. Every morning there was nothing. Finally, she found a letter. In that letter was written, "Mamaleh, I didn't write to you before because I didn't have nothing to write about." "So," she says, "why didn't you write and tell me?"

You know this group of ours reminds me of that letter. When I first heard about this group, I thought to myself, "What can I learn? What can I hear that I don't know, about life in the Old Country, of the struggles, the life in the poor towns, in the bigger towns, of the rich people and the poor people? What is there to learn, I'm eighty-eight, that I haven't seen myself?" Then I think, "What can I give to anybody else? I'm not an educated woman. It's a waste of time."

That was my impression. But then I came here and heard all those stories. I knew them, but you know it was laid down deep, deep in your mind, with all those troubles mixed. You know it's there but you don't think of it, because sometimes you don't want to live in your past. Who needs all these foolish stories?

But finally, this group brought out such beautiful memories, not always so beautiful, but still, all the pictures came up. It touched the layers of the kind that it was on those dead people already. It was laying on them like layers, separate layers of earth, and all of a sudden in this class I feel it coming up like lava. It just melted away the earth from all those people. It melted away, and they became alive. And then to me it looked like they were never dead.

Then I felt like the time my mother got that letter. "Why don't you come and tell me?" "Well, I have nothing to say," I think. But I start to say it and I find something. The memories come up in me like lava. So I felt I enriched myself. And I am hoping maybe I enriched somebody else. All this, it's not only for us. It's for the generations.

NOTES

1. It is necessary to pause here to clarify some terms that I use. Technically, Center life is a part-culture or subculture, surrounded as it is by a larger, overlapping dominant outside society in which Center members also participate. The term "culture" is used to refer to Center life, however, because it is less cumbersome and because it emphasizes the uniqueness, the intensity, and significance of the Center members' common attitudes and practices, developed out of a shared past, common language, and religion.

   The term *shtetl* is surrounded by considerable confusion. Some writers have used it to refer to the territorial units in which Jews lived outside of cities in nineteenth-century Eastern Europe. Of those who stress the territorial dimension, some refer to shtetls as villages, settlements, and towns. Others, Irving Howe for example, prefer that it be preserved for units smaller than towns. Some writers mean shtetl to refer to the legally organized communities in Eastern Europe governed by Jewish regulatory organs known as *kehilla*. Many use it to signify a particular way of life or state of

mind, equating shtetl with Yiddishkeit. Much of the confusion stems from the fact that the most widely read work on the subject, *Life Is with the People: The Culture of the Shtetl* by Mark Zborowski and Elizabeth Herzog, is a valuable though seriously flawed work, as Barbara Kirshenblatt-Gimblett has pointed out. The book is an ethnography based on reconstructed materials rather than first-hand observations, and is generally agreed to be overly general, idealized, and static. Since its appearance three decades ago, many authors have used the term shtetl very broadly: to signify contemporary Jewish ghettoes in the New World, life in the Pale of Settlement in the Old World, and all manifestations of immigrant cultures historically based on Eastern European life, regardless of enormous regional and national variations.

   Center old people also used the term shtetl to refer to their childhood culture, whether they had lived primarily in cities in Eastern Europe or not. They too idealized these memories and generalized about them, minimizing internal and external variations in the culture. Nevertheless, I have adopted their usage, employing the word to mean their childhood experiences, memories, and the culture of Yiddishkeit. To distinguish between the elders' recollections and actual experiences was not my purpose, nor was it possible. Rather I wished to render their interpretation of their past and present lives.

   "Shtetl life" or Yiddishkeit are terms that can and often have been equated with Robert Redfield's concept of *folk culture*. In this notion, Redfield points to a small community that is isolated, stable, homogeneous, and in which members share a strong sense of identity with each other and the community. Their behavior is highly personalized and their world is dominated by the family. In outlook their attitudes are more sacred than secular. Local traditions are strong and cherished. The Center people's life in the present, and in the past, resembled Redfield's folk culture in all the features just mentioned, and is applicable with a few exceptions: Most notably, Redfield had a non-literate group in mind and these people are certainly literate. And unlike people in a folk society as Redfield understands it, Center folk had extensive contacts with outsiders: intellectual, economic, and legal. But in terms of the importance of intimate relationships, strong common identity, and possessing its own language, religion, values, social institutions, and shared common identity, one may speak of Center life and Yiddishkeit—in the Old and New World—as constituting a valid example of a folk culture.

2. Mother tongue.

3. Most beautiful.

4. The word *Holocaust* referring in this setting in Hitler's destruction of six million Jews, mostly Eastern European, was not used casually by these people.

5. Irving Howe, *The World of Our Fathers*, p. 8.

6. Claude Lévi-Strauss, *The Savage Mind*, p. 17.

7. A dreidel is a top used for a Chanukah game; a menorah is the branched candelabra also used for Chanukah; a shofar is the Ram's Horn blown on the Jewish New Year.

8. The land of Israel; the Promised Land.

9. The "Enlightenment" or "Awakening."

10. Will Herberg, *Protestant-Catholic-Jew: An Essay in American Religious Sociology.*

11. In doing fieldwork, an anthropologist "becomes the phenomenon" being studied, by taking on the reality of the observed peoples. But some part of oneself is usually held back for self-protection, and justified methodologically as providing the objectivity necessary for scientific observation. Hugh Mehan and Houston Wood, in a discussion of the paradox of belonging and not-belonging to an observed culture, lament this "methodological aloofness," stating that it is unacceptable because it prevents the fieldworker from effectively knowing the people being studied by preventing the researcher from "becoming one of them." They urge a greater involvement. "The researcher cannot hold back. The researcher who holds back in the name of objectivity never comes to respect [the] reality [being studied] or be respected by its practitioners." "Membership," they insist,

"cannot be simulated." See *The Reality of Ethnomethodology*, p. 227.

12. See the author's *Peyote Hunt: The Sacred Journey of the Huichol Indians.*

13. A little story or folk tale.

14. For further discussion of the complex question of survivor's guilt, see the following in particular: Robert Jay Lifton, *Death in Life: Survivors of Hiroshima;* Terrence Des Pres, *The Survivor: An Anatomy of Life in the Death Camps;* Dorothy Rabinowitz, *New Lives: Survivors of the Holocaust Living in America;* Bruno Bettelheim, "Reflections: Surviving," *The New Yorker,* August 2, 1976, pp. 31–52.

15. Elie Wiesel and Bruno Bettelheim point out that survivors and all those who have "borne witness" are ultimately an embarrassment to a world that would find it much easier if they simply weren't around. See Bettelheim, "Reflections," p. 52. Says Des Pres, we protect ourselves by discrediting the unbearable tales told by survivors. "The survivor, then, is a disturber of the peace. He is a runner of the blockade men erect against knowledge of 'unspeakable' things." Des Pres, *Survivor,* p. 45. "Thus we undermine the survivor's authority by pointing to his guilt. If he is guilty, then perhaps it is true that the victims of atrocity collaborate in their own destruction; in which case blame can be imputed to the victims themselves. And if he is guilty, then the survivor's suffering…is deserved; in which case a balance between *that* pain and our own is restored." Ibid., p. 44.

16. Himself a survivor, Bettelheim points to what he considers one of the deepest lessons learned from having lived through the concentration camps, not that life is meaningless but that it is the very opposite—full of meaning. The discovery of one's humanity can occur through the experience of survival guilt. He says, "And our feeling of guilt for having been so lucky as to survive the hell of the concentration camp is a most significant part of this meaning—testimony to a humanity that not even the abomination of the concentration camp can destroy." Bettelheim, "Reflections," p. 52. Viktor

E. Frankl's classic work, *Man's Search for Meaning,* makes the same point.

17. Lifton, *Death in Life,* p. 526.

18. Des Pres, *Survivors,* p. 43.

19. *Enemies, A Love Story.* For further discussion of difficulties experienced by Jews in writing about themselves—and other Jews—see Philip Roth, "Writing About Jews," *Reading Myself and Others,* pp. 135–153.

20. The film, also entitled *Number Our Days,* is a thirty-minute 16mm color sound documentary, produced and directed by Lynne Littman for KCET, Community Television of Southern California, Los Angeles. It received many awards, including an Academy Award for Best Short Documentary in 1977.

21. Victor Turner, *Dramas, Fields and Metaphors: Symbolic Action in Human Society.*

22. The interpretation of culture as a reflecting surface, part of the developing area of reflexive sociology, was explored by Barbara Babcock, Victor Turner, and others who attended a conference entitled "Cultural Frames and Reflections: Ritual, Drama and Spectacle," held in August 1977 at Burg-Wartenstein, Austria, sponsored by the Wenner-Gren Foundation for Anthropological Research, convened by Turner, Babcock, and myself. I am indebted to Barbara Babcock who introduced me to this subject. Her dissertation presents an excellent summary.

23. Sally F. Moore and Barbara G. Myerhoff, "Introduction: Forms and Meanings" in *Secular Ritual,* pp. 3–24. Also, Roy A. Rappaport, "Ritual Sanctity and Cybernetics," *American Anthropologist* 73 (1): pp. 59–76.

24. Lifton, *Death in Life,* p. 534. In fact many of the Center folk had spent only part of their childhood in shtetls. But even those who had not resided within them for most of their early life had come to regard the shtetl as their place of origin and were inclined to use the shtetl as a symbol for Yiddishkeit, a cultural form that did indeed embrace everyone.

25. Freud, *Death, Grief and Mourning.*

26. Left-winger.

27. Fellow countrymen.

28. Andrew Erlich is presently exploring the therapeutic functions of storytelling among the elderly. His forthcoming dissertation will present the results of his study. Robert Butler (1969), Barbara Myerhoff, and Virginia Tufte (1975) have published articles on the benefits of autobiographical work among the elderly. Kenneth Koch's work with the elderly, using a collective poetry writing class, seems to have many similarities with the discourse and emotions aroused in these Living History classes. See his *I Never Told Anybody: Teaching Poetry in a Nursing Home.* For works that give evidence of the significance of storytelling as a powerful and necessary human activity, see Reynolds Price, *A Palpable God: Thirty Stories Translated from the Bible with an Essay on the Origins and Life of Narrative.* I am especially indebted to Jerome Rothenberg's collections of poetry and essays that emphasize the importance of orally transmitted tales, "in which the word is renewed by being re-sounded." These ideas are set forth in *A Big Jewish Book: Poems and Other Visions of the Jews from Tribal Times to Present* and in an unpublished essay entitled "The Poetics of Performance," delivered at the Burg-Wartenstein Conference, Austria, 1977. One of the greatest practitioners and appreciators of the significance of oral traditions among the Jews is Elie Wiesel, especially in *Souls on Fire: Portraits and Legends of Hasidic Masters.*

29. Hasidism was a form of popular Judaism, an intensely personal, often mystical revitalization movement influential in Europe in the eighteenth and nineteenth centuries. Because of the fervor of its expression and emotional appeal to the poor and uneducated, it was opposed by the established rabbinate in many communities who regarded it as a threat to orthodoxy, order, and authority. Among the Hasidim, " ...Torah took the form of an inexhaustible fountain of storytelling," according to Gershom G. Scholem whose work *Major Trends in Jewish Mysticism* is a definitive study of the subject.

REFERENCES

Babcock, Barbara. 1975. *Mirrors, Masks, and Metafiction: Studies in Narrative Reflexivity.* Doctoral dissertation. Department of English, University of Chicago, 1975.

Bettelheim, Bruno. 1943. "Individual and Mass Behavior in Extreme Situations." *Journal of Abnormal and Social Psychology* 38(4): 417–452.

———. "Reflections: Surviving." 1976. *The New Yorker* (August 2): 31–52.

Butler, Robert N. 1968. "The Life Review: An Interpretation of Reminiscence in the Aged." In *Middle Age and Aging.* Bernice L. Neugarten (ed.). Chicago: Chicago University Press.

Des Pres, Terrence. 1977. *The Survivor: An Anatomy of Life in the Death Camps.* New York: Pocket Books.

Frankl, Victor E. 1973. *Man's Search for Meaning: An Introduction to Logotherapy.* Translated by Ilse Lasch. New York: Pocket Books.

Freud, Sigmund. 1965. *Death, Grief and Mourning.* New York: Doubleday.

Herberg, Will. 1955. *Protestant-Catholic-Jew: An Essay in American Religious Sociology.* New York: Anchor Books.

Howe, Irving. 1976. *World of Our Fathers.* New York: Harcourt, Brace, Jovanovich.

Kirshenblatt-Gimblett, Barbara. 1976. "The *Shtetl* Model in East European Jewish Ethnology," paper presented at the American Anthropological Association meeting, Washington, D.C.

Koch, Kenneth. 1977. *I Never Told Anybody: Teaching Poetry Writing in a Nursing Home.* New York: Random House.

Lévi-Strauss, Claude. 1966. *The Savage Mind.* Translated by G. Weidenfeld and Nicolson Ltd. Chicago: University of Chicago Press.

Lifton, Robert Jay. 1967. *Death in Life: Survivors of Hiroshima.* New York: Simon and Schuster.

Mehan, Hugh and Wood, Houston. 1975. *The Reality of Ethnomethodology.* New York: John Wiley and Sons.

Moore, Sally F. and Myerhoff, Barbara G. 1977. "Introduction: Forms and Meanings." In *Secular Ritual.* Sally F. Moore and Barbara G. Myerhoff (eds.). Amsterdam: Van Gorcum.

Myerhoff, Barbara G. 1974. *Peyote Hunt: The Sacred Journey of the Huichol Indians.* Ithaca: Cornell University Press.

Myerhoff, Barbara G., and Tufte, Virginia. "Life History as Integration: Personal Myth and Aging." *The Gerontologist.*

Price, Reynolds. 1978. *A Palpable God: Thirty Stories Translated from the Bible with an Essay on the Origins and Life of Narrative.* New York: Atheneum.

Rabinowitz, Dorothy. 1976. *New Lives: Survivors of the Holocaust Living in America.* New York: Avon Books.

Rappaport, Roy. 1971. "Ritual Sanctity and Cybernetics." *American Anthropologist* 73(1): 59–76.

Redfield, Robert. 1960. *The Little Community and Peasant Society and Culture.* Chicago: The University of Chicago Press.

Roth, Philip. 1977. "Writing About Jews," *Reading Myself and Others.* New York: Bantam Books.

Rothenberg, Jerome. 1978. *The Big Jewish Book: Poems and Other Visions of the Jews from Tribal Times to the Present.* New York: Doubleday.

———. 1977. "The Poetics of Performance." Paper delivered to the Burg-Wartenstein Conference on "Cultural Frames and Reflections: Ritual, Drama and Spectacle," sponsored by Wenner-Gren Foundation for Anthropological Research. Austria.

Scholem, Gershom G. 1961. *Major Trends in Jewish Mysticism.* New York: Schocken Books.

Singer, Isaac Bashevis. 1973. *Enemies, A Love Story.* Greenwich: Fawcett Crest.

Turner, Victor W. 1974. *Dramas, Fields and Metaphors: Symbolic Action in Human Society.* Ithaca: Cornell University Press.

Wiesel, Elie. 1973. *Souls on Fire: Portraits and Legends of Hasidic Masters.* Marion Wiesel (trans.). New York: Vintage Books.

Zborowski, Mark and Herzog, Elizabeth. 1952. *Life Is with the People: The Culture of the Shtetl.* New York: Schocken Books.

49

PHILIPPE BOURGOIS

VIOLATING APARTHEID IN THE UNITED STATES

from *In Search of Respect* (1996)

In 1985, the anthropologist Philippe Bourgois and his wife moved into a tenement apartment in East Harlem—a poor neighborhood whose population was mostly Puerto Rican and African American. This selection gives a snapshot of the trials and tribulations inherent in a white male ethnographer trying to win the trust and acceptance of a group of Puerto Rican men deeply embedded in the illegal and violent crack trade.

We love listening to you talk. It makes us laugh. You sound just like a television advertisement.

—giggling eight-year-old

My research on the streets of Spanish Harlem almost came to a disastrous end just after the halfway point when I inadvertently "disrespected" Ray, the man who owned the crackhouses where I spent much of my time between 1985 and 1990. It was just after midnight, and Ray was visiting his most profitable sales point to make sure the manager of the late-night shift had opened punctually. Business was booming and the heavyset, thirty-two-year-old Puerto Rican crack entrepreneur was surrounded by his coterie of employees, friends, and wanna-be acquaintances—all eager for his attention. We were on the corner of 110th Street by the entrance to the Lexington Avenue subway station right in front of the abandoned four-story tenement building occupied by Ray's dealers. He had camouflaged the ground floor as an after-hours bootleg social club and pool hall. Ray and many of his employees had grown up in this very tenement before its Italian owner burned it down to collect its insurance value. Their corner has long been nicknamed "La Farmacia" because of the unique diversity of psychoactive substances available: from standard products like heroin, Valium, powder cocaine, and crack to more recherché, offbeat items like mescaline and angel dust.[1]

Learning Street Smarts

In retrospect I wince at my lack of street smarts for accidentally humiliating the man who was crucial not only to my continued access to the crack scene, but also to my physical security. Perhaps, despite my two and a half years of crackhouse experience at that point, I was justified in being temporarily seduced by the night's friendly aura. Ray was leaning on the front bumper of his gold Mercedes smiling and chatting—happy with life. His followers and employees were also happy because Ray had just treated us all to a round of beers and had promised to order some lobster takeout from the lone surviving hole-in-the-wall Chinese restaurant down the block. We all loved it when Ray was in one of his good moods; it made the man capable of unpredictable largesse, which contrasted dramatically with his usual churlishness. The night was young, and comfortably warm. The emaciated junkies, crackheads, and intravenous coke freaks who gather on La Farmacia's corner twenty-four hours a day, seven days a week, had retreated respectfully across the street, occasionally eyeing our closely knit group enviously. We controlled the space.

Perhaps it was also only normal for me to want to bask in my increasingly close and privileged relationship with the "main man." Earlier that week Ray had confided to me the intimate details of his stickup artist past. According to his account, he had specialized in holding up drug spots until he

was ambushed by a hidden lookout while fleeing with $14,000 from a high-volume heroin outlet. It ended with a rooftop shoot-out and a four-and-a-half-year prison sentence for him. His sister posted bail following his arrest by recovering the $14,000 wad of bills that he had managed to stuff into a half-empty can of roofing tar just before his arrest.

Perhaps my guard was also down because Ray had just made a point, in front of everyone, of buying me a bottle of Heineken's instead of the fifteen-cents-cheaper can of Budweiser that everyone else had received. He had said loudly and clearly for everyone to hear, "Felipe, you drink Heineken's don't tcha'?" I felt even more privileged when I saw that he had purchased a Heineken for himself as well, as if to distinguish us from the run-of-the-mill street drinkers by our distinctively green imported bottles.

Surrounded by all this good feeling and security, I thought it might be a good moment to share my minor media coup from earlier that day: a photograph of me on page 4 of the *New York Post* standing next to Phil Donahue following a prime-time television debate on violent crime in East Harlem.[2] I hoped this would impress Ray and his entourage, raising my credibility as a "real professor," capable of accessing the mainstream world of white-dominated daytime television. I was eager to legitimize my presence because there were still a few people in Ray's network who suspected that I was an imposter—nothing more than a fast-talking closet drug addict, or a pervert—pretending to be a "stuck-up professor." Worse yet, my white skin and outsider class background kept some people convinced to the very end of my residence in the neighborhood that I was really a narcotics agent on a long-term undercover assignment.

I noticed Ray stiffen uncharacteristically as I proudly pushed the newspaper into his hands—but it was too late to stop. I had already called out loudly for everyone to hear "Yo! Big Ray! Check out this picture of me in the papers!" A half-dozen of the voices surrounding the large man were already urging him to read the caption on the photo. There was an eager silence as he fumbled awkwardly with the newspaper, not quite knowing how to hold the pages open without having them flap loudly in the gentle breeze. I tried to help by pointing directly to the lines where the caption began. Flustered, he feigned indifference and tried to throw the newspaper into the gutter, but the voices of his admirers were calling out aggressively now for him to read the blurb under my picture. "Come on Ray! What's the matter? What's it say? Read it! Read it!" Unable to save face, he desperately angled the paper to get a fuller beam from the streetlight above us, and screwed his face into an expression of intense concentration. I suddenly realized what the problem was: Ray did not know how to read.

Unfortunately, he tried. He painfully stumbled through the entire caption—ironically entitled "The Calm After the Storm"—his face contorted into an expression akin to that of a dyslexic second-grader who has been singled out for ridicule by his teacher. The eager silence of his followers was broken by embarrassed, muffled giggles. Ray's long-buried and overcompensated childhood wound of institutional failure had burst open. He looked up; regained his deadpan street scowl, threw down the paper, and screamed, "Fuck you Felipe! I don't care about this shit! Get out of here! All of you's!" He then somewhat clumsily pushed his oversized body into his Mercedes, revved the motor, and screeched his tires as he sped away from the corner impervious to the red light, or to the Auschwitz-like survivors on La Farmacia's far curb who dodged his flying wheels and continued to hawk Valium, adulterated heroin, cocaine, and animal tranquilizers.[3]

Primo, my closest friend on the streets...and the manager of Ray's other crackhouse, known as the "Game Room," located in a bogus video arcade two doors down from the rat-infested tenement where I lived with my wife and infant child—turned to me with a worried expression, "Yo, Felipe! You dissed the fat nigga'." Someone else picked the crumpled newspaper out of the gutter and started to read the offending article and to comment on the quality of the photograph. Most of the other hangers-on simply lost interest, disappointed that there would be no more freebees from the head drug dealer that night. They straggled back inside the crackhouse to listen to rap music, play pool, and watch anxious addicts pour through the doors clutching handfuls of dollar bills.

The Parameters of Violence, Power, and Generosity

Ray recovered his dignity by redefining his anger as a legitimate concern over the potential breach of security that my exposure in the press represented. The next time I ran into him as he was delivering a fresh shipment of crack vials and picking up the midshift's sales at the Game Room next to my house, he pulled me aside gruffly, speaking in a loud voice for all to hear:

> Felipe, let me tell you something, people who get people busted—even if it's by mistake—sometimes get found in the garbage with their heart ripped out and their bodies chopped up into little pieces...or else maybe they just get their fingers stuck in electrical sockets. You understand what I'm saying?

He then hurried out to his double-parked Lincoln Continental with black-tinted windows, stumbling clumsily over a curled linoleum fragment in the Game Room entrance. To my dismay, his teenage girlfriend, who was waiting impatiently chewing gum in her powerful lover's car, chose this moment to look up from her scowl and eyeball me intensely. Terrified lest Ray think that on top of everything else I was flirting with his new girlfriend, I stared at the ground and lamely hung my head.

Primo was worried. He had known Ray all his life. As a child, Ray who is ten years older than Primo, had been the leader of two loosely knit youth gangs that Primo and most of Ray's other employers had been involved with in their early teens: the TCC (The Cheeba [marijuana] Crew)[4] and *la Mafia Boba* (the Sly Mafia).[5] He had taught Primo how to steal car radios and burglarize downtown businesses. I tried to laugh off Ray's warning and recover some of my flustered dignity by cracking one of the misogynist jokes they frequently used to dismiss their boss's nasty mood swings: "The fat yak is on the rag. He'll get over it. Chill out man." But Primo shook his head somewhat apologetically; he pulled me out of the Game Room onto the curb to tell me in a hushed voice, that I should make myself scarce around the Game Room for the next few weeks. "You don't understand Felipe, that nigga' is crazy. He's respected on the streets. People know about him. He was wild when he was a kid. He's got juice." When I interrupted Primo somewhat confrontationally in a loud voice with "You mean you're scared of Ray?" Primo responded with what at that stage in our friendship was still a rare admission of vulnerability.

Hell yeah! I know that nigga' since I was little. He was weird man. Used to think he would rape me or something. Because he's a big nigga', and I'm a little guy back then. I'm only fifteen, boy. And he used to talk crazy shit like, "One of these days I'm gonna get that ass." And I used to wonder if that was true. I never used to dare to be alone with him.

To press his point Primo camouflaged his memories of childhood terror by proceeding casually with an account of how Ray

and his best childhood friend, Luis, once raped an old male transient in the empty lot next to the Game Room. I had turned my tape recorder off, unconsciously enforcing the taboo on public discussions of rape. Caesar, however, Primo's best friend who was working as lookout at the Game Room, joined us outside and insisted I document the tale. He mistook my expression of shock to be a sign of fear that someone passing by on the street might be suspicious or angry at seeing a "white boy" holding out a tape recorder to two Puerto Rican men.

CAESAR: Take the recorder out, ain't no one going to do nothing to you here Felipe.

PRIMO: Yeah! They fucked some dirty old man bum in the butt. They followed him in the yard over there [pointing to the garbage strewn rubble to our right].

CAESAR: Yeah! Yeah!

PRIMO: Ray and Luis takes turns boning the man in the ass right over there [walking halfway into the lot to mark the spot].

CAESAR: Real crazy. Yeah! Ray's a fuckin' pig; Ray's a wild motherfucker. He's got juice. You understand Felipe? Juice!...On the street that means respect.

Ignoring Caesar's outburst, Primo proceeded to explain how Ray at that very moment was debating whether or not to have Luis—his fellow rapist, childhood friend, and employee—killed rather than having to spend money on legal fees following Luis's recent arrest while delivering a bundle[6] of crack to the Game Room crackhouse. Coincidentally, the cost of a murder contract was the same as the fee demanded by Luis's lawyer: $3,000. Even though Luis—who was also Primo's first cousin—had grown up as Ray's best friend, he was no longer trusted because of his crack habit. He hustled money compulsively from everyone around him, and, worse yet, he had a reputation as a *chiota,* a stool pigeon. It was rumored that several years earlier he had broken down under police interrogation following an arrest for burglary and reported his own godmother's husband for fencing stolen objects.

These assertions and rumors of Ray's ruthlessness and even cruelty were an integral part of his effectiveness at running his network of crackhouses smoothly. Regular displays of violence are essential for preventing tip-offs by colleagues, customers, and professional holdup artists. Indeed, upward mobility in the underground economy of the street-dealing world requires a systematic and effective use of violence against one's colleagues, one's neighbors, and, to a certain extent, against oneself. Behavior that appears irrationally violent, "barbaric," and ultimately self-destructive to the outsider, can be reinterpreted according to the logic of the underground economy as judicious public relations and long-term investment in one's "human capital development."[7] Primo and Caesar explained this to me in less academic terms early on in my relationship to them.

> PRIMO: It's not good to be too sweet sometimes to people, man, because they're just gonna take advantage of you. You could be a nice and sweet person in real life but you gotta have a little meanness in you and play street. Like, "Get the fuck outta my face." Or "I don't give a fuck." That way you don't let nobody fuck with you later.
>
> CAESAR: Yeah, like me. People think that I'm wild.
>
> PRIMO: Out here, you gotta be a little wild in the streets.
>
> CAESAR: You've got to be a little wild for this neighborhood, Felipe. [gunshots] What did I tell you? You can't be allowing people to push you around, then people think that you're a punk

and shit like that. And that's the whole point: making people think you're cool so that nobody bothers you. You don't really want to be a bully or violent or nothing. But you can't let people push you around, because when the other guys see that, they want to do the same thing too. You get that reputation, like, "That nigga's soft." And there's a way of not having really big fights or nothing, but having the rep—like "That dude's cool; don't mess with him"—without even having to hit nobody. And then there's the other way of just total violence.

Fully aware of the potential consequences of Ray's public warning in front of the crackhouse, I gave him a wide berth. Primo and his lookout Caesar cooperated fully to protect me. We worked out a modus vivendi so that I could continue visiting them at the Game Room during working hours without risking a confrontation with Ray. Primo "hired" one of the addicts on the corner to warn with a whistle whenever he saw Ray's car approaching so that I could slip out of the crackhouse to the safety of my apartment building two doors down.

After several weeks of maintaining this cautious low profile at the Game Room, I was still not rehabilitated. Primo warned me that Ray had foreboding dreams about me:

> Ray dreamt you was some kind of agent— like an FBI or CIA agent—no it was more like you was from Mars or something, that you was sent here to spy on us.

Everyone took this symbolic warning seriously because dreams have a powerful significance in Puerto Rican culture. Meshed with the Afro-Caribbean religious practices of *Santería,* their import may even be greater in the hybrid "Nuyorican culture" of second- and third-generation New York–born Puerto Ricans in the inner city.

My camouflaged visits to the crackhouse continued for almost three more months until finally one night Ray arrived on foot instead of by car, surprising us all in the midst of an uproarious conversation. Primo and I were trying to calm the lookout, Caesar, who had drunk too much rum and coincidentally was venting his resentment of Ray's authoritarianism. Caesar, who was nicknamed "C-Zone" because of the frequency of his drug and alcohol binges, had to be watched closely and taken seriously because of his propensity for gratuitous violence. In our attempts to quiet Caesar down, we had been ineffectively warning him of Ray's rules against obstreperous behavior in his crackhouses.

CAESAR: Ray's been riffin' [complaining]? He's gonna come in and say I'm not allowed no more to associate?
PRIMO: Don't worry. Just don't make no noises. Don't worry about it.
CAESAR: I'll tell you about Ray. He's the fattest, laziest, son of a bitch in the fuckin' East. 'Cause he's a drink-Budweiser, be-fat-motherfucker. [pausing to vomit in the trash can at the entrance] He's one of those motherfuckers that whenever the fuck, he feel good, everybody else gonna watch out.He don't wanta let anybody make money. Well. I teach that nigga' ... Ah kill that fat-assed Michelin man. The only reason I don't kill that fat son of a bitch is because I'm going to fuck him up.[facing me] You recording this shit, Felipe? Fuck you man![turning back to Primo] You talking a lotta shit too, Primo, because you're scared of that fat motherfucker. But ah' kill him. Ah' kill that fat motherfucker. I kill him.... He's just a black, ugly nigga', a black-a-claus, a fat yak.[spinning back to me again] I'm scared if I'm sober. I wouldn't talk this shit...[pointing to the tape recorder] but since I drunk, I kill that fat son of a

bitch.Understand? [screaming directly into the microphone] Ah' kill that motherfucker!
PRIMO: [changing his tone somewhat aggressively] You wouldn't do shit.
CAESAR: [in an almost sober tone] I would too. I would even murder someone. That shit is like wild. Ah'm'a nut case man. What's the matter? You never thought about that shit, man?
PRIMO: You must be a simpleton to do something like that.
CAESAR: Just think! I should become a wild murderer, man.
PRIMO: You believe that shit, Philippe?
PHILIPPE: Yes. I believe it. I just don't want to be around when be does the killing.

Right at this point, just as we were on the verge of coaxing Caesar into laughing to defuse his mounting rage, Ray stepped into the Game Room unannounced. My racing adrenaline immediately subsided when Ray merely smiled at me and cracked an insignificant, hostile joke about how skinny I looked and how awkwardly my pants fit. We all laughed with relief—even Caesar, who had suddenly become as subdued and bewildered as me.

Over the next few months my relationship with Ray gradually improved until by the end of a year I had achieved the same levels of confidence with the man that I had originally enjoyed prior to my gaffe in exposing his illiteracy. I remember with relief when he began greeting me, once again, with his usual question. "How's that book comin' Felipe? Finished yet?" thereby communicating to everyone within earshot that I had his formal permission to be prying into his personal business.

Ray's followers did not remain loyal to him solely out of fear and violence. Some of the older members of his network genuinely liked him. He was capable of reciprocating friendship. For example, Candy, an old childhood friend of his and one of only two women who sold for him during the years I frequented his crackhouses, described him affectionately:

> He was like a Gumby Bear as a kid. He was always a nice kid.
> [pausing thoughtfully] He was wild; but not wild in the sense for you to hate him.
> We were like brothers and sisters. He always helped me out.
> And don't get me wrong, when he gave me money he always did it out of the goodness of his own heart.

The Barriers of Cultural Capital

Whether Ray was a Gumby Bear, a violent pervert, or an omnipotent street don "with juice," my long-term relationship with the man ultimately uncovered a vulnerability that he kept hidden in his street persona. In his private conversations with me over his aspirations for the future, he often seemed naive or even learning-disabled. He was completely incapable of fathoming the intricate rules and regulations of legal society despite his brilliant success at directing a retail network for crack distribution. To borrow the French sociologist Pierre Bourdieu's analytical category, Ray lacked the "cultural capital" necessary to succeed in the middle-class—or even the working-class—world. Ironically, by the time I left New York in August 1991, my relationship to Ray became problematic once again, but this time because he trusted me too much. He expected me to serve as his cultural broker to the outside world, ultimately demanding that I help him launder his money. It began with a harmless phone call: "Felipe, do you know how I can get a picture I.D.?"

Despite all his cars, and the wads of cash padding his pockets, Ray did not even have a driver's license or any other form of legal identification. He was helpless outside the cocoon of El Barrio's streets. He had no concept of how to deal with bureaucracies. New York City's Department of Motor Vehicles rejected the photocopy of his birth certificate when he applied for a license, insisting that he needed a picture I.D. I explained to him what a passport was, and how to obtain one. Soon he was asking me to accompany him through all the bureaucratic hoops that kept him from being able to operate as a legal entrepreneur. He wanted me to come with him to police auctions to review the lists of tax-defaulted and drug-bust confiscated buildings that the City of New York sponsors several times a year. His dream was to buy an abandoned building, renovate it, and establish a legal business. Careful not to offend the man in any way, I always concocted excuses to avoid unwittingly becoming a facilitator to his money-laundering schemes, which inevitably failed miserably as soon as he encountered institutionalized bureaucracies or any kind of formal paperwork.

The first legal business Ray attempted to establish was a Laundromat. He was unable to wade through the bureaucratic maze of permits, however, and gave up after a few weeks. He then bought the lease on a bodega, a corner grocery store, and thought he had obtained the rights to its second-hand liquor license and health permit, but ran afoul of the bureaucracy once again and abandoned the project. His most successful foray into the legal economy was his purchase of the lease on a former garment factory a few blocks uptown from the Game Room, He converted it into a "legitimate" social club, renting the space out for parties and selling beer without a liquor license. He was proud of this new operation and considered it legal because he kept it rigorously "clean." He expressly forbade drugs from being sold on the premises. New York City closed the social club down in 1992, following the implementation of the Peoples with

Disabilities Act, as it was not wheelchair accessible.

Confronting Race, Class, and the Police

Ray represented only one of the many complex personal relationships and ethical contradictions I had to balance while living in the crack-dealer scene. Before I even was able to establish my first relationship with a crack dealer I had to confront the overwhelming reality of racial and class-based apartheid in America. When I first moved into my irregularly heated tenement opposite a massive conglomeration of high-rise, subsidized housing projects sheltering more than five thousand families,[8] I was painfully aware of my outsider status whenever I initially attempted to access any street-dealing scenes. The first time I walked home from the subway station I went down a side street that happened to be a heroin "copping corner" where a half dozen different "companies" competed with each other to sell ten-dollar glassine bags with official, ink-stamped logos. I was greeted by a hail of whistles and echoing shouts of *bajando* [coming down]"—the coded alarms that lookouts posted on dealing corners use to announce the approach of a potential undercover agent to the "pitchers" who make the actual hand-to-hand sales. Everyone began scattering in front of me as if I had the plague; all of a sudden the block was desolate. I felt as if I was infested with vermin, as if my white skin signaled the terminal stage of some kind of contagious disease sowing havoc in its path. On this occasion my feelings were hurt; I had been feeling lonely and had walked a block out of my way to reach this particularly busy corner precisely because of the exciting bustle of activity surrounding it. In my hopeful naiveté I had thought that the eager knots of pedestrians coming and

going signaled the location of one of the street fairs that often grace East Harlem streets like a splash of charm in springtime—relics from a small-town past.

In the long run it was not my conspicuous profile as a potential undercover narcotics agent that became my biggest obstacle to accessing crackhouses and copping corners but, rather, my white drug addict profile. I was almost never harassed by the street sellers; at worst, they simply fled from me or ignored me. On the other hand, I was repeatedly stopped, searched, cursed, and humiliated by New York City police officers on the beat. From their perspective there was no reason for a white boy to be in the neighborhood unless he was an undercover cop or a drug addict, and because I am skinny they instantly assumed the latter. Only one time was I able successfully to impersonate a narcotics officer when stopped by angry police officers. I was in a corner grocery store-cum-numbers joint on my block, buying an ice-cream sandwich and a beer with one of Primo's part-time crack dealer lookouts, when a heavyset white undercover police officer pushed me across the ice-cream counter, spreading my legs and poking me around the groin. As he came dangerously close to the bulge in my right pocket, I hissed in his ear, "It's a tape recorder." He snapped backward, releasing his left hand's grip on my neck, whispering a barely audible "Sorry." Apparently he thought he had inadvertently intercepted an undercover officer from another unit because before I could get a close look at his face he had exited. Meanwhile the marijuana sellers stationed in front of the bodega, observing that the undercover had been rough with me when he searched through my pants, suddenly felt safe and relieved, confident that I was a white drug addict rather than an undercover; and one of them—the tallest and burliest with flashing eyes that suggested recent ingestion of angel dust—promptly came barreling through the door to mug everyone waiting in line at the cash register.

Many of my approximately bimonthly encounters with the police did not end so smoothly. My first encounter with the police was my worst. It was 2:00 A.M. and I was on a notorious crack-copping corner three blocks from where I lived, chatting with a street dealer who was the former boyfriend of one of my neighbors. He had told me to wait with him because his shift had just ended and as soon as the night manager collected the receipts he was going "to go party" and he wanted me to accompany him. I was eager to please him; happy that I had finally found an entrée into this new and particularly active crack scene. He was already introducing me to his colleagues and competitors as a long lost friend and neighbor of his "ex-girl," thereby finally dispelling their conviction that I was a police officer. All of a sudden a patrol car flashed its lights, tooted its siren, and screeched to a halt next to us. To my surprise the officers called out to me and not to my crack-dealing acquaintance: "Hey, white boy! Come ovah' hea'h." For the next fifteen minutes I found myself shouted at, cursed, and generally humiliated in front of a growing crowd of crack dealer/addict spectators. My mistake that night was to try to tell the police officers the truth when they asked me, "What the hell you doin' hea'h?" When they heard me explain, in what I thought was a police voice, that I was an anthropologist studying poverty and marginalization, the largest of the two officers in the car exploded:

> What kind of a fuckin' moron do you think I am. You think I don't know what you're doin'? You think I'm stupid? You're babbling, you fuckin' drug addict. You're dirty white scum! Go buy your drugs in a white neighborhood! If you don't get the hell out of here right now, motherfucka', you're gonna hafta repeat your story in the precinct. You want me to take you in? Hunh?...Hunh? Answer, me motherfucka'!

After ineffectual protests that merely prompted further outrage, I was reduced to staring at the ground, mumbling "Yes sir," and shuffling obediently to the bus stop to take the next transportation downtown. Behind me I heard: "If I see you around here later, white boy, ah'm'a' take you in!"[9]

I eventually learned how to act appropriately. By my second year on the street my adrenaline would no longer pump in total panic when police officers pushed me against a wall and made me stand spread-eagled to be patted down for weapons and drugs. My accent proved to be a serious problem in these encounters because patrol officers in East Harlem are almost always white males from working-class backgrounds with heavy Irish- or Italian-American dictions. In contrast to the Puerto Rican and African-American children on my block, who used to marvel at what they called my "television advertisement voice," the police officers assumed I was making fun of them, or putting on airs when I spoke politely to them in complete sentences. I learned that my only hope was to shorten my encounters with the patrol officers by staring at the ground, rapidly handing over my driver's license, and saying "yes-sir-officer" or "no-sir-officer" in minimalist, factual phrases. When I tried to sound sincere, friendly—or even polite—I risked offending them.

Conversely, on the occasions when the police tried to be polite to me their actions only reinforced my sense of violating hidden apartheid laws. On one occasion a squad car overtook me as I was riding my bicycle, to make sure I was not lost or insane: "You know where ya going? This is Harlem!" Another time as I was sitting on my stoop at sunset to admire the spectacular colors that only New York City's summer smog can produce, a patrolman on the beat asked me, "What're you doing here?" I quickly showed him my driver's license with my address to prove I had a right to be loitering in public. He laughed incredulously. "You mean to tell me you live here! What'sa' matter with you?" I explained apologetically that the rent was inexpensive. Trying to be helpful, he suggested I look for cheap rent in Queens, a multiethnic, working-class borough of mixed ethnicity near New York City's airports.

Racism and the Culture of Terror

It is not merely the police who enforce inner-city apartheid in the United States but also a racist "common sense" that persuades whites, and middle-class outsiders of all colors, that it is too dangerous for them to venture into poor African-American or Latino neighborhoods. For example, when I moved to East Harlem, virtually all of my friends, whether white, black, or Latino/a, berated me for being crazy and irresponsible. Those who still visited me would often phone me in advance to make sure I would meet them downstairs as they descended from their taxis. Indeed, most people still consider me crazy and irresponsible for having "forced" my wife and infant son to live for three and a half years in an East Harlem tenement. When we left the neighborhood in mid-1990, several of my friends congratulated us, and all of them breathed a sigh of relief.[10]

Most people in the United States are somehow convinced that they would be ripped limb from limb by savagely enraged local residents if they were to set foot in Harlem. While everyday danger is certainly real in El Barrio, the vast majority of the 110,599 people—51 percent Latino/Puerto Rican, 39 percent African-American, and 10 percent "other"—who lived in the neighborhood, according to the 1990 Census,

are not mugged with any regularity—if ever. Ironically, the few whites residing in the neighborhood are probably safer than their African-American and Puerto Rican neighbors because most would-be muggers assume whites are either police officers or drug addicts—or both—and hesitate before assaulting them. Primo's primary lookout at the Game Room crackhouse, Caesar, was the first person to explain this to me:

> Felipe, people think you're a *fed* [federal agent] if anything. But that's good; it makes them stay away from you.
>
> Think about it: If you was selling shit on the street and you see a white guy coming by, you wouldn't really want to bother with him.
>
> But then again, some people also think, "he's white and he's in the neighborhood, so he must be crazy." If they didn't, they'd just come up to you and crack you in the face and take your wallet.
>
> You're lucky. Look at me, I'm Puerto Rican. If I was to walk into Bensonhurst,[11] they would figure, "we could beat the shit out of this dude." They might think that I got to be crazy or something but they will test me or kick my ass.

During all the years I spent on the streets of El Barrio walking around at all hours of the night, I was mugged only once—and that was at 2:00 A.M. in a store where everyone else was also robbed at the same time. My wife, who is Costa Rican, was never mugged and she circulated freely throughout the neighborhood—although she was cautious after dark. During the span of these same years, at least a half-dozen of our friends living downtown in safer neighborhoods were mugged. I do not mean to overstate the safety of El Barrio; my seventy-year-old Filipino landlord was mugged in the hallway of our apartment building in broad daylight while walking out of his ground-floor apartment.... Everyone is conscious of the real possibility of assault. Even the toughest of the drug dealers in Ray's network would ask a friend to accompany them for protection when they were carrying money or drugs after dark.

Violence cannot be reduced to its statistical expression, which would show that most murders and beatings in any given inner-city neighborhood remain confined to a small subgroup of individuals who are directly involved in substance abuse and the underground economy, or who are obviously vulnerable, such as frail, elderly persons. Street culture's violence pervades daily life in El Barrio and shapes mainstream society's perception of the ghetto in a manner completely disproportionate to its objective danger. Part of the reason is that violent incidents, even when they do not physically threaten bystanders, are highly visible and traumatic. For example, during my first thirteen months of residence in El Barrio I witnessed a slew of violent incidents:

- A deadly shotgun shooting outside my apartment window of a drug-dealing woman (who also happened to be the mother of a three-year-old child).
- A bombing and a machine-gunning of a numbers joint by rival factions of the local Mafia—once again, within view of my window.[12]
- A shoot-out and police car chase in front of a pizza parlor where I happened to be eating a snack with my wife.
- The aftermath of the fire-bombing of a heroin house by an unpaid supplier around the block from where I lived.
- A half-dozen screaming, clothes-ripping fights.

None of these particular incidents came close to threatening me physically, but their traumatic nature and prominent public visibility contributed to a sense of an omnipresent threatening reality that extended far beyond the statistical possibility of

becoming a victim.[13] To analyze the very different contexts of South America and Nazi Germany, anthropologist Michael Taussig has coined the term "culture of terror" to convey the dominating effect of widespread violence on a vulnerable society.[14] In contemporary Spanish Harlem one of the consequences of the "culture of terror" dynamic is to silence the peaceful majority of the population who reside in the neighborhood. They isolate themselves from the community and grow to hate those who participate in street culture—sometimes internalizing racist stereotypes in the process. A profound ideological dynamic mandates distrust of one's neighbors.[15] Conversely, mainstream society unconsciously uses the images of a culture of terror to dehumanize the victims and perpetrators and to justify its unwillingness to confront segregation, economic marginalization, and public sector breakdown.

I had a professional and personal imperative to deny or "normalize" the culture of terror during the years I lived in El Barrio. Many local residents employ this strategy. They readjust their daily routines to accommodate the shock of everyday brutality in order to maintain their own sense of sanity and safety. To be successful in my street ethnography, I had to be relaxed and enjoy myself on the street. I had to feel comfortable while hanging out surrounded by friends and basking in relaxed conversation. This is not difficult during daylight hours or even during the early evening, when El Barrio streets often feel warm and appealing. Children are running every which way playing tag and squealing with delight; one's neighbors are out strolling and often pause to strike up a friendly conversation; a loudspeaker pulses salsa music from a tenth-story housing project window so that everyone on the street below can step in tune for free. In short, there is a sense of community in the neighborhood despite the violence. In fact, most residents even know the nicknames of their more hostile or suspicious neighbors.

Having grown up in Manhattan's Silk Stocking district just seven blocks downtown from El Barrio's southern border delineated by East 96th Street, I always appreciated the shared sense of public space that echoes through Spanish Harlem's streets on warm sunny days. In the safe building where I grew up downtown, neighbors do not have nicknames, and when one shares the elevator with them, they usually do not even say hello or nod an acknowledgment of existence.[16] I enjoyed the illusion of friendly public space that the working-class majority in El Barrio are often able to project during daylight hours. It was the dealers themselves who frequently shattered my sense of optimism and insisted that I respect the violent minority who really controlled the streets when push came to shove. In one particular instance toward the end of my residence I had commented to Caesar in the Game Room that the neighborhood felt safe. His outraged comical response was particularly interesting in that it traced the full ambiguous cycle of the culture of terror by demonstrating the instrumental brutality of the people who were supposed to be protecting us. Both the criminals and the police play by the rules of the culture of terror:

CAESAR: Yo Pops [waving Primo over], listen to this. [turning to me] Felipe thinks the block is chill.

Well let me tell you Felipe, what happened earlier today, because all day it was wild on this block. I didn't even have to watch HBO today. I just had to look out the window and I had a full array of murder and beat down and everything. There was even a fire. I saw an assortment of all kinds of crap out there.

It all started when two crackheads— an older man and a black dude—yoked this girl. They beat her down and took

her jewelry. Punched her in the eye; just cold bashed her. She was screaming and the old guy kicked her some more. It was in the daytime like around two.

Then the cops came and caught the muggers and beat them down. There was at least twenty cops stomping out them two niggas because they resisted.

And they should never have attempted that shit because they got the beat-down of their lives. The cops had a circus with the black kid's face. Hell yeah! They were trying to kill that kid. That's why they needed two ambulances.

Homeboy got hurt! Both of them was in stretchers bleeding hard. It wasn't even a body there. It was just a blob of blood that was left over. The cops had pleasure in doing it.

It was not a normal beat-down like: throw-you-up-on-a-car extra hard. I'm talking about "take your turn, buddy" [grinning]; hold 'em right here [punching] and BOOM and BOOM. And this guy goes BOOM [pretending to fall unconscious].

Even 'Buela [grandma] saw it from the window next to me. And she was yelling and someone else was yelling, "Abuse! Abuse! Police brutality!"

If I woulda had a little video camera I woulda sent it to Al Sharpton.[17] Because it was a black dude that they did that beat-down to. Coulda caused a major political scandal and Sharpton woulda been right up here with that wack perm he's got.

PHILIPPE: How does it make you feel to see the cops doing that?

CAESAR: I was feeling really sorry for myself because I was thinking about getting hit. I could feel the pain they was feeling 'cause I know what it is to be beat down by cops. They don't let up; they be trying to kill you, man! They do it with pleasure [grinning].

That's stress management right there. That's release of tension. That's my-wife-treated-me-dirty-you'll-pay. That's terrorism with a badge. That's what that is.

The cops look forward to that. They get up in the morning and go, "Yeah, Ah'm'a' gonna kick some minority ass today." [rubbing his hands together and licking his lips]

I could tell that attitude, because I would be the same if I was a police officer. 'Cause you take the badge for granted. The badge gets to your head. You know what I'm saying? Makes you feel like you're invincible; like you could do whatever you goddamn well please.

I would have the same attitude. I'm going to hurt somebody today. I don't care if he's white or Puerto Rican. And I'm going to have pleasure in doing it. I'm full into it. And I would be a happy married man because I wouldn't fight with my wife.

I don't even know why they have human police officers. They should just put animals out there patrolling the streets. Word up! 'Cause they're worse than animals. It's like they're animals with a mind.

Internalizing Institutional Violence

Although we did have to worry about the danger of police brutality, it was not one of our primary daily concerns. There was always a strong undercurrent of anxiety over the risk of arrest, but we were considerably less worried about being brutalized by the police if they raided the crackhouse compared to what we risked at the hands of our fellow inmates in the holding pen. Judges in Manhattan almost never send anyone to prison for selling or buying small quantities of drugs the first time they are arrested. A hand-to-hand sale of crack to an undercover officer usually results in a two- to four-year suspended felony sentence.

I have never even heard of a simple customer being brought to trial—much less being convicted of anything. The problem in an arrest is that one usually has to wait in a municipal jail holding pen for forty-eight to seventy-two hours before being arraigned by the judge in the special Narcotics Court.[18]

Our fate in these overcrowded "bullpens" was a frequent subject of anxious discussion. I captured one such debate on my tape recorder. Caesar's non-drug-using cousin, Eddie, was reminding all of us in the Game Room that we risked being sodomized in jail if the police picked us up in a sweep that night. Eddie's father was African-American, and Caesar made sure to racialize his retort as well as demonstrate his superior technical knowledge of the likelihood of sexual assault in a New York City holding pen.

EDDIE: Yo Caesar, don't you come crying to me when they take that ass a yours downtown and bust your cherry. [laughter]

CAESAR: [businesslike] Unnh-uhh! They don't rape niggas in the bullpen no more 'cause a' AIDS. You don't even get raped on Riker's [New York City's biggest municipal jail] no more.

You get raped when you go upstate where they got them big, black, brick-Georgia, Georgia-Tech Bulldog, Black Muslim ham bocks that been in the slammer twenty years.

They be runnin' that little ass a' yours. [jumping to within an eighth of an inch of Eddie's face] Because they bigger than you. They been lifting weights. They big and they take your shit. [spinning around into my face] And they take your arm like this [twisting my arm] and they put it down and they dog it. [spinning around and seizing Eddie in a full nelson] And they jerk it around. [pumping his crotch against Eddie's rear] And you like: [switching roles to grab at his head and pull his hair, shrieking] AHHUUHH.

Because they got their large mammoth, lamabada-blada, Alabama black snake with its magnets out plunging you. Alabama black snake found its way to the assets boy!

[pausing to gauge our hesitant laughter] And they black. And they cruddy. And they smell black. And they big. And they smell like James Brown. And they spit their stuff in your shit. And you gotta be like a lamb and wash drawers and shit, and socks. And you get juiced because you give the biggest niggas' *bolos* [penises] blow jobs. And that's your man [hugging Eddie violently].

And if you're a new nigga' [jumping into my face] and you're a fag and you like it and he want to dog you, you get the big black bogeyman and shit. And they take your ass and stuff it with some mad concrete. They fill your canyon. Word!

And if the faggots like you, they get you in trouble. [spinning back around to face me] And they try to mush 'em, "All right motherfucker, you don't wanta fuck me? I'm back with the black bohemians."

[swinging around again into Primo's face] And they're taking that ass and they make you a fag. And people out on the street, be recognizing *you*! [swinging his face around yet again to within an eighth of an inch of my nose]

I was especially sensitive to Caesar's harangue that night because the New York City police had just deployed their new elite Tactical Narcotics Teams—appropriately nicknamed TNT—in El Barrio.[19] TNT was founded in 1989 to assuage popular outrage during the height of the national just-say-no-to-drugs hysteria.[20] TNT's specific directive was to bust the small, street-level dealer rather than the wholesale supplier. A week earlier, at 2:00 A.M., TNT had arrived in U-Haul trucks to block off both ends of a notorious crack-copping block a few streets down from the Game Room. They rounded up everyone loitering on the sidewalk and even dragged people out of private apartments in the few still-inhabited tenements on the block.

The night of Caesar and Eddie's jousting over jailhouse rape, I had forgotten my driver's license. Not carrying a picture identification is a sure guarantee for inciting police wrath. The recording from this session ends with my voice cursing Caesar through cackles of nervous background laughter:

PHILIPPE: Outta' my face Caesar! What the fuck's the matter with you! You'a fucking pervert, or what?

PRIMO: I'm outta here. You guys have made me *petro* [paranoid]. I'll be right back though, I'm just going upstairs to get my I.D.

Accessing the Game Room Crackhouse

In my first months on the block, I was not debating complex theoretical points about how the United States legitimizes inner-city segregation, or how victims enforce the brutality of their social marginalization. I was primarily concerned with how to persuade the manager of the crackhouse on my block that I was not an undercover police officer. I remember vividly the night I first went to the Game Room. My neighbor Carmen—a thirty-nine-year-old grandmother who I had watched over the past three months become addicted to crack and transform herself into a homeless ninety-nine-pound harpie abandoning her two-year-old twin grandchildren—brought me over to the manager of the Game Room and told him in Spanish, "Primo, let me introduce you to my neighbor, Felipe; he's from the block and wants to meet you." Excited at the possibility of finally accessing a crackhouse scene, my heart dropped when Primo shyly giggled and turned his back on me as if to hide his face. Staring out into the street, he asked Carmen in English, loud enough for me to hear clearly, "What precinct did you pick him up at?" I hurriedly mumbled an embarrassed protest about not being "an undercover" and about wanting to write a book about "the street and the neighborhood." I had the good sense not to impose myself, however, and instead slunk into the background onto the hood of a nearby parked car after buying a round of beers. Even in my largesse I managed to prolong the awkwardness by purchasing the wrong kind of beer—an unstreetwise brand whose taste Primo did not like. He was only drinking 16-ounce bottles of a new brand of malt liquor called Private Stock, which was being marketed on Harlem billboards featuring beautiful, brown-skinned women draped in scanty leopard skins and flashing bright, white teeth, to attract a fresh generation of young, inner-city street alcoholics.

Despite my inauspicious first evening, it took less than two weeks for Primo to warm up to my presence. I was aided by having to pass the Game Room literally every day, and usually several times a day, in order to reach the supermarket, the bus stop, or the subway. Primo would usually be standing outside his pseudo video arcade surrounded by a little clique of teenage girls vying for his attention. At first we just nodded politely to each other, but after a week he called out, "Hey guy, you like to drink beer, don't you?" and we shared a round of Private Stocks with Maria, his fifteen-year-old girlfriend, and his current lookout, Benito—anglicized and commodity fetishized into "Benzie"—a short, loud-voiced twenty-year-old whose exaggerated street swagger hid the limp caused by the dumdum bullet lodged in his left femur.

A few hours, and beers, later my pulse quickened when Primo invited me into the back of the Game Room to where the crack supply was hidden behind a false linoleum panel, and he laid out a dime bag of powder cocaine. It was the "We Are the World" brand, which was sold across the avenue under a half-block-long mural celebrating the late-1980s rock concert of the same title for famine relief in Ethiopia. "You like to sniff too?" Worried that I was going to ruin rapport—or, worse yet, confirm my suspected police officer status—for turning down his offer, I discovered to my surprise that both Primo and his lookout, Benzie, were thrilled to be hanging out with someone who was "such good people" that he did not even "sniff." This was my first encounter with the profound moral—even righteous—contradictory code of street ethics that equates any kind of drug use with the work of the devil, even if almost everybody on the street is busy sniffing, smoking, shooting, or selling.

Primo, Benzie, Maria, and everyone else around that night had never been tête-à-tête with a friendly white before, so it was with a sense of relief that they saw I hung out with them out of genuine interest rather than to obtain drugs or engage in some other act of *perdición*. The only whites they had ever seen at such close quarters had been school principals, policemen, parole officers, and angry bosses. Even their schoolteachers and social workers were largely African-American and Puerto Rican. Despite his obvious fear, Primo could not hide his curiosity. As he confided in me several months later, he had always wanted a chance to "conversate" with an actual live representative of mainstream, "drug-free" white America.

Over the next few weeks, I regularly spent a few hours at the Game Room crackhouse chatting with Primo and whoever else was on duty that shift—either little Benzie or Caesar. To my surprise, I became an exotic object of prestige; the crackhouse habitués actually wanted to be seen in public with me. I had unwittingly stepped into a field of power relations where my presence intimidated people. My next challenge, consequently, was to break through the impressions-management game playing that inverse power relationships inevitably entail. For example, I had triggered within Primo a wave of internalized racism whereby he enthusiastically presented himself as superior to "the *sinvergüenza mamao'* [shameless scum] all around us here." He kept trying to differentiate himself "from all these illiterate Puerto Ricans" who "work in *factorías.*" I was especially embarrassed when he began letting me know how good he thought it was for the development of his mind to be talking with me. At the same time, however, he still thought I might be an undercover police officer. Almost a month after I met him, he said, "I don't care if tomorrow you come and arrest me, I want to talk to you. You're good people." It was not until three years later that Primo would casually describe me to others as "the white nigga' who always be hangin' with me." As a matter of fact, I still remember the night when I first graduated to "honorary nigga'" status. Primo had imbibed more alcohol than usual, and I had walked him up to his girlfriend Maria's sister's high-rise project apartment to make sure he would not get mugged in the stairway, because the elevators were broken as usual.[21] Upon our safe arrival, swaying in the doorway, he grabbed me by the shoulders to thank me: "You're a good nigga', Felipe. You're a good nigga'. See you tomorrow."

It was not until two years later at 2 A.M. in the stairwell of Primo's mother's high-rise project, where Primo and Benzie had gone to sniff a "speedball" (combination of heroin and cocaine), during New Year's week that they told me what their first impressions of me at the Game Room had been. Primo had tipped open a $10 glassine envelope of heroin and dipped his housekey into the white powder in order to lift a dab to his left nostril. He sniffed deeply, repeating the motion deftly two more times to his right nostril before sighing and reaching out for me to hand him the 40 ounce bottle of Ole English malt liquor I was swigging from. Benzie, meanwhile, was crushing the contents of

a $15 vial of cocaine inside a folded dollar bill by rolling it between his thumbs and forefingers, which gets rid of any clumps and crystals and makes it easier to sniff. He then dipped a folded cardboard matchbook cover into the inch-long pile of white powder and sniffed dryly twice before laying it down gently in the corner of the stair he was sitting on:

PRIMO: When I first met you, Felipe, I was wondering who the hell you were, but, of course, I received you good because you sounded interesting; so, of course, I received you good. [reaching for the cocaine] *Te recibí como amigo, con respeto* [I welcomed you as a friend, with respect].

BENZIE: [interrupting and handing me the malt liquor bottle] Felipe, I'm going to tell you the honest truth—and he knows it. [pointing to Primo] The first time I met you I thought that you was in a different way.... But I would really rather not tell you. [sniffing from the heroin packet with Primo's key]

PHILIPPE: [drinking] It's all right don't worry; you can tell me. I won't get angry.

BENZIE: Yeah...well...[turns to Primo to avoid eye contact with me, and sniffs again] yeah, you remember? I used to tell you, you know, the way he used to talk. The way he used to be. That I thought maybe...you know.... How you call it? That some people are bisexual. Even though you had a wife. I thought you was like...dirty.

It was really 'cause of the way you talk and 'cause of the way you act. You always asking a lot of questions, and a lot of gay people be like that—you know, trying to find out the way you are.

But then after a while, when I got to know you [grabbing the bottle from me], I saw the way you was hanging; and I got to know you better; but still, I always had that thought in my head,

"Man, but, but this nigga's a faggot." [drinking]

PRIMO: [cutting Benzie short] Damn, shut up man! You're going to give Felipe a *complejo* [complex]. [putting his arm over my shoulder]. It was just 'cause you was white. He was thinking, *"Quién es éste blanquito?"* [Who is this white boy?]

PHILIPPE: So was it my accent? My voice? The way I move my body?

BENZIE: Yeah, like your accent...

PRIMO: [interrupting] I told him you were an anfropologist, and that the way you speak is just like intelligent talk. I mean you just speak your way. And maybe, we don't understand a few words, but it's all right.

But when you talk Spanish, then you really be sounding different. Then you really be sounding different. You know, when you talk Spanish, you sound like an *Español* [Spaniard].

Even my mother thought you was gay, but that was because she was only talking to you through the phone. [gunshots] One day she asks me [in Spanish], "Who's this little white boy who's always calling here? Is he a *pato* [faggot] or something?" [*Quién es este blanquito que siempre llama aquí? Es pato a algo así?*]

And I said [once again in Spanish], "No! What are you talking about? He is a professor. He speaks Spanish and English and French." [*No! De qué tú hablas? El es profesor. Habla español, inglés, y francés.*]

At the time I heard this, I could not stop myself from feeling some kind of vain personal pique at having been misidentified sexually, because by that time I fancied myself to be at least minimally streetwise. In retrospect I am relieved that during the first few years of my fieldwork I thoroughly misread street cues and did not suspect I was giving off "dirty sexual pervert" vibes. Being self-conscious about my sexual image

in the homophobic context of street culture might have interfered with my ability to initiate comfortable relationships with the crack dealers.

African-American/Puerto Rican Relations on the Street

Racial tension in El Barrio is not just focused around whites. Ray's network was intensely internally segregated. It was almost exclusively composed of second-generation. New York–born Puerto Ricans.[22] Although Ray himself would be classified as "black" by Anglo society—as would almost half of his employees—most were explicitly hostile to African-Americans. Only two of the approximately two-dozen, dealers I met working for Ray were African-American. Both had hispanicized their nicknames: Sylvester, for example, was called Gato, the Spanish word for car. The other African-American dealer, who went by the name Juán, confided to me in private that he found the atmosphere at the social club crackhouse on La Farmacia's corner distinctly hostile:

> Blacks and Puerto Ricans really don't get along here. See that plaque there, that says "Latin Family"? Well, some people take that seriously. It's a lot of racism. When I come through the door I have to have an aim and a purpose. If I go and I sit in a seat and I cross my legs, all of a sudden they'll be gathering together, speaking in Spanish, like "Yo, who's that?" They'll even tell you in English, "Yo, you better be chill."

Caesar was more explicit about racial tension in the Game Room—at least when he was drinking.

> I'm Klu Klux Klan. Ah' kill black people. You know why I hate black people? Because they're black, they stink; they smell like shit. And they're lazy

motherfuckers. I swear to God I hate their fucking guts.

I even hate Puerto Ricans that afro. I hate them like any other black man. [running his hands through Primo's hair] Fuck Primo too, because he's got an afro and he's black. I kill him.

[facing me] I hate whites too. I kill them all. But not you Felipe. You all right, you a good nigga'. But if you didn't hang out with us I'd kill you.

You know why I hate *moyos* [racist Puerto Rican term for blacks] because it was a black man who killed my sister—stabbed her eighteen times in the projects.

They get me pissed off, because why did they got to do these things to me? I'm already fucked up as it is. I hate everybody.

For all his explicit racism, Caesar emulated African-American street culture, which has an almost complete hegemony over style in the underground economy.

I used to want to be black when I was younger. I wanted to be with that black style. 'Cause they're badder. Like *malos* [bad]. Yeah: *Malo malos!* More rowdier.

I liked'ed evil black kids the most because I was learning how to be schemish and steal fruit from the fruit stand and stuff like that.

Plus black people like to dress hard—like rugged. You know what I'm saying? Look wild, like *black*. Black, just being *black*. Cool.

'Cause the Spanish people I used to hang with, their style was kind of wimpy, you know.

Look, right now, it's the *moyos* be bringing in the marked necks and the A.J.'s.

That be the *moyos* with the fly clothes.

Regardless of the complexities of racial tension, class polarization, and everyday street style, in the long term everyone in Ray's network came to accept me—and most people appeared genuinely to like having me around. Of course, there were dozens of other people on the periphery of Ray's scene, or in other dealing networks, who never grew to trust me. This was especially true of African-American sellers and younger Puerto Rican teenage dealers, whose relationship to white society is more self-consciously oppositional–hostile than that of their parents or even their older brothers. Nevertheless, I felt comfortable in my role as "professor" and "anthropologist" writing a book. On several occasions it almost became problematic when marginal members of Ray's network, and even outsiders, accosted me angrily for never tape-recording them, claiming that they "deserved to be at least a chapter" in my book. I had originally worried that the main characters in this book might resent the fact that an outsider was going to use their life stories to build an academic career. My long-term goal has always been to give something back to the community. When I discussed with Ray and his employees my desire to write a book of life stories "about poverty and marginalization" that might contribute to a more progressive understanding of inner-city problems by mainstream society, they thought I was crazy and treated my concerns about social responsibility with suspicion. In their conception everyone in the world is hustling, and anyone in their right mind would want to write a best seller and make a lot of money. It had not occurred to them that they would ever get anything back from this book project, except maybe a good party on publication day. On several occasions my insistence that there should be a tangible political benefit for the community from my research project spawned humiliating responses:

CAESAR: Felipe, you just talking an immense amount of shit. Because we talk huge amounts of crap that don't mean a goddamned thing—into the air.

Like, like we on Oprah Winfrey or the Donahue Show—which doesn't mean shit. That's not going to help the community. It's not going to help us. It's not going to change the world in an eensy-weensy bit at all. It's just talk. Flap the lip.

Of course, I hope Caesar is wrong; but maybe his cynicism is more realistic than my academic idealism.

About halfway through my research, the main characters in this book, with whom I have developed deeper relations, began following the details of my writing habits and urging me to make speedier progress. They wanted to be part of "a best seller." For example, when I came down with a debilitating tendinitis in my wrists and forearms from spending too many hours at my word processor, Caesar and Primo became genuinely worried and disappointed. I realized that our relationships had developed an almost psychotherapeutic dimension.

CAESAR: [grabbing my arms and twisting them] Don't be giving up on us, Felipe. Don't be fuckin' up. We could beat you up for this.

[turning to Primo] I think Felipe is going out of his mind. I think we're going to have to put pressure on him.

[giggling] You're our role model here. You can't be fuckin' around. We could beat you down for shit like that. Word up!

I ain't lettin' you leave us until I get something in writing with your name on it, as a lifetime reference. You gonna have to give me at least a chapter, regardless. I know my words is going to be in your chapters because my stories is so good that you can't leave them out.

[hugging me] I think the students are becoming more advanced than the teacher here, educational-wise. I think Felipe's in a deep depression. I think he's got a writer's block thing.

NOTES

1. The corner of 110th Street and Lexington is featured periodically in the national and local press as "A Devil's Playground" or as "the worst and druggiest corner" in the city. In 1990 alone, it boasted photo spreads in *National Geographic* (Van Dyk, May 1990), *The American Lawyer* (Frankel and Freeland, March 1990), and the *New York Daily News* (October 19, 1990:1). When I looked up the legal real estate records for Ray's Social Club, I found that the City of New York had seized it from its original Italian owner for tax default and donated it to Operation Open City, a nonprofit affordable housing coalition. Budget cuts prevented the nonprofit organization from developing the site. Instead, Ray continued paying rent for the space to the elderly Italian landlord who no longer legally owned the property.

2. May 4, 1989:4.

3. Ironically, the only real survivors of the holocaust on La Farmacia's corner are the two Palestinian refugee families that own the bodegas catty-corner to Ray's social club–crackhouse. These Middle Eastern exiles have even expanded into local real estate, buying the few still standing tenements along the avenue. They do a brisk business in beer, candy, and drug paraphernalia—including glass crack-pipe stems, and plastic crack and cocaine vials.

4. "Cheeba" is a New York term for marijuana.

5. *La Mafia Boba* is difficult to translate. Literally, *boba* or *bobo* means "slow-witted," but Primo's gang used the term ironically to convey their ability to prey on people unawares:

> Like they think we're *bobos* but we're *guapos* [aggressive, streetwise]. We know what we're doing. Ray used to start shouting *"le Mafia boba a botellazo* [to the bottles]!" And we start grabbing bottles and throwing them at whoever—like if we used to see a faggot, or a punk, or whatever—someone we just didn't like.

6. In New York City, a "bundle" refers to an established quantity of prepackaged drugs ready for individual retail sale. The number

of packets in a bundle changes depending on the drug and its cost, i.e., a bundle of heroin is ten $10 glassine envelopes, whereas a bundle of crack is twenty-five vials when they cost $5 each and fifty-five vials when they are worth $3 each. Payments to street sellers are usually made as a percentage of the profit on each bundle sold. For example, in the housing projects opposite the Game Room the lookout and the server who sold crack at $3 a vial shared $20 for every bundle of fifty-five vials they sold.

7. See Bourgois 1989b. When the Jamaican owner of a gold pawnshop that sold powder cocaine around the corner from the Game Room shot one of his employees in the kneecaps for skimming from a night's receipts, Primo told me, "Jamaicans don't fuck around—they're not like Puerto Ricans." Indeed, on the street Jamaican drug dealers enjoyed a reputation for extreme brutality (cf. Gunst 1995).

8. It is part of an immense swath of uninterrupted housing projects that covers a thirty-two-square-block perimeter, extending from East Harlem through Central Harlem, with an approximate population of 17,800.

9. It was not until two years later that I finally gained full access to that particular crack corner by befriending the owner, Tito, a twenty-one-year-old who shot his older brother in the spine and paralyzed him for life in a struggle over control of the block. Tito was an extraordinarily talented graffiti artist. He covered the six bricked-up abandoned tenements on his block with huge spray-painted murals depicting his glory in the drug-dealing world—including comic character self-portraits of himself covered in gold chains.... He lived in one of the abandoned buildings with his grandmother. His father had been killed and Tito introduced me to his cocaine-addicted mother, who happened to be visiting on one occasion. She nervously tried to hide the needle-mark scabs covering the top of her hands. With the warm encouragement of Tito's grandmother I tried to connect Tito to downtown art galleries. We encountered only a cold reception in the New York City art world, and halfway through the process Tito lost control of his block and disappeared in a cloud of angel dust.

10. I moved to El Barrio in March 1985, and we moved out in September 1990. Economic constraints forced us to spend several academic semesters outside New York City, so our actual length of physical residence in the neighborhood was a total of 3.5 years—two of which (1988–90) were uninterrupted. During the first year after moving out of El Barrio, from September 1990 to August 1991, we lived nearby in West Harlem (along Morningside Park) and I continued to spend at least two nights a week with Ray's crack dealers. Since moving to San Francisco in late 1991, I have maintained telephone contact with several of the dealers, and I never visit New York City without seeing Primo. During the spring and part of the summer of 1994, I spent almost two months in New York City, visiting Primo and other East Harlem friends regularly.

11. Bensonhurst is a working-class Italian-American neighborhood in Brooklyn. On August 23, 1989, a group of young white men in the neighborhood killed Yusuf Hawkins, a sixteen-year-old African-American who had come to Bensonhurst to buy a used car advertised in the local newspapers. They thought he was dating an Italian-American woman who lived on the block (*New York Times*, August 25, 1989:A1, B2).

12. The Puerto Rican faction of the Mafia eventually wrested control of East Harlem's numbers racket from the Genovese crime family. The new Puerto Rican director of this $30 million gambling empire was eventually arrested in 1994 (*New York Times*, April 21, 1994:A13).

13. In one case, a stray bullet ricocheted off the curb next to us while we lounged in front of the Game Room. I hesitated including this particular incident for fear of oversensationalizing my experience of neighborhood violence in a self-celebratory macho manner. In fact, we did not feel as if we were in imminent danger of getting shot. At the same time, the transcriptions of my tape recordings are frequently punctuated by

gunshots. In my original round of editing, I was so close to the material that I did not transcribe the sound of gunshots, treating them instead like static interference or traffic noises.

14. Taussig 1987.

15. Based on his research on Chicago's Southside, the French sociologist Loïc Wacquant (1993) calls this "the depacification of everyday life." He links it to structural economic as well as political factors, such as the breakdown of state-provided infrastructure and social services in the wake of deindustrialization. See also John Devine's (1996) discussion of the culture of violence in New York's "lower tier," inner-city high schools.

16. My childhood census tract was listed as the richest in all of New York City in the 1990 census. Its average household income ($249,556) was more than eleven times higher than the average household income (just over $21,000) of my census tracts in El Barrio and its median household income was more than thirteen times higher (*New York Times*, March 20, 1994:A6; *1990 Census of Population and Housing Block Statistics*).

17. Al Sharpton is an African-American inner-city reverend in New York City who caught the attention of the media for his flamboyant denunciations of racism and his community-level mobilizations in the early 1990s.

18. See, for example, *New York Times*, March 23, 1990:A1, B4.

19. *New York Times*, November 16, 1988:A1, B5. The TNT strategy was declared a failure and discontinued in early 1994.

20. Caesar was acutely aware of the hype and hypocrisy driving the anti-drug hysteria that swept the United States in the late 1980s and early 1990s along with the "family values" and abortion debates.

> I could be some dumb scumbag ho' that have a lot of money to push my campaign. And all I gotta say is "Drugs!" and they'll elect me immediately.
>
> Abortion and drugs is the best thing for politicians in America, man.

> Why you think they gettin' elected? Look at Idaho with all them bureaucrat delegates making all these promises about stopping abortion and all that.
>
> Over here in New York they got a drug problem, and all you gotta say is "I'm gonna stop the flow of drugs. Hire more police!" and you got the job, man.

In the mid-1990s, the words "violent crime," "unwed welfare mothers," or "illegal immigrants" could be substituted verbatim for "drugs" in Caesar's harangue.

21. That particular year, the neighboring housing projects where Maria lived had the highest murder rates of all the Housing Authority projects in Manhattan.

22. See Rodríguez 1989:chap. 3 for a discussion of race relations among Puerto Ricans.

REFERENCES

Bourgois, Philippe. 1989. *Ethnicity at Work: Divided Labor on a Central American Banana Plantation*. Studies in Atlantic History and Culture Series. Baltimore: Johns Hopkins University Press.

Devine, John. (in press). *The New Panopticon: The Construction of Violence in Inner City High Schools*. Chicago: University of Chicago Press.

Frankel, Alison, and Lisa Freeland. 1990. "Is Street-Level Enforcement a Bust?" *The American Lawyer* (March): 100–109.

Gunst, Laurie. 1995. *Born Fi' Dead: A Journey Through the Jamaican Posse Underworld*. New York: Holt.

New York Daily News. 1990. "Devil's Playgrounds." (October 19): 1.

New York Post. 1989. "Calm After the Storm." (May 4): 4.

New York Times. 1988. "Crackdown on Drug Sellers Is Expanded to East Harlem." (November 16): A1, B5. George James.

New York Times. 1989. "Black Youth Is Killed by Whites; Brooklyn Attack Is Called Racial." (August 25): A1, B2.

New York Times. 1990. "Trapped in the Terror of New York's Holding Pens." (March 23): A1, B4. William Glaberson.

New York Times. 1994. "Two Census Tracts, at the Extremes." (March 20): A6. Sam Roberts.

New York Times. 1994. "Using Fax Spells Arrest for Numbers Ring." (April 21): A13. Selwyn Raab.

Rodríguez, Clara E. 1989. *Puerto Ricans: Born in the U.S.A.* Winchester, Mass.: Unwin Hyman.

Taussig, Michael. 1987. *Shamanism, Colonialism, and the Wild Man: A Study in Terror and Healing.* Chicago: University of Chicago Press.

Van Dyk, Jere. 1990. "Across the Line in East Harlem." *National Geographic* 177(5): 52–75.

Wacquant, Loïc. 1993. "Décivilisation et démonisation: la mutation du ghetto noir americain." In *L'Amerique des français,* pp. 103–125. Christine Faure and Tom Bishop (eds.). Paris: Editions François Bourin.

50

HAKIM HASAN

AFTERWORD

from *Sidewalk* (1999)

Sometimes the data talks back. Hakim Hasan, a book vendor in Greenwich Village, was a key figure in Mitchell Duneier's *Sidewalk*. Following the completion of the book, Duneier asked Hasan to write an afterword about his experiences being a research "subject" (which Duneier did not see until the book went to press).

The streets that are the focus of these pages are places of metropolitan refuge, where the identities of the men and women who work and live are hidden in public space. In the pedestrian's eye these men and women are reduced to a horrific *National Geographic* photograph come to life. It is as if they were born on these streets and have no past, or other life experiences.

My decision to leave the corporate world and sell books on Sixth Avenue was incomprehensible to my family and friends. One of my black former co-workers saw me selling books one evening, walked over to me and asked with comic disbelief. "So this is what you are doing now?" I did not want to answer this embarrassing question, so I replied, "No. I'm just watching the stuff for a friend of mine. He went to the bathroom."

In effect, I want into exile on the street. I began the process of exile long before I arrived on Sixth Avenue. In an attempt to avoid the everyday formalities of corporate life, in 1988 I began working as a legal proofreader on the night shift in the word-processing department of the law firm Robinson, Silverman. Nothing made the futility of my efforts more evident to me than an incident that occurred one evening when I had no work to do because of an upcoming holiday. I sat at a secretary's work station and read a copy of *Business Week*. A white attorney walked over to me. He leaned over my shoulder, saying not a word, and began to read. The crumbs from the popcorn he was eating fell on my head. I thought to myself. "Man, I should stand up and slap this guy senseless." In the moments that it took for me to weigh this option, I imagined paramedics working on his limp body and a phalanx of television reporters and police officers interviewing my co-workers in the corridor. I did not say a word to him. My silence was simply another in a series of concessions I made to those who provided me with my daily bread.

I was abruptly fired during an employee-review meeting in 1991 by the director of administrative services, a middle-aged white woman. Why? I had been accused of being incompetent, she said, by an attorney she refused to identify. I still remember the cadence of her words: "I'm so sorry, but we're going to have to let you go," as if it were a refrain to a song: and I recall the way I sat in a chair opposite her desk, statue-still, paralyzed by their unforeseen and immediate implications. I recall the way she stared at my face and the way my silence prompted her to say, "You seem to be taking this so calmly."

The director of administrative services was not my supervisor. How did she conclude that I was incompetent? What were her criteria? I worked on the night shift and saw her rarely—only when she was working late. The night-shift proofreaders and word processors had very little contact with her or the members of the legal staff, as it was my supervisor's responsibility to deal with them.

Prior to this meeting, my supervisor and I traded the normal office banter. She never gave me any verbal or written notification, during the time she was my supervisor, that my work was not satisfactory, nor was she present at the meeting.

Incompetent? What about these three years, working under deadlines and enormous pressure, proofreading legal documents inside a room the size of a prison cell with three other proofreaders? The director of administrative services believed the expression on my face was one of calm. It was an expression of shock. That night I left this insular world in order to salvage

whatever was left of myself and forge a new identity.

Mitchell Duneier recalls that he was thoroughly surprised when, during our first conversation at my book-vending table, I told him that I had a Rolodex. His surprise was a matter of social context. But what if I had not mentioned the word Rolodex to Mitch? Because the word Rolodex is associated with people who work in offices, and because I was perceived as a "street person," my use of it stood out. It caused a shift in Mitch's perceptions of me. I am now inclined to suggest that this book would not have been written if it had not been for this conversation, which challenged his assumptions about me and my social status.

In the first chapter Mitch recalls his difficulty in convincing me to become a subject—at that time the sole subject—of the book. Indeed, I found myself hearing the decree of my mother, whenever she had to leave my siblings and me at home alone: *Do not open the door for anyone while I'm gone.*

If I defied the maternal decree and opened *this* door, on what basis would I weigh Mitch's intentions? How could I prevent him from appropriating me as mere data, from not giving me a voice in how the material in his book would be selected and depicted? How does a subject take part in an ethnographic study in which he has very little faith and survive as something more than a subject and less than an author?

Because I believe my disastrous experience in the corporate world was the effect of racism (a claim many whites these days liken to that of the proverbial boy who cried "Wolf!"), I asked myself. "Can I expect Mitch, as a white sociologist, to understand why that experience led me to work as a book vendor on Sixth Avenue in the first place?" The idea of race as a lived experience could not be avoided; at the same time, if I made the mistake of denying Mitch *his* humanity on the basis of race, without giving him a fair chance, there would have been no way for me to know whether he could write about my life accurately.

I did not know how Mitch would construct an account of my life on these blocks. Would he conduct his research as a descendant of a sociological tradition which historically has found it all but impossible to write and theorize about blacks, especially poor blacks, as complex human beings? I worried this way, oddly enough, even after reading Mitch's book *Slim's Table,* despite its insights into the lives of working-class black men, because my life, not the lives of the men depicted in that book, was at stake.

Over several weeks, I talked with Mitch informally at my book-vending table, and whenever possible at a restaurant where we could speak candidly without being interrupted. These exploratory conversations revolved around the basic facts of my life and, more to the point, the circumstances that prompted me to become a street bookseller, and they were emotionally charged. Mitch did not react to what I had to say with the cool, clinical detachment I had imagined to be the sociologist's stock-in-trade. He listened attentively. I came to respect his sensitivity, and soon I trusted him to write about my life.

After reading the original manuscript three years ago, I concluded that the events and conversations that took place at my book-vending table could not convey, by themselves, the complexity of the social structure that existed on these blocks. I sent Mitch a long, handwritten letter outlining my concerns. I expected him to think I had overstepped my bounds as "subject." True, I knew Mitch's research agenda had been shaped by my reference to Jane Jacobs's intriguing idea of the "public character." But, since I was a subject, how far did my right to theorize go?

Not long afterward we spoke on the telephone—I from a public telephone as I watched my table, he from his office. Mitch told me that he appreciated my sociological insights and that he was grateful for the letter. He wondered aloud if it might be productive for us to co-teach a seminar where we would discuss the issues raised by the book with students and each other. Shortly thereafter, Mitch received permission to invite me as a paid lecturer to co-teach a ten-week undergraduate seminar with him. This course marked the beginning of a process whereby the other men and women on Sixth Avenue would no longer be mere data.

I literally found myself selling books on Sixth Avenue one day and on the next seated opposite Mitch at a huge conference table at the University of California at Santa Barbara. This was new terrain, since I had no formal experience whatsoever teaching in a university environment. Up until that point, I had jokingly told Mitch that the sidewalk had been my classroom, so to speak, and that I was contemplating charging tuition.

The nineteen students whom Mitch and I had selected on an "instructor approval" basis to enroll in this seminar represented diverse ethnic backgrounds and demonstrated a keen interest in the way the seminar was structured, as well as a willingness to tackle an arduous series of reading assignments. Race, of course, was an unavoidable component of our meetings. This was due to the choice of reading materials and to the issues that emanated from the street.

We encouraged class participation based upon the assigned reading materials so that individual seminars would not be reduced to "rap sessions." The reading material we assigned was twofold: some books provided structural and conceptual understanding of issues of street life (*The Death and Life of Great American Cities, Streetwise, Urban Fortunes,* and *The Homeless*), others were "black books" that working and middle-class blacks purchased at my book-vending table (*Pimp, Dopefiend, Volunteer Slavery, Africa: Mother of Civilization, Makes Me Wanna Holler, Breaking Bread, Race Matters,* and *Confronting Authority,* to name a few).

Co-teaching this seminar with Mitch was not easy. Not only was there a tremendous amount of preparation involved, but it gave me a firsthand understanding of the magnitude of his responsibilities as a college professor. Teaching undergraduates, where a professor must contend with the occasionally base intellectual instincts of some students, is a difficult enterprise. Standards and critical thinking are of the utmost importance.

I was given an office in which to work and conduct meetings with students during my office hours. Before each of the first four seminars, I would sit in my office stricken with such anxiety that I would find myself taking two Tylenols to help ease the onslaught of a headache, even though I had spent years at my book-vending table conversing with ordinary and famous people day after day.

And yet I adapted easily to this new social context. The seminar proceeded wonderfully, with Alice and Marvin visiting us in the middle of the academic quarter for two weeks. What became evident from the questions and responses of students was the shortcomings of the book. Why were the lives of the magazine vendors not included in the first draft? What about the panhandlers? What about homelessness? Why didn't these people simply find jobs? What did the whites have to say to these people? What were their interactions like with neighborhood residents? How did I get my books ? Could a white professor really be trusted to write about black men without succumbing to stereotypes? These were difficult questions, and Mitch and I talked about them at length in between sessions. As a result of the seminar and our conversations, Mitch began writing this book all over again, returning to Sixth Avenue to document the lives of the other men.

My telephone communiqués back to New York proved to be meaningless as Alice recounted the general assessment of my trip to me. The men on Sixth Avenue could hardly believe that I was actually co-teaching a class with Mitch. They thought I was in Santa Barbara vacationing and enjoying the high life.

The social hierarchy of the book vendors and magazine vendors was characterized by long-standing antagonisms (as described in the chapter on the space wars), and I had a good but far from perfect relationship with the magazine vendors. In order for Mitch to gain access, he needed a sponsor among them—both to help him gain their trust and to ensure his safety. This is why Marvin was crucial. As a sponsor, he had greater credibility than I would have had, because he and Mitch had had no prior relationship.

Marvin and I briefed Mitch on what to expect and avoid as he initially moved about these blocks conducting fieldwork. Many of these men believed that Mitch was "rich" (that is the word I often heard) and they were prepared to take advantage of him. On these blocks, life is measured on a day-to-day basis, often in terms of the money one can obtain from people of goodwill. In those early days of fieldwork, the question of whether or not Mitch was really writing a book about the meaning of their lives was secondary. Their question was: How much money can I get out of him?

Some of them had earned as much as one hundred dollars apiece selling magazines the day before, but had spent that money on crack or alcohol before dawn. They invariably asked Mitch for money to buy breakfast, which had a variety of shaded meanings: a two-dollar ham, egg, and cheese sandwich from Gray's Papaya, a bottle of St. Ides malt liquor, or a hit or two of crack.

As far as money goes, none of these men were aware that Mitch had covered all of the costs associated with the research for this book out of his salary. He did not have a research grant, and would not wait to get one before conducting his research. Marvin was shocked when I told him this, but I knew that it would not have mattered if I told it to the other men.

Mitch eventually learned how to say no to requests for money from seemingly desperate people. He established goodwill through his seriousness of purpose and sincerity as a sociologist. I watched him gain access to the magazine vendors as I periodically peeked around the corner from my table and sometimes looked from the second-floor window of Userfriendly (a pay-by-the-hour computer center, now closed). I could see him working for Marvin and slowly but assuredly easing his way into the life that existed at that table. There was an "invisible" social world there unknown to most pedestrians and, as I would later learn, even to me. Through intensive fieldwork, Mitch managed to document this subtle and complex social structure. It is fair to say, in retrospect, that his reception among these men was actually far easier than I anticipated it would be.

Alfred Robinson, who was among the "first generation" of men to make their lives on Sixth Avenue, told me that Mitch would have become a "victim" on these streets had there not been a consensus among the men and women that what he was trying to do was important. In the end, any sociologist who simply believes that time spent in the field qualifies him as "one of the boys" is not only sadly mistaken but in grave trouble. The street is the street. Make no mistake about it. Mitch understood this from the outset. He never pretended to be anything other than he was: a human being and sociologist attempting to understand the meaning of our lives.

Not one of these men or women (including myself) had any coordinates for this kind of undertaking but in order for Ovie Carter to photograph these men and women, they had to put their faith in him too. People who work and live on the street, as a general rule, do not like, let alone permit, photographs to be taken of them. Some do not like the idea of their lives being reduced to a tourist attraction, while others see photographs as an aspect of police surveillance. Many think that unless they "get paid" the photographer is "getting over" on them.

Ovie is a black staff photographer for the *Chicago Tribune*. He is a soft-spoken man who has spent over twenty-five years photographing the inner city, with a particular focus on problems like drug abuse. This would be the third major project on which he and Mitch would collaborate. I can say with assurance that Ovie's status as a black man was not the sole criterion for his admission into the lives of these men and women. Jamaane, for example, initially expressed his reluctance to be photographed. I recall Ovie talking to Jamaane about his reluctance in front of Store 24 (now Go Sushi) on Greenwich Avenue, the very block I work on. It was an intense yet cordial conversation. Within fifteen minutes, Jamaane changed his mind. Jamaane, who is a man of great integrity, had come to respect Ovie and his intentions as they related to this project. The wealth of Ovie's Chicago experience photographing men and women very much like those on Sixth Avenue had never really occurred to me in my own assessment of how he would manage to be accepted on these blocks. Compared to Mitch's, his rapport with the men and women was almost instantaneous.

When Mitch had written another draft of this book and photographs had been carefully selected, he came back to New York, rented a room at the Washington Square Hotel, and brought each and every man and woman involved with this project there. He read chapters of the book to them and solicited their opinions. This was not easy, but it proved (particularly when everyone involved had heard their own words) that the book was a work in progress that portrayed their lives accurately. Mitch had made his own judgments after listening to everyone first.

There was no way for me to know that my desire to survive as something more than a subject and less than an author *would* influence the way this book was conceived and written. Let me elaborate my determination to participate in this project forced me to discover that a dialogue with Mitch, in his capacity *as a social scientist,* was possible. This was no small achievement. This was a departure from the "scholar knows best" paradigm. The romanticized idea of "the subject's voice" that I often hear about from graduate students studying at New York University and the New School for Social Research who come to my table is one thing. The radical willingness of the social scientist to listen is quite another.

Mitch's research compelled me to realize that I knew less about the lives of the men and women on these streets than I thought, although I had spent years working right next to them. For instance, I was quite surprised to learn that a sub-group of these men had actually known one another for over fifteen years and had "migrated" to Sixth Avenue after having lived in and around Pennsylvania Station. Because of social distinctions that exist between the magazine and book vendors, I was not privy to this fascinating information. Had Mitch failed to talk to each and every man who inhabited these blocks, there would have been no way to determine, let alone document, their shared history and their migration from Penn Station to Sixth Avenue. The story of their migration raised profound questions for me, since it demonstrated their tremendous adaptability and ability to create a milieu in public space in which they could survive. Perhaps, in the final analysis, migration of any kind is a story of survival and adaptability. But this seems never to occur to people who encounter these persons, including policy makers, who think street vendors can be eliminated with laws that cut vending space or ordinances that make the world less comfortable for them.

When I read the first draft of the chapter "A Scene from Jane Street," I found it unimaginable that Billy Romp and his family are allowed to live in a camper on Jane Street (an unusually narrow street, no less) and that residents think so much of the Romps that they give them keys to their apartments. I explained to Mitch, I have never been offered keys to any resident's apartment, and even if I were, I doubt that I would have accepted. The limitations that I place upon trust would not allow me to do so. Maybe this is not important. What is important is the keys, which symbolize that the Romps are accepted by the residents.

The juxtaposition of Ishmael being told by the police officers that he could not sell his magazines on Christmas day and Billy Romp selling his Christmas trees made me angry. Let me say something about the comparison between Billy Romp and me as public characters: while it is admirable that he is widely accepted on Jane Street, and undeniable that his presence creates a sense of "eyes upon the street," the role I came to play on Sixth Avenue is markedly different from his. Without the signs of race, class, and family stability (I have no children) that might have allowed me to gain immediate acceptance on Sixth Avenue, I had to earn my place there through my wit, presence, and perseverance. There is no indication that I, or any of the other men and women, have ever been accepted altogether on Sixth Avenue.

Despite the fact that it was a labor of love, working on the Avenue for over seven years took a toll on me. Two days after Alice handed me a letter on the sidewalk notifying me that our relationship was over and that she was romantically involved with another vendor on *our* block, I decided to leave Sixth Avenue. While this news was a precipitating factor, I had endured poverty and the lack of health insurance long enough, and the prospect of entering middle age with no financial security was frightening. I had to leave.

My departure from Sixth Avenue was no easier than my arrival. One does not spend seven years working on the sidewalk and make a swift foray back into the formal economy. I thought that I could. My attempt now to move into publishing, public school education, or urban policy research is marred still by bitterness and my contempt for corporate whites who thwarted my ability to simply earn a living, which is what brought me to Sixth Avenue in the first place. This conflict between my aspirations and my bitterness is the essence of my story. It has not been resolved. It may never be.

I am still trying to understand how Mitch and the people whose lives he documented developed relationships on several New York City streets where race and class conflicts derail most efforts to transcend such barriers. Does this mean that people sometimes find ways—the will, actually—to work through their phobias and prejudices on these streets? Is it a matter of being willing to listen to one another with respect? Does it hinge on the sheer willpower of a subject, in this case myself, who was determined not to be reduced to a theoretical formulation or mere "data"? Given the vast inequalities, racial misunderstandings, and violence found on the street at every turn, I believe there was some measure of good luck involved here—the kind of luck that scholars and "subjects" of different races, classes, and genders will need when they encounter one another "in the field."

New York
August 1999

51

SUDHIR VENKATESH

THE HUSTLER AND
THE HUSTLED

from *Gang Leader for a Day* (2008)

In *Gang Leader for a Day*, Sudhir Venkatesh looks back after twenty years at his own experiences as an urban ethnographer in Chicago's Robert Taylor Homes.

Four years deep into my research, it came to my attention that I might get into a lot of trouble if I kept doing what I'd been doing.

During a casual conversation with a couple of my professors, in which I apprised them of how J.T.'s gang went about planning a drive-by shooting—they often sent a young woman to surreptitiously cozy up to the rival gang and learn enough information to prepare a surprise attack—my professors duly apprised *me* that I needed to consult a lawyer. Apparently the research I was doing lay a bit out of bounds of the typical academic research.

[The sociologist William Julius (Bill)] Wilson told me to stop visiting the projects until I got some legal advice. I tried to convince Wilson to let me at least hang out

around the Boys & Girls Club, but he shot me a look indicating that his position was not negotiable.

I did see a lawyer, and I learned a few important things.

First, if I became aware of a plan to physically harm somebody, I was obliged to tell the police. Meaning I could no longer watch the gang plan a drive-by shooting, although I could speak with them about drive-bys in the abstract.

Second, there was no such thing as "researcher-client confidentiality," akin to the privilege conferred upon lawyers, doctors, or priests. This meant that if I were ever subpoenaed to testify against the gang, I would be legally obligated to participate. If I withheld information, I could be cited for contempt. While some states offer so-called shield laws that allow journalists to protect their confidential sources, no such protection exists for academic researchers.

It wasn't as if I had any intention of joining the gang in an actual drive-by shooting (nor would they ever invite me). But since I could get in trouble just for driving around with them while they *talked* about shooting somebody, I had to rethink my approach. I would especially have to be clearer with J.T. We had spoken several times about my involvement; when I was gang leader for a day, for instance, he knew my limits and I understood his. But now I would need to tell him, and perhaps a few others, about the fact that I was legally obligated to share my notes if I was ever subpoenaed.

This legal advice was ultimately helpful in that it led me to seriously take stock of my research. It was getting to be time for me to start thinking about the next stage: writing up my notes into a dissertation. I had become so involved in the daily drama of tagging along with Ms. Bailey and J.T. that I'd nearly abandoned my study of the broader underground economy my professors wanted to be the backbone of my research.

So I returned to Robert Taylor armed with two objectives: let people know about my legal issues and glean more details of the tenants' illegal economic activities.

I figured that most people would balk at revealing the economics of hustling, but when I presented the idea to J.T., Ms. Bailey, and several others, nearly everyone agreed to cooperate. Most of the hustlers liked being taken seriously as businesspeople—and, it should be said, they were eager to know if they earned more than their competitors. I emphasized that I wouldn't be able to share the details of anyone else's business, but most people just shrugged off my caveat as a technicality that could be gotten around.

So with the blessing of J.T. and Ms. Bailey, I began devoting my time to interviewing the local hustlers: candy sellers, pimps and prostitutes, tailors, psychics, squeegee men.

I also told J.T. and Ms. Bailey about my second problem, my legal obligation to share notes with the police.

"You mean you didn't know this all along?" Ms. Bailey said. "Even *I* knew that you have to tell police what you're doing—unless you give them information on the sly."

"Oh, no!" I protested. "I'm not going to be an informant."

"Sweetheart, we're all informants around here. Nothing to be ashamed of. Just make sure that you get what you need, I always say. And don't let them beat you up."

"I'm not sharing my data with them—that's what I mean."

"You mean you'll go to prison?"

"Well, not exactly. I just mean I won't share my data with them."

"Do you know what being in contempt means?"

When I didn't reply, Ms. Bailey shook her head in disgust. I had seen this look before: she was wondering how I had qualified for higher education given my lack of street smarts.

"Any nigger around here can tell you that you got two choices," she said. "Tell them what they want or sit in Cook County Jail."

I was silent, trying to think of a third option.

"I'll ask you again," she said. "Will you give up your information, or will you agree to go to jail?"

"You need to know that? That's important to you?"

"Sudhir, let me explain something to you. You think we were born yesterday around here. Haven't we had this conversation a hundred times? You think we don't know what you do? You think we don't know that you keep all your notebooks in Ms. Mae's apartment?"

I shuddered. Ms. Mae had made me feel so comfortable in her apartment that I'd never even entertained the possibility that someone like Ms. Bailey would think about—and perhaps even page through—my notebooks.

"So why let me hang out?" I asked.

"Why do you *want* to hang out?"

"I suppose I'm learning. That's what I do, study the poor."

"Okay, well, you want to act like a saint, then you go ahead," Ms. Bailey said, laughing. "Of course you're learning! But you are also *hustling*. And we're all hustlers. So when we see another one of us, we gravitate toward them. Because we need other hustlers to survive."

"You mean that people think I can do something for them if they talk to me?"

"They *know* you can do something for them!" she yelped, leaning across the table and practically spitting out her words. "And they know you *will*, because you need to get your information. You're a hustler, I can see it. You'll do anything to get what you want. Just don't be ashamed of it."

I tried to turn the conversation back to the narrow legal issue, but Ms. Bailey kept on lecturing me.

"I'll be honest with you," she said, sitting back in her chair. "If you *do* tell the police, everyone here will find you and beat the shit out of you. So that's why we know you won't tell nobody." She smiled as if she'd won the battle.

So who should I be worried about? I wondered. *The police or Ms. Bailey and the tenants?*

When I told J.T. about my legal concerns, he looked at me with some surprise. "I could've told you all that!" he said. "Listen, I'm never going to tell you anything that's going to land me in jail—or get me killed. So it don't bother me what you write down, because I can take care of myself. But that's really not what you should be worried about."

I waited.

"What you should be asking yourself is this: 'Am I going to be on the side of black folks or the cops?' Once you decide, you'll do whatever it takes. You understand?"

I didn't.

"Let me try again. Either you're with us—you feel like you're in this with us and you respect that—or you're just here to look around. So far these niggers can tell that you've been with us. You come back every day. Just don't change, and nothing will go wrong, at least not around here."

J.T.'s advice seemed vague and a bit too philosophical. Ms. Bailey's warning—that I would get beat up if I betrayed confidences—made more sense. But maybe J.T. was saying the same thing, in his own way.

I decided to focus my study of the underground economy on the three high-rise buildings that formed the core of J.T.'s territory. I already knew quite a bit—that squatters fixed cars in the alleys, people sold meals out of their homes, and prostitutes took clients to vacant apartments—but I had never asked people how much money they made, what kind of expenses they incurred, and so on.

J.T. was far more enthusiastic about my project than I'd imagined he would be, although I couldn't figure out why.

"I have a great idea," he told me one day. "I think you should talk to all the pimps. Then you can go to all the whores. Then I'll let you talk to all the people stealing cars. Oh, yeah! And you also have folks selling stolen stuff. I mean, there's a whole bunch of people you can talk to about selling shoes or shirts! And I'll make sure they cooperate with you. Don't worry, they won't say no."

"Well, we don't want to force anyone to talk to me," I said, even though I was excited about meeting all these people. "I can't *make* anyone talk to me."

"I know," J. T. said, breaking into a smile. "But *I* can."

I laughed. "No, you can't do that. That's what I'm saying. That wouldn't be good for my research."

"Fine, fine," he said. "I'll do it, but I won't tell you."

J.T. arranged for me to start interviewing the pimps. He explained that he taxed all the pimps working in or around his buildings: some paid a flat fee, others paid a percentage of their take, and all paid in kind by providing women to J.T.'s members at no cost. The pimps had to pay extra, of course, if they used a vacant apartment as a brothel; they even paid a fee to use the stairwells or a parking lot.

As I began interviewing the pimps, I also befriended some of the freelance prostitutes like Clarisse who lived and worked in the building. "Oh, my ladies will love the attention," Clarisse said when I asked for help in talking to these women. Within two weeks I had interviewed more than twenty of them.

Between these conversations and my interviews with the pimps, some distinctions began to emerge. The prostitutes who were managed by pimps (these women were known as "affiliates") had some clear advantages over the "independents" who worked for themselves. The typical affiliate was beaten up far less frequently—about once a year, as against roughly four times a year for the independents. The affiliates also earned about twenty dollars per week more than the independents, even though their pimps took a 33 percent cut. (Twenty dollars wasn't a small sum, considering that the average Robert Taylor prostitute earned only about one hundred dollars per week.) And I never heard of an affiliate being killed in the line of work, whereas in one recent two-year stretch three independents were killed.

But the two types of prostitutes had much in common. Both groups had high rates of heroin and crack use, and they were bound to the projects, where the demand for sex came mostly from low-income customers. At the truck stops on the other side of the Dan Ryan Expressway—barely a mile away from Robert Taylor but a different ecosystem entirely—a different set of pimps catered to a clientele of white truckers who paid more than the typical black customer in a housing project. Around Robert Taylor a prostitute usually earned ten to twenty dollars for oral sex, sometimes as little as twenty-five dollars for intercourse, and at least fifty dollars for anal sex. But if she was in need of drugs, she would drop her price significantly or accept a few bags of drugs in lieu of any cash.

Once my prostitute research was under way, I asked Ms. Bailey if she would help me meet female hustlers who sold something other than sex. I had casual knowledge of any number of off-the-books businesses: women who sold food out of their apartments or catered parties; women who made clothing, offered marital counseling or baby-sitting; women who read horoscopes, styled hair, prepared taxes, drove gypsy cabs, and sold anything from candy to used appliances to stolen goods. But since most of these activities were conducted out of public view, I needed Ms. Bailey to open some doors.

She was cautious. For the first week, she selectively introduced me to a few women but refused to let me meet others. I'd suggest a name, and she'd mull it over. "Well," she'd say, "let me think about whether I want you to meet with her." Or, just as often, "No, she's not good. But I got someone else for you." Once, after Ms. Bailey introduced me to a psychic, I asked if many other psychics worked in the building. "Maybe, maybe," she said, then changed the subject and left the room.

I eventually figured out why she was reluctant to let me explore the underground economy. As it turned out, tenant leaders like Ms. Bailey always got their cut from such activities. If you sold food out of your kitchen or took in other people's children to baby-sit, you'd better give Ms. Bailey a few dollars, or you might find a CHA manager knocking on your door. If you occasionally cut hair in your apartment, it was probably a good idea to give Ms. Bailey a free styling once in a while. In these parts

Ms. Bailey was like the local IRS—and probably a whole lot more successful at collecting her due.

So the people she let me talk to were the ones she probably trusted most not to speak out of line. But I didn't have much choice: Without Ms. Bailey's say-so, *no one* was going to speak with me about any illegal activities.

Truth be told, nearly everyone Ms. Bailey introduced me to had a fascinating story to tell. One of the most fascinating women I met was Cordella Levy, a close friend of Ms. Bailey. She was sixty-three years old and had lived in public housing her entire life, the past thirty years in Robert Taylor. (She had a Jewish surname, she said, because her grandmother had married a Jewish man; someone else in her family, however, told me that they were descended from black Hebrew Israelites.) Cordella had raised seven children, all but one of whom had moved out of Robert Taylor. Although she used a walking crutch to get around, Cordella had the fight of a bulldog inside her.

She now ran a small candy store inside her apartment. All day long she sat on a stool by the door and waited for children to stop by. Her living room was barren except for the candy: boxes and boxes of lollipops, gum, and candy bars stacked invitingly on a few tables. If you peeked around the corner, you could see into the back bedroom, where Cordella had a TV, couches, and so on. But she liked to keep her candy room sparse, she told me, because if customers saw her furniture, they might decide to come back and rob her.

"You know," she told me, "I didn't always sell candy."

"You mean you didn't go to school for this?" I joked.

"Sweetheart, I never made it past the fourth grade. Black folks weren't really allowed to go to school in the South. What I meant was that I used to be somebody different. Ms. Bailey didn't tell you?" I shook

my head. "She told me you wanted to know how I used to hustle."

"I'd love to hear," I said Cordella seemed itching to tell her story.

"Sweetheart, I've made money around here every which way you can. You know, I started out working for Ms. Bailey's mother, Ella Bailey. Ella was a madam, used to have parties in the building. Oh, Lord! She could throw a party!"

"Ms. Bailey's mother was a madam?" I laughed. "That explains a lot!"

"Yes, sir, and when she passed, I took over from her. Three apartments on the fourteenth floor. Cordella's Place, they used to call it. Come in for a drink, play some cards, make a friend, have a nice time."

"Make a friend? Is that what they used to call it?"

"Ain't nothing wrong with friendship. And then I started making clothes, and then I sold some food, drove people around for a while to the store. My mother taught me how to sew wedding dresses, so I was doing a lot of—"

"Wait!" I said. "Slow down, please. Let's get back to helping people make friends. I'm curious why you stopped running the parties. What happened? I ask because all the people doing that today are men: J.T. and the pimps. I haven't heard about any women."

"That's because they took over. The men ruined everything for us. The first one was J.T.'s mama's cousin, Miss Mae's cousin. He just decided to start harassing all the women who were making money. I think it was around 1981. He would beat us up if we didn't pay him money to work out of the building. I had to pay him a few dollars each week to manage my women and throw my parties. He nearly killed my friend because she wouldn't give him money for doing hairstyling in her apartment. He was real awful. On heroin, used to carry around a big gun, like he was in the movies. And he was a very violent man."

"So what happened, he took over your parties?"

"Well, all of a sudden, he told me I had to give him fifty percent of what I was making, and he'd protect me—keep the cops away. But I knew he couldn't keep any cops away. The man was a thug and wasn't even no good at that. I figured I had been doing it for a while, and so I just gave up and let him have the whole thing. But what I'm saying is that the women ran things around here, before the gangs and the rest of them took over. It was different, because we also helped people."

"How?"

"See, people like me had a little power. I could get your apartment fixed or get you out of jail, because the cops were my best customers. These folks today, like J.T., they can't do that."

"What about Ms. Bailey?"

"Yeah, she can, but she's just one person. Imagine if you had about fifty people like her doing their thing! Now, that was a sight. Fifty women, all powerful women with no shame. It was a different time. It was a time for women, a place for women."

For several days after I interviewed Cordella, I kept thinking of what she said: "It was a time for women, a place for women." Her nostalgia reminded me of how Catrina, Ms. Bailey's assistant, spoke so reverently of women helping each other in the building.

I spent the next three months focused on meeting the matriarchs of the high-rises. There were plenty to choose from: more than 90 percent of the four thousand households in Robert Taylor were headed by a female. Whenever Ms. Bailey introduced me to an elderly dressmaker or a grandmother who offered day care to working parents, I tried to solicit stories about the past as well as details of her current enterprise.

Many of these women had protested for civil rights in the 1960s and campaigned for black political candidates in the 1970s; they took the need to fight for their community very seriously. But during the 1980s and 1990s, as their plight was worsened by gangs, drugs, and even deeper poverty, they struggled just to keep their families together. By then the housing authority had grown corrupt and unsupportive, the police were largely unresponsive, and the tribe of strong women had been severely marginalized.

While the official statistics said that 96 percent of Robert Taylor's adult population was unemployed, many tenants did have part-time legitimate jobs—as restaurant workers, cabdrivers, cleaning ladies in downtown corporate offices, and nannies to middle-class families. But nearly all of them tried to hide any legitimate income from the CHA, lest they lose their lease or other welfare benefits.

There were also working men living in Robert Taylor, perhaps a few dozen in each building. But they stayed largely out of sight, again because of the CHA limits on how much money a tenant family could earn. Sometimes a man would leave home for a few weeks just to keep the CHA inspectors off guard. So when I or someone else they didn't recognize came into an apartment, the men might head for the back room. They didn't attend many tenant meetings, and for the most part they let the women handle the battle for better living conditions. The absence of men in Robert Taylor had made it that much easier for the gang members and pimps to essentially have the run of the place.

As I began compiling statistics on the illicit earnings generated by women throughout Robert Taylor, it became obvious that all their illicit earnings combined hardly constituted a lucrative economy. Selling food or candy out of your apartment might net you about twenty dollars per week. (Cordella Levy managed to do better than that, having persuaded a local grocery store to sell her candy wholesale in return for steering her customers to that store for their groceries.) Day care brought in five or ten dollars per day per child, but business wasn't steady. A woman could earn more selling sex, but that was risky in a few ways.

One of the favored moneymaking options, therefore, was to take in a boarder, which could generate a hundred dollars a month. There was never any shortage of people who needed a place to stay.

But I also discovered something more interesting, and probably more important, than the money that changed hands in these various transactions. Many households participated in a vast web of exchange in which women borrowed, bartered, and pooled their resources to survive. One woman might offer day care for a large group of women, another might have a car and contribute by driving folks to buy groceries, and other women might take turns cooking for various families. In some cases the members of a network maintained a fixed formula of exchange: If you cook my family five dinners, I'll take care of your kids for two days.

Often a network of women would share their apartments as well. Let's say there were five women on one floor whose apartments had maintenance problems (which, given the condition of the buildings, wasn't uncommon). There was little chance that the CHA would respond to all their repair requests, and the women couldn't afford to pay five different bribes to Ms. Bailey or the CHA building manager. These women would pool their money to make sure they *could* pay the necessary bribes so that at least one apartment in their network had hot water and at least two had working refrigerators and stoves; perhaps one of them would also pay for pirated cable TV. Everyone would shower in one apartment, cook in another apartment, keep their food elsewhere, sit in the one air-conditioned room to watch the one TV with cable, and so on. To have your own apartment with all utilities functioning was a luxury that few people expected in Robert Taylor.

I met most of the neighborhood's male hustlers by hanging out in the local parking lot with C-Note. He let people know that it was safe to speak with me. There were always a lot of men milling around, talking and drinking, who represented the diversity of the neighborhood hustlers: carpenters who did inexpensive home repairs, freelance preachers, truck drivers who worked off the books for local factories, car thieves, rappers and musicians, cooks and cleaners. All of them made their money under the table.

Most of them had once held legitimate jobs that they lost out of either misfortune or misbehavior. Until a few years earlier, they could have gotten a few hundred dollars a month in welfare money, but by 1990, Illinois and many other states eliminated such aid for adult men. The conservative revolution launched by President Ronald Reagan would lead eventually to a complete welfare overhaul, culminating in the 1996 directive by President Bill Clinton that made welfare a temporary program by setting time limits on just about every form of public aid—for men, women, and children.

For men like the ones in Robert Taylor, the welfare changes only exacerbated their poverty. They all learned to keep track of which restaurants and churches offered free food and which abandoned buildings were available for sleeping. Like the women, the men also had a network: One would cook while another looked for work while yet another tried to find a place for all of them to sleep. If they heard of a vacant apartment, they'd pool their resources to bribe the CHA building manager, gang leader, tenant leader, or whoever else happened to have the key. These men also passed along information to cops in exchange for "get out of jail free" promises, and they could always make a few dollars from CHA janitors—who regularly paid off hustlers to clean the buildings when they felt like taking a day off.

C-Note introduced me to Porter Harris, a bone-thin man, sixty-five years old, who spent much of his time scouring the South Side for recyclable junk. When I met him, he was pushing a shopping cart filled with wire, cans, and metal scrap, trolling the tall grass between the high-rises and the railroad tracks. Years ago, Porter told me, *he* was the one who dictated where various hustlers in Robert Taylor could work, sell, and trade, much as C-Note did now. But he'd had to leave because of a battle with a gang leader.

"Booty Caldwell, real name was Carter," he told me in a southern drawl. "That was the one who kicked me out of here for good." Porter picked at his few remaining teeth with a blade of grass. He wore a floppy straw hat that made him look as if he'd stepped out of a faded photograph from the Old South. "There were about ten of us. I controlled Forty-seventh Street to Fifty-first. I had this whole area—you couldn't sell your *soul* without letting me know about it, yessir."

"Sounds like a good living," I said, smiling. "You were the king of hustlers?"

"Lord, king, and chief. Call it what you want, I ran that area. And then one day it all was taken away. By Booty Caldwell. He was part of the El Rukn gang." By the late 1960s, El Rukn had become the most powerful gang in Chicago. They were widely credited with uniting many independent gangs, making peace treaties and cooperative arrangements that resulted in a few El Rukn "supergangs." But a federal indictment in the mid-1980s weakened El Rukn, allowing other gangs, including the Black Kings, to take over the burgeoning crack trade.

From Porter, C-Note, and others, I learned that the most profitable hustling jobs for men were in manual labor: you could earn five hundred dollars a month fixing cars in a parking lot or roughly three hundred dollars a month cleaning up at the local schools. The worst-paying jobs, meanwhile, often required the longest hours: gathering up scrap metal or aluminum (a hundred dollars a month) or selling stolen clothes or cigarettes (about seventy-five dollars a month). While just about every hustler I interviewed told me that he was hoping for a legit job and a better life, I rarely saw anyone get out

of the hustling racket unless he died or went to jail.

One day, after I'd spent hours interviewing Porter and some of the other male hustlers, I was summoned to Ms. Bailey's office. I'd been so busy that I hadn't seen her in a while. It was probably a good idea, I thought, to have a catch-up session.

I said hello to Catrina on my way in, and she gave me a smile. She was assuming more and more duties and seemed to be acting nearly as a junior officer to Ms. Bailey. Inside, J.T. and Ms. Bailey were laughing together and greeted me heartily.

"Mr. Professor!" J.T. said. "My mother says you haven't been by in a month! What, you don't like us anymore? You found somebody who cooks better?"

"You better not piss off Ms. Mae," Ms. Bailey said. "You'll never be able to come back in the building again."

"Sorry, all this interviewing has kept me really busy," I said, exasperated. "I just haven't had time to do much of anything else."

"Well, then, sit down, baby," Ms. Bailey said. "We won't keep you long. We just wanted to know who you've been meeting. We're curious about what you've learned."

"Hey, you know what, I could actually use the chance to tell you what I've been finding," I said, taking out my notebooks. "I've been meeting so many people, and I can't be sure whether they're telling me the truth about how much they earn. I suppose I want to know whether I'm really understanding what it's like to hustle around here."

"Sure," J.T. said. "We were just talking about that. You used to ask us to find you people. Now you do it yourself. We feel like you don't need us no more." He started laughing, and so did Ms. Bailey.

"Yeah," Ms. Bailey said. "Don't leave us behind, Mr. Professor, when you start to be successful! Go ahead, tell me who you've been talking to. If you tell us who you met and what they're doing, maybe we can check for you and see if folks are being straight."

For the next three hours, I went through my notebooks and told them what I'd learned about dozens of hustlers, male and female. There was Bird, the guy who sold license plates, Social Security cards, and small appliances out of his van. Doritha the tax preparer. Candy, one of the only female carpenters in the neighborhood. Prince, the man who could pirate gas and electricity for your apartment. J.T. and Ms. Bailey rarely seemed surprised, although every now and then one of them perked up when I mentioned a particularly enterprising hustler or a woman who had recently started taking in boarders.

I finally left, riding the bus home to my apartment. I was grateful for having had the opportunity to discuss my findings with two of the neighborhood's most formidable power brokers. As I looked out the bus windows, I realized just how much I owed Ms. Bailey and J.T. If it weren't for the two of them, and a few other people like C-Note and Autry, I wouldn't ever have made any progress in learning how things really worked around Robert Taylor.

I spent the next few weeks turning the information in my notebooks into statistical tables and graphs that showed how much different hustlers made. I figured that J.T. would appreciate this data at least as much as my professors would, since he was always talking about the importance of data analysis within his managerial technique. So I headed over to Robert Taylor to show him my research.

In the parking lot, I ran into C-Note, who was in his usual spot with a few other squatters, fixing flat tires and washing cars.

"Hey, what's up, guys?" I shouted out. "Long time—how you been?"

Nobody replied. They looked at me, then turned away. I walked closer and stood a few feet from them. "What's up?" I said. "Everything all right?"

One of the men, Pootie, picked up a tool and started to loosen a tire from the rim. "Man, sometimes you just learn the hard way," he said to no one in particular. "That's life, isn't it? Sometimes you realize you can't trust nobody. They could be a cop, a snitch—who knows?"

C-Note simply shrugged. "Mm-hmm," he said.

"Yup, you just learn you can't trust *nobody*," Pootie continued. "You tell them something, and then they turn on you. Just like *that*! You can't predict it. Especially if they're not from around here."

Once again C-Note shrugged. "Mm-hmm," he muttered. "You got that right."

They kept ignoring me, so I walked over to J.T.'s building. A young woman I knew named Keisha was standing on the grass with her kids. They looked like they were waiting for a ride.

"Hey, Keisha," I said. "How are you doing?"

"How am I *doing*?" she asked, shaking her head. "I was doing a lot better before I started talking to *you*." She picked up her things and walked her kids a few yards away.

In the lobby some of J.T.'s gang members were hanging out. We shook hands and said hello. I went upstairs to see Ms. Bailey and J.T., but neither of them was home.

Down in the lobby again, I could feel people staring at me, but I couldn't figure out why. I felt myself growing paranoid. Did people suddenly think I was a cop? What was up with Pootie, C-Note, and Keisha? I decided to go back home.

I spent a few days trying to track down J.T., but nobody knew where he was. I couldn't wait any longer, so I went back to Robert Taylor and found C-Note in the parking lot. He and two other men were working on a car.

"C-Note, please," I begged, "what did I do? Tell me."

C-Note stood up and wiped the oil off a wrench. He motioned for the two other men to leave us alone. One of them gave me a nasty look and muttered something that sounded equally nasty, but I couldn't quite make it out.

"You need to learn to shut your mouth," C-Note finally said.

"Shut my mouth? I don't know what you're talking about."

"Don't play with me. All that shit I told you. All them niggers I introduced you to. If you told me you were going to tell J.T. they were making that money, I wouldn't have told you nothing."

My heart sank. I thought of my long debriefing with J.T. and Ms. Bailey. I had given them breakdowns on each hustler's earnings: how much every one of them made, when and where they worked, what they planned for the future. I didn't hand over my written data, but I'd done the next-best thing.

"J.T. is all *over* these niggers," C-Note said. He looked disgusted and spit on the ground. I could tell he was angry but that he wasn't comfortable expressing it to me. Until now our relationship had been based on trust; I rarely, if ever, spoke to anyone about what I learned from C-Note.

"He's taxing every one of them now," he said. "And he beat the shit out of Parnell and his brother because he thought they were hiding what they were doing. They weren't, but you can't convince J.T. of nothing. When he gets his mind to something, that's it. And then he tells Jo-Jo and his guys that they can't come around no more because *they* were hiding things from him. Jo-Jo's daughter lives up in here. So now he can't see *her*." C-Note kept talking, getting angrier and angrier as he listed all the people that J.T. was cracking down on. "There's no way he could've found out if you didn't say nothing."

There was an awkward silence. I thought about lying, and I began to drum up an excuse. But something came over me.

During the years I'd been in this community, people were always telling me that I was different from all the journalists and other outsiders who came by, hunting up stories. They didn't eat dinner with families or hang around at night to share a beer; they typically asked a lot of questions and then left with their story, never to return. I prided myself on this difference.

But now it was time to accept my fate. "I was sitting in Ms. Bailey's office," I told C-Note. "She and J.T. always help me, just like you. And I fucked up. I told them things, and I had no idea that they would use that information. Man, I had no idea that it would even be useful to them."

"That has to be one of the stupidest things I *ever* heard you say." C-Note began putting away his tools.

"Honestly, C-Note, I had no idea when I was talking to them—"

"No!" C-Note's voice grew sharp. "You knew. Yes you did. But you were too busy thinking about your own self. That's what happened. You got some shit for your professors, and you were getting high on that. I know you ain't *that* naïve, man."

"I'm sorry, C-Note. I don't know what else to say. I fucked up."

"Yeah, you fucked up. You need to think about *why* you're doing your work. You always tell me you want to help us. Well, we ain't never asked for your help, and we sure don't need it now."

C-Note walked away toward the other men. They stood quietly drinking beer and watching me. I headed toward the building. I wanted to see if Ms. Bailey was in her office.

Then an obvious thought hit me: If J.T. had acted on my information to tax the male street hustlers, Ms. Bailey might have started taxing the women I told her about. Worse yet, she might have had some of them evicted for hiding their income. How could I find out what had happened because of my stupidity? As I stood in the grassy expanse, staring up at the high-rise,

I tried to think of someone who might possibly help me. I needed a tenant who was relatively independent of Ms. Bailey, someone who might still trust me enough to talk. I thought of Clarisse.

I hustled over to the liquor store and bought a few bottles of Boone's Farm wine. Clarisse wasn't going to talk for free.

I walked quickly through the building lobby and took the stairs up. I didn't want to get trapped in the elevator with women who might be angry with me for selling them out to Ms. Bailey. Clarisse opened her door and greeted me with a loud burst of laughter.

"Oooh! Boy, you fucked up this time, you surely did."

"So it's all over the building? Everyone knows?"

"Sweetheart, ain't no secrets in this place. What did Clarisse tell you when we first met? *Shut the fuck up.* Don't tell them nothing about who you are and what you do. Clarisse should have been there with you. You were spying for Ms. Bailey?"

"Spying! No way. I wasn't spying, I was just doing my research, asking questions and—"

"Sweetheart, it don't matter what you call it. Ms. Bailey got pissed off and went running up in people's houses, claiming they owed her money. I mean, you probably doubled her income, just like that. And you're really not getting *any* kickbacks? Just a little something from her?"

"Wait a minute," I said. "How do they know I was the one who gave Ms. Bailey the information?"

"Because, you fool, she *told* everyone! Even if she didn't tell them, she was running around saying, 'You made twenty-five dollars last month,' 'You made fifty dollars last week,' 'You made ten dollars this week, and you owe me ten percent plus a penalty for not telling me.' I mean, the only folks we told all this information to was you!"

"But did she charge you, too?"

"No, no! She don't charge the hos, remember? J.T. already charges us."

I sat and listened with my head down as Clarisse listed all the women who'd been confronted by Ms. Bailey. I had a sinking feeling that I'd have a hard time coming back to this building to continue my research. I also had to face the small matter of managing to leave here today still in one piece.

Clarisse sensed my anxiety. As she talked—laughing heartily all the while, at my expense—she started massaging my shoulder. "Don't worry, little baby! You probably never had an ass whuppin', have you? Well, sometimes that helps clear the air. Just don't take the stairs when you leave, 'cause if you get caught there, they may never find your body."

I must have looked truly frightened, for Clarisse stopped laughing and took a sincere tone.

"Folks forgive around here," she said gently. "We're all religious people, sweetheart. We have to put up with a lot of shit from our own families, so nothing you did to us will make things much worse."

At that moment, sitting with Clarisse, I didn't think that even the Good Lord himself could, or would, help me. It was embarrassing to think that I had been so wrapped up in my desire to obtain good data that I couldn't anticipate the consequences of my actions. After several years in the projects, I had become attuned to each and every opportunity to get information from the tenants. This obsession was primarily fueled by a desire to make my dissertation stand out and increase my stature in the eyes of my advisers. After I'd talked with C-Note and Clarisse, it was clear to me that other people were paying a price for my success.

I began to feel deeply ambivalent about my own reasons for being in the projects. Would I really advance society with my research, as Bill Wilson had promised I could do if I worked hard? Could I change our stereotypes of the poor by getting so deep inside the lives of the families? I suddenly felt deluged by these kinds of questions.

Looking back, I was probably being a little melodramatic. I had been so naïve up to this point about how others perceived my presence that any sort of shake-up at all was bound to send me reeling.

I couldn't think of a way to rectify the situation other than to stop coming to Robert Taylor entirely. But I was close to finishing my fieldwork, and I didn't want to quit prematurely. In the coming weeks, I spoke to Clarisse and Autry a few times for advice. Both suggested that the tenants I had angered would eventually stop being so angry, but they couldn't promise much more than that. When I asked Autry whether I'd be able to get back to collecting data, he just shrugged and walked off.

I eventually came back to the building to face the tenants. No one declined to speak with me outright, but I didn't exactly receive a hero's welcome either. Everyone knew I had J.T.'s support, so it was unlikely that anyone would confront me in a hostile manner. When I went to visit C-Note in the parking lot, he simply nodded at me and then went about his work, talking with customers and singing along with the radio. It felt like people in the building looked at me strangely when I passed by, but I wondered if I was just being paranoid. Perhaps the best indicator of my change in status was that I wasn't doing much of anything *casual*—hearing jokes, sharing a beer, loaning someone a dollar.

One sultry summer day not long after my fiasco with the hustlers, I attended the funeral of Catrina, Ms. Bailey's dutiful assistant. On the printed announcement, her full name was rendered as Catrina Eugenia Washington. But I knew this was not her real name.

Catrina had once told me that her father had sexually abused her when she was a teenager, so she ran away from home. She wound up living in Robert Taylor with a distant relative. She changed her name so her father wouldn't find her and enrolled in a GED program at DuSable High School. She took a few part-time jobs to help pay for rent and groceries. She was also saving money to go to community college; she was trying to start over. I never did find out her real name.

As a kid she had wanted to study math. But her father, she told me, said that higher education was inappropriate for a young black woman. He advised her instead just to get married and have children.

Catrina had a love of knowledge and would participate in a discussion about nearly anything. I enjoyed talking with her about science, African-American history, and Chicago politics. She always wore a studious look, intense and focused. Working as Ms. Bailey's assistant, she received just a few dollars a week. But, far more significant, she was receiving an apprenticeship in Chicago politics. "I will do something important one day," she liked to tell me, in her most serious voice. "Like Ms. Bailey, I *will* make a difference for black people. Especially black women."

By this time Catrina had been living in Robert Taylor for a few years. But over the July Fourth holiday, she decided to visit her siblings in Chicago's south suburbs, an area increasingly populated with African-American families who'd made it out of the ghetto. From what I was told, her father heard that she was visiting and tracked her down. A skirmish followed. Catrina got caught between her brother, who was protecting her, and her angry father. A gun went off, and the bullet hit Catrina, killing her instantly. No one around Robert Taylor knew if either the brother or the father had been arrested.

The funeral was held in the back room of a large African Methodist Episcopal church on the grounds of Robert Taylor. The hot air was stifling, the sun streaming in shafts through dusty windows. There were perhaps fifty people in attendance, mostly women from Ms. Bailey's building. A few members of Catrina's family were also there, but they came surreptitiously because they didn't want her father to hear about the funeral. Ms. Bailey stationed herself at the room's entrance, welcoming the mourners. She looked as if she were presiding over a tenant meeting: upright, authoritarian, refusing to cry while consoling those who were. She had the air of someone who did this regularly, who mourned for someone every week.

Sitting in a corner up front was T-Bone, his head down, still as stone. He and Catrina had been seeing each other for a few months. Although T-Bone had a steady girlfriend—it wasn't uncommon for gang members, or practically any other young man in the projects, to have multiple girlfriends—he and Catrina had struck up a friendship and, over time, become lovers. I sometimes came upon the two of them studying together at a local diner. T-Bone was about to leave his girlfriend for Catrina when she was killed.

Any loss of life is mourned in the projects, but there are degrees. Young men and women who choose a life of drugs and street gangs may, understandably, not be long for this world. When one of them dies, he or she is certainly mourned, but without any great sense of shock; there is a general feeling that death was always a good possibility. But for someone like Catrina, who had refused to follow such a path, death came with a deep sense of shock and disbelief. She was one of thousands of young people who had escaped the attention of social workers, the police, and just about everyone else. Adults in the projects pile up their hopes on people like Catrina, young men and women who take a sincere interest in education, work, and self-betterment. And I guess I did, too. Her death left me with a sting that would never fade.

The essays that Catrina used to write covered the difficulties of family life in the projects, the need for women to be independent, the stereotypes about poor people. Writing seemed to provide Catrina a sense of relief,

as though she were finally acknowledging the hurdles of her own past; it also helped her develop a strong, assertive voice, not unlike that of her hero, Ms. Bailey.

In tribute to Catrina, I thought I'd try to broaden this idea by starting a writing workshop for young women in the building who were interested in going back to school. I brought up the possibility with Ms. Bailey. "Good idea," she said, "but take it slow, especially when you're dealing with *these* young women."

I was nervous about teaching the workshop, but I was also eager. My relationship with tenants up to this point had largely been a one-way street; after all this time in Robert Taylor, I felt as though I should give something back. On a few occasions, I had managed to solicit donations from my professors, fifty or a hundred dollars, for some kind of program in the neighborhood. This money might do a great deal of good, but it seemed to me a fairly impersonal way of helping. I was hoping to do something more direct.

In the past I hadn't been drawn to standard charitable activities like coaching basketball or volunteering at a school, because I wanted to differentiate myself from the people who helped families and ran programs in the community. I had heard many tenants criticize the patronizing attitudes of such volunteers. The writing workshop, however, seemed like a good fit. Having hung out in the community for several years, I believed I could avoid the kind of fate—exclusion, cold stares, condescending responses—that often greeted the people who rode into town to do good.

I was also still reeling from the fact that I had alienated so many people around J.T.'s territory. I was feeling guilty, and I needed to get people back on my side again.

Of all the people in the projects, I had the least experience spending time with young women, particularly single mothers. I was a bit nervous, particularly because Ms. Bailey, Ms. Mae, and other older women warned me not to get too close to the young women. They felt that the women would begin looking to me as a source of support.

In the beginning the group convened wherever we could—in someone's apartment, at a diner, outside under a tree. At first there were five women in the group, and then we grew to roughly a dozen as more people heard about it. The meetings were pretty casual, and attendance could be spotty, since the women had family and work obligations.

From the outset it was an emotional experience. The women wrote and spoke openly about their struggles. Each of them had at least a couple of children, which generally meant at least one "baby daddy" who wasn't in the picture. Each of them had a man in her life who'd been either jailed or killed. They spoke of in-laws who demanded that the women give up their children to the father's family, some of whom were willing to use physical force to claim the children.

Their material hardships were overwhelming. Most of them earned no more than ten thousand dollars a year, a combination of welfare payments and food stamps. Some worked part-time, and others took in boarders who paid cash or, nearly as valuable, provided day care so the young women could work, run errands, or just have a little time for themselves.

The most forceful stories were the tales of abuse. Every single woman had been beaten up by a boyfriend (who was usually drunk at the time), some almost fatally. Every one of them had lived in fear for days or weeks, waiting for the same man to return.

One cold autumn evening, we congregated at a local diner. We found a large table in the back, where it was quiet. The owner was by now accustomed to our presence, and he didn't mind that we stayed for hours. If business was particularly good, he'd feed us all night long and then waive the tab. He and I had struck up a friendship—I often came to the diner to write up my field notes—and he liked the fact that I was trying to help tenants.

The theme of this week's essay was "How I Survive." Tanya was the first to read from her journal. She was twenty years old, a high-school dropout with two children. She'd stayed with her mother after the first child was born but eventually got her own apartment in the same building, then had a second baby. She didn't know the whereabouts of the first father; the second had died in a gang shooting. In her essay she bragged about how she earned twice her welfare income by taking in boarders.

"But sometimes it doesn't go so well, Sudhir," said one of the other women, Sarina, who liked to be the voice of reason. She stared down Tanya as she spoke. Sarina had three children, the fathers of whom were, respectively, in jail, dead, and unwilling to pay child support. So she, too, had taken in boarders. "I remember when my brother came into the house, he started dealing dope and they caught him. Almost took my lease away."

"Yeah, but that's just because you didn't pay the building manager enough money," Tanya said. "Or I think that it was because you didn't sleep with him!"

"Well, I'm not doing either one of those things," Sarina said in a moralistic tone, shaking her head.

"You got some nerve," interrupted Keisha. "Sarina, you put your ass out there for any man who comes looking." At twenty-six, Keisha was one of the oldest women in the group. Even though she had grown angry with me for sharing information about hustlers with Ms. Bailey, she hadn't held the grudge for long. She had two daughters and was the best writer in the group, a high-school graduate now planning to apply to Roosevelt College. "Hell, there ain't no difference between some ho selling her shit and you taking some man in your house for money."

"Hey, *that's* survival!" Tanya said. "I mean, that's what we're here to talk about, right?"

"Okay," I jumped in, trying to establish some order. "What's the best way for you to take care of whatever you need to? Give me the top ten ways you survive."

Sarina began. "Always make sure you know someone at the CHA you can turn to when you can't make rent. It helps, because you could get evicted."

"Yeah, and if you have to sleep with a nigger downtown, then you got to do it," said Keisha. "Because if you don't, they *will* put your kids on the street."

Sarina went on, ignoring Keisha. "You got to make sure you can get clothes and food and diapers for your kids," she said. "Even if you don't have money. So you need to have good relations with stores."

"Make sure Ms. Bailey's always getting some dick!" Keisha shouted, laughing hard.

"You know, one time I had to let her sleep with *my* man so I wouldn't get kicked out of the building," Chantelle said.

"That's awful," I said.

"Yeah," Chantelle said. "And he almost left me, too, when he found out that Ms. Bailey could get him a job and would let him stay up there and eat all her food." Chantelle was twenty-one. Her son had learning disabilities, so she was struggling to find a school that could help him. She worked part-time at a fast-food restaurant and depended on her mother and grandmother for day care and cash.

Chantelle's hardships weren't uncommon in the projects. Unfortunately, neither was her need to appease Ms. Bailey. The thought that a tenant had to let the building president sleep with her partner was alarming to me. But among these women such indignities weren't rare. To keep your own household intact, they said, you had to keep Ms. Bailey happy and well paid. As I heard more stories similar to Chantelle's, I found myself growing angry at Ms. Bailey and the other LAC officials. I asked Chantelle and the other women why they didn't challenge Ms. Bailey. Their answer made perfect sense: When it became obvious that the

housing authority supported a management system based on extortion and corruption, the women decided their best option was to shrug their shoulders and accept their fate.

I found it unconscionable that such a regime existed, but I wasn't going to confront Ms. Bailey either. She was too powerful. And so while the women's anger turned into despair, my disgust began to morph into bitterness.

The women's list of survival techniques went well beyond ten. Keep cigarettes in your apartment so you can pay off a squatter to fix things when they break. Let your child pee in the stairwell to keep prostitutes from congregating there at night. Let the gangs pay you to store drugs and cash in your apartment. (The risk of apprehension, the women concurred, was slim.)

Then there were all the resources to be procured in exchange for sex: groceries from the bodega owner, rent forgiveness from the CHA, assistance from a welfare bureaucrat, preferential treatment from a police officer for a jailed relative. The women's explanation for using sex as currency was consistent and pragmatic: If your child was in danger of going hungry, then you did whatever it took to fix the problem. The women looked pained when they discussed using their bodies to obtain these necessities; it was clear that this wasn't their first—or even their hundredth—preference.

"Always know somebody at the hospital," Tanya blurted out. "Always have somebody you can call, because that ambulance never comes. And when you get there, you need to pay somebody, or else you'll be waiting in line forever!"

"Yes, that's true, and the people at the hospital can give you free baby food," Sarina said. "Usually you need to meet them in the back alley. And I'd say you should keep a gun or a knife hidden, in case your man starts beating you. Because sometimes you have to do something to get him to stop."

"You've had to use a knife before?" I asked. No one had spoken or written about this yet. "How often?"

"Many times!" Sarina looked at me as if I'd grown up on Mars. "When these men start drinking, you can't talk to them. You just need to protect yourself—and don't forget, they'll beat up the kids, too."

Keisha started to cry. She dropped her head into her lap and covered up so no one could see. Sarina leaned over and hugged her.

"The easiest time is when they're asleep," Tanya said. "They're lying there, mostly because they've passed out drunk. That's when it runs through your mind. You start thinking, 'I could end it right here. I could kill the motherfucker, right now. Then he can't beat me no more.' I think about it a lot."

Keisha wiped her eyes. "I stabbed that nigger because I couldn't take it no more. Wasn't anybody helping me. Ms. Bailey said she couldn't do nothing, the police said they couldn't do nothing. And this man was coming around beating me and beating my baby for no reason. I couldn't think of any other way, couldn't think of nothing else to do...."

She began to sob again. Sarina escorted her to the bathroom.

"She sent her man to the hospital," Tanya quietly explained. "Almost killed him. One night he was asleep on the couch—he had already sent *her* to the hospital a few times, broke her ribs, she got stitches and bruises all over her body. She grabbed that knife and kept putting it in his stomach. He got up and ran out the apartment. I think one of J.T.'s boys took him to the hospital. He's a BK."

Because the boyfriend was a senior gang member, Tanya said, J.T. refused to pressure him to stop beating Keisha. She still lived in fear that the man would return.

One day Ms. Bailey called and asked that I come to a building-wide meeting with her tenants. She hadn't invited me to such a meeting in more than a year, so I figured something important was afoot.

I hadn't been keeping up with Ms. Bailey's tenant meetings in part because I'd already amassed sufficient information on these gatherings and also because, in all honesty, I'd grown uncomfortable watching the horse-trading schemes that she and other tenant leaders used to manage the community.

My own life was also starting to evolve. I had moved in with my girlfriend, Katchen, and we were thinking about getting married. Visiting our relatives—mine in California and hers in Montana—took time away from my fieldwork, including much of our summers and vacations. My parents were thrilled, and they pushed me to think seriously about starting a family along with a career. Katchen was applying to law school; neither of us was ready for children just yet.

And then there was the matter of my dissertation, which I still had to write. I began to meet more regularly with Bill Wilson and other advisers to see whether I could plausibly move toward wrapping up my graduate study.

Ms. Bailey's office was packed for the meeting when I arrived, with a few dozen people in attendance, all talking excitedly. As usual, most of them were older women, but there were also several men standing in the back. I recognized a couple of them as the partners of women in the building; it was unusual to see these men at a public meeting. Ms. Bailey waved me up front, pointing me to the chair next to hers.

"Okay," she said, "Sudhir has agreed to come here today so we can clear this up."

I was taken aback. Clear *what* up? Everyone was suddenly staring at me, and they didn't look happy.

"Why are you sleeping with my daughter?" shouted a woman I didn't recognize. "Tell me, goddamn it! Why are you fucking my baby?"

"Answer the woman!" someone else hollered. I couldn't tell who was talking, but it didn't matter: I was in a state of shock.

One man, addressing me as "Arab," told me I should get out of the neighborhood for good and especially leave alone their young women. Other people joined in:

"Nigger, get out of here!"

"Arab, go home!"

"Get the fuck out, Julio!"

Ms. Bailey tried to restore order. Amid the shouting she yelled out that I would explain myself.

I was still confused. "Let Sudhir tell you why he's meeting them!" Ms. Bailey said, and then I understood: It was the writing workshop. People had seen me picking up the young women and driving away with them. Apparently they thought I was sleeping with them, or maybe pimping them out.

As I cried to explain the writing workshop, I kept getting drowned out. I began to feel scared. I had seen how a mob of tenants nearly tore apart the Middle Eastern shopkeeper who'd slept with Boo-Boo's daughter.

Ms. Bailey finally made herself heard above the riot. "He's trying to tell you that he's just helping them with homework!"

That quieted everyone down a little bit. But still, I was stung: Why weren't any of the women from the workshop in attendance? Why hadn't anyone come to defend me, to tell the truth?

After a few more minutes, things having calmed down a bit, Ms. Bailey told me to leave. There was other business to take care of, she said, laughing—at me—and clearly enjoying herself at my expense.

Leaving the building that night, I wondered how much more time I could afford to spend in J.T.'s territory. It was hard to think of any tenants who *weren't* angry with me.

52

ANNETTE LAREAU

REFLECTIONS ON LONGITUDINAL ETHNOGRAPHY AND THE FAMILIES' REACTIONS TO UNEQUAL CHILDHOODS

from *Unequal Childhoods* (2011)

In this courageous contribution, Annette Lareau describes her subjects' reactions to the way they were represented in her long-term study of poor and middle-class family life in Philadelphia. Highlighting their sense of betrayal, she makes it possible for us to end this volume with her insistence that we never lose sight of the emotional costs that ethnography can have for subjects and investigators alike.

You slurred us, Annette; you made us look like poor white trash. (Ms. Yanelli's reaction to reading *Unequal Childhoods*)

In qualitative research, the way the researcher acts in the field is inextricably connected to data quality. Thus, by tradition qualitative researchers often share the "story behind the story."[1] Throughout my career, I have contributed to this tradition by sharing the missteps that are inevitable in a research project.[2] As part of the second edition, I once again share some of the more problematic details, which otherwise would remain private, of my methodological decisions and my experience conducting the longitudinal research. I also summarize and discuss the reactions of the families to the book.

I present this information for three reasons. First, it may help readers assess the quality, and limits, of these data. Second, it may relieve novice researchers to know that seasoned researchers make mistakes in the field; such knowledge may spur them to develop a more realistic view of field work. Third, I seek to use my experience as a springboard to reflect on broader methodological issues that confront many researchers. For example, the topic of longitudinal ethnography is relatively recent in the literature.[3] I take up some of the problems that surface in longitudinal ethnography that, I believe, have not been sufficiently acknowledged. In particular, the follow-up to an ethnographic study is likely to rely much more on interviews than on observations; this form of data collection is severely limited. Also, ethnographic studies that are large and ambitious face more complications in a follow-up than do ethnographic studies that are more manageable in size.

Another area I address involves relations between the researcher and research participants. There is an extensive body of methodological writings on this topic.[4] But little attention has been paid to the issue of sharing research results with research participants. Participants seem frequently to feel angry and betrayed when they read research results.[5] This response needs stronger emphasis and more sustained discussion in methodological writings.... I think conducting ethnographic research is important, and researchers should do everything possible to forewarn and protect study participants, including offering them assistance as they respond to social-science portrayals of their lives. But researchers also need to retain control over key aspects of their projects. It is a delicate process to forge meaningful relationships with research participants while simultaneously maintaining the critical analytic framework necessary to

undergird an argument. There are neither easy answers nor one-size-fits-all guidelines. An essential first step for researchers, however, is to more directly acknowledge the emotional cost of ethnographic work for study participants.

The Limits of the Longitudinal Follow-up to *Unequal Childhoods*

...I kept in touch with the children over the years by sending an annual holiday card with five dollars tucked into the envelope. When, approximately ten years after the start of the original study, I decided to do a follow-up, some of the families were easy to reach.[6] Others, particularly the McAllisters, were extremely difficult to find. Still, the many hours spent searching paid off: I tracked down everyone. I began reinterviewing the families in the spring and summer of 2003. I generally just called the house, spoke with the mother, and requested her son's or daughter's cell phone number and e-mail address. I contacted the young adults directly; now that they were older, they could decide for themselves if they wanted to be interviewed. I offered the youths a hefty honorarium ($75), since I felt it was critical that each one agree to participate in the follow-up. I also offered an honorarium of $50 to each of the other family members who agreed to an interview. In each family, I completed the family-member interviews after I had interviewed the youth. My sense is that all of the young people and family members would have participated in the follow-up without the incentive of an honorarium, but I cannot be certain of that. Since the book was not published until the early fall of 2003, the families had not read it at the time I first reestablished contact. Most seemed glad to hear from me. Some had given up on the possibility that a book would ever appear; they were pleased to hear it was coming out. Generally, people greeted me warmly, as if I were an old friend. However, as I explain below, after they had read their description in the book, some families' feelings changed.[7]

The fact that I was able to reach 100 percent of the families is a strength of the follow-up study, as is the fact that I gained the cooperation of all of the young adults and most of the parents. Nonetheless, even this small study was labor intensive. In the end, I conducted nearly forty follow-up interviews. Then I arranged to have the interviews transcribed; next came coding and analyzing the data; and finally, the struggle to write up my findings. In short, the project was a major undertaking in which I invested significant time and energy. Nevertheless, I am fundamentally dissatisfied with the data set. Because my criticisms are conceptual they are relevant for other studies.

Social scientists see a longitudinal follow-up to an ethnography as having many potential virtues, including the ability to assess the degree to which original theoretical conclusions are sustained over time. The in-depth interviews I conducted were revealing, but they provide few surprises in terms of the youths' and families' trajectories. Over time, the inequalities in family life grew, rather than shrank. Although some of the working-class and poor families made important gains, the power of social class remained considerable. Hence, the follow-up supports the basic argument of the original study. These are interesting findings, and they may help satisfy readers' curiosity about what happened as the youngsters profiled in the text grew into adulthood. But, like all other longitudinal studies based solely on interviews, the follow-up has important limitations. The research design precluded collecting the deeper, richer, and, I believe, ultimately more valuable data that come from participant-observation of the rituals of daily life. The original study, because it involved participant-observation across multiple settings, embedded the

families and kids in a social context. The longitudinal follow-up isolated the young adults and families from the social context.

This is a crucial methodological difference.[8] With no observations of daily life (and no interviews with educators or other key people), the longitudinal follow-up lacks the critical institutional information and triangulation of data that characterized the original study. This severely limits its value. The lack of institutional checks weakens the interview findings. There was no way for me to confirm the young adults' portrayal of events; and it was impossible to ascertain the accuracy of information conveyed by family members about key life transitions. And, particularly compared to the observational data collected in the original study, the interviews shed less light on a fundamental point: that differences in social class matter because they provide unequal advantages in key institutions.

What I Wish I Could Have Done

In hindsight, I wish I had visited the kids when most were in their senior year of high school to do observations; gather school transcripts, SAT scores, and college applications; and conduct interviews with key teachers, coaches, and counselors. But even as wishful thinking, it is hard to imagine. It would have been too formidable a task, for a variety of reasons. The nine youths featured most prominently in the book attended eight different high schools; the full sample of twelve covered ten different high schools. In the years since I began the original study, the paperwork requirements for doing research have escalated. Applications to the committee for the protection of human subjects (commonly known as an Institutional Review Board, or IRB) are much more detailed than in earlier years. The IRB must review and approve researchers' interview guides, consent forms, letters of solicitation to recruit participants, etc. Moreover, the application process for research in schools is cumbersome; the permissions alone typically take many weeks. Likewise, negotiating access with districts, principals, and families involves countless hours and a wide array of challenges.

As Mitchell Duneier has pointed out, many of the best ethnographic studies have been doctoral dissertations.[9] These projects were not carried out by seasoned researchers but by novices who, despite their inexperience, have tremendous advantages. One is that frequently they are at a life stage that allows them to spend an enormous number of hours in the field. This immersion is often crucial for the establishment of rapport with participants and the subsequent development of rich theoretical insights. In the youths' last year in high school (2001–2), I was still writing *Unequal Childhoods*. The following year, although I continued to think about beginning another round of observations and interviews for all of the youths, I faced many professional and personal obstacles to undertaking a labor-intensive study. I had significant teaching, advising, and professional responsibilities.[10] The normal obligations of family life were heightened by the upheaval associated with the unexpected need for immediate and extensive home repair work. In addition, I faced personal challenges that year, with the deaths of my mother and a close family friend. Qualitative research intrudes further into the researcher's personal life than does quantitative research, in that vital aspects of qualitative research are interpersonal rather than distanced. Despite my desire to reconnect with the twelve kids and to gather information about the key institutions in their lives, the prospect of launching another major study seemed overwhelming.

As with the initial study, a key problem presented by the follow-up was that the project was too big. With ethnographies, the more typical approach is to focus on one site—or even one family.[11] With twelve families in the original study, *Unequal Childhoods* was too ambitious; subsequently, the longitudinal follow-up was also overly ambitious, which created complications at every point. If there had been only three families in the original study, I might have managed to gain access to the schools, follow kids around, and re-immerse myself in participant-observation. Doing that kind of follow-up with twelve (or even nine) families was not feasible.

There are fortunately, some aspects of the longitudinal follow-up about which I remain enthusiastic. It was very helpful to examine the youths' trajectory over time. The evidence of continuity rather than deflection in the trajectories is striking. Still, as I have tried to make clear here, there are very significant differences between the information yielded by interviews and the information yielded by participant-observation. Given the labor-intensive nature of participant-observation and the increased institutional demands on researchers, interviews are more common, but, despite some valuable features, interviews are inevitably less revealing about the rituals of daily life than are observations.[12]

The Cost of Research: Reactions to the Book

The process whereby I learned what families thought about *Unequal Childhoods* unfolded over several months. As previously noted, the longitudinal follow-up consisted of in-depth interviews with all of the young adults, their parents, and, in most cases, one sibling. In some cases, such as with the Marshall family, I finished all of the interviews with the family members in the summer and then dropped off a copy of the book in the fall. Other times, I brought the book to the interview, and then when I came back to do another interview, I listened to how the families felt about the book. Some of the time, I heard what family members thought during telephone conversations (usually when I was calling to arrange another interview). Other times we were face-to-face. Sometimes I simply dropped by unannounced a week or so after having dropped off a copy of the book, just to see what the family thought. I usually brought food, such as a cake or a pie, when I came.[13] In a few cases, I brought a tape recorder and taped the family members' reactions to the book. "I want to be sure that I understand exactly what you are saying," I would say. "Is it okay if I tape?" I also told the families that the second edition was going to include a new section, where I would summarize their reactions. In asking their permission to tape, I explained that I wanted the new section to be as accurate as possible.[14]

There were many different reactions to the book. The Brindles, McAllisters, and Marshalls seemed fundamentally "okay" with it. Similarly, the Carrolls, Greeleys, and Irwins, the families who were discussed in the tables and appendices but who were not portrayed in detail in the text, did not have complaints. However, the other six of the twelve families, the Drivers, Handlons, Tallingers, Taylors, Williamses, and Yanellis, were deeply troubled by the book. One family, the Williamses, severed ties with me, as did one mother, Ms. Tallinger. The complaints varied. Some families felt that I had made them "look bad." Some disputed the accuracy of the claims. Others felt that the portraits failed to grasp core elements of family members' subjective experience. I invited each of the families to write a summary of how they felt about the book or to edit what I wrote. Only Ms. Taylor wrote something; in addition, the Tallingers edited my draft.[15] As the summaries of their reactions...reveal, there is no obvious pattern by class (or race) in how families reacted....

Reaction of the Middle-Class Families

The Tallinger Family (white boy/middle-class)
The Tallingers objected to the portrayal of their family. At a fundamental level, they felt that I did not "get it" in terms of how much they *enjoyed* the activities that kept their family so busy. It was fun for all of them. Mr. Tallinger reported that the children had wonderful memories of their participation in activities. It was not labor. The parents also vehemently objected to any hint that they might have favored one child (Garrett) and his activities over another. Indeed, they clearly recalled emphasizing the extent to which they worked to find activities that Spencer might enjoy. A committed conservative, Mr. Tallinger also objected to the book's concluding chapter, which he found "socialistic." Ms. Tallinger appeared to feel as if the family had been misused; she indicated in an e-mail message that she preferred not to communicate with me any longer. Garrett gave his father a holiday gift of Malcolm Gladwell's *Outliers*, which discusses *Unequal Childhoods*. After reading it, Mr. Tallinger wrote me a friendly e-mail.[16]

The Handlon Family (white girl/middle-class) The Handlons also were not happy about the book. On the phone, Ms. Handlon said tersely, "I felt it was written by three women who were here for three weeks and who didn't have kids." Mr. Handlon elaborated that he and his wife felt that *Unequal Childhoods* uncritically adopted the perspective of Melanie's teacher as the only legitimate point of view and thus failed to accurately chronicle the Handlons' actual experience with educators. Ms. Handlon felt that I had failed to grasp the reality of having children, especially having a child who, every single day, was unhappy about having to go to school. When I interviewed Mr. Handlon, he conveyed this same idea by telling me a story about his choir leader. Until this woman had children of her own, he said, she did not fully understand why choir would not be every choir member's top priority. For Mr. and Ms. Handlon, a similar kind of inexperience marred *Unequal Childhoods.* They too felt that I just "didn't get it."

Moreover, Mr. Handlon, stressing "we deliberately kept a slower pace" so that the children would have time to play outside, objected to the portrayal of their family life as hectic. References to their house being messy also felt critical to the Handlons. Mr. Handlon reported, too, that Melanie was devastated by the description of her as "chubby." He wondered out loud, "What does it really add" to the description? He said it was particularly insulting since another girl was described as "pretty." He recalled that the physical description of his daughter was a powerful negative experience that led Melanie to "shut down" (i.e., withdraw from a conversation about the book).[17] Still, Mr. Handlon did acknowledge that the description of their Christmas Eve felt accurate and that, to this day, when it is hard for Melanie to get a word in edgewise in the busy conversational space of the Handlon family, Melanie will sometimes brandish the point that they are not letting her finish, just as was written in the book.

The Williams Family (African American boy/middle-class) A few months after I had interviewed Alexander, I stopped by the Williamses' house to drop off a copy of the book. It was a Saturday afternoon. Mr. Williams was in the yard, raking leaves. He seemed pleased to hold the book in his hand and to see that (after many years) the project had come to fruition. I told him that I wanted to interview him. He seemed open to it. Smiling, he said that the previous spring would have been a better time for the interview, since his wife was traveling frequently. I e-mailed Ms. Williams to set up an interview, but there was never a good time. (Once, I happened to call just as a pipe was bursting and water was flooding the first floor of their home.) I sent an e-mail every three months or so for almost two years. Ms. Williams would say that she

was busy or not available then, but that she would give me a call.

By December 2005, I was thinking of making one final attempt to schedule interviews with Mr. and Ms. Williams. I e-mailed Ms. Williams to ask if there would be time to set up an interview. She wrote to say that the family did not wish to have any further involvement with the project. The note indicated that they felt that objectivity had been "lost" in the "subjective details," with the result that none of them had been portrayed in an "honest manner." They felt that the "training" and "maturity" of the researchers was inadequate and not up to professional standards. Ms. Williams asked me not to contact them and, especially, not to contact Alexander in the future; she reported that Alexander also had grave concerns about the portrait. She acknowledged that the family's decision likely would be "troubling" to me but asked that I honor their request.

I e-mailed Ms. Williams (with the subject line "confirmation that I will honor your request") and indicated that I would certainly honor their request, including no longer sending a holiday card and small gift to Alexander. I also apologized for any difficulty the book had caused them. She replied immediately with a brief note wishing me a wonderful holiday season.[18]

The Marshall Family (African American girl/middle-class) As with many of the families, I postponed the task of delivering the book to the Marshalls because I was extremely anxious about how they might react to it. I had interviewed all four family members in the summer, but it was November—and the book had been published in September—before I dropped by the Marshall home. I came in the evening, without calling ahead, bringing along a copy of the book. Ms. Marshall answered the door. As we stood, just inside, near the door, she told me in a friendly tone that she had found the book at Barnes and Noble and had already read it. (She had not wanted to wait.) I told her that I was sorry it had taken me so long to get it to her. I asked her what she thought. Shifting from foot to foot and looking somewhat sheepish and embarrassed, she said, "I thought, 'Is that really me?' And then I thought, 'Yes.'" She did not have any complaints. We then went upstairs to see Mr. Marshall, who was recuperating from a leg injury. I told them that some of the families were distressed by the book. Always a jovial and expansive man, Mr. Marshall could not see why that would happen since, in his view, "It complimented everyone!" Somewhat later Stacey wrote me an e-mail. She told me that she had read the description of her family and that it made her "appreciate" how much her mom did for her.[19] Unlike some other families, the Marshalls seemed comfortable with the book's portrayal of them.

Reaction of the Working-Class Families

The Driver Family (white girl/working-class) Wendy Driver, Ms. Driver, and Wendy's stepfather Mack all vehemently objected to the book. The complaints were largely about the interpretation of events and a representation that made them look bad. For example, during my interview with Wendy, she focused on a passage in the book where her parents are described as listening to her but not turning her statements into a teachable moment. She read aloud from the book, in heated tones:

> [When she asks] her family members, one by one, if they knew what a mortal sin is, her mom says, "Tell us what it is. You're the one who went to CCD."...[They] looked at her as she spoke but neither acknowledged her answer. They waited her out and then returned to watching TV.[20]

Then, speaking angrily, Wendy told me:

> First of all, I *know* for a fact that my mother would never say anything like that to me. They would tell me, like I said,

to go get the book and we will, you know, find it, and if they don't find it, that you can call my grandma and find it....They wouldn't blow it off and sit there and just watch TV. When it came to CCD, school work, any kind of work, they took it serious. They just never blew it off the way the book is saying.

Wendy felt the portrayal suggested that her family ignored her. "So you're basically saying, I'm standing there speaking and they're going like, 'Yeah, okay. Sure, yeah,' and watching TV. And basically ignoring what I'm saying."

Similarly, in the description of the racialized character of their family, Wendy complained that I wrote that they drove past a mall to go to one in a white neighborhood....She felt that made the family look racist:

> Basically [you are] saying we're a white family that would rather go to the mall farther away than the closest mall because there's no black people there. We didn't go to one mall because they were all white or because it was all black.

She also noted that she had had a Black friend in elementary school.

In addition, in *Unequal Childhoods*, the terms *working-class* and *poor* frequently appear in the same sentence. Wendy found that juxtaposition profoundly insulting:

> It made it seem that we were working class but then again we were poor. I've never considered us poor. My mom had a roof over our heads and food on the table every night for us since I was little. I never remember my mom ever telling me, "We can't have dinner tonight," because we didn't have no....Maybe sometime we wouldn't want what she had in the refrigerator, and like, "Mom, can we go out this week?" "No, we're kind

of short this week." "Oh, ok. Well, let's eat spaghetti or something."

Wendy felt that the book erased the differences between working-class and poor families, and that this made her family seem poor.

The most upsetting piece, however, was the portrayal of her mother's role in her schooling. Wendy was certain that her mother had been very active in fighting the school. She fundamentally rejected the book's version:

> It says right here, it says that the teacher said she was very loving, but "they are disappointed in Ms. Driver's failure to take a more active, interventionist role in Wendy's education."...My mom stuck around....My mom—I mean, my teachers, I know none of my teachers would say that because my mom [was] fighting with the teachers.

Wendy was insistent that her teachers would not have characterized her mother that way:

> I can remember all my teachers in grade school. And I cannot imagine any of my teachers saying that about my mom. Maybe they'd be like, "She's a bitch," because she comes up too much, or maybe, "She's a nag," because she's always constantly on the phone with them. I mean my mom in high school had a fight with one of my teachers because she [the teacher] didn't want me to graduate, she didn't want me to be there. And she fought with them every day. I mean, I just cannot imagine any of my teachers saying that.

Wendy's mother and stepfather, in different ways, also expressed anger and disappointment with the way they had been represented in the book. Ms. Driver denied that she felt obligated to take her children to the emergency room lest they be turned in to protective services. Wendy's stepfather was livid over the family portrait, in part because he perceived his wife and stepdaughter as having been injured by the book. Similarly, in her conversation with me, Ms. Driver focused more on how worried she was over Wendy's reaction to the book and less on her own feelings.

The Taylor Family (African American boy/working-class) As I did with all of the families, when I called Ms. Taylor to schedule an interview, I said that I wanted to "come for a visit" to see how things were going. I added that I wanted to do a follow-up interview, for which she would receive an honorarium. Researchers are required to create complex paper trails (e.g., interview consent forms, receipts for honorariums), but interviewees typically have only their recollections of events. As I did with all of the families, I subsequently sent Ms. Taylor a summary of her reaction to the book. She objected to what I had written, particularly (as she alludes to below) to a statement that she had found the visits to be "fun." Per her request, I have withdrawn my summary of her reaction to the book. With her permission, I have substituted her e-mail message to me (edited slightly for length and punctuation). She summarizes the position expressed by many of the families: her family was misused.

> Hello Annette,
> Unfortunately, I do not wish to have anything that I've said [about my reaction to the book] printed....In fact, you did not come to visit, but instead you came to further observe me and my family for your own gain, and you did it under false pretense by calling it a visit and, once inside and settled, pulling out your tape recorder.
> Your observation is just that, your own, and when you put it in print it becomes factual to others who may read it, and that is unfortunate.

I did not allow you to come into my home and judge my family because I thought it would be fun. I did it because I somehow believed, as a very young mother separated from her husband and scared to death of what in the world would become of my children's future, that you may somehow have been able to help us.

You, on the other hand, were only in this for your own reward. So, if you want to print something, print what I really feel and print it in my writing and from my perspective.

By the way, here's another suggestion for the researchers of the future: If you want to complete research on families from different backgrounds, cultures, races, and educational levels, do it with fairness to all and include people from those backgrounds to help understand just what is going on, because if you have never been there, you can't begin to understand what is there.

Regards,
Celeste R. Taylor

The Yanelli Family (white boy/working-class)
The reaction of the Yanelli family developed over time. At first, the interaction among us was very difficult for everyone, as my notes show:

I had dropped by with the book to the Yanellis about ten days ago. I called and then went by tonight. They are very, very hurt. They feel as if the book portrays them as child abusers. Little Billy said that he thought that I "twisted" things and (looking down) said that he was "ashamed." He said that he had been looking forward to showing people about the book but now he felt that he couldn't show it to anyone. Big Billy looked angry. He preferred not to discuss it, but at one point when I was in the kitchen

talking to Linda, [he] called out, "You slurred us, Annette; you made us look like poor white trash."

Ms. Yanelli thought that the chapter [on them] was "the grand finale," since it came last. She was particularly upset that they were the last chapter since she thought it made it worse. I talked with them, taped the mom's feedback, and then hung out. It was tense but okay but still tense.

In the interview, Ms. Yanelli said she felt that the book was highly critical of her and her family, that it "looked down" on them. She thought that the description of the Tallingers as having a "glass of wine" sounded "better" than that of Mr. Yanelli as "having a beer." She also reported that she did not feel powerless with the school. She felt that she had fought the school and had shown determination and strength. In addition, Ms. Yanelli categorically denied that certain events had taken place. She said that she had never in her life purchased a lottery ticket, for example. Also, she felt that "the headline" (i.e., the chapter title, "Beating with a Belt, Fearing 'the School': Little Billy Yanelli") stressed the child abuse issue.

In part, the Yanelli family's reactions were related to their expectations. During a phone conversation, Ms. Yanelli told me, "I thought it was going to be like the book that Oprah had."[21] I was distressed each time I encountered a family that reacted negatively to the book, but the Yanellis' wounded feelings were especially difficult because I felt particularly close to this family.[22] Fortunately, a quirk of fate led to a shift in their views. Ms. Yanelli cleans the house of a sociologist whom I know slightly (we work at different universities). One day, he happened to be home while she was cleaning. She saw that he had *Unequal Childhoods* on his bookshelf. She told him that she was in the book and described how disappointed she and the rest of her family were with the book.

Later, when I called the Yanellis (just to say hello and keep in touch), Ms. Yanelli told me that he had "explained" the book to her, saying that it was about things that were not right in society, with some people having more than others. She said that he had "made her" understand the book, and now she and her family were "fine with it."[23]

Reaction of the Poor Families

The Brindle Family (white girl/poor) The Brindles' lives were in a different and largely better place when I followed up with them than they had been during the initial study. In a phone conversation, Ms. Brindle said that the book "brought back" the earlier period. She said, "It made me laugh, it made me cry." It made her feel as if they had moved along and things had gotten better. Ms. Brindle said, "There was one thing that did bother me. Why did you say that we were the most disturbed family in the book?" Stuttering and somewhat flustered, I said that at the time, Jenna had just been diagnosed as HIV-positive, they were being evicted, and things seemed generally difficult. Ms. Brindle did not reply. (Since we were on the telephone, I could not see her facial expression.) In her interview, Katie did not express criticisms of the book's portrayal of her family. She seemed to have been most struck by the descriptions of her interest in performing plays and her dramatic side. Referring to them, she told me that she thought that she could have been an actress and that she wished that had happened. Overall, the Brindles did not seem to be troubled by the book. This surprised me a great deal. As I have noted, with each family, the possibility of a negative reaction worried me. The Brindles were of special concern because their life situation had been so difficult during the study period. I did not want them to think that I was judging them. The considerable distance that they had traveled in terms of economic security seemed to contribute to their positive assessment of the book. They saw their lives as now being in a different place.

The McAllister Family (African American boy/poor) The housing project where the McAllister family had lived when we first met was torn down, and I lost touch with them for a number of years. After several failed attempts to track them down, I tried searching on the internet for the name of Harold's father. I found an address and phone number for a person with that name and ended up speaking with Harold's older brother. He gave me Ms. McAllister's number. I called and spoke with her, and then I went by her house.

Ms. McAllister was surprised to see me reappear in their lives after several years. They had wondered what had happened to me and "the book." Of all the people portrayed in *Unequal Childhoods,* she seemed the most excited to discover that the book had been published and that they were in it. She was visibly pleased. She seemed excited and proud that there was a book about her family. She held her copy and, flipping the pages in awe, said, "I'm going to show it to my sisters."

I hung out at the house for a while and played with the kids while she read. She thought parts were hilarious, including the section about my walking through their neighborhood and people thinking I was a dope dealer or a welfare person, as well as the section about the family reunion when Greg, one of the research assistants, had trouble spotting me. Ms. McAllister had quipped, "She the only white person here and you can't find her?" The quote and the memory it evoked made her laugh out loud. She pronounced her verdict on the book: "I don't have no problem with it."

A bit later, in a much more somber tone, Ms. McAllister said, "So we communicate without words." She seemed to be pondering the idea that her family was being evaluated during the study observations. I nodded and said, "At least that is the way it seemed compared to other families." While reading more, she said, clearly surprised, "You wrote down my words with the kids?" I nodded. I told her that I was worried it might bother her and that some of the families were fine with the book, but some were bothered by it. She dismissed this thought. She said, "I know my family is crazy."

Enduring Challenges

In reassessing the book for the second edition, I have concluded that relatively small changes in wording or emphasis could have made the text more accurate and less hurtful to family members. For example, weight is always a sensitive issue. Rather than describing Melanie Handlon as "chubby," which is evocative but also evaluative, I should have used more neutral language. I could have noted that according to weight tables for children her age and height, she would have been considered overweight. In recounting the Driver family's response to Wendy's catechism question, I should have been clearer that her parents and brother listened to her carefully when she asked them if they knew what a mortal sin was (such attention is a form of acknowledgment) but did not transform her question into a teachable moment. The original text makes it seem, as Wendy angrily pointed out, as if her family members had ignored her. In the case of the Yanellis, it is likely that Ms. Yanelli was buying the lottery ticket for Billy's dad and not for herself; I should have kept track of that detail. Thus, there are some issues that could have been handled differently. Overall, though, most families seemed to feel that the book resonated with their experiences. Accuracy was not the crux of the problem. The problem was how the families felt about the way they were portrayed.

"Traumatic for Both Sides"

Michael Burawoy correctly notes that a revisit by an ethnographer to a research site to learn the reaction of the study participants (what he terms a "valedictory revisit") is rare and often traumatic:

> When the ethnographer returns to the participants, armed with the results of the study, whether in draft or published form [t]he purpose is...to ascertain the participants' responses to the reported research....This is the moment of judgment, when previous relations are reassessed, theory is put to the test, and accounts are reevaluated. It can be traumatic for both sides, and for this reason it is all too rare.[24]

As Burawoy suggests, it is not uncommon for some study participants to be surprised and very unhappy when they read a researcher's written portrayal of them.[25] When I recruited the families for the original study, I told them I would be writing a book. At the very beginning of the study, when they were signing consent forms, for example, family members often asked if they would be getting a copy of the book. At that point, feeling that it was the least I could do, given their willingness to open up their lives to me, I promised to provide copies. As the study progressed, I began to worry about how the families might react to the book. One impetus for the study was my desire to correct what I considered the superficial and overly romantic view of child rearing that dominated the literature. I wanted to present a realistic view of family life. Still, as I grew emotionally attached to the family members, I worried about the necessity of objectifying them in the writing process. I was concerned that what I planned to write might hurt their feelings.[26]

When I was still in their homes, sitting around in the kitchen chatting, collecting the original data, I did try to warn the families that the final product probably would not be to their liking. "You know, when someone takes a picture of someone and everyone else thinks it is fine, but the person really doesn't like it?" I would say. They would nod, somewhat uncertainly. I would then continue, "Well, that is how it will probably be with the book. You probably won't like it." Still, I think that the families and I were *both* surprised by the level of pain, hurt, and dismay—the very kind of reaction Burawoy notes—that the book created for many. One mother said, "I know that you warned us." But seeing the results in print made the findings painfully real.

This likely negative, even "traumatic," aspect of research has not been fully integrated into methodological writings, despite striking examples from well-known—even classic—studies. Arthur Vidich was hung in effigy after *Small Town in Mass Society* was published; communities featured in the early sociological studies such as *Yankee City* also expressed ire. William Foote Whyte reported the tense reaction, particularly on the part of Doc, to *Street Corner Society*.[27] More recently, a few researchers have vividly described the anger and hurt expressed by ethnographic study participants, but these descriptions have tended to focus on the researcher's decision not to reveal her or his intention to write a book or the researcher's decision to conceal key information which would have mattered to study participants.[28]

Considering the Alternatives

To help mitigate problems study participants experience, some researchers suggest that ethnographers should share the study results prior to publication, so that participants can articulate their concerns.[29] This viewpoint is both optimistic and problematic. It raises complex questions regarding the balance between what researchers owe study participants and how much control the researcher ought to retain over what is written.

Some people argue that having participants read draft text and give feedback provides "buy in" on the part of respondents.[30] Writers on this subject have also recommended various forms of "member checks." These range from sharing certain information with participants in order to confirm the accuracy of small details to asking respondents to validate the researcher's analysis and conclusions. Checks of the former type generally are of little consequence to a study's main argument or to the relationship with the study participants, particularly if they can be managed in informal, verbal interactions (e.g., stopping by to say hello and checking the information in the midst of a broader conversation about other issues). But checks that involve sharing the written report of a prepublication draft can bring significant perils.

Although the voices of study participants are crucial, they represent only one piece of a complex puzzle. Who should decide the focus of what the researcher writes?[31] Study participants are likely to want certain issues to be developed and recast to reflect their own views. If a researcher requests the time and energy of respondents to read text and provide feedback, then the researcher should plan to incorporate that feedback. But academics face constraints from disciplinary standards, editorial boards, and publishers about the shape of the argument or the length of a piece; as a result, researchers can find that they have solicited input that they cannot or do not want to incorporate. They have issued a contradictory invitation to their respondents, saying, essentially, "I know this text may upset you, but I would love for you to take the time to read it and give me your considered opinion. You may have a different understanding of the events; your input is valuable. But, you also need to know that I have to have the final say on the piece. I may, or may not, be able to make the changes you suggest." Arguably, this kind of highly constrained request for input is yet another tax on study participants; in some circumstances, it could be more an act of tokenism than a sincere request for honest feedback that could radically reshape the publication.

Some researchers have successfully negotiated this process. They have shared their work and argued with participants over the portraits. They have made changes. They have used the prepublication stage to "work through" conflict. Ethnographers such as Hugh Mehan, Tim Black, Mark Warren, and others have managed to make clear their sincere interest in respondents' feedback, but also make clear that the goal is to correct inaccuracies and not to reshape the written representation.[32] Some advocates of prepublication discussions in which subjects provide their interpretation of events feel these sessions offer the potential additional advantage of helping researchers deepen and improve their analyses.

In many instances, researchers who have been most successful in soliciting input from respondents without relinquishing control over the published text were studying organizations and organizational policies. Often, work in these areas draws on stable data collected from written memoranda, published documents, and public records, as well as the more volatile evidence supplied by human subjects. Many researchers who study organizations strive for compromise, "toning down" their analyses to accommodate respondents' concerns. This approach has costs, however. The portraits often become less sharply focused, particularly with respect to weaknesses or problems in an organization.[33]

Generally, organizational dynamics are more public, and certainly less personal, than child rearing. In studies of more private settings, it is easy for people to feel criticized, even when that is not the researcher's intent. Ultimately, many decisions researchers make are dependent on the particular content as well as on the researchers' own sensibilities. They cannot be mandated. In my case, I worried that showing a draft of the manuscript to the families would make the book hard to complete. I was not primarily concerned about issues of accuracy. The research assistants and I were in the homes

frequently, and we took very detailed notes, sought disconfirming evidence, carried out in-depth interviews, and made every effort to make only claims that were buttressed with ample data. But if, as I anticipated, the families did object to how they were portrayed, I would feel deeply conflicted. I would want to stand by my analysis but also please the participants. The result would be paralysis; I would find myself unable to move the book to closure. (Researchers vary in how easy they find writing and/or wrapping up a project. I find both steps challenging.) What if some participants found their portrait so painful that they requested that I drop that chapter? What would I do then? For example, even now, the Yanellis continue to find their portrait quite painful. If I had shown it to them ahead of time, they would have demanded that it be removed from the book or that it be radically restructured to eliminate their sense that they had been made to look like child abusers. If I had taken out the chapter, the book would have been weaker. If I had dropped the discussion of discipline, the central argument of the chapter would have been gutted. If I had proceeded to publish despite the Yanellis' intense objections, I would have severely damaged our relationship.[34]

Of course, in making choices, and in finding a balance that is "right for them," researchers are not free agents.[35] They need to meet certain critically important ethical obligations: they must inform people that they are being studied, get their explicit agreement to participate in the research, tell them in advance that the results will be published, and protect the confidentiality of information respondents would prefer to remain private.[36] Following the Golden Rule, ethnographers should not ask study participants to do anything that they would not be willing to do themselves or have their own children do. Still, finding a balance that is "right for them" raises a quagmire of ethical challenges for researchers. All possible pathways have problems. In my own case, I have concluded that sharing research results with study participants in order to gain their approval should be optional. Since sharing research results has numerous drawbacks for all parties (despite some potential advantages), it should not be required any more than other researchers or journalists should be required to gain approval from their informants and participants before publication.[37] In my view, for better or worse, a research project is controlled by the researcher. It is the researcher, not the research participants, who frames the research topic, asks the questions, figures out the probes, decides what information to record, selects what to analyze, chooses the quotes to highlight, and does the writing.[38]

To Expect Forgiveness Is to Expect Too Much

It is exceedingly rare for researchers to give a finished book to research participants and *then go back to them to learn how they feel about it,* as I did, Nancy Scheper-Hughes, who did the same, describes in her book *Saints, Scholars, and Schizophrenics: Mental Illness in Rural Ireland,* the pain and anger her book caused in an Irish village. In her view, some of the pain was an inevitable and inextricable part of the project, given that ethnographic research requires the public exposure of personal warts: "Any ethnography ultimately stands or falls on the basis of whether or not it resonates: it should ring true, strike a familiar (even if occasionally painful) chord. It should not leave the 'native' reader cold and confused. Angry and hurt, perhaps, but not confused or perplexed." Doing ethnography raises difficult ethical questions, as Scheper-Hughes further notes: "To whose advantage or for whose good do we cast what is so often a critical gaze on the contradictions and paradoxes implicit in the character of human relations, institutions, and organizations?"[39] From Scheper-Hughes's writings, and from my own experience, I reluctantly conclude that some of this anger and hurt is the "price of doing business" in writing ethnography and having the research participants read the results. For some, it is a high price to pay. To act as if there is no price—to act as if ethnographic research is "free"—is to be naïve. Indeed, some would say the failure to acknowledge to oneself the cost of research goes beyond naïveté and shades into ethically irresponsible behavior. Ethnographers must acknowledge the difficult, angst-inducing questions about whether the price is worth it.[40]

Accepting that there are costs for those who participate in a research project is only the first step. It is also important that ethnographers think carefully about how to reduce that price. If I were to do *Unequal Childhoods* again, before I asked potential participants to sign a consent form, I would explain in more detail what research entails. Notably, as Ms. Taylor said, it is not a "story" but an analysis. I would give individuals who expressed interest in participating in my study a book such as *The Second Shift* and encourage them to look it over carefully. I would say something like, "This is what my book is going to look like. Is this okay?"[41] I would not promise participants a copy of my study's published results, as I did with the *Unequal Childhoods* families. Instead, I would create a color brochure or newsletter that would include a prominent thank you to the research participants and would highlight project results that would be of interest to general readers. (The brochure could also be used as an informative handout for journalists, research groups, or other generalists.) This level of information is all most people really want; they are interested in whether the project came to a close and whether the research revealed anything significant. By giving each family a book, I was in a sense forcing the respondents to look at themselves from others' perspectives.

Some, such as the Yanellis, interpreted the way their lives were portrayed in the text as demeaning and false—a "slur." Some readers, on the other hand, have told me that the Yanelli chapter made them understand how families who use corporal punishment could see the school as a threatening and powerful force. These readers said they found that insight truly helpful. But the fact that I, and some readers, may disagree with a family's interpretation is *irrelevant to the family* and thus does nothing to lessen their pain.[42] That is the key point.

There could be class differences in the likelihood of study participants seeking out the book on their own: middle-class respondents are likely to have the educational skills that would allow them to do so, and some may be more motivated to find the book than others. Still, the feelings that result from bringing study participants a copy of the book, and thus compelling them to consider a portrait of themselves that does not match their own self-vision, are likely to be more troublesome than those that arise after participants who actively sought out a copy of the research results read those results. If participants sought out and read the research report(s) and become very upset as a result, then, as with the families of *Unequal Childhoods,* I would try to engage them in a process in which we worked through the problems together. I would not withdraw from them (although, admittedly, this is a strong temptation). I would not ignore their feelings. Instead, I would directly and clearly interact with them about those feelings—that is, if they were willing to continue to see me. I would drop by from time to time, bringing bakery cakes and perhaps some wine or beer, to say hello and to see how they were doing. Even if research participants are blisteringly angry, I believe that it is still possible, in some cases, to be engaged in conversation in a way that can lead to a diffusion of anger.[43] If the respondents are willing to continue a relationship with the researcher, clearly acknowledging

their position and doing so at repeated intervals may eventually lead to people's anger subsiding. I also think it is fitting for a researcher to invest time and energy in return visits, given that she or he is the cause of the respondents' anger.

With the *Unequal Childhoods* participants, my efforts were rewarded. Some participants' anger did diffuse over time. I continue to send cards and little gifts to the Yanellis, I give them big hugs whenever I see them, and they in turn greet me warmly.[44] Others have been less forgiving. To expect forgiveness is to expect too much.

Concluding Thoughts

In the appendix to his classic sociological study *Street Corner Society,* William F. Whyte describes the anger and sense of betrayal that many of the "boys" felt toward him after the publication of his book. "The trouble is, Bill, you caught people with their hair down," one of the men tells him.[45] The entire point of ethnography is to catch people in the routines of daily life, to reveal taken-for-granted aspects of their experience, and to make the background foreground. But researchers have often underestimated the level of anger and the sense of betrayal that can surface when they share their research results with participants. The dual process of seeking to reduce feelings of anger and pain while also accepting that such emotions may occur remains an enduring challenge.

NOTES

1. See William Foote Whyte, *Street Corner Society.*
2. See Annette Lareau, "Common Problems in Fieldwork: A Personal Essay," in *Home Advantage.* See also Annette Lareau and Jeffrey Shultz, eds., *Journeys through Ethnography....*
3. Michael Burawoy, "Revisits"; Linda M. Burton, Diane Purvin, and Raymond

Garrett-Peters, "Longitudinal Ethnography"; Nancy Scheper-Hughes, "Ire in Ireland"; Jay MacLeod, *Ain't No Making It*. See also Michael Burawoy, "Public Ethnography as Film."

4. See Norman K. Denzin and Yvonna S. Lincoln, *The SAGE Handbook of Qualitative Research;* Caroline Ramazanoğlu and Joan Holland, *Feminist Methodology;* Diane L. Wolf, ed., *Feminist Dilemmas in Fieldwork;* Martyn Hammersley and Paul Atkinson, *Ethnography;* Dorothy Smith, *Institutional Ethnography;* Paul ten Have, *Understanding Qualitative Research and Ethnomethodology;* Joan Cassell, "Risks and Benefits to Subjects of Fieldwork." For a vigorous defense of the position that ethnographers should collaborate and "co-construct" ethnographies with research participants, see Luke Eric Lassiter, *The Chicago Guide to Collaborative Ethnography*.

5. Whyte, *Street Corner Society;* Scheper-Hughes, "Ire in Ireland"; Arthur J. Vidich and Joseph Bensman, *Small Town and Mass Society;* Carolyn Ellis, "Emotional and Ethical Quagmires in Returning to the Field"; Arlene Stein, "Sex, Truths, and Audiotape."

6. The original research was done in 1993–95. Some families had kept in touch with me over the years since then. I attended Wendy Driver's high school graduation party, for example; I got a prom picture and graduation notice for Tyrec Taylor. I also received announcements of high school graduation and college enrollment for Garrett Tallinger and Stacey Marshall.

7. Williams, Marshall, Handlon (mother and Melanie), Irwin, Greeley, Carroll, Brindle, Tallinger (Garrett), and Yanelli family-member interviews were completed before they received the book. The interviews with Ms. McAllister and the Tallinger parents took place on the day I delivered the book. The Driver, Taylor, and Handlon (father) interviews occurred after they had read the book. Some of the interviews took place as late as 2005. Then, in 2009 and 2010, I began contacting the families to share my summary of their reaction; as I note elsewhere, I invited them to submit their own reactions. In 2010, as the second edition was going to press,

I confirmed the employment status of all the young adults except Alex Williams and Harold McAllister. Although I did not ask them directly, most people appeared to have read only the chapter about their family. Conversations with the Tallingers, Ms. Yanelli, and Ms. Marshall, however, revealed that they had read the entire book.

8. Indeed, the follow-up does not meet the definition Michael Burawoy gave to ethnographic revisits: "An ethnographic revisit occurs when an ethnographer undertakes participant observation, that is, studying others in their space and time, with a view to comparing his or her site with the same one studied at an earlier point in time, whether by him or herself or by someone else." "Revisits," p. 646.

9. Mitchell Duneier, "Transparency in Ethnography."

10. At the time, I was at Temple University, where I regularly taught a class of 110 students, with the equivalent of one 20-hour per week teaching assistant. I taught one weekly discussion section, and I did one-third of the grading of essay midterms, papers, and finals. At the University of Pennsylvania, where I teach the same kind of course, I have two teaching assistants, each working twenty hours per week, and a smaller enrollment (100 students).

11. See Mario Luis Small, "How Many Cases Do I Need?," on the size of projects.

12. Although beyond the scope of this chapter, there have been new calls for "scientific standards" in qualitative research. See reports by the Sociology Program of the National Science Foundation: Charles Ragin, Joane Nagel, and Patricia White, *Workshop on Scientific Foundations of Qualitative Research;* and Michèle Lamont and Patricia White, *Workshop on Interdisciplinary Standards for Systematic Qualitative Research;* as well as the critical essay by Howard Becker, "How to Find Out How to Do Qualitative Research," on these NSF reports. Some researchers have responded to this pressure for standards by assembling very large-scale qualitative interview studies (e.g., 300 cases) where the

principal investigator herself or himself does proportionally little interviewing. In addition, many of these studies do not include any participant-observation. With this approach, qualitative researchers are seeking to avoid the limitations of qualitative research (i.e., small, purposive samples). But, too often, the results of these kinds of large-scale studies are unsatisfying; they do not provide the "thick description" that is a hallmark of ethnographic work; see Clifford Geertz, *Interpretations of Cultures.* Nor do they provide sufficient attention to the meaning of events. For a critical assessment of these issues, see Annette Lareau, *Doing Ethnography in the Real World.* Of course, there are many different types of qualitative work; see the review of various approaches in Denzin and Lincoln, *SAGE Handbook of Qualitative Research,* as well as discussions of ethnography in Smith, *Institutional Ethnography;* Shulamit Reinharz and Lynn Davidman, *Feminist Methods in Social Research;* Hammersly and Atkinson, *Ethnography;* Iddo Tavory and Stefan Timmermans, "Two Cases of Ethnography"; Michael Buroway, *The Extended Case Method.* See also Elinor Ochs et al., "Video Ethnography and Ethnoarchaeological Tracking"; Stephen A. Matthews, Linda M. Burton, and James Detwiler, "Geo-ethnography."

13. In developing and sustaining ethnographic relationships, it is helpful to bring food, provide reciprocity in some way, or (if possible) offer an honorarium for participation. If cost is an issue, there are also inexpensive options such as framed photos, CDs burned at home, or photo albums.

14. I taped conversations, conducted separately, with Wendy Driver, Ms. Driver, Mr. Handlon, and Ms. Yanelli. Mr. Yanelli refused to be taped, although he did listen from the living room as I taped my discussion with Ms. Yanelli in the kitchen.

15. After drafting a brief summary of each family's reaction to the book, I mailed four of the nine families a package with a copy of my draft of their reaction and a letter inviting them to either write their own summary of how they reacted (which I promised would be reproduced, unedited, in the second edition of the book) or edit my version. As a friendly gesture, I also included a box of chocolates. I had working addresses for all the families except the Drivers and McAllisters. The McAllisters had moved again, and the telephone numbers I had were no longer in service. I tried to reach them by leaving a message on a relative's answering machine, but this strategy was not successful. The Drivers also had moved; I could not reach them via Facebook, telephone white pages, or Google. (Later, Wendy contacted me via Facebook. She updated me on her family and work status. When I suggested that we get together, however, she declined.) Rather than mailing a package to the Yanellis, I went to see the family (bringing my draft summary, beer, and chocolate). Mr. Yanelli said my draft was "on the money," an accurate statement of their feelings "at that time." I called the Brindles and left a message; Ms. Brindle immediately returned my call. I later e-mailed the description to her eldest daughter, who read it to her over the phone. Ms. Brindle approved it. I also e-mailed Ms. Taylor. At her suggestion, and with her permission, I replaced my summary with her response to me. For clarification, I added an introductory note and edited her message, particularly for length. The responses of the remaining families varied. The Marshalls contacted me in a warm e-mail: both Ms. Marshall and Stacey wrote to me (separately), saying that they were "comfortable" with the portrait. The Tallingers also responded. Mr. Tallinger edited the summary I had drafted; his edits made it clearer and more precise. His e-mail message was friendly and humorous (he said that they were doing "concerted cultivation" on me). I spoke with Ms. Handlon by phone. She was cool. She said that she had received the package and had given it to Melanie. I indicated that the letter was addressed to her and her husband as well as to Melanie. She said that she would look at it. She did not get back to me. The Williamses did not reply either.

16. Ms. Tallinger ended contact in 2004. In January 2010, though, she responded, in a friendly manner, to a follow-up e-mail I had sent to the family about a package I had sent to the home (with a box of chocolates and a description of the family's reaction to the book). Correspondence regarding the Tallingers' reaction was handled exclusively by Mr. Tallinger, however.

17. I did not hear directly from Melanie about how she felt about the book or its description of her. However, she came home while I was interviewing her father. I was sitting on the floor, talking across the coffee table to Mr. Handlon. I stood up and, as Melanie stood next to the piano, told her that I had learned that the book had upset her and that I was very sorry about that. She (keeping her face impassive) nodded but did not chat. My efforts to draw her out were not successful. She disappeared into the back of the house, and I continued my interview with her father.

18. The Williamses' reaction is more vague than the reactions of the other families. My suspicion is that they were offended by an endnote in the first edition.... In the note, a fieldworker expresses discomfort with a mock game of peek-a-boo in which the parents treat Alexander as if he were a very young child. In addition, from the beginning, Mr. Williams had been unenthusiastic about being in the study; he saw it (correctly enough) as an "invasion of privacy." The family's portrait may have made him feel vindicated. Given the e-mail exchange with Ms. Williams, I agonized over whether I should contact them again. In the end, I felt I needed to give them a chance to say their piece (if they wished). I sent them the same sort of package I mailed to the other families, inviting them to summarize their reaction to the book (or edit my draft). I enclosed a CD with a copy of my summary and their e-mail. I received no response.

19. When Stacey was at college a couple of years later, her roommate was reading the book for a class. Stacey revealed that she was in the book.

20. Although Wendy had the book open at this time, the transcription of the tape shows that she made a number of minor modifications as she read the piece aloud. Thus, the quote does not follow the text exactly. Also, in the original field note, this quotation was longer and made it clear that her mother, stepfather, and brother stopped what they were doing, looked at her, and then (after she was finished speaking) returned to looking at the television. Wendy was upset because she felt that the attention her family gave to her was not sufficiently emphasized in the text.

21. At the time, *The Oprah Winfrey Show* featured a monthly discussion of a book selected by Oprah. The book Ms. Yanelli was referring to was *Anna Karenina*. Somewhat differently, one colleague told me that ethnography is not "wedding photography." In retrospect, I think that indeed many of the families thought that the portrait would be similar to a written version of wedding photography, showing the family in the best possible light.

22. For example, throughout this process, I showed normal symptoms of being in a stressful situation, including having trouble sleeping.

23. I ran into the Yanellis in a store a few years later. They were warm and friendly; they looked happy. Billy now had his own apartment. "He even keeps it clean," his mother marveled. He was working regularly. He was doing well. Mr. and Ms. Yanelli were delighted that their older son and his girlfriend had recently made them grandparents; they looked forward to spending time with the baby.

24. Burawoy, "Revisits," p. 672.

25. It should be emphasized that not all study participants come away with negative feelings. Some report truly enjoying being in studies. Their involvement makes them feel special; they are excited by the prospect of being discussed in a book; and they draw comfort from being able to talk about private concerns with a nonjudgmental listener. Similarly, despite the very real and painful costs that participation in ethnographic studies can exact from individuals, these

costs are surely less than are incurred in other spheres. In medical research, needy individuals in the control group cannot benefit from an experimental drug until after the clinical trial has ended and the drug has been approved. In a recent case of two cousins participating in the same medical study, one died waiting for the treatment to be approved. See Harmon, "Target Cancer."

26. My experience leads me to urge that the costs of being a study participant be explicitly acknowledged prior to the beginning of a research project. They could be covered in the consent form, under a statement such as "the research could make you uncomfortable" or "the conclusions of the research report may not match your understanding of your life."

27. See Vidich and Bensman, *Small Town in Mass Society,* particularly the Afterword with its description of the negative reaction of the community, including his being hung in effigy. Similarly, in the introduction to a special issue assessing *Street Corner Society,* Peter Adler and the other editors report that "virtually all of Cornerville felt hurt by the publication of *Street Corner Society*" in 1943 (p. 5). William Lloyd Warner, who studied "Yankee City" (Newburyport, Mass.) in 1949 was famously mocked by John Phillips Marquand through the character of Malcolm Bryant in Marquand's novel *Point of No Return.* Studies have also been critically assessed decades later; see W. A. Marianne Boelen, "Street Corner Society," and the vigorous defense of Whyte by Angelo Ralph Orlandella, "Boelen May Know Holland..."

28. See Ellis, "Emotional and Ethical Quagralres"; Stein, "Sex, Truths, and Audiotape"; Scheper-Hughes, "Ire in Ireland."

29. See, for example, the extensive literature on action research or advocacy research. This tradition has a more extensive following in the field of education than in sociology, although there are advocates in sociology as well. See Jack Whitehead and Jean McNiff, *Action Research.* Some researchers, including Nancy Scheper-Hughes, have called for avoiding the use of pseudonyms.

30. For example, Mitchell Duneier, in the appendix to his book *Sidewalk,* provides a comical description of his (vain) efforts to gain the attention and approval of the Greenwich Village street vendors be studied as he read aloud sections of the draft that involved them.

31. Some researchers have sought to resolve these questions by more directly privileging the voices of the respondents. Publishing portions of an unedited interview transcript is one approach. Others provide an analysis, but see a primary purpose of the piece as an opportunity to tell the stories of underrepresented groups. See, among others, Eddah Mutua Kombo, "Their Words, Actions, and Meaning." Still, it was the researcher, not the respondent, who conceptualized the study, decided what questions to ask, and edited (most of) the transcript for publication. This also does not address the issue of the researcher's career advancement. If a researcher genuinely shares control of the writing with respondents, then it will be harder to comply with the criteria for publication in peer-reviewed journals. Some ethnographers have retreated into the study of themselves, creating the subfield of autoethnography. See Carolyn Ellis and Arthur E. Bochner, "Analyzing Analytic Autoethnography." Others have engaged in community-based research. Alisa Lincoln reported, for example, a study where an ethnographer co-authored a piece with eighteen clients who had a major mental illness. The piece could not be published until every single co-author signed off. In some cases, the refusal of clients to approve a publication could harm a young scholar's career (personal communication, January 27, 2011). See also Lassiter, *Collaborative Ethnography.*

32. Hugh Mehan commented, "I have been in similar situations—trying to depict events honestly while at the same time trying to ensure that the voices of the participants are rendered accurately. For our book [Mchan et. al.,] *Constructing School Success,* I had promised the AVID folks access to

the [manuscript] before publication. The AVID director reacted extremely negatively about certain points—which led to a succession of Friday afternoon sessions going over portions of the ms that she found offensive. We discussed. We argued. We settled on changes—ones that were not so volatile, but did not alter the argument. I made some acknowledgement of that situation in introductory material" (personal communication, August 31, 2009). Tim Black followed a similar approach for his book, *When a Heart Turns Rock Solid.* In a talk on his research on community organizers (which does not use pseudonyms), Mark Warren emphasizes the importance of building collaborative relationships with the groups he studies. This is not always easy, and sometimes the process of recruiting organizations to the study can be seen as "seduction" and the sharing of the results, especially when the results expose problems, as "betrayal." He describes the interactions as "hot and heavy" with one organization, though it was much less contentious with other organizations. As he wrote, "Even in the more contentious cases, the team worked hard to reach some consensus on what was acceptable." Personal communication, October 31, 2010. See Warren, "A Collaborative Approach to Ethnographic Case Study Research."

33. See Rubén Gaztambide-Fernández's *Best of the Best* for a thoughtful account of the experience of privilege in an elite boarding school. Gaztambide-Fernández offers insight regarding the experience of students, but his work contains little about the foibles, missteps, or inadequacies of the institution. He reports that was not deliberate, but rather "it reflects the fact that the book is not about the school itself, but about how the students construct elite identifications. I wanted to understand what the school does best: convince students that they are 'the best of the best.'" Personal communication, October 17, 2010.

34. As I have already explained, the Yanellis and I did repair our relationship. I doubt that would have been possible, however, if I had published the gist of the analysis *after* knowing their objections. I continue to send holiday cards to Billy, as well as to the other young adults and families that wish to remain in touch with me (and for whom I have addresses). I now send food or tuck a somewhat larger bill ($20) into the envelope; and, if the young adults have children, I send gift cards from a store such as Target for them.

35. The phrase of finding a balance that is "right for them" is from Shana Maier and Brian Monahan, "How Close Is Too Close?"

36. Some publishers now demand to know whether respondents gave written permission for the interviews or field notes to be published, particularly if the respondents' identities could be deduced by readers. As a result, consent forms should include an explicit statement that study participants are giving permission for the information to be published and that while every effort will be made to keep the information confidential, the participants understand that there is always the possibility that someone could recognize them in the publication.

37. Of course, persons portrayed in newspaper articles or, for that matter, on reality television, often are livid about those portrayals. Arlene N. Morgan, a dean at the Columbia School of Journalism, reported from her career as a reporter that it was "good common sense to meet with a person and give him or her a chance to write a letter to the editor or come in to meet with the editors in charge." She adds, "Being more proactive to signal what is in a story is...[what] I would recommend.... Prepare and prepare some more and if it does not damage the story, think hard before you publish." Personal communication, October 27, 2010. For the journalist code of ethics, see Gene Foreman, *The Ethical Journalist.* For an example of one family's reactions to a reality show, see Jacques Steinberg, "One Show's Unexpected Lessons in Reality."

38. Participatory research is an exception. In that tradition, research participants are involved

in each of these steps. See Whitehead and McNiff, *Action Research,* as well as, in a somewhat different vein, Binaya Subedi and Jeong-eun Rhee, "Negotiating Collaborating across Differences." On the role of the researcher in conducting the research and reporting on it, see, among others, Maier and Mocahan, "How Close Is Too Close?"; Cassell, "Risks and Benefits to Subjects of Fieldwork"; Katherine Irwin, "Into the Dark Heart of Ethnography"; Jack Katz, "On the Rhetoric and Politics of Ethnographic Method"; John Van Maanen, *Tales of the Field.* There are also many efforts to create new forms for the presentation of ethnography, including poetry and performance art. See Michal M. McCall and Howard S. Becker, "Performance Science"; Carl Bagley, "Educational Ethnography as Performance Art."

39. Nancy Scheper-Hughes, *Saints, Scholars, and Schizophrenics,* 2nd ed., pp. xviii, xvi–xvii.

40. Researchers seek to resolve this complex ethical dilemma in various ways. Duneier, for example, has allocated his royalties from *Sidewalk* to the men profiled in the book. But the actual amount is very modest, often less than $25 per man per year. In addition, introducing a payment after the research is over for work done earlier changes the relationship between a researcher and participants. In *When a Heart Turns Rock Solid,* Timothy Black directly labels ethnographic research as a form of exploitation. Compared to sociologists, anthropologists have a much richer literature on methodological dilemmas in fieldwork. See, for example, Paul Rabinow, *Reflections on Doing Fieldwork in Morocco*; Margery Wolf, *A Thrice-Told Tale.*

41. See Arlie Hochschild, *The Second Shift.* If I continue my research focus on the reproduction of inequality, then I would not want to give my own book to potential participants, since it would reveal too much about the research question of the study. However, given widespread internet access, it is likely that some potential research participants would do a search on my name; they are very likely to learn of my research

interests that way. (Other researchers, though, could use *Unequal Childhoods* as an example of a final product.)

42. It is importance to remember that researchers and subjects not only have different interests in the final product, but they are engaged in different endeavors: study participants are living their lives; researchers are engaged in analysis.

43. This kind of dialog is not easy to achieve. It requires a willingness to listen to people's highly critical and angry statements. Here the key is not to argue, or be defensive, or insist on explaining the original ideas. Rather, the goal is to listen very carefully to others' statements, clearly conveying that you have heard not only their words but the emotions behind them. Acknowledging these respondents' concerns word for word demonstrates that you have heard and understood their position. Then, by continuing to come back to visit, you confirm the sincerity of your concern about them and their feelings. I term this "staying in relationship with them" through the anger. It is quite difficult to do. But it is not impossible.

44. Indeed, when I went by the house to share my summary of their reaction to the book (included above), both Mr. and Ms. Yanelli noted that their views had changed. Mr. Yanelli said the summary was "on the money," an accurate statement of their feelings "at that time." When I told Ms. Yanelli on the telephone that I had a draft of their reaction to the book, she asked, "When? At first or now?" In addition, Ms. Yanelli was aware that others had different views. (Ms. Yanelli had given the book to a relative to read; the relative liked the portrait.) Still, the portrait of the family clashes with Ms. Yanelli's view of herself and her family and thus remains a source of pain. During our visit, over six years after the book appeared, Ms. Yanelli became tearful as she discussed it.

45. William Foote Whyte, "On the Evolution of *Street Corner Society,*" p. 66. Paul ten Have makes a similar point in *Understanding Qualitative Research and Ethnomethodology.*

He notes that "Doc" read "every page" of Whyte's book before it was published, but that it can be difficult to predict how research participants will feel later. As ten Have writes, "The feeling of being 'used' by the researcher may be hard to avoid" (p. 116).

REFERENCES

Adler, Patricia A., Peter Adler, and John M. Johnson. 1992. "Street Corner Society Revisited: New Questions about Old Issues." *Journal of Contemporary Ethnography* 21(1): 3–10.

Bagley, Carl. 2008. "Educational Ethnography as Performance Art: Towards a Sensuous Feeling and Knowing." *Qualitative Research* 8, 1: 53–72.

Becker, Howard S. 2009. "How to Find Out How to Do Qualitative Research." *International Journal of Communication* 3: 545–553.

Black, Timothy. 2009. *When a Heart Turns Rock Solid: The Lives of Three Puerto Rican Brothers on and off the Streets.* New York: Pantheon.

Boelen, W. A. Marianne. 1992. "Street Corner Society: Cornerville Revisited." *Journal of Contemporary Ethnography* 21(1): 11–51.

Burawoy, Michael. 2009. *The Extended Case Method: Four Countries, Four Decades, Four Great Transformations, and One Theoretical Tradition.* Berkeley: University of California Press.

———. 2009. "Public Ethnography as Film: Michael Apted and the Up! Series." *Ethnography* 10(3): 317–319.

———. 2003. "Revisits: An Outline of a Theory of Reflexive Ethnography." *American Sociological Review* 68(5): 645–679.

Burton, Linda M., Diane Purvin, and Raymond Garrett-Peters. 2009. "Longitudinal Ethnography: Uncovering Domestic Abuse in Low-Income Women's Lives." *The Craft of Life Course Research*, pp. 70–92. Glen H. Elder Jr. and Janet Zollinger Giele (eds.). New York: Guilford Press.

Cassell, Joan. 1978. "Risks and Benefits to Subjects of Fieldwork." *The American Sociologist* 13 (August): 134–143.

Denzin, Norman K., and Yvonna S. Lincoln. 2005. *The SAGE Handbook of Qualitative Research.* 3rd ed. Thousand Oaks, Calif.: Sage.

Duneier, Mitchell. 1999. *Sidewalk.* New York: Farrar, Straus and Giroux.

———. 2011. "Transparency in Ethnography." *Sociological Methodology* 41.

Ellis, Carolyn. 1995. "Emotional and Ethical Quagmires in Returning to the Field." *Journal of Contemporary Ethnography* 24(1): 68–98.

Ellis, Carolyn S., and Arthur P. Bochner. 2006. "Analyzing Analytic Autoethnography: An Autopsy." *Journal of Contemporary Ethnography* 35(4): 429–449.

Foreman, Gene. 2010. *The Ethical Journalist: Making Responsible Decisions in Pursuit of the News.* New York: Wiley-Blackwell.

Gaztambide-Fernández, Rubén A. 2009. *The Best of the Best: Becoming Elite at an American Boarding School.* Cambridge, Mass.: Harvard University Press.

Geertz, Clifford. 1973. *The Interpretation of Cultures: Selected Essays.* New York: Basic Books.

Hammersley, Martyn, and Paul Atkinson. 2007. *Ethnography: Principles in Practice.* 3rd ed. London: Routledge.

Harmon, Amy. 2010. "Target Cancer: New Drugs Stir Debates on Rules of Clinical Trials." *New York Times* (September 19): 1.

Hochschild, Arlie, with Anne Machung. 1989. *The Second Shift: Working Parents and the Revolution at Home.* New York: Avon.

Irwin, Katherine. 2006. "Into the Dark Heart of Ethnography: The Lived Ethics and Inequality of Intimate Field Relationships." *Qualitative Sociology* 29(2): 155–175.

Katz, Jack. 2004. "On the Rhetoric and Politics of Ethnographic Method." *ANNALS of the American Academy of Political and Social Science* 595(1): 280–308.

Kombo, Eddah Mutua. 2009. "Their Words, Actions, and Meaning: A Researcher's Reflection on Rwandan Women's Experience of Genocide." *Qualitative Inquiry* 15(2): 308–323.

Lamont, Michèle, and Patricia White. 2009. *Workshop on Interdisciplinary Standards for Systematic Qualitative Research.* Washington: National Science Foundation. Available at www.nsf.gov/sbe/ses/soc/ISSQR_workshop_rpt.pdf. Accessed February 24, 2011.

Lareau, Annette. 2010. *Doing Ethnography in the Real World: A Companion Guide.* Unpublished manuscript. Department of Sociology, University of Pennsylvania.

———. 2000. *Home Advantage.* 2nd ed. Lanham, Md.: Rowman and Littlefield.

Lareau, Annette, and Jeffrey Shultz (eds.). 1996. *Journeys through Ethnography: Realistic Accounts of Fieldwork.* Boulder, Colo.: Westview Press.

Lassiter, Luke Eric. 2005. *The Chicago Guide to Collaborative Ethnography.* Chicago: University of Chicago Press.

MacLeod, Jay. 2008 [1995]. *Ain't No Makin' It: Aspirations and Attainment in a Low-Income Neighborhood.* 3rd ed. Boulder, Colo.: Westview Press.

Maier, Shana L., and Brian A. Monahan. 2010. "How Close Is Too Close? Balancing Closeness and Detachment in Qualitative Research." *Deviant Behavior* 31(1): 1–32.

Marquand, John Phillips. 1949. *Point of No Return.* Boston: Little Brown.

Matthews, Stephen A., Linda M. Burton, and James Detwiler. 2005. "Geo-ethnography: Coupling Geographic Information Analysis Techniques with Ethnographic Methods in Urban Research." *Cartographica* 40(4): 75–90.

McCall, Michal M., and Howard S. Becker. 1990. "Performance Science." *Social Problems* 37(1): 117–132.

Mehan, Hugh, Lea Hubbard, Irene Villanueva, and Angela Lintz. 1996. *Constructing School Success: The Consequences of Untracking Low-achieving Students.* Cambridge and New York: Cambridge University.

Ochs, Elinor, Anthony P. Graesch, Angela Mittmann, Thomas Bradbury, and Rena Repetti. 2006. "Video Ethnography and Ethnoarchaeological Tracking."

In *The Work-Family Handbook: Multi-Disciplinary Perspectives and Approaches to Research,* pp. 387–409. Marcie Pitt-Catsouphes, Ellen Ernst Kossek, and Stephen A. Sweet. Mahwah (eds.). N.J.: Lawrence Erlbaum Associates.

Orlandella, Angelo Ralph. 1992. "Boelen May Know Holland, Boelen May Know Barzini, But Boelen 'Doesn't Know Diddle about the North End!'" *Journal of Contemporary Ethnography* 21(1): 69–79.

Rabinow, Paul. 2007. *Reflections on Fieldwork in Morocco.* 2nd ed. Berkeley: University of California Press.

Ragin, Charles, Joane Nagel, and Patricia White. 2004. *Workshop on Scientific Foundations of Qualitative Research.* Washington, D.C.: National Science Foundation. Available at www.nsf.gov/pubs/2004/nsf04219/nsf04219.pdf. Accessed February 24, 2011.

Ramazanoğlu, Caroline, and Janet Holland. 2002. *Feminist Methodology: Challenges and Choices.* Thousand Oaks, Calif.: Sage.

Reinharz, Shulamit, and Lynn Davidman. 1992. *Feminist Methods in Social Research.* New York: Oxford University Press.

Scheper-Hughes, Nancy. 2000. "Ire in Ireland." *Ethnography* 1(1): 117–140.

———. 2001. *Saints, Scholars, and Schizophrenics: Mental Illness in Rural Ireland.* 2nd ed. Berkeley: University of California Press.

Small, Mario Luis. 2009. "How Many Cases Do I Need?: On Science and the Logic of Case Selection in Field-Based Research." *Ethnography* 10(1): 5–38.

Smith, Dorothy E. 2005. *Institutional Ethnography: A Sociology for People.* Oxford: AltaMira Press.

Stein, Arlene. 2010. "Sex, Truths, and Audiotape: Anonymity and the Ethics of Exposure in Public Ethnography." *Journal of Contemporary Ethnography* 39: 554–568.

Steinberg, Jacques. 2005. "One Show's Unexpected Lessons in Reality." *New York Times* (March 16): E1.

Subedi, Binaya, and Jeong-eun Rhee. 2008. "Negotiating Collaboration across Differences." *Qualitative Inquiry* 14(6): 1070–1092.

Tavory, Iddo, and Stefan Timmermans. 2009. "Two Cases of Ethnography: Grounded Theory and the Extended Case Method." *Ethnography* 10(3): 243–263.

ten Have, Paul. 2004. *Understanding Qualitative Research and Ethnomethodology*. Thousand Oaks, Calif.: Sage.

Van Maanen, John. 1988. *Tales of the Field: On Writing Ethnography*. Chicago: University of Chicago Press.

Vidich, Arthur J., and Joseph Bensman. 2000. *Small Town in Mass Society: Class, Power, and Religion in a Rural Community*, rev. ed. Champaign: University of Illinois Press.

Warner, William Lloyd, J. O. Low, Paul S. Lunt, and Leo Srole. 1963. *Yankee City*. New Haven: Yale University Press.

Warren, Mark. 2010. "A Collaborative Approach to Ethnographic Case Study Research: The Community Organizing and School Reform Project at Harvard University." Paper presented at a colloquium, Department of Sociology, University of Pennsylvania.

Whitehead, Jack, and Jean McNiff. 2006. *Action Research: Living Theory*. Thousand Oaks, Calif.: Sage.

Whyte, William Foote. 1996. "On the Evolution of Street Corner Society." In *Journeys through Ethnography: Realistic Accounts of Fieldwork*, pp. 9–73. Annette Lareau and Jeffrey Shultz (eds.). Boulder, Colo.: Westview Press.

———. 1993 [1943]. *Street Corner Society: The Social Structure of an Italian Slum*. 4th ed. Chicago: University of Chicago Press.

Wolf, Diane L. (ed.) 1996. *Feminist Dilemmas in Fieldwork*. Boulder, Colo.: Westview Press.

Wolf, Margery. 1992. *A Thrice-Told Tale: Feminism, Postmodernism, and Ethnographic Responsibility*. Stanford, Calif.: Stanford University Press.

CREDITS

Printed in the USA/Agawam, MA
June 17, 2020

756731.033